→ Nicholson W9-ARV-028

LONDON STREETFINDER

London Streetfinder
© Robert Nicholson Publications Limited
1984
Based upon the Ordance Survey Map
with the sanction of the Controller of Her
Majesty's Station Office. Crown
Copyright reserved.

**Buyer's Guide and Information
Service**
© Robert Nicholson Publications Limited
1984

All other maps
© Robert Nicholson Publications Limited

London Underground map by kind
permission of London Transport.

Designed by Robert Nicholson and
Romek Marber

Published and distributed by
Robert Nicholson Publications Ltd
17 Conway Street
London W1P 6JD

Great care has been taken throughout
this book to be accurate but the
publishers cannot accept responsibility
for any errors which appear, or their
consequences.

Printed in Great Britain by
The Guernsey Press Co. Ltd.,
Guernsey, Channel Islands

ISBN 0 900568 98 4

Symbols

† Church

✚ Hospital

🚗 Car park

🏛 Historic buildings

🏚 Small buildings

🎒 Schools

⬤ Sports stadium

⊖ London Underground station

🎣 British Rail station

🚌 Coach station

✈ Air terminal

⇌ British Rail terminal

PO Post Office

Pol Police station

➞ One ways (central area only)

⋮⋮⋮⋮ Footpath

300 ▶
◀ 400 Figure indicating the direction
of street numbering and the
approximate position

Outer area
☐☐☐☐ ½ mile
☐☐☐ ½ km

Large scale Central area
☐☐☐☐☐ ½ mile
☐☐☐ ½ km

ROBERT NICHOLSON PUBLICATIONS
(GEOGRAPHIA)

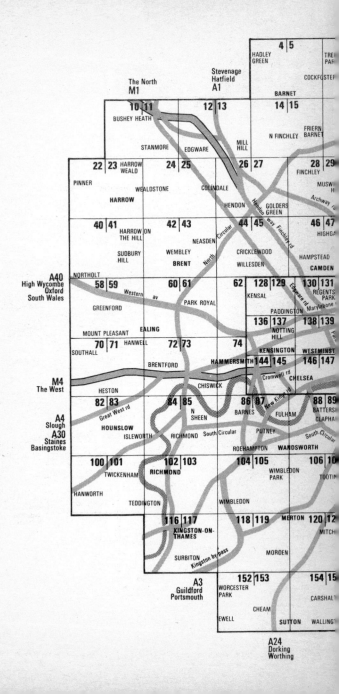

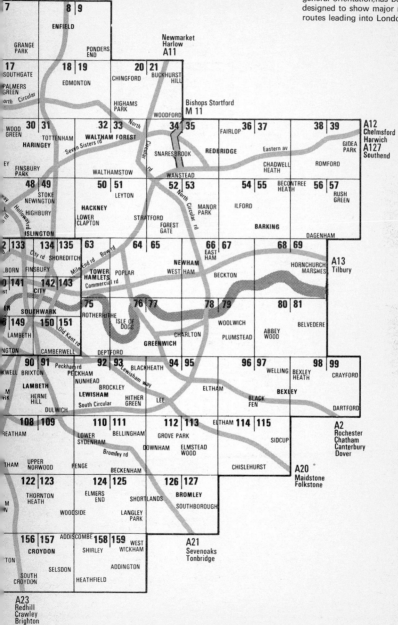

Key to map pages

This general map, apart from giving map numbers and general orientation, has been designed to show major road routes leading into London.

Cambridge
A10

7

8 | 9

ENFIELD

GRANGE PARK

PONDERS END

Newmarket
Harlow
A11

17 SOUTHGATE

PALMERS GREEN

North Circular

18 | 19

EDMONTON

20

CHINGFORD

21 BUCKHURST HILL

HIGHAMS PARK

WOODFORD

Bishops Stortford
M 11

30 | 31

WOOD GREEN

TOTTENHAM

HARINGEY

Seven Sisters rd

FINSBURY PARK

32 33

WALTHAM FOREST

North Circular rd

WALTHAMSTOW

34 | 35

SNARESBROOK

WANSTEAD

FAIRLOP

36 | 37

REDBRIDGE

Eastern av

CHADWELL HEATH

38 | 39

GIDEA PARK

ROMFORD

A12
Chelmsford
Harwich
A127
Southend

48 | 49

STOKE NEWINGTON

HIGHBURY

Holloway rd

ISLINGTON

50 | 51

LEYTON

HACKNEY

LOWER CLAPTON

52 | 53

STRATFORD

FOREST GATE

North Circular rd

MANOR PARK

54 | 55

ILFORD

BARKING

BECONTREE HEATH

56 | 57

RUSH GREEN

DAGENHAM

2 | 133

134 | 135

City rd SHOREDITCH

BORN FINSBURY

Mile End rd

63

Bow rd

TOWER HAMLETS

Commercial rd

POPLAR

64 | 65

NEWHAM

WEST HAM

66 | 67

EAST HAM

BECKTON

68 | 69

HORNCHURCH MARSHES

A13
Tilbury

0 | 141

142 | 143

CITY

SOUTHWARK

75

ROTHERHITHE

ISLE OF DOGS

76 | 77

78 | 79

WOOLWICH

80 | 81

BELVEDERE

149

150 | 151

LAMBETH

Old Kent rd

CAMBERWELL

NGTON

DEPTFORD

CHARLTON

GREENWICH

PLUMSTEAD

ABBEY WOOD

90 | 91

KWELL BRIXTON

LAMBETH

HERNE HILL

DULWICH

Peckham rd

PECKHAM

NUNHEAD

92 | 93

BROCKLEY

LEWISHAM

South Circular

HITHER GREEN

Lewisham way

BLACKHEATH

LEE

94 | 95

ELTHAM

96 | 97

WELLING

BEXLEY HEATH

BEXLEY

BLACK FEN

98 | 99

CRAYFORD

DARTFORD

108 | 109

REATHAM

LOWER SYDENHAM

110 | 111

BELLINGHAM

Bromley rd

DOWNHAM

112 | 113

GROVE PARK

ELMSTEAD WOOD

ELTHAM

114 | 115

SIDCUP

CHISLEHURST

A2
Rochester
Chatham
Canterbury
Dover

THAM

UPPER NORWOOD

PENGE

122 | 123

THORNTON HEATH

WOODSIDE

BECKENHAM

124 | 125

ELMERS END

SHORTLANDS

LANGLEY PARK

126 | 127

BROMLEY

SOUTHBOROUGH

A20
Maidstone
Folkstone

156 | 157

CROYDON

SOUTH CROYDON

SELSDON

ADDISCOMBE

158 | 159

SHIRLEY

WEST WICKHAM

ADDINGTON

HEATHFIELD

A21
Sevenoaks
Tonbridge

A23
Redhill
Crawley
Brighton

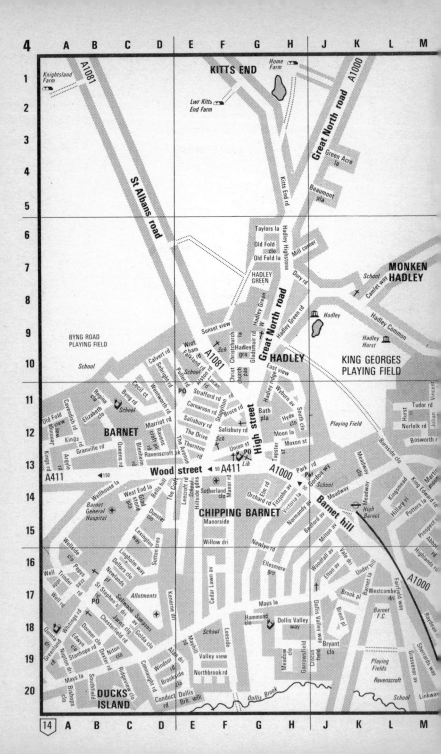

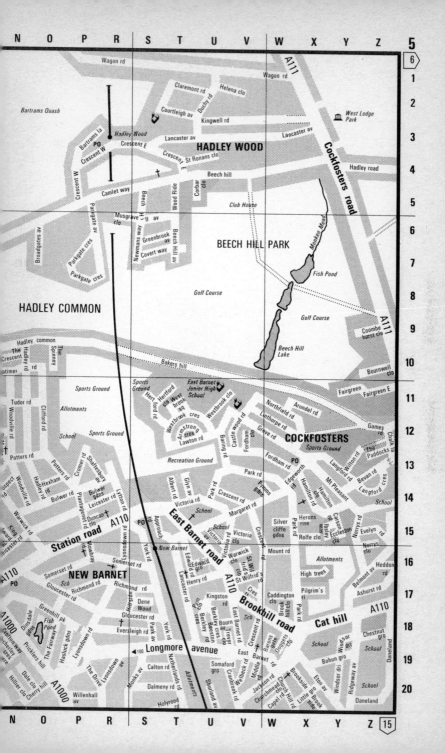

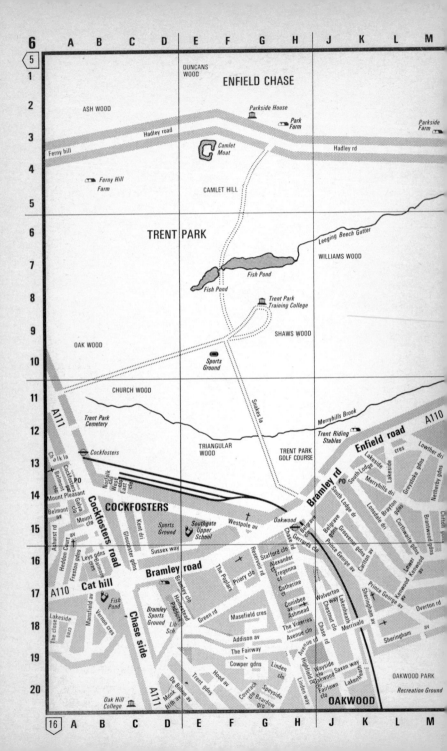

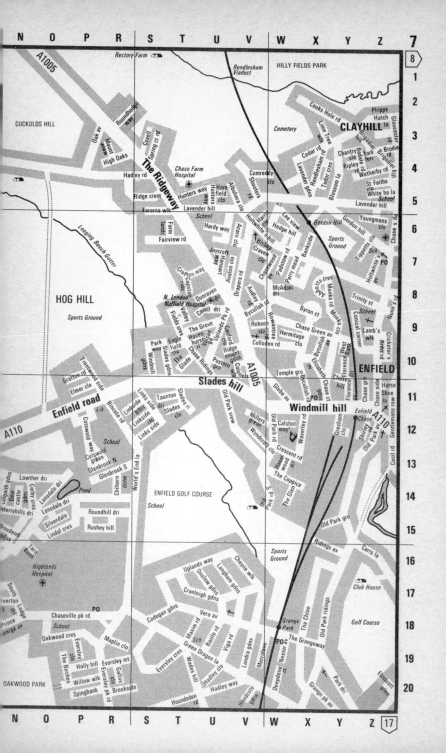

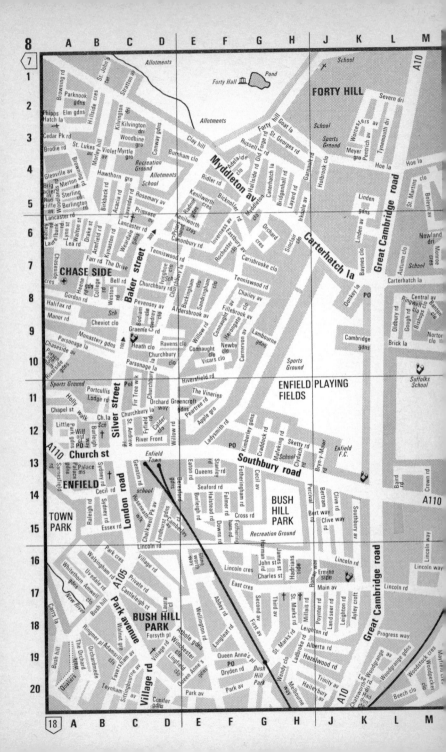

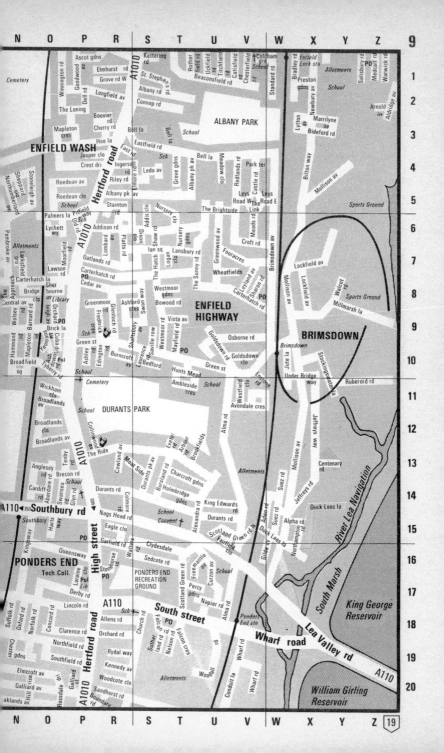

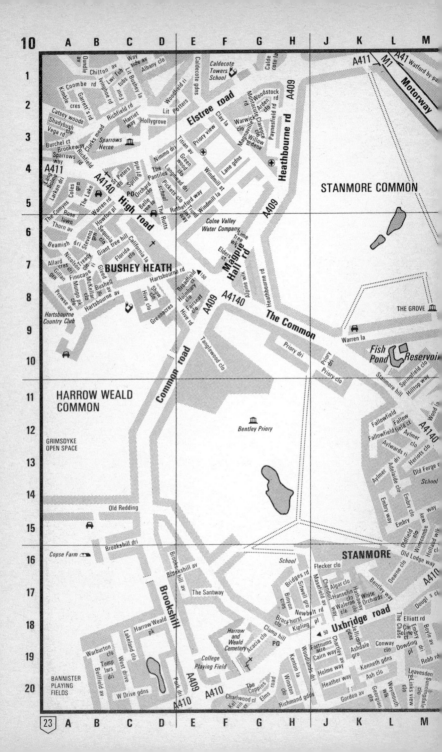

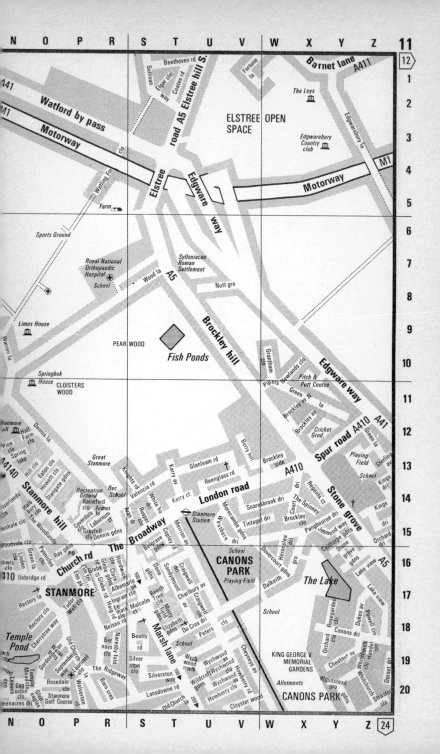

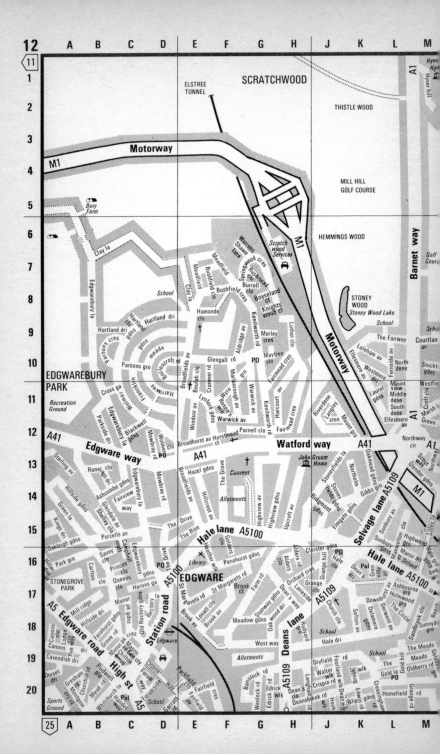

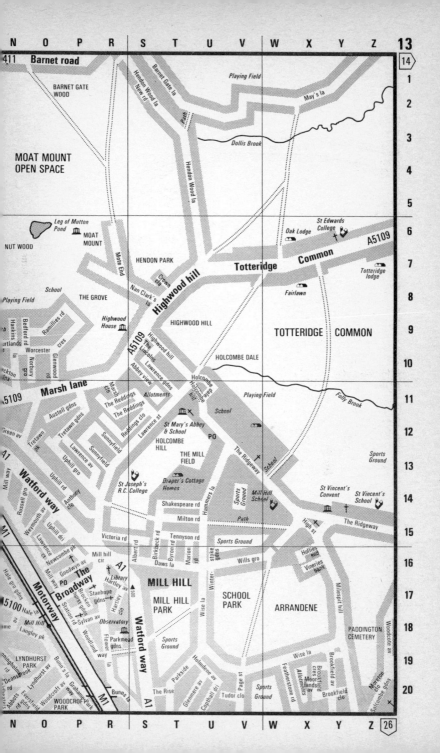

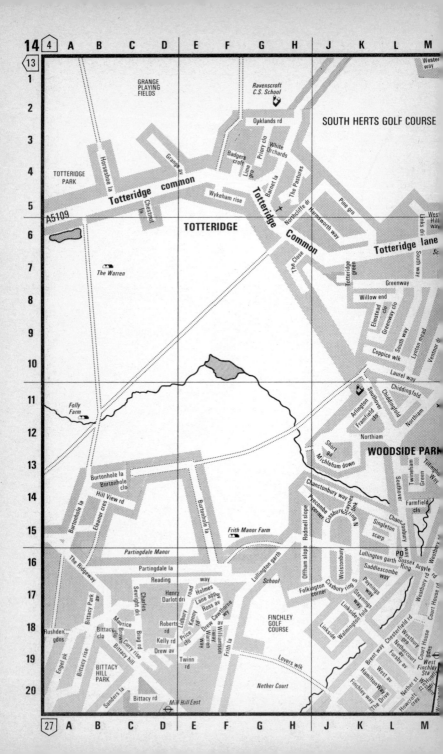

A B C D E F G H J K L M

Wester way

GRANGE PLAYING FIELDS

Ravenscroft C.S. School

Oaklands rd

SOUTH HERTS GOLF COURSE

White Orchards

Priory clo

Badgers croft

Lime gro

Banter la

The Pastures

TOTTERIDGE PARK

Horseshoe la

Grange av

Totteridge common

Chestnut la

Wykeham rise

Pine gro

Norcliffe dr

Hemsworth way

A5109

TOTTERIDGE

Totteridge Common

West Hill way

Totteridge lane

Sc

The Warren

The Close

Totteridge green

South way

Greenway

Willow end

Elmstead clo

Greenway clo

South way

Lynton mead

Ventnor dr

Coppice wlk

Laurel way

Chidding fold

Folly Farm

Arlington

Southover

Chiddingfold

Northam

Framfield clo

Short rd

Mychleham down

Northam

WOODSIDE PARK

Burtonhole la

Burtonhole clo

Hill View rd

Burtonhole la

Eleanor cres

Burtonhole la

Frith Manor Farm

Chanctonbury way

Pyecombe corner

Cissbury ring

Saames link

Spring link

Southover

Twineham Green

Farmfield clo

Chanctonbury

Singleton scarp

Partingdale Manor

Rodmell slope

Offham slope

Lullington garth

School

Wolstonbury

Singleton scarp

PO

Lullington garth

Sussex Ring

Argyle

The Ridgeway

Partingdale la

Reading

way

Holmes

Lane app

Charles Sewright dri

Henry Darlot dri

Price clo

Kenny rd

Drew av

Cawthorne way

Ross av

Folkington corner

Cissbury ring S

Poynings way

Stayings way

Saddlescombe way

Westbury rd

Nethercourt av

Fursby av

Court House rd

Bittacy Park av

Maurice Brown clo

Curry rise

Bittacy hill

Roberts rd

Kelly rd

Lidbury rd

Frith la

Linkside

Walmington fold

Linkside

Chesterfield rd

Westbury

Court House av

Rushden gdns

Bittacy clo

Drew av

Twinn rd

FINCHLEY GOLF COURSE

Brent way

West av

Hamilton way

Court House av

West Finchley Sta

Engel pk

Bittacy rise

Bittacy hill

Lovers wlk

Hamilton Way

Howcroft cres

Finchley way

The Drive

West Hund

BITTACY HILL PARK

Sanders la

Bittacy rd

Mill Hill East

Nether Court

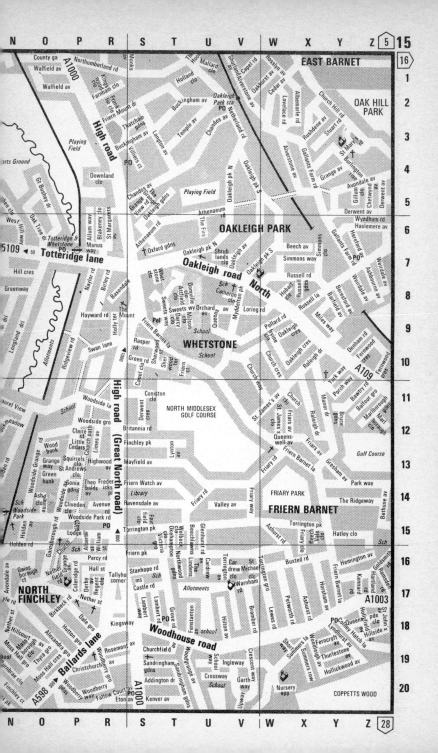

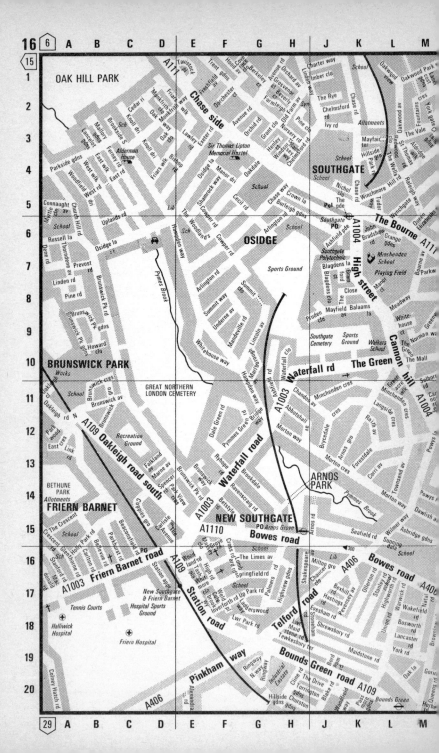

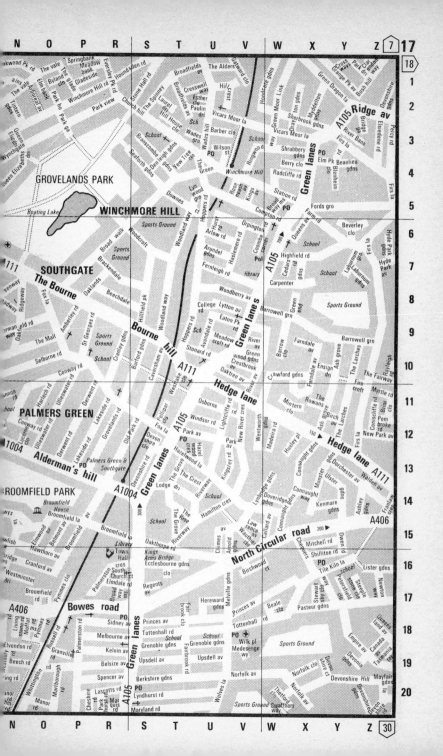

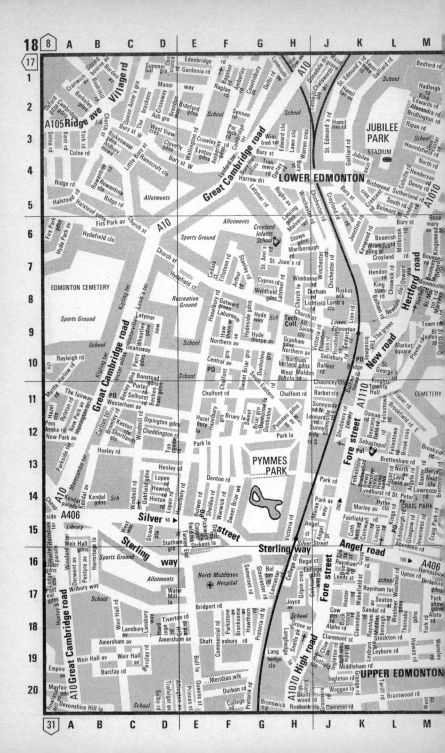

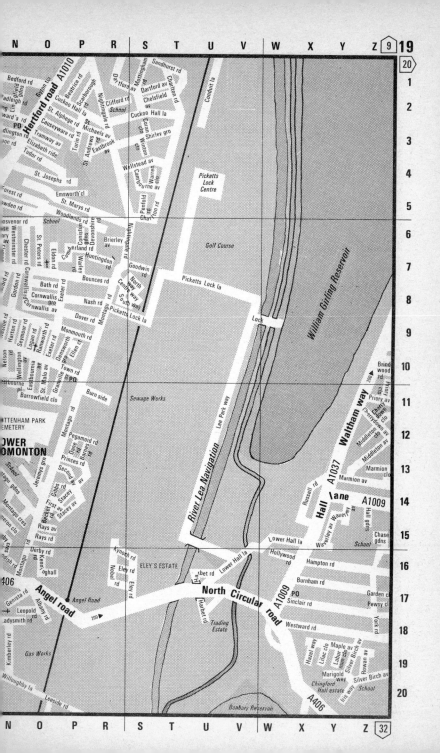

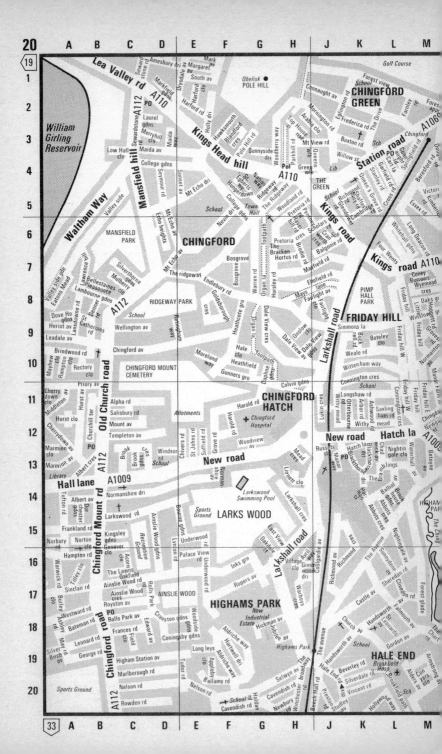

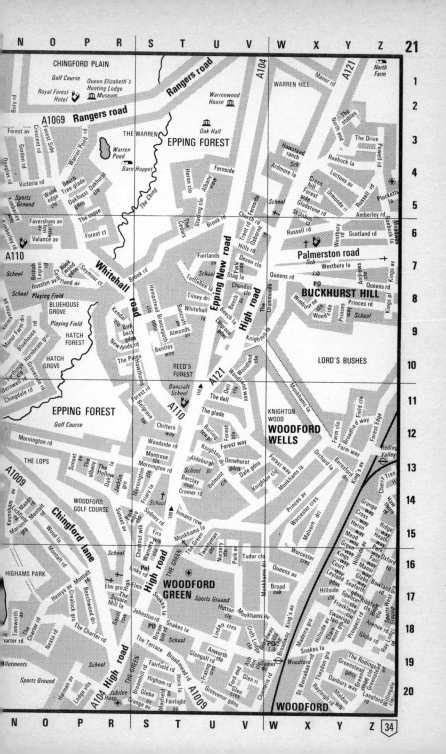

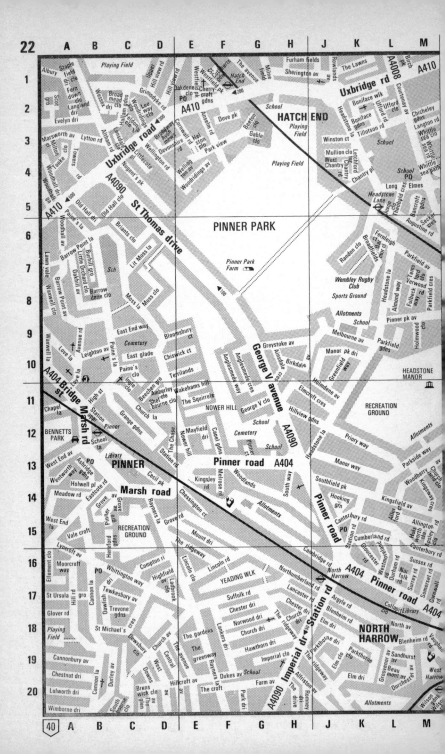

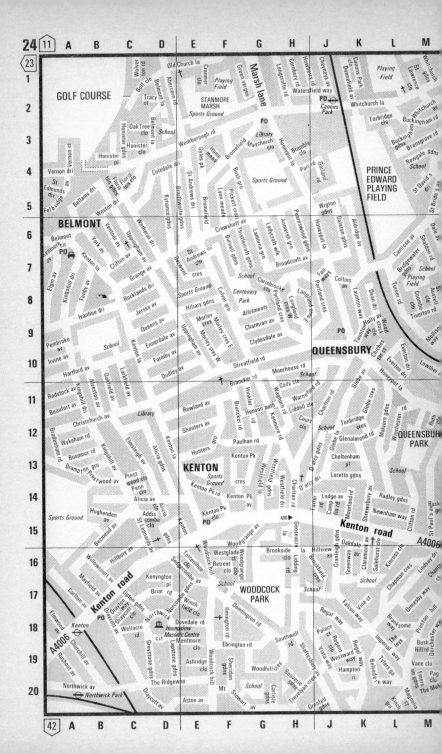

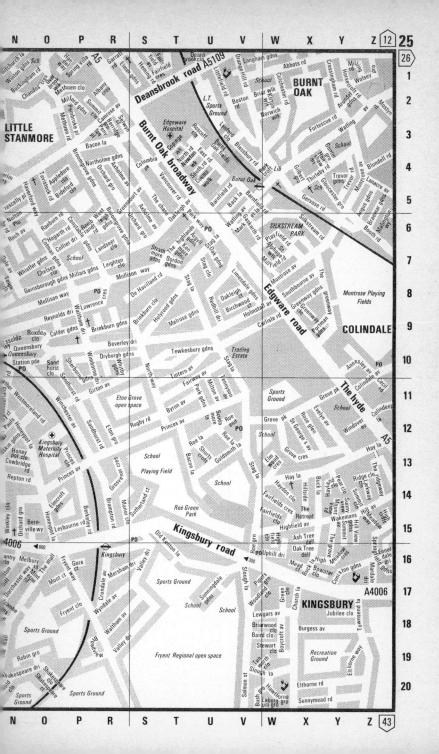

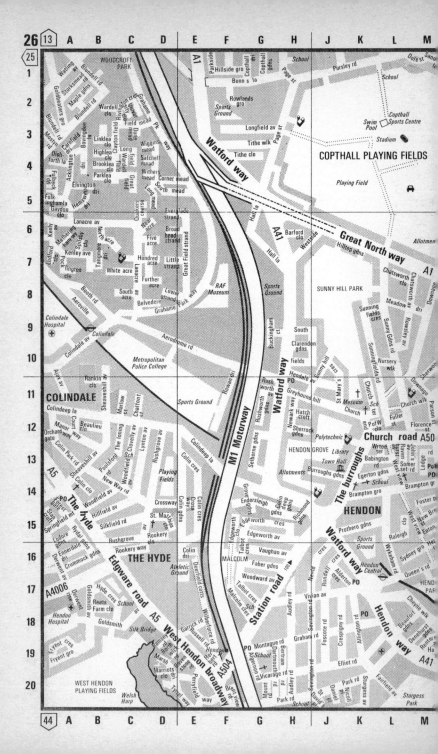

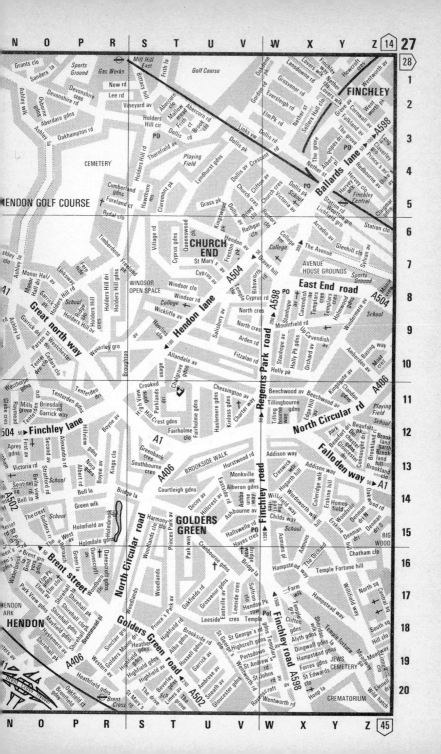

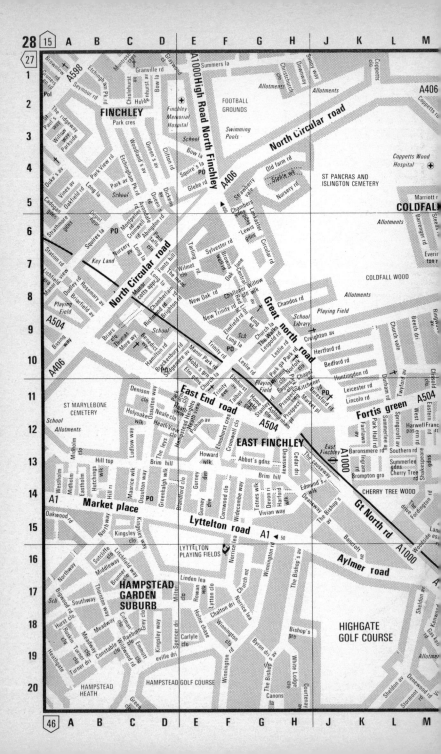

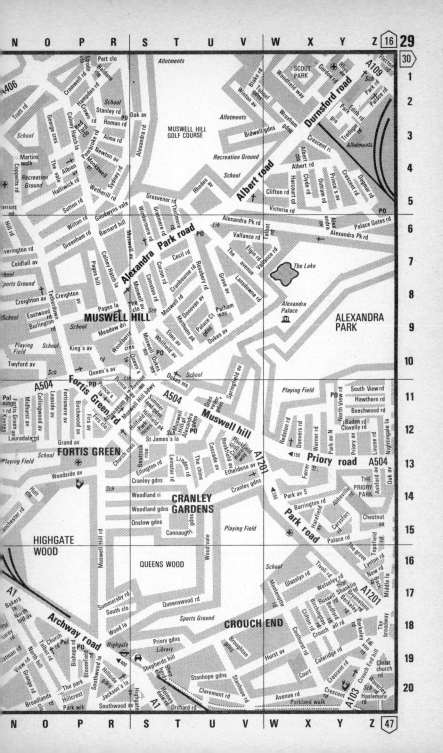

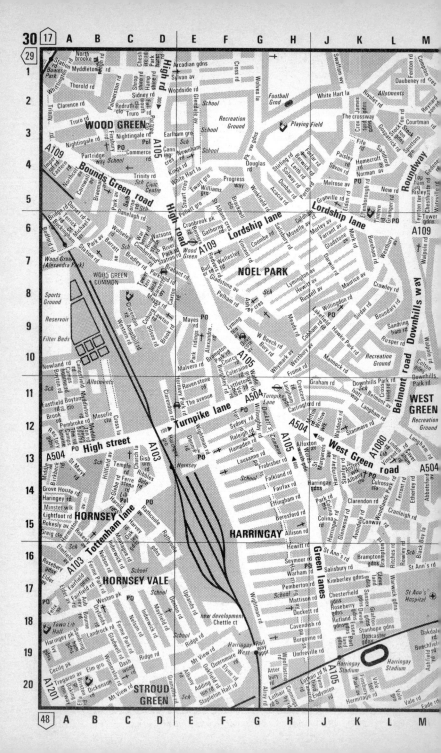

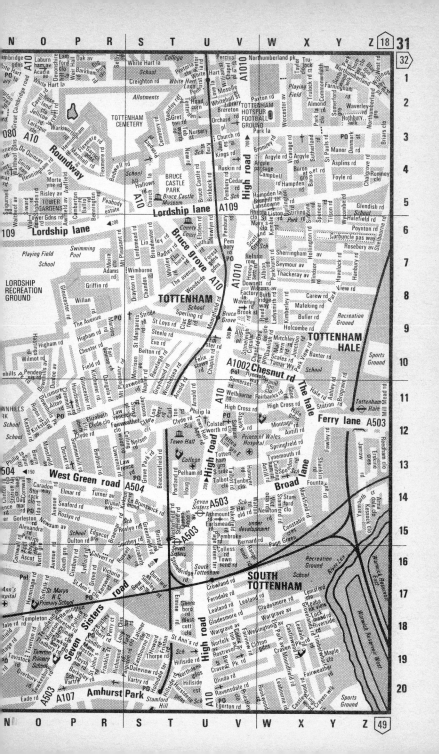

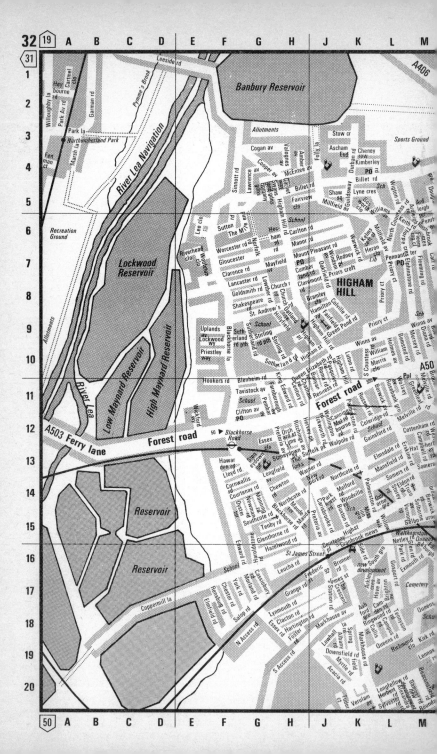

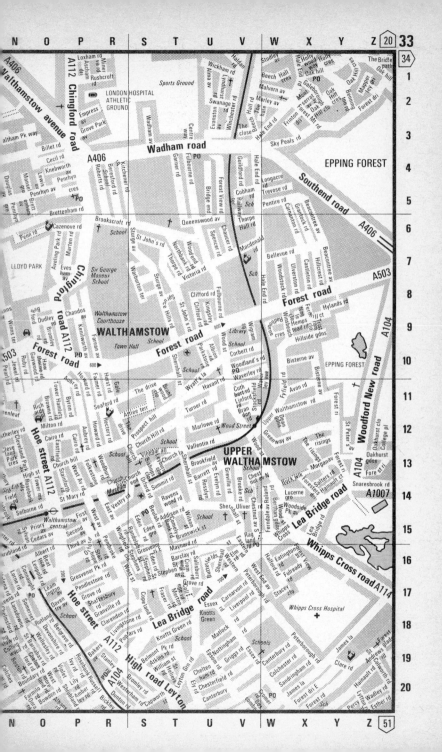

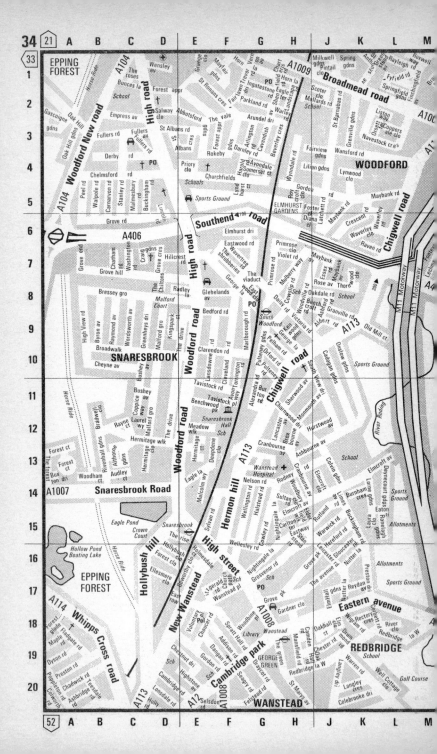

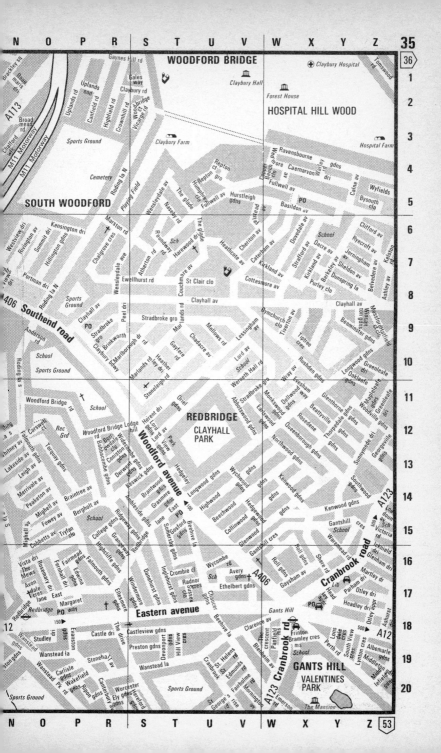

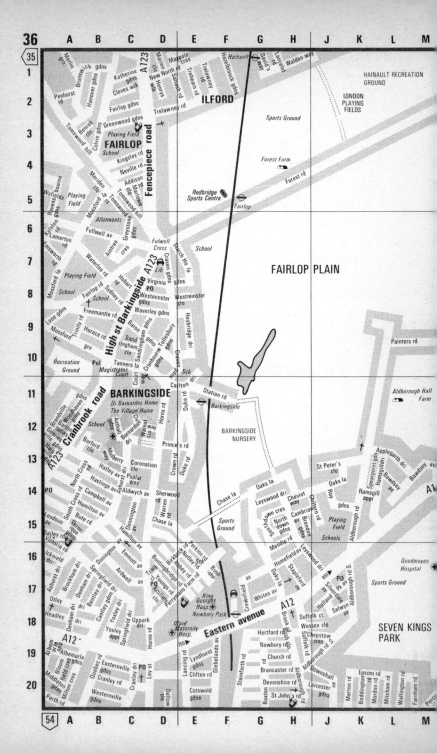

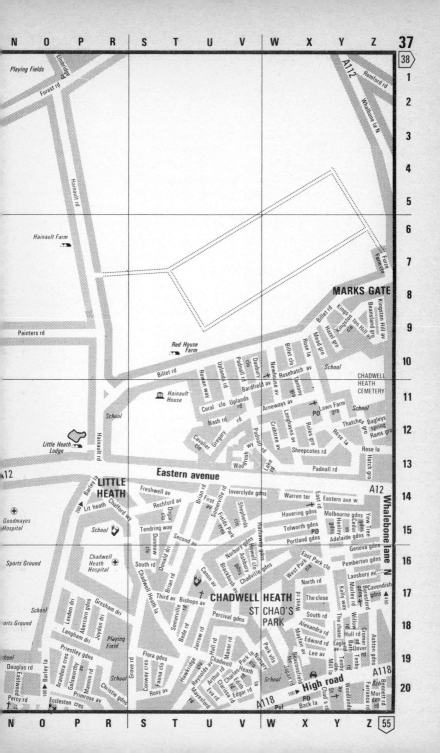

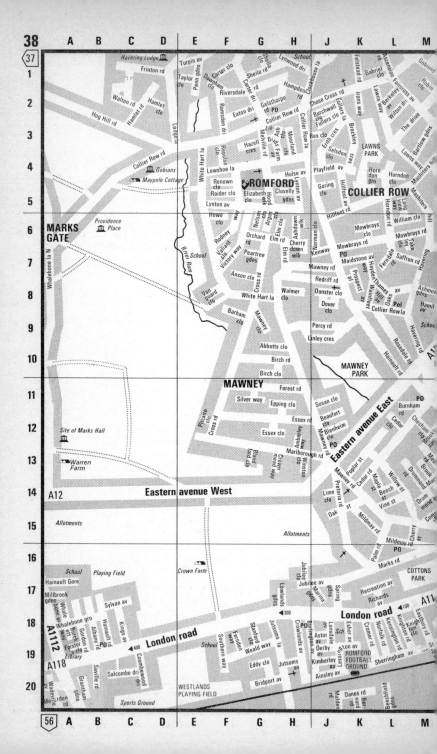

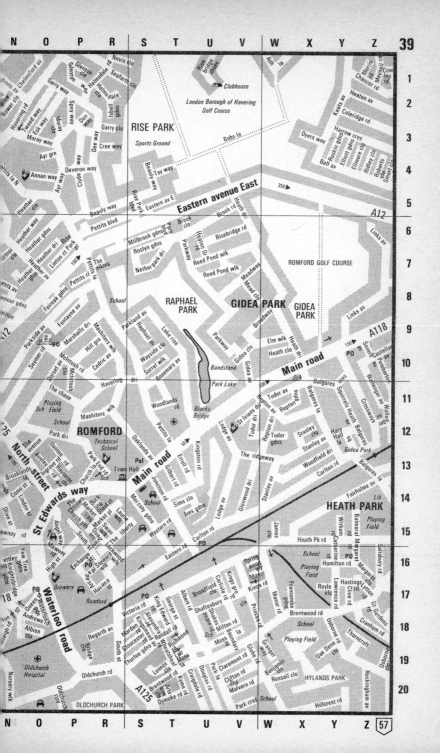

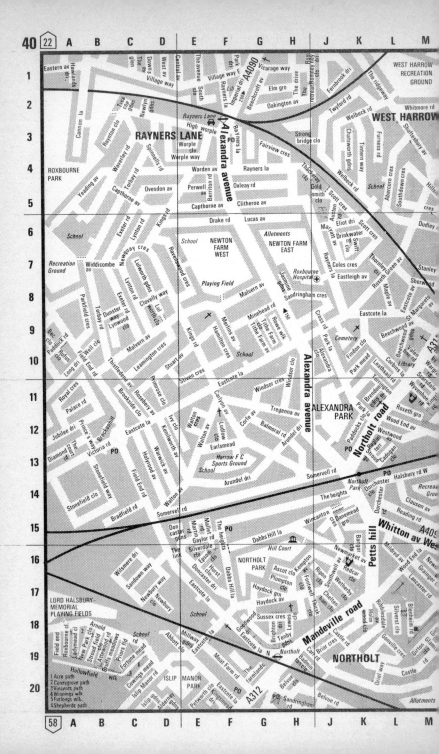

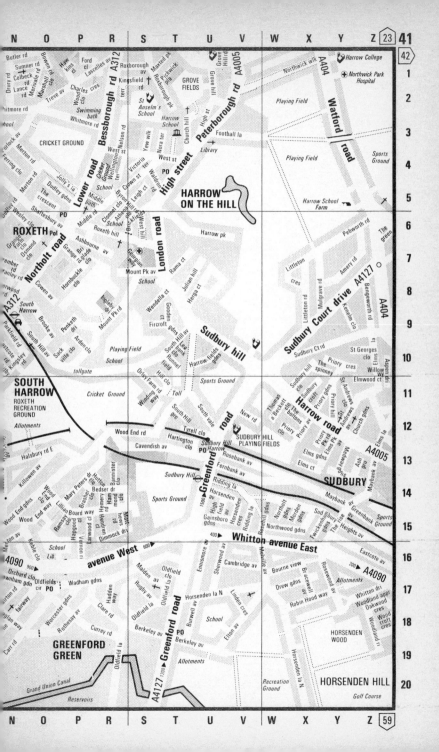

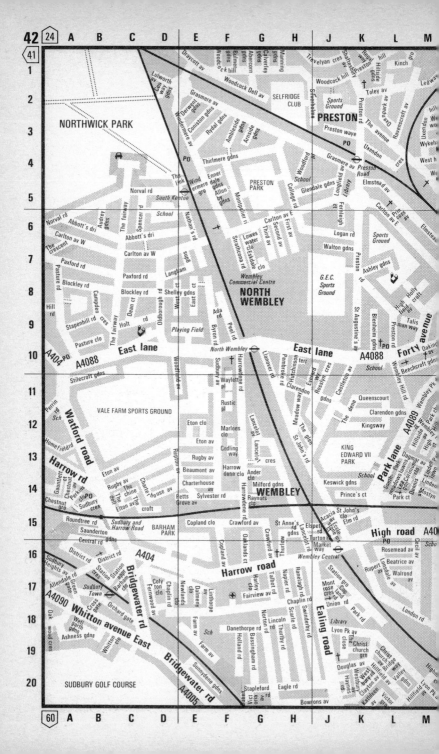

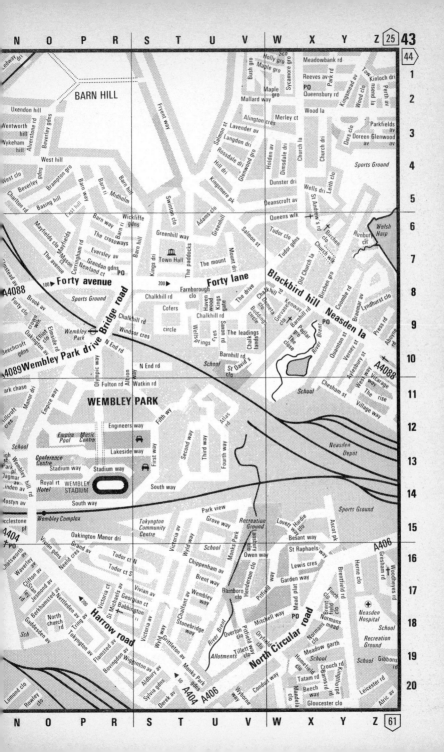

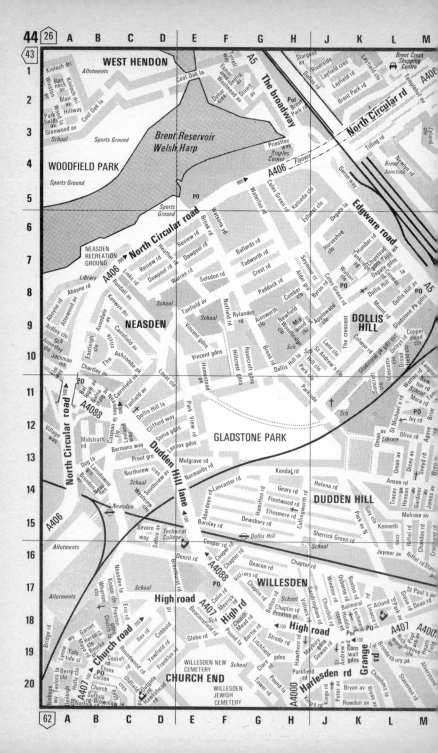

GOLDERS GREEN
CHILDS HILL
GOLDERS HILL PARK
CRICKLEWOOD
FORTUNE GREEN
WEST HAMPSTEAD
BRONDESBURY
KILBURN GRANGE PARK

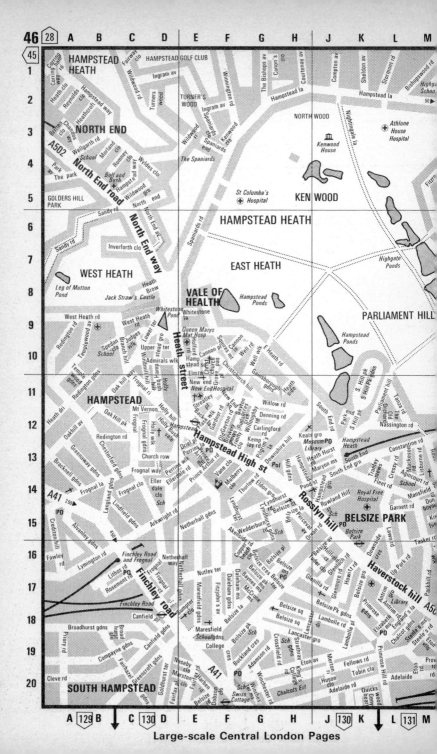

Large-scale Central London Pages

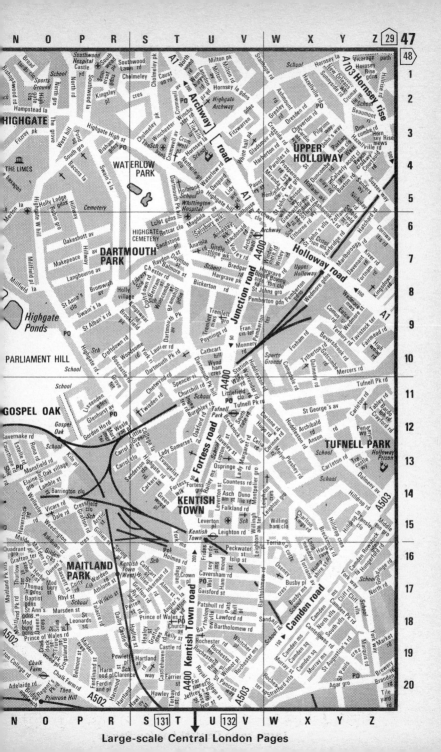

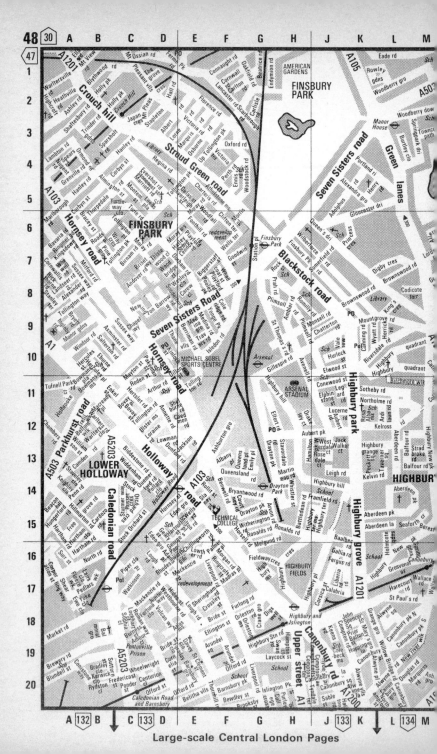

A B C D E F G H J K L M

1 2 3 4 5 6 7 8 9 10 11 12 13 14 15 16 17 18 19 20

Eade rd

A105

Rowley gdns

A50

Woodberry gro

Woodberry dow

Manor House

Springpark dri

Burtley clo

Seven Sisters road

Green lanes

Alexandra gro

Henry

Gloucester dri

AMERICAN GARDENS

FINSBURY PARK

Connaught rd

Cornwall rd

Lancaster rd

Carlton

Beatrice rd

Oakfield rd

Endymion rd

Carlisle

Ossian rd

Ferme PK

Terr PK

Mt View

Ellr

A1201

Waltersville

Heathville

Highcroft

Ashley rd

Shaftesbury rd

Trinder rd

Hanley rd

Crouch hill

Blythwood rd

Holly pk

Holly

Japan cres

Albert

Stapleton

Crouch Hill

Mt Pleas

Lone

Mt Pleasant grove

Hall rd

Florence rd

Victoria rd

Oxford rd

Marquis rd

Osborne

Perth

Woodstock rd

Ennis rd

Victoria rd

Stroud Green road

Regina rd

Tollington pk

Charteris

Woodall

Clifton ter

Clifton

Evershot rd

Tollington

Dalmeny

Marriott

Mornington

Woodfall

Roads

Fonthill rd

Playford

Durham

Wray

Wesley rd

Biggerstaff

Goodwin

St

Station pl

Finsbury Park

Rock

Prah rd

Somerfield rd

Queen's dri

Wilberforce

Finsbury Pk

Blackstock road

Digby cres

Brownswood rd

Brownswood rd

Codicote terr

Library

King's

FINSBURY PARK

Hornsey road

A103

Marlborough

Bavaria

Ringmer

Kingsdown

Cornwallis

Landseer rd

Stanley

Tollington way

Manor gdns

Windsor rd

Salterton rd

Hercules

Elbourne

Bowman

Thorpedale

Biscay

Mingard

Roads

Tollington pk

Tollington

Pine

Birnam rd

Risley

Thane

Wood

Andover rd

Seven Sisters Road

Wray

Carew

Barrow

Iron

New

Sch

Hornsey Road

Roden

Hertslet rd

Arthur rd

Chapel

Axminster

Sussex way

Bovey

Sussex way

Tollington

Bowman's

Enkel

Shelburne rd

Ulster ms

Loraine

Lowman

Lowman

Dunford

Jackson

Arsenal

Gillespie rd

MICHAEL SOBEL SPORTS CENTRE

Tollington ter

Highbury hill

ARSENAL STADIUM

Conewood st

Leg

Elphin stone rd

ard rd

Lucerne rd

Mountgrove rd

Riversdale

Wyatt rd

Chatterton

Monsell rd

Plimsoll rd

Romilly rd

Ambler rd

St Thomas's rd

Highbury

quadrant

quadrant

Codicote terr

Sotheby rd

Northolme rd

Kelross

Ritchmore wlk

Highbury grange

Calabria

Highbury park

Baalbec rd

Kelvin rd

HIGHBUR

Aberdeen

Aberdeen pk

Aberdeen la

Seaforth

Beres

Parkhurst road

A503

LOWER HOLLOWAY

Tufnell Park rd

Holmcote

Chambers

William

son st

Camden

Biddestone

Widdenham

Roman

Holloway road

Bride rd

Beacon

Hungerford

Hilmarton

Cardozo

Hartham

Free

Hartham

Caledonian road

Sussex

Stock Orchard

Eden gro

Holloway rd

Hornsey rd

TECHNICAL COLLEGE

Witherington rd

Ronalds rd

Ronalds rd

Melgund rd

A103

Ashburton gro

Albany

Queens

Queensland

Benwell rd

Drayton pk

Drayton Park

Emily rd

Martin

Bryantwood rd

Drayton pk

Bavaria

Arvon

Framfield rd

Leigh rd

Highbury hill

Battledean rd

Highbury ter

Highbury grove

A1201

HIGHBURY FIELDS

Fieldway cres

Highbury

Gaskin

Morgan rd

Ringcroft

Liverpool rd

Mackenzie

Sheringham rd

Crossley

Furlong rd

Bride st

Orleston rd

Orleston

Cran Digs

Ellington st

Highbury and Islington

Highbury Stn rd

Laycock rd

Upper street

A1

Market rd

redevelopment

Caledonian road

Piper clo

Watkinson

Mackenzie rd

Junction

West garden

Madras

Pol

Yoke

Pedlars wk

Ewe clo

North rd

Bride st

Burnsbury

Sophia

Vulcan

Arundel sq

Barnsbury

Belitha vlls

Bewdley st

Bingfield st

Offord rd

Offord rd

Barnsbury rd

Islington Stn

Brooksby

Laycock

Copenhagen st

Sheen

Shearling

Caledonian Road and Barnsbury

Market rd

Brewery rd

Blundell st

Pentonville Prison

Bradley

Suttie

A5203

Wheelwright

Centurion

Frederica st

Ponder

Ward

Canonbury rd

St Paul's rd

Harecourt rd

Wallace

Canonbury pk N

Canonbury pk S

Alwyne pl

St Mary's path

Willow Bridge rd

Alwyne rd

Canonbury pk

Grosvenor av

John Spencer sq

Compton

Keens

Grange

Canonbury

New

Marquess

Douglas rd

Sable

A200

Upper street

A1

Large-scale Central London Pages

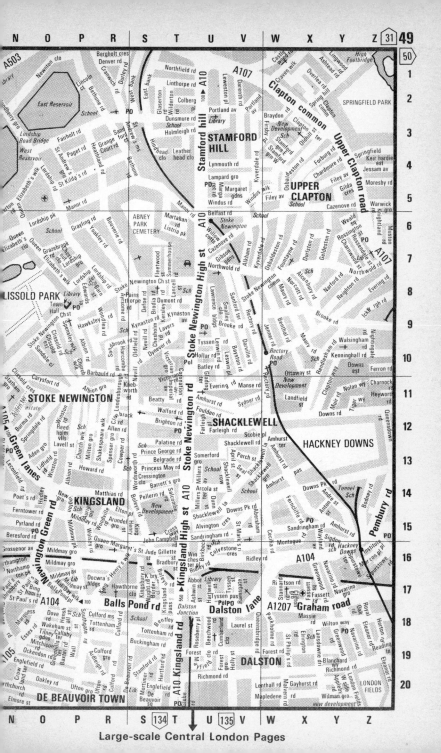

Large-scale Central London Pages

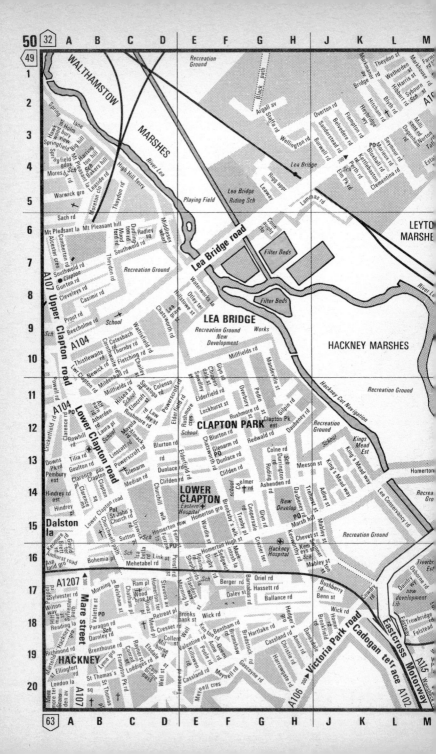

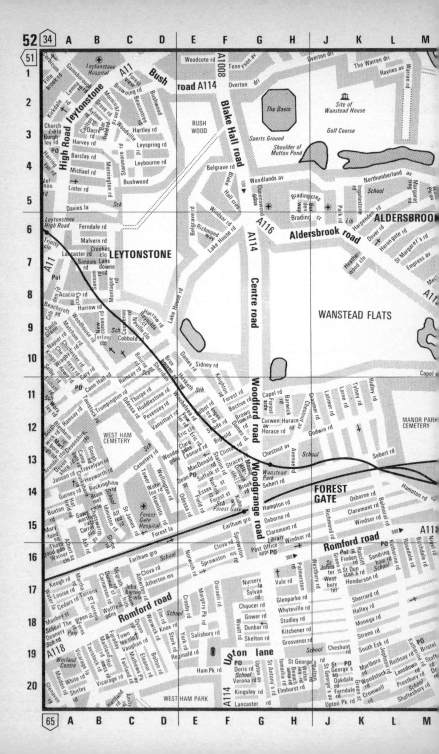

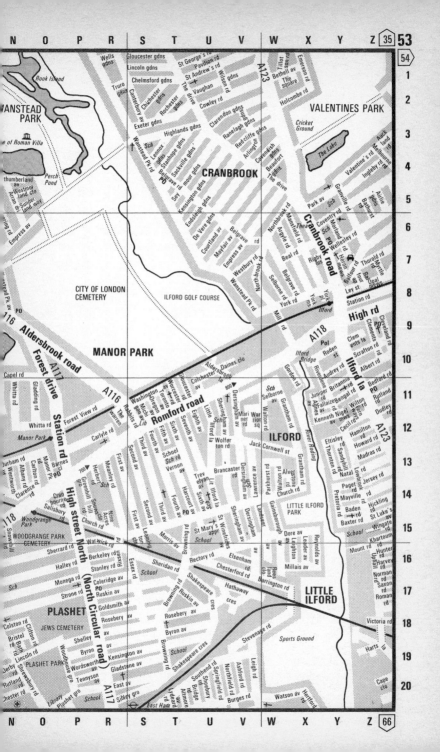

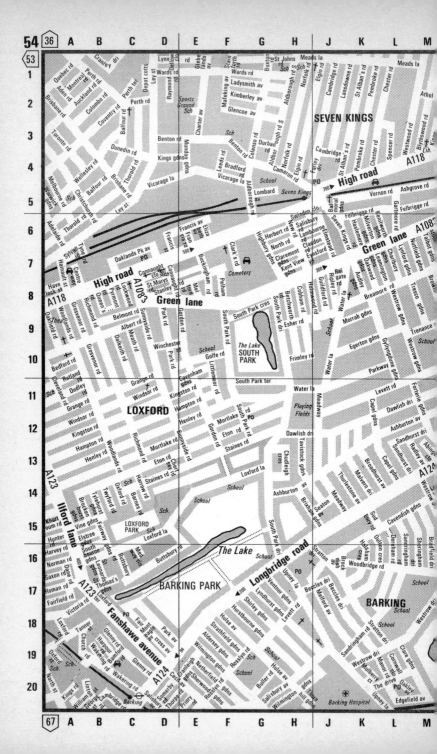

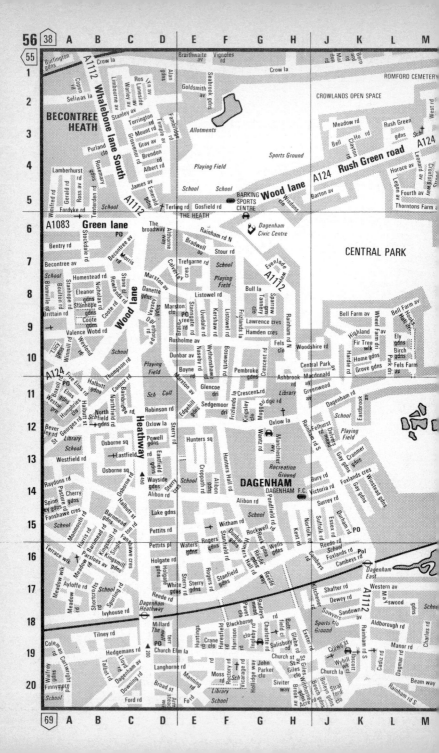

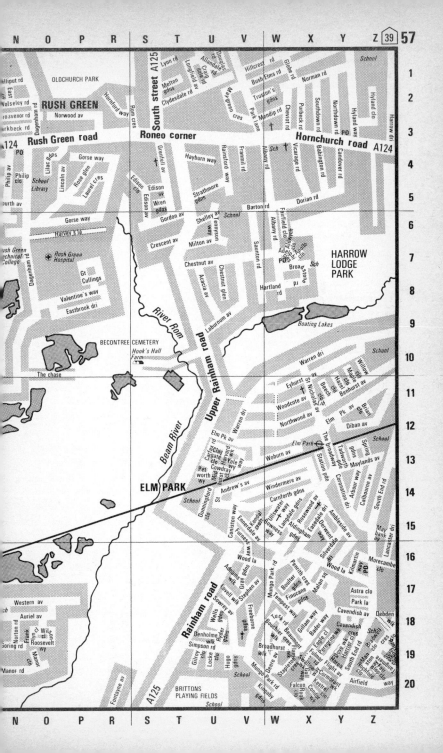

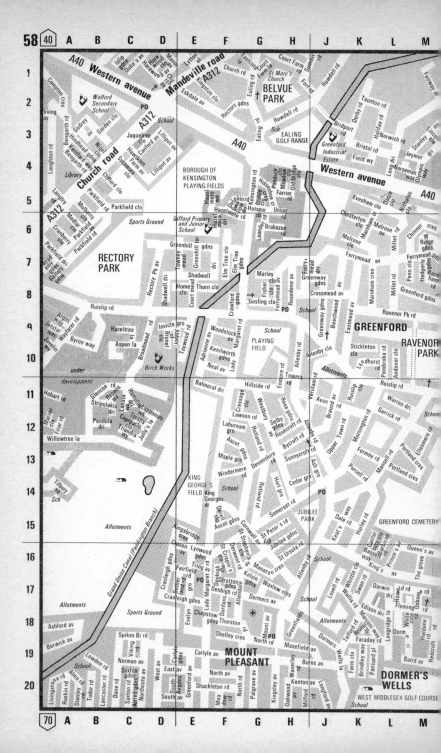

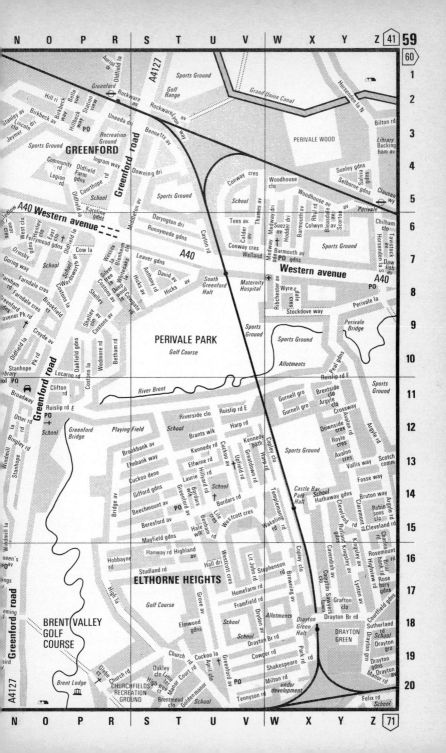

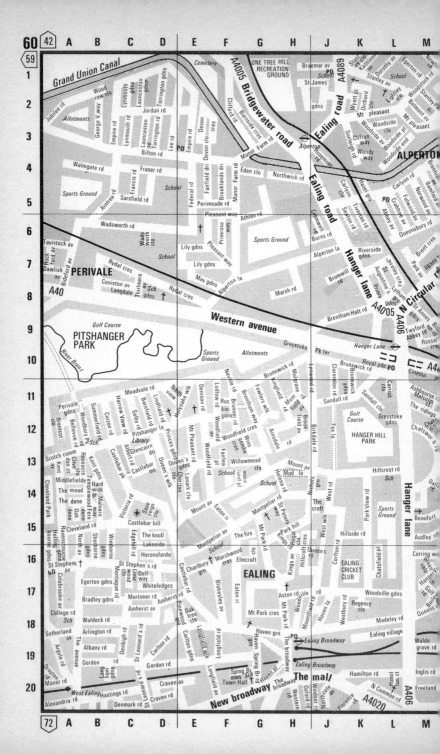

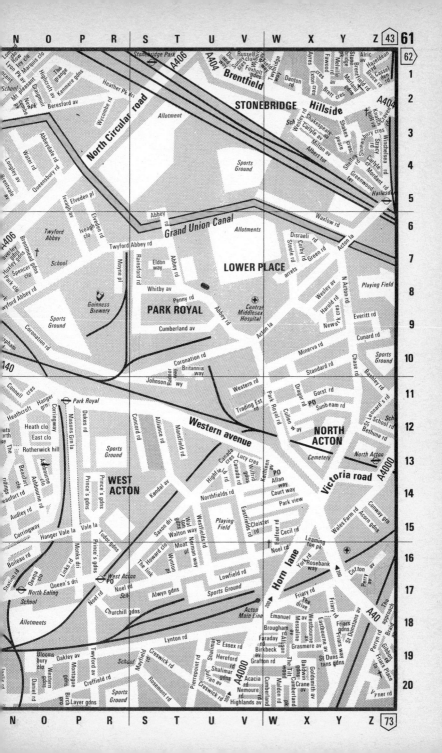

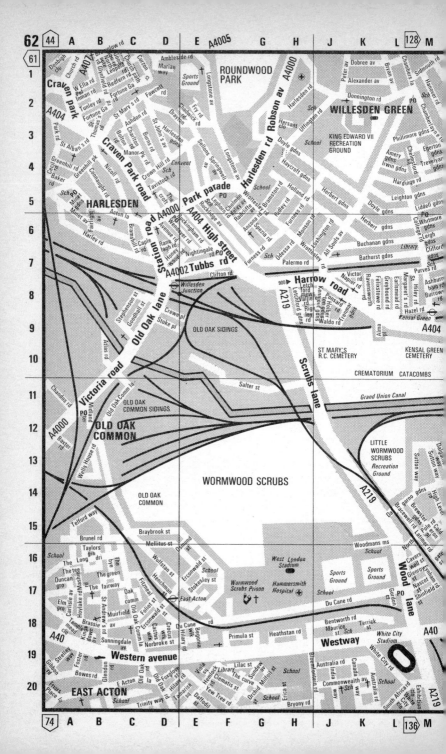

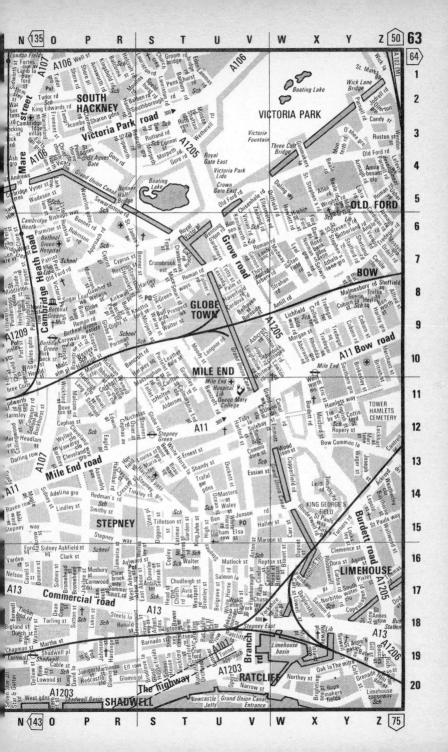

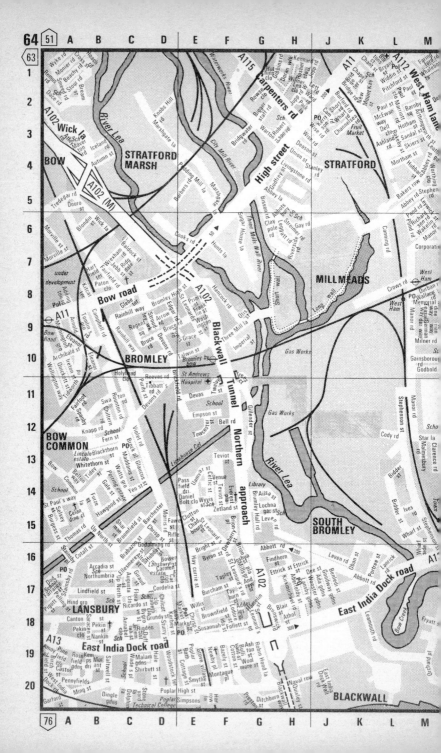

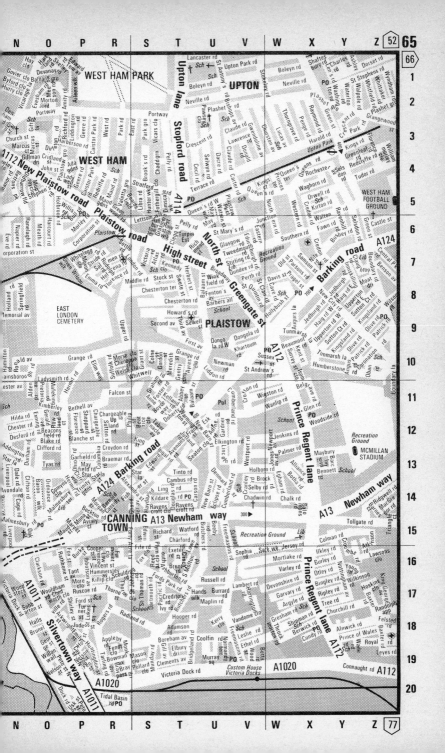

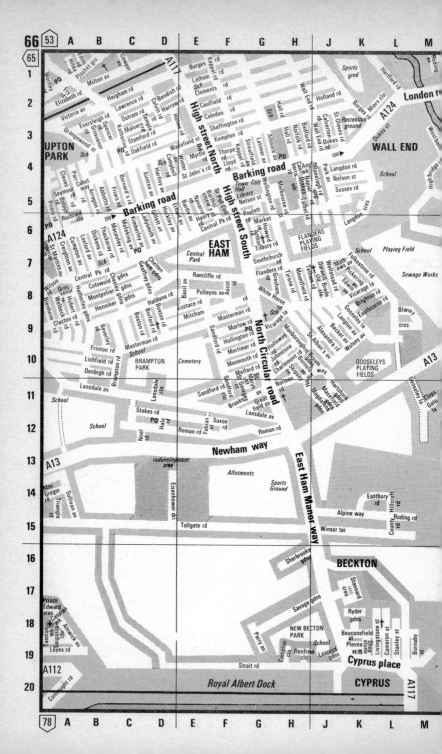

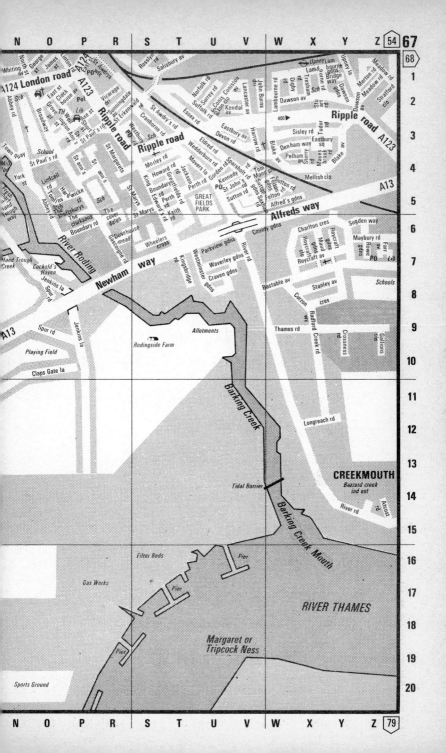

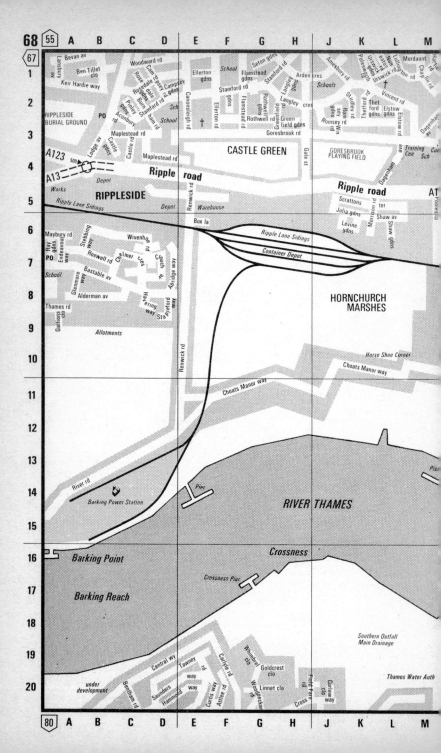

A B C D E F G H J K L M

1
2
3
4
5
6
7
8
9
10
11
12
13
14
15
16
17
18
19
20

Lansbury av
Bevan av
Kingsway
Ben Tillet clo
Keir Hardie way
Woodward rd
Can Erwall rd
Campsey
Ellerton gdns
School
Seton gdns
Flamstead gdns
Stamford rd
Arden cres
Amesbury rd
Schools
Mordaunt
Chaplin rd
Urswick rd

RIPPLESIDE BURIAL GROUND
PO
Rosedale clo
Rydens
Pinley gdns
Stamford rd
Aconbury
Burnham rd
Sch
Ellerton gdns
Stamford rd
School
Ellerton Pl
Flamstead gdns
Rothwell gdns
Langley gdns
Langley cres
Rothwell rd
Greenfield gdns
Green field gdns
Goresbrook rd
Studley rd
Romsey rd
Thetford gdns
Vincent rd
Elstow rd
Dagenham
Training Cen
Car
Sch

A123
500
Maplestead rd
Castle gdns
Lodge av
Castle rd
Maplestead rd
CASTLE GREEN
Gale st
GORESBROOK PLAYING FIELD
Dagenham ave

A13
Depot
Ripple road
Ripple road
AT

Works
RIPPLESIDE
Depot
Warehouse
Scrattons ter
Julia gdns
Levine gdns
Morrison rd
Shaw av
Shaw gdns
Pooleslg

Ripple Lane Sidings
Renwick rd
Box la

Maybury rd
Rav gdns
PO
Endeavour way
Stebbing way
Roxwell rd
Wivenhoe rd
Celmer cres
Couch ave
Abridge way
Ripple Lane Sidings
Container Depot

School
Glenmore way
Bastable av
Alderman av
Havering way
Stapleford way
HORNCHURCH MARSHES

Thames rd
Galleons clo
Allotments

Renwick rd
Horse Shoe Corner
Choats Manor way

Choats Manor way

RIVER THAMES

River rd
Barking Power Station
Pier
Pier

Barking Point
Crossness

Barking Reach
Crossness Pier

Southern Outfall Main Drainage

Central wy
Tawney way
Curtis way
Saunders way
Hammond way
Bonham rd
Atllee rd
Carlyle rd
Whinbeck clo
Goldcrest clo
Linnet clo
Woodpecker
Fried Fare rd
Cross
Curlew way
Thames Water Auth

under development

A B C D E F G H J K L M

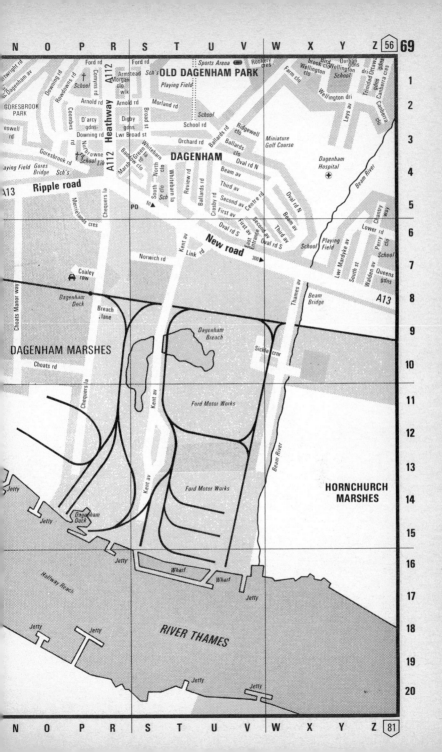

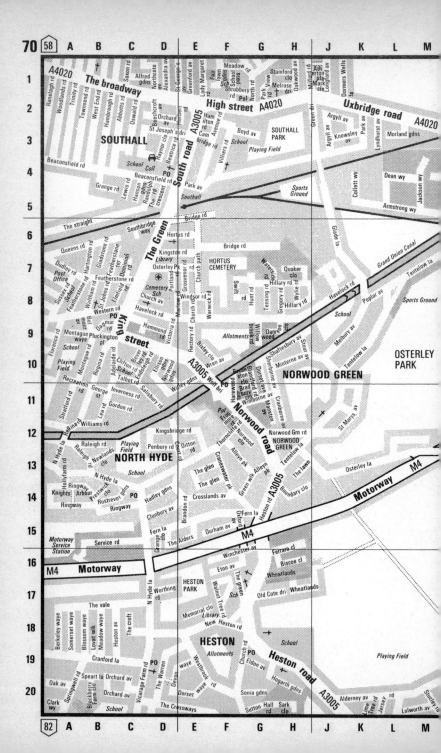

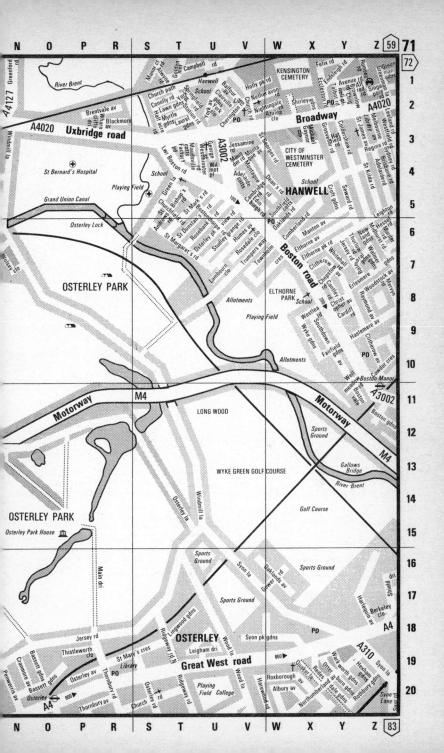

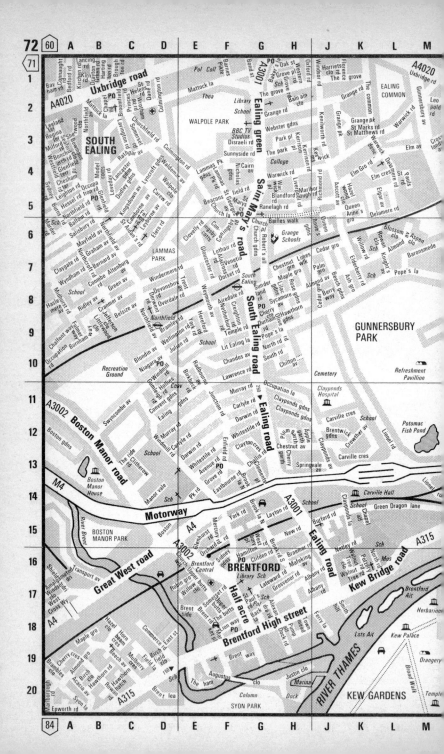

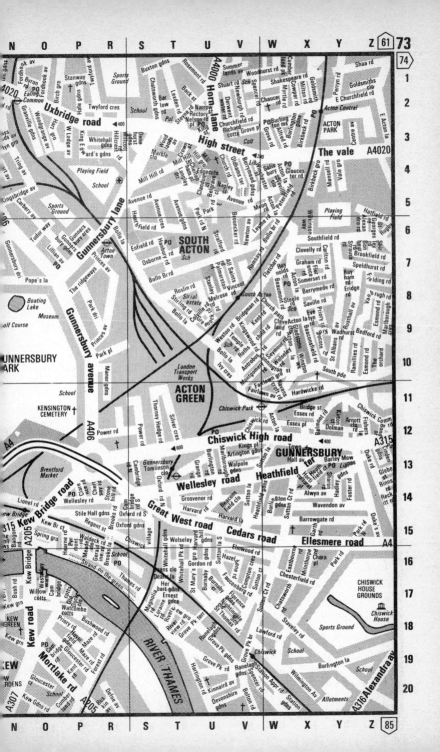

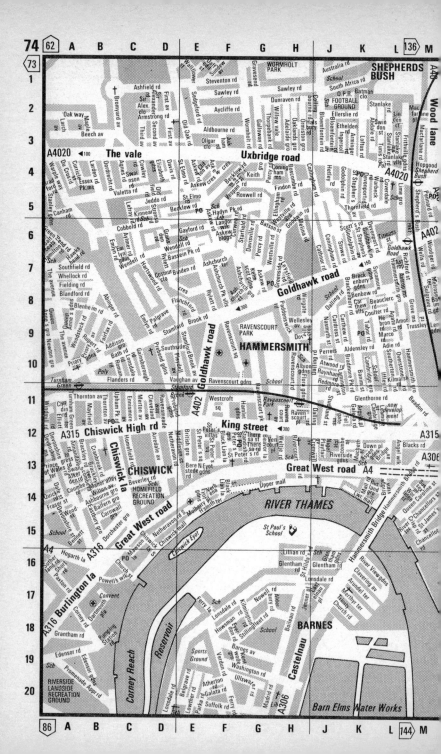

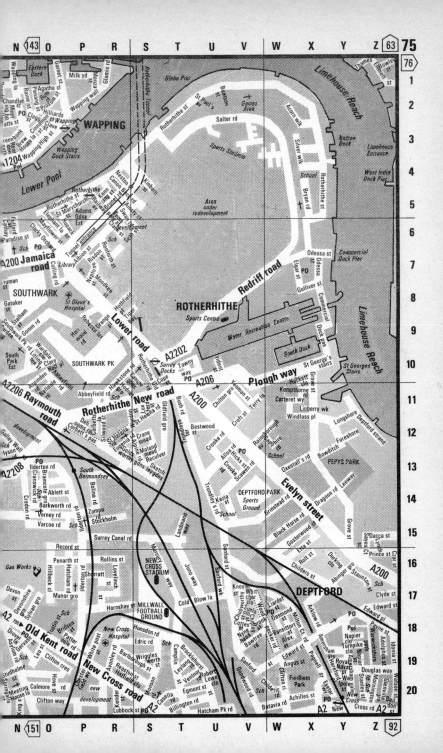

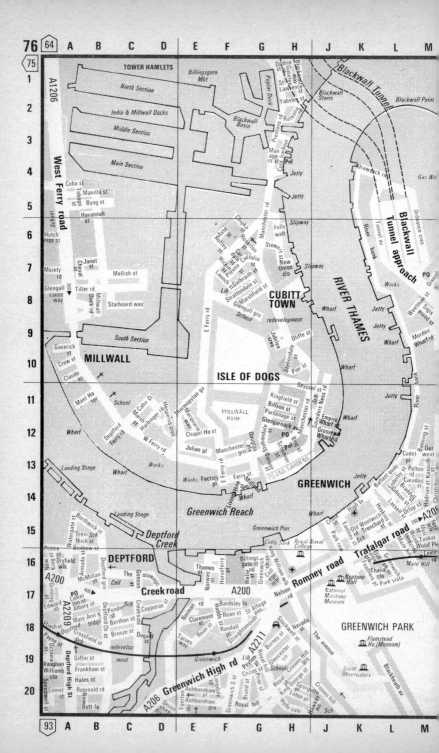

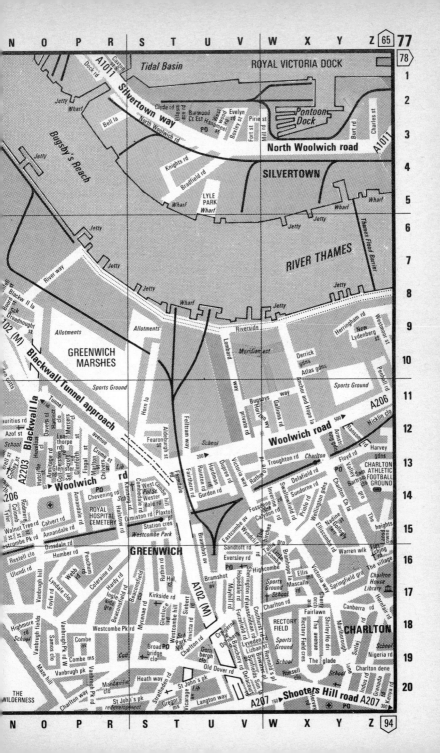

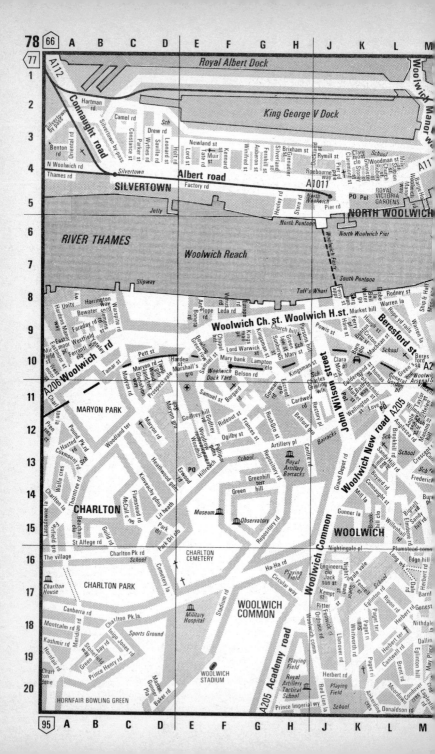

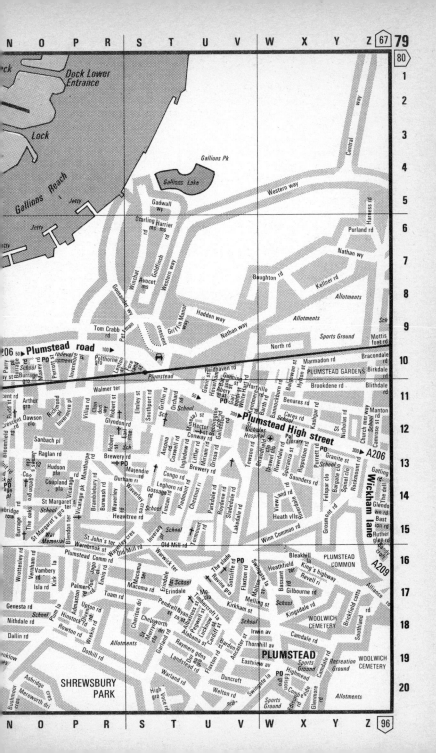

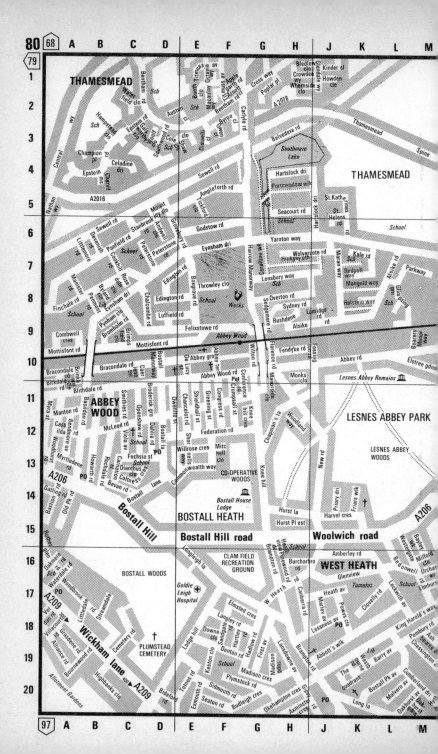

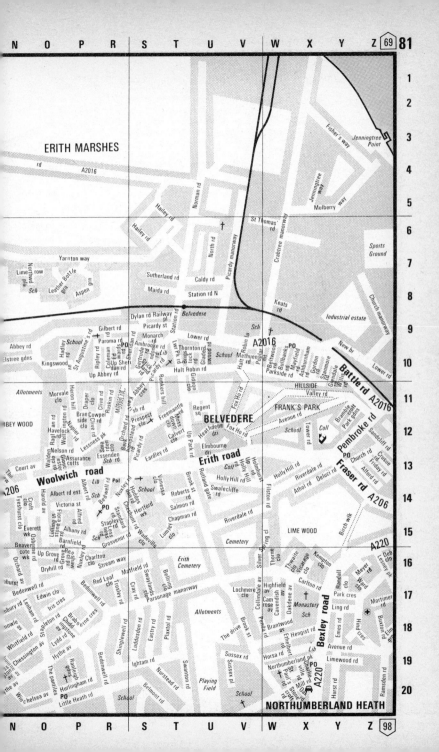

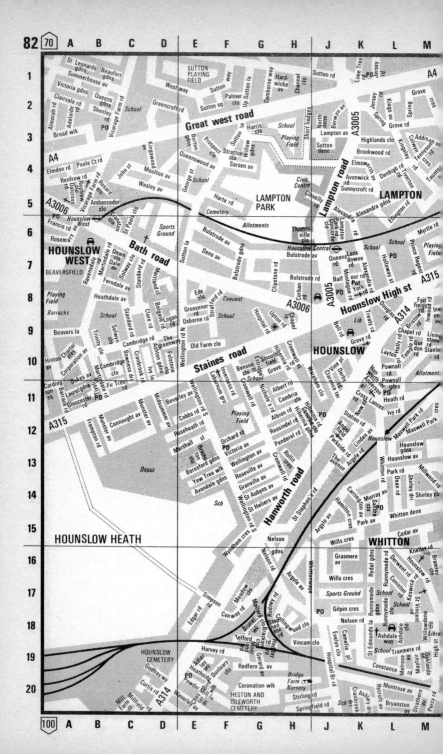

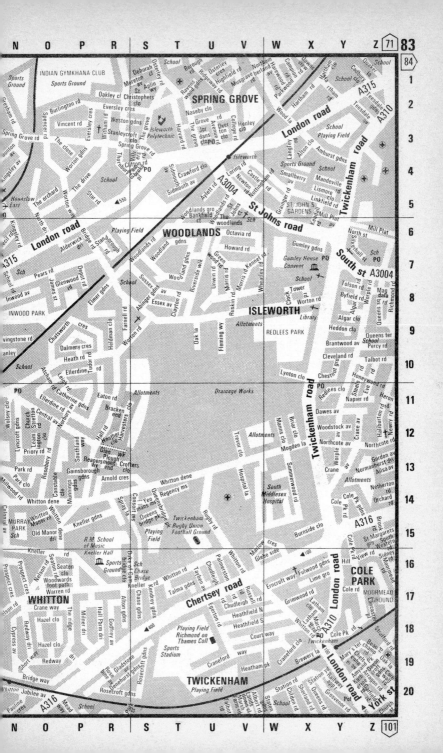

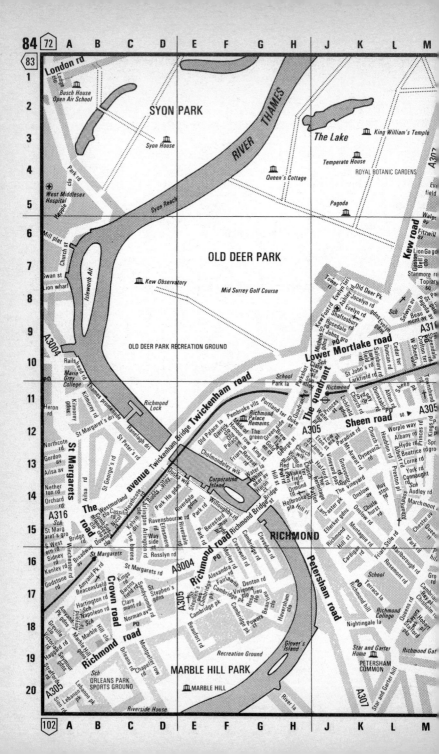

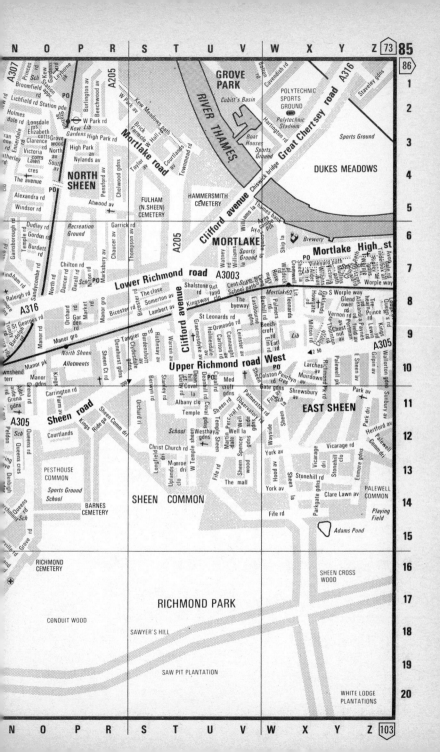

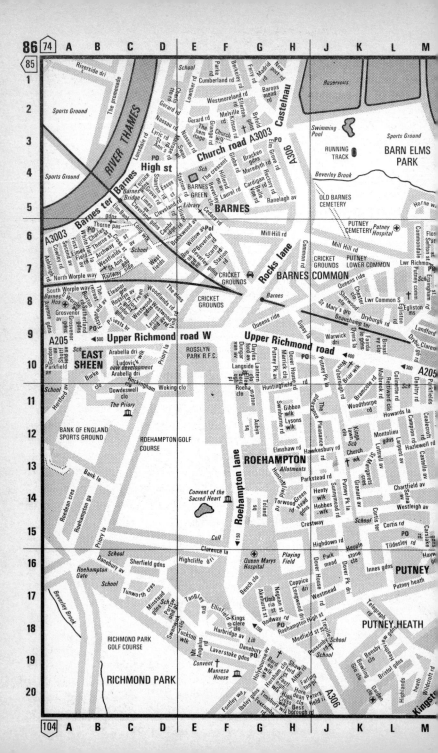

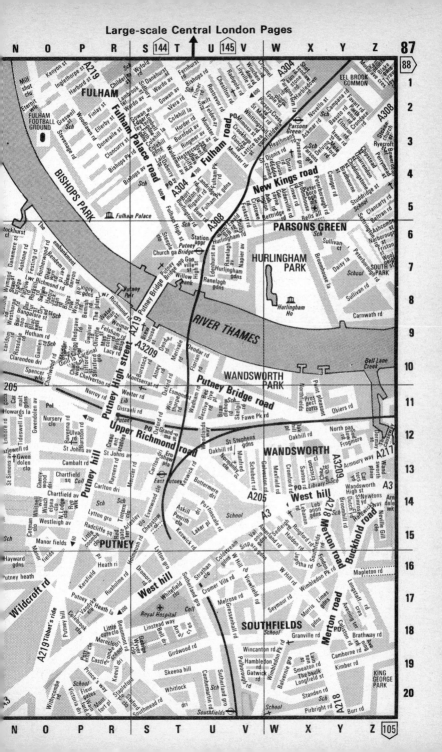

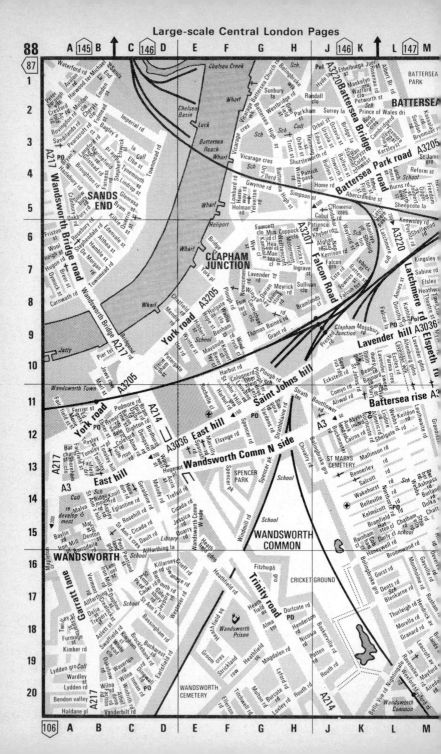

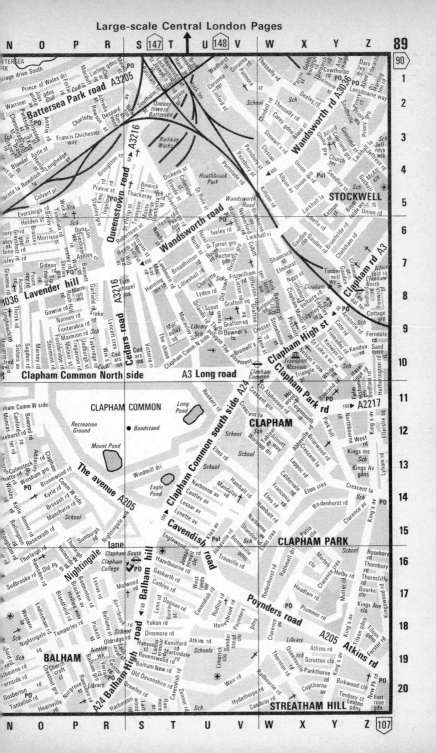

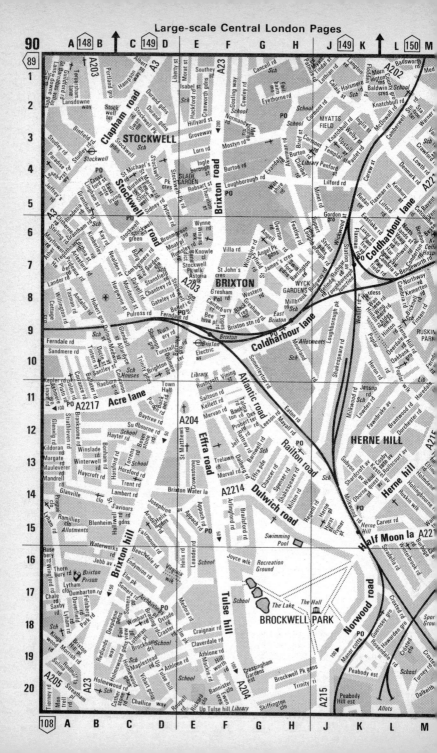

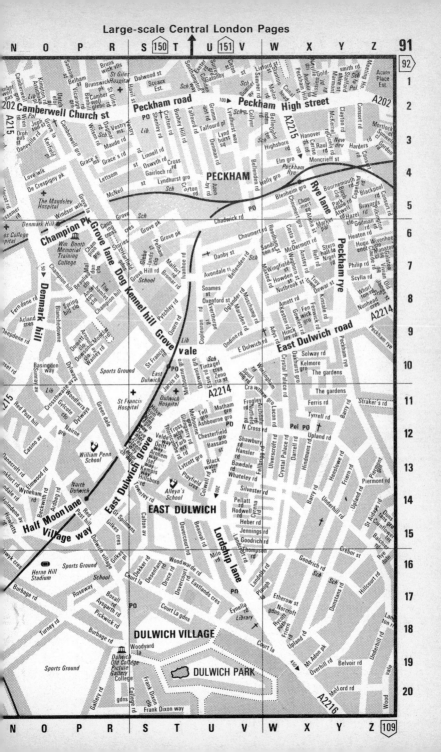

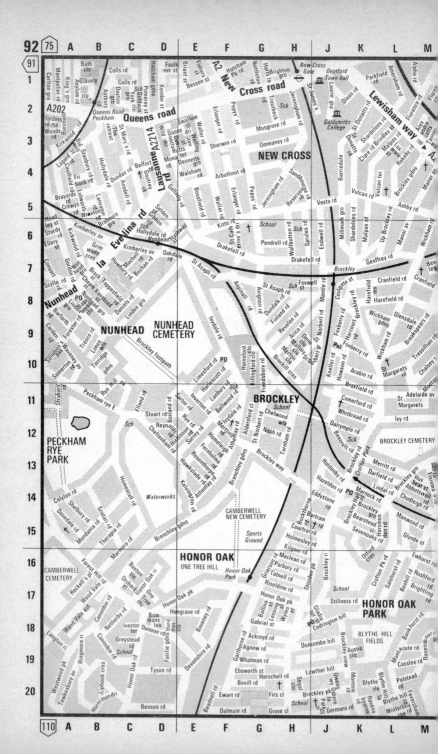

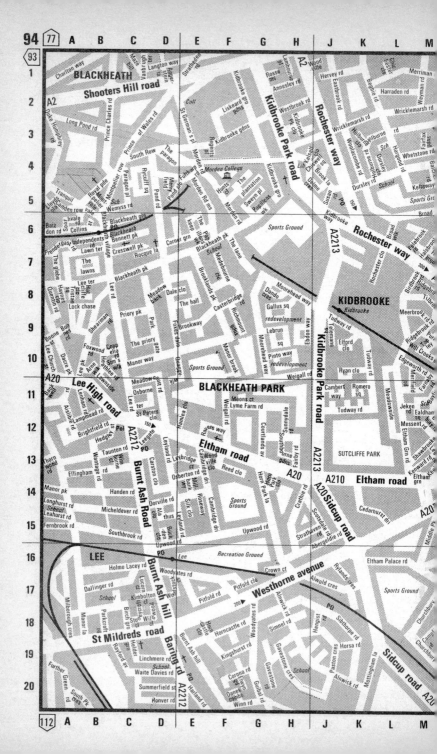

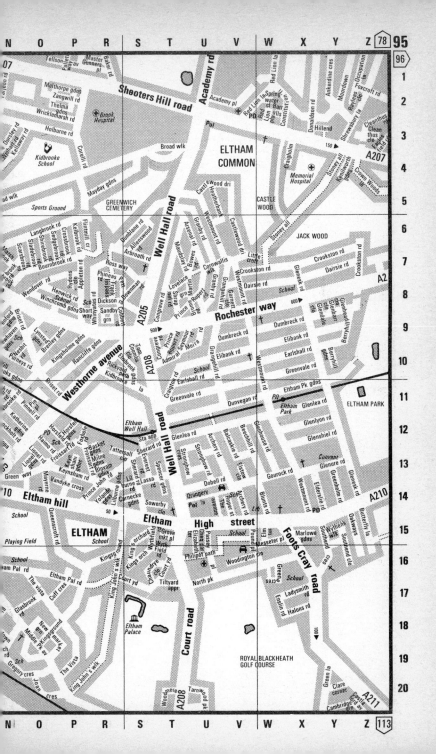

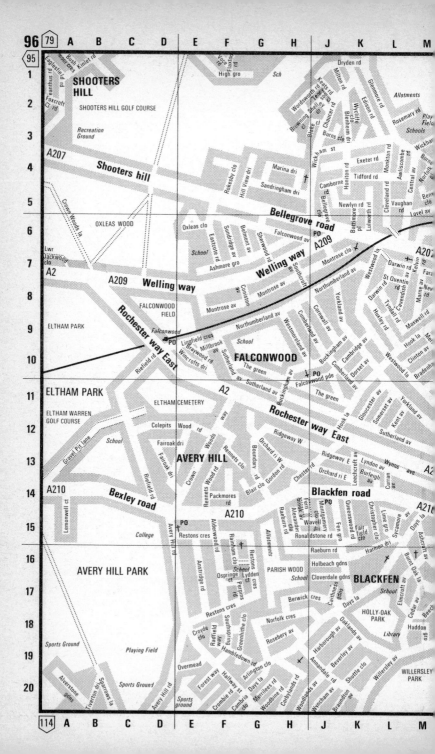

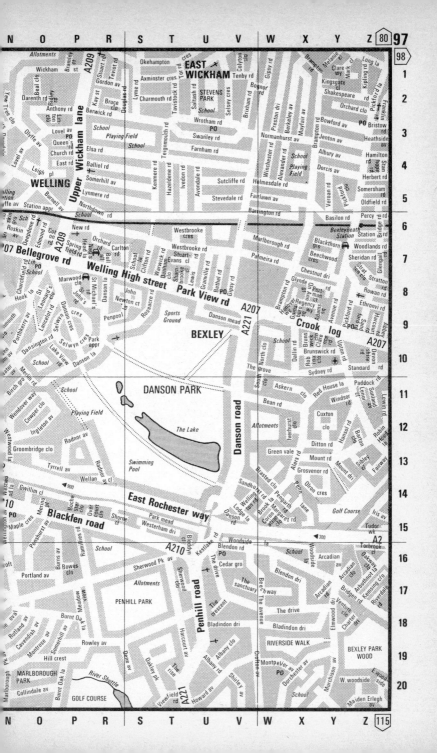

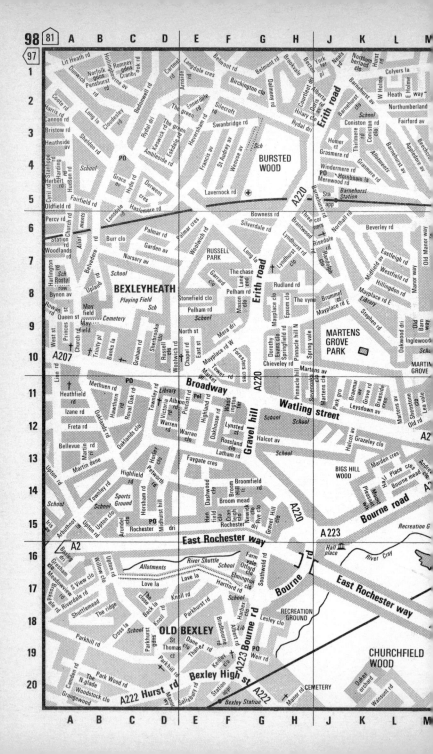

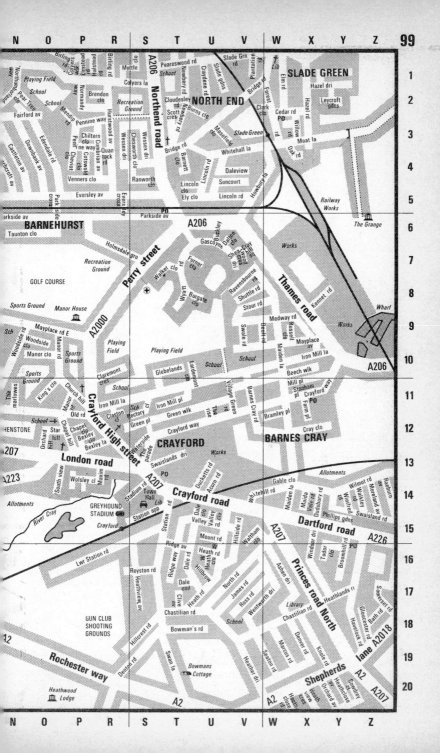

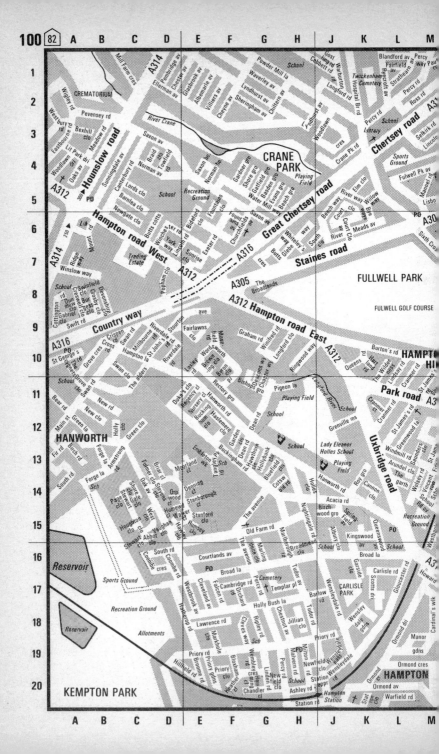

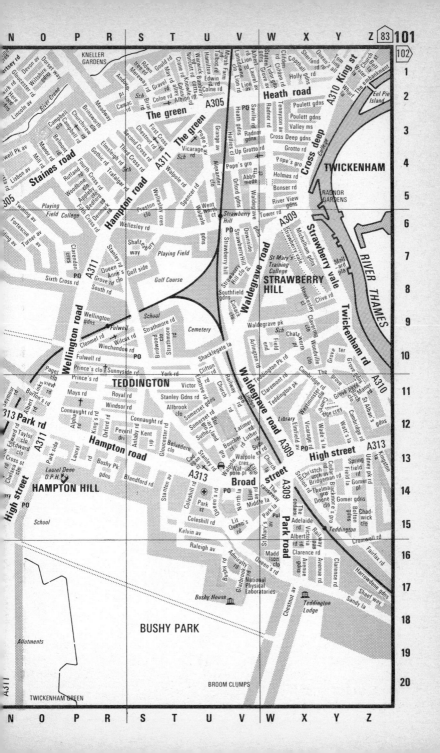

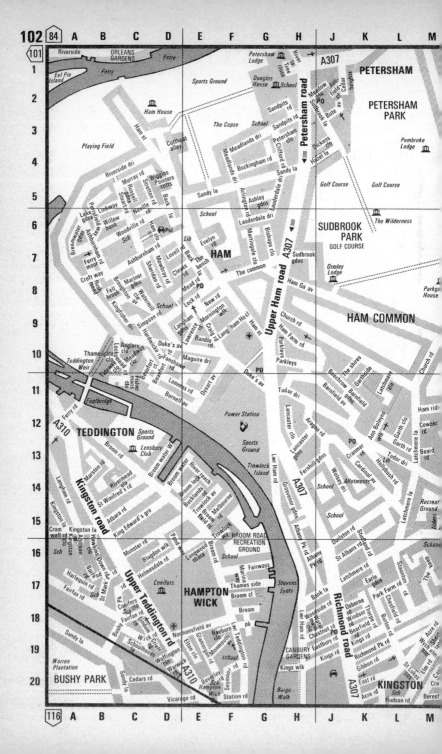

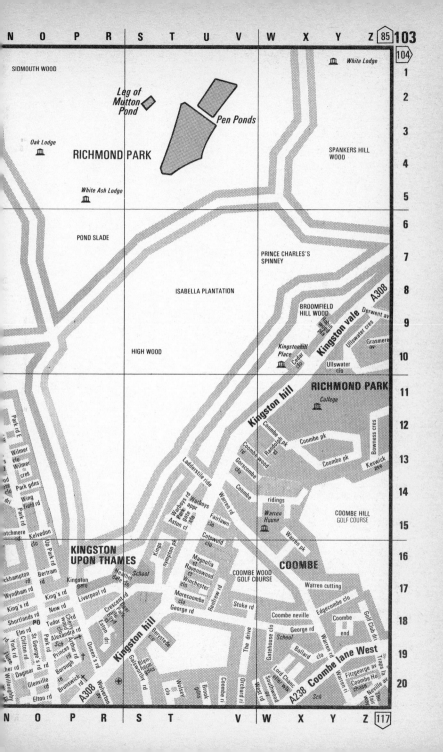

SIDMOUTH WOOD

White Lodge

Leg of Mutton Pond

Pen Ponds

Oak Lodge

RICHMOND PARK

SPANKERS HILL WOOD

White Ash Lodge

POND SLADE

PRINCE CHARLES'S SPINNEY

ISABELLA PLANTATION

BROOMFIELD HILL WOOD

A308

Kingston vale

Derwent av

Ullswater cres

Grasmere av

HIGH WOOD

Kingstonhill Place

Cedar

Ullswater clo

Ullswater

RICHMOND PARK

Kingston hill

College

Bowness cres

Coombe hi rd

Coombe pk

Randolph rd

Coombe pk

Coombewood

Keswick ave

Lauderdale ride

Gorscombe clo

Coombe

Warren rd

ridings

COOMBE HILL GOLF COURSE

Warren House

Warren pk

Park rd E

Wilmer clo

Wilmer cres

Park gdns

Wing field rd

Park rd

Wadboys rd Wadboys

app

Park gate clo

Aston ct

Fairlawn clo

dri

Kelvedon clo

Cotswold clo

atchmere rd

ckhampton rd

Bertram rd

KINGSTON UPON THAMES

Kings nympton pk

School

Magnolia ct

Ravenswood clo

Winchester clo

COOMBE

COOMBE WOOD GOLF COURSE

Warren cutting

Wyndham rd

King's gate

Kingston gate

Heather dale clo

Morecoombe clo

Renfrew rd

Stoke rd

Coombe neville

Edgecombe clo

Coombe end

Golf Club dri

King's rd

Liverpool rd

New rd

George rd

The drive

Coombe neville

George rd

Warren

Shortlands rd

PO

Tudor drd

Crd

Cherry

Orch

Crescent rd

Exton dri

School

Gatehouse clo

Ballard clo

Coombe lane West

Elm rd

Clifton rd

St George's rd

Park rd

Sch

Alexandra rd

Princes rd

Berystede

Kingston hill

Lord Chanc

after walk

Fitzgeorge av

Coombe Ho

chase

her rd

Dagnar rd

York rd

Queen s rd

Borough

Galsworthy rd

Blen heim gdns

Traps

Neville av

Willoughby

Glenville rd

Brunswick rd

A308 Wolverton

Wolsey clo

Brook gdns

Coombe ri

West rd

Southwood

A238 Coombe lane West

Warren ri

Elton rd

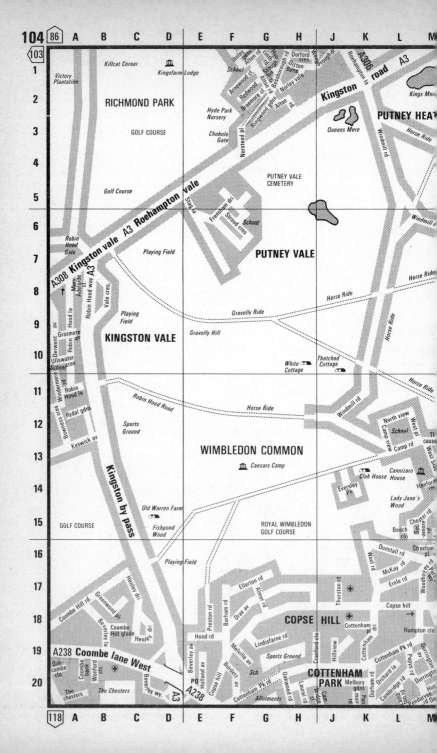

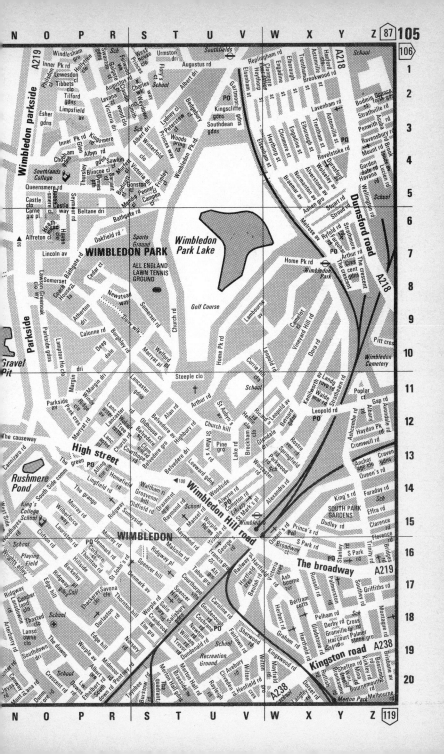

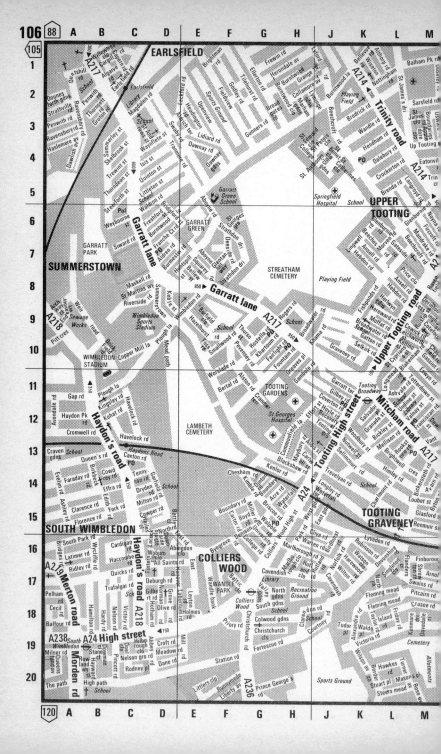

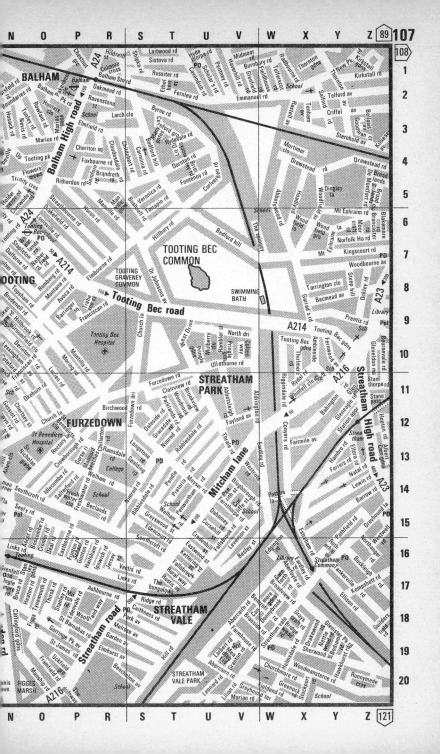

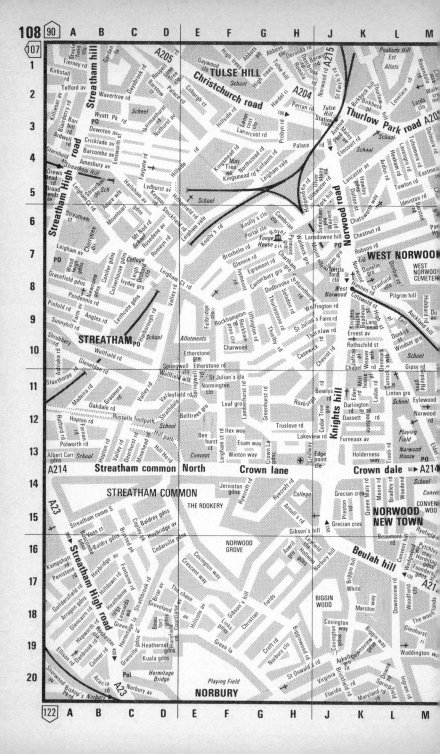

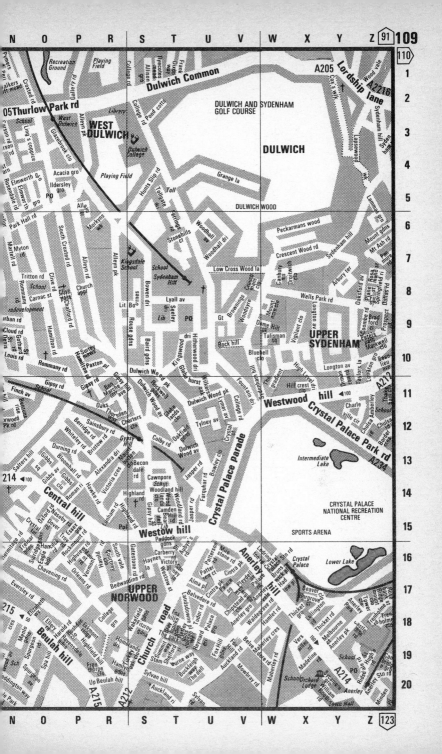

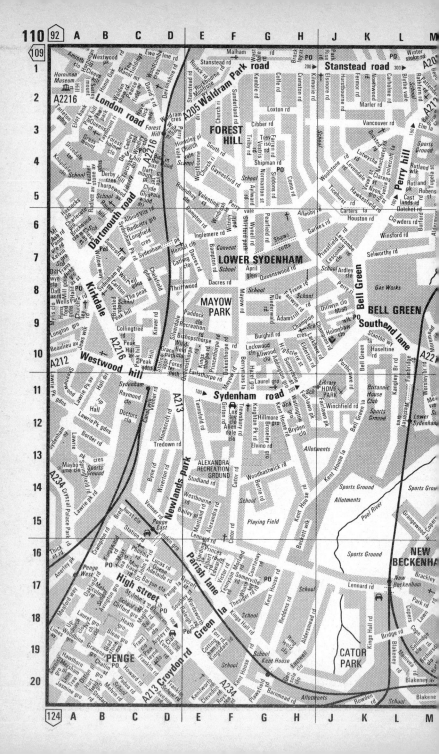

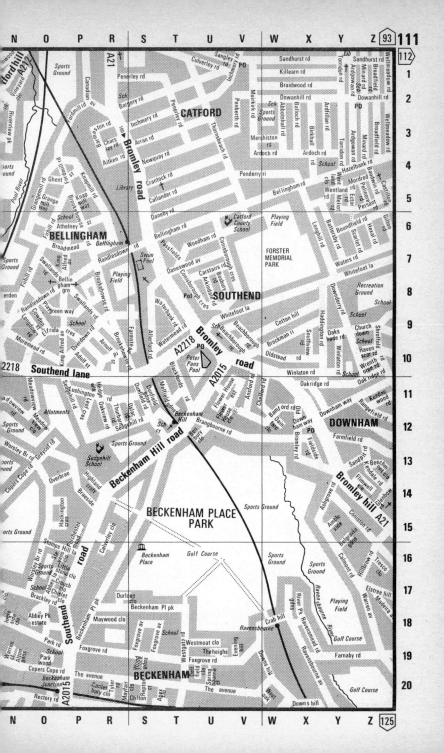

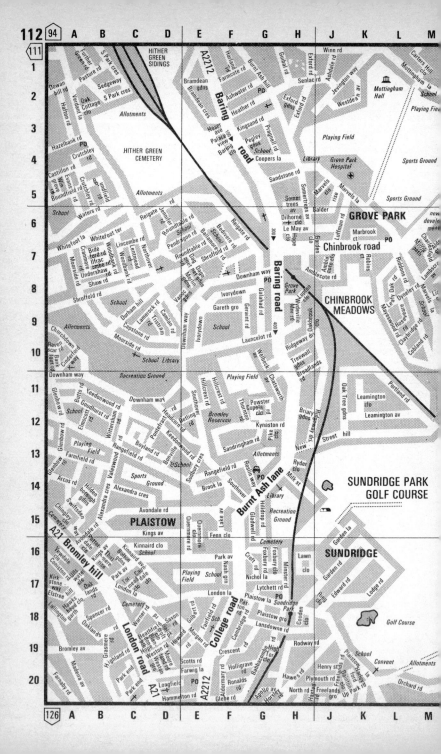

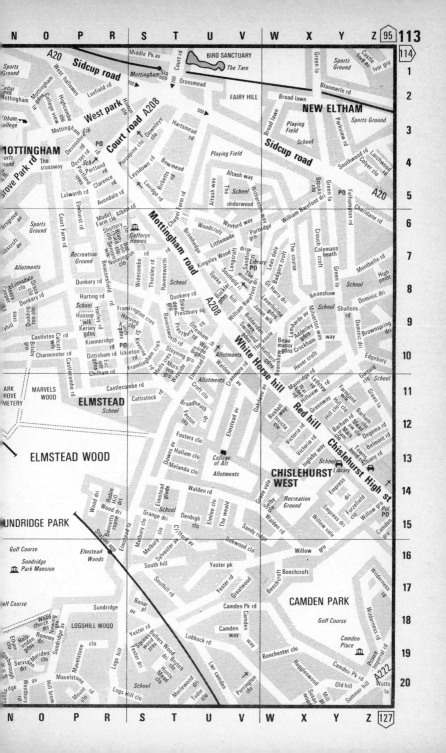

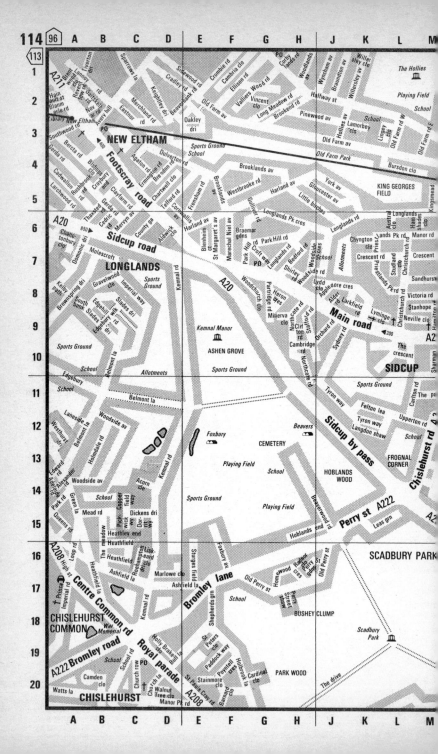

A21

NEW ELTHAM

Footscray road

Sidcup road

LONGLANDS

A20

Sports Ground

ASHEN GROVE

Sports Ground

Kemnal Manor

School

Edgebury

Belmont la

Woodside av

Foxbury

CEMETERY

Playing Field

School

Sports Ground

Playing Field

Kemnal rd

Sidcup by pass

FROGNAL CORNER

HOBLANDS WOOD

Beaverwood rd

Perry st A222

Hoblands end

Leas grn

SCADBURY PARK

Chislehurst rd

Centre Common rd

CHISLEHURST COMMON

War Memorial

A222 Bromley road

Royal parade

Bromley lane

Old Perry st

School

BUSHEY CLUMP

Scadbury Park

PARK WOOD

The drive

CHISLEHURST

King Georges Field

Old Farm Park

Old Farm av

Bursdon clo

Main road

SIDCUP

The crescent

Sports Ground

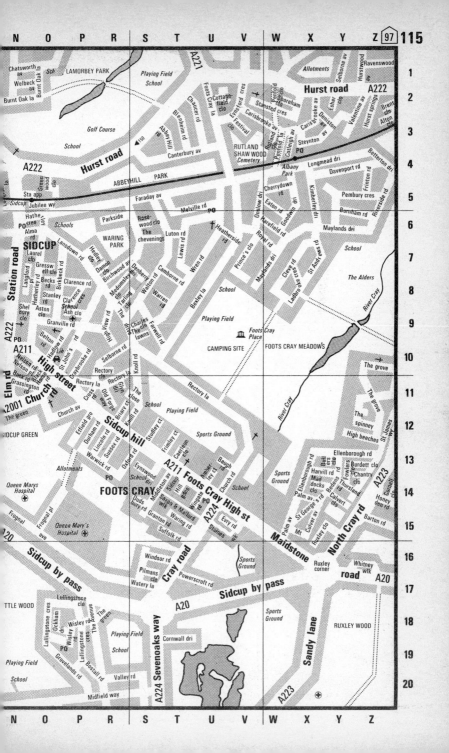

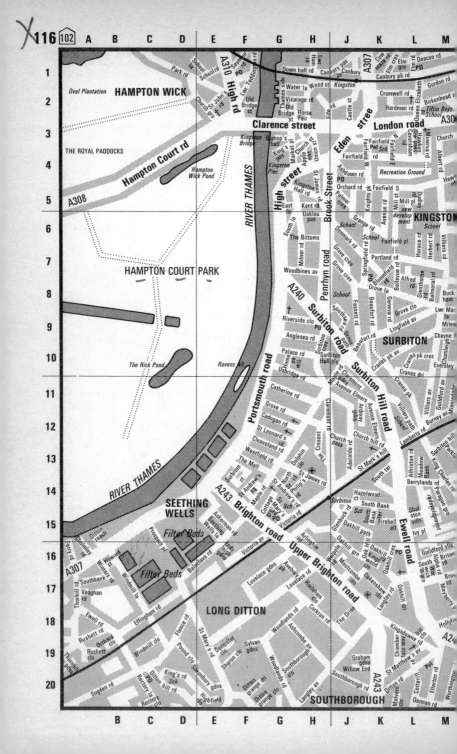

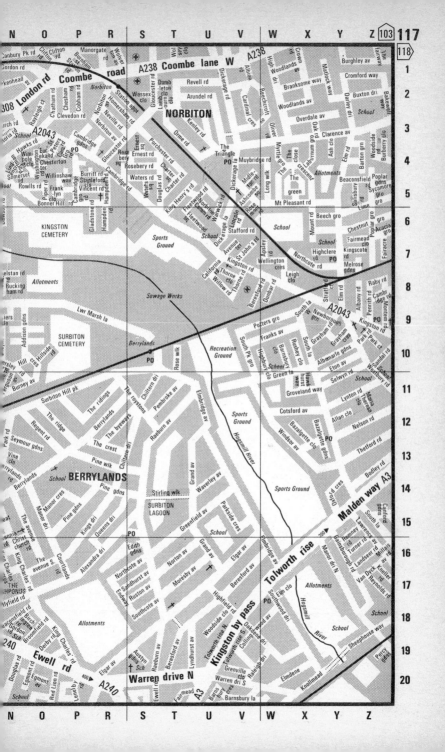

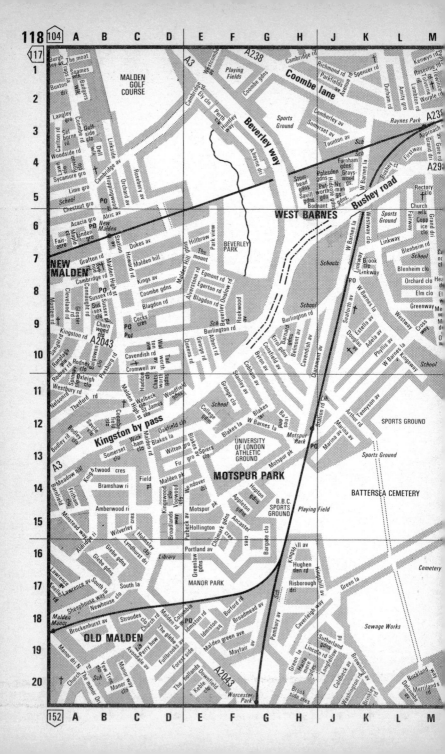

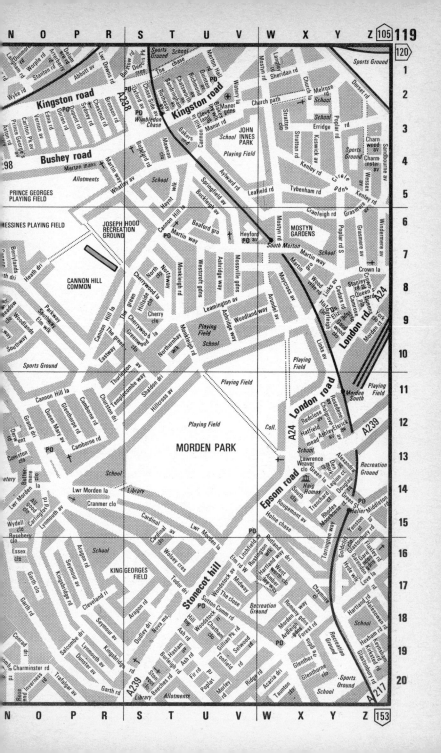

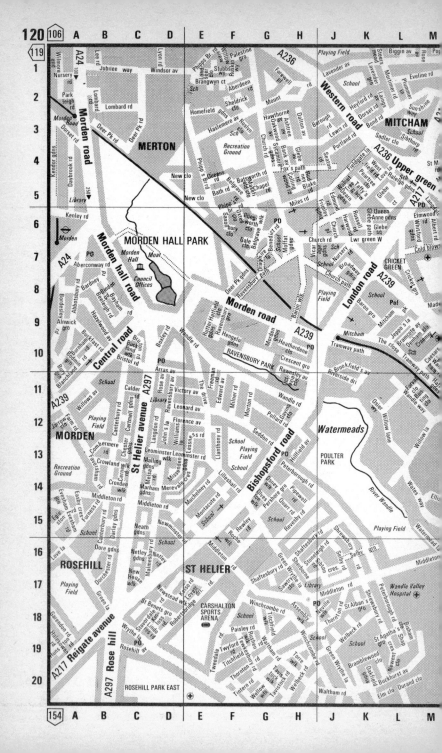

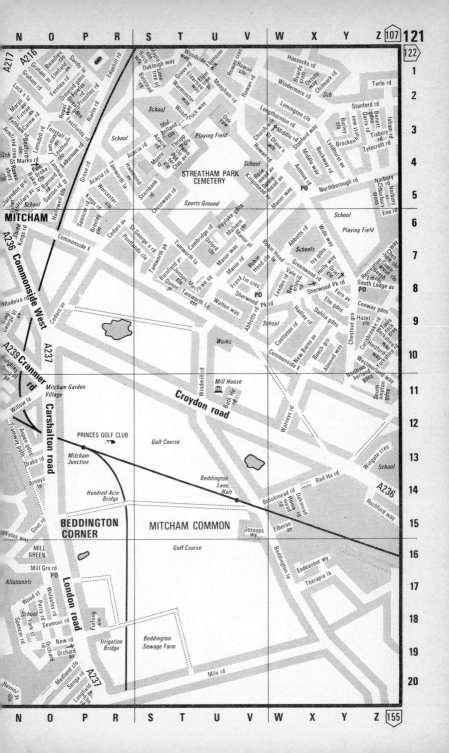

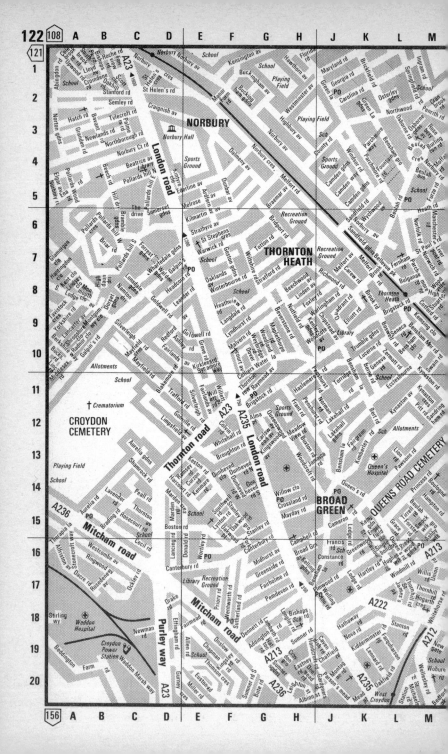

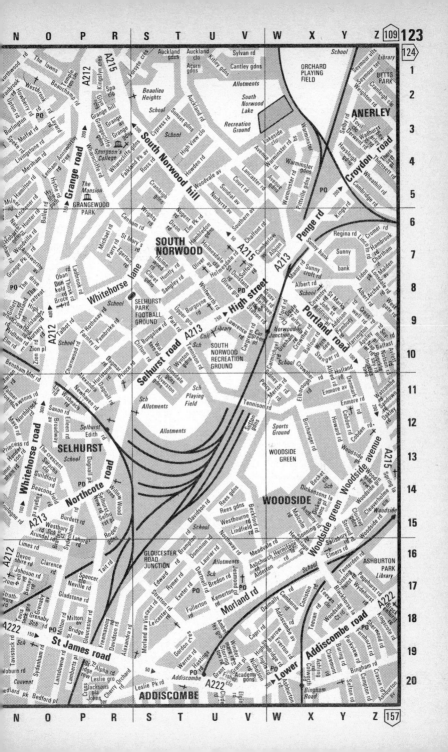

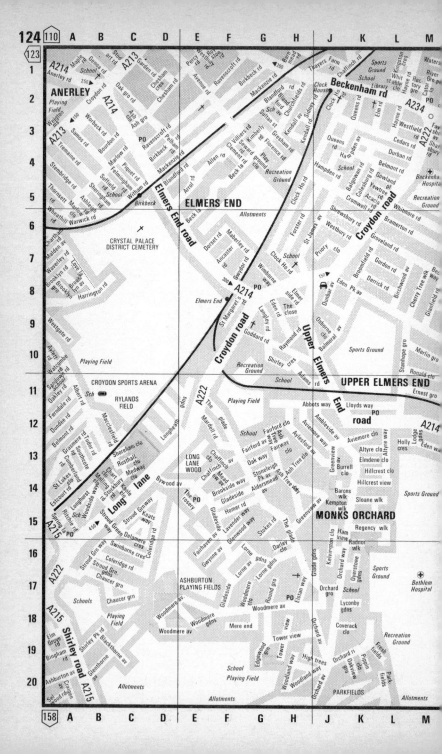

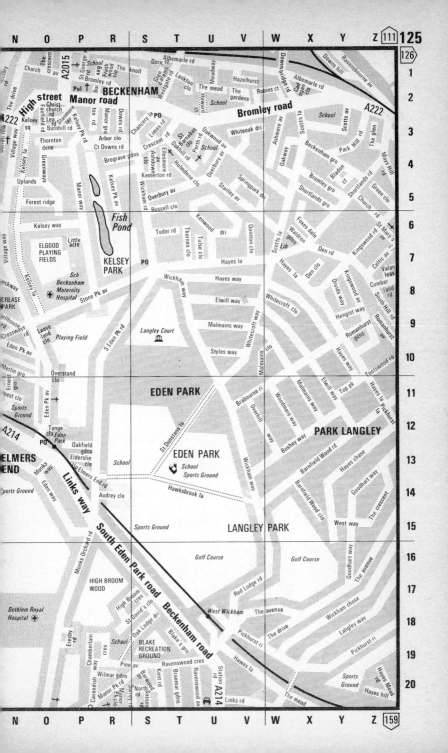

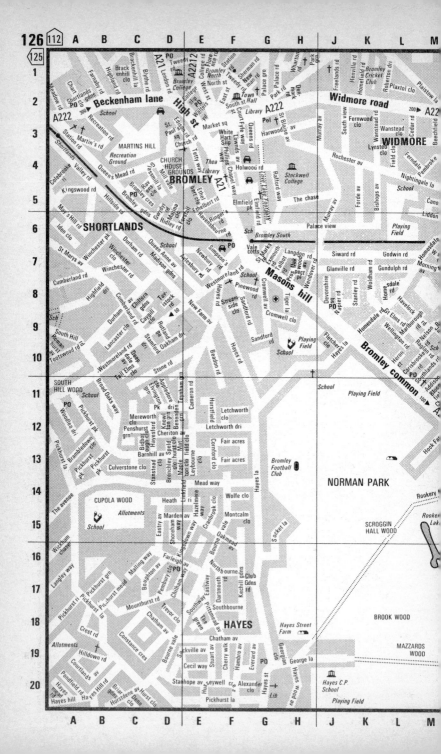

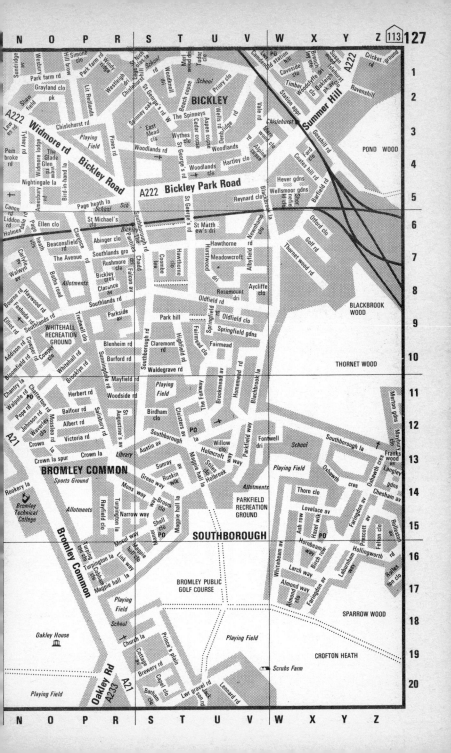

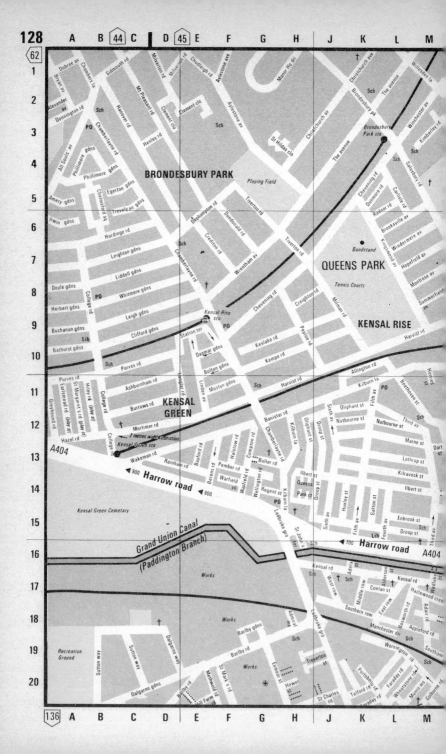

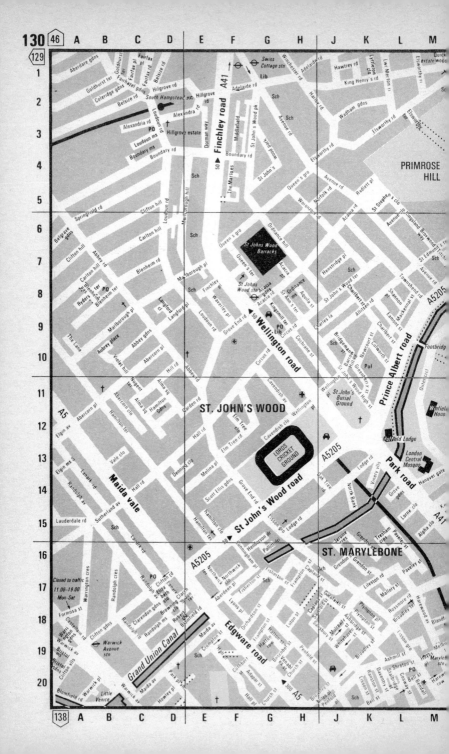

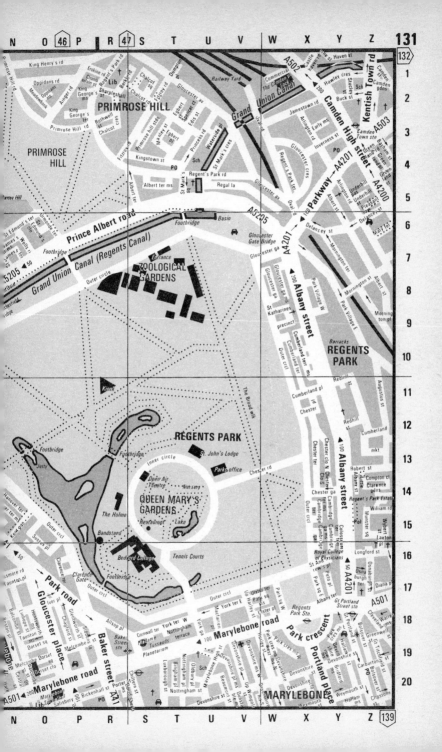

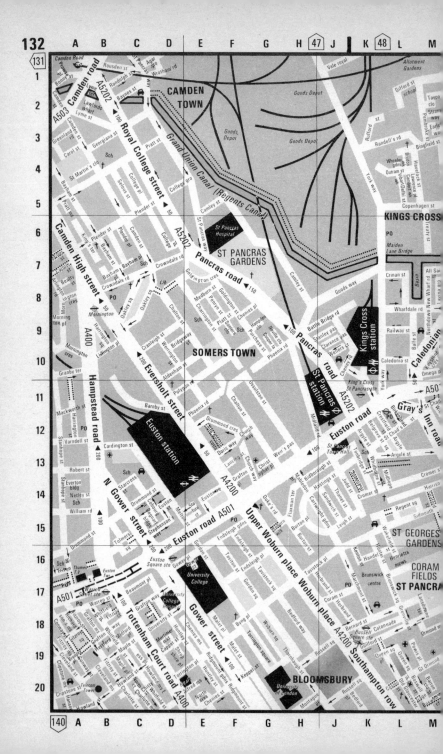

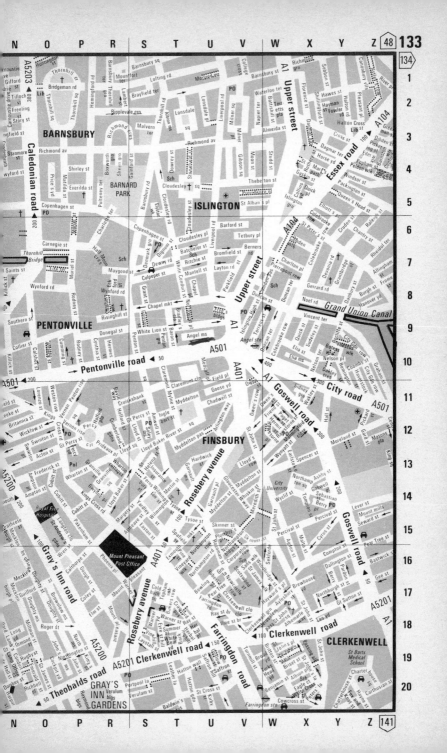

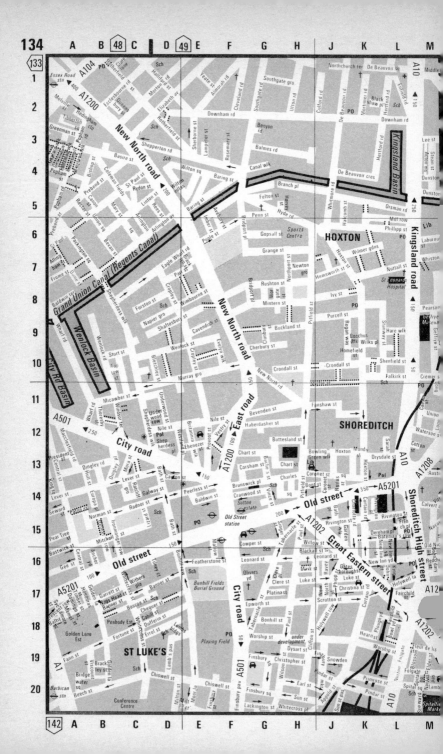

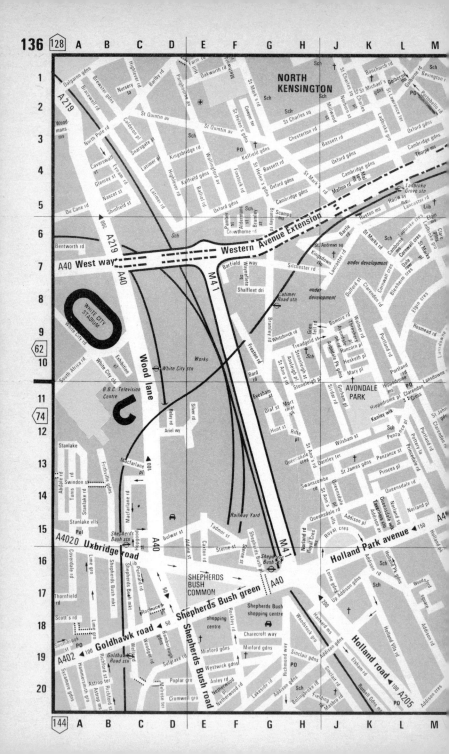

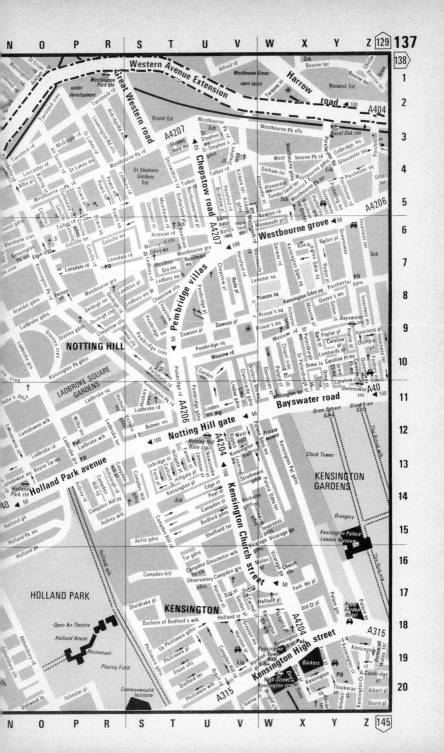

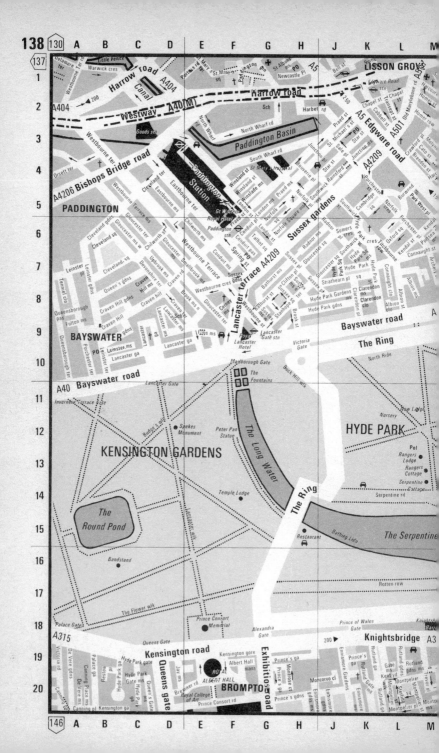

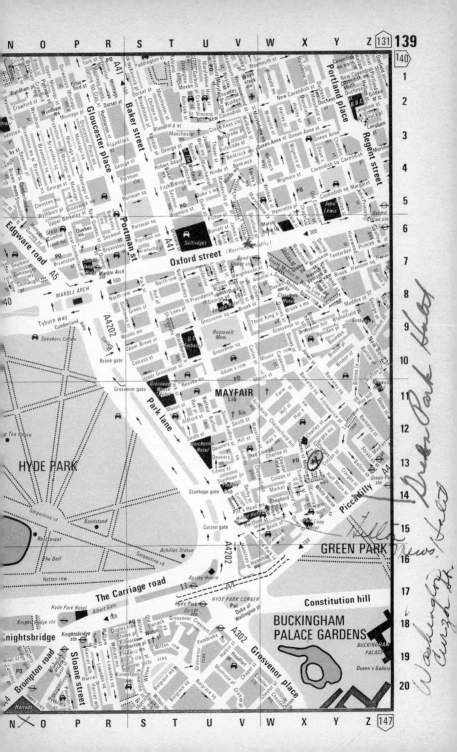

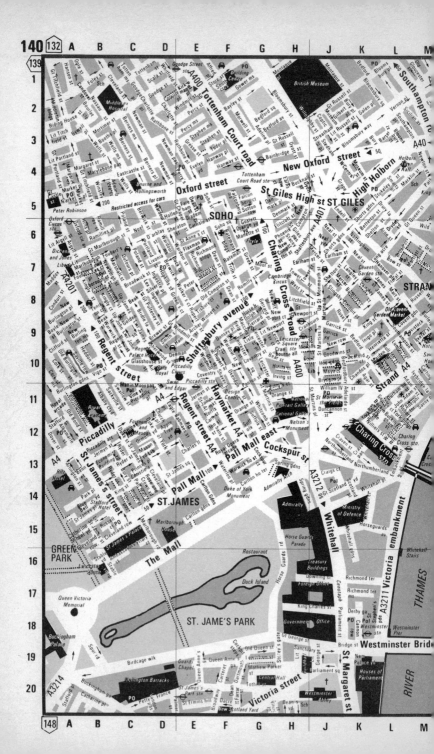

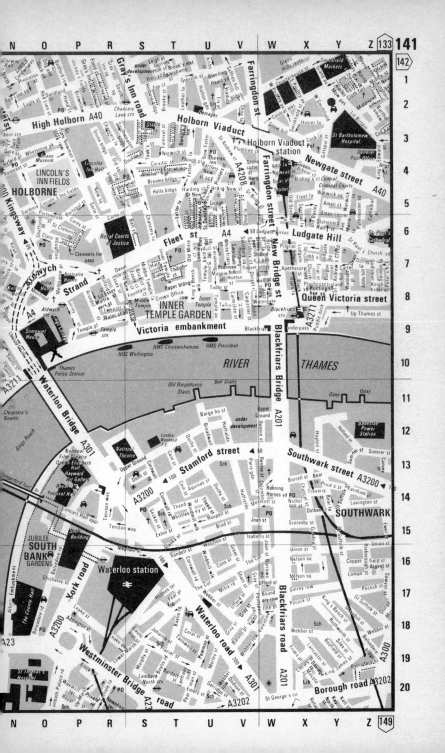

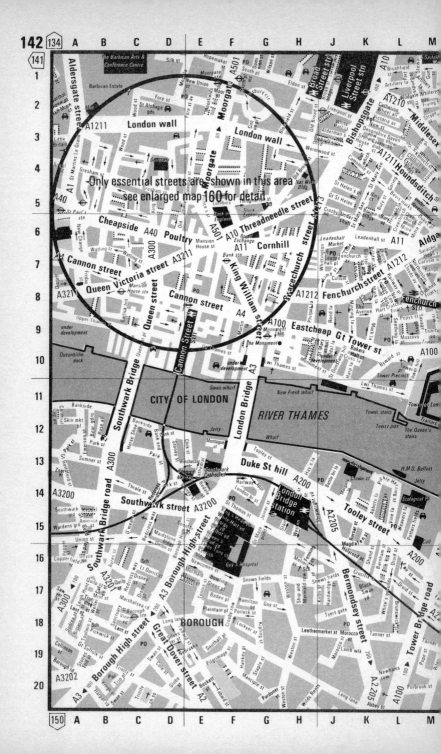

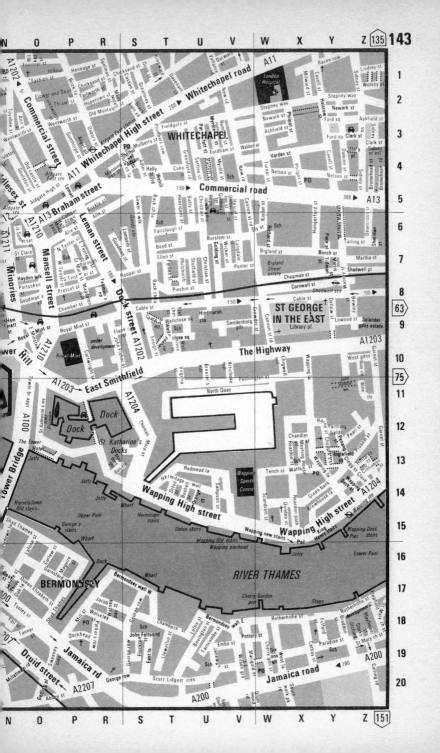

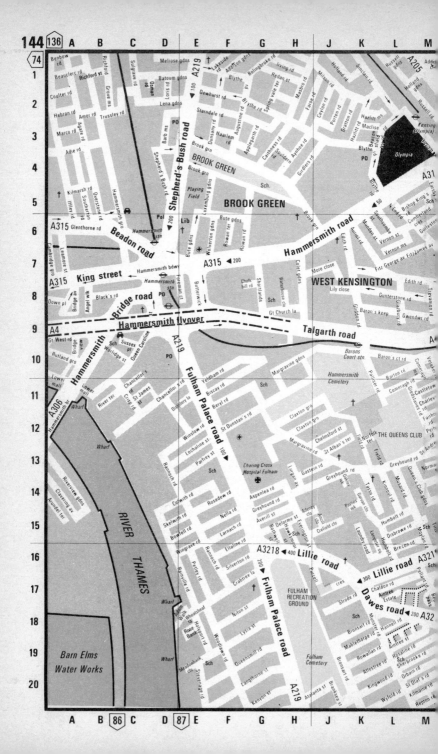

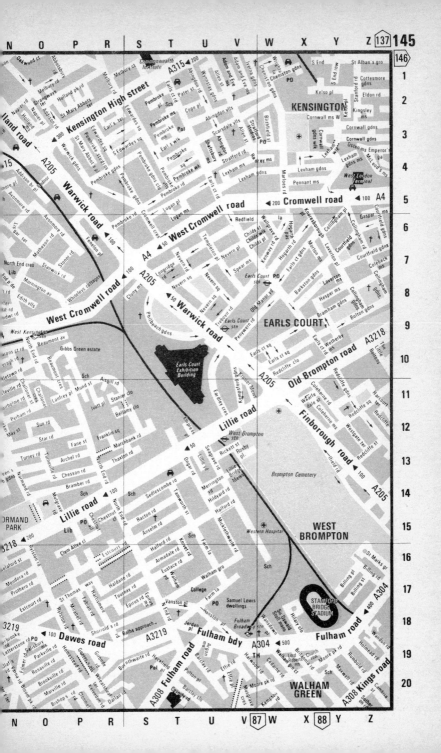

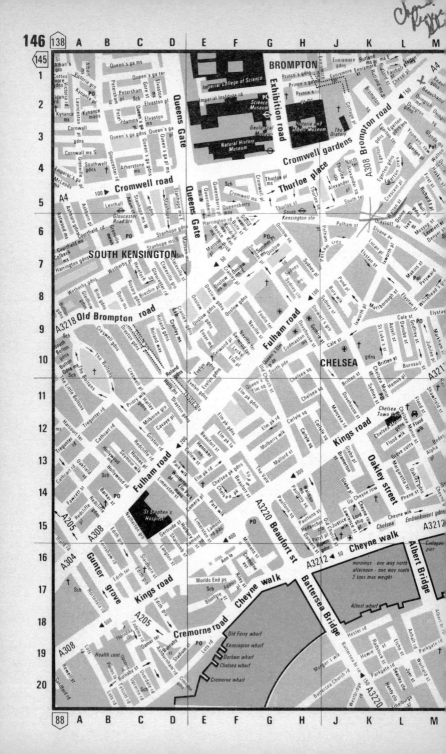

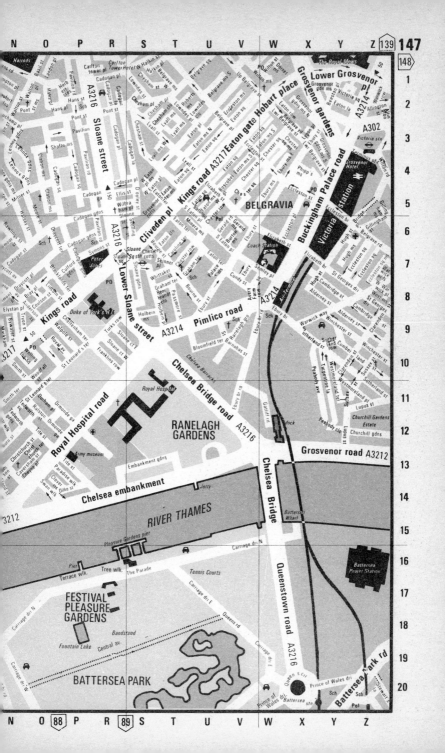

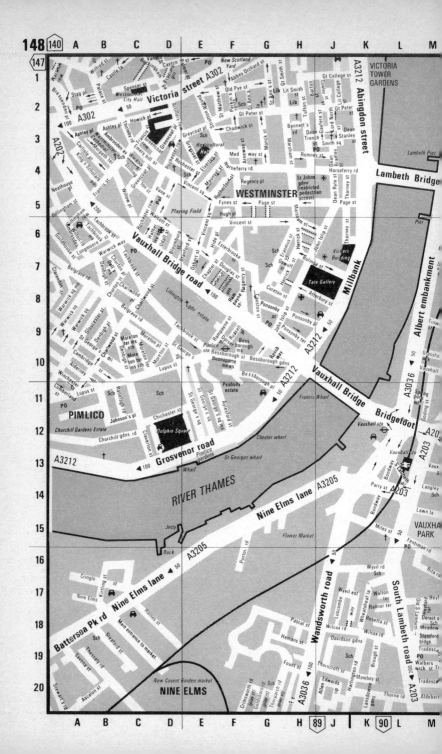

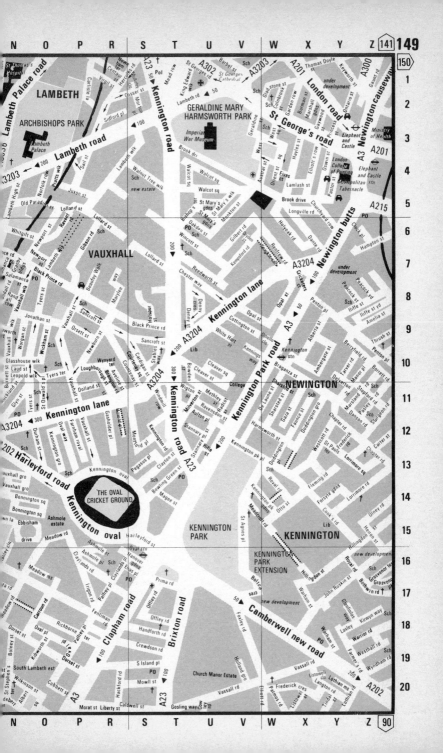

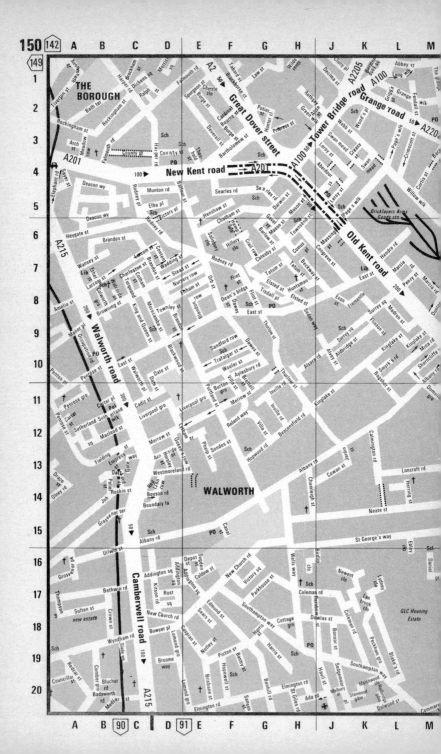

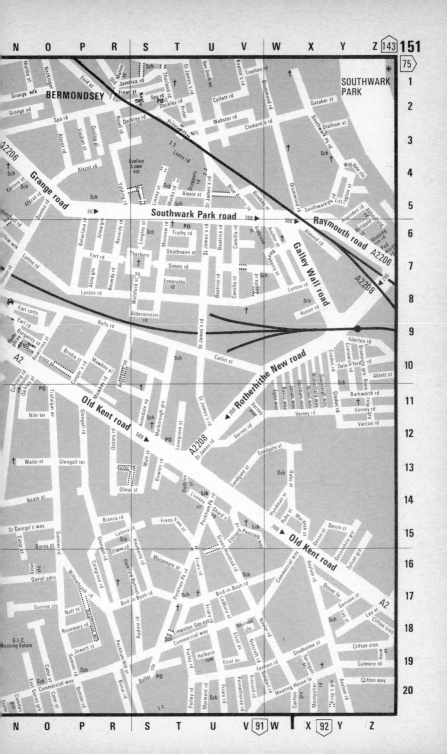

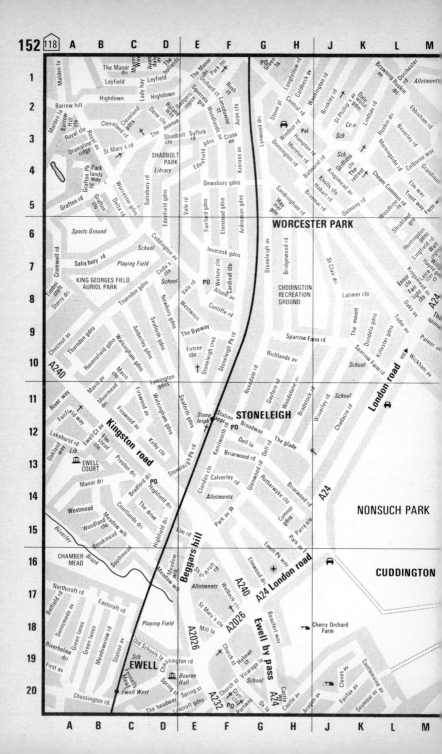

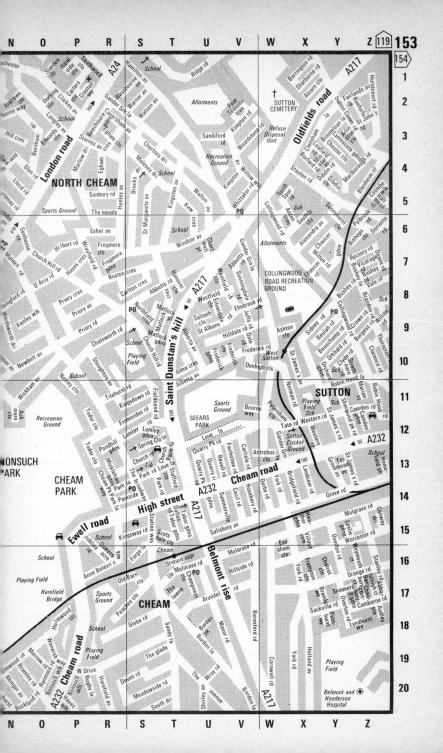

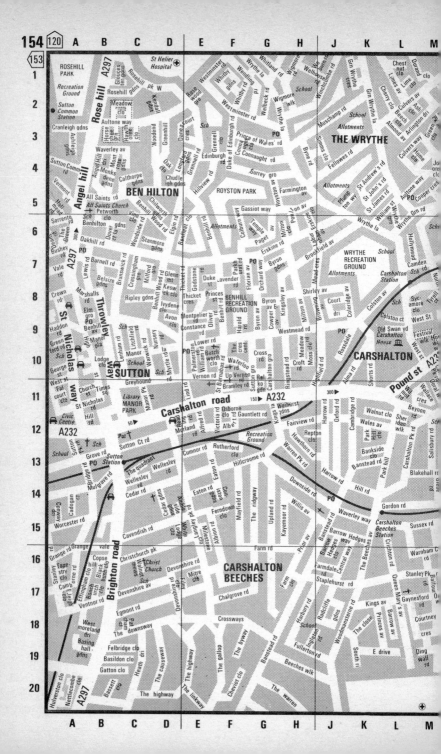

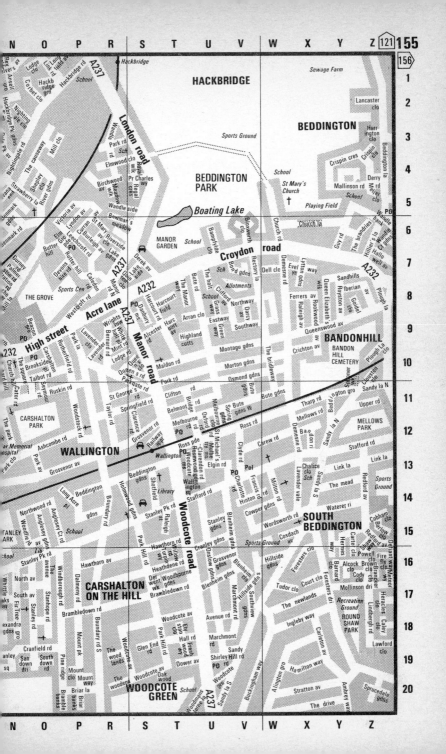

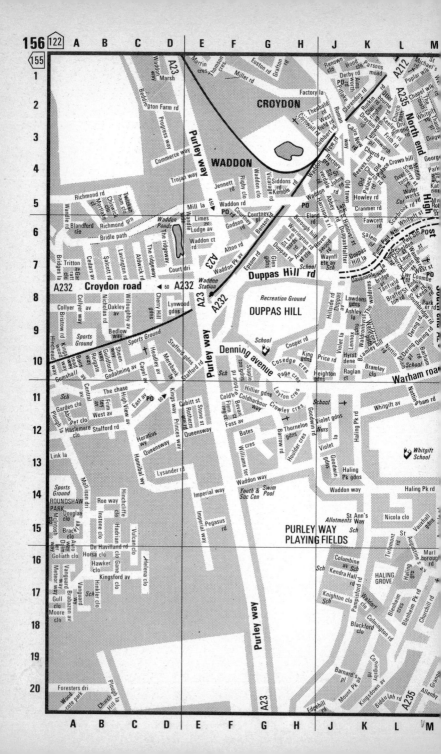

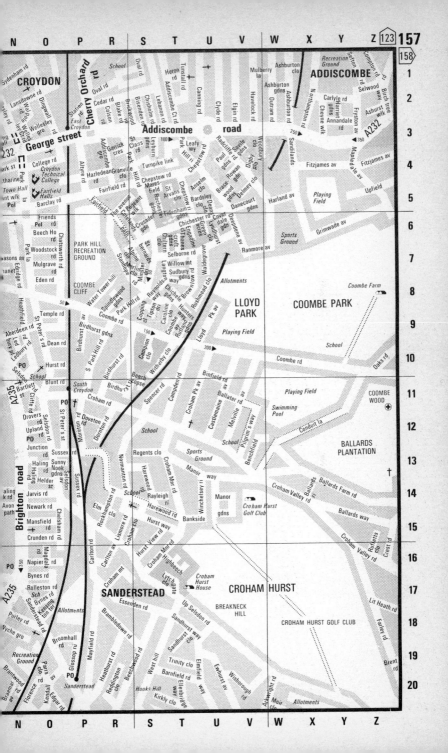

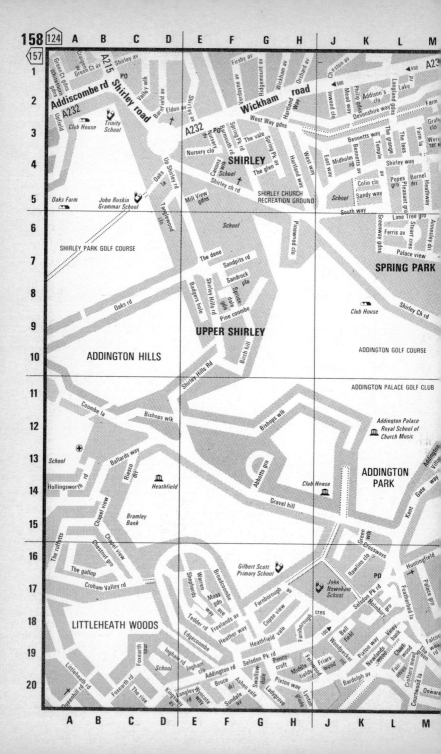

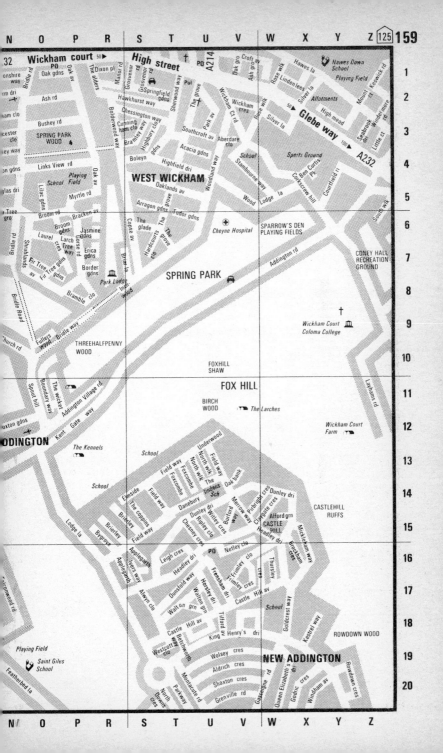

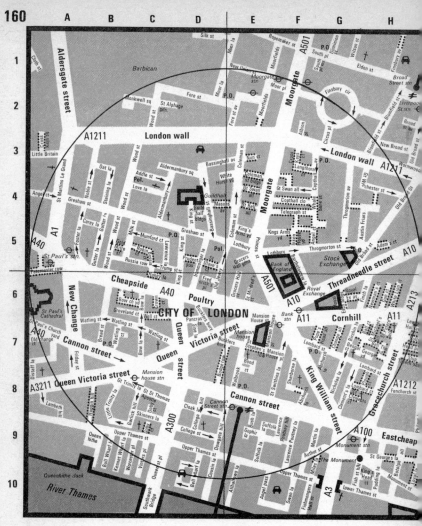

Enlargement of crowded city area for extra clarity

NICHOLSON

LONDON INFORMATION SERVICE

CONTENTS

Emergency and late night help	ii
Telephone Services	iii
Lost Property	iii
Police Stations	iv
Tourist Information	vi
Car Hire	vi
Coach Hire	vii
Cycle Hire	vii
Taxis and Minicabs	vii
Air Services	vii
Rail Terminals	viii
London Underground Map	ix
Day Bus Map (Central London)	x
Night Bus Map (Central London)	xi
Shopping Map (Central London)	xii
Theatres and Cinemas Map (Central London)	xiii
Public Transport	xiv
Hotel Booking Agents	xv
High Commissions	xv
Embassies	xvi

Emergency and late night help

Accident?
When in an accident with another vehicle you must stop and exchange names, addresses and insurance details with the other party. There is no need to call the police to the scene of the accident unless a person is seriously injured, in which case dial 999 immediately. In the case of a person being injured but able to walk away or where the other driver fails to stop, then this must be reported to the nearest police station within 24 hours.

Arrested?
Always keep calm and remain polite. You do not have to say anything in answer to any allegations that are made but it is sensible to give your name and address. Ask to phone your solicitor or phone Release 01-603 8654 (open 24 hours) who will give you advice and get a solicitor if necessary. Appeals for legal representation, legal aid and bail can be made in court.

All-night prescription
Your local police station keeps a list of chemists and doctors available at all hours. Or try:
Bliss Chemist
54 Willesden La NW6. 01-624 8000. 24 hrs. daily.
V.J. Hall
85 Shaftesbury Av W1. 01-437 3174. *OPEN 09.30–23.00 Mon–Sat, 12.00–22.00 Sun.*
Warman-Freed
45 Golders Green Rd NW11. *OPEN 08.00–24.00 daily, including Xmas.*

Bombs
If you see a suspicious looking package.
1–**DON'T TOUCH IT**
2–*Get people away from the area*
3–*Inform personnel in charge of the premises*
4–*Dial 999 and tell the police where it is.*

Broken Down?
AA Breakdown service
01-954 7373. *24 hrs.*
RAC Breakdown service
0923 33555 (north of the Thames). 01-681 3611 (south of the Thames, and Kent, Surrey, Sussex). *24 hrs.*

Desperate?
New Horizon
1 Macklin St WC2. 01-242 0010. Advice, referral and day centre *Mon–Fri*, for the young homeless in the West End.

Transport
The underground system closes down about midnight although the night bus service is good and extends to the suburbs. There are fewer taxis around late at night and prices increase after midnight. Minicabs operate 24-hr services and the Yellow Pages are full of them. Affluent late-night arrivals may try:
Avis Rent-a-Car
68 North Row, Marble Arch W1. 01-629 7811. *24-hr service from Heathrow and Gatwick airports.*
Godfrey Davis Europe Car
London Heathrow Airport. 01-897 0811. Desks in each terminal. *24-hr service Mon–Sun.*

24 hour emergency casualty
In an emergency dial 999 and ask for the ambulance service or make your own way to a casualty hospital (see 'Hospitals' under Social Services section). If at all practicable, go to your doctor as casualty hospitals are for serious emergencies only.

Piccadilly Advice Centre
Subway 4, Piccadilly Circus underground station W1. 01-930 0066. Information on housing and jobs for young people new to London or homeless. *OPEN 10.00–21.00 Mon–Thur, 13.00–21.00 Fri–Sun.*

Samaritans
St Stephen's Church Crypt, Walbrook EC4. 01-283 3400. Just phone or walk in and talk out your problem. *24-hr telephone service.*

Emergency birth?
Phone the hospital at which the mother is registered – if any, or phone one of the maternity hospitals under the 'Hospitals' section. If all else fails, dial 999 – the ambulance men are trained to cope.

Late post?
Post Office
St Martin's Pl, Trafalgar Sq WC2. 01-930 9580. *OPEN 08.00–20.00 Mon–Sat, 10.00–17.00 Sun & B. Hols.*

Locked out?
The police keep a list of local locksmiths or try the Yellow Pages for a 24-hr service or a willing locksmith who will come out after hours.

Lost your car keys?
If you know the number of your key (keep a note of it somewhere in your wallet) the AA or RAC can probably help (phone numbers under 'Broken down?') if a nearby garage or the police can't.

No cash?
Cash dispensing machines outside major branches of most banks operate 24 hours. Ask your bank about obtaining the special card, and a list of branches with dispensers. There are now many places (in small shops, arcades, etc), open till late in the evening, which call themselves Bureax de Change and will change travellers cheques. Some are quite unscrupulous and charge a very high commission for the service. It is always best to change money in a proper bank or well-known and established Bureau de Change. The following open longer hours than usual.
Brent Cross Shopping Centre
NW4 Barclays Bank (01-202 3311) *OPEN 09.30–20.00 Mon–Fri, 09.30–18.00 Sat.*
Chequepoint
37 Coventry St W1. 01-839 5072. Also 236 Earl's Court Rd SW5, 01-370 3238; Marble Arch W1, 01-723 1005; 126 Bayswater Rd W2, 727 4212. Will cash cheques backed by a cheque card. Higher percentage charge made between *24.00 & 08.00. OPEN 24 hrs Mon–Sun.*
London Gatwick Airport
Lloyds Bank (Crawley 37559) and Midland Bank (Crawley 26934) operates a *24-hr service Mon–Sun on alternate weeks.*
London Heathrow Airport
Barclays Bank (01-897 7551) in Terminal 3 arrivals area. Midland Bank (01-897 3351) in Terminal 1 *OPEN 24 hrs Mon–Sun.* Midland Bank in Terminal 2, *OPEN 24 hrs. Mon–Sun.* Barclays Bank in Terminal 3 departures area. *OPEN 06.30–21.30 Mon–Sun.*
Luton Airport
Barclays Bank (Luton 30700) *OPEN Easter–Sep 06.00–23.00. Oct–Easter 07.00–23.00 Fri–Mon, 07.00–19.00 Tue–Thur.*

No petrol?
Stuck in the middle of the night? The following have 24-hr service unless otherwise stated.
Cavendish Motors
Cavendish Rd NW6. 01-459 0046.
Chelsea Cloisters Garage
Sloane Av SW3. 01-589 1226.
Chiswick Flyover Service Station
1 Great West Rd W4. 01-994 1119.

Emergency and late night help—continued

Esso Garages
115–117 Maida Vale W9. 01-286 7321.
Fountain Garage
Mawson La W4. 01-994 2446.
Park Lane Underground Garage
Park La, Hyde Park W1. 01-262 1814. *24-hr* parking. Petrol *OPEN 08.00–22.00 Mon–Sun.*
Station Supreme
63 Fortune Green Rd NW6. 01-435 2211.

Nowhere to park?
Blue signs direct you to NCP car parks, a lot of which are open 24 hrs. Notice boards at the entrance give details of time and charges. Most parking meters and single yellow lines along London streets cease to be applicable as from *18.30 Mon–Fri, 13.30 Sat and all day Sun;* but do read the signs on the meters or affixed to nearby lamp posts which give times of operation. Parking on double yellow lines, on the pavement and double-banked parking is forbidden at all times, and you may emerge to find your car has been towed away or that a clamp has rendered it immobile. Collecting your car (or having the clamp removed) is costly and inconvenient. Fines for illegal parking are stiff and worth avoiding at all costs.

Telephone services

All London telephone numbers begin with 01- followed by seven figures. If already in London do not dial the 01, only the seven following figures. If dialling from London to an exchange elsewhere, you must find the code of the exchange. The codes are listed in a booklet called Telephone Dialling Codes *or the operator will tell you. If dialling from a coin box telephone, dial as normal and when a connection is made, rapid pips will sound; insert money – either 5p or 10p. Pips will repeat at intervals and more money must then be inserted to continue the connection. The newer push-button phones take 2p and 10p coins, but you put your money in* first. *Details of all telephone services are in the booklet – this is a summary.*

Emergency calls Dial 999 and ask for police, fire or ambulance service.
Directory enquiries 142 for London postal addresses, 192 for other British addresses.
Transfer charge (collect) calls or difficulty in getting through to a number – 100 for the operator.
Telemessages 190 for inland, 193 for international.
International calls You can now dial direct to many countries. Codes are listed in the *Telephone Dialling Codes* booklet or ask the operator.

Recorded services:
Children's London 246 8007.
Discline 160.
Financial Times Cityline 246 8026.
Golden Hitline 246 8044.
Leisureline tourist information 246 8041.
London Traveline 246 8021.
Puffin Storyline *from 18.00.* 246 8000.
Raceline 168.
Recipeline 246 8071.
Sportsline 246 8020.
Starline *08.00–18.00.* 246 8000.
Time 123.
Weatherline 246 8091.

Lost property

British Rail
All Regions except Southern
Property held at station where handed in for 3 days, then sent to central depot in west London. Enquire at local station. North of border to Glasgow central depot, Glasgow 332 9811.
Southern Region
Covering Blackfriars, Cannon Street, Charing Cross, Holborn Viaduct, London Bridge, Victoria and Waterloo. Apply at the nearest railway station. Property will be held there for 2 days and then sent to the central holding depot at
Waterloo Station
York Rd SE1. 01-928 5151.

London Transport
Lost Property Office
200 Baker St W1 (next to Baker St Station). For enquiries about lost property please call in person (or send another person with written authority) or apply by letter. No telephone enquiries. *OPEN 09.30–17.30 Mon–Fri. CLOSED nat hols.*

Sealink
Enquiries to 01-387 1234.

Air Travel
This is held by each individual airline. Property lost in the main airport buildings enquire: British Airport Police Lost Property Office, London Airport, Heathrow, Middx. 01-745 7727/8.

Taxis
Apply 15 Penton St N1 or nearest police station.

Lost anywhere
Apply to the nearest police station. Lost property found in the street is usually taken there.

Lost children
Will be cared for by the railway police if lost on British Rail, otherwise ask at the nearest police station if lost elsewhere.

Lost dogs
May have been taken to Battersea Dogs Home, 4 Battersea Pk Rd SW8. 01-622 4454. Unwanted dogs should be taken to the same address by the owner or by a representative with a letter. *OPEN 09.30–16.30 Mon–Fri, 14.00–16.00 Sat & Sun.* (Purchasing or viewing Mon–Fri only.)

Police Stations

*Stations not continuously manned

Acton 73 T2
250 High Street, W3
Addington 159 O12
Addington Village Road
Albany Street 131 Y15
60 Albany Street, NW1
Arbour Square 63 R16
East Arbour Street, E1

Barking 67 P2
6 Ripple Road
Barkingside 36 B10
1 High Street
Barnes 86 E6
92-102 Station Road, SW13
Barnet 4 H14
26 High Street
Battersea 88 J1
112 Battersea Bridge Road, SW11
Belvedere 81 R13
2 Nuxley Road
Bethnal Green 63 N9
458 Bethnal Green Road, E2
Bexleyheath 98 E11
49 Broadway
*****Bishopsgate** 142 K3
182 Bishopsgate, EC2
Blackwell 76 H3
19 Coldharbour, E14
Bow 64 A8
111 Bow Road, E3
Bow Street 140 L7
28 Bow Street, WC2
Brentford 72 G17
The Half Acre
Brixton 90 F8
367 Brixton Road, SW9
*****Brockley** 92 J9
4 Howson Road, SE4
Bromley 126 G2
Widmore Road

*****Camberwell** 91 02
22a Camberwell Church Street, SE5
Cannon Row 140 K18
1 Cannon Row, SW1
Carter Street 150 B11
292 Walworth Road, SE17
Catford 111 T8
333 Bromley Road, SE6
Chadwell Heath 55 V1
14 Wangey Road
Chelsea 146 L7
2 Lucan Place, SW3
Chingford 20 H4
Kings Head Hill, E4
Chislehurst 113 Z14
47 High Street
Chiswick 73 Z12
209 Chiswick High Road, W4
City Road 134 C12
4 Shepherdess Walk, N1
Clapham 89 X4
51 Union Grove, SW8

Croydon 157 N5
71 Park Lane

Dagenham 56 K16
561 Rainham Road South
Dalston 49 U18
39 Dalston Lane, E8
Deptford 75 Y18
116 Amersham Vale, SE14

Ealing 73 T2
67 Uxbridge Road, W5
Earsfield 106 C6
522 Garratt Lane, SW17
East Dulwich CB46 77
173-183 Lordship Lane, SE22
East Ham 66 F5
4 High Street, South E6
Edgware 12 C20
Whitchurch Lane
Edmonton 18 K13
320 Fore Street, N9
Eltham 95 T14
20 Well Hall Road, SE9
Enfield 8 C11
Baker Street

Finchley 28 A2
193 Ballards Lane, N3
Forest Gate 52 K16
370 Romford Road, E7
Fulham 145 S19
Heckfield Place, SW6

Gerald Road 147 U6
5 Gerald Road, SW1
Gipsy Hill 109 R15
16 Central Hill, SE19
Golders Green 27 W18
1069 Finchley Road, NW11
Greenford 59 N11
21 Oldfield Lane
Greenwich 76 G19
31 Royal Hill, SE10

Hackney 50 B14
2 Lower Clapton Road, E5
*****Ham** 102 D6
Ashburnham Road
Hammersmith 144 D6
226 Shepherds Bush Road, W6
Hampstead 46 G13
26½ Rosslyn Hill, NW3
Harlesden 62 A2
76 Craven Park, NW10
Harrow 4107
74 Northolt Road
Harrow Road 129 S19
325 Harrow Road, W9
Hendon 26 M13
133 Brent Street North, NW4
Highbury Vale 48 K9
211 Blackstock Road, N5
Highgate 29 P18
407 Archway Road, N6
*****Holborn** 020 O20
70 Theobalds Road, WC1
*****Holloway** 48 C9
284 Hornsey Road, N7

Hornsey 30 C14
98 Tottenham Lane, N8
Hounslow 82 K8
5 Montague Road
Hyde Park 138 L12
North of Serpentine, W2

Ilford 53 X9
40 High Road
Isle of Dogs 76 H12
West Ferry Road, E14
*****Islington** 133 X1
277 Upper Street, N1

Kennington Road 149 S1
49 Kennington Road, SE1
Kensington 145 T3
72 Earl's Court Road, W8
Kentish Town 47 T16
12a Holmes Road, NW5
*****Kingsbury** 25 O16
3 The Mall, Kenton
*****Kingston upon Thames** 116 H5
5 High Street
Kings Cross Road 133 P13
76 Kings Cross Road, WC1

Lavender Hill 88 M8
176 Lavender Hill, SW11
Lee Road 94 C12
418 Lee High Road, SE12
*****Leman Street** 143 P7
74 Leman Street, E1
Lewisham 93 T12
2 Ladywell Road, SE13
Leyton 51 U5
215 Francis Road, E10
Leytonstone 52 A7
470 High Road, E11
*****Limehouse** 64 A19
29 West India Dock Road, E14

*****Marylebone** 139 R7
1-9 Seymour Street, W1
Mill Hill 12 K16
11 Deans Drive
Mitcham 120 L8
58 Cricket Green
Muswell Hill 29 N11
Fortis Green, N2

New Malden 118 C9
184 High Street
*****New Southgate** 16E 16
High Road, N11
*****Norbury** 122 C3
1516 London Road, SW16
North Woolwich 78 K5
Albert Road, E16
Norwood Green 70 F11
190 Norwood Road, Southall
Notting Hill 137 P12
101 Ladbroke Road, W11

Paddington Green 129 S12
4 Harrow Road, W2
Peckham 91 Y1
177 Peckham High Street, SE15

Penge 110 E18
175 High Street, SE20
Plaistow 65 U11
444 Barking Road, E13
Plumstead 79 X12
216 Plumstead High Street, SE18
Ponders End 9 P17
204 High Street
Putney 87 O11
215 Upper Richmond Road,
SW15

Richmond 84 H13
8 Red Lion Street
Rochester Row 148 D5
63 Rochester Row, SW1
Roehampton 86 G19
117 Danebury Avenue, SW15
Romford 39 S12
19 Main Road
*****Rotherhithe** 75 R8
99 Lower Road, SE16

St. Anns Road 31 O17
289 St. Anns Road, N15
St John's Wood 130 K10
20½ New Court Street, NW8
Shepherds Bush 136 A15
252 Uxbridge Road, W12
Shooters Hill 95 U3
Shooters Hill, SE18
Snow Hill 141 X3
5 Snow Hill, EC1
Southall 70 G2
67 High Street
Southgate 16 J5
25 Chase Side, N14
South Norwood 123 V9
83 High Street, SE25
Southwark 142 B20
323 Borough High Street, SE1

Stoke Newington 49 U10
33 Stoke Newington High Street
N16
Streatham 108 C20
101 Streatham High Road, SW16
Surbiton 116 M19
299 Ewell Road, Tolworth
Sutton 154 C12
6 Carshalton Road West
Sydenham 110 B7
179 Dartmouth Road, SE26

Teddington 101 W15
18 Park Road
*****Thamesmead** 80 G5
1 Tavy Bridge, SE2
Tooting 107 N15
Mitcham Road, SW17
Tottenham 31 V10
398 High Road, N17
Tottenham Court Road
140 E1
56 Tottenham Court Road, W1
Tower Bridge 143 N16
209 Tooley Street, SE1
Twickenham 83 Y20
41 London Road

Vine Street 140 C11
10 Vine Street, W1

Wallington 155 V13
84 Stafford Road
Walthamstow 32 L10
360 Forest Road, E17
*****Wandsworth** 87 X13
146 High Street, SW18
Wanstead 34 E18
Spratt Hall Road, E11
Wapping 75 N3
98 Wapping High Street, E1

Waterloo Pier 141 O10
Victoria Embankment, WC2
Wealdstone 23 U10
78 High Street
*****Welling** 97 P7
60-62 High Street
*****Wembley** 42 F17
603 Harrow Road
Westcombe Park 77 S14
11 Combedale Road, SE10
*****West End Central** 140 A10
27 Savile Row, W1
West Ham 64 L1
18 West Ham Lane, E15
West Hampstead 45 X14
21 Fortune Green Road, NW6
West Hendon 44 H2
West Hendon, Broadway,
Edgware Road, NW9
West Wickham 159 T1
9 High Street
Whetstone 15 S9
1170 High Road, N20
Willesden Green 44 K18
96 High Road, NW10
Wimbledon 105 W15
15 Queens Road, SW19
Winchmore Hill 17 V7
687 Green Lanes, N21
Woodford Green 21 S16
509 High Road
Wood Green 30 D3
347 High Road, N22
Wood Street 160 C3
37 Wood Street, EC2
Woolwich 78 J11
29 Market Street, SE18
*****Worcester Park** 152 H3
154 Central Road

NB. Because of differences in the revision schedules not all the police stations listed here are shown on the actual map pages.

Tourist information

British Rail Travel Centre
4–12 Lower Regent St SW1. Personal callers only. British Rail's shop window in the West End. Booking centre for rail travel in Britain and rail-and-sea journeys to the Continent and Ireland. Several languages spoken. Smaller offices at: 14 Kingsgate Pde, Victoria St SW1, 407 Oxford St W1, 170b Strand WC2, 87 King William St EC4, Heathrow Airport.

City of London Information Centre
St Paul's Churchyard EC4. 01-606 3030. Information and advice with specific reference to the 'Square Mile'. Free literature. Essential to get monthly *Diary of Events* which lists a big choice of free entertainment in the City. *OPEN Apr–Sept 10.00–16.00 Mon–Sat; Oct–Mar 10.00–14.30. CLOSED 13.00–14.00.*

Daily Telegraph Information Bureau
Telephone only. 01-353 4242.

General information service available *09.30–17.30 Mon–Sat.*

Guildhall Library
Aldermanbury EC2. 01-606 3030. Will tell you anything historical about London. *OPEN 09.30–17.00 Mon–Fri.*

London Transport Travel Information Centres
London Transport offices for enquiries on travel (underground, buses and Green Line coaches) and general tourist information. Their booklet *How to get there* is essential. Also free maps of underground and buses and tourist maps in French, German, Italian, Spanish and Dutch.
St James's Park Underground Station
01-222 1234. *24-hr telephone service.*
Euston Underground Station
Heathrow Central Underground Station
King's Cross Underground Station

Oxford Circus Underground Station
Piccadilly Circus Underground Station
Victoria Underground Station
ALL OPEN 08.30–21.30 Mon–Sun.

National Tourist Information Centre
Main forecourt Victoria Station SW1. Gives travel and tourist information on London and England. Most languages spoken. Also instant hotel reservations, theatre and tour bookings, sales of tourist tickets, guide books and maps. *OPEN 09.00–20.30, 08.30–22.00 Jul & Aug.* Telephone information service: 01-730 3488.
Harrods, Knightsbridge SW1
Heathrow Central Underground Station
Selfridges, Oxford St W1
Tower of London, West Gate E1

Car hire

Self-drive car hire
Prices differ greatly from company to company and depending on make of car and the season. There is a basic daily, weekly or monthly charge, sometimes inclusive of mileage, and you will also have to leave a deposit. Normally you will have to be over 21 and have held a licence, valid for use in the UK, for at least a year.

Avis Rent-a-Car
35 Headford Pl SW1. 01-245 9862. For bookings anywhere in London. *OPEN 07.00–20.00 Mon–Sun.* World-wide reservations at Trident House, Station Rd, Hayes, Middx. 01-848 8765.

Budget
01-441 5882 for your nearest branch in London. *OPEN 08.30–18.00 Mon–Fri, 09.00–12.30 Sat.*

Car Hire Centre
23 Swallow St SW1. 01-734 7661. Free reservation centre for most British car-hire groups. Arrange hire in GB and world-wide.

J. Davy
820 Bath Rd, Cranford, Middx. 01-897 6088. *OPEN 08.30–18.00 Mon–Fri, 08.30–12.00 Sat. CLOSED Sun.*

Eaton Self-Drive Car Hire
48 Ebury Bri Rd SW1. 01-730 3554. *OPEN 08.00–18.00 Mon–Fri, 08.00–13.00 Sat. CLOSED Sun.*

Godfrey Davis (Eurocar)
Davis House, Wilton Rd SW1. 01-834 8484. For London bookings. *OPEN 08.00–20.00.* Central reservations at Bushey House, High St, Bushey, Watford, Herts. 01-950 5050. *OPEN 08.30–19.00.*

Hertz, Rent a Car
Radnor House, 1272 London Rd SW16. 01-679 1799. Daimlers particularly. Self or chauffeur driven. Stations throughout GB and Continent.

Kenning
84–90 Holland Pk Av W11. 01-727 0123. Self-drive cars. Stations throughout GB at airports and abroad. *OPEN 08.00–18.00 Mon–Sun.*

Sportshire
6 Kendrick Pl, Reece Mews SW7. 01-589 8309. MGB, Morgan, TR7, Golf and Range Rovers for hire. *OPEN 09.30–18.30 Mon–Fri, Sat until 13.00.*

Swan National
305–7 Chiswick High Rd W4. 01-995 4665. Phone here for your

nearest branch. *OPEN 08.30–18.00 Mon–Fri.*

Travelwise Car Hire
77 Pavilion Rd SW1. 01-235 0751. *OPEN 08.00–19.00 Mon–Fri, 08.00–17.00 Sat, 09.00–12.00 Sun.*

Chauffeur drive
A-1 Cars
King's Cross WC1. 01-278/437 5225. Black and white Rolls-Royces, Daimlers and Mercedes. Personal body guards and multilingual drivers. *OPEN 24 hrs.*

Patrick Barthropp
1 Dorset Mews, Wilton St SW1. 01-245 9171. Bentleys, Silver Spirits and Silver Spurs with liveried chauffeurs. *OPEN 07.30–22.30 Mon–Sun.*

Belvedere
296 Fulham Rd SW10. 01-589 0034/581 0071. Luxury saloons, limousines and Rolls-Royces. *OPEN 24 hrs.*

Arthur Monk
Monk House, 823 Western Rd NW10. 01-965 5333. Chauffeur-driven Volvo saloons and 12-passenger minibuses for hire. Also 18–35 seaters and 29 seaters. *OPEN 07.00–19.30 Mon–Fri. 24-hr telephone service.*

Coach hire

Capital Coaches
Sipson Rd, W. Drayton, Middx.
01-897 6131.
Greens
213a Hoe St E17. 01-520 1138.

Grey-Green Coaches
53–55 Stamford Hill N16. 01-800 4549.
London Transport
Private Hire Office, 55 Broadway SW1. 01-222 5600.

National Travel (London)
Victoria Coach Station, 164 Buckingham Palace Rd SW1. 01-461 2222.
Sheenway Coaches
66 Stanley Rd SW14. 01-876 4243.

Cycle hire

The bike offers an alternative form of transport worth considering when it costs 40p to travel one stop on the tube. Danger to health through breathing noxious fumes is not nearly as great as the benefit gained from the exercise of cycling. Test the experience for yourself by hiring a bike, or contact the London Cycling Campaign (01-928 7220) for information.

Bell Street Bikes
Bell St NW1. 01-724 0456.
Bicycle Revival
17–19 Elizabeth St SW1. 01-730 6716. And at 28 North End Pde, North End Rd W14. 01-602 4499.

Dial-a-Bike
2 Denbigh Mews SW1. 01-834 0756.
Rent-a-Bike
41–42 Floral St WC2. 01-836 7830.
Saviles Cycle Stores
97–99 Battersea Rise SW11. 01-228 4279. No advance bookings.

Taxis and minicabs

Taxis
The famous London black taxi cabs can be hailed in the street; they are available for hire if the yellow light above the windscreen is lit. All black taxis have meters which the driver must use on all journeys within the Metropolitan Police District (most of Greater London and Heathrow Airport); for longer journeys the price should be negotiated with the driver beforehand. There is also a minimum payable charge which is shown on the meter when you hire the cab. Expect to pay extra for large luggage, journeys between 20.00–06.00, at weekends and nat hols. There are over 500 ranks throughout London, including all major hotels and British Rail stations. For your nearest rank, look in the telephone book under 'Taxi'; some of the more central are:
Islington, Liverpool Rd N1. 01-837 2394.
Lancaster Gate W2. 01-723 9907.
Moorgate EC2. 01-606 4526.
68 Queen's Gdns W2. 01-402 9771.
Russell Sq WC1. 01-636 1247.
St George's Sq SW1. 01-834 1014.
Sloane Sq SW1. 01-730 2664.
South Kensington, Harrington Rd SW7. 01-589 5242.
Warwick Av W9. 01-286 2566 or try:

Computer-Cab. 01-286 0286.
Owner Drivers Radio Taxi Service. 01-286 4848.
Radio Taxicabs. 01-272 0272. 24 hrs.

Mini cabs
These cannot be hailed in the street, and in any case they are indistinguishable from private cars. Unlike the black cabs they are not licensed and neither do their drivers take the same stringest tests, but they are cheaper on longer runs. Negotiate the price with the company, for any journey, when you phone. Your nearest mini-cab office is listed in Yellow Pages.

Air services

Check-in facilities for most major airlines are now based at the airports. For information contact airline booking offices. See Telephone directories for details.
British Caledonian
Central London Air Terminal, Victoria Station SW1. 01-834 9411. OPEN summer 06.00–22.00, winter to 21.00.

Airport bus services
London Transport
A1 Heathrow, Victoria, Cromwell Rd.

A2 Heathrow, Bayswater, Paddington.
A3 Heathrow, Kensington, Hyde Park Corner, Euston.
Flightline
747 Gatwick, Heathrow
757 Luton, Victoria
767 Heathrow, Victoria
777 Gatwick, Victoria

Cheap air tickets
Considerable savings can be made on full price air tickets – any travel agent can give details of arrangements which vary according to destination. ABC (Advance Booking Charter) and APEX (Advance Purchase Excursion) return tickets are available to many world-wide destinations in-including N. America and Australia; tickets for these must be bought 21 or 30 days in advance and neither outward or return dates can be altered. The classified ads in Time Out are a source of other less official cheap flights. If you are a student, special rates are available – check with the student travel office.

Rail terminals

British Rail Travel Centre
4–12 Lower Regent St SW1. Personal callers only. And at 14 Kingsgate Pde, Victoria St SW1, 87 King William St EC4, 407 Oxford St W1, 170b Strand WC2, Heathrow Airport. Booking centre for rail travel in Britain, rail and sea journeys to the Continent and Ireland, motorail and rail package holidays and tours. Several languages spoken.

Blackfriars
Queen Victoria St EC4. Information 01-928 5100. South and south east London suburbs. Built in 1864, rebuilt 1977. *CLOSED Sat & Sun.*

Broad Street
Liverpool St EC2. Information 01-387 7070. North London line to Richmond and peak hour trains to Watford. Built in 1865 by William Baker. Only three platforms now used.

Cannon Street
Cannon St EC4. Information 01-928 5100. South east London suburbs, Kent, E. Sussex. Built 1866; rebuilt with office block above in 1965. *CLOSED Sat & Sun.*

Charing Cross
Strand WC2. Information 01-928 5100. South east London suburbs, Kent. Built 1864. Trains from here go over Hungerford Bridge.

Euston
Euston Rd NW1. Information 01-387 7070. Fast trains to Birmingham, Liverpool, Manchester, Glasow, Inverness, Northampton. Suburban line to Watford. The original station was built in 1837, designed by Robert Stephenson. It had a famous Doric portico which was 72 ft high. The station was completely rebuilt in 1968 and is now a modern functional terminal.

Fenchurch Street
Railway Pl, Fenchurch St EC3. Information 01-283 7171. Trains to Tilbury and Southend. Built 1841.

Holborn Viaduct
Holborn Viaduct EC1. Information 01-928 5100. South and south east London suburbs. Built 1874, rebuilt 1963. *CLOSED Sat & Sun.*

King's Cross
Euston Rd N1. Information 01-278 2477. Fast trains to Leeds, York, Newcastle, Edinburgh, Aberdeen. Built by Lewis Cubitt in 1851, it has a surprisingly modern appearance and the recently added concourse blends in well. The clock on the tower was taken from the original Crystal Palace in Hyde Park.

Liverpool Street
Liverpool St EC2. Information 01-283 7171. East and north east London suburbs, fast trains to Cambridge, Colchester, Norwich and Harwich harbour. Built 1874–5.

London Bridge
Borough High St SE1. Information 01-928 5100. South and south east London suburbs, Kent, Sussex, East Surrey. First opened in 1836, expanded in 1839 and 1864.

Marylebone
Boston Pl NW1. Information 01-387 7070. Suburban lines to Amersham, High Wycombe, Banbury, Aylesbury. The last of the main-line terminals to be built in 1899.

Moorgate
Moorgate EC2. Information 01-278 2477. Recently opened for suburban services to Welwyn Garden City and Hertford. Constructed in 1904 as an underground station with tunnels to Drayton Park and thence overground. The tube tunnels are 16ft diameter, the largest in London.

Paddington
Praed St W2. Information 01-262 6767. Fast trains to Bath, Bristol, Cardiff, Hereford, Swansea, Devon and Cornwall. Some 125 mph services. Built in 1854 by Brunel, it was the London terminus of his Great Western Railway and one of his dreams was to run a service from Paddington to America – by rail to Bristol and high-speed steamship across the Atlantic. The railway hotel, built by Hardwick, is a superb edifice in French renaissance style.

St Pancras
Euston Rd NW1. Information 01-387 7070. Fast trains to Nottingham, Leicester, Sheffield, Derby; suburban to Luton, Bedford, St Albans. Designed by Sir George Gilbert Scott, opened in 1868. An imposing building in mock Gothic style and resembling a cathedral more than a station. The frontage was a grand hotel but is now used for offices. Inside the station, the roof is 100 ft high.

Victoria
Terminus Pl, Victoria St SW1. Information 01-928 5100. South and south east London suburbs, Kent, Sussex, East Surrey. Fast trains to Brighton. Built in two parts; Brighton side in 1860, Dover side in 1862. The concourse and platforms are being modernised.

Waterloo
York Rd SE1. Information 01-928 5100. South west London suburbs. West Surrey, Hampshire, Dorset. Fast trains to Portsmouth, Southampton, Bournemouth. Built 1848, partly modernised 1922. There is also a separate Waterloo (East) station where all trains from Charing Cross stop.

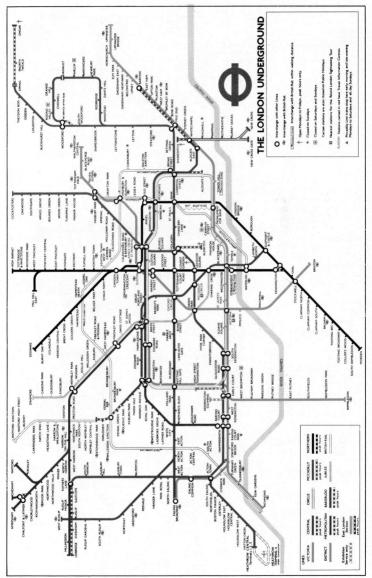

London Transport Underground Map Registered User Number 85/067

ix

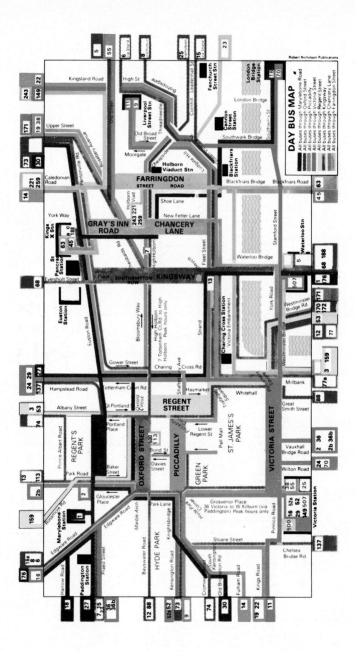

X

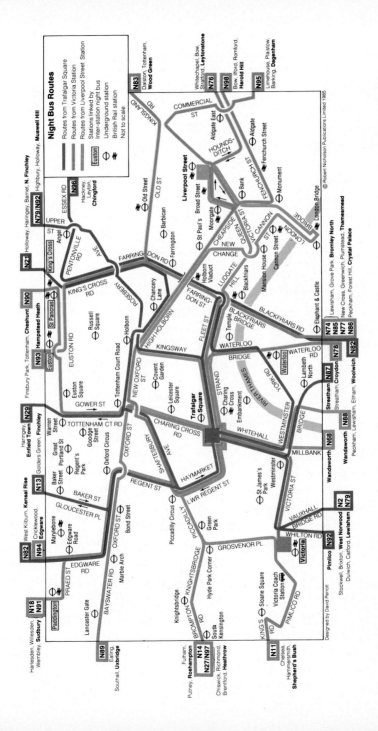

Night Bus Routes

Routes from Trafalgar Square
Routes from Victoria Station
Routes from Liverpool Street Station
Stations linked by inter-station night bus
Underground station
British Rail station
Not to scale

© Robert Nicholson Publications Limited 1985

Designed by David Perrott

xi

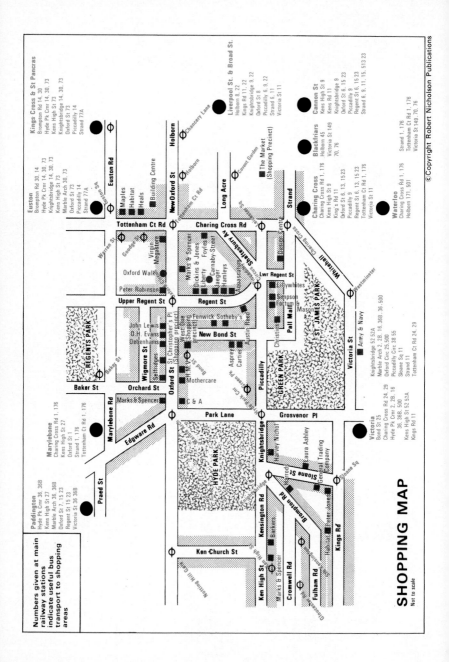

SHOPPING MAP

Not to scale

© Copyright Robert Nicholson Publications

Numbers given at main railway stations indicate useful bus transport to shopping areas

Paddington
Hyde Pk Crnr 36, 36B
Kens High St 27
Marble Arch 36, 36B
Oxford 7, 15, 23
Regent St 15 23
Victoria St 36 36B

Marylebone
Charing Cross Rd 1, 176
Kens High St 27
Oxford St 1
Strand 1, 176
Tottenham Ct Rd 1, 176

Euston
Brompton Rd 30, 14
Hyde Pk Crnr 14, 30, 73
Knightsbridge 14, 30, 73
Kens High St 73
Oxford St 73
Piccadilly 14
Strand 77A

Kings Cross & St Pancras
Brompton Rd 14, 30
Hyde Pk Crnr 14, 30, 73
Kens High St 73
Knightsbridge 14, 30, 73
Oxford St 73
Piccadilly 14
Strand 77A

Liverpool St. & Broad St.
Holborn 8, 22
Kings Rd 11, 22
Knightsbridge 9, 22
Oxford St 8
Piccadilly 9, 22
Strand 6, 11
Victoria St 11

Cannon St
Kens High St 9
Kens Rd 11
Knightsbridge 9
Oxford St 6, 15, 23
Piccadilly 9
Regent St 6, 15, 23
Strand 6, 9, 11, 15, 513, 23

Blackfriars
Holborn 45
Victoria St 149, 70, 76

Charing Cross
Charing Cross Rd 1, 176
Kens High St 9
King's Rd 11
Oxford St 6, 13, 1523
Piccadilly 9
Regent St 6, 13, 15, 23
Strand 1, 176
Victoria St 11

Waterloo
Charing Cross Rd 1, 176
Holborn 171, 501

Strand 1, 176
Tottenham Ct Rd 1, 176
Victoria St 149, 70, 76

Victoria
Bond St 25
Charing Cross Rd 24, 29
Hyde Pk Crnr 2, 2B, 16
36, 36B, 500
Kens High St 52 52A
Kings Rd 11

Knightsbridge 52 52A
Marble Arch 2, 2B, 16, 36B, 36, 500
Oxford Circ 25 500
Sloane Sq 11
Strand 11
Tottenham Ct Rd 24, 29

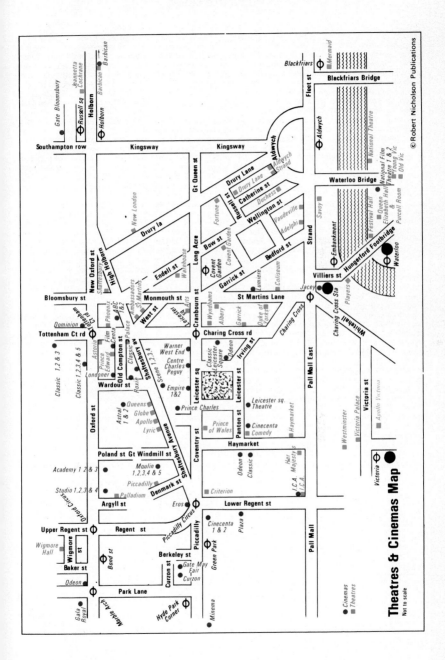

Theatres & Cinemas Map
Not to scale

© Robert Nicholson Publications

● Cinemas
■ Theatres

xiii

Public transport

London has a fairly good system of public transport, its worst failing being the poor service during the night. There are three different services – red buses, the underground (tube) and British Rail overground trains. The system is supposed to be integrated so that all three connect with each other wherever practicable, but bus and train timetables don't always coincide. To find your way around, use the underground and bus maps in this book.

London Transport
Travel Information Centre, St James's Park Station SW1. 01-222 1234. LT operates buses and the underground. Other travel information centres at these underground stations: Euston, Heathrow, King's Cross, Oxford Circus, Piccadilly Circus and Victoria.

The underground
For the stranger to London, this is the simplest way of getting around. Very efficient in central London and very quick. Few lines run south of the river where BR offers a better service. For journeys starting from the centre, tubes run *05.30–00.15 Mon–Sat, 07.30–23.30 Sun*. Start 30 minutes earlier if coming from the suburbs or if you have to change; all tube stations have a notice showing the times of first and last trains. Fares are graduated according to zones and for the regular traveller, weekly, monthly, quarterly or annual Travelcards provide considerable savings. Travelcards can be used on both the underground and buses. To save queuing at ticket offices, keep some 10p, 20p and 50p coins handy to use in ticket machines. Cheap day returns are available if you start your journey after *10.00 Mon–Fri or anytime Sat & Sun*.

Buses
Slower, especially in the rush hours, but more pleasant and you see so much more. They cover the whole of Greater London. They run *06.00–24.00 Mon–Sat, 07.30–23.30 Sun*. Start 30 minutes earlier if outside the centre. First and last times of bus routes are indicated on bus stops but buses are not always reliable so don't depend on these. Again fares are graduated, apart from a few flat-fare routes, notably the Red Arrow buses in the centre. Return tickets are not available. On some buses you pay the driver as you get on but others (including all those with the entrance at the back of the bus) have a conductor who collects the fares as the bus goes along. Both give change but do not like being handed notes, especially large ones. If you are waiting at a request stop you must raise or wave your arm to make the bus stop for you. If already on a bus and you wish to alight at a request stop, you must ring the bell once, in good time. At other bus stops, called compulsory stops, this is not necessary. There are now all-night buses serving London every night, with a greatly extended service to the suburbs as well. Consult *Buses for Night Owls* for night buses, available from LT and Br travel information centres.

British Rail trains
See rail terminals below. BR run intercity trains to all over Britain but also run many suburban lines, especially in South London. These trains generally run *06.00–24.00 Mon–Sat, 07.00–22.30 Sun*. There are some one-off trains during the early hours; check with your station to see if there is a suitable one. Fares on BR trains are graduated and cheap day returns are available but not Mon–Fri on busy trains during rush hours (*approx 08.00–09.30 and 16.30–18.00*). Many BR stations connect with the underground.

Green Line coaches
Enquiries 01-222 1234. These are express buses run by London Country bus company. Most run from central London to outlying areas such as Windsor. The main point for these is Eccleston Bridge, Victoria SW1, others from Regent St just north of Oxford Circus. Two unique services: route 700 from Victoria to Windsor Castle, special express via M4 motorway; route 747 from Crawley via Gatwick & Heathrow airports to Luton airport. Services generally run every hour. Green Line can be used for travel within central London but the bus stops are quite far apart and the fares are high for short journeys.

Coaches
Victoria Coach Station
164 Buckingham Palace Rd SW1. 01-730 0202. The main provincial coach companies operate from here, travelling all over Britain and Continent. Booking necessary.

Hotel booking agents

Acommodation Service of the National Tourist Information Centre
Tourist Information Centre, main forecourt, Victoria Station SW1. No phone. They give information and make bookings. *OPEN 09.00–20.30 Mon–Sat. Longer hours in summer.* Also at Heathrow.

Balcombe Bureau
86 Balcombe St NW1. 01-262 6688. Hotel reservations in London and Britain. All classes of hotels. Also holiday flats arranged. *OPEN 08.00–18.00 Mon–Sat.*

Concordia
19 Churton St SW1. 01-834 7673. All kinds of hotels. *OPEN 09.30–17.00 Mon–Fri. London free.*

Eco-Res
3 Spring St W2. 01-262 2601. Hotel bookings in London and throughout Britain. Specialise in exhibitions. *OPEN 09.30–18.00 Mon–Fri.*

Expotel Hotel Reservations
Dial 01-568 8765 to make hotel reservations. Covers the whole of Great Britain. *OPEN 09.00–17.30 Mon–Fri. Free.*

Hotel Booking Service
Cashmere House, 13–14 Golden Sq W1. 01-437 5052. Excellent and knowledgeable service to business firms and general public. All types of hotel reservations in London, UK and worldwide. *OPEN 09.30–17.30 Mon–Fri, 09.30–13.00 Sat. Charge for private bookings.*

Hotel Finders
20 Bell La NW4. 01-202 7000. All kinds of hotels. *OPEN 09.00–18.00 Mon–Sat. Free.*

Hotel Guide
Faraday House, 8–10 Charing Cross Rd WC2. 01-836 7677. Hotel Accommodation service. *OPEN 09.00–17.30 Mon–Fri. Free.*

Hotel Pacc Group Services Ltd
10 Lower Belgrave St SW1. 01-730 7148. Hotel accommodation for groups (10 people or more) in London and Europe. Facilities for coach and tour operators and conference organisers. *OPEN 09.30–17.30 Mon–Fri.*

Room Centre
IEC Hotel Bookings Ltd, 9 Argyll St W1. 01-437 9733. Free worldwide hotel and conference booking service. *OPEN 09.30–17.30 Mon–Fri.*

High Commissions

All these offices deal with emigration. A full list of high commissions is in the London Diplomatic List, *available from the* HMSO Bookshop, 49 High Holborn WC1.

Australia
Australia House, Strand WC2. 01-438 8000.

Bahamas
39 Pall Mall SW1. 01-930 6967.

Bangladesh
28 Queen's Gate SW7. 01-584 0081.

Barbados
6 Upper Belgrave St SW1. 01-235 8686.

Canada
MacDonald House, 1 Grosvenor Sq W1. 01-629 9492.

Cyprus
93 Park St W1. 01-499 8272.

Ghana
13 Belgrave Sq SW1. 01-235 4142.

Guyana
3 Palace Ct, Bayswater Rd W2. 01-229 7684.

India
India House, Aldwych WC2. 01-836 8484.

Jamaica
50 St James's St SW1. 01-499 8600.

Kenya
45 Portland Pl W1. 01-636 2371.

Malaysia
45 Belgrave Sq SW1. 01-235 8033.

Malta
16 Kensington Sq W8. 01-938 1712.

New Zealand
New Zealand House, 80 Haymarket SW1. 01-930 8422.

Nigeria
Nigeria House, 9 Northumberland Av WC2. 01-839 1244.

Sierra Leone
33 Portland Pl W1. 01-636 6483.

Singapore
5 Chesham St SW1. 01-235 9067/8.

Sri Lanka (Ceylon)
13 Hyde Park Gdns W2. 01-262 1841.

Tanzania
43 Hertford St W1. 01-499 8951.

Trinidad & Tobago
42 Belgrave Sq SW1. 01-245 9351.

Zambia
2 Palace Ga W8. 01-589 6655.

Embassies

All have Consulates in the same building unless a separate address is given. They all deal with emigration. A full list of embassies is in the London Diplomatic List, *available from the HMSO Bookshop, 49 High Holborn WC1.*

Austria
18 Belgrave Mews West SW1.
01-235 3731.

Belgium
103 Eaton Sq SW1. 01-235 5422.

Brazil
32 Green St W1. 01-499 0877.
Consulate: 6 Deanery St W1.
01-499 7441.

Bulgaria
186–188 Queen's Gate SW7.
01-584 9400.

Chile
12 Devonshire St W1.
01-580 6392.
Consulate: 01-580 1023.

China
31 Portland Pl W1. 01-636 5726.

Cuba
167 High Holborn WC1.
01-240 2488.

Czechoslovakia
25 Kensington Palace Gdns W8.
01-229 1255.
Consulate: 28 Kensington Palace
Gdns W8. 01-727 9431.

Denmark
55 Sloane St SW1. 01-235 1255.

Egypt
75 South Audley St W1.
01-499 2401.

Finland
38 Chesham Pl SW1. 01-235 9531.

France
58 Knightsbridge SW1.
01-235 8080.
Consulate: 24 Rutland Gate SW7.
01-581 5292

Germany
23 Belgrave Sq SW1. 01-235 5033.

Greece
1a Holland Park W11.
01-727 8040.

Hong Kong
6 Grafton St W1. 01-499 9821.

Hungary
35 Eaton Pl SW1. 01-235 4048.
Consulate: 35b Eaton Pl SW1.
01-235 2664.

Iceland
1 Eaton Ter SW1. 01-730 5131.

Iran
Consulate: 50 Kensington Ct W8.
01-937 5225.

Iraq
21–2 Queen's Gate SW7.
01-584 7141.

Ireland
17 Grosvenor Pl SW1.
01-235 2171.
Passport office: 01-245 9033.

Israel
2 Palace Grn, Kensington Palace
Gdns W8. 01-937 8050.

Italy
14 Three Kings Yd W1.
01-629 8200.
Passport office: 38 Eaton Pl SW1.
01-235 9371.

Japan
46 Grosvenor St W1. 01-493 6030.

Jordan
6 Upper Philimore Gdns W8.
01-937 3685.

Kuwait
46 Queen's Gate SW7.
01-589 4533.

Lebanon
21 Kensington Palace Gdns.
01-229 7265.
Consulate: 15 Palace Gdns
Mews W8. 01-727 6696.

Luxembourg
27 Wilton Cres SW1. 01-235 6961.

Mexico
8 Halkin St SW1. 01-235 6393.

Morocco
49 Queen's Gate Gdns.
01-584 8827.

Netherlands
38 Hyde Pk Gate SW7.
01-584 5040.

Norway
25 Belgrave Sq SW1. 01-235 7151.

Pakistan
35 Lowndes Sq SW1.
01-235 2044.

Peru
52 Sloane St SW1. 01-235 1917.
Consulate: 01-235 6867.

The Philippines
1 Cumberland House, Kensington
Rd W8. 01-937 3646.

Poland
47 Portland Pl W1. 01-580 4324.
Consulate: 73 New Cavendish St
W1. 01-636 4533.

Portugal
11 Belgrave Sq SW1.
01-235 5331.
Consulate: 62 Brompton Rd
SW3. 01-581 8722.

Romania
4 Palace Grn, Kensington Palace
Grn W8. 01-937 9666.

Saudi Arabia
30 Belgrave Sq SW1. 01-235 0831.
Consulate: 01-235 0303.

South Africa
South Africa House, Trafalgar Sq
WC2. 01-930 4488.
Consulate: 8 Duncannon St WC2.
01-839 2211.

Spain
24 Belgrave Sq SW1.
01-235 5555.
20 Draycott Pl SW3. 01-581 5921.

Sweden
11 Montague Pl WC1.
01-724 2101.

Switzerland
18 Montagu Pl W1. 01-723 0701.

Tunisia
29 Prince's Gate SW7.
01-584 8117.

Turkey
43 Belgrave Sq SW1.
01-235 5252.
Consulate: Rutland Gdns SW7.
01-589 0360.

USA
24 Grosvenor Sq W1.
01-499 9000.

USSR
13 Kensington Palace Gdns W8.
01-229 3628.
Consulate: 5 Kensington Palace
Gdns W8. 01-229 3215.

Venezuela
1 Cromwell Rd SW7.
01-584 4206.
Consulate: 71a Park Mansions,
Brompton Rd SW1.
01-589 9916 (Visas Dept).

Yugoslavia
5 Lexham Gdns W8. 01-370 6105.
Consulate: 7 Lexham Gdns W8.

Alphabetical system

This has been programmed for computer typesetting and is consistent throughout the index in the following order.

Postal districts are in alphabetical order followed by numerical order
High av **NW1**
High av **WC1**
High av **WC2**

Outer districts follow postal districts in alphabetical order
High av **Dgnhm**
High av **Mitch**
High av **Wemb**

Strict alphabetical order is followed — disregarding any spacing between separate words
Highendon st
High Hill st
High st

New 'quick-reference' index
Our new quick-reference thumb-guide on the back cover brings you to the right letter immediately. So your Street Finder is faster and easier to use than ever.

Abbreviations

Outer districts

Barking **Bark**
Barnet **Barnt**
Beckenham **Becknhm**
Belvedere **Blvdr**
Bexley **Bxly**
Bexley Heath **Bxly Hth**
Boreham Wood **Borhm wd**
Bromley **Brom**
Brentford **Brentf**
Buckhurst Hill **Buck Hl**
Carshalton **Carsh**
Chislehurst **Chisl**
Croydon **Croy**
Dagenham **Dgnhm**
Dartford **Drtfrd**
East Molesey **E. Molesey**
Edgware **Edg**
Enfield **Enf**
Feltham **Felt**
Greenford **Grnfd**
Hampton **Hampt**
Hornchurch **Hornch**
Hounslow **Hounsl**
Ilford **Ilf**
Isleworth **Islwth**
Kingston **Kingst**
Mitcham **Mitch**
Morden **Mrdn**
New Malden **New Mald**
Orpington **Orp**
Pinner **Pinn**
Rainham **Rainhm**
Richmond **Rich**
Romford **Rom**
Ruislip **Ruis**
Sidcup **Sidcp**
Southall **S'hall**
South Croydon **S Croy**
Surbiton **Surb**
Teddington **Tedd**
Thornton Heath **Thntn Hth**
Twickenham **Twick**
Stanmore **Stanm**
Wallington **Wallgtn**
Wembley **Wemb**
West Wickham **W. Wckm**
Woodford Green **Wdfd Grn**
Worcester Park **Worc pk**

Streets etc

Alley **all**
Approach **appr**
Arcade **arc**
Avenue **av**
Bank **bank**
Boulevard **blvd**
Bridge **br**
Broadway **bdwy**
Buildings **bldgs**
Church **ch**
Churchyard **chyd**
Circle **crcl**
Circus **cir**
Close **clo**
Common **comm**
Cottages **cotts**
Court **ct**
Crescent **cres**
Drive **dri**
East **east**
Embankment **emb**
Estate **est**
Gardens **gdns**
Gate **ga**
Great **gt**
Green **grn**
Grove **gro**
Hill **hill**
House **ho**
Junction **junc**
Lane **la**
Little **lit**
Lower **lwr**
Manor **mnr**
Mansions **mans**
Market **mkt**
Mews **ms**
Mount **mt**
North **north**
Palace **pal**
Parade **p'de**
Park **pk**
Passage **pas**
Path **pth**
Place **pl**
Rise **ri**
Road **rd**
Slope **slope**
South **south**
Square **sq**
Station **sta**
Street **st**
Terrace **ter**
Upper **up**
Villas **villas**
Walk **wlk**
Way **way**
West **west**
Yard **yd**

A

108 G 1 Abbess clo SW2
29 Y 14 Abbeville rd N8
89 V 15 Abbeville rd SW4
60 L 5 Abbey av Wemb
58 D 9 Abbey clo Grnfd
81 S 11 Abbey cres Erith
61 O 3 Abbeydale rd Wemb
75 P 11 Abbeyfield rd SE 16
151 Z 5 Abbeyfield rd SE 16
130 C 9 Abbey gdns NW8
80 E 10 Abbey gro SE2
115 T 3 Abbey Hill rd Sidcp
64 G 5 Abbey la E15
111 O 17 Abbey la Becknhm
148 F 1 Abbey Orchard st SW1
111 O 17 Abbey Pk estate Becknhm
64 L 5 Abbey rd E15
129 Y 4 Abbey rd NW6
130 B 7 Abbey rd NW8
61 T 5 Abbey rd NW10
61 T 7 Abbey rd NW10
106 D 19 Abbey rd SW19
67 N 2 Abbey rd Bark
80 K 10 Abbey rd Blvdr
81 N 9 Abbey rd Blvdr
97 Z 9 Abbey rd Bxly Hth
156 J 5 Abbey rd Croy
8 F 17 Abbey rd Enf
36 E 16 Abbey rd Ilf
65 T 11 Abbey st E13
143 O 20 Abbey st SE1
150 L 1 Abbey st SE1
80 F 10 Abbey ter SE2
60 M 7 Abbey ter Wemb
13 S 10 Abbey view NW7
80 F 10 Abbey Wood rd SE2
100 C 15 Abbot clo Hampt
64 G 5 Abbotsbury clo E15
137 N 19 Abbotsbury clo W14
137 N 18 Abbotsbury rd W14
120 A 8 Abbotsbury rd Mrdn
30 M 14 Abbotsford av N15
34 E 2 Abbotsford gdns Wdfd Grn
55 O 7 Abbotsford rd Ilf
20 L 14 Abbots cres E4
28 G 13 Abbots gdns N2
16 H 12 Abbotshall av N14
111 W 3 Abbotshall rd SE6
142 K 14 Abbots la SE1
153 Z 17 Abbotsleigh clo Sutton
107 V 11 Abbotsleigh rd SW16
108 G 1 Abbots pk SW2
129 W 3 Abbot's pl NW6
13 N 20 Abbots rd NW7
25 W 1 Abbots rd Edgw
87 N 8 Abbotstone rd SW15
49 T 17 Abbot st E8
124 H 11 Abbots way Becknhm
92 M 13 Abbotswell rd SE4
35 U 11 Abbotswood gdns Ilf
107 W 5 Abbotswood rd SW2
119 P 1 Abbott av SW20
40 D 18 Abbott clo Grnfd
64 K 16 Abbott rd E14
38 G 10 Abbotts clo Rom
7 X 8 Abbotts cres Enf
42 A 6 Abbotts dri Wemb
158 G 13 Abbotts grn Croy
51 U 1 Abbotts Pk rd E10
101 V 4 Abbottsmede clo Twick
66 B 5 Abbotts rd E6
4 M 16 Abbotts rd Barnt
25 X 1 Abbotts rd Edg
121 X 6 Abbotts rd Mitch
70 C 2 Abbotts rd S'hall
153 V 7 Abbotts rd Sutton
80 J 19 Abbotts wlk Bxly Hth
160 F 8 Abchurch la EC4
74 K 3 Abdale rd W12
136 A 14 Abdale rd W12
150 J 4 Abedour st SE1
63 X 10 Aberavon rd E3
107 V 18 Abercairn rd SW16
120 A 7 Aberconway rd Mrdn
27 T 2 Abercorn clo NW7
130 C 11 Abercorn clo NW8
40 L 4 Abercorn cres Harrow
42 G 1 Abercorn gdns Harrow
37 P 18 Abercorn gdns Rom
130 C 10 Abercorn pl NW8
27 U 2 Abercorn rd NW7
24 D 2 Abercorn rd Stanm
88 K 5 Abercrombie st SW11
159 V 3 Aberdare clo W Wkhm
129 Z 1 Aberdare gdns NW6
130 A 1 Aberdare gdns NW6
27 O 2 Aberdare gdns NW7
9 O 14 Aberdare rd Enf
48 K 15 Aberdeen la N5
48 K 15 Aberdeen pk N5
130 F 17 Aberdeen pl NW8
48 L 13 Aberdeen rd N5
18 L 15 Aberdeen rd N18
44 E 14 Aberdeen rd NW10
120 F 2 Aberdeen rd SW19
157 N 9 Aberdeen rd Croy
23 V 9 Aberdeen rd Harrow
93 X 5 Aberdeen ter SE3
55 P 6 Aberdour rd Ilf
64 H 17 Aberfeldy st E14
107 X 17 Aberfoyle rd SW16
94 J 15 Abergeldie rd SE12
93 Z 11 Abernethy rd SE13
49 V 15 Abersham rd E8
79 U 11 Abery st SE18
106 E 16 Abingdon clo SW19
28 D 6 Abingdon rd N3
122 A 1 Abingdon rd SW16
145 U 1 Abingdon rd W8
148 K 2 Abingdon st SW1
145 U 2 Abingdon vlls W8
153 N 20 Abinger av Sutton
127 P 6 Abinger clo Brom
54 M 13 Abinger clo Ilf
156 A 12 Abinger clo Wallgtn
83 S 8 Abinger gdns Islwth
75 Y 16 Abinger gro SE8
74 B 8 Abinger rd W4
151 Z 10 Ablett st SE1
75 O 14 Ablett st SE16
118 G 4 Aboyne dri SW20
43 Z 9 Aboyne rd NW10
44 B 8 Aboyne rd NW10
106 E 5 Aboyne rd SW17
68 D 7 Abridge way Bark
88 K 12 Abyssinia rd SW11
31 O 1 Acacia av N17
72 A 20 Acacia av Brentf
57 U 8 Acacia av Hornch
42 J 15 Acacia av Wemb
10 G 19 Acacia clo Harrow
119 W 20 Acacia dri Sutton
130 G 8 Acacia gdns NW8
159 U 4 Acacia gdns W Wkhm
109 P 4 Acacia gro SE21
117 Z 6 Acacia gro New Mald
118 A 6 Acacia gro New Mald
130 G 8 Acacia pl NW8
52 A 8 Acacia rd E11
32 J 19 Acacia rd E17
30 G 5 Acacia rd N22
130 G 8 Acacia rd NW8
108 B 20 Acacia rd SW16
61 V 20 Acacia rd W3
8 C 5 Acacia rd Enf
100 J 14 Acacia rd Hampt
121 R 4 Acacia rd Mitch
123 V 20 Academy gdns Croy
58 A 7 Academy gdns Grnfd
95 U 2 Academy pl SE18
78 G 19 Academy rd SE18
95 U 1 Academy rd SE18
89 N 8 Acans rd SW11
45 W 3 Accommodation rd NW11
88 A 2 Acfold rd SW6
45 W 14 Achilles rd NW6
75 X 20 Achilles st SE14
137 O 1 Acklam rd W10
26 A 4 Acklington dri NW9
87 X 3 Ackmar rd SW6
63 Z 14 Ackroyd dri E3
92 G 18 Ackroyd rd SE23
91 N 8 Acland cres SE5
44 L 17 Acland rd NW2
129 W 1 Acol rd NW6
68 C3 Aconbury rd Dgnhm
114 C 13 Acorn clo Chisl
20 C 16 Acorn clo E4
7 V 6 Acorn clo Enf
123 T 1 Acorn gdns SE19
61 Z 15 Acorn gdns W3
99 U 14 Acorn rd Drtfrd
75 W 2 Acorn wlk SE16
90 C 11 Acre la SW2
155 R 8 Acre la Wallgtn
40 A 18 Acre path Grnfd
106 G 14 Acre rd SW19
56 H 20 Acre rd Dgnhm
102 K 20 Acre rd Kingst
88 D 14 Acris st SW18
61 Z 6 Acton la NW10
73 W 5 Acton la W3
73 W 4 Acton la W3
73 W 12 Acton la W4
134 M 3 Acton ms E8
133 O 13 Acton st WC1
105 Z 3 Acuba rd SW18
64 J 17 Ada gdns E14
65 P 4 Ada gdns E15
128 M 18 Adair rd W10
140 B 4 Adam & Eve ct W1
145 V 1 Adam & Eve ms W8
146 C 5 Adam ct SW7
144 E 18 Adam wlk
43 U 6 Adams clo NW9
160 H 5 Adam's ct EC2
75 P 5 Adams gdns SE16
65 T 18 Adamson rd E16
46 G 19 Adamson rd NW3
48 D 16 Adams pl N7
8 B 19 Adamsrill Clo Enf
110 H 9 Adamsrill rd SE26
31 R 7 Adams rd N17
124 H 11 Adams rd Becknhm
139 V 10 Adams row W1
97 Y 9 Adams sq Bxly Hth
140 L 10 Adams st WC2
135 V 7 Ada pl E2
108 B 5 Adare wlk SW16
150 H 20 Ada rd SE5
42 F 9 Ada rd Wemb
135 V 5 Ada st E8
113 X 9 Adderley gdns SE9
89 O 13 Adderley gro SW11
23 V 5 Adderley rd Harrow
64 F 18 Adderley st E14
15 S 20 Addington dr N12
110 G 10 Addington gro SE26
158 K 12 Addington palace Croy
158 L 14 Addington park Croy
64 A 8 Addington rd E3
65 N 13 Addington rd E16
30 E 20 Addington rd N4
122 G 19 Addington rd Croy
158 E 20 Addington rd S Croy
159 W 7 Addington rd W Wkhm
150 D 16 Addington sq SE5
141 P 18 Addington st SE1
158 M 13 Addington Village rd Croy
159 P 11 Addington Village rd Croy
9 S 6 Addis clo Enf
123 W 18 Addiscombe av Croy
24 D 15 Addiscombe clo Harrow
157 T 2 Addiscombe ct Croy
157 R 4 Addiscombe gro Croy
157 U 3 Addiscombe rd Croy
158 B 2 Addiscombe rd Croy
6 E 18 Addison av N14
82 M 3 Addison av Hounsl
145 N 4 Addison Br pl W14
136 M 20 Addison cres W14
144 M 1 Addison cres W14
136 F 20 Addison gdns W14
144 F 1 Addison gdns W14
117 N 9 Addison gdns Surb
74 B 9 Addison gro W4
123 X 9 Addison pl SE25
136 J 15 Addison pl W11
34 F 19 Addison rd E11
33 T 15 Addison rd E17
123 Y 9 Addison rd SE25
136 M 18 Addison rd W14
145 O 2 Addison rd W14
126 M 10 Addison rd Brom
127 N 10 Addison rd Brom
9 R 6 Addison rd Enf
36 C 5 Addison rd Ilf
102 A 15 Addison rd Tedd
158 K 2 Addisons clo Croy
27 X 13 Addison way NW11
141 Y 7 Addle hill EC4
160 C 3 Addle st EC2
118 K 9 Adela av New Mald
118 K 10 Adela av New Mald
92 M 11 Adelaide av SE4
93 N 11 Adelaide av SE4
8 F 4 Adelaide clo Enf
10 K 13 Adelaide clo Stanm
71 V 4 Adelaide cotts W7
37 Y 15 Adelaide gdns Rom
74 H 3 Adelaide gro W12
51 T 9 Adelaide rd E10
46 M 20 Adelaide rd NW3
47 N 20 Adelaide rd NW3
130 H 1 Adelaide rd NW3
71 Z 4 Adelaide rd W13
114 A 14 Adelaide rd Chisl
82 A 2 Adelaide rd Hounsl
54 A 6 Adelaide rd Ilf
85 N 11 Adelaide rd Rich
70 B 10 Adelaide rd S'hall
116 J 13 Adelaide rd Surb
101 X 15 Adelaide rd Tedd
140 J 11 Adelaide st WC2
128 K 17 Adela st W10
63 O 14 Adelina gro E1
135 Z 20 Adelina gro E1
140 G 3 Adeline pl WC1
57 W 7 Adelphi cres Hornch
140 L 11 Adelphi ter WC2
144 H 14 Adeney clo W6
144 U 16 Adeney rd W6
49 O 13 Aden gro N16
93 O 19 Adenmore rd SE6
9 V 15 Aden rd Enf
54 A 2 Aden rd Ilf
49 N 12 Aden ter N16
74 L 9 Adie rd W6
144 A 3 Adie rd W6
65 U 12 Adine rd E13
143 S 4 Adler st E1
50 J 14 Adley st E5
79 P 18 Admaston rd SE18
128 H 18 Admiral ms W10
95 T 9 Admiral Seymour rd SE9
93 O 3 Admirals st SE4
46 D 16 Admirals wlk NW3
101 V 16 Admiralty rd Tedd
57 V 17 Adnams wlk Rainhm
111 P 10 Adolf st SE6
48 J 5 Adolphus rd N4
75 Z 19 Adolphus st SE8
55 X 11 Adomar rd Dgnhm
44 J 3 Adrian av NW2
58 E 10 Adrienne av S'hall
91 W 9 Adys rd SE15
26 E 9 Aerodrome rd NW9
26 B 8 Aeroville NW9
133 O 10 Affleck st N1
88 J 6 Afghan rd SW11
45 W 14 Agamemnon rd NW6
47 Y 20 Agar gro NW1
132 D 1 Agar gro NW1
140 K 10 Agar st WC2
74 L 8 Agate rd W6
144 A 3 Agate rd W6
75 O 2 Agatha clo E1
143 Y 12 Agatha clo E1
114 C 4 Agaton rd SE9
44 M 12 Agave rd NW2
133 W 15 Agdon st EC1
46 L 13 Agincourt rd NW3
53 X 11 Agnes av Ilf
55 X 11 Agnes gdns Dgnhm
74 C 4 Agnes rd W3
63 Y 16 Agnes st E14
92 G 18 Agnew rd SE23
55 Y 11 Aidan clo Dgnhm
65 O 1 Aileen wlk E15
84 A 13 Ailsa av Twick
83 Z 13 Ailsa av Twick
84 A 13 Ailsa av Twick
84 B 13 Ailsa rd Twick
64 G 14 Ailsa st E14
131 P 2 Ainger ms NW8
131 P 2 Ainger rd NW3
22 H 10 Ainsdale cres Pinn
60 H 13 Ainsdale rd W5
38 J 19 Ainsley av Rom
63 N 8 Ainsley st E2
135 W 14 Ainsley st E2
20 C 17 Ainslie Wood cres E4
20 D 15 Ainslie Wood gdns E4
20 C 17 Ainslie Wood rd E4
89 R 19 Ainslie wk SW12
75 R 5 Ainsty st SE16
44 H 9 Ainsworth clo NW2
63 P 1 Ainsworth rd E9
156 K 1 Ainsworth rd Croy
66 C 5 Aintree av E6
36 B 7 Aintree cres Ilf
60 B 5 Aintree rd Grnfd
144 L 18 Aintree st SW6
133 N 2 Airdie clo N1
74 D 12 Airedale av W4
88 M 20 Airedale rd SW12
89 N 19 Airedale rd SW12
72 F 8 Airedale rd W5
57 Z 20 Airfield way Hornch
137 S 15 Airlie gdns W8
53 Z 5 Airlie gdns Ilf
140 D 10 Air st W1
55 P 5 Airthrie rd Ilf
94 A 12 Aislible rd SE12
111 R 4 Aitken rd SE6
26 A 10 Ajax av NW9
45 W 14 Ajax rd NW6
86 G 17 Akehurst st SW15
46 G 16 Akenside rd NW3
116 E 15 Akerman rd Surb
79 T 18 Alabama st SE18

72 F 7 Alacross rd W5
4 D 19 Alan dri Barnt
56 D 1 Alan gdns Rom
105 T 12 Alan rd SW19
94 D 15 Alanthus clo SE12
141 T 16 Alaska st SE1
93 R 15 Albacore cres SE13
27 T 18 Alba gdns NW11
3 K 14 Albany clo N15
85 U 11 Albany clo SW14
97 U 19 Albany clo Bxly
10 D 1 Albany clo Bushey
25 Z 4 Albany ct NW9
25 R 2 Albany cres Edg
140 B 11 Albany ctyd W1
9 U 2 Albany park Enf
9 R 5 Albany Pk av Enf
9 T 4 Albany Pk av Enf
9 T 4 Albany Pk rd Enf
102 H 16 Albany Pk rd Kingst
84 L 14 Albany pass Rich
48 F 13 Albany pl N7
33 O 20 Albany rd E10
53 O 13 Albany rd E12
32 J 18 Albany rd E17
30 E 20 Albany rd N4
19 O 18 Albany rd N18
150 M 20 Albany rd SE1
150 H 13 Albany rd SE5
150 D 15 Albany rd SE17
105 Z 12 Albany rd SW19
60 B 19 Albany rd W13
81 P 15 Albany rd Blvdr
97 U 19 Albany rd Bxly
72 J 17 Albany rd Brentf
113 Z 13 Albany rd Chisl
9 S 2 Albany rd Enf
57 W 8 Albany rd Hornch
117 Y 8 Albany rd New Mald
84 L 12 Albany rd Rich
38 B 18 Albany rd Rom
131 X 8 Albany st NW1
21 P 13 Albany the Wdfd Grn
21 U 4 Albany view Buck Hl
137 N 4 Alba pl W11
79 T 18 Albatross st SE18
36 A 19 Albemarle appr Ilf
100 E 2 Albemarle av Twick
35 Z 19 Albemarle gdns Ilf
36 A 19 Albemarle gdns Ilf
11 R 17 Albemarle pk Stanm
15 X 2 Albemarle rd Barnt
125 X 1 Albemarle rd Becknhm
117 Y 10 Albemarle rd New Mald
140 A 12 Albemarle st W1
133 W 18 Albemarle way EC1
27 V 14 Alberon gdns NW11
153 U 10 Alberta av Sutton
8 J 19 Alberta rd Enf
98 J 2 Alberta rd Erith
149 X 9 Alberta st SE17
20 B 14 Albert av E4
146 M 17 Albert br SW11
88 L 1 Albert Br rd SW11
146 M 18 Albert Br rd SW11
147 N 20 Albert Br rd SW11
107 Z 13 Albert Carr gdns SW16
108 A 13 Albert Carr gdns SW16
29 X 3 Albert clo N22
20 V 13 Albert cres E4
105 T 2 Albert dri SW19
141 N 17 Albert emb SE1
148 M 8 Albert emb SE1
63 S 18 Albert gdns E1
105 P 20 Albert gro SW20
138 F 19 Albert Hall mans SW7
146 A 1 Albert ms W8
27 Y 4 Albert pl N3
31 U 9 Albert pl N17
137 Z 20 Albert pl W8
51 U 6 Albert rd E10
78 D 4 Albert rd E16
33 O 16 Albert rd E17
34 J 9 Albert rd E18
48 D 3 Albert rd N4
31 R 18 Albert rd N15
29 V 5 Albert rd N22
27 P 13 Albert rd NW4
129 R 9 Albert rd NW6
13 S 16 Albert rd NW7
113 R 6 Albert rd SE9
110 E 16 Albert rd SE20
123 Z 8 Albert rd SE25
124 B 11 Albert rd SE25
60 C 13 Albert rd W5
5 S 14 Albert rd Barnt
81 P 14 Albert rd Blvdr
98 F 18 Albert rd Bxly
127 P 12 Albert rd Brom
56 D 4 Albert rd Dgnhm
101 O 12 Albert rd Hampt
23 N 11 Albert rd Harrow
82 H 11 Albert rd Hounsl
53 Z 10 Albert rd Ilf
54 C 9 Albert rd Ilf
120 M 6 Albert rd Mitch
8 E 10 Albert rd New Mald
84 L 13 Albert rd Rich
39 T 17 Albert rd Rom
154 F 12 Albert rd Sutton
101 X 15 Albert rd Tedd
83 V 20 Albert rd Twick
101 V 1 Albert rd Twick
81 P 14 Albert Rd est Blvdr
52 A 16 Albert sq E15
90 C 1 Albert sq SW8
149 N 20 Albert sq SW8
15 P 15 Albert st N12
131 Z 8 Albert st NW1
131 S 4 Albert ter NW1
61 X 4 Albert ter NW10
131 S 4 Albert Ter ms NW1
29 O 4 Albion av N10
89 W 4 Albion av SW8
138 L 8 Albion clo W2
39 O 18 Albion clo Rom
135 O 2 Albion dri E8
74 H 10 Albion gdns W6
49 R 11 Albion gro N16
133 T 2 Albion ms N1
45 V 20 Albion ms NW6
138 L 7 Albion ms W2
133 W 19 Albion pl EC1
160 F 2 Albion pl EC2
123 W 7 Albion pl SE25
33 U 9 Albion rd E17
49 P 10 Albion rd N16
31 W 7 Albion rd N17
98 D 11 Albion rd Bxly Hth
82 H 12 Albion rd Hounsl
117 V 1 Albion rd Kingst
154 E 15 Albion rd Sutton
101 T 2 Albion rd Twick
135 O 1 Albion sq E8
75 P 7 Albion st SE16
138 L 8 Albion st W2
122 H 20 Albion st Croy
135 N 1 Albion ter E8
110 C 6 Albion Vlls rd SE26
93 U 9 Albion way SE13
43 R 10 Albion way Wemb
7 U 5 Albuhera clo Enf
97 Y 4 Albury av Bxly Hth
71 W 20 Albury av Islwth
22 A 1 Albury dri Pinn
76 B 17 Albury st SE8
127 V 7 Albyfield Brom
93 P 4 Albyn rd SE4
50 A 6 Alcester cres E5
155 S 9 Alcester rd Wallgtn
155 Y 16 Alcock clo Wallgtn
49 X 8 Alconbury rd E5
153 X 2 Alcorn clo Sutton
56 K 18 Aldborough rd Dgnhm
54 H 1 Aldborough rd Ilf
36 K 15 Aldborough Rd north Ilf
36 K 15 Aldborough Rd south Ilf
54 F 5 Aldborough Rd south Ilf
74 F 3 Aldbourne rd W12
150 J 9 Aldbridge st SE17
43 S 19 Aldbury av Wemb
18 B 3 Aldbury ms N9
148 M 20 Aldebert ter SW8
149 N 20 Aldebert ter SW8
21 T 13 Aldeburgh pl Wdfd Grn
77 S 12 Aldeburgh st SE10
65 N 11 Alden av E15
132 D 10 Aldenham st NW1
74 K 9 Aldensley rd W6
89 R 18 Alderbrook rd SW12
74 G 17 Alderbury rd SW13
151 O 16 Alder clo SE15
44 H 8 Alder gro NW2
68 B 8 Alderman av Bark
160 C 4 Aldermanbury EC2
160 C 4 Aldermanbury sq EC2
17 O 13 Aldermans hill N13
136 F 6 Aldermans st W10
142 J 3 Aldermans wlk EC2
112 F 20 Aldermary rd Brom
151 S 9 Alderminster rd SE1
110 M 6 Aldermoor rd SE6
70 K 20 Alderney av Hounsl
40 D 20 Alderney gdns Grnfd
63 T 11 Alderney rd E1
147 X 8 Alderney st SW1
148 A 10 Alderney st SW1
85 X 7 Alder rd SW14
114 J 8 Alder rd Sidcp
20 M 19 Alders av Wdfd Grn
8 E 8 Aldersbrook av Enf
102 M 15 Aldersbrook dri Kingst
53 V 10 Aldersbrook la E12
52 H 6 Aldersbrook rd E11
53 R 11 Aldersbrook rd E12
12 H 16 Alders clo Edg
92 G 12 Aldersford clo SE4
54 E 18 Aldersey gdns Bark
142 A 1 Aldersgate st EC1
160 A 1 Aldersgate st EC1
112 M 7 Aldersgrove av SE9
113 N 6 Aldersgrove av SE9
129 R 3 Aldershot rd NW6
124 G 14 Aldersmead av Croy
110 H 18 Aldersmead rd Becknhm
128 L 16 Alderson st W10
12 H 16 Alders rd Edg
17 U 1 Alders the N21
100 C 11 Alders the Felt
70 E 15 Alders the Hounsl
159 R 1 Alders the W Wkhm
26 J 17 Alderton cres NW4
90 L 9 Alderton rd SE24
123 V 16 Alderton rd Croy
87 W 5 Alderville rd SW6
83 P 7 Alderwick dri Hounsl
86 F 15 Alderwood rd SE9
139 T 11 Aldford st W1
142 M 6 Aldgate EC3
143 O 5 Aldgate High st E1
136 E 16 Aldine st W12
57 X 15 Aldingham gdns Hornch
106 H 13 Aldis st SW17
45 X 15 Aldred rd NW6
106 D 7 Aldren rd SW17
159 V 1 Aldrich cres Croy
20 F 19 Aldriche way E4
106 E 3 Aldrich ter SW18
12 F 9 Aldridge av Edg
9 Z 2 Aldridge av Enf
24 K 6 Aldridge av Stanm
118 A 16 Aldridge ri New Mald
137 R 3 Aldridge rd vlls W11
16 L 3 Aldridge wlk N14
107 V 11 Aldrington rd SW16
114 D 6 Aldwick clo SE9
156 C 7 Aldwick rd Croy
93 T 16 Aldworth gro SE13
51 Z 20 Aldworth rd E15
64 L 1 Aldworth rd E15
64 M 1 Aldworth rd E15
141 O 7 Aldwych WC2
36 C 14 Aldwych av Ilf
57 W 7 Aldwych clo Hornch
97 X 13 Alers rd Bxly Hth
62 K 1 Alexander av NW10
128 A 2 Alexander av NW10
126 G 20 Alexander clo Brom
96 H 15 Alexander clo Sidcp
101 U 4 Alexander clo Twick
6 G 16 Alexander ct N14
137 W 4 Alexander ms W2
146 J 4 Alexander pl SW7
48 A 8 Alexander rd N4
97 W 4 Alexander rd Bxly Hth
114 A 14 Alexander rd Chisl
146 J 4 Alexander sq SW7
137 W 5 Alexander st W2
29 Y 6 Alexandra av N22
89 O 2 Alexandra av SW11
73 Z 20 Alexandra av W4
40 F 4 Alexandra av Harrow
70 D 1 Alexandra av S'hall
153 X 6 Alexandra av Sutton
40 J 10 Alexandra clo Harrow
92 M 3 Alexandra cotts SE14
112 C 14 Alexandra cres Brom
112 B 14 Alexandra cres Brom
109 R 13 Alexandra dri SE19
117 R 16 Alexandra dri Surb
29 T 12 Alexandra gdns N10
155 N 18 Alexandra gdns Carsh
82 K 5 Alexandra gdns Hounsl
48 K 5 Alexandra gro N4
15 O 18 Alexandra gro N12
29 W 9 Alexandra palace N22
29 Z 9 Alexandra park N22
40 J 11 Alexandra park Harrow
29 T 6 Alexandra Pk rd N22
123 P 11 Alexandra pl SE25
66 J 9 Alexandra rd E6
51 U 10 Alexandra rd E10
32 L 20 Alexandra rd E17
34 G 11 Alexandra rd E18
30 F 9 Alexandra rd N8
29 S 3 Alexandra rd N10
16 E 20 Alexandra rd N11
31 O 15 Alexandra rd N15
27 P 13 Alexandra rd NW4
130 C 3 Alexandra rd NW8
110 E 15 Alexandra rd SE26
85 Z 8 Alexandra rd SW14
105 V 15 Alexandra rd SW19
73 Z 6 Alexandra rd W4
72 G 17 Alexandra rd Brentf
123 R 19 Alexandra rd Croy
9 T 15 Alexandra rd Enf
82 K 7 Alexandra rd Hounsl
103 P 18 Alexandra rd Kingst
106 K 19 Alexandra rd Mitch
85 N 5 Alexandra rd Rich
37 X 18 Alexandra rd Rom
39 S 18 Alexandra rd Rom
84 F 17 Alexandra rd Twick
119 Y 13 Alexandra sq Mrdn
65 R 14 Alexandra st E16
75 W 18 Alexandra st SE14
60 A 20 Alexandria rd W13
151 T 5 Alexis st SE16
50 B 11 Alfearn rd E5
159 W 15 Alford gdns Croy
159 W 15 Alford grn Croy
89 Y 3 Alford rd SW8
81 Z 13 Alford rd Erith
30 H 13 Alfoxton av N15
58 C 20 Alfred gdns S'hall
70 C 1 Alfred gdns S'hall
132 E 20 Alfred ms W1
140 E 1 Alfred pl W1
52 C 15 Alfred rd E15
123 Y 10 Alfred rd SE25
137 U 1 Alfred rd W2
73 W 3 Alfred rd W3
71 Y 1 Alfred rd W13
81 P 14 Alfred rd Belvdr
116 L 7 Alfred rd Kingst
154 E 12 Alfred rd Sutton
89 R 2 Alfreda st SW11
67 W 5 Alfreds gdns Bark
63 Z 8 Alfred st E3
67 T 6 Alfreds way Bark
105 O 7 Alfreton clo SW19
122 A 16 Alfriston av Croy
22 H 20 Alfriston av Harrow
89 N 13 Alfriston rd SW11
116 L 13 Alfriston rd Surb
83 Y 9 Algar clo Islwth
10 J 17 Algar clo Stanm
83 Y 8 Algar rd Islwth
106 B 2 Algarve rd SW18
26 G 19 Algernon rd NW4
129 S 5 Algernon rd NW6
93 R 7 Algernon rd SE13
93 P 11 Algiers rd SE13
56 F 14 Albion gdns Dgnhm
150 H 2 Alice st SE1
24 C 14 Alicia av Harrow
24 D 14 Alicia clo Harrow
24 D 14 Alicia gdns Harrow
143 R 6 Alie st E1
43 V 3 Alington cres NW9
155 W 20 Alington gro Wallgtn
88 J 11 Aliwal rd SW11
74 B 13 Alkerden rd W4
49 V 7 Alkham rd N16
117 Y 12 Allan clo New Mald
27 T 10 Allandale av N3
57 U 1 Allandale rd Hornch
51 N 20 Allanmouth rd E9
61 W 13 Allan way W3
10 A 7 Allard cres Bushey
90 C 10 Allardyce st SW4
101 T 11 Allbrook clo Tedd
156 M 20 Allenby av S Croy
58 J 10 Allenby clo Grnfd
110 H 6 Allenby rd SE23
58 H 10 Allenby rd S'hall
58 F 17 Allendale av S'hall
110 F 12 Allendale clo SE26
42 A 17 Allendale rd Grnfd
89 Z 1 Allen Edwards dri SW8
148 J 20 Allen Edwards dri SW8
63 X 5 Allen rd E3
49 R 12 Allen rd N16
124 E 4 Allen rd Becknhm
122 E 19 Allen rd Croy
9 R 18 Allens rd Enf
145 U 1 Allen st W8
95 S 6 Allenswood rd SE9
22 L 14 Allerford ct Harrow
111 S 10 Allerford rd SE6
48 M 6 Allerton rd N16
49 N 6 Allerton rd N16
144 K 19 Allestree rd SW6
109 P 6 Alleyn cres SE21
55 T 7 Alleyndale rd Dgnhm

A

109 P 3	Alleyn pk SE21
70 F 13	Alleyn rd S'hall
109 P 7	Alleyn rd SE21
88 B 17	Allfarthing la SW18
119 O 15	Allgood clo Mtcm
31 S 4	All Hallows rd N17
65 X 13	Alliance rd E13
79 Z 17	Alliance st SE18
80 A 19	Alliance st SE18
61 S 12	Alliance rd W3
133 Z 7	Alliance st N1
134 A 7	Allingham st N1
105 P 13	Allington clo SW19
26 K 18	Allington rd NW4
128 K 10	Allington rd W10
22 M 15	Allington rd Harrow
147 Z 2	Allington st SW1
93 V 2	Allison clo SE10
109 S 1	Allison rd N8
30 H 15	Allison rd N8
61 W 19	Allison rd W3
130 K 8	Allitsen rd NW8
89 W 12	Allnutt way SW4
75 U 13	Alloa rd SE8
55 O 6	Alloa rd Ilf
47 E 5	Allonby gdns Wemb
63 W 9	Alloway rd E3
18 H 9	All Saints clo N9
106 D 16	All Saints rd SW19
73 V 7	All Saints rd W3
137 O 3	All Saints rd W11
154 B 5	All Saints rd Sutton
133 N 7	All Saints st N1
133 N 7	All Saints st N1
31 R 18	Allsop pl NW1
62 J 6	All Souls av NW10
128 A 4	All Souls av NW10
139 Z 2	All Souls pl W1
1 P 6	Allum way N20
110 G 10	Allwood clo SE26
33 U 1	Alma av E4
50 C 12	Almack rd E5
153 T 10	Alma cres Sutton
151 P 6	Alma gro SE1
62 K 9	Alma pl NW10
109 T 17	Alma pl SE19
122 G 12	Alma pl Thntn Hth
29 R 3	Alma rd N10
88 C 11	Alma rd NW3
154 K 10	Alma rd Carsh
6 U 12	Alma rd Enf
115 O 6	Alma rd Sidcp
58 A 20	Alma rd S'hall
23 R 3	Alma row Har
130 D 11	Alma sq NW8
51 X 16	Alma st E15
47 T 17	Alma st NW5
88 G 18	Alma ter SW18
133 W 3	Almedia st N1
88 K 12	Almeric rd SW11
104 G 17	Almer rd SW20
48 B 4	Almington st N4
72 J 8	Almond av W5
46 L 6	Almond av W5
154 L 3	Almond av Carsh
127 W 17	Almond clo Brom
72 A 19	Almond gro Brentf
31 X 2	Almond rd N17
151 X 6	Almond rd SE16
21 T 9	Almonds av Buck Hl
127 W 17	Almond way Brom
7 L 8	Almond way Harrow
121 Y 10	Almond way Mitch
82 A 2	Almorah rd Hounsl
134 E 2	Almorah st N1
6 A 18	Alnwick av E16
120 A 9	Alnwick grdn Mrdn
65 Y 18	Alnwick rd E16
94 H 17	Alnwick rd SE12
60 G 7	Alperton la Wemb
129 N 16	Alperton st W10
129 N 1	Alpha clo NW1
129 U 8	Alpha pl NW6
146 M 13	Alpha pl SW3
20 C 11	Alpha rd E4
18 J 18	Alpha rd N18
92 M 1	Alpha rd SE14
123 R 20	Alpha rd Croy
9 W 15	Alpha rd Enf
116 M 16	Alpha rd Surb
101 P 12	Alpha rd Tedd
91 X 5	Alpha rd SE15
157 S 7	Alpine clo Croy
127 W 3	Alpine copse Brom
75 S 12	Alpine rd SE16
66 K 14	Alpine way E6
10 G 8	Alpine wlk Stanm
41 Z 1	Alric av N Mald
118 B 6	Alric av New Mald
43 Z 20	Alrick av W10
30 G 20	Alroy rd N4
150 H 10	Alsace rd SE17
151 O 5	Alscot rd SE1
80 J 9	Alsike rd Belvdr
152 F 8	Alsom av Worc Pk
18 M 18	Alston rd N18
11 H 11	Alston rd SW17
4 E 10	Alston rd Barnt
113 U 5	Altash way SE9
18 H 20	Altair clo N17
72 B 7	Altenburg av W13
88 L 10	Altenburgh gdns SW11
105 U 17	Alt gro SW19
22 B 3	Altham rd Pinn
88 B 6	Althea st SW6
117 N 7	Altheston rd Kingst
34 B 13	Althorne gdns E18
D 6	Althorne way Dgnhm
23 O 16	Althorpe rd Harrow
106 K 1	Althorp rd SW17
53 T 20	Altmore av E6
66 G 4	Altmore av E6
23 W 2	Alton av Stanm
115 Z 3	Alton clo Bxly
83 X 3	Alton clo Islwth
111 N 19	Alton gdns Becknhm
83 R 17	Alton gdns Twick
31 O 11	Alton rd N17
86 H 19	Alton rd SW15
104 G 1	Alton rd SW15
156 F 6	Alton rd Croy
84 L 11	Alton rd Rich
84 C 16	Alton st E14
124 A 15	Altyre clo Becknhm
157 P 4	Altyre rd Croy
124 L 12	Altyre way Becknhm
46 B 15	Alvanley gdns NW6
105 X 5	Alverstone av SW19
15 V 2	Alverstone av Barnt
96 A 20	Alverstone gdns SE9
53 W 14	Alverstone rd E12
44 M 20	Alverstone rd NW2
118 E 8	Alverstone rd New Mald
43 N 3	Alverstone rd Wemb
123 S 11	Alverston gdns SE25
24 B 11	Alveston av Harrow
150 J 9	Alvey st SE17
49 U 19	Alvington cres E8
94 J 17	Alwald cres SE12
73 X 4	Alwyn av W4
159 S 17	Alwyn clo Croy
48 K 19	Alwyne la N1
48 K 19	Alwyne pl N1
105 V 14	Alwyne rd SW19
71 S 1	Alwyne rd W7
48 L 18	Alwyne rd N1
48 K 20	Alwyne vlls N1
61 T 17	Alwyn gdns W3
27 X 18	Alyth gdns NW11
71 Z 17	Amalgamated dr Brentf
143 V 5	Amazon st E1
82 C 5	Ambassador clo Hounsl
140 C 15	Ambassadors ct SW1
32 H 4	Amber av E17
27 Z 10	Amberden av N3
149 X 10	Ambergate st SE17
22 D 11	Amberley clo Pinn
115 U 13	Amberley ct Sidcp
18 F 4	Amberley gdns Enf
152 C 9	Amberley gdns Epsom
109 Z 11	Amberley gro SE26
123 U 18	Amberley gro Croy
93 P 20	Amberley rd E10
17 P 9	Amberley rd N13
80 K 16	Amberley rd SE2
129 W 19	Amberley rd W9
21 Y 5	Amberley rd Buck Hl
18 F 1	Amberley rd Enf
119 W 17	Amberley way Mrdn
38 H 12	Amberley way Rom
51 X 18	Amber st E15
118 B 15	Amberwood ri New Mald
112 J 7	Amblecote clo SE12
112 J 7	Amblecote rd SE12
48 H 9	Ambler rd N4
111 X 15	Ambleside Brom
107 X 10	Ambleside av SW16
124 J 12	Ambleside av Becknhm
57 Y 15	Ambleside av Hornch
7 T 11	Ambleside cres Enf
35 S 14	Ambleside gdns Ilf
154 D 14	Ambleside gdns Sutton
42 F 3	Ambleside gdns Wemb
62 D 1	Ambleside rd NW10
98 D 4	Ambleside rd Bxly Hth
155 Y 20	Ambrey way Wallgtn
81 S 9	Ambrooke rd Belvdr
148 B 3	Ambrosden av SW1
27 U 20	Ambrose av NW11
151 V 6	Ambrose st SE16
149 Z 8	Amelia st SE17
141 Y 5	Amen corner EC4
107 N 14	Amen corner SW17
141 Y 5	Amen ct EC4
143 N 8	America sq EC3
142 A 15	America st SE1
87 N 15	Amerland rd SW18
75 X 18	Amersham gro SE14
18 B 19	Amersham rd N18
92 L 1	Amersham rd SE14
123 N 13	Amersham rd Croy
23 S 18	Amersham rd Harrow
75 Y 19	Amersham vale SE14
62 L 3	Amery gdns NW10
128 A 5	Amery gdns NW10
41 Y 7	Amery rd Harrow
108 B 4	Amesbury av SW2
20 D 1	Amesbury dri E4
127 O 5	Amesbury rd Brom
68 J 1	Amesbury rd Dgnhm
119 N 19	Ames clo Worc Pk
51 X 13	Amethyst rd E15
60 C 17	Amherst av W13
60 D 17	Amherst rd W13
83 Y 4	Amhurst gdns Islwth
31 R 20	Amhurst pk N16
92 W 13	Amhurst pas E8
49 Z 15	Amhurst rd E8
52 A 16	Amhurst rd E8
49 U 11	Amhurst rd N16
49 W 12	Amhurst ter E5
55 P 12	Amidas gdns Dgnhm
63 P 11	Amiel st E1
88 L 8	Amies st SW11
118 L 2	Amity gro SW20
65 O 2	Amity rd E15
64 E 7	Ammiel ter E3
89 O 15	Amner rd SW11
74 L 8	Amor rd W6
144 B 2	Amor rd W6
91 W 8	Amott rd SE15
80 F 5	Ampleforth rd SE2
133 N 13	Ampton pl WC1
133 N 14	Ampton st WC1
110 A 1	Amroth clo SE23
8 B 17	Amwell clo Enf
133 S 12	Amwell st EC1
84 A 18	Amyand la Twick
84 A 18	Amyand Pk gdns Twick
83 Z 19	Amyand Pk rd Twick
84 B 17	Amyand Pk rd Twick
93 N 13	Amyruth rd SE4
89 N 3	Analy st SW11
47 U 6	Anatola rd N19
118 F 15	Ancaster cres New Mald
124 F 7	Ancaster rd Becknhm
79 V 19	Ancaster st SE18
144 J 15	Ancill clo W6
105 Z 13	Anchorage clo SW19
77 X 11	Anchor And Hope la SE7
151 W 6	Anchor st SE16
92 G 6	Ancona rd NW10
79 T 12	Ancona rd SE18
90 A 8	Andalus rd SW9
42 G 13	Ander clo Wemb
82 K 11	Anderson pl Hounsl
35 O 9	Anderson rd Ilf
147 O 8	Anderson st SW3
91 P 8	Anderton clo SE5
58 L 10	Andover clo Grnfd
129 X 9	Andover pl NW6
101 R 2	Andover rd Twick
9 Y 14	Andre st E8
98 M 14	Andrew clo Bxly
89 Y 1	Andrew pl SW8
89 Y 1	Andrew pl SW8
21 Y 7	Andrews clo Buck Hl
153 N 2	Andrews clo Worc Pk
135 X 6	Andrews rd E8
64 G 17	Andrew st E14
80 D 6	Andwell rd SE2
109 V 18	Anerley gro SE19
109 W 17	Anerley hill SE19
109 Y 18	Anerley pk SE20
110 A 17	Anerley pk SE20
109 Y 17	Anerley Park rd SE20
109 Y 20	Anerley rd SE20
124 A 1	Anerley rd SE20
109 Z 20	Anerley Station rd SE20
109 W 17	Anerley vale SE19
143 P 3	Angel all E1
18 H 15	Angel clo N18
160 A 4	Angel ct EC1
160 F 5	Angel ct EC2
140 C 14	Angel ct SW1
82 K 12	Angelfield Hounsl
154 A 5	Angel hill Sutton
154 B 4	Angel Hill dri Sutton
51 X 18	Angel la E15
90 G 6	Angell rd SW9
133 T 9	Angel ms N1
90 G 7	Angel Pk gdns SW19
160 F 10	Angel pass EC4
18 H 15	Angel pl N18
19 O 17	Angel rd N18
9 O 14	Angel rd Enf
23 U 18	Angel rd Harrow
142 A 4	Angel st EC1
74 L 12	Angel wlk W6
144 B 8	Angel wlk W6
39 O 15	Angel way Rom
94 D 1	Angerstein la SE3
55 U 4	Angle green Dgnhm
102 C 10	Anglers clo Rich
47 T 1	Anglers la NW5
78 M 12	Anglesea av SE18
78 L 12	Anglesea rd SE18
116 G 9	Anglesea rd Kingst
135 T 17	Anglesea st E1
15 O 15	Anglesey Ct rd Carsh
155 O 15	Anglesey gdns Carsh
9 O 13	Anglesey rd Enf
22 G 10	Anglesmede way Pinn
108 B 9	Angles rd SW16
66 H 4	Anglia wk E6
63 Y 6	Anglo rd E3
25 Z 5	Angus gdns NW9
65 Y 10	Angus rd E13
75 X 19	Angus st SE14
146 L 19	Anhalt rd SW11
78 L 20	Ankerdine cres SE18
95 Y 1	Ankerdine cres SE18
101 S 12	Anlaby rd Tedd
64 C 18	Anley rd W14
11 P 15	Anmer lodge Stanm
64 C 18	Anmersh gro Stanm
77 P 14	Annandale rd SE10
74 A 13	Annandale rd W4
157 Y 3	Annandale rd Croy
96 J 19	Annandale rd Sidcp
39 O 4	Annan way Rom
102 K 12	Anne Boleyns wlk Kingst
153 R 16	Anne Boleyns wlk Sutton
25 Z 10	Annesley av NW9
44 A 10	Annesley clo NW10
158 M 6	Annesley dri Croy
94 G 2	Annesley rd SE3
47 U 6	Annesley wlk N19
65 S 11	Anne st E13
23 T 6	Annette clo Harrow
48 D 12	Annette rd N7
63 Z 4	Annie Besant clo E3
29 N 11	Annington rd N2
50 H 19	Annis rd E9
146 F 16	Ann la SW10
139 S 19	Anns clo SW1
143 O 2	Anns pl E1
88 C 17	Ann's Pk rd SW18
123 N 7	Annsworthy av Thntn Hth
123 P 4	Annsworthy cres Thntn Hth
92 C 5	Ansdell rd SE15
137 Y 20	Ansdell st W8
137 Y 20	Ansdell ter W8
155 N 1	Ansell gro Carsh
106 K 7	Ansell rd SW17
157 U 4	Anselm clo Croy
145 S 15	Anselm rd SW6
22 E 3	Anselm rd Pinn
128 B 7	Ansford rd Brom
136 H 10	Ansleigh pl W11
38 F 7	Anson clo Rom
47 X 13	Anson rd N7
44 L 14	Anson rd NW2
45 P 14	Anson rd NW2
91 X 7	Anstey rd SE15
30 X 16	Anstey wlk N15
96 E 16	Anstridge rd SE9
78 E 8	Antelope rd SE18
63 W 8	Anthill rd E3
13 P 14	Anthony clo NW7
123 X 15	Anthony rd SE25
59 S 7	Anthony rd Grnfd
97 O 2	Anthony rd Welling
31 W 13	Antill rd N15
63 S 17	Antill ter E1
153 W 6	Anton cres Sutton
49 Y 16	Anton st E8

46 L 17	Antrim gro NW3
46 L 18	Antrim rd NW3
153 W 19	Antrobus clo Sutton
73 V 10	Antrobus rd W4
21 U 19	Anworth clo Wdfd Grn
85 W 6	Anyscombe pth SW14
111 S 20	Apex clo Becknhm
83 S 1	Aplin way Islwth
112 G 20	Apollo av Brom
57 W 7	Apollo clo Hornch
146 F 17	Apollo pl SW10
141 W 7	Apothecary st EC4
90 E 14	Appach rd SW2
20 E 19	Appleby clo E4
31 N 16	Appleby clo N15
101 P 5	Appleby clo Twick
49 Y 20	Appleby rd E8
65 R 18	Appleby rd E16
135 N 8	Appleby st E2
98 L 4	Appledore av Bxly Hth
106 L 3	Appledore clo SW17
126 D 11	Appledore clo Brom
25 O 4	Appledore clo Edg
114 J 8	Appledore cres Sidcp
128 M 18	Appleford rd W10
72 H 12	Applegarth Brentf
159 S 16	Applegarth Croy
36 L 13	Applegath dri Ilf
80 F 1	Applegarth rd SE2
142 G 3	Applegarth rd W14
8 E 12	Apple gro Enf
116 H 4	Apple mkt Kingst
118 F 14	Appleton gdns New Mald
95 P 7	Appleton rd SE9
140 D 12	Apple Tree yd SW1
44 J 9	Applewood clo NW2
134 J 20	Appold st EC2
63 P 7	Approach rd E2
118 M 3	Approach rd SW20
5 S 15	Approach rd Barnt
27 O 15	Approach the NW4
61 Z 17	Approach the W3
9 N 8	Approach the Enf
27 N 13	Aprey gdns NW4
59 U 19	April clo W7
110 F 7	April glen SE23
49 V 13	April st E8
22 M 15	Apsley clo Harrow
123 Z 9	Apsley rd SE25
17 W 7	Apsley rd New Mald
130 H 8	Aquila st NW8
141 T 14	Aquinas st SE1
86 C 10	Arabella dri SW15
20 H 2	Arabia clo E4
92 K 10	Arabin rd SE4
152 H 20	Aragon av Epsom
102 H 12	Aragon rd Kingst
119 P 16	Aragon rd Mrdn
37 O 19	Arandora cres Brom
11 S 14	Aran dri Stanm
63 V 7	Arbery rd E4
17 N 2	Arboreal av N14
125 R 3	Arbor clo Becknhm
20 K 11	Arbor rd E4
63 R 11	Arbor sq E1
9 T 12	Arbour rd Enf
57 Y 14	Arbour way Hornch
95 S 7	Arbroath rd SE9
109 Y 8	Arbury ter SE26
97 Z 16	Arbuthnot la Bxly
98 A 15	Arbuthnot la Bxly
82 F 4	Arbuthnot rd SE14
39 R 17	Arcade pl Rom
142 J 2	Arcade the EC2
27 X 6	Arcadia av N3
97 Y 16	Arcadian av Bxly
97 Y 16	Arcadian clo Bxly
30 E 1	Arcadian gdns N22
97 Y 17	Arcadian rd Bxly
64 B 16	Arcadia st E14
149 O 2	Archbishops park SE11
90 D 17	Archbishops pl SW2
91 V 11	Archdale rd SE22
145 P 13	Archel rd W14
23 W 9	Archer clo Harrow
123 Z 8	Archer rd SE25
140 E 9	Archer st W1
138 M 7	Archery clo W2
95 U 12	Archery rd SE9
139 W 11	Archibald ms W1
47 X 12	Archibald rd N7
64 A 10	Archibald st E3
150 A 3	Arch st SE1
47 V 6	Archway clo N19
106 A 9	Archway clo SW20
47 V 6	Archway mall N19
46 U 6	Archway rd N6
47 U 3	Archway rd N6
86 B 7	Archway st SW13
49 U 14	Arcola st E8
47 R 15	Arctic st NW5
112 A 14	Arcus rd Brom
91 O 14	Ardbeg rd SE24
10 G 2	Arden clo Bushey Watf
41 P 10	Arden clo Harrow
55 W 20	Arden cres Dgnhm
68 H 1	Arden cres Dgnhm
27 V 9	Arden rd N3
122 E 5	Ardfern av SW16
111 Y 3	Ardfillan rd SE6
93 Y 19	Ardgowan rd SE6
111 Y 3	Ardgowan rd SE6
48 L 12	Ardilaun rd N5
119 X 19	Ardleigh gdns Sutton
32 L 5	Ardleigh rd E17
49 P 18	Ardleigh rd N1
32 M 5	Ardleigh ter E17
44 A 9	Ardley clo NW10
110 J 7	Ardley clo SE6
21 W 4	Ardlui rd SE27
116 J 12	Ardmay gdns Surb
93 X 15	Ardmere rd SE13
21 W 4	Ardmore la Buck Hl
111 W 4	Ardock rd SE6
152 F 5	Ardrossan gdns Worc Pk
36 C 17	Ardwell av Ilf
108 A 3	Ardwell rd SW2
45 X 12	Ardwick rd NW2
50 G 2	Argall av E10
141 Z 16	Argent st SE1
145 U 19	Argon ms SW6
38 G 6	Argus clo Rom
58 A 9	Argus way Grnfd
82 J 15	Argyle av Hounsl
16 H 16	Argyle av Hounsl
59 Y 11	Argyle av W13
74 K 11	Argyle pl W6
63 S 11	Argyle rd E1
51 Z 13	Argyle rd E15
14 L 16	Argyle rd N12
15 N 17	Argyle rd N12
31 W 4	Argyle rd N17
18 L 13	Argyle rd N18
59 Z 12	Argyle rd W13
60 A 19	Argyle rd W13
4 A 13	Argyle rd Barnt
22 J 17	Argyle rd Harrow
82 K 13	Argyle rd Hounsl
53 W 6	Argyle rd Ilf
132 L 12	Argyle sq WC1
70 J 2	Argyll av S'hall
25 T 7	Argyll gdns Edg
137 U 20	Argyll rd W8
140 A 6	Argyll st W1
92 H 9	Arica rd SE4
45 X 18	Ariel rd NW6
136 D 12	Ariel way W12
89 Y 9	Aristotle rd SW4
108 J 19	Arkell gro SE19
111 U 8	Arkindale rd SE6
32 K 17	Arkley cres E17
75 X 17	Arklow rd SE14
46 D 15	Arkwright rd NW3
157 V 20	Arkwright rd S Croy
58 A 8	Arkwright st E16
90 A 7	Arlesford rd SW9
87 S 14	Arlesley clo SW15
90 F 15	Arlingford rd SW2
14 K 12	Arlington N12
134 D 6	Arlington av N1
96 G 19	Arlington clo Sidcp
153 Y 3	Arlington clo Sutton
84 C 14	Arlington clo Twick
154 L 3	Arlington dri Carsh
73 V 13	Arlington gdns W4
53 V 3	Arlington gdns Ilf
16 G 6	Arlington rd N14
131 Y 5	Arlington rd NW1
132 A 8	Arlington rd NW1
60 B 18	Arlington rd W13
122 F 5	Arlington rd Rich
116 H 15	Arlington rd Surb
101 V 10	Arlington rd Tedd
84 C 15	Arlington rd Twick
34 G 13	Arlington rd Wdfd Grn
134 C 6	Arlington sq N1
140 A 13	Arlington st W1
133 U 12	Arlington way EC1
17 U 6	Arlow rd N21
31 Z 14	Armadale clo N15
145 T 16	Armadale rd NW6
76 B 16	Armada st SE8
63 Y 4	Armagh rd E3
121 N 3	Armfield cres Mitch
8 B 6	Armfield rd Enf
74 K 3	Arminger rd W12
77 O 13	Armitage rd SE10
45 U 4	Armitage rd NW11
87 Y 13	Armoury way SW18
56 D 20	Armstead wlk Dgnhm
69 R 1	Armstead wlk Dgnhm
20 M 19	Armstrong av Wdfd Grn
5 T 12	Armstrong cres Barnt
77 Y 12	Armstrong gdns SE7
74 D 2	Armstrong rd W3
100 C 13	Armstrong rd Felt
70 K 5	Armstrong wy S'hall
5 S 18	Arnal cres SW 18
87 Z 14	Arndale wlk SW18
140 L 6	Arne st WC2
94 B 10	Arne wlk SE3
37 W 11	Arneways av Rom
148 F 3	Arneway st SW1
140 F 2	Arnewood clo SW15
121 N 13	Arneys la Mitch
93 W 19	Arngask rd SE6
91 S 13	Arnhem way SE22
9 Z 2	Arnold av Enf
135 N 14	Arnold cir E2
25 N 20	Arnold clo Harrow
83 R 13	Arnold cres Islwth
17 U 15	Arnold gdns N13
64 A 9	Arnold rd E3
31 T 11	Arnold rd N15
16 M 17	Arnold rd SW17
69 P 2	Arnold rd Dgnhm
69 R 1	Arnold rd Dgnhm
40 B 18	Arnold rd Grnfd
16 K 12	Arnos gro N14
16 J 15	Arnos rd N11
80 F 1	Arnott clo SE2
74 C 3	Arnott clo W4
91 Y 12	Arnould av SE5
91 P 9	Arnould av SE5
42 G 3	Arnside gdns Wemb
98 E 2	Arnside rd Bxly Hth
150 D 13	Arnside st SE17
111 R 10	Arnulf st SE6
108 H 15	Arnulls rd SW16
90 D 15	Arodene rd SW2
108 A 18	Arpley rd SE20
159 S 5	Arragon gdns SW16 W Wkhm
66 B 4	Arragon rd E6
83 Z 20	Arragon rd Twick
155 T 8	Arran cl Wallgtn
5 N 5	Arran dri E12
111 S 3	Arran rd SE6
120 D 10	Arras av Mrdn
124 E 5	Arrol rd Becknhm
64 D 9	Arrow rd E3
95 T 6	Arsenal rd SE9
105 N 19	Artebery rd SW20
39 T 20	Artesian clo Hornch
137 T 6	Artesian rd W2
64 M 3	Arthingworth st E15
79 O 11	Arthur gro SE18
66 G 8	Arthur rd E6
8 D 11	Arthur rd N7
18 F 7	Arthur rd N9
105 W 7	Arthur rd SW19
103 P 19	Arthur rd Kingst
6 K 12	Arthur rd New Mald
32 U 19	Arthur rd Rom
160 F 9	Arthur st EC4
143 V 10	Artichoke hill E1
91 O 2	Artichoke pl SE5
36 D 17	Artillery clo Ilf
142 L 1	Artillery la E1
142 M 2	Artillery pas E1
78 H 12	Artillery pl SE18
2 D 2	Artillery row SW1
119 W 9	Asbaston av Mrdn
42 A 13	Arundel clo E15
58 C 15	Arundel clo Bxly
156 H 7	Arundel clo Croy
100 L 13	Arundel clo Hampt
17 F 14	Arundel dri Harrow
34 G 2	Arundel dri Wdfd Grn
17 U 7	Arundel gdns N21
137 N 8	Arundel gdns W11
25 Y 2	Arundel gdns Edg
25 Y 2	Arundel gdns Edg
55 N 6	Arundel gdns Ilf
49 R 15	Arundel gro N16
8 F 19	Arundel pl N1
5 X 12	Arundel rd Barnt
123 O 15	Arundel rd Croy
117 U 2	Arundel rd Kingst
153 U 17	Arundel rd Sutton
48 F 19	Arundel sq N1
141 P 8	Arundel st WC2
74 K 17	Arundel ter SW12
144 A 14	Arundel ter SW12
74 K 17	Arundel ter SW13
48 G 15	Arvon rd N5
148 B 20	Ascalon st SW8
38 L 1	Ascension rd Rom
33 P 1	Ascham dri E4
32 J 3	Ascham end E17
47 V 14	Ascham st NW5
123 V 17	Ashurch rd Croy
40 G 16	Ascot clo Grnfd
9 P 1	Ascot gdns Enf
43 Y 15	Ascot pk NW10
66 F 8	Ascot rd E6
31 O 16	Ascot rd N15
18 K 13	Ascot rd N18
107 N 15	Ascot rd SW17
72 J 5	Ascot av W5
34 H 13	Ashbourne av E18
15 Z 7	Ashbourne av N20
53 V 14	Ashbourne av NW11
81 N 19	Ashbourne av Bxly Hth
41 R 7	Ashbourne av Harrow
107 R 17	Ashbourne av Mitch
15 O 14	Ashbourne clo N5
61 O 13	Ashbourne clo W5
12 L 17	Ashbourne gro NW7
91 O 12	Ashbourne gro SE22
74 B 14	Ashbourne gro W4
60 M 11	Ashbourne rd W5
61 O 13	Ashbourne rd W5
105 W 17	Ashbourne ter SW19
27 V 14	Ashbourne way NW11
24 E 19	Ashbridge clo Harrow
34 A 20	Ashbridge rd E11
130 K 18	Ashbridge st NW8
47 X 5	Ashbrook rd N19
56 H 10	Ashbrook rd Dgnhm
146 A 5	Ashburn gdns SW7
23 W 20	Ashburnham av Harrow
28 G 12	Ashburnham clo N2
23 X 20	Ashburnham gdns Harrow
76 E 20	Ashburnham gro SE10
76 E 20	Ashburnham pl SE10
62 M 8	Ashburnham rd NW10
128 C 11	Ashburnham rd NW10
146 D 19	Ashburnham rd SW10
81 X 10	Ashburnham rd Erith
102 C 7	Ashburnham rd Rich
146 A 5	Ashburn pl SW7
123 Z 20	Ashburton av Croy
54 G 14	Ashburton av Ilf
157 W 1	Ashburton clo Croy
157 W 2	Ashburton gdns Croy
48 F 13	Ashburton gro N7
65 T 17	Ashburton rd E16
123 W 20	Ashburton rd Croy
157 W 2	Ashburton rd Croy
65 S 6	Ashburton ter E13
37 V 16	Ashbury gdns Rom
89 N 6	Ashbury rd SW11
48 M 20	Ashby gro N1
31 W 15	Ashby rd N15
92 L 5	Ashby rd SE4
93 N 5	Ashby rd SE4
133 X 3	Ashby st EC1
122 M 15	Ashby wlk Croy
74 A 10	Ashchurch ct W4
74 F 8	Ashchurch gro W12
74 F 7	Ashchurch Pk vlls W12
74 F 8	Ashchurch Pk vlls W12
74 F 7	Ashchurch ter W12
154 L 2	Ashcombe av Carsh
117 X 3	Ash clo New Mald
38 G 3	Ash clo Rom
124 C 3	Ash clo SE20
115 P 9	Ash clo Sidcp
10 K 19	Ash clo Stanm
116 G 18	Ashcombe av Surb
12 B 14	Ashcombe gdns Edg
44 C 10	Ashcombe pk NW2
105 Y 12	Ashcombe rd SW19
155 O 12	Ashcombe rd Carsh
117 V 5	Ashcombe sq New Mald
87 Z 6	Ashcombe rd SW6
96 M 15	Ashcroft av Sidcp
97 N 16	Ashcroft cres Sidcp
63 V 9	Ashcroft rd E3
82 L 18	Ashdale clo Twick
10 K 19	Ashdale gro Stanm
112 J 1	Ashdale rd SE12
82 L 18	Ashdale way Twick
21 V 19	Ashdon clo Wdfd Grn
62 C 3	Ashdon rd NW10
125 S 4	Ashdown clo Becknhm

47 O 15	Ashdown cr NW5	
9 O 10	Ashdown rd Enf	
116 J 4	Ashdown rd Kingst	
38 H 6	Ashdown wlk Rom	
50 G 14	Ashenden rd E5	
99 W 16	Ashen dri Drtfrd	
105 X 5	Ashen gro SW19	
158 G 20	Ashen vale S Croy	
102 J 1	Ashfield clo Rich	
102 J 2	Ashfield clo Rich	
114 C 17	Ashfield la Chisl	
6 K 6	Ashfield p'de N9	
30 M 19	Ashfield rd N4	
16 G 11	Ashfield rd N14	
74 C 1	Ashfield rd W3	
63 O 16	Ashfield st E1	
143 W 3	Ashfield st E1	
29 Z 14	Ashford av N8	
9 R 8	Ashford cres Enf	
32 K 18	Ashford gro E17	
53 V 20	Ashford rd E6	
34 J 8	Ashford rd E18	
45 O 12	Ashford rd NW2	
135 X 5	Ash gro E8	
17 X 12	Ash gro N13	
45 R 13	Ash gro NW2	
124 C 3	Ash gro SE 20	
72 K 7	Ash gro W5	
18 D 2	Ash gro Enf	
58 J 13	Ash gro S'hall	
159 V 1	Ash gro W Wckm	
41 Y 13	Ash gro Wemb	
111 Y 14	Ashgrove rd Ilf	
54 L 5	Ashgrove rd Ilf	
55 N 4	Ashgrove rd Ilf	
87 W 5	Ashington rd SW6	
39 W 1	Ash la Rom	
108 A 10	Ashlake rd SW16	
139 T 1	Ashland pl W1	
64 K 3	Ashland rd E15	
78 M 12	Ashland pl SE18	
102 J 1	Ashleigh clo Rich	
154 A 3	Ashleigh gdns Croy	
124 B 5	Ashleigh rd SE20	
86 A 7	Ashleigh rd SW14	
48 A 2	Ashley N19	
35 Z 8	Ashley av Ilf	
119 Y 12	Ashley av Mrdn	
27 N 7	Ashley clo NW4	
89 P 7	Ashley cr SW11	
G 8	Ashley cres N22	
82 K 20	Ashley gdns Twick	
17 Y 14	Ashley gdns N13	
102 G 5	Ashley gdns Rich	
42 K 7	Ashley gdns Wemb	
27 N 7	Ashley la NW4	
156 J 8	Ashley la Croy	
148 B 3	Ashley pl SW1	
20 A 18	Ashley rd E4	
65 Y 1	Ashley rd E7	
31 Y 1	Ashley rd N17	
106 A 15	Ashley rd SW19	
9 P 10	Ashley rd Enf	
100 H 20	Ashley rd Hampt	
84 K 8	Ashley rd Rich	
122 D 10	Ashley rd Thntn Hth	
27 N 2	Ashley wlk NW7	
123 X 20	Ashling rd Croy	
51 Y 13	Ashling rd E15	
87 N 6	Ashlone rd SW6	
6 H 18	Ashmed N14	
93 O 4	Ashmead rd SE8	
125 W 3	Ashmere av Becknhm	
153 N 12	Ashmere clo Sutton	
90 A 11	Ashmere gro SW2	
130 L 19	Ashmill st NW1	
149 O 15	Ashmole estate SE11	
91 R 16	Ashmole rd SW8	
149 R 16	Ashmole rd SW8	
96 F 7	Ashmore gro Welling	
129 O 11	Ashmore rd W9	
31 U 14	Ashmount rd N15	
47 W 2	Ashmount rd N19	
38 M 8	Ashmour gdns Rom	
39 N 8	Ashmour gdns Rom	
42 A 19	Ashness gdns Grnfd	
88 M 13	Ashness rd SW11	
24 E 19	Ashridge clo Harrow	
9 O 20	Ashridge cres SE18	
18 M 15	Ashridge gdns N13	
17 N 16	Ashridge gdns N13	
22 B 13	Ashridge gdns Pinn	
119 U 8	Ashridge way Mrdn	
52 B 15	Ash rd E5	
159 O 2	Ash rd Croy	
119 T 19	Ash rd Sutton	
127 W 15	Ash row Brom	
49 X 1	Ashstead rd E5	
153 W 9	Ashton clo Sutton	
82 D 10	Ashton gdns Hounsl	
37 Z 19	Ashton gdns Rom	
51 X 16	Ashton rd E15	
64 G 19	Ashton st E14	
120 H 3	Ashtree av Mitch	
124 H 13	Ash Tree clo Croy	
25 X 15	Ash Tree dell NW9	
124 H 14	Ash Tree way Croy	
35 Z 18	Ashurst dri Ilf	
36 C 13	Ashurst dri Ilf	
15 X 17	Ashurst rd N12	
5 Z 17	Ashurst rd Barnt	
6 A 15	Ashurst rd Barnt	
157 Z 2	Ashurst wlk Croy	
106 L 11	Ashville rd E11	
51 W 8	Ashville rd E11	
112 F 2	Ashwater rd SE12	
18 D 16	Ashwell gro N18	
49 T 17	Ashwin st E8	
20 K 11	Ashwood rd E4	
129 Y 13	Ashworth rd W9	
97 X 11	Askern clo Bxly Hth	
74 F 6	Askew bldgs W12	
74 E 4	Askew cres W12	
74 G 7	Askew rd W12	
74 F 3	Askham rd W12	
87 T 14	Askill dri SW15	
88 B 18	Aslett st SW18	
45 U 14	Asmara rd NW2	
157 A 1	Asmuns hill NW11	
27 X 15	Asmuns hill NW11	
27 W 15	Asmuns pl NW11	
72 L 6	Aspen clo W5	
127 U 3	Aspen copse Brom	
41 Z 10	Aspen dri Harrow	
74 K 13	Aspen gdns W6	
121 N 12	Aspen gdns Mitch	
81 P 7	Aspen grn Blvdr	
144 G 14	Aspenlea rd W6	
92 F 8	Aspinall rd SE4	
75 O 10	Aspinden rd SE16	
151 Y 5	Aspinden rd SE16	
50 A 16	Aspland gro E8	
88 B 14	Aspley rd SW18	
81 Y 4	Asplins rd N17	
143 S 4	Assam st E1	
63 P 13	Assembly pas E1	
120 H 18	Assembly wlk Carsh	
81 P 13	Assurance cotts Blvdr	
23 R 5	Astall clo Harrow	
92 B 1	Astbury rd SE15	
146 L 9	Astell st SW3	
76 F 6	Aste st E14	
36 C 12	Asthall gdns Ilf	
89 O 3	Astle st SW11	
45 N 12	Astley av NW2	
133 Z 1	Astleys row N1	
24 E 20	Aston av Harrow	
103 T 15	Aston clo Kingst	
115 O 9	Aston clo Sidcp	
119 N 3	Aston rd SW20	
63 V 16	Aston rd W5	
63 U 16	Aston st E14	
105 X 2	Astonville st SW18	
38 J 18	Astor av Rom	
90 E 7	Astoria wlk SW9	
57 Y 17	Astra clo Hornch	
74 L 7	Astrop ms W6	
136 B 20	Astrop ms W6	
74 L 7	Astrop ter W6	
136 B 20	Astrop ter W6	
146 A 6	Astwood ms SW5	
75 N 20	Asylum rd SE15	
92 A 1	Asylum rd E15	
151 X 16	Asylum rd SE15	
144 J 20	Atalanta st SW6	
102 C 15	Atbara rd Tedd	
83 O 10	Atcham rd Hounsl	
67 Z 14	Atcost rd Bark	
88 B 20	Atheldene rd SW18	
111 P 6	Athelney st SE6	
63 X 7	Athelstan gro E3	
48 F 5	Athelstane ms N4	
117 N 8	Athelstan rd Kingst	
23 R 8	Athelstone rd Harrow	
41 R 5	Athena clo Harrow	
29 R 11	Athenaeum pl N10	
15 S 6	Athenaeum rd N20	
92 F 13	Athenlay rd SE15	
129 S 18	Athens gdns W9	
50 B 12	Atherden rd E5	
89 Z 7	Atherfold rd SW9	
90 A 7	Atherfold rd SW9	
146 C 4	Atherstone ms SW7	
105 P 9	Atherton dri SW19	
70 J 1	Atherton pl S'hall	
52 C 17	Atherton rd E7	
74 E 20	Atherton rd SW13	
35 S 7	Atherton rd Ilf	
88 K 5	Atherton st SW11	
90 E 19	Athlone rd SW2	
47 N 19	Athlone st NW5	
60 G 6	Athlon rd Wemb	
8 D 18	Athole gdns Enf	
81 X 14	Athol rd Erith	
54 M 2	Athol rd Ilf	
55 N 1	Athol rd Ilf	
64 H 18	Athol st E14	
93 O 13	Athurdon rd SE4	
65 Y 15	Atkinson rd E16	
33 S 19	Atkins rd E10	
89 Z 19	Atkins rd SW12	
90 F 10	Atlantic rd SW19	
77 X 10	Atlas gdns SE7	
48 D 18	Atlas ms N7	
65 S 7	Atlas rd E13	
62 B 10	Atlas rd NW10	
43 U 12	Atlas rd Wemb	
64 A 3	Atley rd E3	
87 S 10	Atney rd SW15	
15 T 8	Attfield clo N20	
30 G 19	Atterbury rd N4	
148 H 8	Atterbury st SW1	
44 A 9	Attewood av NW10	
40 A 19	Attewood rd Grnfd	
68 F 20	Attlee rd SE2	
33 S 11	Attlee ter E17	
133 R 15	Attneave st WC1	
90 E 20	Atwater clo SW2	
91 Y 5	Atwell rd SE15	
85 R 5	Atwood av Rich	
74 J 10	Atwood rd W6	
78 G 3	Auberon st E16	
48 H 12	Aubert pk N5	
48 J 12	Aubert rd N5	
130 C 9	Aubrey pl NW8	
33 P 11	Aubrey rd E17	
30 B 18	Aubrey rd N8	
137 P 14	Aubrey rd W8	
137 R 15	Aubrey wlk W8	
109 N 11	Auburn hill SE27	
86 G 12	Aubyn sq SW15	
123 U 1	Auckland clo SE19	
123 T 1	Auckland gdns SE19	
108 M 9	Auckland hill SE27	
17 N 20	Auckland ri SE19	
51 R 9	Auckland rd E10	
123 U 3	Auckland rd SE19	
123 T 3	Auckland rd SE19	
88 J 12	Auckland rd SW11	
53 Z 3	Auckland rd Ilf	
54 A 2	Auckland rd Ilf	
117 N 8	Auckland rd Kingst	
149 N 11	Auckland rd SE11	
34 C 14	Audley ct E18	
54 K 8	Audley gdns Ilf	
153 Z 18	Audley pl Sutton	
26 H 19	Audley rd NW4	
60 M 15	Audley rd W5	
61 N 14	Audley rd W5	
7 V 8	Audley rd Enf	
139 V 13	Audley sq W1	
125 R 14	Audley gdns Becknhm	
42 B 6	Audley gdns Wemb	
53 Y 10	Audrey rd Ilf	
135 T 8	Audrey st E2	
65 X 9	Augurs la E13	
101 N 5	Augusta rd Twick	
64 C 17	Augusta st E14	
144 F 3	Augustine rd W14	
2 M 5	Augustine rd Harrow	
72 E 19	Augustus clo Brentf	
105 S 1	Augustus st SW19	
131 Z 11	Augustus st NW1	
52 R 13	Aulay st SE1	
154 L 4	Aultone way Carsh	
154 B 2	Aultone way Sutton	
12 U 12	Aulton pl SE11	
123 G 13	Aurelia gdns Croy	
128 B 14	Aurelia rd Croy	
57 O 18	Auriel av Dgnhm	
49 R 15	Auriga ms N5	
59 R 1	Auriol dri Grnfd	
144 K 6	Auriol rd W14	
13 O 11	Austell gdns NW7	
80 E 3	Austen clo SE18	
40 J 6	Austen rd Harrow	
57 S 13	Austin av Brom	
92 K 19	Austin clo SE23	
160 G 5	Austin friars EC2	
89 O 3	Austin st E2	
34 M 14	Austin st E2	
114 L 6	Austral clo Sidcp	
62 J 19	Australia rd W12	
114 B 2	Austral rd W12	
149 W 4	Austral st SE11	
117 S 19	Austyn gdns Surb	
1 L 7	Autumn clo Enf	
64 B 4	Autumn st E3	
7 U 7	Avalon clo Enf	
59 Y 13	Avalon cr W13	
88 A 1	Avalon rd SW6	
9 Y 12	Avalon rd W13	
106 M 14	Avarn rd SW17	
G 16	Avebury pk Surb	
51 X 3	Avebury rd E11	
109 V 19	Avebury rd SW19	
134 F 6	Avebury st N1	
29 O 13	Aveley rd Rom	
149 R 10	Aveline st SE11	
33 O 6	Aveling Park rd E17	
141 Y 6	Ave Maria la EC4	
48 H 10	Avenell rd N5	
87 Z 18	Avening rd SW18	
87 Y 18	Avening terr SW18	
65 T 12	Avenons rd E13	
6 H 18	Avenue clo N14	
44 L 19	Avenue clo NW2	
130 L 6	Avenue clo NW8	
73 S 5	Avenue cres W3	
116 J 11	Avenue elmers Surb	
123 W 5	Avenue gdns SE25	
86 A 8	Avenue gdns SW14	
73 T 5	Avenue gdns W3	
101 X 16	Avenue gdns Tedd	
29 S 11	Avenue ms N10	
108 J 3	Avenue Pk rd SE27	
52 H 13	Avenue rd E7	
29 W 20	Avenue rd N6	
15 R 14	Avenue rd N12	
6 G 20	Avenue rd N14	
16 G 1	Avenue rd N14	
31 O 16	Avenue rd N15	
130 J 4	Avenue rd NW8	
62 D 6	Avenue rd NW10	
110 D 20	Avenue rd SE20	
124 E 2	Avenue rd SE20	
123 V 4	Avenue rd SE25	
121 X 4	Avenue rd SW16	
118 K 2	Avenue rd SW20	
73 S 5	Avenue rd W3	
71 Y 1	Avenue rd W13	
81 W 11	Avenue rd Blvdr	
97 Y 9	Avenue rd Bxly Hth	
72 E 13	Avenue rd Brentf	
81 Y 19	Avenue rd Erith	
83 U 3	Avenue rd Islwth	
116 K 6	Avenue rd Kingst	
118 B 7	Avenue rd New Mald	
22 A 9	Avenue rd Pinn	
55 S 2	Avenue rd Rom	
70 F 2	Avenue rd S'hall	
101 X 16	Avenue rd Tedd	
155 U 18	Avenue rd Wallgtn	
21 Z 18	Avenue rd Wdfd Grn	
117 O 15	Avenue S the Surb	
117 V 7	Avenue ter New Mald	
20 J 15	Avenue the E4	
34 J 17	Avenue the E11	
142 B 8	Avenue the EC3	
27 Y 7	Avenue the N3	
30 E 11	Avenue the N8	
29 U 7	Avenue the N10	
16 P 15	Avenue the N11	
31 P 9	Avenue the N17	
128 J 4	Avenue the NW6	
77 X 18	Avenue the SE7	
95 U 14	Avenue the SE9	
76 J 19	Avenue the SE10	
89 P 13	Avenue the SW4	
74 A 9	Avenue the W4	
60 A 19	Avenue the W13	
4 E 13	Avenue the Barnt	
111 U 20	Avenue the Becknhm	
97 W 18	Avenue the Bxly	
127 O 7	Avenue the Brom	
155 O 16	Avenue the Carsh	
157 R 5	Avenue the Croy	
100 F 14	Avenue the Hampt	
23 V 4	Avenue the Harrow	
82 J 13	Avenue the Hounsl	
115 R 18	Avenue the Orp	
22 E 19	Avenue the Pinn	
85 N 4	Avenue the Rich	
39 O 13	Avenue the Rom	
153 U 20	Avenue the Sutton	
84 D 14	Avenue the Twick	
125 W 18	Avenue the W Wkhm	
126 A 14	Avenue the Wemb	
42 K 3	Avenue the Wemb	
43 O 7	Avenue the Wemb	
152 D 3	Avenue the Worc Pk	
108 H 16	Averill st W6	
144 G 15	Averill st W6	
147 V 8	Avery Farm row SW1	
35 V 16	Avery gdns Ilf	
114 B 2	Avery hill Sidcp	
96 B 16	Avery Hill park SE9	
96 D 20	Avery Hill rd SE9	
139 X 8	Avery row W1	
65 P 14	Aviary clo E13	
124 K 12	Aviemore clo Becknhm	
124 K 12	Aviemore way Becknhm	
92 G 8	Avignon rd SE4	
110 B 17	Avington gro SE20	
63 T 17	Avis sq E1	
107 P 8	Avoca rd SW17	
79 S 8	Avocet ms SE18	
154 D 8	Avon clo Sutton	
152 F 2	Avon clo Worc Pk	
15 N 17	Avondale av N12	

44 B 9 Avondale av NW2
15 Y 4 Avondale av Barnt
118 C 19 Avondale av Worc Pk
34 G 4 Avondale ct E18
9 V 11 Avondale cres Enf
35 O 17 Avondale cres Ilf
82 E 14 Avondale gdns Hounsl
136 K 11 Avondale park W11
136 J 10 Avondale Pk gdns W11
136 J 9 Avondale Pk rd W11
91 U 7 Avondale ri SE15
65 N 14 Avondale rd E16
51 N 1 Avondale rd E17
28 C 5 Avondale rd N3
17 U 9 Avondale rd N13
30 K 15 Avondale rd N15
113 R 5 Avondale rd N19
85 Z 7 Avondale rd SW14
105 Z 12 Avondale rd SW19
106 A 12 Avondale rd SW19
112 C 15 Avondale rd Brom
23 X 9 Avondale rd Harrow
156 M 15 Avondale rd S Croy
97 U 5 Avondale rd Welling
151 S 11 Avondale sq SE1
75 R 19 Avonley rd SE14
22 D 3 Avon mews Pinn
145 N 4 Avonmore pl W14
145 N 5 Avonmore pl W14
150 A 1 Avonmouth st SE1
157 N 14 Avon path S Croy
33 X 11 Avon rd E17
93 O 7 Avon rd SE4
58 J 11 Avon rd Grnfd
77 F 11 Avon way E18
82 K 4 Avonwick rd Hounsl
H 16 Avril way E4
31 P 5 Awfield av N17
96 L 4 Awliscombe rd Welling
67 O 3 Axe st Bark
25 R 4 Axholme av Edg
80 H 20 Axminster cres Welling
97 S 1 Axminster cres Welling
48 B 9 Axminster rd N7
139 T 2 Aybrook st W1
127 W 8 Aycliffe clo Brom
72 H 12 Aycliffe rd W12
126 E 7 Aylesbury rd Brom
133 W 17 Aylesbury st EC1
43 Y 10 Aylesbury st NW10
124 H 13 Aylesford av Becknhm
148 F 11 Aylesford st SW1
45 O 20 Aylestone av NW6
128 F 2 Aylestone av NW6
123 Z 10 Aylett rd SE25
124 A 10 Aylett rd SE25
83 U 5 Aylett rd Islwth
6 K 18 Ayley croft Enf
10 L 12 Aylmer clo Stanm
10 K 13 Aylmer dri Stanm
52 B 2 Aylmer rd E11
68 K 16 Aylmer rd N2
74 C 6 Aylmer rd W12
55 X 11 Aylmer rd Dgnhm
110 G 5 Aylward rd SE23
119 V 5 Aylward rd SW20
10 L 13 Aylwards ri Stanm
63 R 16 Aylward st E1
144 H 3 Aynhoe rd W14
65 T 10 Aynscombe la SW14
65 V 6 Ayres clo E13
61 X 1 Ayres cres NW10
142 B 16 Ayres st SE1
38 O 4 Ayr grn Rom
49 R 8 Ayrsome rd N16
38 O 4 Ayr way Rom
91 P 17 Aysgarth rd SE21
90 D 5 Aytoun rd SW19
71 W 2 Azalea clo W7
91 U 4 Azenby rd SE15
77 N 12 Azof st SE10

B

48 J 15 Baalbec rd N5
35 P 12 Babbacombe gdns Ilf
112 G 19 Babbacombe rd Brom
43 R 17 Babbington ri Wemb
26 K 13 Babington rd NW4
107 Y 11 Babington rd SW16
55 T 14 Babington rd Dgnhm

57 X 4 Babington rd Hornch
140 E 12 Babmaes st SW1
134 G 13 Baches st N1
143 T 5 Back Ch la E1
133 T 18 Back hill EC1
29 Z 17 Back la N8
46 E 12 Back la NW3
98 C 18 Back la Bxly
72 G 18 Back la Brentf
25 V 5 Back la Edg
102 D 5 Back la Rich
37 X 20 Back la Rom
115 N 10 Back rd Sidcp
73 T 2 Back st W3
150 M 3 Bacon gro SE1
25 P 3 Bacon la Edg
47 P 4 Bacons la N6
135 R 16 Bacon st E2
63 R 8 Bacton st E2
69 S 4 Baddow clo Dgnhm
142 F 17 Baden pl SE1
29 Z 12 Baden rd N8
53 Y 14 Baden rd Ilf
57 X 18 Bader way Rainhm
152 E 2 Badgers copse Worc Pk
14 F 4 Badgers croft N20
113 W 7 Badgers croft SE9
158 E 8 Badgers hole Croy
118 A 2 Badgers wlk New Mald
33 N 9 Badis rd E17
40 H 19 Badminton clo Grnfd
23 S 14 Badminton clo Har
89 P 17 Badminton rd SW12
90 L 1 Badsworth rd SE5
150 B 20 Badsworth rd SE5
88 C 3 Bagleys la SW6
37 Z 12 Bagleys spring Rom
18 F 1 Bagshot rd Enf
150 K 10 Bagshot st SE17
75 Z 20 Baildon st SE8
110 E 15 Bailey pl SE26
36 A 15 Bailey rd Ilf
72 H 5 Bailles wlk W5
56 C 11 Bainbridge rd Dgnhm
136 G 3 Bainbridge st WC1
58 M 19 Baird av S'hall
25 V 18 Baird clo NW9
109 S 10 Baird gdns SE21
8 K 4 Baird rd Enf
93 Z 6 Baizdon rd SE3
94 A 6 Baizdon rd SE3
121 N 4 Baker la Mitch
62 A 4 Baker rd NW10
78 D 20 Baker rd SE7
95 R 1 Baker st SE18
142 K 14 Bakers all SE1
33 R 19 Bakers av E17
119 T 3 Bakers end SW20
50 B 4 Bakers hill E5
29 N 17 Bakers la N6
72 G 1 Bakers la W5
139 T 4 Bakers ms W1
64 L 5 Bakers row E15
133 T 17 Bakers row EC1
81 R 19 Baker st NW1
139 S 2 Baker st W1
8 D 6 Baker st Enf
117 Z 2 Bakewell way New Mald
16 K 8 Balaams la N14
65 U 11 Balaam st E13
151 P 6 Balaclava rd SE16
116 D 16 Balaclava rd Surb
63 S 2 Balchen rd SE3
95 V 12 Balcaskie rd SE9
94 M 4 Balchen rd SE3
91 Z 15 Balchier rd SE22
131 N 18 Balcombe st NW1
63 R 1 Balcorne st E9
112 J 6 Balder ri SE12
139 U 7 Balderton st W1
64 C 7 Baldock st E3
108 B 16 Baldry gdns SW16
90 K 2 Baldwin cres SE5
61 X 20 Baldwin gdns W3
133 S 20 Baldwins gdns EC1
134 E 14 Baldwin st EC1
134 A 8 Baldwin ter N1
74 B 14 Balfern gro W4
88 J 4 Balfern st SW11
132 L 9 Balfe st NW1
53 Z 7 Balfour appr Ilf
71 V 2 Balfour av W7
72 Z 11 Balfour gro N20
18 K 10 Balfour ms N1
139 U 11 Balfour ms W1
139 U 11 Balfour pl W1
48 M 13 Balfour rd N5
18 J 10 Balfour rd N9
123 X 10 Balfour rd SE12
106 A 18 Balfour rd SW19
61 W 15 Balfour rd W3

72 A 6 Balfour rd W13
127 P 11 Balfour rd Brom
154 M 17 Balfour rd Carsh
23 R 16 Balfour rd Harrow
52 K 7 Balfour rd Hounsl
37 Z 7 Balfour rd Ilf
54 C 3 Balfour rd Ilf
150 D 5 Balfour st SE17
20 J 6 Balgonie rd E4
39 Y 11 Balgores cres Rom
39 X 11 Balgores la Rom
39 Y 12 Balgores sq Rom
118 B 10 Balgowan clo New Mald
124 K 4 Balgowan rd Becknhm
79 X 11 Balgowan st SE18
89 R 19 Balham gro SW12
89 R 19 Balham High rd SW12
107 P 3 Balham High rd SW17
89 S 16 Balham hill SW12
89 S 19 Balham New rd SW12
106 M 1 Balham Pk rd SW12
107 O 2 Balham Pk rd SW12
18 L 8 Balham rd N9
107 R 1 Balham Stn rd SW12
112 E 7 Ballamore rd Brom
88 C 11 Ballance rd E9
52 C 11 Ballantyne st SW18
103 X 19 Ballard clo Kingst
69 V 3 Ballards clo Dgnhm
157 V 14 Ballards Farm rd Croy
27 Z 3 Ballards la N3
157 X 14 Ballards ri S Croy
44 G 7 Ballards rd NW2
69 V 2 Ballards rd Dgnhm
158 C 13 Ballards way Croy
157 Y 15 Ballards way S Croy
76 L 13 Ballast quay SE10
90 B 11 Ballater rd SW2
157 U 11 Ballater rd S Croy
160 H 7 Ball ct EC3
92 C 17 Ballina st SE23
89 N 15 Ballingdon rd SW11
20 K 14 Balliol av E4
31 P 5 Balliol rd N17
136 E 5 Balliol rd W10
97 R 4 Balliol rd Welling
111 X 3 Balloch rd SE6
44 B 11 Ballogie av NW10
49 O 17 Balls Pond pl N1
49 R 17 Balls Pond rd N1
72 H 2 Balmain clo W5
63 Y 7 Balmer rd E3
134 G 3 Balmes rd N1
124 J 9 Balmoral av Becknhm
71 Y 7 Balmoral gdns W13
54 J 5 Balmoral gdns Ilf
48 B 18 Balmoral gro N7
52 L 14 Balmoral rd E7
51 S 8 Balmoral rd E10
44 K 17 Balmoral rd NW2
40 G 12 Balmoral rd Harrow
116 L 8 Balmoral rd Kingst
39 Y 15 Balmoral rd Worc Pk
152 J 4 Balmoral rd Worc Pk
6 B 16 Balmoral cres Barnt
47 T 2 Balmore st N19
87 N 11 Balmuir gdns SW15
44 B 12 Balnacraig av NW10
106 F 17 Baltic clo SW19
134 A 18 Baltic st EC1
96 K 5 Baltimore pl Welling
87 W 20 Balvernie gro SW18
136 D 18 Bamborough gdns W12
60 M 5 Bamford av Wemb
51 S 15 Bamford ct E15
54 B 19 Bamford rd Bark
111 W 11 Bamford rd Brom
155 U 6 Bamfylde clo Wallgtn
110 E 6 Bampton rd SE23
101 U 2 Banbury cotts Twick
140 K 8 Banbury ct WC2
153 Z 17 Banbury ct Sutton
63 T 1 Banbury rd E9
88 K 4 Banbury rd SW11
77 V 19 Banchory rd SE3
28 K 15 Bancroft av N2
21 T 9 Bancroft av Buck Hl
22 M 10 Bancroft gdns Harrow
63 T 11 Bancroft rd E1
23 N 6 Bancroft rd Har
155 X 12 Bandon ri Wallgtn
87 O 8 Bangalore st SW15
40 K 15 Bangor clo Grnfd
73 N 15 Bangor rd Brentf
74 K 10 Banim st W6

128 G 12 Banister rd NW10
120 G 4 Bank av Mitch
142 D 12 Bank end SE1
83 U 5 Bankfield ct Islwth
112 A 10 Bankfoot rd Brom
92 L 18 Bankhurst rd SE6
86 B 13 Bank la SW15
102 J 17 Bank la Kingst
142 A 11 Bankside SE1
7 X 7 Bankside Enf
157 T 15 Bankside S Croy
154 K 13 Bankside clo Carsh
98 B 10 Banks la Bxly Hth
47 S 3 Bank the N6
90 F 12 Bankton rd SW2
94 A 11 Bankwell rd SE13
23 Z 17 Bannersfield la Harrow
134 B 18 Banner st EC1
76 M 12 Banning st SE10
41 R 13 Bannister clo Grnfd
90 F 20 Bannister rd SW2
79 W 11 Bannockburn rd SE18
18 F 10 Banstead gdns N9
154 K 13 Banstead st Carsh
92 B 8 Banstead st SE15
156 A 10 Banstead way Wallgtn
12 G 20 Banstock rd Edg
8 M 8 Banton cl Enf
8 M 9 Banton cl Enf
75 V 18 Bantree rd SE14
F 19 Bantry st SE5
47 O 17 Baptist gdns NW5
49 R 10 Barbauld rd N16
148 V 1 Barbel st SE1
17 U 3 Barber clo N21
65 U 8 Barbers all E13
64 E 5 Barbers rd E15
58 L 15 Barbican rd Grnfd
144 D 3 Barb ms W6
18 J 11 Barbut clo N9
88 A 13 Barchard st SW18
23 R 6 Barchester rd Harrow
64 D 15 Barchester st E14
21 T 14 Barclay oval Wdfd Grn
52 B 4 Barclay rd E11
65 Y 13 Barclay rd E13
13 T 16 Barclay rd E17
18 B 19 Barclay rd N18
145 V 19 Barclay rd SW6
107 O 5 Barclay rd Croy
108 B 4 Barcombe av SW2
79 U 19 Barden st SE18
37 V 11 Bardfield av Rom
120 B 8 Bardney rd Mrdn
158 K 20 Bardolph av Croy
47 Z 12 Bardolph rd N7
85 N 9 Bardolph rd Rich
6 G 10 Bard rd W10
63 O 13 Bardsey pl E1
157 T 4 Bardsley clo Croy
76 F 17 Bardsley la SE10
129 N 15 Barfett st W10
15 Y 8 Barfield av N20
52 B 3 Barfield rd E11
127 X 5 Barfield way Brom
26 H 6 Barford clo NW4
133 U 6 Barford st N1
92 A 8 Barforth rd SE15
79 Y 13 Bargate clo SE18
118 G 16 Bargate clo New Mald
78 M 4 Barge Ho rd E16
141 U 11 Barge Ho st SE1
11 S 2 Bargery rd SE6
109 X 17 Bargrove clo SE6
110 M 2 Bargrove cres SE6
127 G 20 Barham clo Brom
113 Z 12 Barham clo Chisl
38 F 9 Barham clo Rom
42 C 17 Barham clo Wemb
104 F 18 Barham rd SW20
113 Y 12 Barham clo Chisl
156 M 10 Barham rd S Croy
112 F 4 Barham clo SE12
94 D 19 Baring rd SE12
94 E 18 Baring rd SE12
112 F 2 Baring rd SE12
5 U 12 Baring rd Barnt
123 Y 19 Baring rd Croy
134 E 5 Baring st N1
146 B 14 Barker st SW10
31 P 1 Barkham rd N17
65 Y 14 Barking By pass E16
67 T 6 Barking By pass Bark
64 E 17 Barking park Bark
66 F 4 Barking rd E6
65 S 12 Barking rd E16
145 X 7 Barkston gdns SW5
50 O 14 Barkworth rd SE16

Bar—Bea

B

151 Y 11 Barkworth rd SE16
75 R 19 Barlborough st SE14
128 F 19 Barlby gdns W10
128 F 19 Barlby rd W10
55 O 2 Barley la Ilf
37 R 14 Barley la Rom
141 Y 1 Barley Mow pass EC1
73 Y 13 Barley Mow pass W4
155 Z 16 Barlow clo Wallgtn
139 Z 10 Barlow pl W1
73 T 2 Barlow rd W3
100 J 17 Barlow rd Hampt
150 G 6 Barlow st SE17
111 R 3 Barmeston rd SE6
22 L 6 Barmor clo Harrow
59 X 6 Barmouth av Grnfd
88 D 17 Barmouth rd SW18
158 F 3 Barmouth rd Croy
50 F 15 Barnabas ter E9
50 G 15 Barnabas rd E8
36 C 12 Barnardo dri Ilf
63 S 19 Barnardo st E1
114 F 20 Barnard clo Chisl
155 Y 16 Barnard clo Wallgtn
118 G 9 Barnard gdns New Mald
65 O 1 Barnard gro E15
29 R 6 Barnard hill N10
88 K 10 Barnard rd SW11
9 N 9 Barnard rd Enf
121 O 4 Barnard rd Mitch
141 T 3 Barnards Inn EC4
158 J 19 Barnard's pl S Croy
64 L 2 Barnby sq E15
64 L 2 Barnby st E15
132 C 11 Barnby st NW1
78 J 10 Barn clo SE18
11 R 20 Barn cres Stanm
98 L 6 Barnehrst av Bxly Hth
98 K 2 Barnehurst clo Erith
98 J 5 Barnehurst rd Bxly Hth
144 A 19 Barn Elms Water Works SW13
74 F 19 Barnes av SW13
53 O 13 Barnes clo E12
65 Z 14 Barnes ct E16
99 V 11 Barnes Cray rd Drtfrd
118 H 12 Barnes end New Mald
86 C 4 Barnes High st SW13
72 F 1 Barnes pickle W5
54 C 14 Barnes rd Ilf
19 P 13 Barnes rd N18
63 U 17 Barnes st E14
86 B 5 Barnes ter SW13
13 T 1 Barnet Ga la Barnt
135 S 13 Barnet gro E2
4 J 14 Barnet hill Barnt
14 G 5 Barnet la E6
4 K 16 Barnet la Barnt
1 X 1 Barnet la Brhm Wd
12 L 7 Barnet la NW7
99 T 4 Barnet rd Erith
118 A 14 Barnfield New Mald
158 D 2 Barnfield av Croy
102 J 11 Barnfield av Kingst
121 T 7 Barnfield av Mitch
102 K 11 Barnfield gdns Rich
79 N 16 Barnfield rd SE18
60 C 11 Barnfield rd W5
81 P 15 Barnfield rd Blvdr
25 U 5 Barnfield rd Edg
157 T 20 Barnfield rd S Croy
125 X 14 Barnfield Wood clo W Wkhm
125 X 13 Barnfield Wood rd Becknhm
58 M 7 Barnham av Grnfd
59 N 8 Barnham rd Grnfd
142 L 16 Barnham st SE1
43 S 7 Barn hill Wemb
126 C 13 Barnhill av Brom
43 W 9 Barnhill rd Wemb
100 C 5 Barnlea clo Felt
56 C 15 Barnmead gdns Dgnhm
110 G 20 Barnmead rd Becknhm
56 B 15 Barnmead rd Dgnhm
43 R 5 Barn ri Wemb
117 X 10 Barnsbury clo New Mald
117 U 20 Barnsbury cres Surb
48 E 19 Barnsbury gro N7
117 V 20 Barnsbury la Surb
48 F 20 Barnsbury pk N1
133 S 5 Barnsbury rd N1
133 S 1 Barnsbury sq N1
133 V 1 Barnsbury st N1
133 R 1 Barnsbury ter N1

129 P 16 Barnsdale rd W9
129 S 17 Barnsdale av W9
63 N 12 Barnsley st E1
135 X 7 Barnsley st E1
43 X 20 Barns rd NW10
49 P 8 Barn st N16
43 P 5 Barn way Wemb
90 G 13 Barnwell rd SW2
77 T 2 Barnwood ct E16
135 O 11 Baroness rd E2
31 X 4 Baronet gro N17
31 X 4 Baronet rd N17
36 C 9 Baron gdns Ilf
120 K 8 Baron rd Dgnhm
54 V 3 Baron rd Dgnhm
144 L 10 Barons Ct rd W14
145 N 10 Barons Ct rd W14
84 C 17 Baronsfield rd Twick
5 W 18 Barons ga Barnt
144 K 8 Barons keep W14
86 G 2 Baronsmead rd SW13
72 M 7 Baronsmede W5
68 K 13 Baronsmere rd N2
141 V 18 Barons pl SE1
84 C 15 Barons the Twick
133 T 9 Barons wlk Croy
124 K 13 Barons wlk Croy
65 O 14 Baron wlk E15
120 H 9 Baron wlk Mitch
23 T 1 Barons mead Harrow
76 G 13 Barque st E14
82 A 11 Barrack rd Hounsl
23 R 10 Barrat wy Harrow
30 B 6 Barratt av N22
28 M 6 Barrenger rd N10
33 U 13 Barrett rd E17
61 X 7 Barretts Green rd NW10
48 T 13 Barretts gro N16
139 V 6 Barrett st W1
92 J 4 Barriedale SE14
107 P 9 Barringer sq SW17
47 O 14 Barrington rd NW5
53 W 17 Barrington rd E12
29 W 14 Barrington rd N8
90 H 7 Barrington rd SW9
97 W 6 Barrington rd Bxly Hth
153 X 1 Barrington rd Sutton
132 M 19 Barron clo WC1
154 L 18 Barrow av Carsh
17 W 10 Barrow clo N21
22 B 8 Barrowdene clo Pinn
17 W 9 Barrowell grn N21
9 O 11 Barrowfield clo N9
73 X 15 Barrowgate rd W4
154 J 15 Barrow Hedgs clo Carsh
154 J 15 Barrow Hedges way Carsh
152 A 2 Barrow hill Worc Pk
152 A 2 Barrow Hill clo Worc
130 J 10 Barrow Hill rd NW8
22 A 8 Barrow Point av Pinn
22 A 6 Barrow Point la Pinn
107 Z 14 Barrow rd SW16
156 G 12 Barrow rd Croy
95 W 2 Barr vlls SE18
31 V 19 Barry av N15
80 L 19 Barry av Bxly Hth
91 X 14 Barry rd SE22
110 C 18 Barson clo SE20
108 M 6 Barston rd SE27
108 C 1 Barstow cres SW12
140 L 3 Barter st WC1
141 Z 2 Bartholomew clo EC1
88 D 12 Bartholomew clo SW18
160 F 6 Bartholomew la EC2
142 A 2 Bartholomew pl EC1
47 W 17 Bartholomew rd NW5
150 F 3 Bartholomew sq EC1
47 U 18 Bartholomew vlls NW5
79 W 11 Barth rd SE18
136 E 5 Bartle av E6
136 J 6 Bartle rd N1
141 U 4 Bartlett ct EC4
157 N 11 Bartlett st S Croy
38 M 3 Barton gdns Rom
34 J 5 Barton av Rom
97 Z 12 Barton clo Bxly Hth
117 Z 4 Barton grn New Mald
36 A 12 Barton meadows Ilf
31 N 4 Barton pk E15
14 L 10 Barton rd W14
97 V 5 Barton rd Hornch
115 Z 15 Barton rd Sidcp
148 H 2 Barton st SW1
92 J 14 Bartram rd SE4
5 P 3 Bartrams la Barnt

52 H 11 Barwick rd E7
125 S 20 Barwood av W
100 G 5 Basden gro Felt
55 P 20 Basedale rd Dgnhm
61 Z 11 Baskley rd NW10
66 E 8 Basil av E6
35 W 5 Basildon av Ilf
154 B 19 Basildon clo Sutton
80 B 11 Basildon rd SE2
97 Y 6 Basildon rd Bxly Hth
139 O 19 Basil st SW3
91 O 10 Basingdon way SE5
98 A 16 Basing dri Bxly
154 B 18 Basinghall gdns Sutton
160 D 4 Basinghall st EC2
45 U 4 Basing hill NW11
43 O 5 Basing hill Wemb
137 O 4 Basing st W11
27 Z 10 Basing way N3
28 A 9 Basing way N3
134 B 3 Basire st N1
88 J 18 Baskerville rd SW18
95 P 13 Basket gdns SE9
23 R 5 Baslow clo Harrow
89 P 7 Basnett rd SW11
91 U 12 Bassano st SE22
79 W 17 Bassant rd SE18
74 E 7 Bassein Pk rd W12
154 B 20 Bassett clo Sutton
71 O 19 Bassett gdns Islwth
136 J 3 Bassett rd W10
47 P 17 Bassett st NW5
58 K 16 Bassett way Grnfd
160 D 3 Bassinghall av EC2
88 D 18 Bassingham rd SW18
42 G 19 Bassingham rd Wemb
67 W 8 Bastable av Bark
68 B 7 Bastable av Bark
79 Z 15 Bastion rd SE2
80 A 14 Bastion rd SE2
133 Z 16 Bastwick st EC1
134 A 16 Bastwick st EC1
87 Y 2 Basuto rd SW6
75 W 20 Batavia rd SE14
133 N 6 Batchelor st N1
20 B 18 Bateman rd E4
140 F 6 Batemans bldgs W1
134 L 15 Batemans row EC2
140 F 6 Bateman st W1
156 F 12 Bates cres Croy
63 Y 19 Bate st E14
105 P 7 Bathgate rd SW19
92 A 1 Bath clo SE15
121 V 11 Bath Ho rd Mitch
134 J 14 Bath pl EC1
4 G 11 Bath pl Barnt
53 N 19 Bath rd E12
19 O 8 Bath rd N9
74 B 10 Bath rd W4
99 Z 18 Bath rd Drtfrd
82 D 7 Bath rd Hounsl
37 V 18 Bath rd Rom
134 D 14 Bath st EC1
127 O 7 Baths rd Brom
150 A 2 Bath ter SE1
62 K 7 Bathurst gdns NW10
128 A 10 Bathurst gdns NW10
138 G 8 Bathurst ms W2
53 Z 5 Bathurst rd Ilf
138 G 8 Bathurst st W2
78 K 11 Bathway SE18
49 U 10 Batley rd N16
8 A 6 Batley rd Enf
74 K 2 Batman clo W12
74 M 8 Batoum gdns W6
144 D 1 Batoum gdns W6
74 H 6 Batson st W12
120 F 5 Batsworth rd Mitch
88 K 9 Batten clo SW11
111 Y 6 Battersby rd SE6
146 J 18 Battersea br SW11
88 K 2 Battersea Br rd SW11
146 J 19 Battersea Br rd SW11
88 G 1 Battersea Church rd SW11
146 J 20 Battersea Church rd SW11
88 G 2 Battersea High st SW11
88 M 1 Battersea park SW11
147 M 1 Battersea park SW11
148 A 18 Battersea Pk rd SW8
88 J 11 Battersea Pk rd SW11

89 O 2 Battersea Pk rd SW11
147 Z 20 Battersea Pk rd SW11
88 J 11 Battersea ri SW11
133 W 2 Battishill st N1
132 C 2 Battle Bridge rd NW1
142 J 14 Battle Bridge la SE1
106 D 15 Battle clo SW19
48 H 15 Battledean rd N5
81 Y 1 Battle rd Erith
143 T 5 Batty st E1
111 Z 5 Baudwin rd SE6
115 U 13 Baugh rd Sidcp
87 X 19 Baulk the SW18
122 B 3 Bavant rd SW16
48 A 7 Bavaria rd N4
90 M 5 Bavent rd SE5
91 V 13 Bawdale rd SE22
56 L 14 Bawdsey av Ilf
15 Y 11 Bawtry rd N20
15 R 8 Baxendale N20
135 S 11 Baxendale st E2
65 Z 17 Baxter rd E16
49 P 19 Baxter rd N1
31 X 10 Baxter rd N17
18 M 13 Baxter rd N18
62 A 12 Baxter rd NW10
53 Y 15 Baxter rd Ilf
144 J 14 Bayonne rd development W6
94 M 11 Bayfield rd SE9
128 C 13 Bayford rd NW10
63 N 1 Bayford st E8
132 B 7 Bayham pl NW1
73 Y 3 Bayham rd W4
72 A 1 Bayham rd W13
120 B 8 Bayham rd Mrdn
131 Z 3 Bayham st NW1
132 A 4 Bayham st NW1
140 F 2 Bayley st WC1
80 M 15 Bayley wk Blvdr
88 A 15 Baylin rd SW18
141 S 19 Baylis rd SE1
8 K 7 Baynes clo Enf
46 G 17 Baynes ms NW3
132 C 2 Baynes st NW1
49 V 10 Bayston rd N16
137 W 11 Bayswater rd W2
138 K 9 Bayswater rd W2
63 Z 14 Baythorne st E3
90 D 12 Baytree rd SW2
117 X 13 Bazalgette clo New Mald
117 X 13 Bazalgette gdns New Mald
64 F 19 Bazely st E14
7 U 18 Bazile rd N21
78 B 15 Beacham clo SE7
111 V 10 Beachborough rd Brom
52 A 8 Beachcroft rd E11
47 Y 4 Beachcroft way N19
100 H 5 Beach gro Felt
64 A 1 Beachy rd E3
155 O 9 Beacon gro Carsh
48 A 15 Beacon hill N7
93 W 15 Beacon rd SE13
77 S 17 Beaconsfield clo SE3
73 U 14 Beaconsfield clo W4
51 U 8 Beaconsfield rd E10
65 O 12 Beaconsfield rd E16
32 M 20 Beaconsfield rd E17
18 J 12 Beaconsfield rd N9
16 C 15 Beaconsfield rd N11
31 T 14 Beaconsfield rd N15
44 E 18 Beaconsfield rd NW10
77 R 17 Beaconsfield rd SE3
113 R 18 Beaconsfield rd SE9
150 D 13 Beaconsfield rd SE17
73 X 9 Beaconsfield rd W4
72 F 5 Beaconsfield rd W5
127 O 6 Beaconsfield rd Brom
123 O 14 Beaconsfield rd Croy
9 U 1 Beaconsfield rd Enf
117 Z 5 Beaconsfield rd New Mald
70 D 4 Beaconsfield rd S'hall
117 N 18 Beaconsfield rd Surb
84 B 17 Beaconsfield rd Twick
66 K 18 Beaconsfield st E6
39 S 20 Beaconsfield ter Rom
144 K 3 Beaconsfield Ter rd W14
87 V 3 Beaconsfield wlk SW6
33 Y 7 Beacontree av E18
52 C 2 Beacontree rd E11

B

108 K 9 Beadman st SE27
92 F 20 Beadnell rd SE23
74 M 11 Beadon rd W6
144 C 6 Beadon rd W6
126 E 10 Beadon rd Brom
119 V 6 Beaford gro SW20
140 B 8 Beak st W1
97 O 2 Beal clo Well
17 W 17 Beale clo N13
63 Y 5 Beale pl E3
63 X 4 Beale rd E3
65 S 5 Beale st E13
53 W 7 Beal rd Ilf
69 V 4 Beam av Dgnhm
35 Y 9 Beaminster gdns Ilf
92 K 14 Beamish dri Bushey
18 L 6 Beamish rd N9
56 M 20 Beam way Dgnhm
97 W 11 Beam rd Bxly Hth
113 X 10 Beanshaw SE9
37 Z 9 Beansland gro Rom
141 W 4 Bear all EC4
109 T 15 Beardell st SE19
6 G 20 Beardow clo N14
102 M 13 Beard rd Kingst
65 R 5 Beardsfield E13
102 K 18 Bearfield rd Kingst
142 B 12 Bear gdns SE1
141 Y 14 Bear la SE1
100 A 11 Bear rd Felt
92 K 14 Bearstead ri SE4
140 G 10 Bear st WC2
122 C 4 Beatrice av SW16
42 L 16 Beatrice av Wemb
33 O 16 Beatrice E17
48 G 1 Beatrice rd N4
19 P 2 Beatrice rd N9
151 U 6 Beatrice rd SE1
84 L 13 Beatrice rd Rich
70 D 3 Beatrice rd S'hall
65 S 12 Beatrice st E13
75 U 1 Beatson st SE16
92 S 13 Beattock rise N10
49 T 11 Beatty rd N16
11 S 18 Beatty rd Stanm
43 T 2 Beatty st NW1
35 X 12 Beattyville gdns Ilf
146 M 2 Beauchamp pl SW3
52 H 20 Beauchamp rd E7
123 P 2 Beauchamp rd SE19
88 K 10 Beauchamp rd SW11
153 Y 9 Beauchamp rd Sutton
83 Z 19 Beauchamp rd Twick
141 T 1 Beauchamp st EC1
86 K 8 Beauchamp ter SW15
74 L 8 Beauclerc rd W6
144 A 1 Beauclerc rd W6
23 Z 11 Beaufort av Harrow
24 A 11 Beaufort av Harrow
61 N 13 Beaufort clo W5
38 J 12 Beaufort clo Rom
102 C 10 Beaufort ct Rich
27 Y 12 Beaufort dri NW11
26 L 19 Beaufort gdns NW4
146 M 1 Beaufort gdns SW3
147 N 2 Beaufort gdns SW3
108 D 18 Beaufort gdns SW16
82 B 1 Beaufort gdns Hounsl
53 W 4 Beaufort gdns Ilf
60 M 15 Beaufort rd W5
61 N 13 Beaufort rd W5
116 J 10 Beaufort rd Kingst
102 D 10 Beaufort rd Rich
83 W 19 Beaufort rd Twick
12 E 18 Beaufort st SW3
146 E 12 Beaufort st SW3
146 H 16 Beaufort st SW3
152 G 18 Beaufort way Epsom
31 T 2 Beaufoy rd N17
149 P 8 Beaufoy wlk
109 Z 10 Beaulah av SE26
109 Z 19 Beaulah hill SE19
109 Z 10 Beaulieu av SE26
110 A 10 Beaulieu av SE26
26 B 12 Beaulieu clo NW9
91 P 7 Beaulieu clo SE5
121 O 1 Beaulieu clo Mitch
84 G 17 Beaulieu clo Twick
17 Y 4 Beaulieu gdns N21
39 R 5 Beauly way Rom
113 W 10 Beaumanor gdns SE9
35 N 2 Beaumaris dri Wdfd Grn
145 O 9 Beaumont av W8
22 L 19 Beaumont av Harrow
84 M 9 Beaumont av Rich
42 E 14 Beaumont av Wemb
145 O 10 Beaumont cres W14
57 X 18 Beaumont cres Rainhm

63 S 13 Beaumont gro E1
139 U 1 Beaumont ms W1
132 C 17 Beaumont pl WC1
4 J 4 Beaumont pl Barnt
47 J 2 Beaumont ri N19
51 R 2 Beaumont rd E10
65 W 9 Beaumont rd E13
108 L 15 Beaumont rd SE19
87 R 18 Beaumont rd SW19
73 W 8 Beaumont rd W4
63 T 13 Beaumont sq E1
131 V 20 Beaumont st W1
139 V 1 Beaumont st W1
91 U 15 Beauval rd SE22
114 D 2 Beaverbank rd Sidcp
109 X 17 Beaver clo SE20
81 O 16 Beavercote wk Blvdr
82 A 9 Beavers la Hounsl
114 J 14 Beaverwood rd Chisl
74 G 12 Beavor la W6
79 U 12 Bebbington rd SE18
54 J 17 Beccles dri Bark
63 Z 19 Beccles st E14
40 A 9 Bec clo Harrow
18 C 11 Beckenham gdns N9
125 X 4 Beckenham gro Brom
111 S 13 Beckenham Hill rd Becknhm
126 A 3 Beckenham la Brom
111 T 16 Beckenham pl Becknhm
111 P 18 Beckenham Pl pk Becknhm
111 T 15 Beckenham Pl pk Becknhm
124 K 2 Beckenham rd Becknhm
125 U 18 Beckenham rd W Wkhm
66 J 9 Becket av E6
123 X 14 Becket clo SE25
19 O 14 Becket rd N18
23 W 16 Becketfold Harrow
110 H 15 Beckett wlk SE26
110 H 15 Beckett wlk Becknhm
123 V 15 Beckford rd Croy
124 E 6 Becks la Becknhm
74 E 5 Becklow rd W12
135 X 4 Beck rd E8
115 O 8 Becks rd Sidcp
65 R 18 Beckton rd E16
124 H 8 Beckway Becknhm
125 N 8 Beckway Becknhm
121 X 4 Beckway rd SW16
150 H 7 Beckway st SE17
91 O 14 Beckwith rd SE24
107 R 14 Beclands rd SW17
107 Y 8 Becmead av SW16
24 B 15 Becmead av Harrow
109 S 13 Becondale rd SE19
55 T 8 Becontree av Dgnhm
56 A 7 Becontree av Dgnhm
87 U 11 Bective rd SW15
52 G 11 Bective rd E7
87 U 11 Bective rd SW15
66 E 15 Becton pl E6
98 H 1 Becton pl Erith
7 Y 4 Bedale av Enf
142 E 24 Bedale st SE1
51 V 16 Beddingfield rd E15
122 B 19 Beddington Farm rd Croy
156 C 2 Beddington Farm rd Croy
155 P 14 Beddington gdns Carsh
155 Y 11 Beddington gdns Wallgtn
121 W 16 Beddington la Croy
155 Z 3 Beddington la Wallgtn
155 U 4 Beddington park Wallgtn
36 K 20 Beddington rd Ilf
115 Y 14 Bedens rd Sidcp
37 T 18 Bede rd Rom
4 J 15 Bedford av Barnt
140 J 10 Bedfordbury WC2
121 N 4 Bedford clo Mitch
29 P 3 Bedford clo N10
140 K 10 Bedford ct WC2
137 U 15 Bedford gdns W8
107 V 6 Bedford hill SW16
122 M 20 Bedford pk Croy
144 M 17 Bedford pass SW6
132 K 20 Bedford pl WC1
140 K 1 Bedford pl WC1
123 O 20 Bedford pl Croy
66 H 3 Bedford rd E6
33 O 8 Bedford rd E17
34 E 9 Bedford rd E18
28 J 10 Bedford rd N2
29 Y 17 Bedford rd N8

18 M 1 Bedford rd N9
19 N 2 Bedford rd N9
31 R 13 Bedford rd N15
30 A 6 Bedford rd N22
13 N 9 Bedford rd NW7
89 Z 8 Bedford rd SW9
73 Z 9 Bedford rd W4
72 A 1 Bedford rd W13
9 S 10 Bedford rd Enf
23 N 17 Bedford rd Harrow
53 Z 10 Bedford rd Ilf
54 A 10 Bedford rd Ilf
114 H 7 Bedford rd Sidcp
101 P 5 Bedford rd Twick
153 N 4 Bedford rd Worc Pk
141 O 1 Bedford row WC1
140 G 2 Bedford sq WC1
140 K 9 Bedford st WC2
132 H 18 Bedford st WC2
105 T 2 Bedgebury rd SW19
94 M 11 Bedgebury rd SE9
112 F 6 Bedivere rd Brom
80 M 16 Bedonwell rd SE2
O 16 Bedonwell rd Blvdr
81 R 17 Bedonwell rd Bxly Hth
98 C 2 Bedonwell rd Bxly Hth
41 P 14 Bedser clo Grnfd
109 R 17 Bedwardine rd SE 19
31 R 4 Bedwell rd N17
81 R 14 Bedwell rd Blvdr
65 U 15 Beeby rd E16
15 X 6 Beech av N20
74 B 3 Beech av W3
72 B 19 Beech av Brentf
21 V 8 Beech av Buck Hl
96 M 17 Beech av Sidcp
86 G 17 Beech clo SW15
104 L 15 Beech clo SW19
154 L 2 Beech clo Carsh
8 L 20 Beech clo Enf
57 X 11 Beech clo Hornch
121 Z 8 Beech clo Mitch
157 S 10 Beechcopse S Croy
127 T 2 Beech copse Brom
113 W 17 Beechcroft Chisl
45 V 1 Beechcroft av NW1
40 G 2 Beechcroft av Harrow
117 W 2 Beechcroft av New Mald
70 D 2 Beechcroft av S'hall
42 M 10 Beechcroft gdns Wemb
43 N 10 Beechcroft gdns Wemb
34 H 8 Beechcroft rd E18
98 W 9 Beechcroft rd SW14
106 J 3 Beechcroft rd SW17
17 R 8 Beechdale N21
90 D 16 Beechdale rd SW2
28 L 9 Beech dri N2
22 D 11 Beechen glen Pinn
154 K 16 Beeches Av the Carsh
106 K 6 Beeches rd SW 17
179 T 20 Beeches rd Sutton
154 H 19 Beeches wlk Carsh
51 W 15 Beechey pl E15
38 L 20 Beechfield gdns Rom
31 N 18 Beechfield rd N4
110 M 1 Beechfield rd SE6
126 M 3 Beechfield rd Brom
72 J 8 Beech gdns W5
56 J 20 Beech gdns Dgnhm
121 X 10 Beech gro Mitch
117 Y 6 Beech gro New Mald
33 W 1 Beech Hall cres E4
20 J 20 Beech Hall rd E4
33 V 2 Beech Hall rd E4
5 U 4 Beech Hill Barnt
5 S 5 Beech Hill av Barnt
5 V 7 Beech Hill pk Barnt
95 V 12 Beechhill rd SE9
157 O 6 Beech Ho rd Croy
21 U 9 Beech la Buck Hl
15 U 15 Beech lawns N12
9 N 2 Beechmore rd SW11
112 Z 13 Beechmont clo Brom
73 R 3 Beechmore gdns Sutton
89 N 2 Beechmore rd SW8
59 S 14 Beechmount av W7
107 R 9 Beecholme av Mitch
50 A 9 Beecholme rd E5
17 N 19 Beech rd N11
122 B 4 Beech rd SW16
98 M 4 Beechcroft av Bxly Hth
102 J 11 Beechrow Rich
134 A 20 Beech st EC1
38 L 14 Beech st Rom
11 S 17 Beech Tree clo Stanm
21 O 4 Beech Tree glade E4

15 X 15 Beach Vale clo N12
12 M 18 Beam wlk NW7
99 X 10 Beam wlk Drtford
43 X 20 Beech way NW10
100 J 5 Beech way Twick
97 W 17 Beechway Bxly
27 W 11 Beechwood av N3
58 J 8 Beechwood av Grnfd
40 L 9 Beechwood av Harrow
85 P 2 Beechwood av Rich
122 H 8 Beechwood av Thtn Hth
12 M 16 Beechwood clo NW7
97 Y 7 Beechwood cres Bxly Hth
21 P 17 Beechwood dri Wdfd Grn
40 L 9 Beechwood gdns Harrow
35 U 14 Beechwood gdns Ilf
34 E 11 Beechwood pk E18
49 U 18 Beechwood rd E8
29 Y 11 Beechwood rd N8
157 R 19 Beechwood rd S Croy
45 Z 8 Beechworth clo NW3
92 J 12 Beecroft rd SE4
35 T 15 Beehive la Ilf
90 F 9 Beehive pl SW19
120 B 8 Beeleigh rd Mrdn
127 X 2 Bean cl E4
86 H 20 Beesborough rd SW15
147 Y 2 Beeston pl SW1
5 U 19 Beeston rd Barnt
11 T 1 Beethoven rd Borhm Wd
128 L 11 Beethoven st W10
22 G 3 Beeton clo Pinn
94 K 2 Begbie rd SE3
152 E 15 Beggars hill Epsom
62 E 18 Begonia wlk W12
89 T 17 Bekesbourne st E1
63 U 18 Bekesbourne st E1
112 D 18 Belcroft clo Brom
55 U 1 Belfairs dri Rom
44 U 9 Belfast rd N16
123 Z 10 Belfast rd SE25
48 B 12 Belfont wlk N7
78 H 12 Belford gro SE18
92 C 4 Belford rd SE15
49 T 13 Belfrade rd N16
6 H 15 Belgrave clo N14
73 U 4 Belgrave clo W3
6 J 15 Belgrave gdns N14
129 Z 7 Belgrave gdns NW8
130 A 6 Belgrave gdns NW8
11 S 15 Belgrave gdns Stanm
139 S 20 Belgrave ms north SW1
147 U 1 Belgrave ms S SW1
147 U 1 Belgrave ms W SW1
147 U 3 Belgrave pl SW1
51 U 3 Belgrave rd E10
52 F 4 Belgrave rd E11
65 X 11 Belgrave rd E13
33 O 18 Belgrave rd E17
123 V 8 Belgrave rd SE25
147 A 7 Belgrave rd SW1
148 C 8 Belgrave rd SW1
74 E 20 Belgrave rd SW13
82 D 8 Belgrave rd Hounsl
53 T 4 Belgrave rd Ilf
120 F 5 Belgrave rd Mitch
139 T 20 Belgrave sq SW1
147 U 1 Belgrave sq SW1
63 U 17 Belgrave st E1
21 S 11 Belgrave ter Wdfd Grn
120 G 6 Belgrave wlk Mitch
147 W 2 Belgravia wlk SW1
111 X 16 Belgravia gdns Brom
132 K 12 Belgrove st WC1
91 P 1 Belham st SE5
90 J 8 Belinda rd SW9
48 E 20 Belitha vlls N1
145 R 11 Bellamy clo SW6
24 B 5 Bellamy dri Stanm
20 F 20 Bellamy rd E4
89 R 18 Bellamy st SW12
43 S 4 Bellasis av SE2
39 Y 4 Bell av Rom
87 S 18 Bell dri SW18
90 E 8 Bellefields rd SW9
110 K 8 Belle gdns SE26
96 J 5 Bellegrove clo Welling
91 V 4 Bellenden rd SE15
20 B 7 Bellestaines E4
88 L 14 Belleville rd SW11
59 P 2 Bellevue Grnfd
10 C 5 Bellevue la Bushey

122	L 7	Bellevue pk Thrtn
33	W 7	Bellevue rd E17
16	B 16	Bellevue rd E17
86	G 5	Bellevue rd SW13
88	K 20	Belle Vue rd SW17
106	K 1	Bellevue rd SW17
60	A 12	Bellevue rd W13
98	A 13	Bellevue rd Bxly Hth
116	K 8	Bellevue rd Kingst
106	E 7	Bellevue st SW17
56	K 9	Bell Farm av Dgnhm
158	K 18	Bell field Croy
10	B 20	Bellfield av Harrow
152	A 18	Bellfield rd Epsom
110	J 12	Bell green SE26
110	K 10	Bell Green la SE26
96	G 5	Bellgrove rd Welling
97	O 7	Bellgrove rd Welling
63	V 8	Bellhaven st E3
56	K 3	Bell Ho rd Dgnhm
111	P 8	Bellingham grn SE6
111	S 6	Bellingham rd SE6
160	H 7	Bell Inn yd EC3
142	M 2	Bell la E1
143	N 3	Bell la E1
77	R 2	Bell la E16
27	N 14	Bell la NW4
9	U 4	Bell la Enf
101	Z 1	Bell la Twick
77	N 12	Bellot st SE10
81	T 16	Bellring clo Blvdr
64	F 12	Bell rd E3
8	C 7	Bell rd Enf
82	J 9	Bell rd Hounsl
87	X 5	Bells all SW6
4	D 14	Bells hill Barnt
130	K 20	Bell st NW1
138	J 1	Bell st NW1
108	E 12	Belltrees gro SE16
27	O 14	Bell View rd NW4
78	K 8	Bell Water ga SE18
160	D 10	Bell Wharf la EC4
92	F 11	Bellwood rd SE15
130	L 5	Bell yd WC2
18	L 5	Belmont av N9
17	O 15	Belmont av N13
30	L 11	Belmont av N17
5	Z 17	Belmont av Barnt
4	A 14	Belmont av Barnt
118	H 10	Belmont av New Mald
70	B 9	Belmont av S'hall
98	G 6	Belmont av Welling
60	M 2	Belmont av Wemb
24	A 6	Belmont cir Harrow
89	W 8	Belmont clo SW4
6	A 14	Belmont clo Barnt
21	U 13	Belmont clo Wdfd Grn
93	X 8	Belmont gro SE13
93	Y 8	Belmont hill SE13
114	B 10	Belmont la Chisl
24	D 3	Belmont la Harrow
93	V 10	Belmont Pk clo SE13
93	X 10	Belmont pk SE13
33	S 19	Belmont Pk rd E10
153	V 18	Belmont ri Sutton
30	L 12	Belmont rd N17
124	A 13	Belmont rd SE25
89	W 8	Belmont rd SW8
73	X 12	Belmont rd SW19
124	L 4	Belmont rd Becknhm
113	Z 2	Belmont rd Chisl
81	S 20	Belmont rd Erith
98	F 1	Belmont rd Erith
23	X 10	Belmont rd Harrow
54	C 9	Belmont rd Ilf
101	P 3	Belmont rd Twick
155	T 11	Belmont rd Wallgtn
47	P 19	Belmont st NW1
89	Y 2	Belmore st SW8
50	C 17	Belsham st E9
17	N 13	Belsize av N13
46	J 16	Belsize av NW3
72	C 8	Belsize av W13
46	H 15	Belsize ct NW3
46	G 16	Belsize cres NW3
154	B 7	Belsize gdns Sutton
46	K 17	Belsize gro NW3
36	F 18	Belsize la NW3
46	G 16	Belsize ms NW3
46	F 18	Belsize la NW3
46	J 17	Belsize Pk gdns NW3
46	G 17	Belsize Pk ms NW3
46	J 18	Belsize pl NW3
46	E 20	Belsize rd NW6
129	Z 3	Belsize rd NW6
130	D 1	Belsize rd NW6
23	P 1	Belsize rd Harrow
46	H 18	Belsize sq NW3
46	G 17	Belsize ter NW3
78	F 10	Belson rd SE18
105	P 6	Beltane dri SW19

52	J 20	Belton rd E7
51	Z 12	Belton rd E11
31	S 10	Belton rd N17
44	G 17	Belton rd NW2
115	O 9	Belton rd Sidcp
64	A 14	Belton way E3
87	Z 5	Beltran rd SW6
81	W 10	Beltwood rd Blvdr
26	C 8	Belvedere NW9
105	T 12	Belvedere av SW19
35	Z 8	Belvedere av Ilf
141	Z 19	Belvedere bldgs SE1
101	T 13	Belvedere clo Tedd
51	O 19	Belvedere gro SW19
105	S 13	Belvedere gro SW19
141	Z 19	Belvedere pl SE1
50	J 3	Belvedere rd E10
141	O 18	Belvedere rd SE1
80	H 3	Belvedere rd SE2
109	U 17	Belvedere rd SE19
98	B 7	Belvedere rd Bxly Hth
105	S 12	Belvedere sq SW19
24	K 19	Belvedere way Harrow
113	R 6	Belvoir clo SE9
91	Y 9	Belvoir rd SE22
40	H 20	Belvue clo Grnfd
58	H 2	Belvue pk Grnfd
40	J 20	Belvue rd Grnfd
45	R 20	Bembridge clo NW6
132	M 2	Bemerton st N1
87	P 8	Bemish rd SW15
32	L 9	Bemsted rd E17
79	X 11	Benares rd SE18
74	K 8	Benbow rd W6
144	A 1	Benbow rd W6
76	B 15	Benbow st SE8
111	U 12	Benbury clo Brom
157	V 13	Bench Fld S Croy
102	E 7	Bench the Rich
107	W 17	Bencroft rd NW16
159	X 4	Ben Curtis pk Wkhm
130	M 20	Bendall ms NW1
9	U 1	Bendemeer rd SW15
66	D 2	Bendish rd E6
80	A 12	Bendmore av SE2
88	A 20	Bendon valley SW18
90	E 7	Benedict clo W3
120	G 7	Benedict rd Mitch
28	C 9	Benedict way W3
126	D 12	Beneden grn Brom
121	Z 3	Benett gdns SW16
154	D 6	Benfleet clo Sutton
160	G 7	Bengal ct EC3
53	Y 11	Bengal rd Ilf
23	R 7	Bengarth dri Harrow
58	A 3	Bengarth rd Grnfd
90	L 7	Bengeworth rd SE5
41	Z 8	Bengeworth rd Harrow
11	N 5	Benhale clo Stanm
88	F 9	Benham clo SW11
59	U 15	Benham rd W7
154	B 9	Benhill av Sutton
91	P 2	Ben Hill rd SE5
150	G 20	Benhill rd SE5
154	E 6	Benhill rd Sutton
154	C 5	Benhill Wood rd Sutton
154	B 6	Benhilton gdns Sutton
108	E 12	Benhurst ct SW16
57	Y 11	Benhurst av Hornch
93	Y 18	Benin st SE13
133	W 20	Benjamin st EC1
18	M 13	Benjamin clo Hornch
39	W 19	Benjamin clo Hornch
63	U 15	Ben Jonson rd E1
151	U 1	Ben Smith wy SE16
64	J 17	Benledi st E14
88	K 13	Bennerley rd SW11
140	A 13	Bennet st SW1
96	M 5	Bennet clo Welling
99	S 3	Bennet gro SE13
94	C 6	Bennet pk SE3
65	X 13	Bennett rd E13
37	Z 20	Bennett rd Rom
158	K 4	Bennetts av Croy
65	U 7	Bennetts av Grnfd
113	R 15	Bennetts copse Chisl
74	A 15	Bennett st W4
158	K 3	Bennetts way Croy
148	H 3	Bennetts yd SW1
13	N 19	Benningholme rd Edg
31	P 5	Bennington rd N17
33	Y 2	Bennington rd Wdfd Grn
50	J 17	Benn st E9
36	B 3	Benrek clo Ilf
86	K 19	Bensby clo SW15

122	L 10	Bensham clo Thntn Hth
122	L 3	Bensham gro Thntn Hth
122	J 10	Bensham la Thntn Hth
123	N 10	Bensham Mnr rd Thntn Hth
65	Z 7	Benson av E6
82	G 10	Benson clo Hounsl
92	D 20	Benson rd SE23
156	G 6	Benson rd Croy
49	X 10	Benthal rd N16
50	F 18	Bentham rd E9
68	C 20	Bentham rd SE2
80	C 1	Bentham rd SE18
68	B 1	Ben Tillet clo Bark
139	V 3	Bentinck ms W1
139	V 4	Bentinck st W1
36	B 17	Bentley dri Ilf
10	G 12	Bentley priory Stanm
49	S 18	Bentley rd N1
10	K 17	Bentley way Stanm
21	S 9	Bentley way Wdfd Grn
78	A 3	Benton rd E16
54	D 3	Benton rd Ilf
108	M 11	Bentons la SE27
109	N 11	Bentons ri SE27
55	Z 7	Bentry clo Dgnhm
55	Z 7	Bentry rd Dgnhm
56	A 7	Bentry rd Dgnhm
62	J 19	Bentworth rd W12
136	A 6	Bentworth rd W12
48	F 14	Benwell rd N7
63	Z 8	Benworth st E3
134	G 3	Benyon rd N1
88	M 13	Berber rd SW11
114	A 4	Bercta rd SE9
128	F 13	Berends rd NW10
15	Y 8	Beresford av N20
59	S 15	Beresford av W7
117	T 19	Beresford av Surb
84	F 15	Beresford av Twick
61	P 2	Beresford av Wemb
7	Y 13	Beresford dri Buck Hl
8	D 14	Beresford gdns Enf
82	E 14	Beresford gdns Hounsl
37	Z 17	Beresford gdns Rom
20	M 4	Beresford rd E4
33	R 4	Beresford rd E17
28	J 11	Beresford rd N2
49	N 15	Beresford rd N5
30	H 15	Beresford rd N8
23	O 16	Beresford rd Harrow
102	M 20	Beresford rd Kingst
103	N 20	Beresford rd Kingst
117	V 8	Beresford rd New Mald
153	N 11	Beresford rd Sutton
78	M 10	Beresford sq SE18
78	L 9	Beresford st SE18
48	M 15	Beresford ter N5
74	E 13	Berestede rd W6
50	E 17	Berger rd E9
50	F 17	Berger rd E9
35	P 14	Bergholt av Ilf
49	R 1	Berholt cres N16
97	X 2	Berkeley av Bxly Hth
41	S 18	Berkeley av Grnfd
37	Y 7	Berkeley av Ilf
38	L 2	Berkeley av Rom
71	Z 18	Berkeley clo Brentf
16	G 1	Berkeley ct N14
18	A 2	Berkeley gdns N21
137	V 14	Berkeley gdns W8
139	R 5	Berkeley ms W1
105	P 17	Berkeley pl SW19
53	R 16	Berkeley rd E12
29	Y 17	Berkeley rd N8
31	P 19	Berkeley rd N15
25	P 14	Berkeley rd NW9
86	F 1	Berkeley rd SW13
139	Y 11	Berkeley sq W1
139	Z 12	Berkeley st W1
70	A 18	Berkeley waye Hounsl
81	N 12	Berkhampstead rd Blvdr
81	S 12	Berkhampstead rd Blvdr
43	O 18	Berkhamsted av Wemb
5	U 18	Berkley cres Barnt
131	R 11	Berkley rd NW1
17	S 20	Berkshire gdns N13
18	M 17	Berkshire gdns N18
50	M 16	Berkshire rd E9
51	N 17	Berkshire rd E9
121	Z 10	Berkshire way Mitch
122	A 10	Berkshire way Mitch

44	C 13	Bermans way NW10
150	K 1	Bermondsey sq SE1
142	J 17	Bermondsey st SE1
143	U 18	Bermondsey Wall east SE16
143	S 18	Bermondsey Wall west SE16
72	B 7	Bernard av W13
65	R 14	Bernard Cassidy st E16
105	W 12	Bernard gdns SW19
31	V 15	Bernard rd N15
38	K 20	Bernard rd Rom
56	K 1	Bernard rd Rom
155	R 9	Bernard rd Wallgtn
32	K 18	Bernard st WC1
11	R 19	Bernays clo Stanm
90	D 9	Bernays gro SW9
158	M 4	Bernel dri Croy
122	K 10	Berne rd Thntn Hth
140	C 2	Berners ms W1
140	D 4	Berners pl W1
133	V 6	Berners rd N1
30	E 6	Berners rd N22
140	C 3	Berners st W1
123	N 17	Berney rd Croy
25	O 15	Bernville way SE6
21	N 11	Bernwell rd E4
109	P 12	Berridge rd SE19
48	E 9	Berriman rd N7
40	E 5	Berriton rd Harrow
17	W 4	Berry clo N21
44	A 20	Berry clo NW10
149	Y 10	Berryfield rd SE17
95	Y 9	Berryhill SE9
11	V 13	Berry hill Stanm
95	Y 10	Berryhill gdns SE9
119	N 7	Berrylands SW20
117	R 12	Berrylands Surb
116	N 13	Berrylands rd Surb
117	N 13	Berrylands rd Surb
55	V 10	Berryman clo Dgnhm
110	F 10	Berrymans la SE26
73	V 4	Berrymead gdns W3
73	X 8	Berrymede rd W4
133	X 14	Berry pl EC1
103	T 18	Berrystede clo Kingst
133	X 16	Berry st EC1
72	J 8	Berry way W5
106	F 11	Bertal rd SW17
33	W 15	Berthan gdns E17
76	C 18	Berthon st SE8
44	G 18	Bertie rd NW10
110	G 14	Bertie rd SE26
105	X 18	Bertram cotts SW19
26	H 19	Bertram rd NW4
8	J 14	Bertram rd Enf
103	O 17	Bertram rd Kingst
47	S 8	Bertram st N19
93	R 7	Betrand st SE13
25	R 3	Bertridge grn Edg
122	K 12	Bert rd Thntn Hth
8	J 14	Berт way Enf
96	H 17	Berwick clo Sidcp
65	X 18	Berwick rd E16
32	M 14	Berwick rd E17
30	H 4	Berwick rd N22
97	R 3	Berwick rd Welling
140	C 5	Berwick st W1
82	J 2	Berwyn av Hounsl
108	J 1	Berwyn rd SE21
85	S 10	Berwyn rd Rich
144	F 11	Beryl rd W6
103	T 18	Berystede clo Kingst
45	S 11	Besant rd NW2
43	W 15	Besant way NW10
107	V 16	Besley st SW16
148	G 10	Bessborough gdns SW1
148	F 10	Bessborough ms SW1
148	F 10	Bessborough pl SW1
104	G 1	Bessborough rd SW15
41	R 2	Bessborough rd Harrow
148	G 10	Bessborough st SW1
148	G 10	Bessborough way SW1
90	M 6	Bessemer rd SE5
91	N 5	Bessemer rd SE5
92	E 1	Besson st SE14
75	T 12	Besson st SE14
154	F 10	Betchworth clo Sutton
54	H 8	Betchworth rd Ilf
158	T 18	Betchworth way Croy
59	R 10	Betham rd Grnfd
23	T 14	Bethecar rd Harrow
65	P 11	Bethell av E16
53	W 1	Bethell av Ilf
97	U 8	Bethel rd Welling
110	M 19	Bethersden clo Becknhm

135 U 14 Bethnal Green rd E2
135 Z 11 Bethnel Green museum E2
15 Z 14 Bethume av N11
49 S 4 Bethune rd N16
61 Z 12 Bethune rd NW10
149 Z 17 Bethwin rd SE5
150 C 17 Bethwin rd SE15
20 M 13 Betoyne av E4
16 F 14 Betstyle rd N11
115 Z 4 Betterton dri Sidcp
140 K 5 Betterton st WC2
87 W 5 Bettridge rd SW8
65 V 19 Betts rd E16
122 M 4 Beulah av Thntn Hth
12 E 10 Beulah clo Edg
122 M 4 Beulah cres Thntn Hth
122 M 15 Beulah gro Croy
108 K 16 Beulah hill SE19
33 T 14 Beulah rd E17
105 V 17 Beulah rd SW19
153 Y 9 Beulah rd Sutton
99 W 9 Beult rd Drtford
68 A 1 Bevan av Bark
156 F 11 Bevan ct Croy
80 C 14 Bevan rd SE2
5 Z 13 Bevan rd Barnt
134 B 6 Bevan st N1
134 G 12 Bevenden st N1
104 E 19 Beverley av SW20
82 F 11 Beverley av Hounsl
96 J 19 Beverley av Sidcp
17 Y 6 Beverley clo N21
88 E 10 Beverley clo SW11
86 F 5 Beverley clo SW13
92 M 7 Beverley ct SE4
34 H 3 Beverley cres Wdfd Grn
25 R 9 Beverley dri Edg
27 T 20 Beverley gdns NW11
86 E 7 Beverley gdns SW13
23 Y 5 Beverley gdns Stanm
43 O 3 Beverley gdns Wemb
104 B 18 Beverley la Kingst
118 F 7 Beverley park New Mald
20 K 19 Beverley rd E4
66 B 9 Beverley rd E6
123 Z 3 Beverley rd SE20
86 E 6 Beverley rd SW13
74 C 14 Beverley rd W4
98 L 6 Beverley rd Bxly Hth
55 Z 12 Beverley rd Dgnhm
56 A 12 Beverley rd Dgnhm
102 E 20 Beverley rd Kingst
121 W 8 Beverley rd Mitch
118 F 9 Beverley rd New Mald
70 C 10 Beverley rd S'hall
152 L 3 Beverley rd Worc Pk
104 C 20 Beverley way new Mald
118 G 3 Beverley way SW20
16 H 2 Beverley ct N14
47 Y 10 Beversbrook rd N19
90 C 12 Beverstone rd SW2
122 H 9 Beverstone rd Thntn Hth
107 N 13 Bevill Allen SW17
107 N 13 Bevill Allen clo SW17
136 M 1 Bevington rd W10
137 N 2 Bevington rd W10
125 P 3 Bevington rd Becknhm
143 U 18 Bevington st SE16
133 R 11 Bevin way WC1
142 L 5 Bevis marks EC3
7 N 14 Newcastle gdns Enf
48 F 20 Bewdley st N1
89 S 4 Bewick st SW8
63 O 19 Bewley st E1
143 Z 8 Bewley st E1
108 J 11 Bewleys rd SE27
100 A 3 Bexhill clo Felt
16 J 17 Bexhill rd N11
92 L 17 Bexhill rd SE4
85 W 8 Bexhill rd SW14
99 P 12 Bexley clo Dartford
18 B 11 Bexley gdns N9
98 F 20 Bexley High st Bxly
99 P 12 Bexley la Drtford
115 U 8 Bexley la Sidcp
96 Z 14 Bexley rd SE9
154 L 11 Beynon rd Carsh
151 R 14 Bianca rd SE15
27 V 8 Bibsworth rd N3
85 S 8 Bicester rd Rich
131 P 20 Bickenhall st W1
106 M 14 Bickersteth rd SW17
47 U 8 Bickerton rd N19
127 U 5 Bickler Pk rd Brom
127 R 8 Bickley cres Brom
33 R 20 Bickley rd E10
127 P 4 Bickley rd Brom
106 L 13 Bickley st SW17
90 M 8 Bicknell rd SE5
8 F 5 Bicknoller rd Enf
126 C 12 Bidborough clo Brom
132 H 13 Bidborough st WC1
88 E 11 Bidcot st SW11
113 V 9 Biddenden way SE9
64 L 14 Bidder st E16
48 C 13 Biddestone rd N7
129 Y 14 Biddulph rd W9
156 L 20 Biddulph rd S Croy
60 A 7 Bideford av Grnfd
25 O 5 Bideford clo Edg
18 E 2 Bideford gdns Enf
112 B 7 Bideford rd Brom
9 X 3 Bideford av Enf
100 E 6 Bideford rd Felt
80 D 20 Bideford rd Welling
29 V 3 Bidwell gdns N11
92 A 3 Bidewell st SE15
31 R 1 Bigbury clo N17
64 G 2 Biggerstaff rd E15
48 E 7 Biggerstaff st N4
120 L 1 Biggin av Mitch
108 K 17 Biggin hill SE19
108 K 19 Biggin way SE19
108 H 19 Bigginwood rd SW16
87 O 8 Biggs row SW15
50 A 3 Big hill E5
63 N 18 Bigland st E1
147 W 7 Bigland st E1
78 M 14 Big Nell rd SE18
52 F 13 Bignold rd E7
28 A 17 Bigwood rd NW11
37 W 10 Billet clo Rom
32 J 5 Billet rd E17
33 O 3 Billet rd E17
37 V 10 Billet rd Rom
92 G 10 Billingford clo SE4
145 Y 17 Billing pl SW10
145 Z 16 Billing rd SW10
76 G 16 Billingsgate st SE10
145 Y 17 Billing st SW6
75 T 20 Billington rd SE14
142 K 7 Billiter sq EC3
142 K 7 Billiter st EC3
76 G 11 Billson st E14
113 O 10 Bilsby gro SE9
59 Z 3 Bilton rd Grnfd
60 D 3 Bilton rd Grnfd
9 X 4 Bilton way Enf
146 B 8 Bina gdns SW5
7 R 12 Bincote rd Enf
74 E 7 Binden rd W12
120 B 8 Bindon gd Mrdn
90 A 3 Binfield rd SW4
157 U 10 Binfield rd S Croy
132 M 3 Bingfield st N1
133 N 3 Bingfield st N1
131 T 19 Bingham pl W1
123 Y 20 Bingham rd Croy
49 O 17 Bingham st N1
65 X 17 Bingley rd E16
59 N 12 Bingley rd Grnfd
139 V 8 Binney st SW1
73 Z 13 Binns rd W4
10 H 17 Binyon cres Stanm
113 T 5 Birbetts rd SE9
123 X 12 Birchanger rd SE25
17 Y 12 Birch av N13
72 B 19 Birch clo Brentf
38 G 10 Birch clo Rom
91 Y 5 Birch clo SE15
101 Y 11 Birch clo Tedd
55 V 1 Birchdale gdns Rom
52 M 15 Birchdale rd E7
43 X 6 Birchen clo NW9
43 X 8 Birchen gro NW9
7 P 19 Birches the N21
77 W 15 Birches the SE7
72 D 18 Birchfield clo Brentf
64 A 19 Birchfield st E14
56 L 10 Birch gdns Dgnhm
94 C 18 Birch gro SE12
61 P 20 Birch gro W3
73 O 2 Birch gro W3
97 N 11 Birch gro Welling
158 G 10 Birch hill Croy
98 G 1 Birchington clo Bxly Hth
29 X 17 Birchington rd N8
129 V 4 Birchington rd NW6
117 O 18 Birchington rd Surb
160 G 7 Birchin la EC3
88 M 18 Birchlands av SW12
89 N 18 Birchlands av SW12
22 L 1 Birch pk Harrow
48 L 11 Birchmore wlk N5
100 A 13 Birch rd Felt
38 G 10 Birch rd Rom
127 X 16 Birch row Brom
157 Z 2 Birch Tree way Croy
81 Y 15 Birch wlk Erith
121 S 1 Birch wlk Mitch
29 P 11 Birchwood av N10
124 L 8 Birchwood av Becknhm
115 R 7 Birchwood av Sidcp
155 R 4 Birchwood av Wallgtn
17 V 16 Birchwood ct N13
25 V 8 Birchwood ct Edg
100 J 15 Birchwood gro Hampt
107 R 11 Birchwood rd SW17
151 R 17 Bird-In-Bush rd SE15
127 O 4 Bird-In-Hand la Brom
94 M 8 Birdbrook rd SE3
140 C 19 Birdcage wlk SW1
127 S 12 Birdham clo Brom
157 P 9 Birdhurst av S Croy
157 P 9 Birdhurst gdns S Croy
157 R 11 Birdhurst ri S Croy
88 C 12 Birdhurst rd SW18
106 J 16 Birdhurst rd SW19
157 R 10 Birdhurst rd S Croy
110 D 4 Bird In The Hand SE23
150 J 15 Birdlip clo SE15
38 G 3 Birds Farm av Rom
139 V 6 Bird st W1
82 E 20 Bird wlk Twick
69 Y 2 Birdwood clo Dgnhm
61 W 19 Birkbeck av W3
59 O 3 Birkbeck av Grnfd
21 R 9 Birkbeck gdns Wdfd Grn
73 X 4 Birkbeck gro W3
108 K 2 Birkbeck hill SE21
108 K 2 Birkbeck pl SE21
49 U 16 Birkbeck rd E8
30 A 13 Birkbeck rd N8
15 O 17 Birkbeck rd N12
31 U 5 Birkbeck rd N17
13 S 16 Birkbeck rd NW7
106 B 14 Birkbeck rd SW19
73 X 3 Birkbeck rd W3
72 E 10 Birkbeck rd W5
124 D 4 Birkbeck rd Becknhm
8 B 5 Birkbeck rd Enf
36 D 16 Birkbeck rd Ilf
57 N 3 Birkbeck rd Rom
115 O 7 Birkbeck rd Sidcp
63 O 10 Birkbeck st E2
135 Y 14 Birkbeck st E2
59 O 2 Birkbeck way Grnfd
22 H 10 Birkdale av Pinn
79 Z 10 Birkdale rd SE2
80 A 11 Birkdale rd SE2
60 J 12 Birkdale rd W5
116 M 2 Birkenhead av Kingst
117 N 2 Birkenhead av Kingst
111 X 3 Birkhall rd SE6
89 Y 20 Birkwood clo SW12
15 R 8 Birley rd N20
89 O 6 Birley st SW11
99 R 1 Birling rd Erith
48 C 7 Birnam rd N4
31 T 15 Birstall rd N15
144 F 11 Biscay rd W6
70 H 16 Biscoe clo Hounsl
93 X 9 Biscoe way SE13
157 S 2 Bisenden rd Croy
120 L 18 Bisham clo Carsh
47 R 3 Bishop gdns N6
7 V 7 Bishop Craven clo Enf
114 B 4 Bishops clo SE9
23 W 6 Bishop Ken rd Harrow
144 L 5 Bishop Kings rd W14
16 D 4 Bishop rd N14
65 U 2 Bishops av E13
87 R 4 Bishops av SW6
126 K 5 Bishops av Brom
37 T 18 Bishops av Rom
28 H 16 Bishops av the N2
46 G 2 Bishops av the N2
138 B 4 Bishops Bridge rd W2
33 S 13 Bishops clo E17
4 A 20 Bishops clo Barnt
8 M 9 Bishops clo Enf
102 G 6 Bishops clo Rich
153 Z 6 Bishops clo Sutton
141 X 4 Bishops ct EC4
141 R 4 Bishops ct WC2
120 G 13 Bishopsford rd Mrdn
142 K 3 Bishopsgate EC2
142 J 3 Bishopsgate chyd EC2
28 H 18 Bishops gro N2
100 G 11 Bishops gro Hampt
116 G 3 Bishops hall Kingst
87 O 4 Bishops park SW6
87 R 4 Bishops Pk rd SW6
108 A 20 Bishops Pk rd SW16
122 B 1 Bishops Pk rd SW16
29 P 19 Bishops rd N6
87 U 1 Bishops rd SW6
145 O 20 Bishops rd SW6
71 T 5 Bishops rd W7
122 H 18 Bishops rd Croy
149 T 5 Bishops ter SE11
110 E 9 Bishopsthorpe rd SE26
134 B 4 Bishops st N1
158 G 12 Bishops wlk Croy
63 O 6 Bishops way E2
135 Y 8 Bishops way E2
44 A 20 Bishops way NW10
46 M 1 Bishopswood rd N6
47 N 2 Bishopswood rd N6
119 N 20 Bisley clo Worc Pk
61 N 9 Bispham rd NW10
60 M 9 Bispham rd Wemb
70 E 9 Bisley clo S'hall
64 G 5 Bisson rd E15
33 X 10 Bisterne av E17
14 B 18 Bittacy clo NW7
14 C 19 Bittacy hill NW7
27 S 2 Bittacy hill NW7
14 B 19 Bittacy Hill park NW7
14 B 18 Bittacy Park av NW7
14 A 19 Bittacy rise NW7
14 D 20 Bittacy rd NW7
142 A 18 Bittern st SE1
116 H 6 Bittoms the Kingst
134 H 16 Blackall st EC2
70 B 20 Blackberry Farm clo Hounsl
43 W 8 Blackbird hill NW9
56 G 18 Blackborne rd Dgnhm
30 M 16 Black Boy la N15
127 V 5 Blackbrook la Brom
139 T 10 Blackburnes ms W1
45 Z 18 Blackburn rd NW6
37 V 17 Blackbush av Rom
154 B 16 Blackbush clo Sutton
135 N 20 Black Eagle st E1
87 O 8 Blackett st SW15
96 K 14 Blackfen rd Sidcp
97 P 15 Blackfen rd Sidcp
156 K 18 Blackford clo S Croy
141 W 10 Blackfriars br EC4
141 X 8 Blackfriars la EC4
141 W 17 Blackfriars rd SE1
141 V 9 Blackfriars underpass EC4
93 Z 1 Blackheath av SE10
94 C 6 Blackheath gro SE3
93 T 2 Blackheath hill SE10
94 E 7 Blackheath pk SE3
93 U 4 Blackheath ri SE13
93 R 2 Blackheath rd SE10
93 Z 4 Blackheath vale SE3
94 A 3 Blackheath vale SE3
94 B 6 Blackheath village SE3
150 F 2 Black Horse ct SE1
32 F 9 Blackhorse la E17
123 Y 17 Blackhorse la Croy
32 G 14 Blackhorse rd E17
75 W 15 Black Horse rd SE8
115 O 10 Black Horse rd Sidcp
111 T 11 Blacklands rd SE6
147 O 7 Blacklands ter SW3
156 A 14 Blackley clo Croy
74 F 12 Black Lion la W6
143 S 2 Black Lion yd E1
71 R 2 Blackmore av S'hall
101 Y 14 Blackmores gro Tedd
50 G 2 Black path E10
91 Z 5 Blackpool rd SE15
149 O 7 Black Prince rd SE11
134 L 2 Blackshaw pl N1
106 H 13 Blackshaw rd SW17
74 M 12 Blacks rd W6
144 B 8 Blacks rd W6
48 H 7 Blackstock rd N4
45 N 14 Blackstone rd NW2
142 K 17 Black Swan yd SE1
124 B 19 Blackthorn av Croy
20 K 13 Blackthorne dri E4
97 Y 7 Blackthorn gro Bxly Hth
64 B 13 Blackthorn st E3
90 G 9 Black Tree ms SW19
77 O 9 Blackwall la SE10
64 H 20 Blackwall tunnel E14
77 P 11 Blackwall tunnel approach SE10
64 F 9 Blackwall tunnel northern approach E14
64 H 20 Blackwall way E14
76 H 1 Blackwall way E14
91 U 13 Blackwater st SE22

B

23 P 2 Blackwell clo Harrow
12 C 12 Blackwell gdns Edg
150 S 10 Blackwood st SE17
97 V 18 Bladindon dri Bxly
125 Y 4 Bladon ct Brom
16 J 8 Blagdens clo N14
16 J 7 Blagdens la N14
118 F 7 Blagdon house New
   Mald
93 R 16 Blagdon rd SE13
118 C 9 Blagdon rd New
   Mald
102 D 16 Blagdon wlk Tedd
137 N 2 Blagrove rd W10
44 A 2 Blair av NW9
96 G 14 Blair clo Sidcp
108 A 3 Blairderby rd SW2
64 H 18 Blair st E14
67 W 4 Blake av Bark
87 Z 1 Blake gdns SW6
52 F 5 Blake Hall cres E11
52 F 5 Blake Hall rd E11
154 M 13 Blakehall rd Carsh
76 L 5 Blakeley cotts SE10
107 Z 6 Blackemore rd N15
122 D 11 Blakemore rd Thntn
   Hth
110 M 20 Blakeney av
   Becknhm
15 P 6 Blakeney clo N20
110 L 19 Blackeney rd
   Becknhm
106 M 10 Blakenham rd SW17
107 N 9 Blakenham rd SW17
65 O 12 Blake rd E16
16 J 20 Blake rd N11
29 V 2 Blake rd N11
157 R 2 Blake rd Croy
120 H 5 Blake rd Mitch
118 E 13 Blakes av New Mald
125 T 19 Blakes grn W Wkhm
118 D 13 Blakes la new Mald
6 F 17 Blakesley av W5
119 U 3 Blakesley wlk SW20
150 L 19 Blakes rd SE15
118 G 12 Blakes ter New Mald
18 C 3 Blakesware gdns N9
113 R 6 Bianchard clo SE9
49 Y 19 Blanchard way E8
91 O 8 Blanchedowne SE5
65 P 12 Blanche st E16
120 A 11 Blanchland rd Mrdn
89 P 17 Blandfield rd SW12
124 G 2 Blandford av
   Becknhm
100 L 1 Blandford av Twick
28 E 14 Blandford clo N2
156 A 6 Blandford clo Croy
38 G 13 Blandford clo Rom
20 F 3 Blandford cres E4
74 A 8 Blandford rd W4
72 H 5 Blandford rd W5
124 D 4 Blandford rd
   Becknhm
70 F 11 Blandford rd S'hall
101 S 14 Blandford rd Tedd
130 M 17 Blandford sq NW8
137 T 3 Blandford st W1
66 L 9 Blaney cres E6
113 Y 2 Blanmerle rd SE9
114 A 2 Blanmerle rd SE9
146 F 17 Blantyre st SW10
93 Y 18 Blashford st SE 13
23 U 14 Blawith rd Harrow
31 Z 1 Blaydon clo N15
79 X 16 Bleakhill la SE 18
110 B 18 Blean gro SE20
59 X 6 Bleasdale av Grnfd
59 Y 6 Bleasdale av Grnfd
97 U 15 Bledlow clo Bxly
80 H 1 Bledlow clo SE2
59 N 6 Bledlow ri Grnfd
141 U 1 Bleeding Heart yd
   EC1
107 V 14 Blegborough rd
   SW16
97 W 17 Blendon dri Bxly
112 D 18 Blendon pth Brom
150 E 9 Blendon rd SE17
97 U 16 Blendon rd Bxly
79 P 15 Blendon ter SE18
35 V 19 Blenheim av Ilf
17 Y 4 Blenheim clo N21
118 L 1 Blenheim clo SW20
59 R 7 Blenheim clo Grnfd
38 J 12 Blenheim clo Rom
155 V 16 Blenheim clo Wallgtn
114 E 6 Blenheim ct Sidcp
136 L 7 Blenheim cres W11
137 N 6 Blenheim cres W11
136 L 17 Blenheim cres S
   Croy
96 K 3 Blenheim dri Welling
45 N 15 Blenheim gdns NW2

90 B 15 Blenheim gdns SW2
103 S 19 Blenheim gdns
   Kingst
155 V 15 Blenheim gdns
   Wallgtn
42 K 9 Blenheim gdns
   Wemb
30 E 8 Blenheim gro SE15
91 W 5 Blenheim gro SE15
156 L 17 Blenheim Pk rd S
   Croy
130 B 8 Blenheim pas NW8
66 A 8 Blenheim rd E6
52 A 12 Blenheim rd E15
32 G 10 Blenheim rd E17
30 E 8 Blenheim rd N22
130 C 7 Blenheim rd NW8
110 C 18 Blenheim rd SE20
118 L 7 Blenheim rd SW20
74 B 8 Blenheim rd W4
4 C 13 Blenheim rd Barnt
127 R 9 Blenheim rd Brom
115 T 6 Blenheim rd Grnfd
22 K 8 Blenheim rd Har
22 J 17 Blenheim rd Harrow
115 T 3 Blenheim rd Sidcp
153 Z 4 Blenheim rd Sutton
139 X 7 Blenheim st W1
130 B 8 Blenheim ter NW8
88 L 17 Blenkarne rd SW11
25 V 4 Blessbury rd Edg
93 X 9 Blessington clo SE13
93 X 9 Blessington rd SE13
134 C 10 Bletchley st N1
105 P 4 Blincoe clo SW19
93 R 3 Bliss cr SE13
93 T 1 Blisset st SE10
55 P 18 Blithbury rd Dgnhm
79 Z 11 Blithdale rd SE2
80 B 11 Blithdale rd SE2
145 W 3 Blithfield st W8
42 A 8 Blockley rd Wemb
74 J 3 Bloemfontein av
   W12
62 H 19 Bloemfontein rd
   W12
74 J 3 Bloemfontein rd
   W12
130 E 18 Blomfield rd W9
129 Z 20 Blomfield rd W9
130 E 16 Blomfield rd W9
143 H 3 Blomfield st EC2
137 Z 1 Blomfield st EC2
56 A 8 Blomville rd Dgnhm
89 N 4 Blondel st SW11
72 C 10 Blondin av W5
64 B 6 Blondon st E3
148 D 6 Bloomburg st SW1
36 A 19 Bloomfield cres Ilf
139 Y 8 Bloomfield pl W1
29 P 19 Bloomfield rd N6
79 N 13 Bloomfield rd SE18
126 M 11 Bloomfield rd Brom
127 N 10 Bloomfield rd Brom
116 K 8 Bloomfield rd Kingst
147 U 9 Bloomfield ter SW1
108 J 7 Bloom gro SE27
130 P 13 Bloomhall rd SE19
145 N 20 Bloom Pk rd SW6
61 O 19 Bloomsbury clo W5
140 L 3 Bloomsbury ct Pinn
22 E 9 Bloomsbury ct Pinn
140 L 1 Bloomsbury pl WC1
140 K 1 Bloomsbury sq WC1
140 H 2 Bloomsbury st WC1
140 K 3 Bloomsbury way
   WC1
89 X 3 Blore clo SW8
72 L 6 Blossom clo W5
7 X 5 Blossom la Enf
134 M 19 Blossom st E1
70 B 18 Blossom waye
   Hounsl
63 W 16 Blount st E14
95 P 13 Bloxham gdns SE9
50 K 4 Bloxhall rd E10
100 F 19 Bloxam cres Hampt
155 V 6 Bloxworth clo Wallgtn
150 B 20 Blucher rd SE5
91 X 1 Blue Anchor la SE16
151 X 5 Blue Anchor la SE16
109 V 10 Bluebell clo SE26
140 B 14 Blue Bell yd SW1
100 G 13 Bluefield clo Hampt
21 N 9 Bluehouse rd E4
25 Z 4 Blundell rd Edg
26 A 3 Blundell rd Edg
48 A 20 Blundell st N7
157 O 11 Blunt rd S Croy
95 W 14 Blunts rd SE9
50 D 13 Blurton rd E5
92 L 19 Blythe clo SE6
92 L 20 Blythe hill SE6

92 L 19 Blythe Hill la SE6
110 L 1 Blythe Hill la SE6
144 F 1 Blythe rd W14
144 K 3 Blythe rd W14
126 C 1 Blythe rd W14
110 L 2 Blythe vale SE6
50 L 2 Blythe rd E17
54 M 4 Blythswood rd Ilf
48 B 1 Blythwood rd N4
133 N 6 Boadicea st N1
80 M 10 Boarers Manor way
   Blvdr
151 P 18 Boathouse wlk SE15
39 U 3 Bobs la Rom
103 N 17 Bockhampton rd
   Kingst
135 X 4 Bocking st E8
63 N 3 Bocking st E9
8 C 9 Bodiam clo Enf
107 Y 19 Bodiam rd SW16
105 R 5 Bodicott clo SW19
118 A 13 Bodley clo New Mald
117 Z 13 Bodley rd New Mald
118 C 12 Bodley rd New Mald
120 A 10 Bodmin gro Mrdn
105 Z 2 Bodmin st SW18
118 H 5 Bodnant gdns New
   Mald
49 Z 14 Bodney rd E5
97 V 2 Bognor rd Welling
50 B 16 Bohemia pl E8
5 Y 19 Bohun gro Barnt
74 H 18 Boileau rd SW13
60 M 17 Boileau rd W5
61 N 16 Boileau rd W5
93 P 4 Bolden st SE4
159 R 3 Bolderwood way W
   Wykhm
8 M 5 Boleyn av Enf
56 J 20 Boleyn gdns Dgnhm
159 S 4 Boleyn gdns W
   Wkhm
66 A 5 Boleyn rd E6
65 V 1 Boleyn rd E7
49 S 14 Boleyn rd N16
75 P 14 Boleyn rd N16
88 K 16 Bilingbroke gro
   SW11
136 H 20 Bolingbroke rd W14
144 G 1 Bolingbroke rd W14
88 H 1 Bolingbroke wlk
   SW11
73 T 7 Bollo Br rd W3
73 R 6 Bollo la W3
73 V 10 Bollo la W3
149 N 18 Bolney st SW8
131 Z 19 Bolsover st W1
121 S 2 Bolstead rd Mitch
141 U 5 Bolt ct EC4
149 N 18 Bolton cres SE5
128 F 10 Bolton gdns NW10
146 A 8 Bolton gdns SW5
112 C 16 Bolton gdns Brom
101 Y 15 Bolton gdns Tedd
146 A 10 Bolton gdns ms SW5
52 D 19 Bolton rd E15
18 G 17 Bolton rd N18
129 Z 6 Bolton rd NW8
62 C 3 Bolton rd NW10
73 V 20 Bolton rd W4
85 W 1 Bolton rd W4
146 B 10 Boltons the SW10
41 X 12 Boltons the Wemb
139 Y 13 Bolton st W1
151 V 5 Bombay st SE16
136 J 8 Bonar rd W11
113 S 18 Bonar pl Chisl
151 R 20 Bonar rd SE15
113 W 19 Bonchester clo Chisl
154 B 11 Bonchurch clo
   Sutton
136 K 1 Bonchurch rd W10
72 A 4 Bonchurch rd W13
108 E 7 Bond ct EC4
155 V 7 Bond gdns Wallgtn
120 K 3 Bond st N65
   Bond st W1
   see under
   New & Old Bond St
51 X 15 Bond st E15
73 Z 12 Bond st W4
72 G 1 Bond st W5
148 K 14 Bondway SW8
78 E 8 Boneta rd SE18
93 V 10 Bonfield rd SE13
90 B 13 Bonham rd SW2
72 A 7 Bonham rd Dgnhm
73 Y 7 Bonheur rd W4
134 G 18 Bonhill st EC2
22 K 3 Boniface gdns
   Harrow
22 K 2 Boniface wlk Harrow
109 R 11 Bon Marche ter
   SE 27

117 O 5 Bonner Hill rd Kingst
63 P 6 Bonner rd E2
23 X 17 Bonnersfield clo
   Harrow
23 Z 17 Bonnersfield la
   Harrow
23 Y 17 Bonnersfield la
   Harrow
63 S 7 Bonner st E2
89 V 15 Bonneville gdns
   SW4
149 N 14 Bonnington sq SW8
132 A 1 Bonny st NW1
101 W 5 Bonser rd Twick
150 J 18 Bonsor st SE15
112 D 13 Bonville rd Brom
18 J 16 Booker rd N18
94 A 9 Boones rd SE13
93 Z 10 Boone st SE13
94 A 9 Boone st SE13
77 N 8 Boord st SE10
47 X 6 Boothby rd N19
80 F 2 Booth clo SE2
25 X 6 Booth rd NW9
26 B 8 Booth rd NW9
140 B 3 Booths pl W1
134 H 14 Boot st N1
59 U 14 Bordars rd W7
59 T 14 Bordars wlk W7
18 B 1 Borden av Enf
86 G 19 Borden wlk SW15
109 Z 12 Border cres SE26
159 P 7 Border gdns Croy
106 K 20 Border ga Mitch
110 B 13 Bord rd SE26
120 A 9 Bordesley rd Mrdn
16 J 19 Bordham rd N11
65 T 18 Boreham av E16
51 T 3 Boreham clo E10
30 K 6 Boreham rd N22
78 F 11 Borgard rd SE18
92 D 11 Borland rd SE15
102 B 17 Borland rd Tedd
87 N 8 Borneo st SW15
142 B 19 Borough High st SE1
156 H 6 Borough hill Croy
141 X 20 Borough rd SE1
142 A 19 Borough rd SE1
83 T 1 Borough rd Islwth
103 P 19 Borough rd Kingst
120 J 3 Borough rd Mitch
149 Z 10 Borrett rd SE17
88 B 15 Borrodaile rd SW18
23 Y 8 Borrowdale av
   Harrow
35 R 12 Borrowdale clo Ilf
51 Z 13 Borthwick rd E15
52 A 12 Borthwick rd E15
26 D 19 Borthwick rd NW9
76 B 15 Borthwick st SE8
32 K 11 Borwick av E17
111 U 8 Bosbury rd SE6
47 N 10 Boscastle rd NW5
147 V 4 Boscobel pl SW1
130 G 19 Boscobel st NW8
33 V 20 Boscombe av E10
108 B 16 Boscombe gdns
   SW16
107 N 15 Boscombe rd SW17
105 Z 19 Boscombe rd SW19
74 H 4 Boscombe rd W12
119 N 19 Boscombe rd Worc
   Pk
20 F 7 Bosgrove E4
143 N 16 Boss st SE1
80 E 14 Bostall heath SE2
80 C 15 Bostall hill SE2
80 F 15 Bostall Hill rd SE2
80 F 14 Bostall House lodge
   SE2
80 D 12 Bostall la SE2
80 D 10 Bostall manorway
   SE2
80 L 20 Bostall Pk av Bxly
   Hth
115 P 19 Bostall rd Orp
98 A 8 Bostall row Bxly Hth
71 Z 12 Boston gdns Brentf
72 B 13 Boston gdns Brentf
72 B 13 Boston Manor House
   Brentf
72 B 12 Boston Mnr rd Brentf
72 D 15 Boston Pk rd Brentf
131 N 18 Boston pl NW1
66 C 9 Boston rd E6
33 N 19 Boston rd E17
71 X 9 Boston rd W7
72 D 15 Boston rd Croy
25 V 2 Boston rd Edg
135 S 7 Boston st E2
72 D 7 Bostonthorpe rd W7
71 Y 11 Boston vale W7
133 N 20 Boston st WC1
122 L 9 Boswell rd Thntn Hth

132 M 20 Boswell st WC1
32 K 5 Bosworth clo E17
16 L 18 Bosworth rd N11
128 L 18 Bosworth rd W10
4 M 12 Bosworth rd Barnt
56 F 10 Bosworth rd Dgnhm
20 K 9 Boteley clo E7
65 X 13 Botha rd E13
144 G 15 Bothwell st W6
160 H 9 Botolph all EC3
119 S 4 Botsford rd SW20
137 V 6 Botts ms W2
137 U 6 Botts pass W11
101 V 13 Boucher clo Tedd
57 W 18 Bouchier wlk Rainhm
126 C 17 Boughton av Brom
79 W 7 Boughton rd SE18
63 U 18 Boulcott st E1
122 M 13 Boulogne rd Croy
123 N 14 Boulogne rd Croy
57 X 17 Boulter gdns Rainhm
56 A 8 Boulton rd Dgnhm
18 M 7 Bounces la N9
19 P 8 Bounces rd N9
106 M 3 Boundaries rd SW12
107 N 2 Boundaries rd SW12
70 H 14 Boundary clo S'hall
65 Z 11 Boundary la E13
150 D 14 Boundary la SE17
130 C 4 Boundary ms NW8
65 Z 7 Boundary rd E13
33 O 20 Boundary rd E17
19 R 1 Boundary rd N9
30 L 8 Boundary rd N22
30 D 4 Boundary rd NW8
106 F 15 Boundary rd SW19
106 G 14 Boundary rd SW19
67 O 6 Boundary rd Bark
67 S 5 Boundary rd Bark
9 R 20 Boundary rd Enf
39 V 18 Boundary rd Rom
155 R 18 Boundary rd S Wallgtn
96 G 13 Boundary rd Sidcp
155 R 14 Boundary rd Wallgtn
141 W 17 Boundary row SE1
159 O 11 Boundary way Croy
111 Y 6 Boundfield rd SE6
112 A 5 Boundfield rd SE6
16 J 19 Bounds Green rd N11
30 R 4 Bounds Green rd N22
140 E 7 Bourchier st W1
139 X 9 Bourdon pl W1
124 B 3 Bourdon rd SE20
139 X 9 Bourdon st W1
89 Z 17 Bourke clo SW2
44 B 19 Bourke clo NW10
140 B 2 Bourlet clo W1
31 O 13 Bourn av N15
5 U 18 Bourn av Barnt
95 O 7 Bournbrook rd SE3
16 M 7 Bourne av N14
20 E 15 Bourne gdns E4
17 S 9 Bourne hill N13
98 L 14 Bourne mead Bxly
91 X 4 Bournemouth rd SE 15
105 Z 20 Bournemouth rd SW19
52 C 10 Bourne rd E7
30 B 18 Bourne rd N8
98 K 15 Bourne rd Bxly
126 M 8 Bourne rd Brom
127 N 8 Bourne rd Brom
99 N 13 Bourne rd Drtford
147 S 6 Bourne st SW1
156 J 3 Bourne st Croy
137 X 1 Bourne ter W2
16 L 6 Bourne the N14
7 O 19 Bourne the N14
126 D 19 Bourne vale Brom
107 Z 10 Bournevale rd SW16
41 W 16 Bourne view Grnfd
153 V 12 Bourne way Sutton
9 A 3 Bourne Way Bushey Watf
80 A 19 Bournewood rd SW2
93 N 18 Bournville rd SE6
5 Z 10 Bournwell clo Barnt
92 E 55 Bousfield rd SE4
88 J 11 Boutflower rd SW11
24 H 20 Bouverie gdns Harrow
138 H 4 Bouverie pl W2
49 R 6 Bouverie rd N16
23 O 20 Bouverie rd Harrow
141 U 7 Bouverie st EC4
9 R 3 Bouvier rd Enf
48 C 11 Bovay st N7
48 C 11 Bovay st N7
92 E 18 Boveney rd SE23
92 G 20 Bovill rd SE23

43 R 19 Bovingdon av Wemb
47 W 8 Bovingdon clo N19
26 A 3 Bovingdon la NW9
88 A 3 Bovingdon rd SW6
25 X 16 Bowater clo NW9
77 W 19 Bowater pl SE3
78 B 8 Bowater rd SE18
160 B 6 Bow Church yd EC4
63 Y 13 Bow Common la E3
64 A 13 Bow Common la E3
33 N 20 Bowden rd E17
149 T 10 Bowden st SE11
75 X 12 Bowditch SE8
109 S 8 Bowen dri SE21
23 O 20 Bowen rd Harrow
41 O 1 Bowen rd Harrow
64 D 16 Bowen st E14
93 Z 1 Bower av SE10
39 N 2 Bower clo Rom
87 Z 3 Bowerdean st SW6
63 S 18 Bower st E1
97 P 16 Bowes clo Sidcp
16 G 15 Bowes rd N11
17 N 17 Bowes rd N13
62 A 20 Bowes rd W3
55 U 13 Bowes rd Dgnhm
144 E 15 Bowfell rd W6
97 Y 3 Bowford av Bxly Hth
89 X 11 Bowland rd SW4
21 Z 17 Bowland rd Wdfd Grn
160 C 7 Bow la EC4
28 D 1 Bow la N12
151 S 13 Bowles rd SE1
109 U 13 Bowley clo SE19
75 Z 1 Bowley st E14
86 K 19 Bowling Grn clo SW15
133 U 17 Bowling Grn la EC1
142 E 17 Bowling Green pl SE1
79 E 9 Bowling Green row SE 18
149 T 13 Bowling Green st SE11
134 H 12 Bowling Green wlk N1
11 N 16 Bowls clo Stanm
65 R 19 Bowman av E16
72 A 3 Bowmans clo W13
92 D 18 Bowmans lea SE23
155 R 6 Bowmans meadow Wallgtn
48 B 11 Bowmans ms N7
48 A 11 Bowmans ms N7
48 A 11 Bowmans pl N7
99 T 18 Bowmans rd Drtford
113 T 4 Bowmead SE9
103 Z 12 Bowness cres SW15
104 A 12 Bowness cres SW15
82 C 10 Bowness dri Hounsl
93 S 19 Bowness rd SE6
98 G 6 Bowness rd Bxly Hth
57 W 15 Bowness way Hornch
89 O 13 Bowood rd SW11
9 T 8 Bowood rd Enf
63 Y 10 Bow rd E3
64 C 8 Bow rd E3
42 H 20 Bowrons av Wemb
51 Z 15 Bow st E15
140 L 7 Bow st WC2
150 D 18 Bowyer pl SE5
91 R 17 Boxall rd SE21
56 A 11 Boxall rd Dgnhm
80 E 8 Boxgrove rd SE2
120 D 10 Boxley rd Mrdn
77 V 3 Boxley st E16
24 A 13 Boxmoor rd Harrow
23 O 3 Boxtree la Harrow
133 R 4 Boxworth gr N1
78 L 13 Boyard rd SE18
65 T 12 Boyce way E13
59 W 18 Boycroft av NW9
103 R 18 Boyd clo Kingst
106 F 15 Boyd rd SW19
143 T 7 Boyd st E1
141 Y 19 Boyfield st SE1
112 C 13 Boyland rd Brom
10 M 18 Boyle av Stanm
140 A 9 Boyle st W1
27 R 12 Boyle rd NW4
27 R 13 Boyne av NW4
93 W 8 Boyne rd SE13
56 E 10 Boyne rd Dgnhm
137 O 13 Boyne Ter ms W11
12 G 7 Boyseland ct Edg
150 D 14 Boyston st SE17
30 A 11 Boyton clo N8
30 B 17 Boyton rd N8
30 D 7 Brabant rd N22
156 A 17 Brabazon av Wallgtn
58 G 6 Brabazon rd Grnfd
64 C 16 Brabazon st E14

81 P 18 Brabourne cres Bxly Hth
125 V 11 Brabourne ri Becknhm
92 B 6 Braburn gro SE15
81 X 17 Bracewell av Grnfd
62 L 14 Bracewell rd W10
136 B 2 Bracewell rd W10
157 V 5 Bracewood gdns Croy
48 B 6 Bracey st N4
89 P 17 Bracken av SW12
159 P 6 Bracken av Croy
74 K 7 Brackenbury gdns W6
28 D 10 Brackenbury rd N2
74 K 8 Brackenbury rd W6
17 R 7 Brackendale N21
83 R 11 Bracken end Islwth
86 G 4 Bracken gdns SW13
40 B 12 Brackenhill Ruis
126 C 1 Brackenhill clo Brom
126 C 1 Brackenhill la Brom
18 C 2 Brackens the Enf
20 G 7 Brackens the E4
74 B 12 Brackley rd W4
111 O 17 Brackley rd Becknhm
35 N 1 Brackley sq Ilf
34 M 1 Brackley sq Wdfd Grn
134 B 19 Brackley st EC1
74 B 13 Brackley ter W4
45 Y 13 Bracknell clo NW3
73 F 5 Bracknell clo N22
46 A 13 Bracknell gdns NW3
45 Z 13 Bracknell way NW3
79 Z 10 Bracondale rd SE2
80 C 10 Bracondale rd SE2
98 F 18 Bradbourne rd Bxly
87 Y 4 Bradbourne st SW6
70 F 10 Bradbury clo S'hall
49 T 16 Bradbury st N16
85 N 6 Braddon rd Rich
76 L 13 Braddyll st SE10
96 M 10 Bradenham av Welling
97 N 10 Bradenham av Welling
24 A 12 Bradenham rd Harrow
129 X 18 Braden st W9
54 M 16 Bradfield dri Bark
77 T 4 Bradfield rd E16
40 C 15 Bradfield rd Ruis
9 N 10 Bradfield sq Enf
152 C 14 Bradford rd Epsom
109 Z 9 Bradford rd SE26
74 A 4 Bradford rd W3
54 F 4 Bradford rd Ilf
93 R 17 Bradgate SE6
52 H 5 Brading cres E11
52 K 7 Brading cres E12
90 D 18 Brading rd SW2
122 B 15 Brading rd Croy
129 R 12 Bradiston rd W9
48 B 20 Bradley clo N7
60 B 17 Bradley gdns W13
30 C 7 Bradley rd N22
108 L 14 Bradley rd SE19
9 X 1 Bradley rd Enf
133 T 9 Bradleys bldgs N1
11 O 10 Broadmead SW8
74 K 10 Bradmore Pk rd W6
50 G 19 Bradstock rd E9
152 H 11 Bradstock rd Epsom
141 U 15 Brad st SE1
56 E 6 Bradwell av Dgnhm
34 B 12 Bradwell clo E18
57 Z 19 Bradwell clo Hornch
18 K 14 Bradwell ms N18
63 N 14 Brady st E1
135 X 20 Brady st E1
30 B 5 Braemar av N22
43 Y 8 Braemar av NW10
105 X 5 Braemar av SW19
98 K 11 Braemar av Bxly Hth
157 N 20 Braemar av S Croy
122 G 5 Braemar av Thntn Hth
60 J 1 Braemar av Wemb
25 Z 6 Braemar gdns NW9
114 F 6 Braemar gdns Sidcp
125 T 20 Braemar gdns W Wkhm
65 R 13 Braemar rd E13
31 R 15 Braemar rd N15
72 H 16 Braemar rd Brentf
152 J 5 Braemar rd Worc Pk
104 F 2 Braemore clo Worth Hl
55 N 7 Braemore ct Ilf
54 K 8 Braemore rd Ilf
105 T 20 Braeside SW19
111 P 14 Braeside Becknhm
81 O 12 Braeside clo Blvdr
98 K 11 Braeside cres Bxly Hth

107 V 18 Braeside rd SW16
156 L 8 Brafferton rd Croy
149 W 10 Braganza st SE17
14 C 18 Brag rd NW7
143 P 5 Braham st E1
61 Z 18 Braid av W3
100 C 4 Braid clo Felt
111 X 2 Braidwood rd SE6
142 K 14 Braidwood st SE1
90 G 15 Brailsford rd SW2
35 M 4 Braintree av Ilf
56 E 9 Braintree rd Dgnhm
63 P 10 Braintree st E2
56 E 1 Braithwaite av E2
24 E 5 Braithwaite gdns Stanm
15 V 18 Bramber rd N12
145 P 14 Bramber rd W14
155 O 20 Bramble banks Carsh
79 P 14 Bramblebury rd SE18
24 H 4 Bramble clo Stanm
159 P 8 Bramble clo Croy
81 Y 11 Bramblecroft Erith
126 A 13 Brambledown clo Brom
155 P 17 Brambledown rd Carsh
157 R 18 Brambledown rd S Croy
122 C 6 Bramble gdns SW18
72 A 20 Brambles clo Brentf
120 K 20 Bramblewood clo Carsh
20 L 14 Bramblings the E4
120 L 9 Bramcote av Mitch
75 O 13 Bramcote gro SE16
151 Z 10 Bramcote gro SE16
86 K 11 Bramcote rd SW15
112 E 2 Bramdean cres SE12
112 E 2 Bramdean gdns SE12
124 L 6 Bramerton rd Beck
146 J 13 Bramerton st SW3
88 L 14 Bramfield rd SW11
16 K 7 Bramford ct N14
88 C 11 Bramford rd SW18
145 Y 8 Bramham gdns SW5
77 W 16 Bramhope la SE7
88 H 7 Bramlands clo SW11
156 K 10 Bramley clo S Croy
32 J 8 Bramley clo E17
6 D 17 Bramley clo N14
82 M 16 Bramley clo Twick
35 X 18 Bramley cres Ilf
97 P 1 Bramley ct Welling
156 K 9 Bramley hill S Croy
99 W 12 Bramley pl Drtford
6 D 17 Bramley rd N14
72 D 9 Bramley rd W5
136 G 9 Bramley rd W11
6 L 13 Bramley rd Enf
153 N 19 Bramley rd Sutton
154 F 11 Bramley rd Sutton
136 G 6 Bramley st W10
159 S 3 Bramley way W Wkhm
52 B 15 Brammel clo E15
26 K 14 Brampton gdns N15
26 K 14 Brampton gro NW4
23 Z 12 Brampton gro Harrow
42 O 4 Brampton gro Wemb
30 F 10 Brampton Park rd N8
66 C 10 Brampton rd E6
30 L 16 Brampton rd N15
25 R 15 Brampton rd NW9
80 G 16 Brampton rd SE18
80 G 18 Brampton rd Bxly Hth
97 X 1 Brampton rd Bxly Hth
123 T 16 Brampton rd Croy
118 B 14 Bramshaw ri New Mald
50 F 19 Bramshaw rd E9
47 T 8 Bramshill gdns NW5
62 C 6 Bramshill rd NW10
77 U 16 Bramshot av SE7
62 G 5 Bramston rd NW10
53 U 13 Brancaster dri E12
107 Z 6 Brancaster rd SW16
21 S 9 Brancaster rd Ilf
45 C 10 Branch hill NW3
134 G 4 Branch pl N1
63 V 19 Branch rd E14
155 Z 16 Brancker clo Wallgtn
24 F 10 Brancker rd Harrow
150 D 9 Brandar st SE17
87 V 11 Brandlehow rd SW15

B

Page	Ref	Name
33	V 12	Brandon rd E17
47	Z 20	Brandon rd N7
70	E 14	Brandon rd S'hall
153	Z 8	Brandon rd Sutton
150	C 7	Brandon st SE17
58	B 6	Brandon st SE17
93	Y 10	Brandram rd SE13
107	R 4	Brandreth rd SW17
155	Z 6	Brandries the Wallgtn
76	G 20	Brand st SE10
36	A 12	Brandville clo Enf
153	X 17	Brandy way Sutton
111	U 12	Brangbourne rd Brom
149	R 10	Brangton rd SE11
120	E 1	Brangwyn cres SW19
144	J 20	Branksea st SW6
18	F 18	Branksome av N18
90	A 12	Branksome av SW2
105	Y 20	Branksome av SW19
24	L 18	Branksome way Harrow
117	X 2	Branksome way New Mald
17	S 3	Branscombe gdns N21
93	R 8	Branscombe st SE13
24	M 3	Bransgrove rd Edg
85	N 5	Branstone rd Rich
133	Z 4	Branston wlk N1
59	U 12	Brants wlk W7
81	W 18	Brantwood av Erith
83	Y 9	Brantwood av Islwth
35	S 11	Brantwood clo E17
6	M 15	Brantwood gdns Enf
35	S 14	Brantwood gdns Ilf
18	L 20	Brantwood rd N17
90	L 12	Brantwood rd SE24
98	H 6	Brantwood rd Bxly Hth
157	N 20	Brantwood rd S Croy
41	P 14	Brasher clo Grnfd
89	O 6	Brassey sq SW11
62	B 18	Brassie av W3
58	B 9	Brasted clo SE26
97	W 13	Brasted clo Bxly Hth
87	Z 18	Brathway rd SW18
123	O 15	Bratten ct Croy
58	J 11	Braund av Grnfd
96	K 20	Braundton av Sidcp
114	J 1	Braundton av Sidcp
129	O 15	Bravington pl W9
129	O 12	Bravington rd W9
129	O 16	Bravington rd W9
92	K 11	Braxfield rd SE4
108	C 15	Braxted pk SW16
91	Z 5	Brayards rd SE15
92	A 5	Brayards rd SE15
62	D 15	Braybrook st W12
109	T 18	Braybrooke gdns SE19
89	W 6	Brayburne av SW4
49	W 2	Braydon rd E5
65	R 19	Bray dri E16
133	S 2	Brayfield ter N1
65	R 19	Bray pass E16
147	N 8	Bray pl SW3
6	L 14	Brayton gdns Enf
96	E 10	Braywood rd SE9
69	R 8	Breach la Dgnhm
160	B 7	Bread st EC4
92	M 9	Breakspears rd SE4
93	N 6	Breakspears rd SE4
66	J 10	Bream gdns E6
104	G 2	Breamore clo SW15
54	K 8	Breamore rd Ilf
55	N 7	Breamore rd Ilf
141	S 4	Breams bldgs EC4
64	A 2	Bream st E3
102	A 6	Breamwater gdns Rich
86	L 9	Breasley clo SW15
146	C 8	Breachin pl SW7
47	V 15	Brecknock rd N7
144	L 15	Brecon rd W6
9	O 13	Brecon rd Enf
66	J 8	Brede clo E6
47	V 7	Bredgar rd N19
90	M 6	Bredon rd SE5
123	U 17	Bredon rd Croy
110	B 15	Bredhurst clo SE20
88	A 7	Breer st SW6
143	U 10	Breezes hill E1
41	N 7	Brember rd Harrow
138	D 20	Bremner rd W7
126	D 13	Brenchley clo Brom
127	X 1	Brenchley clo Chisl
9	D 15	Brenchley gdns SE23
106	L 5	Brenda rd SW17
44	A 14	Brendon av NW10
99	P 2	Brendon clo Erith
40	K 11	Brendon gdns Harrow
36	H 15	Brendon gdns Ilf
114	D 4	Brendon rd SE9
56	D 4	Brendon rd Dgnhm
138	M 4	Brendon st W1
18	D 2	Brendon way Enf
121	P 6	Brenley clo Mitch
95	O 9	Brenley gdns SE9
115	Z 2	Brent clo Bxly
60	A 12	Brentcot clo W13
60	M 7	Brent crs NW10
61	V 1	Brentfield NW10
43	X 17	Brentfield clo NW10
27	P 20	Brentfield gdns NW11
43	Y 17	Brentfield rd NW10
61	Y 1	Brentfield rd NW10
72	G 18	Brentford high Brentf
27	O 16	Brent grn NW4
60	K 9	Brentham Hall rd W5
60	F 11	Brentham way W5
50	B 19	Brenthouse rd E9
44	E 17	Brenthurst rd NW10
72	D 20	Brentlea Brentf
59	T 20	Brentmead clo W7
61	N 7	Brentmead gdns NW10
27	P 18	Brentmead pl NW11
63	V 17	Brenton st E14
44	H 2	Brent Park rd NW4
4	J 18	Brent pl Barnt
65	T 16	Brent rd E16
78	L 19	Brent rd SE18
72	E 18	Brent rd Brentf
157	Z 19	Brent rd S Croy
72	E 17	Brent side Brentf
59	Y 11	Brentside clo W13
27	O 15	Brent st NW4
71	P 2	Brentvale av S'hall
60	M 4	Brentvale av Wemb
61	N 5	Brentvale av Wemb
26	F 20	Brent View rd NW9
14	K 20	Brent way N3
72	G 19	Brent way Brentf
43	U 17	Brent way Wemb
72	J 12	Brentwick gdns Brentf
114	A 1	Brentwood clo SE9
39	X 18	Brentwood rd Rom
31	V 2	Brereton rd N17
148	A 2	Bressenden pl SW1
34	C 8	Bressey gro E18
61	Y 2	Brett cres NW10
150	F 10	Brettell st SE17
33	O 5	Brettenham av E17
33	O 5	Brettenham av E17
18	M 13	Brettenham rd N18
18	K 12	Brettenham rd east N18
55	Y 20	Brett gdns Dgnhm
50	A 16	Brett rd E8
148	D 1	Brewers grn SW1
84	G 12	Brewers la Rich
140	D 9	Brewer st W1
83	X 19	Brewery la Twick
47	Z 19	Brewery rd N1
48	A 19	Brewery rd N7
79	R 13	Brewery rd SE18
127	S 19	Brewery rd Brom
143	Y 14	Brewhouse la E1
87	S 9	Brewhouse st SW15
133	W 17	Brewhouse yd EC1
55	R 17	Brewood rd Dgnhm
62	M 14	Brewster gdns W10
136	B 2	Brewster rd E10
51	S 4	Brewster rd E10
57	Y 11	Brian clo Hornch
37	U 14	Brian rd Rom
22	C 6	Briants clo Pinn
92	E 1	Briant st SE14
108	D 17	Briar av SW16
59	Z 16	Briarbank rd W13
155	P 20	Briar banks Carsh
17	Z 11	Briar clo N13
100	D 14	Briar clo Hampt
83	W 12	Briar clo Islwth
40	J 19	Briar cres Grnfd
45	X 10	Briardale gdns NW3
126	B 20	Briar gdns Brom
155	P 20	Briar la Carsh
159	R 7	Briar la Croy
44	M 11	Briar rd NW2
122	B 7	Briar rd SW16
24	D 17	Briar rd Harrow
101	S 2	Briar rd Twick
28	B 9	Briars clo N3
31	Z 3	Briars clo N17
86	K 10	Briar wlk SW15
25	W 2	Briar wlk Edg
25	W 18	Briarwood clo NW9
89	X 12	Briarwood rd SW4
152	F 13	Briarwood rd Epsom
115	R 12	Briary ct Sidcp
112	H 12	Briary gdns Brom
18	F 12	Briary la N9
141	S 8	Brick ct WC2
85	S 3	Brick Farm clo Rich
79	Y 18	Brickfield cotts SE18
64	D 10	Brickfield rd E3
58	B 10	Brick-Field rd SW19
122	K 2	Brickfield rd Thntn Hth
41	R 6	Brickfields Harrow
143	P 2	Brick la E1
8	L 9	Brick la Enf
9	O 9	Brick la Enf
139	W 15	Brick st W1
157	S 2	Brickwood rd Croy
141	W 6	Brick la EC4
48	D 19	Bride st N7
141	W 7	Bridewell pl EC4
131	Y 19	Bridford ms W1
47	N 20	Bridge appr NW3
74	K 12	Bridge av W6
144	A 8	Bridge av W6
59	R 14	Bridge av W7
9	N 8	Bridge clo Enf
59	P 19	Bridge clo Rom
88	F 6	Bridge ct SW11
33	U 4	Bridge end E17
153	X 14	Bridgefield rd Sutton
148	L 12	Bridgefoot SE1
17	Y 3	Bridge ga N21
65	T 18	Bridgeland rd E16
27	S 14	Bridge la NW11
88	K 3	Bridge la SW11
133	O 2	Bridgeman rd N1
101	X 14	Bridgeman rd Tedd
130	J 9	Bridgeman st NW8
8	H 5	Bridgenhall rd Enf
97	Y 17	Bridgen rd Bxly
88	C 9	Bridgend rd SW18
147	Y 5	Bridge pl SW1
123	P 18	Bridge pl Croy
53	T 20	Bridge rd E6
64	K 2	Bridge rd E15
50	K 2	Bridge rd E17
18	K 10	Bridge rd N9
30	A 6	Bridge rd N22
44	A 18	Bridge rd NW10
110	L 18	Bridge rd Becknhm
97	Z 6	Bridge rd Bxly Hth
99	T 3	Bridge rd Erith
99	V 1	Bridge rd Erith
83	P 6	Bridge rd Hounsl
70	E 5	Bridge rd S'hall
154	B 14	Bridge rd Sutton
84	A 15	Bridge rd Twick
99	T 3	Bridge rd W Erith
155	T 11	Bridge rd Wallgtn
43	R 9	Bridge rd Wemb
123	P 19	Bridge row Croy
85	A 7	Bridges la Croy
87	W 2	Bridges pl SW6
105	Z 16	Bridges rd SW19
106	A 16	Bridges rd SW19
10	H 17	Bridges rd Stanm
140	K 18	Bridge st SW1
73	Y 11	Bridge st W4
22	A 10	Bridge st Pinn
84	G 14	Bridge st Rich
64	K 1	Bridge ter E15
23	U 11	Bridge the Harrow
74	L 13	Bridgeview W6
44	A 9	Bridge view W6
144	M 7	Bridgewater gdns Edg
42	C 17	Bridgewater rd Grnfd
42	C 17	Bridgewater rd Wemb
134	A 14	Bridgewater sq EC1
16	G 12	Bridge way N11
27	V 16	Bridge way NW11
67	X 1	Bridgeway Bark
83	O 20	Bridge way Twick
42	L 19	Bridgeway Wemb
132	D 9	Bridgeway st NW1
107	X 18	Bridgewood rd SW 16
152	H 7	Bridgewood rd Worc Pk
106	D 6	Bridgford st SW18
73	W 8	Bridgman rd W4
64	F 3	Bridgwater rd E15
140	C 8	Bridle la W1
156	B 6	Bridle path Croy
156	O 1	Bridle rd Croy
159	P 9	Bridleway Croy
155	W 10	Bridleway the Wallgtn
18	M 2	Bridlington rd N9
19	N 3	Bridlington rd N9
38	G 20	Bridport av Rom
134	F 6	Bridport pl N1
134	F 8	Bridport pl N1
18	E 18	Bridport rd N18
58	K 3	Bridport rd Grnfd
122	K 6	Bridport rd Thntn Hth
75	O 18	Bridson st SE15
137	U 5	Bridstow pl W2
90	H 3	Brief st SE5
159	R 15	Brierley Croy
19	R 6	Brierley av N6
123	Y 9	Brierley clo SE25
51	X 12	Brierley rd E11
107	T 4	Brierley rd SW12
7	A 8	Brigadier av Enf
7	Y 3	Brigadier hill Enf
94	B 12	Brightfield rd SE12
92	M 17	Brightling rd SE4
63	X 20	Brightlingsea pl E14
106	E 1	Brightman rd SW18
32	L 17	Brighton av E17
40	G 18	Brighton dri Grnfd
92	H 1	Brighton gro SE14
66	K 8	Brighton rd E6
49	T 12	Brighton rd N16
157	N 13	Brighton rd S Croy
116	E 14	Brighton rd Surb
154	B 17	Brighton rd Sutton
90	D 10	Brighton ter SW9
93	X 15	Brighton ter SE13
9	U 5	Brightside the Enf
64	E 16	Bright st E14
106	L 13	Brightwell cres SW17
41	P 7	Briglade clo Harrow
81	T 10	Brigstock rd Blvdr
122	L 9	Brigstock rd Thntn Hth
76	H 12	Brig st E14
28	D 13	Brim hill N2
80	C 9	Brimpsfield clo SE2
9	W 7	Brimsdown av Enf
92	L 3	Brindley st SE14
58	K 19	Brindley way S'hall
19	Z 10	Brindwood rd E4
20	A 10	Brindwood rd E4
80	B 10	Brinkburn clo SE2
25	S 9	Brinkburn clo Edg
25	R 9	Brinkburn gdns Edg
152	J 2	Brinkley rd Worc Pk
78	M 20	Brinklow cres SE18
79	N 19	Brinklow cres SE18
35	R 9	Brinkworth rd Ilf
27	O 11	Brinsdale rd NW4
9	W 7	Brinsdown av Enf
23	P 7	Brinsley rd Harrow
101	P 2	Brinsworth clo Twick
105	X 19	Brisbane av SW19
51	S 8	Brisbane rd E10
71	Z 4	Brisbane rd W13
54	A 2	Brisbane rd Ilf
150	E 20	Brisbane st SE5
106	G 15	Briscoe rd SW19
95	N 8	Briset rd SE9
133	W 19	Briset st EC1
48	C 7	Briset way N7
86	L 19	Bristol gdns SW15
129	Z 19	Bristol gdns W9
130	A 19	Bristol gdns W9
129	Z 19	Bristol ms W9
130	A 19	Bristol ms W9
52	M 19	Bristol rd E12
53	N 18	Bristol rd E12
58	K 3	Bristol rd Grnfd
120	C 10	Bristol rd Mrdn
30	B 20	Briston gro N8
109	R 12	Bristow rd SE19
97	Z 3	Bristow rd Bxly Hth
98	A 3	Bristow rd Bxly Hth
156	A 9	Bristow rd Croy
82	M 9	Bristow rd Hounsl
15	S 12	Britannia clo N12
145	X 19	Britannia rd SW6
53	V 11	Britannia rd Ilf
116	M 16	Britannia rd Surb
117	N 16	Britannia rd Surb
133	Y 4	Britannia row N1
133	N 12	Britannia st WC1
134	E 12	Britannia st WC1
61	T 10	Britannia way NW10
74	E 12	British gro W4
74	E 14	British Grove pass W6
21	O 7	British Legion rd E4
140	H 2	British Museum WC1
63	Z 10	British st E3
56	A 9	Brittain rd Dgnhm
46	A 3	Britten clo NW11
146	J 10	Britten st SW3
133	W 19	Britton st EC1
54	H 14	Brixham gdns Ilf
97	V 2	Brixham rd Welling
78	L 4	Brixham st E16
54	C 16	Brixton hill SW2
90	A 19	Brixton Hill pl SW2
90	F 5	Brixton rd SW9
149	T 18	Brixton rd SW9
90	F 9	Brixton Stn rd SW9

Ref	Name
90 E 14	Brixton Water la SW2
139 X 9	Broadbent st W1
77 S 19	Broadbridge clo SE3
158 F 17	Broadcoombe S Croy
140 L 6	Broad ct WC2
24 H 7	Broadcroft av Stanm
44 L 10	Broadfield clo NW2
10 E 8	Broadfield ct Bushey Watf
93 Z 20	Broadfield rd SE6
111 Z 3	Broadfield rd SE6
22 K 6	Broadfields Harrow
17 T 1	Broadfields av N21
12 E 14	Broadfields av Edg
39 U 17	Broadfield gdns NW6
21 Y 12	Broadfield way Buck Hl
5 O 7	Broadgates av Barnt
106 G 3	Broadgates rd SW18
122 H 16	Broad Grn av Croy
26 D 6	Broadhead strand NW9
113 U 11	Broadheath dri Chisl
89 T 7	Broadhinton rd SW4
12 E 12	Broadhurst av Edg
54 K 13	Broadhurst av Ilf
46 B 18	Broadhurst clo NW6
45 Z 19	Broadhurst gdns NW6
46 B 18	Broadhurst gdns NW6
57 W 19	Broadhurst wlk Rainhm
107 Z 4	Broadlands av SW16
108 A 5	Broadlands av SW16
9 O 12	Broadlands av Enf
47 N 1	Broadlands Av clo N6
29 O 20	Broadlands clo N6
107 Z 5	Broadlands clo SW16
9 O 12	Broadlands clo Enf
29 N 20	Broadlands rd N6
112 H 10	Broadlands rd Brom
100 G 8	Broadlands the Felt
118 D 15	Broadlands way New Mald
31 W 14	Broad la N15
100 F 16	Broad la Hampt
113 W 2	Broad lawn SE9
23 W 5	Broadlawns ct Harrow
130 H 20	Bradley st NW8
130 L 18	Bradley ter NW8
111 P 7	Broadmead SE6
118 F 18	Broadmead av Worc Pk
100 H 16	Broadmead clo Hampt
22 C 2	Broadmead clo Pinn
58 D 10	Broadmead rd Grnfd
21 S 18	Broadmead rd Wdf Gn
34 K 2	Broadmead rd Wdfd Gn
35 N 3	Broadmead rd Wdfd Gn
126 B 11	Broad Oaks way Brom
139 S 2	Broadstone pl W1
57 W 7	Broadstone rd Hornch
56 D 20	Broad st Dgnhm
69 S 2	Broad st Dgnhm
101 V 14	Broad st Tedd
160 H 2	Broad St av EC2
142 J 2	Broad St bldgs EC2
25 P 19	Broadview NW9
107 W 17	Broadview rd SW16
34 B 10	Broad wlk E18
17 R 6	Broad wlk N21
94 L 6	Broad wlk SE3
95 T 3	Broad wlk SE18
82 A 3	Broad wlk Hounsl
45 V 1	Broad Walk la NW1
11 U 12	Broadwalk SE1
31 S 6	Broadwater rd N17
106 H 9	Broadwater rd SW17
65 U 7	Broadway E13
51 Y 20	Broadway E15
140 F 20	Broadway SW1
105 W 16	Broadway ct SW19
71 W 2	Broadway W7
72 A 2	Broadway W13
67 O 3	Broadway Bark
98 E 11	Broadway Bxly Hth
152 G 12	Broadway Epsom
59 N 11	Broadway Grnfd
39 W 9	Broadway Rom
123 O 12	Broadway av Croy
84 A 16	Broadway av Twick
18 W 18	Broadway clo Wdfd Grn
120 J 7	Broadway gdns Mitch
135 U 5	Broadway mkt E8
17 R 17	Broadway ms N13
17 W 5	Broadway ms N21
20 H 19	Broadway the E4
29 Z 18	Broadway the N8
18 K 9	Broadway the N9
13 P 17	Broadway the NW7
44 G 2	Broadway the NW9
105 X 16	Broadway the SW19
60 H 19	Broadway the W5
55 C 6	Broadway the Dagnhm
23 U 7	Broad Way the Harrow
57 Y 13	Broadway the Hornch
22 D 3	Broadway the Pinn
70 C 1	Broadway the S'hall
15 S 15	Broadway the Stanm
153 S 14	Broadway the Sutton
21 W 18	Broadway the Wdfd Grn
140 C 7	Broadwick st W1
133 V 19	Broad yd EC1
54 J 16	Brockdish av Bark
23 Z 18	Brockenhurst Croy
118 B 18	Brockenhurst Worc Pk
13 P 17	Brockenhurst gdns NW7
54 B 14	Brockenhurst gdns Ilf
121 Y 3	Brockenhurst way SW16
105 V 13	Brockham clo SW19
159 X 16	Brockham cres Croy
20 D 19	Brockham dri SW2
36 A 17	Brockham dri Ilf
150 C 1	Brockham st SE1
10 H 18	Brockhurst clo Stanm
92 H 10	Brockill cres SE4
88 C 19	Brocklebank rd SW18
75 T 19	Brocklehurst st SE14
123 Z 10	Brocklesby rd SE25
11 X 11	Brockley av Stanm
11 X 11	Brockley Av north Stanm
11 X 14	Brockley clo Stanm
38 K 3	Brockley cres Rom
92 C 9	Brockley footpath SE15
92 L 4	Brockley gdns SE4
92 K 14	Brockley gros SE4
93 N 12	Brockley gros SE4
92 K 14	Brockley Hall rd SE4
11 U 9	Brockley hill Stanm
92 J 20	Brockley pk SE23
92 J 16	Brockley ri SE23
110 H 1	Brockley rd SE23
92 J 8	Brockley rd SE4
110 H 1	Brockley rd SE4
11 W 13	Brockley view SE23
92 K 18	Brockley view SE23
92 G 13	Brockley way SE4
111 W 9	Brockman ri Brom
64 C 13	Brock pl E3
65 C 14	Brock rd E13
153 S 4	Brocks dri Sutton
92 B 7	Brock st SE15
90 H 18	Brockwell park SE24
90 H 20	Brockwell Pk gdns SE24
80 D 11	Broderick gro SE2
49 T 8	Brodia rd N16
20 H 7	Brodie rd E4
7 Z 3	Brodie rd Enf
8 A 4	Brodie rd Enf
151 P 10	Brodie st SE1
63 S 19	Brodlove la E1
106 K 3	Brodrick rd SW17
144 E 4	Brograve gdns Becknhm
31 Y 11	Brograve rd N17
135 R 4	Broke rd E8
24 E 5	Brokesley st E3
63 O 17	Bromehead st E1
63 O 7	Bromehead st E1
9 V 10	Bromells rd SW4
95 U 8	Bromer rd SE5
91 T 7	Bromer rd SE5
89 Y 6	Bromfelde rd SW4
89 Z 5	Bromfelde wy SW4
133 U 7	Bromfield st N1
5 P 18	Bromhall rd Dgnhm
5 U 7	Bromhedge SE9
80 B 9	Bromholm rd SE2
112 A 19	Bromley av Brom
126 L 11	Bromley comm Brom
127 P 16	Bromley comm Brom
126 C 5	Bromley cres Brom
126 C 5	Bromley gdns Brom
125 X 5	Bromley gro Brom
64 G 14	Bromley Hall rd E14
64 D 8	Bromley High st E3
111 Z 15	Bromley hill Brom
112 A 16	Bromley hill Brom
114 E 18	Bromley la Chisl
132 A 19	Bromley pl W1
33 S 20	Bromley rd E10
33 O 9	Bromley rd E17
31 W 3	Bromley rd N17
18 B 12	Bromley rd N18
111 T 6	Bromley rd SE6
125 V 2	Bromley rd Becknhm
114 B 19	Bromley rd Chisl
63 O 17	Bromley st E1
82 E 13	Brompton clo Hounsl
28 K 13	Brompton gro N2
147 N 1	Brompton pl SW3
139 O 19	Brompton rd SW3
146 K 3	Brompton rd SW3
146 K 2	Brompton sq SW3
101 Z 15	Bromwell rd Tedd
102 A 15	Bromwell rd Tedd
47 R 8	Bromwich av N6
74 B 2	Bromyard av W3
44 L 19	Brondesbury pk NW6
45 O 20	Brondesbury pk NW6
128 K 2	Brondesbury rd NW2
129 U 7	Brondesbury rd NW6
129 T 7	Brondesbury vills NW2
31 W 5	Bronhill ter N17
144 J 19	Bronsart rd SW6
119 R 3	Bronson rd SW20
76 C 18	Bronze st SE8
56 H 20	Brook av Dgnhm
12 F 18	Brook av Edg
43 O 8	Brook av Wemb
59 S 13	Brookbank av W7
93 P 8	Brookbank rd SE13
27 U 3	Brook clo NW7
118 K 7	Brook clo SW20
39 T 6	Brook clo Rom
20 C 13	Brook cres E4
18 L 13	Brook cres N9
12 F 17	Brook ct Edg
33 N 11	Brookdale rd E17
93 R 17	Brookdale rd SE6
98 A 17	Brookdale rd Bxly
79 Y 11	Brookdene rd SE18
149 T 3	Brook dri SE11
149 X 5	Brook dri SE11
23 O 12	Brook dri Harrow
41 O 9	Brooke av Harrow
111 P 6	Brookehowse rd SE6
114 H 2	Brookend rd Sidcp
33 V 14	Brooke rd E17
49 X 9	Brooke rd N16
141 T 2	Brooke st EC1
10 A 3	Brooke way Bushey Watf
33 U 13	Brookfield av E17
60 H 12	Brookfield av W5
154 H 7	Brookfield av Sutton
13 Y 20	Brookfield clo NW7
59 O 8	Brookfield ct Grnfd
13 X 20	Brookfield cres NW7
24 J 16	Brookfield cres Harrow
47 R 9	Brookfield pk NW5
20 L 20	Brookfield path Wdfd Grn
50 J 18	Brookfield rd E9
18 L 11	Brookfield rd East N9
73 Z 7	Brookfield rd W4
9 T 13	Brookfields Enf
120 J 10	Brookfields av Mitch
20 C 13	Brook gdns E4
86 E 7	Brook gdns SW13
103 U 20	Brook gdns Kingst
144 E 4	Brook grn W6
5 W 17	Brookhill clo Barnt
78 K 15	Brook Hill clo SE18
78 L 12	Brookhill rd SE18
5 W 18	Brookhill rd Barnt
83 O 11	Brookhouse gdns E4
27 Z 13	Brookland clo NW11
27 Z 13	Brookland garth NW11
27 Z 13	Brookland hill NW11
27 Z 12	Brookland ri NW11
38 M 12	Brookland appr Rom
105 Z 4	Brooklands av SW16
114 G 4	Brooklands av Sidcp
58 N 14	Brooklands clo Rom
39 N 13	Brooklands la Rom
94 E 7	Brooklands pk SE3
38 M 14	Brooklands rd Rom
94 J 4	Brook la SE3
97 V 14	Brook la Bxly
112 E 14	Brook la Brom
72 G 14	Brook la north Brentf
26 B 4	Brooklea clo NW9
124 B 8	Brooklyn av SE25
124 A 8	Brooklyn rd SE25
127 P 10	Brooklyn rd Brom
152 B 15	Brookmead Epsom
127 U 11	Brookmead av Brom
15 N 12	Brookmeadow N12
121 W 14	Brookmead rd Croy
138 E 8	Brook Ms north W2
93 O 2	Brookmill rd SE8
4 K 17	Brook pl Barnt
52 G 14	Brook rd E7
30 A 12	Brook rd N8
30 D 9	Brook rd N22
44 E 6	Brook rd NW2
21 U 6	Brook rd Buck Hl
36 H 18	Brook rd Ilf
39 U 5	Brook rd Rom
122 K 7	Brook rd Thntn Hth
122 K 8	Brook rd Thntn Hth
83 Z 15	Brook rd Twick
72 G 15	Brook Rd south Brentf
6 F 11	Brooks av E6
51 S 14	Brooks clo E15
50 E 18	Brooksbank st E9
48 G 20	Brooksby st N1
113 X 5	Brooks clo SE9
33 R 6	Brookscroft rd E17
10 D 19	Brooks hill Harrow
10 D 17	Brookshill av Harrow
10 C 18	Brooks Hill dri Bushey Watf
7 R 20	Brookside N21
5 X 20	Brookside Barnt
155 O 10	Brookside Carsh
4 D 20	Brookside clo Barnt
24 H 16	Brookside clo Harrow
40 C 11	Brookside clo Harrow
118 H 20	Brookside cres Worc Pk
18 M 13	Brookside rd N9
47 V 8	Brookside rd N19
27 U 18	Brookside rd NW11
16 B 3	Brookside south Barnt
14 J 19	Brookside wlk N3
27 U 13	Brookside wlk NW11
124 F 14	Brookside way Croy
73 R 15	Brooks la W4
141 T 1	Brook's mkt EC1
139 X 8	Brooks ms W1
65 S 4	Brooks rd E13
73 R 15	Brooks rd W4
31 V 9	Brook st N17
139 Y 7	Brook st W1
138 H 9	Brook st W2
81 U 16	Brook st Erith
116 H 4	Brook st Kingst
128 L 6	Brooksville av NW6
98 H 1	Brookvale Erith
107 T 11	Brookview SW16
145 O 19	Brookville rd SW6
12 K 20	Brook wlk Edg
94 E 9	Brookway SE3
86 E 6	Brookwood av SW13
105 X 1	Brookwood rd SW18
82 K 1	Brookwood rd Hounsl
127 S 14	Broom clo Brom
102 F 17	Broom clo Tedd
100 E 19	Broome rd Hampt
150 D 19	Broome way SE5
17 P 15	Broomfield av N13
17 O 14	Broomfield house N13
17 R 15	Broomfield la N13
17 N 13	Broomfield park N13
72 B 2	Broomfield pl W13
17 O 17	Broomfield rd N13
72 C 2	Broomfield rd W13
124 K 7	Broomfield rd Beck
74 E 4	Broomfield rd Bxly Hth
85 N 1	Broomfield rd Rich
59 W 11	Broomfield rd Rom
117 O 18	Broomfield rd Surb
102 E 15	Broomfield rd Tedd
64 C 15	Broomfield st E14
159 P 6	Broom gdns Croy
25 P 4	Broomgrove gdns Edg
90 D 6	Broomgrove rd SW9
157 O 18	Broomhall rd S Croy
98 E 17	Broom Hill ri Bxly Hth
87 Y 14	Broomhill rd SW18
99 Y 16	Broomhill rd Drtfrd
55 O 6	Broomhill rd Ilf

B

21 S 18	Broomhill rd Wdfd Grn	
21 S 20	Bromhill rd Wdfd Grn	
87 X 7	Broomhouse la SW6	
87 X 5	Broomhouse rd SW6	
153 Y 3	Broomloan la Sutton	
102 E 14	Broom lock Tedd	
98 F 14	Broom mead Bxly Hth	
102 F 18	Broom pk Tedd	
159 O 6	Broom rd Croy	
102 B 13	Broom rd Tedd	
45 W 6	Broomsleigh st NW6	
102 D 14	Broom water Tedd	
102 D 13	Broomwater west Tedd	
89 P 13	Broomwood rd SW4	
88 L 16	Broomwood rd W5	
110 G 12	Broseley gro SE26	
135 T 3	Brougham rd E8	
61 W 18	Brougham rd W3	
148 X 19	Brough st SW8	
27 R 10	Broughton av N3	
102 C 8	Broughton av Rich	
29 V 18	Broughton gdns N6	
88 B 4	Broughton rd SW6	
72 C 1	Broughton rd W13	
122 F 13	Broughton rd Thntn Hth	
89 R 4	Broughton st SW8	
73 V 6	Brouncker rd W3	
155 Z 16	Brown clo Wallgtn	
64 E 18	Brownfield st E14	
139 V 7	Brown Hart gdns W1	
93 V 19	Brownhill rd SE6	
59 W 17	Browning av W7	
154 J 8	Browning av Sutton	
118 K 19	Browning av Worc Pk	
96 H 2	Browning clo SE18	
30 D 17	Browning clo W9	
100 E 10	Browning clo Hampt	
52 C 2	Browning rd E11	
53 T 18	Browning rd E12	
8 A 2	Browning rd Enf	
150 B 8	Browning st SE17	
54 M 8	Brownlea gdns Ilf	
111 T 11	Brownlee rd SE6	
33 O 17	Brownlow ms WC1	
52 G 12	Brownlow rd E7	
135 R 3	Brownlow rd E8	
28 A 1	Brownlow rd N3	
16 M 18	Brownlow rd N11	
44 B 20	Brownlow rd NW10	
62 B 1	Brownlow rd NW10	
71 Y 2	Brownlow rd W13	
157 U 8	Brownlow rd Croy	
141 P 2	Brownlow rd WC1	
142 K 5	Browns bldgs EC3	
113 Z 9	Brownspring dri SE9	
114 A 8	Brownspring dri SE9	
33 O 11	Browns rd E17	
116 M 17	Browns rd Surb	
139 N 5	Browns st W1	
28 F 7	Brownswell rd N2	
48 K 8	Brownswood rd N4	
89 P 14	Broxash rd SW11	
84 H 12	Broxbourne av E18	
52 D 10	Broxbourne st E7	
108 F 7	Broxholm rd SE27	
110 K 3	Broxted rd SE6	
130 M 7	Broxwood way NW8	
31 S 4	Bruce Castle museum N17	
31 T 4	Bruce Castle pk N17	
31 U 5	Bruce Castle rd N17	
97 R 2	Bruce clo Wellng	
158 F 20	Bruce dri S Croy	
15 Y 12	Bruce gdns N20	
31 T 6	Bruce gro N17	
64 D 9	Bruce rd E3	
64 E 9	Bruce rd E3	
61 Z 1	Bruce rd NW10	
123 O 8	Bruce rd SE25	
4 F 12	Bruce rd Barnt	
23 T 8	Bruce rd Harrow	
107 N 17	Bruce rd Mitch	
107 N 8	Brudenell rd SW17	
88 B 19	Bruffs meadow Grnfd	
98 J 8	Brummel clo Bxly Hth	
60 J 7	Brumwil rd Wemb	
58 D 9	Brunel clo Grnfd	
58 K 18	Brunel pl S'hall	
75 R 5	Brunel rd SE16	
62 B 15	Brunel rd W3	
65 O 18	Brunel st E16	
31 R 14	Brunel wlk N15	
143 N 2	Brune st E1	
28 C 17	Brunner clo NW11	
32 J 6	Brunner rd E17	
60 F 11	Brunner rd W5	
16 B 11	Brunswick av N11	
97 X 9	Brunswick clo Bxly Hth	
22 C 20	Brunswick clo Pinn	
142 L 18	Brunswick ct SE1	
16 B 11	Brunswick cres N11	
60 J 10	Brunswick gdns W5	
137 W 15	Brunswick gdns W8	
36 B 1	Brunswick gdns Ilf	
16 B 12	Brunswick gro N11	
139 P 5	Brunswick ms W1	
91 P 1	Brunswick pk SE5	
16 B 9	Brunswick Pk gdns N11	
134 F 14	Brunswick pl N1	
109 W 16	Brunswick pl SE20	
51 T 4	Brunswick rd E10	
16 B 8	Brunswick rd N11	
31 S 15	Brunswick rd N15	
60 K 10	Brunswick rd W5	
97 X 10	Brunswick rd Bxly Hth	
103 P 20	Brunswick rd Kingst	
154 C 7	Brunswick rd Sutton	
8 G 20	Brunswick sq N17	
132 L 17	Brunswick sq WC1	
33 T 16	Brunswick st E17	
91 R 1	Brunswick vlls SE5	
16 E 13	Brunswick wy N11	
63 W 18	Brunton pl E14	
60 J 7	Brunwill rd W5	
142 L 1	Brushfield st E1	
143 N 1	Brushfield st E1	
88 G 11	Brussels rd SW11	
132 L 9	Bruton clo Chisl	
139 Y 10	Bruton la W1	
139 Y 9	Bruton pl W1	
120 C 10	Bruton rd Mrdn	
139 Y 10	Bruton st W1	
52 Z 14	Bruton way W13	
44 K 20	Bryan av NW10	
62 L 1	Bryan av NW10	
128 A 1	Bryan av NW10	
75 X 5	Bryan rd SE16	
88 A 34	Bryans alley SW6	
70 F 10	Bryanston av Twick	
82 L 20	Bryanston av Twick	
29 Y 17	Bryanstone rd N8	
139 O 3	Bryanston Ms east W1	
139 O 3	Bryanston Ms west W1	
139 N 3	Bryanston pl W1	
139 O 4	Bryanston sq W1	
139 R 6	Bryanston st W1	
4 J 19	Bryant ct Barnt	
64 L 1	Bryant st E15	
48 E 14	Bryantwood rd N7	
16 J 12	Brycedale cres N14	
55 T 12	Bryce rd Dgnhm	
110 H 12	Bryden clo SE20	
132 L 4	Brydon wk N1	
140 J 10	Brydges pl WC2	
51 X 14	Brydges rd E15	
48 A 8	Bryett rd N7	
8 J 13	Bryn-Y-Mawr rd Enf	
88 M 3	Brynmaer rd SW11	
62 H 20	Bryony rd W12	
62 K 7	Buchanan gdns NW10	
128 A 9	Buchanan gdns NW10	
92 C 7	Buchan rd SE15	
88 D 19	Bucharest rd SW18	
94 D 15	Buckden clo SE12	
120 B 10	Buckfast rd Mrdn	
135 T 14	Buckfast st E2	
138 H 10	Buck Hill wlk W2	
87 Y 16	Buckhold rd SW18	
120 L 20	Buckhurst av Carsh	
63 O 12	Buckhurst st E1	
135 Y 12	Buckhurst st E1	
140 L 12	Buckingham arcade WC2	
15 R 3	Buckingham av N20	
59 Z 3	Buckingham av Grnfd	
122 G 1	Buckingham av Thntn Hth	
96 H 11	Buckingham av Welling	
8 E 8	Buckingham clo Enf	
100 E 12	Buckingham clo Hampt	
26 G 9	Buckingham ct NW4	
24 L 3	Buckingham gdns Edg	
122 F 2	Buckingham gdns Thntn Hth	
148 D 1	Buckingham ga SW1	
92 J20	Buckingham la SE23	
139 Z 19	Buckingham palace SW1	
140 A 19	Buckingham Palace SW1	
139 X 18	Buckingham Palace gdns SW1	
147 X 6	Buckingham Palace rd SW1	
51 R 9	Buckingham rd E10	
34 K 15	Buckingham rd E11	
52 B 14	Buckingham rd E15	
34 C 6	Buckingham rd E18	
49 S 19	Buckingham rd N1	
30 B 7	Buckingham rd N22	
62 E 6	Buckingham rd NW10	
24 M 2	Buckingham rd Edg	
25 N 1	Buckingham rd Edg	
107 F 13	Buckingham rd Hampt	
23 R 15	Buckingham rd Harrow	
54 E 7	Buckingham rd Ilf	
116 M 8	Buckingham rd Kingst	
117 N 8	Buckingham rd Kingst	
122 A 10	Buckingham rd Mitch	
102 G 4	Buckingham rd Rich	
54 L 11	Buckingham st WC2	
155 V 20	Buckingham way Wallgtn	
46 G 19	Buckland cres NW3	
51 T 6	Buckland rd E10	
153 N 20	Buckland rd Sutton	
102 E 14	Bucklands rd Tedd	
134 G 9	Buckland st N1	
120 C 10	Buckland wlk Mrdn	
118 L 20	Buckland way Worc Pk	
25 X 16	Buck la NW9	
119 V 5	Buckleigh av SW20	
127 Z 16	Buckleigh rd SW16	
109 T 19	Buckleigh way SE19	
113 U 18	Buckleigh gdns SE9	
100 D 7	Bucklersbury EC4	
143 R 5	Buckle st E1	
99 U 6	Buckley clo Drtfrd	
129 P 2	Buckley rd NW6	
88 J 12	Buckmaster rd SW11	
140 H 4	Bucknall st WC2	
90 D 11	Buckner rd SW2	
129 N 12	Buckner rd W1	
20 K 9	Buckrell rd E4	
18 K 18	Buckstone rd N18	
131 Y 2	Buck st NW1	
92 H 14	Buckthorne rd SE4	
33 W 14	Buck wlk E17	
43 V 9	Buddings crcl Wemb	
84 D 14	Budds alley Twick	
160 D 7	Budge row EC4	
80 G 20	Budleigh gdns Welling	
51 N 8	Budoch dri Ilf	
87 U 8	Buer rd SW6	
77 V 10	Bugsby rd SE7	
77 V 11	Bugsbys way SE7	
122 L 7	Bulganak rd Thntn Hth	
148 J 7	Bulinga st SW1	
97 R 7	Bull adj Welling	
63 S 9	Bullards pl E1	
81 W 10	Bullbanks rd Blvdr	
38 J 4	Bullen st SW11	
151 S 19	Buller clo SE15	
31 X 9	Buller rd N17	
30 E 7	Buller rd N22	
128 G 13	Buller rd NW10	
54 G 20	Buller rd Bark	
123 O 6	Buller rd Thntn Hth	
115 X 13	Bullers clo Sidcp	
113 T 19	Bullers Wood dri Chisl	
12 D 16	Bullescroft rd Edg	
141 L 9	Bull Inn ct WC2	
64 G 19	Bullivant st E14	
18 E 15	Bull la N18	
114 D 19	Bull la Chisl	
56 G 8	Bull la Dgnhm	
65 P 5	Bull rd E15	
145 P 5	Bulls gdns SW3	
150 H 7	Bulls Head pas EC3	
160 B 9	Bull wharf EC4	
42 F 1	Bulmer gdns Harrow	
137 S 12	Bulmer ms W11	
82 F 6	Bulstrode av Hounsl	
82 E 7	Bulstrode gdns Hounsl	
139 V 3	Bulstrode pl W1	
82 H 7	Bulstrode rd Hounsl	
139 V 3	Bulstrode st W1	
51 X 3	Bulwer Ct rd E11	
5 P 14	Bulwer gdns Barnt	
51 X 3	Bulwer rd E11	
18 E 15	Bulwer rd N18	
5 P 14	Bulwer rd Barnt	
136 D 15	Bulwer st W12	
34 C 1	Bunces la Wdfd Grn	
143 Y 7	Bunch st E1	
123 S 9	Bungalow rd SE25	
107 S 17	Bungalows the SW16	
134 D 16	Bunhill row EC1	
81 S 11	Bunkers hill Blvdr	
13 P 19	Bunns la NW7	
26 F 1	Bunns la NW7	
63 U 6	Bunsen st E3	
36 D 16	Buntingbridge rd Ilf	
120 M 11	Bunting clo Mitch	
78 K 9	Bunton st SE18	
32 J 10	Bunyan rd E17	
148 F 10	Buonaparte mews SW1	
150 E 2	Burbage clo SE1	
90 M 15	Burbage rd SE24	
91 O 17	Burbage rd SE24	
117 Z 4	Burberry clo New Mald	
31 W 8	Burbridge rd N17	
64 F 17	Burcham st E14	
80 H 16	Burcharbro rd SE2	
10 A 3	Burchel ct Bushey Watf	
51 R 3	Burchell rd E10	
92 A 3	Burchell rd SE15	
38 A 18	Burchett way Rom	
38 J 2	Burchwall clo Rom	
88 G 20	Burcote rd SW18	
85 S 9	Burdenshott av Rich	
52 H 5	Burden way E11	
49 T 18	Burder clo N1	
115 Z 13	Burder rd N1	
14 F 20	Burdett av SW20	
63 Y 15	Burdett rd E14	
123 P 15	Burdett rd Croy	
85 O 6	Burdett rd Rich	
141 T 20	Burdett st SE1	
153 V 20	Burdon la Sutton	
153 U 18	Burdon pk Sutton	
106 E 9	Burfield clo SW17	
55 U 11	Burford clo Dgnhm	
36 B 12	Burford clo Ilf	
17 S 10	Burford gdns N13	
66 C 9	Burford rd E6	
64 J 2	Burford rd E15	
110 M 6	Burford rd SE6	
72 J 15	Burford rd Brentf	
127 R 10	Burford rd Brom	
153 X 4	Burford rd Sutton	
118 F 18	Burford rd Worc Pk	
159 V 15	Burford way Croy	
151 N 9	Burgandy st SE1	
99 T 8	Burgate clo Drtfrd	
53 V 20	Burges rd E6	
66 E 1	Burges rd E6	
66 K 2	Burges rd E6	
25 Y 18	Burgess av NW9	
100 B 8	Burgess clo Felt	
45 W 11	Burgess hill NW2	
51 Y 13	Burgess rd E15	
153 Z 9	Burgess rd Sutton	
64 A 15	Burgess st E14	
150 E 2	Burge st SE1	
150 F 3	Burge st SE1	
110 G 9	Burghill rd SE26	
105 R 9	Burghley av SW19	
117 Y 1	Burghley av New Mald	
118 A 1	Burghley av New Mald	
121 N 10	Burgley pl Mitch	
52 A 3	Burghley rd E11	
30 F 10	Burghley rd N8	
47 U 11	Burghley rd NW5	
133 Z 8	Burgh st N1	
141 Y 7	Burgon st EC4	
93 R 1	Burgos gro SE10	
30 H 19	Burgoyne rd N4	
123 U 8	Burgoyne rd SE25	
90 C 7	Burgoyne rd SW9	
110 D 18	Burham clo SE20	
22 B 7	Burhill gro Pinn	
86 B 10	Burke clo SW15	
65 P 16	Burke st E16	
88 M 14	Burland rd SW11	
96 K 13	Burland rd Sidcp	
16 G 5	Burleigh av Wallgtn	
8 E 14	Burleigh av Enf	
119 T 19	Burleigh rd Sutton	
140 M 8	Burleigh st WC2	
8 B 12	Burleigh way Enf	
20 A 17	Burley clo E4	
121 Y 3	Burley clo SW16	
65 X 16	Burley rd E16	
140 A 11	Burlington arc W1	
85 P 2	Burlington av Rich	
38 H 18	Burlington av Rom	
140 A 11	Burlington gdns W1	

73	X 3	Burlington gdns W3
73	W 14	Burlington gdns W4
55	Z 1	Burlington gdns Rom
56	A 1	Burlington gdns Rom
73	Y 19	Burlington la W4
74	A 17	Burlington la W4
73	W 3	Burlington ms W3
87	T 5	Burlington pl SW 6
21	U 12	Burlington pl Wdfd Grn
15	Y 4	Burlington ri Barnt
29	O 9	Burlington rd N10
31	X 5	Burlington rd N17
87	J 5	Burlington rd SW6
73	U 13	Burlington rd W4
8	A 5	Burlington rd Enf
83	P 2	Burlington rd Islwth
118	F 9	Burlington rd New Mald
122	M 4	Burlington rd Thntn
123	N 3	Burlington rd Thntn Hth
21	U 12	Burlin pl Wdfd Grn
149	X 2	Burman st SE1
49	O 12	Burma rd N16
106	D 7	Burmester rd SW17
73	U 17	Burnaby cres W4
73	U 16	Burnaby gdns W4
66	M 19	Burnaby st E6
146	B 20	Burnaby st SW10
146	D 19	Burnaby st SW10
15	N 19	Burnbrae clo N12
107	V 1	Burnbury rd SW12
9	R 10	Burncroft av Enf
102	D 11	Burnell av Rich
96	L 3	Burnell av Well
97	O 5	Burnell av Welling
24	F 7	Burnell gdns Stanm
154	B 7	Burnell rd Sutton
66	H 10	Burnels av E6
48	C 19	Burness clo N7
138	K 1	Burne st W2
149	N 10	Burnett st SE11
116	L 12	Burney av Surb
117	N 11	Burney av Surb
76	G 19	Burney st SE10
87	T 3	Burnfoot av SW6
8	E 4	Burnham clo Enf
34	K 14	Burnham cres E11
27	N 13	Burnham ct NW4
153	O 3	Burnham dri Worc Pk
19	X 17	Burnham rd E4
68	C 2	Burnham rd Dgnhm
120	A 10	Burnham rd Mrdn
38	L 11	Burnham rd Rom
115	X 5	Burnham rd Sidcp
63	P 8	Burnham st E2
117	P 1	Burnham st Kingst
72	A 9	Burnham way W13
125	O 3	Burnhill rd Becknm
44	F 15	Burnley rd NW10
90	C 4	Burnley rd SW9
146	L 10	Burnsall st SW3
97	O 16	Burns av Sidcp
58	J 19	Burns av S'hall
99	U 2	Burns clo Erith
96	J 3	Burns clo Welling
19	P 10	Burn side N9
4	L 13	Burnside clo Barnt
83	X 15	Burnside clo Twick
60	G 3	Burnside cres Wemb
55	U 3	Burnside rd Dgnhm
63	V 8	Burnside st E3
62	C 3	Burns rd NW10
88	L 4	Burns rd SW11
72	A 5	Burns rd W13
60	J 6	Burns rd Wemb
94	F 20	Burnt Ash hill SE12
112	G 1	Burnt Ash hill SE12
112	G 14	Burnt Ash la Brom
94	C 13	Burnst Ash rd SE12
25	T 4	Burnt Oak bdwy Edg
25	U 3	Burnt Oak fields Edg
96	M 16	Burnt Oak la Sidcp
97	O 20	Burnt Oak la Sidcp
114	M 3	Burnt Oak la Sidcp
106	H 2	Burntwood clo SW18
106	H 2	Burntwood Grange rd SW18
106	D 6	Burntwood la SW17
79	O 10	Burrage gro SE18
78	M 14	Burrage pl SE18
79	N 14	Burrage pl SE18
79	O 10	Burrage rd SE18
65	U 17	Burrard rd E16
45	Y 13	Burrard rd NW6
98	C 6	Burr clo Bxly Hth
124	J 14	Burrell clo Becknhm
12	G 7	Burrell clo Edg
125	N 3	Burrell row Becknhm
141	X 13	Burrell st SE1
117	R 4	Burritt rd Kingst
26	J 13	Burroughs gdns NW4
26	K 13	Burroughs the NW4
141	W 16	Burrows ms SE1
62	M 8	Burrows rd NW10
128	D 11	Burrows rd NW10
87	Y 20	Burr rd SW18
142	J 15	Bursar st SE1
114	L 4	Bursdon clo Sidc
9	S 13	Bursland rd Enf
143	U 6	Burslem st E1
87	S 10	Burstock rd SW15
87	P 12	Burston rd SW15
105	S 20	Burstow rd SW20
119	S 1	Burstow rd SW20
145	S 19	Burthwaite rd SW6
48	L 3	Burtley clo N4
82	E 3	Burton gdns Hounsl
150	F 11	Burton gro SE17
14	B 14	Burtonhole clo NW7
14	B 13	Burtonhole la NW7
147	V 6	Burton mews SW1
132	H 15	Burton pl WC1
34	G 11	Burton rd E18
129	R 2	Burton rd NW6
90	F 4	Burton rd SW9
90	H 3	Burton rd SW19
102	L 18	Burton rd Kingst
64	L 1	Burtons ct E15
100	K 10	Burtons rd Hampt
101	O 11	Burtons rd Hampt
132	H 15	Burton st WC1
77	Y 3	Burt rd E16
79	R 14	Burwash rd SE18
41	T 18	Burwell av Grnfd
63	N 18	Burwell clo E1
50	J 3	Burwell rd E10
138	L 5	Burwood pl W2
142	K 5	Bury ct EC3
120	A 10	Bury gro Mrdn
18	G 4	Bury Hall villas N9
140	K 2	Bury pl WC1
21	N 2	Bury rd E4
30	G 10	Bury rd N22
56	J 14	Bury rd Dgnhm
142	K 5	Bury st EC3
18	K 5	Bury st N9
140	C 13	Bury st SW1
18	E 4	Bury st west N9
146	J 8	Bury wlk SW3
47	X 17	Busby ms NW5
47	X 17	Busby pl NW5
50	J 17	Bushberry rd E9
36	F 16	Bush clo Ilf
10	B 8	Bushell grn Bushey Watf
143	T 14	Bushell st E1
113	W 11	Bushell way Chisl
57	W 1	Bush Elms rd Hornch
34	C 10	Bushey av E18
118	L 4	Bushey ct SW20
91	T 2	Bushey Hill rd SE5
153	Z 7	Bushey la Sutton
101	S 18	Bushey park Tedd
65	Y 6	Bushey rd E13
31	R 18	Bushey rd N15
118	L 4	Bushey rd SW20
119	P 4	Bushey rd SW20
159	O 3	Bushey rd Croy
153	Z 8	Bushey rd Sutton
154	A 7	Bushey rd Sutton
125	W 13	Bushey way Becknhm
12	E 8	Bushfield clo Edg
12	F 8	Bushfield cres Edg
25	W 20	Bush gro NW9
43	V 1	Bush gro NW9
24	F 4	Bush gro Stanm
55	V 11	Bushgrove rd Dgnhm
55	V 12	Bushgrove rd Dgnhm
17	Y 2	Bush hill N21
18	A 1	Bush hill N21
8	B 18	Bush hill Enf
18	B 1	Bush Hill rd N21
24	M 19	Bush hill rd Harrow
160	E 9	Bush la EC4
79	N 20	Bushmoor cres SE18
96	A 1	Bushmoor cres SE18
107	S 5	Bushnell rd SW17
52	D 1	Bush rd E11
75	T 11	Bush rd SE8
73	N 17	Bush rd Rich
55	V 11	Bushway Dgnhm
52	D 2	Bushwood E11
73	P 18	Bushwood rd Rich
8	G 15	Bushy Hill park Enf
101	U 17	Bushyhouse Tedd
101	R 13	Bushy Pk gdns Tedd
102	B 18	Bushy Pk rd Tedd
101	V 16	Bushy rd Tedd
63	U 19	Butcher row E14
65	T 17	Butcher rd E16
102	J 2	Bute av Rich
144	E 6	Bute gdns W6
155	V 11	Bute gdns Wallgtn
155	V 11	Bute Gdns west Wallgtn
122	G 20	Bute rd Croy
36	B 15	Bute rd Ilf
155	U 7	Bute rd Wallgtn
146	F 6	Bute st SW7
23	R 20	Butler av Harrow
55	P 11	Butler rd Dgnhm
23	P 20	Butler rd Harrow
41	N 1	Butler rd Harrow
63	R 8	Butler st E2
33	U 16	Butterfields E17
95	Z 15	Butterfly la SE9
155	O 6	Butter hill Carsh
155	P 7	Butterhill Wallgtn
119	N 14	Buttermere clo Mrdn
87	U 13	Buttermere dri SW15
144	E 8	Butterwick W6
134	G 12	Buttesland st N1
56	H 18	Buttfield clo Dgnhm
79	N 12	Buttmarsh clo SE18
54	C 16	Buttsbury rd Ilf
100	C 6	Butts cotts Felt
100	G 7	Butts cres Felt
112	A 11	Butts rd Brom
72	F 18	Butts the Brentf
15	X 16	Buxted rd N12
92	C 16	Buxton clo SE23
35	N 1	Buxton clo Wdfd Grn
153	R 7	Buxton cres Sutton
34	A 14	Buxton dri E11
117	Z 2	Buxton dri New Mald
118	A 2	Buxton dri New Mald
73	S 1	Buxton gdns W3
20	K 3	Buxton rd E4
66	D 9	Buxton rd E6
51	Z 15	Buxton rd E15
52	A 15	Buxton rd E15
32	K 15	Buxton rd E17
47	Y 4	Buxton rd N19
44	K 17	Buxton rd NW2
86	B 8	Buxton rd SW13
81	Z 18	Buxton rd Erith
36	G 20	Buxton rd Ilf
54	G 1	Buxton rd Ilf
122	H 13	Buxton rd Thntn Hth
135	R 18	Buxton st E1
88	C 5	Byam st SW6
121	X 1	Byards croft SW16
58	H 13	Bycroft rd S'hall
110	E 17	Bycroft st SE20
7	X 9	Bycullah av Enf
7	V 9	Bycullah rd Enf
106	G 16	Byegrove rd SW19
62	B 16	Bye the W3
100	K 5	Bye ways Twick
117	R 12	Byeways the Surb
85	V 8	Byeway the SW14
152	E 9	Byeway the Epsom
23	U 5	Bye Way the Harrow
86	G 3	Byfeld gdns SW13
83	Y 8	Byfield rd Islwth
65	N 1	Byford clo E15
159	R 15	Bygrove Croy
64	C 18	Bygrove st E14
17	O 1	Byland clo N21
80	B 8	Bylands clo SE2
110	D 14	Byne rd SE26
154	H 3	Byne rd Carsh
157	O 17	Bynes rd S Croy
132	F 18	Byng pl WC1
4	C 11	Byng rd Barnt
76	B 5	Byng st E14
98	A 8	Bynon av Bxly Hth
107	T 2	Byrne rd SW12
53	P 19	Byron av E12
34	B 9	Byron av E18
25	T 11	Byron av NW9
118	G 10	Byron av New Mald
154	G 9	Byron av Sutton
154	G 9	Byron Av east Sutton
80	F 3	Byron clo SE18
100	F 10	Byron clo Hampt
7	X 9	Byron ct Enf
28	G 18	Byron dri N2
154	G 7	Byron gdns Sutton
41	R 5	Byron Hill rd Harrow
51	R 3	Byron rd E10
33	P 11	Byron rd E17
44	J 8	Byron rd NW2
13	T 16	Byron rd NW7
73	O 1	Byron rd W5
23	T 18	Byron rd Harrow
23	W 10	Bryon rd Harrow
42	E 9	Byron rd Wemb
64	F 16	Byron st E14
19	O 1	Byron terr N9
58	B 9	Byron way Grnfd
35	Z 5	Bysouth clo Ilf
106	M 14	Byton rd SW17
142	K 10	Byward st EC3
147	N 9	Bywater st SW3
154	F 18	Byway the Sutton
140	A 3	Bywell pl W1
124	D 14	Bywood av Croy

B

C

C

138	K 2	Cabbell st NW1
143	X 8	Cable st E1
66	B 5	Cabot way E6
88	J 5	Cabul rd SW11
62	D 18	Cactus wlk W12
5	W 17	Caddington clo Barnt
45	S 10	Caddington rd NW2
76	L 12	Cadeb pl SE10
93	W2	Cade rd SE10
88	C 17	Cader rd SW18
56	L 19	Cadiz rd Dgnhm
150	C 11	Cadiz st SE17
110	C 3	Cadley ter SE23
125	X 2	Cadogan clo Becknhm
40	K 13	Cadogan clo Harrow
101	U 13	Cadogan clo Tedd
154	A 14	Cadogan ct Sutton
34	J 10	Cadogan gdns E18
28	A 5	Cadogan gdns N3
7	S 18	Cadogan gdns N21
147	P 5	Cadogan gdns SW3
147	P 5	Cadogan ga SW3
147	R 2	Cadogan la SW1
147	S 3	Cadogan la SW1
147	R 1	Cadogan pl SW1
116	G 12	Cadogan rd Surb
147	O 4	Cadogan sq SW1
147	N 7	Cadogan st SW3
50	K 18	Cadogan ter E9
31	V 18	Cadoxton av N15
114	A 4	Cadwallon rd SE9
48	E 12	Caedmon rd N7
115	T 12	Caerleon clo Sidcp
80	C 10	Caerleon ter SE2
121	Z 7	Caernarvon clo Mitch
35	W 4	Caernarvon dri Ilf
134	M 11	Caesar st E2
104	F 13	Caesars camp SW19
120	M 10	Caesars wlk Mitch
121	N 10	Caesars wlk Mitch
76	C 11	Cahir st E14
129	N 15	Caird st W10
72	G 4	Cairn av W5
112	C 17	Cairndale clo Brom
44	C 11	Cairnfield av NW2
88	K 12	Cairns rd SW11
10	J 19	Cairn way Stanm
156	J 3	Cairo New rd Croy
33	O 12	Cairo rd E17
65	P 4	Caistor pk E15
65	P 3	Caistor Park rd E15
89	R 19	Caistor rd SW12
96	J 17	Caithness gdns Sidcp
144	G 3	Caithness rd W14
107	S 18	Caithness rd Mitch
48	K 17	Calabria rd N5
90	J 1	Calais st SE5
57	Z 14	Calbourne av Hornch
89	N 19	Calbourne rd SW12
113	O 10	Calcott wlk SE9
118	J 19	Caldbeck av Worc Pk
10	E 1	Caldecote gdns Bushey Watf
10	G 1	Caldecote la Bushey Watf
91	N 4	Caldecot rd SE5
59	V 6	Calder av Grnfd
8	D 12	Calder clo Enf
25	O 9	Calder gdns Edg
62	M 15	Calderon pl W10
136	C 3	Calderon pl W10
51	V 11	Calderon rd E11
120	C 11	Calder rd Mrdn
89	X 13	Caldervale rd SW4
78	K 10	Calderwood st SE18
150	E 16	Caldew st SE5
149	P 20	Caldwell st SW9
81	U 7	Caldy rd Blvdr
142	B 17	Caleb st SE1
132	M 9	Caledonian rd N1
133	N 4	Caledonian rd N1
48	C 15	Caledonian rd N7
132	L 10	Caledonia st N1
66	F 2	Caledon rd E6
155	P 7	Caledon rd Wallgtn
146	J 9	Cale st SW3
155	Z 18	Caley clo Wallgtn
10	C 7	California la Bushey Watf
117	U 7	California rd New Mald
49	O 18	Callaby ter N1

111 S 5 Callander rd SE6
17 W 15 Callard av N13
129 O 1 Callcott rd NW6
137 T 13 Callcott st W8
32 L 18 Callis rd E17
146 E 13 Callow st SW3
150 K 13 Calmington rd SE5
111 Y 16 Calmont rd Brom
35 Y 4 Calne av Ilf
105 P 9 Calonne rd SW19
133 O 10 Calshot st N1
7 W 12 Calshot way Enf
11 Y 16 Calthorpe gdns Edg
154 C 4 Calthorpe gdns Sutton
133 P 16 Calthorpe st WC1
91 S 14 Calton av SE21
5 S 19 Calton rd Barnt
111 R 16 Calverley clo Becknhm
56 D 7 Calverley cres Dgnhm
42 G 1 Calverley gdns Harrow
47 Y 4 Calverly gro N19
152 F 14 Calverley rd Epsom
134 M 14 Calvert av E2
81 T 12 Calvert clo Blvdr
115 X 14 Calvert clo Sidcp
66 J 3 Calverton rd E6
77 O 14 Calvert rd SE10
4 D 10 Calvert rd Barnt
131 T 3 Calvert st NW1
135 N 18 Calvin st E1
77 W 14 Calydon rd SE7
101 R 2 Camac rd Twick
87 P 13 Cambalt rd SW15
32 M 12 Cambell rd E17
8 D 15 Camberley ave Enf
118 J 3 Camberley av SW20
8 D 15 Camberley cl Enf
132 L4 Cambert wk N1
94 J 11 Cambert way SE9
91 O 2 Camberwell Church st SE5
91 P 2 Camberwell glebe SE5
91 N 1 Camberwell grn SE5
91 O 2 Camberwell grn SE5
149 W 18 Camberwell New rd SE5
91 N 2 Camberwell pas SE5
150 C 17 Camberwell rd SE5
90 L 2 Camberwell Stn rd SE5
56 K 16 Cambeys rd Dgnhm
72 C 5 Camborne av W13
104 J 20 Cambridge clo SW20
136 L 6 Camborne ms W11
87 Y 19 Camborne rd SW18
123 W 18 Camborne rd Croy
119 P 12 Camborne rd Mrdn
115 T 8 Camborne rd Sidcp
153 Z 17 Camborne rd Sutton
154 A 16 Camborne rd Sutton
96 J 4 Camborne rd Welling
82 G 1 Camborne way Hounsl
19 S 4 Cambourne av N9
89 W 20 Cambray rd SW12
82 H 11 Cambria clo Hounsl
96 F 20 Cambria clo Sidcp
114 F 1 Cambria clo Sidcp
36 H 15 Cambrian av Ilf
108 H 6 Cambrian clo SE27
51 N 2 Cambrian rd E10
84 M 17 Cambrian rd Rich
90 L 7 Cambria rd SE5
145 Z 20 Cambria st SW6
129 V 7 Cambridge av NW6
41 V 16 Cambridge av Grnfd
118 B 4 Cambridge av New Mald
96 K 10 Cambridge av Welling
140 G 7 Cambridge cir WC2
104 J 20 Cambridge clo SW20
82 C 10 Cambridge clo Hounsl
73 O 17 Cambridge cotts Rich
63 N 7 Cambridge cres E2
135 W 9 Cambridge cres E2
101 X 11 Cambridge cres Tedd
94 E 13 Cambridge dri SE12
31 N 1 Cambridge gdns N17
18 A 2 Cambridge gdns N21
129 V 9 Cambridge gdns NW6
136 K 4 Cambridge gdns W10
8 K 9 Cambridge gdns Enf
117 P 3 Cambridge gdns Kingst
131 X 15 Cambridge ga NW1
131 Y 15 Cambridge Ga ms NW1
95 Y 20 Cambridge grn SE9
109 Z 19 Cambridge gro SE20
74 K 10 Cambridge gro W6
144 A 7 Cambridge gro W6
117 P 4 Cambridge Grove rd Kingst
117 P 5 Cambridge Gro rd Kingst
63 O 9 Cambridge Heath rd E2
135 Y 5 Cambridge Heath rd E8
63 N 3 Cambridge Ldge vlls E9
34 F 19 Cambridge pk E11
84 E 17 Cambridge pk Twick
50 D 19 Cambridge pass E9
137 Z 19 Cambridge pl W8
20 K 5 Cambridge rd E4
34 D 20 Cambridge rd E11
129 U 12 Cambridge rd NW6
123 Z 5 Cambridge rd SE20
88 L 3 Cambridge rd SW11
86 D 6 Cambridge rd SW13
104 L 20 Cambridge rd SW20
118 H 1 Cambridge rd SW20
71 V 5 Cambridge rd W7
54 B 20 Cambridge rd Bark
112 F 18 Cambridge rd Brom
154 K 11 Cambridge rd Carsh
100 F 17 Cambridge rd Hampt
22 J 16 Cambridge rd Harrow
82 C 9 Cambridge rd Hounsl
54 J 2 Cambridge rd Ilf
117 R 5 Cambridge rd Kingst
121 U 6 Cambridge rd Mitch
117 Z 8 Cambridge rd New Mald
118 B 8 Cambridge rd New Mald
73 O 19 Cambridge rd Rich
114 H 10 Cambridge rd Sidcp
70 E 3 Cambridge rd S'hall
101 X 11 Cambridge rd Tedd
84 G 15 Cambridge rd Twick
73 S 13 Cambridge Rd north W4
73 S 14 Cambridge Rd south W4
79 N 14 Cambridge row SE18
138 K 5 Cambridge sq W2
147 Y 8 Cambridge st SW1
148 A 10 Cambridge st SW1
131 X 14 Cambridge ter NW1
18 F 3 Cambridge ter Enf
131 Y 14 Cambridge Ter ms NW1
65 T 13 Cambus rd E16
79 X 19 Camdale rd SE18
91 U 1 Camden av SE5
114 B 20 Camden clo Chisl
131 Z 1 Camden gdns NW1
153 Z 12 Camden gdns Sutton
122 J 4 Camden gdns Thntn Hth
151 N 20 Camden gro SE15
113 Z 15 Camden gro Chisl
131 Y 2 Camden High st NW1
132 A 6 Camden High st NW1
109 T 15 Camden Hill rd SE19
63 W 17 Camden Hurst st E14
47 Z 16 Camden la N7
47 X 18 Camden ms NW1
113 X 17 Camden pk Chisl
47 Y 18 Camden Pk rd NW1
113 Y 20 Camden Pk rd Chisl
133 V 8 Camden pas N1
113 Y 19 Camden place Chisl
34 H 18 Camden rd E11
32 K 18 Camden rd E17
47 X 18 Camden rd N7
48 A 14 Camden rd N7
132 A 2 Camden rd NW1
98 A 20 Camden rd Bxly
154 L 7 Camden rd Carsh
153 Z 11 Camden rd Sutton
94 A 5 Camden row SE3
47 X 19 Camden sq NW1
131 Z 1 Camden st NW1
132 A 2 Camden st NW1
133 V 18 Camden wlk N1
113 V 18 Camden way Chisl
122 J 5 Camden way Thntn Hth
82 J 18 Camelia pl Twick
78 B 2 Camel rd E16
146 E 14 Camera pl SW10
105 X 9 Camelot clo SW19
15 U 8 Cameron clo N12
19 N 15 Cameron clo N18
15 V 8 Cameron clo N20
110 M 5 Cameron rd SE6
126 E 11 Cameron rd Brom
122 J 15 Cameron rd Croy
54 H 4 Cameron rd Ilf
66 L 19 Cameron st E6
151 V 6 Camilla rd SE16
112 D 9 Camlan rd Brom
135 N 16 Camlet st E2
4 L 8 Camlet way Barnt
5 R 5 Camlet way Barnt
132 E 5 Camley st NW1
142 K 4 Camomile st EC3
87 Y 2 Campana rd SW6
36 B 14 Campbell av Ilf
101 O 3 Campbell clo Twick
12 C 15 Campbell Croft Edg
64 B 9 Campbell rd E3
66 D 4 Campbell rd E6
52 A 13 Campbell rd E15
31 W 4 Campbell rd N7
71 T 1 Campbell rd W7
122 H 15 Campbell rd Croy
101 P 3 Campbell rd Twick
47 W 10 Campdale rd N7
55 T 10 Campden cres Dgnhm
42 B 8 Campden cres Wemb
137 V 16 Campden gro W8
137 S 16 Campden hill W8
137 S 14 Campden hill gdns W8
137 R 13 Campden Hill pl W8
137 T 15 Campden Hill rd W8
137 R 14 Campden Hill sq W8
137 U 16 Campden Ho clo W8
157 T 11 Campden rd S Croy
137 U 14 Campden st W8
105 S 5 Campden clo SW19
143 O 6 Camperdown st E1
94 M 18 Campfield rd SE9
95 N 18 Campfield rd SE9
157 S 10 Campion clo S. Croy
66 H 19 Campion clo E6
86 L 12 Campion rd SW15
83 W 1 Campion rd Islwth
45 P 10 Campion ter NW2
24 J 14 Camplin rd Harrow
75 T 19 Camplin st SE14
104 L 13 Camp rd SW19
30 A 11 Campsbourne rd N8
30 B 12 Campsbourne the N8
68 D 2 Campsey gdns Dgnhm
68 D 1 Campsey rd Dgnhm
93 U 13 Campshill pl SE13
93 U 13 Campshill rd SE13
32 L 18 Campus rd E17
104 L 12 Camp view SW19
24 L 6 Camrose av Edg
25 R 2 Camrose av Edg
81 W 17 Camrose av Erith
119 Y 9 Camrose clo SW19
79 Z 12 Camrose st SE2
17 Z 18 Canada av N18
61 U 13 Canada cres W3
61 U 13 Canada rd W3
62 K 20 Canada way W12
93 P 20 Canadian av SE6
111 P 2 Canadian av SE6
63 V 11 Canal clo E1
91 W 1 Canal head SE15
63 W 12 Canal rd E3
150 E 15 Canal st SE5
134 G 3 Canal walk N1
110 D 12 Canal wlk SE26
69 Z 2 Canberra clo Dgnhm
69 Z 1 Canberra cres Dgnhm
66 H 4 Canberra rd E6
77 Y 18 Canberra rd SE7
78 A 17 Canberra rd SE 18
80 H 17 Canberra rd Bxly Hth
102 M 19 Canbury av Kingst
109 W 8 Canbury ms SE26
116 K 1 Canbury Pk rd Kingst
117 N 1 Canbury Pk rd Kingst
116 H 1 Canbury pas Kingst
116 J 1 Canbury pl Kingst
90 G 1 Cancell rd SW9
88 J 5 Candahar rd SW11
31 P 18 Candler st N15
57 Y 4 Candover rd Hornch
140 A 1 Candover st W1
140 B 2 Candover st W1
63 Z 3 Candy st E3
46 D 19 Canfield gdns NW6
46 C 18 Canfield pl NW6
35 P 2 Canfield rd Wdfd Grn
58 D 3 Canford av Grnfd
7 U 9 Canford clo Enf
117 Z 15 Canford gds New Mald
89 N 12 Canford rd SW11
123 S 6 Canham rd SE25
74 A 5 Canham rd W3
107 W 18 Canmore gdns SW16
51 Z 12 Can Hall rd E11
30 D 4 Canning cres N22
91 R 6 Canning cross SE5
138 A 20 Canning pas W8
138 B 20 Canning Place ms W8
64 L 6 Canning rd E15
32 K 12 Canning rd E17
48 K 9 Canning rd N5
157 U 2 Canning rd Croy
23 U 10 Canning rd Harrow
55 S 18 Cannington rd Dgnhm
104 M 13 Cannizard house SW19
105 N 13 Cannizard rd SW19
22 A 19 Cannonbury av Pinn
118 M 7 Cannon clo SW20
119 N 7 Cannon clo SW20
100 K 14 Cannon clo Hampt
16 L 9 Cannon hill N14
45 Z 14 Cannon hill NW6
119 R 8 Cannon Hill la SW10
46 F 9 Cannon la NW3
22 B 20 Cannon la Pinn
40 A 3 Cannon la Pinn
46 F 10 Cannon pl NW3
16 M 11 Cannon rd N14
17 N 11 Cannon rd N14
98 A 3 Cannon rd Bxly Hth
140 K 18 Cannon row SW1
11 X 20 Cannons park Stanmore
142 A 7 Cannon st EC4
160 E 8 Cannon st EC4
143 W 9 Cannon St rd E1
142 D 10 Cannon St station EC4
37 V 17 Canon av Rom
75 R 4 Canon Beck rd SE16
92 B 17 Canonbie rd SE23
48 L 20 Canonbury gro N1
48 J 20 Canonbury la N1
48 L 18 Canonbury Pk north N1
48 L 19 Canonbury Pk south N1
48 K 19 Canonbury pl N1
48 J 19 Canonbury rd N1
8 D 6 Canonbury rd Enf
48 J 20 Canonbury st N1
48 L 20 Canonbury st N1
133 Y 1 Canonbury vlls N1
126 M 5 Canon rd Brom
127 N 5 Canon rd Brom
46 G 1 Canons clo N2
12 A 18 Canons clo Edg
11 Y 18 Canons dr Edg
12 A 19 Canons dri Edg
28 G 20 Canons la N2
55 R 20 Canonsleigh rd Dgnhm
68 E 2 Canonsleigh rd Dgnhm
24 K 1 Canons Park clo Edg
134 B 5 Canon st N1
158 F 4 Canons wlk Croy
135 W 13 Canrobert st E2
47 X 18 Cantelowes rd NW1
35 R 20 Canterbury av Ilf
53 S 2 Canterbury av Ilf
115 T 3 Canterbury av Sidcp
111 P 20 Canterbury clo Becknhm
58 K 15 Canterbury clo Grnfd
90 F 8 Canterbury ct SW19
108 G 8 Canterbury gro SE27
33 U 20 Canterbury rd E10
129 T 9 Canterbury rd NW6
122 G 16 Canterbury rd Croy
100 C 4 Canterbury rd Felt
22 M 16 Canterbury rd Harrow
23 N 16 Canterbury rd Harrow
120 B 12 Canterbury rd Mrdn
129 S 10 Canterbury ter NW6
123 V 1 Cantley gdns SE19
36 B 18 Cantley gdns Ilf
71 X 8 Cantley rd W7
64 B 18 Canton st E14
63 Z 12 Cantrell rd E3
78 L 19 Cantwell rd SE18
75 R 10 Canute gdns SE16
141 Z 13 Canvey st SE1
53 Z 20 Cape clo Bark
31 W 11 Cape rd N15

156 C 10 Capel av Wallgtn
15 S 10 Capel clo N20
127 S 20 Capel clo Brom
54 K 12 Capel gdns Ilf
22 F 12 Capel gdns Pinn
52 M 10 Capel rd E7
53 O 11 Capel rd E12
9 W 20 Capel rd Barnt
15 V 1 Capel rd Barnt
139 S 19 Capeners clo SW1
106 B 1 Capern rd SW18
62 C 6 Capel rd NW10
132 D 19 Capper st WC1
58 C 12 Caprea clo Grnfd
123 V 18 Capri rd Croy
7 T 8 Capstan ride Enf
112 C 9 Capstone rd Brom
40 E 5 Capthrone av Harrow
11 N 20 Capuchin clo Stanm
33 S 20 Capworth st E10
51 R 1 Capworth st E10
76 M 13 Caradoc st SE10
31 O 14 Caradon way N15
109 T 16 Carberry rd SE19
73 O 5 Carbery av W3
63 Y 17 Carbis rd E14
31 Y 6 Carbuncle Pas way N17
131 Z 19 Carburton st W1
76 F 7 Cardale st E14
92 A 9 Cardale rd SE15
71 Y 8 Cardiff rd W7
9 O 14 Cardiff rd Enf
79 U 18 Cardiff st SE18
55 N 6 Cardigan gdns Ilf
63 Z 6 Cardigan rd E3
86 G 4 Cardigan rd SW13
106 C 16 Cardigan rd SW19
84 K 16 Cardigan rd Rich
149 S 10 Cardigan st SE11
119 S 15 Cardinal av Mrdn
102 K 14 Cardinal av Tedd
150 F 3 Cardinal Bourne st SE1
A 11 Cardinal Cap all SE1
114 G 20 Cardinal clo Chisl
115 S 15 Cardinal clo Mrdn
117 V 3 Cardinal cres New Mald
87 P 9 Cardinal pl SW15
100 M 18 Cardinals wlk Hampt
152 F 8 Cardinal clo Worc Pk
X 3 Cardinal way N19
82 A 11 Cardington sq Hounsl
132 B 13 Cardozo rd N7
48 B 15 Cardozo rd N7
15 U 16 Cardrew av N12
15 V 16 Cardrew clo N12
74 J 9 Cardros st W6
78 H 11 Cardwell rd SE18
48 D 8 Carew clo N7
31 X 8 Carew rd N17
72 D 5 Carew rd W13
121 N 3 Carew rd Mitch
J 7 Carew rd Thntn Hth
155 W 12 Carew rd Wallgtn
90 K 4 Carew st SE5
89 W 3 Carew gdns SW8
160 B 4 Carey la EC2
148 D 7 Carey pl SW1
55 Z 12 Carey rd Dgnhm
141 R 5 Carey st WC2
57 U 13 Carfax rd Hornch
106 B 1 Cargill rd SW18
123 V 9 Cargreen pl SE25
123 V 10 Cargreen rd SE25
110 L 2 Carholme rd SE23
121 Z 9 Carisbrooke Mitch
115 V 2 Carisbrooke av Bxly
8 G 7 Carisbrooke clo Enf
24 G 7 Carisbrooke clo Stanm
32 J 15 Carisbrooke rd E17
126 L 10 Carisbrooke rd Brom
47 S 14 Carkers la NW5
155 N 18 Carleton av Wallgtn
47 Z 11 Carleton rd N1
63 Z 7 Carlile clo E3
107 N 18 Carlingford gdns Mitch
30 H 12 Carlingford rd N15
45 G 12 Carlingford rd NW3
119 O 15 Carlingford rd Mrdn
142 M 7 Carlisle av EC3
24 A 18 Carlisle av W3
24 G 20 Carlisle gdns Harrow
35 P 19 Carlisle gdns Ilf
141 R 20 Carlisle la SE1
149 P 1 Carlisle la SW1
148 A 3 Carlisle pl SW1
51 P 5 Carlisle rd E10
48 G 2 Carlisle rd N4
128 L 5 Carlisle rd NW6

25 W 9 Carlisle rd NW9
100 K 17 Carlisle rd Hampt
39 U 17 Carlisle rd Rom
153 V 13 Carlisle rd Sutton
140 E 5 Carlisle st W1
139 V 9 Carlos pl W1
132 A 7 Carlow st NW1
6 K 16 Carlton av N14
24 A 17 Carlton av Harrow
157 R 16 Carlton av S Croy
42 G 6 Carlton Av east Wemb
42 C 7 Carlton Ave west Wemb
47 Y 7 Carlton clo NW3
12 B 16 Carlton clo Edg
153 S 8 Carlton cres Sutton
87 R 14 Carlton dri SW15
36 D 11 Carlton dri Ilf
140 E 14 Carlton gdns SW1
60 E 19 Carlton gdns W5
92 A 1 Carlton gro SE15
151 X 20 Carleton gro SE15
129 Z 9 Carlton hill NW8
130 C 6 Carlton hill NW8
140 G 13 Carlton House ter SW1
119 O 3 Carlton Park av SW20
52 B 3 Carlton rd E11
53 O 13 Carlton rd E12
32 H 6 Carlton rd E17
48 F 2 Carlton rd N4
16 B 16 Carlton rd N11
31 T 12 Carlton rd N15
85 U 9 Carlton rd SW14
73 Y 7 Carlton rd W4
60 D 19 Carlton rd W5
81 X 17 Carlton rd Erith
118 A 3 Carlton rd New Mald
39 Y 13 Carlton rd Rom
14 M 11 Carlton rd Sidcp
157 P 16 Carlton rd S Croy
97 R 7 Carlton rd Welling
63 T 11 Carlton sq E1
140 E 12 Carlton st SW1
18 B 12 Carlton ter N18
34 H 15 Carlton ter E11
110 B 8 Carlton ter SE26
147 N 1 Carlton Tower pl SW1
129 S 10 Carlton vale NW6
106 H 13 Carlwell st SW17
61 X 3 Carlyle av NW10
127 N 7 Carlyle av Brom
58 T 19 Carlyle av S'hall
28 E 19 Carlyle clo N2
53 R 12 Carlyle rd E12
68 F 20 Carlyle rd SE2
72 F 11 Carlyle rd W5
157 Y 2 Carlyle rd Croy
146 H 12 Carlyle sq SW3
40 G 13 Carlyon av Harrow
60 J 4 Carlyon clo Wemb
60 L 4 Carlyon rd Wemb
87 N 11 Carmalt gdns SW15
137 V 17 Carmel ct W8
23 N 5 Carmelite clo Harrow
23 O 8 Carmelite rd Harrow
141 V 8 Carmelite st EC4
23 N 6 Carmelite wlk Harrow
23 O 7 Carmelite way Harrow
64 D 11 Carmen st E14
88 G 9 Carmichael clo SW11
123 W 10 Carmichael rd SE25
107 S 4 Carminia rd SW17
140 B 8 Carnaby st W1
109 O 8 Carnac st SE27
33 X 5 Carnanton rd E17
8 F 10 Carnarvon av Enf
33 U 17 Carnarvon rd E10
52 B 17 Carnarvon rd E15
34 B 6 Carnarvon rd E18
4 E 11 Carnarvon rd Barnt
90 C 13 Carnecke st SE2
95 S 14 Carnecke gdns SE9
105 N 6 Carnegie pl SW19
133 O6 Carnegie st N1
26 A 3 Carnfield dr NW9
57 W 14 Carnforth gdns Hornch
107 W 17 Carnforth rd SW16
133 N 1 Carnoustie dr N1
87 Y 8 Carnoustie rd SW6
88 A 8 Carnoustie rd SW6
122 K 2 Carolina la Thntn Hth
137 Y 10 Caroline clo W2
157 S 9 Caroline clo Croy
10 M 18 Caroline ct Stanm

137 Y 9 Caroline pl W2
137 Y 10 Caroline Pl ms W2
105 U 18 Caroline rd SW19
63 T 18 Caroline st E1
147 T 6 Caroline ter SW1
44 K 16 Caroline wlk SW6
132 A 4 Carol st NW1
51 A 19 Carpenters rd E15
64 G 2 Carpenters rd E15
139 W 10 Carpenter st W1
147 U 17 Carriage Dri east SW11
147 V 15 Carriage Dri north SW11
89 N 1 Carriage Dri south SW11
147 N 19 Carriage Dri west SW11
60 L 11 Carrick clo W5
31 P 3 Carrick gdns N17
82 K 14 Carrington av Hounsl
85 P 11 Carrington rd Rich
139 X 14 Carrington st W1
52 B 15 Carrol clo E15
47 N 5 Carrol clo NW5
47 R 13 Carrol pl NW5
52 E 14 Carron clo E14
142 O 17 Carroun rd SW8
55 R 20 Carrow rd Dgnhm
32 M 7 Carr rd E17
40 H 19 Carr rd Grnfd
41 U 18 Carr rd Grnfd
7 Z 16 Carrs la N21
8 A 17 Carrs la Enf
63 W 15 Carr st E14
154 G 10 Carshalton gro Sutton
154 L 9 Carshalton house Carsh
154 M 10 Carshalton Pk rd Carsh
155 O 10 Carshalton pl Carsh
121 O 12 Carshalton rd Mitch
154 E 11 Carshalton rd Sutton
86 M 15 Carslake rd SW15
65 T 14 Carson rd E16
109 N 3 Carson rd SE21
5 Y 15 Carson rd Barnt
111 U 7 Carstairs rd SE6
94 D 13 Carston clo SE12
35 O 12 Carswell ct Ilf
93 U 18 Carswell rd SE6
38 F 1 Carter clo Rom
155 Y 15 Carter clo Wallgtn
38 G 2 Carter dri Rom
140 F 19 Carteret st SW1
75 W 11 Carteret wy SE8
8 L 7 Carterhatch la Enf
9 N 8 Carterhatch la Enf
9 P 8 Carterhatch la Enf
141 Y 7 Carter la EC4
150 B 11 Carter pl SE17
65 U 4 Carter rd E13
106 F 15 Carter rd SW19
153 P 2 Carters clo Worc pk
112 M 1 Carters Hill clo SE9
149 Z 12 Carter st SE17
150 A 12 Carter st SE17
130 J 5 Carters la SE23
87 P 13 Carters yd SW18
74 J 8 Carthew rd W6
74 K 8 Carthew vlls W6
133 Z 20 Carthusian st EC1
140 M 10 Carting la WC2
20 L 4 Cart la E4
32 A 1 Carton clo N17
120 C 12 Cartmell gdns Mrdn
98 D 1 Cartmel rd Bxly Hth
132 D 14 Cartwright gdns WC1
56 A 19 Cartwright rd Dgnhm
69 N 1 Cartwright rd Dgnhm
143 P 19 Cartwright st E1
90 L 15 Carver rd SE24
72 J 12 Carville cres Brentf
52 B 10 Cary rd E11
49 O 11 Carysfort rd N8
29 U 12 Carysfort rd N16
75 T 20 Casella rd SE14
108 H 10 Casewick rd SE27
50 B 8 Casimir rd E5
91 O 12 Casino av SE24
135 Y 17 Caslon pl E1
44 B 12 Casman clo NW10
150 E 18 Caspian st SE5
66 A 18 Caspian wk E16
21 Z 1 Casselden rd NW10
145 U 20 Cassidy rd SW5
80 A 12 Cassilda rd SE2
84 C 14 Cassilis rd Twick
32 G 17 Cassiobury rd E17
16 H 19 Cassland rd E9

123 N 9 Cassland rd Thntn Hth
92 L 19 Cassies rd SE6
143 S 1 Casson st E1
54 K 1 Castalia st E14
76 G 7 Castalia st E14
39 Z 10 Castella av Rom
129 X 15 Castellain rd W9
130 A 18 Castellain rd W9
39 Z 10 Castello av Rom
86 M 13 Castello av SW15
74 H 18 Castelnau SW13
86 H 2 Castelnau SW13
74 J 17 Castelnau gdns SW13
94 F 8 Casterbridge rd SE3
111 Z 5 Castillon rd SE6
112 A 4 Castillon rd SE6
110 L 5 Castlands rd SE6
20 K 17 Castle av E4
152 H 20 Castle av Epsom
60 C 15 Castlebar hill W5
60 C 13 Castlebar ms W5
60 B 13 Castlebar pk W5
E 16 Castlebar rd W5
15 S 17 Cstle clo N10
105 O 5 Castle clo SW19
87 R 19 Castlecombe dri SW19
113 P 11 Castlecombe rd SE9
160 G 7 Cstle st EC3
109 Z 19 Castledine rd SE20
35 R 18 Castle dri Ilf
95 Z 20 Castleford av SE9
113 Z 1 Castleford av SE9
68 B 3 Castle gdns Dgnhm
84 M 9 Castlegate Rich
47 S 19 Castlehaven rd NW1
131 X 1 Castlehaven rd NW1
159 U 18 Castle Hill av Croy
148 B 1 Castle la SW1
8 C 17 Castleleigh ct Enf
157 U 11 Castlemaine S Croy
152 K 19 Castlemaine av Epsom
155 N 3 Castleragh st W1
15 S 17 Castle rd N12
47 T 19 Castle rd NW1
68 C 4 Castle rd Dgnhm
9 V 4 Castle rd Enf
40 J 19 Castle rd Grnfd
64 M 19 Cstle rd Grnfd
83 V 4 Castle rd Islwth
65 Z 6 Castle st E6
66 A 6 Castle st E6
16 J 2 Castle st Kingst
98 M 3 Castleton av Bxly Hth
99 N 4 Castleton av Bxly Hth
42 J 12 Castleton av Wemb
33 X 7 Castleton rd E17
54 O 4 Castleton rd Ilf
121 W 9 Castleton rd Mitch
144 M 11 Castletown rd W14
145 N 10 Castletown rd W14
105 O 5 Castle way SW19
152 H 20 Castle way Epsom
95 V 4 Castlewood dri SE9
31 X 20 Castlewood rd N16
5 V 12 Castlewood rd Barnt
47 P 1 Castle yd N6
64 A 19 Castor st E14
135 V 5 Cat & Mutton bridge E8
35 V 7 Caterham av Ilf
93 W 3 Caterham rd SE13
150 G 7 Catesby st SE17
93 P 19 Catford bdwy SE6
111 N 1 Catford hill SE6
93 P 19 Catford rd SE6
51 X 8 Cathall rd E11
51 Y 9 Cathall rd E11
75 N 16 Cathay st SE16
43 X 18 Cathay st SE16
47 U 10 Cathart hill N19
44 A 13 Cathcart rd SW10
47 S 16 Cathart st NW5
141 Z 5 Cathedral pl EC4
142 E 13 Cathedral st SE1
48 M 10 Catherall rd N5
6 H 17 Catherine ct N14
83 P 11 Catherine gdns Hounsl
93 R 1 Catherine gro SE10
88 B 20 Catherine pl SW1
39 Y 16 Catherine rd Rom
116 G 11 Catherine rd Surb
141 N 8 Catherine st WC2
142 K 2 Catherine Wheel all E1
140 B 15 Catherine Wheel yd SW1
5 X 18 Cat hill Barnt

6 A 17 Cat hill Barnt
89 T 17 Cathles rd SW12
74 J 7 Cathnor rd W12
9 V 1 Catistield rd Enf
110 D 7 Catling clo SE23
151 U 10 Catlin st SE16
91 V 1 Caton st SE5
124 M 1 Cator la Becknhm
124 M 2 Cator la Becknhm
89 Y 9 Cato rd SW4
110 J 19 Cator park Becknhm
F 15 Cator rd SE26
155 N 11 Cator rd Carsh
151 S 15 Cator rd SE15
151 O 17 Cator rd SE15
138 M 3 Cato st W1
10 A 5 Catsey woods Bushey Watf
113 S 11 Cattistock rd SE9
140 M 2 Caton st WC1
66 E 2 Caulfield rd E6
92 A 4 Caulfield rd SE15
28 H 13 Causeway the N2
87 Z 12 Causeway the SW18
104 M 12 Causeway the SW19
105 N 12 Causeway the SW19
155 O 4 Causeway the Carsh
154 B 19 Causeway the Sutton
101 W 14 Causeway the Tedd
19 O 3 Causeyware rd N9
47 T 1 Causton rd N6
148 G 8 Causton st SW1
89 T 14 Cautley av SW4
37 T 12 Cavalier clo Rom
146 O 12 Cavaye pl SW10
7 U 8 Cavell dri Enf
31 O 2 Cavell rd N17
63 N 16 Cavell st E1
143 Y 4 Cavell st E1
27 X 8 Cavendish av N3
130 G 11 Cavendish av NW8
59 Y 16 Cavendish av W13
81 W 17 Cavendish av Erith
41 T 13 Cavendish av Harrow
57 Y 18 Cavendish av Hornch
118 H 10 Cavendish av New Mald
97 N 18 Cavendish av Sidcp
96 M 8 Cavendish av Welling
34 G 3 Cavendish av Wdfd Grn
130 G 12 Cavendish clo NW8
45 U 19 Cavendish clo NW8
142 K 3 Cavendish ct EC2
57 Y 18 Cavendish cres Hornchurch
51 V 3 Cavendish dri E11
12 A 19 Cavendish dr Edg
54 L 15 Cavendish gdns Bark
53 W 3 Cavendish gdns Ilf
37 Z 17 Cavendish gdns Rom
139 Y 1 Cavendish ms north W1
139 Y 1 Cavendish ms south W1
139 Y 1 Cavendish pl W1
20 H 20 Cavendish rd E4
30 H 18 Cavendish rd N4
19 N 16 Cavendish rd N18
45 U 19 Cavendish rd NW6
107 T 1 Cavendish rd SW4
89 T 16 Cavendish rd SW19
106 H 17 Cavendish rd SW19
106 J 17 Cavendish rd SW19
85 W 1 Cavendish rd W4
4 A 12 Cavendish rd Barnt
2 J 19 Cavendish rd Croy
118 C 10 Cavendish rd New Mald
154 C 15 Cavendish rd Sutton
139 Y 4 Cavendish sq W1
134 E 9 Cavendish st N1
125 P 20 Cavendish way W Wckm
54 E 10 Cavenham gdns Ilf
118 H 18 Caverleigh way Worc Pk
65 W 8 Cave rd E13
17 T 10 Caversham av N13
153 R 2 Caversham av Sutton
30 L 13 Caversham rd N15
12 A 17 Caversham rd NW5
147 N 13 Caversham rd SW3
136 B 4 Caverswall st W12
62 L 16 Caverswall st W12
127 W 1 Caveside clo Chisl
71 Z 10 Cawdor cres W7
109 T 14 Cawnpore st SE19
64 A 7 Caxton gro E3
30 D 8 Caxton rd N22
106 C 13 Caxton rd SW19
136 E 16 Caxton rd W12
148 S 11 Caxton st SW1

65 P 19 Caxton St north E16
77 R 1 Caxton St south E16
14 E 18 Cawthorne way NW7
126 C 9 Caygill clo Brom
59 U 7 Cayton rd Grnfd
134 D 14 Cayton st EC1
33 O 6 Cazenove rd E17
49 Y 5 Cazenove rd N16
54 D 20 Cecil av Bark
8 G 14 Cecil av Enf
42 M 16 Cecil av Wemb
140 H 10 Cecil ct WC2
4 C 10 Cecil ct Barnt
30 A 19 Cecile pk N8
49 W 15 Cecilia rd E8
121 N 11 Cecil pl Mitch
120 M 9 Cecil pla Mitch
52 A 8 Cecil rd E11
65 T 4 Cecil rd E13
33 O 3 Cecil rd E17
28 T 7 Cecil rd N10
16 F 5 Cecil rd N14
25 Z 11 Cecil rd N10
62 A 4 Cecil rd SW19
106 A 18 Cecil rd SW19
61 W 15 Cecil rd W3
122 C 16 Cecil rd Croy
7 Z 13 Cecil rd Enf
8 B 14 Cecil rd Enf
23 S 10 Cecil rd Hounsl
83 N 6 Cecil rd Hounsl
53 Y 12 Cecil rd Ilf
55 X 1 Cecil rd Rom
153 V 14 Cecil rd Sutton
126 E 19 Cecil way Brom
15 W 1 Cedar av Barnt
9 P 8 Cedar av Enf
37 Y 15 Cedar av Rom
96 M 17 Cedar av Sidcp
82 M 15 Cedar av Twick
103 X 10 Cedar clo SW15
38 L 12 Cedar clo Rom
105 P 8 Cedar ct SW19
28 H 13 Cedar dri N2
154 D 14 Cedar gdns Sutton
72 J 7 Cedar gro W5
97 V 16 Cedar gro Bxly
54 E 14 Cedar gro S'hall
102 J 1 Cedar heights Ric
94 K 14 Cedarhurst dri SE9
113 N 2 Cedar mt SE9
4 F 17 Cedar Lawn av Barnt
145 W 19 Cedarne rd SW6
1 V 1 Cedar Park gdns Rom
8 A 3 Cedar Park rd Enf
6 C 2 Cedar ri N14
31 V 4 Cedar rd N17
45 N 12 Cedar rd NW2
126 L 3 Cedar rd Brom
7 X 4 Cedar rd Enf
99 W 2 Cedar rd Erith
38 K 14 Cedar rd Rom
154 C 14 Cedar rd Sutton
13 Y 13 Cedar rd Tedd
33 O 15 Cedars av E17
156 B 7 Cedars av Croy
121 P 8 Cedars av Mitch
27 O 10 Cedars clo NW4
18 E 7 Cedars ct N9
89 R 10 Cedars ms SW4
54 A 18 Cedars rd E15
18 K 9 Cedars rd N9
17 W 7 Cedars rd N21
89 S 10 Cedars rd SW4
86 F 5 Cedars rd SW13
73 V 15 Cedars rd W4
124 L 3 Cedars rd Becknhm
156 B 7 Cedars rd Croy
120 C 20 Cedars rd Kingst
119 Y 8 Cedars rd Mrdn
1 T 6 Cedars the Buck HI
101 X 15 Cedars the Tedd
84 L 10 Ceder ter Rom
108 J 12 Cedar Tree gro SE27
7 T 10 Cedarville gdns SW16

80 C 19 Cemetery rd SE2
149 R 1 Centaur st SE1
9 X 13 Centenary rd Enf
28 F 7 Central av N2
51 X 7 Central av E11
28 F 8 Centrl av N2
18 F 10 Central av N9
147 R 19 Central av SW1
8 M 8 Central av Enf
9 N 8 Central av Enf
83 O 12 Central av Hounsl
22 D 19 Central av Pinn
156 B 11 Central av Wallgtn
96 M 4 Central av Welling
109 P 14 Central hill SE19
141 W 2 Central mkt EC1
56 L 7 Central park Rom
56 H 10 Central Park av Dgnhm
65 Z 7 Central Pk rd E6
F 6 Central Pk rd E6
59 Y 8 Central pde Grnfd
28 B 10 Central rd Mrdn
42 B 15 Central rd Wemb
152 H 2 Central rd Worc Pk
85 V 7 Central School path SW14
27 Z 17 Central sq NW11
133 Z 12 Central st EC1
134 A 16 Central st EC1
79 Y 3 Central way SE18
154 J 16 Central way Carsh
80 A 4 Central wy SE18
68 C 20 Central wy SE2
73 Y 3 Centre av W3
114 B 17 Centre common rd Chisl
78 H 13 Centre rd SE18
69 V 5 Centre rd Dgnhm
63 N 7 Centre rd E2
135 W 9 Centre st E2
33 T 3 Centre way E4
19 S 8 Centre way N9
54 B 7 Centre way N9
48 C 20 Centurion clo N7
32 H 11 Cephas av E1
63 R 12 Cephas av E1
63 O 12 Cephas st E1
135 Z 17 Cephas st E1
59 X 12 Ceres rd SE18
91 X 3 Cerise rd SE15
120 C 14 Cerne rd Mrdn
144 J 2 Ceylon rd W14
35 U 9 Chadacre av Ilf
52 J 12 Chadacre rd Epso
64 E 15 Chadbourn st E14
65 S 4 Chadd gdns E15
127 S 7 Chadd dri Brom
37 V 16 Chadville gdns Rom
55 U 5 Chadway Dgnhm
55 R 1 Chadwell av Rom
37 S 17 Chadwell Heath la Rom
133 U 11 Chadwell st EC1
20 L 12 Chadwick av E4
101 Z 15 Chadwick clo Tedd
34 A 20 Chadwick rd E11
62 E 2 Chadwick rd NW10
91 U 5 Chadwick rd SE15
148 F 3 Chadwick st SW1
65 V 14 Chadwin rd E13
124 F 13 Chaffinch av Croy
124 F 13 Chaffinch clo Croy
124 K 1 Chaffinch rd Becknhm
37 S 14 Chafford way Rom
131 P 18 Chagford st NW1
8 F 8 Chailey av Enf
50 C 10 Chailey st E5
133 R 8 Chalbury wlk N1
80 D 8 Chalcombe rd SE2
153 X 16 Chalcot clo Sutton
131 R 3 Chalcot cres NW1
46 L 18 Chalcote gdns NW3
131 S 2 Chalcot rd NW1
131 T 1 Chalcot sq NW1
93 Z 13 Chalcroft rd SE13
124 L 17 Chaldon rd SW6
90 A 17 Chale rd SW2
43 T 18 Chalfont av Wemb
26 C 11 Chalfont ct NW9
18 F 10 Chalfont grn N9
48 E 17 Chalfont rd N7
18 F 11 Chalfont rd N9
123 V 6 Chalfont rd SE25
72 A 9 Chalfont way W13
109 P 8 Chalford rd SE21
35 N 3 Chalford wlk Wdfd Grn

47 O 20 Chalk Farm rd NW1
43 R 9 Chalkhill rd Wemb
144 G 8 Chalk hill rd W6
43 V 9 Chalklands Wemb
5 Z 12 Chalk la Barnt
6 A 13 Chalk la Barnt
65 W 14 Chalk rd E13
8 C 15 Chalkwell Pk av Enf
155 X 13 Chalice clo Wallgtn
9 D 20 Challice way SW2
110 B 19 Challin st SE20
72 G 13 Challis rd Brentf
28 F 8 Challoner clo N2
145 O 11 Challoner cres W14
145 O 11 Challoner st W14
92 M 10 Chalsey rd SE4
28 F 18 Chalton dri N2
132 D 8 Chalton st NW1
125 P 19 Chamberlain cres W Wckm
28 D 8 Chamberlain rd N2
18 J 9 Chamberlain rd N9
131 P 1 Chamberlain st NW1
116 K 19 Chamberlain way Surb
62 M 2 Chamberlayne rd NW10
128 D 7 Chamberlayne rd NW10
28 F 5 Chambers gdns N2
44 L 20 Chambers la NW10
62 L 1 Chambers la NW10
128 B 1 Chambers la NW10
48 A 11 Chambers rd N7
143 T 18 Chambers st SE16
143 P 8 Chamber st E1
135 O 13 Chambord st E2
110 H 9 Champion cres SE26
91 P 6 Champion gro SE5
91 O 7 Champion hill SE5
91 R 8 Champion hill SE5
80 B 4 Champion pl SE18
110 J 9 Champion rd SE26
153 T 17 Champneys clo Sutton
109 N 6 Chancellor gro SE21
108 M 5 Chancellor gro SE24
74 M 15 Chancellors rd W6
144 C 10 Chancellors rd W6
144 D 11 Chancellors rd W6
74 M 14 Chancellors rd W6
80 E 11 Chancelot rd SE2
141 X 14 Chancel st SE1
141 R 3 Chancery la WC2
125 S 3 Chancery la Becknhm
114 A 6 Chanctonbury clo Chisl
153 Z 17 Chanctonbury gdns Sutton
14 J 14 Chanctonbury way N12
65 S 14 Chandler av E16
100 G 20 Chandler clo Hampt
75 N 2 Chandler st E1
143 X 12 Chandler st E1
33 P 8 Chandos av N14
16 H 11 Chandos av N14
15 S 5 Chandos av N15
15 U 3 Chandos av N20
72 F 10 Chandos av W5
21 V 8 Chandos clo Buck HI
25 N 2 Chandos cres Edg
140 K 10 Chandos pl WC2
51 W 14 Chandos rd E15
28 H 8 Chandos rd N2
31 S 8 Chandos rd N17
44 M 15 Chandos rd NW2
62 A 11 Chandos rd NW10
23 O 16 Chandos rd Harrow
139 Y 3 Chandos st W1
46 A 3 Chandos way NW11
160 G 7 Change all EC3
82 H 2 Channel clo Hounsl
64 J 3 Channelsea rd E15
90 D 8 Chantrey rd SW9
7 Y 3 Chantry clo Enf
24 M 16 Chantry clo Harrow
115 Z 14 Chantry clo Sidcp
126 M 11 Chantry la Brom
127 N 11 Chantry la Brom
22 K 4 Chantry pl Harrow
22 K 4 Chantry rd Harrow
133 Y 6 Chantry st N1
69 Z 5 Chantry way Rainhm
64 K 1 Chant st E15
99 P 12 Chapel all Brent
99 P 12 Chapel clo Drtfrd
28 H 10 Chapel ct N2
142 E 17 Chapel ct SE1
133 T 6 Chapel Farm rd SE9
78 F 9 Chapel hill SE18
99 P 12 Chapel hill Drtfrd
76 E 12 Chapel Ho st E14

C

22 A 11 Chapel la Pinn
55 W 1 Chapel la Rom
133 S 8 Chapel mkt N1
133 T 8 Chapel pl N1
31 V 1 Chapel pl N17
139 X 5 Chapel pl W1
108 K 10 Chapel rd SE27
72 B 2 Chapel rd W13
98 E 10 Chapel rd Bxly Hth
82 M 9 Chapel rd Hounsl
120 F 5 Chapel rd Mitch
84 C 19 Chapel rd Twick
137 W 10 Chapel side W2
64 K 1 Chapel st E15
138 K 2 Chapel st NW1
139 V 19 Chapel st SW1
8 A 11 Chapel st Enf
158 B 15 Chapel view S Croy
48 C 9 Chapel way N7
196 M 2 Chapel wlk Croy
126 F 4 Chapel way Brom
31 U 10 Chaplin rd N17
44 H 18 Chaplin rd NW2
55 Z 20 Chaplin rd Dgnhm
68 M 1 Chaplin rd Dgnhm
42 H 18 Chaplin rd Wemb
24 L 17 Chapman cres Harrow
81 T 14 Chapman rd Blvdr
72 E 19 Chapman rd Croy
80 G 12 Chapmans la SE2
63 N 19 Chapman st E1
143 X 8 Chapman st E1
F 16 Chapter rd NW2
72 E 19 Chapter rd SE17
52 F 14 Chapter st E7
148 E 7 Chapter st SW1
100 G 11 Chapter way Hampt
73 X 16 Chara pl W4
9 T 13 Charcroft gdns Eng
74 A 11 Chardin rd W4
49 X 4 Chardmore rd N16
136 G 18 Charecroft way W12
65 T 15 Charford rd E16
65 R 11 Chargeable la E13
6 P 12 Chargeable st E16
140 G 7 Charing Cross rd WC2
130 K 9 Charlbert st NW8
11 T 17 Charlbury av Stanm
54 L 7 Charlbury gdns Ilf
60 E 16 Charlbury gro W5
113 Z 6 Charldane rd SE9
110 A 6 Charlecote gro SE26
55 Y 11 Charlecote rd Dgnhm
66 H 10 Charlemont rd E6
15 S 9 Charles clo Sidcp
41 P 2 Charles cres Harrow
112 M 7 Charlesfield SE9
78 J 10 Charles Grinling wlk SE18
140 E 12 Charles li st SW1
130 J 9 Charles la NW8
65 Y 1 Charles rd E7
59 Z 6 Charles rd W13
56 M 19 Charles rd Dgnhm
37 V 19 Charles rd Rom
14 C 17 Charles Sevright dri NW7
H 14 Charles sq N1
77 Z 3 Charles st E16
86 B 6 Charles st SW13
139 W 12 Charles st W1
8 G 17 Charles st Enf
150 C 7 Charleston st SE17
109 Y 12 Charleville cir SE26
144 M 11 Charleville cir SE26
N 10 Charleville rd W14
81 X 19 Charlieville rd Erith
106 L 14 Charlmont rd SW17
89 P 2 Charlotte Despard av SW8
132 C 20 Charlotte ms W1
89 U 7 Charlotte pl SW4
140 D 2 Charlotte pl W1
134 K 14 Charlotte rd EC2
86 D 2 Charlotte rd SW13
56 G 18 Charlotte rd Dgnhm
155 V 14 Charlotte rd Wallgtn
132 C 20 Charlotte st W1
140 D 2 Charlotte st W1
133 R 6 Charlotte ter N1
Y 14 Charlton ch la SE7
81 R 16 Charlton clo blvdr
67 X 6 Charlton cres Bark
77 Z 19 Charlton dene SE7
78 A 20 Charlton dene SE18
78 A 17 Charlton house SE18
47 X 15 Charlton Kings rd NW5
78 B 17 Charlton park SE18
78 C 18 Charlton Pk la SE7
78 B 16 Charlton Pk rd SE7

133 W 7 Charlton pl N1
19 T 1 Charlton rd N9
62 C 3 Charlton rd NW10
77 U 18 Charlton rd SE3
77 W 17 Charlton rd SE7
24 J 11 Charlton rd Harrow
43 N 5 Charlton rd Wemb
77 P 20 Charlton way SE3
94 A 1 Charlton way SE3
93 Y 2 Charlton way SE10
158 L 19 Charlwood Croy
10 G 20 Charlwood clo Harrow
148 C 8 Charlwood pl SW1
87 O 10 Charlwood rd SW15
148 B 9 Charlwood st SW1
97 S 2 Charmaith rd Welling
24 G 9 Charmian av Stanm
119 Z 4 Charminster av SW19
113 O 10 Charminster rd SE9
49 Z 11 Charnock rd E5
119 Z 3 Charnwood av SW19
118 B 9 Charnwood clo New Mald
34 G 12 Charnwood dri E18
123 P 10 Charnwood rd SE25
49 Y 7 Charnwood st E5
156 A 2 Charrington rd Croy
132 E 8 Charrington st NW1
111 R 4 Charsley rd SE6
124 B 13 Chart clo Croy
126 A 2 Chart clo Brom
54 E 3 Charter av Ilf
82 A 10 Charter cres Hounsl
97 X 19 Charter dri Bxly
42 C 14 Charterhouse av Wemb
133 Y 13 Charterhouse sq EC1
133 Y 20 Charterhouse st EC1
141 W 1 Charterhouse st EC1
48 E 5 Charteris rd N4
129 R 5 Charteris rd NW6
21 W 19 Charteris rd Wdfd Grn
34 G 3 Charteris rd Wdfd Grn
117 T 5 Charter rd Kingst
20 M 18 Charter Rd the Wdfd Grn
21 P 18 Charter Rd the Wdfd Grn
109 S 12 Charters clo SE19
117 T 4 Charter sq Kingst
27 V 11 Charter way N3
16 J 1 Charter way N14
86 L 14 Chartfield av SW15
87 P 14 Chartfield av SW15
87 P 13 Chartfield rd SW15
108 H 7 Chartham gro SE27
123 Z 7 Chartham rd SE25
44 B 10 Chartley av NW2
10 J 19 Chartley av Stanm
134 G 13 Chart st N1
114 D 5 Chartwell clo SE9
153 U 7 Chartwell pl Sutton
110 A 20 Chartwell wy SE20
108 F 10 Charwood SE27
87 P 10 Charwood ter SW15
7 X 1 Chase Ct gdns Enf
7 X 9 Chase Green av Enf
38 J 2 Chase Cros rd Rom
106 M 10 Chasefield rd SW17
107 N 11 Chasefield rd SW17
19 Z 16 Chase gdns E4
83 S 17 Chase gdns Twick
7 Z 11 Chase grn Enf
7 Y 10 Chase hill Enf
36 D 15 Chase la Ilf
63 V 17 Chaseley st E14
7 T 10 Chase ridings Enf
6 H 15 Chase rd N14
16 K 2 Chase rd N14
61 Y 10 Chase rd NW10
7 V 9 Chase side Enf
119 S 2 Chase Side av SW20
8 A 9 Chaseside av Enf
8 A 7 Chaseside cres Enf
89 T 9 Chase the E12
89 T 9 Chase the SW4
108 E 17 Chase the SW16
119 T 1 Chase the SW20
98 G 7 Chase the Bxly Hth
126 H 5 Chase the Brom
25 S 5 Chase the Edg
57 T 9 Chase the Hornch
22 D 12 Chase the Pinn
22 D 13 Chase the Pinn
37 Y 18 Chase the Rom
39 O 11 Chase the Rom
57 O 10 Chase the Rom
1 L 18 Chase the Stanm
156 B 11 Chase the Wallgtn
7 O 18 Chaseville Pk rd N21

16 G 5 Chase way N14
7 V 7 Chasewood av Enf
99 X 17 Chastian st Dart
47 N 16 Chaston st NW5
60 K 6 Chatfield pl Croy
88 E 9 Chatfield rd SW11
122 J 19 Chatfield rd Croy
126 D 18 Chatham av N1
27 Z 16 Chatham clo NW11
119 V 18 Chatham clo Sutton
50 C 17 Chatham pl E9
32 H 11 Chatham rd E17
34 C 7 Chatham rd E18
88 L 15 Chatham rd SW11
117 O 2 Chatham rd Kingst
150 F 5 Chatham st SE17
26 L 8 Chatsworth av NW4
119 T 2 Chatsworth av SW20
112 G 11 Chatsworth av Brom
115 O 1 Chatsworth av Sidcp
43 N 16 Chatsworth av Wemb
26 L 8 Chatsworth clo NW4
83 P 9 Chatsworth cres Hounsl
8 K 20 Chatsworth dri Eng
18 J 1 Chatsworth dri Eng
18 J 1 Chatsworth dri Eng
73 S 2 Chatsworth gdns W3
40 K 4 Chatsworth gdns Harrow
118 D 11 Chatsworth gdns New Mald
101 X 9 Chatsworth pl Tedd
60 M 12 Chatsworth ri W5
50 D 9 Chatsworth rd E5
52 B 15 Chatsworth rd E15
45 M 18 Chatsworth rd E17
73 W 17 Chatsworth rd W4
60 M 12 Chatsworth rd W5
157 O 7 Chatsworth rd Croy
153 R 9 Chatsworth rd Sutton
108 K 6 Chatsworth way SE27
48 J 9 Chatterton rd N4
127 N 11 Chatterton rd Brom
88 M 14 Chatto rd SW11
89 N 13 Chatto rd SW11
85 R 6 Chaucer av Rich
3 J 16 Chaucer clo N11
35 U 17 Chaucer gdns Ilf
153 Y 6 Chaucer grn Croy
C 17 Chaucer grn Croy
52 G 18 Chaucer rd E7
34 F 18 Chaucer rd E11
35 U 6 Chaucer rd E17
90 G 14 Chaucer rd SE24
73 W 2 Chaucer rd W3
39 Z 1 Chaucer rd Rom
115 U 3 Chaucer rd Sidcp
153 X 7 Chaucer rd Sutton
96 J 2 Chaucer rd Welling
18 J 10 Chauncey clo N9
95 T 16 Chaundrve clo SE9
152 L 4 Cheasm Comm rd Worc Pk
153 P 20 Cheam rd Sutton
153 R 13 Cheam Pk way Sutton
153 P 20 Cheam rd Sutton
92 B 7 Cheam rd SE15
142 B 6 Cheapside EC2
160 B 6 Cheapside EC2
18 A 14 Cheapside N13
18 C 12 Cheddington rd N18
65 P 17 Chedworth clo E16
111 W 11 Chelford rd Brom
68 C 7 Chelmer cres Bark
50 F 14 Chelmer rd E9
39 O 1 Chelmsford av Rom
53 S 1 Chelmsford gdns Ilf
51 Y 3 Chelmsford rd E11
33 N 18 Chelmsford rd E17
34 B 4 Chelmsford rd E18
16 H 4 Chelmsford rd N14
62 L 4 Chelmsford sq NW10
128 B 5 Chelmsford sq NW10
144 J 12 Chelmsford st
147 W 13 Chelsea br SW1
147 U 11 Chelsea Br rd SW1
25 O 7 Chelsea clo Edg
101 N 13 Chelsea clo Hampt
147 R 14 Chelsea emb SW3
146 L 15 Chelsea Embankment gdns SW3
146 K 12 Chelsea Mnr gdns SW3
146 L 14 Chelsea Manor st SW3
146 F 14 Chelsea Pk gdns SW3
146 H 10 Chelsea sq SW3
19 S 2 Chelsfield av N9

110 D 8 Chelsfield gdns SE26
89 Y 7 Chelsham rd SW4
157 O 15 Chelsham rd S Croy
79 S 18 Chelsworth dri SE18
83 Y 19 Cheltenham av Twick
40 J 17 Cheltenham clo Grnfd
66 D 7 Cheltenham gdns E6
73 T 4 Cheltenham pl W3
24 J 13 Cheltenham pl Harrow
33 U 19 Cheltenham rd E10
92 D 12 Cheltenham rd SE15
147 P 9 Cheltenham ter SW3
87 P 10 Chelverton rd SW15
85 R 4 Chelwood gdns Rich
92 G 11 Chelwood wlk SE4
116 M 10 Chemleigh wlk Surb
65 R 10 Chenappa clo E13
10 J 17 Chenduit way Stanm
132 J 10 Cheney rd NW1
64 A 4 Cheney row E17
52 A 10 Cheneys rd E11
132 E 18 Chenies ms WC1
132 F 8 Chenies pl NW1
132 E 20 Chenies st WC1
145 W 1 Cheniston gdns W8
145 X 1 Cheniston gdns W8
87 S 15 Chepstow cl SW15
137 T 8 Chepstow cres W11
36 J 19 Chepstow cres Ilf
58 F 18 Chepstow gdns S'hall
137 U 7 Chepstow pl W2
157 T 5 Chepstow ri Croy
137 U 4 Chepstow rd W2
71 X 7 Chepstow rd W7
157 S 4 Chepstow rd Croy
137 R 9 Chepstow vlls W11
95 U 15 Cheq per SE9
69 R 5 Chequers la Dgnhm
134 D 18 Chequer st EC1
17 X 15 Chequers way N13
134 G 9 Cherbury st N1
71 X 2 Cherington rd W7
126 D 12 Cheriton av Brom
35 V 6 Cheriton av Ilf
60 D 14 Cheriton clo W5
79 S 18 Cheriton dri SE18
107 P 4 Cheriton sq SW17
72 G 8 Cherry clo W5
154 L 2 Cherry clo Carsh
119 S 9 Cherry clo Mrdn
72 A 19 Cherry cres Brentf
22 E 1 Cherrycroft gdns Pinn
19 Z 11 Cherrydown av E4
20 A 12 Cherrydown av E4
19 Z 11 Cherrydown clo E4
20 A 11 Cherrydown clo E4
115 W 5 Cherrydown rd Sidcp
38 H 7 Cherrydown wk Rom
56 A 14 Cherry gdns Dgnhm
143 W 19 Cherry Gdn st SE6
72 H 13 Cherry garth Brentf
5 O 20 Cherry hill Barnt
156 D 8 Cherry Hill gdns Croy
77 X 17 Cherry orchard SE7
157 P 1 Cherry orchard Croy.
123 R 20 Cherry Orchard rd Croy
9 R 3 Cherry rd Enf
38 M 15 Cherry st Rom
21 Z 13 Cherry Tree ri Buck Hl
108 B 7 Cherrytree dr SW16
28 L 13 Cherry Tree rd N2
124 M 8 Cherry Tree wlk Becknhm
11 O 18 Cherrytree way Stanm
28 L 14 Cherry Tree woods N2
126 F 19 Cherry wlk Brom
103 P 18 Cherrywood clo Kingst
87 O 13 Cherrywood dri SW15
119 S 8 Cherrywood la Mrdn
153 T 4 Chertsey dri Sutton
51 X 5 Chertsey rd E11
73 P 14 Chertsey rd W4
54 D 13 Chertsey rd Ilf
83 W 17 Chertsey rd Twick
100 L 3 Chertsey rd Twick
101 N 1 Chertsey rd Twick
107 N 12 Chertsey st SW17
80 B 4 Chervil ms SE8
88 B 2 Cheryls clo SW6
110 A 6 Cheseman st SE26
102 L 18 Chesfield rd Kingst
127 Z 14 Chesham av Brom
147 S 2 Chesham clo SW1
38 M 12 Chesham clo Rom
124 D 11 Chesham cres SE20

C

147 S 2	Chesam pl SW1
124 D 2	Chesham rd SE20
106 F 13	Chesham rd SW19
117 P 2	Chesham rd Kingst
43 Y 11	Chesham st NW10
147 S 1	Chesham st SW1
147 S 3	Chesham st SW1
72 A 4	Chesham ter W13
121 Z 7	Cheshire clo Mitch
17 P 20	Cheshire rd N22
30 C 1	Cheshire rd N22
135 S 16	Cheshire st E2
89 S 9	Chesholm rd N16
52 J 19	Cheshunt rd E7
81 R 14	Cheshunt rd Blvdr
87 U 1	Chesilton rd SW6
66 C 8	Chesley gdns E6
159 U 15	Chesney cres Croy
89 N 2	Chesney st SW11
31 W 10	Chesnut rd N17
27 V 11	Chessington av N3
80 M 19	Chessington av Bxly Hth
81 N 19	Chessington av Bxly Hth
81 O 19	Chessington av Bxly Hth
22 E 14	Chessington ct Pinn
152 B 20	Chessington rd Epsom
159 S 3	Chessington way W Wckm
145 P 13	Chesson rd W14
82 E 20	Chester av Hounsl
84 M 15	Chester av Rich
100 D 1	Chester av Twick
139 W 20	Chester clo SW1
86 K 8	Chester clo SW15
153 Y 3	Chester clo Sutton
131 X 13	Chester Clo north NW1
131 X 13	Chester Clo south NW1
147 S 6	Chester cotts SW1
18 H 17	Chester dri Harrow
30 K 17	Chesterfield gdns N4
139 W 13	Chesterfield gdns W1
91 U 12	Chesterfield gro SE22
139 W 12	Chesterfield hill W1
33 U 20	Chesterfield rd E10
14 L 18	Chesterfield rd N3
73 W 17	Chesterfield rd W4
4 B 18	Chesterfield rd Barnt
9 V 1	Chesterfield rd Enf
139 W 13	Chesterfield rd W1
75 P 20	Chesterfield way SE15
93 X 1	Chesterfield wlk SE10
46 B 13	Chesterford gdns NW3
53 U 17	Chesterford rd E12
9 N 19	Chester gdns Enf
120 C 13	Chester gdns Mrdn
131 X 14	Chester ga NW1
139 W 20	Chester pl NW1
131 X 11	Chester pl NW1
34 J 19	Chester rd E11
53 N 20	Chester rd E12
65 N 12	Chester rd E16
32 F 17	Chester rd E17
19 N 7	Chester rd N9
31 R 9	Chester rd N17
47 S 7	Chester rd N19
131 V 13	Chester rd NW1
104 M 15	Chester rd SW19
54 L 2	Chester rd Ilf
96 H 13	Chester rd Sidcp
147 T 7	Chester row SW1
147 U 5	Chester row SW1
147 V 4	Chester sq SW1
147 W 3	Chester Sq ms SW1
139 W 20	Chester st SW1
104 A 20	Chesters the New Mald
87 X 13	Chesterton clo SW18
58 K 6	Chesterton clo Grnfd
128 D 15	Chesterton rd E13
136 H 3	Chesterton rd W10
65 S 8	Chesterton ter E13
117 P 4	Chesterton ter Kingst
149 T 7	Chester way SE11
148 G 12	Chester Wharf SW1
30 M 5	Chesthunte rd N17
145 R 15	Chestnut all SW6
52 G 13	Chestnut av E7
29 Z 15	Chestnut av N8
33 V 14	Chestnut av SE17
85 Y 9	Chestnut av SW14
72 H 12	Chestnut av Brentf
11 Y 19	Chestnut av Edg
152 A 9	Chestnut av Epsom
100 G 18	Chestnut av Hampt
57 U 7	Chestnut av Hornch
101 W 18	Chestnut av Tedd
42 A 14	Chestnut av Wemb
33 V 13	Chestnut Av north E17
6 J 18	Chestnut clo N14
49 O 6	Chestnut clo N16
154 L 1	Chestnut clo Carsh
145 R 15	Chestnut ct SW6
34 E 19	Chestnut dri E11
97 X 8	Chestnut dri Bxly Hth
23 V 3	Chestnut dri Harrow
22 A 19	Chestnut dri Pinn
57 U 8	Chestnut glen Hornch
31 N 19	Chestnut gro N17
72 G 7	Chestnut gro W5
89 O 19	Chestnut gro W12
107 P 1	Chestnut gro SW12
5 Z 18	Chestnut gro Barnt
83 Y 10	Chestnut gro Islwth
121 Y 9	Chestnut gro Mitch
117 Z 6	Chestnut gro New Mald
118 A 5	Chestnut gro New Mald
158 B 16	Chestnut gro S Croy
42 A 14	Chestnut gro Wemb
14 C 5	Chestnut la N20
79 U 14	Chestnut ri SE18
108 K 6	Chestnut rd SE27
119 R 3	Chestnut rd SW20
102 J 18	Chestnut rd Kingst
101 S 3	Chestnut rd Twick
21 S 16	Chestnut wlk Wdfd Grn
158 J 1	Cheston av Croy
99 S 3	Chesworth clo Erith
150 E 2	Chettle clo
30 E 18	Chettle ct N8
107 N 5	Chetwode rd SW17
47 S 11	Chetwynd av Barnt
146 L 1	Cheval pl SW7
76 A 7	Cheval st E14
128 G 9	Chevening rd NW6
77 R 14	Chevening rd SE10
107 O 16	Chevening rd SE19
115 S 6	Chevenings the Sidcp
47 X 3	Cheverton rd N19
50 H 15	Chevet st E9
99 P 4	Cheviot clo Bxly Hth
8 B 9	Cheviot clo Enf
154 F 20	Cheviot clo Sutton
45 R 7	Cheviot gdns NW2
58 K 6	Cheviot ga Grnfd
108 J 10	Cheviot rd SE27
57 W 2	Cheviot rd Hornch
36 H 14	Cheviot way Ilf
32 H 14	Chewton rd E17
34 B 10	Cheyne av E18
100 F 2	Cheyne av Twick
146 M 14	Cheyne gdns SW3
116 M 9	Cheyne hill Surb
117 N 9	Cheyne hill Surb
147 O 13	Cheyne pl SW3
146 K 15	Cheyne row SW3
7 V 16	Cheyne wlk N21
26 M 18	Cheyne wlk NW4
146 K 16	Cheyne wlk SW3
146 L 15	Cheyne wlk SW3
146 F 17	Cheyne wlk SW10
157 X 3	Cheyne wlk Croy
11 V 19	Cheyneys av Edg
24 J 1	Cheyneys av Edg
157 T 8	Chichele gdns Croy
45 P 13	Chichele rd NW2
22 M 2	Chicheley gdns Harrow
23 N 3	Chicheley rd Harrow
141 O 16	Chicheley st SE1
94 L 1	Chichester clo SE3
24 L 10	Chichester ct Stanm
53 S 2	Chichester gdns Ilf
141 R 5	Chichester rents WC2
52 A 10	Chichester rd E11
18 J 5	Chichester rd N9
129 U 9	Chichester rd NW6
129 Z 20	Chichester rd W9
157 U 6	Chichester rd Croy
148 D 11	Chichester rd W2
143 R 1	Chicksand st E1
14 L 11	Chiddingfold N12
87 Y 4	Chiddingfold SW6
81 P 18	Chiddingstone av Bxly Hth
98 G 10	Chieveley rd Bxly Hth
71 Y 2	Chignell pl W13
143 X 10	Chigwell hill E1
34 H 10	Chigwell rd E18
64 D 18	Chilcot clo E14
107 S 4	Childebert rd SW17
75 W 20	Childeric rd SE14
87 R 1	Childerley st SW6
75 X 16	Childers st SE8
145 V 6	Childs pl SW5
145 V 6	Childs st SW5
145 V 6	Childs st SW5
27 W 15	Childs way NW11
59 Z 6	Chilham clo Grnfd
113 R 10	Chilham clo SE9
126 D 17	Chilham way Brom
107 P 13	Chillerton rd SW17
48 E 16	Chillingworth rd N7
118 F 15	Chilmark gdns New Mald
121 X 2	Chilmark rd SW16
100 G 2	Chiltern av Twick
99 P 3	Chiltern clo Bxly Hth
157 T 6	Chiltern clo Croy
7 R 14	Chiltern dene Enf
113 S 13	Chiltern dri Surb
45 P 8	Chiltern gdns NW2
126 C 8	Chiltern gdns Brom
8 B 12	Chiltern rd E3
36 J 14	Chiltern rd Ilf
131 S 19	Chiltern st W1
139 S 2	Chiltern st W1
21 T 12	Chiltern way Wdfd Grn
72 G 10	Chilton av W5
10 B 1	Chilton av Bushey Watf
75 U 11	Chilton gro SE8
12 C 19	Chilton rd Edg
85 P 7	Chilton rd Rich
34 D 8	Chiltons the E18
83 R 15	Chilton st E2
154 D 5	Chilworth gdns Sutton
138 E 6	Chilworth ms W2
138 D 6	Chilworth st W2
77 R 13	Chilvers st SE10
17 U 15	Chimes av N13
112 H 7	Chinbrook rd SE12
9 N 10	Chine the N10
7 X 18	Chine the N21
42 C 14	Chine the Wemb
20 M 11	Chingdale rd E4
21 N 11	Chingdale rd E4
20 C 9	Chingford av E4
21 O 14	Chingford la Wdfd Grn
20 B 16	Chingford Mount rd E4
21 N 12	Chingford rd E4
33 P 2	Chingford rd E4
112 A 15	Chingley clo Brom
58 M 6	Chinnor cres Grnfd
59 N 6	Chinnor cres Grnfd
76 F 6	Chipka st E14
75 V 18	Chipley st SE14
50 F 10	Chippendale st E5
43 U 16	Chippenham av Wemb
129 U 15	Chippenhm ms W9
129 T 18	Chippenhm ms W9
122 J 9	Chipstead av Thntn Hth
44 L 7	Chipstead gdns NW2
109 V 18	Chipstead clo SE19
87 Y 3	Chipstead st SW6
63 V 5	Chisenhalle rd E3
84 M 17	Chisholm rd Rich
28 C 2	Chisholm rd N3
113 Z 14	Chislehurst High st Chisl
127 S 1	Chislehurst rd Chisl
84 K 14	Chislehurst rd Rich
14 M 13	Chislehurst rd Sidcp
31 R 18	Chislet rd N15
94 H 4	Chiswell sq SE3
134 E 20	Chiswell st EC1
74 C 13	Chiswick la NW4
74 D 15	Chiswick la NW4
85 V 4	Chiswick br W4
156 B 5	Chiswick clo Croy
73 Z 11	Chiswick Comm rd W4
73 U 12	Chiswick High rd W4
74 B 12	Chiswick High rd W4
74 D 15	Chiswick mall W4
18 L 8	Chiswick rd N9
73 V 12	Chiswick rd W4
22 E 10	Chiswick st Pinn
73 S 15	Chiswick Village W4
55 V 5	Chittys la Dgnhm
132 C 20	Chitty st W1
88 H 13	Chivalry rd SW11
20 E 13	Chivers rd E4
68 F 11	Choats Manor way Dgnhm
69 N 10	Choats rd Dgnhm
105 O 4	Chobhams gdns
51 W 15	Chobham rd E15
47 S 1	Cholmeley cres N6
47 S 1	Cholmeley pk N6
116 A 16	Cholmley rd Surb
62 F 5	Cholmondeley av NW10
84 F 13	Cholmondeley wlk Rich
143 Y 13	Choppins ct E1
91 X 5	Choumert gro SE15
91 V 6	Choumert rd SE15
91 X 5	Choumert sq SE15
64 C 15	Chrisp st E14
64 D 15	Chrisp st E14
64 E 18	Chrisp st E14
15 P 19	Christchurch av N12
45 U 19	Christchurch av NW6
128 J 3	Christchurch av NW6
23 Z 12	Christchurch av Harrow
24 B 12	Christchurch av Harrow
101 X 13	Christchurch av Tedd
42 L 19	Christchurch av Wemb
28 H 1	Christchurch clo N12
106 G 19	Christchurch clo SW19
23 Z 12	Christchurch gdns Harrow
42 K 19	Christchurch grn Wemb
46 F 10	Christchurch hill NW3
4 F 10	Christchurch la Barnt
154 C 16	Christchurch pk Sutton
46 F 10	Christchurch pas NW3
4 F 10	Christchurch pas NW3
29 T 19	Christchurch rd N8
108 E 2	Christchurch rd SW2
85 S 12	Christ Church rd SW14
106 G 19	Christchurch rd SW19
125 O 2	Christchurch rd Becknhm
54 A 5	Christchurch rd Ilf
114 L 8	Christchurch rd Sidcp
117 N 16	Christchurch rd Surb
63 O 4	Christchurch sq E9
147 N 13	Christchurch rd SW3
147 O 13	Christchurch ter SW3
76 M 14	Christchurch way SE10
108 G 18	Christian fields SE16
143 U 7	Christian st E1
37 R 20	Christie gdns Rom
50 H 19	Christie rd E9
134 J 17	Christina st EC2
71 Y 8	Christopher av W7
96 K 15	Christopher clo Sidcp
55 V 14	Christopher gdns Dgnhm
132 G 13	Christopher pl NW1
134 G 19	Christopher st EC2
75 V 17	Chubworthy st SE14
54 H 13	Chudleigh cres Ilf
154 D 4	Chudleigh gdns Sutton
128 E 1	Chudleigh rd NW6
92 M 14	Chudleigh rd SE4
93 N 13	Chudleigh rd SE4
83 V 17	Chudleigh rd Twick
63 T 17	Chudleigh st E1
109 Z 12	Chulsa rd SE26
150 H 14	Chumleigh st SE5
116 M 10	Chumleigh Such
109 P 8	Church appr SE21
20 K 18	Church av E4
47 T 18	Church av NW1
85 Y 9	Church av SW14
125 O 1	Church av Becknhm
58 D 1	Church av Grnfd
22 D 19	Church av Pinn
115 P 11	Church av Sidcp
70 D 8	Church av S'hall
8 D 10	Churchbury clo Enf
8 C 12	Churchbury la Enf
94 M 17	Churchbury rd SE9
95 N 19	Churchbury rd SE9
8 D 8	Churchbury rd Enf
15 X 11	Church clo N20
137 W 16	Church clo W8
12 J 18	Church clo Edg
141 T 7	Church ct WC2
63 S 1	Church cres E9
27 V 5	Church cres N3

Grid	Name
29 R 13	Church cres N10
15 W 10	Church cres N20
89 P 19	Churchcroft cl SW12
111 Z 9	Churchdown Brom
112 A 9	Churchdown Brom
43 X 3	Church dri NW9
22 G 18	Church dr Harrow
159 Z 6	Church dri W Wckm
33 R 14	Church end E17
26 K 11	Church end NW4
141 X 7	Church entry EC4
153 T 13	Church Farm la Sutton
22 M 13	Churchfield clo Harrow
73 V 3	Churchfield rd W3
71 S 5	Churchfield rd W7
72 C 3	Churchfield rd W13
97 N 8	Churchfield rd Welling
34 F 4	Churchfields E18
100 F 6	Churchfields av Felt
124 H 2	Churchfields rd Becknhm
72 G 6	Church gdns W5
41 Y 12	Church gdns Wemb
87 S 6	Church ga SW6
93 S 12	Church gro SE13
113 E 2	Church gro Kingst
33 P 13	Church hill E17
17 R 2	Church hill N21
78 H 9	Church hill SE18
105 W 12	Church hill SW19
155 N 10	Church hill Carsh
156 B 20	Church hill Croy
99 P 11	Chruch hill Drtfrd
41 T 3	Chruch hill Harrow
33 S 12	Church hill rd E17
5 W 20	Church Hill rd Barnt
15 X 1	Church Hill rd Barnt
16 A 5	Church Hill rd Barnt
116 J 12	Church Hill rd Surb
153 S 10	Church Hill rd Sutton
24 A 16	Churchill av Harrow
147 Z 12	Churchill Gdns SW1
61 R 18	Churchill gdns W3
148 A 12	Churchill Garden's Estate SW1
148 B 12	Churchill Gdns rd SW1
23 U 13	Churchill pl Harrow
57 Y 17	Churchill rd E16
44 J 18	Churchill rd NW2
47 T 11	Churchill rd NW5
12 A 20	Churchill rd Edg
156 M 17	Churchill rd S Croy
20 B 12	Churchill ter E4
50 D 14	Churchill wlk E9
51 Z 4	Church la E11
34 A 3	Church la E11
33 T 13	Church la E17
28 G 9	Church la N2
30 C 13	Church la N8
18 H 8	Church la N9
25 X 18	Church la N17
31 S 4	Church la N17
31 S 5	Church la N17
43 W 4	Church la NW9
B 18	Church la NW10
107 O 12	Church la NW10
119 X 2	Church la SW19
72 F 5	Church la W5
127 R 18	Church la Brom
114 D 20	Church la Chisl
J 20	Church la Dgnhm
8 B 12	Church la Enf
23 V 6	Church la Harrow
22 C 11	Church la Pinn
101 W 13	Church la Tedd
155 X 6	Church la Wallgtn
110 A 9	Churchley rd SE26
149 U 20	Church Manor Estate SW9
79 Z 12	Church Mnr way SE2
81 Z 8	Church Mnr way Erith
5 W 20	Churchmead clo Barnt
44 G 18	Church Mead rd NW10
107 W 20	Churchmore rd SW16
28 F 17	Church mt N2
116 J 12	Church pas Surb
33 R 14	Church path E17
15 P 13	Church path N12
44 B 20	Church path NW10
83 O 11	Church Stretton rd Hounsl
85 Y 7	Church path SW14
119 W 2	Church path SW19
73 W 8	Church path W4
71 S 2	Church path W7
156 L 2	Church path Croy
120 J 8	Church path Mitch
39 P 14	Church path Rom
70 E 7	Church path S'hall
140 D 17	Church pl SW1
72 G 6	Church pl W5
120 J 6	Church pl Mitch
110 F 2	Church ri SE23
51 N 3	Church rd E10
53 W 14	Church rd E12
32 G 8	Church rd E17
29 O 18	Church rd N6
31 T 3	Church rd N17
26 M 12	Church rd NW4
44 C 19	Church rd NW4
109 S 20	Church rd SE19
86 F 3	Church rd SW13
105 R 13	Church rd SW19
73 V 4	Church rd W3
59 T 19	Church rd W7
71 V 2	Church rd W7
98 A 9	Church rd Bxly Hth
125 Y 5	Church rd Brom
126 E 3	Church rd Brom
21 V 5	Church rd Buck Hl
156 K 4	Church rd Croy
156 K 7	Church rd Croy
159 N 10	Church rd Croy
9 S 18	Church rd Enf
81 Y 13	Church rd Erith
58 B 4	Church rd Grnfd
70 F 19	Church rd Hounsl
36 G 19	Church rd Ilf
71 S 20	Church rd Islwth
83 R 1	Church rd Islwth
116 M 3	Church rd Kingst
117 N 3	Church rd Kingst
120 G 4	Church rd Mitch
84 K 12	Church rd Rich
102 M 10	Church rd Rich
115 O 11	Church rd Sidcp
115 W 13	Church rd Sidcp
70 E 8	Church rd S'hall
11 P 16	Church rd Stanm
153 S 13	Church rd Sutton
101 U 11	Church rd Tedd
155 W 5	Church rd Wallgtn
97 P 4	Church rd Welling
118 C 18	Church rd Worc Pk
46 C 13	Church row NW 3
114 C 20	Church row Chisl
144 X 19	Church row SW6
65 N 3	Church st E15
78 L 4	Church st E16
18 D 6	Church st N9
76 G 17	Church st SE10
130 G 20	Church st W2
74 C 16	Church st W4
156 K 4	Church st Croy
56 H 19	Church st Dgnhm
152 F 19	Church st Epsom
84 A 7	Church st Islwth
116 H 3	Church st Kingst
154 B 11	Church st Sutton
83 Z 20	Church st Twick
101 Z 1	Church st Twick
65 N 3	Church St north E15
83 O 11	Church Stretton rd Hounsl
26 L 11	Church ter NW4
93 Y 9	Church ter SE13
89 Y 4	Church ter SW8
84 H 13	Church ter Rich
28 L 9	Church vale la
110 E 4	Church vale SE23
101 P 3	Churchview rd Twick
49 P 13	Church wlk N16
45 W 9	Church wlk NW2
26 M 11	Church wlk NW4
43 X 7	Church wlk NW9
88 X 5	Church wlk SW13
86 K 13	Church wlk SW15
121 V 3	Church wlk SW16
118 M 5	Church wlk SW20
72 E 16	Church wlk Brentf
84 H 12	Church wlk Rich
15 V 10	Church way N20
132 F 12	Church way NW1
12 D 19	Church way Edg
50 B 15	Churchwell path E9
149 X 5	Churchyard row SE11
65 V 3	Churston av E13
119 R 12	Churston dri Mrdn
16 H 20	Churston gdns N11
148 B 7	Churton pl SW1
148 B 8	Churton st SW1
114 K 6	Chyngton clo Sidcp
110 G 3	Cibber rd SE23
88 D 15	Cicada rd SW18
91 X 3	Cicely rd SE15
112 A 10	Cinderford way Brom
60 M 10	Cinema pde W5
75 O 3	Cinnamon st E1
143 Z 13	Cinnamon st E1
119 V 16	Cinna pk SE19
119 Y 5	Circle gdns SW19
4 C 10	Circle the NW2
12 L 19	Circle the NW7
28 G 7	Circular rd N2
31 V 9	Circular rd N17
78 H 16	Circular rd way SE18
139 N 1	Circus ms W1
160 G 2	Circus pl EC2
130 G 10	Circus rd NW8
76 G 19	Circus rd SE10
129 X 20	Cirencester st W2
14 K 15	Cissbury Ring north N12
14 K 16	Cissbury Ring south N12
31 P 16	Cissbury rd N15
133 Y 10	City Gdn row N1
133 Y 11	City rd EC1
134 C 12	City rd EC1
36 C 3	Civic way Ilf
147 O 4	Clabon ms SW1
75 R 5	Clack st SE16
66 A 9	Clacton rd E6
32 H 18	Clacton rd E17
31 U 9	Clacton rd N17
27 Z 5	Claigmar gdns N3
12 J 2	Claire ct N12
82 A 2	Clairvale rd Hounsl
107 T 11	Clairvale rd SW16
71 U 2	Clairville gdns W7
10 G 18	Clamp hill Stanm
87 Z 5	Clancarty rd SW6
73 U 4	Clandon clo W3
152 E 14	Clandon clo Epsom
27 Y 11	Clandon gdns N3
54 H 7	Clandon rd Ilf
93 O 3	Clandon st SE4
137 V 10	Clanricarde gdns W2
89 R 10	Clapham common SW4
89 P 10	Clapham Comm North side SW4
89 U 12	Clapham Comm South side SW4
89 N 11	Clapham Comm West side SW4
89 X 9	Clapham High st SW4
89 X 8	Clapham Manor st SW4
89 X 10	Clapham rd SW8
149 R 18	Clapham rd SW8
89 Y 8	Clapham rd SW9
90 C 2	Clapham rd SW9
66 M 11	Claps Gate la E6
67 O 10	Clapsgate la Bark
49 W 2	Clapton comm E5
50 B 14	Clapton Pk est E5
50 B 14	Clapton pas E5
50 C 14	Clapton sq E5
49 X 3	Clapton ter N16
49 X 11	Clapton way E5
78 J 10	Clara pl SE18
95 Y 20	Clare corner SE9
135 V 10	Claredale st E2
52 E 13	Clare gdns E7
136 M 6	Clare gdns W11
54 L 19	Clare gdns Bark
75 O 10	Clarehall pl SE16
134 B 1	Clare lane N1
85 Y 14	Clare Lawn av SW14
141 O 6	Clare mkt WC2
24 K 16	Claremont av Harrow
118 N 10	Claremont av New Mald
78 K 3	Claremont clo N1
133 T 11	Claremont clo N1
99 R 10	Claremont cres Drtfrd
54 G 7	Claremont gdns Ilf
116 J 10	Claremont gdns Surb
21 Y 18	Claremont gro Wdfd Grn
27 T 5	Claremont pk N3
52 K 15	Claremont rd E7
51 W 9	Claremont rd E11
32 J 8	Claremont rd E17
29 U 20	Claremont rd N6
45 N 2	Claremont rd NW2
129 N 10	Claremont rd W9
59 Y 14	Claremont rd W13
5 T 2	Claremont rd Barnt
122 S 10	Claremont rd Brom
123 Y 19	Claremont rd Croy
23 U 8	Claremont rd Harrow
39 V 19	Claremont rd Hornch
319 V 19	Claremont rd Hornch
116 H 11	Claremont rd Surb
101 W 11	Claremont rd Tedd
84 C 17	Claremont rd Twick
133 S 10	Claremont sq N1
78 K 4	Claremont st E16
18 J 18	Claremont st N18
76 E 18	Claremont st SE10
45 N 3	Claremont way NW2
89 Y 14	Clarence av SW4
127 R 8	Clarence av Brom
35 V 18	Clarence av Ilf
117 Y 3	Clarence av New Mald
10 G 3	Clarence clo Bushey Watf
89 Y 16	Clarence cres SW4
115 P 8	Clarence cres Sidcp
131 Z 14	Clarence gdns NW1
131 P 16	Clarence gdns NW1
86 E 15	Clarence la SW15
50 A 14	Clarence ms E5
132 J 9	Clarence pas NW1
50 A 14	Clarence pl E5
50 A 12	Clarence rd E5
53 N 14	Clarence rd E12
64 M 13	Clarence rd E16
32 F 7	Clarence rd E17
31 N 14	Clarence rd N15
30 A 2	Clarence rd N22
129 O 2	Clarence rd NW6
113 R 5	Clarence rd SE9
105 Z 15	Clarence rd SW19
106 A 15	Clarence rd SW19
73 P 14	Clarence rd W4
97 X 9	Clarence rd Bxly Hth
127 P 7	Clarence rd Brom
123 O 16	Clarence rd Croy
9 P 18	Clarence rd Enf
85 O 3	Clarence rd Rich
115 P 8	Clarence rd Sidcp
153 Z 10	Clarence rd Sutton
101 X 16	Clarence rd Tedd
155 S 12	Clarence rd Wallgtn
116 H 3	Clarence st Kingst
84 J 10	Clarence st Rich
131 O 16	Clarence ter NW1
82 J 10	Clarence ter Hounsl
47 R 20	Clarence way NW1
138 K 8	Clarendon cl W2
101 P 7	Clarendon cres Twick
136 L 11	Clarendon Cross W11
86 M 9	Clarendon dri SW15
87 N 10	Clarendon dri SW15
26 H 19	Clarendon gdns NW4
130 C 18	Clarendon gdns W9
53 V 2	Clarendon gdns Ilf
42 H 11	Clarendon gdns Wemb
121 N 5	Clarendon gro Mitch
138 K 8	Clarendon ms W2
138 K 8	Clarendon pl W2
93 V 9	Clarendon ri SE13
51 X 2	Clarndon rd E11
23 R 18	Clarendon rd E17
34 E 10	Clarendon rd E18
30 D 11	Clarendon rd N8
30 K 14	Clarendon rd N15
18 K 18	Clarendon rd N18
30 C 9	Clarendon rd N22
106 H 18	Clarendon rd SW19
60 J 10	Clarendon rd W5
136 K 8	Clarendon rd W11
137 N 13	Clarendon rd W11
156 K 2	Clarendon rd Croy
23 T 19	Clarendon rd Harrow
155 U 13	Clarendon rd Wallgtn
148 A 8	Clarendon st SW1
147 Y 10	Clarendon st SW1
130 D 17	Clarendon ter W9
17 Z 1	Clarendon way N21
110 K 4	Clarens st SE6
33 Y 19	Clare rd E11
44 C 19	Clare rd NW10
92 K 3	Clare rd SE14
41 R 18	Clare rd Grnfd
82 C 9	Clare rd Hounsl
63 N 7	Clare st E2
135 X 9	Clare st E2
123 S 7	Claret gdns SE25
146 D 7	Clareville gro SW7
146 D 7	Clareville st SW7
97 Y 1	Clare way Bxly Hth
139 X 12	Clarges ms W1
139 Y 13	Clarges st W1
90 H 4	Claribel rd SW9
27 V 11	Clarindon gdns N3
110 D 19	Clarins st SE20
37 U 20	Clarissa rd Rom
135 N 4	Clarissa st E8
153 P 2	Clarkes av Worc Pk
99 W 2	Clark clo Erith
139 V 1	Clarke's pl W1
10 B 3	Clarks mead Bushey Watfd

C

65 O 16 Clarkson rd E16
67 P 6 Clarkson the Bark
75 O 6 Clarks orchard SE16
143 Z 18 Clarks orchard SE16
142 J 4 Clarks pl EC3
54 F 7 Clark st Ilf
63 O 16 Clark st E1
143 Z 3 Clark st E1
70 A 20 Clark way Hounsl
99 R 11 Claston cl Drtfd
51 U 5 Claude rd E10
65 U 4 Claude rd E13
91 Z 7 Claude rd SE15
76 A 10 Claude st E14
105 R 2 Claudia pl SW19
65 Y 7 Claughton rd E13
92 Z 5 Clausen wy Grnfd
40 L 14 Clauson av Grnfd
90 F 19 Claverdale rd SW2
74 K 16 Clavering av SW13
144 A 14 Clavering av SW13
101 X 9 Clavering clo Twick
53 N 6 Clavering rd E12
27 Z 4 Claverley gro N3
148 C 12 Claverton st SW1
75 O 3 Claverton st E1
143 Z 13 Claverton st E1
144 H 11 Claxton gro W6
121 T 4 Clay av Mitch
112 M 9 Claybridge rd SE12
35 R 10 Claybury bdwy Ilf
35 V 1 Claybury Hall Wdfd Grn
35 R 2 Claybury rd Wdfd Grn
114 B 5 Clayfarm rd SE9
57 V 13 Claygate clo Hornch
159 W 15 Claygate cres Croy
72 A 7 Claygate rd W13
8 E 3 Clayhall av Ilf
35 U 5 Clayhall av Ilf
8 C 2 Clay hill Enf
113 N 9 Clayhill cres SE9
149 R 16 Claylands pl SW8
10 F 3 Clay la Bushey Watf
12 B 7 Clay la Edg
119 X 17 Claymore clo Sutton
66 G 6 Claypole rd E6
72 J 13 Clayponds av Brentf
72 H 11 Clayponds gdns W5
72 K 14 Clayponds la Brentf
51 S 16 Clays la ct E15
51 T 14 Clays la E15
139 R 2 Clay st W1
42 K 20 Clayton av Wemb
72 G 13 Clayton cres Brentf
26 B 3 Clayton field NW9
91 Y 2 Clayton rd SE15
83 T 8 Clayton rd Islwth
56 K 4 Clayton rd Rom
111 Y 13 Clayton st SE11
95 Z 3 Cleanthus clo SE18
95 Z 2 Cleanthus rd SE18
96 A 2 Cleanthus rd SE18
63 R 17 Clearbrook way E1
110 B 1 Cleave hill SE23
116 G 12 Cleaveland rd Surb
123 Z 14 Cleaverholme clo SE25
149 U 10 Cleaver sq SE11
149 U 10 Cleaver st SE11
87 O 9 Clegg pl SW15
75 O 3 Clegg st E1
143 Y 13 Clegg st E1
65 T 6 Clegg st E13
62 F 20 Clematis st W12
145 O 15 Clem Attlee ct SW6
93 Y 16 Clemence st E14
128 E 2 Clement clo NW6
55 T 18 Clementhorpe rd Dgnhm
50 K 5 Clementina rd E10
105 S 13 Clement rd SW19
124 F 4 Clement rd Becknhm
65 T 19 Clements av E16
141 P 6 Clements Inn pas WC2
160 G 8 Clement's la EC3
72 G 13 Clements pl Brentf
66 E 2 Clements rd E6
151 V 3 Clements rd SE16
53 Z 9 Clements rd Ilf
79 P 11 Clendon way SE18
153 X 3 Clensham la Sutton
139 O 5 Clenston ms W1
49 N 18 Clephane rd N1
134 G 16 Clere pl EC2
134 G 17 Clere st EC2
133 V 17 Clerkenwell clo EC1
133 V 17 Clerkenwell grn EC1
133 W 17 Clerkenwell rd EC1
63 P 2 Clermont rd E9
49 U 8 Clevedon pas N16

110 E 20 Clevedon rd SE20
117 P 3 Clevedon rd Kingst
84 G 15 Clevedon rd Twick
119 U 3 Clevedon rd SW20
79 D 11 Cleveland av W4
73 W 9 Cleveland av W4
100 E 17 Cleveland av Hampt
30 L 17 Cleveland gdns N4
45 P 6 Cleveland gdns NW2
86 C 5 Cleveland gdns SW13
138 B 6 Cleveland gdns W2
152 C 2 Cleveland gdns Worc
63 P 12 Cleveland gro E1
152 B 20 Cleveland ms W1
60 A 14 Cleveland park W13
33 N 13 Cleveland Park av E17
33 N 13 Cleveland Park cres E17
140 D 13 Cleveland rd SW13
119 R 17 Cleveland rd Mrdn
34 F 10 Cleveland rd E18
134 F 2 Cleveland rd N1
86 D 5 Cleveland rd SW13
59 Y 15 Cleveland rd W13
60 B 15 Cleveland rd W13
53 Z 9 Cleveland rd Ilf
54 A 11 Cleveland rd Islwth
83 Y 10 Cleveland rd Islwth
118 A 8 Cleveland rd New Mald
96 L 5 Cleveland rd Welling
152 C 3 Cleveland rd Worc Pk
140 B 15 Cleveland row SW1
138 B 7 Cleveland sq W2
131 Z 18 Cleveland st W1
132 A 19 Cleveland st W1
138 C 4 Cleveland ter W2
63 P 12 Cleveland way E1
60 K 7 Cleveley cres W5
50 A 8 Cleveleys rd E5
45 Z 20 Cleve rd NW6
46 A 20 Cleve rd NW6
115 W 7 Cleve rd Sidcp
152 J 19 Cleves av Epsom
66 A 4 Cleves rd E6
102 D 7 Cleves rd Rich
36 C 2 Cleves wlk Ilf
100 F 18 Cleves way Hampt
23 P 5 Clewer cres Harrow
50 D 14 Clifden rd E5
72 F 16 Clifden rd Brentf
83 X 20 Clifden rd Twick
101 W 1 Clifden rd Twick
157 O 11 Cliffe rd S Croy
85 U 6 Clifford av SW14
113 T 15 Clifford av Chisl
35 Z 6 Clifford av Ilf
58 B 5 Clifford clo Grnfd
128 C 9 Clifford gdns NW10
110 C 18 Clifford gro SE20
65 O 13 Clifford rd E13
33 U 8 Clifford rd E17
123 W 9 Clifford rd E25
19 R 2 Clifford rd W9
5 O 12 Clifford rd Barnt
102 H 4 Clifford rd Rich
60 F 3 Clifford rd Wemb
140 A 9 Clifford st W1
44 D 12 Clifford way NW1
47 Y 17 Cliff rd NW1
93 P 4 Cliff ter SW4
93 O 9 Cliffview rd SE13
47 Y 7 Cliff vlls NW1
65 P 13 Cliff wlk E16
32 G 12 Clifton av E17
27 V 4 Clifton av N3
74 E 4 Clifton av W12
24 C 7 Clifton av Stanm
43 N 17 Clifton av Wemb
75 O 19 Clifton cres SE15
151 Z 18 Clifton cres SE15
31 W 18 Clifton gdns N15
27 X 18 Clifton gdns NW11
130 B 18 Clifton gdns W9
6 M 15 Clifton gdns Enf
49 X 17 Clifton gro E8
129 Y 8 Clifton hill NW6
130 C 5 Clifton hill NW8
110 M 3 Clifton Park av SW20
119 N 3 Clifton Park av SW20
138 H 7 Clifton pl W2
75 W 19 Clifton ri SE14
50 O 18 Clifton rd E12
65 N 13 Clifton rd E16
28 A 18 Clifton rd N3
29 X 18 Clifton rd N8
29 W 5 Clifton rd N22

62 F 7 Clifton rd NW10
123 S 10 Clifton rd SE25
105 O 15 Clifton rd SW19
130 D 17 Clifton rd W9
59 O 11 Clifton rd Grnfd
24 L 15 Clifton rd Harrow
39 V 19 Clifton rd Hornch
36 E 20 Clifton rd Ilf
83 S 4 Clifton rd Islwth
103 O 19 Clifton rd Kingst
117 O 1 Clifton rd Kingst
114 M 9 Clifton rd Sidcp
70 C 10 Clifton rd S'hall
101 U 10 Clifton rd Tedd
155 T 11 Clifton rd Wallgtn
97 S 7 Clifton rd Welling
134 H 19 Clifton st EC2
48 F 6 Clifton ter N4
130 A 20 Clifton vlls W9
75 O 20 Clifton way SE15
151 Z 20 Clifton way SE15
60 K 3 Clifton way Wemb
65 T 16 Clinch ct E16
16 H 19 Cline rd N11
142 D 12 Clink st SE1
96 M 9 Clinton av Welling
63 V 9 Clinton rd E3
52 F 13 Clinton rd E7
31 N 14 Clinton rd N14
93 U 11 Clipper wy SE13
131 Z 20 Clipstone ms W1
132 A 20 Clipstone st W1
28 M 10 Clissold clo N2
49 N 11 Clissold cres N16
49 O 9 Clissold est N16
49 N 8 Clissold park N16
49 O 9 Clissold rd N16
40 G 5 Clitheroe av Harrow
90 A 6 Clitheroe rd SW9
71 X 7 Clitherow av W7
72 C 13 Clitherow rd Brentf
45 N 5 Clitterhouse cres NW2
45 N 5 Clitterhouse rd NW2
18 J 19 Clive av N18
99 T 7 Clive av Drtfrd
15 P 14 Cliveden clo N12
147 S 6 Cliveden pl SW1
105 U 20 Cliveden rd SW19
60 A 13 Cliveden rd W13
20 L 17 Clivedon rd E4
109 O 8 Clive pass SE27
109 O 8 Clive rd SE21
106 J 15 Clive rd SW19
81 P 12 Clive rd Blvdr
8 J 14 Clive rd Enf
9 Y 17 Clive rd Rom
101 X 8 Clive rd Twick
8 J 15 Clive way Enf
160 D 8 Cloak la EC4
57 O 2 Clockhouse av Bark
38 H 2 Clockhouse la Rom
124 H 5 Clock Ho rd Becknhm
149 Y 6 Clock pl SE17
83 X 8 Clock Tower rd Islwth
123 Z 14 Cloister gdns SE25
12 J 16 Cloister gdns Edg
45 U 8 Cloister rd NW2
73 V 15 Cloister rd W3
127 T 12 Cloisters av Brom
49 R 12 Clonbrock rd N16
87 R 3 Cloncurry st SW6
31 P 11 Clonmell rd N17
87 W 1 Clonmel rd SW6
145 P 20 Clonmel rd SW6
101 P 10 Clonmel rd Tedd
105 W 2 Clonmore st SW18
41 R 5 Clonmore st N1
45 X 11 Clorane gdns NW3
33 V 3 Close the E4
29 S 8 Close the N10
16 K 8 Close the N14
14 H 7 Close the N20
6 A 18 Close the Barnt
124 H 9 Close the Becknhm
98 C 17 Close the Bxly
154 K 18 Close the Carsh
23 N 8 Close the Harrow
83 P 3 Close the Islwth
120 K 10 Close the Mitch
117 X 4 Close the New Mald
85 S 7 Close the Rich
37 X 17 Close the Rom
115 R 11 Close the Sidcp
119 V 17 Close the Sutton
42 J 18 Close the Wemb
43 W 10 Close the Wemb
141 Y 1 Cloth ct EC1
141 Y 2 Cloth fair EC1
142 L 4 Clothier st E1
142 A 1 Cloth st EC1
160 A 1 Cloth st EC1

107 R 4 Cloudesdale rd SW17
133 T 6 Cloudesley pl N1
133 T 5 Cloudesley rd N1
98 C 2 Cloudesley rd Bxly Hth
99 T 2 Cloudesley rd Erith
133 T 4 Cloudesley sq N1
133 T 5 Cloudesley st N1
155 Z 20 Clouston clo Wallgtn
26 C 12 Clovelly av NW9
18 D 3 Clovelly gdns Enf
38 H 5 Clovelly gdns Rom
29 Y 12 Clovelly rd N8
73 X 7 Clovelly rd W4
72 E 6 Clovelly rd W5
80 K 17 Clovelly rd Bxly Hth
40 D 8 Clovelly way Harrow
96 J 16 Cloverdale gdns Sidcp
51 X 8 Clover clo E11
147 O 13 Clover ms SW3
52 F 16 Clove rd E7
110 L 6 Clowders rd SE6
11 V 20 Cloyster wood Edg
126 G 17 Club Gardens rd Brom
135 N 16 Club row E2
70 D 14 Clunbury av S'hall
145 S 8 Cluny ms SW5
150 J 1 Cluny pl SE1
64 E 15 Clutton st E14
8 H 13 Clyach rd Enf
31 S 12 Clyde cir N15
51 P 2 Clyde pl E10
77 T 2 Clyde rd E16
31 T 12 Clyde rd N15
29 X 4 Clyde rd N22
123 U 20 Clyde rd Croy
157 L 12 Clyde rd Croy
153 Y 10 Clyde rd Sutton
155 V 13 Clyde rd Wallgtn
9 S 16 Clydesdale Enf
24 G 9 Clydesdale av Stanm
85 S 10 Clydesdale gdns Rich
137 P 5 Clydesdale rd W11
57 T 2 Clydesdale rd Hornch
5 Z 17 Clyde st SE8
110 D 4 Clyde ter SE23
110 D 5 Clyde vale SE23
39 P 4 Clyde way Rom
89 W 3 Clyston st SW8
86 M 12 Coalcroft rd SW15
69 R 7 Coaley row Dgnhm
127 X 4 Coates Hill rd Brom
11 T 2 Coates ct Borehm Wd
135 U 8 Coate st E2
95 R 8 Cobbett rd SE9
100 J 1 Cobbett rd Twick
35 O 15 Cobbetts av Ilf
149 O 20 Cobbett st SW8
52 C 9 Cobbold rd E11
44 D 18 Cobbold rd NW10
74 C 6 Cobbold rd W12
141 X 7 Cobbs ct EC4
82 E 12 Cobbs rd Hounsl
142 M 3 Cobb st E1
52 A 8 Cobden rd E11
123 Y 12 Cobden rd SE25
118 G 10 Cobham av New Mald
127 P 16 Cobham clo Brom
88 K 15 Cobham clo SW11
33 V 5 Cobham clo Edg
30 J 9 Cobham rd N22
54 H 8 Cobham rd Ilf
117 P 2 Cobham rd Kingst
112 M 10 Cobland rd SE12
63 Y 9 Coborn rd E3
63 Y 8 Coborn rd E3
63 Y 9 Coborn st E3
151 N 15 Coburg rd SE5
132 C 14 Coburg st NW1
155 Z 15 Cobham clo Wallgtn
39 D 9 Coburg rd N22
105 U 18 Cochrane rd SW19
130 H 10 Cochrane st NW8
6 A 14 Cockfosters p'de Barnt
5 X 4 Cockfosters rd Barnt
6 A 13 Cockfosters rd Barnt
142 L 3 Cock hill E1
141 X 3 Cock la EC1
140 F 19 Cockpit steps SW1
133 O 19 Cockpit yd WC1
108 E 2 Coburgh st WC1
140 G 13 Cockspur st SW1
135 P 18 Code st E1
118 C 9 Cocks cres New Mald
92 J 18 Codrington hill SE23
137 N 7 Codrington ms W11
24 H 11 Cody clo Harrow

C

155 Z 17 Cody clo Wallgtn
48 L 7 Codicote terr N4
64 L 12 Cody rd E16
43 T 9 Cofers crcl Wemb
32 G 3 Cogan av E17
63 Y 17 Copenhagen pl E14
141 T 13 Coin st SE1
109 N 2 Cokers la SE21
143 T 5 Coke st E1
129 V 4 Colas ms NW6
146 A 7 Colbeck ms SW7
41 N 1 Colbeck rd Harrow
49 T 2 Colberg pl N16
152 M 3 Colborne ay Worc Pk
153 N 2 Colborne way Worc Pk
154 F 6 Colburn way Sutton
109 T 13 Colby rd SE19
53 U 10 Colchester av E12
33 V 20 Colchester rd E10
33 N 20 Colchester rd E17
25 W 2 Colchester rd Edg
133 S 17 Coldbath sq EC1
75 T 17 Cold Blow la SE14
120 M 7 Cold blows Mitch
71 Y 3 Coldershaw rd W13
29 N 7 Coldfall av N10
30 H 6 Coldham ct N22
76 H 4 Cold harbour E14
90 H 9 Coldharbour la SW9
156 F 11 Coldharbour rd Croy
156 G 11 Coldharbour way Croy
42 F 13 Colding way Wemb
87 V 16 Coldstream gdns SW18
80 D 3 Cole clo SE18
145 Z 7 Colebeck ms SW5
63 R 11 Colebert av E1
87 P 17 Colebrook clo SW15
60 A 17 Colebrooke av W13
34 K 20 Colebrooke dri E11
126 A 4 Colebrook ri Brom
133 X 7 Colebrook row N1
33 N 14 Colebrook rd E17
122 A 1 Colebrook rd SW16
16 F 17 Colebrook way N11
47 P 17 Coity rd NW5
48 J 19 Colebeck ms N1
24 D 4 Coledale dri Stanm
88 C 12 Coleford rd SW18
51 W 13 Colegrave rd E15
151 R 16 Colegrove rd SE15
145 Y 12 Coleherne ms SW10
145 X 11 Coleherne rd SW10
87 S 3 Colehill gdns SW6
87 S 3 Colehill la SW6
134 B 4 Coleman fields N1
50 H 17 Coleman rd SE5
150 K 8 Coleman rd SE5
81 R 10 Coleman rd Blvdr
55 Z 19 Coleman rd Dgnhm
56 A 19 Coleman rd Dgnhm
113 X 7 Colemans heath SE9
142 E 5 Coleman st EC2
160 E 4 Coleman st EC2
160 E 3 Coleman St bldgs EC2
50 D 11 Colenso rd E5
54 G 4 Colenso rd Ilf
83 Y 14 Cole Pk gdns Twick
83 Y 15 Cole Pk rd Twick
83 Y 18 Cole Pk rd Twick
96 D 12 Colepits Wood rd SE9
30 F 10 Coleraine rd N8
77 R 16 Coleraine rd SE3
53 R 17 Coleridge av E12
154 K 8 Coleridge av Sutton
89 T 4 Coleridge clo SW8
130 B 2 Coleridge gdns NW6
32 L 12 Coleridge rd E17
48 F 8 Coleridge rd N4
29 X 19 Coleridge rd N8
15 P 17 Coleridge rd N12
124 C 16 Coleridge rd Croy
39 Y 3 Coleridge rd Rom
27 X 14 Coleridge wlk NW11
83 Y 17 Cole rd Twick
124 K 5 Colesburg rd Becknhm
40 K 2 Coles cres Harrow
10 B 6 Coles grn Bushey Watf
44 H 5 Coles Green rd NW2
101 U 15 Coleshill rd Tedd
88 K 4 Colestown st SW11
142 D 19 Cole st SE1
144 H 7 Colet gdns W14
133 P 17 Coley st WC1
110 G 1 Colfe rd SE23
30 J 14 Colina ms N15

30 J 15 Colina rd N15
26 B 14 Colin clo NW9
158 K 4 Colin clo Croy
26 E 15 Colin cres NW9
25 Z 11 Colindale av NW9
26 B 19 Colindale av NW9
26 H 14 Colin Deep gdns NW9
26 F 13 Colin Deep la NW9
26 F 13 Colin Deep la NW9
26 A 13 Colin Park rd NW9
44 F 17 Colin rd NW10
55 R 6 Colinton rd Ilf
87 Y 18 Coliston rd SW18
106 H 3 Collamore av SW18
22 L 16 Collapit clo Harrow
76 G 16 College appr SE10
23 T 4 College av Harrow
23 U 2 College clo Harrow
46 F 19 College cres NW3
133 V 1 College cross N1
20 D 4 College gdns E4
18 H 16 College gdns N18
91 R 20 College gdns SE21
8 B 8 College gdns Enf
35 R 15 College gdns Ilf
118 E 12 College gdns New Mald
106 H 4 College gdns SW17
109 R 18 College gdns SE19
132 D 5 College gro NW1
160 D 8 College hill EC4
23 U 3 College Hill Harrow
23 V 4 College Hill rd Harrow
47 S 12 College la NW5
18 F 20 College Pk rd N17
33 Z 12 College pl E17
132 C 4 College pl NW1
33 T 17 College pl E17
18 F 20 College rd N17
17 U 8 College rd N21
66 F 19 College rd NW10
128 B 8 College rd NW10
91 R 19 College rd SE21
109 S 1 College rd SE21
106 G 16 College rd SW19
60 A 18 College rd W13
112 F 18 College rd Brom
126 E 1 College rd Enf
157 O 4 College rd Croy
8 B 8 College rd Enf
23 T 3 College rd Harrow
23 U 19 College rd Harrow
83 V 3 College rd Islwth
42 H 5 College rd Wemb
126 E 2 College slip Brom
160 D 9 College st EC4
83 X 8 College ter E3
27 W 6 College ter N3
113 O 3 College view SE9
50 D 18 Collent st E9
77 O 13 Collerston rd SE10
31 U 16 Colless rd N15
70 K 4 Collet wy S'hall
151 U 2 Collett rd SE16
28 P 7 Collier dri Edg
38 H 3 Collier Row la Rom
38 C 4 Collier Row rd Rom
133 N 9 Collier st N1
122 G 10 Colliers Water la Thntn Hth
106 G 16 Colliers Wood High st SW19
81 V 17 Collindale av Erith
97 O 20 Collindale av Sidcp
74 J 2 Collinbourne rd W12
145 Z 12 Collingham gdns SW5
145 Y 6 Collingham pl SW5
110 C 9 Collingtree rd SE26
29 O 19 Collingwood av N10
117 V 18 Collingwood av Surb
82 H 18 Collingwood clo Twick
33 N 18 Collingwood rd E17
31 S 12 Collingwood rd N15
120 G 5 Collingwood rd Mitch
153 W 5 Collingwood rd Sutton
63 N 12 Collingwood st E1
53 X 17 Collingwood st E1
24 K 7 Collins av Stanm
142 A 19 Collinson st SE1
48 C 12 Collins rd N5
94 B 6 Collins st SE3
133 X 5 Collins yd N1
9 P 12 Collinwood av Enf
35 V 5 Collinwood gdns Ilf
92 C 1 Colls rd SE15

156 A 8 Collyer av Croy
91 V 2 Collyer pl SE15
156 A 8 Collyer rd Croy
55 R 6 Collynton rd Ilf
135 R 16 Colman clo E2
65 Y 15 Colman rd E16
135 R 16 Colman clo E2
63 T 11 Colman clo E1
23 P 3 Colmer pl Harrow
108 B 19 Colmer rd SW16
9 R 14 Colmore rd Enf
149 W 2 Colnbrook st SE1
50 H 13 Colne rd E5
18 A 3 Colne rd N21
101 U 2 Colne rd Twick
55 S 10 Colne st E13
29 P 2 Colney Hatch la N10
15 Y 18 Colney Hatch la N11
16 A 20 Colney Hatch rd N11
88 G 10 Cologne rd SW11
54 B 2 Colombo rd Ilf
141 W 15 Colombo st SE1
77 N 14 Colomb st SE10
7 V 10 Colonels wlk Enf
83 N 15 Colonial av Twick
132 K 18 Colonnade WC1
131 Y 15 Colosseum ter NW1
157 R 2 Colson rd Croy
107 V 10 Colson way SW16
31 V 12 Colsterworth rd N15
154 K 8 Colston av Carsh
53 N 18 Colston rd E12
85 W 10 Colston rd SW14
80 C 13 Coltness cres SE2
30 M 10 Colton gdns N17
23 U 14 Colton rd Har
25 S 4 Columbia av Edg
118 E 18 Columbia av Worc Pk
135 S 10 Columbia rd E2
65 R 13 Columbia rd E13
156 J 16 Columbine av S Croy
93 T 5 Columbine way SE13
101 T 2 Colus all Twick
49 U 16 Colvestone cres E8
137 P 6 Colville gdns W11
137 R 6 Colville ms W11
18 L 4 Colville rd N9
140 D 2 Colville pl W1
51 V 9 Colville rd E11
32 J 8 Colville rd E17
73 U 8 Colville rd W3
154 L 9 Colston ct Carsh
137 P 5 Colville rd W11
137 R 7 Colville rd W11
137 O 6 Colville sq W11
137 O 5 Colville Sq ms W11
137 P 6 Colville ter W11
20 H 11 Colvin gdns E4
34 J 13 Colvin gdns E11
36 B 3 Colvin gdns Ilf
66 D 2 Colvin rd E6
72 F 12 Colvin rd Thntn Hth
74 K 11 Colvin st W6
91 U 14 Colwall rd SE22
144 E 14 Colwith rd W6
106 G 18 Colwood gdns SW19
150 B 8 Colworth gro SE17
33 Z 19 Colworth rd E11
34 A 20 Colworth rd E11
123 X 20 Colworth rd Croy
59 X 6 Colwyn av Grnfd
82 M 3 Colwyn cres Hounsl
44 K 9 Colwyn rd NW2
113 Z 4 Colyer clo SE9
98 M 1 Colyers clo Erith
99 S 1 Colyers la Erith
99 P 7 Colyers wlk Erith
97 V 1 Colyton clo Welling
42 C 17 Colyton clo Wemb
92 A 14 Colyton rd SE22
18 H 17 Colyton way N18
77 P 19 Combe av SE3
44 A 8 Comber clo NW2
150 B 20 Comber gro SE5
90 C 7 Combermere rd SW9
50 A 6 Comberton rd E5
120 B 13 Comberton rd Mrdn
79 X 20 Combesides SE18
103 Y 14 Combe Wood Golf course Kingst
38 C 19 Commonwood dri Rom
80 A 9 Combwell cres SE2
33 T 15 Comely Bank rd E17
144 M 10 Comeragh ms W14
144 L 11 Comeragh rd W14
145 N 10 Comeragh rd W14
92 K 11 Comerford rd SE4
76 A 20 Comet st SE8

30 B 4 Commerce rd N22
30 D 4 Commerce rd N22
72 C 18 Commerce rd Brentf
75 X 8 Commercial Dock pas SE16
131 W 1 Commercial pl NW1
63 O 17 Commercial rd E1
143 U 5 Commercial rd E1
18 F 19 Commercial rd N18
143 O 2 Commercial st E1
150 M 20 Commercial way SE15
151 T 18 Commercial way SE15
77 N 13 Commerell st SE10
63 V 13 Commodore st E1
86 M 6 Commondale SW15
106 H 13 Commonfield la SW17
106 H 13 Commonfield pas SW17
86 H 7 Common rd SW13
10 D 11 Common rd Stanm
121 P 7 Commonside east Mitch
121 N 8 Commonside west Mitch
72 K 2 Common the W5
102 F 7 Common the Rich
10 H 9 Common the Stanm
62 K 20 Commonwealth av W12
137 S 20 Commonwealth institute W8
31 X 1 Commonwealth rd N17
80 E 13 Commonwealth way SE2
51 X 16 Community rd E15
59 P 4 Community rd Grnfd
110 H 5 Como rd SE23
38 M 15 Como rd Rom
39 N 14 Como st Rom
45 Z 19 Compayne gdns NW6
46 B 19 Compayne gdns NW6
66 A 6 Compton av E6
48 J 19 Compton av N1
46 J 1 Compton av N6
131 Z 14 Compton cl NW1
59 V 13 Compton clo W13
31 N 2 Compton cres N17
73 V 17 Compton cres W4
58 A 1 Compton cres Grnfd
22 D 16 Compton ri Pinn
48 K 19 Compton rd N1
17 V 5 Compton rd N21
128 G 13 Compton rd NW10
105 V 14 Compton rd SW19
123 Z 20 Compton rd Croy
157 Z 1 Compton rd Croy
65 R 5 Compton st E13
133 X 16 Compton st EC1
48 H 19 Comper st N1
7 V 4 Comreddy clo Enf
150 H 6 Comus pl SE17
47 X 9 Comus rd N19
88 J 11 Comyn rd SW11
65 O 14 Comyns clo E16
69 P 1 Comyns rd Dgnhm
10 A 6 Comyns the Bushey Watf
90 B 10 Concanon rd SW2
141 P 14 Concert Hall appr SE1
82 J 6 Concord clo Hounsl
61 S 12 Concord rd W3
9 O 18 Concord rd Enf
89 W 2 Condell rd SW8
51 O 19 Conder st E14
90 L 7 Conderton rd SE5
57 X 20 Condor wk Hornch
78 M 20 Condover cres SE18
4 D 20 Conduct rd Barnt
140 K 8 Conduit ct WC2
19 U 2 Conduit la N9
9 V 20 Conduit la Enf
157 X 12 Conduit la S Croy
138 F 7 Conduit ms W2
138 F 6 Conduit pas W2
138 G 6 Conduit pl W2
78 M 13 Conduit rd SE18
79 N 13 Conduit rd SE18
37 S 11 Conduit st W1
140 A 8 Conduit st W1
43 V 20 Conduit way NW10
48 J 11 Conewood st N5
108 M 1 Coney ash SE21
20 M 7 Coney Burrows E4
80 G 10 Conference rd SE2
79 T 13 Congo rd SE18

79	N 13	Congeton gro SE18
80	F 11	Congress rd SE2
95	S 8	Congreve rd SE9
150	J 7	Congreve st SE17
7	Y 9	Conical corner Enf
8	D 20	Conifer av Enf
108	B 8	Conifer gdns SW16
102	C 18	Conifers clo Tedd
87	X 4	Coniger rd SW6
156	K 19	Coningby rd S Croy
74	H 4	Coningham ms W12
74	J 6	Coningham rd W12
72	F 6	Coningsby cotts W5
20	D 18	Coningsby gdns E4
72	F 6	Coningsby rd W5
93	T 5	Conington rd SE13
6	H 17	Conisbee ct N14
111	U 7	Conisborough cres SE6
17	Z 12	Coniscliffe rd N13
67	U 2	Coniston av Bark
60	B 8	Coniston av Grnfd
96	G 8	Coniston av Welling
15	S 11	Coniston clo N20
67	U 2	Coniston clo Bark
98	K 3	Coniston clo Bxly Hth
119	N 13	Coniston clo Mrdn
48	A 20	Conistone way N7
25	Y 16	Coniston gdn W9
19	A 6	Coniston gdns N9
35	R 19	Coniston gdns Ilf
154	F 14	Coniston gdns Sutton
42	E 3	Coniston gdns Wemb
29	S 7	Coniston rd N10
18	J 20	Coniston rd N17
98	K 3	Coniston rd Bxly Hth
111	Y 15	Coniston rd Brom
112	A 17	Coniston rd Brom
123	A 17	Coniston rd Croy
82	L 17	Coniston rd Twick
57	V 15	Coniston way Hornch
128	L 17	Conlan st W10
44	C 19	Conley rd NW10
77	N 13	Conley st SE10
20	J 2	Connaught av E4
85	V 9	Connaught av SW14
16	A 5	Connaught av Barnt
8	F 9	Connaught av Enf
82	C 12	Connaught av Hounsl
50	G 6	Connaught clo E10
138	L 7	Connaught clo W2
8	F 10	Connaught clo Enf
54	D 7	Connaught clo Ilf
154	F 3	Connaught clo Sutton
27	Z 13	Connaught dri NW11
29	T 15	Connaught gdns N10
17	W 15	Connaught gdns N13
54	D 8	Connaught la Ilf
139	N 7	Connaught ms W2
139	N 7	Connaught pl W2
20	L 4	Connaught rd E4
51	Y 4	Connaught rd E11
65	Z 20	Connaught rd E16
66	A 20	Connaught rd E16
78	B 3	Connaught rd E16
33	N 16	Connaught rd E17
48	F 1	Connaught rd N4
62	B 5	Connaught rd NW10
72	A 1	Connaught rd W13
4	D 20	Connaught rd Barnt
23	W 5	Connaught rd Harrow
54	D 8	Connaught rd Ilf
118	B 8	Connaught rd New Mald
84	L 13	Connaught rd Rich
156	G 4	Connaught rd Sutton
101	S 12	Connaught rd Tedd
138	M 7	Connaught sq W2
139	N 6	Connaught sq W2
78	L 14	Connaught st SE18
138	M 6	Connaught st W2
17	X 14	Connaught way N13
60	M 10	Connell cres W5
61	N 11	Connell cres W5
3	H 20	Conningsby rd N4
20	K 10	Connington cres E4
9	S 2	Connop rd Enf
56	C 17	Connor rd Dgnhm
63	S 3	Connor st E9
71	S 2	Conolly rd W7
119	N 19	Conrad dr Worc Pk
50	X 9	Conrad st E9
91	Z 5	Consert rd SE15
92	A 7	Consert st SE15
118	G 18	Consfield av New Mald
83	S 14	Consort ms Islwth
91	Z 2	Consort rd SE15
141	U 19	Cons st SE1
28	B 19	Constable clo NW11
83	O 13	Constable clo Hounsl
31	X 15	Constable cres N15
25	O 6	Constable gdns Edg
126	C 19	Constance cres Brom
122	J 16	Constance rd Croy
18	D 1	Constance rd Enf
154	E 9	Constance rd Sutton
82	L 19	Constance rd Twick
78	C 3	Constance st E16
46	L 13	Constantine rd NW3
139	Y 17	Constitution hill SW1
95	W 2	Constitution ri SE18
150	C 7	Content st SE17
72	D 11	Convent gdns W5
137	N 6	Covent gdns W11
108	L 16	Convent hill SE19
10	L 19	Conway clo Stanm
59	V 4	Conway cres Grnfd
37	S 19	Conway cres Rom
154	A 14	Conway dri Sutton
153	Z 15	Conway dri Sutton
8	D 3	Conway gdns Enf
121	Z 9	Conway gdns Mitch
42	D 2	Conway gdns Wemb
61	Z 14	Conway gro W3
17	O 10	Conway rd N14
30	K 15	Conway rd N15
44	L 8	Conway rd NW2
79	U 12	Conway rd SE18
105	N 20	Conway rd SW20
82	F 18	Conway rd SW20
42	J 19	Conway st W1
46	K 20	Conybeare NW3
25	M 19	Conyers clo Wdfd Grn
107	W 12	Conyers rd SW16
112	H 18	Cooden clo Brom
80	C 7	Cookhill rd SE22
7	X 2	Cooks Hole rd Enf
64	E 6	Cooks rd E3
149	X 13	Cooks rd SE17
65	U 19	Coolfin rd E16
20	J 16	Coolgardie av E4
29	X 18	Coolhurst rd N8
44	B 3	Cool Oak la NW9
129	O 15	Coomassie rd W9
157	T 9	Coombe av Croy
104	A 20	Coombe bank New Mald
24	M 9	Coombe clo Edg
82	H 12	Coombe clo Hounsl
17	V 6	Coombe corner N21
100	D 16	Coombe cres Hampt
103	Y 18	Coombe end Kingst
118	B 12	Coombe Field clo New Mald
118	G 20	Coombe gdns SW20
118	C 8	Coombe gdns New Mald
103	Y 14	Coombe hill Kingst
104	C 18	Coombe Hill glade SW20
104	A 18	Coombe Hill rd Kingst
103	Z 20	Coombe Ho chase Kingst
5	Z 9	Coombehurst clo Barnt
118	H 1	Coombe la SW20
158	B 12	Coombe la Croy
117	U 1	Coombe la Kingst
103	Y 19	Coombe La west Kingst
104	C 19	Coombe La west Kingst
25	C 7	Coombe lea Brom
103	X 18	Coombe neville Kingst
118	A 3	Coombe pk Croy
157	X 8	Coombe park Croy
103	X 13	Coombe pk Kingst
103	V 13	Coombe ridings Kingst
103	V 20	Coombe ri Kingst
30	G 7	Coombe rd N22
43	Y 8	Coombe rd NW10
109	Z 9	Coombe rd SE26
74	B 14	Coombe rd W4
72	B 8	Coombe rd W13
10	B 1	Coombe rd Bushey Watford
157	W 10	Coombe rd Croy
100	D 16	Coombe rd Hampt
117	P 1	Coombe rd Kingst
118	A 3	Coombe rd New Mald
69	P 3	Coombes rd Dgnhm
153	Z 5	Coombe wlk Sutton
38	C 20	Coombe Wood dri Rom
103	W 13	Coombe Wood rd Kingst
133	Y 10	Coombs st N1
32	G 4	Cooper av E17
154	M 5	Cooper cres Carsh
44	F 16	Cooper rd NW10
156	H 9	Cooper rd Croy
34	L 3	Coopersale clo Wdfd Grn
50	G 15	Coopersale rd E9
51	S 3	Coopers la E10
132	G 9	Coopers la NW1
112	G 4	Coopers la SE12
151	P 10	Coopers la SE1
142	M 8	Coopers row EC3
65	P 16	Cooper st E16
25	U 5	Cooms wlk Edg
56	B 9	Coote gdns Dgnhm
98	A 2	Coote rd Bxly Hth
56	B 9	Coote rd Dgnhm
33	S 17	Copeland rd E17
91	Y 5	Copeland rd SE15
63	Y 17	Copenhagen pl E14
133	S 6	Copenhagen st N1
132	L 5	Copenhagen st WC1
56	A 1	Copen rd Dgnhm
145	U 2	Cope pl W8
110	M 18	Copers Cope rd Becknhm
110	O 20	Copers Cope rd Becknhm
75	T 10	Cope st SE16
133	Z 4	Copford wlk N1
134	A 3	Copford wlk N1
25	T 3	Copinge Wlk Edg
42	F 16	Copland av Wemb
42	F 16	Copland clo Wemb
42	J 17	Copland rd Wemb
91	U 9	Copleson rd SE15
59	W 12	Copley clo W7
108	C 15	Copley pk SW16
11	T 15	Copley rd Stanm
63	T 15	Copley st E1
94	C 10	Coppelia rd SE3
76	D 17	Copperas st SE8
46	F 16	Copperbeach clo NW3
63	W 13	Copperfield rd E3
141	Z 16	Copperfield st SE1
142	A 16	Copperfield st SE1
18	E 15	Copperfield ms N18
35	W 4	Copper Beach clo Ilf
44	L 9	Coppermead clo NW2
32	D 18	Coppermill la E17
106	C 10	Copper Mill la SW17
28	K 1	Coppetts clo N12
28	M 2	Coppetts rd N10
29	N 4	Coppetts rd N10
118	M 6	Coppice dri SW20
86	H 17	Coppice dri SW15
7	W 13	Coppice the Enf
14	L 10	Coppice wlk N20
34	C 11	Coppice way E18
114	D 14	Copperfield way Chisl
16	D 14	Coppies gro N11
159	S 15	Coppins the Croy
10	G 20	Coppins the Stanm
157	S 8	Copping clo Croy
159	S 6	Copse av W Wckm
14	E 20	Copse hill SW20
154	B 16	Copse hill Sutton
21	P 6	Copse the E4
158	G 18	Copse view S Croy
160	G 3	Copthall av EC2
160	F 4	Copthall clo EC2
13	U 20	Copthall dri NW7
26	G 1	Copthall gdns NW7
26	G 1	Copthall gdns NW7
101	X 1	Copthall gdns Twick
89	X 20	Copthorne av SW12
140	J 2	Coptic st WC1
80	G 7	Coralline wlk SE2
141	T 8	Coral st SE1
132	J 17	Coram st WC1
29	N 9	Coran clo N9
82	H 8	Corban rd Hounsl
5	T 5	Corbar clo Barnt
155	O 2	Corbet clo Wallgtn
135	O 19	Corbet pl E1
34	K 18	Corbett rd E11
3	V 10	Corbett rd E17
88	H 6	Coppock rd SW11
75	P 12	Corbetts pas SE16
52	A 1	Corbicum rd E11
105	P 16	Corbiere st SW19
40	L 10	Corbins la Harrow
63	N 5	Corbridge cres E2
7	N 6	Corby cres Enf
96	H 20	Corbylands rd Sidcp
114	H 1	Corbylands rd Sidcp
48	A 5	Corbyn st N4
41	X 7	Corby rd NW10
64	D 19	Cordelia st E14
63	U 18	Cordova rd E3
37	U 11	Coral clo Rom
95	P 3	Corelli rd SE3
40	F 12	Corfe av Harrow
63	N 10	Corfield st E2
135	X 15	Corfield st E2
60	J 16	Corfton rd W5
75	P 12	Corbetts la SE16
47	W 12	Corinne rd N19
116	H 17	Corkran rd Surb
159	X 5	Corkscrew hill W Wckm
140	A 10	Cork st W1
140	A 10	Cork St ms W1
138	J 1	Corlett st NW1
90	H 3	Cormont rd SE5
93	Y 12	Cordwell rd SE13
24	H 1	Cornbury rd Edg
24	H 1	Cornbury rd Edg
48	D 19	Cornelia st N7
115	Z 14	Cornell clo Sidcp
94	D 7	Corner gm SE3
26	D 3	Corner mead NW9
74	B 18	Corney rd W4
91	Z 15	Cornflower ter SE22
126	E 13	Cornford clo Brom
107	T 3	Cornford gro SW12
142	G 6	Cornhill EC3
160	G 7	Cornhill EC3
110	A 20	Cornmill la SE20
93	T 8	Cornmill la SE13
55	W 3	Cornwall av W5
50	B 10	Cornthwaite rd E5
63	O 9	Cornwall av E9
27	Z 2	Cornwall av N3
30	B 5	Cornwall av N22
58	G 15	Cornwall av S'hall
96	J 9	Cornwall av Welling
54	L 19	Cornwall clo Bark
136	L 7	Cornwall cres W11
115	T 18	Cornwall dri Orp
44	K 19	Cornwall gdns NW10
145	Z 3	Cornwall gdns SW7
146	A 3	Cornwall gdns SW7
145	Y 3	Cornwall Gdns wlk SW7
74	B 15	Cornwall gro W4
19	N 8	Cornwallis av N9
19	O 8	Cornwallis av N9
114	D 5	Cornwallis av SE9
19	O 8	Cornwallis gro N9
32	G 14	Cornwallis rd E17
48	A 7	Cornwallis rd N4
47	Z 6	Cornwallis rd N19
55	X 13	Cornwallis wlk SE9
95	U 7	Cornwallis wlk SE9
146	A 3	Cornwall Ms south SW7
145	X 2	Cornwall Ms west W8
48	F 2	Cornwall rd N4
31	O 5	Cornwall rd N15
18	K 15	Cornwall rd N18
141	T 14	Cornwall rd SE1
156	H 3	Cornwall rd Croy
22	M 17	Cornwall rd Harrow
22	E 3	Cornwall rd Pinn
153	W 19	Cornwall rd Sutton
83	Z 20	Cornwall rd Twick
63	N 19	Cornwall st E1
131	S 8	Cornwall ter NW1
28	F 14	Cornwood clo N2
63	P 17	Cornwood dri E1
55	S 16	Cornworthy rd Dgnhm
94	F 19	Corona rd SE12
49	T 11	Coronation av N16
42	L 13	Corinium clo Wemb
97	W 15	Coronation clo Bxly
36	C 13	Coronation clo Ilf
57	Y 14	Coronation dri Hornch
65	Z 10	Coronation rd E13
61	O 9	Coronation rd NW10
82	G 20	Coronation wlk Twick
134	J 13	Coronet st N1
82	A 10	Corporation av Hounsl
133	U 16	Corporation row EC1
64	M 7	Corporation st E15
65	P 6	Corporation st E15
72	X 16	Corporation st N7
48	E 11	Corrall rd N7
90	A 11	Corrance rd SW2
16	L 13	Corri av N14
45	Z 2	Corrina ct NW11
57	X 20	Cormorant wlk Hornch
45	Z 2	Corringham ct NW2
45	X 1	Corringham rd NW11
46	A 1	Corringham rd NW11
43	P 7	Corringham rd Wemb
45	Z 2	Corringway NW11

C

Ref	Street
46 A 1	Corringway NW11
60 M 16	Corringway W5
61 O 11	Corringway W5
107 U 15	Corsehill st SW16
134 G 13	Corsham st N1
48 J 17	Corsica st N5
87 W 5	Cortayne rd SW8
86 L 15	Cortis rd SW15
86 L 15	Cortis ter SW15
89 V 1	Corunna rd SW8
89 U 1	Corunna ter SW8
90 L 13	Cosbycote av SE24
155 X 15	Cosdach av Wallgtn
156 H 10	Cosedge cres Croy
132 L 20	Cosmo pl WC1
74 D 7	Cosmur clo W12
149 S 2	Coser st SE1
91 W 6	Costa st SE15
59 R 8	Costons av Grnfd
59 O 8	Costons la Grnfd
130 L 20	Cosway st NW1
64 B 16	Cotall st E14
106 M 9	Coteford st SW17
107 N 10	Coteford st S'W17
157 S 6	Coteland Croy
5 C 9	Cotesbach rd E5
55 T 13	Cotesmore gdns Dgnhm
122 M 8	Cotford rd Thntn Hth
150 C 7	Cotham st SE17
97 C 20	Cotherstone rd SW2
115 W 3	Cotleigh av Bxly
45 Y 20	Cotleigh rd NW6
39 X 18	Cotleigh rd Rom
28 C 18	Cotman clo NW11
87 O 15	Cotman clo SW15
25 O 7	Cotman gdns Edg
97 O 6	Coton rd Welling
117 X 12	Cotsford av New Mald
99 P 4	Cotswold clo Bxly Hth
103 U 14	Cotswold clo Kingst
66 B 8	Cotswold gdns E6
45 P 6	Cotswold gdns NW2
36 E 20	Cotswold gdns NW2
45 S 5	Cotswold ga NW2
7 P 13	Cotswold grn Enf
100 G 14	Cotswold rd Hampt
108 K 8	Cotswold st SE17
7 P 12	Cotswold way Enf
127 S 19	Cottage av Brom
115 U 2	Cottagefield clo Sidcp
150 H 18	Cottage grn SE5
89 Z 8	Cottage gro SW9
90 A 8	Cottage gro SW19
116 G 15	Cottage gro Surb
146 J 2	Cottage pl SW3
64 E 19	Cottage st E14
104 K 18	Cottenham dri SW20
104 G 20	Cottenham Pk rd SW20
104 K 18	Cottenham pl SW20
32 M 12	Cottenham rd E17
116 L 20	Cotterill rd Surb
75 V 18	Cottesbrook st SE14
35 V 7	Cottesmore av Ilf
145 Z 1	Cottesmore gdns W8
146 A 1	Cottesmore gdns W8
110 E 19	Cottingham rd SE20
100 A 8	Cottington rd Felt
149 V 9	Cottington st SE11
63 Y 12	Cottisford rd E3
61 Y 16	Cotton av W3
111 W 9	Cotton hill Brom
64 F 19	Cotton st E14
39 N 16	Cottons app Rom
29 X 18	Couch Hall rd N8
35 T 7	Couchmore av Ilf
43 X 19	Couch rd NW10
92 J 8	Coulgate st SE4
147 O 8	Coulson st SW3
74 K 8	Coulter rd W6
144 A 2	Coulter rd W6
150 A 20	Councillor st SE5
142 E 15	Counter st SE1
47 V 14	Countess rd NW5
18 G 1	Countisbury av Enf
100 B 9	Country way Felt
67 V 6	County gdns Bark
114 C 6	County ga SE9
15 O 1	County ga Barnt
90 L 1	County gro SE5
66 L 15	County rd E6
122 J 4	County rd Thntn Hth
150 C 3	County st SE1
150 D 3	County st SE1
79 O 14	Coupland pla SE18
70 N 8	Courcy rd N8
89 Y 3	Courland gro SW9
89 Y 3	Courland st SW8
113 X 7	Course the SE9
13 A 2	Court av SE2
24 H 12	Court clo Harrow
155 X 17	Court clo Wallgtn
100 J 6	Court Clo av Twick
125 R 3	Court Downs rd Becknhm
156 D 7	Court dri Croy
31 X 14	Court dri Stanm
154 J 8	Court dri Sutton
46 H 1	Courtenay av N6
47 Z 4	Courtland rd N19
22 L 2	Courtenay av Harrow
23 N 6	Courtenay av Harrow
23 N 6	Courtenay gdns Har
23 N 7	Courtenay gdns Harrow
28 H 20	Courtenay av N6
52 C 9	Courtenay rd E11
32 G 14	Courtenay rd E17
110 G 16	Courtenay rd SE20
153 N 5	Courtenay rd Worc Pk
149 S 10	Courtenay sq SE11
149 S 10	Courtenay st SE11
58 G 1	Court Farm la Grnfd
113 O 6	Court Farm rd SE9
58 H 1	Court Farm rd Grnfd
23 W 17	Courtfield av Harrow
23 X 16	Courtfield cres Harrow
145 Y 6	Courtfield gdns SW5
145 Z 6	Courtfield gdns SW5
59 Z 17	Courtfield gdns SW5
159 Y 5	Courtfield ri W Wckhm
146 A 6	Courtfield rd SW7
93 U 12	Courthill rd SE13
47 N 13	Courthope rd NW3
105 R 13	Courthope rd SW19
59 P 5	Courthope rd Grnfd
105 T 17	Courthope vlls SE19
M 19	Court House gdns N3
14 M 18	Court House rd N12
21 P 8	Courtland av E4
108 D 18	Courtland av SW16
126 A 20	Courtland av Brom
53 T 6	Courtland av Ilf
85 P 12	Courtlands Rich
94 G 12	Courtlands av SE12
12 M 9	Courtlands av NW7
13 N 9	Courtlands av NW7
16 E 16	Courtlands av Hampt
85 T 3	Courtlands av Rich
152 C 14	Courtlands dri Epsom
117 P 16	Courtlands rd Surb
117 P 17	Courtlands rd Surb
91 V 18	Court la SE21
91 T 17	Court La gdns SE21
91 T 17	Court Lane gdns SE21
98 H 2	Courtleet dri Erith
5 T 3	Courtleigh av Barnt
27 T 14	Courtleigh gdns NW11
30 M 2	Courtman rd N17
31 N 3	Courtman rd N17
90 M 16	Courtmead clo SE24
58 E 8	Court mead Grnfd
137 S 5	Courtnell st W2
109 R 16	Courtney clo SE19
154 M 18	Courtney cres Carsh
156 G 5	Courtney pl Croy
32 J 15	Courtney pl E17
48 G 14	Courtney rd N7
106 J 18	Courtney rd SW19
16 F 5	Courtrai rd SE23
92 H 15	Court rd SE9
58 U 17	Court rd SE9
113 S 3	Court rd SE9
123 V 5	Court rd SE25
116 B 5	Court rd Kingst
70 E 13	Court rd S'hall
29 X 19	Courtside N8
16 F 2	Court st Brom
158 M 20	Courtswood la Croy
24 A 15	Court the Ruislip
26 B 12	Court way NW9
61 W 14	Court way W3
36 C 11	Court way Ilf
83 W 18	Court way Twick
21 Y 16	Court way Wdfd Grn
95 S 17	Court yd SE9
95 S 16	Court yd SE9
160 D 10	Courza la EC4
77 W 18	Couthurst rd SE3
85 U 11	Coval gdns SW14
85 T 10	Coval la SW14
85 U 10	Coval rd SW14
7 S 3	Covell Enf
140 L 8	Covent gdn WC2
116 L 16	Covent hill SE19
63 N 12	Coventry rd E1
135 Y 17	Coventry rd E1
123 X 8	Coventry rd SE25
53 X 5	Coventry rd Ilf
54 B 3	Coventry rd Ilf
135 Y 15	Coventry st E2
140 E 10	Coventry st W1
6 F 20	Coverack clo N14
16 F 1	Coverack clo N14
124 J 18	Coverack clo Croy
11 P 15	Coverdale clo Stanm
157 U 6	Coverdale gdn Croy
45 N 19	Coverdale rd NW2
74 L 4	Coverdale rd W12
136 A 16	Coverdale rd W12
67 R 6	Coverdales the Bark
106 J 11	Coverton rd SW17
5 S 7	Covert way Barnt
108 J 19	Covington gdns SW16
108 E 16	Covington way SW16
108 J 18	Covington way SW16
150 J 13	Cowan st SE5
25 N 13	Cowbridge rd Harrow
133 X 20	Cowcross st EC1
111 O 9	Cowden st SE6
133 N 3	Cowdenbeath pth N1
57 V 13	Cowdray way Hornch
8 D 9	Cowdrey clo Enf
99 Z 20	Cowdrey ct Drtfd
106 B 14	Cowdrey rd SW19
50 K 17	Cowdry rd E9
41 O 8	Cowen av Harrow
59 R 7	Cowgate rd Grnfd
106 M 9	Cowick rd SW17
107 N 10	Cowick rd SW17
40 C 19	Cowings mead Grnfd
9 R 13	Cowland av Enf
59 P 7	Cow la Grnfd
116 K 1	Cowleaze rd Kingst
51 Z 9	Cowley la E11
34 G 16	Cowley rd E11
149 J 20	Cowley rd SW9
86 A 7	Cowley rd SW13
90 F 2	Cowley rd SW19
54 C 4	Cowley rd W3
53 U 2	Cowley rd Ilf
39 Z 1	Cowley rd Rom
148 J 1	Cowley st SW1
54 C 4	Cowper av E6
154 G 9	Cowper av Sutton
127 O 10	Cowper clo Brom
97 O 12	Cowper clo Welling
6 F 19	Cowper gdns N14
155 V 14	Cowper gdns Wallgtn
16 E 5	Cowper rd N14
49 R 13	Cowper rd N16
18 J 18	Cowper rd N18
106 D 15	Cowper rd SW19
73 X 2	Cowper rd W3
59 V 19	Cowper rd W7
81 P 11	Cowper rd Blvdr
127 N 10	Cowper rd Brom
102 M 12	Cowper rd Kingst
134 G 15	Cowper st EC2
72 E 2	Cowper ter W10
34 H 8	Cowslip rd E18
89 X 1	Cowthorpe rd SW8
89 Y 1	Cawthorpe rd SW8
78 A 13	Coxmount rd SE7
141 Z 3	Cox's ct EC1
143 N 18	Coxsons wy SE1
109 Y 2	Coxs wk SE21
79 T 13	Coxwell rd SE18
111 W 18	Crab hill Becknhm
37 W 12	Crabtree av Rom
40 K 5	Crabtree av Wemb
51 S 15	Crabtree ct E15
144 F 17	Crabtree la SW6
81 W 7	Crabtree Mnr way Belvdr
8 G 13	Craddock rd Enf
47 O 19	Craddock st NW5
114 D 2	Cradley rd SE9
39 U 20	Craigdale rd Hornch
57 U 1	Craigdale rd Hornch
124 A 20	Craigen av Croy
158 A 1	Craigen av Croy
77 U 19	Craigerne rd SE3
34 C 7	Craig gdns E18
95 X 3	Craigholm SE9
61 O 2	Craigmuir pk Wemb
90 E 18	Craignair rd SW2
122 D 2	Craignish av SW16
18 M 15	Craig Park rd N18
102 E 9	Craig rd Rich
140 J 13	Craigs ct SW1
95 T 11	Craigton rd SE9
11 T 17	Craigwell av Stanm
11 T 16	Craigwell dri Stanm
150 F 6	Crail row SE17
139 U 2	Cramer st W1
110 B 16	Crampton rd SE20
58 A 6	Crampton st SE17
58 A 6	Cranberry clo Grnfd
135 T 18	Cranberry st E1
70 H 11	Cranborne av S'hall
36 D 11	Cranborne gdns Ilf
53 P 14	Cranborne rd E12
67 S 3	Cranbourne av Bark
140 H 9	Cranbourne all WC2
34 H 13	Cranbourne av E11
27 U 16	Cranbourne gdns NW11
51 U 12	Cranbourne rd E15
29 T 8	Cranbourne rd N10
140 H 9	Cranbourn st WC2
126 E 15	Cranbrook clo Brom
82 K 20	Cranbrook dri Twick
63 S 7	Cranbrook estate E2
32 K 15	Cranbrook mews E17
30 E 6	Cranbrook pk N22
53 U 19	Cranbrook rise Ilf
95 N 7	Cranbrook rd SE3
93 O 2	Cranbrook rd SE8
105 S 18	Cranbrook rd SW19
74 B 13	Cranbrook rd W4
5 V 20	Cranbrook rd Barnt
98 C 1	Cranbrook rd Bxly Hth
52 C 10	Cranbrook rd Hounsl
35 W 1	Cranbrook rd Ilf
36 A 12	Cranbrook rd Ilf
53 W 2	Cranbrook rd Ilf
122 M 2	Cranbrook rd Thntn Hth
88 A 5	Cranbury rd SW6
61 X 20	Crane av W3
56 F 19	Crane clo Dgnhm
87 Y 13	Crane av Islwrth
141 U 5	Crane ct EC4
89 W 19	Craneford clo Twick
83 U 19	Craneford way Twick
48 G 18	Crane gro N7
75 S 12	Crane mead SE16
100 G 4	Crane park Twick
100 J 4	Crane Pk rd Twick
101 T 1	Crane rd Twick
116 K 10	Crane dri Surb
116 K 11	Cranes pk Surb
116 K 10	Cranes Pk av Surb
116 L 10	Cranes Pk cres Surb
70 F 13	Craneswater pk S'hall
76 J 15	Crane st SE10
83 O 17	Crane way Twick
92 L 7	Cranefield rd SE4
155 O 19	Cranfield rd Carsh
108 L 8	Cranfield vlls SE27
17 O 16	Cranford av N13
104 H 19	Cranford clo SW20
63 T 19	Cranford Cottages E1
70 B 19	Cranford la Hounsl
63 T 19	Cranford st E1
39 Z 18	Cranhurst rd Hornch
44 M 15	Cranhurst rd NW2
123 Z 2	Cranleigh clo Bxly
98 F 15	Cranleigh clo Bxly
7 T 17	Cranleigh gdns N21
135 S 5	Cranleigh gdns Bark
54 E 19	Cranleigh gdns Bark
24 J 16	Cranleigh gdns Harrow
103 N 15	Cranleigh gdns Kingst
58 D 17	Cranleigh gdns S'hall
154 A 3	Cranleigh gdns Sutton
30 L 14	Cranleigh rd N15
119 X 6	Cranleigh rd SW19
132 C 9	Cranleigh st NW1
36 C 20	Cranleigh dri Ilf
54 C 1	Cranley dri Ilf
29 S 14	Cranley gdns N10
17 R 10	Cranley gdns N13
149 D 9	Cranley gdns SW7
155 U 15	Cranley gdns Wallgtn
146 D 9	Cranley ms SW7
146 F 7	Cranley pl SW7
65 V 14	Cranley rd E13
36 B 20	Cranley rd Ilf
89 Y 7	Cranmar ct SW4
72 B 8	Cranmer av W13
119 R 14	Cranmer clo Mrdn
24 E 1	Cranmer clo Stanm
100 K 11	Cranmer ct Hampt
120 L 9	Cranmer Farm clo Mitch
56 K 13	Cranmer gdns Dgnhm
52 J 11	Cranmer rd E7
156 K 5	Cranmer rd Croy
12 E 10	Cranmer rd Edg
100 L 11	Cranmer rd Hampt
102 K 13	Cranmer rd Kingst
121 N 10	Cranmer rd Mitch

C

C
D

143 N 7 Crosswall EC3
15 U 19 Crossway N16
49 T 15 Crossway N16
26 D 14 Crossway NW9
26 E 14 Crossway NW9
68 J 20 Crossway SE2
118 M 9 Crossway SW20
59 Y 11 Crossway W13
55 T 10 Cross way Dgnhm
18 D 2 Crossway Enf
21 Y 14 Cross way Wdfd Grn
7 Y 1 Crossways N21
39 Z 11 Crossways Rom
158 K 16 Crossways S Croy
154 F 18 Crossways Sutton
125 N 9 Crossways rd
Becknhm
121 S 5 Crossways rd Mitch
70 E 20 Crossways the
Hounsl
43 R 7 Crossways the
Wemb
30 K 3 Crossway the N22
113 O 4 Crossway the SE9
23 U 6 Cross Way the
Harrow
68 D 7 Crouch av Bark
111 P 16 Crouch clo Becknhm
113 X 7 Crouch croft SE19
29 Z 19 Crouch End hill N8
29 Y 18 Crouch Hall rd N8
48 A 1 Crouch hill N4
109 V 8 Crouchmans clo SE21
107 P 13 Crowborough rd
SW17
80 H 1 Crowden way SE2
143 W 9 Crowder st E1
16 M 3 Crowland gdns N14
31 V 16 Crowland rd N15
123 N 9 Crowland rd Thntn
Hth
38 H 18 Crowlands av Rom
49 N 20 Crowland ter N1
120 B 13 Crowland wlk Mrdn
56 H 1 Crow la Rom
156 H 11 Crowley cres Croy
141 T 8 Crown-Office row
EC4
13 S 7 Crown clo NW7
13 T 7 Crown clo NW7
160 C 6 Crown ct EC4
94 G 16 Crown ct SE12
140 M 7 Crown ct WC2
108 L 14 Crown dale SE19
132 B 8 Crowndale rd NW1
36 F 17 Crownfield av Ilf
51 W 13 Crownfield rd E15
156 L 4 Crown hill Croy
62 D 4 Crownhill rd NW10
35 R 3 Crownhill rd Wdfd
Grn
16 H 5 Crown la N14
108 G 14 Crown la SW16
127 O 13 Crown la Brom
119 Z 7 Crown la Mrdn
127 O 13 Crown la Spur Brom
108 G 13 Crown La gdns
SW16
38 H 13 Crownmead way
Rom
140 C 14 Crown pas SW1
47 T 17 Crown pl NW5
29 P 2 Crown rd N10
8 M 14 Crown rd Enf
30 D 13 Crown rd Ilf
119 Z 6 Crown rd Mrdn
117 X 1 Crown rd New Mald
153 Z 9 Crown rd Sutton
154 A 8 Crown rd Sutton
84 C 17 Crown rd Twick
150 B 18 Crown st SE5
73 T 3 Crown st W3
56 J 19 Crown st Dgnhm
41 S 4 Crown st Harrow
90 E 13 Crownstone rd SW2
84 M 9 Crown ter Rich
43 O 8 Crown wlk Wemb
96 A 7 Crownwoods la SE9
95 Z 4 Crown Woods la
SE18
96 F 12 Crownwoods way
SE9
24 F 6 Crowshott av Stanm
64 L 8 Crows rd E15
72 K 12 Crowther av Brentf
43 O 8 Crown wlk Wemb
123 X 10 Crowther rd SE25
120 C 14 Croxden wlk Mrdn
30 K 3 Croxford gdns N22
56 L 4 Croxford way Rom
129 R 13 Croxley rd W9
90 L 19 Croxted clo SE21
91 N 2 Croxted rd SE21
90 L 18 Croxted rd SE24

59 O 9 Croyde av Grnfd
24 H 3 Crowther clo Stanm
122 H 19 Croydon gro Croy
65 R 12 Croydon rd E13
110 D 20 Croydon rd SE20
123 Z 4 Croydon rd SE20
124 L 6 Croydon rd Becknhm
156 B 8 Croydon rd Croy
121 T 11 Croydon rd Mitch
155 V 7 Croydon rd Wallgtn
18 J 5 Croyland rd N9
129 P 15 Croyland rd N9
50 G 16 Crozier ter E9
142 K 17 Crucifix la SE1
133 Y 6 Cruden st N1
133 R 11 Cruickshank st WC1
52 B 14 Cruikshank rd E15
26 B 16 Crummock gdns
NW9
80 F 11 Crumpsall st SE2
25 R 17 Crundale av NW9
157 O 15 Crunden rd S Croy
96 E 18 Croyde clo Sidcp
106 M 18 Crusoe rd Mitch
142 L 8 Crutched friars EC3
112 A 4 Crutchley rd SE6
157 S 6 Crusader gdn Croy
109 U 12 Crystal st SE19
103 Y 12 Crystal Palace park
SE26
109 V 13 Crystal Palace pde
SE19
91 W 10 Crystal Palace rd
SE22
109 W 16 Crystal Palace Stn rd
SE19
109 O 15 Crystal ter SE19
9 O 9 Cuba dri Enf
76 A 4 Cuba st E14
133 O 14 Cubitt st WC1
156 E 11 Cubitt st Croy
89 V 7 Cubitt terr SW4
59 S 13 Cuckoo av W7
59 S 13 Cuckoo dene W7
19 P 2 Cuckoo Hall la N9
59 U 19 Cuckoo la W7
152 D 7 Cudas clo Epsom
152 D 6 Cuddington av Worc
Pk
93 T 18 Cudham st SE6
63 N 11 Cudworth st E1
135 X 16 Cudworth st E1
95 P 17 Cuff cres SE9
147 O 7 Culford gdns SW3
49 R 19 Culford gro N1
49 R 18 Culford ms N1
49 R 18 Culford rd N1
134 J 2 Culford rd N1
7 N 13 Culgaith gdns Enf
61 W 12 Cullen way NW10
75 O 7 Culling rd SE16
143 Z 20 Culling st SE16
23 X 13 Cullington clo
Harrow
44 H 15 Cullingworth rd
NW10
7 V 9 Culloden rd Enf
142 J 7 Cullum st EC3
156 K 18 Culmington rd S
Croy
107 R 1 Culmore cross SW4
75 O 20 Culmore rd SE14
151 Z 19 Culmore rd SE15
89 O 13 Culmstock rd SW11
59 T 5 Culpepper st N1
30 L 14 Culross clo N15
139 S 9 Culross st W1
24 F 8 Culver gro Stanm
108 C 8 Culverhouse gdns
SW16
11 N 14 Culverlands clo
Stanm
93 R 20 Culverley rd SE6
111 U 1 Culverley rd SE6
154 L 2 Culvers av Carsh
155 N 1 Culvers av Carsh
155 N 2 Culvers retreat
Carsh
126 C 13 Culvestone clo Brom
154 L 3 Culvers way Carsh
89 O 5 Culvert pl SW11
31 R 16 Culvert rd N15
89 N 4 Culvert rd SW11
130 K 10 Culworth st NW8
123 W 7 Cumbedow av SE25
61 T 9 Cumberland av
NW10
96 K 10 Cumberland av
Welling
49 U 18 Cumberland clo
E8
105 N 18 Cumberland clo
SW20

84 B 15 Cumberland clo
Twick
144 M 5 Cumberland cres
W14
80 M 20 Cumberland dri Bxly
Hth
98 A 1 Cumberland dri Bxly
Hth
27 R 4 Cumberland gdns
NW4
133 R 12 Cumberland gdns
WC1
139 N 5 Cumberland mans
W1
131 Z 12 Cumberland mkt
NW1
61 X 20 Cumberland pk W3
73 W 1 Cumberland pk W3
131 X 12 Cumberland pl NW1
53 N 14 Cumberland rd E12
65 V 11 Cumberland rd E13
32 H 7 Cumberland rd E17
19 P 7 Cumberland rd N9
30 D 6 Cumberland rd N22
86 E 1 Cumberland rd
SW13
61 W 20 Cumberland rd W3
71 W 6 Cumberland rd W7
125 Z 8 Cumberland rd Brom
126 C 8 Cumberland rd Brom
22 K 15 Cumberland rd
Harrow
73 O 20 Cumberland rd Rich
25 N 11 Cumberland rd
Stanm
147 Y 10 Cumberland st SW1
148 A 11 Cumberland st SW1
131 W 10 Cumberland ter NW1
131 X 10 Cumberland Terr ms
NW1
124 A 13 Cumberland va SE25
31 P 5 Cumberton rd N17
99 R 4 Cumbrian av Bxly
Hth
45 R 7 Cumbrian gdns NW2
133 O 9 Cumming st N1
152 H 15 Cumnor gdns Epsom
154 E 13 Cumnor rd Sutton
61 Z 9 Cunard rd NW10
65 X 18 Cundy rd E16
147 V 7 Cundy st SW1
152 F 8 Cunliffe rd Worc Pk
107 V 14 Cunliffe st SW16
159 S 3 Cunningham clo W
Wckm
23 P 15 Cunningham pk
Harrow
130 F 16 Cunningham pl NW8
31 W 13 Cunningham rd N15
73 W 10 Cunnington st W4
89 R 1 Cupar rd SW11
112 G 12 Cupola clo Brom
148 G 8 Cureton st SW1
68 J 20 Curlew clo SE2
143 O 16 Curlew st SE1
107 U 5 Curlverden rd SW12
108 L 11 Curnicks la SE27
155 P 6 Curran av Wallgtn
96 L 14 Currant av Sidcp
41 P 18 Currey rd Grnfd
74 A 4 Curricle st W3
105 V 10 Currie Hill clo SW19
14 C 18 Curry rise NW7
141 S 4 Cursitor st EC4
134 K 14 Curtain rd EC2
6 L 15 Curthwaite gdns Enf
73 O 1 Curtis rd Hounsl
150 M 4 Curtis st SE1
68 E 20 Curtis way SE2
62 F 20 Curve the W12
52 G 12 Curwen av E7
74 F 6 Curwen rd W12
9 U 17 Curzon av Enf
23 Y 5 Curzon av Stanm
44 B 20 Curzon cres NW10
62 C 1 Curzon cres NW10
67 X 8 Curzon cres Bark
139 V 14 Curzon pl W1
29 S 7 Curzon rd N10
60 B 12 Curzon rd W5
122 E 14 Curzon rd Thntn Hth
139 W 13 Curzon st W1
101 V 8 Cursack clo Twick
81 Z 13 Cusack rd Erith
90 M 5 Cutcombe rd SE5
33 V 11 Cuthbert rd E17
18 K 15 Cuthbert rd N18
156 J 3 Cuthbert rd Croy
130 F 20 Cuthbert st W2
142 L 4 Cutler st E1
102 D 3 Cutthroat all Rich
97 X 12 Cuxton clo Bxly Hth
135 O 16 Cygnet st E2
100 A 10 Cygnets the Felt

133 P 9 Cynthia st N1
83 N 18 Cypress av Twick
132 C 19 Cypress pl W1
123 T 3 Cypress rd SE25
23 P 7 Cypress rd Harrow
27 U 7 Cyprus av N3
27 T 6 Cyprus gdns N3
63 P 7 Cyprus pl E2
63 R 7 Cyprus pl E2
66 K 19 Cyprus place E6
27 V 8 Cyprus rd N3
18 G 7 Cyprus rd N9
63 R 7 Cyprus st E2
93 V 15 Cyrena rd SE22
98 A 5 Cyril rd Bxly Hth
133 X 15 Cyrus st EC1
75 Z 16 Czar st SE8

D

40 J 14 Dabbs Hill la Grnfrd
93 T 2 Dabia cres SE10
75 Z 15 Dacca st SE8
64 A 2 Dace rd E3
35 X 7 Dace av Ilf
58 L 5 Dacre clo Grnfd
93 Z 10 Dacre gdn SE13
93 Z 7 Dacre pk SE13
94 A 10 Dacre pk SE13
93 Z 8 Dacre pl SE13
52 B 3 Dacre rd E11
65 U 4 Dacre rd E13
122 A 17 Dacre rd Croy
110 E 7 Dacres rd SE23
140 F 20 Dacre st SW1
74 E 1 Daffodil st W12
62 E 20 Daffodil st W12
107 N 7 Dafforne rd SW1
68 M 3 Dagenham av
Dgnhm
68 K 4 Dagenham av
Dgnhm
69 N 1 Dagenham av
Dgnhm
69 U 1 Dagenham av
Dgnhm
69 U 1 Dagenham Old park
Dgnhm
50 M 3 Dagenham rd E10
56 J 11 Dagenham rd Dgnhm
57 N 4 Dagenham rd Rom
42 L 13 Dagmar av Wemb
43 N 13 Dagmar av Wemb
128 E 10 Dagmar gdns NW10
133 X 3 Dagmar pas N1
31 O 14 Dagmar rd N15
29 V 4 Dagmar rd N22
91 R 3 Dagmar rd SE5
123 R 10 Dagmar rd SE25
56 L 19 Dagmar rd Dgnhm
70 C 9 Dagmar rd S'hall
133 X 3 Dagmar ter N1
123 P 13 Dagnall pk SE25
123 R 11 Dagnall rd SE25
89 N 3 Dagnall st SW11
89 T 17 Dagnan rd SW12
112 F 14 Dagonet gdns Brom
112 E 7 Dagonet rd Brom
121 X 9 Dahlia gdns Mitch
80 O 12 Dahlia rd SE2
107 U 15 Dahomey rd SW16
156 A 15 Dailmer way Wallgtn
53 V 10 Daines clo E12
111 W 12 Dainford clo Brom
112 K 19 Dainton clo Brom
50 L 17 Daintry way E9
95 Y 7 Dairsie rd SE9
105 W 9 Dairy wlk SW19
87 Y 3 Daisy la SW6
34 H 8 Daisy rd E18
90 F 13 Dalberg rd SW2
88 C 11 Dalby st SW18
47 N 18 Dalby st NW5
82 A 5 Dalcross rd Hounsl
24 M 6 Dale av Edg
25 N 7 Dale av Hounsl
82 C 7 Dale av Hounsl
106 K 4 Dalebury rd SW17
94 D 8 Dale clo SE3
5 N 20 Dale clo Barnt
90 U 14 Dale clo Drtfrd
99 U 17 Dale end Drtfrd
21 V 13 Dale gdns Wdfd Grn
16 F 12 Dale Green rd N11
46 F 17 Daleham gdns NW3
46 F 17 Daleham ms NW3
154 M 3 Dale Park av Carsh
155 N 3 Dale Park av Carsh
109 N 20 Dale Park rd SE19

65	N 15	Dale rd E16
47	O 15	Dale rd NW5
99	U 16	Dale rd Drtfrd
58	K 15	Dale rd Grnfd
153	V 9	Dale rd Sutton
78	M 17	Dale rd SE18
107	V 9	Daleside rd SW16
74	A 14	Dale st W4
136	L 6	Dale row W11
99	V 4	Daleview Erith
20	H 9	Dale View av E4
20	G 9	Dale View cres E4
20	H 9	Dale View gdns E4
31	S 19	Daleview rd N15
152	L 2	Dalewood gdns Worc Pk
50	F 17	Daley st E9
62	L 14	Dalgarno gdns W10
128	C 20	Dalgarno gdns W10
136	A 1	Dalgarno gdns W10
62	M 12	Dalgarno way W10
128	D 19	Dalgarno way W10
63	X 17	Dalgleish st E14
11	W 17	Dalkeith gro Stanm
90	M 20	Dalkeith rd SE21
54	C 10	Dalkeith rd Ilf
44	H 1	Dallas rd NW4
109	Z 8	Dallas rd SE26
110	A 8	Dallas rd SE26
60	M 14	Dallas rd W5
153	T 14	Dallas rd Sutton
94	B 17	Dallinger rd SE12
74	J 8	Dalling rd W6
133	X 16	Dallington st EC1
78	M 18	Dallin rd SE18
79	N 18	Dallin rd SE18
97	X 10	Dallin rd Bxly Hth
63	W 5	Daling wy E3
92	F20	Dalmain rd SE23
123	W 17	Dalmally rd Croy
47	Z 14	Dalmeny av N7
122	F 4	Dalmeny av SW16
42	E 17	Dalmeny clo Wemb
83	P 9	Dalmeny cres Hounsl
47	X 10	Dalmeny rd N1
5	S 20	Dalmeny rd Barnt
98	G 2	Dalmeny rd Bxly Hth
155	P 17	Dalmeny rd Carsh
152	K 5	Dalmeny rd Worc Park
115	R 7	Damon clo Sidcp
108	M 3	Dalmore rd SE21
92	J 12	Dalrymple rd SE4
24	J 6	Dalston gdns Stanm
50	A 15	Dalston la E5
49	V 18	Dalston la E8
120	H 3	Dalton av Mitch
99	U 6	Dalton clo Drtfrd
91	S 1	Dalton st SE5
108	K 5	Dalton st SE27
150	L 20	Dalwood st SE15
90	C 8	Dalyell rd SW9
103	T 19	Dalziel Of Wooler home Kingst
146	C 19	Damer ter SW10
52	F 12	Dames rd E7
63	N 17	Damien st E1
143	Y 4	Damien st E1
70	H 9	Damsonwood clo S'hall
108	B 19	Danbrook rd SW16
37	V 10	Danbury clo Rom
155	S 8	Danbury ms Wallgtn
133	Y 8	Danbury st N1
21	Y 20	Danbury way Wdfd Grn
91	U 7	Danby st SE15
87	V 3	Dancer rd SW6
85	P 7	Dancer rd Rich
94	G 8	Dando cres SE3
86	B 16	Danebury av SW15
159	U 14	Danebury Croy
111	S 5	Daneby rd SE6
98	E 19	Dane clo Bxly
157	V 5	Dane Court gdns Croy
91	N 13	Danecroft rd SE24
35	S 17	Danehurst gdns Ilf
87	S 1	Danehurst st SW6
5	Z 20	Daneland Barnt
40	K 15	Danemead gro Grnfd
87	N 7	Danemere st SW15
63	X 6	Dane pl E3
19	P 13	Dane rd N18
106	D 20	Dane rd SW19
72	D 2	Dane rd W13
54	A 16	Dane rd Ilf
58	C 20	Dane rd S'hall
94	F 20	Danescombe SE12
154	D 3	Danescourt cres Sutton
27	R 16	Danescroft av NW4
27	R 16	Danescroft gdns NW4
50	H 18	Danesdale rd E9
23	S 11	Danes ga Harrow
38	K 20	Danes rd Rom
111	T 7	Daneswood av SE6
42	F 18	Danethorpe rd Wemb
56	D 8	Danette gdns Dgnhm
91	N 3	Daneville rd SE5
34	E 19	Dangan rd E11
64	E 14	Daniel Bolt clo E14
150	M 16	Daniel gdns SE15
151	O 17	Daniel gdns SE15
26	J 20	Daniel pl NW4
61	O 20	Daniel rd W5
92	C 8	Daniels rd SE15
140	F 9	Dansey pl W1
97	O 9	Dansington rd Welling
97	O 9	Danson cres Welling
07	P 10	Danson la Welling
97	V 9	Danson mead Welling
149	Y 12	Danson rd SE17
97	U 15	Danson rd Bxly
97	V 12	Danson rd Bxly Hth
149	X 6	Dante rd SE11
146	L 9	Danube st SW3
29	W 12	Danvers rd N8
146	H 15	Danvers st SW3
20	G 10	Daphne gdns E4
88	B 17	Daphne st SW18
140	D 6	Darblay st W1
155	V 8	Darcy av Wallgtn
15	T 9	Darcy clo N20
24	H 14	Darcy dri Harrow
69	P 2	Darcy gdns Dgnhm
24	J 13	Darcy gdns Harrow
121	Z 3	Darcy rd SW16
153	O 8	Darcy rd Sutton
55	Z 10	Dare gdns Dgnhm
85	P 7	Darell rd Rich
49	V 2	Darenth rd N16
97	O 2	Darenth rd Welling
92	K 13	Darfield rd SE4
87	O8	Darfur st SW15
109	V 17	Dargate cl SE19
88	G 8	Darien rd SW11
145	R 20	Darlan rd SW6
105	R 18	Darlaston rd SW19
124	H 16	Darley clo Croy
117	Y 3	Darley dri New Mald
18	G 4	Darley rd N9
93	O 7	Darling rd SE4
63	N 13	Darling row E1
135	Y 19	Darling row E1
108	K 12	Darlington rd SE27
88	L 15	Darly clo SW11
50	B 19	Darnley rd E9
34	G 4	Darnley rd Wdfd Grn
136	J 13	Darnley ter W11
91	X 13	Darrell rd SE22
89	Z 1	Darsley dri SW8
19	R 1	Dartford av N9
99	Y 15	Dartford rd Drtfrd
150	B 13	Dartford st SE17
93	V 3	Dartmouth gro SE10
93	V 3	Dartmouth hill SE10
47	T 9	Dartmouth Pk av NW5
47	T 5	Dartmouth Pk hill NW5
47	S 10	Dartmouth Pk rd NW5
74	B 18	Dartmouth pl W4
110	D 4	Dartmouth pl SE23
65	S 17	Dartmouth rd E16
45	O 17	Dartmouth rd NW2
26	G 19	Dartmouth rd NW4
110	C 5	Dartmouth rd SE26
126	F 17	Dartmouth rd Brom
93	V 3	Dartmouth row SE10
140	F 19	Dartmouth st SW1
123	U 17	Dartnell rd Croy
129	N 12	Dart st W10
49	V 10	Darville rd N16
66	J 7	Darwell clo E6
58	L 17	Darwin dri S'hall
30	J 7	Darwin rd N22
72	F 12	Darwin rd W5
96	L 8	Darwin rd Welling
150	G 5	Darwin st SE17
59	T 6	Daryngton dri Grnfd
98	E 14	Dashwood clo Bxly Hth
30	C 19	Dashwood rd N8
108	K 12	Dassett rd SE27
91	P 2	Datchelor pl SE5
110	L 6	Datchet rd SE6
150	D 10	Date st SE17
50	H 12	Daubeney rd E5
30	L 2	Daubeney rd N17
88	C 15	Daulte rd SW18
156	J 7	Daveant la Croy
47	Z 7	Davenant rd N19
143	T 2	Davenant st E1
93	T 16	Davenport rd SE6
115	Y 4	Davenport rd Sidcp
33	O 17	Daventry av E17
130	K 20	Daventry st NW1
77	O 12	Davern clo SE10
49	E 19	Davey clo N7
151	O 15	Davey st SE15
59	T 8	David av Grnfd
141	X 19	Davidge st SE1
131	S 20	David ms W1
55	X 6	David rd Dgnhm
148	J 18	Davidson gdns SW1
123	U 15	Davidson rd Croy
110	C 2	Davids rd SE23
51	Y 16	David st E15
36	G 1	Davids way Ilf
52	A 5	Davies la E11
139	W 8	Davies ms W1
139	W 8	Davies st W1
55	R 16	Davington gdns Dgnhm
55	R 15	Davington rd Dgnhm
74	D 4	Davis rd W3
65	W 7	Davis st E13
74	G 6	Davisville rd W12
83	X 11	Dawes av Islwth
144	K 17	Dawes rd SW6
145	P 18	Dawes rd SW6
150	F 8	Dawes st SE17
150	G 9	Dawes st SE17
16	M 14	Dawlish av N13
17	N 15	Dawlish av N13
106	A 4	Dawlish av SW18
59	Z 7	Dawlish av Grnfd
60	A 7	Dawlish av Grnfd
54	H 12	Dawlish dri Ilf
22	B 17	Dawlish dri Pinn
51	T 5	Dawlish rd E10
31	W 9	Dawlish rd N17
45	P 17	Dawlish rd NW2
106	E 4	Dawnay gdns SW18
106	E 3	Dawnay rd SW18
82	B 7	Dawn clo Hounsl
44	E 7	Dawpool rd NW2
13	T 16	Daws la NW7
67	W 2	Dawson av Bark
67	Y 2	Dawson av Bark
67	Y 2	Dawson gdns Bark
137	U 9	Dawson pl W2
45	N 13	Dawson rd NW2
117	N 6	Dawson rd Surb
135	O 9	Dawson st E2
120	A 4	Daybrook rd SW19
86	G 9	Daylesford av SW15
108	C 2	Daysbrook rd SW2
96	G 20	Days la Sidcp
92	C 1	Dayton gro SE15
44	G 16	Deacon rd NW2
116	M 1	Deacon rd Kingst
100	G 11	Deacons way Hampt
150	B 4	Deacon way SE17
107	O 15	Deal rd SW17
135	S 19	Deal st E1
86	L 10	Dealtry rd SW15
148	J 4	Dean Bradley st SW1
42	C 9	Dean ct Wemb
63	O 17	Deancross st E1
143	Z 6	Deancross st E1
24	K 8	Dean dri Stanm
139	U 13	Deanery ms W1
51	Z 18	Deanery rd E15
52	A 19	Deanery rd E15
139	U 13	Deanery st W1
140	F 20	Dean Farar st SW1
33	W 12	Dean gdns E17
85	T 10	Dean hill ct SW14
85	U 10	Deanhill rd SW14
44	M 17	Dean pl NW2
157	O 9	Dean rd Croy
100	F 13	Dean rd Hampt
82	L 14	Dean rd Hounsl
148	J 4	Dean Ryle st SW1
25	U 1	Deansbrook clo Edg
25	U 1	Deansbrook clo Edg
13	N 20	Deansbrook rd NW7
12	H 20	Deansbrook rd Edg
13	N 20	Deansbrook rd Edg
150	F 8	Deans bldgs SE17
73	T 16	Deans clo W4
157	U 5	Deans clo Croy
12	H 20	Deans clo Edg
141	Y 7	Deans ct EC4
43	V 5	Deanscroft av NW9
12	K 16	Deans dri Edg
73	T 16	Deans la W4
12	H 18	Deans la Edg
139	X 4	Deans ms W1
71	W 4	Deans rd W7
153	Z 7	Deans rd Sutton
154	A 6	Deans rd Sutton
148	J 3	Dean Stanley st SW1
52	E 14	Dean st E7
140	F 7	Dean st W1
28	G 13	Deansway N2
18	E 10	Deansway N9
12	G 17	Deans way Edg
140	H 20	Deans yd SW1
148	J 3	Dean Trench st SW1
12	K 20	Dean wlk Edg
70	L 4	Dean wy S'hall
10	L 17	Dearne clo Stanm
120	J 5	Dearn gdns Mitch
64	H 3	Deason st E15
57	Z 18	Debden wlk Hornch
134	J 2	De Beauvoir cres N1
49	R 20	De Beauvoir rd N1
134	J 20	De Beauvoir rd N1
49	S 20	De Beauvoir sq N1
134	K 1	De Beauvoir sq N1
6	D 20	De Bohun av N14
75	P 12	Debnams rd SE16
83	S 1	Deborah clo Islwth
81	Z 16	Debrabant clo Erith
106	D 17	Deburgh rd SW19
150	J 1	Decima st SE1
27	U 14	Decoy av NW11
91	O 4	De Crespigny pk SE5
89	X 2	Deeley rd SW8
61	O 17	Deena clo W3
105	R 10	Deepdale SW19
126	C 10	Deepdale av Brom
157	V 7	Deepdene av Croy
34	F 13	Deepdene clo E18
7	W 20	Deepdene ct N21
90	C 18	Deepdene gdns SW2
91	N 9	Deepdene rd SE5
97	O 6	Deepdene rd Welling
59	R 8	Deepwood la Grnfd
108	H 1	Deerbrook rd SE24
90	L 9	Deerdale rd SE24
57	W 19	Deere av Rainhm
26	F 16	Deerfield cotts NW9
26	F 17	Deerfield cotts NW9
45	P 19	Deerhurst rd NW2
108	C 13	Deerhurst rd SW16
85	W 9	Dee rd Rich
103	R 18	Deer Park clo Kingst
120	C 3	Deer Pk rd SW19
106	F 7	Deeside rd SW17
64	J 16	Dee st E14
39	P 3	Dee way Rom
155	Z 16	Defiant way Wallgtn
73	R 20	Defoe av Rich
49	S 8	Defoe rd N16
110	H 8	De Frene rd SE26
113	Y 13	Degema rd Chisl
44	F 2	Dehar cres NW9
156	B 16	De Havilland rd Croy
25	S 8	De Havillan rd Edg
156	B 16	De Havillard rd Croy
91	S 16	Dekker rd SE21
77	V 20	Delacourt rd SE3
77	X 13	Delafield rd SE7
151	Y 10	Delaford rd SE1
145	N 16	Delaford st SW6
124	C 15	Delamere cres Croy
12	K 18	Delamere gdns NW7
119	P 1	Delamere rd SW20
72	L 4	Delamere rd W5
138	A 1	Delamere st W2
138	A 1	Delamere ter W2
129	Y 20	Delamere ter W9
131	X 6	Delancey st NW1
149	W 11	De Laune st SE17
129	W 16	Delaware rd W9
91	N 16	Delawyk cres SE24
118	L 20	Delacombe av Worc Pk
91	S 12	Delft way SE22
18	G 1	Delhi rd Enf
132	L 5	Delhi st N1
88	B 18	Delia st SW18
64	L 3	Dell clo E15
155	W 7	Dell clo Wallgtn
21	U 11	Dell clo Wdfd Grn
111	U 20	Dellfield clo Becknhm
152	F 12	Dell la Epsom
4	C 16	Dellors clo Barnt
36	D 20	Dellow clo Ilf
54	D 1	Dellow clo
63	N 20	Dellow st E1
143	Y 8	Dellow st E1
9	P 2	Dell rd Enf
152	G 12	Dell rd Epsom
148	B 7	Dell's ms SW1
79	Z 14	Dell the SE2
109	U 19	Dell the SE19
72	E 16	Dell the Brentf
42	C 14	Dell the Wemb
21	U 11	Dell the Wdfd Grn
118	B 4	Dell wlk New Mald
60	C 17	Dell way W13
35	X 11	Dellwood gdns Ilf
90	D 10	Delmare clo SW19
94	J 4	Delme cres SE3

157 V 5 Delmey clo Croy
93 N 2 Deloraine st SE4
144 H 15 Delorme st W6
152 C 5 Delta rd Worc Pk
135 R 12 Delta st E2
81 Y 13 Deluci rd Erith
80 E 10 De Lucy st SE17
56 J 12 Delversmead Dgnhm
149 Y 10 Delverton rd SE17
87 X 3 Delvino rd SW6
155 W 7 Demesne rd Wallgtn
43 V 9 Demeta clo Wemb
107 Z 5 De Montford rd SW16

88 B 7 De Morgan rd SW6
116 E 19 Dempster clo Surb
88 C 12 Dempster rd SW18
115 S 8 Denberry dri Sidcp
44 A 20 Denbigh clo NW10
62 A 1 Denbigh clo NW10
137 R 8 Denbigh clo W11
113 T 15 Denbigh clo Chisl
58 F 17 Denbigh clo S'hall
153 V 10 Denbigh clo Sutton
85 N 14 Denbigh gdns Rich
148 B 9 Denbigh pl SW1
66 B 10 Denbigh rd E6
137 R 8 Denbigh rd W11
60 C 19 Denbigh rd W13
82 L 4 Denbigh rd Hounsl
58 F 17 Denbigh rd S'hall
148 C 10 Denbigh st SW1
137 R 8 Denbigh ter W11
127 V 2 Denbridge rd Brom
125 X 7 Den clo Becknhm
82 E 7 Dene av Hounsl
97 S 19 Dene av Sidcp
92 H 9 Dene clo SE4
126 C 20 Dene clo Brom
152 D 2 Dene clo Worc Pk
11 S 16 Dene gdns Stanm
26 M 19 Denehurst gdns NW4

73 S 3 Denehurst gdns W3
85 R 10 Denehurst gdns Rich
83 R 19 Denehurst gdns Twick

21 U 13 Denehurst gdns Wdfd Grn
16 A 7 Dene the W13
60 A 14 Dene the W13
158 E 7 Dene the Croy
42 J 12 Dene the Wemb
5 S 17 Dene wood Barnt
28 M 20 Denewood rd N6
120 L 9 Denham clo Mitch
97 T 8 Denham clo Welling
36 A 18 Denham dri Ilf
15 Y 10 Denham rd N20
67 W 3 Denham way Bark
129 R 12 Denholme rd W9
57 U 18 Denholme wk Rainhm
28 C 11 Denison clo N2
106 F 16 Denison rd SW19
60 E 11 Denison rd W5
115 Y 3 Deniston av Bxly
17 S 4 Denleigh gdns N21
27 Z 15 Denman dri NW11
27 Z 14 Denman dri north NW11

27 Z 15 Denman Dri south NW11

91 U 3 Denman st SE15
140 E 9 Denman st W1
105 S 17 Denmark av SW19
119 Y 13 Denmark ct Mrdn
155 N 5 Denmark gdns Carsh
133 S 7 Denmark gro N1
91 O 10 Denmark hill SE5
140 G 5 Denmark pl WC2
30 E 12 Denmark rd N8
129 R 9 Denmark rd NW6
90 L 4 Denmark rd SE5
123 Y 11 Denmark rd SE25
105 R 16 Denmark rd SW19
126 H 2 Denmark rd Brom
155 N 6 Denmark rd Carsh
60 C 20 Denmark rd Grnfd
116 J 6 Denmark rd Kingst
101 R 6 Denmark rd Twick
51 Y 10 Denmark st E11
65 U 13 Denmark st E13
31 Y 3 Denmark st N17
115 V 3 Denmark st WC2
108 L 10 Denmark wk SE27
122 H 19 Denmead rd Croy
116 L 20 Denmead rd Surb
20 B 8 Denner rd E4
28 P 5 Dene ter E8
122 G 18 Dennett rd Croy
92 D 3 Dennetts dri SE14
92 E 4 Dennetts gro SE14
156 G 10 Denning av Croy
130 D 14 Denning clo NW8

100 E 14 Denning clo Hampt
46 G 12 Denning rd NW3
45 Y 16 Dennington Pk rd NW6

42 L 14 Dennis av Wemb
11 R 15 Dennis gdns Stanm
11 O 12 Dennis la Stanm
119 S 1 Dennis Pk cres SW2

107 N 20 Dennis Reeve clo Mitch
149 U 8 Dennis cres SE11
55 S 20 Denny gdns Dgnhm
18 M 5 Denny rd N9
149 T 8 Denny st SE11
125 X 7 Den rd Brom
64 M 2 Densham rd E15
65 N 3 Densham rd E15
110 H 20 Densole clo Becknhm
19 P 10 Densworth gro N9
30 E 17 Denton rd N8
18 F 14 Denton rd N18
61 W 2 Denton rd NW10
99 S 19 Denton rd Drtfrd
84 G 17 Denton rd Twick
80 F 19 Denton rd Welling
88 B 15 Denton st SW18
88 L 17 Dents rd SW11
49 R 1 Denver rd N16
99 X 19 Denver rd Drtfrd
54 M 6 Denyers st SW3
44 E 16 Denzil rd NW10
87 U 9 Deodar rd SW15
28 B 6 Depot appr N3
54 C 1 Depot cotts Ilf
83 P 7 Depot rd Hounsl
150 E 16 Depot st SE5
93 O 1 Deptford br SE4
93 O 1 Deptford bdwy SE4
76 B 17 Deptford Ch st SE8
76 B 12 Deptford Ferry rd E14

76 B 16 Deptford grn SE8
76 A 17 Deptford high st SE8
75 Y 12 Deptford strand SE8
31 O 4 De Quiney st N17
15 P 17 Derby av N11
23 P 5 Derby av Harrow
38 J 19 Derby av Rom
140 K 17 Derby ga SW1
110 C 4 Derby hill SE23
110 B 4 Derby hill cres SE23
63 S 3 Derby rd E9
52 M 20 Derby rd E12
53 N 19 Derby rd E12
34 B 4 Derby rd E18
30 K 13 Derby rd N15
19 O 16 Derby rd N18
85 T 10 Derby rd SW14
105 Y 18 Derby rd SW19
156 J 1 Derby rd Croy
9 P 7 Derby rd Enf
54 K 8 Derby rd Grnfd
82 K 10 Derby rd Hounsl
117 O 18 Derby rd Surb
153 W 14 Derby rd Sutton
135 U 14 Derbyshire st E2
139 V 14 Derby st W1
134 K 15 Dereham pl EC2
134 L 14 Dereham pl EC2
54 L 16 Dereham rd Bark
155 S 7 Derek av Wallgtn
43 S 20 Derek av Wemb
135 V 4 Dericote st E8
156 L 9 Dering pl Croy
156 M 9 Dering rd Croy
139 X 6 Dering st W1
106 M 8 Derinton rd SW17
107 N 10 Derinton rd SW17
93 W 12 Dermody gdns SE13
93 W 12 Dermody rd SE13
108 H 1 Deronda rd SE24
77 X 10 Derrick gdns SE7
124 L 8 Derrick rd Becknhm
155 Z 4 Derry rd Wallgtn
137 X 19 Derry st W8
53 V 12 Dersingham av E12
53 V 14 Dersingham av E12
53 V 16 Dersingham av E12
45 T 9 Dersingham rd NW2
18 A 17 Derwent av N18
12 L 18 Derwent av NW7
26 A 16 Derwent av NW9
103 Z 9 Derwent av SW15
104 A 10 Derwent av SW15
15 Y 5 Derwent av Barnt
15 S 11 Derwent cres N20
98 D 5 Derwent cres Bxly Hth

24 E 7 Derwent cres Stanm
35 R 13 Derwent gdns Ilf
42 E 2 Derwent gdns Wemb
91 T 10 Derwent gro SE22
26 A 17 Derwent rise NW9

17 P 11 Derwent rd N13
123 Y 3 Derwent rd SE20
72 C 8 Derwent rd W5
119 N 12 Derwent rd Mrdn
58 F 16 Derwent rd S'hall
82 L 16 Derwent rd Twick
76 M 12 Derwent st SE10
155 S 17 Derwent wk Wallgtn
73 V 2 Derwentwater rd W3
57 Y 15 Derwent way Hornch
129 X 20 Desborough st W2
91 S 16 Desenfans rd SE21
65 N 12 Desford rd E16
75 W 17 Desmond st SE14
47 U 4 Despar rd N19
112 E 12 Detling rd Brom
155 N 5 Devana end Carsh
25 C 19 Devany clo Pinn
104 M 20 Devas rd SW20
105 N 20 Devas rd SW20
64 F 11 Devas st E3
80 B 6 Devenish rd SE2
91 S 16 Deventer cres SE22
138 A 19 De Vere gdns W8
53 T 5 De Vere gdns Ilf
150 E 3 Deverell st SE1
138 A 20 De Vere ms W8
141 R 7 Devereux ct WC2
88 M 16 Devereux rd SW11
39 P 4 Devereux way Rom
101 O 1 Devon av Twick
31 W 9 Devon clo N17
21 V 7 Devon clo Buck Hl
60 E 3 Devon clo Grnfd
60 E 3 Devon cres Grnfd
83 Z 19 Devoncroft gdns Twick

30 K 18 Devon gdns N4
17 V 19 Devonia gdns N18
133 X 7 Devonia rd N1
35 T 19 Devonport gdns Ilf
74 K 4 Devonport rd W12
87 O 1 Devonport st E1
28 G 14 Devon ri N2
67 U 3 Devon rd Bark
153 S 19 Devon rd Sutton
17 S 12 Devonshire clo N13
131 X 20 Devonshire clo W1
17 Y 19 Devonshire ct N18
27 P 1 Devonshire cres NW7

76 D 20 Devonshire dri SE10
93 S 1 Devonshire dri SE10
17 Z 20 Devonshire gdns N18

17 Z 2 Devonshire gdns N21

73 U 20 Devonshire gdns W4
75 N 17 Devonshire gro SE15
151 Y 19 Devonshire gro SE15
23 A 20 Devonshire Hill la N17

31 O 1 Devonshire Hill la N17

17 X 20 Devonshire la N18

74 A 13 Devonshire ms W4
17 X 20 Devonshire Ms north W1

131 W 20 Devonshire Ms south W1

131 V 19 Devonshire Ms west W1

45 X 9 Devonshire pl NW2
131 X 19 Devonshire pl W1
131 V 19 Devonshire Pl ms W1

52 A 13 Devonshire pl E15
65 W 17 Devonshire rd E16
33 O 18 Devonshire rd E17
19 P 6 Devonshire rd N9
17 Z 20 Devonshire rd N18
27 N 1 Devonshire rd NW7
113 P 4 Devonshire rd SE9
92 E 19 Devonshire rd SE23
110 D 2 Devonshire rd SE23
116 L 16 Devonshire rd SW19
74 A 13 Devonshire rd W4
72 D 8 Devonshire rd W5
97 Z 10 Devonshire rd Bxly Hth

116 N 16 Devonshire rd Croy
100 B 8 Devonshire rd Felt
23 O 18 Devonshire rd Harrow

36 G 20 Devonshire rd Ilf
22 D 3 Devonshire rd Pinn
58 G 13 Devonshire rd S'hall
154 D 16 Devonshire rd Sutton
155 O 7 Devonshire rd Wallgtn

142 K 3 Devonshire row EC2
131 Y 19 Devonshire Row ms W1

142 L 3 Devonshire sq EC2
126 J 8 Devonshire sq Brom
131 X 19 Devonshire st W1
74 A 15 Devonshire st W4
138 C 7 Devonshire ter W2
158 K 2 Devonshire way Croy
159 N 1 Devonshire way Croy
64 C 11 Devons rd E3
75 N 17 Devon st SE15
151 X 15 Devon st SE15
70 E 19 Devon waye Hounsl
139 V 2 De Walden st W1
91 X 8 Dewar st SE15
22 C 19 Dewsbury clo Pinn
133 S 7 Dewey rd N1
56 J 18 Dewey rd Dgnhm
106 M 12 Dewey st SW17
144 F 2 Dewhurst rd W14
152 F 4 Dewsbury gdns Worc Pk

44 G 15 Dewsbury rd NW10
90 G 12 Dexter rd SE24
4 B 19 Dexter st Barnt
31 N 4 Deyncourt rd N17
34 L 14 Deynecourt gdns E11

140 E 5 Diadem ct W1
40 A 13 Diamond rd Pinn
59 X 1 Diamond ter SE10
34 H 6 Diana clo E18
131 Z 17 Diana pl NW1
32 M 9 Diana rd E17
80 C 13 Dianthus clo SE2
57 Y 12 Diban av Hornch
133 Z 3 Dibden st N1
153 Y 4 Dibdin clo Sutton
153 Y 4 Dibdin rd Sutton
44 L 13 Dicey av NW2
28 D 5 Dickens av N3
102 J 3 Dickens clo Rich
14 C 14 Dickens dri Chisl
18 E 16 Dickens la N18
30 B 20 Dickenson rd N8
123 X 14 Dickensons la SE25
123 X 15 Dickensons pl SE25
66 E 6 Dickens rd E6
150 C 1 Dickens sq SE1
89 T 4 Dickens st SW8
117 V 4 Dickerage la New Mald

117 V 2 Dickerage la Kingst
95 R 8 Dickson rd SE9
48 K 7 Digby cres N4
52 M 2 Digby gdns Dgnhm
157 V 4 Digby pla Croy
50 F 16 Digby rd E9
67 W 1 Digby rd Bark
63 R 9 Digby st E2
63 S 15 Diggon st E1
88 C 12 Dighton rd SW18
133 S 6 Dignum st N1
48 G 18 Digswell st N7
112 H 6 Dilhorne clo SE12
147 P 14 Dilke st SW3
48 D 11 Dillon pl N7
110 A 7 Dillwyn clo SE26
110 J 8 Dillwyn clo SE26
104 H 1 Dilton gdns SW15
74 K 11 Dimes pl W6
41 R 15 Dimmock dri Grnfd
52 F 14 Dimond clo E7
65 S 5 Dimsdale wlk E15
43 W 4 Dinsdale rd NW4
18 J 1 Dimsdale dri Enf
6 B 20 Dingle gdns E14
107 X 5 Dingley la SW16
88 B 13 Dingley pl EC1
134 B 13 Dingley pl EC1
156 M 3 Dingwall av Croy
157 N 3 Dingwall av Croy
27 X 19 Dingwall gdns New Mald

88 C 19 Dingwall rd SW18
154 M 19 Dingwall rd Carsh
157 O 2 Dingwall rd Croy
135 V 9 Dinmont st E2
123 T 10 Dinsdale gdns SE25
5 O 18 Dinsdale gdns Barnt
77 O 15 Dinsdale rd SE3
89 S 18 Dinsmore rd SW12
106 G 14 Dinton rd SW19
103 N 17 Dinton rd Kingst
65 O 3 Dirleton rd E15
145 L 15 Disbrowe rd W6
26 A 4 Dishorth la NW9
142 C 17 Disney pl SE1
142 C 17 Disney st SE1
9 S 6 Dison clo Enf
80 E 3 Disraeli clo SE18
52 F 17 Disraeli rd E7
61 X 6 Disraeli rd NW10
87 R 11 Disraeli rd SW15

72 F 3 Disraeli rd W5
135 O 11 Diss st E2
142 A 8 Distaff la EC4
160 A 8 Distaff la EC4
144 E 11 Distillery la W6
42 B 16 District rd Wemb
93 R 2 Ditch all SE10
64 G 20 Ditchburn st E14
113 R 10 Dittisham rd SE9
116 F 20 Ditton Grange clo Surb
116 F 20 Ditton Grange dri Surb
116 C 20 Ditton Hill rd Surb
110 A 20 Ditton pl SE20
116 A 15 Ditton reach Surb
97 Y 13 Ditton rd Bxly Hth
70 E 13 Ditton rd S'hall
116 K 20 Ditton rd Surb
159 R 1 Dixon pl W Wckm
92 K 1 Dixon rd SE14
123 T 6 Dixon st SE25
143 W 19 Dixons all SE1
23 Z 7 Dobbin clo Harrow
95 U 13 Dobell rd SE9
62 K 1 Dobree av NW10
128 A 1 Dobree av NW10
46 F 20 Dobson clo NW6
160 C 9 Doby ct EC4
143 P 18 Dockhead SE1
78 J 3 Dockland st E16
151 S 2 Dockley rd SE16
65 P 20 Dock rd E16
77 P 1 Dock rd E16
72 H 18 Dock rd Brentf
110 C 12 Doctors clo SE26
49 R 17 Docwras bldgs N1
108 H 8 Dodbrooke rd SE27
149 X 12 Doddington gro SE17
149 W 13 Doddington pl SE17
141 V 20 Dodson st SE1
63 Z 17 Dod st E14
64 A 17 Dod st E14
106 C 19 Doel clo SW19
141 P 1 Dog and Duck yd WC1
5 W 19 Doggets clo Barnt
93 O 19 Dogget rd SE6
91 S 8 Dog Kennel hill SE5
44 B 18 Dog la NW10
65 T 11 Doherty rd E13
141 X 14 Dolben st SE1
87 V 6 Dolby rd N5
26 M 1 Dole st NW7
149 P 11 Dolland st SE11
27 V 4 Dollis av N3
4 E 20 Dollis Brook wlk Barnt
44 L 8 Dollis Hill av NW2
44 H 10 Dollis Hill la NW2
27 V 3 Dollis pk N3
27 T 3 Dollis rd NW7
4 H 18 Dollis Valley way Barnt
73 Y 12 Dolman rd W4
90 B 19 Dolman st SW4
116 B 20 Dolphin clo Surb
64 C 20 Dolphin la E14
58 F 5 Dolphin rd Grnfd
148 D 12 Dolphin sq SW1
133 N 20 Dombey st WC1
109 V 9 Dome Hill pk SE26
91 P 9 Domett clo SE5
134 A 17 Domingo st EC1
123 U 16 Dominion rd Croy
70 C 7 Dominion rd S'hall
142 G 1 Dominion st EC2
160 G 1 Dominion st EC2
113 Z 8 Domonic dri SE9
114 A 7 Domonic dri SE9
15 T 8 Domville rd N20
150 M 11 Domville gro SE5
37 T 16 Donald dri Rom
65 V 4 Donald rd E13
122 E 16 Donald rd Croy
129 P 6 Donaldson rd NW6
78 L 20 Donaldson rd SE18
95 X 2 Donaldson rd SE18
40 E 17 Doncaster dri Grnfd
30 L 19 Doncaster dri N4
40 D 15 Doncaster gdns Grnfd
18 M 3 Doncaster rd N9
133 R 9 Donegal st N1
87 R 3 Doneraile st SW6
65 V 9 Dongola rd E13
31 R 11 Dongola rd N17
65 U 9 Dongola rd west E13
8 K 8 Donkey la Enf
51 X 13 Donmow rd E15
24 K 1 Donnefield av Edg
146 L 5 Donne pl SW3
121 T 8 Donne pl Mitch

55 T 6 Donne rd Dgnhm
36 C 15 Donington av Ilf
62 K 2 Donnington rd NW10
128 A 3 Donnington rd NW10
24 G 18 Donnington rd Harrow
152 H 3 Donnington rd Worc Pk
107 W 18 Donnybrook rd SW16
29 T 8 Donovan av N10
39 P 3 Don way Rom
101 X 14 Doone clo Tedd
141 S 13 Doon st SE1
154 M 11 Doral way Carsh
79 U 19 Doran gro SE18
64 H 1 Doran wlk E15
105 X 10 Dora rd SW19
63 Y 16 Dora st E14
17 Y 13 Dorchester av N13
97 X 19 Dorchester av Bxly
22 L 20 Dorchester av Harrow
40 L 14 Dorchester clo Grnfd
16 F 2 Dorchester ct N14
20 B 14 Dorchester gdns E4
27 Y 12 Dorchester gdns NW11
74 B 15 Dorchester gro W4
90 L 12 Dorchester rd SE24
40 L 14 Dorchester rd Grnfd
120 B 17 Dorchester rd Mrdn
152 L 1 Dorchester rd Worc Pk
153 N 1 Dorchester rd Worc Pk
24 M 18 Dorchester way Harrow
25 N 17 Dorchester way Harrow
97 Y 4 Dorcis av Bxly Hth
74 B 4 Dordrecht rd W3
53 W 15 Dore av E12
43 Y 3 Doreen av NW9
120 B 16 Dore gdns Mrdn
58 X 5 Dorian rd Hornch
75 Y 16 Dorking clo SE8
153 O 2 Dorking clo Worc Pk
57 X 5 Dorian rd Hornch
87 W 4 Doria rd SW6
125 S 1 Doric ct Becknhm
132 F 13 Doric way NW1
119 P 3 Dorien rd SW20
98 J 2 Doris av Erith
52 F 20 Doris rd E7
88 H 17 Doricote rd SW18
130 F 4 Dorman way NW8
87 Z 12 Dormay st SW18
52 B 17 Dormer clo E15
4 B 18 Dormer clo Barnt
58 G 17 Dormers S'hall
58 L 18 Dormers ri S'hall
58 J 19 Dormers Wells la S'hall
70 K 1 Dormers Wells la S'hall
77 U 19 Dornbergh clo SE3
77 U 19 Dornberg rd SE3
87 T 4 Dorncliffe rd SW6
45 W 16 Dornfell st NW6
107 T 4 Dornton rd SW12
157 P 12 Dornton rd S Croy
60 L 1 Dornton av by Wemb
98 G 10 Dorothy Evans clo Bxly Hth
55 S 13 Dorothy gdns Dgnhm
88 L 8 Dorothy rd SW11
141 T 1 Dorrington st EC1
18 F 15 Dorrit ms N18
114 C 15 Dorrit way Chisl
43 Y 3 Dors clo NW9
39 O 10 Dorset av Rom
70 G 10 Dorset av S'hall
96 K 10 Dorset av Welling
141 V 7 Dorset bldgs EC4
131 O 19 Dorset clo NW1
11 Z 20 Dorset dri Edg
12 A 20 Dorset dri Edg
122 B 8 Dorset gdns Mitch
147 W 1 Dorset ms SW1
147 W 17 Dorset pl E15
148 F 9 Dorset ri EC4
141 V 7 Dorset ri EC4
65 Z 1 Dorset rd E7
57 P 13 Dorset rd N15
30 A 6 Dorset rd N22
71 P 4 Dorset rd SE9
105 X 20 Dorset rd SW19
119 Z 2 Dorset rd SW19
120 A 3 Dorset rd SW19
72 F 7 Dorset rd W5

124 E 6 Dorset rd Becknhm
23 O 18 Dorset rd Harrow
120 K 3 Dorset rd Mitch
131 P 18 Dorset sq NW1
149 P 19 Dorset st SW8
139 S 1 Dorset st W1
148 M 18 Dorset st Sch SW8
101 O 7 Dorset way Twick
70 E 20 Dorset way Hounsl
74 H 9 Dorville cres W6
94 D 14 Dorville rd SE12
79 P 19 Dothill rd SE18
133 N 17 Doughty ms WC1
133 O 17 Doughty st WC1
32 M 5 Douglas av E17
33 N 4 Douglas av E17
118 K 9 Douglas av New Mald
42 K 19 Douglas av Wemb
156 A 14 Douglas clo Stanm
10 M 27 Douglas clo Stanm
159 N 5 Douglas dri Croy
102 G 1 Douglas house Rich
76 G 12 Douglas pl E14
148 F 8 Douglas pth SW1
20 M 4 Douglas rd E4
21 N 4 Douglas rd E4
65 T 14 Douglas rd E16
48 L 19 Douglas rd N1
30 G 4 Douglas rd N22
129 P 3 Douglas rd NW6
39 U 19 Douglas rd Hornch
57 U 1 Douglas rd Hounsl
82 L 8 Douglas rd Hounsl
37 N 19 Douglas rd Ilf
117 T 5 Douglas rd Kingst
117 N 19 Douglas rd Surb
97 R 2 Douglas rd Welling
119 Y 14 Douglas sq Mrdn
148 F 7 Douglas st SW1
75 Z 19 Douglas way SE8
105 Z 2 Dounceforth gdns SW18
106 A 2 Dounceforth gdns SW18
137 Z 20 Douro pl W8
64 A 5 Douro st E3
30 G 10 Dovecote av N22
35 X 6 Dovedale av Ilf
97 N 3 Dovedale clo Welling
106 M 19 Dovedale ri Mitch
92 A 15 Dovedale rd SE22
24 E 18 Dovedale rd Harrow
20 A 8 Dove House gdns E4
67 R 6 Dovehouse mead Bark
146 J 11 Dovehouse st SW3
146 B 8 Dove ms SW5
52 F 2 Dove pk Pinn
57 Y 19 Dove wlk Hornch
38 J 8 Dover clo Rom
122 G 16 Dovercourt av Thntn Hth
11 W 16 Dovercourt gdns Stanm
154 B 6 Dover Ct la Sutton
91 T 15 Dovercourt rd SE22
90 B 18 Doverfield rd SW2
86 H 10 Doverhouse rd SW15
17 W 14 Doveridge gdns N13
49 O 18 Dove rd N1
135 T 7 Dove row E2
86 K 16 Dover Pk dri SW15
52 K 6 Doverd rd E12
19 P 9 Dover rd N9
109 O 15 Dover rd SE19
37 Z 19 Dover rd Rom
139 Z 11 Dover st W1
140 A 12 Dover st W1
157 P 12 Doveton rd S Croy
63 P 12 Doveton st E1
86 D 11 Dowdeswell clo SW15
111 X 2 Dowanhill rd SE6
112 A 2 Dowanhill rd SE6
106 B 19 Dowman cl SW19
10 L 18 Dowding st Stanm
155 T 19 Dower av Wallgtn
160 D 9 Dowgate hill EC4
150 J 18 Dowla st SE5
89 V 9 Downers la SW4
26 M 8 Downage NW4
99 O 4 Downalde av Bxly Hth
111 Y 8 Downderry rd Brom
80 F 18 Downe clo Welling
84 B 15 Downes clo Twick
17 T 5 Downes ct N21
118 E 20 Downfield Worc Pk
116 G 1 Down Hall rd Kingst
38 F 2 Downham clo Rom
134 E 2 Downham rd N1
111 Y 2 Downham way Brom

112 A 11 Downham way Brom
31 O 10 Downhills av N17
31 L 11 Downhills Pk rd N17
31 O 11 Downhills Pk rd N17
30 M 9 Downhills way N17
12 L 17 Downhurst av NW7
23 O 10 Downing clo Harrow
59 S 4 Downing dri Grnfd
56 C 20 Downing rd Dgnhm
69 O 1 Downing rd Dgnhm
140 J 16 Downing st SW1
15 R 4 Downland clo N20
129 N 11 Downland st W13
113 T 3 Downleys clo SE9
95 S 8 Downman rd SE9
73 K 12 Down pl W6
144 A 8 Down pl W6
102 B 16 Down rd Tedd
113 T 13 Downs av Chisl
22 D 20 Downs av Pinn
125 W 1 Downs Br rd Becknhm
49 Y 10 Downs est E5
51 V 12 Downsell rd E15
32 J 19 Downsfield rd E17
36 J 19 Downshall av Ilf
111 W 20 Downs hill Becknhm
125 X 1 Downs hill Becknhm
46 G 13 Downshire Hill NW3
106 D 16 Downside clo SW19
101 V 6 Downside Twick
46 K 16 Downside cres NW3
59 Y 12 Downside cres W13
154 H 14 Downside rd Sutton
49 Z 11 Downs la N16
50 A 13 Downs Pk rd E5
49 X 14 Downs Pk rd E8
49 Y 12 Downs Pk rd E5
125 R 2 Downs rd Becknhm
8 F 15 Downs rd Enf
108 L 20 Downs rd Thntn Hth
105 O 19 Downs rd SW20
139 W 15 Down st W1
83 X 1 Downs view Islwth
108 K 19 Downsview gdns SE19
128 L 17 Downsview rd SE19
154 C 18 Downsway the Sutton
108 B 3 Downton av SW2
28 H 1 Downway N12
133 T 4 Downrey st N1
31 V 8 Downsett rd N17
91 P 10 Dowson clo SE5
142 B 16 Doyce st SE1
62 H 3 Doyle gdns NW10
128 A 3 Doyle gdns NW10
123 X 9 Doyle rd SE25
147 S 5 D'oyley st SW1
47 T 7 Doynton st N19
150 A 13 Draco st SE17
122 G 7 Dragmire la Mitch
75 X 14 Dragoon rd SE8
62 X 11 Dragor rd NW10
92 F 6 Drakefell rd SE14
107 X 18 Drakefield rd SW17
48 H 12 Drakeley ct N5
52 B 13 Drake rd SE4
121 N 13 Drake rd Croy
122 D 17 Drake rd Croy
40 F 6 Drake rd Harrow
8 B 6 Drake st Enf
66 H 5 Drakes wlk E6
107 X 18 Drakewood rd SW16
81 P 12 Draper clo Blvdr
51 V 13 Drapers rd E15
7 V 8 Drapers rd Enf
151 T 4 Drappers rd SE16
76 K 4 Drawdock rd SE10
79 W 13 Draxad clo SE18
104 F 18 Drax av SW20
105 T 14 Draxmont appr SW19
34 G 19 Draycot rd E11
146 K 3 Draycott av SW3
147 N 7 Draycott av SW3
24 B 18 Draycott av Harrow
224 B 18 Draycott av Harrow
24 C 18 Draycott clo Harrow
147 N 7 Draycott clo SW3
12 P 17 Draycott pl SW3
147 N 6 Draycott ter SW3
146 J 16 Drayford clo W9
137 V 18 Draysons ms W8
52 Z 20 Drayton av W13
59 V 19 Drayton av W13
17 W 2 Drayton gdns N21
146 B 9 Drayton gdns SW10
59 Z 19 Drayton gdns W13
59 Z 19 Drayton grn W13
72 B 1 Drayton Green rd W13
59 Z 19 Drayton gro W13
72 B 1 Drayton Gr rd W13
48 G 15 Drayton pk N5

D

51 X 3 Drayton rd E11
31 S 8 Drayton rd N17
62 E 3 Drayton rd NW10
60 A 19 Drayton rd W13
156 K 2 Drayton rd Croy
24 C 17 Drayton waye Harrow
77 O 9 Dreadnought st SE10
47 X 2 Dresden rd N19
93 O 14 Dressington av SE4
14 D 19 Drew av NW7
41 W 17 Drew gdns Grnfd
78 D 3 Drew rd E16
107 X 4 Drewstead rd SW16
108 A 5 Drewstead rd SW16
63 W 5 Driffield rd E3
107 P 20 Driftway the Mitch
40 K 6 Drinkwater rd Harrow
20 K 3 Drive the E4
33 S 11 Drive the E17
34 E 9 Drive the E18
14 L 20 Drive the N3
28 L 14 Drive the N6
16 H 20 Drive the N11
27 S 20 Drive the NW11
45 T 1 Drive the NW11
122 C 6 Drive the SW6
104 M 18 Drive the SW20
61 X 7 Drive the W3
54 L 20 Drive the Bark
4 E 12 Drive the Barnt
5 P 20 Drive the Barnt
125 N 2 Drive the Beckenham
97 W 18 Drive the Bxly
21 Y 3 Drive the Buck Hl
114 J 19 Drive the Chisl
12 E 15 Drive the Edg
8 C 7 Drive the Enf
152 C 14 Drive the Epsom
81 V 18 Drive the Erith
22 H 20 Drive the Harrow
40 H 2 Drive the Harrow
35 R 18 Drive the Ilf
53 T 2 Drive the Ilf
83 P 4 Drive the Islwth
103 V 19 Drive the Kingst
120 E 11 Drive the Mrdn
38 L 3 Drive the Rom
39 N 2 Drive the Rom
115 R 9 Drive the Sidcp
116 J 18 Drive the Surb
123 N 8 Drive the Thntn Hth
125 W 18 Drive the W Wckm
155 X 20 Drive the Wallgtn
43 V 8 Drive the Wemb
107 X 7 Dr Johnson av SW17
109 X 8 Droitwich clo SE26
23 V 1 Dromey gdns Harrow
87 S 16 Dromore rd SW15
55 T 14 Dronfield gdns Dgnhm
128 J 14 Droop st W10
128 M 15 Droop st W10
75 N 18 Drover la SE15
151 Y 17 Drover la SE15
157 N 12 Drovers rd S Croy
91 T 16 Druce rd SE21
142 L 16 Druid st SE1
143 O 19 Druid st SE1
125 Y 8 Druids way Brom
152 A 3 Drumaline ridge Worc Pk
38 M 14 Drummond av Rom
132 E 12 Drummond cres NW1
23 W 2 Drummond dri. Stanm
34 K 18 Drummond rd E11
143 W 20 Drummond rd SE16
151 W 1 Drummond rd SE16
156 L 2 Drummond rd Croy
38 L 13 Drummond rd Rom
140 L 5 Drummond rd Rom
132 D 15 Drummond st NW1
140 L 5 Drury la WC2
23 N 20 Drury rd Harrow
41 N 2 Drury rd Harrow
7 O 8 Dryad st SW15
25 R 10 Dryburgh gdns NW9
86 M 9 Dryburgh rd SW15
59 V 18 Dryden av W7
149 U 7 Dryden Ct Housing est SE11
149 V 6 Dryden ct SE11
106 C 14 Dryden rd SW19
8 F 19 Dryden rd Enf
23 W 6 Dryden rd Harrow
96 K 1 Dryden rd Welling
140 L 6 Dryden st WC2
43 V 18 Dryfield clo NW10
12 J 19 Dryfield rd Edg
76 A 16 Dryfield wlk SE8
23 O 8 Dryhill rd Blvdr
30 B 18 Drylands rd N8

20 E 1 Drysdale av E4
93 T 3 Drysdale rd SE13
134 L 13 Drysdale st N1
62 E 18 Du Cane rd W12
136 A 5 Du Cane rd W12
135 P 14 Ducat st E2
139 X 2 Duchess ms W1
137 T 18 Duchess of Bedford's wlk W8
139 Y 2 Duchess st W1
5 U 2 Duchy rd Barnt
141 T 12 Duchy st SE1
89 B 10 Ducie st SW4
30 H 18 Duckett rd N4
99 T 13 Ducketts rd Drtfrd
63 U 13 Duckett st E1
140 D 7 Duck la W1
9 V 15 Duck Lees la Enf
39 P 14 Duckling Stool ct Rom
84 D 13 Ducks wlk Twick
11 U 18 Du Cros dri Stanm
74 A 4 Du Cros rd W3
44 E 14 Dudden Hill la NW10
113 N 9 Duddington clo SE9
24 D 10 Dudley av Harrow
119 S 18 Dudley dri Mrdn
72 C 5 Dudley gdns W13
41 O 5 Dudley gdns Harrow
33 O 9 Dudley rd E17
28 A 8 Dudley rd N3
129 N 8 Dudley NW6
105 Y 15 Dudley rd SW19
40 M 6 Dudley rd Harrow
41 N 5 Dudley rd Harrow
53 Z 11 Dudley rd Ilf
54 A 11 Dudley rd Ilf
116 L 5 Dudley rd Kingst
85 O 6 Dudley rd Rich
70 A 7 Dudley rd S'hall
138 F 2 Dudley st W2
50 C 6 Dudmaston ms E5
146 H 9 Dudmaston ms SW3
99 X 14 Dudsbury rd Drtfrd
115 S 14 Dudsbury rd Sidcp
134 D 18 Dufferin st EC1
23 W 16 Duffield clo Harrow
88 K 7 Duffield st SW11
64 C 18 Duff st E14
140 C 7 Dufours pl W1
76 C 18 Dugald st SE8
93 Z 2 Duke Humphrey rd SE3
94 A 2 Duke Humphrey rd SE3
83 R 16 Duke of Cambridge clo Twick
154 F 4 Duke of Edinburgh rd Sutton
139 V 17 Duke of Wellington pl W1
140 D 12 Duke Of York st SW1
73 Z 13 Duke rd W4
36 E 13 Duke rd W4
36 E 13 Duke rd Ilf
27 Z 4 Dukes av N3
28 A 4 Dukes av N3
29 U 9 Dukes av N10
73 Z 15 Dukes av W4
11 Z 18 Dukes av Edg
40 D 20 Dukes av Grnfd
58 C 1 Dukes av Grnfd
23 T 12 Dukes av Harrow
82 A 10 Dukes av Hounsl
102 F 11 Dukes av Kingst
102 G 11 Dukes av Kingst
118 C 7 Dukes av New Mald
100 D 11 Dukes clo Hampt
137 V 17 Dukes la W8
29 T 10 Dukes ms N10
139 U 4 Dukes ms W1
98 K 20 Dukes orchard Bxly
150 M 6 Dukes pl EC3
66 J 3 Dukes rd E6
61 P 12 Dukes rd W3
132 G 14 Dukes rd WC1
110 F 10 Dukesthorpe rd SE26
139 U 7 Duke st W1
84 H 12 Duke st Rich
154 E 8 Duke st Sutton
142 G 13 Duke St hill SE1
140 C 12 Duke St St James's SW1
48 E 5 Dulas st N4
136 J 8 Dulford st W11
88 M 14 Dulka rd SW11
114 D 4 Dulverton rd SE9
109 T 1 Dulwich comm SE21
91 U 19 Dulwich pk SE21
90 G 14 Dulwich rd SE24
91 P 15 Dulwich village SE21

109 S 11 Dulwich Wood av SE19
109 T 11 Dulwich Wood pk SE19
156 J 8 Dumas av Croy
90 B 17 Dumbarton rd SW2
117 T 2 Dumbleton clo Kingst
95 V 9 Dumbreck rd SE9
49 T 8 Dumont rd N16
131 T 1 Dumpton pl NW1
122 F 5 Dunbar av SW16
124 J 8 Dunbar av Becknhm
56 E 10 Dunbar av Dgnhm
56 F 15 Dunbar av Dgnhm
52 G 18 Dunbar rd E7
30 H 5 Dunbar rd N22
108 L 7 Dunbar rd SE27
117 W 8 Dunbar rd New Mald
95 S 6 Dunblane st SE9
135 V 16 Dunbridge st E2
5 P 15 Duncan clo Barnt
62 A 17 Duncan gro W3
140 J 11 Duncannon st WC2
135 V 4 Duncan rd E8
84 L 10 Duncan rd Rich
133 V 8 Duncan st N1
133 W 9 Duncan ter N1
63 N 18 Dunch st E1
92 J 18 Duncombe hill SE23
47 X 4 Duncombe rd N19
93 Y 16 Duncrievie rd SE13
79 U 20 Duncroft SE18
92 G 8 Dundalk rd SE4
92 C 4 Dundas rd SE15
65 V 7 Dundee rd E13
124 A 12 Dundee rd SE25
143 X 15 Dundee st E1
152 K 9 Dundela gdns Worc Pk
128 F 6 Dundonald rd NW10
105 U 20 Dundonald rd SW19
51 S 9 Dunedin rd E10
54 C 3 Dunedin rd Ilf
108 K 7 Dunelm gro SE27
63 S 17 Dunelm st E1
111 S 11 Dunfield gdns SE6
111 S 11 Dunfield rd SE6
48 D 13 Dunford rd N7
86 F 9 Dungarvan av SW15
122 F 13 Dunheved clo Thntn Hth
122 G 14 Dunheved Rd south Thntn Hth
122 F 14 Dunheved Rd west Thntn Hth
18 G 10 Dunholme grn N9
18 G 12 Dunholme la N9
18 G 12 Dunholme rd N9
123 O 8 Dunkeld rd SE25
55 S 6 Dunkeld rd Dgnhm
113 O 8 Dunkery rd SE9
108 L 9 Dunkirk st SE27
143 S 1 Dunk st E1
50 D 13 Dunlace rd E5
82 F 19 Dunleasry clo Hounsl
159 W 14 Dunley dri Croy
31 O 10 Dunloe av N17
134 M 9 Dunloe st E2
135 P 9 Dunloe st E2
151 P 3 Dunlop pl SE16
100 A 8 Dunmow clo Felt
128 K 5 Dunmore rd NW6
105 O 20 Dunmore rd SW20
119 N 1 Dunmore rd SW20
37 S 15 Dunmow clo Rom
134 A 3 Dunmow wlk N1
57 U 14 Dunningford clo Hornch
26 C 3 Dunn mead W9
49 U 14 Dunn st E8
47 V 14 Dunollie rd NW5
92 D 18 Dunoon rd SE23
7 U 8 Dunraven dri Enf
74 H 2 Dunraven rd W12
139 S 8 Dunraven st W1
144 E 3 Dunsany rd W14
123 T 10 Dunsdale rd SE2
159 T 17 Dunsfold way Croy
35 Y 8 Dunsmure rd N16
35 V 8 Dunspring la Ilf
131 V 20 Dunstable ms W1
84 K 11 Dunstable rd Rich
104 L 16 Dunstall rd SW20
45 X 5 Dunstan rd NW11
91 Z 15 Dunstans gro SE22
91 Y 17 Dunstans rd SE22
119 P 19 Dunster av Mrdn
4 D 15 Dunster clo Barnt
38 A 8 Dunster clo Rom
43 V 4 Dunster dri NW9
129 P 1 Dunster gdns NW6
40 B 9 Dunster way Harrow
135 N 5 Dunston rd E8

89 P 6 Dunston rd SW11
134 M 4 Dunston st E8
33 R 20 Dunton rd E10
150 M 8 Dunton rd SE1
131 O 5 Dunton st SE1
39 O 13 Dunton rd Rom
106 A 1 Duntshill rd SW18
95 V 11 Dunvegan rd SE9
98 B 2 Dunwich rd Bxly Hth
139 R 18 Duplex ride SW1
99 P 3 Dupont rd SW20
63 X 16 Dupont st E14
156 K 7 Duppas Hill la Croy
156 G 7 Duppas Hill la Croy
156 G 7 Duppas Hill rd Croy
156 J 7 Duppas Hall terr Croy
156 H 7 Duppas rd Croy
77 U 13 Dupree rd SE7
120 L 20 Durand clo Carsh
154 M 1 Durand clo Carsh
90 D 2 Durand gdns SW9
61 U 1 Durand way NW10
9 R 11 Durants park Enf
9 S 13 Durants Pk av Enf
9 R 14 Durants rd Enf
135 T 10 Durant st E2
69 Y 3 Durban gdns Dgnhm
69 Y 2 Durban gdns Dgnhm
64 M 8 Durban rd E15
32 K 4 Durban rd E17
18 F 20 Durban rd N17
108 M 9 Durban rd SE27
109 N 9 Durban rd SE27
124 L 4 Durban rd Becknhm
54 G 3 Durban rd Ilf
58 F 17 Durdans rd S'hall
55 W 14 Durell gdns Dgnhm
55 V 14 Durell rd Dgnhm
126 C 9 Durham av Brom
70 F 15 Durham av Hounsl
140 L 11 Durham Ho st WC2
147 O 11 Durham pl SW3
79 R 14 Durham ri SE18
53 N 13 Durham rd E12
65 O 12 Durham rd E16
22 L 11 Durham rd N2
48 D 7 Durham rd N7
7 J 8 Durham rd N9
114 K 20 Durham rd SW20
118 L 2 Durham rd SW20
72 G 9 Durham rd W5
126 C 6 Durham rd Brom
56 J 15 Durham rd Dgnhm
22 L 16 Durham rd Harrow
115 P 12 Durham rd Sidcp
63 U 15 Durham row E1
149 O 12 Durham st SE11
137 W 4 Durham ter W2
122 F 13 Durheve Rd north Thntn Hth
111 R 17 Durlden clo Becknhm
22 B 19 Durley av Pinn
99 R 1 Durley rd N16
49 X 7 Durlston rd E5
102 J 15 Durlston rd Kingst
31 T 17 Durnford st N15
109 P 13 Durning rd SE19
105 Y 4 Durnsford av SW19
99 Y 1 Durnsford rd N11
87 U 3 Durrell rd SW6
104 M 19 Durrington av SW20
114 M 20 Durrington Pk rd SW20
50 G 13 Durrington rd E5
94 K 4 Dursley clo SE3
95 N 2 Dursley gdns SE3
94 K 4 Dursley rd SE3
95 K 2 Dursley rd SE3
135 W 20 Durward st E1
43 V 1 Durweston ms W1
139 R 1 Durweston ms W1
139 P 1 Durweston st W1
4 H 7 Dury rd Barnt
87 V 18 Dutch yd SW18
76 H 1 Duthie st E14
15 S 10 Dutton st SE10
57 Z 19 Duxford clo Hornch
141 T 3 Dyers bldgs EC1
51 Y 5 Dyers Hall rd E11
51 X 5 Dyers la SW15
39 X 3 Dyers way Rom
81 S 8 Dylan rd Blvdr
55 W 9 Dylways SE5
35 W 9 Dymchurch clo Ilf
105 P 5 Dymes pth SW19
88 A 7 Dymock st SW6
37 T 20 Dymoke rd Hornch
112 L 8 Dyneley rd SE12
129 N 1 Dyne rd NW6
49 S 10 Dynevor rd N16
84 K 13 Dynevor rd Rich
45 Y 20 Dynham rd NW6
140 H 3 Dyott st WC1

D

E

102 E 11 Dysart av Kingst
134 H 19 Dysart st EC2
34 A 19 Dyson rd E11
52 C 18 Dyson rd E15
19 N 17 Dysons rd N18

E

30 M 20 Eade rd N4
31 O 20 Eade rd N4
48 L 1 Eade rd N4
28 G 11 Eagans clo N2
37 Y 19 Eagle av Rom
9 R 15 Eagle clo Enf
57 X 18 Eagle clo Hornch
57 X 18 Eagle clo Hornch
133 W 20 Eagle ct EC1
109 O 16 Eagle hill SE19
34 E 14 Eagle la E11
140 D 11 Eagle pl SW1
42 H 20 Eagle rd Wemb
78 M 20 Eaglesfield rd SE18
95 Z 3 Eaglesfield rd SE18
96 A 1 Eaglesfield rd SE18
141 O 2 Eagle st WC1
34 H 2 Eagle ter Wdfd Grn
63 P 12 Eaglet pl E1
134 D 7 Eagle Wharf rd N1
94 M 11 Ealdham sq SE9
72 G 2 Ealing grn W5
72 D 11 Ealing Pk gdns W5
72 J 16 Ealing rd Brentf
58 G 7 Ealing rd Grnfd
42 J 17 Ealing rd Wemb
60 J 6 Ealing rd Wemb
60 L 18 Ealing village W5
130 L 9 Eamont st NW8
99 T 10 Eardemont clo Drtfrd
145 U 11 Eardley cres SW5
107 X 17 Eardley rd SW16
81 S 13 Eardley rd Blvdr
51 N 9 Earl cotts SE1
87 N 9 Earldom rd SW15
102 K 17 Earle gdns Kingst
52 F 16 Earlham gro E7
30 D 3 Earlham rd N22
140 J 6 Earlham st WC2
79 S 12 Earl ri SE13
151 N 9 Earl rd SE1
85 W 9 Earl rd SW14
145 T 10 Earls Ct Exhibition
building SW5
145 X 7 Earls Ct gdns SW5
145 T 2 Earls Ct rd W8
145 W 10 Earls Ct sq SW5
23 T 12 Earls cres Harrow
132 M 3 Earlsferry way N1
88 D 19 Earlsfield rd SW18
106 C 1 Earlsfield rd SW18
95 V 10 Earlshall rd SE9
40 F 13 Earlsmead Harrow
31 U 15 Earlsmead rd N15
62 L 8 Earlsmead rd NW10
128 A 11 Earlsmead rd NW10
145 R 3 Earls ter W8
110 E 11 Earlsthorpe rd SE26
133 W 13 Earlstoke st EC1
63 N 3 Earlston gro E9
134 H 20 Earl st EC2
145 T 3 Earls wlk W8
122 G 12 Earlswood av Thnton
Hth
35 W 12 Earlswood gdns Ilf
77 N 14 Earlswood st SE10
131 X 3 Early ms NW1
140 H 4 Earnshaw ct WC2
144 M 5 Earsby st W14
120 A 15 Easby cres Mrdn
55 S 16 Easebourne rd
Dgnhm
57 X 15 Easedale dri Hornch
139 V 4 Easleys ms W1
63 S 17 East Abour st E1
62 B 20 East Acton la W3
73 Z 3 East Acton la W3
53 R 20 East av E12
33 R 14 East av E17
53 D 20 East av S'hall
156 C 11 East av Wallgtn
101 N 13 Eastbank rd Hampt
5 V 18 East Barnet rd Barnt
61 Y 19 Eastbourne av W3
85 V 8 Eastbourne gdns
SW14
138 D 5 Eastbourne ms W2
66 K 8 Eastbourne rd E6
31 S 19 Eastbourne rd E15
107 P 16 Eastbourne rd SW17
73 X 16 Eastbourne rd W4
72 T 14 Eastbourne rd Brentf

100 A 3 Eastbourne rd Felt
138 D 5 Eastbourne ter W2
19 O 10 Eastbournia av N9
19 P 3 Eastbrook av N9
56 K 12 Eastbrook av Dgnhm
57 P 8 Eastbrook dri Rom
94 J 1 Eastbrook rd SE3
67 V 3 Eastbury av Bark
8 F 6 Eastbury av Enf
74 B 14 Eastbury gro W4
66 K 14 Eastbury E6
102 J 19 Eastbury Kingst
38 M 18 Eastbury rd Rom
67 X 3 Eastbury sq Bark
140 C 4 Eastcastle st W1
142 H 9 Eastcheap EC3
160 H 9 Eastcheap EC3
73 Y 2 East Churchfield rd
W3
61 O 12 East clo W5
6 C 14 East clo Barnt
59 O 6 East clo Grnfd
77 V 15 Eastcombe av SE7
41 Z 16 Eastcote av Grnfd
40 L 8 Eastcote av Harrow
40 E 17 Eastcote la Grnfd
58 G 1 Eastcote la Grnfd
40 E 11 Eastcote la Harrow
40 G 18 Eastcote la N
Grnfd
41 N 10 Eastcote rd Harrow
22 B 14 Eastcote rd Pinn
96 F 6 Eastcote rd Welling
90 B 5 Eastcote st SW9
42 E 8 East cres N11
16 A 12 East cres N11
8 G 17 East cres Enf
152 B 17 Eastcroft rd Epsom
50 L 16 Eastcross E9
93 X 11 Eastdown pk SE13
154 K 19 East drive Carsh
91 R 14 East Dulwich gro
SE22
91 V 10 East Dulwich rd
SE22
28 C 10 East End rd N2
27 Y 8 East End rd N3
22 C 9 East End way Pinn
69 V 6 East entrance Dgnhm
34 K 17 Eastern av Ilf
35 T 18 Eastern av Ilf
36 F 18 Eastern av Ilf
40 A 1 Eastern av Pinn
37 T 13 Eastern av Rom
39 V 5 Eastern av Rom
38 J 13 Eastern Av east
Rom
37 Y 14 Eastern Av west
Rom
38 M 10 Eastern Av west
Rom
65 V 6 Eastern rd E13
33 V 15 Eastern rd E17
28 M 12 Eastern rd N2
30 A 4 Eastern rd N22
93 O 11 Eastern rd SE4
39 T 16 Eastern rd Rom
38 B 19 Easternville gdns Ilf
76 E 9 East Ferry rd E14
56 D 13 Eastfield gdns
Dgnhm
33 O 12 Eastfield rd E17
30 A 11 Eastfield rd N8
61 V 14 Eastfield rd W3
56 C 13 Eastfield rd Dgnhm
9 S 3 Eastfield rd Enf
121 P 3 Eastfields rd Mitch
106 J 13 East gdns SW17
22 C 10 East glade Pinn
66 H 14 East Ham Manor way
E6
141 U 5 East Harding st EC4
46 G 10 East Heath rd NW3
88 B 13 East hill SW18
43 P 5 East hill Wemb
28 B 14 Eastholm N11
98 L 1 East holme Erith
56 K 18 East India Dock rd
E14
64 J 20 East India Dock
Wall rd E14
90 K 6 Eastlake rd SE5
19 U 17 Eastlands cres SE21
143 S 20 East la SE1
116 G 5 East la Kingst
42 D 10 East la Wemb
40 K 8 Eastleigh av Harrow
44 B 10 Eastleigh clo NW2
154 A 17 Eastleigh clo Sutton
98 L 7 Eastleigh rd Bxly Hth
68 G 19 Eastleigh wlk SW15
58 K 9 Eastmead av Grnfd
127 S 3 East Mead clo Brom
108 M 4 Eastmearn rd SE21

109 N 4 East Mearn rd SE21
143 O 9 East minster E1
78 A 9 Eastmoor pl SE7
78 A 10 Eastmoor st SE7
76 K 15 Eastney st SE10
122 H 19 Eastney rd Croy
114 C 2 Eastnor rd SE9
133 S 15 Easton st WC1
37 X 16 East Park clo Rom
141 Z 1 East pas EC1
108 L 9 East pl SE27
141 X 1 East Poultry av EC1
65 R 3 East rd E15
134 F 12 East rd N1
106 E 15 East rd SW19
17 S 16 East rd Barnt
25 U 4 East rd Edgw
9 R 3 East rd Enf
102 K 20 East rd Kingst
37 X 14 East rd Rom
57 N 2 East rd Rom
97 P 4 East rd Welling
98 F 15 East Rochester way
Bxly Hth
98 K 18 East Rochester way
Bxly Hth
97 T 15 East Rochester way
Sidcup
34 D 17 East row E11
128 L 17 East row W10
126 D 15 Eastry av Brom
81 S 18 Eastry rd Erith
85 V 14 East Sheen av SW14
27 U 14 Eastside rd NW11
143 R 11 East smithfield E1
150 K 7 East st SE1
150 C 10 East st SE17
150 G 8 East st SE17
67 O 2 East st Bark
67 P 1 East st Bark
98 E 10 East st Bxly Hth
72 D 19 East st Brentf
126 F 2 East st Brom
151 N 19 East Surrey gro
SE15
143 P 6 East Tenter st E1
20 G 15 East view E4
4 H 10 East view Barnt
79 V 19 Eastview av SE18
27 U 17 Eastville av NW11
16 B 4 East wlk Barnt
50 L 18 Eastway E9
51 N 14 Eastway E9
34 H 15 Eastway E11
126 E 17 Eastway Brom
119 R 10 Eastway Mrdn
155 U 9 Eastway Wallgtn
110 H 19 Eastwell clo Becknhm
34 G 8 Eastwood clo E18
34 F 6 Eastwood rd E18
29 O 8 Eastwood rd N10
37 N 20 Eastwood rd Ilf
55 N 2 Eastwood rd Ilf
97 Z 20 East woodside Bxly
107 U 16 Eastwood st SW16
33 W 16 Eatington rd E10
147 T 6 Eaton clo SW1
11 O 13 Eaton clo Stanm
103 S 18 Eaton dri Kingst
38 F 3 Eaton dri Rom
55 Y 20 Eaton gdns Dgnhm
147 V 3 Eaton gate SW1
147 Y 9 Eaton gro N19
147 Y 2 Eaton la SW1
147 U 1 Eaton la SW1
147 V 3 Eaton Ms north SW1
147 V 4 Eaton Ms south SW1
147 U 5 Eaton Ms west SW1
17 U 9 Eaton Pk rd N21
147 U 2 Eaton pl SW1
34 L 14 Eaton ri E11
60 F 17 Eaton ri W5
26 M 15 Eaton rd NW4
90 H 12 Eaton rd SW9
8 E 13 Eaton rd Enf
83 R 11 Eaton rd Hounsl
115 W 5 Eaton rd Sidcp
154 E 14 Eaton rd Sutton
147 W 2 Eaton row SW1
147 U 3 Eaton sq SW1
147 T 6 Eaton Ter SW1
147 T 5 Eaton ter ms SW1
106 M 4 Eatonville rd SW17
107 N 4 Eatonville rd SW17
107 N 4 Eatonville vlls SW17
149 O 15 Ebbisham drive SE11
152 M 2 Ebbisham rd Worc
Pk
94 H 9 Ebdon way SE3
45 X 10 Ebenezer rd NW2
134 E 13 Ebenezer st N1

121 U 1 Ebenezer wlk SW16
150 L 15 Ebley clo SE15
87 S 18 Ebner st SW18
134 M 16 Ebor st E2
24 F 19 Ebrington rd Harrow
45 R 13 Ebsfleet rd NW2
92 G 19 Ebsworth st SE23
48 B 10 Eburne rd N7
147 W 9 Ebury br SW1
147 V 11 Ebury Br rd SW1
147 W 4 Ebury ms SW1
147 W 4 Ebury Ms east SW1
147 V 7 Ebury sq SW1
147 V 6 Ebury st SW1
17 S 16 Ecclesbourne clo
N13
17 S 16 Ecclesbourne gdns
N13
134 B 2 Ecclesbourne rd N1
122 L 11 Ecclesbourne rd
Thntn Hth
88 L 9 Eccles rd SW11
147 Y 5 Eccleston br SW1
5 Y 15 Eccleston clo Barnt
37 O 20 Eccleston cres Rom
55 P 1 Eccleston cres Rom
42 K 15 Ecclestone ct Wemb
42 J 15 Ecclestone ms
Wemb
42 K 15 Ecclestone mews
Wemb
43 N 15 Ecclestone pl Wemb
147 V 2 Eccleston ms SW1
147 Y 6 Eccleston pl SW1
71 X 2 Eccleston rd W13
147 Z 7 Eccleston sq SW1
147 Z 7 Eccleston Sq ms
SW1
147 X 5 Eccleston st SW1
20 D 6 Echo heights E4
135 R 18 Eckersley st E1
133 R 7 Eckford st N1
88 J 10 Eckstein rd SW11
65 U 14 Eclipse rd E13
111 Y 5 Ector rd SE6
129 U 18 Edbrooke rd W9
87 W 4 Eddiscombe rd SW6
38 G 19 Eddy clo Rom
92 J 14 Eddystone rd SE4
100 E 8 Ede clo Hounsl
63 T 1 Edenbridge rd E9
18 E 1 Edenbridge rd Enf
63 T 1 Edenbridge rd E9
18 E 1 Edenbridge rd Enf
60 F 4 Eden clo Wemb
107 T 15 Edencourt rd SW16
99 O 4 Edendale rd Bxly Hth
152 E 4 Edenfield gdns Worc
Pk
33 S 15 Eden gro E17
48 D 15 Eden gro N7
30 U 7 Edenham av SW6
125 T 13 Eden park Becknhm
124 K 8 Eden Pk av Becknhm
125 P 10 Eden Pk av Becknhm
33 S 15 Eden rd E17
108 K 11 Eden rd SE27
124 G 8 Eden rd Becknhm
157 O 8 Eden rd Croy
74 B 19 Edensor gdns W4
74 A 19 Edensor rd W4
116 J 9 Eden st Kingst
107 P 18 Edenvale clo Mitch
88 C 6 Edenvale st SW6
124 M 12 Eden way Becknhm
125 O 14 Eden way Becknhm
122 E 5 Ederline av SW16
133 Z 4 Eder wlk N1
87 S 2 Edgarley ter SW6
64 D 9 Edgar rd E3
64 D 9 Edgar rd E3
82 E 18 Edgar rd Hounsl
37 V 20 Edgar rd Rom
157 O 20 Edgar rd S Croy
113 N 19 Edgeborough way
Chisl
113 Z 10 Edgebury Chisl
114 A 10 Edgebury Chisl
114 B 9 Edgebury wlk Chisl
103 X 18 Edgecombe clo
Kingst
158 E 18 Edgecombe S Croy
73 U 4 Edgecote W3
31 R 15 Edgecot gro N15
54 L 20 Edgefield av Bark
78 M 16 Edge hill SE18
105 O 19 Edge hill SW19
27 X 11 Edge Hill av N3
128 G 13 Edgehill gdns Dgnhm
60 C 15 Edgehill rd W13
114 B 9 Edgehill rd Chisl
121 R 1 Edgehill rd Mitch
156 H 20 Edgehill rd S Croy
89 X 8 Edgeley la SW4

89	X 8	Edgeley rd SW4
88	A 11	Edgel st SW18
108	J 13	Edgepoint clo SE27
137	U 14	Edge st W8
124	G 19	Edgewood grn Croy
26	G 15	Edgeworth av NW4
26	F 15	Edgeworth clo NW4
26	G 15	Edgeworth cres NW4
94	L 10	Edgeworth rd SE9
95	N 11	Edgeworth rd SE9
5	X 13	Edgeworth rd Barnt
107	W 16	Edgington rd SW16
12	C 16	Edgwarebury gdns Edg
11	X 3	Edgwarebury house Borhm Wd
11	Y 3	Edgwarebury la Borhm Wd
12	B 8	Edgwarebury la Edg
12	B 12	Edgwarebury la Edg
12	C 14	Edgwarebury la Edg
12	A 10	Edgwarebury park Edg
12	C 20	Edgware High st Edg
44	L 6	Edgware rd NW2
25	W 9	Edgware rd NW9
26	D 18	Edgware rd NW9
130	F 19	Edgware rd W2
138	K 3	Edgware rd W2
139	N 6	Edgware rd W2
12	A 18	Edgwar rd Edg
11	T 4	Edgware way Edg
12	B 17	Edgware way Edg
65	V 7	Edinburgh rd E13
32	M 16	Edinburgh rd E17
18	L 15	Edinburgh rd N18
71	V 5	Edinburgh rd W7
154	E 4	Edinburgh rd Sutton
80	D 7	Edington rd SE2
9	P 10	Edington rd Enf
57	T 4	Edison av Hornch
57	S 4	Edison clo Hornch
58	K 17	Edison dri S'hall
79	X 20	Edison gro SE18
29	Z 19	Edison rd N8
79	Y 20	Edison rd S18
79	Y 20	Edison rd SE18
126	D 3	Edison rd Brom
96	K 2	Edison rd Welling
131	U 2	Edis st NW1
117	S 16	Edith gdns Surb
146	B 15	Edith gro SW10
90	B 7	Edithna st SW9
66	A 1	Edith rd E6
51	X 14	Edith rd E15
29	Y 2	Edith rd N11
123	P 12	Edith rd SE25
106	B 15	Edith rd SW19
144	J 6	Edith rd W14
145	N 8	Edith rd W14
37	V 20	Edith rd Rom
146	B 17	Edith ter SW10
145	O 8	Edith vlls W14
120	J 5	Edmund rd Mitch
97	O 6	Edmund rd Welling
150	F 18	Edmund st SE5
28	H 14	Edmunds wlk N2
119	O 3	Edna rd SW20
88	J 3	Edna st SW11
12	G 20	Edrick rd Edg
12	G 20	Edrick wlk Edg
75	S 18	Edric rd SE14
157	N 7	Edridge rd Croy
20	C 18	Edward av E4
120	F 11	Edward av Mrdn
18	H 3	Edward clo N9
101	N 13	Edward clo Hampt
153	O 3	Edward clo Worc Pk
145	R 3	Edwardes sq W8
5	T 16	Edward gro Barnt
75	Z 17	Edward pl SE8
32	G 16	Edward rd E17
110	F 16	Edward rd SE20
5	T 16	Edward rd Barnt
112	J 17	Edward rd Brom
114	A 13	Edward rd Chisl
123	T 16	Edward rd Croy
101	N 12	Edward rd Hampt
23	N 11	Edward rd Harrow
37	X 18	Edward rd Rom
48	H 19	Edwards cotts N1
49	P 8	Edwards la N16
139	T 6	Edwards ms W1
133	N 6	Edwards sq N1
81	R 9	Edwards rd Blvdr
65	S 13	Edward st E16
75	Z 17	Edward st SE8
76	A 17	Edward st SE8
65	O 1	Edward Tem av E15
35	P 16	Edwina gdns Ilf
66	K 8	Edwin av E6
81	O 17	Edwin clo Bxly Hth
12	K 20	Edwin rd Edg
101	U 1	Edwin rd Twick
63	R 12	Edwin st E1
65	S 15	Edwin st E16
4	A 18	Edwyn clo Barnt
145	U 19	Effie pl SW6
145	U 19	Effie rd SW6
154	B 17	Effingham clo Sutton
30	H 14	Effiningham rd N8
94	C 13	Effingham rd SE12
122	D 18	Effingham rd Croy
116	C 18	Effingham rd Surb
106	J 12	Effort st SW17
90	G 13	Effra pde SW2
90	E 13	Effra rd SW2
105	Z 14	Effra rd SW19
106	B 14	Effra rd SW19
131	T 3	Egbert pl NW1
131	T 2	Egbert st NW1
146	L 4	Egerton cres SW3
76	E 20	Egerton dri SE10
93	S 1	Egerton dri SE10
26	K 13	Egerton gdns NW4
62	M 3	Egerton gdns NW10
128	C 5	Egerton gdns NW10
146	K 4	Egerton gdns SW3
60	B 17	Egerton gdns W13
54	K 10	Egerton gdns Ilf
146	L 3	Egerton Gdns ms SW3
146	L 3	Egerton pl SW3
31	U 20	Egerton rd N16
123	R 7	Egerton rd SE25
118	E 8	Egerton rd New Mald
83	U 17	Egerton rd Twick
60	L 1	Egerton rd Wemb
146	K 3	Egerton ter SW3
153	R 3	Egham clo Sutton
153	R 4	Egham cres Sutton
65	W 14	Egham rd E13
88	C 14	Eglantine rd SW18
120	A 15	Egleston rd Mrdn
20	K 2	Eglington rd E4
78	M 19	Eglinton hills SE18
78	K 17	Eglinton rd SE18
86	L 8	Egliston ms SW15
86	L 8	Egliston rd SW15
117	O 20	Egmont av Surb
118	E 7	Egmont rd New Mald
117	O 20	Egmont rd Surb
154	C 18	Egmont rd Sutton
75	T 20	Egmont st SE14
108	G 7	Egremont rd SE27
53	U 11	Eighth av E12
123	P 12	Eileen rd SE25
66	D 14	Eisenhower dri E6
47	N 14	Elaine gro NW5
89	N 7	Eland rd SW11
156	H 5	Eland rd Croy
150	C 5	Elba pl SE17
121	W 15	Elberon av Croy
88	C 4	Elbe st SW6
123	W 11	Elborough rd SE25
105	X 2	Elborough st SW18
65	T 19	Elbury dri E16
146	L 19	Elcho st SW11
151	V 18	Elcot av SE15
30	A 17	Elder av N8
72	K 7	Elderberry rd W5
50	D 12	Elderfield rd E5
34	H 15	Elderfield wlk E11
108	M 13	Elder rd SE27
10	F 7	Elders ct Bushey Watf
125	P 13	Elderslie clo Becknhm
95	X 14	Elderslie rd SE9
134	M 19	Elder st E1
110	H 10	Elderton rd SE26
121	U 1	Eldertree pl Mitch
121	T 2	Eldertree way Mitch
158	D 2	Eldon av Croy
70	G 19	Eldon av Hounsl
46	G 14	Eldon gro NW3
123	Z 8	Eldon pk SE25
32	L 14	Eldon rd E17
19	O 7	Eldon rd N9
30	K 5	Eldon rd N22
145	Z 2	Eldon rd W8
146	A 2	Eldon rd W8
142	H 1	Eldon st EC2
160	G 1	Eldon st EC2
61	S 7	Eldon way NW10
67	U 3	Eldred rd Bark
14	B 15	Eleanor cres NW7
56	A 8	Eleanor gdns Dgnhm
86	C 8	Eleanor gro SW13
49	Z 18	Eleanor rd E8
52	D 19	Eleanor rd E15
17	N 20	Eleanor rd N11
64	A 9	Eleanor st E3
64	B 10	Eleanor st E3
90	E 10	Electric av SW9
149	Z 3	Elephant and Castle SE1
75	O 5	Elephant la SE16
143	Z 17	Elephant la SE16
150	A 4	Elephant rd SE17
72	D 6	Elers rd W13
19	R 16	Eley rd N18
90	M 13	Elfindale rd SE24
91	N 14	Elfindale rd SE24
101	V 13	Elfin gro Tedd
94	J 9	Elford clo SE9
48	G 12	Elfort rd N5
111	O 9	Elfrida cres SE6
63	R 19	Elf row E1
59	U 13	Elfwine rd W7
122	A 5	Elgar av SW16
72	K 5	Elgar av W5
117	R 19	Elgar av Surb
11	S 2	Elgar clo Borehm Wd
75	W 7	Elgar st SE16
129	T 17	Elgin av W9
130	A 14	Elgin av W9
24	A 7	Elgin av Harrow
136	M 8	Elgin cres W11
137	N 7	Elgin cres W11
136	M 5	Elgin ms W11
129	Z 12	Elgin Ms north W9
130	A 13	Elgin Ms south W9
29	V 7	Elgin rd N22
123	U 20	Elgin rd Croy
157	V 2	Elgin rd Croy
54	J 1	Elgin rd Ilf
154	J 1	Elgin rd Sutton
155	U 13	Elgin rd Wallgtn
113	N 19	Elham clo Chisl
149	S 16	Elias pl SE11
133	W 9	Elia st N1
95	V 10	Elibank rd SE9
65	P 10	Elim way E13
110	A 3	Eliot bank SE23
40	J 6	Eliot dri Harrow
93	V 5	Eliot hill SE13
93	V 5	Eliot pk SE13
93	Y 5	Eliot pl SE13
55	W 13	Eliot rd Dgnhm
93	X 5	Eliot vale SE13
31	P 12	Elizabethan pl N15
134	D 2	Elizabeth av N1
7	X 10	Elizabeth av Enf
54	E 6	Elizabeth av Ilf
147	X 7	Elizabeth br SW1
64	D 17	Elizabeth clo E14
130	D 17	Elizabeth clo W9
4	B 12	Elizabeth clo Barnt
38	G 5	Elizabeth clo Rom
31	R 12	Elizabeth Clyde clo N15
85	O 2	Elizabeth cotts Rich
74	D 4	Elizabeth gdns W3
11	T 18	Elizabeth gdns Stanm
46	L 18	Elizabeth ms NW3
31	P 12	Elizabeth pl N15
19	O 3	Elizabeth ride N9
66	A 2	Elizabeth rd E6
31	S 16	Elizabeth rd N15
147	W 6	Elizabeth st SW1
95	U 15	Elizabeth ter SE9
109	O 18	Elizabeth wy SE19
65	U 12	Elkington rd E13
39	P 7	Elkins the Rom
144	F 15	Ellaline rd W6
19	N 16	Ellanby cres N18
92	C 11	Elland rd SE15
30	B 20	Ella rd N8
22	A 16	Ellement clo Pinn
86	F 10	Ellenborough pl SW15
30	K 5	Ellenborough rd N20
115	Y 13	Ellenborough rd Sidcp
157	T 20	Ellenbridge way S Croy
127	O 6	Ellen clo Brom
19	P 10	Ellen ct N9
143	T 7	Ellen st E1
101	V 14	Elleray rd Tedd
87	P 2	Ellerby st SW6
46	D 14	Ellerdale clo NW3
46	D 14	Ellerdale rd NW3
93	R 9	Ellerdale st SE13
83	O 11	Ellerdine rd Hounsl
84	J 15	Ellerker gdns Rich
74	J 2	Ellerslie rd W12
89	Z 12	Ellerslie sq SW4
68	E 1	Ellerton gdns Dgnhm
86	F 2	Ellerton rd SW13
88	F 20	Ellerton rd SW13
106	G 1	Ellerton rd SW18
104	G 17	Ellerton rd SW20
68	F 2	Ellerton rd Dgnhm
116	M 20	Ellerton rd Surb
109	O 18	Ellery rd SE19
92	A 6	Ellery st SE15
12	K 10	Ellesmere av NW7
125	S 4	Ellesmere av Becknhm
34	D 16	Ellesmere clo E11
35	R 17	Ellesmere gdns Ilf
4	G 16	Ellesmere gro Barnt
63	V 5	Ellesmere rd E3
77	T 2	Ellesmere rd E16
44	H 15	Ellesmere rd NW10
73	X 15	Ellesmere rd W4
58	M 12	Ellesmere rd Grnfd
84	D 15	Ellesmere rd Twick
64	C 17	Ellesmere st E14
50	A 19	Ellingford rd E8
51	X 13	Ellingham rd E15
74	G 5	Ellingham rd W12
29	S 13	Ellington rd N10
82	L 5	Ellington rd Hounsl
48	F 18	Ellington st N7
51	Z 20	Elliot clo E15
43	O 9	Elliot clo Wemb
26	K 19	Elliot rd NW4
126	M 9	Elliot rd Brom
127	N 9	Elliot rd Brom
122	K 9	Elliott rd Thntn Hth
39	Y 4	Elliott gdns Rom
149	W 20	Elliott rd SW9
149	W 20	Elliott rd SW9
74	A 11	Elliott rd W4
10	M 18	Elliott rd Stanm
149	X 4	Elliotts row SE11
77	Y 15	Elliscombe rd SE7
86	F 17	Ellisfield dri SW15
77	X 16	Ellis ms SE7
70	D 10	Ellison gdns S'hall
86	E 5	Ellison rd SW13
107	Y 18	Ellison rd SW16
108	A 19	Ellison rd SW16
114	F 2	Ellison rd Sidcp
120	M 14	Ellis rd Mitch
147	R 4	Ellis st SW1
39	Y 4	Ellmore clo Rom
107	Y 13	Ellora rd SW16
63	N 9	Ellsworth st E2
135	X 12	Ellsworth st E2
31	P 14	Elmar rd N15
72	L 4	Elm av W5
17	O 2	Elm bank N14
86	C 5	Elm Bank gdns SW13
59	S 13	Elmbank way W7
81	U 12	Elmbourne dr Blvdr
107	R 7	Elmbourne rd SW17
117	W 16	Elmbridge av Surb
37	P 1	Elmbridge rd Ilf
95	S10	Elmbrook gdns SE9
153	V 8	Elmbrook rd Sutton
34	J 18	Elm clo E11
27	O 17	Elm clo NW4
113	M 8	Elm clo SW20
120	L 20	Elm clo Carsh
22	J 19	Elm clo Harrow
38	G 6	Elm clo Rom
157	P 14	Elm clo S Croy
117	W 17	Elm clo Surb
100	K 5	Elm clo Twick
108	K 3	Elmcourt rd SE27
72	K 4	Elm cres W5
116	K 1	Elm cres Kingst
34	H 14	Elmcroft av E11
45	W 1	Elmcroft av NW11
9	N 20	Elmcroft av Enf
96	L 17	Elmcroft av Sidcp
34	J 13	Elmcroft clo E11
60	G 16	Elmcroft clo W5
45	R 1	Elmcroft cres NW11
22	J 11	Elmcroft cres Harrow
25	P 14	Elmcroft gdns NW9
50	C 11	Elmcroft st E5
17	R 17	Elmdale rd N13
117	X 20	Elmdene Surb
124	K 13	Elmdene clo Becknhm
78	M 15	Elmdene rd SE18
82	A 4	Elmdon rd Hounsl
22	J 18	Elm dri Harrow
7	P 11	Elmer clo Enf
25	S 2	Elmer gdns Edg
83	R 8	Elmer gdns Islwth
93	U 19	Elmer rd SE6
124	D 6	Elmers End rd Becknhm
124	H 8	Elmer Side rd Becknhm
123	Y 16	Elmers rd SE25
30	A 16	Elmfield av N8
121	O 1	Elmfield av Mitch
101	X 12	Elmfield av Tedd
126	F 5	Elmfield pk Brom
20	J 7	Elmfield rd E4
32	E 17	Elmfield rd E17
27	F 9	Elmfield rd N2
28	F 9	Elmfield rd N2
107	P 3	Elmfield rd SW17
126	G 5	Elmfield rd Brom
70	C 8	Elmfield rd S'hall
157	U 19	Elmfield way S Croy

28	E 10	Elm gdns N2
8	A 2	Elm gdns Enf
121	X 6	Elm gdns Mitch
12	K 15	Elmgate gdns Edg
62	A 17	Elm grn W3
30	B 19	Elm gro N8
45	R 12	Elm gro NW2
91	W 4	Elm gro SE15
105	S 18	Elm gro SW19
81	Z 18	Elm gro Erith
40	G 2	Elm gro Harrow
116	L 1	Elm gro Kingst
154	B 9	Elm gro Sutton
21	R 17	Elm gro Wdfd Grn
23	X 15	Elmgrove cres Harrow
23	Y 15	Elmgrove gdns Harrow
155	P 6	Elm Gro pde Wallgtn
86	G 4	Elm Grove rd SW13
72	K 4	Elmgrove rd W5
124	A 18	Elm Grove rd Croy
34	J 18	Elm Hall gdns E11
80	M 17	Elmhurst Blvdr
81	N 16	Elmhurst Blvdr
28	F 11	Elmhurst av N2
107	R 19	Elmhurst av Mitch
34	F 6	Elmhurst dri E18
52	H 20	Elmhurst rd E7
31	T 7	Elmhurst rd N17
113	P 6	Elmhurst rd SE9
89	X 7	Elmhurst st SW4
98	F 17	Elmington clo Bxly
150	E 20	Elmington rd SE5
150	G 20	Elmington rd SE5
93	S 8	Elmira st SE13
110	M 3	Elm la SE6
113	U 15	Elmlee clo Chisl
79	S 12	Elmley st SE18
51	V 10	Elmore rd E11
9	S 4	Elmore rd Enf
49	N 20	Elmore st N1
90	C 17	Elm pk SW2
90	E 18	Elm pk SW2
11	P 17	Elm pk Stanm
31	W 18	Elm Park av N15
57	Y 12	Elm Park av Hornch
27	O 17	Elm Pk gdns NW4
146	F 11	Elm Pk gdns SW10
146	F 12	Elm Pk la SW3
146	D 14	Elm Park mans SW10
50	J 4	Elm Pk rd E10
27	W 2	Elm Pk rd N3
17	X 4	Elm Pk rd N21
123	T 6	Elm Pk rd SE25
146	E 13	Elm Pk rd SW3
146	F 10	Elm pl SW7
52	D 18	Elm rd E7
33	V 16	Elm rd E10
51	V 7	Elm rd E11
33	V 16	Elm rd E17
85	W 9	Elm rd SW14
4	G 14	Elm rd Barnt
124	L 2	Elm rd Becknhm
152	E 15	Elm rd Epsom
99	W 1	Elm rd Erith
102	M 19	Elm rd Kingst
103	O 18	Elm rd Kingst
116	L 1	Elm rd Kingst
117	Y 4	Elm rd New Mald
38	G 7	Elm rd Rom
114	M 2	Elm rd Sidcp
123	N 10	Elm rd Thntn Hth
121	P 20	Elm rd Wallgtn
42	K 15	Elm rd Wemb
119	V 16	Elm Rd west Sutton
46	E 10	Elm row NW3
29	T 9	Elms av N10
27	O 17	Elms av NW4
7	Z 20	Elmscott gdns N21
18	A 1	Elmscott gdns N21
112	A 12	Elmscott rd Brom
41	X 13	Elms ct Wemb
89	X 14	Elms cres SW4
32	L 12	Elmsdale rd E17
56	A 11	Elms gdns Dgnhm
41	X 13	Elms gdns Wemb
86	H 13	Elmshaw rd SW15
28	F 12	Elmhurst cres N2
28	F 12	Elmshurst cres N2
228	F 12	Elmshurst cres N2
159	S 14	Elmside Croy
43	O 9	Elmside rd Wemb
41	Z 9	Elms la Harrow
41	Z 12	Elms la Wemb
24	C 13	Elmsleigh av Harrow
101	R 4	Elmsleigh rd Twick
138	E 9	Elms ms W2
41	Y 12	Elms Pk av Wemb
89	U 13	Elms rd SW4
10	G 20	Elms rd Harrow
23	S 2	Elms rd Harrow
113	V 12	Elmstead av Chisl
42	K 5	Elmstead av Wemb
43	N 7	Elmstead av Wemb
14	K 8	Elmstead clo N20
152	B 12	Elmstead clo Epsom
80	F 17	Elmstead cres Bxly Hth
152	F 5	Elmstead gdns Worc Pk
113	T 14	Elmstead glade Chisl
113	U 10	Elmstead la Chisl
99	P 1	Elmstead rd Erith
54	J 7	Elmstead rd Ilf
86	D 8	Elms the SW13
87	W 1	Elmstone rd SW6
133	P 17	Elm st WC1
82	K 4	Elmsworth av Hounsl
45	X 9	Elm ter NW2
95	W 15	Elm ter SE9
23	R 3	Elm ter Harrow
11	P 17	Elm ter Stanm
130	F 12	Elm Tree clo NW8
58	F 7	Elm Tree clo Grnfd
58	G 7	Elm Tree gdns Grnfd
130	F 13	Elm Tree rd NW8
101	U 11	Elmtree rd Tedd
45	Z 8	Elm wlk NW3
118	M 8	Elm walk SW20
119	O 9	Elm wlk SW20
39	W 9	Elm wlk Rom
43	Z 11	Elm way NW10
44	A 11	Elm way NW10
152	M 4	Elm way Worc Pk
17	O 15	Elmwood av N13
23	Z 16	Elmwood av Harrow
24	A 18	Elmwood av Harrow
155	R 4	Elmwood clo Wallgtn
41	Z 11	Elmwood ct Wemb
25	W 13	Elmwood cres NW9
97	Y 18	Elmwood dri Bxly
152	G 16	Elmwood dri Epsom
59	T 18	Elmwood gdns W7
91	O 14	Elmwood rd SE24
73	V 16	Elmwood rd W4
122	J 17	Elmwood rd Croy
120	M 6	Elmwood rd Mitch
109	N 4	Elmworth gro SE21
109	N 4	Elmworth gro SE21
129	Y 18	Elnathan ms W9
32	L 7	Elphinstone rd E17
48	J 11	Elphinstone st N5
49	X 18	Elrington rd E8
97	R 4	Elsa rd Welling
63	U 15	Elsa st E1
50	D 18	Elsdale st E9
31	U 6	Elsden rd N17
53	V 16	Elsenham rd E12
105	V 3	Elsenham st SW18
51	Z 11	Elsham rd E11
52	A 11	Elsham rd E11
136	K 19	Elsham rd W14
17	Z 3	Elsiedene rd N21
92	M 13	Elsiemaud rd SE4
91	U 10	Elsie rd SE22
110	J 2	Elsinore rd SE23
88	M 7	Elsley rd SW11
89	N 7	Elsley rd SW11
82	D 8	Elsma ter Hounsl
88	M 9	Elspeth rd SW11
42	J 15	Elspeth rd Wemb
119	Y 12	Elsrick av Mrdn
124	H 17	Elstan way Croy
150	G 8	Elsted st SE17
95	V 13	Elstow clo SE9
68	L 2	Elstow gdns Dgnhm
68	L 3	Elstow rd Dgnhm
19	N 7	Elstree gdns N9
80	M 10	Elstree gdns Blvdr
81	N 10	Elstree gdns Blvdr
112	A 17	Elstree gdns Blvdr
54	B 15	Elstree gdns Ilf
11	T 2	Elstree hills Boreham Wd
11	S 5	Elstree rd Boreham Wd
111	Z 17	Elstree hill Brom
10	E 3	Elstree rd Bushey Watf
93	R 6	Elswick rd SE13
88	C 3	Elswick st SW6
130	L 1	Elsworthy ri NW3
130	J 4	Elsworthy rd NW8
130	L 3	Elsworthy ter NW3
88	F 12	Elsynge rd SW18
95	E 14	Eltham common SE18
94	N 13	Eltham grn SE9
94	L 12	Eltham Grn rd SE9
95	T 14	Eltham High st SE9
95	N 14	Eltham hill SE9
95	S 18	Eltham palace SE9
94	L 16	Eltham Pal rd SE9
95	N 16	Eltham Pal rd SE9
96	A 11	Eltham pk SE9
95	X 11	Eltham Pk gdns SE9
94	F 12	Eltham rd SE12
150	E 8	Eltham st SE17
87	Y 2	Elthiron rd SW6
71	X 6	Elthorne av W7
71	X 6	Elthorne Pk rd W7
25	Y 20	Elthorne rd NW9
25	Y 19	Elthorne way NW9
93	Y 16	Elthruda rd SE13
53	Y 12	Eltisley rd Ilf
4	J 17	Elton av Barnt
41	V 18	Elton av Grnfd
42	C 14	Elton av Wemb
102	E 19	Elton clo Kingst
49	R 14	Elton pl N16
103	O 20	Elton rd Kingst
88	D 10	Eltringham st SW18
146	C 2	Elvaston ms SW7
146	C 2	Elvaston pl SW7
6	P 5	Elveden pl NW10
61	P 6	Elveden rd NW10
17	N 18	Elvendon rd N13
93	R 5	Elverson rd SE4
148	E 4	Elverton st SW1
26	A 4	Elvington dri NW9
126	C 11	Elvington grn Brom
110	G 13	Elvino rd SE26
125	U 8	Elwill way Becknhm
135	R 12	Elwin st E2
48	J 10	Elwood st N5
94	F 19	Elwyn gdns SE12
9	T 5	Ely clo Erith
118	E 2	Ely clo New Mald
56	L 9	Ely gdns Dgnhm
35	R 20	Ely gdns Ilf
30	F 19	Elyne rd N4
141	U 2	Ely pl EC1
33	U 20	Ely rd E10
123	O 11	Ely rd Croy
155	T 18	Elystan clo Wallgtn
146	M 8	Elystan pl SW3
147	N 8	Elystan pl SW3
146	K 7	Elystan st SW3
133	S 5	Elystan wk N1
61	W 18	Emanuel av W3
147	S 13	Embankment gdns SW3
140	L 13	Embankment pl WC2
87	O 6	Embankment the SW15
101	Z 1	Embankment the Twick
143	V 19	Emba st SE16
93	R 10	Embleton rd SE13
100	E 13	Embleton wlk Hampt
20	L 14	Embry clo Stanm
10	M 18	Embry dri Stanm
10	L 15	Embry way Stanm
88	B 2	Emden st SW6
56	D 5	Emerald gdns Dgnhm
133	N 19	Emerald st WC1
24	M 20	Emerson gdns Harrow
35	W 20	Emerson rd Ilf
53	X 1	Emerson rd Ilf
142	A 12	Emerson st SE1
148	C 3	Emery Hill st SW1
141	T 20	Emery st SE1
81	Y 18	Emes rd Erith
48	G 13	Emily pl N7
65	P 18	Emily st E16
74	B 6	Emlyn gdns W12
74	B 6	Emlyn rd W12
107	V 2	Emmanuel rd SW12
65	P 8	Emma rd E13
135	V 8	Emma st E2
75	Z 1	Emmsett st E14
36	C 16	Emmott av Ilf
63	V 12	Emmott clo E1
28	C 19	Emmott clo NW11
145	Z 4	Emperors ga SW7
146	A 4	Emperors ga SW7
17	Y 18	Empire av N18
60	E 3	Empire rd Grnfd
18	A 19	Empire sq N18
43	O 11	Empire way Wemb
76	J 11	Empire Wharf rd E14
33	P 2	Empress av E4
52	M 7	Empress av E12
53	N 7	Empress av E12
53	V 7	Empress av Ilf
34	C 2	Empress av Wdfd Grn
113	Y 14	Empress dri Chisl
145	U 12	Empress pl SW5
150	B 13	Empress st SE17
64	F 12	Empson st E3
19	O 5	Emsworth clo N9
36	A 7	Emsworth rd Ilf
108	C 4	Emsworth st SW2
89	R 5	Emu rd SW8
121	Z 6	Ena rd SW16
122	A 5	Ena rd SW16
128	L 15	Enbrook st W10
106	A 9	Endeavour way SW19
68	A 7	Endeavour way Bark
121	X 16	Endeavour wy Croy
140	J 5	Endell st WC2
76	L 13	Enderby st SE10
23	S 6	Enderley rd Harrow
26	G 14	Endersleigh gdns NW4
20	F 8	Endlebury rd E4
89	O 17	Endlesham rd SW12
132	F 15	Endsleigh gdns WC1
53	U 5	Endsleigh gdns Ilf
116	E 16	Endsleigh gdns Surb
132	F 16	Endsleigh pl WC1
71	Y 1	Endsleigh rd W13
70	D 10	Endsleigh rd S'hall
132	F 15	Endsleigh st WC1
46	E 7	Endway NW3
117	R 17	Endway Surb
92	J 6	Endwell rd SE4
30	J 20	Endymion rd N4
48	G 2	Endymion rd N4
90	C 16	Endymion rd SW2
6	M 12	Enfield cres Enf
134	L 1	Enfield rd N1
73	S 6	Enfield rd W3
72	F 13	Enfield rd Brentf
6	L 12	Enfield rd Enf
7	O 12	Enfield rd Enf
139	N 1	Enford st W1
157	T 6	Engadine clo Croy
105	W 2	Engadine st SW18
93	T 10	Engate st SE13
122	K 15	Englefield clo Croy
14	A 19	Engel pk NW7
78	J 16	Engineers clo SE18
43	P 12	Engineers way Wemb
46	L 18	Englands la NW3
7	T 10	Englefield clo Enf
49	N 19	Englefield rd N1
93	T 20	Engleheart rd SE6
89	T 15	Englewood rd SW12
142	J 13	English Grounds SE1
63	Y 12	English st E3
151	P 1	Enid st SE16
48	B 11	Enkel st N7
123	Y 11	Enmore av SE25
85	Z 13	Enmore gdns SW14
123	Y 11	Enmore rd SE25
87	N 12	Enmore rd SW15
58	H 10	Enmore rd S'hall
57	V 15	Ennerdale av Hornch
24	D 9	Ennerdale av Stanm
25	Z 16	Ennerdale dri NW9
26	B 16	Ennerdale dri NW9
42	E 4	Ennerdale gdns Wemb
98	E 2	Ennerdale rd Bxly Hth
85	N 3	Ennerdale rd Rich
93	W 14	Ennersdale rd SE13
74	C 11	Ennismore av W4
41	U 16	Ennismore av Grnfd
138	J 20	Ennismore gdns SW7
146	J 1	Ennismore gdns SW7
138	H 20	Ennismore Gdns ms SW7
136	K 20	Ennismore ms SW7
146	J 1	Ennismore ms SW7
146	K 1	Ennismore st SW7
146	J 1	Ennismore ter SW7
48	F 4	Ennis rd N4
79	R 16	Ennis rd SE18
152	L 8	Ennor ct Worc Pk
17	X 10	Ensign dri N13
143	T 9	Ensign st E1
95	W 17	Enslin rd SE9
146	E 9	Ensor ms SW7
9	V 11	Enstone rd Enf
63	O 10	Entick st E2
145	S 17	Epirus ms SW6
145	S 17	Epirus rd SW6
38	H 11	Epping clo Rom
21	U 3	Epping forest Buck Hl
21	U 8	Epping New rd Buck Hl
87	W 2	Epple rd SW6
98	H 9	Epsom clo Bxly Hth
40	E 16	Epsom clo Grnfd
33	U 19	Epsom rd E10
156	G 7	Epson rd Croy
36	K 20	Epsom rd Ilf
119	W 14	Epsom rd Mrdn
80	C 3	Epstein rd SE18
72	A 20	Epworth rd Brentf
134	G 17	Epworth st EC2
148	H 6	Erasmus st SW1
62	D 18	Erconwald st W12

159 P 7	Erica gdns Croy	137 U 19	Essex vlls W8
62 H 20	Erica st W12	63 V 13	Essian st E1
52 E 12	Eric clo E7	25 N 9	Essoldo way NW9
87 X 13	Ericcson clo SW18	50 M 4	Estate way E10
52 E 13	Eric rd E7	124 A 14	Estcourt rd SE25
44 C 19	Eric rd NW10	145 N 17	Estcourt rd SW6
55 X 1	Eric rd Rom	118 K 9	Estella av New Mald
63 X 11	Eric st E3	47 N 13	Estelle rd NW3
73 Y 8	Eridge rd W4	148 F 6	Esterbrooke st SW1
79 T 17	Erindale SE18	88 J 7	Este rd SW11
79 T 17	Erindale ter SE18	17 U 12	Esther clo N21
38 J 3	Erith cres Rom	33 Z 20	Esther rd E11
80 L 84	Erith marshes Blvdr	107 X 16	Estreham rd SW16
81 U 13	Erith rd Blvdr	82 G 10	Estridge clo Hounsl
98 G 8	Erith rd Bxly Hth	106 M 10	Eswyn rd SW17
98 J 3	Erith rd Erith	107 N 12	Eswyn rd SW17
92 F 2	Erlanger rd SE14	28 B 1	Etchingham Pk rd N3
71 Y 7	Erlesmere gdns W13	51 U 12	Etchingham rd E15
93 R 10	Ermine rd E13	115 P 12	Etfield gro Sidcp
31 T 17	Ermine rd N17	126 E 5	Ethelbert clo Brom
8 J 16	Ermine side Enf	35 V 17	Ethelbert gdns Ilf
114 C 4	Ermington rd SE9	105 P 20	Ethelbert rd SW20
66 E 6	Ernald av E6	126 E 5	Ethelbert rd Brom
83 W 17	Erncroft way Twick	81 W 19	Ethelbert rd Erith
108 K 9	Ernest av SE27	107 T 2	Ethelbert st SW4
125 N 11	Ernest clo Becknhm	88 K 1	Ethelburga st SW11
73 T 17	Ernest gdns W4	146 L 20	Ethelburga st SW11
124 M 11	Ernest gro Becknhm	29 U 13	Etheldene av N10
125 N 11	Ernest gro Becknhm	74 J 3	Ethelden rd W12
65 O 13	Ernest rd E16	65 V 19	Ethel rd E16
117 S 4	Ernest rd Kingst	150 B 7	Ethel st SE17
117 S 3	Ernest sq Kingst	30 L 14	Etherley rd N15
63 U 13	Ernest st E1	91 W 17	Etherow st SE22
104 L 17	Ernie rd SW20	108 E 10	Etherstone grn SW16
87 T 13	Ernshaw pla SW15		
86 M 7	Erpingham rd SW15	108 E 10	Etherstone rd SW16
119 Y 3	Erridge rd S19	151 V 15	Ethnard rd SE15
129 R 17	Errington rd W9	97 Z 8	Ethronvi rd Bxly Hth
118 G 10	Errol gdns New Mald	51 N 6	Etloe rd E10
39 T 13	Erroll rd Rom	15 R 20	Eton av N12
134 D 18	Errol st EC1	46 H 19	Eton av NW3
154 H 6	Erskine clo Sutton	70 F 16	Eton av Hounsl
31 Z 13	Erskine cres N17	117 V 10	Eton av New Mald
87 T 13	Ernshaw pla SW15	42 E 13	Eton av Wemb
27 Y 15	Erskine hill NW11	47 N 19	Eton College rd NW3
131 R 1	Erskine ms NW1	42 E 12	Eton ct Wemb
32 L 12	Erskine rd E17	25 R 12	Eton gro NW9
131 R 1	Erskine rd NW1	93 Z 8	Eton gro SE13
154 G 7	Erskine rd Sutton	46 M 19	Eton vlls NW3
108 G 13	Esam way SW16	54 D 13	Eton rd Ilf
113 R 10	Escott gdns SE9	84 J 12	Eton rd Rich
78 H 11	Escreet gro SE18	46 M 19	Eton vlls NW3
38 K 18	Esher av Rom	50 H 11	Etropol rd E5
153 R 6	Esher av Sutton	75 X 15	Etta st SE8
115 Y 2	Esher clo Bxly	64 H 16	Ettrick st E14
105 O 3	Esher gdns SW19	112 A 5	Eugenia rd SE16
78 E 13	Erwood rd SE18	117 O 4	Eureka rd Kingst
54 H 9	Esher rd Ilf	134 B 14	Europa pl EC1
58 E 2	Eskdale av Grnfd	78 F 8	Europe rd SE18
42 G 7	Eskdale clo Wemb	68 E 8	Eustace rd E6
98 D 4	Eskdale rd Bxly Hth	145 T 18	Eustace rd SW6
121 N 5	Esher ms Mitch	55 X 1	Eustace rd Rom
65 U 12	Esk rd E13	132 E 15	Euston rd NW1
109 P 18	Eskmontridge SE19	122 E 20	Euston rd Croy
39 O 3	Esk way Rom	156 G 1	Euston rd Croy
44 F 1	Esmar cres NW9	132 E 14	Euston sq NW1
151 T 8	Esmeralda rd SE1	132 D 13	Euston station NW1
129 P 5	Esmond rd NW6	132 D 14	Euston st NW1
73 Z 10	Esmond rd W4	90 G 4	Evandale rd SW9
87 T 11	Esmond rd SW18	47 T 13	Evangelist rd NW5
88 A 18	Esparto st SW18	100 G 5	Evans gro Felt
81 R 13	Essenden rd Blvdr	112 A 5	Evans rd SE6
157 R 17	Essenden rd S Croy	33 U 2	Evanston av E4
129 U 15	Esendine rd W9	35 P 18	Evanston gdns Ilf
83 T 8	Essex av Islwth	92 C 6	Evelina rd SE15
32 G 12	Essex clo E17	110 D 19	Evelina rd SE20
119 N 16	Essex clo Mrdn	120 L 2	Eveline rd Mitch
38 G 20	Essex clo Rom	25 X 12	Evelyn av NW9
86 D 4	Essex ct SW13	82 J 18	Evelyn clo Twick
141 S 7	Essex ct WC2	22 A 2	Evelyn dri Pinn
30 K 18	Essex gdns N4	146 E 10	Evelyn gdns SW7
109 P 15	Essex gro SE19	84 L 9	Evelyn gdns Rich
15 N 20	Essex Pk ms W3	73 N 3	Evelyn gro W5
74 B 4	Essex Pk ms W3	58 E 17	Evelyn gro S'hall
73 X 12	Essex pl W4	77 V 2	Evelyn rd E16
20 M 5	Essex rd E4	33 U 14	Evelyn rd E17
33 V 19	Essex rd E10	106 A 14	Evelyn rd SW19
53 S 16	Essex rd E12	73 X 9	Evelyn rd W4
32 H 18	Essex rd E17	5 Z 15	Evelyn rd Barnt
34 J 7	Essex rd E18	84 K 8	Evelyn rd Rich
49 N 8	Essex rd N1	102 E 6	Evelyn rd Rich
133 Y 4	Essex rd N1	75 W 13	Evelyn st SE8
44 C 19	Essex rd NW10	84 J 8	Evelyn ter Rich
51 X 1	Essex rd SE11	134 E 10	Evelyn wlk N1
61 U 19	Essex rd W3	155 X 7	Evelyn way Wallgtn
73 X 11	Essex rd W4	140 E 4	Evelyn yd W1
67 T 3	Essex rd Bark	111 V 19	Evening hil Becknhm
56 H 15	Essex rd Dgnhm	56 H 7	Evenlode way Dgnhm
8 B 15	Essex rd Enf		
38 H 12	Essex rd Rom	87 S 3	Evenwood clo SW15
55 S 2	Essex rd Rom	16 G 19	Everard av Brom
51 X 1	Essex Rd south E11	42 H 11	Everard way Wemb
52 E 14	Essex st E7	74 F 18	Everdon rd SW13
141 R 8	Essex st WC2	64 F 14	Everest pla E14
95 S 13	Everest rd SE9	112 H 2	Exford rd SE12
81 O 15	Everett wk Blvdr	136 B 10	Exhibition clo W12
20 D 5	Everglade strand NW9	138 G 19	Exhibition rd SW7
		146 G 2	Exhibition rd SW7
133 P 5	Everilda st N1	62 M 20	Exhibition rd W12
49 U 11	Evering rd N16	128 H 20	Exmoor st W10
28 M 7	Everington rd N10	133 T 16	Exmouth mkt EC1
29 N 6	Everington rd N10	32 L 16	Exmouth rd E17
144 H 15	Everington st W6	126 G 7	Exmouth rd Brom
61 Z 9	Everitt rd NW10	80 E 20	Exmouth rd Welling
48 E 5	Eversleigh st N4	63 P 17	Exmouth st E1
51 Z 12	Eve rd E11	65 O 12	Exning rd E16
65 N 7	Eve rd E11	150 J 8	Exon st SE17
31 T 9	Eve rd N17	61 X 2	Exton cres NW10
83 Z 11	Eve rd Islwth	55 U 14	Exton gdns Dgnhm
37 U 20	Eve rd Rom	141 T 15	Exton st SE1
13 N 20	Eversfield gdns NW9	90 G 2	Eyethorne rd SW9
		57 W 11	Eyhurst av Hornch
84 M 4	Eversfield rd Rich	44 H 6	Eyhurt clo NW2
84 N 4	Eversfield rd Rich	108 M 11	Eylewood rd SE27
120 A 14	Eversham grn Mrdn	91 V 17	Eynella rd SE22
132 C 10	Eversholt st NW1	136 B 4	Eynham rd W12
48 C 4	Evershot rd N4	62 M 17	Eynham rd W12
66 B 3	Eversleigh rd E6	115 V 2	Eynsford cres Bxly
27 W 2	Eversleigh rd N3	54 J 7	Eynsford rd Ilf
89 O 5	Eversleigh rd SW8	80 F 6	Eynsham dri SE2
5 S 18	Eversleigh rd Barnt	115 S 13	Eynswood dri Sidcp
99 P 5	Eversley av Bxly Hth	74 E 14	Eyot gdns W6
43 P 7	Eversley av Wemb	133 S 18	Eyre St hill EC1
7 P 19	Eversley clo N21	135 P 11	Ezra st E2
7 T 19	Eversley cres N21		
99 R 5	Eversley cros SW9 Hth		
83 R 2	Eversley cres Islwth		
7 R 19	Eversley mt N21		
7 T 20	Eversley Pk rd N21		
17 R 1	Eversley Pk rd N21		**F**
104 J 14	Eversley pk SW19	26 G 16	Faber gdns NW4
77 V 16	Eversley rd SE7	145 P 17	Fabian rd SW6
109 O 17	Eversley rd SE19	66 F 12	Fabian st E6
116 M 10	Eversley rd Surb	31 V 8	Factory la N17
117 N 10	Eversley rd Surb	156 N 6	Factory la Croy
158 M 6	Eversley way Croy	76 F 13	Factory pl E14
91 U 8	Everthorpe rd SE15	78 E 4	Factory rd E16
132 A 14	Everton bldg NW1	71 T 3	Factory yd W7
24 L 10	Everton dri Stanm	117 Z 7	Fairacre New Mald
123 W 19	Everton rd Croy	118 A 6	Fairacre New Mald
29 P 19	Evesby rd W Wckm	126 F 13	Fair acres Brom
		158 L 19	Fairacres Croy
33 P 7	Evesham av E17	90 H 2	Fairbairn grn SW9
58 K 5	Evesham clo Grnfd	31 X 11	Fairbanks rd N17
153 W 16	Evesham clo Sutton	31 R 10	Fairbourne rd N17
65 O 2	Evesham rd E15	47 Y 7	Fairbridge rd N19
120 A 15	Evesham rd Mrdn	17 T 18	Fairbrook clo N13
35 X 11	Evesham way Ilf	17 T 18	Fairbrook rd N13
89 P 6	Evesham wlk SW11	94 H 13	Fairby rd SE12
115 O 15	Evry rd Sidcp	134 L 17	Fairchild st EC2
87 X 18	Ewanrigg ter Wdfd Grn	143 T 6	Fairclough st E1
		54 C 18	Faircross av Bark
30 E 5	Ewart gro N22	38 L 2	Faircross av Rom
7 F 20	Ewart rd SE23	86 K 9	Fairdale gdns SW15
48 A 18	Ewe clo N7	152 J 20	Fairfax av Epsom
152 G 16	Ewell By-pass Epsom	94 M 3	Fairfax gdns SE3
116 A 18	Ewell rd Surb	47 D 20	Fairfax pl NW6
117 P 20	Ewell rd Surb	130 C 1	Fairfax pl NW6
153 R 15	Ewell rd Sutton	30 H 14	Fairfax rd N8
110 D 1	Ewelme rd SE23	46 E 20	Fairfax rd NW6
90 F 20	Ewen cres SW2	130 C 1	Fairfax rd NW6
90 F 20	Ewen cres SW2	74 B 9	Fairfax rd W4
141 Z 15	Ewer st SE1	101 Z 16	Fairfax rd Tedd
157 U 20	Ewhurst av S Croy	102 C 18	Fairfax rd Tedd
153 N 20	Ewhurst clo Sutton	26 L 20	Fairfield av NW4
92 M 16	Ewhurst rd SE4	12 E 20	Fairfield av Edg
93 N 16	Ewhurst rd SE4	25 S 1	Fairfield av Edg
110 M 4	Exbury rd SE6	100 L 1	Fairfield av Twick
93 U 5	Excelsior gdns SE13	15 S 14	Fairfield clo N12
117 O 4	Excelsior rd SE13	9 U 16	Fairfield clo Enf
L 4	Exchange bldngs E1	57 W 6	Fairfield clo Hornch
140 L 10	Exchange ct WC2	96 K 15	Fairfield clo Sidcp
29 P 16	Exchange st Rom	12 E 20	Fairfield cres Edg
53 S 2	Exeter gdns Ilf	88 B 13	Fairfield dri SW18
65 T 16	Exeter rd E16	60 E 4	Fairfield dri Grnfd
33 N 15	Exeter rd E17	23 N 11	Fairfield dri Harrow
19 O 9	Exeter rd N9	116 K 3	Fairfield east Kingst
16 E 3	Exeter rd N14	30 B 17	Fairfield gdns N8
45 S 17	Exeter rd NW2	71 Y 10	Fairfield gdns W7
123 T 17	Exeter rd Croy	28 A 15	Fairfield pl Kingst
56 H 19	Exeter rd Dgnhm	116 K 3	Fairfield north Kingst
9 T 12	Exeter rd Enf	157 S 6	Fairfield path Croy
100 E 7	Exeter rd Felt	116 K 6	Fairfield pl Kingst
40 C 6	Exeter rd Harrow	64 B 7	Fairfield rd E3
91 U 1	Exeter rd SE5	32 J 8	Fairfield rd E17
151 N 20	Exeter rd SE15	30 B 17	Fairfield rd N8
96 K 4	Exeter rd Welling	18 K 15	Fairfield rd N18
140 M 9	Exeter rd WC2	125 O 2	Fairfield rd Becknhm
141 N 9	Exeter rd WC2	98 B 5	Fairfield rd Bxly Hth
75 X 20	Exeter way SE14	112 E 18	Fairfield rd Brom
112 H 2	Exford gdns SE12	157 R 5	Fairfield rd Croy
		54 A 17	Fairfield rd Ilf
		116 J 4	Fairfield rd Kingst
		58 E 16	Fairfield rd S'hall
		21 S 19	Fairfield rd Wdfd Grn
		25 W 15	Fairfield clo NW9
		25 W 14	Fairfields cres NW9

116	K 5	Fairfield south Kingst	
82	M 8	Fairfields rd Hounsl	
88	A 11	Fairfield st SW18	
4	L 17	Fairfield way Barnt	
152	A 12	Fairfield way Epsom	
116	K 4	Fairfield west Kingst	
64	B 11	Fairfoot rd E3	
98	M 2	Fairford av Bxly Hth	
99	N 2	Fairford av Bxly Hth	
124	G 13	Fairford clo Becknhm	
152	E 5	Fairford gdns Worc Pk	
5	Y 10	Fairgreen Barnt	
5	Y 11	Fairgreen east Barnt	
124	E 16	Fairhaven av Croy	
46	C 20	Fairhazel gdns NW6	
130	C 2	Fairhazel gdns NW6	
39	Y 14	Fairholme av Rom	
27	T 12	Fairholme clo N3	
27	U 12	Fairholme gdns N3	
145	N 11	Fairholme rd W14	
122	G 17	Fairholme rd Croy	
23	V 17	Fairholme rd Harrow	
35	V 20	Fairholme rd Ilf	
153	V 13	Fairholme rd Sutton	
49	P 3	Fairholt rd N16	
146	L 1	Fairholt st SW7	
52	C 19	Fairland av Buck Hl	
21	U 7	Fairlands av Buck Hl	
153	Z 2	Fairlands av Sutton	
122	d 10	Fairlands av Thntn Hth	
70	F 1	Fairlands gdn S'hall	
77	X 18	Fairlawn SE7	
28	K 12	Fairlawn av N2	
73	W 11	Fairlawn av W4	
97	W 5	Fairlawn av Bxly Hth	
6	J 20	Fairlawn clo N14	
100	E 9	Fairlawn clo Feth	
103	U 15	Fairlawn clo Kingst	
34	F 2	Fairlawn dri Wdfd Grn	
70	F 1	Fairlawn gdns S'hall	
73	W 10	Fairlawn gro W4	
110	J 12	Fairlawn pk SE26	
105	V 19	Fairlawn rd SW19	
84	F 17	Fairlawns Twick	
60	F 13	Fairlea pl W5	
92	D 19	Fairlie gdns SE23	
152	L 8	Fairlight av Worc Pk	
20	J 8	Fairlight av E4	
82	B 6	Fairlight av NW10	
21	T 20	Fairlight av Wdfd Grn	
20	J 8	Fairlight clo E4	
106	H 10	Fairlight rd SW17	
52	Z 19	Fairlop clo	
57	Z 19	Fairlop clo Hornch	
36	C 2	Fairlop gdns Ilf	
36	H 7	Fairlop plain Ilf	
51	X 2	Fairlop rd E11	
36	B 8	Fairlop rd Ilf	
127	U 18	Fairmead Brom	
117	T 20	Fairmead Brom	
127	U 20	Fairmead clo Brom	
117	Z 7	Fairmead clo New Mald	
12	H 11	Fairmead cres Edg	
35	P 16	Fairmead gdns Ilf	
47	Z 9	Fairmead rd N19	
122	E 18	Fairmead rd Croy	
107	X 12	Fairmile av SW16	
90	D 15	Fairmount rd SW2	
96	D 13	Fairoak dri SE9	
39	O 8	Fairoak gdns Rom	
10	E 8	Fairseat clo Bushey Watf	
134	A 3	Fairstead wlk N1	
142	M 16	Fair st SE1	
143	N 19	Fair st SE1	
77	T 13	Fairthorn rd SE7	
42	G 17	Fairview av Wemb	
32	H 5	Fairview clo E17	
40	G 3	Fairview cres Harrow	
34	J 4	Fairview gdns Wdfd Grn	
60	C 18	Fairview pl SW2	
31	V 18	Fairview rd N15	
122	B 1	Fairview rd SW16	
77	H 6	Fairview rd Enf	
154	H 12	Fairview rd Sutton	
12	C 14	Fairview way Edg	
97	N 10	Fairwater av Welling	
118	L 6	Fairway SW20	
97	Z 13	Fairway Bxly Hth	
21	Z 16	Fairway Wdfd Grn	
25	T 10	Fairway av NW9	
46	C 1	Fairway clo NW11	
124	H 13	Fairway clo Croy	
58	M 2	Fairway dr Grnfd	
58	B 15	Fairway gdns Ilf	
24	J 7	Fairways Stanm	
102	G 16	Fairways Tedd	
17	Z 10	Fairway the N13	
6	E 19	Fairway the N14	
18	A 11	Fairway the N18	
12	L 9	Fairway the NW7	
82	B 17	Fairway the W3	
5	O 19	Fairway the Barnt	
127	T 11	Fairway the Brom	
41	N 17	Fairway the Grnfrd	
103	Z 20	Fairway the Kingst	
117	Z 1	Fairway the New Mald	
42	C 5	Fairway the Wemb	
31	R 12	Fairweather clo N15	
31	X 19	Fairweather rd N16	
110	H 8	Fairwyn rd SE26	
127	R 7	Falcon av Brom	
140	G 5	Falconberg ct W1	
140	F 5	Falconberg ms W1	
9	T 18	Falcon cres Enf	
129	P 11	Falconer ms W9	
88	J 7	Falcon gro SW11	
88	L 8	Falcon la SW11	
88	L 9	Falcon la SW11	
9	S 18	Falcon rd Enf	
100	F 17	Falcon rd Hampt	
65	S 11	Falcon st E13	
88	K 8	Falcon ter SW11	
24	K 18	Falcon way Harrow	
57	X 20	Falcon way Hornch	
96	H 6	Falconwood av Welling	
96	J 10	Falconwood pde Welling	
158	M 18	Falconwood rd Croy	
159	N 20	Falconwood rd Croy	
154	A 11	Falcourt clo Sutton	
134	L 10	Falkirk st N1	
27	Y 3	Falkland av N3	
16	D 13	Falkland av N11	
123	S 4	Falkland Pk av SE25	
30	H 14	Falkland rd N8	
47	V 4	Falkland rd NW5	
4	E 10	Falkland rd Barnt	
53	X 11	Fallaize av Ilf	
27	Y 13	Falloden way NW11	
15	R 20	Fallow Court av N12	
10	K 12	Fallowfield Stanm	
10	L 12	Fallowfield ct Stanm	
107	T 17	Fallsbrook rd SW16	
33	P 10	Falmer rd E17	
31	N 15	Falmer rd N15	
8	F 14	Falmer rd Enf	
20	L 17	Falmouth av E4	
30	C 2	Falmouth clo N22	
35	P 16	Falmouth gdns Ilf	
35	N 2	Falmouth gdns Wdfd Grn	
150	B 3	Falmouth rd SE1	
150	E 1	Falmouth rd SE1	
51	Y 15	Falmouth rd E15	
110	L 10	Fambridge rd SE26	
56	D 3	Fambridge rd Dgnhm	
145	P 12	Fane st W14	
134	A 19	Fann st EC1	
54	C 18	Fanshawe av Bark	
56	A 15	Fanshawe cres Dgnhm	
102	D 10	Fanshawe rd Rich	
134	J 11	Fanshaw st N1	
86	M 7	Fanthorpe st SW15	
115	S 5	Faraday av Sidcp	
48	D 19	Faraday clo N7	
52	B 19	Faraday rd E15	
78	B 9	Faraday rd SE18	
105	Z 14	Faraday rd SW19	
106	A 14	Faraday rd SW19	
61	W 18	Faraday rd W3	
128	L 20	Faraday rd W10	
58	K 18	Faraday rd S'hall	
97	M 7	Faraday rd Well	
97	N 8	Faraday rd Welling	
127	X 3	Fard clo Brom	
140	X 3	Fareham st W1	
120	G 2	Farewell pl Mitch	
127	X 16	Faringdon av Brom	
64	M 1	Faringford rd E15	
95	N 1	Farjeon rd SE3	
126	D 16	Farleigh av Brom	
49	U 12	Farleigh pl N16	
49	V 12	Farleigh rd N16	
54	J 4	Farley av	
123	X 9	Farley pl SE25	
93	T 17	Farley rd SE6	
157	Z 18	Farley rd S Croy	
86	H 19	Farlington pl SW15	
87	N 8	Farlow rd SW15	
88	B 10	Farlton rd SW18	
45	T 10	Farm av NW2	
108	A 9	Farm av SW16	
22	G 20	Farm av Harrow	
42	E 18	Farm av Wemb	
21	Y 12	Farm clo Buck Hl	
69	W 1	Farm clo Dgnhm	
58	W 19	Farm clo S'hall	
154	H 16	Farm clo Sutton	
132	F 1	Farmcote rd SE12	
77	T 14	Farmdale rd SE7	
146	J 16	Farmdale rd Carsh	
158	M 2	Farm dri Croy	
159	N 2	Farm dri Croy	
51	R 3	Farmer rd E17	
149	Y 19	Farmers rd SE5	
137	T 13	Farmer st W8	
14	L 14	Farmfield clo N12	
111	Y 12	Farmfield rd Brom	
112	A 13	Farmfield rd Brom	
107	V 19	Farmhouse rd SW16	
33	N 20	Farmilo rd E17	
50	M 1	Farmilo rd E17	
154	H 5	Farmington av Sutton	
7	T 6	Farmlands Enf	
62	G 19	Farmlands the Grnfd	
113	Y 11	Farmland wlk Chisl	
145	V 16	Farm la SW6	
158	M 3	Farm la Croy	
16	G 2	Farmleigh N14	
137	S 13	Farm pl W8	
99	X 11	Farm pl Drtfrd	
17	X 5	Farm rd N21	
12	G 17	Farm rd Edg	
120	A 12	Farm rd Mrdn	
154	G 16	Farm rd Sutton	
111	S 9	Farmstead rd SE6	
23	R 6	Farmstead rd Harrow	
139	W 11	Farm st W1	
98	G 16	Farm vale Bxly	
27	X 17	Farm wlk NW11	
21	Y 13	Farm way Buck Hl	
55	T 11	Farmway Dgnhm	
152	M 5	Farm way Worc Pk	
53	N 4	Farm way Worc Pk	
94	M 11	Farnaby rd SE9	
111	Y 19	Farnaby rd Brom	
112	A 20	Farnaby rd Brom	
126	B 1	Farnaby rd Brom	
33	R 10	Farnan av E17	
108	A 12	Farnan rd SW16	
32	G 11	Farnborough av E17	
158	H 17	Farnborough av S Croy	
43	T 8	Farnborough clo Wemb	
158	H 18	Farnborough cres S Croy	
134	U 18	Farncombe st SE16	
17	X 9	Farndale av N13	
59	N 8	Farndale cres Grnfd	
83	R 8	Farnell rd Islwth	
15	R 2	Farnham clo N20	
118	J 4	Farnham gdns New Mald	
141	Y 14	Farnham pl SE1	
34	M 20	Farnham rd Ilf	
97	U 4	Farnham rd Welling	
97	P 12	Farnham royal SE11	
31	Y 2	Farningham rd N17	
20	L 2	Farnley rd E4	
123	P 9	Farnley rd SE25	
144	H 2	Faroe rd W14	
7	S 5	Farorna wlk Enf	
109	U 14	Farquhar rd SE19	
105	Y 7	Farquhar rd SW19	
122	L 19	Farquharon rd Croy	
37	Z 20	Farrance rd Rom	
55	Z 1	Farrance rd Rom	
64	A 17	Farrance st E14	
30	J 6	Farrant av N22	
67	Z 6	Farr av Bark	
110	G 4	Farren rd SE23	
29	X 13	Farrer rd N8	
24	J 14	Farrer rd Harrow	
88	H 5	Farrier clo Grnfd	
47	U 20	Farrier st NW1	
133	U 17	Farringdon rd EC1	
133	U 18	Farringdon rd EC1	
141	W 5	Farringdon st EC4	
8	B 7	Farr rd Enf	
21	N 10	Farthing clo E4	
143	V 12	Farthing fields E1	
115	S 9	Farwell rd Sidcp	
112	E 20	Farwig la Brom	
143	O 2	Fashion st E1	
127	N 8	Fashoda rd Brom	
49	X 17	Fassett rd E8	
116	J 3	Fassett rd Kingst	
49	X 17	Fassett sq E8	
73	V 17	Fauconberg rd W4	
92	D 1	Faulkner st SE15	
35	S 20	Fauna clo Rom	
149	X 11	Faunce st SE17	
87	X 2	Favart rd SW6	
21	O 6	Faversham av E4	
8	B 19	Faversham av Enf	
92	M 21	Faversham rd SE6	
124	M 3	Faversham rd Becknhm	
120	B 14	Faversham rd Mrdn	
88	G 6	Fawcett clo SW11	
62	C 2	Fawcett rd NW10	
156	K 6	Fawcett rd Croy	
146	A 14	Fawcett st SW10	
87	V 11	Fawe Pk rd SW15	
64	D 15	Fawe st E14	
31	Y 12	Fawley rd N17	
45	Z 16	Fawley rd NW6	
46	A 16	Fawley rd NW6	
90	K 12	Fawnbrake av SE24	
65	X 6	Fawn rd E13	
61	Y 1	Fawood av NW10	
98	E 13	Faygate cres Bxly Hth	
108	C 4	Faygate rd SW2	
107	V 12	Fayland av SW16	
77	S 12	Fearon st SE10	
158	L 17	Featherbed la Croy	
159	N 20	Featherbed la Croy	
76	K 16	Feathers pl SE10	
110	B 4	Featherstone av SE23	
13	X 20	Featherstone rd NW7	
70	A 8	Featherstone rd S'hall	
134	E 16	Featherstone st EC1	
70	C 7	Featherstone ter S'hall	
90	H 6	Featley rd SW9	
60	E 5	Federal rd Grnfd	
80	F 12	Federation rd SE2	
23	Z 5	Felbridge av Stanm	
24	A 5	Felbridge av Stanm	
108	F 9	Felbridge clo SW16	
154	C 19	Felbridge clo Sutton	
54	L 5	Felbrigge rd Ilf	
93	R 16	Felday rd SE13	
87	U 2	Felden st SW6	
22	C 3	Feldon clo Pinn	
74	J 11	Felgate ms W6	
113	Y 5	Felhampton rd SE9	
56	J 12	Felhurst rd Dgnhm	
30	A 17	Felix av N8	
59	Z 20	Felix rd W13	
71	X 1	Felix rd W13	
18	L 12	Felixstowe rd N9	
31	U 10	Felixstowe rd N17	
62	K 8	Felixstowe rd NW10	
80	E 9	Felixstowe rd SE2	
63	N 6	Felix st E2	
135	X 9	Felix st E2	
91	V 13	Fellbrigg rd SE22	
135	Y 18	Fellbrigg st E1	
102	B 8	Fellbrook Rich	
154	J 4	Fellowes rd Carsh	
46	K 19	Fellows rd NW3	
156	M 5	Fell rd Croy	
77	T 12	Felltram way SE7	
89	Z 11	Felmersham clo SW4	
124	C 4	Felmingham rd SE20	
90	B 17	Felsberg rd SW2	
56	G 10	Fels clo Dgnhm	
56	L 10	Fels Farm av Dgnhm	
86	M 78	Felsham rd SW15	
87	R 9	Felsham rd SW15	
79	Y 14	Felspar clo SE18	
35	V 6	Felstead av Ilf	
34	G 20	Felstead rd E11	
65	Z 18	Felstead rd E16	
38	K 1	Felstead rd Rom	
50	M 18	Felstead st E9	
121	N 3	Feltham rd Mitch	
127	Z 15	Felton clo Brom	
67	W 5	Felton gdns Bark	
114	K 11	Felton lea Sidcp	
114	K 12	Felton lea Sidcp	
72	C 5	Felton rd W13	
67	V 5	Felton rd Bark	
134	G 5	Felton st N1	
36	D 3	Fencepiece rd Ilf	
142	J 7	Fenchurch av EC3	
142	L 7	Fenchurch bldgs EC3	
142	J 8	Fenchurch st EC3	
142	M 8	Fenchurch st station EC3	
142	K 7	Fen ct EC3	
150	L 2	Fendall st SE1	
65	R 18	Fendt clo E16	
80	H 9	Fendyke rd Blvdr	
145	R 6	Fenelon pl W14	
96	J 14	Fen gro Sidcp	
32	A 4	Fenman st N17	
112	E 15	Fenn clo Brom	
152	C 20	Fennells mead Epsom	
78	K 17	Fennel st SE18	
50	D 15	Fenn st E9	
15	T 18	Fenstanton av N12	
65	P 19	Fen st E16	
148	R 18	Fentiman rd SW8	
90	C 5	Fenton clo SW9	
113	T 12	Fenton clo Chisl	
30	H 17	Fenton rd N17	

65 U 8 Fentons av E13
78 J 17 Fenwick clo SE18
91 X 8 Fenwick gro SE15
89 Z 8 Fenwick pl SW9
91 X 8 Fenwick rd SE15
47 P 20 Ferdinand p NW1
47 P 20 Ferdinand rd NW1
117 N 11 Ferguson av Surb
48 J 16 Fergus rd N5
48 D 1 Ferme Pk rd N4
30 B 16 Ferme Pk rd N8
110 K 2 Fermor rd SE23
129 P 18 Fermoy rd W9
58 K 13 Fermoy rd Grnfd
121 Y 8 Fern av Mitch
41 V 14 Fernbank av Wemb
96 H 14 Fernbrook av Sidcp
40 J 2 Fernbrook dri Harrow
93 Y 15 Fernbrook rd SE13
94 A 15 Fernbrook rd SE13
49 W 14 Ferncliffe rd E8
15 Y 18 Ferncroft av N12
45 Z 11 Ferncroft av NW3
126 L 4 Ferndale Brom
33 W 15 Ferndale av E17
8 C 8 Ferndale av Hounsl
52 J 20 Ferndale rd E7
52 B 6 Ferndale rd E11
31 V 17 Ferndale rd N15
124 A 12 Ferndasle rd SE28
89 Z 9 Ferndale rd SW4
90 D 9 Ferndale rd SW9
38 L 7 Ferndale rd Rom
23 V 13 Ferndale ter Harrow
60 B 14 Fern dene W13
90 M 10 Ferndene rd SE24
91 N 8 Ferndene rd SE24
38 F 19 Fernden way Rom
22 A 2 Ferndown clo Pinn
154 F 14 Ferndown clo Sutton
91 N 19 Ferndown rd SE9
16 B 4 Ferney rd Barnt
5 P 16 Fernhall dri Ilf
122 L 7 Fernham rd Thntn Hth
129 P 11 Fernhead rd W9
33 X 8 Fernhill ct E17
102 H 13 Fernhill gdns Kingst
78 G 3 Fernhill st E16
92 F 13 Fernholme rd SE15
12 B 18 Fernhurst gdns Edg
87 T 1 Fernhurst rd SW6
123 Z 19 Fernhurst rd Croy
70 D 15 Fern la Hounsl
107 T 2 Fernlea rd SW12
121 C 2 Fernlea rd Mitch
156 E 8 Fernleigh clo Croy
22 L 6 Fernleigh ct Harrow
42 J 6 Fernleigh ct Wemb
17 U 7 Fernleigh rd N21
133 S 13 Fernsbury st WC1
146 B 16 Fernshaw rd SW10
45 Y 6 Fernside NW3
27 P 7 Fernside NW4
21 U 4 Fernside Buck Hl
21 V 5 Fernside Buck Hl
12 L 10 Fernside av NW7
89 N 19 Fernside rd SW12
52 B 18 Ferns rd E15
64 B 3 Fern st E3
107 V 15 Fernthorpe rd SW16
49 O 14 Ferntower rd N5
53 Y 12 Fernways Ilf
107 Y 10 Fernwood av SW16
42 C 17 Fernwood av Wemb
126 K 2 Fernwood clo Brom
15 Z 10 Fernwood cres N20
158 J 19 Fernwood Croy
6 B 3 Ferry hill Barnt
70 A 10 Ferrano clo Hounsl
78 A 10 Ferranti clo SE18
155 X 8 Ferrers av Wallgtn
107 Y 13 Ferrers rd SW16
30 C 14 Ferrestone rd N8
88 B 11 Ferrier st SW18
41 N 4 Ferring clo Harrow
109 S 6 Ferrings rd SE21
158 L 6 Ferris av Croy
91 X 11 Ferris rd SE22
28 E 5 Ferron rd E5
78 J 8 Ferry appr SE18
31 Y 12 Ferry la N17
74 E 17 Ferry la SW13
72 J 18 Ferry la Brentf
73 N 17 Ferry la Rich
58 L 7 Ferrymead av Grnfd
58 N 8 Ferrymead dri Grnfd
59 O 6 Ferrymead gdns Grnfd
102 B 7 Ferrymoor Rich
63 M 8 Ferry pl SE 18
86 G 1 Ferry rd SW13
16 A 16 Ferry rd Surb
102 A 12 Ferry rd Tedd

76 F 13 Ferry st E14
87 O 7 Festing rd SW15
115 V 3 Festival clo Bxly
154 M 9 Festival wlk Carsh
141 T 4 Fetter la EC4
76 A 18 Finch st SE8
20 C 19 Field clo E4
126 L 4 Field clo Brom
21 Y 11 Field clo Buck Hl
141 R 1 Field ct WC1
40 A 19 Field end Grnfd
101 W 10 Field end Tedd
107 W 20 Fieldend rd SE17
60 C 14 Field End rd Ruis
68 H 20 Field Fare rd SE2
126 K 4 Fieldgate la Mitch
143 T 3 Fieldgate st E1
107 W 2 Fieldhouse rd SW12
101 N 8 Fielding la Twick
74 A 7 Fielding rd W3
73 Z 8 Fielding rd W4
136 H 20 Fielding rd W14
150 B 13 Fielding st SE17
110 C 1 Fieldings the SE23
72 D 19 Field la Brentf
101 Y 13 Field la Tedd
26 C 3 Field mead NW9
133 U 10 Field pl EC1
118 C 14 Field pl New Mald
52 E 14 Field rd E7
33 N 14 Field rd E17
31 P 10 Field rd N17
144 L 13 Field rd W6
153 S 11 Fieldsend rd Sutton
111 X 13 Fieldside rd Brom
37 V 15 Fields Park cres Rom
133 N 11 Field st WC1
106 F 2 Fieldview SW18
58 K 4 Field wy Grnfd
61 W 1 Field way NW10
159 S 15 Field way Croy
159 T 13 Field way Croy
55 S 11 Fieldway Dgnhm
48 G 16 Fieldway cres N5
65 S 15 Fife rd E16
56 K 3 Fife rd N22
85 V 14 Fife rd SW14
116 H 3 Fife rd Kingst
133 O 7 Fife st E1
53 T 12 Fifth av E12
128 K 15 Fifth av W10
101 P 6 Fifth Cross rd Twick
43 S 12 Fifth wy Wemb
107 O 18 Figgs rd Mitch
49 W 5 Filey av N16
154 D 16 Filey rd E15
8 F 8 Fillebrook av Enf
51 Y 3 Fillebrook rd E11
53 A 1 Fillebrook rd E11
87 T 1 Filmer rd SW6
91 N 19 Filmer rd SW6
81 W 13 Filston rd Erith
145 X 12 Finborough rd SW10
100 M 16 Finborough rd SW17
80 A 8 Finchale rd SE2
109 N 11 Finch av SE27
43 X 17 Finch clo NW10
34 M 1 Finchingfield av Wdfd Grn
160 G 6 Finch la EC2
15 N 20 Finchley ct N12
27 O 12 Finchley la NW4
15 S 12 Finchley pk N12
130 E 8 Finchley pl NW8
46 D 18 Finchley rd NW3
130 F 3 Finchley rd NW8
27 W 15 Finchley rd NW11
45 X 4 Finchley rd NW11
27 Y 1 Finchley way N3
141 P 19 Finck st SE1
52 K 16 Finden rd E7
64 G 16 Findhorn st E14
87 X 16 Findon clo SW18
40 K 10 Findon clo Harrow
18 L 5 Findon rd N9
74 G 4 Findon rd W12
77 P 13 Fingal st SE10
92 G 3 Finland rd SE4
87 P 2 Finlay st SW6
63 N 11 Finnis st E2
135 X 15 Finnis st E2
55 Z 20 Finnymore rd Dgnhm
55 Z 20 Finnymore rd Dgnhm
160 H 1 Finsbury av EC2
142 G 2 Finsbury cir EC2
160 G 2 Finsbury cir EC2
134 J 19 Finsbury mkt EC2
48 J 3 Finsbury pk N4
58 K 20 Finsbury Pk av N4
48 H 7 Finsbury Pk rd N4
134 F 20 Finsbury pav EC2
30 B 3 Finsbury rd N22
134 G 20 Finsbury sq EC2

134 E 20 Finsbury st EC2
90 M 9 Finsen rd SE5
136 F 4 Finstock rd W10
57 W 17 Finucane gdns Rainhm
10 B 7 Finucane rd Bushey Watford
92 B 4 Firbank rd SE15
41 S 9 Fircroft gdns Harrow
106 M 6 Fircroft rd SW17
116 K 15 Firebell all surb
155 Z 16 Firefly clo Wallgtn
118 E 13 Fir gro New Mald
111 N 9 Firhill rd SE6
100 A 13 Fir rd Felt
119 U 20 Firs rd Sutton
29 P 12 Firs av N10
85 W 11 Firs av SW14
158 F 1 Firsby av Croy
49 V 3 Firsby rd N16
29 P 12 Firs clo N10
92 G 20 Firs clo SE23
17 Y 10 Firscroft N13
17 Y 3 Firs la N21
18 B 6 Firs Park av N21
18 A 6 Firs Park gdns N21
109 Z 8 Fir st SE26
53 R 13 First av E12
65 T 10 First av E13
33 P 14 First av E17
19 P 15 First av N18
27 N 13 First av NW4
86 A 7 First av SW14
74 D 2 First av W3
74 D 3 First av W3
129 N 16 First av W10
69 V 5 First av Dgnhm
8 G 18 First av Enf
152 A 19 First av Epsom
37 V 14 First av Rom
80 G 19 First av Welling
42 H 6 First av Wemb
101 S 3 First Cross rd Twick
15 U 6 Firs the N20
60 F 15 Firs the W5
146 M 4 First st SW3
1 Firstway SW20
21 S 15 Firs wth Wdfd Grn
152 C 11 Firswood av Epsom
152 C 12 Firswood av Epsom
87 S 3 Firth gdns SW6
121 N 2 Firtree av Mitch
152 E 10 Firtree clo Epsom
39 O 9 Fir Tree clo Rom
159 O 7 Fir Tree gdns Croy
155 N 18 Fir Tree gro Carsh
82 C 11 Fir Tree rd Hounsl
56 K 10 Fir Tree rd Epsom
8 C 11 Fir Tree wlk Enf
123 U 20 Fisher clo Croy
58 G 8 Fisher clo Grnfd
23 K 6 Fisher rd Harrow
92 E 1 Fishers ct SE14
73 Z 12 Fishers la W4
65 R 14 Fisher st E16
140 M 2 Fisher st WC1
81 T 3 Fisher's way Blvdr
130 F 17 Fisherton st NW8
102 C 11 Fishermans rd Rich
160 F 10 Fishmongers Hall st EC4
106 K 8 Fishponds rd SW17
160 G 10 Fish St hill EC3
144 L 7 Fitz-George av W14
27 V 10 Fitzalan rd N3
103 Z 19 Fitzgeorge av Kingst
86 B 9 Fitzgerald av SW14
52 F 13 Fitzgerald rd E11
85 Y 7 Fitzgerald rd SW14
139 T 4 Fitzhardinge st W1
88 H 16 Fitzhugh gro SW18
144 M 6 Fitz James av W14
157 Z 4 Fitzjames av Croy
4 H 14 Fitzjohn av Barnt
46 F 17 Fitzjohn's av NW3
139 X 12 Fitzmaurice pl W1
62 D 17 Fitzneal st W12
132 B 18 Fitzroy ct W1
109 S 18 Fitzroy gdns SE19
132 A 19 Fitzroy ms W1
46 M 5 Fitzroy pk N6
47 N 3 Fitzroy pk N6
131 T 2 Fitzroy rd NW1
132 A 18 Fitzroy sq W1
132 B 19 Fitzroy st W1
55 T 15 Fitzstephen rd Dgnhm
47 V 3 Fitzwarren gdns N19
84 M 6 Fitzwilliam av Rich
85 N 6 Fitzwilliam av Rich
89 V 7 Fitzwilliam rd SW4
100 M 13 Fitz Wygram clo Hampt
26 C 6 Five acre NW9

56 A 11 Five Elms rd Dgnhm
149 W 4 Fives ct SE11
31 O 19 Fladbury rd N15
34 A 18 Fladgate rd E11
23 Z 18 Flambard rd Harrow
63 V 17 Flamborough st E14
57 W 19 Flamingo Hornch
68 G 1 Flamstead gdns
78 C 14 Flamstead rd SE7
55 T 20 Flamstead rd Dgnhm
68 F 2 Flamstead rd Dgnhm
43 P 19 Flamsted av Wemb
74 E 8 Flanchford rd W12
106 L 17 Flanders cr SW17
66 G 2 Flanders rd E6
74 C 10 Flanders rd W4
50 E 17 Flanders way E9
143 R 9 Flank st E1
46 E 12 Flask wlk NW3
119 Z 16 Flaxley rd Mrdn
140 E 6 Flaxman ct W1
90 L 5 Flaxman SE5
132 H 14 Flaxman ter WC1
79 R 19 Flaxton rd SE18
96 F 1 Flaxton rd SE18
10 H 17 Flecker clo Stanm
116 D 19 Fleece rd Surb
48 A 17 Fleece wk N7
32 L 6 Fleeming clo E17
32 M 7 Fleeming rd E17
141 X 5 Fleet la EC4
44 H 15 Fleet rd NW3
141 T 6 Fleet st EC4
44 H 15 Fleetwood rd NW10
117 W 5 Fleetwood rd New Mald
117 W 6 Fleetwood sq New Mald
49 S 7 Fleetwood st N16
77 Z 16 Felching rd SE7
156 F 11 Fleming ct Croy
106 L 18 Fleming mead Mitch
149 X 13 Fleming st SE17
58 M 17 Fleming wy S'hall
83 U 9 Fleming wy Islwth
50 K 3 Flempton rd E10
126 J 9 Fletcher clo Brom
52 U 1 Fletcher la E10
73 W 7 Fletcher rd W4
143 T 8 Fletcher st E1
50 C 16 Fletching rd E5
29 Z 1 Fletton rd N11
134 M 19 Fleur De Lis st E1
87 P 20 Fleur gates SW19
31 R 4 Flexmere rd N17
111 Z 13 Flimwell clo Brom
95 P 6 Flintmill clo SE3
150 K 9 Flinton st SE17
150 G 8 Flint st SE17
140 H 5 Flitcroft st WC2
143 S 19 Flockton st SE16
90 K 1 Flodden rd SE5
146 L 11 Flood st SW3
146 K 12 Flood wlk SW3
64 C 17 Flora clo E14
74 H 10 Flora gdns W6
37 S 19 Flora gdns Rom
140 L 7 Flora st Blvdr
81 P 14 Flora st Blvdr
7 Y 11 Florence av Enf
120 D 12 Florence av Mrdn
92 M 1 Florence cotts SE4
7 Y 10 Florence dri Enf
73 V 17 Florence gdns W4
65 Z 3 Florence rd E6
52 G 10 Florence rd E13
48 E 2 Florence rd N4
80 G 10 Florence rd N4
92 M 2 Florence rd SE14
106 A 15 Florence rd SW19
73 X 7 Florence rd W4
60 V 20 Florence rd W5
72 J 1 Florence rd W5
124 G 4 Florence rd Becknhm
126 F 1 Florence rd Brom
103 N 19 Florence rd Kingst
70 A 9 Florence rd S'hall
157 N 20 Florence rd S Croy
65 P 12 Florence st E16
133 X 2 Florence st N1
26 L 12 Florence st NW4
92 M 1 Florence ter SE14
154 F 7 Florian av Sutton
87 U 10 Florian rd SW15
10 C 7 Florida clo Bushey Watford
108 J 20 Florida rd Thntn Hth
122 J 1 Florida rd Thntn Hth
115 T 13 Florida st E2
24 C 4 Floriston clo Stanm
24 C 4 Floriston gdns Stanm
105 S 1 Florys ct SW19
86 M 15 Floss st SW15

F

111	V 12	Flower House clo SE6
111	V 11	Flower House est SE6
13	R 18	Flower la NW7
107	O 4	Flowers ms SW17
77	Y 13	Floyd rd SE7
93	Z 10	Fluyder st SE13
140	B 1	Foley st W1
134	M 20	Folgate sq E1
134	L 20	Folgate st EC2
62	C 18	Foliot st W12
66	K 7	Folkestone rd E6
33	R 13	Folkestone rd E17
18	K 14	Folkestone rd N18
26	A 5	Folkingham la NW9
14	H 17	Folkington corner N12
64	F 18	Follett st E14
5	T 11	Folly house Barnt
32	J 3	Folly la E17
76	H 6	Folly wall E14
108	C 17	Fontaine rd SW16
89	P 9	Fontarabia rd SW8
39	P 9	Fontayne av Rainhm
57	R 20	Fontayne av Rainhm
107	U 4	Fontenoy rd SW4
	M 6	Fonteyne gdns Ilf
48	E 6	Fonthill rd N4
86	F 20	Fontley way SW15
28	D 7	Fonts hill N2
40	H 17	Fontwell clo Grnfd
23	T 1	Fontwell clo Harrow
127	V 12	Fontwell dri Brom
41	V 3	Football la Harrow
115	V 15	Footscray High st Sidcp
115	U 3	Footscray la Sidcp
115	U 9	Footscray place Sidcp
95	X 15	Footscray rd SE9
114	B 4	Footscray rd SE9
143	T 8	Forbes st E1
49	X 4	Ford clo Harrow
41	P 1	Ford clo Harrow
126	K 5	Forde av Brom
93	W 20	Fordel rd E6
21	V 20	Ford end Wdfd Grn
21	S 21	Fordham clo Barnt
5	W 13	Fordham clo Barnt
143	V 3	Fordham st E1
73	O 1	Fordhook av W5
129	R 14	Fordingley rd W9
28	M 14	Fordington rd N6
111	O 3	Fordmill rd SE6
63	X 6	Ford rd E3
56	C 20	Ford rd Dgnhm
69	P 1	Ford rd Dgnhm
69	R 1	Ford rd Dgnhm
17	X 5	Fords gro N21
65	T 17	Fords Park rd E16
68	N 16	Ford sq E1
143	Y 3	Ford sq E1
65	P 17	Ford st E16
45	S 13	Fordwych rd NW2
93	U 14	Fordyce rd SE13
56	A 5	Fordyke rd Dgnhm
27	R 5	Foreland ct NW4
79	S 10	Foreland st SE18
144	D 7	Foreman st W6
77	Y 12	Foreshore SE8
20	M 2	Forest appr E4
34	D 1	Forest appr Wdfd Grn
34	D 16	Forest clo E11
21	U 12	Forest clo Wdfd Grn
21	P 6	Forest clo E4
34	A 13	Forest ct E11
16	K 13	Forestdale N14
53	O 10	Forest dri E12
33	Z 2	Forest dri Wdfd Grn
33	X 20	Forest Dri east E10
51	V 1	Forest Dri west E10
21	Z 12	Forest edge Buck Hl
92	A 9	Forest rd SE15
155	X 16	Foresters clo Wallgtn
98	F 10	Foresters cres Bxly Hth
33	X 14	Foresters dri E17
155	Y 17	Foresters dri Wallgtn
156	A 20	Foresters dri Wallgtn
31	U 7	Forest gdns N17
26	A 14	Forest gate NW9
20	M 17	Forest glade E4
33	Z 18	Forest glade E11
34	A 18	Forest glade E11
49	U 19	Forest gro E8
92	B 16	Forest Hill rd SE22
110	B 4	Forestholme clo SE23
35	W 1	Forest house Wdfd Grn
51	Z 16	Forest la E15
52	D 15	Forest la E15
33	X 2	Forest Mt rd Wdfd Grn
142	D 2	Fore st EC2
160	D 2	Fore st EC2
18	H 19	Fore st N18
18	J 17	Fore st N18
160	E 2	Fore St av EC2
125	O 5	Forest ridge Becknhm
110	D 10	Forester path SE26
33	Y 11	Forest ri E17
33	Z 13	Forest ri E17
52	F 11	Forest rd E7
49	T 19	Forest rd E8
33	X 20	Forest rd E11
51	V 1	Forest rd E11
51	Z 16	Forest rd E15
32	C 13	Forest rd E17
33	O 10	Forest rd E17
19	N 5	Forest rd N9
99	W 2	Forest rd Erith
36	H 4	Forest rd Ilf
73	P 19	Forest rd Rich
38	H 11	Forest rd Rom
119	X 18	Forest rd Sutton
21	S 11	Forest rd Wdfd Grn
52	G 11	Forest side E7
21	X 5	Forest side Buck Hl
118	D 19	Forest side Worc Pk
52	F 15	Forest st E7
34	A 13	Foresi the E11
20	K 1	Forest view E4
52	C 1	Forest view E4
33	X 16	Forest view av E10
53	P 12	Forest View rd E12
33	U 4	Forest View rd E17
26	E 20	Forest way Sidcp
21	U 12	Forest way Wdfd Grn
21	W 13	Forest way Wdfd Grn
30	H 4	Forfar rd N22
89	P 1	Forfar rd SW11
100	B 13	Forge la Felt
153	S 16	Forge la Sutton
24	D 10	Formby av Stanm
129	Z 18	Formosa st W9
130	A 18	Formosa st W9
65	P 16	Formount clo E16
27	X 19	Forres gdns NW11
122	C 7	Forstal clo Brom
126	E 6	Forstal clo Brom
139	N 5	Forset st W1
111	W 7	Forster Memorial park SE6
31	U 9	Forster rd N17
89	Z 18	Forster rd SW2
124	H 6	Forster rd Bcknhm
122	L 15	Forster rd Croy
134	C 8	Forston st N1
123	S 1	Forsyte cres SE18
149	X 14	Forsyte gdns SE17
8	D 18	Forsyth pl Enf
54	L 11	Forterie gdns Ilf
63	N 1	Fortescue av E8
101	N 6	Fortescue av Twick
106	G 19	Fortescue rd Edg
25	X 2	Fortescue rd Edg
65	P 18	Fortess gro NW5
47	U 12	Fortess rd NW5
47	T 14	Fortess wlk NW5
89	O 9	Forthbridge rd SW11
28	K 12	Fortis green N2
29	N 12	Fortis Green av N2
29	P 11	Fortis Green rd N10
29	P 11	Fortismere av N10
47	Z 7	Fortnam rd N19
10	J 18	Fortnums av Stanm
151	R 7	Fort rd SE1
58	H 2	Fort rd Grnfd
89	Z 20	Fortrose gdns SW12
142	L 1	Fort st E1
77	V 3	Fort st E16
48	D 19	Fortuna clo N7
62	C 1	Fortune Ga rd NW10
45	Y 14	Fortune Green rd NW6
11	V 1	Fortune la Borehamwood
40	B 19	Fortunes mead Grnfd
134	B 19	Fortune st EC1
65	R 15	Forty Acre la E16
42	M 9	Forty av Wemb
43	O 8	Forty av Wemb
43	N 8	Forty clo Wemb
8	H 2	Forty hill Enf
43	T 8	Forty la Wemb
12	D 19	Forumside Edg
12	C 20	Forum way Edg
120	M 11	Forval clo Mitch
137	Z 10	Fosbury ms W2
98	A 20	Foscote rd NW4
87	V 5	Foskett rd SW6
156	F 12	Foss av Croy
77	W 14	Fossdene rd SE7
59	Z 14	Fosse way W13
93	P 9	Fossil rd SE13
80	M 20	Fossington rd Blvdr
106	E 10	Foss rd SW17
55	U 5	Fossway Dgnhm
34	J 5	Foster clo E18
160	B 4	Foster la EC2
26	M 14	Foster pl NW4
65	S 11	Foster rd E13
33	H 18	Foster rd E17
42	A 19	Foster rd W3
73	Y 14	Foster rd W4
113	T 12	Fosters clo Chisl
65	S 5	Fosters clo E13
8	F 13	Fotheringham rd E4
140	B 7	Foubert's pl W1
49	U 11	Foulden rd N16
146	G 9	Foulis ter SW7
107	N 8	Foulser rd SW17
123	N 7	Foulsham rd Thntn Hth
108	L 17	Founders gdns SE19
141	S 18	Fountain ct WC2
109	V 11	Fountain dri SE19
110	H 10	Fountain rd SW17
122	K 4	Fountain rd Thntn Hth
100	F 6	Fountains av Felt
100	F 5	Fountains clo Felt
16	M 2	Fountains cres N14
17	N 1	Fountains cres N14
31	X 14	Fountayne rd N15
49	W 7	Fountayne rd N16
148	H 19	Fount st SW8
9	V 7	Fouracres Enf
12	J 19	Fourland wlk Edg
143	O 1	Fournier st E1
153	V 2	Four season cres Sutton
53	S 12	Fourth av E12
128	L 12	Fourth av W10
56	M 5	Fourth av Rom
57	N 5	Fourth av Rom
101	P 4	Fourth Cross rd Twick
43	U 13	Fourth way Wemb
10	C 2	Four tubs Bushey Watf
20	L 6	Fowey av Ilf
35	O 15	Fowey av Ilf
88	G 8	Fowler clo SW11
52	E 12	Fowler rd E7
121	P 2	Fowler rd Mitch
115	X 13	Fowlers av Sidcp
60	G 11	Fowlers wlk W5
88	K 7	Fownes st SW11
133	Y 20	Fox And Knot st EC1
92	K 8	Foxberry rd SE4
93	W 14	Foxborough gdns SE4
107	R 4	Foxbourne rd SW17
114	F 16	Foxbury av Chisl
114	F 16	Foxbury av Sidcp
112	G 16	Foxbury clo Brom
112	G 16	Foxbury rd Brom
63	R 11	Fox clo E1
65	R 20	Fox clo E16
159	T 14	Foxcombe Croy
86	G 20	Foxcombe rd SW15
129	V 19	Foxcote ms NW9
17	Z 14	Foxct EC1
95	Z 2	Foxcroft rd SE18
96	A 2	Foxcroft rd SE18
158	C 20	Foxearth rd S Croy
158	C 19	Foxearth spur S Croy
94	D 8	Foxes dale SE3
125	X 6	Foxes dale Brom
62	D 19	Foxglove st W12
16	M 12	Fox gro N14
17	N 12	Foxgrove N14
111	S 18	Foxgrove av Becknhm
111	U 19	Foxgrove rd Becknhm
47	X 9	Foxham rd N19
10	V 19	Fox hill SE19
109	V 19	Fox Hill SE19
109	Y 18	Fox Hill gdns SE19
95	P 12	Foxhole rd SE9
59	N 10	Foxholt gdns NW10
81	V 12	Fox Ho rd Blvdr
56	K 14	Foxlands cres Dgnhm
56	K 16	Foxlands rd Dgnhm
17	O 8	Fox la N13
60	J 12	Fox lane W5
149	V 18	Foxley rd SW9
122	H 8	Foxley rd Thntn Hth
88	L 3	Foxmore st SW11
120	H 4	Fox's path Mitch
65	O 16	Fox st E16
94	H 7	Foxwell st SE4
94	B 10	Foxwood rd SE3
31	Y 4	Foyle rd N17
77	O 17	Foyle rd SE7
14	K 12	Framfield clo N12
48	J 14	Framfield rd N5
59	V 17	Framfield rd W7
107	O 19	Framfield rd Mitch
113	S 10	Framlingham cres SE9
153	X 15	Frampton clo Sutton
50	C 20	Frampton Pk rd E9
82	B 12	Frampton rd Hounsl
130	H 17	Frampton st NW8
93	O 13	Francemary rd SE4
20	C 18	Frances rd E4
78	G 12	Frances st SE18
106	D 7	Franche Ct rd SW17
98	F 4	Francis av Bxly Hth
23	Y 15	Francis av Harrow
54	E 6	Francis av Ilf
106	M 12	Franciscan rd SW17
107	O 10	Franciscan rd SW17
89	P 3	Francis Chichester way SW11
105	U 16	Francis clo SW19
51	T 4	Francis rd E10
28	M 12	Francis rd N2
122	J 16	Francis rd Croy
60	C 4	Francis rd Grnfd
23	Z 15	Francis rd Harrow
82	A 6	Francis rd Hounsl
54	E 6	Francis rd Ilf
155	V 14	Francis rd Wallgtn
51	Y 16	Francis st E15
148	B 4	Francis st SW1
54	D 6	Francis st Ilf
47	V 9	Francis ter N19
148	H 11	Francis Wharf SW1
12	C 10	Francklin gdns Edg
12	C 10	Francklyn gdns Edg
39	W 17	Francombe gdns Rom
89	W 14	Franconia rd SW4
91	S 20	Frank Dixon clo SE21
91	T 20	Frank Dixon way SE21
109	T 1	Frank Dixon way SE21
90	M 13	Frankfurt rd SE24
91	N 13	Frankfurt rd SE24
76	B 19	Frankham st SE8
21	Y 17	Frankland clo Wdfd Grn
20	A 15	Frankland rd E4
15	R 2	Frankland clo N20
121	V 8	Frankland cres Mitch
95	R 8	Franklin pas SE9
110	D 20	Franklin rd SE20
97	Z 2	Franklin rd Bxly Hth
117	P 5	Franklin rd Kingst
145	R 12	Franklin sq SW6
147	R 10	Franklin row SW3
64	E 9	Franklin st E3
31	R 19	Franklin st N15
57	N 18	Franklyn clo Dgnhm
117	O 5	Franklyn rd Walton
44	D 19	Franklyn rd NW10
117	W 9	Franks av New Mald
65	T 12	Frank st E13
127	Z 13	Frankswood av Brom
91	X 1	Frankton rd SE15
17	Z 14	Franlaw cres N13
57	V 4	Franmil rd Hornch
110	C 19	Frant clo SE20
110	S 7	Fransfield gro SE26
	H 11	Frant rd Thntn Hth
33	T 17	Fraser rd E17
18	L 11	Fraser rd N9
60	D 4	Fraser rd Grnfd
74	A 14	Fraser st W4
81	Z 14	Frason rd E18
21	U 18	Frating cres Wdfd Grn
141	T 19	Frazier st SE1
151	S 1	Frean st SE16
20	K 2	Frederica rd E4
48	B 20	Frederica st N7
139	N 7	Frederick clo W2
153	V 10	Frederick clo Sutton
149	W 20	Frederick cres SW9
9	P 9	Frederick cres Enf
153	U 10	Frederick gdns Sutton
78	M 13	Frederick pl SE18
79	N 13	Frederick pl SE18
149	Y 12	Frederick rd SE17
153	V 10	Frederick rd Sutton
160	D 6	Frederick's pl EC2
	R 14	Fredericks pl N12
133	O 13	Frederick st WC1
39	S 18	Frederic ms SW1
32	H 17	Frederic st E17
57	V 18	Freebone gdns Rainham
88	M 5	Freedom st SW11
48	N 15	Freegrove rd N7

27 R 7	Freeland pk NW4
60 M 19	Freeland rd W5
158 F 18	Freelands av S Croy
112 J 20	Freelands gro Brom
26 J 1	Freelands rd Brom
112 J 20	Freelands rd Brom
133 N 2	Feeling st N1
120 E 11	Freeman rd Mrdn
9 T 16	Freemantle av Enf
81 T 11	Freemantle rd Blvdr
36 B 8	Freemantle rd Ilf
65 U 15	Freemasons rd E16
123 R 18	Freemasons rd Croy
135 Z 4	Freemont st E9
109 R 19	Freethorpe clo SE18
89 P 9	Freke rd SW11
150 K 8	Freemantle SE17
63 O 3	Fremont st E9
134 L 14	French pl EC2
92 G 10	Frensbury rd SE4
114 F 5	Frensham dri SW15
159 U 17	Frensham dri Croy
114 E 5	Frensham rd SE9
151 T 15	Frensham rd SE15
88 K 5	Frere st SW11
124 L 19	Freshfields Croy
16 F 1	Freshfield dr N14
106 D 6	Freshwater rd SW18
107 P 14	Freshwater clo SW17
55 W 3	Freshwater rd Dgnhm
37 S 14	Freshwell av Rom
67 N 5	Fresh Wharf rd Bark
155 T 19	Freshwood wy Wallgtn
6 A 16	Freston gdns Barnt
27 V 7	Freston pk N3
136 F 9	Freston rd W11
98 A 12	Freta rd Bxly Hth
106 G 1	Frewin rd SW18
58 A 14	Friar rd Grnfd
15 X 12	Friars av N20
15 W 12	Friars av N20
61 Y 18	Friars gdns W3
84 F 13	Friars la Rich
141 X 19	Friars pl SE1
61 Z 19	Friars Place la W3
62 A 20	Friars Place la W3
66 B 4	Friars rd E6
84 K 16	Friars Stile rd Rich
141 X 7	Friar st EC4
16 D 2	Friars wlk N14
16 D 4	Friars wlk N14
80 K 14	Friars wlk SE2
23 U 3	Friars wlk Harrow
61 Y 19	Friars way W3
158 J 19	Friarswood S Croy
15 X 15	Friary clo N12
140 C 15	Friary ct SW1
21 S 14	Friary la Wdfd Grn
15 W 14	Friary park N12
15 W 13	Friary rd N12
151 U 18	Friary rd SE15
61 X 17	Friary rd W3
15 V 14	Friary way N12
20 L 8	Friday hill E4
20 M 11	Friday Hill east E4
20 L 9	Friday Hill west E4
81 Z 13	Friday rd Erith
106 L 19	Friday rd Mitch
142 A 7	Friday st EC4
47 U 16	Frideswide pl NW5
93 N 4	Friendly st SE4
157 O 6	Friends rd Croy
133 W 12	Friend st EC1
15 S 9	Friern Barnet la N11
16 C 17	Friern Barnet rd N11
15 T 10	Friern ct N20
15 R 3	Friern Mount dri N20
15 S 16	Friern pk N12
91 W 18	Friern rd SE22
15 S 14	Friern Watch av N12
105 T 5	Frimley av SW19
159 V 16	Frimley clo Croy
115 T 13	Frimley ct Sidcp
159 V 17	Frimley cres Croy
120 J 6	Frimley gdns Mitch
54 H 10	Frimley rd Ilf
33 X 2	Frinton dri Wdfd Grn
35 W 18	Frinton mews Ilf
66 B 9	Frinton rd E6
31 T 19	Frinton rd N15
107 P 16	Frinton rd SW17
38 D 1	Frinton rd Rom
115 Z 4	Frinton rd Sidcp
37 Z 6	Friston st SW6
88 A 6	Friston st SW6
118 A 14	Fritham clo New Mald
27 T 2	Frith ct NW7
14 F 19	Frith la NW7
77 T 1	Frith la NW7
51 W 11	Frith rd E11
156 L 3	Frith rd Croy
140 F 7	Frith st W1
74 L 3	Frithville gdns W12
136 B 13	Frithville gdns W12
56 G 9	Frizlands la Dgnhm
30 G 13	Frobisher rd N8
91 V 17	Frogley rd SE22
87 V 12	Frogmore SW18
153 R 7	Frogmore clo Sutton
70 F 12	Frogmore ct S'hall
153 R 7	Frogmore gdns Sutton
46 C 12	Frognal NW3
23 V 14	Frognal av Harrow
115 O 15	Frognal av Sidcp
46 C 14	Frognal clo NW3
46 D 17	Frognal ct NW3
46 C 12	Frognal gdns NW3
46 B 14	Frognal la NW3
115 O 15	Frognal pl Sidcp
46 C 11	Frognal ri NW3
46 C 13	Frognal way NW3
95 P 12	Froissart rd SE9
30 H 10	Frome rd N15
133 Z 7	Frome st N1
134 A 7	Frome st N1
153 S 11	Fromondes rd Sutton
89 T 5	Froude st SW8
31 O 3	Fryatt rd N17
64 M 18	Fryat st E14
25 P 18	Fryent clo NW9
26 A 19	Fryent cres NW9
26 A 19	Fryent gro NW9
25 P 17	Fryent way NW9
43 S 2	Fryent way NW9
133 U 8	Frye's bldgs N1
142 M 2	Frying Pan all E1
66 A 2	Fry rd E6
62 E 2	Fry rd NW10
157 Z 3	Fryston av Croy
80 C 13	Fuchsia st SE2
26 A 4	Fulbeck dri NW9
22 M 8	Fulbeck way Harrow
33 T 4	Fulbourne rd E17
47 V 11	Fulbrook rd N19
75 N 6	Fulford st SE16
143 Y 18	Fulford st SE16
145 T 18	Fulham bdy SW6
87 T 5	Fulham High st SW6
87 P 5	Fulham palace SW6
87 R 3	Fulham Palace rd SW6
144 H 18	Fulham Palace rd SW6
144 E 11	Fulham Palace rd W6
87 U 5	Fulham Pk gdns SW6
87 U 4	Fulham Pk rd SW6
146 G 9	Fulham rd SW3
87 U 3	Fulham rd SW6
145 T 19	Fulham rd SW6
118 D 19	Fullbrooks av Worc Pk
55 S 11	Fuller rd Dgnhm
34 C 3	Fullers av Wdfd Grn
38 J 2	Fullers clo Rom
38 J 2	Fullers la Rom
34 B 3	Fullers rd E18
26 L 12	Fuller st NW4
159 O 9	Fullers wood Croy
123 U 13	Fullerton rd SE25
88 C 13	Fullerton rd SW18
154 H 18	Fullerton rd Carsh
36 B 6	Fullwell av Ilf
100 K 8	Fullwell park Twick
57 X 19	Fulmar rd Hornch
88 B 2	Fulmead st SW6
33 X 2	Fulmer clo Hampt
72 A 9	Fulmer way W13
140 K 2	Fulready rd E10
82 D 10	Fulstone clo Hounsl
94 E 5	Fulthorp rd SE3
138 A 9	Fulton ms W2
43 R 11	Fulton rd Wemb
35 W 4	Fulwell av Ilf
100 L 4	Fulwell Pk av Twick
101 N 4	Fulwell Pk av Twick
101 P 10	Fulwell rd Tedd
60 L 5	Fulwood av Wemb
83 X 16	Fulwood gdns Twick
141 R 2	Fulwood pl WC1
105 R 1	Fulwood wlk SW19
22 G 1	Furham fields Pinn
151 T 20	Furley rd SE15
121 P 18	Furlong clo Mitch
48 F 18	Furlong rd N7
40 C 19	Furlongs wlk Grnfd
88 A 18	Furmage st SW18
154 C 17	Furneaux av SE27
99 T 7	Furner clo Drtfd
62 G 7	Furness rd NW10
88 B 4	Furness rd SW6
40 L 3	Furness rd Harrow
120 B 15	Furness rd Mrdn
57 V 15	Furness way Hornch
141 T 3	Furnival st EC4
50 D 15	Furrow la E9
14 L 19	Fursby av N3
26 D 8	Further acre NW9
94 A 20	Further Green rd SE6
12 A 1	Further Green rd SE6
107 S 12	Furzedown dri SW17
107 T 11	Furzedown rd SW17
37 Z 7	Furze Farm clo Rom
113 Z 14	Furzefield clo Chisl
77 V 18	Furzefield rd SE3
122 M 5	Furze rd Thntn Hth
64 B 14	Furze st E3
126 F 3	Fyfe way Brom
33 W 9	Fyfield rd E17
90 G 7	Fyfield rd SW9
8 C 12	Fyfield rd Enf
34 L 1	Fyfield rd Wdfd Grn
148 F 5	Fynes st SW1

G

99 W 13	Gable clo Dartford
22 G 3	Gable clo Pinn
100 A 9	Gabriel clo Felt
38 K 1	Gabriel clo Rom
92 G 18	Gabriel st SE23
43 O 18	Gaddesden av Wemb
79 T 5	Gadwall wy SE6
65 N 3	Gage rd E16
132 M 20	Gage st WC1
133 R 4	Gainford st N1
41 T 17	Gainsboro gdns Grnfd
97 X 9	Gainsboro sq Bxly Hth
55 P 11	Gainsborough Dgnhm
53 W 14	Gainsborough av E12
15 N 17	Gainsborough ct N12
46 G 11	Gainsborough gdns NW3
45 U 1	Gainsborough gdns NW11
25 O 7	Gainsborough gdns Edgw
83 P 13	Gainsborough gdns Islwth
52 A 1	Gainsborough rd E11
64 M 10	Gainsborough rd E15
65 N 10	Gainsborough rd E15
15 O 16	Gainsborough rd N12
74 C 10	Gainsborough rd W4
117 Y 15	Gainsborough rd New Mald
85 N 9	Gainsborough rd Rich
32 K 13	Gainsford rd E17
143 O 17	Gainsford st SE1
122 K 13	Gainsford st SE1
91 S 4	Gairloch rd SE5
47 U 17	Gaisford st NW5
114 B 2	Gaitskell rd SE9
112 G 8	Galahad rd Brom
74 F 20	Galata rd SW13
91 Z 7	Galatea sq SE15
76 F 7	Galbraith st E14
120 F 6	Gale clo Mitch
33 X 2	Galeborough av Wdfd Grn
74 K 11	Galena rd W6
100 C 14	Gale clo Hampt
88 D 17	Galesbury rd SW18
63 N 10	Gales gdns E2
64 B 14	Gale st E3
55 V 20	Gale st Dgnhm
68 H 4	Gale st Dgnhm
35 S 1	Gales way Wdfd Grn
105 R 1	Galgate clo SW19
15 Y 6	Gallants Farm rd Barnt
58 A 7	Gallery gdns Grnfd
87 R 20	Gallery rd SE21
109 P 2	Gallery rd SE21
151 W 7	Galley Wall rd SE15
75 N 12	Galley Wall rd SE16
19 N 20	Galliard av Enf
9 P 20	Galliard ct Enf
18 K 4	Galliard rd N9
19 O 1	Galliard rd N9
18 J 16	Galliard rd N5
67 Z 10	Gallions clo Bark
77 W 11	Gallions rd SE7
154 F 19	Gallop Sutton
158 B 16	Gallop the S Croy
79 U 12	Gallosson rd SE18
74 Z 2	Galloway rd W12
7 R 20	Gallus clo N21
94 G 8	Gallus sq SE3
122 B 10	Galpin's rd Thntn Hth
37 P 20	Galsworthy av Rom
45 T 12	Galsworthy rd NW2
103 S 19	Galsworthy rd Kingst
128 K 15	Galton st W10
6 A 14	Galva clo Barnt
87 W 13	Galveston rd SW15
134 C 14	Galway st EC1
89 T 5	Gambetta st SW8
141 X 15	Gambia st SE1
106 H 11	Gambole rd SW17
5 Z 12	Games rd Barnet
86 M 15	Gamlen rd SW15
64 J 3	Gam rd E15
153 W 13	Gander Grn la Sutton
156 B 16	Ganton clo Croy
140 B 7	Ganton st W1
35 V 15	Gantshill cres Ilford
105 Z 11	Gap rd SW19
106 A 11	Gap rd SW19
139 U 1	Garbutt pl W1
98 D 6	Garden av Bxly Hth
107 R 19	Garden av Mitch
12 C 19	Garden city Edg
19 Z 16	Garden cl E4
90 D 7	Garden clo SW9
58 B 3	Garden clo Grnfd
100 F 13	Garden clo Hampt
156 A 11	Garden clo Wallgtn
112 H 6	Garden clo SE12
86 K 20	Garden clo SW15
63 U 7	Gardeners rd E3
18 E 1	Gardenia rd Enf
108 B 1	Garden la SW2
112 J 15	Garden la Brom
137 U 10	Garden ms W2
130 E 11	Garden rd NW8
124 C 1	Garden rd SE20
112 J 17	Garden rd Brom
85 P 9	Garden rd Rich
72 F 9	Gareth gro Brom
65 P 13	Garfield rd E13
89 P 8	Garfield rd SW11
106 D 14	Garfield rd SW19
9 R 16	Garfield rd Enf
83 Z 20	Garfield rd Twick
64 A 20	Garford st E14
79 U 11	Garibaldi st SE18
79 T 19	Garland rd SE18
24 J 4	Garland rd Stanm
142 C 9	Garlick Hill EC4
160 B 8	Garlick hill EC4
110 J 6	Garlie's rd SE23
45 U 18	Garlinge rd NW2
32 B 2	Garman rd N17
133 T 13	Garnault ms EC1
133 U 14	Garnault pl EC1
4 H 14	Garnault rd Enf
33 T 4	Garner rd E17
135 U 9	Garner st E2
44 A 18	Garnet rd NW10
123 N 9	Garnet rd Thntn Hth
63 O 20	Garnet st E1
75 O 1	Garnet st E1
143 Z 10	Garner st E1
95 V 8	Garnett clo SE9
46 L 14	Garnett rd NW3
32 G 4	Garnet way E17
107 X 8	Garrard's rd SW16
98 F 8	Garrard clo Bxly Hth
113 Z 10	Garrard clo Chisl
156 A 7	Garratt clo Croy
106 G 9	Garratt la SW17
88 A 14	Garratt la SW18
12 D 20	Garratt rd Edgw
25 R 1	Garratt rd Edgw
3 J 11	Garratt ter SW17
10 B 3	Garretts rd Bushey Watf
134 B 17	Garrett st EC1

F
G

27 U 19 Garrick av NW11
84 F 12 Garrick cl Rich
157 R 3 Garrick cres Croy
27 N 9 Garrick dri NW4
31 P 3 Garrick gdns N17
27 O 8 Garrick pk NW4
26 E 18 Garrick rd Kingst
58 L 12 Garrick rd Grnfd
85 R 6 Garrick rd E8
140 J 9 Garrick st WC2
27 O 12 Garrick way NW4
140 J 9 Garrick yd WC2
39 R 3 Garry clo Rom
39 O 2 Garry way Rom
100 K 16 Garside clo Hampt
25 N 18 Garside Gdn
100 L 14 Garth Hampt
102 L 12 Garth clo Kingst
119 O 17 Garth clo Mrdn
92 F 18 Garthorne rd SE23
45 U 8 Garth rd NW2
73 X 15 Garth rd W4
102 L 13 Garth rd Kingstn
119 O 18 Garth rd Mrdn
102 K 11 Garthside Rich
25 N 18 Garth the Harrow
15 V 20 Garth way N12
105 V 2 Gartmoor gdns SW19
54 L 5 Gartmore rd Ilf
144 K 14 Garvan clo W6
65 W 12 Garvary rd E16
137 W 7 Garway rd W2
34 A 2 Gascoigne gdns Wdfd Grn
135 N 12 Gascoigne pl E2
67 R 6 Gascoigne rd Bark
159 W 20 Gascoigne rd Croy
129 T 1 Gascony av NW6
99 U 6 Gascoyne dr Drtfrd
50 G 19 Gascoyne rd E9
76 H 1 Gaselee st E14
149 R 12 Gasholder pl SE11
89 T 17 Gaskarth rd SW12
25 V 6 Gaskarth rd Edg
28 M 18 Gaskell rd N6
89 Z 5 Gaskell st SW4
133 X 4 Gaskin st N1
63 N 11 Gaston pl E2
106 M 10 Gassiot rd SW17
107 N 11 Gassiot rd SW17
154 G 5 Gassiot way Sutton
144 H 13 Gastein rd W6
84 L 7 Gaston Bell clo Rich
121 O 5 Gaston rd Mitch
151 X 2 Gataker st SE16
47 Y 10 Gatcombe rd N19
130 J 17 Gateforth st NW8
103 W 19 Gatehouse clo Kingst
90 D 8 Gately rd SW9
138 L 19 Gate ms SW7
18 K 14 Gate rd N18
134 J 16 Gatesborough st EC2
106 L 7 Gateside rd SW17
108 S 16 Gatestone rd SE19
141 N 3 Gate st WC2
150 C 13 Gateway SE17
100 G 5 Gatfield gro Felt
30 F 6 Gathorne rd N22
63 T 7 Gathorne st E2
147 W 11 Gatliff rd SW1
79 Z 13 Gatling rd SE2
80 A 14 Gatling rd SE2
91 U 1 Gatonby St SE5
154 C 19 Gatton clo Sutton
106 K 9 Gatton rd SW17
17 V 1 Gatward clo N21
87 Y 19 Gatward grn N9
89 X 6 Gauden clo SW4
89 X 7 Gauden rd SW4
41 Z 14 Gauntlett ct Wemb
42 A 14 Gauntlett ct Wemb
154 C 17 Gauntlett rd Sutton
149 Z 1 Gaunt rd SE11
92 C 4 Gautrey rd SE15
150 G 6 Gavell rd SE17
76 A 9 Gaverick st E14
94 H 19 Gavestone cres SE12
94 G 18 Gavestone rd SE12
75 N 8 Gataker st SE16
120 G 12 Gavina clo Mrdn
79 U 11 Gavin st SE18
63 P 8 Gawber st E2
A 15 Gawsworthy clo E15
14 K 14 Gay clo NW2
26 A 5 Gaydon clo NW9
35 T 9 Gayfere rd Ilf
148 J 2 Gayfere st SW1
74 E 6 Gayford rd W12
56 J 13 Gay gdns Dgnhm
49 X 20 Gayhurst rd E8
40 E 15 Gaylor rd Grnfd
110 F 4 Gaynesford rd SE23

154 M 17 Gaynesford rd Carsh
35 R 1 Gaynes Hill rd Wdfd Grn
64 H 6 Gay rd E15
35 W 17 Gaysham av Ilf
46 F 12 Gayton cres NW3
46 F 12 Gayton rd NW3
23 W 19 Gayton rd Harrow
88 M 16 Gayton rd SW11
108 E 1 Gaywood clo SW2
33 O 10 Gaywood rd E17
149 X 2 Gaywood st SE1
149 W 11 Gaza st SE17
36 A 12 Geariesville gdns Ilf
44 H 14 Geary rd NW10
48 D 15 Geary st N7
30 M 4 Gedeney rd N17
31 N 3 Gedeney rd N17
143 O 20 Gedling pl SE1
65 P 3 Geere rd E15
139 V 6 Gees ct W1
133 Z 16 Gee st EC1
134 A 16 Gee st EC1
113 S 6 Gefferys homes SE9
134 M 3 Geffrye museum E2
134 M 9 Geffrye st E2
151 W 19 Geldart rd SE15
49 Y 7 Geldstone rd E5
92 P 5 Gellatly rd SE14
38 G 2 Gelstorpe rd Rom
18 L 10 General Gordon pl SE18
93 X 1 General Wolfe rd SE10
78 M 17 Genesta rd SE18
79 N 17 Genesta rd SE18
37 Y 16 Geneva gdns Rom
116 K 8 Geneva rd Kingst
12 L 10 Geneva rd Thntn Hth
20 C 15 Genever clo E4
19 N 18 Genista rd N18
86 M 13 Genoa av SW15
87 N 14 Genoa av SW15
124 B 1 Genoa rd SE20
8 C 13 Genotin rd Enf
7 Z 12 Gentlemans row Enf
65 T 10 Gentry gdns E13
92 K 7 Geoffrey rd SE4
146 G 3 Geological museum SW7
140 L 13 George ct WC2
29 O 3 George cres N10
142 F 15 George Inn yd SE1
34 G 8 George la E18
93 S 16 George la SE13
126 H 19 George la Brom
20 B 19 George rd E4
103 V 19 George rd Kingst
118 E 10 George rd New Mald
143 S 19 George row SE16
48 E 15 George's rd N7
65 O 18 George st E16
139 T 3 George st W1
71 U 3 George st W7
54 B 20 George st Bark
67 N 1 George st Bark
156 M 4 George st Croy
157 O 3 George st Croy
82 E 4 George st Hounsl
84 H 12 George st Rich
39 T 17 George st Rom
70 B 11 George st S'hall
154 A 10 George st Sutton
76 H 20 Georgette pl SE10
22 F 10 Georg V av Pinn
22 G 11 George V clo Pinn
35 Z 12 Georgeville gdns Ilf
60 B 3 George Wyver clo SW18
87 S 18 George W way Grnfd
139 V 8 George wyd W1
132 B 3 Georgiana st NW1
126 H 19 Georgian clo Brom
10 K 20 Georgian clo Stanm
43 R 17 Georgian ct Wemb
41 S 7 Georgian way Harrow
122 J 2 Georgia rd Thntn Hth
112 G 9 Geraint rd Brom
149 U 2 GERALDINE MARY HARMSWORTH PARK SE11
88 C 14 Geraldine rd SW18
73 P 16 Geraldine rd W4
149 V 3 Geraldine st SE1
147 V 6 Geraldine ms SW1
65 O 12 Gerald rd E16
147 U 6 Gerald rd SW1
58 A 5 Gerald rd Dgnhm
82 A 3 Gerard av Hounsl
82 D 2 Gerard rd SW13
23 Z 18 Gerard rd Harrow
114 A 4 Gerda rd SE9
64 M 9 Germander way E15

63 V 7 Gernon rd E3
44 J 4 Geron way NW2
6 H 15 Gerrards clo N14
64 H 1 Gerrard pl W1
133 X 8 Gerrard rd N1
140 G 8 Gerrard st W1
141 U 20 Gerridge st SE1
81 S 9 Gertrude rd Belv
146 D 15 Gertrude st SW10
43 W 9 Gervase clo Wemb
25 X 5 Gervase rd Edgw
25 X 5 Gervase rd Edg
75 N 18 Gervase st SE14
151 Y 17 Gervase st SE15
111 O 4 Ghent st SE6
10 B 7 Giant Tree hill Bushey
64 H 1 Gibbins rd E15
92 D 5 Gibbon rd SE15
61 Z 19 Gibbon rd W3
62 A 19 Gibbon rd W3
102 K 19 Gibbon rd Kingst
43 Z 19 Gibbons rd NW10
86 H 12 Gibbon wlk SW15
109 O 13 Gibbs av SE19
109 P 13 Gibbs clo SE19
12 K 14 Gibbs grn Edg
145 P 9 Gibbs Green estate W14
19 P 14 Gibbs rd N18
109 O 13 Gibbs sq SE19
63 R 11 Gibson clo E1
49 U 7 Gibson gdns N16
108 H 15 Gibson's hill SW16
49 U 8 Gibson sq N1
76 L 14 Gibson st SE10
39 V 9 Gidea clo Rom
39 V 8 Gidea park Rom
81 U 10 Gideon rd Blvdr
89 O 7 Gideon rd SW11
39 V 10 Gideon rd SW11
47 W 6 Giesbach rd N19
18 D 18 Giffard rd N18
76 B 19 Giffin st SE8
59 S 14 Gifford gdns W7
132 L 2 Gifford st N1
133 N 1 Gifford st N1
65 N 3 Gift la E15
25 W 4 Gilbert gro Edg
140 J 2 Gilbert pl WC1
142 V 6 Gilbert rd SE11
106 C 17 Gilbert rd SE19
81 R 9 Gilbert rd Belvdr
112 E 18 Gilbert rd Brom
39 T 13 Gilbert rd Rom
51 Y 13 Gilbert st E15
139 V 7 Gilbert st W1
106 J 11 Gilbey rd SW17
79 X 17 Gilbourne rd SE18
9 V 16 Gilda av Enf
49 Y 5 Gilda cres N16
139 Z 2 Gildea st W1
47 O 16 Gilden cres NW5
109 T 10 Giles coppice SE19
91 R 15 Giles cres SE21
91 R 16 Giles pl SE21
57 X 18 Gillam way Rainham
10 A 7 Gillan grn Bushey Watf
65 S 19 Gill av E16
64 G 12 Gillender st E3
48 G 10 Gillespie rd N5
66 D 6 Gillett av E6
5 S 16 Gillette st N16
123 N 9 Gillett rd Thntn Hth
19 V 19 Gillian Pk rd Sutton
93 P 12 Gillian st SE13
47 R 15 Gillies st NW5
148 Z 5 Gillingham ms SW1
45 S 10 Gillingham rd NW2
147 Z 5 Gillingham row SW7
148 A 5 Gillingham st SW1
65 O 3 Gillman dri E15
62 Z 19 Gill st E14
15 Y 5 Gillum clo Barnt
93 W 10 Gilmore rd SE13
85 Z 10 Gilpin av SW14
72 H 11 Gilpin cres N18
82 K 17 Gilpin cres Twick
57 H 12 Gilpin rd E5
57 T 19 Gilroy clo Rainhm
123 O 9 Gisland rd Thntn Hth
88 B 4 Glastead rd SW6
126 C 12 Gilston rd SW10
111 Z 6 Gilston rd SW10
141 X 3 Gitspur st EC1
93 S 15 Gipsey hill SE19
86 H 9 Gipsy la SW15
58 M 10 Gipsy la E27
109 O 11 Gipsy rd SE27
80 H 20 Gipsy rd Welling
97 W 1 Gipsy rd Welling
108 M 11 Gipsy Rd gdns SE27

144 H 4 Girdlers rd W1J
47 U 7 Girdlestone wlk N19
87 T 18 Girdwood rd SW18
145 R 19 Gironde st SW6
64 C 17 Girsud st E14
25 R 11 Girton av NW9
40 M 19 Girton clo Grnfd
159 N 4 Girton gdns Croy
110 F 12 Girton rd SE26
40 M 18 Girton rd Grnfd
41 N 17 Girton rd Grnfd
30 C 13 Gisburn rd N8
65 P 7 Given Wilson wlk E13
53 O 13 Gladding rd E12
124 H 16 Glade gdns Croy
70 J 6 Glade la S'hall
17 O 1 Glade the N21
17 P 1 Gladeside N21
124 F 17 Gladeside Croy
31 V 17 Gladeside rd N15
81 U 10 Gladeswood rd Belvdr
77 X 19 Glade the SE7
127 O 4 Glade the Brom
124 H 15 Glade the Croy
7 T 10 Glade the Enf
152 H 12 Glade the Epsom
35 T 5 Glade the Ilf
153 T 19 Glade the Sutton
159 T 6 Glade the W Wkhm
21 U 12 Glade the Wdfd Grn
92 J 18 Gladiator st SE23
49 U 11 Glading ter N16
47 V 4 Gladsmuir rd N19
4 G 10 Gladsmuir rd Barnt
53 R 19 Gladstone av E12
30 J 6 Gladstone av N22
83 R 19 Gladstone av Twick
73 X 19 Gladstone clo W4
44 G 12 Gladstone park NW2
44 L 10 Gladstone pk Gdn est NW2
44 L 9 Gladstone Pk gdns NW2
4 C 14 Gladstone pla Barnt
105 X 18 Gladstone rd SW19
21 X 5 Gladstone rd Buck Hl
123 P 17 Gladstone rd Croy
117 R 6 Gladstone rd Kingst
70 B 7 Gladstone rd S'hall
149 W 1 Gladstone st SE1
89 T 1 Gladstone ter SW8
23 V 10 Gladstone wy Harrow
30 C 19 Gladwell rd N8
112 G 15 Gladwell rd Brom
87 O 7 Gladwyn rd SW15
45 Y 19 Gladys rd NW6
63 R 20 Glamis pl E1
63 R 18 Glamis rd E1
75 R 1 Glamis rd E1
40 M 19 Glamis way Grnfd
122 A 7 Glamorgan clo Mitch
102 E 19 Glamorgan rd Kingst
124 M 8 Glanfield rd Beckenhm
11 U 13 Glanleam rd Stanm
90 A 14 Glanville rd SW2
126 J 7 Glanville rd Brom
100 F 2 Glasbrook av Twick
49 T 2 Glasserton rd N16
106 M 15 Glasford st SW17
65 U 6 Glasgow rd E13
18 L 15 Glasgow rd N18
95 O 17 Glassbrook rd SE9
141 Y 18 Glasshill st SE1
63 S 19 Glass House fields E1
140 C 10 Glasshouse st W1
148 M 9 Glasshouse wlk SE11
149 N 9 Glasshouse wlk SE11
29 W 17 Glasslyn rd N8
126 D 5 Glassmill la Brom
63 N 10 Glass st E2
135 Y 15 Glass st E2
119 Z 16 Glastonbury rd Mrdn
45 W 16 Glastonbury st NW6
64 C 13 Glaucus st E3
101 U 17 Glazbrook rd Tedd
144 L 9 Glazebury rd W14
109 O 3 Glazebrook clo SE21
7 W 11 Glebe av Enf
24 J 10 Glebe av Harrow
36 A 14 Glebe av Mitch
21 S 20 Glebe av Wdfd Grn
120 L 5 Glebe cl Mitch
11 P 16 Glebe ct Stanm
27 N 12 Glebe cres NW4
24 K 11 Glebe cres Harrow
118 B 16 Glebe gdns New Mald
109 T 10 Glebe hurst SE19

G

91 S 7	Glebelands clo SE5
109 T 11	Glebelands av SE19
99 T 10	Glebelands Drtfrd
34 E 8	Glebelands av E18
36 F 19	Glebelands av Ilf
54 E 1	Glebelands av Ilf
24 J 12	Glebe la Harrow
120 K 6	Glebe path Mitch
146 J 13	Glebe pl SW3
43 U 20	Glebe rd E8
28 E 5	Glebe rd N3
30 C 14	Glebe rd N8
44 E 18	Glebe rd NW10
86 F 4	Glebe rd SW13
112 F 20	Glebe rd Brom
154 M 13	Glebe rd Carsh
155 N 14	Glebe rd Carsh
56 H 19	Glebe rd Dgnhm
11 R 16	Glebe rd Stanm
11 R 17	Glebe rd Stanm
153 S 18	Glebe rd Sutton
83 W 16	Glebe side Twick
120 K 6	Glebe sq Mitch
73 Z 13	Glebe st W4
24 C 8	Glebe ter E3
32 Z 7	Glebe the SE3
94 A 7	Glebe the SE3
118 D 19	Glebe the Worc Pk
100 G 7	Glebe way Felt
159 Y 3	Glebe way W Wkhm
21 Y 17	Glebe way Wdfd Grn
146 A 8	Gledhow gdns SW5
144 L 11	Gledstanes rd W14
10 B 7	Gleed Bushey Watf
10 B 7	Gleed av Bushey Watf
78 C 10	Glenalyon way SE18
105 P 4	Glen Albyn rd SW19
24 K 12	Glenalmond rd Harrow
50 C 13	Glenarm rd E5
52 A 20	Glenavon rd E15
95 Y 8	Glenbarr clo SE9
111 Z 14	Glenbow rd Brom
112 A 13	Glenbow rd Brom
7 P 13	Glenbrook North Enf
7 R 13	Glenbrook South Enf
45 X 16	Glenbrook rd NW6
116 J 15	Glenbuck rd Surb
106 M 6	Glenburnie rd SW17
106 K 16	Glenburnie rd SW17
60 C 13	Glencairn dri W5
108 B 18	Glencairn rd NW10
54 F 2	Glencoe av Ilf
56 E 11	Glencoe dri Dgnhm
58 B 12	Glencoe rd Grnfd
21 V 20	Glen cres Wdfd Grn
30 E 2	Glendale av N22
12 B 15	Glendale av Edg
55 S 1	Glendale av Edg
95 X 8	Glendale clo SE9
105 V 12	Glendale dri SW19
42 J 5	Glendale gdns Wemb
81 Y 10	Glendale rd Erith
80 H 1	Glendale way SE2
90 C 9	Glendall st SW9
87 P 7	Glendarvon st SW15
31 Z 5	Glendish rd N17
12 M 14	Glendor gdns NW7
146 K 5	Glendower pl SW7
85 Y 8	Glendower rd E4
79 Z 14	Glendower rd SW14
62 B 20	Glendown rd SE2
155 S 18	Glendun rd W3
107 V 11	Glen End rd Carsh
11 O 20	Gleneagle rd SW16
107 Z 10	Gleneagles Stanm
108 D 10	Gleneldon ms SW16
90 A 12	Gleneldon rd SW16
95 Y 13	Glenelg rd SW2
93 W 20	Glenesk rd SE9
107 V 1	Glenfarg rd SE6
72 B 5	Glenfield rd SW4
59 S 14	Glenfield rd W13
77 P 13	Glenfinlas way
72 A 4	Glenforth st SE10
76 A 8	Glenfield ter W13
76 F 8	Glengall causeway E14
129 T 4	Glengall gro E14
129 T 4	Glengall pass NW6
151 P 12	Glengall rd NW6
97 Z 7	Glengall rd SE15
12 F 6	Glengall rd Bxly Hth
21 U 19	Glengall rd Edg
151 P 13	Glengall rd Wdfd Grn
156 G 7	Glengall ter SE15
92 A 14	Glen gdns Croy
91 U 12	Glengarnock av E14
31 U 18	Glengarry rd SE22
95 Y 8	Glenham dri Ilf
97 Y 7	Glenhead clo SE9
	Glenhill clo N7

95 W 12	Glenhouse rd SE9
47 P 12	Glenhurst av NW5
108 M 17	Glenhurst ri SE19
15 U 15	Glenhurst rd N12
72 E 15	Glenhurst rd Brentf
46 J 17	Glenhurst rd NW3
107 Y 19	Glenister Pk rd SW16
77 P 13	Glenister rd SE10
78 K 4	Glenister st E16
95 X 11	Glenlea rd SE9
46 J 16	Glenloch rd NW3
9 R 9	Glenloch rd Enf
77 T 18	Glenluce rd SE3
95 X 12	Glenlyon rd SE9
13 T 20	Glenmere av NW7
107 Y 11	Glen mews SW16
46 J 17	Glenmore rd NW3
96 K 2	Glenmore rd Welling
79 X 20	Glenmore way Bark
68 A 8	Glenmount
154 D 7	Glenn mt Sutton
108 F 7	Glennie rd SE27
54 B 18	Glenny rd Bark
52 H 17	Glanpark rd E7
21 V 19	Glen ri Wdfd Grn
80 L 8	Glimpsing grn Belvdr
65 X 11	Glen rd E13
88 C 5	Glenrosa st SW6
95 X 10	Glenroy st W10
62 M 16	Glenroy st W12
92 L 8	Glensdale rd SE4
95 X 12	Glenshiel rd SE9
108 F 7	Glentanner way SW17
74 J 16	Glentham gdns SW13
74 J 16	Glentham rd SW13
125 Z 3	Glen the Brom
158 G 4	Glen the Croy
7 W 1	Glen the Enf
22 C 20	Glen the Pinn
70 F 13	Glen the S'hall
42 H 12	Glen the Wemb
124 B 19	Glenthorne av Croy
119 X 19	Glenthorne clo Sutton
35 Y 11	Glenthorne gdns Ilf
119 X 19	Glenthorne gdns Sutton
32 H 15	Glenthorne rd E17
16 B 16	Glenthorne rd N11
74 K 11	Glenthorne rd W6
144 A 6	Glenthorne rd W6
116 L 8	Glenthorne rd Kingst
119 P 12	Glenthorne rd Mrdn
39 P 1	Glenton clo Rom
93 Y 10	Glenton rd SE13
39 P 2	Glenton way Rom
131 P 18	Glentworth st NW1
95 X 13	Glenure rd SE9
95 X 13	Glenview rd SE9
80 K 16	Glenview SE2
127 O 4	Glenview rd Brom
8 A 4	Glenville av Enf
75 Z 20	Glenville gro SE8
103 O 20	Glenville rd Kingst
58 B 12	Glencoe rd Grnfd
43 Z 3	Glen wk Islwth
44 A 3	Glenwood av NW9
23 W 16	Glenwood clo Harrow
39 V 14	Glenwood dri Rom
39 V 15	Glenwood gdns Ilf
43 V 4	Glenwood gro NW9
13 O 10	Glenwood rd N15
30 K 15	Glenwood rd N15
110 M 1	Glenwood rd SE6
11 N 1	Glenwood rd SE6
152 G 13	Glenwood rd Epsom
83 P 8	Glenwood rd Hounsl
124 F 15	Glenwood way Croy
64 E 8	Glergion way E3
144 K 9	Giddar rd W14
78 K 8	Globe la SE18
63 P 7	Globe rd E2
63 B 15	Globe rd E15
39 V 19	Globe rd Hornch
57 W 1	Globe rd Hornch
21 Z 18	Globe rd Wdfd Grn
142 D 20	Globe st SE1
58 P 8	Globe ter E2
139 X 7	Globe yd W1
157 P 19	Glossop rd S Croy
118 B 9	Gloster rd New Mald
131 T 2	Gloucester av NW1
114 J 5	Gloucester av Sidcp
96 K 11	Gloucester av Welling
76 G 19	Gloucester cir SE10
43 X 20	Gloucester clo NW10
73 O 20	Gloucester ct Rich
131 X 4	Gloucester cres NW1

48 K 6	Gloucester dri N4
27 Y 3	Gloucester dri NW11
27 U 20	Gloucester gdns NW11
6 C 15	Gloucester gdns Barnt
53 S 1	Gloucester gdns Ilf
154 B 1	Gloucester gdns Sutton
131 W 7	Gloucester ga NW1
131 W 7	Gloucester Ga ms NW1
25 X 5	Gloucester ho Edg
138 D 6	Gloucester ms W2
138 C 6	Gloucester Ms w W2
131 O 18	Gloucester pl NW1
139 P 2	Gloucester pl W1
139 P 2	Gloucester Pl ms W1
51 N 2	Gloucester rd E10
34 J 16	Gloucester rd E11
53 T 11	Gloucester rd E12
32 F 7	Gloucester rd E17
31 P 11	Gloucester rd N17
18 G 17	Gloucester rd N18
146 C 8	Gloucester rd SW7
73 X 4	Gloucester rd W3
72 E 7	Gloucester rd W5
5 O 17	Gloucester rd Barnt
5 R 18	Gloucester rd Barnt
81 O 13	Gloucester rd Blvdr
123 P 18	Gloucester rd Croy
99 Z 18	Gloucester rd Dartfd
100 L 17	Gloucester rd Enf
22 K 16	Gloucester rd Harrow
82 A 11	Gloucester rd Hounsl
117 R 4	Gloucester rd Kingst
73 P 19	Gloucester rd Richm
39 S 19	Gloucester rd Rom
101 S 13	Gloucester rd Tedd
101 N 1	Gloucester rd Twick
138 H 7	Gloucester sq W2
148 B 8	Gloucester sq SW1
138 C 6	Gloucester ter W2
137 U 16	Gloucester wlk W8
133 U 14	Gloucester way EC1
22 A 18	Glover rd Pinn
89 N 8	Glycena rd SW11
5 T 14	Glyn av Barnt
123 P 2	Glyn clo SE25
152 F 20	Glyn clo Epsom
146 M 3	Glynde ms SW3
97 X 8	Glynde rd Bxly Hth
92 M 15	Glynde st SE4
79 R 12	Glyndon rd SE18
115 S 11	Glyn rd Sidcp
62 B 1	Glynfield rd NW10
50 F 11	Glyn rd E5
9 P 14	Glyn rd Enf
153 O 4	Glyn rd Worc Pk
149 N 11	Glyn st SE11
110 C 5	Glynwood dri SE23
145 P 19	Goater's all SW6
8 H 3	Goat la Enf
121 N 15	Goat rd Mitch
143 N 16	Goat st SE1
38 M 1	Gobions av Rom
39 N 2	Gobions av Rom
156 B 10	Godalming av Wallgtn
64 C 16	Godalming rd E14
64 M 10	Godbold rd E15
124 G 9	Goddard rd Becknhm
83 R 18	Godfrey av Twick
78 E 12	Godfrey hill SE18
78 F 12	Godfrey rd SE18
64 G 4	Godfrey st E15
146 L 9	Godfrey st SW3
82 D 19	Godfrey wy Hounsl
106 F 2	Godley rd SW18
141 Z 7	Godliman st EC4
91 Z 6	Godman rd SE15
74 J 4	Godolphin rd W12
58 B 3	Godrey av Grnfd
159 X 20	Godric cres Croy
156 F 6	Godson rd Croy
133 S 9	Godson st N1
154 E 7	Godstone rd Sutton
84 A 17	Godstone rd Twick
80 E 6	Godstow rd SE2
52 J 12	Godwin rd E7
126 L 7	Godwin rd Brom
93 Y 3	Goffers rd SE3
155 Y 8	Goidel clo Wallgtn
136 L 1	Golborne ms W10
136 L 1	Golborne rd W10
128 M 20	Golborne rd W10
4 C 18	Golda clo Barnt
12 M 19	Goldbesters gro Edg
13 N 20	Goldbesters gro Edg
26 A 2	Goldbesters gro Edg
119 Y 16	Goldcliff clo Mrdn

159 X 18	Goldcrest way Croy
68 G 19	Goldcrest cl SE2
84 G 13	Golden ct Rich
134 B 17	Golden la EC1
59 T 20	Golden manor W7
71 T 1	Golden manor W7
140 C 9	Golden sq W1
12 F 15	Golders clo Edg
45 U 1	Golders gdns NW11
45 W 2	Golders Green cres NW11
27 T 18	Golders Green rd NW11
45 V 1	Golders Green rd NW11
45 Z 6	Golders Hill park NW3
46 A 5	Golders Hill park NW3
27 R 19	Golders Manor dri NW11
45 Z 5	Golders Pk clo NW11
27 O 15	Golders ri NW4
45 W 2	Golders way NW11
79 T 7	Goldfinch rd SE18
74 K 6	Goldhawk ms W12
74 G 8	Goldhawk rd W12
136 B 19	Goldhawk rd W12
12 L 19	Gold hill Edg
46 D 20	Goldhurst ter NW6
129 Y 2	Goldhurst ter NW6
130 B 1	Goldhurst ter NW6
127 N 13	Goldie st SE5
143 U 7	Golding st E1
132 E 7	Goldington cres NW1
132 F 8	Goldington st NW1
12 L 20	Gold la Edg
129 T 18	Goldney rd W9
143 U 5	Goldney ter E1
148 G 19	Goldsboro' clo SW8
20 F 8	Goldsborough cres E4
89 Y 1	Goldsborough rd SW8
9 V 10	Goldsdown clo Enf
9 U 9	Goldsdown rd Enf
53 R 17	Goldsmith av E12
26 B 17	Goldsmith av NW9
61 X 20	Goldsmith av W3
56 E 2	Goldsmith av Rom
40 J 5	Goldsmith clo Harrow
25 V 13	Goldsmith la NW9
51 P 4	Goldsmith rd E10
32 G 8	Goldsmith rd E17
15 Z 16	Goldsmith rd N11
91 X 1	Goldsmith rd SE15
73 X 1	Goldsmith rd W3
73 Z 1	Goldsmiths clo W3
135 T 9	Goldsmith's row E2
135 U 7	Goldsmith's sq E2
79 V 14	Goldsmith st SE18
75 R 12	Goldsworthy gdns SE16
122 D 8	Goldwell rd Thntn Hth
92 C 2	Goldwin clo SE15
24 C 2	Golf clo Stanm
103 Z 18	Golf Club clo Kingst
54 F 10	Golfe rd Ilf
60 N 17	Golf rd W5
127 X 7	Golf rd Brom
101 S 7	Golf side Twick
118 A 3	Golfside rd New Mald
156 A 16	Goliath clo Wallgt
77 Y 15	Goilogly ter SE7
101 Y 14	Gomer gdns Tedd
101 Y 14	Gomer pl Tedd
75 N 9	Gomm rd SE16
156 A 10	Gomshall av Wallgtn
45 V 14	Gondar gdns NW6
76 C 17	Gonson st SE8
106 S 5	Gonston clo SW19
40 L 19	Gonville sq SW6
87 T 7	Gonville st SW6
51 V 10	Goodall rd E11
41 T 9	Gooden ct Harrow
105 U 8	Goodenough rd SW19
140 C 1	Goodge pl W1
140 D 1	Goodge st W1
62 C 9	Goodhall st NW10
125 Y 14	Goodhart way W Wkhm
142 Z 16	Goodlinge rd N7
107 Y 3	Goodman cr SE2
142 R 8	Goodman rd E10
143 R 6	Goodman st E1
48 C 8	Goodman's yd E1
55 N 3	Goodmayes av Ilf
55 N 3	Goodmayes av Ilf

G

55 O 4 Goodmayes rd Ilf
91 V 15 Goodrich rd SE22
62 B 1 Goodson rd NW10
132 J 8 Goods way NW1
64 J 17 Goodway gdns E14
115 W 6 Goodwin dri Sidcup
156 J 13 Goodwin gdns Croy
19 S 7 Goodwin rd N9
74 H 5 Goodwin rd W12
156 H 12 Goodwin rd Croy
140 J 9 Goodwin ct WC2
48 F 7 Goodwin st N4
9 P 1 Goodwood clo Enf
119 Y 9 Goodwood clo Mrdn
40 G 18 Goodwood dri Grnfd
75 V 20 Goodwood rd SE14
13 P 16 Goodwyn av NW7
29 R 5 Goodwyns vale N10
27 O 16 Goodyers gdns NW4
24 H 15 Gooseacre la Harrow
79 R 8 Goosander way SE18
66 K 9 Gooseley la E6
133 U 11 Goose yd EC1
160 E 9 Gophir la EC4
134 G 6 Gospall st N1
20 L 18 Gordon av E4
86 A 10 Gordon av SW13
57 T 6 Gordon av Hrnch
10 K 20 Gordon av Stanm
11 O 19 Gordon av Stanm
83 Z 13 Gordon av Twick
84 A 13 Gordon av Twick
97 R 2 Gordon av Welling
93 N 13 Gordonbrook rd SE4
L 17 Gordon ct W12
123 T 19 Gordon cres Croy
105 Z 4 Gordondale rd SW19
9 J 5 Gordon gro SE5
7 Y 6 Gordon hill Enf
47 P 12 Gordon Ho rd NW5
137 V 17 Gordon pl W8
21 N 4 Gordon rd E4
34 E 19 Gordon rd E11
53 W 10 Gordon rd E12
51 U 13 Gordon rd E15
34 H 5 Gordon rd E18
27 V 2 Gordon rd N3
19 N 8 Gordon rd N9
29 X 1 Gordon rd N11
91 Z 3 Gordon rd SE15
92 A 7 Gordon rd SE15
73 U 16 Gordon rd W4
60 D 19 Gordon rd W5
67 U 4 Gordon rd Bark
124 L 7 Gordon rd Becknhm
81 X 10 Gordon rd Blvdr
154 L 14 Gordon rd Carsh
4 A 8 Gordon rd Enf
23 T 10 Gordon rd Harrow
82 M 9 Gordon rd Hounsl
54 E 9 Gordon rd Ilf
116 M 2 Gordon rd Kingst
117 N 1 Gordon rd Kingst
117 N 19 Gordon rd Kingst
85 O 6 Gordon rd Rich
38 A 19 Gordon rd Rom
96 H 13 Gordon rd Sidcp
70 C 11 Gordon rd S'hall
132 F 17 Gordon sq WC1
65 T 10 Gordon st E13
132 E 16 Gordon st WC1
4 J 14 Gordon way Barnt
25 P 16 Gore ct NW9
63 O 4 Gore rd E9
118 M 3 Gore rd SW20
129 U 8 Gorefield pla NW6
69 P 4 Gorsebrook rd Dgnhm
69 P 4 Gorebrook rd Dgnhm
146 C 1 Gore st SW7
136 J 11 Gorham pl W11
38 J 5 Goring clo Rom
55 T 13 Goring gdns Dgnhm
16 M 19 Goring rd N11
17 N 19 Goring rd N11
16 M 19 Goring rd Dgnhm
142 L 5 Goring st EC3
59 N 7 Goring way Grnfd
31 O 15 Gorleston rd N15
144 M 6 Gorleston st W14
107 P 19 Gorringe Pk av Mitch
103 V 14 Gorscombe clo Kingst
107 P 13 Gorse ri NW11
159 P 6 Gorse rd Croy
57 P 4 Gorse way Rom
61 X 11 Gorst rd NW10
88 L 17 Gorst rd SW11
135 N 11 Gorsuch pl E2
89 N 20 Gosberton rd SW12
56 E 5 Gosfield rd Dgnhm
139 Z 1 Gosfield st W1
35 T 15 Gosford gdns Ilf
140 G 5 Goslett yd W1

58 G 8 Gosling clo Grnfd
90 F 2 Gosling way SW9
149 T 20 Gosling way SW9
30 L 3 Gospatrick rd N17
31 N 4 Gospatrick rd N17
32 L 16 Gosport rd E17
79 S 14 Gossage rd SE18
135 P 13 Gosset st E2
127 X 3 Gosshill rd Chisl
75 W 15 Gosterwood st SE8
100 J 1 Gostling rd Twick
122 F 7 Goston gdns Thntn Hth
133 X 14 Goswell pl EC1
133 Y 15 Goswell rd EC1
101 R 4 Gothic rd Twick
112 B 12 Goudhurst rd Brom
52 B 13 Gough rd E15
8 L 9 Gough rd Enf
141 U 5 Gough sq EC4
133 P 16 Gough st WC1
101 T 1 Gould rd Twick
50 A 16 Gould ter E9
143 O 4 Goulston st E1
50 A 13 Goulston rd E1
31 S 17 Gourley pl N15
31 S 17 Gourley st N15
95 W 13 Gourock rd SE9
65 N 1 Govier clo E15
87 S 2 Gowan av SW6
44 J 19 Gowan rd NW10
132 E 16 Gower ct WC1
140 F 1 Gower ms W1
52 G 18 Gower rd E1
71 W 17 Gower rd Isl
132 C 16 Gower st NW1
132 C 15 Gower st WC1
143 S 5 Gower's wlk E1
124 L 4 Gowland pl Becknhm
91 W 8 Gowlett rd SE5
89 O 8 Gowrie rd SW11
98 C 4 Grace av Bxly Hth
142 H 8 Gracechurch st EC3
160 H 8 Gracechurch st EC3
113 N 8 Grace clo SE9
107 T 12 Gracedale rd SW16
108 A 8 Gracefield gdns SW16
110 D 10 Grace path SE26
64 H 1 Grace rd E15
122 L 15 Grace rd Croy
143 T 9 Grace's all E1
91 P 3 Grace's ms SE5
91 R 3 Grace's rd SE5
64 E 9 Grace st E3
109 W 11 Gradient, The SE26
8 C 9 Graeme rd Enf
85 T 9 Graemesdyke av SW14
59 V 7 Grafton clo W13
152 B 2 Grafton clo Worc Pk
47 S 18 Grafton cres NW1
30 K 18 Grafton gdns N4
55 Z 6 Grafton gdns Dgnhm
132 B 18 Grafton ms W1
152 B 4 Grafton Pk rd Worc Pk
132 F 13 Grafton pl NW1
47 S 17 Grafton rd NW5
61 V 19 Grafton rd W3
156 G 17 Grafton rd Croy
55 Z 6 Grafton rd Dgnhm
7 P 11 Grafton rd Enf
23 O 17 Grafton rd Harrow
118 B 7 Grafton rd New Mald
152 A 5 Grafton rd Worc Pk
89 V 8 Grafton sq SW4
139 Z 10 Grafton st W1
47 N 16 Grafton ter NW5
132 B 18 Grafton way W1
47 T 18 Grafton way NW5
72 B 7 Graham av W13
121 O 1 Graham av Mitch
158 M 2 Graham clo Croy
159 N 3 Graham clo Croy
13 P 20 Grahame park way NW7
26 D 8 Grahame park way NW9
116 J 19 Graham gdns Surb
74 J 9 Graham mansions W6
49 X 18 Graham rd E8
65 S 10 Graham rd E13
30 J 11 Graham rd N15
26 H 19 Graham rd NW4
105 W 19 Graham rd SW19
73 X 7 Graham rd W4
98 C 10 Graham rd Bxly Hth
100 F 9 Graham rd Hampt
23 T 9 Graham rd Harrow
121 N 1 Graham rd Mitch
133 Z 10 Graham st N1
147 T 7 Graham ter SW1

150 F 6 Grail row SE17
40 M 16 Grainger clo Grnfd
30 L 5 Grainger rd N22
83 W 5 Grainger rd Islwth
51 Y 7 Graimer clo E11
45 S 4 Grampian gdns NW2
106 L 12 Granada st SW17
86 K 14 Granard av SW15
88 M 18 Granard rd SW12
149 N 7 Granby bldgs SE11
95 U 6 Granby rd SE9
59 R 15 Granby st E2
132 A 10 Granby ter NW1
141 X 1 Grand av EC1
29 P 12 Grand av N10
117 U 16 Grand av Surb
43 P 16 Grand av Wemb
78 J 13 Grand Depot rd SE18
118 M 3 Grand dri SW20
119 O 12 Grand dri SW20
87 S 12 Grand Par ms SW15
122 A 3 Grandison rd SW16
89 N 13 Grandison rd SW1
88 M 12 Grandison rd SW4
152 M 4 Grandison rd Worc Pk
63 V 11 Grand wk E1
88 H 2 Granfield st SW11
15 P 17 Grange av N12
14 D 4 Grange av N20
123 R 3 Grange av SE25
15 Y 4 Grange av Barnt
24 C 7 Grange av Stanm
101 U 3 Grange av Twick
21 S 20 Grange av Wdfd Grn
34 W 1 Grange av Wdfd Grn
123 R 3 Grange Cliffe gdns SE25
2 J 17 Grange clo Edg
70 D 15 Grange clo Hounsl
118 F 11 Grange clo New Mald
114 M 6 Grange clo Sidcp
34 E 1 Grange clo Wdfd Grn
141 P 6 Grange ct WC2
49 R 3 Grangecourt rd N16
113 S 15 Grange dri Chisl
41 O 6 Grange Farm clo Harrow
123 R 3 Grange gdns SE25
22 C 12 Grange gdns Pinn
15 L 6 Grange gdns N14
65 K 18 Grange gro N1
123 R 2 Grange hill SE25
12 J 16 Grange hill Edg
95 V 8 Grangehill rd SE9
109 V 4 Grange la SE21
111 O 5 Grangemill rd SE6
111 O 5 Grangemill way SE6
72 K 3 Grange pk W5
7 X 20 Grange Pk av N21
17 Y 1 Grange Pk av N21
51 P 4 Grange Pk rd E10
123 N 7 Grange Pk rd Thntn Hth
51 O 4 Grange rd E10
65 R 10 Grange rd E13
32 H 17 Grange rd E17
29 N 19 Grange rd N6
15 K 20 Grange rd N17
44 K 19 Grange rd NW10
150 L 2 Grange rd SE1
123 P 5 Grange rd SE25
86 F 3 Grange rd SW13
73 T 13 Grange rd W4
72 G 2 Grange rd W5
12 M 20 Grange rd Edg
23 Y 17 Grange rd Harrow
41 P 7 Grange rd Harrow
54 A 11 Grange rd Ilf
116 J 6 Grange rd Kingst
70 B 4 Grange rd S'hall
156 M 20 Grange rd S Croy
153 Z 16 Grange rd Sutton
154 A 16 Grange rd Sutton
39 W 19 Grange way Rom
134 G 7 Grange st N1
15 S 5 Grange the N20
150 M 1 Grange the SE1
109 P 14 Grange the SW19
158 L 3 Grange the Croy
61 O 1 Grange the Wemb
154 B 16 Grange vale Sutton
15 S 5 Grange View rd N20
150 L 2 Grange wlk SE1
15 O 13 Grange way N1
129 S 1 Grangeway NW6
21 Y 14 Grangeway Wdfd Grn
35 R 15 Grangeway gdns Ilf
7 X 19 Grangeway the N21
98 A 20 Grangeway Bxly

110 M 15 Grangewood la Becknhm
65 Z 3 Grangewood st E6
66 B 3 Grangewood st E6
127 N 2 Grange yd SE1
18 H 9 Granham gdns N9
79 Y 13 Granite st SE18
51 Z 7 Granleigh rd E11
71 N 19 Granmore av Islwth
50 A 20 Gransden av E8
74 G 6 Gransden rd W12
133 Y 7 Grantbridge st N1
16 G 3 Grant clo N14
11 W 10 Grantham clo Edg
38 A 20 Grantham gdns Rom
139 W 15 Grantham pl W1
53 W 11 Grantham rd E12
90 A 5 Grantham rd SW9
74 A 18 Grantham rd W4
63 T 10 Grantle st E1
33 X 5 Grantock rd E17
107 V 19 Granton rd SW16
55 N 5 Granton rd Ilf
17 T 15 Granton rd Sidcp
123 V 20 Grant pl Croy
123 U 20 Grant rd Croy
23 U 9 Grant rd Harrow
88 G 9 Grant rd SW11
27 N 1 Grants clo NW7
65 S 10 Grant st E13
133 S 8 Grant st N1
129 X 14 Grantully rd W9
19 P 11 Granville av N9
82 G 14 Granville av Hounsl
108 C 19 Granville gdns SW16
73 O 2 Granville gdns W5
93 V 8 Granville gro SE13
45 T 10 Granville ms NW2
93 U 6 Granville pk SE13
139 S 9 Granville pl W1
33 R 17 Granville rd E17
34 J 8 Granville rd E18
30 D 20 Granville rd N4
28 D 1 Granville rd N12
17 O 18 Granville rd N22
30 J 5 Granville rd N22
45 V 7 Granville rd NW2
129 T 10 Granville rd NW6
87 X 18 Granville rd SW18
105 Y 18 Granville rd SW19
4 B 13 Granville rd Barnt
53 Y 5 Granville rd Ilf
115 O 9 Granville rd Sidcp
97 U 8 Granville rd Welling
133 R 13 Granville sq WC1
133 P 13 Granville st WC1
140 J 4 Grape st WC1
80 A 18 Grasbrook rd SE19
103 Z 10 Grasmere av SW15
105 A 9 Grasmere av SW15
115 Y 6 Grasmere av SW19
61 X 19 Grasmere av W3
82 J 16 Grasmere av Hounsl
42 J 4 Grasmere av Wemb
23 Z 8 Grasmere gdns Harrow
35 S 14 Grasmere gdns Ilf
29 S 6 Grasmere rd N10
18 J 20 Grasmere rd N17
124 A 13 Grasmere rd SE25
108 B 11 Grasmere rd SW16
65 S 6 Grasmere rd E13
108 G 1 Gras Mere rd SW16
98 K 4 Grasmere rd Bxly Hth
112 B 19 Grasmere rd Brom
115 N 11 Grassington rd Sidcp
110 B 3 Grassmount SE23
27 V 5 Grass pk N3
155 U 8 Grass way Wallgtn
4 M 19 Grasvenor av Barnt
144 K 2 Gratton rd W14
45 O 10 Gratton ter NW2
27 W 7 Gravel hill N3
98 G 13 Gravel hill Bxly Hth
158 H 14 Gravel la E1
142 M 4 Gravel la E1
101 S 2 Gravel rd Twick
98 G 16 Gravel Hill clo Bxly Hth
114 B 8 Gravelwood clo Chisl
138 J 10 Graveney rd SW17
74 G 1 Gravesend rd W12
56 C 4 Gray av Dgnhm
57 V 16 Gray gdns Rainhm
117 Y 9 Grayham cres New Mald
117 X 9 Grayham rd New Mald
127 O 2 Grayling clo Brom
49 P 6 Grayling rd N16
107 X 18 Grayscroft rd SW16
141 P 1 Gray's Inn pl WC1
133 O 16 Gray's Inn rd WC1
141 N 1 Gray's Inn sq WC1

Map	Grid	Name	Map	Grid	Name	Map	Grid	Name	Map	Grid	Name
141	V 18	Gray st SE1	46	B 13	Greenaway gdns NW3	54	D 8	Green la Ilf	24	K 16	Greenway Harrow
89	N 6	Grayshott rd SW11	75	N 3	Green bank E1	55	O 5	Green la Ilf	B2	D 9	Greenway Hounsl
118	J 4	Grayswood gdns New Mald	143	Y 14	Green bank E1	119	X 14	Green la Mrdn	155	U 9	Greenway Wallgtn
28	D 1	Graywood ct N12	15	O 13	Green bank N12	120	B 17	Green la Mrdn	21	Y 15	Green way Wdfd Grn
49	O 7	Grazebrook rd N16	41	Y 15	Greenbank av Wemb	117	W 11	Green la New Mald	33	W 12	Greenway av E17
98	K 12	Grazeley clo Bxly Hth	53	S 13	Greenbank cres NW4	11	O 16	Green la Stanm	48	M 7	Greenway av N4
10	R 11	Grazeley clo SE19	78	B 19	Greenbank rd SE7	122	J 2	Green la Thntn Hth	14	L 9	Greenway clo N20
160	E 4	Gt Bell all EC2	130	K 10	Greenberry st NW8	118	H 19	Green la Worc Pk	25	X 9	Greenway clo NW9
109	V 8	Gt Brownings SE21	5	S 6	Greenbrook av Barnt	122	K 2	Green La gdns Thntn Hth	25	X 8	Greenway gdns NW9
15	O 5	Gt Bushey dri N20	25	W 17	Green clo NW9	48	L 4	Green lanes N4	158	K 6	Greenway gdns Croy
18	B 11	Gt Cambridge rd N9	28	C 20	Green clo NW11	30	H 16	Green lanes N8	58	J 8	Greenway gdns Grnfd
31	N 3	Gt Cambridge rd N17	125	Z 5	Green clo Brom	49	N 12	Green lanes N16	23	U 6	Greenway gdns Harrow
8	L 5	Gt Cambridge rd Enf	154	M 3	Green clo Carsh	17	X 4	Green lanes N21	25	E 2	Greenways E2
139	Z 5	Great Castle st W1	100	C 12	Green clo Hampt	152	B 18	Green lanes Epsom	25	O 4	Greenways Becknhm
140	A 5	Gt Casle st W1	148	C 4	Greencoat pl SW1	118	E 16	Greenlaw gdns New Mald	25	Y 8	Greenway the SE9
131	N 20	Gt Central st NW1	148	D 3	Greencoat pl SW1	78	H 9	Greenlaw st SE18	23	U 6	Greenway the Harrow
140	E 5	Gt Chapel st W1	148	D 3	Greencoat row SW1	35	Z 10	Greenleafe dri Ilf	22	E 19	Greenway the Pinn
85	X 2	Gt Chertsy rd W7	158	A 1	Green Ct av Croy	65	Y 4	Greenleaf rd E6	131	Z 18	Greenwell st W1
100	H 6	Gt Chertsy rd Felt	25	R 5	Greencourt av Edg	32	M 11	Greenleaf rd E17	76	G 16	Greenwich Ch st SE10
144	G 8	Gt Church la W0	158	A 1	Green Ct gdns Croy	33	N 11	Greenleaf rd E17	76	F 19	Greenwich High rd SE10
38	J 1	Gt College st W1	46	D 19	Greencroft gdns NW6	71	Z 1	Green Man gdns W13	76	L 18	Greenwich park SE10
148	J 1	Gt College st SW1	129	Y 1	Greencroft gdns NW6	71	Z 1	Green Man la W13	93	S 2	Greenwich South st SE10
57	P 7	Gt Cullings Rom	8	E 11	Greencroft gdns Enf	133	Z 3	Greenman st N1	56	H 11	Greenwood av Dgnhm
139	O 6	Gt Cumberland ms W1	82	D 2	Greencroft rd Hounsl	134	A 2	Greenman st N1	9	U 7	Greenwood av Enf
139	P 6	Gt Cumberland pl W1	91	R 11	Green dale SE5	17	W 2	Green Moor link N21	10	E 4	Greenwood clo Bushey Watf
150	F 2	Gt Dover st SE1	7	T 19	Green Dragon la N21	105	O 8	Green Oak wy SW19	119	S 9	Greenwood clo Mrdn
59	V 13	Greatdown rd E7	17	X 1	Green Dragon la N21	107	X 20	Greenock rd SW16	115	O 4	Greenwood clo Sidcp
51	X 18	Gt Eastern rd E15	62	K 14	Green Dragon la Brentf	73	U 9	Greenock rd W4	20	H 16	Greenwood dri E4
134	J 15	Gt Eastern st EC2	70	J 2	Green dri S'hall	139	Y 16	Green park SW1	17	V 10	Greenwood gdns N13
126	L 8	Gt Elms rd Brom	17	X 8	Green end N21	99	S 12	Green pl Drtfrd	36	C 3	Greenwood gdns Ilf
66	G 11	Greatfield av E6	74	A 6	Greenend rd W4	32	J 9	Green Pond rd E17	100	L 12	Greenwood la Hampt
93	O 11	Greatfield clo SE4	76	M 7	Greenfell st SE10	6	D 19	Green rd N14	104	B 17	Greenwood pk Kingst
26	D 7	Great Field strand NW9	77	N 8	Greenfell st SE10	15	S 10	Green rd N20	47	T 14	Greenwood pl NW5
67	T 4	Greatfields rd Bark	117	T 15	Greenfield av Surb	140	D 8	Green's ct W1	49	X 16	Greenwood rd E8
39	Z 18	Gt gardens rd Rom	45	T 9	Greenfield gdns NW2	78	L 10	Green s end SE18	65	S 5	Greenwood rd E13
140	H 18	Gt George st SW1	68	H 3	Greenfield gdns Dgnhm	55	T 5	Greenside Dgnhm	122	K 16	Greenwood rd Croy
142	A 13	Gt Guilford st SE1	143	U 4	Greenfield rd E1	84	G 12	Greenside Rich	83	U 7	Greenwood rd Islwrth
113	W 8	Gt Harry dri SE9	31	S 15	Greenfield rd N15	74	A 6	Greenside rd W11	121	X 7	Greenwood rd Mitch
133	O 19	Gt James st WC1	68	G 3	Greenfield rd Dgnhm	74	G 7	Greenside rd W12	61	Y 4	Greenwood ter NW10
140	B 6	Gt Marlborough st W1	58	H 18	Greenfields S'hall	122	G 16	Greenside rd Croy	154	K 1	Green Wrythe cres Carsh
142	G 15	Gt Maze pond SE1	22	J 10	Greenfield way Harrow	21	Z 20	Greenstead av Wdfd Grn	120	H 17	Green Wrythe la Carsh
140	H 8	Gt Newport st WC2	59	T 14	Greenford av W7	34	K 1	Greenstead av Wdfd Grn	23	O 4	Greer rd Harrow
28	G 8	Gt North rd N2	70	E 1	Greenford av S'hall	34	L 1	Greenstead av Wdfd Grn	141	V 16	Greer st SE1
74	J 14	Gt North rd W6	58	M 8	Greenford gdns Grnfd	21	Y 19	Greenstead clo Wdfd Grn	17	T 20	Gregor ms SE3
4	H 8	Gt North rd Barnt	59	N 8	Greenford gdns Grnfd	86	H 14	Greenstead gdns SW15	95	O 19	Gregory cres SE9
26	L 6	Gt North way NW4	41	T 19	Greenford rd Grnfd	21	Y 19	Greenstead gdns Wdfd Grn	137	W 18	Gregory rd W8
27	P 9	Gt North way NW4	59	O 10	Greenford rd Grnfd	52	K 20	Green st E7	65	X 19	Gregory rd E16
143	S 2	Greatorex st E1	71	N 1	Greenford rd S'hall	65	X 2	Green st E13	70	H 8	Gregory rd S'hall
132	M 19	Gt Ormond st WC1	154	A 9	Greenford rd Sutton	139	S 8	Green st W1	37	U 12	Gregory rd Rom
133	N 19	Gt Ormond st WC1	42	A 17	Greengate Grnfd	9	P 9	Green st Enf	30	A 15	Greig clo N8
133	P 12	Gt Percy st WC1	65	V 8	Greengate st E13	34	H 19	Green the E11	123	O 18	Grenaby av Croy
148	G 2	Gt Peter st SW1	28	D 14	Greenhalgh wlk N2	52	A 18	Green the E15	123	O 18	Grenaby rd Croy
148	J 2	Gt Peter st SW1	29	P 6	Greenham rd N10	16	K 10	Green the N9	77	Z 20	Grenada rd SE7
139	Z 2	Gt Portland st W1	34	C 9	Greenheys dri E18	16	L 10	Green the N14	63	Z 20	Grenada st E14
140	A 4	Gt Portland st W1	78	G 14	Green hill SE18	17	V 4	Green the N21	78	H 4	Grenadier st E16
140	D 8	Gt Pulteney st W1	21	X 4	Greenhill Buck Hl	105	O 13	Green the SW19	85	N 11	Grena gdns Rich
140	M 5	Gt Queen st WC2	154	D 3	Greenhill Sutton	62	B 17	Green the W3	85	N 11	Grena rd Rich
140	J 2	Gt Russell st WC1	43	U 6	Greenhill Wemb	126	E 18	Green the Brom	43	P 7	Grendon gdns Wemb
2	J 14	Gt Scotland yd SW1	23	V 17	Greenhill cres Harrow	158	M 19	Green the Croy	57	T 4	Grenfell av Hornch
140	G 20	Gt Smith st SW1	58	E 6	Greenhill gdns Dgnhm	70	F 17	Green the Hounsl		J 20	Grenfell gdns Harrow
148	H 1	Gt Smith st SW1	59	P 14	Greenhill gro E12	119	R 9	Green the Mrdn	76	H 9	Grenfell rd W11
91	R 14	Gt Spilmans SE21	62	A 4	Greenhill pk NW10	119	S 9	Green the Mrdn	107	N 17	Grenfell rd Mitch
142	J 5	Gt St Helen's EC3	5	O 18	Greenhill pk Barnt	117	X 5	Green the N Mald	17	S 18	Grenoble gdns N13
160	C 8	Gt St Thomas apostle EC4	62	A 4	Greenhill rd NW10	78	R 18	Green the Orp	107	N 17	Grennell clo Sutton
141	Y 15	Gt Suffolk st SE1	23	U 18	Greenhill rd Harrow	84	G 12	Green the Rich	154	E 3	Grennell clo Sutton
142	A 19	Gt Suffolk st SE1	78	G 13	Greenhill ter SE18	70	C 8	Green the S'hall	154	E 4	Grennell rd Sutton
133	V 17	Gt Suffolk st EC1	49	O 19	Greenhills Ter N1	154	A 6	Green the Sutton	117	V 20	Grenville clo Surb
160	F 4	Gt Swan all EC2	141	X 1	Green Hills rents E1	101	T 2	Green the Twick	34	K 3	Grenville gdns Wdfd Grn
131	Z 19	Gt Titchfield st W1	58	E 7	Greenhill ter Grnfd	96	J 11	Green the Welling	146	B 6	Grenville ms SW7
140	A 2	Gt Titchfield st W1	43	T 6	Greenhill way Wemb	47	Z 6	Green the Wemb	100	J 12	Grenville ms Hampt
142	J 9	Gt Tower st EC3	96	F 18	Greenhithe clo Sidcp	21	T 16	Green the Wdfd Grn	12	K 16	Grenville pl NW7
160	C 8	Gt Trinity la EC4	95	Y 13	Greenholm rd SE9	60	M 16	Green vale W5	146	A 4	Grenville pl SW7
141	O 3	Gt Turnstile WC1	95	Y 14	Greenholm rd SE9	97	W 13	Green vale Bxly Hth	48	A 15	Grenville rd N4
129	R 19	Gt Western rd W9	151	V 15	Green Hundred rd SE15	24	F 1	Green verges Stanm	159	V 20	Grenville rd Croy
137	S 2	Gt Western rd W11	108	G 12	Greenhurst rd SE27	124	J 14	Greenview av Becknhm	132	L 18	Grenville rd WC1
144	A 9	Gt West rd W6	80	F 11	Greening st SE2	124	H 15	Greenview av Croy	15	Y 13	Gresham av N20
72	B 17	Gt West rd Brentf	131	Z 4	Greenland pl NW1	20	H 4	Green wlk E4	98	A 16	Gresham clo Bxly
82	E 3	Gt West rd Hounsl	131	Z 4	Greenland rd NW1	27	P 14	Green wlk NW4	7	Y 12	Gresham clo Enf
71	U 19	Gt West rd Islwrth	132	A 3	Greenland rd NW1	150	H 2	Green wlk SE1	37	R 18	Gresham dri Rom
73	T 15	Great West rd NW4	4	A 19	Greenland st NW1	99	T 11	Green wlk Drtfrd	45	T 3	Gresham gdns NW11
160	H 3	Gt Winchester st EC2	131	Z 4	Greenland st NW1	70	G 14	Green wlk S'hall	66	G 7	Gresham rd E6
140	E 9	Gt Windmill st W1	27	P 16	Green la NW4	158	K 15	Green wlk S Croy	65	W 18	Gresham rd E16
113	V 17	Greatwood Chisl	95	Y 19	Green la SE9	16	W 9	Greenway N14	43	Z 16	Gresham rd NW10
106	H 10	Greaves pl SW17	113	X 4	Green la SE9	17	N 7	Greenway N14	93	W 10	Gresham rd SE25
108	K 15	Grecian cres SE19	110	E 18	Green la SE20	14	L 7	Greenway N20	90	G 8	Gresham rd SW9
140	E 9	Greek st W1	108	T 19	Green la SW16	15	N 8	Greenway N20	124	G 3	Gresham rd Becknhm
95	W 16	Greenacres SE9	71	T 4	Green la W7	95	N 13	Green way SE9	12	A 20	Gresham rd Edg
157	U 6	Greenacres Croy	114	A 14	Green la Dgnhm	118	M 8	Greenway SW20	83	N 21	Gresham rd Hounsl
11	N 20	Greenacres dri Stanm	56	B 6	Green la Dgnhm	127	S 14	Green way Brom			
4	J 3	Green Acre la Barnt	11	Z 12	Green la Edg	113	X 11	Greenway Chisl			
5	L 11	Greenacre wlk N14	12	A 14	Green la Edg	55	U 5	Greenway Dgnhm			
10	D 8	Greenacres Bushey Watf	100	A 12	Greeen la Felt						
141	X 4	Green Arbour ct EC1									
12	N 12	Green av NW7									
13	N 12	Green av NW7									
72	C 8	Green av W13									

G

G
H

Ref	Name
142 C 5	Gresham st EC2
160 C 4	Gresham st EC2
31 N 14	Gresham clo N14
47 W 2	Gresley rd N19
87 V 17	Gressenhall rd SW18
140 E 3	Gresse st W1
115 O 1	Gresswell clo Sidcp
87 O 2	Greswell st SW6
31 T 3	Gretton rd N17
84 A 18	Greville clo Twick
129 W 6	Greville ms NW6
Y 8	Greville pl NW6
33 U 13	Greville rd E17
129 Z 8	Greville rd NW6
85 N 15	Greville rd Rich
141 T 1	Greville st EC1
28 C 18	Grey clo NW11
148 E 3	Greycoat pl SW1
148 E 3	Greycoat st SW1
111 O 12	Greycot rd Becknhm
135 O 19	Greyeagle st E1
11 P 15	Greyfell clo Stanm
26 H 11	Greyhound hill NW4
107 Z 15	Greyhound la SW16
31 T 10	Greyhound rd N17
62 L 8	Greyhound rd NW10
128 A 12	Greyhound rd NW10
144 G 14	Greyhound rd SW6
144 J 13	Greyhound rd W6
154 D 10	Greyhound rd Sutton
58 B 11	Greyhound rd Sutton
107 V 20	Greyhound ter SW16
92 C 18	Greystead rd SE23
22 H 10	Greystoke av Pinn
60 L 12	Greystoke gdns W5
60 H 9	Greystoke Pk ter W5
141 T 4	Greystoke pl EC4
6 L 14	Greystoke gdns Enf
24 D 19	Greystoke gdns Harrow
36 C 6	Greystoke gdns Ilf
107 T 15	Greyswood st SW16
92 G 16	Grierson rd SE23
79 T 9	Griffin Mnr way SE18
31 R 8	Griffin rd N17
79 T 11	Griffin rd SE18
152 K 4	Griffiths clo Worc Pk
105 Z 17	Griffiths rd SW19
126 L 2	Griggs pl SE1
150 L 1	Grigg's clo E10
33 V 19	Griggs rd E10
135 P 17	Grimsby st E2
22 D 2	Grimsdyke rd Pinn
87 V 6	Grimston rd SW6
157 Y 6	Grimwade av Carsh
92 B 6	Grimwade cres SE15
83 X 17	Grinwood rd Twick
75 Z 17	Grinling pl SE8
76 A 17	Grinling pl SE8
75 W 14	Grinstead rd SE8
43 T 19	Grittleton av Wemb
129 T 16	Grittleton rd W9
110 A 4	Grizedale ter SE23
154 K 2	Grn Wrythe la Carsh
160 E 6	Grocers Hall ct EC2
160 E 5	Grocers Hall gdns EC2
97 O 13	Groombridge clo Welling
63 T 1	Groombridge rd E9
88 F 19	Groom cres SW18
107 O 9	Groomfield clo SW17
139 V 20	Groom pl SW1
65 V 15	Grooms rd E16
79 Y 14	Grosmont rd SE18
48 L 17	Grosvenor av N5
49 N 16	Grosvenor av N5
86 A 8	Grosvenor av SW14
33 O 3	Grosvenor av Carsh
22 L 19	Grosvenor av Harrow
147 S 5	Grosvenor cotts SW1
16 H 1	Grosvenor ct N14
25 R 13	Grosvenor cres NW9
139 T 19	Grosvenor cres SW1
139 T 18	Grosvenor Cres ms SW1
147 X 1	Grosvenor Gdn ms SW1
147 X 2	Grosvenor gdns SW1
86 A 9	Grosvenor gdns SW13
102 H 14	Grosvenor gdns Kingst
155 U 16	Grosvenor gdns Wallgtn
21 U 20	Grosvenor gdns Wdfd Grn
147 X 2	Grosvenor Gdns Ms north SW1
147 X 3	Grosvenor Gdns Ms south SW1
105 S 14	Grosvenor hill SW19
139 X 9	Grosvenor hill W1
149 Z 17	Grosvenor pk SE5
150 A 17	Grosvenor pk SE5
33 P 16	Grosvenor Pk rd E17
139 W 19	Grosvenor pl SW1
33 S 16	Grosvenor rise east E17
66 B 3	Grosvenor rd E6
52 H 19	Grosvenor rd E7
51 U 3	Grosvenor rd E10
34 G 17	Grosvenor rd E11
27 W 1	Grosvenor rd N3
19 N 5	Grosvenor rd N9
29 S 5	Grosvenor rd N10
123 W 8	Grosvenor rd SE25
147 Y 13	Grosvenor rd SW1
73 T 14	Grosvenor rd W4
71 X 3	Grosvenor rd W7
81 R 15	Grosvenor rd Belvdr
97 X 13	Grosvenor rd Bxly Hth
72 H 17	Grosvenor rd Brentf
56 C 3	Grosvenor rd Dgnhm
82 E 8	Grosvenor rd Hounsl
54 A 9	Grosvenor rd Ilf
84 K 13	Grosvenor rd Rich
70 E 7	Grosvenor rd Rom
83 Y 20	Grosvenor rd S'hall
159 S 1	Grosvenor rd W Wkhm
155 S 12	Grosvenor rd Wallgtn
139 V 9	Grosvenor sq SW1
149 Z 16	Grosvenor ter SE5
150 B 15	Grosvenor ter SE5
76 J 12	Grosvenor Wharf Rd E14
93 Z 5	Grotes pl SE3
106 B 3	Groton rd SW18
139 U 1	Grotto pas W1
101 W 4	Grotto rd Twick
27 Y 2	Grove av N3
29 U 8	Grove av N10
59 U 17	Grove av W7
22 B 14	Grove av Pinn
153 Y 14	Grove av Sutton
101 W 1	Grove av Twick
80 D 6	Grovebury rd SE2
100 B 11	Grove clo Felt
116 L 9	Grove clo Kingst
92 G 20	Grove clo SE23
146 L 12	Grove cotts SW3
34 D 7	Grove cres E18
25 X 13	Grove cres NW9
91 R 5	Grove cres SE5
100 B 10	Grove cres Felt
116 J 7	Grove cres Kingst
51 Y 18	Grove Crescent rd E15
47 X 5	Grovesdale rd N19
34 A 7	Grove end E18
130 F 14	Grove End rd NW8
25 G 14	Grove gdns NW4
130 K 14	Grove gdns NW8
56 K 10	Grove gdns Dgnhm
9 T 4	Grove gdns Enf
101 Z 10	Grove gdns Tedd
51 V 4	Grove Green rd E11
34 B 7	Grove hill E18
41 U 2	Grove hill Harrow
91 S 7	Grve Hill rd SE5
41 U 1	Grve Hill rd Harrow
86 E 15	Grove house SW15
30 A 14	Grove House rd N8
108 D 18	Groveland av SW16
160 C 6	Groveland ct EC4
124 L 6	Groveland rd Becknhm
17 P 4	Grovelands park N21
17 T 12	Grovelands rd N13
31 X 18	Grovelands rd N15
115 P 19	Grovelands rd Orp
117 X 11	Grovelands way New Mald
91 N 2	Grove la SE5
116 K 8	Grove la Kingst
95 T 15	Grove Market pl SE9
74 L 8	Grove ms W6
144 B 2	Grove ms W6
34 G 17	Grove pk E11
25 W 12	Grove pk NW9
91 S 6	Grove pk SE5
85 V 1	Grove park W4
33 P 2	Grove Park av E4
73 V 19	Grove Park dr W4
73 U 19	Grove Park gdns W4
31 S 13	Grove Park rd N15
112 M 6	Grove Park rd SE9
113 N 5	Grove Park rd SE9
73 T 18	Grove Park rd W4
73 T 18	Grove Park ter W4
101 Y 11	Grove pass Tedd
116 K 10	Grove path Surb
46 F 11	Grove pl NW3
73 V 3	Grove pl W3
72 H 1	Grove pl W5
67 O 2	Grove pl Bark
63 V 7	Grove rd E3
27 F 13	Grove rd E4
52 B 2	Grove rd E11
33 P 17	Grove rd E17
34 C 6	Grove rd E18
16 F 15	Grove rd N11
15 T 18	Grove rd N12
31 P 16	Grove rd N15
44 L 17	Grove rd NW2
86 D 4	Grove rd SW13
106 D 18	Grove rd SW19
72 H 1	Grove rd W5
73 W 3	Grove rd W3
5 V 12	Grove rd Barnt
81 P 16	Grove rd Blvdr
98 K 11	Grove rd Bxly Hth
72 F 14	Grove rd Brentf
12 B 18	Grove rd Edg
82 G 10	Grove rd Hounsl
93 U 3	Grove rd Islwth
121 P 4	Grove rd Mitch
22 D 15	Grove rd Pinn
85 N 15	Grove rd Rich
37 S 19	Grove rd Rom
55 S 1	Grove rd Rom
116 G 11	Grove rd Surb
84 M 16	Grove rd Rich
153 Y 14	Grove rd Sutton
154 B 13	Grove rd Sutton
122 E 10	Grove rd Thntn Hth
101 R 8	Grove rd Twick
9 R 1	Grove rd west Enfield
9 R 1	Grove rd west Enfield
20 M 9	Groveside rd E4
21 O 10	Groveside rd E4
18 H 18	Grove st N18
75 X 10	Grove st SE8
47 R 11	Grover ter NW5
101 Y 10	Grove ter Tedd
51 Y 18	Grove the E15
27 X 3	Grove the N3
48 D 1	Grove the N4
47 O 3	Grove the N6
17 T 13	Grove the N13
45 T 1	Grove the NW11
25 Y 16	Grove the SE9
72 G 2	Grove the W5
97 W 10	Grove the Bxly Hth
12 F 13	Grove the Edg
7 T 9	Grove the Enf
58 M 17	Grove the Grnfd
83 T 3	Grove the Islwth
73 Z 11	Grove the Sidcp
101 Y 11	Grove the Tedd
159 T 6	Grove the W Wkhm
159 U 1	Grove the W Wkhm
91 T 9	Grove vale SE22
113 W 14	Grove vale Chisl
64 E 19	Grove villas E14
90 E 3	Groveway SW9
53 V 11	Grove way Dgnhm
43 U 15	Grove way Wemb
85 O 3	Grovewood Rich
91 U 2	Grummant rd SE15
64 D 18	Grundy st E14
28 A 1	Gruneisen rd N3
90 K 13	Gubyon av SE24
48 E 3	Guerin sq E3
94 G 20	Guibal rd SE12
112 G 1	Guibal rd SE12
107 Z 18	Guildersfield rd SW16
108 A 17	Guildersfield rd SW16
116 M 11	Guildford av Surb
93 S 1	Guildford gro SE10
33 V 4	Guildford rd E17
90 A 1	Guildford rd SW8
123 O 14	Guildford rd Croy
54 J 8	Guildford rd Ilf
115 L 15	Guildford vlls Surb
156 B 10	Guildford rd Wallgtn
142 C 4	Guildhall EC2
160 D 4	Guildhall bldgs EC2
148 A 6	Guildhouse st SW1
78 B 15	Guild rd SE18
32 K 5	Guildsway E17
133 N 18	Guildford pl WC1
132 K 19	Guildford st WC1
133 O 17	Guildford st WC1
87 W 4	Guion rd SW6
156 A 17	Gull clo Wallgtn
57 X 19	Gull way Hornch
114 G 5	Gulliver rd Sidcp
75 X 8	Gulliver st SE16
72 D 11	Gumleigh rd W5
83 X 7	Gumley gdns Islwth
126 L 7	Gundulph rd Brom
63 X 3	Gunmakers la E3
78 K 14	Gunner la SE18
73 P 9	Gunnersbury av W3
72 M 2	Gunnersbury av W5
73 P 6	Gunnersbury cres W3
73 N 7	Gunnersbury dri W5
73 P 6	Gunnersbury gdns W3
73 R 6	Gunnersbury la W3
72 K 9	Gunnersbury park W3
20 F 10	Gunners gro E4
106 G 3	Gunners rd SW18
79 U 10	Gunning st SE18
49 S 11	Gunstor rd N16
142 M 1	Gun st E1
146 B 16	Gunter gro SW10
25 X 4	Gunter gro Edgw
144 L 8	Gunterstone rd W14
145 N 8	Gunterstone rd W14
143 P 3	Gunthorpe st E1
107 P 16	Gunton rd SW17
77 U 14	Gurdon rd SE7
59 X 11	Gurnell gro W13
122 D 20	Gurney cres Croy
62 E 14	Gurney dri N2
51 Z 14	Gurney rd E15
52 A 14	Gurney rd E15
155 N 7	Gurney rd Carsh
151 O 16	Gurnies clo SE15
146 J 9	Guthrie st SW3
160 B 5	Gutter la EC2
121 P 2	Guyatt gdns Mitch
155 Y 6	Guy rd Wallgtn
93 T 13	Guyscliffe rd SE13
142 G 17	Guy st SE1
87 P 9	Gwalior rd SW15
87 C 11	Gwendolen av SW15
87 O 12	Gwendolen clo SW15
65 V 3	Gwendoline av E13
144 M 9	Gwendwr rd W14
145 N 8	Gwendwr rd W14
97 O 14	Gwillim clo Sidcp
124 F 7	Gwydor rd Becknhm
126 D 5	Gwydyr rd Brom
126 E 16	Gwynne av Croy
133 P 14	Gwynne pl WC1
88 G 4	Gwynne st SW11
148 M 10	Gye st SE11
9 P 11	Glycoe clo SE5
24 E 4	Gyles pk Stanm
54 L 10	Gyllyngdune gdns Ilf

H

Ref	Name
78 H 16	Ha-Ha rd SE18
144 F 3	Haarlem rd W14
134 G 12	Haberdasher st N1
106 C 16	Haccombe rd SW19
155 O 2	Hackbridge grn Wallgtn
155 N 2	Hackbridge Pk gdns Carsh
155 P 1	Hackbridge rd Wallgtn
90 E 2	Hackford rd SW9
149 R 20	Hackford rd SW9
111 O 15	Hackington cres Becknhm
50 A 19	Hackney gro E8
135 T 9	Hackney rd E2
118 C 11	Haddon clo New Mald
79 U 9	Hadden way SE18
41 R 17	Hadden way Grnfd
X 9	Haddington rd Brom
8 K 20	Haddon clo Enf
96 M 18	Haddon gro Sidcp
154 R 18	Haddon rd Sutton
76 F 17	Haddo st SE10
63 P 11	Hadleigh clo E1
18 M 2	Hadleigh rd N9
19 N 2	Hadleigh rd N9
63 P 10	Hadleigh st E2
7 U 19	Hadley clo N21

5 N 9 Hadley Common Barnt
5 O 10 Hadley Common Barnt
4 K 9 Hadley Common Barnt
73 Y 13 Hadley gdns W4
70 D 14 Hadley gdns S'hall
4 G 8 Hadley green West Barnt
4 H 9 Hdley Green rd Barnt
4 G 10 Hadley gro Barnt
4 H 6 Hadley highstone Barnt
4 J 8 Hadley house Barnt
4 G 11 Hadley ridge Barnt
5 O 10 Hadley rd Barnt
6 G 3 Hadley rd Barnt
5 Y 4 Hadley road Barnt
81 O 9 Hadley rd Belvdr
7 R 4 Hadley rd Enf
121 X 9 Hadley rd Mitch
47 S 18 Hadley st NW1
7 T 20 Hadley way N21
109 W 17 Hadlow pl SE19
115 O 10 Hadlow rd Sidcp
80 G 19 Hadlow rd Welling
156 B 15 Hadrian clo Croy
4 H 16 Hadrians ride Enf
76 M 14 Hadrian st SE10
74 F 5 Hadyn Pk rd W12
88 K 11 Hafer rd SW11
112 A 2 Hafton rd SE6
84 A 19 Haggard rd Twick
135 N 2 Haggerston rd E8
135 U 14 Hague st E2
11 R 17 Haig rd E13
65 Y 8 Haig Rd east E13
65 X 8 Haig Rd west E13
106 C 15 Hailes cl SW19
8 H 20 Haileybury av Enf
81 R 6 Haileybury rd Belvdr
108 C 5 Hailsham av SW16
116 H 17 Hailsham rd SW17
107 P 16 Hailsham rd SW17
18 A 15 Hailsham ter N16
95 O 12 Haimo rd SE9
33 X 14 Hainault ct E17
38 A 17 Hainault gore Rom
37 S 11 Hainault house Rom
33 Z 20 Hainault rd E11
38 B 18 Hainault rd Rom
38 L 10 Hainault rd Rom
114 A 2 Hainault st SE9
54 A 7 Hainault st Ilf
92 G 10 Hainsford clo SE4
108 M 8 Hainthorpe rd SE27
56 B 11 Halbutt gdns Dgnhm
56 B 11 Halbutt st Dgnhm
134 J 6 Halcomb st N1
98 H 12 Halcot av Bxly Hth
63 O 16 Halcrow st E1
88 A 20 Haldane pl SW18
66 D 8 Haldane rd E6
145 R 17 Haldane rd SW16
20 G 20 Haldan rd E4
21 O 1 Haldane clo N10
58 M 18 Haldene rd S'hall
87 W 15 Haldon rd SW18
20 G 10 Hale clo E4
12 J 16 Hale clo Edg
12 K 19 Hale dri NW7
20 J 19 Hale End rd E4
33 W 8 Hale End rd E17
33 V 8 Hale End rd Wdfd Grn
31 Z 6 Halefield rd N17
31 X 11 Hale gdns N17
73 P 2 Hale gdns W3
12 M 16 Hale Gro gdns NW7
13 N 17 Hale Gro gdns NW7
12 L 16 Hale la NW7
13 O 17 Hale la NW7
12 E 16 Hale la Edg
66 D 12 Hale rd E6
31 X 11 Hale rd N17
76 A 20 Hales st SE8
119 Z 18 Halesowen rd Mrdn
120 A 19 Halesowen rd Mrdn
93 P 7 Halesworth rd SE13
33 W 2 Hale the N4
31 X 11 Hale the N17
59 U 15 Hale wk NW7
26 M 18 Haley rd NW4
72 F 17 Half acre Brentf
71 S 2 Half Acre rd W7
142 A 2 Half Moon ct EC1
56 L 15 Half Moon la SE24
90 L 15 Half Moon la SE24
143 O 5 Halfmoon pass E1

139 Y 14 Half Moon st W1
33 W 16 Halford rd E10
145 T 15 Halford rd SW6
84 J 13 Halford rd Rich
96 F 20 Halfway st Sidcp
114 J 2 Halfway st Sidcp
83 Z 12 Haliburton rd Twick
49 O 17 Haliday wlk N1
8 A 8 Halifax rd Enf
58 L 3 Halifax rd Grnfd
110 A 8 Halifax st SE26
156 C 16 Haling gro S Croy
156 K 13 Haling Pk gdns S Croy
156 M 14 Haling Pk rd S Croy
157 N 14 Haling Pk rd S Croy
157 O 13 Haling rd S Croy
139 S 20 Halkin ms SW1
147 S 1 Halkin pl SW1
139 U 19 Halkin st SW1
113 T 13 Halkin clo Chisl
44 G 14 Hallam gdns Pinn
131 Y 20 Hallam ms W1
131 Y 19 Hallam st W1
139 Z 1 Hallam st W1
110 B 11 Hall dri SE26
59 U 16 Hall dri W7
52 K 18 Halley rd E7
53 P 15 Halley rd E7
63 V 15 Halley st E14
11 N 12 Hall Fm clo Stanm
83 R 18 Hall Farm dri Twick
19 Z 14 Hall gdns E4
134 D 1 Halliford st N1
90 B 15 Halliwell rd SW2
29 O 4 Halliwick rd N10
19 Y 14 Hal la E4
20 B 14 Hal la E4
26 G 7 Hall la NW4
153 Z 5 Hallmead rd Sutton
154 A 5 Hallmead rd Sutton
155 Z 7 Hallowell av Wallgtn
121 O 5 Hallowell clo Mitch
130 F 19 Hall pl W2
98 L 14 Hall Pl cres Bxly
66 G 3 Hall rd E6
51 X 12 Hall rd E15
130 C 14 Hall rd NW8
83 R 12 Hall rd Islwth
37 U 18 Hall rd Rom
155 T 18 Hall rd Wallgtn
53 X 11 Hall st EC1
15 P 16 Hall st N12
113 N 4 Hall view SE9
65 O 17 Hallsville rd E16
65 O 18 Hallsville rd E16
27 V 15 Hallswelle rd NW11
94 E 8 Hallside rd SE3
49 P 17 Hallway wlk N1
95 X 17 Halons rd SE9
150 G 7 Halpin pl SE17
94 M 6 Halsbrook rd SE3
95 P 11 Halsbrook rd SE3
11 O 15 Halsbury clo Stanm
74 H 3 Halsbury rd W12
41 O 13 Halsbury Rd east Grnfd
40 L 14 Halsbury Rd west Grnfd
147 N 6 Halsey st SW3
54 K 16 Halsham cres Bark
90 K 2 Halsmere rd SE5
18 A 5 Halstead gdns N21
34 G 15 Halstead rd E11
18 A 5 Halstead rd N21
8 E 14 Halstead rd Enf
99 P 1 Hastead rd Erith
128 F 13 Halstow rd NW10
78 C 14 Halstow rd SE10
133 Y 3 Halton Cross st N1
48 J 20 Halton rd N1
133 Y 2 Halton rd N1
81 V 10 Halt Robin la Belvdr
81 T 10 Halt Robin rd Belvdr
89 V 14 Hambalt rd SW4
123 U 6 Hambledon gdns SE25
87 V 19 Hambledon rd SW18
96 F 19 Hambledown rd Sidcp
88 B 7 Hamble st SW6
126 F 19 Hambro av Brom
123 Z 6 Hambrook rd SE25
73 V 3 Hambro rd SW16
70 B 2 Hamborough rd S'hall
102 D 6 Ham clo Rich
56 G 9 Hamden cres Dgnhm
64 G 18 Hamelin st E14
66 J 10 Hameway E6
102 H 9 Ham Farm rd Rich
52 C 17 Hamfrith rd E15
102 H 8 Ham Ga av Rich
102 C 2 Ham house Rich

18 K 2 Hamilton av N9
36 B 14 Hamilton av Ilf
38 M 9 Hamilton av Rom
39 N 8 Hamilton av Rom
153 S 1 Hamilton av Sutton
31 W 11 Hamilton clo N17
130 E 15 Hamilton clo NW8
5 X 14 Hamilton clo Barnt
60 L 20 Hamilton ct W5
17 U 14 Hamilton cres N13
40 F 9 Hamilton cres Harrow
82 K 14 Hamilton cres Hounsl
130 D 11 Hamilton gdns NW8
139 V 16 Hamilton mans W1
48 H 13 Hamilton Pk west N5
139 V 16 Hamilton rd E15
65 N 10 Hamilton rd E15
32 J 9 Hamilton rd E17
28 D 10 Hamilton rd N2
18 J 3 Hamilton rd E9
44 G 14 Hamilton rd NW10
45 R 1 Hamilton rd NW11
120 O 9 Hamilton rd SE27
106 B 18 Hamilton rd SW19
74 A 7 Hamilton rd W4
60 L 19 Hamilton rd W5
5 X 14 Hamilton rd Barnt
97 Z 4 Hamilton rd Bxly Hth
72 G 16 Hamilton rd Brentf
23 U 15 Hamilton rd Harrow
53 Z 12 Hamilton rd Ilf
39 Y 16 Hamilton rd Rom
70 E 2 Hamilton rd S'hall
114 M 9 Hamilton rd Sidcp
123 N 5 Hamilton rd Thntn Hth
101 U 1 Hamilton rd Twick
129 Z 9 Hamilton ter NW8
130 B 12 Hamilton ter NW8
14 K 20 Hamilton way N3
155 X 19 Hamilton way Wallgtn
94 D 13 Hamlea clo SE12
39 D 2 Hamlet clo Rom
74 F 11 Hamlet gdns W6
109 W 18 Hamlet rd SE19
38 C 2 Hamlet rd Rom
91 R 7 The hamlet SE5
63 Y 11 Hamlets way E3
109 R 19 Hamlyn gdns SE19
112 E 20 Hammelton rd Brom
13 U 14 Hammers la NW1
65 R 17 Hammersley av E16
74 K 15 Hammersmith br W6
14 A 11 Hammersmith br W6
74 L 13 Hammersmith Br rd W6
144 B 10 Hammersmith Br yd W6
144 D 7 Hammersmith bdwy W6
144 D 9 Hammersmith flyover W6
74 L 7 Hammersmith gro W6
136 A 20 Hammersmith gro W6
144 C 5 Hammersmith gro W6
144 H 6 Hammersmith rd W6
64 G 14 Hammersmith ter W6
143 N 9 Hammett st EC3
121 R 4 Hammond av Mitch
4 F 18 Hammond clo Barnt
41 R 14 Hammond clo Grnfd
9 N 10 Hammond rd Enf
70 D 9 Hammond rd S'hall
47 U 17 Hammond st NW5
68 D 20 Hammond way SE2
12 E 9 Hammonds clo Edg
52 E 20 Ham Pk rd E7
124 K 4 Hampden av Becknhm
139 O 6 Hampden Gurney st W1
31 W 5 Hampden la N17
132 G 9 Hampden pl NW1
30 G 13 Hampden pl N8
29 P 1 Hampden pl N10
31 X 4 Hampden rd N17
28 D 16 Hampden rd Becknhm
23 O 5 Hampden rd Harrow
117 R 5 Hampden rd Kingst
88 H 2 Hampden rd Rom
16 E 6 Hampden way N14
110 A 20 Ham Pk rd SE13
28 M 17 Hampshire clo N18
30 D 1 Hampshire rd N22
47 X 16 Hampshire st NW5
90 C 1 Hampson way SE8
80 B 3 Hampstead clo SE18

27 X 19 Hampstead gdns NW11
46 J 14 Hampstead grn NW3
46 D 11 Hampstead gro NW3
46 G 6 Hampstead heath NW3
28 E 11 Hampstead heights N2
46 F 13 Hampstead High st NW3
46 H 13 Hampstead Hill gdns NW3
46 K 2 Hampstead la N6
47 N 2 Hampstead la N6
132 B 11 Hampstead rd NW1
46 E 10 Hampstead sq NW3
27 X 16 Hampstead way NW11
46 C 4 Hampstead way NW11
104 L 18 Hampton clo SW20
129 T 13 Hampton clo NW6
48 H 18 Hampton ct N1
116 C 8 Hampton Court park Kingst
100 C 10 Hampton la Felt
24 K 19 Hampton ri Harrow
19 X 16 Hampton rd E4
20 A 16 Hampton rd E4
52 G 15 Hampton rd E7
51 X 5 Hampton rd E11
122 M 14 Hampton rd Croy
54 B 13 Hampton rd Ilf
101 R 13 Hampton rd Tedd
101 R 6 Hampton rd Twick
152 H 3 Hampton rd Worc Pk
100 G 9 Hampton Rd east Felt
100 C 6 Hampton Rd west Felt
149 Z 6 Hampton st SE17
102 M 11 Ham ridings Rich
114 L 5 Hamshades clo Sidcp
102 C 3 Ham st Rich
72 E 20 Ham the Brentf
124 J 15 Ham view Croy
140 D 9 Ham wy W1
77 U 3 Hanameel st E16
31 Y 7 Hanbury rd N17
73 T 7 Hanbury rd W3
135 S 20 Hanbury st E1
64 F 9 Hancock rd E3
109 O 16 Hancock rd SE19
141 P 2 Hand ct WC2
122 H 19 Handcroft rd Croy
11 Z 19 Handel clo Edg
132 K 16 Handel st WC1
12 C 20 Handel way Edg
25 O 1 Handel way Edg
94 C 14 Handen rd SE12
149 S 18 Handforth rd SW9
63 R 2 Handley rd E9
153 P 1 Handside clo Worc Pk
65 T 17 Hands wlk E16
20 J 19 Handsworth av E4
31 P 11 Handsworth rd N17
67 N 5 Handtrough way Barking
105 Y 1 Hanford clo SW18
104 M 14 Hanford row SW19
61 O 11 Hanger grn W5
60 K 12 Hanger Hill park W5
60 L 14 Hanger la W5
60 M 17 Hanger vale W5
61 O 15 Hanger Vale la W5
141 V 6 Hanging Sword all EC4
142 F 19 Hankey pl SE1
13 N 10 Hankins la NW7
48 A 5 Hanley rd N4
144 L 18 Hannell rd SW6
108 K 8 Hannen rd SE27
63 R 14 Hannibal rd E1
156 C 13 Hannibal wy Croy
50 L 17 Hannington point E9
89 S 8 Hannington rd SW4
153 T 8 Hanover clo Sutton
149 S 16 Hanover gdns SE11
36 B 2 Hanover gdns Ilf
130 M 13 Hanover gdns NW8
91 X 3 Hanover pk SE15
140 L 7 Hanover pl WC2
31 V 13 Hanover rd N15
128 M 2 Hanover rd NW10
128 C 3 Hanover rd NW10
106 E 17 Hanover rd SW19
139 Y 7 Hanover sq W1
139 Z 7 Hanover st W1
156 J 6 Hanover sq Croy
131 N 14 Hanover ter NW1
91 N 15 Hanover Ter ms NW1
97 X 9 Hanover yd Bxly Hth
133 Z 8 Hanover yd N1

7 U 7 Hansait way Enf
136 J 18 Hansard ms W14
7 U 7 Hansart way Enf
139 O 20 Hans cres SW3
10 J 17 Hanselin clo Stanm
25 X 4 Hanshaw dri Edgw
91 V 13 Hansler rd SE22
97 Y 12 Hansol rd Bxly Hth
89 S 19 Hanson cl SW12
70 C 5 Hanson gdns S'hall
132 A 20 Hanson st W1
140 A 1 Hanson st W1
147 O 2 Hans pl SW1
147 N 1 Hans rd SW3
147 P 2 Hans st SW1
140 F 3 Hanaway pl W1
59 T 16 Hanaway rd W7
140 F 4 Hanaway st W1
100 J 14 Hanworth rd Hampt
82 H 14 Hanworth rd Hounsl
82 K 10 Hanworth ter Hounsl
143 T 9 Harads pl E1
46 E 20 Harben rd NW6
65 P 3 Harberson rd E15
89 R 20 Harberson rd SW12
47 V 4 Harberton rd N19
19 U 17 Harbet rd E4
138 H 2 Harbet st W2
98 F 18 Harbex clo Bxly
76 D 12 Harbinger rd E14
87 X 1 Harbledown rd SW6
87 P 1 Harbord st SW6
96 J 18 Harborough av Sidcp
108 D 9 Harborough rd SW16
90 L 7 Harbour rd SE5
68 F 18 Harbridge av SW15
154 H 17 Harbury rd Carsh
88 F 11 Harbut rd SW11
49 R 10 Harcombe rd N16
53 T 14 Harcourt av E12
12 G 11 Harcourt av Edg
97 T 18 Harcourt av Sidcp
155 T 9 Harcourt av Wallgtn
155 T 8 Harcourt field Wallgtn
65 O 6 Harcourt rd E15
9 W 4 Harcourt rd N22
29 W 4 Harcourt rd N22
92 K 8 Harcourt rd SE4
105 Y 19 Harcourt rd SW19
97 Z 9 Harcourt rd Bxly Hth
122 D 14 Harcourt rd Thntn Hth
155 S 8 Harcourt rd Wallgtn
M 2 Harcourt st W1
145 Z 11 Harcourt ter SW10
146 A 12 Harcourt ter SW10
159 T 7 Hardcourts clo W Wkhm
108 G 2 Hardel ri SW2
78 A 9 Hardens manorway SE18
78 D 10 Harders rd SE18
91 Z 2 Harders rd SE15
92 A 2 Harders Rd ms SE15
90 K 8 Hardess st SE24
43 W 15 Hardie clo NW10
56 K 10 Hardie rd Dgnhm
18 D 18 Hardinge rd N18
62 L 4 Hardinge rd NW10
128 C 6 Hardinge rd NW10
89 R 19 Hardinge st E1
98 A 4 Harding rd Bxly Hth
110 E 16 Hardings la SE20
77 U 13 Hardman rd SE7
116 K 2 Hardman rd Kingst
11 R 16 Hardwick clo Stanm
82 H 2 Hardwicke clo Hounsl
17 N 18 Hardwicke rd N13
73 X 11 Hardwicke rd W4
102 C 9 Hardwicke rd Rich
60 B 14 Hardwicke grn W13
133 T 13 Hardwick st EC1
67 O 4 Hardwick st Bark
87 Z 14 Hardwicks way SW18
142 J 17 Hardwidge st SE1
77 R 17 Hardy rd SE3
106 B 18 Hardy rd SW19
7 U 6 Hardy way Enf
94 A 4 Hare And Billet rd SE3
93 X 4 Hare And Billet rd SE3
141 S 7 Hare ct EC4
48 L 17 Harecourt rd N1
90 M 11 Haredale rd SE24
92 D 18 Haredon clo SE23
29 X 15 Harefield av N8
153 R 20 Harefield av Sutton
7 U 5 Harefield clo Enf

92 K 7 Harefield ms SE4
92 L 8 Harefield rd SE4
93 N 8 Harefield rd SE4
108 D 18 Harefield rd SW16
115 W 6 Harefield rd Sidcp
39 Y 12 Hare Hall la Rom
63 N 5 Hare row E2
56 F 19 Haresfield rd Dgnhm
28 J 8 Hare st SE18
134 L 9 Hare wlk N1
130 M 7 Harewood av NW1
131 N 20 Harewood av NW1
58 D 1 Harewood clo Grnfd
35 T 7 Harewood dri Ilf
139 Y 6 Harewood pl W1
106 K 16 Harewood rd SW19
71 V 20 Harewood rd Islwth
83 W 1 Harewood rd Islwth
157 S 14 Harewood rd S Croy
130 M 20 Harewood row NW1
70 F 11 Harewgod ter S'hall
91 R 7 Harfield gdns SE5
20 E 2 Harford clo E4
20 E 2 Harford rd E4
63 U 12 Harford st E1
28 G 14 Harford wlk N2
94 L 4 Hargood rd SE3
47 U 8 Hargrave pk N19
47 X 16 Hargrave pl NW5
47 W 7 Hargrave rd N19
36 A 13 Hargville gdns Ilf
90 B 8 Hargwyne st SW9
30 D 13 Haringey av N8
30 A 19 Haringey pk N8
30 A 14 Haringey rd N8
23 V 6 Harkett clo Harrow
157 W 5 Harland av Croy
114 E 6 Harland av Sidcp
94 E 20 Harland rd SE12
112 F 1 Harland rd SE12
10 O 11 Harlech rd N14
71 Z 17 Harlequin av Brentf
102 A 17 Harlequin rd Tedd
92 F 10 Harlescott rd SE15
62 D 3 Harlesden gdns NW10
44 J 20 Harlesden rd NW10
62 H 2 Harlesden rd NW10
42 G 17 Harley clo Wemb
23 R 13 Harley cres Harrow
112 K 20 Harleyford Brom
149 O 13 Harleyford rd SE11
149 S 15 Harleyford st SE11
146 C 11 Harley gdns SW10
63 Z 9 Harley gro E3
139 W 2 Harley pl W1
130 H 2 Harley rd NW3
62 B 6 Harley rd NW10
23 R 12 Harley rd Harrow
131 W 19 Harley st W1
139 X 2 Harley st W1
98 A 7 Harlington rd Bxly Hth
18 A 10 Harlow rd N13
21 O 20 Harman av Wdfd Grn
45 T 11 Harman clo NW2
20 K 14 Harman clo E4
45 T 11 Harman dri NW2
96 L 15 Harman dri Sidcp
8 G 16 Harman rd Enf
30 A 15 Harmiston av N8
27 T 15 Harmony clo NW11
47 R 20 Harmond pl NW1
47 R 20 Harmond st NW1
149 W 12 Harmsworth st SE17
14 J 6 Harmsworth way N20
79 Z 6 Harness rd SE18
25 X 4 Harnshaw dri Edg
81 O 14 Harold av Belvdr
149 R 12 Harold pl SE11
20 F 12 Harold rd E4
51 Z 4 Harold rd E11
65 X 3 Harold rd E13
30 C 14 Harold rd N8
31 V 14 Harold rd N8
61 X 8 Harold rd NW10
109 R 16 Harold rd SE19
154 F 9 Harold rd Sutton
34 G 4 Harold rd Wdfd Grn
32 G 16 Haroldstone rd E17
141 V 4 Harp all EC4
108 H 5 Harpenden rd E12
142 B 20 Harpenden rd SE1
150 C 1 Harper rd SE1
142 K 10 Harp la EC3
63 S 10 Harpley sq E1
54 B 19 Harpour rd Bark
59 V 12 Harp rd W7
89 O 3 Harpsden st SW11
133 N 20 Harpur st WC1
94 L 2 Harraden rd SE3
57 Y 19 Harrier clo Hornch

79 T 6 Harrier ms SE18
157 X 2 Harriet gdns Croy
139 R 20 Harriet st SW1
139 R 19 Harriet wlk SW1
10 C 3 Harriet way Bush'ey
72 J 1 Harriets clo W5
30 J 14 Harringay gdns N15
30 G 15 Harringay pass N8
30 J 13 Harringay rd N15
30 J 14 Harringay rd N15
155 Z 3 Harrington clo Wallgtn
146 A 7 Harrington gdns SW7
50 B 4 Harrington hill E5
52 A 4 Harrington rd E11
123 Y 9 Harrington rd SE25
124 B 8 Harrington rd SE25
146 E 6 Harrington rd SW7
132 B 9 Harrington sq NW1
132 A 12 Harrington st NW1
18 B 12 Harrington ter N13
78 B 8 Harrington way SE18
77 O 12 Harriott clo SE10
56 F 19 Harrison rd Dgnhm
156 J 5 Harrison's ri Croy
132 M 14 Harrison st WC1
7 V 6 Harris clo Hounsl
82 G 2 Harris clo Hounsl
98 A 2 Harris rd Bxly Hth
56 B 15 Harris rd Dgnhm
50 L 1 Harris rd E17
150 G 19 Harris st SE5
56 R 15 Harrold rd Dgnhm
18 H 1 Harrow av Enf
88 F 5 Harroway rd SW11
138 M 4 Harrowby st W1
139 N 4 Harrowby st W1
39 Z 3 Harrow cres Rom
42 F 14 Harrowdene clo Wemb
101 Z 17 Harrowdene gdns Tedd
42 G 10 Harrowdene rd Wemb
18 G 4 Harrow dri N9
57 Z 3 Harrow dri Hornch
12 D 10 Harrowes meade Edg
41 U 10 Harrowfields gdns Harrow
6 G 19 Harrowgate rd E9
51 Z 9 Harrow grn E11
64 F 20 Harrow la E14
57 V 7 Harrow Lodge park Hornch
80 F 2 Harrow Lodge park Hornch
41 U 6 Harrow pk Harrow
142 M 3 Harrow pl E1
66 D 2 Harrow rd E11
52 D 9 Harrow rd E11
62 J 8 Harrow rd NW10
128 D 14 Harrow rd NW10
129 N 9 Harrow rd W2
28 L 12 Harrow rd W2
129 O 17 Harrow rd W2
67 V 3 Harrow rd Bark
154 J 12 Harrow rd Carsh
54 C 14 Harrow rd Ilf
41 X 12 Harrow rd Wemb
49 P 17 Harrow rd Wemb
23 R 14 Harrow view Harrow
60 C 12 Harrow view rd W5
10 D 18 Harrow Weald pk Harrow
82 F 5 Harrow Hounsl
105 V 17 Hartfield cres SW19
110 B 20 Hartfield gro SE20
105 W 18 Hartfield rd SW19
64 B 7 Hartfield ter E3
23 Z 10 Hartford av Harrow
24 A 10 Hartford av Harrow
98 F 17 Hartford rd Bxly
27 H 14 Hartfort wlk N2
73 O 2 Hart gro W5
58 S 14 Hart gro S'hall
48 A 15 Hartham clo N7
83 X 1 Hartham clo Islwth
16 A 16 Hartham rd N17
31 U 6 Hartham rd N7
83 X 2 Hartham rd Islwth
113 P 8 Harting rd SE9
41 T 12 Hartington clo Harrow
65 V 17 Hartington rd E16
32 H 19 Hartington rd E17
89 Z 1 Hartington rd SW8
148 J 20 Hartington rd SW8
73 U 20 Hartington rd W4
85 W 3 Hartington rd W4
72 B 1 Hartington rd W13
70 B 7 Hartington rd S'hall
84 B 17 Hartington rd Twick
145 R 17 Hartismere rd SW6
50 G 18 Hartlake rd E9

12 C 9 Hartland clo Edg
12 B 9 Hartland dri Edg
52 B 20 Hartland rd E15
65 O 1 Hartland rd E15
15 Z 17 Hartland rd N11
47 R 20 Hartland rd NW1
129 O 7 Hartland rd NW6
100 K 16 Hartland rd Hampt
57 W 8 Hartland rd Hornch
119 Z 18 Hartland rd Mrdn
47 S 19 Hartland rd NW1
158 H 2 Hartland way Croy
158 H 4 Hartland way Croy
119 W 16 Hartland way Mrdn
66 D 4 Hartley av E6
13 R 17 Hartley av NW7
13 R 17 Hartley clo NW7
127 V 4 Hartley clo Brom
52 C 3 Hartley rd E11
126 K 16 Hartley rd Croy
80 F 18 Hartley rd Welling
63 R 8 Hartley st E2
78 A 2 Hartman rd E16
48 D 15 Hartnoll st N7
113 N 20 Harton clo Chisl
19 N 9 Harton rd N9
93 N 1 Harton st SE4
120 L 17 Hatropp av SW4
10 B 8 Hartsbourne av Bushey Watf
10 D 8 Hartsbourne rd Bushey Watf
66 J 11 Hartshorn gdns E6
92 G 1 Harts la SE14
53 Z 18 Harts la Bark
80 H 4 Hartslock dri SE2
113 T 3 Hartsmead rd SE9
142 L 8 Hart st EC3
9 O 15 Harts way Enf
74 C 7 Hartswood rd W12
79 V 11 Hartville rd SE18
20 F 19 Hartwell dri E4
49 U 17 Hartwell st E8
141 S 1 Hart yd EC1
73 U 15 Harvard hill W4
73 V 15 Harvard la W4
93 V 14 Harvard rd SE13
73 T 14 Harvard rd W4
83 T 3 Harvard rd Islwth
80 J 14 Harvel cres SW2
83 R 12 Harvesters clo Islwth
77 Z 13 Harvey gdns SE7
52 B 3 Harvey rd E11
30 C 15 Harvey rd N8
82 F 19 Harvey rd Hounsl
53 Z 16 Harvey rd Ilf
54 A 16 Harvey rd Ilf
134 G 5 Harvey st N1
57 P 6 Harvey's la Rom
115 X 13 Harvill rd Sidcp
128 H 11 Harvist rd NW6
129 N 9 Harvist rd NW6
28 L 12 Harwell pas N2
126 G 3 Harwood av Brom
120 J 6 Harwood av Mitch
145 V 19 Harwood rd SW6
88 A 1 Harwood ter SW6
18 F 8 Haselbury rd N9
89 Z 10 Haselrigge rd SW4
110 K 10 Haseltine rd SE26
7 W 13 Haslewood dri Enf
55 W 13 Haskard rd Dgnhm
55 W 14 Haskard rd Dgnhm
146 M 4 Hasker st SW3
119 T 19 Haslam av Sutton
100 G 20 Haslam clo N1
27 O 18 Haslemere av NW4
106 A 3 Haslemere av SW18
72 A 8 Haslemere av W13
15 Z 6 Haslemere av Barnt
120 F 3 Haslemere av Mitch
71 Z 9 Haslemere Av 1-84 W13
106 A 4 Haslemere clo Hampt
100 F 12 Haslemere clo Wallgtn
156 A 12 Haslemere gdns Wallgtn
27 U 11 Haslemere gdns N3
29 Z 20 Haslemere rd N8
17 V 7 Haslemere rd N21
98 C 5 Haslemere rd Bxly Hth
54 K 6 Haslemere rd Ilf
122 H 11 Haslemere rd Thntn Hth
159 U 17 Hasley dri Croy
5 O 19 Hasluck gdns Barnt
77 V 18 Hassendean rd SW13
50 G 17 Hassett rd E9
110 A 6 Hassocks clo SE26
121 X 1 Hassocks rd SW16
45 O 11 Hassop rd NW2

113 P 9 Hassop wlk SE9
78 B 13 Hasted rd SE18
36 B 14 Hastings av Ilf
16 J 17 Hastings rd N11
31 O 9 Hastings rd N17
60 B 20 Hastings rd W13
123 U 19 Hastings rd Croy
39 Y 17 Hastings rd Rom
132 J 14 Hastings st WC1
92 D 1 Hatcham gdns SE15
75 P 16 Hatcham rd SE15
92 F 1 Hatcham Pk rd SE14
75 P 16 Hatcham rd SE16
47 Z 6 Hatchard rd N19
26 H 11 Hatch croft NW4
37 Z 13 Hatch gro Rom
20 K 13 Hatch la E4
122 A 3 Hatch rd SW16
9 S 7 Hatch the Enf
94 B 8 Hatcliffe clo SE3
77 O 13 Hatcliffe st SE10
35 Z 9 Hatfield clo Ilf
120 E 9 Hatfield clo Mitch
75 R 19 Hatfield clo SE14
119 X 12 Hatfield mead Mrdn
52 A 14 Hatfield rd E15
73 Z 5 Hatfield rd W4
71 Y 3 Hatfield rd W13
55 Z 20 Hatfield rd Dgnhm
68 M 1 Hatfield rd Dgnhm
141 U 12 Hatfields SE1
10 K 17 Hathaway clo Stanm
53 U 17 Hathaway cres E12
59 Y 14 Hathaway gdns W13
37 V 15 Hathaway gdns Rom
122 K 18 Hathaway rd Croy
119 Y 9 Hatherleigh clo Mrdn
115 O 6 Hatherley cres Sidcp
66 B 8 Hatherley gdns E6
137 X 5 Hatherley gro W2
33 N 12 Hatherley rd E7
32 M 13 Hatherley rd E17
85 N 3 Hatherley rd Rich
115 O 8 Hatherley rd Sidcp
148 D 6 Hatherley st SW1
113 W 10 Hathern gdns SE9
100 D 18 Hatherop rd Hampt
92 D 6 Hathway st SE15
36 B 13 Hatley av Ilf
15 Y 15 Hatley clo N11
48 E 7 Hatley rd N4
88 L 15 Hatston clo SW11
133 T 20 Hatton gdn EC1
141 U 1 Hatton gdn EC1
120 M 11 Hatton gdns Mitch
122 G 19 Hatton rd Croy
130 G 19 Hatton row W2
130 G 18 Hatton st NW8
133 T 19 Hatton wall EC1
139 X 7 Haunch Of Venison rd W1
39 R 17 Havana cl Rom
105 Z 4 Havana rd SW19
76 B 5 Havannah st E14
33 U 11 Havant rd E17
57 V 13 Havard wlk Hornch
23 U 19 Havelock pl Harrow
31 Y 7 Havelock rd N17
106 C 12 Havelock rd SW19
81 O 12 Havelock rd Blvdr
L 8 Havelock rd Brom
V 2 Havelock rd Croy
89 Y 18 Havelock rd Drtfrd
23 T 10 Havelock rd Harrow
70 D 8 Havelock rd S'hall
132 M 4 Havelock st N1
54 A 8 Havelock st Ilf
89 T 1 Havelock ter SW8
110 C 2 Havelock wlk SE23
105 O 6 Haven clo SW19
60 G 18 Haven grn W5
7 T 10 Havenhurst ri Enf
60 J 17 Haven la W5
60 G 19 Haven pl W5
131 Y 1 Haven st NW1
43 U 18 Havenwood Wemb
73 P 19 Haverfield gdns Rich
63 U 8 Haverfield rd E3
25 N 5 Haverford way Edg
20 H 6 Haverhill rd SW4
107 V 1 Haverhill rd SW4
107 V 2 Haverhill rd SW12
39 P 11 Havering dri Rom
37 W 14 Havering gdns Rom
38 M 9 Havering rd Rom
39 N 3 Havering rd Rom
63 S 18 Havering st E1
68 D 8 Havering way Bark
14 K 17 Haversham clo Twick
46 K 17 Haverstock hill NW3
50 H 5 Haverstock rd NW5
133 Y 10 Haverstock st N1
91 S 1 Havil st SE5
126 J 20 Havil st SE5

150 J 20 Havil st SE5
90 L 18 Hawarden gro SE24
32 F 13 Hawarden rd E17
51 W 3 Hawbridge rd E11
125 V 19 Hawes la W Wkham
159 X 1 Hawes la W Wkham
18 L 19 Hawes rd N18
112 H 20 Hawes rd Brom
133 X 2 Hawes st N1
64 B 14 Hawgood st E3
30 K 9 Hawke Park rd N22
156 B 16 Hawker clo Croy
109 P 14 Hawke rd SE19
76 J 20 Hawkes ms SE10
86 J 13 Hawkesbury rd SW15
110 K 5 Hawkesfield rd SE23
101 X 8 Hawkesley clo Twick
116 L 4 Hawkes pass Kingst
106 L 20 Hawkes rd Mitch
107 Y 19 Hawkhurst rd SW16
117 X 11 Hawkhurst way New Mald
159 S 2 Hawkhurst way W Wkhm
102 B 15 Hawkins Clo Tedd
41 P 1 Hawkins cres Harrow
37 T 19 Hawkridge clo Rom
125 T 14 Hawksbrook la Becknhm
112 A 18 Hawkshead clo Brom
44 D 20 Hawkshead rd NW10
74 A 7 Hawkeshead rd W4
92 B 13 Hawkslade rd SE15
49 P 8 Hawksley rd N16
49 P 9 Hawksley rd N16
144 H 15 Hawksmoor st W6
20 F 3 Hawksmouth E4
116 M 4 Hawks rd Kingst
117 N 4 Hawks rd Kingst
75 R 10 Hawkstone rd SE16
50 A 3 Hawkwood mt E5
40 A 1 Hawlands dri Pinn
100 E 15 Hawley clo Hampt
131 Y 1 Hawley cres NW1
108 K 5 Hawley gdns SE27
47 S 20 Hawley rd NW1
47 S 20 Hawley rd NW1
93 R 17 Hawstead rd SE6
21 W 3 Hawsteadranch Buck Hl
155 P 16 Hawthorn av Carsh
17 O 16 Hawthorn av N13
122 H 1 Hawthorn av Thntn Hth
100 F 13 Hawthorn clo Hampt
22 G 19 Hawthorn dri Harrow
120 G 3 Hawthorne av W5
127 T 7 Hawthorne clo Brom
49 R 17 Hawthorne clo N1
154 C 3 Hawthorne clo Sutton
25 W 20 Hawthorne gro NW7
33 O 10 Hawthorne rd E17
127 U 6 Hawthorne rd Brom
58 C 4 Hawthorne Farm av Grnfd
72 H 8 Hawthorn gdns W5
110 A 19 Hawthorn gro SE20
8 C 4 Hawthorn gro Enf
72 C 20 Hawthorn hatch Brentf
27 S 5 Hawthorn ms NW7
29 Y 11 Hawthorn rd N8
18 F 18 Hawthorn rd N18
44 H 19 Hawthorn rd NW10
98 B 12 Hawthorn rd Bxly Hth
72 B 20 Hawthorn rd Brentf
21 Z 14 Hawthorn rd Buck Hl
154 H 12 Hawthorn rd Sutton
155 T 15 Hawthorn rd Wallgtn
21 S 10 Hawthorns Buck Hl
18 F 9 Hawthorn way N9
130 K 1 Hawtrey rd NW3
112 H 20 Haxted rd Brom
57 U 4 Hayburn way Hornch
65 N 1 Hay clo E15
62 H 4 Haycroft gdns NW10
90 B 13 Haycroft rd SW2
64 E 16 Haycurrie st E14
65 S 14 Hayday rd E16
137 N 5 Hayden's pl W11
38 K 7 Hayden way Rom
40 G 17 Haydock av Grnfd
25 W 14 Haydon clo NW9
105 Z 12 Haydon Pk rd SW19
106 A 12 Haydon Pk rd SW19
55 V 7 Haydon rd Dgnhm
20 B 18 Haydon's rd SW19
143 O 7 Haydon wlk EC3
125 Y 13 Hayes chase W Wkhm
27 V 15 Hayes cres NW11
153 P 7 Hayes cres Sutton

126 D 12 Hayesford Pk dri Brom
126 A 20 Hayes hill Brom
126 B 20 Hayes hill rd Brom
125 Z 20 Hayes hill W Wkhm
125 U 7 Hayes la Becknhm
126 G 14 Hayes la Brom
126 A 20 Hayes mead Brom
125 Z 20 Hayes Mead rd W Wkhm
130 M 19 Hayes pl NW1
126 F 10 Hayes rd Brom
126 G 20 Hayes st Brom
153 P 20 Hayes walk Sutton
125 U 8 Hayes way Becknhm
126 H 20 Hayes Wood av Brom
63 S 14 Hayfield pass E1
63 R 13 Hayfield yd E1
105 P 13 Haygarth pl SW19
139 Z 11 Hay hill W1
25 X 14 Hayland clo NW9
25 X 13 Hay la NW9
149 X 3 Hayles st SE11
133 X 2 Hayman st N1
140 F 11 Haymarket SW1
152 G 2 Haymer gdn Worc Pk
151 S 15 Haymerle rd SE15
124 L 2 Hayne rd Becknhm
94 A 8 Haynes clo SE13
109 S 16 Haynes la SE19
42 K 20 Haynes rd Wemb
133 Y 20 Haynes st EC1
121 Z 1 Hayne st EC1
119 T 5 Haynt wlk SW20
142 H 13 Hays la SE1
123 Y 4 Hayslegh gdns SE20
139 W 11 Hay's ms W11
39 O 13 Haysoms clo Rom
90 C 12 Hayter rd SW2
141 P 13 Hayward Art gallery SE1
98 M 13 Hayward clo Bxly Hth
106 B 20 Hayward clo SW19
86 M 16 Hayward gdns SW15
87 N 16 Hayward gdns SW15
15 P 8 Hayward rd N20
133 W 17 Hayward's pl EC1
26 A 5 Haywood rd NW9
97 N 8 Haywood rd Brom
111 Z 4 Hazelbank rd SE6
112 A 4 Hazelbank rd SE6
89 T 16 Hazelbourne rd SW12
36 F 1 Hazelbrouck gdns Ilf
8 F 12 Hazelbury grn N9
18 F 12 Hazelbury la N9
18 A 11 Hazel clo N13
91 Y 5 Hazel clo SE15
72 B 18 Hazel clo Brentf
57 V 11 Hazel clo Hornch
121 Z 9 Hazel clo Mitch
83 O 18 Hazel clo Twick
62 Z 1 Hazeldean rd NW10
73 V 16 Hazeldene rd W4
55 P 6 Hazeldene rd Ilf
97 T 5 Hazeldene rd Welling
92 J 13 Hazeldene rd SE4
99 X 2 Hazel dri Erith
12 E 13 Hazel gdns Edg
110 G 11 Hazel gro SE26
18 J 1 Hazel gro Enf
37 X 9 Hazel gro Rom
60 K 5 Hazel gro Wemb
125 V 1 Hazelhurst Becknhm
16 E 9 Hazelhurst rd SW17
102 J 4 Hazela Rich
38 G 3 Hazell cres Rom
47 X 2 Hazelville rd N19
58 F 6 Hazelmere dri Grnfd
129 S 6 Hazelmere rd NW6
58 F 5 Hazelmere rd Grnfd
126 E 14 Hazelmere way Brom
62 L 8 Hazel rd NW10
58 B 12 Hazel rd NW10
99 X 2 Hazel rd Erith
58 B 9 Hazeltree la Grnfd
127 X 15 Hazel wlk Brom
19 X 19 Hazel way E4
87 N 12 Hazelwell rd SW15
120 B 9 Hazelwood av Mrdn
72 K 5 Hazelwood clo W5
J 14 Hazelwood ct Surb
17 T 13 Hazelwood cres N13
17 T 13 Hazelwood la N13
32 H 16 Hazelwood rd E17
8 J 19 Hazelwood rd Enf
A 4 Hazelbury rd SW6
157 N 4 Hazledean rd Croy
118 H 19 Hazlemere gdns Worc Pk
87 N 12 Hazlewell rd SW15

128 M 17 Hazlewood cres W10
129 N 18 Hazlewood cres W10
144 K 2 Hazlitt ms W14
144 K 3 Hazlitt rd W14
31 U 2 Headcorn rd N17
112 D 12 Headcorn rd Brom
122 D 8 Headcorn rd Thntn Hth
139 V 19 Headford pl SW1
106 E 2 Headington rd SW18
89 X 17 Headlam rd SW4
63 N 12 Headlam st E1
35 Y 17 Headley appr Ilf
156 D 10 Headley av Wallgtn
159 T 16 Headley dri Croy
35 Y 16 Headley dri Ilf
36 A 18 Headley dri Ilf
92 A 6 Headley st SE15
23 P 11 Headstone dri Harrow
23 O 12 Headstone gdns Harrow
22 L 8 Headstone la Harrow
22 M 11 Headstone manor Harrow
23 S 18 Headstone rd Harrow
152 D 13 Headway the Epsom
93 N 2 Heald st SE4
47 S 18 Healey st NW1
150 G 8 Hearn bldgs SE17
73 P 15 Hearne rd W4
134 K 18 Hearn st EC2
89 O 20 Hearnville rd SW12
83 V 19 Heatham pk Twick
80 J 17 Heath av Bxly Hth
10 G 8 Heathbourne rd Stanm
16 C 8 Heath brow NW3
46 A 2 Heath clo NW11
61 O 12 Heath clo W5
8 C 9 Heath clo Enf
39 W 10 Heath clo Rom
99 V 20 Heathclose av Drtfrd
99 W 20 Heathclose rd Drtfrd
35 U 7 Heathcote ave Ilf
20 F 9 Heathcote gro E4
84 C 14 Heathcote rd Twick
133 N 15 Heathcote st WC1
121 Z 1 Heathcroft NW10
46 B 3 Heathcroft NW11
61 N 12 Heathcroft W5
82 B 8 Heathdale av Hounsl
108 C 18 Heathdene rd SW16
81 U 12 Heathdene rd Blvdr
155 T 16 Heathdene rd Wallgtn
45 Z 13 Heath dri NW3
46 A 12 Heath dri NW3
118 M 8 Heath dri SW20
119 N 8 Heath dri SW20
39 W 8 Heath dri Rom
154 C 19 Heath dri Sutton
39 O 7 Heather av Rom
95 V 5 Heatherbank SE9
100 F 20 Heather clo Hampt
39 N 5 Heather clo Rom
103 R 17 Heatherdale clo Kingst
81 V 13 Heathdene rd Blvdr
120 H 10 Heatherdene clo Mitch
99 V 19 Heather dri Drtfrd
39 O 7 Heather dri Rom
27 S 19 Heather gdns NW11
39 O 6 Heather gdns Rom
153 X 14 Heather gdns Sutton
39 N 7 Heather glen Rom
35 S 9 Heatherley dri Ilf
61 R 2 Heather Park dri Wemb
161 R 2 Heather Pk dri Wemb
44 D 7 Heather rd NW2
112 F 2 Heather rd SE12
108 D 19 Heatherset gdns SW16
115 V 6 Heatherside rd Sidcp
12 E 16 Heather wlk Edg
39 N 6 Heather way Rom
158 F 18 Heather way S Croy
10 J 20 Heather way Stanm
52 H 6 Heatherwood clo E12
20 G 10 Heathfield E4
114 C 16 Heathfield Chisl
134 D 11 Heathfield S Croy
88 G 17 Heathfield ave SW18
73 X 13 Heathfield ct W4
27 P 20 Heathfield gdns NW11
88 F 15 Heathfield gdns SW18
73 V 14 Heathfield gdns W4
114 B 17 Heathfield la Chisl

83 V 17 Heathfield north Twick
44 N 19 Heathfield pk NW2
88 F 16 Heathfield rd SW18
73 S 6 Heathfield rd W3
98 A 11 Heathfield rd Bxly Hth
112 D 18 Heathfield rd Brom
157 N 9 Heathfield rd Croy
83 V 18 Heathfield south Twick
88 F 18 Heathfield sq SW18
79 W 16 Heathfield ter SE18
73 W 13 Heathfield ter W4
158 G 18 Heathfield vale S Croy
101 V 2 Heath gdns Twick
27 A 19 Heathgate NW11
28 A 19 Heathgate NW11
110 B 18 Heath gro SE20
46 J 13 Heath Hurst rd NW3
157 R 19 Heathhurst rd S Croy
49 P 3 Heathland rd N16
99 V 1 Heathlands ri Drtfrd
93 H 7 Heath la SE3
94 B 10 Heath la SE3
114 C 15 Heathey end Chisl
87 W 3 Heathmans rd SW6
O 6 Heath mead SW19
39 X 15 Heath Pk rd Rom
87 R 16 Heath ri SW15
126 O 14 Heath ri Brom
99 R 7 Heath rd SW8
89 T 6 Heath rd SW8
99 T 17 Heath rd Drtfrd
23 N 20 Heath rd Harrow
82 L 11 Heath rd Hounsl
83 P 10 Heath rd Hounsl
55 Y 1 Heath rd Romford
122 M 5 Heath rd Thntn Hth
101 W 2 Heath rd Twick
6 H 11 Heath side NW3
82 E 19 Heathside Hounsl
97 Z 3 Heathside av Bxly Hth
98 A 4 Heathside av Bxly Hth
62 H 18 Heathstan rd W12
46 D 10 Heath st NW3
28 D 11 Heathview N2
28 E 12 Heath view N2
99 S 17 Heathview av Drtfrd
99 S 12 Heath View clo N2
80 H 16 Heathview dri SE2
99 X 20 Heathview cres Drtfrd
86 L 19 Heathview gdns SW15
122 F 8 Heathview rd Thntn Hth
48 A 2 Heathville rd N4
79 W 15 Heath vlls SE18
88 M 8 Heathwall st SW11
77 S 20 Heath way SE3
158 M 5 Heathway Croy
56 C 12 Heathway Dgnhm
69 R 2 Heathway Dgnhm
98 L 2 Heath way Erith
21 Z 15 Heath way Wdfd Grn
78 D 13 Heathwood gdns SE18
99 O 20 Heathwood lodge Bxly
39 Y 2 Heaton av Rom
39 U 6 Heaton Grange rd Rom
51 V 16 Heaton pl E15
91 Y 6 Heaton rd SE15
107 O 17 Heaton rd Mitch
88 G 6 Heaver clo SW11
99 S 14 Heavitree rd SE18
107 K 7 Hebdon rd SW17
65 O 14 Heber rd NW2
91 V 15 Heber rd SE22
74 L 9 Hebron rd W6
144 A 2 Hebron rd W6
32 H 6 Hecham rd E17
145 T 19 Heckfield pl SW6
63 T 19 Heckford st E1
79 U 12 Hector st SE18
83 Y 9 Heddon clo Islwth
6 A 15 Heddon Court av Bark
5 Z 16 Heddon rd Barnt
140 B 10 Heddon st W1
7 W 6 Hedge hill Enf
17 V 11 Hedge la N13
35 T 13 Hedgeley Ilf
55 W 20 Hedgeman's rd Dgnhm
56 C 19 Hedgemans rd Dgnhm
55 Y 19 Hedgemans way Dgnhm

58 M 7 Hedgerly gdns Grnfd
50 H 18 Hedgers gro E9
35 V 14 Hedgewood gdns Ilf
94 B 12 Hedgley st SE12
134 A 2 Hedingham clo N1
55 P 19 Hedingham rd Dgnhm
115 R 7 Hedley clo Sidcp
49 O 14 Hedley rw N5
8 A 8 Heene rd Enf
66 C 2 Heigham rd E6
156 J 10 Heighton gdns Croy
41 Y 15 Heights av Grnfd
77 Z 15 Heights the SE7
40 F 15 Heights the Grnfd
89 Y 16 Helby rd SW4
94 C 19 Helder gro SE12
157 O 13 Helder st S Croy
83 R 9 Heldman clo Islwth
156 C 16 Helena clo Croy
60 G 14 Helena ct W5
65 R 7 Helena rd E13
33 N 17 Helena rd E17
44 J 14 Helena rd NW10
60 H 14 Helena rd W5
5 U 2 Helens clo Barnt
45 X 4 Helenslea av NW11
78 M 11 Helen st SE18
90 D 15 Helix gdns SW2
90 E 16 Helix rd SW2
105 V 12 Helme clo SW19
134 B 15 Helmet row EC1
39 R 2 Helmsdale clo Rom
107 W 19 Helmsdale rd SW16
39 R 1 Helmsdale rd Rom
135 X 1 Helmsley pl E8
22 W 3 Helston clo Pinn
77 O 13 Helvelius clo SE10
110 L 5 Helvetia st SE6
148 H 18 Hemans st SW8
90 A 7 Hamberton st SW8
41 P 14 Hemery clo Grnfrd
133 P 2 Hemingford rd N1
153 N 8 Hemingford rd Sutton
25 S 1 Heming rd Edg
15 Y 16 Hemington av N11
86 E 3 Hermitage the SW3
62 E 20 Hemlock rd W12
100 G 20 Hemming clo Hampt
135 U 17 Hemming st E1
150 F 6 Hemp row SE17
21 S 8 Hempstead clo Buck Hl
33 X 9 Hempstead rd E17
150 F 6 Hemp wlk SE17
63 N 2 Hemsley st E8
45 Y 20 Hemstal rd NW6
26 A 5 Hemswell dri NW9
134 J 7 Hemsworth st N1
146 L 10 Hemus pl SW3
142 L 5 Henage la EC3
62 D 17 Henchman st W12
26 H 10 Hendale av NW4
43 V 17 Henderson clo NW10
130 F 16 Henderson dri NW8
52 K 17 Henderson rd E7
18 M 4 Henderson rd N9
88 H 18 Henderson rd SW18
123 N 13 Henderson rd Croy
106 K 4 Hendham rd SW17
27 V 6 Hendon av N3
27 U 9 Hendon la N3
13 S 7 Hendon park NW7
27 V 17 Hendon Pk row NW11
18 K 7 Hendon rd N9
45 T 6 Hendon way NW2
26 L 18 Hendon way NW4
13 T 4 Hendon Wood la NW7
41 P 15 Hendren clo Grnfd
150 K 7 Hendre rd SE1
88 M 18 Hendrick av SW12
143 P 1 Heneage st E1
98 E 15 Henfield clo Bxly
47 W 5 Henfield pl N19
105 V 20 Henfield rd SW19
119 V 1 Henfield rd SW19
120 F 9 Hengelo gdns Mitch
94 J 18 Hengist rd SE12
81 X 18 Hengist rd Erith
125 Y 9 Hengist way Brom
92 E 17 Hengrave rd SE23
46 E 12 Heniker ms SW3
153 R 5 Henley av Sutton
59 O 6 Henley clo Grnfd
83 V 3 Henley clo Islwth
16 G 3 Henley ct N14
14 D 17 Henry Darlot dri NW7
104 C 18 Henley dri Kingst
37 Y 15 Henley gdns Rom

78 H 5 Henley rd E16
18 D 13 Henley rd N18
128 D 3 Henley rd NW10
54 B 13 Henley rd Ilf
89 O 4 Henley st SW11
110 E 7 Hennel clo SE23
66 C 8 Henniker gdns E6
146 E 13 Henniker ms SW3
51 Y 15 Henniker rd E15
31 P 3 Henningham rd N17
88 H 3 Henniker st SW11
139 W 5 Henrietta pl W1
140 K 9 Henrietta st WC2
51 V 15 Henrietta st E15
143 T 6 Henriques st E1
87 O 8 Henry Jackson rd SW18
66 E 6 Henry rd E6
48 K 5 Henry rd N4
5 T 17 Henry rd Barnt
113 N 8 Henry Cooper wy SE9
21 P 16 Henrys av Wdfd Grn
92 M 13 Henryson rd SE4
93 N 13 Henryson rd SE4
112 J 20 Henry st Brom
36 D 2 Henrys wlk Ilf
110 A 9 Hensford gdns SE26
49 P 18 Henshall st N1
55 X 9 Henshawe rd Dgnhm
150 E 5 Henshaw st SE17
91 Y 13 Henslowe rd SE22
44 L 14 Henson av NW2
24 G 11 Henson path Harrow
130 J 7 Henstridge pl NW8
146 L 20 Henty clo SW11
86 J 14 Henty wlk SW15
126 J 1 Henville rd Brom
112 J 14 Henwick rd SE9
75 P 9 Henwood rd SE16
84 A 4 Hepple clo Islwth
86 K 16 Hepple Stone clo SW15
81 N 19 Hepscott rd E9
55 N 15 Hepworth gdns Bark
108 B 19 Hepworth rd SW16
155 Z 17 Heracles clo Wallgtn
63 O 10 Herald st E2
135 Y 15 Herald st E3
133 T 18 Herbal hill EC1
133 U 18 Herbal pl EC1
147 O 1 Herbert cres SW1
62 J 5 Herbert gdns NW10
128 A 8 Herbert gdns NW10
73 T 17 Herbert gdns W4
55 W 1 Herbert gdns Rom
53 R 14 Herbert rd E12
32 L 20 Herbert rd E17
18 M 8 Herbert rd N9
16 M 20 Herbert rd N11
31 W 15 Herbert rd N15
26 E 19 Herbert rd NW9
78 J 19 Herbert rd SE18
105 W 18 Herbert rd SW19
97 Z 4 Herbert rd Bxly Hth
48 A 5 Herbert rd Bxly Hth
127 P 11 Herbert rd Brom
54 G 6 Herbert rd Ilf
116 L 7 Herbert rd Kingst
70 E 2 Herbert rd S'hall
65 T 8 Herbert st E13
47 O 17 Herbert st SE18
78 L 18 Herbert ter SE18
132 J 17 Herbrand st WC1
48 B 10 Hercules pl N7
149 R 1 Hercules st N7
48 A 10 Hercules st N7
15 Y 6 Hereford av Barnt
35 S 20 Hereford gdns Ilf
22 B 15 Hereford gdns Pinn
101 N 2 Hereford gdns Twick
137 V 6 Hereford ms W2
75 Y 19 Hereford pl SE14
151 R 16 Hereford Retreat SE15
34 J 15 Hereford rd E11
137 V 5 Hereford rd W2
61 U 19 Hereford rd W3
72 E 9 Hereford rd W5
146 C 7 Hereford sq SW7
135 T 15 Hereford st E2
35 S 12 Herent dri Ilf
17 U 17 Hereward gdns N13
106 K 8 Hereward rd SW17
73 T 1 Herga ct Harrow
23 V 12 Herga rd Harrow
20 A 9 Heriot av N4
47 N 14 Heriot pl NW5
26 M 15 Heriot rd NW4
27 N 15 Heriot rd NW4
10 L 13 Heriots clo Stanm
99 W 3 Heriot way E4
106 K 8 Herlwyn gdns SW17
71 Z 6 Hermes st N1
155 Y 15 Hermes way Wallgtn

30 A 15 Hermiston av N8
34 C 13 Hermitage clo Enf
7 W 9 Hermitage clo Enf
34 E 13 Hermitage ct E18
45 Y 9 Hermitage gdns NW2
108 M 16 Hermitage gdns SE19
18 B 17 Hermitage la NW2
45 X 9 Hermitage la NW2
108 C 19 Hermitage la SW16
123 X 16 Hermitage la Croy
30 K 20 Hermitage rd N4
31 N 18 Hermitage rd N4
108 M 16 Hermitage rd SE19
109 D 14 Hermitage rd SE19
138 F 2 Hermitage st W2
84 J 14 Hermitage the Rich
34 C 12 Hermitage wlk E18
143 T 14 Hermitage wall E1
23 Z 5 Hermitage way Stanm
65 P 13 Hermit rd E16
133 W 12 Hermit st EC1
34 F 14 Hermon hill E11
88 C 14 Hermond rd SW8
43 Y 16 Herne clo NW10
90 L 14 Herne hill SE24
90 L 9 Herne Hill rd SE24
18 K 14 Herne ms N18
90 J 14 Herne pl SE24
32 K 7 Heron clo E17
44 B 19 Heron clo NW10
126 L 10 Heron ct Brom
84 G 14 Heron ct Rich
114 H 8 Herons clo Sidcp
106 H 1 Herondale av SW15
57 Y 19 Heron Flight av Hornch
57 Y 20 Heron Flight av Hornch
8 F 9 Herongate clo Enf
52 L 7 Herongate rd E12
81 P 12 Heron hill Belvdr
53 Y 2 Heron mews Ilf
157 T 1 Heron rd Croy
90 K 10 Heron rd SE24
83 Z 11 Heron rd Twick
84 A 11 Heron rd Twick
21 T 4 Herons clo Buck Hl
60 D 16 Heronsforde W13
12 C 17 Herons ga Edg
11 W 16 Heronslea dri Stanm
5 X 15 Herons rise Barnt
21 Y 15 Heron way Wdfd Grn
48 L 9 Herrick rd N5
148 H 7 Herrick st SW1
128 M 11 Herries st W10
77 Y 9 Herringham rd SE7
78 A 8 Herringham rd SE7
150 L 14 Herring st SE5
62 H 3 Hersant clo NW10
92 G 19 Herschell rd SE23
86 G 15 Hersham clo SW15
9 P 9 Hertfield st Enf
85 Z 12 Hertford av SW13
86 A 11 Hertford av SW13
5 T 11 Hertford clo Barnt
132 B 19 Hertford pl W1
66 L 1 Hertford rd E6
49 T 20 Hertford rd N1
28 J 10 Hertford rd N2
18 L 8 Hertford rd N9
53 X 20 Hertford rd Bark
5 S 11 Hertford rd Barnt
36 G 18 Hertford rd Ilf
139 V 14 Hertford st W1
81 S 14 Hertford wlk Blvdr
121 Z 10 Hertford way Mitch
48 C 11 Hertslet rd N7
27 Y 4 Hervey clo N3
32 J 12 Hervey pk rd E17
94 G 2 Hervey rd SE3
94 G 2 Hervey rd SE3
27 Y 5 Hervey wlk N3
136 J 10 Hesketh pl W11
52 E 11 Hesketh rd E7
107 N 2 Heslop rd SW12
145 Y 8 Hesper ms SW5
76 D 11 Hesperus cres E14
71 Z 6 Hessel rd W13
72 A 5 Hessel rd W13
143 V 5 Hessel st E1
87 T 3 Hesterscombe av SW6
18 J 17 Hester rd SW11
146 K 18 Hester rd SW11
70 C 18 Heston rd Hounsl
70 G 15 Heston rd Hounsl
70 H 19 Heston rd Hounsl
92 M 2 Heston st SE4
93 N 3 Heston st SE4
89 Z 11 Hetherington rd SW4

Page	Grid	Name
109	T 18	Hetley gdns SE19
74	J 4	Hetley rd W12
74	L 11	Hetton st W6
113	X 10	Hever croft SE9
127	W 4	Hever gdns Brom
79	U 11	Heverham rd SE18
98	E 3	Heversham rd Bxly Hth
128	H 20	Hewer st W10
11	O 13	Hewett clo Stanm
55	V 13	Hewett rd Dgnhm
18	D 14	Hewish rd N18
3	J 8	Hewit av N22
30	H 16	Hewitt rd N8
63	W 6	Hewlett rd E3
47	N 4	Hexagon the N6
111	Z 6	Hexal rd SE6
71	Z 19	Hexham gdns Islwth
108	L 4	Hexham rd SE27
5	O 14	Hexham rd Barnt
119	Z 18	Hexham rd Mrdn
32	A 2	Heybourne rd N17
108	B 17	Heybridge av SW16
36	E 9	Heybridge dri Ilf
50	K 3	Heybridge wy E17
148	M 17	Heyford av SW8
119	V 6	Heyford av SW20
119	W 7	Heyford av Mrdn
120	K 2	Heyford rd Mitch
148	L 17	Heyford ter SW8
150	A 6	Heygate st SE17
63	Y 8	Heylin sq E3
55	T 12	Heynes rd Dgnhm
31		Heysham rd N15
105	W 3	Heythorp st SW18
49	Z 11	Heyworth rd E5
52	B 14	Heyworth rd E15
50	L 2	Hibbert rd E17
23	W 7	Hibbert rd Harrow
88	E 9	Hibbert st SW11
82	H 12	Hibernia gdns Hounsl
82	H 12	Hibernia rd Hounsl
135	O 3	Hiborough ct E8
52	E 12	Hichisson rd SE15
77	Z 12	Hickin clo SE7
76	F 7	Hickin st E14
53	Z 14	Hickling rd Ilf
20	G 18	Hickman av E4
65	T 1	Hickman rd Rom
89	W 8	Hickmore wlk SW4
59	S 8	Hicks av Grnfd
88	H 7	Hicks cl SW11
75	V 13	Hicks st SE8
118	J 5	Hidcote gdns New Mald
148	E 6	Hide pl SW1
23	P 13	Hide rd Harrow
48	E 17	Hides st N7
32	J 10	Higham Hill rd E17
32	H 9	Higham pl E17
31	O 9	Higham rd N17
21	S 20	Higham rd Wdfd Grn
20	F 18	Highams park E4
21	N 16	Highams park E4
20	C 19	Higham Stn av E4
32	J 10	Higham st E17
80	B 20	Highbanks clo Welling
123	W 19	Highbarrow rd Croy
157	S 17	High beech S Croy
115	Z 12	High beeches Sidcp
76	K 14	Highbridge SE10
66	M 4	Highbridge rd Bark
94	M 7	Highbrook rd SE3
95	N 7	Highbrook rd SE3
125	R 17	High Broom cres W Wkhm
122	H 3	Highbury av Thntn Hth
117	W 10	Highbury clo New Mald
159	S 3	Highbury clo W Wkhm
48	H 17	Highbury cres N5
54	G 6	Highbury gdns Ilf
48	K 13	Highbry grange N5
48	K 16	Highbury gro N5
48	G 11	Highbury hill N5
48	G 17	Highbury ms N5
48	M 16	Highbury New pk N5
48	K 11	Highbury pk N5
48	H 17	Highbury rd N5
48	K 10	Highbury quadrant N5
105	T 12	Highbury rd SW19
48	G 19	Highbury Stn rd N1
48	J 15	Highbury ter N5
48	H 15	Highbury Ter ms N5
110	H 10	Highclare st SE25
117	Y 7	Highclere rd New Mald
48	E 16	Highcliffe dri SW15
36	R 16	Highcliffe gdns Ilf
77	W 16	Highcombe SE7
113	P 2	Highcombe clo SE9
25	Z 15	Highcroft NW9
61	O 1	Highcroft av Wemb
27	V 18	Highcroft gdns NW11
48	A 2	Highcroft rd N4
31	V 11	High Cross rd N17
86	H 20	High Cross way SW15
122	B 8	Highdaun dri Mitch
152	C 2	Highdown Worc Pk
86	J 15	Highdown rd SW15
117	W 1	High dri New Mald
21	R 17	High elms Wdfd Grn
25	W 15	Highfield av NW9
27	S 19	Highfield av NW11
81	W 17	Highfield av Erith
41	U 15	Highfield av Grnfd
22	D 16	Highfield av Pinn
42	L 8	Highfield av Wemb
25	W 15	Highfield clo NW9
116	E 20	Highfield clo Surb
6	H 19	Highfield ct N14
126	A 8	Highfield dri Brom
152	D 14	Highfield dri Epsom
159	T 4	Highfield dri W Wkhm
27	S 19	Highfield gdns NW11
109	P 19	Highfield hill SE19
17	W 7	Highfield rd N21
27	T 18	Highfield rd NW11
61	U 13	Highfield rd W3
98	C 14	Highfield rd Bxly Hth
127	T 10	Highfield rd Brom
83	U 1	Highfield rd Islwth
117	U 17	Highfield rd Surb
154	J 10	Highfield rd Sutton
35	R 3	Highfield rd Wdfd Grn
29	S 20	Highgate av N6
47	O 4	Highgate clo N6
47	R 3	Highgate High st N6
47	U 5	Highgate hill N19
47	S 13	Highgate rd NW5
47	O 6	Highgate West hill N6
47	O 7	Highgate West hill N6
79	S 20	Highgro S18
95	F 1	High gro SE18
55	S 14	Highgrove rd Dgnhm
50	B 3	High Hill ferry E5
140	K 4	High Holborn WC1
141	P 2	High Holborn WC1
59	T 16	Highland av W7
56	K 9	Highland av Dgnhm
155	T 9	Highland cotts Wallgtn
111	R 13	Highland croft Becknhm
109	R 15	Highland rd SE19
98	E 12	Highland rd Bxly Hth
112	B 19	Highland rd Brom
125	B 1	Highland rd Brom
61	V 20	Highlands av W3
82	U 3	Highlands clo Hounsl
53	T 2	Highlands gdns Ilf
86	L 20	Highlands heath SW15
4	M 16	Highlands rd Barnt
25	T 6	Highlands the Edg
59	R 17	High la W7
113	O 6	Highla clo NW9
109	X 10	High Level dri SE26
62	M 14	High Lever rd W10
136	C 1	Highlever rd W10
79	X 20	Highmead SE18
23	U 15	High mead Harrow
159	Y 3	High mead W Wkhm
42	M 20	Highmead cres Wemb
25	X 16	High Meadow cres NW9
77	N 18	Highmore rd SE3
7	R 4	High oaks Enf
85	P 3	High Park av Rich
85	P 3	High Park rd Rich
106	B 20	High path SW19
113	Z 7	High point SE9
34	E 7	High rd E18
16	E 16	High rd N11
28	E 1	High rd N12
31	V 4	High rd N17
15	R 11	High rd N20/N12
30	D 6	High rd N22
44	J 18	High rd NW10
10	C 5	High rd Bushey Watf
23	S 3	High rd Harrow
53	Y 9	High rd Ilf
54	B 8	High rd Ilf
116	F 4	High rd Kingst
37	X 20	High rd Rom
55	O 2	High rd Rom
42	L 16	High rd Wemb
21	S 18	High rd Wdfd Grn
28	G 7	High Rd Finchley N12
33	R 19	High Rd Leyton E10
51	S 5	High Rd Leyton E10
51	U 13	High Rd Leyton E15
51	Y 11	High rd Leytonstone E11
52	B 2	High Rd Leytonstone E11
28	E 2	High Rd N Finchley N12
91	W 3	Highshore rd SE15
34	F 16	High st E11
65	T 7	High st E13
51	X 20	High st E15
64	G 4	High st E15
33	N 13	High st E17
16	K 7	High st N14
13	X 15	High st NW7
62	F 6	High st NW10
110	D 17	High st SE20
123	V 8	High st SE25
87	U 7	High st SW6
105	B 13	High st SW19
73	U 3	High st W3
36	C 9	High st Barkingside Ilf
4	G 12	High st Barnt
125	N 2	High st Becknhm
126	F 5	High st Brom
155	O 9	High st Carsh
114	A 16	High st Chisl
155	M 5	High st Croy
159	S 1	High st Croy
9	P 17	High st Enf
101	N 15	High st Hampt
23	T 7	High st Harrow
41	T 4	High st Harrow
82	K 8	High st Hounsl
82	L 8	High st Hounsl
116	G 6	High st Kingst
118	C 9	High st New Mald
22	B 11	High st Pinn
39	O 16	High st Rom
115	O 10	High st Sidcp
70	G 2	High st S'hall
153	T 14	High st Sutton
154	B 9	High st Sutton
10	X 13	High st Tedd
122	M 8	High st Thntn Hth
123	O 8	High st Thntn Hth
2	M 18	High st Twick
183	W 18	High st Twick
42	M 13	High st Wemb
43	N 13	High st Wemb
116	E 3	High st Hamptonwick Kingst
30	C 13	High st Hornsey N8
66	F 4	High st north E6
53	P 14	High st north E12
66	F 5	High st south E6
112	G 19	High Tor clo Brom
59	S 20	High tree ct W7
5	X 16	High trees Barnt
105	P 1	High trees SW2
124	J 19	High trees Croy
12	M 11	Highview NW7
12	G 14	Highview av Edg
156	C 11	Highview av Wallgtn
123	T 3	High View clo SE19
16	H 17	Highview gdns N11
12	G 14	Highview gdns Edg
27	S 11	High View gdns N3
34	A 9	High View rd E18
109	P 16	Highview rd SE19
72	Z 16	Highview rd W13
115	R 9	High View rd Sidcp
63	S 20	Highway the E1
143	W 10	Highway the E1
23	X 1	Highway the Stanm
154	D 20	Highway the Sutton
31	T 16	Highweek rd N15
15	R 13	Highwood av N12
35	U 14	Highwood gdns Ilf
12	M 15	Highwood gdns NW7
13	S 10	Highwood wall NW7
13	R 9	Highwood house NW7
47	Z 10	Highwood rd N19
40	E 3	High worple Harrow
121	N 5	Hilary av Mitch
145	X 18	Hilary clo SW6
98	H 2	Hilary clo Bxly Hth
20	D 20	Hilary rd W12
153	P 6	Hilbert rd Sutton
109	C 19	Hilborough clo SW19
66	A 1	Hilda rd E6
65	N 12	Hilda rd E16
112	B 14	Hildenborough gdns Brom
107	R 1	Hildreth st SW12
145	U 14	Hildyard rd SW6
62	L 8	Hiley cres NW10
128	B 11	Hiley rd NW10
130	D 2	Hilgrove rd NW6
24	E 8	Hilliary gdns Stanm
70	H 7	Hiliary rd S'hall
70	H 8	Hilliary rd S'hall
4	L 15	Hilliary rd Barnt
75	O 16	Hillbeck cl SE15
151	Z 16	Hillbeck clo SE16
59	P 3	Hillbeck way Grnfd
107	O 9	Hillbrook rd SW17
127	P 2	Hill brow Brom
113	O 20	Hill brow Chisl
99	U 17	Hill brow Drtfrd
118	E 7	Hillbrow New Mald
111	Z 16	Hillbrow rd Brom
24	C 16	Hillbury av Harrow
107	T 6	Hillbury rd SW17
44	J 10	Hill clo NW2
27	Z 18	Hill clo NW11
113	Y 12	Hill clo Chisl
41	T 11	Hill clo Harrow
11	N 3	Hill clo Stanm
108	E 18	Hillcrest av SW16
40	H 15	Hill court Grnfd
15	N 18	Hillcourt av N12
91	Z 17	Hillcourt rd SE22
15	N 7	Hill cres N20
23	Y 16	Hill cres Harrow
117	O 10	Hill cres Surb
153	N 3	Hill cres Worc Pk
29	P 20	Hillcrest N6
17	U 2	Hillcrest N21
97	O 19	Hill crest Sidcp
27	U 14	Hillcrest av NW11
12	E 14	Hillcrest av Edg
124	K 13	Hillcrest clo Becknhm
27	S 11	Hill Crest gdns N3
44	F 10	Hillcrest gdns NW2
33	Y 7	Hillcrest rd E17
34	D 7	Hillcrest rd E18
109	X 11	Hillcrest rd SE26
73	R 3	Hillcrest rd W3
60	L 13	Hillcrest rd W5
112	E 11	Hillcrest rd Brom
99	S 18	Hillcrest rd Drtfrd
39	Y 20	Hillcrest rd Hornch
57	V 1	Hillcrest rd Hornch
124	K 14	Hilcrest view Becknhm
22	E 20	Hillcroft av Pinn
60	H 16	Hillcroft cres W5
42	M 12	Hillcroft cres Wemb
43	N 12	Hillcroft cres Wemb
66	L 14	Hillcroft rd E6
154	G 13	Hillcroome rd Sutton
119	S 11	Hillcross av Mrdn
153	V 9	Hilldale rd Sutton
108	B 19	Hilldown rd SW16
126	B 19	Hilldown rd Brom
43	U 4	Hill dri NW9
47	Y 15	Hilldrop cres N7
47	Y 14	Hilldrop rd N7
112	G 15	Hilldrop rd Brom
95	X 2	Hill end SE18
95	Y 3	Hillend SE18
12	A 16	Hillerdon av Edg
86	F 4	Hillersdon av SW13
150	F 6	Hillery clo SE17
128	E 20	Hill Farm rd W10
136	E 1	Hill Farm rd W10
30	B 13	Hillfield av N8
26	B 15	Hillfield av NW9
120	H 13	Hillfield av Mrdn
42	M 20	Hillfield av Wemb
23	N 13	Hillfield clo Harrow
46	J 16	Hillfield ct NW3
29	S 12	Hillfield pk N10
17	S 9	Hillfield pk N21
29	S 12	Hillfield Park ms N10
45	X 14	Hillfield rd NW6
100	D 19	Hillfield rd Hampt
38	K 5	Hillfoot av Rom
38	J 5	Hillfoot rd Rom
137	T 13	Hillgate pl W8
137	T 13	Hillgate st W8
39	P 9	Hill gro Rom
23	W 1	Hill Ho av Stanm
17	T 2	Hill House clo N21
108	D 13	Hill Ho rd SW16
75	O 2	Hilliards ct E1
143	Z 13	Hilliards ct E1
5	N 20	Hillier clo Barnt
156	G 11	Hillier gdns Croy
89	N 16	Hillier rd SW11
98	M 15	Hillier rd SW11
155	Z 6	Hilliers la Wallgtn

H

98 L 8 Hillingdon rd Bxly Hth
149 X 16 Hillingdon st SE5
150 A 14 Hillingdon st SE17
35 O 7 Hillington gdns Wdfd Grn
50 A 18 Hillman st E8
48 A 14 Hillmarton rd N7
110 G 12 Hillmore gro SE26
108 D 13 Hill path SW16
78 E 13 Hillreach SE18
9 N 20 Hill rise Enf
19 N 1 Hill rise N9
28 B 14 Hill ri NW11
59 O 2 Hill ri Grnfd
84 H 14 Hill ri Rich
110 A 2 Hill ri SE23
47 Z 1 Hillrise rd N19
29 N 6 Hill rd N10
130 D 10 Hill rd NW8
154 K 14 Hill rd Carsh
23 Y 16 Hill rd Harrow
107 T 19 Hill rd Mitch
22 A 17 Hill rd Pinn
154 A 11 Hill rd Sutton
42 A 8 Hill rd Wemb
91 S 13 Hillsboro rd SE22
25 X 14 Hillside NW9
61 W 2 Hillside NW10
105 P 16 Hillside SW19
5 S 17 Hillside Barnt
15 Z 18 Hillside av N11
42 L 12 Hillside av Wemb
21 Z 16 Hillside av Wdfd Grn
21 Z 18 Hillside av Wdfd Grn
119 S 8 Hillside clo Mrdn
21 Y 17 Hillside clo Wdfd Grn
8 B 2 Hillside cres Enf
40 M 5 Hillside cres Harrow
12 B 18 Hillside dri Edg
31 U 20 Hillside est N15
33 X 9 Hillside gdns E17
29 R 19 Hillside gdns N6
16 H 20 Hillside gdns N11
4 E 14 Hillside gdns Barnt
12 A 14 Hillside gdns Edg
42 K 1 Hillside gdns Harrow
155 V 17 Hillside gdns Wallgtn
16 K 3 Hillside gro N14
26 F 1 Hillside gro NW7
31 T 19 Hillside rd N15
108 F 3 Hillside rd SW2
60 J 15 Hillside rd W5
156 J 8 Hillside rd Croy
99 V 15 Hillside rd Drtfrd
58 G 11 Hillside rd S'hall
117 O 10 Hillside rd Surb
153 V 16 Hillside rd Sutton
137 R 13 Hillsleigh rd W8
140 B 6 Hills pl W1
21 V 6 Hills rd Buck Hl
50 E 8 Hillstowe st E5
139 V 12 Hill st W1
84 H 14 Hill st Rich
26 J 6 Hilltop gdns NW4
28 B 13 Hill top NW11
119 T 18 Hill top Sutton
45 Y 19 Hilltop rd NW6
10 L 11 Hilltop way Stanm
104 J 19 Hillview SW20
24 J 16 Hillview av Harrow
35 T 18 Hill View cres Ilf
96 G 4 Hill View dri Welling
27 P 12 Hillview gdns NW4
25 Y 15 Hill View gdns NW9
22 H 11 Hillview gdns Harrow
14 B 14 Hill View rd NW7
113 X 11 Hillview rd Chisl
22 D 1 Hillview rd Pinn
154 E 4 Hillview rd Sutton
83 Y 16 Hillview rd Twick
47 P 7 Hillway N6
44 A 2 Hillway NW9
90 F 9 Hillworth rd SW2
59 U 14 Hillyard rd W13
90 E 3 Hillyard st SW9
32 G 8 Hillyfield E17
93 N 9 Hilly Fields cres SE4
7 X 1 Hilly Fields park Enf
50 C 11 Hilsea st E5
15 U 18 Hilton av N12
91 S 11 Hilversum cres SE22
106 K 14 Himley rd SW17
156 C 14 Hinchcliffe clo Croy
91 W 9 Hinckley rd SE15
141 U 5 Hind ct EC4
81 Z 18 Hind cres Erith
139 V 4 Hinde ms W1
23 R 17 Hindes rd Harrow
139 U 4 Hinde st W1
64 B 17 Hind gro E14
49 S 3 Hindhead clo N16
58 B 3 Hindhead gdns Grnfd
156 A 10 Hindhead way Croy
91 X 13 Hindmans rd SE22
143 U 8 Hindmarsh clo E1
50 A 15 Hindrey pl E5
50 A 14 Hindrey rd est E5
110 D 3 Hindsley pl SE23
156 B 17 Hinkler clo Croy
24 G 11 Hinkler rd Harrow
80 H 7 Hinksey pth SE2
79 P 18 Hinstock rd SE18
82 A 10 Hinton av Hounsl
113 R 2 Hinton clo SE9
18 D 14 Hinton rd N18
90 K 9 Hinton rd SE24
155 V 14 Hinton rd Wallgtn
136 L 11 Hippodrome ms W11
136 L 11 Hippodrome pl W11
50 K 3 Hitcham rd E17
63 W 6 Hitchin sq E3
108 E 5 Hitherfield rd SW16
55 Y 7 Hitherfield rd Dgnhm
93 V 14 Hither green la SE13
23 O 4 Hitherwell dri Harrow
109 U 10 Hitherwood dri SE19
10 D 8 Hive clo Bushey
10 E 9 Hive rd Bushey Watf
107 X 5 Hoadly rd SW16
15 W 8 Hobart clo N20
123 N 6 Hobart gdns Thnton Hth
147 W 2 Hobart pl SW1
84 M 18 Hobart pl Rich
55 X 12 Hobart dri Dgnhm
36 C 8 Hobart rd Ilf
58 A 11 Hobart rd Grnfd
152 J 5 Hobart rd Worc Pk
59 R 16 Hobbayne rd W7
86 J 14 Hobbes wlk SW15
28 E 10 Hobbs grn N2
109 N 11 Hobbs rd SE27
64 C 16 Hobday st E14
114 H 5 Hoblands end Chisl
135 R 20 Hobson pl E1
135 N 14 Hocker st E2
75 X 10 Hocket clo SE8
66 D 6 Hockley av E6
45 U 10 Hocroft av NW2
59 W 6 Hodder dri Grnfd
81 S 14 Hoddesdon rd Blvdr
45 W 3 Hodford rd NW11
75 R 10 Hodnet gro SE16
8 L 4 Hoe la Enf
9 P 3 Hoe la Enf
33 O 12 Hoe st E17
144 J 1 Hofland rd W14
142 K 7 Hogarth ct EC3
122 M 17 Hogarth cres Croy
70 H 20 Hogarth gdns Hounsl
27 W 13 Hogarth hill NW11
74 A 16 Hogarth la W4
145 W 8 Hogarth rd SW5
25 O 6 Hogarth rd Edg
18 E 8 Hoggin rd N9
38 B 2 Hog Hill rd Rom
96 J 16 Holbeach gdns Sidcp
93 R 18 Holbeach rd SE6
151 U 19 Holbeck row SE15
147 S 8 Holbein ms SW1
147 S 9 Holbein pl SW1
62 J 8 Holberton gdns NW10
141 S 2 Holborn bldgs EC4
65 V 13 Holborn rd E13
141 U 3 Holborn viaduct EC1
8 J 4 Holbrook clo Enf
114 G 19 Holbrook la Chisl
47 T 5 Holbrook clo NW5
65 O 5 Holbrook rd E15
127 U 13 Holbrook way Brom
48 B 11 Holbrooke ct N7
84 H 14 Holbrooke pla Rich
94 K 3 Holburne clo SE3
94 M 3 Holburne gdns SE3
94 K 4 Holburne rd SE3
94 L 3 Holburne rd SE3
95 P 3 Holburne rd SE3
13 T 11 Holcombe dale NW7
13 T 11 Holcombe hill NW7
31 W 9 Holcombe rd N17
53 W 2 Holcombe rd Ilf
74 K 12 Holcombe st W6
63 R 1 Holcroft rd E9
15 N 15 Holden av N12
43 W 4 Holden av NW9
92 J 13 Holdenby rd SE4
28 C 2 Holdenhurst av N12
15 N 13 Holden rd N12
89 O 6 Holden st SW11
107 N 5 Holdernesse rd SW17
108 K 13 Holderness way SE27
27 P 9 Holders Hill av NW
27 S 3 Holders Hill circus NW7
27 P 8 Holders Hill crs NW4
27 R 9 Holders Hill dri NW4
27 R 8 Holders Hill gdns NW4
27 S 4 Holders Hill rd NW7
133 P 12 Holford pl WC1
46 E 9 Holford rd NW3
133 R 11 Holford st WC1
88 F 8 Holgate av SW11
56 D 17 Holgate gdns Dgnhm
56 D 16 Holgate rd Dgnhm
13 X 15 Hollies end NW7
104 E 20 Holland av SW20
153 X 19 Holland av Sutton
15 T 1 Holland clo Barnt
144 L1 Holland gdns W14
149 V 19 Holland gro SW9
145 O 2 Holland ms W14
137 P 17 Holland Park W8
137 N 15 Holland pk W11
136 M 15 Holland pk W14
136 J 16 Holland Pk av W11
137 O 14 Holland Pk av W11
36 J 18 Holland Pk av Ilf
136 L 16 Holland Pk gdns W14
137 N 15 Holland Pk ms W11
145 P 2 Holland Pk rd W14
137 W 17 Holland pl W8
66 J 2 Holland rd E6
65 N 8 Holland rd E15
30 A 14 Holland rd N8
62 H 5 Holland rd NW10
123 Y 10 Holland rd SE25
136 K 19 Holland rd W14
145 N 2 Holland rd W14
42 F 19 Holland rd Wemb
118 E 20 Hollands the Worc Pk
152 D 1 Hollands the Worc Pk
137 U 18 Holland st W8
136 L 19 Holland Vlls rd W14
47 X 5 Holland wlk N19
137 R 16 Holland wlk W8
10 M 16 Holland wlk Stanm
49 U 9 Hollar rd N16
140 D 5 Hollen st W1
100 M 14 Holles clo Hampt
15 Y 5 Holles st W1
139 Y 5 Holles st W1
15 Y 19 Hollickwod av N12
56 G 20 Hollidge way Dgnhm
114 J 2 Hollies av Sidcp
101 V 3 Hollies clo Twick
72 D 11 Hollies rd W5
114 L 1 Hollies the Sidcp
89 P 17 Hollies way SW12
112 F 20 Holligrave rd Brom
98 B 1 Hollingbourne av Bxly Hth
60 A 15 Hollingbourne gdns W13
90 L 14 Hollingbourne rd SE24
158 A 14 Hollingsworth rd Croy
48 E 17 Hollingsworth st N7
118 E 15 Hollington cres New Mald
66 F 9 Hollington rd E6
31 X 6 Hollington rd N17
127 Z 16 Hollingworth rd Brom
108 H 16 Hollman gdns SW16
66 H 9 Holloway rd E6
51 Y 9 Holloway rd E11
48 B 13 Holloway Rd N7
47 X 7 Holloway rd N19
82 L 7 Holloway st Hounsl
40 A 19 Hollowfield wlk Grnfd
21 R 13 The Hollow Wdfd Grn
73 N 15 Hollows the Brentf
24 K 8 Holly av Stanm
24 K 9 Holly av Stanm
100 G 13 Hollybank clo Hampt
114 D 19 Holly Brake clo Chisl
23 U 3 Hollybush Harrow
34 D 16 Hollybush clo E11
63 N 8 Hollybush gdns E2
135 Y 12 Hollybush gdns E2
34 D 16 Hollybush hill E11
46 D 11 Holly Bush hill NW3
100 G 18 Holly Bush la Hampt
63 N 8 Hollybush pl E2
102 L 3 Hollybush rd Kingst
65 W 8 Hollybush st E13
46 D 14 Holly Bush vale NW3
100 C 12 Holly clo Felt
44 A 20 Holly clo NW10
124 L 13 Holly cres Becknhm
33 X 1 Holly cres Wdfd Grn
45 Y 10 Hollycroft av NW3
42 M 8 Hollycroft Wemb
92 B 4 Hollydale rd SE15
51 X 9 Hollydown way E11
20 E 2 Holly dri E4
70 A 13 Hollyfarm rd S'hall
15 Z 18 Hollyfield av N11
117 N 17 Hollyfield av N11
116 M 19 Hollyfield rd Surb
117 N 17 Hollyfield rd Surb
43 W 1 Holly gro NE9
91 W 4 Holly gro SE15
10 D 3 Hollygrove Bushey Watf
7 P 16 Holly hill N21
46 D 12 Holly hill NW3
81 X 13 Holly Hill rd Blvdr
93 V 12 Hollyhouse ter SE13
44 A 19 Holly la NW10
47 P 6 Holly Lodge gdns N6
47 O 5 Holly Lodge gdns N6
154 L 7 Hollymead Carsh
146 D 11 Holly ms SW7
93 U 2 Hollymount clo SE10
96 L 18 Hollyoak Wood pk Sidcp
27 W 10 Holly pk N3
48 B 2 Holly pk N4
27 X 10 Holly Pk gdns N3
16 B 15 Holly Park rd N11
71 V 1 Holly Pk rd W7
34 D 20 Holly rd E11
100 M 14 Holly rd Hampt
82 L 9 Holly rd Hounsl
101 X 1 Holly rd Twick
135 O 1 Holly st E8
15 R 9 Holly ter N20
105 P 1 Hollytree clo SW19
46 D 12 Holly wlk NW3
8 A 11 Holly wlk Enf
121 X 7 Holly way Mitch
146 B 13 Hollywood ms SW10
19 W 16 Hollywood rd E4
146 B 13 Hollywood rd SW10
33 X 1 Hollywood Way Wdfd Grn
152 F 19 Holman ct Epsom
88 F 5 Holman rd SW11
9 T 14 Holmbridge gdns Enf
27 R 14 Holmbrook dri NW4
158 L 18 Holmbury gro Croy
50 A 3 Holmbury view E5
87 S 16 Holmbush rd SW15
48 L 16 Holmcote gdns N5
127 U 13 Holmcroft way Brom
27 R 15 Holmdale gdns NW4
45 Y 15 Holmdale rd NW4
114 B 13 Holmdale rd Chisl
31 T 19 Holmdale ter N15
13 U 19 Holmdale av NW7
90 M 13 Holmdene av SE24
91 N 14 Holmdene av SE24
22 J 11 Holmdene av Harrow
125 T 4 Holmdene clo Becknhm
145 Z 19 Holmead rd SW6
10 E 8 Holmebury clo Bushey Watf
94 C 16 Holme Lacey rd SE12
66 E 3 Holme rd E6
32 K 10 Holmes av E17
14 E 17 Holmes av NW7
106 E 18 Holmes rd SW19
10 E 8 Holmesbury clo Bushey Watf
85 U 9 Holmesdale av SW14
123 U 7 Holmesdale clo SE25
34 E 16 Holmesdale ct E18
29 T 20 Holmesdale rd N6
123 U 7 Holmesdale rd SE25
97 W 5 Holmesdale rd Bxly Hth
127 N 6 Holmesdale rd Brom
85 N 2 Holmesdale rd Rich
102 D 16 Holmesdale rd Tedd
92 H 15 Holmesley rd SE23
146 C 13 Holmes pl SW10
47 T 16 Holmes rd NW5
101 W 4 Holmes rd Twick
141 T 17 Holmes ter SE1
10 J 19 Holme way Stanm
114 G 17 Holmewood cres Chisl
123 S 7 Holmewood rd SE25
90 B 20 Holmewood rd SW2
27 P 15 Holmfield av NW4
81 V 13 Holmhurst rd Belv
49 T 3 Holmleigh rd N16
99 R 7 Holmsdale gro Bxly Hth
110 J 9 Holmshaw clo SE26

89 P 16 Holmside rd SW12
118 C 16 Holmsley clo New Mald
25 V 8 Holmstall av Edg
90 C 19 Holmswood gdns SW2
40 K 18 Holmwood clo Grnfd
22 M 9 Holmwood clo Harrow
153 P 18 Holmwood clo Sutton
27 Y 8 Holmwood gdns N3
155 R 14 Holmwood gdns Wallgtn
12 L 17 Holmwood gro NW7
54 H 8 Holmwood rd Ilf
153 N 19 Holmwood rd Sutton
119 W 15 Holne cha Mrdn
28 E 18 Holne chase N2
52 B 19 Holness rd E15
86 M 12 Holroyd rd SW15
80 K 8 Holstein way Blvdr
22 M 15 Holsworth clo Harrow
29 O 14 Holt clo N6
51 S 14 Holt ct E15
63 S 11 Holton st E1
78 D 3 Holt rd E16
42 C 9 Holt rd Wemb
155 U 7 Holt the Wallgtn
7 Z 7 Holtwhites av Enf
7 V 6 Holtwhites hill Enf
22 A 14 Holwell pl Pinn
89 X 11 Holwood pl SW4
126 G 4 Holwood rd Brom
86 G 19 Holybourne av SW15
64 C 10 Holyhead clo E3
28 C 12 Holyoake wlk N2
80 E 11 Holyoake wlk W5
149 W 6 Holyoak rd SE11
144 E 18 Holyport rd SW6
40 C 13 Holyrood av Harrow
25 T 8 Holyrood gdns Edg
5 T 20 Holyrood rd Barnt
142 J 16 Holyrood st SE1
134 L 17 Holywell la EC2
134 J 18 Holywell row EC2
154 L 3 Home clo Carsh
58 E 8 Home clo Grnfd
30 K 4 Homecroft rd N22
110 D 12 Homecroft rd SE26
59 V 17 Homefarm rd W7
36 G 17 Homefield av Ilf
43 X 19 Homefield clo NW10
120 E 2 Homefield gdns Mitch
28 G 11 Homefield gdns N2
105 R 14 Homefield rd SW19
74 C 12 Homefied rd W4
126 K 1 Homefield rd Brom
12 L 20 Homefield rd Edg
42 A 12 Homefield rd Wemb
134 K 10 Homefield st N1
56 K 10 Home gdns Dgnhm
109 R 19 Homelands dri SE19
92 F 12 Homeleigh rd SE15
24 F 3 Home mead Stanm
127 U 11 Homemead rd Brom
121 W 14 Homemead rd Croy
105 V 9 Home Pk rd SW19
116 G 10 Home Pk wlk Kingst
98 J 3 Homer ct Bxly Hth
88 J 4 Home rd SW11
50 J 18 Homer rd E9
124 F 15 Homer rd Croy
138 M 2 Homer row W1
117 R 3 Homersham rd Kingst
138 M 2 Homer st W1
50 E 15 Homerton gro E9
50 F 16 Homerton High st E9
50 M 14 Homerton rd E9
50 D 15 Homerton row E9
50 D 11 Homerton ter E9
126 M 6 Homesdale rd Brom
27 Y 14 Homesfield NW11
92 C 14 Homestall rd SE22
6 D 17 Homestead paddock N14
44 E 10 Homstead pk NW2
145 P 19 Homestead rd SW6
56 A 8 Homestead rd Dgnhm
100 D 14 Homewood clo Hampt
114 H 16 Homewood cres Chisl
134 A 17 Honduras st EC1
45 Z 15 Honeybourne rd NW6
89 U 18 Honeybrook rd SW12
115 Z 14 Honeyden rd Sidcp
160 C 6 Honey la EC2

25 N 13 Honeypot clo NW4
25 O 15 Honeypot la NW9
24 J 6 Honeypot la Stanm
31 V 7 Honeysett rd N17
88 L 16 Honeywell rd SW11
62 D 7 Honeywood rd NW10
83 Z 10 Honeywood rd Islwth
154 M 9 Honeywod wlk Carsh
24 C 3 Honister clo Stanm
24 C 3 Honister gdns Stanm
24 C 4 Honister pl Stanm
129 P 7 Honiston rd NW6
39 N 18 Honiston rd Rom
96 K 4 Honiton rd Welling
93 T 18 Honley rd SE6
92 D 17 Honor Oak pk SE23
92 D 17 Honor Oak ri SE23
92 C 19 Honor Oak rd SE23
110 B 1 Honor Oak rd SE23
6 F 20 Hood av N14
16 F 1 Hood av N14
85 W 13 Hood av SW14
156 J 1 Hood clo Croy
7 V 20 Hoodcote gdns N21
17 V 2 Hoodcote gdns N21
104 E 18 Hood rd SW20
38 G 4 Hood wlk Rom
32 F 11 Hookers rd E17
126 M 12 Hook Farm rd Brom
22 J 14 Hooking grn Harrow
96 J 12 Hook la Welling
97 O 8 Hook la Welling
56 L 9 Hooks Hall dri Dgnhm
15 U 1 Hook the Barnt
12 J 20 Hook wlk Edg
65 T 18 Hooper rd E16
143 S 7 Hooper st E1
27 X 20 Hoop la NW11
45 W 1 Hoop la NW11
112 H 6 Hope clo SE12
21 Z 17 Hope clo Wdfd Grn
77 V 17 Hopedale rd SE7
128 M 7 Hopefield av NW6
112 D 19 Hope pk Brom
88 E 9 Hope st SW11
143 R 2 Hopetown st E1
143 U 5 Hope wlk gdns E1
150 F 19 Hopewell st SE5
140 J 10 Hop gdns WC2
41 P 15 Hopgood cl Grnfd
74 M 4 Hopgood rd W12
136 C 15 Hopgood st W12
140 D 7 Hopkins st W1
17 U 5 Hoppers rd N21
20 M 8 Hoppett rd E4
118 B 5 Hoppingwood av New Mald
118 G 14 Hopton gdns New Mald
107 Z 12 Hopton rd SW16
108 A 12 Hopton rd SW16
141 X 12 Hopton st SE1
150 G 13 Hopwood rd SE17
56 L 4 Horace av Rom
52 H 12 Horace rd E7
36 B 9 Horace rd Ilf
116 L 7 Horace rd Kingst
135 P 10 Horatio st E2
156 C 12 Horatius wy Croy
137 S 11 Horbury cres W11
137 R 11 Horbury ms W11
146 D 15 Horbury st SW10
87 T 2 Horder rd SW6
32 L 17 Hore av E17
77 W 11 Horizon wy SE7
98 D 13 Horley clo Bxly Hth
113 P 9 Horley rd SE9
129 P 19 Hornmead rd W9
72 C 18 Hornbeam cres Brentf
21 N 10 Hornbeam gro E4
98 J 4 Hornbeam la Bxly Hth
127 X 16 Hornbeam way Brom
41 P 7 Hornbuckle clo Harrow
94 F 18 Horncastle clo SE12
94 F 18 Horncastle rd SE12
57 Y 3 Hornchurch rd Hrnch
86 H 20 Horndean clo SW15
38 L 14 Horndon clo Rom
38 K 4 Horndon grn Rom
38 L 5 Horndon rd Rom
86 M 5 Horne way SW15
77 Z 17 Hornfair rd SE7
78 A 19 Hornfair rd SE7
57 R 2 Hornford way Rom
92 B 20 Horniman dri SE23
110 A 1 Horniman dri SE23
110 A 1 Horniman museum SE20
110 A 1 Horniman museum SE23

113 S 9 Horning clo SE9
61 V 18 Horn la W3
73 U 2 Horn la W3
21 T 20 Horn la Wdfd Grn
94 G 13 Horn Park clo SE12
94 F 13 Horn Park la SE12
47 U 3 Hornsey la N6
47 U 1 Hornsey La gdns N6
30 E 11 Hornsey Park rd N8
47 Z 2 Hornsey ri N19
47 Z 3 Hornsey Rise ms N19
47 Z 1 Hornsey Rise gdns N19
48 B 7 Hornsey rd N4
48 D 14 Hornsey st N7
75 R 17 Hornshay st SE15
36 D 12 Horns rd Ilf
137 V 19 Hornton pl W8
137 V 17 Hornton st W8
156 B 16 Horsa clo Croy
94 K 18 Horsa rd SE12
81 W 19 Horsa rd Erith
140 F 8 Horse & Dolphin sq W1
25 Y 2 Horsecroft rd Edg
116 H 2 Horse fair Kingst
76 F 16 Horseferry pl SE10
148 F 4 Horseferry rd SW1
140 K 15 Horseguards av SW1
140 J 15 Horse guards Parade SW1
140 H 16 Horse Guards rd SW1
48 F 15 Horsell rd N5
143 N 16 Horselydown la SE1
41 U 14 Horsenden av Grnfd
41 V 15 Horsenden cres Grnfd
41 U 17 Horsenden La north Grnfd
59 Y 2 Horsenden La north Grnfd
59 Z 7 Horsenden La south Grnfd
104 M 3 Horse ride SW19
142 C 12 Horse Shoe all SE1
44 J 6 Horseshoe clo NW2
58 C 4 Horseshoe cres Grnfd
154 B 3 Horse Shoe grn Sutton
14 B 4 Horseshoe la N20
7 Z 11 Horse Shoe la Enf
139 X 7 Horse Shoe yd W1
133 X 4 Horse yd N1
95 P 12 Horsfeld gdns SE9
95 P 12 Horsfeld rd SE9
90 C 13 Horsford rd SW2
15 Y 17 Horsham av N12
98 C 14 Horsham rd Bxly Hth
159 V 17 Horsley dri Croy
159 U 17 Horsley dri Croy
20 G 8 Horsley rd E4
112 H 20 Horsley rd Brom
150 D 13 Horsley st SE17
92 L 15 Horsmonden rd SE4
146 A 17 Hortensia rd SW10
73 X 14 Horticultural pl W4
45 T 12 Horton av NW2
49 Z 18 Horton rd E8
20 H 7 Hortus rd E4
70 D 6 Hortus rd S'hall
107 N 3 Hosack rd SW17
112 E 3 Hoser av SE12
141 X 2 Hosier la EC1
100 K 2 Hosiotal Br rd Twick
65 Z 17 Hoskins clo E16
76 L 14 Hoskins st SE10
82 J 19 Hospital Br yd Twick
83 V 13 Hospital la Islwth
82 G 9 Hospital rd Hounsl
87 O 9 Hotham rd SW15
106 D 18 Hotham rd SW19
64 L 3 Hotham st E15
75 R 8 Hothfield pl SE16
58 G 5 Hotspur rd Grnfd
149 S 9 Hotspur st SE11
84 L 12 Houblon rd Rich
78 K 9 Hough st SE18
100 C 15 Houghton clo Hampt
31 T 14 Houghton rd N15
141 O 6 Houghton st WC2
156 H 12 Houlder cres Croy
17 R 1 Houndsden rd N21
142 L 4 Houndsditch EC3
18 M 3 Houndsfield rd N9
100 B 4 Hounslow av Felt
82 L 13 Hounslow av Hounsl
82 L 13 Hounslow gdns Hounsl
82 B 5 Hounslow heath Hounsl
82 K 9 Hounslow High st Hounsl

82 M 16 Hounslow rd Twick
140 K 20 Houses of Parliament SW1
110 K 6 Houston rd SE23
32 L 17 Hove av E17
45 R 14 Hoveden rd NW2
75 O 20 Hove st SE15
151 Y 19 Hove st SE15
97 U 20 Howard av Bxly
45 S 11 Howard clo NW2
16 B 9 Howard clo N11
61 S 16 Howard clo W3
100 M 17 Howard clo Hampt
125 U 2 Howard ct Becknhm
66 G 6 Howard rd E6
33 P 10 Howard rd E17
31 S 18 Howard rd N15
49 R 13 Howard rd N16
45 O 13 Howard rd NW2
110 C 20 Howard rd SE20
123 Y 12 Howard rd SE25
67 S 4 Howard rd Bark
112 E 19 Howard rd Brom
53 Z 12 Howard rd Ilf
83 V 7 Howard rd Islwth
118 C 7 Howard rd New Mald
58 L 17 Howard rd S'hall
86 L 12 Howards la SW15
87 N 11 Howards la SW15
65 T 9 Howards rd E13
116 A 17 Howard st Surb
28 E 13 Howard wlk N2
51 S 15 Howarth ct E15
80 B 13 Howarth rd SE2
11 U 20 Howberry clo Edg
11 V 19 Howberry rd Edg
24 H 1 Howberry rd Edg
123 N 2 Howberry rd Thntn Hth
99 V 5 Howbury la Erith
92 C 7 Howbury rd SE15
14 L 20 Howcroft cres N3
27 Y 1 Howcroft cres N3
80 J 1 Howden clo SE2
123 T 4 Howden rd SE25
91 W 7 Howden st SE15
38 F 6 Howe clo Rom
37 V 16 Howell clo Rom
85 X 8 Howgate rd SW14
148 C 2 Howick pl SW1
140 K 19 Howie st SW11
46 K 17 Howitt rd NW3
132 C 20 Howland Ms east W1
132 B 20 Howland st W1
91 N 15 Howletts rd SE24
130 D 20 Howley pl W2
156 K 5 Howley rd Croy
74 G 18 Howsman rd SW13
92 J 10 Howson rd SE4
135 N 7 How's st E2
10 B 6 Howton pl Bushey Watf
134 J 13 Hoxton sq N1
134 J 7 Hoxton st N1
121 U 6 Hoylake gdns Mitch
62 A 18 Hoylake rd W3
151 V 17 Hoyland rd SE15
106 J 11 Hoyle rd SW17
108 M 8 Hubbard rd SE27
64 L 4 Hubbard st E15
90 B 8 Hubert gro SW9
66 A 8 Hubert rd E6
52 C 12 Huddlestone rd E7
44 J 18 Huddlestone rd NW2
47 V 10 Huddleston rd N1
79 O 13 Hudson pl SE18
98 A 5 Hudson rd Bxly Hth
102 L 20 Hudson rd Kingstn
88 D 13 Hugenot pl SW18
160 B 8 Huggin hill EC4
51 Y 14 Hughan rd E15
24 B 14 Hughenden av Harrow
118 H 16 Hughenden rd Worc Pk
51 U 11 Hughendon ter E15
147 Y 7 Hugh ms SW1
148 F 5 Hugh st SW1
147 Y 6 Hugh st SW1
122 L 16 Hughes wlk Croy
57 U 19 Hugo gdns Rainhm
88 A 7 Hugon rd SW6
47 V 12 Hugo rd N19
91 Y 6 Huguenot sq SE15
88 D 14 Huguenot ter SW18
37 Y 18 Hull rd Rom
134 A 13 Hull st EC1
54 F 18 Hulse av Bark
38 H 4 Hulse av Rom
154 A 20 Hulverston clo Sutton
44 K 7 Humber rd NW2
77 O 16 Humber rd SE3
65 Y 10 Humberstone rd E13

H

H

I

144 L 15 Humbolt rd W6
71 V 6 Humes av W7
56 A 12 Humphries clo Dgnhm
35 U 5 Humphrey clo Ilf
151 N 9 Humphrey st SE1
26 C 7 Hundred acre NW9
20 F 4 Hungerdown E4
141 N 13 Hungerford foot br SE1
47 Z 16 Hungerford rd N1
48 A 15 Hungerford rd N7
143 X 6 Hungerford st E1
55 Z 18 Hunsdon clo Dgnhm
75 S 18 Hunsdon rd SE14
63 R 8 Hunslett st E2
120 A 19 Hunston rd Mrdn
150 G 3 Hunter clo SE1
104 M 20 Hunter rd SW20
105 N 20 Hunter rd SW20
53 Z 16 Hunter rd Bark
53 Z 16 Hunter rd Ilf
54 A 15 Hunter rd Ilf
123 N 6 Hunter rd Thntn Hth
107 O 2 Hunters clo Rom
24 E 13 Hunters gro Harrow
56 F 14 Hunters Hall rd Dgnhm
56 E 12 Hunters sq Dgnhm
132 K 16 Hunter st WC1
65 S 5 Hunter wlk E15
157 T 9 Hunters way Croy
7 T 5 Hunters way Enf
122 A 8 Huntingdon clo Mitch
152 M 6 Huntingdon gdns Worc Pk
8 K 10 Huntingdon rd N2
19 R 7 Huntingdon rd N9
65 P 19 Huntingdon st E16
133 O 1 Huntingdon st N1
158 M 16 Huntingfield Croy
86 H 13 Huntingfield rd SW15
56 E 19 Huntings rd Dgnhm
132 D 18 Huntley st WC1
118 F 3 Huntley rd SW20
14 M 19 Huntly dri N3
123 S 7 Huntly rd SE25
135 R 19 Hunton st E1
70 G 8 Hunt rd S'hall
94 F 5 Hunts clo SE3
140 H 10 Hunts ct WC2
64 F 7 Hunts la E15
37 P 1 Huntsman rd Ilf
150 H 8 Huntsman st SE17
113 T 20 Hunts Meadow clo Chisl
9 T 10 Hunts mead Enf
88 D 12 Huntsmoor rd SW18
106 E 7 Huntspill st SW17
109 S 5 Hunts Slip rd SE21
136 H 12 Hunt st W11
131 O 18 Huntsworth ms NW1
58 K 15 Hurley rd Grnfd
87 V 7 Hurlingham gdns SW6
87 X 8 Hurlingham house SW6
87 W 7 Hurlingham park SW6
87 U 6 Hurlingham rd SW6
81 P 20 Hurlingham rd Bxly Hth
48 J 10 Hurlock st N5
123 R 10 Hurlstone rd SE25
107 P 6 Huron rd SW17
93 Z 6 Harren clo SE3
65 N 2 Hurry clo E15
20 B 11 Hurst av E4
29 W 19 Hurst av N6
54 F 18 Hurstbourne gdns Bark
110 A 2 Hurstbourne rd SE23
20 A 12 Hurst clo E4
28 A 18 Hurst clo NW11
126 C 20 Hurst clo Brom
40 E 16 Hurst clo Grnfd
153 Z 2 Hurstcourt rd Sutton
126 C 20 Hurstdene av Brom
31 T 20 Hurstdene gdns N15
126 E 11 Hurstfield Brom
80 H 14 Hurst la SE2
35 V 5 Hurstleigh gdns Ilf
12 F 12 Hurstmead ct Edg
80 H 15 Hurst Pl est SE2
4 L 12 Hurst ri Barnt
33 R 10 Hurst rd E17
17 U 6 Hurst rd N21
98 D 20 Hurst rd Bxly
115 Y 2 Hurst rd Bxly
157 O 10 Hurst rd Croy
98 K 1 Hurst rd Erith
81 Y 20 Hurst rd Erith
115 Z 2 Hurst springs Bxly

90 J 15 Hurst st SE24
157 S 15 Hurst View rd S Croy
157 S 15 Hurst way S Croy
34 J 12 Hurstwood av E18
99 R 3 Hurstwood av Bxly
115 Z 1 Hurstwood av Bxly
127 U 7 Hurstwood dri Brom
27 V 13 Hurstwood rd NW11
46 J 20 Huson clo NW3
126 F 20 Husseywell cres Brom
64 G 1 Hutchins clo E15
76 A 6 Hutchins st E14
28 B 14 Hutchins wlk NW11
42 H 10 Hutchinson ter Wemb
41 P 13 Hutton clo Grnfd
41 R 13 Hutton clo Grnfd
21 V 18 Hutton clo Wdfd Grn
23 N 2 Hutton gdns Harrow
15 P 18 Hutton gro N12
23 O 2 Hutton la Harrow
141 V 7 Hutton st EC4
23 N 1 Hutton wlk Harrow
92 M 13 Huxbear st SE4
55 P 1 Huxley di Rom
61 N 7 Huxley gdns NW10
75 O 13 Huxley pde N18
17 W 12 Huxley pl N13
51 U 7 Huxley rd E10
18 B 13 Huxley rd N18
96 L 9 Huxley rd Welling
18 A 18 Huxley st N18
104 G 1 Hyacinth rd SW13
4 H 12 Hyde clo Barnt
26 B 17 Hyde cres NW9
18 E 6 Hydefield clo N21
18 E 7 Hydefield ct N9
88 J 1 Hyde la SW11
138 K 12 Hyde park W2
139 O 14 Hyde park av N21
17 Z 7 Hyde Park av N21
18 A 6 Hyde Park av N21
139 V 17 Hyde Park Corner W1
138 K 6 Hyde Park cres W2
17 Z 6 Hyde Park gdns N21
138 J 9 Hyde Park gdns W2
138 J 8 Hyde Park Gdns ms W2
138 C 20 Hyde Park ga SW7
138 C 20 Hyde Park Ga ms SW7
138 K 7 Hyde Park sw W2
138 K 7 Hyde Park Sq ms W2
138 K 7 Hyde Park st W2
134 G 5 Hyde rd N1
98 C 5 Hyde rd Bxly Hth
84 L 12 Hyde rd Rich
18 F 9 Hydeside gdns N9
4 J 19 Hydes pl N1
25 Y 11 Hyde the NW9
26 B 15 Hyde the NW9
18 G 9 Hydethorpe av N9
89 V 20 Hydethorpe rd SW12
107 U 1 Hydethorpe rd SW12
76 H 20 Hyde vale SE10
93 W 2 Hyde vale SE10
119 Z 17 Hyde wlk Mrdn
18 G 9 Hydeway N9
73 Y 8 Hylands rd E17
57 Y 3 Hyland clo Hrnch
79 X 10 Hylton st SE18
151 W 14 Hyndman st SE15
55 U 7 Hynton rd Dgnhm
156 K 10 Hyrstdene S Croy
75 N 12 Hyson rd SE16
80 M 20 Hythe av Bxly Hth
81 O 19 Hythe av Bxly Hth
18 K 14 Hythe clo N18
123 O 5 Hythe path SE25
123 O 5 Hythe rd Thntn Hth
12 M 2 Hyver hill NW7

I

9 T 7 Ian sq Enf
65 P 16 Ibbotson av E16
63 R 10 Ibbott st E1
155 Y 8 Iberian av Wallgtn
56 X 19 Ibscott cl Dgnhm
104 F 1 Ibsley gdns SW15
5 Y 15 Ibsley way Barnt
64 B 4 Iceland rd E3
23 S 9 Ickburgh rd E5
113 S 10 Ickleton rd SE9
35 Z 16 Icknield dri Ilf

36 A 16 Icknield dri Ilf
32 J 12 Ickworth rd E17
31 O 14 Ida rd N15
64 F 18 Ida st E14
126 A 6 Iden clo Brom
77 N 10 Idenden cotts SE10
107 O 13 Idlecombe rd SW17
52 B 14 Idmiston rd E15
108 M 5 Idmiston rd SE27
118 E 18 Idmiston rd Worc Pk
118 E 18 Idmiston sq Worc Pk
142 J 10 Idol la EC3
75 Z 19 Idonia st SE8
74 L 10 Iffley rd W6
144 A 5 Iffley rd W6
145 Y 13 Ifield rd SW10
146 A 15 Ifield rd SW10
81 S 19 Ightam rd Erith
128 H 13 Ilbert st W10
137 X 9 Ilchester gdns W2
137 P 20 Ilchester pl W14
55 T 15 Ilchester rd Dgnhm
109 O 5 Ilderslay gro SE21
151 Y 9 Ilderton rd SE15
75 P 17 Ilderton rd SE15
75 O 13 Ilderton rd SE16
44 C 18 Ilex rd NW10
108 F 12 Ilex way SW16
53 Z 11 Ilford la Ilf
54 A 15 Ilford la Ilf
55 P 1 Ilfracombe gdns Rom
112 B 7 Ilfracombe rd Brom
149 Y 8 Iliffe st SE17
149 Z 8 Iliffe St yd SE17
65 X 16 Ilkley rd E16
120 G 6 Illingworth clo Mitch
8 E 16 Illingworth way Enf
24 F 18 Ilmington rd Harrow
88 X 10 Ilminster gdns SW11
116 L 19 Im's clo Surb
134 J 1 Ilsom clo N14
134 E 6 Imber st N1
49 T 11 Imperial av N16
22 G 19 Imperial clo Harrow
22 H 19 Imperial dri Harrow
40 G 2 Imperial dri Harrow
146 E 2 Imperial Institute st SW7
66 A 7 Imperial ms E6
30 A 4 Imperial rd N22
88 C 2 Imperial rd SW6
64 F 10 Imperial st E3
149 U 3 Imperial War Museum SE1
114 C 8 Imperial way Chisl
156 E 15 Imperial way Croy
24 L 19 Imperial way Harrow
111 S 3 Inchmery rd SE6
159 R 8 Inchwood Croy
94 B 6 Independents rd SE3
30 D 18 Inderwick rd N8
143 N 7 India st EC3
62 J 20 India way W12
77 Z 20 Indus rd SE7
65 T 13 ingal rd E13
89 T 2 Ingate pl SW8
123 Y 10 Ingatestone SE25
52 K 5 Ingatestone rd E12
123 Z 10 Ingatestone rd SE25
34 G 2 Ingatestone rd Wdfd Grn
89 R 5 Inglebow rd SW8
74 J 3 Ingersoll rd W12
9 R 4 Ingersoll rd Enf
140 D 7 Ingestre pl W1
52 F 12 Ingestre rd E7
47 T 11 Ingestre rd NW5
158 E 19 Ingham clo S Croy
45 X 13 Ingham rd NW6
158 D 19 Ingham rd S Croy
133 S 12 Inglebert st EC1
90 E 4 Ingleborough st SW9
56 G 19 Ingleby clo Dgnhm
41 R 9 Ingleby rd Dgnhm
48 A 9 Ingleby rd N7
56 G 19 Ingleby rd Dgnhm
53 Y 3 Ingleby rd Ilf
155 X 18 Ingleby way Wallgtn
22 C 11 Ingle clo Pinn
79 T 13 Ingledew rd SE18
143 Y 13 Inglefield sq E1
35 T 17 Inglehurst gdns Ilf
110 E 6 Inglemere rd SE23
107 N 17 Inglemere rd Mitch
111 N 17 Ingleside clo Becknhm
77 R 17 Ingleside gro SE10
87 O 1 Inglethorpe st SW6
97 O 12 Ingleton av Welling
18 J 19 Ingleton rd N18
154 H 18 Ingleton rd Carsh

15 V 20 Ingleway N12
45 Y 16 Inglewood rd NW6
98 M 9 Inglewood rd Bxly Hth
60 M 19 Inglis rd W5
61 N 20 Inglis rd W5
123 V 19 Inglis rd Croy
90 K 3 Inglis st SE5
46 D 1 Ingram av NW11
11 R 17 Ingram clo Stanm
28 K 13 Ingram rd N2
122 L 1 Ingram rd Thntn Hth
108 L 20 Ingram rd Thntn Hth
59 R 4 Ingram way Grnfd
39 O 13 Ingrave rd Rom
88 H 7 Ingrave st SW11
74 A 13 Ingress rd W4
78 C 18 Inigo Jones rd SE7
140 K 9 Inigo pl WC2
47 T 17 Inkerman rd NW5
20 F 16 Inks grn E4
62 A 2 Inman rd NW10
88 C 20 Inman rd SW18
21 T 15 Inmans row Edgd Grn
131 S 13 Inner crcl NW1
105 P 1 Inner Pk rd SW19
141 T 7 Inner Temple la EC4
86 K 16 Innes gdns SW15
65 Y 7 Inniskilling rd E13
55 W 5 Inskip rd Dgnhm
49 Z 16 Institute pl E8
156 B 15 Instone clo Croy
133 S 13 Insurance st WC1
79 S 15 Inverary pl SE18
37 V 14 Inverclyde gdns Rom
152 F 6 Inveresk gdns Worc Pk
46 C 7 Inverforth clo NW3
67 F 18 Inverforth rd N11
97 X 12 Inverhurst clo Bxly Hth
77 W 14 Inverine rd SE7
79 O 11 Invermore pl SE18
8 F 6 Inverness av Enf
137 W 13 Inverness gdns W8
137 Z 8 Inverness ms W2
137 Z 9 Inverness pl W2
18 M 15 Inverness rd N18
82 F 10 Inverness rd Hounsl
70 C 11 Inverness rd S'hall
119 O 20 Inverness rd Worc Pk
131 X 3 Inverness st NW1
137 Z 9 Inverness ter W2
92 E 11 Inverton rd SE15
113 W 12 Invicta clo Chisl
58 C 9 Invicta gro S'hall
77 T 19 Invicta rd SE3
150 G 12 Inville rd SE17
82 M 8 Inwood av Hounsl
83 N 8 Inwood av Hounsl
158 J 2 Inwood clo Croy
82 M 8 Inwood rd Hounsl
88 J 4 Inwood st N1
134 A 3 Inworth wlk N1
93 N 17 Iona clo SE6
31 T 16 Ipplepen rd N15
107 R 16 Ipswich rd SW17
141 Y 7 Ireland yd EC4
87 Y 3 Irene st W6
64 A 10 Ireton st E3
37 Z 15 Iris av Bxly
98 A 15 Iris av Bxly
81 P 17 Iris cres Bxly
1 Y 20 Iris way E4
8 H 5 Irkdale av Enf
99 X 10 Iron Mill pl Drtfd
99 T 11 Iron Mill pl Drtfd
99 T 11 Iron Mill pl SW11
88 B 16 Iron Mill rd SW18
160 D 6 Ironmonger la EC2
134 C 15 Ironmonger row EC1
38 K 2 Irons way Rom
23 Z 10 Irvine av Harrow
24 A 10 Irvine av Harrow
15 W 9 Irvine clo N20
58 A 2 Irving av Grnfd
152 V 19 Irving gr SW19
144 H 1 Irving rd W14
140 H 10 Irving st WC2
79 V 18 Irwin av SE18
62 L 4 Irwin gdns NW10
128 A 6 Irwin gdns NW10
50 C 16 Isabella rd E9
141 V 13 Isabella st SE1
90 E 2 Isabel st SW9
39 R 2 Isbell gdns Rom
91 S 13 Isel way SE22
121 Z 3 Isham rd SW16
106 C 4 Isis st SW18
106 L 19 Island rd Mitch
63 X 19 Island row E14
79 O 17 Isla rd SE18

Ref	Name
127 Y 1	Islehurst clo Chisl
133 W 5	Islington grn N1
133 V 9	Islington High st N1
48 G 20	Islington Pk st N1
12 K 20	Islip gdns Edg
40 C 20	Islip gdns Grnfd
52 C 1	Islip gdns Grnfd
40 C 20	Islip Manor rd Grnfd
47 V 16	Islip st NW5
52 H 20	Ismailia rd E7
65 X 10	Isom clo E13
23 Z 9	Ivanhoe dri Harrow
24 B 8	Ivanhoe dri Harrow
91 T 7	Ivanhoe rd SE5
145 R 11	Ivatt pl SW6
61 P 5	Iveagh av NW10
61 P 6	Iveagh clo NW10
97 T 5	Ivedon rd Welling
15 O 6	Ive Farm clo E10
89 U 6	Iveley rd SW4
5 N 19	Ivere dri Barnt
12 V 1	Iverna gdns W8
45 V 19	Iverson rd NW6
159 S 16	Ivers way Croy
39 U 14	Ives rd Rom
64 L 14	Ives rd E16
146 L 6	Ives st SW3
92 C 18	Ivestor ter SE23
8 D 7	Ivinghoe clo Enf
10 B 2	Ivinghoe rd Bushey Watf
55 P 15	Ivinghoe rd Dgnhm
113 Z 1	Ivor gro SE9
131 O 17	Ivor pl NW1
47 U 20	Ivor st NW1
2 F 6	Ivorydown Brom
140 M 10	Ivybridge la WC2
110 B 18	Ivy Church clo SE20
40 D 12	Ivy clo Harrow
73 U 10	Ivy cres W4
92 F 9	Ivydale rd SE15
155 N 2	Ivydale rd Carsh
108 C 8	Ivydaly gro SW16
154 D 8	Ivydene clo Sutton
135 U 2	Ivydene rd E8
30 A 19	Ivy gdns N8
121 X 7	Ivy gdns Mitch
55 W 18	Ivyhouse rd Dgnhm
56 B 18	Ivyhouse rd Dgnhm
2 D 10	Ivy la Hounsl
108 F 8	Ivymount rd SE27
116 L 15	Ivy pl Surb
65 T 17	Ivy rd E16
33 P 19	Ivy rd E17
16 J 3	Ivy rd N14
44 M 12	Ivy rd NW2
45 N 12	Ivy rd NW2
92 L 11	Ivy rd SE4
92 O 12	Ivy rd SE4
82 L 11	Ivy rd Hounsl
134 J 8	Iv st N1
55 Y 18	Ivy wlk Dgnhm
146 K 8	Ixworth pl SW3
98 A 12	Izane rd Bxly Hth

J

Ref	Name
30 D 8	Jack Barnett wy N22
53 W 13	Jack Cornwell st E12
21 R 14	Jacklin grn Wdfd Grn
44 A 10	Jackman ms NW10
135 V 4	Jackman st E8
48 E 13	Jackson rd N7
67 T 4	Jackson rd Bark
5 V 20	Jackson rd Barnt
127 T 20	Jackson rd Brom
29 R 20	Jacksons la N6
123 P 19	Jacksons pl Croy
78 J 16	Jackson st SE18
48 J 12	Jack Walker ct N5
143 R 17	Jacob st SE1
139 V 3	Jacobs Well ms W1
108 K 10	Jaffray pl SE27
126 M 9	Jaffray rd Brom
79 P 16	Jago clo SE18
143 P 19	Jamaica rd SE1
75 N 7	Jamaica rd SE16
143 X 20	Jamaica rd SE16
122 H 13	Jamaica rd Thntn Hth
63 R 16	Jamaica st E1
44 M 14	James av NW2
56 C 5	James av Dgnhm
39 W 15	James clo Rom
30 K 2	James gdns N22
33 X 20	James la E11
137 U 13	Jameson st W8
31 U 3	James pl N17
99 V 17	James rd Drtfrd
67 O 1	James st Bark
137 V 6	James st W1
140 K 8	James st WC2
8 H 16	James st Enf
83 O 8	James st Hounsl
131 X 2	Jamestown rd NW1
76 B 7	Janet st E14
143 U 19	Janeway st SE16
51 Z 14	Janson clo E15
51 Z 13	Janson rd E15
52 A 14	Janson rd E15
31 S 11	Jansons rd N15
48 C 3	Japan cres N4
37 W 20	Japan rd Rom
58 C 3	Jaqueline clo Grnfd
150 K 13	Jardin st SE5
120 A 12	Jarrow clo Mrdn
31 Z 14	Jarrow rd N15
37 U 18	Jarrow rd Rom
4 C 18	Jarvis clo Barnt
4 C 18	Jarvis clo Barnt
91 T 11	Jarvis rd SE22
157 O 14	Jarvis rd S Croy
159 P 6	Jasmine gdns Croy
159 R 6	Jasmine gdns Croy
40 H 7	Jasmine gdns Harrow
110 A 20	Jasmine gro SE20
39 V 4	Jason ct W1
113 W 9	Jason wlk SE9
9 P 4	Jasper clo Enf
10 U 13	Jasper rd SE19
58 A 10	Javelin wy Grnfd
13 D 19	Jay ms SW7
90 B 16	Jebb av SW2
64 C 7	Jebb st E3
65 X 8	Jedburgh rd E13
8 P 10	Jedburgh st SW8
74 D 5	Jeddo rd W12
72 B 9	Jefferson clo W13
64 F 9	Jefferson est E3
89 Z 4	Jeffreys rd SW4
90 A 5	Jeffreys rd SW4
9 X 14	Jeffreys rd Enf
47 U 20	Jeffreys st NW1
89 Z 3	Jeffreys wlk SW4
9 X 11	Jeffreys way Enf
153 V 9	Jeffs rd Sutton
94 L 11	Jeken rd SE9
97 F 12	Jelf rd SW2
10 K 18	Jellicoe gdns Stanm
31 O 3	Jellicoe rd N17
65 W 12	Jenkins rd E13
74 H 16	Jenner pl SW13
49 W 9	Jenner rd N16
56 F 4	Jennett rd Croy
112 D 6	Jennifer rd Brom
9 V 15	Jennings rd SE22
4 A 12	Jennings way Barnt
81 Y 3	Jenningtree way Blvdr
97 Y 3	Jenton av Bxly Hth
52 L 19	Jephson rd E7
91 O 3	Jephson st SE5
87 X 15	Jephtha rd SW18
120 L 9	Jeppos la Mitch
145 U 18	Jerdan pl SW6
64 C 18	Jeremiah st E14
19 P 14	Jeremys grn N18
140 B 12	Jermyn st SW1
35 Y 7	Jerningham av Ilf
92 H 2	Jerningham rd SE14
77 T 18	Jernsen wy SE19
130 J 15	Jerome cres NW8
31 N 19	Jerome st E1
93 S 7	Jerrard st SE13
24 D 8	Jersey av Stanm
51 W 5	Jersey rd E11
65 X 15	Jersey rd E16
107 R 16	Jersey rd SW17
71 Y 7	Jersey rd W7
70 L 20	Jersey rd Hounsl
53 Z 13	Jersey rd Ilf
71 P 18	Jersey rd Islwth
135 X 13	Jersey rd E2
133 W 18	Jerusalem pass EC1
F 14	Jerviston gdns SW16
43 O 13	Jesmond av Wemb
123 U 17	Jesmond rd Croy
11 Y 15	Jesmond way Stanm
49 Z 4	Jessam av E5
71 V 3	Jessamine rd W7
51 T 5	Jesse rd E10
88 E 15	Jessica rd SW18
90 K 11	Jessop rd SE24
121 V 15	Jessops wy Mitch
79 O 10	Jessup clo SE18
58 A 10	Jetstar way Grnfd
112 J 2	Jevington way SE12
33 N 10	Jewel rd E17
142 M 7	Jewry st EC3
88 B 10	Jews row SW18
110 A 9	Jews wlk SE26
44 I 16	Jaymer av NW2
58 M 4	Jeymer dri Grnfd
59 N 3	Jeymer dri Grnfd
88 D 17	Jeypore rd SW18
100 H 18	Jillian clo Hampt
96 O 19	Joan cres SE9
95 Y 6	Joan gdns Dgnhm
55 Y 6	Joan rd Dgnhm
141 V 15	Joan st SE1
58 C 3	Joave clo Grnfd
84 K 8	Jocelyn rd Rich
141 P 1	Jockeys fields WC1
63 Z 2	Jodrell rd E3
141 S 18	Johanna st SE1
140 L 11	John Adam st WC2
52 C 17	John Barnes wlk E15
16 K 6	John Bradshaw st N14
67 V 2	John Burns dri Bark
49 T 15	John Campbell rd N16
141 V 8	John Carpenter st EC4
143 S 20	John Felton rd SE16
143 R 10	John Fisher st E1
148 H 8	John Islip st SW1
97 S 8	John Newton st Welling
56 G 20	John Parker clo Dgnhm
93 S 2	John Penn st SE13
139 Z 5	John Prince's st W1
143 Y 11	John Rennie wk E1
149 Y 17	John Ruskin st SE5
149 Y 18	John Ruskin st SE5
26 L 12	Johns av NW4
120 D 12	Johns la Mrdn
133 O 18	Johns ms WC1
127 M 12	Johnson rd Brom
123 N 17	Johnson rd Croy
154 M 4	Johnsons clo Carsh
141 U 6	Johnsons ct EC4
148 B 11	Johnsons pl SW1
61 S 11	Johnson wy NW10
63 P 18	Johnson st E1
48 K 18	John Spencer sq N1
143 Y 4	Johns pl E1
123 P 20	Johns ter Croy
66 H 10	Johnstone rd E6
45 O 10	Johnstone ter NW2
21 S 18	Johnston rd Wdfd Grn
65 O 4	John st E15
123 Y 9	John st SE25
133 P 19	John st WC1
8 G 16	John st Enf
82 C 4	John st Hounsl
78 J 10	John Wilson st SE18
93 Y 9	John Woole clo SE13
142 G 14	Joiner st SE1
58 C 12	Jolly's la Grnfd
41 P 4	Jollys la Harrow
149 O 8	Jonathan st SE11
65 W 13	Jones Av rd E13
66 W 13	Jones rd E13
139 X 10	Jones st W1
121 T 8	Jonson clo Mitch
88 U 3	Jordans clo Islwth
81 P 11	Jordan ct SW15
60 D 2	Jordan rd Grnfd
90 D 14	Josephine av SW2
89 U 16	Joseph Powell clo SW12
63 Y 13	Joseph st E3
64 F 16	Joshua st E14
88 M 5	Joubert st SW11
151 P 19	Jowett st SE15
18 H 17	Joyce av N18
90 P 16	Joyce wlk SW2
37 P 18	Joydon dri Rom
7 U 7	Joycroft Enf
38 H 17	Jubilee av E4
83 O 20	Jubilee av Twick
20 G 18	Jubilee av E4
25 Y 18	Jubilee clo NW9
38 H 16	Jubilee clo Rom
18 K 4	Jubilee cres N9
76 G 9	Jubilee cres E14
40 A 12	Jubilee dri Ruisl
58 H 15	Jubilee gdns S'hall
18 L 3	Jubilee park N9
146 M 10	Jubilee pl SW3
60 A 2	Jubilee rd Grnfd
153 P 15	Jubilee rd Sutton
63 P 17	Jubilee st E1
120 B 1	Jubilee way Mitch
115 N 5	Jubilee way Sidcp
132 J 14	Judd st WC1
65 P 18	Jude st E16
46 C 9	Judges wlk NW3
88 K 19	Juer st SW11
68 J 5	Julia gdns Bark
61 U 20	Julian av W3
4 M 11	Julian clo Barnt
41 T 8	Julian hill Harrow
76 E 12	Julian pl E14
40 O 14	Julia st NW5
72 D 9	Julien rd W5
93 T 7	Junction appr SE13
138 K 4	Junction ms W2
138 H 4	Junction pl W2
65 V 6	Junction rd E13
18 K 6	Junction rd N9
31 X 9	Junction rd N17
47 V 8	Junction rd N19
72 F 11	Junction rd N9
23 S 19	Junction rd Harrow
57 T 14	Junction rd Rom
55 X 1	Junction rd Rom
55 Z 1	Junction rd Rom
157 O 12	Junction rd S Croy
53 X 11	Juniper rd Ilf
16 N 8	Juniper st E1
75 T 16	Juno way SE14
48 D 18	Jupiter way N7
64 J 1	Jup rd E15
74 H 2	Jupp Rd west E15
63 Y 10	Jupps rd E3
146 J 15	Justice wlk SW3
9 M 10	Jute la Enf
65 T 12	Jutland rd E13
93 T 19	Jutland rd SE6
72 H 19	Justin clo Brent
38 H 19	Jutsums av Rom
38 H 19	Justums la Rom
22 L 5	Juxon clo Harrow
149 P 5	Juxon st SE11

K

Ref	Name
80 K 6	Kale rd Belvdr
88 G 6	Kambala rd SW11
110 L 10	Kangley Br rd SE26
59 R 5	Karoline gdns Grnfd
79 X 12	Kashgar rd SE18
78 A 18	Kashmir rd SE7
88 M 2	Kassala rd SW11
156 M 4	Katharine st Croy
157 N 4	Katharine st Croy
95 N 12	Katharine gdns SE9
36 C 1	Katherine rd Ilf
36 C 3	Katherine rd E6
52 L 16	Katherine rd E7
83 Z 20	Katherine rd Twick
61 W 13	Kathleen av W3
42 K 20	Kathleen av Wemb
60 K 1	Kathleen av Wemb
60 L 8	Kathleen rd SW11
154 H 15	Kayemoor rd Sutton
45 P 14	Kayes rd NW2
90 B 6	Kay rd SW9
135 T 9	Kay st E2
64 K 1	Kay st E15
97 R 2	Kay st Welling
14 N 6	Kean st WC2
102 X 11	Keary house SW15
39 Y 2	Keats av Rom
46 H 12	Keats gro NW3
81 W 8	Keats rd Belvdr
96 J 1	Keats rd Welling
124 D 15	Keats way Croy
58 J 15	Keat's way Grnfd
41 O 16	Keble clo Grnfd
118 E 20	Keble clo Worc Pk
106 D 9	Keble st SW17
126 F 17	Kechill gdns Brom
111 Z 11	Keedonwood rd Brom
112 B 11	Keedonwood rd Brom
156 L 3	Keeley rd Croy
141 N 5	Keeley st WC2
94 M 13	Keeling rd SE9
95 N 13	Keeling rd SE9
156 M 8	Keen's rd Croy
48 J 18	Keens yd N1
94 E 6	Keep the SE3
102 M 17	Keep the Kingst
151 V 1	Keeton's rd SE16
87 R 19	Keevil dri SW19
48 A 14	Keighley clo N7
114 D 2	Keightley dri SE9
88 L 11	Keildon rd SW11
68 A 1	Keir Hardie way Bark
74 G 4	Keith rd W12
32 L 6	Keith rd E17
67 T 5	Keith rd Bark
95 P 8	Kelbrook st SE3
114 A 8	Kelby path SE9
44 H 5	Kelceda clo NW2
136 E 4	Kelfield gdns W10

I

J

K

65 T 11 Kelland rd E13
94 M 5 Kellaway rd SE3
95 O 3 Kellaway rd SE3
93 Y 13 Kellerton rd SE13
90 F 11 Kellett rd SW2
122 H 16 Kelling gdns Croy
106 L 9 Kellino st SW17
79 X 8 Kellner rd SE18
141 Y 20 Kell st SE1
76 D 18 Kelly rd NW7
47 T 18 Kelly st NW1
37 Y 17 Kelly way Rom
89 Y 5 Kelman clo SW4
91 X 10 Kellmore gro SE22
74 G 7 Kelmscott gdns W12
32 K 6 Kelmscott clo E17
88 L 14 Kelmscott rd SW11
48 K 12 Kelross rd N5
44 H 4 Kelsall clo SE3
125 N 7 Kelsey la Becknhm
125 R 5 Kelsey Pk av Becknhm
125 P 3 Kelsey Pk rd Becknhm
125 O 3 Kelsey sq Becknhm
135 V 15 Kelsey st E2
125 O 6 Kelsey way Becknhm
145 Y 2 Kelso pl W8
120 E 17 Kelso rd Carsh
35 Z 7 Kelston rd Ilf
36 A 6 Kelston rd Ilf
103 O 15 Kelvedon clop Kingst
145 P 20 Kelvedon rd SW6
17 R 18 Kelvin av N13
101 T 15 Kelvin av Tedd
120 F 20 Kelvin cres Harrow
84 C 15 Kelvin dri Twick
58 G 17 Kelvin gdns S'hall
112 L 16 Kelvin gro SE26
124 J 16 Kelvington clo Croy
92 E 14 Kelvington rd SE15
48 K 13 Kelvin rd N5
96 M 7 Kelvin rd Welling
W 6 Kemble rd N17
110 G 2 Kemble rd SE23
156 H 4 Kemble rd Croy
141 N 6 Kemble st WC2
90 L 8 Kemerton rd SE5
123 U 17 Kemerton rd Becknhm
125 S 4 Kemerton rd Becknhm
50 H 16 Kemeys st E9
114 E 9 Kemnal manor Chisl
114 D 13 Kemnal rd Chisl
122 K 15 Kemp grn Croy
128 G 10 Kempe rd NW6
91 S 13 Kemps way SE22
46 G 12 Kemplay rd NW3
55 W 4 Kempt rd Dgnhm
145 V 11 Kempsford gdns SW5
149 U 7 Kempsford rd SE11
107 Z 17 Kempshott rd SW16
108 A 17 Kempshott rd SW16
87 Z 1 Kempson rd SW6
145 W 20 Kempson rd SW6
75 X 11 Kempthorne rd SE8
40 H 16 Kempton av Grnfd
81 X 16 Kempton clo Erith
100 B 20 Kempton pk Felt
68 F 3 Kempton rd E6
124 K 14 Kempton wlk Croy
97 Z 17 Kemsing clo Bxly
122 N 9 Kemsing clo Thntn Hth
77 S 14 Kemsing rd SE10
90 L 4 Kenbury st SE5
18 B 14 Kendal av N18
61 S 14 Kendal av W3
67 U 2 Kendal av Bark
21 R 9 Kendal clo Wdfd Grn
57 V 15 Kendal croft Hornch
111 Z 13 Kendale rd Brom
18 B 14 Kendal gdns N18
124 H 3 Kendall av Becknhm
157 R 20 Kendall av SW4
154 D 2 Kendall gdns Sutton
139 T 3 Kendall pl W1
124 H 3 Kendall rd Becknhm
83 X 5 Kendall rd Islwth
18 A 14 Kendal pde N18
44 H 13 Kendal rd NW10
138 M 6 Kendal st W2
75 R 20 Kender st SE14
89 Y 9 Kendoa rd SW4
120 A 4 Kendor gdns SW19
156 J 16 Kendra Hall rd S Croy
83 S 17 Kendrick gdns Twick
147 F 6 Kendrick ms SW7
146 F 6 Kendrick pl SW7
41 Y 9 Kenelm clo Harrow
4 D 17 Kenerne dri Barnt

4 D 18 Kenerne dri Barnt
89 T 18 Kenilford rd SW12
33 P 9 Kenilworth av E17
105 X 11 Kenilworth av SW19
40 D 12 Kenilworth av Harrow
8 E 6 Kenilworth cres Enf
54 K 6 Kenilworth gdns Ilf
58 F 10 Kenilworth gdns S'hall
95 Y 4 Kenilworth gdns SE9
63 V 6 Kenilworth rd E3
129 R 3 Kenilworth rd NW6
110 E 20 Kenilworth rd SE20
72 J 3 Kenilworth rd W5
12 G 12 Kenilworth rd Edg
152 F 12 Kenilworth rd Epsom
98 F 19 Kenley clo Bxly
122 H 9 Kenley gdns Thntn Hth
119 X 4 Kenley rd SW19
120 X 5 Kenley rd SW19
117 U 3 Kenley rd Kingst
84 A 16 Kenley rd Twick
136 K 12 Kenley wlk W11
153 N 9 Kenley wlk Sutton
106 G 13 Kenlor rd SW17
26 A 6 Kenly av NW9
106 M 19 Kenmare dri Mitch
17 Y 14 Kenmare gdns N13
122 E 14 Kenmare rd Thntn Hth
61 P 1 Kenmere gdns N Wemb
97 T 4 Kenmere rd Welling
62 J 8 Kenmont gdns NW19
23 Z 13 Kenmore av Harrow
22 A 7 Kenmore av Harrow
23 Z 8 Kenmore av Harrow
25 T 7 Kenmore gdns Edg
24 G 12 Kenmore rd Harrow
50 A 16 Kenmure rd E8
64 H 1 Kennard rd E15
15 Z 17 Kennard rd N11
89 N 3 Kennard st SW11
78 F 3 Kennard st E16
9 R 19 Kennedy av Enf
65 T 7 Kennedy clo E13
59 V 12 Kennedy path W7
59 U 13 Kennedy rd W7
67 U 4 Kennedy rd Bark
53 X 11 Kenneth av E9
44 L 15 Kenneth cres NW2
10 K 19 Kenneth gdns Stanm
55 X 1 Kenneth rd Rom
88 F 9 Kennet clo SW11
129 P 17 Kennet rd W9
99 X 8 Kennet rd Drtfrd
83 V 7 Kennet rd Islwth
160 B 9 Kennet Wharf la EC4
49 Y 10 Kenninghall rd E5
19 P 16 Kenninghall rd N18
75 R 5 Kenning st SE16
149 U 9 Kennings way
149 O 12 Kennington gro SE11
149 V 8 Kennington la SE11
149 P 15 Kennington oval SE11
149 U 15 Kennington park SE11
149 W 14 Kennington Pk gdns SE11
149 V 13 Kennington Pk pl SE11
149 V 11 Kennington Pk rd SE11
149 T 11 Kennington rd SE11
14 E 18 Kenny rd NW7
139 S 1 Kenrick pl W1
128 J 16 Kensal rd W10
129 N 18 Kensal rd W10
53 R 18 Kensington av E12
122 F 1 Kensington av Thntn Hth
137 W 18 Kensington Ch ct W8
137 V 14 Kensington Ch st W8
137 W 18 Kensington Ch wlk W8
137 Z 19 Kensington ct W8
137 Z 20 Kensington ct pl W8
35 O 6 Kensington dri Wdfd Grn
53 U 4 Kensington gdns Ilf
137 X 7 Kensington Gdns sq W2
138 B 20 Kensington ga SW7
138 F 19 Kensington gore SW7
137 W 19 Kensington High st W8
145 R 2 Kensington High st W8

137 V 13 Kensington mall W8
137 W 12 Kensington Pal gdns W8
187 Z 15 Kensington Palace London museum W8
137 P 10 Kensington Pk gdns W11
137 N 6 Kensington Pk ms W11
137 O 7 Kensington Pk rd W11
137 T 14 Kensington pl W8
73 D 19 Kensington rd SW7
58 G 5 Kensington rd Grnfd
38 L 18 Kensington rd Rom
137 X 20 Kensington sq W8
157 O 17 Kensington ter S Croy
60 A 15 Kent av W13
69 T 6 Kent av Dgnhm
96 L 11 Kent av Welling
122 A 8 Kent clo Mitch
6 C 15 Kent dri Barnt
101 S 13 Kent dri Tedd
58 B 4 Kentford way Grnfd
60 B 14 Kent gdns W13
158 M 14 Kent Gate way Croy
159 O 12 Kent Gate way Croy
110 J 14 Kent House la Becknhm
110 F 19 Kent House rd Becknhm
142 E 16 Kentish bldgs SE1
81 S 11 Kentish rd Blvdr
131 Z 2 Kentish Town rd NW1
47 T 18 Kentish Town rd NW5
79 W 13 Kentmere rd SE18
23 W 20 Kenton av Harrow
58 H 20 Kenton av S'hall
24 D 15 Kenton gdns Harrow
23 X 5 Kenton la Harrow
24 C 10 Kenton la Harrow
24 F 15 Kenton Pk av Harrow
24 F 13 Kenton Pk clo Harrow
24 E 14 Kenton Pk cres Harrow
24 E 14 Kenton Pk rd Harrow
50 E 18 Kenton rd E9
23 Z 19 Kenton rd Harrow
24 C 17 Kenton rd Harrow
132 K 17 Kenton st WC1
131 N 15 Kent pas NW1
24 A 3 Kent rd N21
73 V 8 Kent rd W4
56 H 15 Kent rd Dgnhm
116 G 5 Kent rd Kingst
73 P 19 Kent rd Rich
125 S 20 Kent rd W Wckm
135 P 7 Kent st E2
65 X 10 Kent st E13
120 M 14 Kent ter NW1
54 H 7 Kent View gdns Ilf
74 G 19 Kentwode grn SW15
138 L 19 Kent yd SW7
15 S 20 Kenver av N12
94 F 4 Kenward rd SE9
38 J 7 Kenway Rom
43 W 8 Kenway Wemb
145 W 7 Kenway rd SW5
92 D 1 Kenwood av SE14
L 17 Kenwood av Enf
46 F 3 Kenwood clo NW3
125 U 6 Kenwood dri Becknhm
35 W 14 Kenwood gdns Ilf
44 J 3 Kenwood house NW3
28 M 17 Kenwood rd N6
18 K 6 Kenwood rd N9
75 H 16 Kenworthy rd E9
44 C 8 Kenwyn dri NW2
89 V 9 Kenwyn rd SW4
118 M 1 Kenwyn rd SW20
77 Z 20 Kenya rd SE7
87 O 1 Kenyngton pl Harrow
87 O 1 Kenyon st SW6
144 G 20 Kenyon st SW6
52 A 17 Keogh rd E15
66 E 1 Kepler rd SW4
66 E 1 Keppel rd E6
55 X 12 Keppel rd Dgnhm
142 A 15 Keppel row SE1
64 D 18 Kerbey st E14
91 O 3 Kerfield pl SE5
72 H 3 Kerrison pl W5
64 J 3 Kerrison rd E15
88 J 7 Kerrison rd SW11
72 H 4 Kerrison rd W5
11 T 13 Kerry av Stanm

65 U 18 Kerry clo E16
11 T 14 Kerry cl Stanm
113 P 9 Kersey gdns SE9
87 P 16 Kersfield rd SW15
56 F 9 Kershaw rd Dgnhm
88 L 3 Kersley ms SW11
49 T 9 Kersley rd N16
88 L 3 Kersley st SW11
31 R 17 Kerswell cl N15
48 B 20 Kerwick clo N7
128 G 9 Keslake rd NW6
91 Z 14 Kessock clo N15
97 U 16 Kestlake rd Bxly
18 C 12 Keston clo N18
80 E 19 Keston clo Welling
31 O 12 Keston rd N17
91 W 8 Keston rd SW11
122 E 13 Keston rd Thntn Hth
57 X 20 Keston rd Croy
90 L 13 Kestrel av SE24
57 X 20 Kestrel clo Hornch
159 X 18 Kestrel way Croy
104 A 12 Keswick av SW15
119 X 4 Keswick av SW19
103 Z 13 Keswick av Kingst
154 D 8 Keswick clo Sutton
35 S 13 Keswick gdns Ilf
42 J 14 Keswick gdns Wemb
72 J 4 Keswick ms W5
87 T 15 Keswick rd SW15
98 D 3 Keswick rd Bxly Hth
82 M 17 Keswick rd W Wckm
159 Z 1 Keswick rd W Wckm
9 S 1 Kettering rd Enf
107 U 16 Kettering st SW16
50 K 4 Kettlebaston rd E10
31 N 6 Kevelioc rd N17
73 O 16 Kew Bridge Brentf
73 O 15 Kew Bridge ct W4
72 L 16 Kew Bridge la Brentf
153 U 5 Kew cres Sutton
84 K 8 Kew Foot rd Rich
72 L 20 Kew Gardens Brentf
85 O 1 Kew Gardens rd Rich
73 N 18 Kew grn Rich
85 S 3 Kew Meadows path Rich
84 C 7 Kew Observatory Rich
72 L 18 Kew palace Brentf
73 N 17 Kew rd Rich
85 N 2 Kew rd Rich
108 D 5 Keymer rd SW2
29 N 12 Keynes clo N2
141 Y 20 Key North st SE1
21 N 14 Keynsham av Wdfd Grn
95 P 22 Keynsham gdns SE9
95 P 13 Keynsham rd SE9
119 Z 19 Keynsham rd Mrdn
132 M 10 Keystone cres N1
149 Y 1 Keyworth st SE1
75 U 14 Kezia st SE8
106 J 10 Khama rd SW17
65 V 10 Khartoum rd E13
106 G 10 Khartoum rd SW17
53 Z 15 Khartoum rd Ilf
54 A 15 Khartoum rd Ilf
88 J 6 Khyber rd SW11
149 O 19 Kibworth st SW8
94 F 3 Kidbrooke gdns SE3
94 F 2 Kidbrooke gro SE3
95 S 11 Kidbrooke la SE9
94 H 3 Kidbrooke la SE3
94 G 2 Kidbrooke Pk rd SE3
122 K 18 Kidderminster rd Croy
45 Y 13 Kidderpore av NW3
45 Z 12 Kidderpore gdns NW3
49 Z 4 Kier Hardie est E5
45 V 20 Kilburn High rd NW6
129 T 3 Kilburn High rd NW6
129 O 10 Kilburn la W10
128 K 11 Kilburn la W10
129 V 12 Kilburn Pk rd NW6
129 V 5 Kilburn pl NW6
129 X 7 Kilburn priory NW6
129 T 5 Kilburn sq NW6
129 V 5 Kilburn vale NW6
137 V 5 Kildare gdns W2
65 T 14 Kildare rd E16
137 V 4 Kildare ter W2
90 A 15 Kildoran rd SW2
55 N 5 Kildowan rd Ilf
92 H 15 Kilgow rd SE23
88 C 5 Kilis st SW6
28 D 16 Killarney rd SW18
111 X 1 Killasser rd SE6
152 L 9 Killester gdns Worc Pk
133 N 10 Killick st N1
107 Z 14 Killieser av SW2

108 A 2 Killieser av SW2
65 R 17 Killip clo E16
41 O 13 Killowen av Grnfd
50 E 19 Killowen rd E9
89 W 5 Killyon rd SW8
144 M 20 Kilmaine rd SW6
74 L 10 Kilmarsh rd W6
144 A 5 Kilmarsh rd W6
122 E 6 Kilmartin av SW16
55 O 7 Kilmartin rd Ilf
57 Y 16 Kilmartin way Hornch
74 F 17 Kilmington rd SW13
84 A 11 Kilmorey gdns Twick
84 B 11 Kilmorey rd Twick
110 H 2 Kilmorie rd SE23
47 P 13 Kiln pl NW5
128 L 13 Kilravock st W10
8 C 3 Kilvington dri Enf
87 S 2 Kimbell gdns SW6
66 L 5 Kimberley av E6
92 B 6 Kimberley av SE15
54 F 2 Kimberley av Ilf
38 J 19 Kimberley av Rom
115 X 5 Kimberley dri Sidcp
30 J 17 Kimberley gdns N4
8 G 13 Kimberley gdns Enf
20 M 5 Kimberley rd E4
21 N 6 Kimberley rd E4
51 X 6 Kimberley rd E11
65 O 12 Kimberley rd E16
32 K 4 Kimberley rd E17
31 X 9 Kimberley rd N17
19 N 19 Kimberley rd N18
128 M 3 Kimberley rd NW6
90 B 6 Kimberley rd SW9
124 G 4 Kimberley rd Becknhm
122 K 13 Kimberley rd Croy
20 M 5 Kimberley way E4
21 N 5 Kimberley way E4
88 A 19 Kimber rd SW18
10 A 2 Kimble cres Bushey Watf
106 G 14 Kimble rd SW19
94 C 17 Kimbolton clo SE12
113 R 9 Kimm gdns SE9
113 R 10 Kimmeridge rd SE9
91 O 1 Kimpton rd SE5
153 V 3 Kimpton rd Sutton
75 S 4 Kinburn st SE16
151 V 20 Kincaid rd SE15
42 L 20 Kinch gro Harrow
42 L 1 Kinch gro Harrow
80 J 1 Kinder clo SE2
143 W 5 Kinder st E1
55 O 4 Kinfauns rd Ilf
108 G 4 Kinfauns rd SW2
57 V 20 Kingaby gdns Rainham
111 O 10 King Alfred av SE6
150 C 9 King And Queen st SE17
116 M 13 King Charles' cres Surb
117 N 16 King Charles' cres Surb
140 J 17 King Charles st SW1
105 S 2 King Charles wlk SW19
63 O 20 King David la E1
45 Y 17 Kingdon rd NW6
156 K 20 Kingdown av S Croy
63 R 1 King Edward rd E9
51 T 4 King Edward rd E10
32 G 11 King Edward rd E17
4 M 14 King Edward rd Barnt
5 N 15 King Edward rd Barnt
39 T 17 King Edward rd Rom
73 R 3 King Edward rd W3
102 C 15 King Edward's gro Tedd
135 Y 3 King Edwards rd E9
18 M 2 King Edwards rd N9
19 N 3 King Edwards rd N9
67 S 5 King Edward's rd Bark
9 U 14 King Edward's rd Bark
141 Z 4 King Edward st EC1
149 T 1 King Edward wlk SW1
60 H 10 Kingfield rd W5
76 G 11 Kingfield st E14
102 C 9 Kingfisher dri Rich
156 H 10 King gdns Croy
65 Z 17 King George av E16
152 B 7 King George Field Aurioil pk Epsom
87 Z 20 King George pk SW18
58 E 14 King Georges dri S'hall

131 P 2 King George's ms NW1
176 H 20 King George st SE10
131 P 2 King George's ter NW1
121 N 8 King George vi Mitch
88 C 18 Kingham clo SW18
80 M 18 King Harold's way Bxly Hth
159 V 18 King Henry's dri Croy
130 K 1 King Henry's rd NW3
131 O 1 King Henry's rd NW3
117 T 5 King Henry's rd Kingst
49 S 15 King Henry st N16
49 R 17 King Henry's wlk N1
141 Z 2 Kinghorn st EC1
141 Y 19 King James st SE1
134 L 16 King John's ct EC2
63 T 15 King John's st E1
95 P 19 King John's wk SE9
150 J 11 Kinglake st SE17
150 L 9 Kinglake st SE17
140 B 8 Kingly ct W1
140 B 7 Kingly st W1
112 G 3 Kingsand rd SE12
160 F 5 King's Arm yd EC2
29 P 10 King's av N10
17 V 5 King's av N21
89 Z 14 King's av SW4
60 H 16 King's av W5
112 B 16 Kings av Brom
154 C 18 King's av Carsh
58 L 16 King's av Grnfd
82 L 2 Kings av Hounsl
118 C 8 Kings av New Mald
118 D 8 Kings av New Mald
38 C 18 Kings av Rom
21 W 18 King's av Wdfd Grn
89 Z 17 Kings Av clo SW4
89 Y 13 Kings Av gdns SW4
141 Y 17 King's Bench st SE1
141 T 8 Kings Bench wlk EC4
73 N 5 Kingsbridge av W3
58 E 15 Kingsbridge av S'hall
136 E 3 Kingsbridge rd W10
67 T 7 Kingsbridge rd Berk
119 P 17 Kingsbridge rd Mrdn
70 D 12 Kingsbridge rd S'hall
49 S 17 Kingsbury rd N1
25 U 15 Kingsbury rd NW9
49 S 17 Kingsbury ter N1
86 F 17 Kingsclere clo SW15
105 V 3 Kingscliffe gdns SW19
51 R 2 Kings clo E10
27 R 13 Kings clo NW4
99 O 11 King's clo Drtfd
46 H 20 King's College rd NW3
73 X 10 Kingscote rd W4
123 Z 18 Kingscote rd Croy
117 Y 7 Kingscote rd New Mald
141 W 8 Kingscote st EC4
65 W 4 Kings ct E13
107 Z 7 Kingscourt rd SW16
127 U 17 Kingscroft rd NW2
133 O 12 Kings Cross rd WC1
132 K 9 Kings Cross station N1
79 X 17 Kingsdale rd SE18
110 F 19 Kingsdale rd SE20
62 B 18 Kingsdown av W3
72 C 5 Kingsdown av W13
136 J 7 Kingsdown clo W11
116 M 19 Kingsdowne rd Surb
52 A 10 Kingsdown rd E11
48 A 7 Kingsdown rd N4
47 Z 8 Kingsdown rd N19
153 S 11 Kingsdown rd Sutton
126 E 15 Kingsdown way Brom
11 Z 14 Kings dri Edg
12 A 14 Kings dri Edg
117 P 15 Kings dri Surb
43 S 7 Kings dri Wemb
85 O 11 Kings Farm av Rich
104 D 1 Kingsfarm lodge SW15
22 L 14 Kingsfield av Harrow
23 N 15 Kingsfield av Harrow
41 S 2 Kingsfield rd Harrow
41 R 2 Kingsfield rd Harrow
156 S 17 Kingsford av Croy
156 B 17 Kingsford av Croy
46 B 15 Kingsford st NW5
54 D 4 Kings gdns Ilf
43 U 8 Kingsgate Wemb
27 Y 10 Kingsgate av N3

97 Y 1 Kingsgate clo Bxly Hth
129 T 2 Kingsgate pl NW6
45 X 20 Kingsgate rd NW6
129 U 2 Kingsgate rd NW6
95 O 18 Kingsground SE9
75 N 20 Kings gro SE15
151 X 20 King's gro SE15
39 V 17 Kings gro Rom
110 F 18 Kings Hall rd SE20
160 H 10 Kings Head ct EC3
20 E 20 Kings Head hill E4
142 F 15 King's Head yd SE1
79 X 17 King's highway SE18
24 B 13 Kingshill av Harrow
118 H 16 Kingshill av Worc Pk
24 B 11 Kingshill dri Harrow
63 P 1 Kingshold rd E9
95 P 9 Kingsholme gdns SE9
94 F 19 Kingshurst rd SE12
130 M 6 Kingsland NW8
49 T 17 Kingsland High st E8
48 T 17 Kingsland pass N1
134 L 6 Kingsland rd E2
42 V 19 Kingsland rd E8
65 Y 9 Kingsland rd E13
86 K 12 Kings lawn clo SW15
154 G 12 Kings la Sutton
59 Y 16 Kingsley av W13
83 N 4 Kingsley av Hounsl
58 G 20 Kingsley av S'hall
54 G 8 Kingsley av Sutton
28 C 15 Kingsley clo N2
56 G 12 Kingsley clo Dgnhm
20 B 15 Kinglsy gdns E4
145 Z 2 Kingsley ms W8
47 R 2 Kingsley pl N6
52 F 20 Kingsley rd E7
33 T 8 Kingsley rd E17
17 U 13 Kingsley rd N13
129 P 3 Kingsley rd NW6
106 C 12 Kingsley rd SW19
72 F 19 Kingsley rd Croy
40 M 11 Kingsley rd Harrow
41 N 10 Kingsley rd Harrow
82 L 4 Kingsley rd Hounsl
83 N 6 Kingsley rd Hounsl
30 C 4 Kingsley rd Ilf
22 E 14 Kingsley rd Pinn
88 M 7 Kingsley st SW11
89 N 6 Kingsley st SW11
28 C 15 Kingsley way N2
113 U 7 Kingsley Wood dri SE9
123 N 1 Kingslyn cres SE19
78 G 9 Kingsman pk SE18
78 G 9 Kingsman st SE18
4 L 14 Kingsmead Barnt
18 M 6 Kingsmead av N9
43 Y 1 Kingsmead av NW9
121 V 5 Kingsmead av Mitch
39 S 18 Kingsmead av Rom
152 J 4 Kingsmead av Worc Pk
114 M 5 Kingsmead clo Sidcp
40 E 20 Kingsmead dri Grnfd
108 F 5 Kingsmead rd SW12
50 K 13 King's Mead way E9
43 U 5 Kingsmere pk NW9
105 R 4 Kingsmere rd SW19
56 B 16 Kingsmill gdns Dgnhm
130 G 9 Kingsmill ter NW8
103 T 16 Kingsnympton pk Kingst
89 Z 13 Kings ms SW4
95 S 15 King's orchard SE9
34 D 9 Kings Park ct E18
116 G 4 Kings pas Kingst
142 B 20 Kings pl SE1
73 V 12 King's pl W4
133 P 19 King's pl WC1
21 Z 8 King's pl Buck Hl
133 Z 13 King sq EC1
85 P 12 Kings Ride ga Rich
20 J 5 Kings rd E4
65 Y 3 Kings rd E6
51 Y 1 King's rd E11
18 L 15 King's rd N17
31 V 3 King's rd N17
30 E 4 King's rd N22
44 J 20 King's rd NW10
123 Y 6 Kings rd SE25
147 T 4 King's rd SW1
146 J 12 King's rd SW3
145 Z 20 King's rd SW6
85 Z 9 King's rd SW14
105 Y 14 King's rd SW19
60 G 15 King's rd W5
4 A 13 Kings rd Barnt
54 A 20 Kings rd Bark
40 E 9 Kings rd Harrow
102 J 19 Kings rd Kingst

103 O 17 Kings rd Kingst
121 P 5 Kings rd Mitch
84 M 12 Kings rd Rich
39 V 17 Kings rd Rom
116 O 20 King's rd Surb
101 P 12 King's rd Tedd
84 C 17 King's rd Twick
148 B 4 King's Scholars' pas SW1
48 L 8 King's cres N4
132 A 6 King's ter NW1
110 E 10 Kingsthorpe rd SE26
153 T 5 Kingston av Sutton
104 B 15 Kingston By-pass SW20
118 B 12 Kingston By-pass New Mald
58 E 2 Kingston clo Grnfd
37 Y 9 Kingston clo Rom
102 A 15 Kingston clo Tedd
124 L 1 Kingston cres Becknhm
116 F 3 Kingston dr Kingst
103 P 17 Kingston gate Kingst
116 H 5 Kingston Hall rd Kingst
103 S 18 Kingston hill Kingst
37 Z 9 Kingston Hill av Rom
103 W 10 Kingston Hill place Rich
101 Z 13 Kingston la Tedd
102 A 15 Kingston la Tedd
18 L 8 Kingston rd N9
86 M 20 Kingston rd SW15
104 H 3 Kingston rd SW15
105 Y 19 Kingston rd SW19
119 P 2 Kingston rd SW20
5 U 17 Kingston rd Barnt
152 C 12 Kingston rd Epsom
54 B 12 Kingston rd Ilf
117 V 7 Kingston rd New Mald
38 U 13 Kingston rd Rom
70 D 7 Kingston rd S'hall
102 B 15 Kingston rd Tedd
103 Y 3 Kingston vale SW15
104 A 8 Kingston vale SW15
131 S 4 Kingston st NW1
65 S 12 Kings st E13
142 C 6 King st EC2
160 D 5 Kings st EC2
28 G 8 King st N2
31 U 3 King st N17
140 C 14 King st SW1
73 U 3 King st W3
74 F 12 King st W6
144 B 7 King st W6
140 K 9 King st WC2
84 G 13 King st Rich
70 C 8 King st S'hall
101 Y 1 King st Twick
15 R 18 Kingsway N12
85 U 8 Kingsway SW14
141 N 5 Kingsway WC2
156 D 11 Kings way Croy
102 H 19 Kings wlk Kingst
9 N 15 Kingsway Enf
23 T 12 Kings way Harrow
118 L 10 Kingsway New Mald
42 K 12 Kingsway Wemb
21 Y 16 Kings way Wdfd Grn
158 D 20 Kingsway av S Croy
22 M 14 Kingsway cres Harrow
140 M 4 Kingsway Hall WC2
153 S 15 Kingsway rd Sutton
47 S 9 Kingswear rd NW5
128 L 7 Kingswood av NW6
81 O 10 Kingswood av Blvdr
125 Y 8 Kingswood av Brom
100 K 15 Kingswood av Hampt
82 D 4 Kingswood av Hounsl
122 G 13 Kingswood av Thntn Hth
15 R 1 Kingswood clo N20
118 D 15 Kingswood clo New Mald
116 K 16 Kingswood clo Surb
109 S 10 Kingswood dri SE19
27 V 5 Kingswood pl N3
93 Z 9 Kingswood pl SE13
110 B 16 Kingswood rd SE20
90 A 18 Kingswood rd SW2
125 Y 6 Kingswood rd Brom
126 A 5 Kingswood rd Brom
54 N 3 Kingswood rd Ilf
55 N 2 Kingswood rd Ilf
89 Z 17 Kingswood rd SW2
105 W 19 Kingswood rd SW19
73 V 9 Kingswood rd W4
156 A 10 Kingswood way Croy
43 Y 20 Kingthorpe rd NW10
143 T 1 Kingward st E1

K

5 U 3 Kingwell rd Barnt
142 F 7 King William st EC4
160 F 8 King William st EC4
76 H 16 King William wlk SE10
144 L 20 Kingswood rd SW6
96 B 1 Kinlet rd SE18
43 Z 1 Kinloch dri NW9
44 A 1 Kinloch dri NW9
48 D 10 Kinloch st N7
120 D 18 Kinloss rd Carsh
27 U 11 Kinloss gdns N3
73 U 20 Kinnaird av W4
112 C 16 Kinnaird av Brom
112 D 16 Kinnaird clo Brom
74 C 5 Kinnear rd W12
139 R 18 Kinnerton Pl north W1
139 R 19 Kinnerton Pl south W1
139 S 20 Kinnerton st SW1
139 S 19 Kinnerton yd SW1
144 L 14 Kinnoul rd W6
152 F 4 Kinross av Worc Pk
24 L 16 Kinross clo Harrow
91 X 8 Kinsale rd SE15
151 N 4 Kintore st SE1
122 D 4 Kintyre clo Brom
78 C 13 Kinveachy gdns SE7
110 D 9 Kinver rd SE26
10 H 18 Kipling pl Stanm
97 Z 1 Kipling rd Bxly Hth
142 G 18 Kipling st SE1
18 C 9 Kipling ter N21/N9
152 D 12 Kirby clo Epsom
142 J 17 Kirby gro SE1
133 U 20 Kirby st EC1
141 U 1 Kirby st EC1
72 A 1 Kirchen rd W13
110 B 9 Kirkdale SE26
52 A 2 Kirkdale rd E11
79 V 18 Kirkham st SE18
35 W 7 Kirkland av Ilf
76 M 9 Kirkland pl SE10
79 O 16 Kirk la SE18
55 S 16 Kirklees rd Dgnhm
122 E 10 Kirklees rd Thntn Hth
105 Z 19 Kirkley rd SW19
57 S 20 Kirkly clo S Croy
140 E 1 Kirkman pl W1
64 H 17 Kirkmichael rd E14
32 M 18 Kirk rd E17
77 S 17 Kirkside rd SE3
63 X 15 Kirks pl E3
31 O 12 Kirkstall av N17
107 Z 1 Kirkstall gdns SW2
107 Z 1 Kirkstall rd SW2
108 A 1 Kirkstall rd SW2
119 Z 19 Kirkstead rd Mrdn
112 A 17 Kirkstone way Brom
31 R 14 Kirkton rd N15
63 R 8 Kirkwall pl E2
47 O 19 Kirkwood pl NW1
92 A 3 Kirkwood rd SE15
72 A 1 Kirn rd W13
148 B 17 Kirtling st SW8
73 V 12 Kirton clo W4
135 P 13 Kirton gdns E2
65 X 5 Kirton rd E13
25 W 2 Kirton wlk Edg
149 Z 18 Kirwyn way
64 B 8 Kitcat ter E3
52 H 18 Kitchener rd E7
33 R 4 Kitchener rd E17
28 H 11 Kitchener rd N2
31 P 10 Kitchener rd N17
56 J 17 Kitchener rd Dgnhm
123 N 5 Kitchener rd Thntn Hth
123 U 1 Kitley gdns SE19
150 D 17 Kitson rd SE5
86 F 3 Kitson rd SW13
92 F 6 Kitto rd SE14
4 H 5 Kitts end rd Barnt
47 Z 7 Kiver rd N19
89 U 15 Klea av SW4
110 A 4 Knapdale clo SE23
111 P 5 Knapmill rd SE6
111 P 5 Knapmill way SE6
44 B 17 Knapp clo NW10
64 B 12 Knapp rd E3
145 X 6 Knaresborough pl SW5
61 Z 3 Knatchbull rd NW10
90 J 3 Knatchbull rd SE5
33 O 4 Knebworth av E17
43 R 11 Knebworth rd N16
80 G 13 Knee hill SE2
80 G 11 Knee Hill cres SE2
83 P 15 Kneller gdns Islwth
83 R 16 Kneller hall Twick
92 J 10 Kneller rd SE4
117 Z 17 Kneller rd New Mald
82 M 16 Kneller rd Twick

83 O 16 Kneller rd Twick
49 Z 6 Knightland rd E5
38 M 18 Knighton clo Rom
156 J 17 Knighton clo S Croy
21 V 13 Knighton clo Wdfd Grn
21 V 13 Knighton dri Wdfd Grn
21 V 9 Knighton la Buck Hl
110 G 12 Knighton Pk rd SE26
52 F 11 Knighton rd E7
38 L 18 Knighton rd Rom
141 Z 8 Knightrider st EC4
70 A 14 Knights arbour S'hall
72 L 7 Knight's av W5
138 L 19 Knightsbridge SW7
139 O 18 Knightsbridge SW7
39 N 16 Knightsbridge gdns Rom
139 N 19 Knightsbridge grn SW7
108 J 12 Knights hill SE27
108 K 9 Knights hill SE27
18 K 10 Knights la N9
116 J 5 Knights pk Kingst
77 T 4 Knights rd E16
11 S 13 Knights rd Stanm
149 W 7 Knights wlk SE11
12 G 8 Knightswood clo Edg
118 B 14 Knightwood cres New Mald
145 T 15 Knivett rd SW6
64 D 2 Knobs Hill rd E15
95 N 12 Knockholt rd SE9
99 X 19 Knole rd Drtfrd
113 W 10 Knole the SE9
60 C 15 Knoll N14
125 R 1 Knoll Becknhm
16 C 3 Knoll dri N14
88 C 14 Knolle rd SW18
117 X 20 Knollmead Surb
98 D 17 Knoll rd Bxly
115 R 12 Knoll rd Sidcp
54 K 4 Knolls clo Worc Pk
108 G 6 Knolly's Clo SW16
108 E 6 Knolly's rd SW16
63 S 8 Knottisford st E2
33 T 18 Knotts Green rd E10
81 N 18 Knowle av Bxly Hth
90 E 7 Knowle clo SW9
101 T 2 Knowle rd Twick
93 W 13 Knowles Hill cres SE13
70 K 3 Knowlsey av S'hall
88 M 6 Knowlsey rd SW11
126 D 12 Knowlton grn Brom
52 D 18 Knox rd E7
139 O 1 Knox st W1
75 V 17 Knoyle st SE14
106 B 12 Kohat rd SW19
76 M 13 Kossuth st SE10
145 V 11 Kramer Mews
108 D 19 Kuala gdns SW16
52 F 14 Kuhn wy E7
45 Y 19 Kylemore rd NW6
23 T 19 Kymberley rd Harrow
39 T 20 Kyme rd Hornch
24 D 5 Kynance gdns Stanm
146 A 2 Kynance ms SW7
146 A 1 Kynance pl SW7
49 T 9 Kynaston av N16
122 L 11 Kynaston av Thntn Hth
23 R 1 Kynaston clo Harrow
122 M 11 Kynaston cres Thntn Hth
49 S 9 Kynaston rd N16
112 G 12 Kynaston rd Brom
18 B 7 Kynaston rd Enf
122 M 10 Kynaston rd Thntn Hth
23 R 1 Kynaston wood Harrow
19 R 16 Kynoch rd N18
89 O 14 Kyrle rd SW11
49 V 4 Kyverdale rd N16

L

31 O 1 Laburnum av N17
154 H 6 Laburnum av Sutton
127 Y 16 Laburnum av Brom
18 F 3 Laburnum av N9
57 U 9 Laburnum av Hornch
19 Y 19 Laburnum clo E4
11 P 15 Laburnum ct Stanm
121 P 4 Laburnum est Mitch
17 Y 7 Laburnum gdns N21
17 Y 7 Laburnum gro N21

25 W 20 Laburnum gro NW9
82 F 11 Laburnum gro Hounsl
117 X 4 Laburnum gro New Mald
58 F 12 Laburnum gro S'hall
106 E 18 Laburnum rd SW19
121 P 4 Laburnum rd Mitch
135 N 5 Laburnum st E2
134 M 6 Laburnum st E8
134 G 20 Lackington st EC2
106 C 16 Lacock clo SW19
91 W 11 Lacon rd SE22
87 R 9 Lacy rd SW15
108 K 11 Ladas rd SE27
136 L 6 Ladbroke cres W11
137 O 9 Ladbroke gdns W11
128 H 16 Ladbroke gro W10
136 K 3 Ladbroke gro W10
137 O 13 Ladbroke gro W11
8 H 19 Ladbroke rd Enf
137 R 11 Ladbroke sq W11
137 P 10 Ladbroke Sq gdns W11
137 R 12 Ladbroke ter W11
137 R 12 Ladbroke wlk W11
22 D 17 Ladbrook clo Pinn
115 X 8 Ladbrooke cres Sidcp
123 P 8 Ladbrook rd SE25
103 U 13 Ladderstile ride Kingst
16 G 17 Ladderswood way N11
93 P 8 Ladycroft rd SE13
24 G 6 Ladycroft wlk Stanm
158 G 20 Ladygrove S Croy
152 C 1 Lady hay Worc Pk
47 V 13 Lady Margaret rd NW5
58 E 14 Lady Margaret rd S'hall
70 E 1 Lady Margaret rd S'hall
40 A 19 Ladymead clo Grnfd
66 C 5 Ladysmith av E6
54 F 2 Ladysmith av Ilf
65 O 10 Ladysmith rd E16
31 W 8 Ladysmith rd N18
19 N 19 Ladysmith rd N18
95 X 17 Ladysmith rd SE9
8 F 12 Ladysmith rd Enf
23 T 8 Ladysmith rd Harrow
47 T 13 Lady Somerset rd NW5
93 S 12 Ladywell rd SE13
65 P 4 Ladywell st E15
143 N 17 Lafone st SE1
123 P 15 Lahore rd Croy
120 K 2 Laings av Mitch
87 X 19 Lainson st SW18
68 B 17 Lairs clo N7
89 S 20 Laitwood rd SW12
107 T 1 Laitwood rd SW12
112 F 15 Lake av Brom
79 V 15 Lakedale rd SE18
30 J 8 Lakefield rd N22
56 D 15 Lake gdns Dgnhm
102 B 6 Lake gdns Rich
155 R 7 Lake gdns Wallgtn
122 J 12 Lakehall gdns Thntn Hth
122 J 12 Lakehall rd Thntn Hth
52 F 6 Lakehouse rd E11
152 A 12 Lakehurst rd Epsom
10 C 19 Lakeland clo Harrow
6 J 17 Lakenheath N14
6 K 20 Lakenheath N14
39 T 9 Lake rise Rom
37 V 13 Lake rd E11
105 U 13 Lake rd SW19
158 L1 Lake rd Croy
87 U 15 Laker pl SW15
60 D 15 Lakeside W13
6 K 13 Lakeside Enf
155 S 7 Lakeside Wallgtn
35 N 13 Lakeside av Ilf
123 W 3 Lakeside clo SE25
48 K 6 Lakeside ct N4
6 A 18 Lakeside cres Barnt
17 P 12 Lakeside rd N13
136 G 20 Lakeside rd W14
144 E 1 Lakeside rd W14
43 P 13 Lakeside way Wembl
10 B 5 Lake the Bushey Watf
11 Z 17 Lake view Edg
108 J 12 Lakeview rd SE27
97 O 10 Lake View rd Welling
11 Z 17 Lakeview View Edg
12 K 10 Laleham av NW7
93 T 18 Laleham rd SE6

87 S 3 Lalor st SW6
13 X 9 Lambarde av SE9
108 G 11 Lamberhurst rd SE27
56 A 4 Lamberhurst rd Dgnhm
85 S 8 Lambert av Rich
65 V 17 Lambert rd E16
15 S 17 Lambert rd N12
90 C 14 Lambert rd SW2
123 P 20 Lamberts pl Croy
116 L 12 Lamberts rd Surb
133 R 2 Lambert st N1
15 S 17 Lambert way N12
148 L 4 Lambeth br SW1
149 N 5 Lambeth High st SE1
160 A 8 Lambeth hill EC4
149 O 7 Lambeth ms SE11
149 O 3 Lambeth palace SE1
141 O 20 Lambeth Palace rd SE1
149 N 2 Lambeth Palace rd SE1
148 M 3 Lambeth Pier SW1
149 P 3 Lambeth rd SE1
122 G 18 Lambeth rd Croy
143 S 6 Lambeth st E1
149 O 7 Lambeth wlk SE11
63 N 1 Lamb la E8
135 Y 1 Lamb la E8
47 O 14 Lamb st NW5
55 R 18 Lambley rd Dgnhm
46 K 18 Lambolle pl NW3
46 J 18 Lambolle rd NW3
71 U 8 Lambourn clo W7
117 T 2 Lambourn clo Kingst
105 V 9 Lambourne av SW19
20 B 8 Lambourne gdns E4
67 X 1 Lambourne gdns Bark
8 G 9 Lambourne gdns Enf
94 H 1 Lambourne pla SE3
51 V 2 Lambourne rd E11
67 W 2 Lambourne rd Bark
54 H 6 Lambourne rd Ilf
89 T 7 Lambourn rd SW4
87 R 2 Lambrook ter SW6
134 D 18 Lambs bldgs EC1
18 J 8 Lambs clo N9
141 N 1 Lambs Conduit pas WC1
133 N 19 Lambs Conduit st WC1
112 M 8 Lambscroft av SE9
113 N 7 Lambscroft av SE9
35 N 2 Lambs ms Wdfd Grn
134 D 19 Lambs pas EC1
18 C 8 Lambs ter N9
134 M 20 Lamb st E1
135 N 20 Lamb st E1
7 Z 9 Lambs wlk Enf
137 S 8 Lambton pl W11
48 A 4 Lambton N19
104 L 20 Lambton rd SW20
118 L 2 Lambton rd SW20
128 L 19 Lamb wlk SE1
112 D 9 Lamerock rd Brom
36 A 6 Lamerton rd Ilf
76 B 17 Lamerton st SE8
31 P 1 Lamford clo N17
74 J 11 Lamington st W6
149 X 4 Lamlash st SE11
121 O 3 Lammas av Mitch
121 O 4 Lammas av Mitch
109 Z 5 Lammas grn SE26
72 F 4 Lammas Pk gdns W5
72 F 4 Lammas Pk rd W5
63 U 1 Lammas rd E9
50 H 5 Lammas rd E10
102 D 11 Lammas rd Rich
89 T 19 Lammermoor rd SW12
146 E 15 Lamont rd SW10
146 E 16 Lamont Rd pas SW10
114 K 3 Lamorbey clo Sidcp
115 P 1 Lamorbey park Bxly
24 G 6 Lamorna gro Stanm
49 U 4 Lampard gro N16
144 N 15 Lampeter sq W6
134 E 4 Lampeter st N1
94 B 12 Lampmead rd SE12
82 J 3 Lampton av Hounsl
78 G 10 Lampton clo Se18
105 O 10 Lampton Ho clo SW19
82 K 5 Lampton park Hounsl
82 J 6 Lampton Park rd Hounsl
26 C 8 Lanacre NW9
26 B 6 Lanacre NW9
25 Z 5 Lanacre av Edg
60 E 14 Lanark clo W5
130 D 17 Lanark pl W9
129 Z 16 Lanark rd W9

130 B 14 Lanark rd W9
58 C 11 Lanata wk Grnfd
92 F 11 Lanbury rd SE15
139 Y 8 Lancashire ct W1
34 H 12 Lancashire av E18
108 K 4 Lancaster av SE27
105 R 12 Lancaster av SW19
67 V 2 Lancaster av Bark
5 T 3 Lancaster av Barnt
112 A 9 Lancaster av Mitch
122 A 9 Lancaster av Mitch
126 B 10 Lancaster clo Brom
102 H 12 Lancaster clo Kingst
155 Z 2 Lancaster clo Wallgtn
46 H 18 Lancaster dri NW3
57 Z 16 Lancaster dri Hornch
105 S 11 Lancaster gdns SW19
72 C 4 Lancaster gdns W13
102 H 13 Lancaster gdns Kingst
138 C 10 Lancaster ga W2
45 H 18 Lancaster gro NW3
138 O 9 Lancaster ms W2
84 J 14 Lancaster pk Rich
105 R 12 Lancaster pl SW19
83 Z 17 Lancaster pl Twick
141 N 9 Lancaster pl WC2
52 F 20 Lancaster rd E7
65 U 1 Lancaster rd E7
52 B 7 Lancaster rd E11
32 F 8 Lancaster rd E 17
48 F 2 Lancaster rd N4
16 L 18 Lancaster rd N11
18 G 17 Lancaster rd N18
44 F 14 Lancaster rd NW10
123 V 5 Lancaster rd SE25
105 R 12 Lancaster rd SW19
136 L 5 Lancaster rd W11
137 O 4 Lancaster rd W11
5 T 17 Lancaster rd Barnt
8 C 6 Lancaster rd Enf
40 L 16 Lancaster rd Grnfd
22 H 17 Lancaster rd Harrow
58 B 20 Lancaster rd S'hall
138 F 8 Lancaster ter W2
129 O 14 Lancefield st W9
49 T 8 Lancell st N16
42 G 12 Lancelot av Wemb
42 G 13 Lancelot cres Wemb
16 B 3 Lancelot gdns Barnt
139 N 19 Lancelot pl SW7
36 G 1 Lancelot rd Ilf
97 O 9 Lancelot rd Welling
42 G 12 Lancelot rd Welling
42 G 12 Lancelot rd Wemb
41 N 2 Lance rd Harrow
29 N 15 Lanchester rd N6
18 H 5 Lancing rd W13
122 D 16 Lancing rd Croy
36 E 19 Lancing rd Ilf
132 F 13 Lancing st NW1
91 V 15 Landcroft rd SE22
91 V 16 Landells rd SE22
49 X 11 Landfield st E5
86 M 9 Landford rd SW15
105 X 11 Landgrove rd SW19
75 T 15 Landmann way SE14
147 O 1 Landon pl SW3
74 F 6 Landor wlk W12
7 V 19 Landra gdns N21
87 U 4 Landridge rd SW6
30 B 18 Landrock rd N8
34 H 2 Landscape rd Wdfd Grn
53 V 15 Landseer av E12
25 R 7 Landseer clo Edg
120 E 1 Landseer clo SW19
48 A 8 Landseer rd N4
8 J 18 Landseer rd Enf
117 Z 16 Lndseer rd New Mald
153 X 14 Landseer rd Sutton
14 E 17 Lane appr NW7
44 J 10 Lane clo NW2
98 F 8 Lane end Bxly Hth
10 F 4 Lane gdns Bushey Watf
108 G 3 Lanercost clo SW12
16 M 1 Lanercost gdns N14
108 G 3 Lanercost rd SW2
114 A 12 Laneside Chisl
12 H 17 Laneside Edg
56 C 2 Laneside av Dgnhm
130 A 10 Lane the NW8
94 F 7 Lane the SE3
63 V 7 Lanfranc rd E3
141 T 20 Lanfranc st SE1
145 O 11 Lanfrey pl W14
47 P 7 Langbourne av N6
95 O 6 Langbrook rd SE3
120 M 5 Langdale av Mitch
98 E 1 Langdale cres Bxly Hth
60 C 8 Langdale gdns Grnfd
57 W 15 Langdale gdns Hornch
76 F 20 Langdale rd SE10
122 F 9 Langdale rd Thntn Hth
143 V 7 Langdale st E1
66 K 5 Langdon cres E6
43 U 3 Langdon dri NW9
47 U 1 Langdon Pk rd N6
85 V 7 Langdon pl SW14
66 J 4 Langdon rd E6
120 C 12 Langdon rd Mrdn
14 K 12 Langdon Shaw Sidcp
130 D 9 Langford clo NW8
5 Z 13 Langford cres Barnt
91 R 8 Langford grn SE5
130 O 9 Langford pl NW8
115 N 7 Langford pl Sidcp
88 B 3 Langford rd SW6
21 Z 20 Langford rd Wdfd Grn
37 P 19 Langham dri Rom
7 U 17 Langham gdns N21
60 B 20 Langham gdns W13
25 V 1 Langham gdns Edg
102 E 9 Langham gdns Rich
42 D 7 Langham gdns Wemb
102 F 9 Langham ho Clo
30 G 10 Langham pde N15
139 Z 3 Langham pl W1
30 L 12 Langham rd N15
119 N 1 Langham rd SW20
12 H 20 Langham rd Edg
102 A 14 Langham rd Tedd
139 Z 2 Langham st W1
18 G 19 Langhedge clo N18
18 H 18 Langhedge la N18
10 A 4 Langholme Watf
56 D 19 Langhorne rd Dgnhm
24 H 8 Langland cres East Stanm
24 H 8 Langland cres West Stanm
46 B 14 Langland gdns NW3
158 L 2 Langland gdns Cry
128 E 11 Langley rd NW10
116 H 20 Langley av Surb
153 O 2 Langley av Worc Pk
140 K 7 Langley ct WC2
125 S 9 Langley court Becknhm
34 K 20 Langley cres E11
68 H 2 Langley cres Dgnhm
12 J 12 Langley cres Edg
34 J 19 Langley dri E11
73 T 4 Langley dri W3
127 Z 14 Langley gdns Brom
68 H 2 Langley gdns Dgnhm
117 Z 3 Langley gro New Mald
118 A 3 Langley gro New Mald
148 M14 Langley la SW8
13 O 18 Langley pk NW7
154 E 15 Langley Pk rd Sutton
105 X 20 Langley rd SW19
119 W1 Langley rd SW19
124 G 9 Langley rd Becknhm
83 W 3 Langley rd Islwth
158 E 20 Langley rd S Croy
116 K 17 Langley rd Surb
80 F 18 Langley rd Welling
140 K 7 Langley st WC2
126 A 16 Langley way W Wckm
125 Y 18 Langley way W Wckm
108 K 9 Langmead SE27
10 D 4 Langmead dri Watford
106 L 5 Langroyd rd SW17
86 F 10 Langside av SW15
16 L 11 Langside cres N14
63 P 11 Lang st E1
160 F 3 Langthorn ct EC2
51 V 10 Langthorne rd E10
144 G 19 Langthorne st SW6
66 K 9 Langton av E6
15 S 3 Langton av N20
133 O 15 Langton clo WC1
91 Z 18 Langton ri SE22
92 A 19 Langton ri SE23
44 M 10 Langton rd NW2
90 K 1 Langton rd SW9
149 Y 20 Langton rd SW9
22 M 3 Langton rd Harrow
23 N 2 Langton rd Harrow
146 D 16 Langton st SW10
77 U 20 Langton way SE3
94 D 1 Langton way SE3
157 T 7 Langton way Croy
129 X 5 Langtry rd NW6
129 Y 5 Langtry rd NW8
58 A 5 Langtry rd Grnfd
102 E 16 Langwood chase Tedd
129 U 16 Lanhill rd W9
93 V 15 Lanier rd SE13
28 G 6 Lankaster gdns N2
22 F 18 Lankers dri Harrow
125 T 1 Lankton clo Becknhm
114 B 2 Lannoy rd SE9
64 L 16 Lanrick rd E14
80 H 9 Lanridge rd SE2
18 C 18 Lansbury av N18
68 A 1 Lansbury av Bark
37 Z 16 Lansbury av Rom
9 T 7 Lansbury rd Enf
18 C 18 Lansbury way N18
64 H 17 Lansby gdns E14
121 O 3 Lansdell rd Mitch
80 H 19 Lansdowne av Welling
105 N 18 Lansdowne clo SW20
101 V 1 Lansdowne clo Twick
137 N 10 Lansdowne cres W11
152 F 2 Lansdowne ct Worc Pk
49 X 18 Lansdowne dri E8
135 V 3 Lansdowne dri E8
90 A 1 Lansdowne gdns SW8
148 K 20 Lansdowne gdns SW8
44 B 14 Lansdowne gro NW10
108 J 6 Lansdowne hill SE27
77 Z 16 Lansdowne la SE7
78 A 16 Lansdowne la SE7
137 N 14 Lansdowne ms W11
109 T 17 Lansdowne pl SE19
136 M 10 Lansdowne ri W11
20 A 9 Lansdowne rd E4
52 A 7 Lansdowne rd E11
33 N 17 Lansdowne rd E17
34 E 10 Lansdowne rd E18
27 X 1 Lansdowne rd N3
29 V 8 Lansdowne rd N10
31 W 5 Lansdowne rd N17
105 N 17 Lansdowne rd SW20
136 M 9 Lansdowne rd W11
137 N 12 Lansdowne rd W11
112 G 18 Lansdowne rd Brom
123 O 20 Lansdowne rd Croy
157 N 2 Lansdowne rd Croy
82 K 7 Lansdowne rd Hounsl
54 K 2 Lansdowne rd Ilf
115 P 7 Lansdowne rd Sidcp
11 S 20 Lansdowne rd Stanm
139 Y 12 Lansdowne row W1
132 M 17 Lansdowne ter WC1
137 O 12 Lansdowne wlk W11
89 Z 2 Lansdowne way SW8
90 A 2 Lansdowne way SW8
52 L 19 Lansdown rd E7
18 L 13 Lansfield av N18
86 G 10 Lantern clo SW15
142 A 18 Lant st SE1
92 B 5 Lanvanor rd SE15
58 C 12 Lapponum wk Grnfd
109 Y 3 Lapsewood wlk SE26
24 D 19 Laptone gdns Harrow
107 U 19 Larbert rd SW16
74 A 3 Larch av W3
85 X 10 Larches av SW14
17 Y 10 Larches the N13
107 R 3 Larch clo SW12
45 N 12 Larch rd NW2
159 P 6 Larch Tree way Croy
127 W 16 Larch way Brom
113 Z 4 Larchwood rd SE9
114 A 5 Larchwood rd SE9
150 D 6 Larcom st SE17
74 B 4 Larden rd W3
110 H 10 Larkbere rd SE26
10 A 5 Larken dri Watf
24 C 10 Larkfield av Harrow
9 N 8 Larkfield gro Enf
84 K 10 Larkfield rd Rich
114 K 8 Larkfield rd Sidcp
89 X 5 Larkhall la SW4
89 V 6 Larkhall ri SW4
63 O 4 Lark row E2
135 Z 6 Lark row E2
20 H 14 Larkshall cres E4
20 H 11 Larkshall rd E4
31 O 2 Larkspur clo N17
20 C 15 Larkswood rd E4
25 Z 14 Larkway clo NW9
144 F 15 Lanarch rd W6
86 L 13 Larpent av SW15
41 P 15 Larwood clo Grnfd
41 R 1 Lascelles av Harrow
51 X 8 Lascelles clo E11
17 R 20 Lascotts rd N22
95 S 13 Lassa rd SE9
76 L 14 Lassell st SE10
34 J 5 Latchett rd E18
102 K 11 Latchmere clo Rich
88 L 6 Latchmere gro SW11
102 L 14 Latchmere la Kingst
88 L 5 Latchmere pas SW11
88 M 8 Latchmere rd SW11
102 K 17 Latchmere rd Kingst
103 N 15 Latchmere rd Kingst
88 L 4 Latchmere st SW11
72 G 17 Lateward rd Brentf
83 X 17 Latham clo Twick
98 F 13 Latham rd Bxly Hth
83 X 18 Latham rd Twick
18 J 2 Lathkill clo Enf
66 E 1 Lathom rd E6
66 G 4 Latimer av E6
152 K 8 Latimer clo Worc Pk
31 S 18 Latimer clo N15
136 C 4 Latimer pl W10
52 J 11 Latimer rd E7
106 A 16 Latimer rd SW19
62 M 15 Latimer rd W10
136 D 5 Latimer rd W10
5 N 10 Latimer rd Barnt
156 J 5 Latimer rd Croy
101 V 12 Latimer rd Tedd
63 T 15 Latimer st E1
151 R 15 Latona rd SE15
18 H 6 Latymer rd N9
18 C 9 Latymer way N9
102 G 6 Lauderdale dri Rich
129 Y 15 Lauderdale rd W9
130 A 15 Lauderdale rd W9
149 N 10 Laud st SE11
156 M 6 Laud st Croy
58 A 4 Laughton rd Grnfd
112 G 10 Launcelot rd Brom
141 S 18 Launcelot st SE1
60 C 2 Launceston gdns Grnfd
146 A 2 Launceston pl W8
60 C 3 Launceston rd Grnfd
76 F 7 Launch st E14
144 K 15 Laundry rd
29 N 12 Lauradale rd N2
8 D 17 Laura clo Enf
34 K 15 Laura clo E18
50 B 12 Laura pl E5
101 V 1 Laurel av Twick
8 A 6 Laurelbank rd Enf
115 N 7 Laurel clo Sidcp
159 O 6 Laurel cres Croy
57 P 5 Laurel cres Rom
17 S 2 Laurel dri N21
20 D 2 Laurel gdns E4
12 K 11 Laurel gdns NW7
71 T 2 Laurel gdns W7
82 A 11 Laurel gdns Hounsl
110 B 18 Laurel gro SE20
110 G 11 Laurel gro SE26
86 F 5 Laurel rd SW13
104 H 20 Laurel rd SW20
101 P 13 Laurel rd Tedd
49 V 18 Laurel st E8
23 V 2 Laurels the Harrow
15 N 11 Laurel view N12
14 L 10 Laurel way N20
34 C 12 Laurel way E18
160 F 9 Laurence Poutney hill EC4
160 F 9 Laurence Poutney la EC4
9 S 10 Laurence rd Enf
92 J 1 Laurie gro SE14
59 T 14 Lauri rd W7
39 R 14 Laurie wlk Rom
47 S 10 Laurier rd NW5
123 U 16 Laurier rd Croy
11 P 19 Laurimel clo Stanm
63 S 1 Lauriston rd E9
105 O 15 Lauriston rd SW19
30 G 13 Lausanne rd N8
92 D 4 Lausanne rd SE15
49 O 13 Lavell st N16
43 V 3 Lavender av NW9
120 J 1 Lavender av Mitch
153 N 5 Lavender av Worc Pk
155 P 9 Lavender clo Carsh
88 M 9 Lavender gdns SW11
7 X 4 Lavender gdns Enf
120 K 2 Lavender gro Mitch
88 L 9 Lavender hill SW11

89 O 8	Lavender hill SW11
7 T 15	Lavender hill Enf
88 G 7	Lavender hill SW11
155 P 10	Lavender rd Carsh
122 B 14	Lavender rd Croy
8 C 5	Lavender rd Enf
154 F 7	Lavender rd Sutton
51 Z 18	Lavender st E15
88 L 10	Lavender sweep SW11
155 X 14	Lavender vale Wallgtn
88 L 10	Lavender wlk SW11
124 F 15	Lavender way Croy
108 L 4	Lavengro rd SE27
105 X 2	Lavenham rd SW18
98 F 5	Lavernock rd Bxly Hth
49 T 9	Laversha rd N16
86 F 19	Laverstoke gdns SW15
145 Y 8	Laverton ms SW5
145 Y 7	Laverton pl SW5
13 S 5	Lavidge rd SE9
132 N 8	Lavina gro N1
72 C 3	Lavington rd W13
156 C 7	Lavington rd Croy
141 Z 14	Lavington st SE1
156 K 8	Lawdons gdns Croy
155 Z 19	Lawford clo Wallgtn
47 V 18	Lawford rd NW5
73 W 18	Lawford rd W4
132 B 2	Lawfords wharf NW1
16 E 3	Lawley rd N14
50 D 12	Lawley st E5
18 H 3	Lawn clo N9
112 H 16	Lawn clo Brom
118 A 4	Lawn clo New Mald
85 N 4	Lawn cres Rich
37 Y 11	Lawn Farm gro Rom
71 T 2	Lawn gdns W7
148 M 14	Lawn la SW8
149 N 15	Lawn la SW8
29 R 20	Lawn rd N6
46 K 15	Lawn rd NW3
110 M 18	Lawn rd Becknhm
11 N 18	Lawn rd Becknhm
94 A 12	Lawnside SE3
20 C 17	Lawns the E4
94 B 7	Lawns the SE3
123 O 1	Lawns the SE19
22 K 1	Lawns the Pinn
115 S 9	Lawns the Sidcp
153 T 17	Lawns the Sutton
3 L 2	Lawns way Rom
94 B 7	Lawn ter SE3
70 H 13	Lawns the S'hall
22 A 7	Lawn va Pinn
53 V 14	Lawrence av E12
32 G 4	Lawrence av N13
17 V 15	Lawrence av N13
13 P 13	Lawrence av NW7
117 Z 15	Lawrence av New Mald
118 A 16	Lawrence av New Mald
49 U 9	Lawrence bldgs N16
31 R 12	Lawrence clo N15
13 O 15	Lawrence ct NW7
56 G 9	Lawrence cres Dgnhm
25 P 8	Lawrence cres Edg
13 S 10	Lawrence gdns NW7
20 B 7	Lawrence hill E4
160 C 5	Lawrence la EC2
132 L 4	Lawrence pl N1
64 A 8	Lawrence rd E3
66 C 2	Lawrence rd E6
65 V 3	Lawrence rd E13
31 R 13	Lawrence rd N15
18 L 14	Lawrence rd N18
123 V 9	Lawrence rd SE25
72 F 10	Lawrence rd W5
100 E 18	Lawrence rd Hampt
102 E 9	Lawrence rd Rich
18 L 13	Lawrence rd N18
39 Y 17	Lawrence rd Rom
65 P 16	Lawrence st E16
13 S 12	Lawrence st NW7
146 J 15	Lawrence st SW3
119 X 13	Lawrence Weaver clo Mrdn
13 S 13	Lawrence yd N15
110 B 11	Lawrie Pk av SE26
A 13	Lawrie Pk cres SE26
110 B 12	Lawrie Pk gdns SE26
110 B 14	Lawrie Pk rd SE26
105 O 8	Lawson clo SW19
9 O 8	Lawson rd Enf
58 G 12	Lawson rd S'hall
65 Z 16	Lawsons clo E16
150 G 1	Law st SE1
63 W 10	Lawton rd E3
51 T 4	Lawton rd E10
30 D 9	Lawton rd N22
5 T 12	Lawton rd Barnt
149 Y 18	Laxley clo
131 Z 16	Laxton pl NW1
8 H 5	Layard rd Enf
123 O 3	Layard rd Thntn Hth
48 G 19	Laycock st N1
61 P 20	Layer gdns W3
44 K 1	Layfield clo NW4
44 J 1	Layfield cres NW4
44 K 2	Layfield rd NW4
159 Z 12	Layhams rd W Wckm
133 S 18	Laystall st EC1
156 H 11	Layton cres Croy
72 G 15	Layton rd Brentf
82 L 10	Layton rd Hounsl
41 T 10	Leabank clo Harrow
31 Y 17	Leabank view N15
31 W 2	Leabourne rd N16
33 T 17	Lea Bridge rd E10
50 E 6	Lea Bridge rd E10
33 X 15	Lea Bridge rd E17
96 K 13	Leachcroft av Sidcp
88 M 18	Leacroft av SW12
20 A 9	Leadale av E4
31 X 18	Leadale rd N15
160 H 7	Leaden Hall av EC3
142 J 6	Leadenhall market EC3
142 J 7	Leadenhall pl EC3
142 K 6	Leadenhall st EC3
53 X 16	Leader av E12
43 V 9	Leadings the Wemb
108 F 11	Leaf gro SE27
108 H 16	Leafield clo SW16
119 W 5	Leafield rd SW20
153 Y 4	Leafield rd Sutton
112 L 8	Leafy Oak rd SE12
157 T 3	Leafy way Croy
42 L 14	Lea gdns Wemb
50 D 9	Leagrave st E5
51 O 3	Lea Hall rd E10
93 X 13	Leahurst rd SE13
94 A 15	Leahurst rd SE13
141 R 18	Leake st SE1
31 U 17	Lealand rd N15
33 O 17	Leamington av E17
112 K 12	Leamington av Brom
119 U 8	Leamington av Mrdn
112 K 11	Leamington clo Brom
83 O 12	Leamington clo Hounsl
42 S 15	Leamington clo E12
40 C 10	Leamington cres Harrow
54 K 7	Leamington gdns Ilf
61 X 16	Leamington pk W3
137 R 3	Leamington rd vlls W11
74 L 11	Leamore st W6
144 A 7	Leamore st W6
64 K 18	Leamouth rd E14
90 E 16	Leander rd SW2
58 G 5	Leander rd Grnfd
122 E 8	Leander rd Thntn Hth
125 O 2	Lea rd Becknhm
8 A 6	Lea rd Enf
70 B 11	Lea rd S'hall
66 J 19	Learoyd gdns E6
113 W 7	Leas dale SE9
114 L 15	Leas grn Chisl
29 O 11	Leaside av N10
5 B 5	Leaside rd E5
51 O 3	Leasowes rd E10
81 P 7	Leather Bottle grn Belvdr
121 O 4	Leather clo Mitch
63 T 10	Leatherdale st E1
64 M 4	Leather gdns E15
49 T 13	Leatherhead rd N16
133 T 19	Leather la EC1
141 T 2	Leather la EC1
142 J 18	Leathermarket st SE1
40 L 10	Leathsail rd Harrow
88 M 11	Leathwaite rd SW11
93 R 5	Leathwell rd SE4
98 M 11	Lea vale Bxly Hth
51 V 12	Lea Valley rd E4
9 Y 19	Lea Valley rd Enf
125 O 9	Leaveland clo Becknhm
59 S 7	Leaver gdns Grnfd
10 M 19	Leavesden rd Stanm
11 N 20	Leavesden rd Stanm
50 G 5	Leaway E10
87 X 14	Lebanon gdns SW18
84 B 20	Lebanon pk Twick
87 X 14	Lebanon rd SW18
157 T 2	Lebanon rd Croy
94 G 9	Lebrun sq SE3
34 M 7	Lechmere appr Ilf
34 M 7	Lechmere av Ilf
44 K 18	Lechmere rd NW2
106 E 2	Leckford rd SW18
80 L 17	Leckwith av Bxly Hth
146 F 10	Lecky st SW7
86 D 9	Leaconfield av SW13
29 N 13	Leconfield rd N5
9 S 4	Leda av E13
137 T 7	Ledbury ms N W11
137 S 8	Ledbury ms W W11
157 N 9	Ledbury pl Croy
137 S 7	Ledbury rd W11
157 N 9	Ledbury rd Croy
151 U 17	Ledbury st SE15
109 W 16	Ledrington rd SE19
42 M 1	Ledway dri Wemb
43 N 1	Ledway dri Wemb
37 X 19	Lee av Rom
155 P 6	Leechcroft rd Wallgtn
94 A 10	Lee Church st SE13
32 E 6	Lee clo E17
50 L 14	Lee Conservancy rd E9
4 E 14	Leecroft rd Barnt
48 D 4	Leeds pla N4
54 F 4	Leeds rd Ilf
18 J 17	Leek st N18
93 V 9	Lee High rd SE13
133 N 12	Leeke st WC1
71 Z 2	Leeland rd W13
72 A 2	Leeland ter W13
54 C 12	Leeland way NW10
94 B 10	Lee pk SE3
19 V 8	Lee Parkway N9
27 R 2	Lee rd NW7
94 C 11	Lee rd SE3
8 K 20	Lee rd Enf
60 D 3	Lee rd Grnfd
120 B 1	Lee rd Mitch
71 Z 2	Leeside rd W13
72 A 2	Leeside ter W13
94 B 10	Leeside rd N9
90 H 12	Leeson rd SE24
139 T 8	Lees pl W1
158 L 3	Lees the Croy
134 M 3	Lee st E8
135 N 3	Lee st E8
94 A 8	Lee ter SE3
93 Z 8	Lee ter SE3
7 W 6	Lee view Enf
105 U 14	Leeward gdns SW19
22 C 2	Leeway clo Pinn
75 Y 13	Leeway SE8
63 Z 4	Lefevre wk E3
64 C 5	Lefroy rd W12
41 J 1	Legard rd N5
94 M 13	Legatt rd SE9
95 N 12	Legatt rd SE9
64 G 6	Legatt rd E15
93 T 12	Legge st SE13
62 F 5	Leghorn rd NW10
79 T 14	Leghorn rd SE18
119 Y 14	Legion ct Mrdn
59 P 4	Legion rd Grnfd
56 L 5	Legion av Rom
140 G 9	Leicester ct WC2
152 M 7	Leicester ct Worc Pk
36 J 20	Leicester gdns Ilf
140 G 9	Leicester pl W1
34 J 16	Leicester rd E11
36 K 11	Leicester rd N2
43 Z 20	Leicester rd NW10
5 R 14	Leicester rd Barnt
123 S 18	Leicester rd Croy
140 G 10	Leicester sq WC2
43 S 11	Leicester st W1
108 A 7	Leigham av SW16
108 B 5	Leigham Ct rd SW16
17 U 19	Leigham dri Islwth
108 E 6	Leigham vale SW16
35 O 13	Leigh av Ilf
117 X 8	Leigh clo New Mald
41 S 5	Leigh ct Harrow
159 T 16	Leigh cres Croy
62 M 6	Leigh gdns NW10
128 C 9	Leigh gdns NW10
A 17	Leigh Hunt st SE1
108 D 7	Leigh Orchard clo SW6
141 T 1	Leigh pl EC1
97 O 4	Leigh pl Welling
53 V 19	Leigh rd E6
51 V 2	Leigh rd E10
48 J 13	Leigh rd N5
83 P 10	Leigh rd Hounsl
132 J 15	Leigh st WC1
53 W 16	Leighton av E12
58 B 10	Leighton av Pinn
25 R 7	Leighton clo Edg
97 W 14	Leighton cres NW5
62 L 5	Leighton gdns NW10
128 C 7	Leighton gdns NW10
47 W 14	Leighton gro NW5
47 W 16	Leighton pl NW5
47 V 15	Leighton rd NW5
71 Z 5	Leighton rd W13
72 A 5	Leighton rd W13
8 H 18	Leighton rd Enf
122 H 20	Leighton st Croy
85 V 9	Leinster av SW14
138 B 7	Leinster gdns W2
138 B 10	Leinster ms W2
138 A 7	Leinster pl W2
29 T 13	Leinster rd N10
129 U 11	Leinster rd NW6
137 W 7	Leinster sq W2
138 B 10	Leinster ter W2
43 Y 4	Leith clo NW9
108 C 9	Leithcote gdns SW16
63 X 14	Leith rd E3
30 H 4	Leith rd N22
129 U 4	Leith yrd NW6
143 R 7	Leman st E1
11 R 17	Lemark clo Stanm
112 H 6	Le May av SE12
76 M 15	Lemmon rd SE10
52 A 2	Lemna rd E11
96 A 15	Lemonwell ct SE9
31 Y 17	Lemsford clo N15
88 B 16	Lemuel st SW18
74 M 9	Lena gdns W6
144 D 2	Lena gdns W6
89 Y 8	Lendal ter SW9
117 P 20	Lenelby rd Surb
94 B 11	Lenham SE12
81 O 17	Lenham rd Bxly Hth
154 B 9	Lenham rd Sutton
123 O 4	Lenham rd Thntn Hth
110 K 17	Lennard rd Becknhm
127 U 20	Lennard rd Brom
122 K 19	Lennard rd Croy
39 T 19	Lennox clo Rom
44 E 13	Lennox gdns NW10
147 N 4	Lennox gdns SW1
53 S 3	Lennox gdns Croy
147 N 4	Lennox Gdns ms SW1
32 M 18	Lennox rd E17
48 E 7	Lennox rd N4
97 Y 11	Lenor clo Bxly Hth
80 G 7	Lensbury way SE18
80 G 8	Lensbury way SE18
65 X 1	Lens rd E7
146 B 5	Lenthall pl SW7
49 W 20	Lenthall rd E8
77 P 13	Lenthorpe rd Brom
112 C 7	Lentmead rd Brom
79 R 10	Lenton st SE18
111 P 12	Leof cres SE6
120 D 13	Leominster rd Mrdn
120 C 13	Leominster wlk Mrdn
120 D 12	Leonard av Mrdn
56 M 4	Leonard av Rom
20 B 19	Leonard rd E4
52 E 13	Leonard rd E7
18 J 12	Leonard rd N9
107 U 20	Leonard rd SW16
78 D 3	Leonard st E16
134 G 16	Leonard st EC2
105 W 12	Leopold av SW19
33 O 16	Leopold rd E17
28 G 9	Leopold rd N2
62 B 1	Leopold rd NW10
105 X 11	Leopold rd SW19
72 M 2	Leopold rd W5
73 N 2	Leopold rd W5
19 N 18	Leopold rd N18
63 Z 14	Leopold st E3
149 N 10	Leopold wlk SE11
75 O 19	Leo st SE14
151 Z 17	Leo st SE15
133 Y 18	Leo yd EC1
89 X 13	Leppoc rd SW4
150 J 3	Leroy st SE1
110 J 7	Lescombe clo SE23
110 J 7	Lescombe rd SE23
98 G 18	Lesley clo Bxly
153 Y 15	Leslie gdns Sutton
123 S 20	Leslie Pk rd Croy
51 V 12	Leslie rd E11
51 N 6	Leslie rd E16
28 G 10	Leslie rd N2
80 L 12	Lesnes Abbey park SE2
80 L 10	Lesnes Abbey remains Blvdr
81 Z 16	Lesney pk Erith
63 U 7	Lessada st E3
89 T 14	Lessar av SW4
106 M 8	Lessingham av SW17
107 N 10	Lessingham av SW17
35 U 9	Lessingham av Ilf
92 G 17	Lessing st SE23
38 K 19	Lessington av Rom
80 L 10	Lessness av Bxly Hth

81 P 12 Lessness pk Blvdr
81 R 15 Lessness rd Blvdr
120 E 13 Lessness rd Mrdn
65 N 11 Lester av E15
49 U 10 Leswin pl N16
49 U 9 Leswin rd N16
62 H 8 Letchfrd gdns NW10
62 H 8 Letchford mews NW10
22 K 4 Letchford ter Har
126 F 11 Letchworth clo Brom
126 F 12 Letchworth dri Brom
106 M 9 Letchworth st SW17
93 T 4 Lethbridge rd SE10
145 N 19 Letterstone rd SW6
87 V 3 Lettice st SW6
64 J 2 Lett rd E15
91 R 4 Lettsom st SE5
65 S 6 Lettsom wlk E13
32 H 16 Leucha rd E17
105 R 2 Levana clo SW19
110 K 4 Levendale rd SE23
64 J 16 Leven rd E14
146 M 6 Leverett st SW3
113 W 9 Leverholem gdns SE9
90 A 4 Leverhurst way SW4
107 V 16 Leverson st SW16
133 Y 14 Lever st EC1
134 A 14 Lever st EC1
47 U 15 Leverton pl NW5
47 U 14 Leverton st NW5
54 H 17 Levett rd Bark
54 H 18 Levett rd Bark
54 K 11 Levett rd Ilf
68 K 6 Levine gdns Bark
47 W 5 Levison way N19
40 H 18 Lewes clo Grnfd
15 W 18 Lewes rd N12
127 N 3 Lewes rd Brom
105 O 2 Lewesdon clo SW19
49 U 2 Leweston pl N16
25 W 18 Lewgars av NW9
85 Z 9 Lewin rd SW14
107 Z 13 Lewin rd SW16
97 Z 11 Lewin rd Bxly Hth
33 O 4 Lewis av E17
43 X 16 Lewis cres NW10
28 G 8 Lewis gdns N2
33 U 9 Lewis gro SE13
93 T 12 Lewisham High st SE13
93 U 6 Lewisham hill SE13
93 T 14 Lewisham pk SE13
93 T 3 Lewisham rd SE13
140 G 19 Lewisham st SW1
93 S 5 Lewisham way SE4
92 L 2 Lewisham way SE14
120 J 3 Lewis rd Mitch
84 H 13 Lewis rd Rich
115 Y 7 Lewis rd Sidcp
70 C 5 Lewis rd S'hall
154 B 7 Lewis rd Sutton
97 U 8 Lewis rd Welling
37 O 18 Lexden dri Rom
73 T 2 Lexden rd W3
121 W 8 Lexden rd Mitch
145 X 4 Lexham gdns W8
145 Y 5 Lexham Gdns ms SW7
145 V 4 Lexham ms W8
145 X 3 Lexham wlk W8
140 D 8 Lexington st W1
4 C 15 Lexington way Barnt
89 Z 20 Lexton gdns SW12
72 D 5 Leyborne av W13
85 O 1 Leyborne pk Rich
126 E 13 Leybourne clo Brom
52 C 4 Leybourne rd E11
25 O 15 Leybourne rd NW9
94 E 13 Leybridge ct SE12
33 T 13 Leyburn clo E17
157 S 3 Leyburn gdns Croy
18 K 19 Leyburn gro N18
18 L 19 Leyburn rd N18
99 X 2 Leycroft gdns Erith
142 M 2 Leyden st E1
143 N 3 Leyden st E1
65 Z 19 Leyes rd E16
66 A 19 Leyes rd E16
152 C 1 Leyfield Worc Pk
9 V 8 Leyland av Enf
17 Y 17 Leyland gdns Wdfd Grn
94 D 13 Leyland rd SE12
75 T 19 Leylang rd SE14
69 Y 2 Leys av Dgnhm
23 R 14 Leys clo Harrow
98 K 11 Leys rd Bxly Hth
113 S 4 Leysdown rd SE9
74 H 7 Leysfield rd W12
6 B 16 Leys gdns Barnt

52 C 3 Leyspring rd E11
9 V 5 Leys Rd East Enf
9 V 5 Leys Rd West Enf
28 D 13 Leys the Harrow
24 L 18 Leys the Harrow
36 D 20 Ley st Ilf
53 Y 8 Ley st Ilf
54 C 5 Ley st Ilf
36 G 14 Leyswood dri Ilf
73 V 6 Leythe rd W3
33 T 20 Leyton Grn rd E10
51 U 8 Leyton Pk rd E10
51 V 14 Leyton rd E15
106 E 18 Leyton rd SW19
51 Y 13 Leytonstone rd E15
64 M 5 Leywick st E15
75 W 17 Liardet st SE14
48 J 17 Liberia rd N5
120 E 1 Liberty av Mitch
106 F 20 Liberty av Mitch
149 R 20 Liberty st SW8
90 D 1 Liberty st SW9
39 R 15 Liberty the Rom
63 Y 4 Libra rd E3
65 S 5 Libra rd E13
141 X 19 Library st SE1
84 J 11 Lichfield gdns Rich
27 Y 5 Lichfield gro N3
28 A 7 Lichfield gro N3
66 B 10 Lichfield rd N9
18 J 8 Lichfield rd N9
45 S 11 Lichfield rd NW2
63 W 9 Lichfield rd E3
55 S 10 Lichfield rd Dgnhm
85 N 2 Lichfield rd Rich
21 N 14 Lichfield rd Wdfd Grn
14 D 19 Lidbury rd NW7
24 H 11 Liddell clo Harrow
62 M 5 Liddell gdns NW10
128 C 7 Liddell gdns NW10
28 M 6 Lidden rd Brom
24 H 16 Lidding rd Harrow
65 P 3 Liddington rd E15
65 U 10 Liddon rd E13
27 N 6 Liddon rd Brom
49 O 13 Lidfield rd N16
106 E 3 Lidiard rd SW18
132 B 10 Lidlington pl NW1
47 S 4 Lidyard rd N19
73 T 13 Liffler rd SE18
87 P 10 Lifford st SW15
17 U 12 Lightcliffe rd N13
30 A 15 Lightfoot rd N8
60 L 2 Lightley clo Wemb
19 Y 19 Lilac clo E4
72 G 8 Lilac gdns W5
159 O 5 Lilac gdns Croy
57 O 4 Lilac gdns Rom
62 F 19 Lilac st W12
95 R 13 Lilburne gdns SE9
95 S 13 Lilburne rd SE9
58 U 16 Lile cres W7
90 J 4 Lilford rd SE5
34 J 4 Lilian gdns Wdfd Grn
107 U 20 Lilian rd SW16
55 T 15 Lillechurch rd Dgnhm
120 F 14 Lilleshall rd Mrdn
12 M 15 Lilley la NW7
73 O 7 Lillian av W3
41 O 15 Lillian Board way Grnfd
74 H 16 Lillie rd SW6
57 V 13 Lillie Bridge Mews
144 H 16 Lillie rd SW6
145 P 14 Little rd SW6
145 T 13 Lillie yd
89 T 7 Lillieshall rd SW4
148 C 7 Lillington gdn estate SW1
58 D 3 Lilliput av Grnfd
57 N 1 Lilliput rd Rom
144 J 8 Lily clo
60 E 7 Lily gdns Wemb
33 P 19 Lily rd E17
87 V 1 Lilyville rd SW6
56 B 2 Limbourne av Dgnhm
88 K 11 Limburg rd SW11
13 N 18 Lime av NW7
154 L 1 Lime clo Carsh
38 K 14 Lime clo Rom
137 V 11 Lime ct W8
14 G 4 Lime gro N20
79 L 4 Lime gro W12
74 L 4 Lime gro W12
136 B 16 Lime gro W12
117 Z 6 Lime gro New Mald
96 L 15 Lime gro Sidcp
83 X 16 Lime gro Twick
81 N 7 Lime row Belvdr
63 Z 20 Limehouse causeway E14
89 U 19 Limerick clo SW12
146 D 14 Limeston st SW10

34 J 14 Limes av E11
15 R 12 Limes av N12
27 T 20 Limes av NW11
86 C 5 Limes av SW13
154 L 1 Limes av Carsh
156 E 6 Limes av Croy
110 A 19 Limes av SE20
16 G 16 Limes av the N11
25 V 8 Limesdale gdns Edg
86 A 7 Limes Field rd SW14
92 E 10 Limesford rd SE15
87 Y 17 Limes gdns SW18
93 U 10 Limes gro SE13
11 N 9 Limes house Stanm
125 S 3 Limes rd Becknhm
123 N 16 Limes rd Croy
32 H 13 Limes st E17
142 J 7 Limes st EC3
72 H 7 Limes wlk W5
92 B 9 Limes wlk SE15
59 T 20 Lime ter W7
159 N 5 Lime Tree gro Croy
121 S 1 Limetree pl Mitch
110 A 20 Lime Tree av SE20
108 D 2 Lime Tree clo SW12
82 K 1 Lime Tree rd Hounsl
70 K 20 Lime Tree rd Hounsl
158 L 6 Lime Tree rd Hounsl
10 F 6 Lime Tree wk Bushey Watf
7 X 3 Lime Tree wlk Enf
60 C 16 Limewood clo W13
81 Y 19 Limewood rd Erith
105 P 3 Limpsfield av SW19
122 D 12 Limpsfield av Thntn Hth
151 T 18 Limpston Gdn estate SE15
44 K 18 Linacre rd NW2
75 X 11 Linberry wk SE8
94 D 19 Linchmere rd SE12
16 G 10 Lincoln av N14
105 O 7 Lincoln av SW19
57 O 4 Lincoln av Rom
100 M 3 Lincoln av Twick
101 O 2 Lincoln av Twick
99 T 5 Lincoln clo Erith
58 N 3 Lincoln clo Grnfd
22 E 16 Lincoln clo Harrow
49 P 2 Lincoln ct N16
8 F 17 Lincoln cres Enf
53 S 1 Lincoln gdns Ilf
129 N 3 Lincoln rd NW6
53 N 19 Lincoln rd E12
65 U 13 Lincoln rd E13
34 D 6 Lincoln rd E18
28 K 11 Lincoln rd N2
123 Z 7 Lincoln rd SE25
8 L 17 Lincoln rd Enf
9 P 18 Lincoln rd Enf
99 U 4 Lincoln rd Erith
100 D 7 Lincoln rd Felt
22 F 16 Lincoln rd Harrow
117 V 6 Lincoln rd New Mald
115 R 12 Lincoln rd Sidcp
42 G 18 Lincoln rd Wemb
118 H 19 Lincoln rd Worc Pk
122 A 10 Lincoln rd Mitch
141 O 5 Lincolns Inn fields WC2
13 S 9 Lincolns the NW7
51 Y 7 Lincoln st E11
147 O 8 Lincoln st SW3
8 M 16 Lincoln way Enf
112 C 7 Lincombe rd Brom
13 S 9 Lincons the NW7
7 O 15 Lindal cres Enf
92 L 14 Lindal rd SE4
38 M 14 Lindbergh rd Wallgtn
128 E 11 Linden av NW10
8 K 6 Linden av Enf
82 K 12 Linden av Hounsl
122 H 8 Linden av Thntn Hth
42 M 14 Linden av Wemb
43 N 14 Linden av Wemb
6 G 19 Linden clo N14
11 N 16 Linden clo Stanm
74 L 2 Linden ct W12
41 V 17 Linden cres Grnfd
117 N 4 Linden cres Kingst
21 U 18 Linden cres Wdfd Grn
137 V 11 Linden gdns W2
73 Z 13 Linden gdns W4
8 K 5 Linden gdns Enf
92 A 8 Linden gro SE15
110 D 16 Linden gro SE20
118 A 6 Linden gro New Mald
101 V 11 Linden gro Tedd
42 L 14 Linden lawns Wemb
26 L 2 Linden lea N2
159 X 2 Linden lees Wkhm

137 U 11 Linden ms W11
29 T 13 Linden rd N10
16 A 8 Linden rd N11
30 L 13 Linden rd N15
100 G 20 Linden rd Hampt
39 O 14 Linden st Rom
6 H 20 Linden way N14
16 H 1 Linden way N14
159 U 13 Lindens the Croy
15 T 16 Lindens the N12
46 B 14 Lindfield gdns NW3
60 D 11 Lindfield rd W5
123 V 15 Lindfield rd Croy
64 B 17 Lindfield st E14
104 G 19 Lindisfarne rd SW20
55 T 9 Lindisfarne rd Dgnhm
51 T 6 Lindley rd E10
63 O 14 Lindley st E1
143 Z 1 Lindley st E1
88 L 12 Lindore rd SW11
120 C 18 Lindores rd Carsh
154 E 11 Lind rd Sutton
88 C 4 Lindrop st SW6
24 M 16 Lindsay dri Harrow
100 L 10 Lindsay rd Hampt
152 K 2 Lindsay rd Worc Pk
67 O 4 Lindsell rd Bark
93 T 1 Lindsell st SE10
122 A 8 Lindsey clo Mitch
55 S 11 Lindsey rd Dgnhm
141 Y 1 Lindsey st EC1
93 P 4 Lind st SE4
102 C 18 Lindum rd Tedd
108 J 13 Lindway SE27
33 V 11 Linford rd E17
89 U 2 Linford st SW8
93 V 11 Lingards rd SE13
114 L 3 Lingey clo Sidcp
116 K 9 Lingfield av Kingst
8 D 19 Lingfield clo Enf
96 E 10 Lingfield cres SE9
19 N 2 Lingfield gdns N9
105 P 14 Lingfield rd SW19
152 M 6 Lingfield rd Worc Pk
90 B 5 Lingham st SW9
4 C 16 Lingholm way Barnt
65 T 14 Ling rd E13
81 Y 17 Ling rd Erith
21 U 9 Lingrove gdns Buck Hl
109 O 3 Lings coppice SE21
106 K 6 Lingwell rd SW17
71 T 18 Lingwood gdns Islwth
49 Y 1 Lingwood rd E5
31 X 20 Lingwood rd N16
131 N 18 Linhope st NW1
14 E 14 Linkfield Brom
83 Y 5 Linkfield rd Islwth
155 Y 13 Link la Wallgtn
156 A 13 Link la Wallgtn
26 B 3 Linklea clo NW9
16 B 13 Link rd N11
69 T 7 Link rd Dgnhm
155 O 1 Link rd Wallgtn
39 Z 6 Links av Rom
14 M 6 Links dri N20
108 F 18 Links gdns SW16
14 J 18 Linkside N12
118 B 4 Linkside New Mald
7 S 12 Linkside clo Enf
8 R 11 Linkside gdns Enf
44 C 8 Links rd NW2
107 R 17 Links rd W3
61 P 16 Links rd W3
125 V 20 Links rd W Wkhm
21 S 16 Links rd Wdfd Grn
7 S 12 Links side Enf
32 H 13 Links the E17
50 D 16 Links the E9
27 V 3 Links view N3
10 L 20 Links View clo Watf
159 O 4 Links View rd Croy
101 O 11 Links View rd Hampt
27 O 8 Linksway NW4
125 P 14 Links way Becknhm
61 S 16 Link the W3
9 V 5 Links the Enf
20 D 16 Link the Grnfd
20 D 4 Link the Wemb
118 L 6 Linkway SW20
127 R 16 Link way Brom
55 U 11 Linkway Dgnhm
102 B 5 Linkway Rich
4 M 20 Linkway the Barnt
154 E 20 Linkway the Sutton
38 J 9 Linley cres Rom
31 S 7 Linley rd N17
27 Z 19 Linnell clo NW11
27 Z 20 Linnell rd NW11
18 K 15 Linnell rd N18
91 S 3 Linnell rd SE5

68 G 20 Linnet clo SE2
20 H 13 Linnett clo E4
90 A 11 Linon rd SW2
50 C 13 Linscott rd E5
151 S 5 Linsey st SE16
45 X 19 Linstead st NW6
87 S 18 Linstead way SW18
42 F 17 Linthorpe av Wemb
49 T 1 Linthorpe rd N16
5 W 12 Linthorpe rd Barnt
97 O 3 Linton clo Well
39 O 7 Linton ct Rom
108 L 11 Linton gro SE27
54 B 20 Linton rd Bark
67 O 1 Linton rd Bark
67 P 1 Linton rd Bark
134 C 5 Linton st N1
87 W 5 Linver rd SW6
29 Z 13 Linzee rd N8
101 V 2 Lion av Twick
95 O 12 Lionel gdns SE9
95 O 12 Lionel rd SE9
72 L 13 Lionel rd Brentf
73 O 14 Lionel rd Brentf
85 N 5 Lion gdns Rich
84 M 6 Lion Ga gdns Rich
18 J 9 Lion rd N9
98 A 10 Lion rd Bxly Hth
122 L 13 Lion rd Croy
101 V 1 Lion rd Twick
112 M 8 Lions clo SE9
113 N 8 Lionsdale clo SE9
72 F 18 Lion way Brentf
84 A 8 Lion wharf Islwth
82 B 19 Liphook cres SE23
63 S 18 Lipton st E1
100 M 5 Lisbon av Twick

101 N 4 Lisbon av Twick
46 M 13 Lisburne rd NW3
91 V 1 Lisford st SE15
145 N 6 Lisgar ter W14
114 C 16 Liskeard clo Chisl
94 F 2 Liskeard gdns SE3
140 G 9 Lisle st W1
83 Y 5 Lismore clo Islwth
31 O 11 Lismore rd N17
157 R 15 Lismore rd S Croy
47 P 12 Lissenden gdns NW5
130 G 15 Lisson gro NW8
130 K 20 Lisson st NW1
7 Z 16 Lister gdns N18
18 A 16 Lister gdns N18
52 A 5 Lister rd E11
31 W 5 Liston rd N17
89 V 8 Liston rd SW4
34 L 2 Liston way Wdfd Grn
56 E 8 Listowel rd Dgnhm
149 X 20 Listowel st SW9
149 X 20 Llstowell clo SW9
49 T 6 Listria pk N16
51 Z 18 Litchfield av E15
119 V 16 Litchfield av Mrdn
44 G 19 Litchfield gdns NW10
154 B 9 Litchfield rd Sutton
140 H 8 Litchfield st WC2
28 C 16 Litchfield way NW11
141 R 8 Lit Essex st WC2
37 Q 13 Lit Heath lodge Rom
46 C 17 Lithos rd NW3
75 O 10 Litlington st SE16
151 Y 5 Litlington st SE16
125 P 7 Little acre Bcknhm
131 Z 14 Little Albany st NW1
140 A 6 Little Argyll st W1
114 H 5 Little birches Sidcp
146 A 11 Little Boltons the SW10
109 S 8 Little Bournes SE21
141 Y 2 Little Britain EC1
142 A 3 Little Britain EC1
160 A 3 Little Britain EC1
89 X 8 Littlebury rd SW4
18 C 4 Little Bury st N9
10 C 1 Little Bushey la Bushey Watf
15 P 12 Little Cedars N12
139 W 20 Little Chester st SW1
148 J 2 Little College st SW1
77 W 16 Littlecombe SE7
87 P 15 Littlecombe clo SW15
87 R 18 Little Cote clo SW19
22 C 3 Little clo P Inn
159 Z 3 Little ct W Wkhm
159 Z 3 Little court W Wkhm
59 V 7 Littlecroft SE9
80 A 17 Littledale SE2
107 T 3 Little Dimocks SW4
142 C 10 Little Dorrit ct SE1
72 F 9 Little Ealing la W5
47 V 11 Littlefield clo N19
25 U 1 Littlefield rd Edg
20 M 3 Little Friday hill E4

140 J 19 Little George st SW1
47 S 12 Little Green st NW5
5 X 20 Little gro Barnt
78 D 14 Little Heath SE7
37 P 14 Little Heath Rom
81 P 20 Little Heath rd Bxly Hth
98 A 1 Little Heath rd Bxly Hth
157 Z 17 Little Heath rd S Croy
158 A 20 Littleheath rd S Croy
53 U 11 Little Ilford la E12
59 V 16 Little John rd W7
140 B 7 Little Marlborough st W1
113 U 7 Littlemede st SE9
54 E 10 Littlemoor rd Ilf
80 A 7 Littlemore rd SE2
22 C 7 Little Moss la Pinn
140 G 9 Little Newport st WC2
141 U 5 Little New st EC4
22 A 7 Little Orchard clo Pinn
100 A 4 Little Park dri Felt
8 A 12 Little Park gdns Enf
21 Z 5 Little Plucketts la Buck Hl
140 A 3 Little Portland st W1
10 D 2 Little Potters Watf
101 V 15 Little Queens rd Tedd
127 P 2 Little Redlands Brom
106 F 20 Littlers clo SW19
140 J 2 Little Russell st WC1
140 H 19 Little Sanctuary SW1
148 H 1 Little Smith st SW7
143 N 6 Little Somerset st E1
111 P 16 Littlestone clo Becknhm
26 D 7 Little Strand NW9
140 B 15 Little St James st SW1
85 W 8 St Leonards SW14
140 A 3 Little Titchfield st W1
21 O 6 Littleton av Ev
41 W 7 Littleton cres Harrow
41 X 8 Littleton rd Harrow
106 D 5 Littleton st SW18
160 B 8 Little Trinity la EC4
138 B 1 Little Venice W2
93 V 15 Littlewood SE13
72 B 9 Littlewood clo W13
150 D 11 Liverpool gro SE17
33 V 17 Liverpool rd E10
65 N 15 Liverpool rd E16
133 U 2 Liverpool rd N1
48 F 17 Liverpool rd N7
72 H 5 Liverpool rd W5
103 R 17 Liverpool rd Kingst
122 M 7 Liverpool rd Thntn Hth
142 J 2 Liverpool st EC2
142 K 2 Liverpool St station EC2
151 T 14 Livesey pl SE15
76 F 14 Livingstone pl E14
64 H 4 Livingstone rd E15
33 R 18 Livingstone rd E17
17 N 18 Livingstone rd N13
88 G 8 Livingstone rd SW11
82 M 9 Livingstone rd Hounsl
83 N 9 Livingstone rd Hounsl
58 A 20 Livingstone rd S'hall
123 N 4 Livingstone rd Thntn Hth
66 L 18 Livingstone st E6
140 D 7 Livonia st W1
134 C 15 Lizard st EC1
77 V 19 Lizban st SE10
45 W 8 Llanelly rd NW2
78 K 18 Llanover rd SE18
42 G 10 Llanover rd Wemb
120 F 13 Llanthony rd Mrdn
45 W 7 Llanvanor rd NW2
17 T 18 Llewellyn st SE16
122 B 1 Lloyd av SW16
132 U 9 Lloyd Baker st WC1
33 N 7 Lloyd park E17
157 V 8 Lloyd park Croy
66 F 4 Lloyd rd E6
32 F 13 Lloyd rd E17
56 C 19 Lloyd rd Dgnhm
153 N 4 Lloyd rd Worc Pk
142 L 7 Lloyds av EC3
94 A 5 Lloyds pl SE3
133 R 13 Lloyds sq WC1
133 V 13 Lloyds row EC1

133 S 12 Lloyd st WC1
124 K 11 Lloyds way Becknhm
93 P 6 Loampit hills SE13
93 S 7 Loampit vale SE13
59 P 10 Locarno rd Grnfd
93 Z 11 Locarno rd SE13
144 E 12 Lochaline st W6
89 N 19 Lochinvar st SW12
64 G 14 Lochnagar st E14
94 N 8 Lock chase SE3
31 S 19 Locke clo Rainhm
23 U 9 Locket rd Harrow
9 X 8 Lockfield av Enf
63 Z 12 Lockhart st E3
48 C 18 Lockhart clo N7
48 C 18 Lockhart ct N7
50 F 12 Lockhurst st E5
39 Y 18 Lockington rd SW8
94 N 15 Lockmead rd N15
92 M 18 Lockmead rd SE13
81 V 17 Lockmere clo Erith
102 E 8 Lock rd Rich
121 N 2 Locks la Mitch
63 Y 15 Locksley st E14
102 B 10 Locksmead rd Rich
54 C 8 Lockwood rd Ilf
110 G 10 Lockwood clo SE26
39 R 16 Lockwood wlk Rom
32 E 7 Lockwood way E17
142 F 18 Lockyer st SE1
50 C 20 Loddiges rd E9
85 Z 8 Lodge av SW14
156 E 6 Lodge av Croy
55 P 13 Lodge av Dgnhm
68 B 3 Lodge av Dgnhm
24 J 14 Lodge av Harrow
39 U 12 Lodge av Rom
18 A 17 Lodge clo N18
12 A 18 Lodge clo Edg
155 O 1 Lodge clo Wallgtn
84 A 1 Lodge clo Islwth
154 B 10 Lodge clo Sutton
6 K 13 Lodge cres Enf
17 T 14 Lodge dri N13
124 M 12 Lodge gdns Becknhm
80 E 18 Lodge hill Welling
35 S 12 Lodge hill Ilf
15 P 15 Lodge la N12
97 V 14 Lodge la Bxly
159 P 15 Lodge la Croy
38 D 3 Lodge la Rom
26 M 12 Lodge rd NW4
130 H 15 Lodge rd NW8
112 K 14 Lodge rd Brom
122 K 15 Lodge rd Croy
122 L 17 Lodge rd Croy
155 R 10 Lodge rd Wallgtn
21 P 20 Lodge vlls Wdfd Grn
26 A 15 Lodore gdns NW9
64 F 13 Lodore st E14
143 U 18 Loftie st SE16
133 N 1 Lofting rd N1
74 K 3 Loftus rd W12
9 T 7 Logan clo Enf
145 T 5 Logan ms W8
145 T 5 Logan pl W8
19 O 9 Logan rd N9
42 J 6 Logan rd Wemb
82 D 7 Logs hill Chisl
113 R 19 Logs hill Chisl
113 S 19 Logs Hill clo Chisl
149 S 7 Lollard st SE11
141 Y 16 Loman st SE1
135 U 19 Lomas st E9
9 R 7 Lombard av Enf
54 G 5 Lombard av Ilf
141 U 7 Lombard la EC1
88 F 5 Lombard rd N11
120 B 2 Lombard rd SW11
160 G 7 Lombard st EC3
77 V 10 Lombard way SE7
137 Y 10 Lombardy pl W2
160 H 8 Lombard ct EC3
43 N 20 Lomond clo Wemb
31 S 14 Lomond clo N15
150 D 19 Lomond gro SE5
150 L 13 Lancroft rd SE5
49 R 11 Londesborough rd N16
142 F 12 London br EC4
142 H 14 London Bridge station SE1
142 F 14 London Br st SE1
135 W 3 London fields E8
49 Y 20 London fields W side E8
50 A 20 London la E8
112 F 17 London la Brom
138 G 5 London ms W2
137 Z 15 London museum W8
65 R 7 London rd E13

149 X 2 London rd SE1
110 B 2 London rd SE23
122 D 4 London rd SW16
66 M 2 London rd Bark
67 O 1 London rd Bark
112 C 19 London rd Brom
99 P 13 London rd Drtfrd
8 C 14 London rd Enf
152 K 11 London rd Epsom
41 T 7 London rd Harrow
83 X 2 London rd Islwth
84 B 1 London rd Islwth
117 N 2 London rd Kingst
107 N 19 London rd Mitch
120 K 8 London rd Mitch
121 P 17 London rd Mitch
119 X 11 London rd Mrdn
38 F 18 London rd Rom
11 U 14 London rd Stanm
153 O 4 London rd Sutton
83 Y 17 London rd Twick
155 S 3 London rd Wallgtn
42 M 17 London rd Wemb
142 L 8 London st EC3
138 G 6 London st W2
142 G 3 London wall EC2
160 C 3 London wall EC2
160 G 3 London wall EC2
140 L 6 Long acre WC2
155 P 14 Long Acre pl Carsh
33 W 4 Longacre rd E17
189 N 9 Longbeach rd SW11
45 V 8 Longberrys NW2
54 G 16 Longbridge rd Bark
55 N 12 Longbridge rd Dgnhm
93 T 12 Longbridge way SE13
113 V 7 Longcroft SE9
24 H 1 Longcroft av Edg
20 M 6 Long Deacon rd E4
111 O 9 Longdown rd SE6
62 B 16 Long dri Grnfd
58 L 4 Long dri W3
40 B 11 Long dri Pinn
22 M 5 Long elmes Harrow
23 N 4 Long elmes Harrow
63 V 10 Longfellow rd E3
32 L 20 Longfellow rd E17
33 N 18 Longfellow rd E17
152 H 1 Longfellow rd Worc Pk
26 C 4 Long field NW9
112 D 20 Longfield Brom
32 G 14 Longfield av E17
26 G 3 Longfield av NW7
60 E 20 Longfield av W5
9 R 2 Longfield av Enf
57 T 1 Longfield av Hornch
121 P 20 Longfield av Wallgtn
155 P 1 Longfield av Wallgtn
42 J 5 Longfield av Wemb
110 C 6 Longfield cres SE26
85 S 13 Longfield dri SW14
67 F 18 Longfield rd W5
87 X 19 Longfield st SW18
60 E 18 Longfield wik W5
58 J 20 Longford av S'hall
70 J 1 Longford av S'hall
100 G 10 Longford clo Hampt
31 R 18 Longford clo N15
154 D 4 Longford gdns Sutton
100 J 2 Longford rd Twick
131 Z 16 Longford st NW1
37 W 12 Longhayes av Rom
124 D 12 Longheath gdns Croy
99 P 3 Longhedge st SW11
111 X 6 Longhill rd SE6
93 X 14 Longhurst rd SE13
94 A 14 Longhurst rd SE13
124 A 14 Longhurst rd Croy
124 B 14 Longhurst rd Croy
15 N 9 Longland dri N20
115 N 6 Longlands av Sidcp
114 H 6 Longlands Pk cres Sidcp
114 J 6 Longlands rd Sidcp
141 Y 1 Long la EC1
28 D 8 Long la N2
27 Z 3 Long la N3
142 D 18 Long la SE1
80 K 20 Long la Bxly Hth
97 Z 1 Long la Bxyl Hth
124 B 14 Long la Croy
124 B 14 Long la Croy
12 E 1 Longleat av Enf
80 L 16 Longleigh la SE2
61 N 4 Longley av Wemb
106 J 14 Longley rd SW17
122 H 18 Longley rd Croy
23 P 14 Longlewy rd Harrow
20 M 14 Long leys E4
151 S 6 Longmead SE13
26 D 16 Long mead NW9

115 X 4 Longmead dri Sidcp
47 X 16 Long meadow NW5
114 G 2 Long Meadow rd Sidcp
106 L 11 Longmead rd SW17
148 B 6 Longmore st SW1
5 R 19 Longmore av Barnt
63 U 10 Longnor rd E1
93 Z 3 Long Pond rd SE3
94 A 2 Long Pond rd SE3
67 X 12 Longreach rd Bark
58 L 18 Longridge la S'hall
145 T 7 Longridge rd SW5
89 U 10 Long rd SW4
140 G 10 Longs ct WC2
75 Y 11 Longshaw rd E4
85 Z 17 Longshore SE8
87 Z 17 Longstaff cres SW18
87 Z 17 Longstaff rd SW18
62 E 3 Longstone av NW10
107 S 13 Longstone rd SW17
134 M 11 Long st E2
121 W 3 Longthornton rd SW16
109 Y 10 Longton av SE26
109 Z 10 Longton gro SE26
110 A 9 Longton gro SE26
148 L 5 Longview way Rom
49 X 5 Longville rd SE11
64 J 8 Long wall E15
50 L 1 Long wlk E15
78 L 16 Long wk SE18
86 C 8 Long wlk SW13
117 W 5 Long wlk New Mald
86 H 17 Longwood dri SW15
35 U 14 Longwood gdns Ilf
133 N 18 Long yd WC1
26 B 12 Loning the NW9
9 O 2 Loning the Enf
66 G 11 Lonsdale av E6
38 J 18 Lonsdale av Rom
42 L 16 Lonsdale av Wemb
22 C 3 Lonsdale clo Pinn
66 D 11 Lonsdale clo E6
35 Y 18 Lonsdale cres Ilf
6 K 14 Lonsdale dri Enf
7 O 14 Lonsdale dri Enf
122 C 8 Lonsdale gdns Thntn Hth
85 O 2 Lonsdale ms Rich
133 U 2 Lonsdale pl N1
34 D 20 Lonsdale rd E11
29 O 6 Lonsdale rd NW6
124 Z 8 Lonsdale rd SE25
74 F 18 Lonsdale rd SW13
86 D 3 Lonsdale rd SW13
74 C 10 Lonsdale rd W4
137 R 7 Lonsdale rd W11
98 B 5 Lonsdale rd Bxly Hth
133 T 2 Lonsdale sq N1
31 T 11 Loobert rd N15
36 A 9 Looe gdns Ilf
114 A 15 Loop rd Chisl
83 D 13 Lopen rd N18
9 P 17 Loraine clo Enf
48 C 13 Loraine rd N7
23 S 17 Loraine rd W4
35 U 10 Lord av Ilf
103 X 20 Lord Chancellor wlk Kingst
135 P 14 Lorden wlk E2
35 S 12 Lord gdns Ilf
129 Y 20 Lord Hills rd W9
148 J 2 Lord North st SW1
100 C 5 Lords clo Felt
108 M 2 Lord clo SE21
130 G 13 Lords Cricket grd NW8
144 W 19 Lord Robert's ms SW6
49 P 7 Lordship gro N16
31 O 6 Lordship la N16
30 G 6 Lordship la N22
91 V 15 Lordship la SE22
48 M 7 Lordship pk N16
49 O 6 Lordship rd N16
146 K 15 Lordship pl Sw3
49 O 4 Lordship rd N16
49 P 8 Lordship ter N16
31 S 6 Lordsmead rd N17
78 E 3 Lord st E16
78 F 9 Lord Warwick st SE18
133 O 11 Lorenzo st WC1
24 J 13 Loretto gdns Harrow
15 V 8 Loring rd N20
83 V 4 Loring rd Islwth
144 D 2 Loris rd W6
124 F 16 Lorn av Croy
130 L 15 Lorne clo NW8
34 K 14 Lorne gdns E11
136 J 17 Lorne gdns W11
124 F 16 Lorne gdns Croy
52 K 11 Lorne rd E7

33 N 17 Lorne rd E17
48 E 3 Lorne rd N4
23 V 8 Lorne rd Harrow
84 L 13 Lorne rd Rich
90 E 4 Lorn rd SW9
23 T 2 Lorraine pk Harrow
149 Y 14 Lorrimore st SE17
149 Z 13 Lorrimore sq SE17
30 J 20 Lothair rd N4
72 F 7 Lothair rd W5
30 H 20 Lothair rd south N4
88 H 8 Lothair st SW11
142 F 5 Lothbury EC2
160 F 5 Lothbury EC2
90 J 1 Lothian rd SW9
149 V 20 Lothian rd SW9
128 L 13 Lothrop st W10
146 S 19 Lots rd SW10
106 M 14 Loubet st SW17
35 Z 14 Loudoun av Ilf
36 A 15 Loudoun av Ilf
130 C 3 Loudon ms NW8
130 D 5 Loudon rd NW8
90 J 9 Loughborough pk SW9
90 F 4 Loughborough rd SW9
90 J 7 Loughborough rd SW9
149 R 10 Loughborough st SE11
48 D 16 Lough rd N7
63 S 13 Louisa st E1
52 A 17 Lousie rd E15
107 O 6 Lousville rd SW17
88 G 13 Louvaine rd SW11
44 D 11 Lovat clo NW2
142 H 10 Lovat la EC3
160 H 10 Lovat la EC3
12 E 18 Lovatt clo Edg
72 B 3 Loveday rd W13
151 T 12 Lovegrove st SE1
127 X 15 Lovelace av Brom
54 M 14 Lovelace gdns Bark
116 F 17 Lovelace gdns Surb
95 T 7 Lovelace grn SE9
108 L 2 Lovelace rd SE21
15 W 2 Lovelace rd Barnt
116 H 17 Lovelace rd Surb
160 C 3 Love la EC2
31 U 2 Love la N17
78 L 11 Love la SE18
124 A 7 Love la SE25
98 D 17 Love la Bxly
120 K 4 Love la Mitch
119 Z 17 Love la Mrdn
120 A 16 Love la Mrdn
22 A 10 Love la Pinn
153 T 13 Love la Sutton
153 U 12 Love la Sutton
96 N 5 Lovel av Well
97 N 4 Lovel av Welling
75 R 16 Lovelinch st SE15
102 D 7 Lovell rd Rich
58 J 17 Lovell rd S'hall
57 V 17 Lovell wlk Rainhm
45 V 18 Loveridge rd NW6
27 X 1 Lovers wlk N3
14 H 19 Lovers wlk NW7
120 E 17 Lovett dri Carsh
43 W 15 Lovett way NW10
91 N 4 Love wlk SE5
53 Y 14 Lowbrook rd Ilf
109 V 7 Low Cross Wood la SE21
19 N 5 Lowden rd N9
90 K 11 Lowden rd SE24
58 B 19 Lowden rd S'hall
65 T 15 Lowe av E16
53 W 17 Lowell st E14
123 W 20 Lwr Addiscombe rd Croy
147 W 2 Lwr Belgrave st SW1
71 T 4 Lwr Boston rd W7
69 R 3 Lwr Broad st Dgnhm
113 U 20 Lower Camden Chisl
127 V 1 Lower Camden Chisl
156 J 13 Lwr Church st Croy
50 B 12 Lwr Clapton rd E5
156 M 7 Lwr Combie st Croy
86 K 5 Lwr Common south SW15
105 P 20 Lwr Downs rd SW20
119 R 1 Lwr Downs rd SW20
18 K 13 Lwr Fore st N9
127 T 20 Lwr Gravel rd Brom
120 K 7 Lwr Green W Mitch
147 Y 1 Lower Grosvenor pl SW1
19 W 15 Lwr Hall la E4
102 G 14 Lwr Ham rd Kingst
116 H 1 Lwr Ham rd Kingst
96 A 7 Lwr Jackwood clo SE9

140 C 9 Lwr James st W1
140 C 9 Lwr John st W1
6 M 16 Lwr Kenwood av N14
16 H 18 Lwr Maidstone rd N11
74 K 14 Lwr mall W6
74 K 14 Lwr mall W6
144 B 11 Lwr mall W6
69 Y 7 Lwr Mardyke av Rainhm
141 R 19 Lower marsh SE1
116 M 8 Lwr Marsh la Kingst
117 R 9 Lwr Marsh la Kingst
130 K 1 Lwr Merton ri NW3
119 P 14 Lwr Morden la Mrdn
84 L 9 Lwr Mortlake rd Rich
16 G 18 Lwr Park rd N11
81 T 9 Lwr Park rd Blvdr
85 S 7 Lwr Richmond rd SW14
87 O 7 Lwr Richmond rd SW15
86 L 7 Lwr Richmond rd SW15
75 R 8 Lower rd SE16
81 U 9 Lower rd Blvdr
81 Z 10 Lower rd Erith
41 P 4 Lower rd Harrow
98 Z 6 Lower rd Rainhm
154 E 9 Lower rd Sutton
147 R 8 Lwr Sloane st SW1
99 P 16 Lwr Station rd Drtfd
26 D 8 Lower strand NW9
102 F 18 Lwr Teddington rd Kingst
116 F 2 Lwr Teddington rd Kingst
46 D 9 Lower ter NW3
142 G 10 Lwr Thames st EC3
160 H 10 Lwr Thames st EC3
10 B 1 Lower tub Watford
42 G 6 Loweswater clo Wemb
45 X 19 Lowfield rd NW6
61 V 17 Lowfield rd W3
20 L 9 Low Hall clo E4
32 J 19 Lowhall la E17
23 T 15 Lowick rd Harrow
38 F 14 Lowlands gdns Rom
23 T 20 Lowlands rd Harrow
48 D 13 Lowman rd N7
147 U 2 Lowndes clo SW1
140 S 7 Lowndes ct W1
147 T 2 Lowndes pl SW1
139 R 19 Lowndes sq SW1
147 S 1 Lowndes sq SW1
126 F 4 Lownds av Brom
63 O 20 Lowood st E1
143 Y 9 Lowood st E1
38 F 4 Lowshoe la Rom
6 M 13 Lowther dri Enf
9 N 14 Lowther dri Enf
92 J 19 Lowther hill SE23
74 E 20 Lowther rd SE13
86 E 2 Lowther rd SW13
103 N 19 Lowther rd Kingst
24 M 10 Lowther rd Stanm
32 G 8 Lowther rd E17
48 E 16 Lowther rd W7
90 M 4 Lowth rd SE5
86 B 7 Loxford av E6
54 G 14 Loxford la Ilf
54 A 18 Loxford rd Bark
54 B 17 Loxford ter Ilf
33 P 1 Loxham rd E4
110 F 12 Loxley clo SE26
88 H 20 Loxley rd SW18
100 E 10 Loxley rd Hampt
110 G 2 Loxton rd SE23
31 S 11 Loxwood rd N17
141 X 20 Lt Turnstile WC1
113 V 19 Lubbock rd Chisl
127 S 18 Lubbock st SE14
88 K 7 Lucan pl SW3
146 K 6 Lucan pl SW3
4 F 10 Lucan rd Barnt
65 W 3 Lucas av E13
40 G 6 Lucas av Harrow
110 D 16 Lucas rd SE20
93 N 3 Lucas st SE4
17 N 12 Lucerne clo N13
33 X 14 Lucerne gro E17
137 B 13 Lucerne ms E8
48 J 12 Lucerne rd N5
122 K 10 Lucerne rd Thntn Hth
151 T 4 Lucey rd SE16
107 O 10 Lucien rd SW17
105 Z 4 Lucien rd SW18
94 C 17 Lucorn clo SE12
21 Y 4 Luctons av Buck Hl
61 V 13 Lucy cres W3
56 A 10 Lucy gdns Dgnhm
81 S 18 Luddesdon rd Erith
26 A 7 Ludford clo NW9

141 X 6 Ludgate broadway EC4
141 W 6 Ludgate cir EC4
141 X 6 Ludgate hill EC4
141 X 7 Ludgate sq EC4
F 12 Ludlow clo Harrow
60 E 11 Ludlow rd W5
28 C 12 Ludlow way N2
86 C 10 Ludwick wlk SW15
75 V 18 Ludwick rd SE14
80 D 8 Luffield rd SE2
112 J 6 Luffman rd SE12
92 A 4 Lugard rd SE15
134 H 17 Luke st EC2
20 J 12 Lukin cres E4
63 P 18 Lukin st E1
115 P 17 Lullingstone clo Orp
115 O 18 Lullingstone cres Orp
81 O 14 Lullingstone rd Blvdr
14 G 17 Lullington garth N12
112 A 18 Lullington garth Brom
109 X 18 Lullington rd SE20
55 Y 20 Lullington rd Dgnhm
68 L 1 Lullington rd Dgnhm
47 T 6 Lulot gdns NW5
70 L 20 Lulworth av Hounsl
82 L 1 Lulworth av Hounsl
42 D 1 Lulworth av Wemb
40 C 9 Lulworth clo Harrow
22 A 20 Lulworth dri Pinn
40 C 8 Lulworth gdns Harrow
113 N 5 Lulworth rd SE9
92 B 5 Lulworth rd SE15
96 K 6 Lulworth rd Welling
81 T 14 Lumley clo Blvdr
140 L 9 Lumley ct WC2
153 S 12 Lumley gdns Sutton
153 S 12 Lumley rd Sutton
139 U 7 Lumley st W1
123 N 5 Luna rd Thntn Hth
109 R 15 Lunham rd SE19
112 H 8 Lupton clo SE12
47 U 13 Lupton st NW5
147 Y 11 Lupus st SW1
148 A 11 Lupus st SW1
144 G 13 Lurgan av W6
89 R 1 Lurline gdns SW11
148 J 17 Luscombe way SW8
62 J 6 Lushington rd NW10
111 P 11 Lushington rd SE6
12 H 9 Luther clo Edg
101 V 12 Luther rd Tedd
90 C 18 Lutman st SW2
76 H 20 Luton pl SE10
32 K 10 Luton rd E17
115 T 6 Luton rd Sidcp
130 H 18 Luton st NW8
43 S 16 Luttrell av SW15
110 K 4 Lutwyche rd SE6
131 T 19 Luxborough st W1
144 E 5 Luxemburg gdns W6
113 R 2 Luxfield rd SE9
75 S 11 Luxford st SE16
92 L 3 Luxmore st SE4
90 K 6 Luxor st SE5
109 T 8 Lyall av SE21
147 T 2 Lyall ms SW1
143 S 3 Lyall Ms w SW1
147 S 3 Lyall st SW1
63 W 7 Lyal rd E3
124 K 18 Lyconby gdns Croy
114 J 8 Lyd clo Sidcp
96 G 16 Lydden ct SW18
88 A 19 Lydden gdns SW18
88 A 20 Lydden rd SW18
81 O 18 Lydd rd Bxly Hth
53 T 20 Lydeard rd E6
31 P 16 Lydford rd N15
45 O 17 Lydford rd NW2
29 R 15 Lydford rd W9
108 D 5 Lydhurst av SW2
150 K 16 Lydney clo SE15
105 T 3 Lydney clo SW19
89 U 8 Ludon rd SW4
113 X 11 Lydstep rd Chisl
88 H 20 Lydstep rd SW18
106 J 1 Lyford rd SW18
147 X 3 Lygon pl SW1
90 A 15 Lyham rd SW2
89 Z 13 Lyham rd SW4
94 G 11 Lyme Farm rd SE12
50 B 19 Lyme gro E9
109 U 12 Lyme av SE19
97 S 2 Lyme rd Welling
153 Y 3 Lymescote gdns Sutton
122 A 2 Lyme st NW1
132 A 2 Lyme st NW1
132 B 2 Lyme ter NW1
114 L 9 Lyminge clo Sidcp
106 J 2 Lyminge gdns SW18
30 H 8 Lymington av N22
121 W 3 Lymington clo SW16

L

152 D 10 Lymington gdns Epsom
45 Z 11 Lymington rd NW6
46 B 16 Lymington rd NW6
55 W 3 Lymington rd Dgnhm
17 V 14 Lynbridge gdns N13
150 K 17 Lynbrook clo SE15
75 Z 15 Lynch wlk SE8
89 R 9 Lyncott cres SW4
22 A 16 Lyncroft av Pinn
45 Z 14 Lyncroft gdns NW6
72 D 4 Lyncroft gdns W13
152 E 20 Lyncroft gdns Epsom
83 N 12 Lyncroft gdns Hounsl
45 W 11 Lyndale NW2
45 W 10 Lyndale av NW2
77 P 17 Lyndale clo SE10
15 Y 18 Lyndhurst av N12
13 O 20 Lyndhurst av NW7
121 X 4 Lyndhurst av S'hall
70 K 3 Lyndhurst av S'hall
117 U 19 Lyndhurst av Surb
100 G 2 Lyndhurst av Twick
100 H 2 Lyndhurst av Twick
43 Z 8 Lyndhurst clo NW10
98 H 7 Lyndhurst clo Bxly Hth
157 Y 6 Lyndhurst clo Croy
51 V 1 Lyndhurst dri E10
118 C 16 Lyndhurst dri New Mald
27 U 4 Lyndhurst gdns N3
46 G 15 Lyndhurst gdns NW3
54 G 17 Lyndhurst gdns Bark
8 D 15 Lyndhurst gdns Enf
36 E 19 Lyndhurst gdns Ilf
91 T 4 Lyndhurst gro SE15
33 U 1 Lyndhurst rd E4
17 S 20 Lyndhurst rd N18
18 K 14 Lyndhurst rd N18
46 G 14 Lyndhurst rd NW3
98 H 7 Lyndhurst rd Bxly Hth
58 K 10 Lyndhurst rd Grnfd
122 F 9 Lyndhurst rd Thntn Hth
91 U 3 Lyndhurst sq SE15
46 F 14 Lyndhurst ter NW3
91 U 2 Lyndhurst way SE15
96 K 13 Lyndon av Sidcp
155 P 6 Lyndon av Wallgtn
81 S 9 Lyndon pl Blvdr
108 J 13 Lyndway SE27
32 K 5 Lyne cres E17
55 X 5 Lynett rd Dgnhm
89 T 15 Lynette av SW4
25 V 3 Lynford clo Edg
12 E 12 Lynford gdns Edg
54 L 7 Lynford gdns Ilf
18 F 4 Lynford ter N9
97 R 5 Lynmere rd Welling
119 O 15 Lynmouth av Mrdn
81 H 1 Lynmouth av Enf
60 C 2 Lynmouth gdns Grnfd
32 H 18 Lynmouth rd E17
27 M 12 Lynmouth rd N2
28 M 12 Lynmouth rd N2
49 U 4 Lynmouth rd N16
60 C 3 Lynmouth rd Grnfd
23 P 9 Lynn clo Harrow
51 Z 8 Lynn rd E11
89 T 17 Lynn rd SW12
54 D 1 Lynn rd Ilf
31 S 1 Lynn st Enf
44 A 19 Lynne way NW10
126 K 3 Lynstead clo Brom
98 F 12 Lynsted clo Bxly Hth
95 O 9 Lynsted gdns SE9
15 T 13 Lynton av N12
26 C 12 Lynton av NW9
59 Y 17 Lynton av W13
59 Z 17 Lynton av W13
38 F 5 Lynton av Rom
83 W 10 Lynton clo Islwth
35 Z 19 Lynton cres Ilf
18 E 4 Lynton gdns Enf
158 H 20 Lynton glade Croy
14 M 9 Lynton mead N20
20 D 16 Lynton rd E4
51 X 12 Lynton rd E11
29 Z 16 Lynton rd N8
129 P 7 Lynton rd NW6
151 X 8 Lynton rd SE1
61 T 18 Lynton rd W3
122 F 15 Lynton rd Croy
40 C 8 Lynton rd Harrow
117 Y 11 Lynton rd New Mald
34 K 4 Lynwood clo E18
40 B 9 Lynwood clo Harrow
38 H 1 Lynwood dri Rom
152 G 3 Lynwood dri Worc Pk
156 D 8 Lynwood gdns Croy
58 E 16 Lynwood gdns S'hall

17 T 4 Lynwood gro N21
106 M 8 Lynwood rd SW17
60 H 10 Lynwood rd W5
24 F 5 Lyon meade Stanm
42 J 18 Lyon Pk av Wemb
81 N 1 Lyon Pk av Wemb
120 D 1 Lyon rd SW19
23 V 19 Lyon rd Harrow
57 T 1 Lyon rd Hornch
5 R 19 Lyonsdown av Barnt
5 R 16 Lyonsdown rd Barnt
130 F 17 Lyons pl NW8
59 T 3 Lyon way Grnfd
86 D 3 Lyric rd SW13
47 W 4 Lysander gro N19
89 R 17 Lysias av SW12
144 G 18 Lysia st SW6
86 H 12 Lysons wlk SW15
112 G 17 Lytchett rd Brom
9 O 6 Lytchett way Enf
157 T 17 Lytchgate clo S Croy
81 T 13 Lytcott gro SE22
63 O 5 Lyte st E2
90 A 17 Lytham clo SW2
6 L 8 Lytham gro W5
150 E 12 Lytham gro W5
28 F 15 Lyttelton clo N2
30 F 11 Lyttelton rd N8
130 K 1 Lyttelton clo NW3
51 S 9 Lyttelton rd E10
17 V 8 Lytton av N13
9 X 3 Lytton av Enf
28 F 19 Lytton clo N2
58 E 1 Lytton clo Grnfd
155 X 7 Lytton gdns Wallgtn
5 S 16 Lytton gro SW15
33 Z 20 Lytton rd E11
8 R 14 Lytton rd Barnt
22 B 3 Lytton rd Pinn
39 Z 17 Lytton rd Rom
77 V 18 Lyveden rd SE10
106 L 16 Lyveden rd SW17

M

109 W 18 Maberley cres SE19
109 W 19 Maberley cres SE19
124 F 6 Maberley rd Becknhm
132 H 14 Mabledon pl NW1
144 K 18 Mablethorpe rd SW6
50 J 15 Mabley st E9
89 Z 4 McAll clo SW4
78 B 16 Macarthur ter SE7
66 C 6 Macaulay rd E6
89 T 9 Macaulay rd SW4
89 T 9 Macaulay rd SW4
80 F 2 Macaulay way SE2
149 S 1 McAuley clo SE1
78 K 9 Macbean st SE18
74 K 12 Macbeth st W6
124 B 12 Macclesfield rd SE25
140 P 9 Macclesfield st W1
56 J 10 Macdonald av Dgnhm
52 E 13 Macdonald rd E7
33 V 7 Macdonald rd E17
16 A 17 Macdonald rd N11
47 V 6 Macdonald rd N19
89 P 1 Macduff rd SW11
63 T 7 Mace st E2
136 C 13 Macfarlane pl W12
74 M 3 Macfarlane rd W12
136 C 14 Macfarlane rd W12
74 M 2 Macfarlane rd W12
131 U 18 Macfarren pl NW1
136 C 13 Macgregor rd E16
66 A 14 Macgregor rd E16
92 C 7 Machell rd SE15
89 T 9 Mackay rd SW4
36 L 9 Mackenzie rd NW8
48 C 17 Mackenzie rd N7
124 D 4 Mackenzie rd Becknhm
46 L 13 Mackenzie rd NW3
90 E 19 Mackie rd SW2
50 F 16 Mackintosh la E9
140 L 4 Macklin st WC2
151 T 5 Macks rd SE16
132 A 11 Mackworth st NW1
50 H 12 Maclaren st E5
92 M 5 Maclean rd SE23
150 B 12 Macleod st SE17
134 K 3 Maclise rd W14
57 X 17 Macoma rd SE18
58 A 17 Macoma ter SE18
76 E 11 Macquarie way E14
8 B 11 Macready pl N7
129 R 12 Macroom rd W9
131 S 19 Madame Tussauds NW8

64 C 13 Maddams st E3
101 V 16 Maddison clo Tedd
115 X 14 Maddocks clo Islwth
139 Z 8 Maddox st W1
140 A 7 Maddox st W1
111 Z 17 Madeira av Brom
112 A 20 Madeira av Brom
21 X 18 Madeira gro Wdfd Grn
51 Y 5 Madeira rd E11
17 W 12 Madeira rd N13
108 B 11 Madeira rd SW16
120 M 8 Madeira rd Mitch
121 N 8 Madeira rd Mitch
60 L 18 Madeley rd W5
109 X 19 Madeline rd SE20
80 G 19 Madison cres Welling
80 G 19 Madison gdns Welling
126 C 6 Madison gdns Brom
48 F 17 Madras pl N7
53 Z 12 Madras rd Ilf
74 G 20 Madrid rd SW13
86 G 1 Madrid rd SW13
150 L 8 Madron st SE17
66 C 6 Mafeking av E6
74 G 20 Mafeking av Brentf
54 F 2 Mafeking av Ilf
86 S 11 Mafeking rd E16
31 X 8 Mafeking rd N17
47 T 6 Mafeking rd Enf
157 O 16 Magdala av N19
83 Z 8 Magdala rd Islwth
66 J 11 Magdalene gdns E6
143 P 8 Magdalen pas E1
88 G 19 Magdalen rd SW18
106 C 3 Magdalen rd SW18
142 K 15 Magdalen st SE1
149 T 14 Magee st SE11
10 G 3 Magnaville rd Bushey Watf
103 U 16 Magnolia clo Kingst
24 L 20 Magnolia ct Harrow
73 S 17 Magnolia rd W4
141 U 8 Magpie all EC4
141 V 7 Magpie all EC4
127 S 16 Magpie Hall clo Brom
127 T 15 Magpie Hall la Brom
10 G 6 Magpie Hall rd Bushey Watf
102 E 10 Maguire dri Rich
143 P 16 Maguire st SE1
20 D 3 Maida av E9
130 E 19 Maida av W9
81 S 8 Maida rd Blvdr
130 C 14 Maida vale W9
99 X 14 Maida Vale rd Drtfrd
20 D 3 Maida way E4
97 Z 20 Maiden Erlegh av Bxly
140 L 9 Maiden la WC2
99 W 10 Maiden la Drtfrd
132 L 7 Maiden Lane bridge N1
52 A 20 Maiden rd E15
93 U 2 Maidenstone hill
84 F 12 Maid Of Honour row Rich
38 K 7 Maidstone av Rom
142 D 15 Maidstone bldgs SE1
16 K 18 Maidstone rd N11
115 Y 11 Maidstone rd Sidcp
153 T 8 Maidstone rd Sidcp
8 K 17 Main av Enf
71 P 7 Main dr W7
113 X 11 Mainridge rd Chisl
39 X 10 Main rd Rom
114 J 8 Main rd Sidcp
100 A 12 Main st Felt
151 T 16 Maisemore st SE15
82 D 9 Maitland clo Hounsl
47 N 18 Maitland Pk rd NW3
47 N 17 Maitland Pk vlls NW5
52 B 19 Maitland rd E15
110 E 15 Maitland rd SE26
50 H 10 Maiwand rd E5
59 S 13 Majendie rd SE18
151 U 1 Major rd SE16
47 O 7 Makepeace av N6
146 L 7 Makins st SW3
64 C 19 Malam gdns E14
57 X 17 Malan sq Rainhm
86 L 11 Malbrook rd SW15
17 R 17 Malcolm ct Stanm
60 M 5 Malcolm ct W5
26 F 17 Malcolm cres NW4
63 O 10 Malcolm pl E2
63 O 11 Malcolm rd E1

110 B 17 Malcolm rd SE20
123 X 15 Malcolm rd SE25
105 T 16 Malcolm rd SW19
34 E 14 Malcolm way E18
123 Z 7 Malden av SE25
124 A 7 Malden av SE25
41 S 17 Malden av Grnfd
47 P 19 Malden cres NW1
118 F 19 Malden Green av Worc Pk
118 C 7 Malden hill New Mald
118 D 8 Malden Hill gdns New Mald
152 A 1 Malden la Worc Pk
118 D 14 Malden pk New Mald
47 N 15 Malden pl NW5
47 O 16 Malden rd NW5
118 C 13 Malden rd New Mald
38 J 20 Malden rd Rom
153 N 7 Malden rd Sutton
117 Z 15 Malden way New Mald
91 R 7 Maldon clo SE5
18 H 10 Maldon rd N9
61 W 20 Maldon rd W3
56 J 1 Maldon rd Rom
155 T 10 Maldon rd Wallgtn
21 Y 20 Maldon wlk Wdfd Grn
132 E 18 Malet pl WC1
132 F 19 Malet st WC1
108 K 3 Maley av SE27
34 D 9 Malford gro E18
91 T 7 Malfort rd SE5
110 F 1 Malham rd SE23
25 Z 6 Malington way NW9
15 U 1 Mallard clo Barnt
101 Y 7 Mallard pla Twick
34 J 2 Mallards rd Wdfd Grn
43 V 2 Mallard way NW9
93 X 16 Malet rd SE13
40 E 15 Mallet rd Grnfd
119 C 13 Malling gdns Mrdn
126 M 8 Malling way Brom
124 B 13 Malling clo Croy
155 Z 4 Mallinson rd Wallgtn
88 K 3 Mallison rd SW11
146 G 13 Mallord st SW3
92 G 10 Mallory clo SE4
3 B 3 Mallory gdns Barnt
27 T 2 Mallow mead NW7
134 E 16 Mallow st EC1
74 K 13 Mall rd W6
16 L 10 Mall the N14
17 O 9 Mall the N14
140 D 15 Mall the SW1
85 V 13 Mall the SW14
60 H 19 Mall the W5
24 M 20 Mall the Harrow
116 F 13 Mall the Surb
125 V 10 Malmains clo Becknhm
125 V 9 Malmains way Becknhm
64 M 13 Malmesbury rd E16
65 N 15 Malmesbury rd E16
34 C 5 Malmesbury rd E18
120 C 16 Malmesbury rd Mrdn
63 Y 8 Malmesbury rd E3
65 O 14 Malmesbury ter E16
92 L 3 Malpas rd SE4
55 V 19 Malpas rd Dgnhm
51 N 2 Malta rd E10
133 X 15 Malta st EC1
143 N 19 Maltby st SE1
91 N 1 Maltby st SE1
136 K 4 Malton ms W10
136 J 4 Malton rd W10
79 V 18 Malton st SE18
141 P 8 Maltravers st WC2
151 S 13 Malt st SE1
88 A 14 Malva clo SW18
33 W 1 Malvern av E4
80 L 20 Malvern av Bxly Hth
40 G 8 Malvern av Harrow
121 V 6 Malvern clo Mitch
116 K 20 Malvern clo Surb
111 T 20 Malvern ct Becknhm
54 K 13 Malvern dri Ilf
21 X 15 Malvern dri Wdfd Grn
45 S 6 Malvern gdns NW2
129 P 11 Malvern gdns W9
24 L 12 Malvern gdns Harrow
129 R 11 Malvern pl W9
66 C 3 Malvern rd E6
49 W 20 Malvern rd E8
135 S 1 Malvern rd E8
52 B 6 Malvern rd E11
30 E 10 Malvern rd N8
31 W 9 Malvern rd N17
129 S 12 Malvern rd NW6

L
M

100 H 19 Malvern rd Hampt
39 V 20 Malvern rd Hornch
122 F 10 Malvern rd Thntn Hth
133 S 3 Malvern ter N1
18 H 6 Malvern ter N9
60 B 14 Malvern way W13
89 R 17 Malwood rd SW12
93 P 13 Malyions ter SE13
76 G 3 Managers st E14
91 Z 6 Manaton clo SE15
58 G 16 Manaton cres S'hall
51 Z 17 Manbey gro E15
51 Z 17 Manbey Pk rd E15
51 Z 18 Manbey rd E15
51 Z 18 Manbey st E15
52 A 18 Manbey st E15
66 H 9 Manborough rd E6
128 K 18 Manchester dri W10
76 F 12 Manchester gro E14
139 T 3 Manchester ms W1
76 G 6 Manchester rd E14
31 P 19 Manchester rd N15
122 M 6 Manchester rd Thntn Hth
139 U 4 Manchester sq W1
139 T 2 Manchester st W1
56 G 13 Manchester way Dgnhm
89 P 14 Manchuria rd SW11
142 F 20 Manciple st SE1
89 U 14 Mandalay rd SW4
43 W 20 Mandela clo NW10
77 R 20 Mandeville clo SE10
139 V 5 Mandeville pl W1
16 F 9 Mandeville rd N14
40 H 19 Mandeville rd Grnfd
58 D 2 Mandeville rd Grnfd
83 Y 4 Mandeville rd Islwth
50 G 10 Mandeville st E5
106 M 6 Mandrake rd SW17
90 A 13 Mandrell rd SW2
140 G 6 Manette st W1
87 V 13 Manfred rd SW15
80 K 8 Mangold way Blvdr
76 B 5 Manilla st E14
140 C 11 Man in Moon pas W1
80 A 8 Manister rd SE2
88 K 6 Manlays yd SW11
131 T 3 Manley st NW1
42 H 1 Manning gdns Harrow
32 G 14 Manning rd E17
56 E 20 Manning rd Dgnhm
143 R 5 Manningtree st E1
37 P 20 Mannin rd Rom
20 J 10 Mannock rd N22
83 W 12 Manns clo Islwth
12 C 19 Manns rd Edg
100 M 5 Manoel rd Twick
74 B 13 Manor alley W4
92 M 4 Manor av SE4
58 D 1 Manor av Grnfd
94 F 10 Manor brook SE3
25 R 14 Manor clo NW9
57 O 19 Manor clo Dgnhm
99 O 10 Manor clo Drtfrd
39 V 16 Manor clo Rom
118 C 20 Manor clo Worc Pk
90 K 19 Manor cotts SE24
28 C 9 Manor Cotts appr N2
28 D 8 Manor Cotts appr N2
16 L 8 Manor ct N14
20 M 10 Manor Court rd W7
59 T 20 Manor Court rd W7
71 S 1 Manor Court rd W7
117 O 14 Manor cres Surb
16 F 4 Manor dri N14
15 Y 11 Manor dri N20
12 L 16 Manor dri NW7
152 B 14 Manor dri Epsom
117 Y 16 Manor dri North Surb
118 A 19 Manor dri North Worc Pk
117 O 15 Manor dri Surb
43 N 11 Manor dri av Wemb
118 B 20 Manor Dr the Worc Pk
152 E 1 Manor Dri the Worc Pk
152 C 1 Manor Dri the Worc Pk
21 N 9 Manor Farm dri E4
122 F 2 Manor Farm rd SW16
60 F 5 Manor Farm rd Wemb
87 O 15 Manor fields SW15
48 A 9 Manor gdns N7
119 V 2 Manor gdns SW20
73 R 10 Manor gdns W3
100 L 18 Manor gdns Hampt
85 O 10 Manor gdns Rich
157 O 14 Manor gdns S Croy

117 R 1 Manorgate rd Kingst
75 O 17 Manor gro SE14
125 R 3 Manor gro Becknhm
85 R 9 Manor gro Rich
85 O 9 Manor gro Rich
27 O 7 Manor Hall av NW4
27 O 8 Manor Hall av NW4
51 O 3 Manor Hall gdns E10
99 O 9 Manor house Hth
45 P 20 Manor Ho dri NW6
128 H 1 Manor Ho dri NW6
94 B 19 Manor la SE12
83 Z 12 Manor la SE13
154 B 10 Manor la Sutton
93 Z 12 Manor la ter SE13
110 C 1 Manor mt SE23
53 R 10 Manor pk E12
93 Y 11 Manor pk SE13
93 Z 12 Manor pk SE13
118 E 17 Manor park New Mald
85 O 10 Manor pk Rich
125 R 20 Manor Pk clo W Wkhm
12 C 19 Manor Pk cres Edg
22 K 10 Manor Pk dri Harrow
12 C 18 Manor Pk gdns Edg
53 O 13 Manor Pk rd E12
28 E 10 Manor Pk rd N2
62 C 4 Manor Pk rd NW10
114 D 20 Manor Pk rd Chisl
154 C 11 Manor Pk rd Sutton
125 R 20 Manor Pk rd W Wkhm
149 Y 10 Manor pl SE17
150 A 9 Manor pl SE17
121 V 7 Manor pl Mitch
154 B 9 Manor pl Sutton
51 O 2 Manor rd E10
65 N 5 Manor rd E15
32 H 6 Manor rd E17
49 P 5 Manor rd N16
31 Y 3 Manor rd N17
17 O 20 Manor rd N22
119 V 3 Manor rd SE25
123 W 8 Manor rd SW20
59 Z 20 Manor rd W13
60 A 20 Manor rd W13
54 L 19 Manor rd Bark
4 F 14 Manor rd Barnt
125 R 2 Manor rd Becknhm
98 H 20 Manor rd Bxly
56 L 19 Manor rd Dgnhm
57 N 19 Manor rd Dgnhm
99 P 9 Manor rd Drtfrd
8 A 9 Manor rd Enf
23 Y 17 Manor rd Harrow
21 X 1 Manor rd Lghtn
122 V 7 Manor rd Mitch
155 R 8 Manor rd North Wallgtn
85 O 19 Manor rd Rich
37 U 19 Manor rd Rom
39 W 17 Manor rd Rom
114 M 6 Manor rd Sidcp
153 U 18 Manor rd Sutton
101 Z 11 Manor rd Tedd
101 O 4 Manor rd Twick
159 R 1 Manor rd W Wkhm
155 S 10 Manor rd Wallgtn
4 F 15 Manorside Barnt
80 G 11 Manorside clo SE2
55 V 7 Manor sq Dgnhm
72 D 14 Manor vale Brentf
27 Z 8 Manor view N3
28 A 8 Manor view N3
20 J 13 Manor way E4
78 M 2 Manor way E16
98 D 20 Manor way Bxly
121 U 7 Manor way Mitch
26 A 12 Manor way NW9
94 D 10 Manor way SE3
125 P 5 Manor way Becknhm
98 L 8 Manor way Bxly Hth
127 S 15 Manor way Brom
157 U 14 Manor way Croy
18 D 1 Manor way Enf
22 K 13 Manor way Harrow
21 Z 16 Manor way Wkfd Grn
118 C 20 Manor way Worc Pk
155 T 8 Manor Way the Wallgtn
86 F 19 Manresa house SW15
146 J 11 Manresa rd SW3
107 P 13 Mansard beeches SW17
33 N 4 Mansel gro E17
73 Y 4 Mansell rd W3
58 L 13 Mansell rd Grnfd
143 O 7 Mansell st E1
105 T 5 Mansel rd SW19

49 V 11 Manse rd N16
31 O 13 Mansfield av N15
6 B 18 Mansfield av Barnt
20 C 5 Mansfield hill E4
139 X 2 Mansfield ms W1
20 B 6 Mansfield pk E4
34 H 19 Mansfield rd E11
12 L 13 Mansfield rd E17
46 M 14 Mansfield rd NW3
47 O 13 Mansfield rd NW3
11 T 12 Mansfield rd NW3
53 X 6 Mansfield rd Ilf
157 O 15 Mansfield rd S Croy
139 X 2 Mansfield st W1
135 U 10 Mansford st E2
107 O 20 Manship rd Mitch
160 F 7 Mansion House pl EC4
142 E 6 Mansion House st EC2
146 D 6 Manson ms SW7
146 E 7 Manson pl SW7
55 U 1 Mansted gdns Rom
123 Manston av S'hall
45 S 14 Manstone rd NW2
57 V 19 Manston way Hornch
79 P 13 Manthorpe rd SE18
100 M 7 Mantilla rd SW17
92 J 8 Mantle rd SE4
71 X 6 Manton av W7
79 Z 11 Manton rd SE2
80 A 11 Manton rd SE2
63 P 10 Mantus clo E1
88 G 6 Mantua clo SW11
15 P 6 Manus way N20
107 R 5 Manville gdns SW17
107 R 5 Manville rd SW17
92 M 15 Manwood rd SE4
107 T 3 Many gates SW12
45 S 17 Mapesbury rd NW2
135 V 16 Mape st E2
19 Y 19 Maple av E4
43 V 1 Maple av W3
40 L 8 Maple av Harrow
57 Y 10 Maple clo Hornch
121 S 1 Maple clo Mitch
117 Z 7 Maple ct New Mald
118 A 6 Maple ct New Mald
97 N 15 Maple cres Sidcp
157 Y 4 Mapledale av Croy
157 Y 4 Mapledale av W Wkhm
49 W 20 Mapledene rd E8
26 A 2 Maple gdns Edg
43 V 1 Maple gro NW9
72 H 7 Maple gro W5
72 B 18 Maple gro Brentf
58 F 13 Maple gro S'hall
35 Z 11 Maplesleafe gdns Ilf
63 N 15 Maple pl E1
132 B 19 Maple pl W1
34 A 9 Maple rd E11
110 C 18 Maple rd SE20
116 F 15 Maple rd Surb
90 C 19 Maplestead rd SW2
68 D 4 Maplestead rd Dgnhm
132 C 19 Maple st W1
38 K 14 Maple st Rom
122 G 9 Maplethorpe rd Thntn Hth
126 E 13 Mapleton clo Brom
88 A 16 Mapleton rd SW18
87 Z 16 Mapleton rd SW18
9 N 10 Mapleton rd Enf
7 R 18 Maplin clo N21
65 U 17 Maplin rd E16
33 Z 1 Mapperley dri Wdfd Grn
80 J 7 Maran way Blvdr
58 A 20 Marban rd W9
51 Y 8 Marbel clo W3
84 B 18 Marble Hill clo Twick
84 A 18 Marble Hill gdns Twick
84 E 19 Marble Hill park Twick
112 K 6 Marbrook ct SE12
48 C 9 Marcellus rd N7
51 Y 8 Marchant rd E11
145 R 19 Marchbank rd SW6
84 M 14 Marchmont rd Rich
85 N 14 Marchmont rd Rich
155 V 17 Marchmont rd Wallgtn
132 K 17 Marchmont st WC1
83 X 18 March rd Twick
60 F 16 Marchwood cres W5
150 A 20 Marchwood clo SE5
100 M 7 Marcia rd SE1
85 K 18 Marconi way S'hall

49 Z 16 Marcon pl E8
74 L 8 Marco rd W6
144 A 3 Marcus rd W6
65 N 4 Marcus ct E15
99 W 19 Marcus rd Drtfd
65 O 4 Marcus st E15
88 B 15 Marcus st SE18
25 Z 17 Mardale dri NW9
74 L 6 Mardale st W12
124 E 12 Mardell rd Croy
126 D 15 Marden av Brom
98 L 13 Marden cres Bxly
122 D 14 Marden cres Croy
31 R 9 Marden rd N17
122 D 15 Marden rd Croy
71 Z 6 Marder rd W13
72 A 6 Marder rd W13
39 S 18 Marden rd Rom
75 O 8 Marden sq SE16
114 F 6 Marechal Niel av Sidcp
157 S 4 Maresfield Croy
46 E 18 Maresfield gdns NW3
50 A 19 Mare st E8
63 N 3 Mare st E8
135 Y 2 Mare st E8
20 E 1 Margaret av E4
39 Y 16 Margaret clo Rom
140 A 4 Margaret ct W1
49 U 5 Margaret gdns N16
49 U 5 Margaret rd N16
5 V 14 Margaret rd Barnt
97 W 15 Margaret rd Bxly
39 Y 16 Margaret rd Rom
139 Z 4 Margaret st W1
140 A 4 Margaret st W1
146 L 13 Margaretta ter SW3
52 L 5 Margaretting rd E12
35 P 17 Margaret way Ilf
90 A 13 Margaret rd SW2
67 M 1 Marg Bonfield av Bark
52 E 18 Margery Pk rd E7
55 X 8 Margery rd Dgnhm
133 R 15 Margery st WC1
105 P 11 Margin dri SW19
144 H 10 Margravine gdns W6
144 H 12 Margravine rd W6
106 H 3 Marham gdns SW18
120 C 14 Marham gdns SW18
58 A 12 Marian clo Grnfd
153 Z 11 Marian ct Sutton
135 V 7 Marian pl E2
62 D 1 Marian way NW10
107 V 20 Marian rd SW16
58 S 13 Maria ter E1
117 Z 11 Maria Theresa clo New Mald
23 P 4 Maricas av Harrow
143 V 19 Marigold st SE16
19 Y 20 Marigold way E4
118 J 13 Marina av New Mald
126 E 6 Marina clo Brom
96 H 4 Marina dri Welling
58 U 17 Marina gdns Rom
102 F 17 Marina way Tedd
88 B 4 Marinefield rd SW6
102 C 8 Marine dri SE18
53 V 12 Mariner rd E12
151 R 1 Mariner st SE16
36 D 1 Marion clo Ilf
21 O 14 Marion gro Wdfd Grn
13 T 16 Marion rd NW7
123 N 11 Marion rd Thntn Hth
93 W 9 Marischal rd SE13
93 W 9 Marishal rd SE13
76 J 17 Maritime museum SE10
63 Y 12 Maritime st E3
107 O 3 Marius pass SW17
107 O 3 Marius rd SW17
89 N 10 Marjorie gro SW11
20 E 1 Mark av E4
70 J 2 Mark clo Bxly Hth
97 Y 1 Mark clo Bxly Hth
140 A 5 Market st W1
78 K 9 Market hill SE18
25 V 5 Market la Edg
25 U 5 Market la Edg
39 P 14 Market link Rom
59 X 14 Market ms W1
91 X 6 Market pl SE15
28 H 11 Market pl N2
28 C 14 Market pl NW11
140 A 5 Market pl W1
98 E 10 Market pl Bxly Hth
72 F 18 Market pl Brentf
116 G 4 Market pl Kingst
39 R 14 Market pl Rom
47 Z 19 Market rd N7
48 A 18 Market rd N7
85 P 9 Market rd Rich

M

M

64 E 18 Market sq E14
18 L 9 Market sq N9
126 E 13 Market sq Brom
66 G 6 Market st E6
78 K 11 Market st SE18
64 E 18 Market way E14
42 J 16 Market way Wemb
20 D 1 Markfield gdns E4
31 X 14 Markfield rd N15
147 N 9 Markham sq SW3
146 M 9 Markham st SW3
100 E 19 Markhole clo Hampt
32 J 18 Markhouse av E17
32 K 18 Markhouse rd E17
50 M 1 Markhouse rd E17
142 K 8 Mark la EC3
50 K 1 Markmanor av E17
30 K 6 Mark rd N22
85 R 8 Marksbury av Rich
38 A 12 Marks hall Rom
38 L 16 Marks rd Rom
51 Z 20 Mark st E15
134 H 16 Mark st EC2
109 Z 9 Markwell clo SE26
55 R 16 Markyate rd Dgnhm
35 S 10 Marlands rd Ilf
35 T 8 Marlands rd Ilf
135 T 2 Marlborough av E8
16 G 10 Marlborough av N14
12 F 11 Marlborough av Edg
15 Z 12 Marlborough clo N20
106 H 16 Marlborough clo SW19
140 B 7 Marlborough ct W1
73 Z 8 Marlborough cres W4
35 R 10 Marlborough dri Ilf
15 Z 10 Marlborough gdns N20
151 T 12 Marlborough gro SE1
130 D 6 Marlborough hill NW8
23 T 13 Marlborough hill Harrow
140 D 15 Marlborough house SW1
77 Y 18 Marlborough la SE7
97 N 20 Marlborough Pk av Sidcp
130 B 9 Marlborough rd pl NW8
20 C 19 Marlborough rd E4
52 K 19 Marlborough rd E7
52 A 13 Marlborough rd E15
34 G 9 Marlborough rd E18
18 H 7 Marlborough rd N9
47 Y 7 Marlborough rd N19
42 A 6 Marlborough rd N19
17 O 20 Marlborough rd N22
30 B 1 Marlborough rd N22
140 D 15 Marlborough rd SW1
106 H 16 Marlborough rd SW19
73 U 13 Marlborough rd W4
72 H 5 Marlborough rd W5
97 W 7 Marlborough rd Bxly Hth
72 A 20 Marlborough rd Brentf
126 M 9 Marlborough rd Brom
55 T 14 Marlborough rd Dgnhm
100 H 15 Marlborough rd Hampt
84 L 16 Marlborough rd Rich
38 H 13 Marlborough rd Rom
156 M 16 Marlborough rd S Croy
153 Z 4 Marlborough rd Sutton
146 K 8 Marlborough st SW3
110 K 2 Marler rd SE23
80 J 17 Marley av Bxly Hth
58 G 7 Marley clo Grnfd
100 G 19 Marlingdene clo Hampt
42 F 12 Marloes clo Wemb
145 W 4 Marloes rd W8
124 A 5 Marlow clo SE20
26 C 11 Marlow clo NW9
83 V 15 Marlow cres Twick
153 P 4 Marlow dri Sutton
114 D 17 Marlow clo Chisl
36 L 5 Marlowe clo Ilf
95 X 15 Marlowe gdns SE9
33 U 12 Marlowe rd E17
121 U 8 Marlowe sq Mitch
130 F 4 Marlowes the NW8
99 N 11 Marlowes the Drtfrd
66 F 9 Marlow rd E6
124 B 4 Marlow rd SE20
70 E 8 Marlow rd S'hall
88 B 11 Marl st SW18
77 R 13 Marlton st SE10

79 X 10 Marmadon rd SE18
19 Y 13 Marmion av E4
20 A 13 Marmion av E4
20 A 13 Marmion clo E4
89 P 8 Marmion ms SW11
89 P 9 Marmion rd SW11
91 Y 1 Marmont rd SE15
151 U 20 Marmont rd SE15
92 C 15 Marmora rd SE22
16 D 13 Marne av N11
96 M 8 Marne av Welling
90 M 3 Marne st SE5
128 L 12 Marne st W10
89 O 10 Marnell way SW11
45 S 11 Marnham av NW2
58 K 8 Marnham cres Grnfd
58 K 6 Marnham cr Grnfd
92 K 14 Marnock rd SE4
63 V 15 Maroon st E14
49 N 18 Marquess rd N1
48 M 20 Marquess rd N1
61 O 1 Marquis clo Wemb
48 E 3 Marquis rd N4
17 R 20 Marquis rd N22
47 Z 19 Marquis rd NW1
86 H 9 Marrick clo SW15
9 X 3 Marrilyne av Enf
26 D 19 Marriots clo NW9
64 L 2 Marriott rd E15
48 C 5 Marriott rd N4
28 M 5 Marriott rd N10
29 N 5 Marriot rd N10
4 D 12 Marriot rd Barnt
105 S 10 Marryat pl SW19
105 P 12 Marryat rd SW19
93 S 10 Marsala rd SE13
18 M 8 Marsden rd N9
91 V 8 Marsden st SE15
47 P 18 Marsden st NW5
41 O 1 Marshall clo Harrow
82 E 12 Marshall clo Hounsl
149 X 2 Marshalls gdns SE1
31 P 4 Marshall rd N17
39 P 9 Marshalls dri Rom
78 E 10 Marshalls gro SE18
38 M 14 Marshalls rd Rom
154 B 8 Marshalls rd Sutton
140 C 7 Marshall st W1
142 C 17 Marshalsea rd SE1
113 Y 12 Marsham clo Chisl
148 H 3 Marsham st SW1
121 N 2 Marsh av Mitch
95 N 7 Marshbrook clo SE18
13 R 11 Marsh clo NW7
26 D 19 Marsh dri NW9
83 V 20 Marsh Farm rd Twick
101 U 1 Marsh Farm rd Twick
76 G 8 Marshfield st E14
64 D 3 Marshgate la E15
69 R 4 Marsh Green rd Dgnhm
50 H 15 Marsh hill E9
51 N 5 Marsh la E10
32 A 3 Marsh la N17
11 S 18 Marsh la NW7
12 M 12 Marsh la NW7
13 O 11 Marsh la NW7
24 G 1 Marsh la Stanm
60 H 8 Marsh rd W5
22 C 14 Marsh rd Pinn
76 C 11 Marsh st E14
149 Y 11 Marsland rd SE17
56 D 8 Marston av Dgnhm
46 E 20 Marston clo NW6
56 D 8 Marston clo Dgnhm
35 R 6 Marston rd Ilf
102 B 13 Marston rd Tedd
108 K 18 Marston way SE19
22 A 3 Marsworth av Pinn
49 T 6 Martaban rd N16
50 A 20 Martell rd SE21
109 N 7 Martell rd SE21
33 P 6 Martel rd E7
9 J 10 Martens av Bxly Hth
98 L 11 Martens av Bxly Hth
98 J 11 Martens clo Bxly Hth
98 J 9 Martens Grove pk Bxly Hth
52 B 17 Martha st E15
63 O 18 Martha st E1
143 Z 7 Martha st E1
23 R 8 Marthorne cres Harrow
143 Z 7 Marth st E1
95 U 8 Martin Bowes rd SE9
156 E 1 Martin cres Croy
65 V 12 Martindale SW14
85 V 12 Martindale rd SW14
82 B 7 Martindale rd SW12
98 B 13 Martin dene Bxly Hth
48 H 13 Martineau rd N5
63 P 20 Martineau st E1
102 G 7 Martingale clo Rich

55 U 13 Martin gdns Dgnhm
119 X 7 Martin gro Mrdn
142 F 9 Martin la EC4
160 F 9 Martin la EC4
98 B 19 Martin ri Bxly Hth
55 V 13 Martin rd Dgnhm
40 E 15 Martin rd Grnfd
4 M 13 Martins mount Barnt
126 A 3 Martins rd Brom
29 N 4 Martins wlk N10
119 R 4 Martin way SW20
119 T 7 Martin way Mrdn
140 L 7 Martlett ct WC2
35 Z 16 Martley dri Ilf
140 L 8 Mart st WC2
112 J 5 Marvels clo SE12
112 K 5 Marvels la SE12
122 M 11 Marvels la Thntn Hth
145 O 20 Marville rd SW6
97 P 8 Marwood clo Welling
104 A 8 Mary Adelaide clo SW15
76 B 18 Mary Anns bldgs SE8
40 J 7 Maryatt av Harrow
78 F 10 Mary bank SE18
25 N 12 Mary clo Stanm
51 Z 15 Maryland pk E15
51 Y 16 Maryland rd E15
17 S 20 Maryland rd N22
108 K 20 Maryland rd Thntn Hth
122 J 1 Maryland rd Thntn Hth
52 A 15 Maryland sq E15
129 V 18 Marylands rd W9
51 Y 16 Maryland st E15
134 A 3 Maryland wlk N1
131 V 19 Marylebone High st W1
139 U 1 Marylebone High st W1
139 W 5 Marylebone la W1
140 B 4 Marylebone pas W1
139 X 1 Marylebone ms W1
131 V 18 Marylebone rd NW1
131 N 19 Marylebone station NW1
139 U 2 Marylebone st W1
149 R 8 Marylee way SE11
78 D 11 Maryon gro SE18
46 J 13 Maryon ms NW3
78 D 12 Maryon rd SE7
41 P 14 Mary Peters dr Grnfd
136 J 10 Mary pl W11
19 Y 9 Marys av Twick
65 P 15 Mary st E16
134 B 5 Mary st N1
131 Z 6 Mary ter NW1
136 J 20 Masbro rd W14
77 X 17 Mascalls rd SE7
87 R 9 Mascotte rd SW15
4 K 10 Mascotts clo NW2
6 G 19 Masefield av NW9
58 H 19 Masefield av S'hall
10 J 17 Masefield av Stanm
99 U 3 Masefield clo Erith
120 F 5 Masefield clo Mitch
6 G 18 Masefield cres NW4
66 J 11 Masefield gdns E6
100 F 9 Masefield rd Hampt
62 A 17 Mashie rd W3
38 M 5 Mashiters hill Rom
39 R 9 Mashiters wlk Rom
106 C 8 Maskell rd SW17
88 K 1 Maskelyn clo SW11
65 S 19 Mason clo E16
43 O 7 Mason ct Wemb
98 F 8 Mason clo Bxly Hth
21 N 14 Mason rd Wdfd Grn
139 Z 7 Masons Arm ms W1
160 D 4 Masons av EC2
157 N 7 Masons av Croy
23 V 12 Masons av Harrow
12 P 12 Masons Grn la W3
78 M 12 Masons hill SE18
11 N 18 Masons hill Brom
106 L 20 Masons pl Mitch
150 H 5 Masons st SE17
140 C 12 Masons yd SW1
16 E 16 Massey rd N11
33 X 6 Massford st E1
49 X 18 Massie rd E8
16 J 6 Massinger st SE17
63 S 11 Massingham st E1
95 R 1 Master Gunners pl SE18
78 D 20 Master Gunner pl SE7
63 U 16 Masters st E6
76 B 11 Mast Ho ter E14
82 M 17 Maswell Park cres Hounsl

82 L 17 Maswell Park rd Hounsl
52 A 9 Matcham rd E11
126 E 13 Matfield clo Brom
81 S 16 Matfield rd Blvdr
91 U 11 Matham gro SE22
140 G 19 Matthew Parker st SW1
66 K 7 Mathews av E6
52 C 19 Mathews Pk av E15
133 O 4 Matilda st N1
153 T 8 Matlock cres Sutton
153 T 9 Matlock gdns Sutton
153 T 8 Matlock pl Sutton
33 U 18 Matlock rd E10
63 U 16 Matlock st E1
117 Y 1 Matlock way New Mald
89 V 6 Matrimony pl SW4
41 R 15 Matthews rd Grnfd
88 L 5 Matthews st SW11
49 R 14 Matthias sq N16
30 H 17 Mattison rd N4
72 E 2 Mattock la W13
91 R 3 Maude av E13
32 H 15 Maude ter E17
15 R 6 Maud gdns E13
67 X 6 Maud gdns Bark
51 U 10 Maud rd E10
65 R 5 Maud rd E13
32 H 15 Maud rd E17
95 U 7 Maudslay rd SE9
71 T 4 Maudsville cotts W7
90 A 13 Mauleverer rd SW2
74 W 7 Maunder rd W7
148 E 4 Maunsel st SW1
30 K 8 Maurice av N22
14 C 18 Maurice Brown clo NW7
62 J 18 Maurice av W12
28 C 14 Maurice wlk NW11
77 N 12 Mauritius rd SE10
49 N 12 Maury rd N16
113 P 19 Mavalstone clo Chisl
113 P 20 Mavelstone rd Chisl
64 A 4 Maverton rd E3
152 B 10 Mavis av Epsom
152 B 10 Mavis clo Epsom
151 P 10 Mawbey pl SE1
151 P 11 Mawbey rd SE1
148 L 20 Mawbey st SW8
38 G 9 Mawney clo Rom
38 J 10 Mawney pk Rom
38 J 7 Mawney rd Rom
39 N 13 Mawney rd Rom
119 T 4 Mawson clo SW20
74 C 15 Mawson la W4
55 Y 14 Maxey rd Dgnhm
79 O 10 Maxey rd SE18
7 T 18 Maxim rd N21
41 T 1 Maxim rd Drtfd
41 W 7 Maxted pk Harrow
145 Y 19 Maxwell rd SW6
96 M 9 Maxwell rd Welling
12 L 15 Melwelton av NW7
12 L 15 Maxwelton clo NW7
95 X 9 May-Place av Drtfrd
90 H 12 Mayall rd SE24
34 J 7 Maybank av E11
57 Z 15 Maybank av Hornch
47 Y 14 Maybank av Wemb
34 K 5 Maybank rd E18
34 J 6 Maybank rd E18
116 M 17 Mayberry pl Surb
110 A 13 Maybourne clo SE26
127 Z 12 Maybury clo Brom
44 J 19 Maybury gdns NW10
45 X 13 Maybury rd E13
67 Y 6 Maybury rd Bark
A 6 Maybury rd Bark
93 S 17 Maybury st SW17
24 G 3 Maychurch clo Stanm
119 W 8 Maycross av Mrdn
96 R 4 Mayday gdns SE3
122 H 15 Mayday rd Thntn Hth
95 O 13 Mayenne st SE9
67 X 4 Mayesbrook rd Ilf
55 O 9 Mayesbrook rd Ilf
37 U 20 Mayesford rd Rom
30 C 7 Mayes rd N22
30 E 9 Mayes rd N22
112 L 9 Mayeswood rd SE12
97 X 2 Mayfair av Ilf
37 X 19 Mayfair av Rom
82 M 19 Mayfair av Twick
118 F 19 Mayfair av Worc Pk
111 R 20 Mayfair ct Becknhm
18 A 20 Mayfair gdns N17
17 Z 20 Mayfair gdns N18
34 F 1 Mayfair gdns Wdfd Grn

May–Mer

139 Z 12 Mayfair pl W1
16 K 3 Mayfair ter N14
98 B 9 Mayfield Bxly Hth
32 G 7 Mayfield av E17
15 S 13 Mayfield av N12
16 J 8 Mayfield av N14
74 B 11 Mayfield av W4
72 B 6 Mayfield av W13
24 B 17 Mayfield av Harrow
21 S 20 Mayfield av Wdfd Grn
49 U 19 Mayfield clo E8
8 M 19 Mayfield cres Enf
122 C 10 Mayfield cres Thntn Hth
22 E 12 Mayfield dri Pinn
27 P 18 Mayfield gdns NW4
59 S 15 Mayfield gdns W7
20 J 7 Mayfield rd E4
135 N 1 Mayfield rd E8
65 P 13 Mayfield rd E13
30 D 18 Mayfield rd N8
105 W 20 Mayfield rd SW19
61 S 19 Mayfield rd W3
81 X 10 Mayfield rd Blvdr
127 R 11 Mayfield rd Brom
157 P 19 Mayfield rd Croy
55 S 5 Mayfield rd Dgnhm
9 Y 9 Mayfield rd Enf
157 P 18 Mayfield rd S Croy
154 F 15 Mayfield rd Sutton
122 C 10 Mayfield rd Thntn Hth
43 O 7 Mayfields Wemb
43 O 6 Mayfields clo Wemb
90 A 6 Mayflowers rd SW9
75 O 6 Mayflower st SE16
143 Z 18 Mayflower st SE16
88 M 20 Mayford clo SW12
88 M 19 Mayford rd SW12
89 N 18 Mayford rd SW12
60 E 7 May gdns Wemb
133 R 7 Maygood st N1
57 U 2 Maygreen cres Hornch
45 V 18 Maygrove rd NW6
20 A 10 Mayhew clo E4
77 V 17 Mayhill rd SE7
4 E 19 Mayhill rd Barnt
57 Z 13 Maylands av Hornch
115 W 7 Maylands dri Sidcp
151 R 15 Maymerle rd SE15
33 T 15 Maynard rd E17
50 C 12 Mayola rd E5
44 B 19 Mayo rd NW10
123 N 12 Mayo rd Croy
110 E 9 Mayow pk SE26
110 F 11 Mayow rd SE26
99 X 10 Mayow rd Bxly Hth
98 G 9 Mayplace av Bxly Hth
78 M 17 May Place la SE18
99 J 9 Mayplace rd east Bxly Hth
99 N 9 Mayplace rd Bxly Hth
98 F 10 Mayplace rd west Bxly Hth
36 D 1 Maypole cres Ilf
20 A 19 May rd E4
65 U 6 May rd E13
101 T 1 May rd Twick
140 J 10 Mays ct WC2
125 Z 4 Mays Hill rd Brom
126 A 5 Mays Hill rd Brom
4 G 18 Mays la Barnt
13 X 2 Mays la Barnt
20 H 8 Mays la E4
88 F 9 Maysoule rd SW11
101 P 11 Mays rd Tedd
145 O 12 May st W14
56 L 18 Mayswood gdns Dgnhm
48 C 10 Mayton st N7
12 G 10 Maytree clo Edg
108 F 4 May Tree wk SW12
51 Y 7 Mayville rd E11
53 Y 14 Mayville rd Ilf
65 U 5 May wlk E13
111 R 18 Maywood clo Becknhm
51 Z 8 Mayville rd E11
94 C 1 Maze hill SE3
76 L 15 Maze hill SE10
77 O 19 Maze hill SE10
129 U 2 Mazenod av NW6
73 P 19 Maze rd Rich
7 W 8 McAdam dri Enf
89 Z 4 McAll clo SW4
149 S 1 McAuley clo SE1
78 C 14 Mccall cres SE7
94 C 10 Mccrone ms NW3
63 Y 5 McCullum rd E3
90 H 6 Mcdermott clo SW11
91 W 6 Mcdermott rd SE15

90 L 2 Mcdowall rd SE5
32 H 4 Mcentee av E17
64 L 3 Mcewan way E15
52 C 16 McGrath rd E15
137 P 3 McGregor rd W11
156 A 15 McIntosh clo Croy
39 P 10 Mcintosh rd Rom
39 P 10 Mcintosh rd Rom
104 L 17 Mckay rd SW20
10 B 8 Mckellar clo Bushey Watf
91 Y 2 Mckerrel rd SE15
80 C 12 Mcleod rd SE2
145 Z 4 Mcleods ms SW7
146 A 4 Mcleods ms SW7
76 B 16 Mcmillan st SE8
73 R 15 Meade clo W4
23 R 5 Meads clo Harrow
39 V 8 Mead clo Rom
25 X 16 Mead ct NW9
26 H 13 Mead cres E4
154 H 7 Mead cres Sutton
149 V 15 Meadcroft rd SE11
12 E 7 Meadfield Edg
17 V 19 Meadfoot rd SW16
37 X 9 Mead gro Rom
102 F 4 Meadlands dri Rich
124 F 14 Meadow av Croy
131 O 2 Meadowbank NW3
17 P 1 Meadowbank N21
94 D 8 Meadow bank SE3
16 L 13 Meadow bank Surb
144 E 19 Meadowbank clo SW6
43 X 1 Meadowbank rd NW9
111 O 12 Meadow clo SE6
118 M 9 Meadow clo SW20
119 N 9 Meadow clo SW20
4 H 19 Meadow clo Barnt
113 Z 12 Meadow clo Enf
9 U 4 Meadow clo Grnfd
58 H 5 Meadow clo Grnfd
82 G 17 Meadow clo Hounsl
102 J 2 Meadow clo Rich
154 B 2 Meadow clo Rich
94 D 11 Meadowcourt rd SE3
127 U 7 Meadowcroft Brom
17 U 9 Meadowcroft rd N13
29 R 9 Meadow dri NW4
26 L 8 Meadow dri NW4
12 G 18 Meadow gdns Edg
43 W 19 Meadow garth NW9
118 A 14 Meadow hill New Mald
149 O 16 Meadow ms SW8
148 M 18 Meadow pl SW8
149 N 16 Meadow rd SW8
106 D 19 Meadow rd SW19
67 Z 2 Meadow rd Bark
126 A 2 Meadow rd Brom
56 A 18 Meadow rd Dgnhm
100 B 3 Meadow rd Felt
22 A 14 Meadow rd Pinn
56 K 2 Meadow rd Rom
58 F 20 Meadow rd S'hall
70 F 1 Meadow rd S'hall
154 H 9 Meadow rd Sutton
150 A 3 Meadow row SE1
94 L 11 Meadowside SE9
153 S 20 Meadowside rd Sutton
114 B 15 Meadow the Chisl
11 N 11 Meadowview clo SE6
97 P 17 Meadowview Sidcp
11 M 11 Meadowview rd SE6
11 N 11 Meadowview rd SE6
28 A 17 Meadowview rd Bxly
152 B 19 Meadow view rd Epsom
122 H 12 Meadow View rd Thntn Hth
34 E 12 Meadow wlk E18
56 A 17 Meadow wlk Dgnhm
152 D 17 Meadow wlk Epsom
155 R 5 Meadow wlk Wallgtn
52 Z 15 Meadow way NW9
42 H 12 Meadow way Wemb
70 B 18 Meadow way Hounsl
102 C 10 Meadway clo Rich
23 T 5 Meadow Way the Harrow
50 D 18 Mead pl E9
122 K 20 Mead pl Croy
43 X 17 Mead plat NW10
114 B 15 Mead rd Chisl
12 B 20 Mead rd Edg
102 E 8 Mead rd Rich
144 T 1 Mead row SE1
36 J 20 Meads la Ilf
54 H 1 Meads la Ilf
30 H 9 Meads rd N22

9 V 6 Meads rd Enf
12 M 19 Meads the Edg
153 R 5 Meads the Sutton
60 A 14 Mead the W13
125 U 2 Mead the Becknhm
125 W 20 Mead the W Wkhm
155 Y 13 Mead the Wallgtn
28 D 7 Mead, the N2
60 C 11 Meadvale rd W5
123 V 16 Meadvale rd Croy
16 L 8 Meadway N14
17 N 8 Meadway N14
27 Z 19 Meadway NW11
28 B 18 Meadway NW11
118 M 9 Meadway SW20
119 N 8 Meadway SW20
4 K 14 Meadway Barnt
125 U 1 Meadway Becknhm
126 E 14 Mead way Brom
21 Z 6 Meadway Buck Hl
158 J 2 Mead way Croy
54 J 11 Meadway Ilf
39 V 7 Meadway Rom
83 P 20 Meadway Twick
21 Y 15 Mead way Wdfd Grn
23 B 13 Meadway clo NW11
4 K 13 Meadway clo Barnt
27 Z 19 Meadway ga NW11
110 A 18 Meaford way SE20
53 R 14 Meanley rd E12
140 E 7 Meard st W1
65 O6 Meath rd E15
54 C 9 Meath rd Ilf
89 R 1 Meath st SW11
133 N 17 Mecklenburg pl WC1
133 N 16 Mecklenburg sq WC1
133 N 15 Mecklenburg st WC1
132 E 8 Medburn st NW1
133 U 10 Medcalf rd N1
9 Z 1 Medcalf rd Enf
85 U 10 Medcroft gdns SE14
94 F 7 Medebourne clo SE3
17 V 14 Medesenge way N13
86 H 18 Medfield st SW15
63 V 8 Medhurst rd E3
50 C 14 Median rd E5
48 E 9 Medina gro N7
48 E 9 Medina rd N7
121 O 19 Medland clo Mitch
58 A 6 Medlar clo Grnfd
90 M 1 Medlar st SE5
150 C 20 Medlar st SE5
45 V 18 Medley rd NW6
115 R 9 Medomsley clo Sidcp
90 E 18 Medora rd SW2
38 M 13 Medora rd Rom
93 R 16 Medusa rd SE6
124 B 13 Medway clo Croy
54 C 16 Medway clo Ilf
59 W 6 Medway dri Grnfd
41 Y 13 Medway gdns Wemb
59 W 7 Medway pde Grnfd
63 W 7 Medway rd E3
99 W 9 Medway rd Drtfrd
148 F 3 Medway st SW1
89 B 10 Medwin st SW4
94 L 8 Meerbrook rd SE3
65 O 1 Meeson rd E15
143 X 13 Meeting Ho all E1
16 L 2 Meeting Ho la E1
75 N 2 Meeting Ho la E1
75 N 20 Meeting Ho la SE15
91 Z 1 Meeting Ho la SE15
151 W 20 Meeting Ho la SE15
50 C 16 Mehetabel rd E9
113 T 13 Melanda clo Chisl
97 Y 1 Melanie clo Bxly Hth
93 S 3 Melba way SE13
87 R 18 Melbourne av N13
71 Z 2 Melbourne av N13
22 K 9 Melbourne av Pinn
155 U 11 Melbourne clo Wallgtn
109 Y 18 Melbourne ct SE20
37 Y 14 Melbourne gdns Rom
91 T 10 Melbourne gro SE22
90 F 3 Melbourne ms SW9
141 O 7 Melbourne pl WC2
66 G 5 Melbourne rd E6
51 P 1 Melbourne rd E10
32 J 12 Melbourne rd E17
105 Z 20 Melbourne rd SW19
53 Z 4 Melbourne rd Ilf
54 A 4 Melbourne rd Ilf
102 F 15 Melbourne rd Tedd
155 T 12 Melbourne rd Wallgtn
8 H 20 Melbourne way Enf
70 K 9 Melbury av S'hall
113 S 15 Melbury clo Chisl

145 R 1 Melbury ct W8
150 J 20 Melbury dr SE5
104 J 20 Melbury gdns SW20
145 O 1 Melbury rd W14
25 O 16 Melbury rd Harrow
130 M 19 Melbury ter NW1
25 N 16 Melcombe gdns Harrow
131 N 19 Melcombe pl NW1
131 P 19 Melcombe st NW1
88 A 2 Meldon clo SW6
55 O 8 Meldrum rd Ilf
111 T 11 Melfield gdns SE6
54 J 17 Melford av Bark
66 G 10 Melford rd E6
51 Z 7 Melford rd E11
32 K 14 Melford rd E17
91 Y 20 Melford rd SE22
54 E 8 Melford rd Ilf
122 J 7 Melfort av Thntn Hth
122 K 7 Melfort rd Thntn Hth
48 G 16 Melgund rd N5
130 X 4 Melina pl NW8
74 H 6 Melina rd W12
142 H 16 Melior pl SE1
142 H 16 Melior st SE1
111 T 4 Melior st SE6
155 Z 4 Meller clo Wallgtn
79 V 17 Melling st SE18
67 X 4 Mellish clo Bark
106 L 13 Mellison rd SW17
62 D 15 Mellitus st W12
35 U 9 Mellows rd Ilf
155 X 11 Mellows rd Wallgtn
113 T 10 Mells cres SE9
76 M 15 Mell st SE10
88 D 14 Melody rd SW18
137 W 8 Melon pl W8
91 W 1 Melon rd SE15
30 J 4 Melrose av N22
44 M 15 Melrose av NW2
44 N 14 Melrose av NW2
122 E 5 Melrose av SW16
105 X 6 Melrose av SW19
58 L 6 Melrose av Grnfd
107 R 18 Melrose av Mitch
L 19 Melrose av Twick
58 K 6 Melrose clo Grnfd
70 H 1 Melrose dri S'hall
144 D 1 Melrose gdns W6
25 T 9 Melrose gdns Edg
117 Y 7 Melrose gdns New Mald
86 D 3 Melrose rd SW13
87 U 17 Melrose rd SW18
119 Y 2 Melrose rd SW19
73 U 8 Melrose rd W3
22 F 13 Melrose rd Pinn
54 M 7 Melrose rd W6
136 D 20 Melrose ter W6
120 C 14 Melsa rd Rom
95 P 2 Melthorpe gdns SE3
57 T 1 Melton gdns Rom
132 D 15 Melton st NW1
104 F 19 Melville av SW20
41 W 16 Melville av Grnfd
157 V 12 Melville av S Croy
17 U 17 Melville gdns N13
32 L 12 Melville rd E17
61 Y 1 Melville rd NW10
86 F 2 Melville rd SW13
38 H 3 Melville rd Rom
115 T 5 Melville rd Sidcp
134 A 2 Melville st N1
110 B 20 Melvin rd SE20
47 W 13 Melyn clo N7
134 X 17 Memel st EC1
64 M 8 Memorial av E15
65 N 9 Memorial av E15
17 N 17 Memorial clo Hounsl
145 N 16 Mendera rd SW6
105 R 5 Mendip clo SW19
45 R 8 Mendip dri NW2
88 D 8 Mendip rd SW11
99 P 3 Mendip rd Bxly Hth
57 W 2 Mendip rd Hornch
36 Y 16 Mendip rd Ilf
16 N 6 Mendora rd SW6
45 S 13 Menelik rd NW2
109 N 18 Menlo gdns SE19
24 E 17 Mentmore clo Harrow
50 A 20 Mentmore ter E8
73 W 5 Meon rd W3
121 U 2 Meopham rd Mitch
23 N 2 Mepham cres Harrow
23 N 2 Mepham gdns Harrow
141 S 1 Mepham st SE1
98 F 9 Mera dri Bxly Hth
93 X 9 Mercator st SE13
63 N 12 Merceron st E1
135 X 18 Merceron st E1
77 P 12 Mercers clo SE10

M

Mer–Mil

47 Y 10 Mercers rd N19
140 J 6 Mercer st WC2
123 N 4 Mercham rd Thntn Hth
63 Z 10 Merchant st E3
111 W 3 Merchiston rd SE6
114 C 2 Merchland rd SE9
93 V 9 Mercia gro SE13
87 S 13 Mercier rd SW15
72 F 15 Mercury rd Brentf
75 S 15 Mercury way SE14
93 R 12 Mercy ter SE13
56 D 10 Merebank la Croy
87 R 18 Mere clo SW19
45 N 14 Meredith av NW2
65 T 10 Meredith st EC1
133 V 14 Meredith st EC1
86 G 4 Meredyth rd SW13
F 18 Mere end Croy
120 D 14 Merevale cres Croy
101 S 1 Mereway rd Twick
127 V 3 Merewood clo Brom
98 J 4 Merewood rd Bxly Hth
126 C 12 Mereworth clo Brom
79 O 20 Mereworth dri SE18
36 B 4 Meriden clo Ilf
113 O 19 Meriden clo Chisl
78 A 18 Meridian rd SE7
18 F 19 Meridian wlk N17
94 C 10 Merifield rd SE9
97 O 15 Merino pl Sidcp
87 T 10 Merivale rd SW15
41 O 2 Merivale rd Harrow
113 T 20 Merlewood dri Chisl
127 U 1 Merlewood dri Chisl
43 W 3 Merley ct NW9
55 S 7 Merlin clo Croy
25 N 4 Merlin cres Edgw
112 E 8 Merlin gdns Brom
124 M 10 Merlin gro Becknhm
125 N 10 Merlin gro Becknhm
36 A 1 Merlin gro Ilf
52 M 7 Merlin rd E12
96 M 7 Merlin rd Well
97 O 10 Merlin rd Welling
40 F 9 Merlins av Harrow
133 T 14 Merlin st WC1
142 E 16 Mermaid st SE1
150 D 1 Merrick sq SE1
7 V 19 Merridene N21
69 P 5 Merrielands cres Dgnhm
118 M 20 Merrilands rd Worc Pk
96 G 20 Merrilees rd Sidcp
94 M 1 Merriman rd SE3
96 N 1 Merriman rd SE3
145 U 13 Merrington rd SW5
11 T 15 Merrion av Stanm
92 L 13 Merritt rd SE4
6 K 18 Merrivale N14
35 O 13 Merrivale av Ilf
153 O 19 Merrow rd Sutton
150 D 12 Merrow st SE17
150 F 11 Merrow st SE17
159 V 14 Merrow way Croy
11 T 18 Merryfield gdns Stanm
94 D 5 Merryfield SE3
20 D 3 Merryhill clo E4
7 N 15 Merryhills dri Enf
32 L 9 Mersey rd E17
25 R 16 Mersham dri NW9
110 A 20 Mersham pl SE20
74 K 17 Merthyr ter SW13
74 C 11 Merton av W4
41 N 15 Merton av Grnfd
92 G 10 Merton clo SE4
127 Z 12 Merton gdns Brom
105 T 20 Merton Hall gdns SW20
105 T 20 Merton Hall rd SW19
119 U 1 Merton Hall rd SW19
106 D 19 Merton High st SW19
47 N 6 Merton la N6
119 P 4 Merton mans SW20
46 J 19 Merton ri NW3
33 T 17 Merton rd E17
123 W 11 Merton rd SE25
87 Y 17 Merton rd SW18
106 A 18 Merton rd SW19
67 Y 1 Merton rd Bark
8 A 4 Merton rd Enf
41 N 4 Merton rd Harrow
36 K 20 Merton rd Ilf
55 Z 1 Merton rd Rom
92 F 12 Merttins rd SE15
90 F 12 Mervan rd SW2
114 C 6 Mervyn av SE9
71 Z 8 Mervyn rd W13

61 X 18 Messaline av W3
94 L 12 Messent rd SE9
95 W 15 Messeter pl SE9
129 U 1 Mesina av NW6
89 P 10 Meteor st SW11
156 N 16 Meteor way Wallgtn
155 Z 17 Meteor way Wallgtn
26 A 6 Metheringham way NW9
149 U 11 Methley st SE11
25 O 2 Methuen clo Edg
25 O 2 Methuen clo Edg
29 T 9 Methuen pk N10
81 V 10 Methuen rd Blvdr
98 B 11 Methuen rd Bxly Hth
25 O 3 Methuen rd Edg
128 F 20 Methwold rd W10
136 F 1 Methwold rd W10
35 O 16 Mews the Ilf
39 P 14 Mews the Rom
87 W 13 Mexfield rd SW15
8 K 3 Meyer gro Enf
81 Y 16 Meyer rd Erith
58 E 20 Meynell cres E9
50 F 20 Meynell rd E9
39 Z 1 Meynell rd Rom
141 W 14 Meynott st SE1
44 F 17 Meyrick rd NW10
88 H 8 Meyrick rd SW11
110 J 8 Miall wlk SE26
134 C 11 Micawber st N1
52 A 4 Michael pl E11
123 R 7 Michael rd SE25
88 B 1 Michael rd SW6
71 X 3 Michael Gaynor clo W7
84 J 9 Michels gro Rich
94 C 15 Micheldever rd SE12
101 X 6 Michelham gdns Twick
53 S 12 Michigan av E12
14 J 13 Mickleham down N12
153 R 13 Mickleham gdns Sutton
159 X 15 Micklenham way Croy
145 U 15 Mickethwaite rd SW6
12 L 11 Middle dene NW7
130 F 3 Middlefield NW8
60 A 14 Middlefielde W13
35 Z 20 Middlefield gdns Ilf
36 A 19 Midlefield gdns Ilf
158 H 20 Middlefields Croy
18 K 19 Middleham gdns N18
18 K 19 Middleham rd N18
29 Z 16 Middle la N8
101 V 14 Middle la Tedd
94 M 15 Middle Park av SE9
95 N 17 Middle Park av SE9
113 S 1 Middle Park av SE9
41 P 5 Middle path Harrow
65 S 8 Middle rd E13
121 W 3 Middle rd SW16
5 V 19 Middle rd Barnt
41 R 5 Middle rd Harrow
128 K 17 Middle row W10
8 K 18 Middlesborough rd N18
74 E 12 Middlesex ct W4
141 Z 2 Middlesex pas EC1
142 M 3 Middlesex st E1
143 N 5 Middlesex st E1
50 D 5 Middlesex wharf E5
141 Z 1 Middle st EC1
156 L 4 Middle st Croy
141 S 7 Middle Temple la EC4
19 Z 12 Middleton av E4
20 A 11 Middleton av E4
59 S 5 Middleton av Grnfd
115 S 14 Middleton av Sidcp
140 A 1 Middleton bldgs W1
19 Y 12 Middleton clo E4
35 Z 19 Middleton gdns Ilf
36 A 20 Middleton gdns Ilf
134 M 1 Middleton gro N7
135 O 1 Middleton ms N7
45 X 1 Middleton rd E8
119 Z 15 Middleton rd NW11
120 C 14 Middleton rd Mrdn
120 J 17 Middleton rd Mrdn
63 N 8 Middleton rd Mrdn
135 W 11 Middleton st E2
93 X 9 Middleton st E2
28 B 17 Middleton way SE13
121 X 4 Middleway NW11
23 V 7 Middle way SW16
Middle Way the Harrow
122 A 10 Middlesex rd Mitch
98 K 7 Midfield av Bxly Hth
115 R 20 Midfield way Orp

132 C 18 Midford pl W1
28 A 14 Midholm NW11
43 R 5 Midholm Wemb
28 A 13 Midholm clo NW11
158 J 4 Midhope rd Croy
57 K 13 Midhope st WC1
29 O 11 Midhurst av N10
G 16 Midhurst av Croy
57 U 13 Midhurst clo Hornch
98 D 15 Midhurst hill Bxly Hth
71 Z 6 Midhurst rd W13
72 A 8 Midhurst rd W13
44 M 3 Midland Brent ter NW2
76 F 14 Midland pl E14
51 U 3 Midland rd E10
H 12 Midland rd NW1
45 O 10 Midland ter NW2
62 B 12 Midland ter NW10
117 V 5 Midleton rd New Mald
107 V 1 Midmoor rd SW12
105 R 19 Midmoor rd SW19
44 B 12 Midstrath rd NW10
82 D 11 Midsummer av NW2
119 V 17 Midway Sutton
44 H 9 Midwood clo NW2
66 K 2 Miers clo E6
35 O 14 Mighell av Ilf
146 C 12 Milborne gro SW10
58 E 9 Milborne st E9
94 A 17 Milborough cres SE12
141 X 19 Milcote st SE1
84 A 6 Mildenhall rd E5
49 O 16 Mildmay av N1
49 O 16 Mildmay gro N1
59 P 15 Mildmay pk N1
49 P 15 Mildmay rd N1
38 K 15 Mildmay rd Rom
49 P 17 Mildmay st N1
40 L 16 Mildred av Grnfd
63 T 12 Mile End pl E1
63 O 13 Mile End rd E1
32 F 6 Mile End the E17
91 U 16 Mile rd SE22
121 U 19 Mile rd Wallgtn
76 F 9 Miles la EC4
13 Y 17 Milespit hill NW7
J 20 Miles pl NW1
116 M 9 Miles rd N8
H 5 Miles rd Mitch
34 K 15 Miles st SW8
154 F 15 Milestone clo Sutton
109 U 16 Milestone rd SE19
15 Y 9 Miles way N20
62 G 20 Milfoil st W12
80 M 15 Milford clo SE2
25 P 3 Milford gdns Edg
42 G 14 Milford gdns Wemb
154 C 7 Milford gdns Sutton
141 R 7 Milford la WC2
141 S 8 Milford la WC2
72 A 3 Milford rd W13
58 H 20 Milford rd S'hall
70 H 1 Milford rd S'hall
143 S 3 Milfred st E1
76 L 4 Milk st E1
160 B 5 Milt st EC2
112 H 14 Milk st Brom
34 J 1 Milkwell gdns Wdfd Grn
90 K 11 Milkwood rd SE24
75 P 1 Milk yd E1
53 W 16 Millais av E11
25 P 7 Millais gdns Edg
51 V 12 Millais rd E11
8 H 18 Millais rd Enf
117 Z 16 Millais rd New Mald
56 D 18 Millard ter Dgnhm
148 K 7 Millbank SW1
E 14 Millbank way SE12
100 C 9 Millbrook av Welling
96 F 10 Millbrook av Welling
38 A 17 Millbrook gdns Rom
39 S 6 Millbrook gdns Rom
18 L 6 Millbrook rd N9
90 H 8 Millbrook rd SW19
155 O 3 Mill clo Carsh
4 H 7 Mill corner Barnt
106 G 15 Miller rd SW19
122 E 20 Miller rd SW19
49 U 13 Millers av E8
7 V 12 Millers grn Enf
49 U 14 Millers ter E8
132 A 7 Miller st NW1
58 L 8 Millet rd Grnfd
82 C 20 Mill Farm cres Hounsl
100 C 1 Mill Farm cres Twick
32 J 5 Millfield av E17
47 N 8 Millfield la N6
47 O 7 Millfield pl N6

82 C 20 Millfield rd Hounsl
50 G 10 Millfields rd E5
110 A 8 Mills gdns
121 O 16 Mill Grn rd Mitch
89 N 3 Millgrove st SW11
13 R 16 Mill Hill cir NW7
14 D 20 Mill Hill East sta NW7
14 D 20 Mill Hill Estate sta NW7
73 U 4 Mill Hill gro W3
13 T 17 Mill Hill pk NW7
86 G 6 Mill Hill rd SW13
73 S 4 Mill Hill rd W3
73 T 4 Mill Hill ter W3
121 U 11 Mill house Mitch
108 K 11 Millhouse pl SE27
50 M 3 Millicent rd E10
25 Y 1 Milling rd Edg
155 N 8 Mill la Carsh
156 E 5 Mill la Croy
152 E 18 Mill la Epsom
37 Y 19 Mill la Rom
21 R 17 Mill la Wdfd Grn
78 K 14 Mill la SE18
133 N 18 Millman st WC1
92 J 6 Millmark gro SE14
9 Y 8 Millmarsh la Enf
31 Z 11 Mill Mead rd N17
63 X 18 Mill pl E14
113 Y 20 Mill pl Chisl
99 X 11 Mill pl Drtfrd
116 K 5 Mill pl Kingst
83 Z 6 Mill plat Islwth
84 A 6 Mill plat Islwth
83 Y 5 Mill Plat av Islwth
12 B 17 Mill ridge Edg
77 W 3 Mill rd E16
106 E 17 Mill rd SW19
81 X 20 Mill rd Erith
53 W 9 Mill rd Ilf
101 O 4 Mill rd Twick
134 L 5 Mill row N1
64 F 16 Mills gro E14
27 O 11 Mills gro NW4
64 F 16 Mills gro E14
87 N 1 Mill Shot clo SW6
154 M 2 Millside Carsh
15 Y 9 Millson clo N20
143 N 20 Millstream rd SE1
143 P 18 Mill st SE1
139 Z 8 Mill st W1
116 K 6 Mill st Kingst
126 D 4 Mill vale Brom
158 E 5 Mill View gdns Croy
76 B 8 Millwall Dock rd E14
63 N 15 Millward st E1
40 E 19 Millway gdns Grnfd
82 M 13 Millwood rd Hounsl
83 N 13 Millwood rd Hounsl
136 J 2 Millwood st W10
128 J 8 Milman rd NW6
146 G 16 Milman st SW10
22 G 1 Milnefield Pinn
95 P 13 Milne gdns SE9
83 P 18 Milner dri Twick
133 V 3 Milner pl N1
64 M 9 Milner rd E15
106 A 19 Milner rd SW19
116 G 7 Milner rd Kingst
120 F 11 Milner rd Mrdn
123 N 5 Milner rd Thntn Hth
55 S 7 Milner rd Dgnhm
133 V 2 Milner sq N1
147 N 4 Milner st SW3
73 X 16 Milnthorpe rd W4
144 J 1 Milson rd W14
66 B 1 Milton av E6
47 V 1 Milton av N6
25 U 11 Milton av NW9
61 X 4 Milton av NW10
4 J 15 Milton av Barnt
123 P 18 Milton av Croy
57 U 6 Milton av Hornch
154 H 8 Milton av Sutton
28 C 17 Milton av N2
154 G 6 Milton clo Sutton
22 A 3 Milton clo Pinn
134 D 20 Milton ct EC2
75 W 18 Milton Ct rd SE14
36 A 19 Milton cres Ilf
16 J 16 Milton gro N11
49 P 13 Milton gro N16
47 U 1 Milton pk N6
E 15 Milton pl N7
33 O 12 Milton rd E17
47 V 1 Milton rd N6
49 P 14 Milton rd N15
30 J 12 Milton rd N15
13 T 15 Milton rd NW7
90 H 14 Milton rd SE24
85 X 9 Milton rd SW14
106 C 15 Milton rd SW19

73 X 2 Milton rd W3
59 W 20 Milton rd W7
81 R 11 Milton rd Blvdr
123 P 18 Milton rd Croy
100 H 19 Milton rd Hampt
23 U 13 Milton rd Harrow
107 P 18 Milton rd Mitch
39 V 18 Milton rd Rom
153 Y 7 Milton rd Sutton
155 W 14 Milton rd Wallgtn
96 J 1 Milton rd Welling
65 T 5 Milton st E13
134 D 20 Milton st EC2
54 K 6 Milverton gdns Ilf
45 N 20 Milverton rd NW6
128 D 1 Milverton rd NW6
149 U 11 Milverton st SE11
113 X 9 Milverton way SE6
143 X 1 Milward st E1
87 V 2 Mimosa st SW6
93 Y 19 Minard rd SE6
111 Z 3 Minard rd SE6
150 M 9 Mina rd SE17
105 Z 20 Mina rd SW19
16 J 11 Minchenden cres N14
142 K 8 Mincing la EC3
109 Z 20 Minden rd SE20
108 C 13 Minehead rd SW16
40 G 9 Minehead rd Harrow
79 T 12 Mineral st SE18
147 U 6 Minera ms SW1
114 G 9 Minerva clo Sidcp
33 R 1 Minerva rd E4
61 X 10 Minerva rd NW10
116 L 3 Minerva rd Kingst
135 W 9 Minerva st E2
62 A 5 Minet av NW10
62 A 5 Minet gdns NW10
90 J 5 Minet rd SW9
136 E 19 Minford gdns W14
64 B 20 Ming st E14
116 M 11 Minniedale Surb
117 N 10 Minniedale Surb
143 N 8 Minories EC3
89 X 3 Minshull st SW8
63 T 2 Minson rd E9
86 D 17 Minstead gdns SW15
118 A 15 Minstead way New Mald
153 Y 4 Minster av Sutton
157 S 7 Minster dri Croy
45 T 15 Minster rd NW2
112 H 17 Minster rd Brom
30 A 14 Minster wlk N8
17 W 11 Mintern clo N13
70 H 10 Minterne av S'hall
25 O 17 Minterne rd Harrow
25 O 17 Mintern rd Harrow
134 G 8 Mintern st N1
155 R 9 Mint rd Wallgtn
142 B 17 Mint st SE1
157 N 5 Mint wlk Croy
156 M 5 Mint wlk Croy
135 W 12 Minto pl E2
145 P 17 Mirabel rd SW6
44 W 4 Miranda rd N19
78 A 10 Mirfield st SE7
79 U 13 Miriam rd SE18
122 M 7 Mirror path SE9
120 D 14 Missenden gdns Mrdn
32 J 15 Mission gro E17
91 X 1 Mission pl SE15
121 T 15 Mitcham common Mitch
107 V 13 Mitcham la SW16
120 L 9 Mitcham pk Mitch
66 E 9 Mitcham rd E6
121 Z 14 Mitcham rd SW16
106 L 12 Mitcham rd SW17
122 C 16 Mitcham rd Croy
36 L 20 Mitcham rd Ilf
88 F 13 Mitchell clo SE2
17 X 15 Mitchell rd N13
134 B 15 Mitchell st EC1
43 W 18 Mitchell way NW10
40 O 19 Michison rd N1
31 W 9 Mitchley rd N17
48 A 7 Mitford rd N4
154 E 16 Mitre clo Sutton
160 B 5 Mitre ct EC2
141 U 17 Mitre rd SE1
142 M 6 Mitre sq EC3
142 L 6 Mitre st EC3
63 Y 19 Mitre the E14
27 Z 10 Moat cres N3
75 Y 8 Moat dri E13
23 O 13 Moat dri Harrow
40 F 19 Moat Farm rd Grnfd
20 D 7 Moat pl SW9
61 T 16 Moat pl W3
99 X 3 Moat la Erith

9 S 13 Moat side Enf
118 A 1 Moat the New Mald
47 N 18 Modbury gdns NW5
47 O 17 Modbury st NW5
87 P 9 Modder pl SW15
72 B 4 Model cotts W13
113 R 6 Model Farm clo SE9
141 W 5 Modern ct EC4
23 X 16 Moelyn mews Harrow
120 G 7 Moffat gdns Mitch
17 N 18 Moffat rd N13
106 K 9 Moffat rd SW17
122 M 4 Moffat rd Thntn Hth
123 N 3 Moffat rd Thntn Hth
83 X 12 Mogden la Islwth
76 A 7 Moiety rd E14
31 R 7 Moira clo N17
95 U 9 Moira rd SE9
157 W 20 Moir clo S Croy
75 S 12 Moland mead SE16
114 B 7 Molescroft SE9
153 S 4 Molesey dri Sutton
87 Y 3 Molesford rd SW6
93 T 8 Molesworth st SE13
9 W 8 Mollison av Enf
9 X 4 Mollison av Enf
156 B 14 Mollison dri Wallgtn
155 Z 17 Mollison dri Wallgtn
25 O 8 Mollison way Edg
24 M 9 Mollison way Edg
138 M 3 Molyneux st W1
81 S 9 Monarch rd Blvdr
92 A 4 Mona rd SE15
8 B 9 Monastery gdns Enf
66 P 15 Mona st E16
148 G 3 Monck st SW1
91 R 9 Monclar rd SE5
138 J 20 Moncorvo clo SW7
91 X 4 Moncrieff st SE15
52 K 18 Monega rd E7
53 P 17 Monega rd E12
64 A 1 Monier rd E3
110 L 19 Monivea rd Becknhm
65 R 19 Monk dri E16
6 D 20 Monkfrith av N14
16 E 1 Monkfrith av N14
16 D 2 Monkfrith clo N14
16 D 2 Monkfrith way N14
21 V 18 Monkhams av Wdfd Grn
21 V 17 Monkhams dri Wdfd Grn
21 X 11 Monkhams la Buck Hl
21 T 15 Monkhams la Wdfd Grn
119 T 8 Monkleigh rd Mrdn
5 S 20 Monks av Barnt
15 S 1 Monks av Barnt
80 H 10 Monks clo SE2
7 X 9 Monks clo Enf
154 B 4 Monksdene gdns Sutton
61 P 16 Monks dri W3
125 O 13 Monks Orchard rd Becknhm
43 U 16 Monks pl Wemb
43 T 19 Monks Park gdns Wemb
7 X 8 Monks rd Enf
78 J 10 Monks st SE18
125 P 16 Monks way Becknhm
29 P 4 Monkswell ct N10
35 W 11 Monkswood gdns Ilf
96 L 4 Monkton rd Welling
149 V 5 Monkton st SE11
27 V 13 Monkville av NW11
160 B 2 Monkwell sq EC2
34 H 11 Monmouth av E18
102 F 19 Monmouth av Kingst
97 N 9 Monmouth rd Welling
122 B 8 Monmouth clo Mitch
137 W 6 Monmouth pl W2
66 F 10 Monmouth rd E6
18 M 8 Monmouth rd N9
19 P 10 Monmouth rd N9
137 W 7 Monmouth rd W2
56 B 15 Monmouth rd Dgnhm
140 J 7 Monmouth st WC2
47 V 10 Monnery rd N19
151 T 6 Monnow rd SE1
32 M 4 Monoux gro E17
48 J 9 Monroe cres Enf
48 J 20 Monsell rd N4
33 X 2 Monserratt av Wdfd Grn
62 H 6 Monson rd NW10
75 S 20 Monson rd SE14
127 P 14 Mons way Brom
92 L 18 Montacute rd SE6
10 G 2 Montacute rd Bushey Watf

159 T 20 Montacute rd Croy
120 E 15 Montacute rd Mrdn
142 E 13 Montague clo SE1
19 N 15 Montague cres N18
155 V 10 Montagu gdns Wallgtn
31 W 12 Montagu rd N15
92 M 10 Montague av SE4
93 N 10 Montague av SE4
71 V 3 Montague av W7
61 P 19 Montague gdns W3
64 F 19 Montague pl E14
64 F 20 Montague pl E14
132 H 20 Montague pl WC1
49 W 15 Montague rd E8
52 B 8 Montague rd E11
30 C 16 Montague rd N8
26 G 19 Montague rd NW4
105 Z 18 Montague rd SW19
71 V 4 Montague rd W7
60 B 17 Montague rd W13
122 J 19 Montague rd Croy
82 K 7 Montague rd Hounsl
84 K 15 Montague rd Rich
70 B 10 Montague rd S'hall
140 J 1 Montague rd WC1
70 B 9 Montague waye S'hall
19 N 14 Montagu gdns N18
139 R 2 Montagu mans W1
139 P 2 Montagu Ms north W1
139 P 4 Montagu Ms south W1
139 P 4 Montagu Ms west W1
139 P 2 Montagu pl W1
140 H 1 Montagu pl W1
19 O 12 Montagu rd N18
139 R 2 Montagu row W1
139 P 3 Montagu sq W1
139 R 4 Montagu st W1
21 O 16 Montalt rd Wdfd Grn
21 P 15 Montalt rd Wdfd Grn
107 O 8 Montana rd SW17
105 O 20 Montana rd SW20
113 Z 7 Montbelle rd SE9
126 F 15 Montcalm clo Brom
78 A 18 Montcalm rd SE7
54 C 18 Monteagle av Bark
89 S 5 Montefiore st SW8
63 Y 3 Monteith rd E3
92 K 19 Montem rd SE23
117 Z 8 Montem rd New Mald
118 A 9 Montem rd New Mald
48 C 5 Montem st N4
29 W 17 Montenotte rd N8
149 S 11 Montford pl SE11
87 R 20 Montford pl SW19
96 J 15 Montgomery clo Sidcp
122 B 9 Montgomery clo Mitch
73 V 10 Montgomery rd W4
12 A 20 Montgomery rd Edg
88 M 16 Montholme rd SW11
143 R 2 Montholme st WC1
86 L 12 Montolieu gdns SW15
60 E 15 Montpelier av W5
97 W 19 Montpelier av Bxly
66 B 8 Montpelier gdns E6
55 T 1 Montpelier gdns Rom
47 V 14 Montpelier gdns NW5
138 M 20 Montpelier ms SW7
138 L 20 Montpelier pl SW7
45 S 1 Montpelier ri NW11
42 F 5 Montpelier ri Wemb
28 C 6 Montpelier rd N3
92 A 1 Montpelier rd SE15
151 X 20 Montpelier rd SE15
60 G 15 Montpelier rd Sutton
154 E 8 Montpelier row SE3
84 C 4 Montpelier row SW7
84 D 19 Montpelier row Twick
138 L 20 Montpelier sq SW7
138 M 20 Montpelier st SW7
45 S 1 Montpelier ter SW7
94 B 5 Montpelier vale SE3
138 L 20 Montpelier wlk SW7
45 S 1 Montpelier way NW11
110 C 16 Montrave rd SE20
141 O 8 Montreal pl WC2
54 A 2 Montreal rd Ilf
90 A 20 Montrell rd SW2
128 M 7 Montrose av Sidcp
25 W 7 Montrose av Edg
99 O 7 Montrose av Welling
82 L 20 Montrose av Twick
96 G 8 Montrose clo Welling
96 J 7 Montrose clo Welling

21 S 13 Montrose clo Wdfd Grn
138 G 20 Montrose ct SW7
28 C 1 Montrose cres N3
42 J 17 Montrose cres Wemb
120 M 5 Montrose gdns Mitch
154 B 4 Montrose gdns Sutton
139 U 20 Montrose pl SW1
93 W 1 Montrose rd Harrow
110 E 2 Montrose wy SE23
33 X 2 Montserrat av Wdfd Grn
87 S 10 Montserrat rd SW15
142 H 10 Monument st EC3
160 H 10 Monument st EC3
75 P 1 Monza st E1
75 R 7 Moodkey st SE16
63 T 10 Moody st E1
4 H 12 Moon la Barnt
54 W 11 Moons ct SE12
133 V 4 Moon st N1
107 Z 6 Moorcroft st SE6
22 A 16 Moorcroft way Pinn
78 L 20 Moordown SE18
95 Y 1 Moordown SE18
156 A 18 Moore clo Wallgtn
31 U 9 Moorefield rd SW16
112 D 19 Mooreland rd Brom
121 S 4 Moore clo Mitch
145 W 20 Moore Pk rd SW6
108 K 14 Moore rd SE19
147 O 5 Moore st SW3
52 U 13 Moore wlk E7
65 O 3 Moorey clo E15
65 O 4 Moorey clo E15
94 H 8 Moorhead way SE3
60 H 11 Moorfield av W5
9 O 7 Moorfield rd Enf
142 E 2 Moorfields EC2
160 E 2 Moorfields EC2
142 E 2 Moorgate EC2
160 E 4 Moorgate EC2
137 T 5 Moorhouse rd W2
24 H 30 Moorhouse rd Harrow
38 H 3 Moorland clo Rom
24 K 15 Moorland rd Harrow
100 D 13 Moorland rd Hampt
90 H 10 Moorland rd SW9
13 X 20 Moorlands av NW7
134 E 20 Moor la EC2
142 D 1 Moor la EC2
160 D 1 Moor la EC2
152 B 11 Moormead dri Epsom
83 Z 16 Moormead rd Twick
142 F 2 Moor pl EC2
160 F 2 Moor pl EC2
112 A 7 Moorside rd Brom
140 G 7 Moor st W1
25 O 17 Moot ct NW9
64 B 19 Morant st E14
44 N 11 Mora rd NW2
45 N 11 Mora rd NW2
134 C 13 Mora st EC1
149 T 8 Morat st SW8
91 E 1 Morat st SW9
88 B 20 Moravian st E2
39 O 3 Moray ms N4
48 D 6 Moray rd N4
48 E 5 Moray rd N4
39 O 3 Moray way Rom
61 Z 4 Mordant rd NW10
58 C 8 Mordaunt st SW9
93 U 3 Morden clo SE13
139 Z 9 Morden ct Mrdn
41 X 15 Morden gdns Grnfd
120 G 9 Morden gdns Mrdn
120 C 7 Morden hall Mrdn
120 D 6 Morden Hall pk Mrdn
120 B 7 Morden Hall rd Mrdn
93 U 3 Morden hill SE13
119 U 13 Morden pk Mrdn
94 E 4 Morden rd SE3
94 F 5 Morden rd SE3
106 A 20 Morden rd SW19
36 K 20 Morden rd Ilf
120 A 3 Morden rd Mitch
37 Z 20 Morden rd Rom
38 A 20 Morden rd Rom
94 E 5 Morden Rd ms SE3
93 S 5 Morden st SE13
119 X 19 Morden way Sutton
96 M 9 Morden Wharf rd SE10
57 Z 16 Morecambe clo Hornch
11 V 14 Morecambe gdns Stanm
150 C 8 Morecambe st SE17
65 E 16 More clo E16
58 G 8 More clo W14
144 J 7 More st W14
18 A 13 Morecombe ter N18

M

103 T 17	Morecoombe clo Kingst
18 J 15	Moree way N18
99 Z 14	Moreland av Drtfrd
133 Y 12	Moreland st EC1
20 E 10	Moreland way E4
68 L 18	Morella rd SW12
110 H 9	Moremead rd SE6
111 O 10	Moremead rd SE6
93 R 18	Morena st SE6
117 T 17	Moresby av Surb
49 Z 5	Moresby rd E5
50 A 4	Moresby rd E5
83 S 1	Moreton av Islwth
50 B 5	Moreton clo E5
31 O 18	Moreton clo N15
13 Z 20	Moreton clo NW7
148 C 9	Moreton pl SW1
31 P 18	Moreton rd N15
157 P 11	Moreton rd S Croy
152 H 3	Moreton rd Worc Pk
148 D 10	Moreton st SW1
148 C 9	Moreton ter SW1
33 Y 13	Morgan av E17
69 R 1	Morgan clo Dgnhm
F 16	Morgan rd N7
112 E 19	Morgan rd Brom
142 J 14	Morgans la SE1
63 W 9	Morgan st E3
65 P 14	Morgan st E16
146 J 19	Morgans wlk SW11
109 R 6	Morkyns wlk SE21
88 A 12	Morie st SW18
50 L 4	Morieux rd E10
107 P 10	Moring rd SW17
123 S 19	Morland av Croy
46 B 4	Morland clo NW11
61 Y 1	Morland gdns NW10
70 L 3	Morland gdns S'hall
133 U 1	Morland ms N1
32 G 17	Morland rd E17
110 F 16	Morland rd SE20
123 T 18	Morland rd Croy
69 T 2	Morland rd Dgnhm
53 Y 6	Morland rd Ilf
154 E 12	Morland rd Sutton
33 W 2	Morley av E4
18 K 14	Morley av N18
J 6	Morley av N22
12 G 9	Morley cres Edg
24 E 9	Morley cres Stanm
24 F 9	Morely Cres east Stanm
24 E 10	Morley Cres west Stanm
8 B 4	Morley hill Enf
51 U 5	Morley rd E10
P 6	Morley rd E15
93 U 11	Morley rd SE13
S 4	Morley rd Bark
37 Y 17	Morley rd Rom
119 V 20	Morley rd Sutton
84 F 16	Morley rd Twick
141 U 19	Morley st SE1
13 Z 20	Morlton clo NW7
91 N 3	Morna rd SE5
50 B 17	Morning la E9
152 L 3	Morningside rd Worc Pk
145 O 8	Mornington av W14
126 M 7	Mornington av Brom
35 V 20	Mornington av Ilf
21 S 13	Mornington clo Wdfd Grn
132 A 8	Mornington cres NW1
64 A 9	Mornington gro E3
131 Z 8	Mornington pl NW1
132 A 9	Mornington pl NW1
90 K 1	Mornington ms W5
20 J 2	Mornington rd E4
52 B 2	Mornington rd E11
75 Z 20	Mornington rd SE8
58 K 12	Mornington rd Grnfd
21 S 13	Mornington rd Wdfd Grn
131 Y 8	Mornington ter NW1
131 Y 7	Mornington ter NW1
102 E 9	Mornington wlk Rich
142 J 19	Morocco st SE1
63 S 4	Morpeth gro E9
63 S 9	Morpeth rd E9
148 B 3	Morpeth ter SW1
54 K 9	Morrab gdns Ilf
7 T 15	Morris av E12
87 X 17	Morris gdns SW18
48 F 6	Morris pl N4
90 A 19	Morris rd SW2
31 S 10	Morrison av N17
68 K 6	Morrison rd Bark
89 O 6	Morrison st SW11
20 D 15	Morris st E14
51 Y 12	Morris rd E15

56 C 7	Morris rd Dgnhm
83 V 7	Morris rd Islwth
39 Z 1	Morris rd Rom
63 N 18	Morris st E1
143 Y 7	Morris st E1
65 R 10	Morse clo E13
129 W 14	Morshead rd W9
113 T 10	Morston gro SE9
89 X 16	Morten clo SW4
31 O 4	Morteyne rd N17
64 L 4	Mortham st E15
107 X 3	Mortimer clo SW16
129 Y 6	Mortimer cres NW6
132 D 18	Mortimer mkt WC1
129 X 6	Mortimer pl NW6
66 F 9	Mortimer rd E6
49 S 20	Mortimer rd N1
134 K 2	Mortimer rd N1
128 D 12	Mortimer rd NW10
60 C 17	Mortimer rd W13
81 Z 17	Mortimer rd Erith
120 L 2	Mortimer rd Mitch
136 H 11	Mortimer sq W11
139 Z 4	Mortimer st W1
140 B 3	Mortimer st W1
47 R 12	Mortimer ter NW5
156 B 5	Mortlake clo Croy
85 Y 6	Mortlake High st SW14
65 W 16	Mortlake rd E16
54 D 13	Mortlake rd Ilf
73 P 19	Mortlake rd Rich
85 S 4	Mortlake rd Rich
91 Z 2	Mortlock clo SE15
16 J 13	Morton cres N14
155 V 10	Morton gdns Wallgtn
145 X 7	Morton ms SW5
149 S 2	Morton pl SE1
65 O 2	Morton rd E15
134 D 2	Morton rd N1
120 F 12	Morton rd Mrdn
16 H 12	Morton way N14
90 F 14	Morval rd SW2
81 O 11	Morvale clo Blvdr
100 L 6	Morven rd SW17
64 A 6	Morville st E3
140 F 2	Morwell st WC1
137 X 8	Moscow pl W2
137 W 9	Moscow rd W2
30 H 6	Moselle av N22
28 D 12	Moselle clo N8
31 V 2	Moselle pl N17
31 V 2	Moselle st N17
15 N 19	Mossborough clo N12
86 K 9	Mossbury rd SW11
154 H 10	Moss clo Carsh
22 D 8	Moss clo Pinn
81 T 12	Mossdown clo Blvdr
35 Z 8	Mossford clo Ilf
36 B 10	Mossford grn Ilf
36 B 5	Mossford la Ilf
63 X 12	Mossford st E3
158 E 17	Moss gdn S Croy
15 O 19	Moss Hall cres N12
15 N 19	Moss Hall gro N12
151 Z 6	Mossington rd SE16
22 C 8	Moss la Pinn
39 V 18	Moss la Rom
110 C 16	Mosslea rd SE20
127 O 12	Mosslea rd Brom
146 M 6	Mossop st SW3
56 F 20	Moss rd Dgnhm
119 V 7	Mossville gdns Mrdn
42 L 14	Mostyn av Wemb
43 N 14	Mostyn av Wemb
128 F 11	Mostyn gdns NW10
63 Z 7	Mostyn gro E3
90 F 3	Mostyn rd SW9
119 W 1	Mostyn rd SW19
25 Z 2	Mostyn rd Edg
26 A 3	Mostyn rd Edg
127 R 15	Mosul way Brom
139 S 20	Motcomb st SW1
13 R 7	Mote end NW7
13 N 17	Motorway M1 NW7
118 G 13	Motspur pk New Mald
113 O 2	Mottingham gdns SE9
112 K 2	Mottingham hall SE9
94 K 19	Mottingham la SE9
112 L 1	Mottingham la SE9
113 N 2	Mottingham la SE9
19 S 1	Mottingham rd N9
113 U 8	Mottingham rd SE9
79 Z 9	Mottisfont rd SE2
80 A 9	Mottisfont rd SE2
63 R 2	Moulins rd E9
82 D 4	Moulton av Hounsl
31 X 19	Moundfield rd N16
113 V 8	Mound The SE9
109 W 8	Mountacre clo SE26

91 X 19	Mount Adon pk SE22
86 E 19	Mount Angelus rd SW15
84 K 13	Mount Ararat rd Rich
109 Z 7	Mount Ash rd SE26
110 A 6	Mount Ash rd SE26
20 C 11	Mount av E5
60 G 14	Mount av W5
58 G 18	Mount av S'hall
79 U 17	Mountbatten clo SE18
109 S 13	Mountbatten clo SE19
23 Y 6	Mountbell rd Stanm
6 B 15	Mount clo Barnt
113 P 20	Mount clo Chisl
155 H 19	Mount clo Wallgtn
J 16	Mountcombe clo Surb
159 Z 2	Mount ct W Wkhm
115 X 15	Mount Culver av Sidcp
97 Y 13	Mount dri Bxly Hth
E 15	Mount dri Harrow
43 V 7	Mount dri Wemb
108 C 6	Mount Earl gdns SW16
20 D 6	Mount Echo av E4
20 E 4	Mount Echo dri E4
107 Y 7	Mt Ephraim la SW16
107 K 5	Mount Ephraim rd SW16
66 H 8	Mountfield rd E6
27 X 9	Mountfield rd N3
60 H 18	Mountfield rd W5
133 R 1	Mountfort ter N1
109 Z 6	Mount gdns SE26
12 K 12	Mount gro Edg
48 K 9	Mount Grove rd N5
49 L 7	Mount house Barnt
126 C 18	Mounthurst rd Brom
80 D 5	Mountjoy clo SE2
133 Y 15	Mount mills EC1
63 T 16	Mt Morres rd E1
108 C 6	Mount Nod rd SW16
155 P 18	Mount pk Wallgtn
41 S 7	Mount Pk av Harrow
156 J 20	Mount Pk av S Croy
60 G 17	Mount Pk cres W5
60 G 15	Mount Pk rd W5
41 R 9	Mount Pk rd Harrow
133 R 17	Mount pleasant west WC1
133 R 18	Mount pleasant east WC1
5 Y 14	Mount pleasant Barnt
6 A 14	Mount pleasant Barnt
60 K 2	Mount pleasant Wemb
61 N 2	Mount pleasant Wemb
48 C 2	Mount Pleasant cres N4
50 B 6	Mount Pleasant hill E5
50 A 4	Mount Pleasant la E5
32 H 7	Mount Pleasant rd E17
31 R 7	Mount Pleasant rd N17
128 C 2	Mount Pleasant rd NW10
93 T 15	Mount Pleasant rd SE13
60 E 13	Mount Pleasant rd W5
117 X 5	Mount Pleasant rd New Mald
48 C 1	Mount Pleasant vils N4
98 K 14	Mount Pleasant wlk Bxly
44 L 9	Mount rd NW2
26 G 20	Mount rd NW4
109 P 16	Mount rd SE19
105 Z 4	Mount rd SW19
5 W 16	Mount rd Barnt
97 X 13	Mount rd Bxly Hth
56 C 3	Mount rd Dgnhm
99 U 15	Mount rd Drtfrd
100 B 7	Mount rd Felt
53 Z 16	Mount rd Ilf
120 G 2	Mount rd Mitch
117 X 6	Mount rd New Mald
139 W 9	Mount row W1
99 W 15	Mountsfield ct SE13
23 X 4	Mountside Stanm
94 W 4	Mounts Pond rd SE3
24 F 20	Mount Stewart av Harrow
139 W 10	Mount st W1
15 R 8	Mount the N20
46 D 10	Mount the NW3
118 E 7	Mount the New Mald
43 U 7	Mount the Wemb
152 K 9	Mount the Worc Pk

12 L 11	Mount view NW7
20 J 3	Mount View E4
30 F 19	Mount View rd N4
48 B 1	Mount View rd N4
25 X 14	Mount View rd NW9
7 R 3	Mount view Enf
108 J 7	Mount vils SE27
155 P 20	Mount way Wallgtn
67 T 4	Movers la Bark
45 T 19	Mowbray rd NW6
109 V 19	Mowbray rd SE19
5 P 16	Mowbray rd Barnt
12 D 13	Mowbray rd Edg
102 D 7	Mowbray rd Rich
38 K 6	Mowbrays clo Rom
38 K 7	Mowbrays rd Rom
63 O 5	Mowlem st E2
135 S 20	Mowll st SW9
65 P 7	Moxon clo E13
139 U 2	Moxon st W1
4 H 13	Moxon st Barnt
51 U 2	Moyers rd E10
144 M 15	Moylan rd W6
61 R 7	Moyne pl NW10
107 U 14	Moyser rd SW16
129 O 14	Mozart st W10
120 E 14	Muchelney rd Mrdn
56 G 12	Muggeridge rd Dgnhm
49 Y 11	Muir rd E5
85 X 10	Muirdown av SW14
62 C 18	Muirfield W3
111 V 2	Muirkirk rd SE6
78 F 3	Muir st E16
20 C 8	Mulberry clo E4
58 K 18	Mulberry clo Grnfd
46 F 14	Mulberry clo NW3
107 U 10	Mulberry clo SW16
54 K 19	Mulberry ct Bark
72 C 19	Mulberry cres Brentf
157 V 1	Mulberry la W Wkhm
155 U 13	Mulberry ms Wallgtn
74 E 14	Mulberry pl W6
143 S 3	Mulberry st E1
146 G 12	Mulberry wlk SW3
81 Y 5	Mulberry way Blvdr
36 C 13	Mulberry way Ilf
34 H 8	Mulberry way E18
44 E 13	Mulgrave rd NW10
60 H 10	Mulgrave rd W5
145 P 14	Mulgrave rd W14
157 O 7	Mulgrave rd Croy
153 V 16	Mulgrave rd Sutton
154 A 14	Mulgrave rd Sutton
41 X 8	Mulgrave rd Wemb
121 T 3	Mulholland rd Mitch
89 Y 17	Mullard rd SW4
85 Y 7	Mullins path SW14
22 J 3	Mullion clo Harrow
130 J 19	Mulready st NW8
88 G 20	Multon rd SW18
160 C 5	Mumford ct EC2
89 N 12	Muncaster rd SW11
92 B 15	Mundania rd SE22
52 S 19	Munday rd E16
144 K 6	Munden st W14
59 C 6	Mundford rd E5
54 E 4	Mundon gdns Ilf
145 P 11	Mund st W14
10 A 8	Mungo Pk clo Bushy Watf
57 W 17	Mungo Pk rd Rainhm
83 P 14	Munnings gdns Islwth
85 T 14	Munroe dri SW14
23 S 1	Munro gdns Harrow
128 M 20	Munro ms W10
62 C 12	Munster av Hounsl
17 X 13	Munster gdns N13
87 U 2	Munster rd SW6
144 K 18	Munster rd W6
102 C 16	Munster rd Tedd
131 Z 14	Munster sq NW1
150 D 5	Munton rd SE17
97 Y 20	Murchison av Bxly
51 U 5	Murchison rd E10
63 W 10	Murdock cottages E3
105 R 4	Murfett clo SW19
133 P 7	Muriel st N1
93 Y 11	Murillo rd SE13
141 S 19	Murphy st SE1
126 J 3	Murray av Brom
82 K 14	Murray av Hounsl
134 E 10	Murray gro N1
47 X 19	Murray ms NW1
105 P 15	Murray rd SW19
72 D 12	Murray rd W5
102 C 4	Murray rd Rich
65 V 8	Murray sq E16
47 W 19	Murray st NW1
144 L 14	Musard rd W6
63 P 17	Musbury st E1
91 V 8	Muschamp rd SE15

154 J 3	Muschamp rd Carsh
142 L 9	Muscovy st EC3
140 J 2	Museum st WC1
5 R 6	Musgrave clo Barnt
87 Z 1	Musgrave cres SW6
145 V 20	Musgrave cres SW6
83 V 1	Musgrave rd Islwth
92 G 3	Musgrave rd SE14
88 G 6	Musjic clo SW11
49 Z 6	Muston rd E5
29 R 6	Muswell av N10
29 T 11	Muswell hill N10
29 R 12	Muswell Hill bdwy N10
29 T 12	Muswell hill pl N10
29 R 16	Muswell Hill rd N10
23 S 9	Muswell ms N10
29 T 9	Muswell rd N10
29 S 8	Muswell av N10
129 V 3	Mutrix rd NW6
117 V 4	Muybridge rd New Mald
90 J 1	Myatt rd SW9
7 S 18	Mycenae rd SE3
17 X 2	Myddelton gdns N21
15 V 8	Myddelton pk N20
133 T 12	Myddelton pas EC1
30 B 11	Myddelton rd N8
30 C 1	Myddelton rd N22
133 T 11	Myddelton sq EC1
133 U 14	Myddelton st EC1
8 E 4	Myddelton av Enf
8 G 5	Myddelton clo Enf
30 B 12	Myddelton rd N8
110 A 9	Mylis clo SE26
133 T 11	Mylne st EC1
80 A 11	Myra st SE2
143 V 4	Myrdle st E1
93 V 8	Myron pl SE13
16 A 5	Myrtle clo Barnt
99 R·1	Myrtle clo Erith
99 S·1	Myrtle clo Erith
A·13	Myrtledene rd SE2
71 T 2	Myrtle gdns W7
8 C 4	Myrtle gro Enf
117 W 4	Myrtle gro New Mald
66 E 4	Myrtle rd E6
32 J 19	Myrtle rd E17
17 Z 11	Myrtle rd N13
73 W 2	Myrtle rd W3
159 P 5	Myrtle rd Croy
100 M 16	Myrtle rd Hampt
82 M 6	Myrtle rd Hounsl
53 Z 7	Myrtle rd Ilf
154 D 10	Myrtle rd Sutton
J 11	Myrtle st N1
151 X 8	Mysore rd SW8
N 9	Mysore rd SW8
88 M 9	Mysore rd SW11
109 N 7	Myton st SE21
72 B 14	M4 motorway Brentf
70 G 15	M4 motorway Hounsl

N

32 G 18	N Access rd E17
77 Y 15	Nadine st SE7
33 X 9	Nagle clo E17
134 C·17	Nags Head ct EC1
97 P 7	Nags Head la Welling
91 P 12	Nairne gro SE24
64 G·15	Nairne st E14
122 C 8	Namton dri Thntn Hth
13 S 8	Nan Clarks la NW7
64 B 19	Nankin st E14
89 P 9	Nansen rd SW11
45 V 6	Nant rd NW2
63 O 8	Nant st E2
87 V 7	Napier av SW6
75 Y 18	Napier clo SE8
134 C 9	Napier gro N1
145 O·2	Napier pl W14
66 H 4	Napier rd E6
51 Z 11	Napier rd E11
52 A 9	Napier rd E11
65 N 6	Napier rd E15
31 S 10	Napier rd N17
62 K 8	Napier rd NW10
123 Z 10	Napier rd SE25
145 N 2	Napier rd W14
81 P 12	Napier rd Blvdr
126 J 8	Napier rd Brom
157 O 16	Napier rd Croy
27	Napier rd Enf
83 Y 11	Napier rd Islwth
42 H 17	Napier rd Wemb
75 Y 18	Napier st SE8
75 Y 19	Napier st SE8

133 V 3	Napier ter N1
84 B 18	Napoleon rd Twick
89 U 14	Narbonne av SW4
87 Z 6	Narborough st SW6
45 X 16	Narcissus rd NW6
11 R 18	Naresby fold Stanm
49 X 8	Narford rd E5
63 U 20	Narrow st E14
73 U 2	Narrow st W3
127 R 14	Narrow way Brom
62 M 17	Nascot st W12
136 B 5	Nascot st W12
46 E 19	Naseby clo NW6
83 U 2	Naseby clo Islwth
109 O 15	Naseby rd SE19
56 E 10	Naseby rd Dgnhm
35 T 5	Naseby rd Ilf
112 F 17	Nash grn Brom
19 P 8	Nash rd N9
92 G 12	Nash rd SE4
37 U 11	Nash rd Rom
74 J 8	Nasmyth st W6
86 D 3	Nassau rd SW13
140 B 2	Nassau st W1
46 L 12	Nassington rd NW3
16 M 17	Natal rd N11
107 Y 13	Natal rd SW16
53 Y 13	Natal rd Ilf
123 N 6	Natal rd Thntn Hth
42 E 6	Nathans rd Wemb
79 V 9	Nathan way SE18
80 A 5	Nathan way SE2
141 P 13	National Film theatre SE1
140 H 11	National Gallery WC2
140 H 11	National Portrait Gallery WC2
141 R 12	National Theatre SE1
20 G 4	Nation way E4
146 F 3	Natural History museum SW7
64 H 20	Naval row E14
49 Y 17	Navarino gro E8
49 Y 16	Navarino rd E8
66 E 5	Navarre rd E6
134 M 15	Navarre st E2
34 L 4	Navestock cres Wdfd Grn
89 X 7	Naylor rd SW4
15 P 8	Naylor rd N20
151 W 18	Naylor rd SE15
32 L 4	N Countess rd E17
58 F 10	Neal av S'hall
90 B 7	Nealden st SW9
28 D 12	Nale clo N2
140 J 6	Neal st WC2
140 J 6	Neal's yd WC2
98 J 1	Neals yd Erith
26 C 6	Near acre NW9
44 B 14	Neasden clo NW10
43 Y 9	Neasden la NW10
44 B 11	Neasden la NW10
44 B 17	Neasden la NW10
55 P 16	Neasham rd Dgnhm
150 K 14	Neate st SE5
151 O 14	Neate st SE5
120 C 15	Neath gdns Mrdn
148 A 4	Neathouse pl SW1
142 D 19	Nebraska st SE1
151 O 1	Neckinger SE1
93 S 4	Nectavine way SE13
137 T 6	Needham rd W11
45 P 10	Needham ter NW2
26 J 16	Neeld cres NW4
43 P 16	Neeld cres Wemb
93 P 19	Nelgarde rd SE6
74 H 6	Nella rd W6
75 O 11	Nelldale rd SE16
151 Z 6	Nelldale rd SE16
38 G 6	Nelson clo NW6
82 G 15	Nelson gdns Hounsl
106 C 20	Nelson Gro rd SW19
133 X 10	Nelson pl N1
73 T 2	Nelson pl N1
115 N 10	Nelson pl Sidcp
20 C 20	Nelson rd E4
34 G 13	Nelson rd E11
30 C 18	Nelson rd N8
19 N 9	Nelson rd N9
31 S 12	Nelson rd N15
76 H 17	Nelson rd SE10
106 B 18	Nelson rd SW19
126 M 9	Nelson rd Brom
9 T 19	Nelson rd Enf
41 S 3	Nelson rd Harrow
117 Z 12	Nelson rd New Mald
118 A 11	Nelson rd New Mald
115 N 10	Nelson rd Sidcp
11 R 18	Nelson rd Stanm
82 G 16	Nelson rd Twick
83 N 17	Nelson rd Twick
141 X 16	Nelson sq SE1

89 X 10	Nelsons row SW4
63 N 16	Nelson st E1
143 W 4	Nelson st E1
66 K 4	Nelson st E6
65 O 19	Nelson st E16
65 P 19	Nelson st E16
133 X 10	Nelson ter N1
61 V 20	Nemoure rd W3
88 J 6	Nepaul rd SW11
23 P 19	Neptune rd Harrow
75 P 7	Neptune st SE16
93 Z 6	Nesbit clo SE3
95 O 9	Nesbit rd SE9
21 O 18	Nesta rd Wdfd Grn
75 R 4	Nestor st SE16
7 W 19	Nestor av N21
151 S 2	Netheravon rd SW16
74 D 15	Netheravon rd W4
74 D 12	Netheravon rd W4
71 V 2	Netheravon rd W7
72 F 9	Netherbury rd W5
6 M 14	Netherby gdns Enf
92 C 18	Netherby rd SE23
27 Y 1	Nether clo N3
L 18	Nether Court av N3
14 L 19	Nethercourt av N3
14 L 19	Nether Court Golf course N3
54 E 19	Netherfield gdns Bark
15 O 16	Netherfield rd N12
107 O 7	Netherfield rd SW17
89 V 6	Netherfield rd SW4
46 E 15	Netherhall gdns NW3
46 D 16	Netherhall way NW3
15 V 2	Netherhall rd NW3
7 T 19	Netherlands rd Barnt
47 T 4	Netherton gdns N6
39 S 7	Netherpark dri Rom
14 L 20	Nether st N3
27 X 3	Nether st N3
15 P 17	Nether st N12
146 C 15	Netherton rd SW10
83 Z 13	Netherton rd Twick
84 A 14	Netherton rd Twick
45 V 19	Netherwood pl W14
45 V 19	Netherwood rd W14
100 N 16	Netherwood st NW6
159 V 16	Netley clo Sutton
153 P 11	Netley clo Sutton
120 C 16	Netley gdns Mrdn
36 E 16	Netley rd Ilf
72 J 14	Netley rd Brentf
120 C 16	Netley rd Mrdn
132 A 14	Netley st NW1
154 A 20	Nettlecombe Sutton
43 P 17	Nettleden av Wemb
108 J 8	Nettleford clo SE27
92 G 1	Nettleton rd SE6
107 Y 19	Nettlewood rd SW16
110 K 4	Neuchatel rd SE6
76 H 18	Nevada st SE10
145 V 6	Nevern pl SW5
145 T 7	Nevern rd SW5
145 T 7	Nevern sq SW5
103 Z 20	Neville av New Mald
129 R 10	Neville clo NW6
114 M 9	Neville clo Sidcp
52 C 9	Neville clo E15
73 W 4	Neville clo W3
132 C 9	Neville clo NW1
28 D 19	Neville dri N2
91 X 1	Neville dri SE15
55 U 8	Neville gdns Dgnhm
87 Z 15	Neville Gill clo SW18
65 T 2	Neville rd E7
60 P 10	Neville rd W5
123 P 17	Neville rd Croy
55 V 8	Neville rd Dgnhm
36 C 4	Neville rd Ilf
117 X 3	Neville rd Kingst
102 C 5	Neville rd Rich
145 T 5	Neville st SW7
146 F 9	Neville ter SW7
120 J 18	Neville wlk Carsh
49 S 9	Nevill rd N16
20 F 6	Nevin dri E4
39 R 1	Nevis clo Rom
107 N 3	Nevis rd SW17
61 Y 9	Newark cres NW10
157 O 14	Newark rd S Croy
143 W 2	Newark st E1
63 N 16	Newark st E1
26 H 11	Newark way NW4
121 X 10	New Barns av Mitch
65 U 12	New Barn st E13
99 T 1	Newbery rd Erith
153 O 19	Newbolt av Sutton
10 H 18	Newbolt rd Stanm
139 Y 7	New Bond st W1
139 Z 10	New Bond st W1

117 Y 9	Newborough grn New Mald
26 M 15	New Brent st NW4
27 N 14	New Brent st NW4
81 Y 10	New br Erith
141 W 7	New Br st EC4
160 H 3	New Broad st EC2
60 F 20	New broadway W5
73 V 2	Newburgh rd W3
140 B 7	Newburgh st W1
140 A 9	New Burlington ms W1
140 A 8	New Burlington pl W1
140 A 9	New Burlington st W1
149 P 9	Newburn st SE11
9 X 2	Newbury av Enf
40 D 17	Newbury clo Grnfd
152 D 8	Newbury gdns Epsom
20 H 20	Newbury rd E4
126 E 7	Newbury rd Brom
36 G 19	Newbury rd Ilf
141 Z 1	Newbury st EC1
40 C 17	Newbury way Grnfd
76 B 20	New butt la SE8
8 F 9	Newby clo Enf
64 F 19	Newby pl E14
89 T 6	Newby st SW8
138 H 1	Newcastle pl W2
133 U 16	Newcastle row EC1
141 W 4	Newcastle st EC4
139 X 1	New Cavendish st W1
142 A 6	New change EC4
160 A 6	New change EC4
150 D 18	New Church rd SE5
150 F 16	New Church rd SE17
65 Y 8	New City rd E13
120 D 4	New clo SW19
100 B 12	New clo Felt
108 B 8	Newcome gdns SW16
13 O 16	Newcombe pk NW7
61 N 2	Newcombe pk Wemb
137 U 13	Newcomen st W8
52 B 9	Newcomen rd E11
88 F 7	Newcomen st SW11
142 E 16	Newcomen st SE1
140 H 5	New Compton st WC2
141 R 8	New ct WC2
130 K 10	Newcourt st NW8
148 E 17	New Covent Garden market SW1
140 G 10	New Coventry st W1
75 P 19	New Cross rd SE14
92 H 1	New Cross rd SE14
18 L 9	Newdale clo N9
63 Y 19	Newell st E14
46 E 11	New end NW3
46 E 11	New End sq NW3
120 L 19	Newent clo Carsh
150 K 16	Newent clo SE15
126 E 8	New Farm av Brom
141 U 3	New Fetter la EC4
100 G 20	Newfield clo Hampt
100 H 19	Newfield clo Hampt
44 H 9	Newfield ri NW2
142 H 10	New Fresh wharf EC3
24 M 4	Newgate gdns Edg
122 M 19	Newgate Croy
100 C 6	Newgate clo Felt
20 M 12	Newgate st E4
141 X 4	Newgate st EC1
143 N 4	New Goulston st E1
142 L 20	Newhams row SE1
66 F 13	Newham way E6
67 T 15	Newham way E16
65 Y 14	Newham way E16
67 S 7	Newham way Bark
95 N 9	Newhaven gdns SE9
123 P 11	Newhaven rd SE25
70 F 18	New Heston rd Hounsl
37 W 10	Newhome av Rom
37 W 10	Newhouse av Rom
118 B 18	Newhouse clo New Mald
120 C 17	New House wlk Mrdn
98 G 15	Newick clo Bxly
50 B 10	Newick rd E5
113 O 18	Newing grn Chisl
48 C 8	Newington Barrow way N7
149 Y 6	Newington butts SE11
149 Z 2	Newington causeway SE1
49 O 14	Newington grn N16

New–Nor

49 O 16 Newington Grn rd N1
134 L 15 New Inn sq EC2
134 K 15 New Inn st EC2
134 K 16 New Inn yd EC2
150 D 4 New Kent rd SE1
87 W 4 New Kings rd SW6
76 A 16 New King st SE8
43 P 7 Newland ct Wemb
8 M 6 Newland dri Enf
71 Y 6 Newland gdns W13
30 A 10 Newland rd N8
11 X 10 Newlands clo Edg
70 B 13 Newlands clo S'hall
42 E 17 Newlands clo Wemb
110 D 13 Newlands pk SE26
4 B 16 Newlands pl Barnt
122 B 3 Newlands rd SW16
21 R 9 Newlands rd Wdfd Grn
155 X 17 Newlands the Wallgtn
78 E 3 Newland st E16
155 K 19 Newlands wood Croy
142 L 8 New London st EC3
77 Z 9 New Lydenberg st SE7
40 C 2 Newlyn gdns Harrow
44 L 4 Newlyn rd NW4
31 U 6 Newlyn rd N17
4 G 15 Newlyn rd Barnt
96 K 5 Newlyn rd Welling
140 D 3 Newman pas W1
65 U 10 Newman rd E13
32 G 14 Newman rd E17
126 G 2 Newman rd Brom
122 C 18 Newman rd Croy
160 H 6 Newmans ct EC4
141 P 3 Newmans row WC2
140 C 2 Newman st W1
5 S 7 Newmans way Barnt
40 K 16 Newmarket av Grnfd
98 P 18 Newmarket grn SE9
120 D 15 Newminster rd Mrdn
64 K 2 New Mount st E15
40 M 16 Newnham clo Grnfd
40 M 16 Newnham gdns Grnfd
41 N 17 Newnham gdns Grnfd
30 E 4 Newnham rd N22
127 V 6 Newnhams clo Brom
141 R 20 Newnham ter SE1
149 R 1 Newnham ter SE1
24 L 14 Newnham way Harrow
134 J 17 New North pl EC2
134 E 9 New North rd N1
36 D 1 New North rd Ilf
132 M 20 New North st WC1
49 O 1 Newnton clo N4
28 F 8 New Oak rd N2
47 Y 1 New Orleans wk N19
140 H 4 New Oxford st WC1
140 K 19 New Palace yd SW1
17 Z 12 New Park av N13
18 A 12 New Park av N13
40 A 19 New Park clo Grnfd
89 Z 20 New Pk rd SW2
107 Y 1 New Pk rd SW2
65 O4 New Plaistow rd E15
65 W 12 Newport av E13
140 G 8 Newport ct WC2
140 G 8 Newport pl WC2
51 V 6 Newport rd E10
32 J 14 Newport rd E17
86 H 1 Newport rd SW13
149 O 6 Newport st SE11
40 C 7 Newquay cres Harrow
111 S 4 Newquay rd SE6
139 R 6 New Quebec st W1
17 V 12 New River cres N13
48 L 18 New River wlk N1
143 V 4 New rd E1
20 F 13 New rd E4
20 J 12 New rd E4
29 Z 16 New rd N8
18 L 10 New rd N9
31 U 3 New rd N17
30 L 5 New rd N22
13 S 2 New rd NW7
27 R 1 New rd NW7
80 J 13 New rd SE2
72 H 15 New rd Brentf
69 U 6 New rd Dgnhm
100 B 11 New rd Hanwell
82 K 11 New rd Hounsl
54 H 6 New rd Ilf
103 P 17 New rd Kingst
121 O 19 New rd Mitch
102 E 8 New rd Rich
97 P 6 New rd Welling
41 V 12 New rd Wemb
140 J 9 New row WC2
83 Z 12 Newry rd Twick
31 O 15 Newsam av N15
148 F 1 New Scotland yard SW1
141 R 5 New sq WC2
142 K 3 New st EC2
120 D 17 Newstead wlk Carsh
105 R 8 Newstead way SW19
112 J 13 New Street hill Brom
141 U 4 New St sq EC4
29 R 3 Newton av N10
73 V 6 Newton av W3
134 H 7 Newton gro N1
74 A 10 Newton gro W4
40 H 7 Newton pk Harrow UC
51 Y 14 Newton rd E15
31 W 14 Newton rd N15
44 M 11 Newton rd NW2
105 U 18 Newton rd SW19
137 W 5 Newton rd W2
23 T 6 Newton rd Harrow
83 V 4 Newton rd Islwth
96 M 8 Newton rd Welling
60 M 1 Newton rd Wemb
140 M 4 Newton st WC2
89 S 2 Newton st SW11
87 Z 14 Newton yd SW18
25 T 4 Newton wlk Edg
17 Z 16 Newton way N18
28 F 9 New Trinity rd N2
76 G 7 New union clo
142 E 1 New Union st EC2
160 E 1 New Union st EC2
34 E 17 New wanstead E11
26 C 14 New Way rd NW9
132 M 8 New Wharf rd N1
72 C 10 Niagra av W5
23 T 15 Nibthwaite rd Harrow
58 L 5 Nicholas clo Grnfd
72 F 4 Nicholas gdns W5
160 G 8 Nicholas la EC3
63 R 12 Nicholas rd E1
156 B 8 Nicholas rd Croy
56 B 8 Nicholas rd Dgnhm
47 Y 4 Nicholay rd N19
82 G 11 Nicholes rd Hounsl
16 J 4 Nichol clo N14
112 G 17 Nichol la Brom
135 S 17 Nicholl st E2
60 J 14 Nichols grn W5
123 V 20 Nicholson rd Croy
141 X 14 Nicholson st SE1
74 C 15 Nicol clo Twick
23 R 7 Nicola clo Harrow
156 L 14 Nicola clo S Croy
62 B 4 Nicolle rd NW10
26 K 26 Nicoll pl NW4
10 A 7 Nicolson dri Bushey Watf
88 H 18 Nicosia rd SW18
110 G 8 Niederwald rd SE26
58 B 4 Nigel clo Grnfd
53 Y 12 Nigel ms Ilf
74 J 12 Nigel Playfair av W6
52 M 15 Nigel rd E7
91 X 7 Nigel rd SE15
77 Z 19 Nigeria rd SE7
20 L 15 Nightingale av E4
20 L 13 Nightingale clo E4
73 V 18 Nightingale clo W4
155 N 3 Nightingale clo Carsh
93 X 13 Nightingale gro SE13
34 G 15 Nightingale la E11
29 Z 13 Nightingale la N8
88 L 19 Nightingale la SW12
89 O 17 Nightingale la SW12
126 L 4 Nightingale la Brom
127 N 5 Nightingale la Brom
84 K 18 Nightingale la Rich
46 J 3 Nightingale la NW11
78 K 16 Nightingale pl SE18
49 Y 10 Nightingale rd E5
19 S 7 Nightingale rd N9
30 C 3 Nightingale rd N22
62 E 7 Nightingale rd NW10
71 V 2 Nightingale rd W7
155 N 4 Nightingale rd Carsh
100 H 15 Nightingale rd Hampt
89 O 18 Nightingale sq SW12
78 K 16 Nightingale vale SE18
89 R 15 Nightingale wlk SW4
65 X 7 Nile rd E13
134 D 12 Nile st N1
151 O 12 Nile ter SE15
91 S 12 Nimegen way SE22
10 D 4 Nimmo dri Bushey Watf
107 T 12 Nimrod rd SW16
53 R 15 Nine Acres clo E12
148 H 15 Nine Elms la SW8
78 M 18 Nithdale rd SE18
79 N 18 Nithdale rd SE18
4 B 19 Nilton clo Barnt
85 P 8 Niton rd Rich
144 G 17 Niton st SW6
19 S 17 Nobel rd N18
160 B 4 Noble st EC2
66 C 12 Noel rd E6
133 X 8 Noel rd N1
61 P 17 Noel rd W3
55 T 11 Noel sq Dgnhm
140 C 6 Noel st W1
49 Y 11 Nolan way E5
25 N 6 Nolton pla Edg
152 L 15 Nonsuch pk Epsom Sutton
153 N 13 Nonsuch pk Epsom Sutton
153 O 19 Nonsuch wlk Sutton
153 P 20 Nonsuch wlk Sutton
27 P 13 Nora gdns NW4
41 T 3 Nora ter Harrow
117 R 3 Norbiton av Kingst
117 U 6 Norbiton Comm rd Kingst
63 X 17 Norbiton rd E14
62 D 19 Norbroke st W12
136 J 2 Norburn st W10
108 C 20 Norbury av SW16
122 E 1 Norbury av SW16
83 P 11 Norbury av Hounsl
108 H 19 Norbury clo SW16
121 Z 4 Norbury Ct rd SW16
122 C 4 Norbury Ct rd SW16
122 C 1 Norbury cres SW16
121 Z 5 Norbury cross SW16
37 V 16 Norbury gdns Rom
13 O 10 Norbury gro NW7
108 J 17 Norbury hill SW16
121 Z 5 Norbury ri SW16
122 A 5 Norbury ri SW16
20 A 15 Norbury rd E4
122 M 4 Norbury rd Thntn Hth
123 N 4 Norbury rd Thntn Hth
24 D 17 Norcombe gdns Harrow
49 W 8 Norcott rd N16
91 W 17 Norcroft gdns SE22
101 T 1 Norcutt rd Twick
17 X 20 Norfolk av N13
31 V 18 Norfolk av N15
28 H 10 Norfolk clo N2
17 X 19 Norfolk clo N13
6 B 14 Norfolk clo Barnt
84 B 15 Norfolk clo Twick
138 L 5 Norfolk cres W2
96 H 18 Norfolk cres Sidcp
98 B 1 Norfolk gdns Bxly Hth
107 Z 6 Norfolk Ho rd SW16
138 H 5 Norfolk pl W2
96 M 4 Norfolk pl Welling
66 H 3 Norfolk rd E6
32 G 7 Norfolk rd E17
130 J 5 Norfolk rd NW8
44 B 20 Norfolk rd NW10
62 B 1 Norfolk rd NW10
106 J 16 Norfolk rd SW19
67 U 2 Norfolk rd Bark
4 M 12 Norfolk rd Barnt
56 H 15 Norfolk rd Dgnhm
9 O 18 Norfolk rd Enf
22 L 16 Norfolk rd Harrow
54 H 1 Norfolk rd Ilf
38 L 18 Norfolk rd Rom
122 M 6 Norfolk rd Thntn Hth
149 O 4 Norfolk row SE11
138 G 5 Norfolk sq W2
138 H 6 Norfolk Sq ms W2
52 F 14 Norfolk st E7
144 K 12 Norfolk ter W6
89 P 20 Norgrove rd SW12
123 U 5 Norhyrst av SE25
136 L 14 Norland pl W11
136 H 15 Norland rd W11
136 L 14 Norland sq W11
104 H 1 Norley vale SW15
51 V 4 Norlington rd E10
30 K 4 Norman av N22
100 C 4 Norman av Felt
58 C 19 Norman av S'hall
84 C 18 Norman av Twick
87 U 13 Normanby clo SW15
44 E 13 Normanby rd NW10
38 J 6 Norman clo Rom
144 M 13 Normand ms W14
145 N 15 Normand pk W14
145 N 13 Normand rd W14
4 H 14 Normandy av Barnt
90 F 2 Normandy rd SW9
65 U 18 Normandy ter E16
99 P 2 Normandy way Erith
63 X 7 Norman gro E3
97 W 3 Normanhurst av Bxly Hth
83 Z 13 Normanhurst dri Twick
108 D 3 Normanhurst rd SW2
100 E 4 Norman ho Felt
126 J 14 Norman pk Brom
66 H 11 Norman rd E6
51 Y 6 Norman rd E11
31 V 15 Norman rd N15
76 E 17 Norman rd SE10
106 D 17 Norman rd SW19
81 U 4 Norman rd Blvdr
57 X 1 Norman rd Hornch
53 Z 16 Norman rd Ilf
54 A 16 Norman rd Ilf
153 W 10 Norman rd Sutton
153 X 11 Norman rd Sutton
122 J 11 Norman rd Thntn Hth
43 X 18 Normans clo NW10
102 E 18 Normansfield av Tedd
20 F 13 Normanshire av E4
20 C 14 Normanshire dri E4
43 X 18 Normans mead NW10
134 B 15 Norman st EC1
105 X 5 Normanton av SW19
20 M 10 Normanton pk E4
21 N 9 Normanton pk E4
157 R 13 Normanton rd S Croy
110 G 5 Normanton st SE23
16 L 9 Norman way N14
17 N 9 Norman way N14
61 T 16 Norman way W3
108 F 11 Normington clo SW16
28 F 17 Norrice lea N2
140 E 11 Norris st SW1
87 R 11 Norroy rd SW15
5 Z 15 Norrys clo Barnt
5 Y 15 Norrys rd Barnt
58 M 4 Norseman way Grnfd
104 F 5 Norstead pl SW15
32 G 18 North Access rd E17
26 B 6 North acre NW9
61 Y 8 North Acton rd NW10
98 J 6 Northall rd Bxly Hth
133 U 16 Northampton bldgs EC1
49 N 6 Northampton gro N1
49 N 16 Northampton pk N1
133 T 16 Northampton rd EC1
157 X 2 Northampton rd Croy
133 X 13 Northampton sq EC1
48 L 20 Northampton st N1
107 Z 16 Northanger rd SW16
139 T 8 North Audley st W1
132 M 9 North av N1
18 L 13 North av N18
60 N 15 North av W13
155 N 16 North av Carsh
22 L 18 North av Harrow
85 O 3 North av Rich
58 F 20 North av S'hall
140 J 14 North bank NW8
33 T 7 Northbank rd E17
51 X 10 North Birbeck rd E11
121 Y 5 Northborough rd SW16
122 C 4 Northborough rd SW16
126 F 16 Northbourne Brom
89 Y 12 Northbourne rd SW4
30 B 1 Northbrooke rd N22
93 Y 12 Northbrook rd SE13
4 F 20 Northbrook rd Barnt
123 N 11 Northbrook rd Croy
53 V 7 Northbrook rd Ilf
133 X 17 Northburgh st EC1
49 O 20 Northchurch rd N1
43 O 18 Northchurch rd Wemb
134 J 1 Northchurch ter N1
19 W 17 North Circular rd E4
66 F 10 North Circular rd E6
53 R 16 North Circular rd E12
28 C 8 North Circular rd N2
27 X 11 North Circular rd N3
17 V 16 North Circular rd N13
18 F 15 North Circular rd N18
44 D 6 North Circular rd NW2
45 N 1 North Circular rd NW2
43 W 18 North Circular rd NW10
61 R 2 North Circular rd NW10

N

60	L 8	North Circular rd Wemb
14	H 5	Northcliffe dr N20
97	W 10	North clo Bxly Hth
69	S 4	North clo Dgnhm
119	S 8	North clo Mrdn
60	L 20	North Common rd W5
60	J 20	Northcote av W5
58	C 19	Northcote av S'hall
70	D 1	Northcote av S'hall
117	S 16	Northcote av Surb
83	Y 12	Northcote av Twick
32	J 14	Northcote rd E17
62	B 1	Northcote rd NW10
88	K 12	Northcote rd SW11
123	O 14	Northcote rd Croy
117	X 7	Northcote rd New Mald
114	H 10	Northcote rd Sidcp
83	Z 12	Northcote rd Twick
84	A 12	Northcote rd Twick
30	A 4	Northcott av N22
32	L 6	North Countess rd E17
115	Y 15	North Cray rd Sidcp
27	V 19	North cres N3
132	E 20	North cres WC1
132	C 20	North ct W1
72	B 7	Northcroft rd W13
152	A 17	Northcroft rd Epsom
91	V 12	North Cross rd SE22
36	A 14	North Cross rd Ilf
12	L 10	North dene NW7
82	J 3	North dene Hounsl
31	U 19	Northdene gdns N15
36	G 15	Northdown gdns Ilf
57	Y 2	Northdown rd Hornch
97	R 5	Northdown rd Welling
159	S 20	North Downs cres Croy
159	T 20	North Downs cres Croy
132	M 10	Northdown st N1
107	U 9	North dri SW16
83	O 6	North dri Hounsl
46	C 5	North end NW3
21	Y 3	North end Buck Hl
156	L 3	North end Croy
46	D 6	North End av NW3
145	N 7	North End cres W14
46	A 4	North End rd NW3
45	Z 4	North End rd NW11
144	L 5	North End rd SW6
145	R 13	North End rd W14
99	S 2	Northend rd Erith
43	R 10	North End rd Wemb
46	C 7	North End way NW3
18	F 9	Northern av N9
119	T 10	Northernhay wlk Mrdn
65	W 5	Northern rd E13
9	X 15	Northern rd Enf
74	E 13	North Eyot gdns W6
63	W 20	Northey st E14
72	B 3	Northfield av W13
153	S 9	Northfield cres Sutton
56	B 12	Northfield gdns Dgnhm
53	V 20	Northfield rd E6
49	T 1	Northfield rd N16
72	A 5	Northfield rd W13
5	W 12	Northfield rd Barnt
56	B 12	Northfield rd Dgnhm
9	P 19	Northfield rd Enf
87	X 11	Northfields SW18
61	U 14	Northfields rd W3
106	C 17	Northfields SW19
98	B 20	North Glade the Bxly
132	B 14	North Gower st NW1
47	O 2	North gro N6
31	O 16	North gro N15
29	N 19	North hill N6
29	N 17	North Hill av N6
70	A 13	North Hyde la S'hall
14	M 12	Northiam N12
63	O 4	Northiam st E8
133	O 19	Northington st WC1
90	L 6	Northlands st SE5
101	V 14	North la Tedd
87	P 14	North Lodge clo SW15
133	P 18	North ms WC1
12	K 14	Northolm Edg
25	P 4	Northolme gdns Edg
48	K 11	Northolme rd N5
41	W 15	Northolt gdns Grnfd
40	K 12	Northolt rd Harrow
20	O 7	Northolt rd Harrow
112	C 2	Northover Brom
95	U 17	North pk SE9
87	Y 12	North pas SW18
106	L 17	North pl Mitch
62	M 15	North Pole rd W10
136	B 3	North Pole rd W10
134	H 7	Northport st N1
14	K 12	Northram N12
47	Z 17	North rd N1
47	P 1	North rd N6
48	B 16	North rd N7
18	M 4	North rd N9
79	W 9	North rd SE18
106	D 15	North rd SW19
72	G 9	North rd W5
81	U 6	North rd Blvdr
72	L 16	North rd Brentf
112	H 20	North rd Brom
99	U 17	North rd Drtfrd
25	T 3	North rd Edg
54	G 7	North rd Ilf
85	O 8	North rd Rich
37	X 16	North rd Rom
70	G 1	North rd S'hall
58	F 20	North rd S'hall
116	G 14	North rd Surb
125	S 20	North rd W Wkhm
139	T 7	North row W1
93	V 4	North several SE3
153	W 5	North Spur rd Sutton
27	Z 17	North sq NW11
108	G 4	Northstead rd SW2
65	T 6	North st E13
27	N 15	North st NW4
89	U 6	North st SW4
54	A 20	North st Bark
67	N 1	North st Bark
98	E 9	North st Bxly Hth
126	E 2	North St Brom
154	M 8	North st Carsh
155	N 9	North st Carsh
83	Y 6	North st Islwth
39	O 14	North st Rom
143	P 6	North Tenter st E1
146	J 4	North ter SW3
142	M 7	Northumberland all EC3
140	K 13	Northumberland av WC2
52	L 4	Northumberland av E12
9	N 5	Northumberland av Enf
71	X 20	Northumberland av Islwth
83	V 1	Northumberland av Islwth
96	G 9	Northumberland av Welling
89	K 1	Northumberland N9
121	Y 11	Northumberland gdns Mitch
31	Z 2	Northumberland gro N17
31	Y 1	Northumberland pk N17
81	X 19	Northumberland pk Erith
137	U 5	Northumberland pl W2
51	N 1	Northumberland rd E17
15	P 1	Northumberland rd Barnt
22	H 16	Northumberland rd Harrow
140	J 12	Northumberland st WC2
99	N 2	Northumberland way Erith
64	B 17	Northumbria st E14
104	L 12	North view SW19
90	D 11	North view W5
44	C 13	North view cres NW10
35	N 7	North View dri Wdfd Grn
29	Y 11	North View rd N8
47	Y 18	North vlls NW1
159	U 13	North wlk Croy
19	S 8	North way N9
25	S 10	North way NW9
27	A 15	Northway NW11
28	B 15	Northway NW11
89	K 1	Northumberland clo Erith
119	S 8	Northway Mrdn
119	T 8	Northway Mrdn
155	V 8	Northway Wallgtn
12	L 12	Northway cir NW7
12	M 13	Northway cres NW7
90	L 8	Northway rd SE5
123	U 16	Northway rd Croy
138	F 3	North Wharf rd W2
23	Z 19	Northwick av Harrow
24	A 20	Northwick av Harrow
24	D 18	Northwick cir Harrow
130	F 17	Northwick clo NW8
42	B 2	Northwick pk Harrow
23	X 18	Northwick Pk rd Harrow
60	H 4	Northwick rd Wemb
130	E 17	Northwick ter NW8
41	W 1	Northwick wlk Harrow
49	Y 7	Northwold rd E5
49	U 7	Northwold rd N16
57	X 12	Northwood av Hornch
15	T 15	Northwood gdns N12
41	W 15	Northwood gdns Grnfd
35	W 12	Northwoods gdns Ilf
16	G 19	Northway N11
47	T 1	Northwood rd N6
110	K 2	Northwood rd SE23
50	O 14	Northwood rd Carsh
122	L 3	Northwood rd Thntn Hth
77	S 3	North Woolwich rd E16
78	A 4	North Woolwich rd E16
81	N 7	Northwood pl Blvdr
123	N 1	Northwood rd Carsh
84	A 7	North Worple way SW14
85	Z 7	North Worple way SW14
117	T 16	Norton av Surb
20	B 15	Norton clo E4
8	M 9	Norton clo Enf
134	L 19	Norton folgate E1
122	A 3	Norton gdns SW16
50	M 3	Norton rd E10
57	N 18	Norton rd Dgnhm
42	G 18	Norton rd Wemb
4	C 5	Norton rd Wemb
63	X 18	Norway pl E14
76	E 16	Norway st SE10
52	E 16	Norwich rd E7
69	S 7	Norwich rd Dgnhm
58	L 3	Norwich rd Grnfd
122	M 7	Norwich rd Thntn Hth
141	T 3	Norwich st EC4
25	W 2	Norwich wlk Edg
57	P 3	Norwood av Rom
60	M 5	Norwood av Wemb
70	F 12	Norwood clo S'hall
22	G 18	Norwood dri Harrow
70	D 10	Norwood gdns S'hall
70	H 12	Norwood Grn rd S'hall
108	K 8	Norwood High st SE27
108	M 12	Norwood Pk rd SE27
109	N 12	Norwood Pk rd SE27
108	J 5	Norwood rd SE27
70	E 10	Norwood rd S'hall
32	L 15	Notley rd E17
150	E 18	Notley st SE5
123	Z 10	Notson rd SE25
65	J 16	Nottingham av E16
140	K 6	Nottingham ct WC2
131	T 19	Nottingham pl W1
33	U 18	Nottingham rd E10
106	L 2	Nottingham rd SW17
83	V 4	Nottingham rd Islwth
156	L 10	Nottingham rd S Croy
156	L 11	Nottingham rd S Croy
131	U 20	Nottingham st W1
137	T 12	Notting Hill ga W11
119	S 18	Nova ms Sutton
122	K 18	Nova rd Croy
114	B 2	Novar rd SE9
87	X 2	Novello st SW6
74	G 17	Nowell rd SW13
22	E 12	Nower hill Pinn
106	M 6	Noyna rd SW17
93	P 8	Nuding clo SE13
48	A 4	Nugent rd N4
123	T 6	Nugent rd SE25
22	C 4	Nugents pk Pinn
130	C 11	Nugent ter NW8
160	E 3	Nun ct EC2
68	L 9	Nuneaton rd Dgnhm
91	V 8	Nunhead cres SE15
92	A 7	Nunhead grn SE15
92	B 8	Nunhead gro SE15
92	A 8	Nunhead la SE15
113	R 7	Nunnington clo SE9
7	Z 8	Nunns rd Enf
4	A 19	Nupton dri Barnt
15	W 20	Nursery app N12
28	C 7	Nursery av N2
98	C 7	Nursery av Bxly Hth
158	E 3	Nursery av Croy
158	E 4	Nursery clo Croy
9	T 6	Nursery clo Enf
37	W 19	Nursery clo Rom
21	U 16	Nursery clo Wdfd Grn
100	E 11	Nursery clo Hampt
87	O 11	Nursery clo SW15
9	T 6	Nursery gdns Enf
52	G 17	Nursery la E7
136	B 2	Nursery la W10
16	H 3	Nursery rd N14
90	D 9	Nursery rd SW9
106	R 19	Nursery rd SW19
120	J 7	Nursery rd Mitch
120	A 1	Nursery rd Mrdn
28	G 5	Nursery rd N2
154	D 9	Nursery rd Sutton
122	D 9	Nursery rd Thntn Hth
150	D 8	Nursery row SE17
31	U 3	Nursery st N17
89	S 7	Nursery st SW8
26	L 10	Nursery wlk NW4
39	N 20	Nursery wlk Rom
81	T 20	Nurstead rd Erith
128	K 12	Nutbourne st W10
91	W 8	Nutbrook st SE15
69	P 3	Nutbrowne rd Dgnhm
151	V 18	Nutcroft rd SE16
18	J 19	Nutfield clo N18
54	L 7	Nutfield gdns Ilf
51	V 12	Nutfield rd E15
44	F 9	Nutfield rd NW2
91	V 11	Nutfield rd SE22
122	H 9	Nutfield rd Thntn Hth
139	N 4	Nutford pl W1
108	D 3	Nuthurst av SW2
46	E 17	Nutley ter NW3
134	L 7	Nuttall st N1
34	K 16	Nutter la E11
11	U 8	Nutt gro Edg
151	P 18	Nutt st SE15
81	R 14	Nuxley rd Blvdr
79	T 18	Nyanza st SE18
85	P 4	Nylands av Rich
118	J 5	Nyman gdns New Mald
75	V 18	Nynehead st SE14
110	K 5	Nyon gro SE6

N

O

O

29	Z 14	Oak av N8
29	S 2	Oak av N10
31	P 1	Oak av N17
159	P 1	Oak av Croy
7	P 3	Oak av Enf
100	D 14	Oak av Hampt
70	A 20	Oak av Hounsl
159	V 10	Oak bank Croy
65	N 15	Oak cres E16
90	L 10	Oakbank gro SE24
112	H 9	Oakbrook clo SE12
88	A 5	Oakbury rd SW6
16	D 3	Oak clo N14
154	D 4	Oak clo Sutton
104	A 19	Oakcombe clo New Mald
62	C 17	Oak common W3
112	A 2	Oak Cottage clo SE6
93	W 5	Oakcroft SE13
16	G 4	Oakdale N14
24	K 15	Oakdale av Harrow
20	G 15	Oakdale rd E4
52	J 20	Oakdale rd E7
51	W 7	Oakdale rd E11
34	J 8	Oakdale rd E18
30	M 18	Oakdale rd N4
31	N 18	Oakdale rd N4
108	B 12	Oakdale rd SW16
92	D 7	Oakdale rd SE15
60	A 14	Oak dene W13
113	V 11	Oakdene av Chisl
81	X 17	Oakdene av Erith
22	E 1	Oakdene clo Pinn
39	V 19	Oak Dene clo Rom
117	V 19	Oakdene dri Surb
27	W 1	Oakden pk N3
149	U 6	Oakden st SE11
116	K 17	Oakenshaw clo Surb
47	P 6	Oakeshott av N6
20	C 16	Oakfield E4
24	B 11	Oakfield av Harrow
118	D 12	Oakfield clo New Mald
27	P 20	Oakfield ct NW11
8	C 14	Oakfield gdns N18
109	T 12	Oakfield gdns SE19

125 P 13	Oakfield gdns Becknhm	
120 K 20	Oakfield gdns Carsh	
59 P 10	Oakfield gdns Grnfd	
66 C 4	Oakfield rd E6	
32 J 7	Oakfield rd E17	
28 A 5	Oakfield rd N3	
30 F 20	Oakfield rd N4	
48 F 1	Oakfield rd N4	
17 N 9	Oakfield rd N14	
110 B 17	Oakfield rd SE20	
105 R 6	Oakfield rd SW19	
122 L 20	Oakfield rd Croy	
54 A 9	Oakfield rd Ilf	
27 V 17	Oakfields rd NW11	
146 A 13	Oakfield st SW10	
47 V 12	Oakford rd NW5	
159 O 1	Oak gdns Croy	
25 U 7	Oak gdns Edg	
45 R 12	Oak gro NW2	
159 V 1	Oak gro W Wkhm	
124 C 2	Oakgrove rd SE20	
34 J 18	Oakhall ct E11	
34 H 19	Oak Hall rd E11	
126 D 10	Oakham dri Brom	
27 P 3	Oakhampton rd NW7	
116 K 16	Oak hill Surb	
33 X 1	Oak hill Wdfd Grn	
33 Z 1	Oak hill Wdfd Grn	
34 A 2	Oak hill Wdfd Grn	
34 B 3	Oak hill Wdfd Grn	
46 A 12	Oakhill av NW3	
22 A 7	Oakhill av Pinn	
33 X 2	Oak Hill clo Wdfd Grn	
116 K 16	Oakhill cres Surb	
33 Y 1	Oak hill cres Wdfd Grn	
116 L 17	Oakhill dri Surb	
34 A 3	Oak hill gdns Wdfd Grn	
16 B 1	Oakhill gro Surb	
116 J 15	Oakhill gro Surb	
46 C 12	Oak Hill pk NW3	
15 Z 1	Oakhill pk Barnt	
116 J 15	Oakhill path Surb	
87 X 12	Oakhill pl SW15	
87 X 12	Oakhill rd SW15	
122 B 2	Oakhill rd SW16	
125 T 4	Oakhill rd Bcknhm	
116 K 16	Oakhill rd Surb	
154 B 6	Oakhill rd Sutton	
33 Y 1	Oak Hill way Wdfd Grn	
98 E 12	Oakhouse rd Bxly Hth	
15 V 1	Oakhurst av Barnt	
80 L 20	Oakhurst av Bxly Hth	
21 P 5	Oakhurst clo E4	
33 Z 12	Oakhurst clo E17	
21 P 5	Oakhurst gdns E4	
23 Z 13	Oakhurst gdns E17	
80 M 20	Oakhurst gdns Bxly Hth	
91 X 10	Oakington gro SE22	
40 G 2	Oakington av Harrow	
42 M 9	Oakington av Wemb	
43 O 9	Oakington av Wemb	
43 P 15	Oakington Mnr dri Wemb	
129 U 17	Oakington rd W9	
3 A 20	Oakington av N8	
17 P 8	Oaklands N21	
82 M 19	Oaklands Twick	
19 N 1	Oaklands av N9	
9 N 20	Oaklands av Enf	
71 W 16	Oaklands av Islwth	
39 S 12	Oaklands av Rom	
96 K 18	Oaklands av Sidcp	
122 F 8	Oaklands av Thntn Hth	
159 T 5	Oaklands av W Wkhm	
98 C 19	Oaklands clo Bxly Hth	
42 F 16	Oaklands ct Wemb	
74 H 3	Oaklands av W12	
54 C 7	Oaklands Park av Ilf	
14 G 2	Oaklands rd N20	
45 O 13	Oaklands rd NW2	
85 X 8	Oaklands rd SW14	
74 W 5	Oaklands rd W7	
98 B 12	Oaklands rd Bxly Hth	
112 B 17	Oaklands rd Brom	
152 A 13	Oakland way Epsom	
63 X 19	Oak la E14	
28 F 7	Oak la N2	
16 L 19	Oak la N11	
83 U 9	Oak la Twick	
83 Z 19	Oak la Twick	
21 R 13	Oak la Wdfd Grn	
28 F 7	Oak la N2	
57 Y 10	Oakleafe gdns Ilf	
116 H 16	Oaklea pas Kingst	
15 V 7	Oakleigh av N20	
25 T 5	Oakleigh av Edg	
16 A 10	Oakleigh clo N11	
25 V 8	Oakleigh ct Edg	
15 X 10	Oakleigh cres N20	
15 S 5	Oakleigh gdns N20	
12 A 15	Oakleigh gdns Edg	
15 V 2	Oakleigh pk Barnt	
127 X 2	Oakleigh Park av Chisl	
15 U 5	Oakleigh Pk north N20	
15 V 4	Oakleigh Pk south N20	
15 U 7	Oakleigh Rd north N20	
16 A 11	Oakleigh Rd north N20	
16 C 13	Oakleigh Rd south N11	
121 S 1	Oakleigh way Mitch	
61 P 19	Oakley av W5	
54 L 20	Oakley av Bark	
156 B 8	Oakley av Croy	
59 S 19	Oakley clo W7	
83 R 2	Oakley clo Islwth	
133 X 10	Oakley cres N1	
114 E 3	Oakley dri Sidcp	
30 C 15	Oakley gdns N8	
146 L 13	Oakley gdns SW3	
127 O 19	Oakley house Brom	
97 S 19	Oakley pk Sidcp	
151 N 11	Oakley pl SE1	
49 O 20	Oakley rd N1	
123 Z 11	Oakley rd SE25	
124 A 11	Oakley rd SE25	
127 P 20	Oakley rd Brom	
23 S 17	Oakley rd Harrow	
132 C 8	Oakley sq NW1	
146 K 14	Oakley st SW3	
144 J 14	Oakley wk W6	
103 O 3	Oak lodge Rich	
125 S 18	Oak Lodge dri W Wkhm	
126 F 15	Oakmead av Brom	
12 K 13	Oakmead gdns Edg	
107 R 2	Oakmead rd SW12	
121 X 14	Oakmead rd Mitch	
80 A 16	Oakmere rd SE2	
111 X 10	Oakridge rd Brom	
81 X 20	Oak rd Erith	
99 X 3	Oak rd Erith	
117 X 3	Oak rd New Mald	
109 P 11	Oaks av SE19	
100 A 4	Oaks av Felt	
38 L 8	Oaks av Rom	
109 Z 8	Oaks av Worc Pk	
20 M 8	Oaks gro E4	
111 Y 9	Oakshade rd Brom	
36 G 14	Oaks la Ilf	
158 D 4	Oaks la Croy	
157 Z 10	Oaks rd Croy	
158 C 8	Oaks rd Croy	
121 U 3	Oak row Mitch	
79 O 15	Oaks the SE18	
72 H 1	Oak st W5	
38 J 14	Oak st Rom	
88 B 19	Oakshaw rd SW18	
154 M 17	Oaks way Carsh	
155 M 17	Oaks way Carsh	
15 S 15	Oakthorpe rd N13	
17 U 10	Oaktree av N13	
60 E 18	Oak Tree clo W13	
24 C 3	Oak Tree clo Stanm	
25 X 16	Oak Tree dell NW9	
15 O 6	Oak Tree dri N20	
112 J 11	Oak Tree gdns Brom	
130 J 14	Oak Tree rd NW8	
124 K 19	Oakview gro Croy	
111 R 12	Oakview rd SE6	
47 O 13	Oak village NW5	
16 D 2	Oak way N14	
118 M 9	Oak way SW20	
119 N 9	Oak way SW20	
74 A 2	Oak way W3	
124 G 12	Oakway Brom	
124 G 13	Oak way Croy	
97 Z 16	Oakway clo Bxly	
95 Y 15	Oakways SE9	
155 T 19	Oakwood Wallgtn	
125 U 3	Oakwood av Bcknhm	
126 H 17	Oakwood av Brom	
120 G 3	Oakwood av Mitch	
58 H 20	Oakwood av S'hall	
70 H 1	Oakwood av S'hall	
6 J 20	Oakwood clo N14	
113 V 16	Oakwood clo Chisl	
145 O 1	Oakwood ct W14	
7 O 18	Oakwood cres N21	
41 Z 17	Oakwood cres Grnfd	
42 A 18	Oakwood cres Grnfd	
98 L 9	Oakwood dri Bxly Hth	
12 G 18	Oakwood dri Edg	
54 K 7	Oakwood gdns Ilf	
137 O 20	Oakwood la W14	
16 M 2	Oakwood Pk rd N14	
17 N 1	Oakwood Pk rd N14	
122 F 15	Oakwood pl Croy	
27 Z 14	Oakwood rd NW11	
28 A 15	Oakwood rd NW11	
104 H 20	Oakwood rd SW20	
122 F 15	Oakwood rd Croy	
16 L 1	Oakwood view N14	
136 E 1	Oakwork rd W10	
32 H 8	Oatland ri E17	
9 P 7	Oatlands rd Enf	
160 B 3	Oat la EC2	
65 Z 10	Oban rd E13	
123 P 7	Oban rd SE25	
28 S 14	Oban st E14	
88 G 10	Oberstein rd SW11	
21 W 20	Oborne pl SE24	
137 U 17	Observatory gdns W8	
85 V 11	Observatory rd SW14	
95 Z 1	Occupation la SE18	
72 G 11	Occupation la W5	
150 A 9	Occupation rd W13	
72 A 10	Occupation rd W13	
72 B 4	Occupation rd W13	
0 U 14	Ocean st E1	
4 O 19	Ockendon rd N1	
115 O 18	Ockham dri Orp	
107 Z 8	Ockley rd SW16	
122 C 17	Ockley rd Croy	
120 H 10	Octavia clo Mrdn	
83 V 6	Octavia rd Islwth	
76 A 19	Octavia st SE8	
88 J 3	Octavia st SW11	
80 E 1	Octavia st SW11	
52 E 14	Odessa rd E7	
62 H 7	Odessa rd NW10	
75 X 7	Odessa st SE16	
88 M 5	Odger st SW11	
113 U 9	Offenham rd SE9	
89 V 8	Offerton rd SW4	
14 H 16	Offham slope N12	
149 S 18	Offley rd SW9	
48 D 20	Offord rd N1	
78 F 12	Ogilby st SE18	
91 V 8	Oglander rd SE15	
140 A 1	Ogle st W1	
56 D 9	Oglethorpe rd Dgnhm	
65 P 13	Ohio rd E13	
107 O 11	Okeburn rd SW17	
15 T 15	Okehampton clo N12	
80 D 20	Okehampton cres SE18	
80 H 20	Okehampton cres Welling	
97 S 1	Okehampton cres Welling	
128 E 6	Okehampton rd NW10	
136 H 19	Olaf st W11	
141 X 5	Old bailey EC4	
153 S 16	Old Barn clo Sutton	
98 L 9	Old Barn way Bxly Hth	
139 T 18	Old Barrack yd SW1	
65 O 4	Oldbarrow field E15	
12 M 19	Oldberry rd Edg	
135 U 12	Old Bethnal Green rd E2	
140 A 11	Old Bond st W1	
42 D 9	Oldborough rd Wemb	
46 F 13	Old Brewery ms NW3	
58 H 5	Old Bridge clo Grnfd	
116 F 2	Old Bridge st Kingst	
142 H 3	Old Broad st EC2	
160 H 3	Old Broad st EC2	
111 X 12	Old Bromley rd Brom	
88 B 9	Old Brompton rd SW5	
141 R 4	Old Bldgs WC2	
74 A 10	Old Burlington st W1	
131 T 19	Oldbury pl W1	
8 L 9	Oldbury rd Enf	
143 O 4	Old Castle st E1	
139 X 5	Old Cavendish st W1	
160 A 7	Old Change ct EC4	
43 X 7	Old Church la NW9	
11 R 20	Old Church la Stanm	
11 T 20	Old Church la Stanm	
24 E 1	Old Church la Stanm	
57 P 1	Old Church la Rom	
39 P 20	Oldchurch ri Rom	
63 T 17	Old Church rd E1	
81 O 11	Old Church rd E4	
39 P 19	Oldchurch rd Rom	
146 J 15	Old Church st SW3	
140 F 7	Old Compton st W1	
70 G 17	Old Cote dri Hounsl	
137 X 17	Old Ct pl W8	
84 F 7	Old Deer pk Rich	
84 K 8	Old Deer Pk gdns Rich	
89 S 20	Old Devonshire rd SW12	
73 P 17	Old Dock clo Rich	
77 U 19	Old Dover rd SE3	
16 H 2	Old Farm av Sidcup	
144 E 2	Old Farm av Sidcup	
82 E 9	Old Farm clo Hounsl	
100 G 15	Old Farm rd Hampt	
28 G 4	Old Farm rd N2	
114 M 3	Old Farm Rd east Sidcp	
114 L 3	Old Farm Rd west Sidcp	
127 V 9	Oldfield clo Brom	
41 T 17	Oldfield clo Stanm	
10 L 15	Oldfield clo Stanm	
59 P 4	Oldfield Farm gdns Grnfd	
75 T 11	Oldfield gro SE16	
41 S 17	Oldfield la Grnfd	
41 S 18	Oldfield la Grnfd	
59 P 5	Oldfield la Grnfd	
49 S 9	Oldfield rd N16	
44 C 20	Oldfield rd NW10	
105 S 14	Oldfield rd SW19	
74 D 5	Oldfield rd W12	
97 Z 5	Oldfield rd Bxly Hth	
98 A 5	Oldfield rd Bxly Hth	
127 U 8	Oldfield rd Brom	
41 O 17	Oldfields cir Grnfd	
153 X 3	Oldfields rd Sutton	
4 G 7	Old Fold clo Barnt	
4 G 7	Old Fold la Barnt	
4 A 12	Old Fold view Barnt	
135 Z 11	Old Ford rd E2	
63 U 5	Old Ford rd E3	
10 M 14	Old Forge Stanm	
10 M 13	Old Forge cl Stanm	
8 G 4	Old Forge rd Enf	
115 R 11	Old Forge way Sidcp	
132 L 20	Old Gloucester st WC1	
140 M 1	Old Gloucester st WC1	
22 C 5	Old Hall clo Pinn	
22 B 5	Old Hall dri Pinn	
73 V 4	Oldhams ter W3	
113 Y 20	Old hill Chisl	
43 X 3	Oldhill st N16	
105 S 12	Old Ho SW19	
151 R 1	Old Jamaica rd SE16	
91 Z 8	Old James st SE15	
142 D 6	Old Jewry EC2	
160 D 6	Old Jewry EC2	
25 T 16	Old Kenton la NW9	
150 K 7	Old Kent rd SE1	
75 O 18	Old Kent rd SE14	
151 X 16	Old Kent rd SE14	
101 L 16	Old Lodge way Stanm	
83 O 15	Old Manor dri Islwth	
98 M 7	Old Manor way Bxly Hth	
145 W 8	Old Manor yd SW5	
138 L 2	Old Marylebone rd NW1	
34 K 9	Old Mill ct E18	
79 S 16	Old Mill rd SE18	
141 T 6	Old Mitre ct EC4	
135 U 20	Old Montague st E1	
143 R 2	Old Montague st E1	
143 M 15	Old Nichol st E2	
135 N 15	Old Nichol st E2	
141 N 1	Old North st WC1	
62 B 12	Old Oak Comm la NW10	
62 C 18	Old Oak Comm la W3	
62 C 9	Old Oak la NW10	
62 D 20	Old Oak rd W3	
74 E 3	Old Oak rd W3	
46 L 11	Old Orchard the NW3	
84 E 12	Old Palace la Rich	
156 K 4	Old Palace rd Croy	
84 F 12	Old Palace yd Rich	
149 O 5	Old Paradise st SE11	
89 P 16	Old Park av SW12	
7 Z 12	Old Park av Enf	
7 Y 15	Old Park gro Enf	
139 W 16	Old Park la W1	
7 X 18	Old Park ridings Enf	
7 R 12	Old Park rd N13	
80 A 14	Old Park rd SE2	
7 W 12	Old Park rd Enf	
7 V 14	Old Park rd South Enf	
7 U 11	Old Park view Enf	
114 G 17	Old Perry st Chisl	
148 F 1	Old Pye st SW1	
139 R 7	Old Quebec st W1	
140 G 19	Old Queen st SW1	

O

12 C 18 Old Rectory gdns Edg
10 C 14 Old redding Harrow
89 R 18 Oldridge rd SW12
93 Z 11 Old rd SE13
94 A 11 Old rd SE13
98 M 12 Old rd Drtfrd
9 P 6 Old rd Enf
152 D 19 Old Schools la Epsom
141 W 5 Old Seacoal la EC4
148 L 18 Old South Lambeth rd SW8
141 R 4 Old sq WC2
127 W 1 Old Station hill Chisl
111 X 10 Oldstead rd Brom
65 W 7 Old st E13
134 J 14 Old st EC1
154 L 9 Old Swan yd Carsh
98 U 8 Old town SW4
156 K 4 Old town Croy
76 K 15 Old Woolwich rd SE10
63 S 15 Oley pl E1
76 H 9 Oliffe st E14
31 V 19 Olinda rd N16
128 K 11 Oliphant st W10
123 U 7 Oliver av SE25
51 P 7 Oliver clo E10
123 V 8 Oliver gro SE25
65 Z 9 Olive rd E13
44 L 12 Olive rd NW2
45 N 13 Olive rd NW2
106 D 18 Olive rd SW19
72 G 8 Olive rd W5
51 P 7 Oliver rd E10
33 V 14 Oliver rd E17
117 W 3 Oliver rd New Mald
154 F 9 Oliver rd Sutton
134 F 17 Olivers yd EC2
39 N 15 Olive st Rom
87 P 9 Olivette st SW15
63 Z 2 Ollerton grn E3
16 K 17 Ollerton rd N11
74 F 3 Ollgar clo W3
151 R 19 Olmar st SE1
149 Z 14 Olney rd SE17
150 C 12 Olney rd SE17
97 X 14 Olron cres Bxly Hth
79 P 18 Olven rd SE18
120 G 14 Oloveston wlk Carsh
97 O 3 Olyffe av Welling
144 L 4 Olympia W14
144 M 3 Olympia rd W14
137 Z 9 Olympia yd W2
58 M 4 Olympic way Grnfd
43 P 10 Olympic way Wemb
44 K 13 Oman av NW2
93 T 13 Omborough way SE13
142 C 15 O'meara st SE1
132 M 10 Omega pl N1
92 G 3 Ommaney rd SE14
91 U 9 Ondine rd SE15
52 C 17 One Tree clo SE23
145 T 13 Ongar rd SW6
37 T 14 Ongar rd Rom
3 O 20 Onra rd E17
94 K 14 Onslow av Rich
20 H 9 Onslow clo E4
115 V 5 Onslow dri Sidcp
34 J 10 Onslow gdns E18
29 S 15 Onslow gdns N10
7 U 17 Onslow gdns N21
146 E 8 Onslow gdns SW7
155 U 15 Onslow gdns Wllgtn
146 F 7 Onslow ms E SW7
136 E 8 Onslow ms W SW7
122 F 19 Onslow rd Croy
118 F 8 Onslow rd New Mald
94 K 14 Onslow rd Rich
146 G 6 Onslow sq SW7
133 U 19 Onslow st EC1
149 Y 2 Ontario st SE1
53 Z 8 Opal mews llf
149 V 8 Opal st SE11
80 C 11 Openshaw rd E20
106 E 2 Openview SW18
91 W 3 Ophir ter SE15
131 O 1 Oppidans ms NW3
131 O 1 Oppidans rd NW3
143 U 14 Orange ct E1
25 V 1 Orange Hill rd Edg
75 P 9 Orange pl SE16
140 F 11 Orange st WC2
140 G 6 Orange yd W1
55 T 14 Orangery la SE9
144 M 19 Orbain rd SW6
88 H 3 Orbel st SW11
6 B 7 Orb st SE17
27 X 10 Orchard av N3
11 U 1 Orchard av N14
15 U 8 Orchard av N20
80 M 16 Orchard av Blvdr

81 N 16 Orchard av Blvdr
124 J 18 Orchard av Croy
124 J 20 Orchard av Croy
158 H 1 Orchard av Croy
99 Y 20 Orchard av Drtfrd
70 C 20 Orchard av Hounsl
121 O 19 Orchard av Mitch
118 C 5 Orchard av New Mald
70 D 2 Orchard av S'hall
118 L 8 Orchard clo SW20
97 Y 2 Orchard clo Bxly Hth
10 C 5 Orchard clo Bushey Watf
11 Y 18 Orchard clo Edg
41 N 17 Orchard clo Enf
116 B 19 Orchard clo Surb
60 K 2 Orchard clo Wemb
92 C 17 Orchard clo SE23
152 E 1 Orchard ct Worc Pk
12 H 17 Orchard cres Edg
8 G 6 Orchard cres Enf
93 X 4 Orchard dri SE3
11 Z 15 Orchard dri Edg
93 S 4 Orchard est SE13
153 X 10 Orchard gdns Sutton
26 A 12 Orchard ga N6
42 B 17 Orchard ga Grnfd
124 J 17 Orchard gro Croy
25 R 5 Orchard gro Edg
25 N 15 Orchard gro Harrow
93 S 3 Orchard hill SE13
155 N 10 Orchard hill Carsh
99 O 12 Orchard hill Drtfrd
104 K 20 Orchard la SW20
21 X 13 Orchard la NW4
109 X 20 Orchard lodge SE20
8 B 19 Orchardmede Enf
64 M 18 Orchard pl E14
31 U 3 Orchard pl N17
124 K 19 Orchard ri Croy
103 V 20 Orchard ri Kingst
85 S 11 Orchard ri Rich
96 J 13 Orchard Ri east Sidcp

96 G 13 Orchard Ri west Sidcp
29 T 20 Orchard rd N6
4 G 14 Orchard rd Barnt
81 R 12 Orchard rd Blvdr
72 E 16 Orchard rd Brentf
112 M 20 Orchard rd Brom
69 T 3 Orchard rd Dgnhm
9 R 18 Orchard rd Enf
100 F 17 Orchard rd Hampt
82 F 12 Orchard rd Hounsl
116 J 5 Orchard rd Kingst
121 O 19 Orchard rd Mitch
85 P 9 Orchard rd Rich
38 G 6 Orchard rd Rom
114 J 9 Orchard rd Sidcp
153 Y 10 Orchard rd Sutton
83 Z 14 Orchard rd Twick
84 A 14 Orchard rd Twick
97 R 6 Orchard rd Welling
130 F 18 Orchardson st NW8
32 H 12 Orchard st E17
139 T 6 Orchard st W1
27 X 16 Orchard the NW11
73 Z 10 Orchard the W4
8 A 19 Orchard the Enf
83 O 5 Orchard the Hounsl
93 X 4 Orchard the SE3
124 J 16 Orchard way Croy
8 D 11 Orchard way Enf
154 G 8 Orchard way Sutton
16 G 3 Orchid rd N14
133 N 19 Orchid st W12
63 Z 7 Ordell rd E3
76 M 5 Ordnance cres SE10
130 G 6 Ordnance hill NW8
65 S 14 Ordnance rd E16
78 J 18 Ordnance rd E16
53 S 11 Oregon av E12
101 V 5 Orford gdns Twick
33 R 15 Orford rd E17
34 G 10 Orford rd E17
20 G 9 Organ la E4
121 X 7 Oriel clo Mitch
35 T 11 Oriel gdns llf
46 E 13 Oriel pl NW3
71 U 7 Oriel rd E9
40 K 20 Oriel way Grnfd
78 A 3 Oriental rd E16
149 W 4 Orient st SE11
79 U 13 Orissa rd SE18
89 N 3 Orkney st SW11
109 P 19 Orleans rd SE19
84 C 19 Orleans rd Twick
48 G 18 Orleston ms N7
48 G 18 Orleston rd N7

41 S 11 Orley Farm rd Harrow
76 L 14 Orlop st SE10
109 Y 11 Ormanton rd SE26
137 Z 7 Orme Ct ms W2
137 X 9 Orme ct W2
137 Y 10 Orme la W2
102 J 7 Ormeley lodge Rich
89 S 20 Ormeley rd SW12
117 T 3 Orme rd Kingst
121 P 2 Ormerod gdns Mitch
59 N 7 Ormesby gdns Grnfd
24 M 17 Ormesby way Harrow
137 X 10 Orme sq W2
74 H 3 Ormiston gro W12
77 S 14 Ormiston rd SE10
100 K 20 Ormond av Hampt
100 L 19 Ormond clo Hampt
100 K 20 Ormond cres Hampt
100 L 18 Ormond dri Hampt
147 O 11 Ormonde ga SW3
85 U 9 Ormonde rd SW14
21 Y 5 Ormonde rd Buck Hl
131 O 6 Ormonde ter NW8
132 M 18 Ormonde ter NW8
A 4 Ormond ms WC1
84 H 14 Ormond rd N4
140 C 12 Ormond rd Rich
135 N 8 Ormond yd SW1
46 H 15 Ormsby st E2
91 N 3 Ornan rd NW3
18 D 12 Orpheus st SE5
17 V 6 Orpington gdns N18
100 D 14 Orpington rd N21
137 Z 4 Orpwood clo Hampt
138 A 4 Orsett ms W2
149 P 9 Orsett ms W2
137 Z 4 Orsett st SE11
138 A 4 Orsett ter W2
34 K 3 Orsett ter W2
134 L 5 Orsett ter Wdfd Grn
143 T 14 Orsman rd N1
88 C 4 Orton st E1
76 X 5 Orville rd SW11
49 N 16 Orwell rd E13
94 E 13 Osbaldeston rd N16
148 E 7 Osberton rd SE12
124 J 9 Osbert st SW1
Osborne clo Becknhm

39 Z 19 Osborne clo Hornch
154 F 12 Osborne clo Sutton
27 O 2 Osborne gdns NW7
122 L 3 Osborne gdns Thntn Hth
32 K 14 Osborne gro E17
76 H 15 Osborne rd E7
50 M 17 Osborne rd E9
51 S 8 Osborne rd E10
48 E 4 Osborne rd N4
17 U 11 Osborne rd N13
44 J 17 Osborne rd W3
73 S 7 Osborne rd W3
81 O 15 Osborne rd Blvdr
21 V 6 Osborne rd Buck Hl
56 C 14 Osborne rd Dgnhm
9 V 9 Osborne rd Enf
39 Y 18 Osborne rd Hornch
82 E 9 Osborne rd Hounsl
102 K 17 Osborne rd Kingst
58 M 17 Osborne rd S'hall
122 L 3 Osborne rd Thntn Hth
56 B 13 Osborne sq Dgnhm
32 J 20 Osborne la SE23
143 P 3 Osborn la E1
94 C 11 Osborn ter SE3
N 3 Oscar st SE8
47 W 16 Osborne cres NW5
63 Y 3 Oshea gro E3
16 F 3 Osidge la N14
87 V 11 Osiers rd SW18
87 R 12 Osier st E1
51 P 8 Osier way E10
120 K 11 Osier way Mitch
111 S 12 Osney rd SE6
31 P 18 Osman clo N15
18 K 12 Osnan rd N9
41 O 7 Osmond clo Harrow
155 V 10 Osmond gdns Wllgtn
32 E 16 Osmund st W12
131 Z 16 Osnaburgh st NW1
131 Z 17 Osnaburgh st NW1
120 G 14 Osney wlk Wallgtn
96 G 16 Ospringe ct SE9
47 U 13 Ospringe rd NW5
48 D 1 Ossian rd N4
139 T 1 Ossington bldgs W1
137 W 11 Ossington st W2
91 R 12 Ossory rd SE1
132 F 10 Ossulston st NW1
28 D 11 Ossulton way N2
90 D 18 Ostade rd SW2
145 Z 3 Osten ms SW5
71 P 19 Osterley av Islwth

83 U 1 Osterley cres Islwth
122 L 2 Osterley gdns Thntn Hth
70 K 13 Osterley la S'hall
70 M 10 Osterley pk S'hall
71 O 15 Osterley Pk house Islwth
70 D 7 Osterley Pk rd S'hall
71 U 6 Osterley Pk View rd W7
49 S 11 Osterley rd N16
71 S 20 Osterley rd Islwth
83 S 1 Osterley rd Islwth
49 R 11 Osterley rd N16
70 C 2 Oswald rd S'hall
158 M 20 Osward Croy
18 L 8 Osward pla N9
106 M 3 Osward SW17
149 X 4 Oswin st SE11
91 S 4 Oswyth rd SE5
98 G 16 Otford clo Bxly
127 X 6 Otford clo Brom
92 K 16 Otford cres SE4
64 F 9 Otis st E3
149 W 9 Othello clo SE11
35 Z 18 Otley appr llf
35 Y 17 Ottley dri llf
36 A 17 Otley dri llf
65 X 16 Otley rd E16
50 E 8 Otley ter E5
68 Z 1 Ottawa gdns Dgnhm
20 K 11 Otterbourne rd E4
156 K 2 Otterbourne rd Croy
71 Y 19 Otterburn gdns Islwth
107 N 15 Otterburn st SW17
111 N 9 Otterden st SE6
59 N 13 Otter rd Grnfd
149 W 14 Otto st SE17
49 X 10 Ottoway st E5
54 K 16 Oulton cres Bark
31 P 15 Oulton rd N15
10 B 1 Oundle av Bushey Watf
106 M 1 Ouseley rd SW1
130 M 11 Outer circle NW1/NW8

131 W 10 Outer circle NW1/NW8
44 D 20 Outgate rd NW10
66 C 3 Outram rd E6
29 X 4 Outram rd N22
157 W 2 Outram rd Croy
132 L 4 Outram st N1
142 K 4 Outwhich st EC3
149 R 14 Oval Cricket ground SE11
131 X 5 Oval rd NW1
157 S 1 Oval rd Croy
69 V 4 Oval Rd north Dgnhm
69 U 6 Oval Rd south Dgnhm
135 W 8 Oval the E2
97 N 18 Oval the Sidcp
149 P 12 Oval way SE11
111 O 13 Overbrae Becknhm
25 O 1 Overbrook wlk Edg
125 T 5 Overbury av Becknhm

125 U 4 Overbury av Becknhm
31 O 19 Overbury rd N15
50 G 11 Overbury st E5
93 P 8 Overcliff rd SE13
97 P 14 Overcourt clo Sidcp
117 X 3 Overdale av New Mald
72 D 8 Overdale rd W5
111 P 9 Overdown rd SE6
91 X 19 Overhill rd SE22
125 V 12 Overhill way Becknhm
49 X 2 Overlea rd E5
96 E 19 Overmead Sidcp
125 O 10 Overstand clo Becknhm
124 K 16 Overstone gdns Croy
74 L 10 Overstone rd W6
144 B 5 Overstone rd W6
43 V 18 Overton clo NW10
83 U 3 Overton clo Islwth
52 G 2 Overton dri E11
52 G 2 Overton dri Rom
55 U 12 Overton dri Rom
50 J 3 Overton rd E10
6 M 18 Overton rd N14
7 N 17 Overton rd N14
80 H 8 Overton rd SE2
90 G 6 Overton rd SW9
153 Y 17 Overton rd Sutton
156 L 4 Overtons clo Croy
40 D 5 Ovesdon av Harrow
146 L 2 Ovington gdns SW3
146 M 2 Ovington ms SW3

O

146 M 2 Ovington sq SW3
146 M 4 Ovington st SW3
147 N 5 Ovington st SW3
80 D 11 Owenite st SE2
80 F 3 Owen clo SE18
17 Y 15 Owen rd N13
43 V 16 Owen way NW10
133 V 11 Owens ct E1
133 V 11 Owens row EC1
92 J 20 Owens way SE23
133 V 11 Owen st EC1
87 S 3 Oxberry av SW6
140 F 10 Oxendon st SW1
91 U 8 Oxenford st SE15
42 L 2 Oxenpark av Wemb
75 W 13 Oxestalls rd SE8
119 S 2 Oxford av SW20
70 F 15 Oxford av Hounsl
140 A 5 Oxford cir W1
18 M 7 Oxford Cir av W1
121 U 7 Oxford clo Mitch
117 Y 14 Oxford cres New Mald
15 S 6 Oxford gdns N20
18 A 2 Oxford gdns N21
73 R 15 Oxford gdns W4
136 J 4 Oxford gdns W10
51 Y 18 Oxford rd E15
48 F 4 Oxford rd N4
19 N 8 Oxford rd N9
129 W 7 Oxford rd NW6
109 O 15 Oxford rd SE15
87 S 12 Oxford rd SW15
60 H 20 Oxford rd W5
72 H 1 Oxford rd W5
154 J 11 Oxford rd Carsh
9 N 18 Oxford rd Enf
23 O 18 Oxford rd Harrow
23 V 11 Oxford rd Harrow
54 C 14 Oxford rd Ilf
115 R 13 Oxford rd Mitch
101 R 12 Oxford rd Tedd
155 U 12 Oxford rd Wallgtn
21 Z 16 Oxford rd Wdfd Grn
73 T 13 Oxford Rd north W4
73 S 14 Oxford Rd south W4
138 L 6 Oxford sq W2
54 A 19 Oxford st Bark
139 T 6 Oxford st W1
140 E 4 Oxford st W1
44 L 7 Oxgate gdns NW2
44 J 6 Oxgate la NW2
127 X 13 Oxhawth cres Brom
152 G 10 Ox la Epsom
96 E 6 Oxleas clo Welling
40 F 4 Oxleay av Harrow
118 A 11 Oxleigh clo New Mald
44 L 9 Oxleys rd NW2
56 H 12 Oxlow la Dgnhm
56 D 12 Oxlow la Dgnhm
120 F 6 Oxted clo Mitch
121 X 2 Oxtoby way SW16
32 F 14 Oyster ter E17

O
P

P

143 Y 7 Pace pl E1
65 T 6 Pacific rd E16
133 Y 4 Packington st N1
134 A 6 Packington st N1
96 P 14 Packmores rd SE9
74 H 8 Paddenswick rd W6
138 G 1 Paddington grn W2
138 F 5 Paddington station W2
139 S 1 Paddington st W1
110 E 9 Paddock clo SE26
58 H 5 Paddock clo Grnfd
109 T 15 Paddock gdns SE19
44 G 8 Paddock gdns NW2
97 Z 11 Paddock rd Bxly Hth
40 A 9 Paddock Ruis
40 L 13 Paddocks clo Harrow
5 Z 13 Paddocks the Barnt
43 T 7 Paddocks the Wemb
114 F 19 Paddock way Chisl
90 K 7 Padfield rd SE5
37 V 10 Padnall rd Rom
7 W 7 Padstow rd Enf
110 C 20 Padua rd SE20
157 R 5 Pageant wlk Croy
146 B 14 Page clo Hampt
24 M 20 Page clo Harrow
100 B 14 Page clo Hampt
156 H 20 Page cres Croy
31 W 15 Page Green rd N15
31 U 16 Page Green st N15
127 R 5 Page Heath la Brom

127 N 6 Page Heath vlls Brom
123 Y 17 Pagehurst rd Croy
29 R 7 Pages hill N10
29 R 8 Pages la N10
13 V 20 Paget rd SE18
26 G 3 Paget st NW7
148 G 5 Paget st SW1
150 L 3 Pages wlk SE1
154 G 6 Paget av Sutton
101 O 10 Paget clo Hampt
78 K 18 Paget rd SE18
49 P 4 Paget rd N16
53 Y 13 Paget rd Ilf
133 W 12 Paget st EC1
78 K 18 Paget ter SE18
75 X 18 Pagnell st SE14
84 M 8 Pagoda av Rich
93 X 6 Pagoda gdns SE3
31 S 19 Paignton rd N15
22 C 10 Paines clo Pinn
121 T 4 Paines la Pinn
49 S 8 Painsthorpe rd N16
36 U 9 Painters rd Ilf
37 O 9 Painters rd Ilf
30 J 4 Paisley rd N22
120 F 19 Paisley rd Carsh
48 C 10 Pakesman st N7
107 O 1 Pakenham clo SW17
133 P 15 Pakenham st WC1
137 Z 17 Palace av W8
137 W 10 Palace ct W2
24 J 18 Palace ct Harrow
29 U 9 Palace Ct gdns N10
137 Y 17 Palace grn W8
137 W 12 Palace Gdns ms W8
137 W 14 Palace Gdns ter W8
138 B 19 Palace ga W8
29 Z 6 Palace Gates rd N22
158 M 17 Palace grn Croy
109 U 18 Palace gro SE19
128 G 1 Palace gro Brom
147 U 7 Palace ms SW1
29 T 5 Palace rd N8
29 Z 2 Palace rd N11
109 V 17 Palace rd SE19
108 D 2 Palace rd SW2
128 G 1 Palace rd Brom
116 G 10 Palace rd Kingst
40 A 11 Palace rd Pinn
109 U 17 Palace sq SE19
148 B 2 Palace st SW1
126 J 6 Palace view Brom
158 L 7 Palace view Croy
112 F 3 Palace view SE12
20 E 16 Palace view rd E4
51 N 3 Palamos rd E10
49 T 12 Palatine rd N16
62 H 7 Palermo rd NW10
120 F 1 Palestine gro SW19
85 Z 12 Palewell Comm dri SW14
85 Y 10 Palewell pk SW14
149 N 17 Palfrey pl SW8
58 G 20 Palgrave av S'hall
74 D 8 Palgrave rd W12
135 N 14 Palissy st E2
95 P 1 Pallett way SE18
144 K 10 Palliser rd W14
130 G 16 Pallitt dri NW8
140 E 13 Pall mall SW1
140 G 12 Pall Mall east SW1
140 C 14 Pall Mall pl SW1
98 E 6 Palmar cres Bxly Hth
98 D 6 Palmar rd Bxly Hth
115 W 15 Palm av Sidcp
97 W 7 Palmeira rd Bxly Hth
152 M 9 Palmer av Sutton
153 N 10 Palmer av Sutton
82 F 2 Palmer clo Hounsl
116 J 5 Palmer cres Kingst
48 F 16 Palmer pl N7
65 W 13 Palmer rd E13
9 O 6 Palmers la Enf
61 T 8 Palmers rd E2
16 G 16 Palmers rd N11
85 W 8 Palmers rd SW14
122 C 3 Palmers rd SW16
17 P 17 Palmerston cres N13
105 Y 18 Palmerston gro SW19
123 N 11 Palmerston gro Thntn Hth
52 H 17 Palmerston rd E7
32 K 14 Palmerston rd E17
17 P 18 Palmerston rd N22
30 C 1 Palmerston rd N22
45 W 20 Palmerston rd NW6
85 V 11 Palmerston rd SW14
105 Y 17 Palmerston rd SW19
73 U 7 Palmerston rd W3
21 W 7 Palmerston rd Buck Hl
155 N 7 Palmerston rd Carsh

23 V 11 Palmerston rd Harrow
154 E 10 Palmerston rd Sutton
83 U 16 Palmerston rd Twick
79 P 17 Palmerston rd SE18
140 D 20 Palmer st SW1
148 E 1 Palmer st SW1
72 J 7 Palm gro W5
38 L 16 Palm of Rom
63 U 8 Palm st E2
136 F 6 Pamber st W10
156 K 17 Pampisford rd S Croy
160 D 7 Pancras la EC4
132 F 7 Pancras rd NW1
45 X 16 Pandora rd NW6
35 W 18 Panfield ms Ilf
80 B 6 Panfield rd SE2
136 D 1 Pangbourne av W10
11 X 15 Pangbourne dri Stanm
5 S 18 Pank av Barnt
104 K 20 Panmuir rd SW20
109 Z 7 Panmure rd SE26
110 A 7 Panmure rd SE26
58 L 19 Pannard pl S'hall
81 O 20 Pantiles the Bxly Hth
127 R 6 Pantiles the Brom
27 W 14 Pantiles the NW11
10 D 4 Pantiles the Bushey Watf
140 G 10 Panton st SW2
117 T 8 Paper bldng EC4
94 E 6 Papillons wk SE3
94 G 5 Papillons wk SE3
48 D 16 Papworth gdns N7
16 K 6 Parade the N14
147 S 16 Parade the SW11
99 S 12 Parade the Drtfrd
94 D 4 Paradise rd SW4
63 O 8 Paradise row E2
143 Y 19 Paradise st SE16
147 P 13 Paradise wlk SW3
116 M 14 Paragon gro Surb
94 C 4 Paragon pl SE3
50 B 18 Paragon rd E9
84 D 4 Paragon the SE3
92 H 16 Parbury rd SE23
122 K 4 Parchmore rd Thntn Hth
122 K 3 Parchmore way Thntn Hth
142 G 20 Pardoner st SE1
133 Y 16 Pardon st EC1
73 T 5 Pard Rd north W3
143 U 4 Parfett st E1
144 E 13 Parfrey st W6
35 Y 17 Parham dri Ilf
29 U 8 Parham way N10
141 V 13 Paris gdn SE1
110 E 17 Parish la SE20
99 P 9 Park appr Welling
66 S 4 Park av E6
51 Z 18 Park av E15
28 C 4 Park av N3
17 U 12 Park av N13
18 J 14 Park av N18
30 C 5 Park av N22
14 L 18 Park av NW2
61 N 8 Park av NW10
46 A 4 Park av NW11
85 Z 11 Park av SW14
54 D 18 Park av Bark
112 F 16 Park av Brom
155 O 13 Park av Carsh
8 E 20 Park av Enf
82 K 15 Park av Hounsl
53 X 5 Park av Ilf
107 S 18 Park av Mitch
70 E 4 Park av S'hall
159 U 3 Park av W Wkhm
60 L 7 Park av Wemb
21 U 16 Park av Wdfd Grn
152 H 15 Park Av east Epsom
29 X 13 Park Av north N8
44 K 15 Park Av north NW10
53 A 2 Park Avenue rd N17
29 W 14 Park Av south N8
152 F 15 Park Av west Epsom
39 T 6 Park blvd Rom
42 M 12 Park chase Wemb
43 N 11 Park chase Wemb
44 H 10 Park clo NW2
61 N 7 Park clo NW10
155 N 13 Park clo Carsh
23 T 3 Park clo Harrow
83 N 13 Park clo Hounsl
31 Y 1 Park ct E15
117 Z 9 Park ct New Mald
42 L 14 Park ct Wemb
28 C 3 Park cres N3
131 X 18 Park cres NW1
81 Y 17 Park cres Erith
23 T 4 Park cres Harrow

39 V 20 Park cres Hornch
131 Y 18 Park Cres Ms east W1
131 W 19 Park Cres Ms west NW1
83 P 20 Park cres Twick
25 W 4 Park croft Edg
94 B 18 Parkcroft rd SE12
79 U 14 Parkdale rd SE18
21 N 20 Park dri N21
17 Y 1 Park dri N21
23 Z 4 Park dri NW11
78 D 15 Park dri SE7
85 Z 11 Park dri SW14
73 P 8 Park dri W3
56 L 10 Park dri Dgnhm
10 D 20 Park dri Harrow
22 F 20 Park dri Harrow
39 P 12 Park dri Rom
78 D 15 Park Dri clo SE7
46 K 12 Park end NW3
112 C 20 Park end Brom
39 R 13 Park End rd Rom
74 E 20 Parke rd SW13
86 F 1 Parke rd SW13
156 M 8 Parker rd Croy
143 R 19 Parkers row SE1
78 C 3 Parker st E16
140 M 4 Parker st WC2
28 E 11 Park Farm clo N2
127 O 1 Park Farm rd Brom
102 L 17 Park Farm rd Kingst
86 A 10 Parkfield av SW14
58 A 6 Parkfield av Grnfd
23 N 8 Parkfield av Harrow
12 E 20 Parkfield clo Edg
58 C 5 Parkfield clo Grnfd
22 M 8 Parkfield cres Harrow
30 B 8 Parkfield cres Ruis
58 A 7 Parkfield dri Grnfd
22 L 10 Parkfield gdns Harrow
44 N 20 Parkfield rd NW10
92 K 1 Parkfield rd SE14
58 B 5 Parkfield rd Grnfd
41 N 9 Parkfield rd Harrow
86 M 11 Parkfields SW15
124 L 19 Parkfields Croy
42 Z 3 Parkfields av NW9
44 A 3 Parkfields av NW9
118 J 1 Parkfields av SW20
103 N 13 Parkfields rd Kingst
133 U 8 Parkfield st N1
127 V 13 Parkfield way Brom
25 U 11 Park gdns NW9
81 Y 11 Park gdns Erith
103 P 14 Park gdns Kingst
28 H 10 Park ga N21
17 O 3 Park ga N21
94 D 9 Parkgate SE3
60 F 13 Park ga W5
5 P 5 Parkgate av Barnt
103 T 14 Park Ga clo Kingst
5 P 7 Parkgate cres Barnt
85 X 14 Parkgate gdns SW14
102 M 7 Parkgate house Rich
146 K 20 Parkgate rd SW11
155 S 11 Parkgate rd Wallgtn
31 Y 5 Park gro E15
29 Y 2 Park gro N11
98 J 11 Park gro Bxly Hth
126 H 1 Park gro Brom
12 A 16 Park gro Edg
51 Z 7 Park Gro rd E11
28 K 12 Park Hall rd N2
109 N 6 Park Hall rd SE21
106 M 6 Parkhall rd SE27
88 H 2 Parkham st SW11
110 B 3 Park hill SE23
89 Y 12 Park hill SW4
60 H 15 Park hill W5
127 T 9 Park hill Brom
154 L 13 Park hill Carsh
84 M 16 Park hill Rich
154 K 12 Parkhill clo Carsh
157 T 4 Park Hill ri Croy
20 H 4 Parkhill rd E4
46 M 16 Park Hill rd NW3
46 M 17 Parkhill rd NW3
98 C 19 Parkhill rd Bxly
125 Y 3 Park Hill rd Croy
157 R 8 Park Hill rd Croy
114 G 6 Park Hill rd Sidcp
155 S 16 Park Hill rd Wallgtn
46 M 15 Parkhill wk NW3
49 W 18 Parkholme rd E8
17 O 2 Park ho N21
84 D 14 Park Ho gdns Twick
125 Y 7 Parkhouse st SE5
98 D 19 Parkhurst gdns Bxly
53 W 14 Parkhurst rd E12

Page	Grid	Name
48	A 12	Parkhurst rd N7
16	C 15	Parkhurst rd N11
31	W 7	Parkhurst rd N17
32	J 14	Parkhurst rd N17
17	R 20	Parkhurst rd N22
90	D 1	Parkhurst rd N22
98	E 18	Parkhurst rd Bxly
154	F 7	Parkhurst rd Sutton
39	S 9	Parkland av Rom
34	G 2	Parkland rd Wdfd Grn
30	D 7	Parkland rd N22
29	X 20	Parkland wlk N6
116	M 13	Parklands Surb
27	S 11	Parklands dri N3
107	T 12	Parklands rd SW16
152	B 5	Parklands way Worc Pk
64	H 2	Park la E15
18	H 12	Park la N9
31	W 3	Park la N17
32	A 3	Park la N17
135	T 11	Park la W1
155	P 9	Park la Carsh
157	N 4	Park la Croy
40	J 9	Park la Harrow
39	U 19	Park la Hornch
57	V 2	Park la Hornch
57	Y 17	Park la Hornch
84	G 11	Park la Rich
37	V 19	Park la Rom
153	R 14	Park la Sutton
101	W 15	Park la Tedd
42	L 14	Park la Wemb
31	X 3	Park La clo N17
42	L 13	Park lawns Wemb
26	B 4	Parklead clo NW9
120	A 2	Parkleigh rd SW19
102	H 10	Parkleys Rich
86	J 16	Parkmead SW15
40	K 10	Park mead Harrow
97	S 15	Park mead Sidcp
13	R 18	Parkmead gdns NW7
21	S 15	Parkmore clo Wdfd Grn
8	A 2	Parknook gdns Enf
62	E 5	Park pde NW10
140	B 14	Park pl SW1
73	R 9	Park pl W3
72	H 3	Park pl W5
100	M 15	Park pl Hampt
42	M 13	Park pl Wemb
48	M 13	Park pl Wemb
130	D 20	Park Pl vlls W2
38	E 10	Park pl ridings N8
23	T 5	Park ri Harrow
110	J 1	Park Ri rd SE23
92	J 20	Park ri SE23
65	Y 3	Park rd E6
51	O 4	Park rd E10
52	J 5	Park rd E12
65	R 3	Park rd E15
32	L 16	Park rd E17
28	H 10	Park rd N2
28	H 11	Park rd N2
29	W 15	Park rd N8
30	Z 2	Park rd N11
16	K 4	Park rd N14
30	J 14	Park rd N15
18	J 13	Park rd N18
131	O 17	Park rd NW1
73	U 4	Park rd NW3
26	K 20	Park rd NW4
130	L 13	Park rd NW8
43	Y 1	Park rd NW9
62	A 3	Park rd NW10
123	T 9	Park rd SE25
90	B 18	Park rd SW2
106	H 15	Park rd SW19
73	Y 16	Park rd W4
59	X 19	Park rd W7
4	H 13	Park rd Barnt
5	X 15	Park rd Barnt
110	M 17	Park rd Becknhm
111	O 19	Park rd Becknhm
126	G 2	Park rd Brom
114	A 14	Park rd Chisl
100	L 11	Park rd Hampt
82	L 13	Park rd Hounsl
83	N 13	Park rd Hounsl
54	D 9	Park rd Ilf
84	A 4	Park rd Islwth
103	O 14	Park rd Kingst
116	D 1	Park rd Kingst
117	Z 9	Park rd New Mald
84	M 15	Park rd Rich
117	N 12	Park rd Surb
153	R 14	Park rd Sutton
153	S 14	Park rd Sutton
101	W 15	Park rd Tedd
58	E 14	Park rd Twick
155	R 3	Park rd Wallgtn
155	T 10	Park rd Wallgtn
42	K 18	Park rd Wemb
103	N 12	Park Rd east Kingst
73	Y 13	Park Rd north W4
103	N 12	Park Rd west Kingst
76	J 15	Park row SE10
61	S 8	Park royal NW10
61	W 2	Park Royal rd NW10
84	H 10	Parkshott Rich
28	A 3	Parkside N3
44	H 11	Parkside NW2
13	T 19	Parkside NW7
26	E 1	Parkside NW7
105	N 9	Park side SW19
101	O 13	Parkside Hampt
115	R 6	Parkside Sidcp
153	S 14	Parkside Sutton
21	V 7	Parkside Buck Hl
105	O 11	Parkside av SW19
99	S 6	Parkside av Bxly Hth
127	R 9	Parkside av Brom
39	N 10	Parkside av Rom
99	O 5	Parkside cross Bxly Hth
117	V 15	Parkside cres Surb
12	B 15	Parkside dri Edg
105	O 10	Parkside gdns SW19
16	A 4	Parkside gdns Barnt
6	G 2	Parkside house Barnt
81	W 10	Parkside rd Blvdr
82	J 12	Parkside rd Housnl
89	N 2	Parkside st SW11
18	A 13	Parkside ter N13
22	M 13	Parkside way Harrow
23	N 12	Parkside way Harrow
131	X 17	Park Sq east NW1
131	W 17	Park Sq ms NW1
131	W 17	Park Sq west NW1
86	H 13	Parkstead rd SW15
18	J 18	Parkstone av N18
33	U 10	Parkstone rd E17
91	Y 5	Parkstone rd SE15
142	B 17	Park st SE1
139	S 7	Park st W1
156	M 4	Park st Croy
101	U 14	Park st Tedd
9	V 4	Park st Enf
152	F 1	Park ter Worc Pk
29	P 20	Park the N6
46	A 4	Park the N11
109	T 18	Park the SE19
110	B 3	Park the SE23
72	G 4	Park the W5
155	N 12	Park the Carsh
114	M 11	Park the Sidcp
22	K 19	Parkthorne clo Harrow
22	J 19	Parkthorne dri Harrow
80	X 19	Parkthorne rd SW12
17	P 2	Park view N21
61	W 14	Park view W3
118	F 6	Park view New Mald
22	F 3	Park view Pinn
43	U 14	Park view Wemb
16	E 14	Park View cres N11
30	G 4	Park View gdns N22
27	O 17	Park View gdns NW4
67	U 7	Park View gdns Bark
35	T 13	Park view gdns Ilf
28	B 4	Park View rd N3
31	X 10	Park View rd N17
44	E 12	Park View rd NW10
113	Y 3	Parkview rd SE9
60	K 14	Park View rd W5
123	Y 19	Parkview rd Croy
70	G 1	Park View rd S'hall
97	U 8	Park View rd Welling
131	Y 9	Park Village east NW1
131	X 8	Park Village west NW1
145	O 19	Parkville rd SW6
76	L 16	Park vista SE10
37	W 19	Park vlls Rom
29	P 20	Park vlls N6
146	D 13	Park wlk SW10
16	M 7	Park way N14
15	Y 14	Park way N20
131	X 5	Parkway NW1
27	T 16	Park way NW11
119	O 9	Park way SW20
111	O 9	Parkway Becknhm
159	T 20	Parkway Croy
25	T 6	Park way Edg
7	S 10	Park way Enf
54	K 10	Parkway Ilf
39	T 7	Park way Rom
21	Z 16	Park way Wdfd Grn
80	L 7	Parkway Belvdr
16	A 12	Park way N20
138	M 5	Park West pl W2
16	A 12	Park wood N20
105	W 13	Parkwood rd SW19
98	B 20	Park Wood rd Bxly
83	W 1	Parkwood rd Islwth
46	L 11	Parliament hill NW3
140	J 19	Parliament sq SW1
140	J 18	Parliament st SW1
88	L 10	Parma cres SW11
135	Z 6	Parmiter pl E2
63	O 6	Parmiter st E2
135	Y 9	Parmiter st E2
12	G 12	Parnell clo Edg
63	Y 2	Parnell rd E3
63	W 17	Parnham st E14
47	W 4	Parolles rd N19
81	R 9	Paroma rd Blvdr
66	A 4	Parr rd E6
24	J 4	Parr rd Stanm
134	D 7	Parr st N1
157	O 19	Parrs clo S. Croy
66	G 19	Parry av E6
152	H 15	Parry clo Epsom
79	N 10	Parry pl SE18
123	R 7	Parry st SE25
148	K 14	Parry st SW8
45	Y 13	Parsifal rd NW6
56	B 16	Parsloes av Dgnhm
55	X 14	Parsloes av Dgnhm
55	X 17	Parsloes pk Dgnhm
8	A 10	Parsonage gdns Enf
8	B 9	Parsonage la Enf
81	T 17	Parsonage Mnr way Blvdr
76	G 12	Parsons grn SE14
87	X 3	Parson grn SW6
12	B 10	Parsons cres Edg
87	W 1	Parsons Grn la SW6
12	C 10	Parsons gro Edg
78	H 9	Parsons mead Croy
122	J 20	Parsons mead Croy
156	K 1	Parsons mead Croy
65	X 7	Parsons rd E13
26	M 12	Parson st NW4
27	O 9	Parson st NW4
87	Y 2	Parthenia rd SW6
30	B 4	Partidge way N22
12	C 16	Partingdale la NW7
47	P 3	Partington clo N19
113	V 6	Partridge grn SE9
114	G 8	Partridge rd Sidcp
89	X 1	Parvin st SW8
148	H 18	Pascal st SW8
93	X 13	Pascoe rd SE13
149	Z 11	Pasley rd SE17
32	J 10	Pasquier rd E17
59	U 15	Passey pl SE9
64	E 14	Passfield dri E14
16	K 20	Pasmore gdns N11
147	T 8	Passmore st SW1
17	X 17	Pasteur gdns N18
18	A 17	Pasteur gdns N18
94	J 19	Paston cres SE12
149	Y 4	Pastor st SE11
42	B 10	Pasture clo Wemb
112	B 1	Pasture rd SE6
56	A 14	Pasture rd Dgnhm
42	A 8	Pasture rd Wemb
14	H 5	Pasture the N20
89	S 1	Patcham ter SW8
154	C 18	Patchett st Sutton
160	A 6	Paternoster row EC4
141	Y 5	Paternoster sq EC4
145	T 2	Pater st W8
107	Y 16	Pathfield rd SW16
106	A 20	Path the SW19
88	J 6	Patience rd SW11
89	X 15	Patio clo SW4
45	V 1	Patmore st SW8
90	H 1	Patmos rd SW9
90	W 20	Patmos rd SW9
88	B 8	Paton clo E3
134	A 14	Paton st EC1
88	H 14	Patrick pass SW11
65	Z 9	Patrick rd E13
53	O 7	Patriot sq E2
135	Y 10	Patriot sq E2
47	V 18	Patshull pl NW5
47	U 18	Patshull rd NW5
84	H 14	Patten all Rich
110	M 2	Pattenden rd SE6
82	J 19	Patten rd SW18
112	B 16	Patterdale clo Brom
75	P 18	Patterdale rd SE15
109	U 17	Patterson ct SE19
109	V 16	Patterson rd SE19
45	X 10	Pattison rd NW2
64	L 2	Paul clo E15
90	K 4	Paulet rd SE5
157	U 4	Paul gdns Croy
24	G 12	Paulhan rd Harrow
17	T 2	Paulin dri N21
81	N 20	Pauline cres Twick
100	M 1	Pauline cres Twick
64	L 2	Paul st E15
141	U 4	Paul st EC2
134	H 18	Paul st EC2
146	H 14	Paultons sq SW3
146	H 15	Paultons sq SW3
47	V 5	Pauntley st N19
130	L 15	Paveley st NW8
89	V 10	Pavement the SW4
56	G 18	Pavet clo Dgnhm
139	P 20	Pavilion rd SW1
147	P 4	Pavilion rd SW1
53	U 1	Pavilion rd Ilf
147	P 3	Pavilion st SW1
110	D 19	Pawleyne clo SE20
110	C 19	Pawleyne rd SE20
65	U 2	Pawsey clo E13
122	L 13	Pawsons rd Croy
42	A 7	Paxford rd Wemb
65	N 4	Paxton clo Rich
109	P 10	Paxton pl SE27
31	W 2	Paxton rd N17
74	A 17	Paxton rd W4
112	F 18	Paxton rd Brom
85	Y 9	Paynesfield av SW14
10	G 3	Paynesfield rd Bushey Watf
76	A 18	Payne st SE8
75	Z 18	Payne st SE8
144	K 14	Paynes wk W6
147	X 11	Peabody av SW1
147	Y 12	Peabody clo SW1
31	R 5	Peabody estate W7
90	K 19	Peabody estate SE24
148	F 11	Peabody estate SW1
90	K 20	Peabody Hill estate SE24
135	T 17	Peace st E1
153	S 17	Peaches clo Sutton
77	P 16	Peachum rd SE3
149	Y 7	Peacock st SE17
149	Z 8	Peacock yd SE17
35	O 14	Peaketon av Ilf
110	C 10	Peak Hill av SE26
110	D 10	Peak Hill gdns SE26
110	C 10	Peak hill S SE26
110	C 8	Peak the SE26
59	Y 10	Peal gdns W13
122	C 14	Peall rd Croy
110	C 2	Pearcefield av SE23
25	Y 14	Pear clo NW9
51	W 7	Pearcroft rd E11
89	T 6	Peardon st SW8
24	H 6	Pearswood gdns Stanm
110	G 6	Pearfield rd SE23
53	N 10	Pearl rd E17
141	T 19	Pearman st SE1
141	T 17	Pear pl SE1
88	B 3	Pearscroft ct SW6
88	A 3	Pearscroft rd SW6
134	M 8	Pearson st E2
135	N 8	Pearson st E2
83	O 7	Pears rd Hounsl
75	O 2	Pears st E1
133	U 17	Pear Tree clo EC1
99	N 2	Pear Tree clo Erith
120	K 4	Peartree clo Mitch
133	U 17	Pear Tree ct EC1
55	P 13	Pear Tree gdns Dgnhm
38	G 7	Peartree gdns Rom
8	E 12	Peartree rd Enf
133	Z 15	Pear Tree st EC1
134	A 15	Pear Tree st EC1
53	R 8	Peary pl E2
41	Y 6	Pebworth rd Harrow
109	X 6	Peckarmans wood SE26
48	K 13	Peckett sq N5
150	K 18	Peckham gro SE15
91	W 2	Peckham High st SE15
91	X 1	Peckham Hill st SE15
151	R 19	Peckham Hill st SE15
151	U 14	Peckham Pk rd SE15
91	S 2	Peckham rye SE5
91	Y 9	Peckham rye SE15
92	B 11	Peckham Rye east SE15
92	A 12	Peckham Rye pk SE22
47	V 16	Peckwater st NW5
48	B 17	Pedlers wk N7
135	R 18	Pedley st E1
50	G 11	Pedro st E5
151	Z 7	Pedworth rd SE16
105	P 2	Peek cres SW19
35	R 8	Peel dri Ilf
63	O 7	Peel gro E2
135	Z 10	Peel gro E2
129	S 10	Peel Precinct ct NW6
34	A 6	Peel rd E18
10	D 10	Peel rd Harrow
42	F 9	Peel rd Wemb
137	U 14	Peel st W8
134	E 14	Peerless st EC1
19	P 12	Pegamoid rd N18

P

149 S 13 Pegasus pl SE11	151 V 15 Pencraig way SE15	133 S 9 Penton st N1
156 F 15 Pegasus rd Croy	50 H 12 Penda rd E5	133 R 10 Pentonville rd N1
112 G 3 Pegley gdns SE12	81 W 18 Penda rd Erith	8 K 4 Pentrich av Enf
79 U 18 Pegwell st SE18	104 L 20 Pendarves rd SW20	18 B 16 Pentry av N18
64 B 18 Pekin clo E14	118 M 1 Pendarves rd SW16	71 N 20 Penwerris av Islwth
64 B 18 Pekin st E14	31 O 10 Pendennis rd N17	105 Z 3 Penwith rd SW18
85 N 12 Peldon av Rich	108 B 8 Pendennis rd SW16	106 A 3 Penwith rd SW18
85 N 12 Peldon ct Rich	82 H 12 Penderel rd Hounsl	107 T 14 Penwortham rd SW16
84 M 12 Peldon pas Rich	111 V 4 Penderry ri SE6	145 V 9 Penywern rd SW5
67 W 4 Pelham av Bark	76 C 18 Pender st E14	136 L 12 Penzance pl W11
91 S 7 Pelham clo SE5	47 Z 18 Penderyn way N7	136 L 13 Penzance st W11
146 J 7 Pelham cres E18	107 T 13 Pendle rd SW16	128 H 9 Peploe rd NW6
146 J 6 Pelham pl SW7	33 P 17 Pendlestone rd E17	142 A 16 Pepper st SE1
34 G 10 Pelham rd Brom	112 D 7 Pendragon rd Brom	4 B 17 Pepys cres Barnt
31 U 13 Pelham rd N15	92 G 6 Pendrell rd SE4	92 F 2 Pepys rd SE14
30 F 8 Pelham rd N22	79 T 17 Pendrell st SE18	124 L 19 Pepys rd SW20
105 Y 18 Pelham rd SW19	58 B 12 Pendula dr Grnfd	118 M 1 Pepys rd SW20
106 A 17 Pelham rd SW19	111 S 1 Penerley rd SE6	L 9 Pepys st EC3
124 D 3 Pelham rd Becknhm	111 T 2 Penerley rd SE6	46 H 15 Perceval av NW3
98 F 8 Pelham rd Bxly Hth	115 W 2 Penfold clo Bxly	49 V 13 Perch st E8
54 F 8 Pelham rd Ilf	115 W 2 Penfold la Bxly	31 V 1 Percival av N17
146 J 6 Pelham st SW7	115 W 4 Penfold la Bxly	37 U 18 Percival gdns Rom
150 B 13 Pelier st SE17	19 S 5 Penfold rd N9	85 V 11 Percival rd SW14
111 Y 5 Pelimore rd SE6	130 H 19 Penfold rd Enf	8 H 14 Percival rd Enf
144 M 16 Pellant rd SW6	95 N 8 Penford gdns SE9	133 W 15 Percival st EC1
30 E 5 Pellatt gro N22	130 J 20 Penford st NW1	80 G 10 Percival st SE2
91 V 14 Pellatt rd SE22	90 J 4 Penford st SE5	133 P 12 Percy cir WC1
49 S 14 Pellerin rd N16	97 W 14 Pengarth rd Bxly	9 T 17 Percy gdns Enf
64 A 17 Pelling st E14	110 D 17 Penge la SE20	117 Z 19 Percy gdns Worc Pk
17 S 11 Pellipar clo N13	65 X 3 Penge rd E13	140 E 3 Percy ms W1
78 F 12 Pellipar gdns SE18	123 X 6 Penge rd SE25	33 Z 20 Percy rd E11
65 T 4 Pelly rd E13	77 Z 10 Penhall rd SE7	65 N 14 Percy rd E16
65 T 6 Pelly rd E13	97 U 18 Penhill rd Bxly	15 R 16 Percy rd N12
76 M 13 Pelton rd SE10	36 A 2 Penhurst rd Ilf	17 Z 3 Percy rd N21
32 G 11 Pembar av E17	108 A 17 Penistone rd SW16	124 E 1 Percy rd SE20
128 F 13 Pember rd NW10	41 P 9 Penketh dri Harrow	123 W 11 Percy rd SE25
39 Z 10 Pemberton av Rom	80 B 8 Penmont rd SE2	74 G 6 Percy rd W12
47 X 8 Pemberton gdns N19	145 X 1 Pennant ms W8	98 G 6 Percy rd Bxly Hth
37 Y 16 Pemberton gdns Rom	32 L 7 Pennant ter E17	98 A 6 Percy rd Hampt
30 H 17 Pemberton rd N4	74 M 5 Pennard rd W12	100 G 17 Percy rd Hampt
47 V 8 Pemberton rd N19	136 C 16 Pennard rd W12	37 N 20 Percy rd Ilf
141 U 5 Pemberton row EC4	58 M 7 Penn clo Grnfd	83 Z 9 Percy rd Islwth
100 D 1 Pemberton av Twick	24 C 14 Penn clo Harrow	121 O 19 Percy rd Mitch
137 S 9 Pembridge cres W11	55 S 5 Penner clo SW19	39 J 9 Percy rd Rom
137 U 11 Pembridge gdns W2	63 O 14 Pennethorne clo E9	82 H 20 Percy rd Twick
137 S 9 Pembridge ms W11	151 V 20 Pennethorne rd SE15	100 K 3 Percy rd Twick
137 U 8 Pembridge pl W2	38 E 1 Penn gdns Rom	36 M 20 Percy rd Ilf
137 T 10 Pembridge rd W11	45 S 5 Pennine dri NW2	140 E 2 Percy st W1
137 U 9 Pembridge sq W2	99 P 3 Pennine way Bxly Hth	100 M 1 Percy st Twick
137 T 8 Pembridge vlls W11	143 V 11 Pennington st E1	133 P 13 Percy yd WC1
9 N 7 Pembroke av Enf	33 O 6 Penn rd E17	57 X 18 Peregrine wlk Hornch
23 Z 9 Pembroke av Harrow	48 A 14 Penn rd N7	44 M 17 Peregrine way SW19
24 A 9 Pembroke av Harrow	134 G 5 Penn st N1	144 M 14 Perham rd W14
17 T 11 Pembroke av Surb	158 H 19 Pennycroft S Croy	144 M 14 Perham rd W14
139 U 18 Pembroke clo SW1	64 A 20 Pennyfields E14	109 N 1 Perifield SE21
121 O 4 Pembroke clo Mitch	61 T 8 Penny rd NW10	60 E 5 Perimeade rd Grnfd
145 S 5 Pembroke gdns	50 A 7 Penpoll rd E8	95 N 11 Periton rd SE9
56 G 10 Pembroke gdns Dgnhm	97 W 9 Penpool la Welling	60 A 11 Perivale gdns W13
145 S 4 Pembroke Gdns clo W8	32 M 6 Penrhyn av E17	59 Z 8 Perivale la Grnfd
102 M 3 Pembroke lodge Rich	33 O 4 Penrhyn av E17	59 T 10 Perivale pk Grnfd
145 M 3 Pembroke ms W8	33 P 4 Penrhyn cres E17	42 A 14 Perkins clo Wemb
145 T 2 Pembroke pl W8	33 N 3 Penrhyn cres SW14	148 F 2 Perkins rents SW1
25 P 3 Pembroke pl Edg	35 N 5 Penrhyn gro E17	36 E 16 Perkins rd Ilf
83 S 4 Pembroke pl Islwth	116 H 8 Penrhyn rd Kingst	93 Y 6 Perks clo SE3
33 R 15 Pembroke rd E17	87 T 14 Penrith clo SW15	96 F 17 Perpins rd SE9
29 P 3 Pembroke rd N10	56 L 16 Penrith cres Hornch	108 H 2 Perran rd SW2
17 Z 12 Pembroke rd N13	31 O 15 Penrith rd N15	45 S 18 Perren st NW5
18 A 12 Pembroke rd N13	117 Z 8 Penrith rd New Mald	74 J 9 Perrers rd W6
31 V 15 Pembroke rd N8	122 M 2 Penrith rd Thntn Hth	42 A 12 Perrin rd Wemb
30 A 12 Pembroke rd N8	107 U 14 Penrith st SW16	46 E 13 Perrins la NW3
123 R 9 Pembroke rd SE25	122 A 11 Penrose gdns SE17	46 D 13 Perrins wlk NW3
145 R 6 Pembroke rd W14	150 A 10 Penrose st SE17	79 P 10 Perrott st SE18
126 M 4 Pembroke rd Brom	150 A 12 Penrose st SE17	61 Y 17 Perry av W3
127 N 4 Pembroke rd Brom	25 R 3 Penrylan pl Edg	69 Z 6 Perry clo Rainhm
81 Y 12 Pembroke rd Erith	132 E 8 Penryn st NW1	31 R 18 Perry ct N15
58 L 10 Pembroke rd Grnfd	150 L 8 Penry st SE1	26 E 20 Perryfield way NW9
54 K 2 Pembroke rd Ilf	89 V 4 Pensbury pl SW8	102 B 6 Perryfield way Rich
42 G 10 Pembroke rd Wemb	89 V 4 Pensbury st SW8	18 C 10 Perry gdns N9
145 T 4 Pembroke sq W8	85 R 4 Pensford av Rich	18 C 10 Perry gdns N9
132 M 3 Pembroke st N1	97 O 15 Penshurst av Sidcp	110 L 5 Perry hill SE6
145 R 3 Pembroke studios W8	12 F 16 Penshurst gdns Edg	118 C 19 Perry how Worc Pk
145 T 4 Pembroke vlls W8	126 C 12 Penshurst grn Brom	36 D 17 Perrymans Farm rd Ilf
84 F 11 Pembroke vlls Rich	63 T 2 Penshurst rd E9	7 W 7 Perry mead Enf
145 T 4 Pembroke wlk W8	31 U 2 Penshurst rd N17	87 Z 4 Perrymead st SW6
118 G 18 Pembury av Worc Pk	98 B 1 Penshurst rd Bxly Hth	61 Z 19 Perryn rd W3
126 D 17 Pembury clo Brom	122 H 11 Penshurst rd Thntn Hth	73 Y 1 Perryn rd W3
115 Y 5 Pembury clo Sidcp	153 X 18 Penshurst way Sutton	110 J 8 Perry ri SE23
50 A 13 Pembury est E5	33 W 5 Pentire rd E17	140 E 5 Perrys pl W1
49 Z 14 Pembury rd E5	45 S 3 Pentland clo NW11	114 K 15 Perry st W3
31 U 5 Pembury rd N17	121 R 6 Pentlands clo Mitch	114 H 16 Perry St gdns Chisl
123 Y 9 Pembury rd SE25	88 B 15 Pentland gdns SW18	114 H 17 Perry Street shaw Chisl
80 M 18 Pembury rd Bxly Hth	88 C 18 Pentland st SW18	110 D 4 Perry vale SE23
81 N 17 Pembury rd Bxly Hth	86 M 10 Pentlow st SW15	112 Z 5 Persant rd SE6
122 H 17 Pemdevon rd Croy	20 H 5 Pentney rd E4	120 G 14 Pershore clo Carsh
63 R 11 Pemell clo E1	107 U 1 Pentney rd SW12	29 R 1 Pert clo N10
75 O 2 Penang st E1	105 R 19 Pentney rd SW19	43 Z 2 Perth av NW9
143 V 13 Penang st E1	133 S 9 Penton gro N1	118 F 3 Perth clo SW20
75 O 16 Penarth st SE15	149 X 8 Penton pl SE17	50 K 4 Perth rd E10
111 V 3 Penberth rd SE6	150 A 10 Penton pl SE17	65 V 8 Perth rd E13
70 D 12 Penbury rd S'hall	133 P 11 Penton ri WC1	48 F 4 Perth rd N4
		30 H 5 Perth rd N22

67 T 5 Perth rd Bark
125 U 3 Perth rd Becknhm
35 X 18 Perth rd Ilf
36 A 20 Perth rd Ilf
54 B 1 Perth rd Ilf
63 R 16 Perth st E1
54 C 2 Perth ter Ilf
40 E 5 Perwell av Harrow
44 J 20 Peter av NW10
62 J 1 Peter av NW10
87 X 4 Peterborough ms SW6
33 W 18 Peterborough rd E10
87 X 4 Peterborough rd SW6
120 H 13 Peterborough rd Carsh
41 U 2 Peterborough rd Harrow
41 V 2 Peterborough rd Harrow
88 A 2 Peterborough vlls SW6
88 D 10 Petergate SW11
11 U 18 Peters clo Stanm
17 V 16 Peters clo N18
86 J 20 Petersfield ri SW15
73 W 5 Petersfield rd W3
143 M 12 Petersham clo Rich
153 W 12 Petersham clo Sutton
146 B 2 Petersham la SW7
102 G 1 Petersham lodge Rich
146 B 2 Petersham ms SW7
102 L 2 Petersham pk Rich
146 C 1 Petersham pl SW7
84 J 17 Petersham rd Rich
102 J 1 Petersham rd Rich
127 Z 7 Peters hill EC4
133 X 20 Peters la EC1
109 Z 9 Peters path SE26
80 D 7 Peterstone rd SE2
105 T 3 Peterstow clo SW19
140 E 7 Peter st W1
49 N 13 Petherton rd N5
144 E 16 Petley rd W6
131 Y 17 Peto pl NW1
65 O 19 Peto st E16
39 R 6 Pettits blvd Rom
39 P 5 Pettits clo Rom
39 N 4 Pettits la North Rom
56 D 16 Pettits rd Dgnhm
39 N 5 Pettits rd Dgnhm
39 N 16 Pettley gdns Rom
79 R 9 Pettman cres SE18
42 E 14 Petts Grove av Wemb
16 K 14 Petts hill Grnfd
78 D 10 Pett st SE18
140 D 20 Petty france SW1
40 E 20 Petworth clo SW1
54 B 2 Petworth clo Sutton
118 J 5 Petworth gdn New Mald
15 X 17 Petworth rd N12
98 D 14 Petworth rd Bxly Hth
88 K 2 Petworth st SW11
57 V 13 Petworth way Hornch
146 M 7 Petyt pl SW3
16 K 17 Petyward SW3
8 C 8 Pevensey av Enf
52 D 12 Pevensey av N11
106 G 10 Pevensey rd SW17
100 B 2 Pevensey rd Felt
101 R 2 Peverill dri Tedd
10 E 4 Pewsy clo E4
76 G 19 Peyton pl SE10
150 E 13 Phelp st SE17
146 L 14 Phene st SW3
145 T 9 Philbeach gdns SW5
143 T 7 Philchurch st E1
57 N 4 Philip av Rom
158 K 2 Philip gdns Croy
31 U 11 Philip la N15
90 U 16 Philipot path SE9
95 N 12 Philippa gdns SE9
91 Y 7 Philip rd SE15
65 X 8 Philip st E13
126 F 4 Phillips way Brom
62 L 3 Phillimore gdns NW10
128 B 4 Phillimore gdns NW10
137 S 19 Phillimore gdns W8
137 T 19 Phillimore pl W8
137 U 20 Phillimore wlk W8
134 L 6 Phillip st N1
142 H 9 Philpot la EC3
160 H 8 Philpot st E1
143 X 4 Philpot st E1

105	O 2	Philsdon clo SW19
95	X 7	Phineas Pett rd SE9
120	E 1	Phipps Br rd SW19
120	E 4	Phipps Br rd SW19
7	Z 2	Phipps Hatch la Enf
8	A 3	Phipps Hatch la Enf
137	X 4	Phipps ms SW1
120	F 1	Phipps ter SW19
134	J 17	Phipp st EC2
93	O 13	Phoebeth rd SE4
133	R 16	Phoenix pl WC1
132	G 10	Phoenix rd NW1
110	C 16	Phoenix rd SE20
140	H 6	Phoenix st WC2
118	K 10	Phyllis av New Mald
81	U 7	Picardy Mnr way Blvdr
81	S 12	Picardy rd Blvdr
81	S 9	Picardy st Blvdr
139	Y 14	Piccadilly W1
140	B 12	Piccadilly W1
140	C 12	Piccadilly arcade SW1
140	E 10	Piccadilly cir W1
140	C 11	Piccadilly pl W1
133	Y 12	Pickard st EC1
66	K 7	Pickering av E6
137	Y 5	Pickering ms W2
133	Z 3	Pickering st N1
10	D 5	Pickets clo Bushey Watf
89	H 4	Pickets st SW12
24	F 5	Pickett croft Stanm
19	U 8	Picketts Lock la N9
97	Y 5	Pickford clo Bxly Hth
97	Z 2	Pickford rd Bxly Hth
97	Y 9	Pickford rd Bxly Hth
126	B 17	Pickhurst grn Brom
125	Z 12	Pickhurst la W Wkhm
126	A 13	Pickhurst la W Wkhm
126	B 17	Pickhurst mead Brom
126	B 13	Pickhurst pk Brom
126	A 18	Pickhurst ri W Wkhm
125	V 19	Pickhurst ri W Wkhm
142	L 14	Pickle Herring st SE1
41	T 1	Pickwick pl Harrow
18	E 15	Pickwick ms N18
91	R 17	Pickwick rd SE21
142	B 18	Pickwick st SE1
114	D 15	Pickwick way Chisl
139	U 5	Picton pl W1
150	F 19	Picton st SE5
79	T 14	Piedmont rd SE18
91	Z 13	Piermont grn SE22
91	Z 13	Piermont rd SE22
78	J 4	Pier av E16
61	T 19	Pierrepoint rd W3
133	W 7	Pierrepont row N1
78	J 4	Pier rd E16
76	H 10	Pier st E14
88	B 10	Pier ter SW18
100	G 11	Pigeon la Hampt
64	A 17	Piggot st E14
112	G 13	Pike clo Brom
142	F 19	Pilgrimage st SE1
108	L 8	Pilgrim hill SE27
46	G 13	Pilgrims la NW3
5	X 17	Pilgrims ri Barnt
141	W 6	Pilgrim st EC4
47	X 3	Pilgrims way N19
157	V 12	Pilgrims way S Croy
91	Z 5	Pilkington rd SE15
115	S 17	Pilmans clo Sidcp
148	E 13	Pimlico gdns SW1
147	U 8	Pimlico rd SW1
5	V 14	Pimms Brook dri Barnt
20	K 8	Pimp Hall pk E4
95	O 11	Pin pl SE9
143	T 8	Pinchin st E1
106	B 20	Pincott rd SW19
98	E 11	Pincott rd Bxly Hth
134	K 20	Pinder st EC2
129	Z 18	Pindock ms W9
125	R 19	Pine av W Wkhm
16	H 3	Pine clo N14
11	N 12	Pine clo Stanm
158	F 9	Pine coombe Croy
64	A 19	Pinefield clo E14
117	R 14	Pine gdns Surb
90	B 3	Pine gro N4
105	U 13	Pine gro SW19
14	K 5	Pine gro N20
155	O 19	Pine ridge Carsh
18	A 8	Pine rd N11
45	N 12	Pine rd NW2
113	R 10	Pines rd Brom
21	R 18	Pines the Wdfd Grn
136	T 16	Pine st EC1
117	R 13	Pine wlk Surb
114	J 2	Pinewood av Sidcp
158	H 6	Pinewood clo Croy
60	E 17	Pinewood gro W13
80	H 16	Pinewood rd SE2
126	F 8	Pinewood rd Brom
108	A 9	Pinfold rd SW16
16	F 19	Pinkham way N11
68	C 2	Pinley gdns Dgnhm
98	H 11	Pinnacle hill Bxly Hth
98	O 12	Pinnell rd SE9
22	G 13	Pinner ct Pinn
23	B 15	Pinner gro Pinn
22	G 5	Pinner gro Pinn
22	L 9	Pinner Pk av Harrow
23	N 8	Pinner Pk av Harrow
23	O 9	Pinner Pk gdns Harrow
22	J 14	Pinner rd Pinn
23	O 19	Pinner rd Harrow
23	N 17	Pinner view Harrow
34	J 1	Pintail clo Wdfd Grn
94	G 10	Pinto way SE3
48	C 17	Piper clo N7
117	O 5	Piper rd Kingst
89	W 17	Pipers grn NW9
11	Y 12	Pipers Grn la Edg
120	H 14	Pipewell rd Carsh
124	K 19	Pippin clo Croy
124	C 4	Piquet rd SE20
159	V 14	Pirbright cres Croy
87	X 20	Pirbright rd SW18
77	V 3	Pirie st E16
38	E 12	Pitcairn clo Rom
105	M 19	Pitcairn rd Mitch
89	S 6	Pitcairn st SW8
64	L 2	Pitchford st E15
134	H 14	Pitfield st N1
43	V 18	Pitfield way NW10
43	W 17	Pitfield way NW10
9	P 5	Pitfield way Enf
94	F 17	Pitfold clo SE12
94	E 17	Pitfold rd SE12
156	J 2	Pitlake Croy
63	T 18	Pitsea pl E1
63	T 18	Pitsea st E1
60	D 12	Pitshanger la W5
60	B 9	Pitshanger pk Grnfd
106	B 19	Pitt cres SW19
106	A 10	Pitt cres SW19
143	N 16	Pitt rd Thrntn Hth
142	K 14	Pitts ct SE1
139	V 14	Pitts Head ms W1
126	E 18	Pittsmead av Brom
137	V 17	Pitt st W8
123	X 5	Pittville gdns SE25
63	Y 17	Pixley st E14
158	H 20	Pixton way Croy
142	F 18	Plaintain pl SE1
65	O 4	Plaistow gro E15
112	G 18	Plaistow gro Brom
112	G 18	Plaistow la Brom
126	M 2	Plaistow la Brom
65	U 5	Plaistow Pk rd E13
65	R 6	Plaistow rd E15
109	Z 8	Plane st SE26
55	W 2	Plantagenet gdns Rom
55	X 2	Plantagenet pl Rom
5	P 14	Plantagenet rd Barnt
99	V 1	Plantation la Erith
94	F 5	Plantation the SE3
65	Y 2	Plashet gro E6
66	A 1	Plashet gro E6
5	O 20	Plashet gro E7
65	U 2	Plashet rd E13
53	S 19	Plassy rd SE6
134	G 17	Platina st EC2
90	A 11	Plato rd SW2
45	Y 11	Platts la NW3
9	R 7	Platts rd Enf
132	F 9	Platt st NW1
87	R 8	Platt the SW15
110	G 20	Plawsfield rd Becknhm
126	L 2	Plaxton clo Brom
77	T 14	Plaxtol pl SE10
81	T 18	Plaxtol rd Erith
38	J 4	Playfield av Rom
91	T 13	Playfield cres SE22
25	W 6	Playfield rd Edg
48	E 6	Platford rd N4
48	E 7	Playford rd N4
48	E 7	Playford rd N4
111	P 9	Playgreen way SE6
124	G 4	Playground clo Becknhm
141	X 7	Playhouse yd EC4
86	J 12	Pleasance rd SW15
86	J 11	Pleasance the SW15
158	L 5	Pleasant gro Croy
133	Y 1	Pleasant pl N1
131	Z 5	Pleasant row NW1
60	F 5	Pleasant way Wemb
20	B 8	Pleasaunce E4
132	B 6	Plender pl NW1
47	W 13	Pleshey rd N7
31	S 17	Plevna cres N15
31	S 17	Plevna cres N15
18	L 10	Plevna rd N9
66	K 18	Plevna st E6
76	F 7	Plevna st E14
109	V 17	Pleydell av SE19
74	E 10	Pleydell av W6
141	U 6	Pleydell ct WC2
141	U 6	Pleydell st EC4
48	G 8	Plimsoll rd N4
160	G 8	Plough ct EC3
91	W 17	Plough la SE22
106	C 11	Plough la SW19
156	Z 8	Plough la Wallgtn
156	A 12	Plough la Wallgtn
156	B 20	Plough la Wallgtn
155	Z 10	Plough La clo Wallgtn
83	R 13	Ploughmans end Islwth
141	T 4	Plough pl EC4
88	G 10	Plough st SW11
88	G 10	Plough ter SW11
75	W 10	Plough way SE16
134	K 18	Plough yd EC2
70	B 9	Pluckington pl S'hall
133	U 15	Plumbers pl EC1
143	T 3	Plumbers row E1
93	T 2	Plumb st SE10
72	H 12	Plum garth Brentf
79	O 18	Plum la SE18
120	L 2	Plummer la Mitch
89	X 18	Plummer rd SW4
40	G 17	Plumpton clo Grnfd
154	K 5	Plumpton way Carsh
78	L 15	Plumstead Comm rd SE18
76	P 16	Plumstead Comm rd SE18
79	W 11	Plumstead High st SE18
79	O 10	Plumstead rd SE18
141	V 3	Plumtree ct EC4
65	S 16	Plymouth rd E16
112	J 20	Plymouth rd Brom
129	N 2	Plympton av NW6
129	N 1	Plympton pl NW8
129	O 1	Plympton rd NW6
130	K 18	Plympton st NW8
80	F 20	Plymstock rd Welling
141	X 17	Pocock st SE1
26	A 7	Pocklington clo NW9
88	C 11	Podmore rd SW18
49	N 14	Poets rd N5
28	D 6	Pointalls clo N3
93	U 2	Point clo SE10
87	X 11	Point Pleasant SW6
140	C 5	Poland st W1
94	L 6	Polebrook rd SE3
20	F 3	Pole Hill rd E4
110	L 4	Polecroft la SE6
118	J 4	Polesden gdns New Mald
55	X 20	Polesworth rd Dgnhm
68	K 1	Polesworth rd Dgnhm
65	S 19	Pollard clo E16
48	D 14	Pollard clo N7
15	W 9	Pollard rd N20
120	G 12	Pollard rd Mrdn
135	U 13	Pollard row E2
122	B 6	Pollards Hill east SW16
122	C 5	Pollards Hill east SW16
122	C 5	Pollards Hill north SW16
122	C 7	Pollards Hill south SW16
122	B 6	Pollards Hill west SW16
135	U 13	Pollard st E2
122	A 5	Pollards Wood rd SW16
139	Z 7	Pollen st W1
92	M 19	Polstead rd SE6
79	R 10	Polthorne gro SE18
108	A 13	Polworth rd SW16
132	D 11	Polygon rd NW1
89	U 9	Polygon the SW4
78	K 11	Polytechnic st SE18
75	P 26	Pomeroy sq SE14
75	R 20	Pomeroy st SE14
92	C 2	Pomeroy st SE14
90	K 7	Pomfret rd SE5
94	E 5	Pond clo SE3
28	D 6	Ponder st N7
126	A 20	Pondfield rd Brom
56	G 14	Pondfield rd Dgnhm
153	R 12	Pondhill gdns Sutton
91	P 15	Pondmead SE21
146	J 7	Pond pl SW3
64	M 6	Pond rd E15
94	D 5	Pond rd SE3
47	P 3	Pond sq N6
46	H 14	Pond st NW3
102	D 16	Pond way Tedd
143	V 7	Ponler st E1
62	J 8	Ponsard rd NW10
50	D 16	Ponsford st E9
148	H 9	Ponsonby pl SW1
86	J 19	Ponsonby rd SW15
148	H 9	Ponsonby ter SW1
112	D 12	Pontefract rd Brom
148	F 16	Ponton rd SW8
147	R 2	Pont st SW1
147	O 2	Pont st ms SW3
141	V 17	Pontypool pl SE1
82	B 4	Poole Ct rd Hounsl
50	E 19	Poole rd E9
68	M 5	Pooles la Dgnhm
48	B 20	Pooles la SW10
48	E 7	Pooles pk N4
48	E 8	Pooles pk N4
134	E 6	Poole st N1
26	B 13	Poolsford rd NW9
63	R 18	Poonah st E1
52	G 20	Pope rd Brom
101	S 3	Popes av Twick
27	Y 3	Popes dri N3
158	L 4	Popes gro Croy
101	V 4	Popes gro Twick
160	F 7	Pope's Head all EC3
72	G 9	Popes la W5
90	F 9	Popes rd SW9
142	M 19	Pope st SE1
100	D 3	Popham cbl Felt
134	A 3	Popham rd N1
133	Y 4	Popham rd N1
134	A 4	Popham st N1
120	M 1	Poplar av Mitch
70	K 8	Poplar av S'hall
63	E 19	Poplar Bath st E14
105	Y 11	Poplar ct SW19
117	Z 4	Poplar gdns New Mald
136	D 20	Poplar gro W6
117	Z 6	Poplar gro New Mald
43	W 9	Poplar gro Wemb
64	D 20	Poplar High st E14
81	V 10	Poplar rd NW8
137	Y 9	Poplar pl W2
80	G 1	Poplar pl SE2
119	Y 6	Poplar rd SW19
119	U 20	Poplar rd Sutton
90	L 9	Poplar rd SE24
36	C 13	Poplar way Ilf
44	M 19	Poplars av NW2
33	R 18	Poplars the E17
6	F 16	Poplars the N14
38	K 13	Poplar st Rom
90	L 10	Poplar wlk SE24
156	M 1	Poplar wlk Croy
141	V 5	Poppins ct EC4
34	A 20	Poppleton rd E11
138	L 6	Porchester pl W2
137	Y 5	Porchester rd Kingst
137	Y 4	Porchester sq W2
137	X 4	Porchester sq W2
138	B 10	Porchester ter W2
137	Z 3	Porchester Ter north W2
15	Y 11	Porch way N20
113	S 4	Porcupine clo SE9
90	D 11	Porden rd SW2
41	N 3	Porlock av Harrow
18	F 3	Porlock rd Enf
142	F 18	Porlock st SE1
113	V 20	Porrington clo Chisl
108	G 6	Portal clo SE27
8	L 11	Portcullis Lodge rd Enf
63	S 10	Portelet rd E1
144	J 2	Porten rd W14
55	U 15	Porters av Dgnhm
131	S 20	Porter st W1
138	E 1	Porteus rd W2
129	N 5	Portgate clo W9
110	J 10	Porthcawe rd SE26
97	N 9	Porthkerry av Welling
87	U 14	Portinscale rd SW15
49	U 2	Portland av N16
118	E 16	Portland av New Mald
97	O 17	Portland av Sidcp
113	P 4	Portland cres SE9
58	L 13	Portland cres Grnfd
24	G 8	Portland cres Stanm
24	J 8	Portland cres Stanm
24	K 19	Portland gdns N4
37	X 15	Portland gdns Rom
90	B 1	Portland gro SW8
140	C 7	Portland ms W1
131	Y 19	Portland pl W1
139	Y 1	Portland pl W1

P

Ref	Name
48 K 4	Portland ri N4
48 K 4	Portland Ri est N4
31 T 13	Portland rd N15
113 R 4	Portland rd SE9
123 Y 10	Portland rd SE25
136 M 12	Portland rd W11
132 L 11	Portland rd Brom
116 K 7	Portland rd Kingst
120 J 3	Portland rd Mitch
70 D 7	Portland rd S'hall
150 E 11	Portland st SE17
84 G 11	Portland ter Rich
85 Y 9	Portman av SW14
139 S 4	Portman clo W1
97 Y 9	Portman ct Bxly Hth
35 N 7	Portman dri Wdfd Grn
25 X 9	Portman gdns NW9
139 S 6	Portman ms W1
63 R 9	Portman pl E2
117 N 4	Portman Kingst
139 S 5	Portman sq W1
139 R 6	Portman st W1
80 H 4	Portmeadow wlk SE2
129 O 11	Portnall rd W9
77 T 10	Portobello ms W11
136 M 2	Portobello rd W10
136 K 19	Portobello rd W11
137 S 10	Portobello rd W11
39 N 7	Portnoi clo Rom
133 S 10	Portpool la EC1
30 D 3	Portree clo N22
64 K 16	Portree st E14
27 W 19	Portsdown av NW11
138 M 6	Portsea ms W2
138 M 6	Portsea pl W2
89 V 4	Portslade rd SW8
116 F 12	Portsmouth rd Surb & Kingst
141 O 5	Portsmouth st WC2
143 O 8	Portsoken st E1
86 D 17	Portswood pl NW5
00 M 4	Portugal gdns Twick
141 P 5	Portugal st WC2
65 O 2	Portway E15
152 G 20	Portway Epsom
7 U 10	Postern grn Enf
52 G 16	Post Office appr E7
150 G 2	Potier st SE1
121 T 4	Potter clo Mitch
87 P 19	Potterne clo SW19
142 L 15	Potters fields SE1
117 W 9	Potters gro New Mald
107 X 14	Potters la SW16
4 L 15	Potters la Barnt
5 O 13	Potters rd Barnt
136 L 12	Pottery la W11
72 K 16	Pottery rd Brentf
143 V 18	Pottery st SE16
63 N 10	Pott st E2
35 X 14	Pott st E2
101 X 2	Poulett gdns Twick
66 G 5	Poulett rd E6
120 J 13	Poulter pk Carsh
134 H 5	Poulton av Sutton
142 D 6	Poultry EC2
142 D 6	Poultry EC2
116 D 19	Pound clo Surb
44 F 19	Pound la NW10
78 B 12	Pound Pk rd SE7
95 V 15	Pound pl SE9
154 L 11	Pound st Carsh
89 O 7	Pountney rd SW11
8 E 20	Powder Mill la Twick
100 G 1	Powder Mill la Twick
11 Z 18	Powell clo Edg
155 Z 16	Powell gdns Wallgtn
56 D 12	Powell gdns Dgnhm
50 A 11	Powell rd E5
21 Z 3	Powell rd Buck Hl
74 B 17	Powells wlk W4
63 B 12	Power rd W4
74 G 18	Powers ct Twick
50 D 11	Powerscroft rd E5
115 T 17	Powerscroft rd Sidcp
45 U 2	Powis gdns NW11
137 P 5	Powis gdns W11
136 R 5	Powis ms W11
132 L 19	Powis pl WC1
64 D 9	Powis rd E3
137 R 6	Powis rd W11
64 L 9	Powis st E15
78 J 9	Powis st SE18
136 R 5	Powis ter W11
47 R 19	Powlett pl NW1
82 L 10	Pownall gdns Hounsl
135 R 4	Pownall rd E8
82 L 10	Pownall rd Hounsl
112 G 12	Powster rd Brom
80 K 18	Powys clo Bxly Hth
16 M 14	Powys la N13
17 N 14	Powys la N13
16 M 13	Powys la N14
89 V 18	Poynders gdns SW4
89 W 18	Poynders rd SW4
47 U 9	Poynings la N19
14 K 17	Poynings way N12
114 F 20	Poyntell cres Chisl
8 J 18	Poynter rd Enf
31 Z 6	Poynton rd N17
88 M 6	Poyntz rd SW11
63 N 7	Poyser st E2
135 X 11	Poyster st E2
138 G 5	Praed ms W2
138 F 6	Praed st W2
65 X 8	Pragel st E13
112 G 3	Pragnell rd SE12
90 A 14	Prague clo SW4
48 G 8	Prah rd N4
89 R 4	Prairie st SW8
132 A 5	Pratt st NW1
132 B 4	Pratt st NW1
149 O 4	Pratts wlk SE11
45 P 3	Prayle gro NW2
74 D 11	Prebend gdns W4
94 A 7	Prebend st N1
94 A 7	Prendergast rd SE3
107 Z 9	Prentis rd SW16
78 A 11	Prentiss ct SE7
118 B 10	Presburg rd New Mald
25 N 5	Prescelly pl Edg
143 O 8	Prescot st E1
127 Y 15	Prescott av Brom
89 X 9	Prescott pl SW4
134 A 13	President st EC1
43 Z 9	Press rd NW10
64 H 20	Prestage st E14
52 L 20	Prestbury rd E7
113 T 9	Prestbury sq SE9
88 J 9	Prested rd SW11
101 S 5	Preston clo Twick
34 K 16	Preston dri E11
97 W 2	Preston dri Bxly Hth
152 C 13	Preston dri Epsom
44 C 18	Preston gdns NW10
9 X 1	Preston gdns Enf
35 S 19	Preston gdns Ilf
24 M 18	Preston hill Harrow
42 K 1	Preston hill Harrow
84 L 13	Preston pl Rich
44 H 18	Preston pl NW2
34 A 20	Preston rd E11
64 G 3	Preston rd E15
108 J 15	Preston rd SW19
104 E 18	Preston rd SW20
42 K 2	Preston rd Harrow
76 G 3	Prestons rd E14
20 J 20	Preston rd E4
42 J 3	Preston waye Harrow
70 B 14	Prestwick clo S'hall
24 B 13	Prestwood av Harrow
24 C 13	Prestwood clo Harrow
122 L 16	Prestwood gdns Croy
32 G 12	Pretoria av E17
31 U 1	Pretoria clo N17
20 H 6	Pretoria cres E4
14 E 18	Pretoria rd N17
51 X 4	Pretoria rd E11
65 O 11	Pretoria rd E16
31 U 1	Pretoria rd N17
107 T 13	Pretoria rd SW16
53 Y 14	Pretoria rd Ilf
38 J 14	Pretoria rd Rom
18 G 18	Pretoria Rd north N18
16 B 7	Prevost rd N11
106 L 8	Price clo SW17
14 E 18	Price clo NW7
156 J 10	Price rd Croy
141 Y 14	Prices st SE1
133 O 4	Prices yd N1
5 O 19	Pricklers hill Barnt
133 R 12	Prideaux pl WC1
90 A 7	Prideaux rd SW9
110 J 7	Pridham Rd east Thntn Hth
114 L 7	Priestfield rd SE23
110 J 7	Priestlands Pk rd Sidcp
31 V 20	Priestley clo W16
37 P 19	Priestley gdns Rom
32 F 9	Priestley way E17
44 G 3	Priestley way NW4
121 P 2	Priestly rd Mitch
39 N 8	Priests av Rom
86 B 9	Priests br SW15
149 T 17	Prima rd SW9
8 C 5	Primrose av Enf
37 P 20	Primrose av Rom
55 R 1	Primrose av Rom
34 H 7	Primrose clo E3
40 D 11	Primrose clo Harrow
46 K 10	Primrose gdns NW3
141 V 7	Primrose hill EC4
46 L 19	Primrose Hill rd NW3
131 N 1	Primrose Hill rd NW3
131 S 3	Primrose Hill stds NW3
51 R 4	Primrose rd E10
34 G 7	Primrose rd E18
134 K 20	Primrose st EC2
60 F 6	Primrose way Wemb
62 F 18	Primula st W12
130 K 11	Prince Albert rd NW1
131 P 6	Prince Albert rd NW1
46 E 13	Prince Arthur ms NW3
46 E 14	Prince Arthur rd NW3
155 S 4	Prince Charles way Wallgtn
94 B 3	Prince Charles rd SE3
138 E 20	Prince Consort rd SW7
136 M 14	Princedale rd W11
66 A 17	Prince Edward cres E9
50 M 17	Prince Edward rd E9
6 H 15	Prince George Av N14
7 N 18	Prince George av N14
49 S 12	Prince George rd N16
119 N 3	Prince Georges rd SW20
106 H 20	Prince Georges rd SW19
78 B 19	Prince Henry rd SE7
114 A 17	Prince Imperial rd Chisl
113 Z 19	Prince Imperial rd Chisl
78 H 20	Prince Imperial way SE18
95 R 13	Prince John rd SE9
135 P 20	Princelet st E1
26 K 12	Prince Of Wales clo NW4
93 O 1	Prince of Wales dri SW8
147 W 20	Prince Of Wales dri SW8
88 L 2	Prince Of Wales dri SW11
147 Y 20	Prince Of Wales dri SW11
65 Y 18	Prince Of Wales rd E16
47 T 18	Prince Of Wales rd NW5
94 C 3	Prince Of Wales rd SE3
154 G 3	Prince Of Wales rd Sutton
74 A 13	Prince Of Wales ter W4
137 Z 19	Prince Of Wales ter W8
65 X 12	Prince Regent la E13
82 L 7	Prince Regent rd Hounsl
123 R 20	Prince rd SE25
95 T 8	Prince Rupert rd SE9
140 C 12	Princes arcade SW1
27 Z 4	Princes av N3
29 R 11	Princes av N10
17 V 17	Princes av N13
29 Y 4	Princes av N22
25 P 13	Princes av NW9
73 R 7	Princes av W3
154 K 18	Princes av Carsh
58 L 16	Princes av Grnfd
21 X 14	Princes av Wdfd Grn
25 P 13	Princes clo NW9
12 B 16	Princes clo Edg
115 V 7	Princes clo Sidcp
107 P 10	Princes clo Tedd
42 K 14	Princes ct Wemb
138 H 20	Princes gdns SW7
146 H 1	Princes gdns SW7
81 R 14	Princes gdns W3
60 D 13	Princes gdns W5
138 G 19	Princes ga SW7
138 K 19	Princes ga SW7
146 H 2	Princes Ga ms SW7
28 R 11	Princes la N10
137 W 9	Princes ms W2
27 T 17	Princes Pk av NW11
140 C 13	Princes pl SW1
136 L 13	Princes pl W11
127 T 19	Princes plain Brom
93 U 5	Princes ri SE13
19 P 13	Princes rd N18
110 F 16	Princes rd SE20
85 Z 8	Princes rd SW14
105 X 15	Princes rd SW19
72 C 2	Princes rd W13
21 Y 8	Princes rd Buck Hl
36 D 13	Princes rd Ilf
103 P 19	Princes rd Kingst
84 M 12	Princes rd Rich
85 N 1	Princes rd Rich
39 V 18	Princes rd Rom
101 P 11	Princes rd Tedd
99 X 17	Princes Rd north Drtfrd
42 L 6	Princess av Wemb
48 K 6	Princess cres N4
49 S 13	Princess May rd N16
137 W 8	Princes sq W2
131 U 3	Princess rd NW1
129 U 9	Princess rd NW6
122 M 14	Princess rd Croy
123 N 12	Princess rd Croy
142 E 5	Princes st EC2
160 E 5	Princes's st EC2
18 E 20	Princes st N17
139 Z 6	Princes st W1
98 A 9	Princes st Bxly Hth
84 J 11	Princes st Rich
154 F 8	Princes st Sutton
65 W 4	Princes ter E13
75 Z 16	Prince st SE8
76 A 16	Prince st SE8
105 S 2	Princes way SW19
21 Y 8	Princes way Buck Hl
156 D 12	Princes way Croy
40 B 12	Princes way Ruis
110 E 10	Princethorpe rd SE26
141 N 1	Princeton st WC1
107 U 10	Pringle gdns SW16
141 U 4	Printers st EC1
141 X 8	Printing Hse sq EC4
77 X 14	Priolo rd SE7
154 H 15	Prior av Sutton
48 K 19	Prior Bolton st N1
150 G 2	Prioress st SE1
32 J 8	Priors croft E17
40 B 19	Priors field Grnfd
8 D 6	Priors mead Enf
93 U 1	Priors Point hill SE10
76 G 20	Priors st SE10
9 Z 11	Priory av E4
20 B 11	Priory av E4
33 O 15	Priory av E17
29 Y 13	Priory av N8
74 B 9	Priory av W4
153 P 8	Priory av Sutton
41 X 12	Priory av Wemb
19 Z 11	Priory clo E4
34 E 4	Priory clo E18
27 V 5	Priory clo N3
6 F 17	Priory clo N14
14 G 3	Priory clo N20
124 J 7	Priory clo Becknhm
127 U 2	Priory clo Chisl
100 F 19	Priory clo Hampt
44 W 12	Priory clo Wemb
32 K 8	Priory ct E17
89 Z 2	Priory ct SW8
109 N 18	Priory cres SE19
153 P 8	Priory cres Sutton
41 Y 10	Priory cres Wemb
80 J 14	Priory dri SE2
10 H 10	Priory dri Stanm
10 J 10	Priory dri Stanm
29 S 18	Priory gdns N6
86 C 8	Priory gdns SW14
74 A 10	Priory gdns W4
60 K 8	Priory gdns W5
100 E 19	Priory gdns Hampt
41 X 11	Priory gdns Wemb
89 Z 3	Priory ga SW8
41 Y 11	Priory hill Wemb
86 D 10	Priory la SW15
89 Y 2	Priory ms SW8
94 C 9	Priory pk SE3
129 S 3	Priory Pk rd NW6
41 X 12	Priory Pk rd Wemb
66 A 5	Priory rd E6
29 X 13	Priory rd N8
46 A 19	Priory rd NW6
106 F 18	Priory rd SW19
73 X 9	Priory rd W4
54 E 20	Priory rd Bark
122 F 17	Priory rd Croy
100 E 19	Priory rd Hampt
83 O 13	Priory rd Hounsl
73 P 18	Priory rd Rich
153 P 9	Priory rd Sutton
64 E 8	Priory st E3
129 X 4	Priory ter NW6
94 D 10	Priory view Bushey Watf
146 C 11	Priory wlk SW10

22 K 12	Priory way Harrow	
135 W 12	Pritchards rd E2	
151 T 2	Priter rd SE16	
151 T 3	Priter way SE16	
18 C 17	Private rd Enf	
90 G 12	Probert rd SW12	
108 H 4	Probyn rd SW2	
141 N 2	Procter st WC1	
30 F 4	Progress way N22	
156 D 3	Progress way Croy	
8 L 19	Progress way Enf	
74 A 20	Promenade Appr rd W4	
86 C 2	Promenade the W4	
81 S 12	Prospect clo Blvdr	
82 F 3	Prospect clo Hounsl	
87 X 11	Prospect cottages SW18	
83 N 16	Prospect cres Twick	
33 S 12	Prospect hill E17	
28 H 12	Prospect pl N2	
31 S 4	Pospect pl N17	
126 H 7	Prospect pl Brom	
38 K 8	Prospect pl Rom	
116 D 15	Prospect pl Surb	
28 H 11	Prospect ring N2	
45 W 9	Prospect rd NW2	
109 Z 9	Prospect rd SE26	
4 M 15	Prospect rd Barnt	
5 N 14	Prospect rd Barnt	
21 Z 17	Prospect rd Wdfd Grn	
78 D 11	Prospect vale SE18	
63 T 8	Prospect walk E2	
47 W 4	Prospero rd N19	
26 K 15	Prothero gdns NW4	
145 N 17	Prothero rd SW6	
44 C 13	Prout gro NW10	
50 A 9	Prout rd E5	
134 A 8	Provence st N1	
139 U 8	Providence ct W1	
133 V 5	Providence pl N1	
38 B 5	Providence place Rom	
46 M 19	Provost rd NW3	
134 E 13	Provost st N1	
10 A 8	Prowse av Bushey Watf	
47 U 20	Prowse pl NW1	
132 A 1	Prowse pl NW1	
16 J 9	Pruden clo N14	
160 D 5	Prudent pas EC2	
75 O 2	Prusom st E1	
143 Z 12	Prusom st E1	
160 H 10	Pudding la EC3	
64 E 5	Pudding Mill la E15	
141 X 9	Puddle dock EC4	
87 V 19	Pulborough rd SW18	
31 P 18	Pulford rd N15	
28 E 12	Pulham av N2	
4 E 10	Puller rd Barnt	
66 E 8	Pulleyns av E6	
86 M 15	Pullman gdns SW15	
50 C 9	Pulross rd SW9	
34 G 10	Pulteney rd E18	
133 R 5	Pulteney ter N1	
145 T 19	Pulton pl SW6	
135 O 19	Puma ct E1	
72 H 18	Pump all Brentf	
141 S 7	Pump st EC4	
74 B 18	Pumping Station rd W4	
156 L 7	Pump Pail north Croy	
156 L 7	Pump Pail south Croy	
63 N 8	Pundersons gdns E2	
75 X 12	Pundersons gdns E2	
118 D 15	Purbeck rd New Mald	
118 E 15	Purbeck rd New Mald	
45 R 6	Purbeck dri NW2	
57 X 2	Purbeck rd Hornch	
142 M 20	Purbrook st SE1	
144 J 17	Purcell cres SW6	
58 K 13	Purcell rd Grnfd	
12 B 15	Purcells av Edg	
134 J 9	Purcell st N1	
132 G 9	Purchese st NW1	
54 C 11	Purdy st E3	
56 B 4	Purland clo Dgnhm	
79 Z 6	Purland rd SE18	
45 S 8	Purley av NW2	
35 X 8	Purley clo Ilf	
48 H 20	Purley pl N1	
18 C 11	Purley rd N9	
157 N 18	Purley rd S Croy	
122 D 19	Purley way Croy	
156 E 4	Purley way Croy	
94 M 9	Purneys rd SE9	
95 N 10	Purneys rd SE9	
79 X 13	Purrett rd SE18	
87 W 2	Purses Cross rd SW6	
26 K 1	Pursley rd NW7	
62 M 7	Purves rd NW10	
128 C 10	Purves rd NW10	
87 S 8	Putney bridge SW6	
87 S 7	Putney Bridge app SW6	
87 U 10	Putney Bridge rd SW15	
86 L 7	Putney comm SW15	
86 L 17	Putney heath SW15	
87 O 16	Putney heath SW15	
104 M 3	Putney heath SW19	
87 P 17	Putney Heath la SW15	
87 R 11	Putney High st SW15	
87 P 14	Putney hill SW15	
86 H 10	Putney Pk av SW15	
86 J 10	Putney Pk la SW15	
14 H 14	Pyecombe corner N12	
100 L 1	Pycroft av Twick	
153 Z 6	Pylbrook rd Sutton	
5 U 17	Pym clo Barnt	
109 N 1	Pymers mead SE21	
16 B 4	Pymes brook Barnt	
17 O 17	Pymmes clo N13	
18 H 12	Pymmes Gdns north N9	
18 H 12	Pymmes Gdns south N9	
16 F 12	Pymmes Green rd N11	
18 G 13	Pymmes park N18	
17 O 18	Pymmes rd N13	
5 W 14	Pymmes gdns Barnt	
80 B 9	Pynham clo SE2	
11 O 16	Pynnacles clo Stanm	
49 N 15	Pyrland rd N5	
85 N 16	Pyrland rd Rich	
108 H 7	Pyrmont gro SE27	
73 P 16	Pyrmont rd W4	
54 B 8	Pyrmont rd Ilf	
108 M 16	Pytchley cres SE19	
91 T 8	Pytchley rd SE22	

Q

39 P 15	Quadrant arc Rom	
47 N 16	Quadrant gro NW5	
84 H 11	Quadrant rd Thntn Hth	
122 J 8	Quadrant rd Thntn Hth	
105 S 20	Quadrant the SW20	
80 K 20	Quadrant the Bxly Hth	
84 J 11	Quadrant the Rich	
154 C 13	Quadrant the Sutton	
94 F 10	Quaggy wlk SE12	
43 Y 10	Quainton st NW10	
71 X 19	Quaker la Islwth	
81 Z 1	Quaker la Islwth	
70 H 7	Quaker rd S'hall	
49 V 18	Quakers course NW9	
135 N 18	Quaker st E1	
8 A 19	Quakers wlk Enf	
141 S 3	Quality ct WC2	
45 O 7	Quantock gdns NW2	
99 R 3	Quantock rd Bxly Hth	
87 Y 4	Quarrendon st SW6	
120 G 14	Quarr rd Carsh	
153 U 13	Quarry Pk rd Sutton	
153 U 13	Quarry ri Sutton	
88 E 15	Quarry rd SW18	
94 E 10	Quarry wlk SE3	
51 P 12	Quartermile la E10	
139 P 6	Quebec ms W1	
36 B 19	Quebec rd Ilf	
54 A 1	Quebec rd Ilf	
110 D 17	Queen Adelaide rd SE20	
126 D 7	Queen Anne av Brom	
120 K 6	Queen Anne gdns Mitch	
139 Y 3	Queen Anne ms W1	
31 T 15	Queen Annes av N15	
101 R 7	Queen Annes clo Twick	
74 A 8	Queen Annes gdns W4	
72 J 6	Queen Annes gdns W5	
8 E 20	Queen Annes gdns Enf	
140 F 19	Queen Annes gt SW1	
74 A 9	Queen Annes gro W4	
72 K 5	Queen Annes gro W5	
18 C 1	Queen Annes gro Enf	
97 Y 8	Queen Ann pl Bxly Hth	
8 F 19	Queen Annes pl Enf	
50 F 19	Queen Anne rd E9	
139 X 3	Queen Anne st W1	
35 X 12	Queenborough gdns Ilf	
74 L 14	Queen Caroline st W6	
144 C 10	Queen Caroline st W6	
17 N 3	Queen Elizabeth dri N14	
159 W 20	Queen Elizabeth dri Croy	
119 Y 8	Queen Elizabeth gdns Mrdn	
141 P 13	Queen Elizabeth hall SE1	
32 H 10	Queen Elizabeth rd E 17	
116 L 3	Queen Elizabeth rd Kingst	
49 N 6	Queen Elizabeths clo N16	
16 M 6	Queen Elizabeths dri N14	
17 N 4	Queen Elizabeths dri N14	
143 O 17	Queen Elizabeth st SE1	
49 N 4	Queen Elizabeth wlk N16	
155 Y 8	Queen Elizabeths wlk Wallgtn	
158 A 20	Queenhill rd S Croy	
160 B 9	Queenhithe EC4	
49 R 16	Queen Margarets gro N16	
119 O 12	Queen Mary av Mrdn	
108 K 14	Queen Mary rd SE19	
134 L 17	Queen Marys av Carsh	
131 S 15	Queen Marys gardens NW1	
153 R 16	Queens acre Sutton	
59 N 16	Queens av Grnfd	
28 D 4	Queens av N3	
29 R 10	Queens av N10	
15 U 9	Queens av N20	
17 X 6	Queens av N21	
58 M 16	Queens av Grnfd	
24 D 9	Queens av Stanm	
21 W 16	Queens av Wdfd Grn	
119 Z 9	Queens pl Mrdn	
146 E 5	Queensberry ms W SW7	
146 E 5	Queensberry pl SW7	
146 F 5	Queensberry way SW7	
138 A 8	Queensborough pas W2	
138 A 10	Queensborough ter W2	
83 T 14	Queensbridge pk Islwth	
49 V 18	Queensbridge rd E8	
24 M 12	Queensbury park Harrow	
43 X 2	Queensbury rd NW9	
60 M 6	Queensbury rd Wemb	
61 O 5	Queensbury rd Wemb	
25 N 10	Queensbury Stn pde Edg	
134 C 2	Queensbury st N1	
147 X 20	Queens clo SW14	
12 C 17	Queens clo Edg	
155 S 10	Queens clo Wallgtn	
144 M 13	Queens Club gdns W14	
145 N 13	Queens Club gdns W14	
84 F 6	Queens cottage Rich	
110 B 3	Queens ct SE23	
42 K 12	Queenscourt Wemb	
65 O 18	Queens cres NW5	
85 N 13	Queens cres Rich	
9 P 15	Queenscroft rd SE9	
136 H 13	Queensdale cres W11	
136 J 14	Queensdale pl W11	
136 H 15	Queensdale rd W11	
136 K 14	Queensdale rd W11	
49 Z 12	Queensdown rd E5	
51 O 1	Queens dri E10	
48 J 6	Queens dri N4	
61 O 7	Queens dri W5	
60 M 18	Queens dri W5	
117 R 15	Queens dri Surb	
146 G 10	Queens Elm pde SW3	
146 G 11	Queens Elm sq SW3	
139 Z 19	Queens Gallery SW1	
27 N 16	Queens gdns NW4	
138 C 8	Queens gdns W2	
60 E 13	Queens gdns SW5	
82 B 12	Queens gdns Hounsl	
69 Z 7	Queens gdns Rainham	
138 C 20	Queens gate SW7	
146 D 3	Queens ga SW7	
146 B 3	Queens Ga gdns SW7	
146 B 1	Queens Ga ms SW7	
146 D 3	Queens Ga pl SW7	
146 D 4	Queens Ga Pl Ms SW7	
146 C 1	Queens Ga ter SW7	
130 F 7	Queens gro NW8	
20 K 5	Queens Grove rd E4	
133 Y 5	Queens Head st N1	
142 E 15	Queens Head yd SE1	
76 L 17	Queens house SE10	
17 Z 18	Queensland av N18	
106 A 20	Queensland av SW19	
48 G 13	Queensland pl N7	
48 F 13	Queensland rd N7	
29 S 10	Queens la N10	
153 N 20	Queensmead Sutton	
126 B 4	Queens Mead rd Brom	
105 O 5	Queensmere clo SW19	
105 O 5	Queensmere rd SW19	
137 Y 8	Queens ms W2	
144 G 19	Queensmill rd SW6	
15 Z 18	Queens Parade N11	
15 Z 18	Queens Parade clo N11	
128 K 7	Queens prk Rich	
15 Y 18	Queens pde N11	
132 K 19	Queen sq WC1	
132 K 19	Queens Sq pl WC1	
86 G 9	Queens ride SW13	
84 M 15	Queens ri Rich	
51 Y 1	Queens rd E11	
65 V 5	Queens rd E13	
32 L 19	Queens rd E17	
33 N 17	Queens rd E17	
28 D 5	Queens rd N3	
18 M 9	Queens rd N9	
16 M 20	Queens rd NW4	
28 M 17	Queens rd NW4	
27 N 16	Queens rd NW4	
92 E 2	Queens rd SE14	
147 V 18	Queens rd SW11	
85 Z 8	Queens rd SW14	
105 Z 14	Queens rd SW19	
106 B 13	Queens rd SW19	
60 J 16	Queens rd W5	
4 C 13	Queens rd Barnt	
124 J 3	Queens rd Becknhm	
126 F 3	Queens rd Brom	
21 W 7	Queens rd Buck Hl	
114 A 15	Queens rd Chisl	
122 K 14	Queens rd Croy	
8 E 13	Queens rd Enf	
65 K 10	Queens rd Hampt	
82 J 7	Queens rd Hounsl	
54 B 8	Queens rd Ilf	
103 R 19	Queens rd Kingst	
119 Z 8	Queens rd Mrdn	
118 E 10	Queens rd New Mald	
84 L 17	Queens rd Rich	
85 N 12	Queens rd Rich	
85 N 14	Queens rd Rich	
70 A 7	Queens rd S'hall	
101 W 16	Queens rd Tedd	
83 X 20	Queens rd Twick	
101 Y 1	Queens rd Twick	
155 S 10	Queens rd Wallgtn	
97 P 3	Queens rd Welling	
120 E 4	Queens rd SW19	
65 U 5	Queens Rd west E13	
150 D 13	Queens row SE17	
83 Z 8	Queens sq Islwth	
18 E 20	Queens st N17	
65 W 4	Queens ter E13	
130 F 7	Queens ter NW8	
83 Z 9	Queens ter Islwth	
110 E 10	Queensthorpe rd SE26	
89 N 6	Queenstown rd SW8	
147 W 17	Queenstown rd SW8	
142 C 9	Queen st EC4	
160 C 7	Queen st EC4	
98 A 9	Queen st Bxly Hth	
156 L 7	Queen st Croy	
39 O 17	Queen st Rom	
139 X 13	Queen st Mayfair W1	
142 C 10	Queen St pl EC4	
160 C 10	Queen St pl EC4	
89 X 19	Queensville rd SW12	
20 J 4	Queens wlk E4	

43	W 6	Queens wlk NW9
60	D 14	Queens wlk W5
23	S 12	Queens wlk Harrow
27	N 15	Queens way NW4
137	Y 6	Queensway W2
156	E 12	Queensway Croy
156	C 13	Queensway Croy
9	P 16	Queensway Enf
15	W 12	Queenswell av N20
33	U 6	Queenswood av E17
100	K 15	Queenswood av Hampt
82	E 4	Queenswood av Hounsl
122	G 12	Queenswood av Thntn Hth
155	X 9	Queenswood av Wallgtn
52	G 5	Queenswood gdns E11
27	T 6	Queenswood pk N3
110	G 8	Queenswood rd SE23
96	K 15	Queenswood rd Sidcp
29	T 17	Queenswood rd N10
42	G 20	Queen Victoria av Wemb
141	Y 8	Queen Victoria st EC4
142	B 8	Queen Victoria st EC4
160	A 8	Queen Victoria st EC4
48	C 14	Quemerford rd N7
94	A 8	Quentin rd SE13
112	E 15	Quernmore clo Brom
30	F 19	Quernmore rd N4
112	E 15	Quernmore rd Brom
88	C 5	Querin st SW6
129	U 4	Ques ms NW6
129	V 3	Quex rd NW6
64	A 10	Quickett st E3
133	X 5	Quick pl N1
74	A 14	Quick rd W4
106	C 17	Quicks rd SW19
133	X 9	Quick st N1
46	K 20	Quickswood NW3
130	M 1	Quickswood NW3
87	P 10	Quill la SW15
142	B 17	Quilp st SE1
135	R 12	Quilter st E2
4	A 18	Quinta dri Barnt
119	U 1	Quinton av SW20
125	V 6	Quinton clo Becknhm
155	R 8	Quinton clo Wallgtn
106	C 5	Quinton st SW18
64	J 20	Quixley st E14
91	T 9	Quorn rd SE22

R

137	V 12	Rabbit row W8
53	R 11	Rabbits rd E12
117	Z 8	Raby rd New Mald
63	V 17	Raby st E14
157	U 5	Racewood gdns Croy
145	S 15	Racton rd SW6
72	E 10	Radbourne av W5
33	W 9	Radbourne cres E17
89	W 19	Radbourne rd SW12
107	W 1	Radbourne rd SW12
62	F 5	Radcliffe av NW10
8	A 5	Radcliffe av Enf
154	J 18	Radcliffe gdns Carsh
17	W 4	Radcliffe rd N21
157	V 3	Radcliffe rd Croy
23	Y 8	Radcliffe rd Harrow
87	P 15	Radcliffe sq SW15
149	U 11	Radcot st SE11
137	N 1	Raddington rd W10
96	F 18	Radfield way Sidcp
93	V 15	Radford rd SE13
67	X 9	Radford way Bark
87	V 1	Radipole rd SW6
65	R 18	Radland rd E16
110	B 5	Radlett av SE23
130	K 5	Radlett pl NW8
54	L 13	Radley av Ilf
24	L 14	Radley gdns Harrow
34	E 8	Radley la E18
145	W 4	Radley ms W8
31	T 7	Radley rd N17
56	G 18	Radleys mead Dgnhm
50	C 6	Radley sq E5
51	N 4	Radlix rd E10
23	S 15	Radnor av Harrow
97	R 13	Radnor av Welling

114	H 16	Radnor clo Chisl
122	A 10	Radnor clo Mitch
35	T 17	Radnor cres Ilf
8	E 5	Radnor gdns Enf
101	V 3	Radnor gdns Twick
138	H 6	Radnor ms W2
138	J 6	Radnor pl W2
128	L 5	Radnor rd SE15
151	S 17	Radnor rd SE15
151	S 18	Radnor rd SE15
23	T 16	Radnor rd Harrow
101	W 2	Radnor rd Twick
134	C 14	Radnor st EC1
145	O 4	Radnor ter W14
148	K 17	Radnor ter SW8
146	M 11	Radnor wlk SW3
147	N 12	Radnor wlk SW3
124	K 16	Radnor wlk Croy
61	S 10	Radnor way NW10
151	T 12	Radsley st SE1
23	Z 11	Radstock av Harrow
24	A 11	Radstock av Harrow
146	K 19	Radstock st SW11
99	Z 14	Raeburn av Drtfrd
117	S 19	Raeburn av Surb
28	C 19	Raeburn clo NW11
102	F 19	Raeburn clo Kingst
25	O 6	Raeburn rd Edg
96	J 16	Raeburn rd Sidcp
90	B 11	Raeburn st SW2
126	G 4	Rafford way Brom
113	X 20	Raggleswood Chisl
155	K 10	Raglan st S Croy
33	V 15	Raglan rd E17
81	O 12	Raglan rd Blvdr
126	M 9	Raglan rd Brom
18	F 2	Raglan rd Enf
47	T 17	Raglan st NW5
46	K 13	Raglan ter Harrow
41	N 18	Raglan way Grnfd
73	U 4	Ragley clo W3
38	F 5	Raider clo Rom
47	U 14	Railey ms NW5
84	A 10	Railshead rd Twick
90	G 12	Railton rd SE24
32	G 19	Railway appr N8
142	F 14	Railway appr SE1
23	V 13	Railway appr Harrow
83	Y 20	Railway appr Twick
155	S 12	Railway appr Wallgtn
75	P 5	Railway av SE16
136	L 5	Railway ms W10
101	X 15	Railway pas Tedd
142	L 8	Railway pl EC3
105	V 16	Railway pl SW19
81	T 8	Railway pl Blvdr
101	V 11	Railway rd Tedd
86	B 7	Railway side SW13
132	L 9	Railway st N1
55	T 2	Railway st Rom
33	V 5	Railway ter E17
93	R 13	Railway ter SE13
43	U 17	Rainbow clo NW10
150	J 17	Rainbow st SE5
75	N 2	Raine st E1
143	Y 12	Raine st E1
96	F 15	Rainham clo SE9
88	K 15	Rainham clo SW11
128	D 13	Rainham rd NW10
56	H 9	Rainham rd North Dgnhm
57	T 18	Rainham rd Rainhm
56	K 19	Rainham rd South Dgnhm
64	C 9	Rainhill way E3
75	V 12	Rainsborough av SE8
11	P 15	Rainsford clo Stanm
61	S 7	Rainsford rd NW10
138	J 4	Rainsford st W2
57	U 4	Rainsford way Hornch
77	U 13	Rainton rd SE7
144	E 16	Rainville rd W6
16	K 12	Raith av N14
76	H 2	Raleana rd E14
101	U 16	Raleigh av Tedd
155	X 8	Raleigh av Wallgtn
26	L 15	Raleigh clo NW4
155	T 15	Raleigh ct Wallgtn
15	X 10	Raleigh dri N20
117	V 20	Raleigh dri Surb
120	L 4	Raleigh gdns Mitch
30	G 13	Raleigh rd N8
16	E 18	Raleigh rd SE20
8	B 15	Raleigh rd Enf
85	N 8	Raleigh rd Rich
70	B 12	Raleigh rd S'hall
133	Z 6	Raleigh st N1
16	L 4	Raleigh way N14
150	C 2	Ralph st SE1
148	O 11	Ralston st SW3
41	T 7	Rama ct Harrow
107	U 10	Rambler clo SW16
40	A 15	Ramillies clo SW2

140	B 5	Ramillies pl W1
13	O 9	Ramillies rd NW7
73	Y 9	Ramillies rd W4
97	P 16	Ramillies rd Sidcp
140	B 6	Ramillies st W1
75	O 11	Ramouth rd SE16
148	F 9	Rampayne st SW1
50	C 17	Ram pl E9
20	A 10	Rampton clo E4
41	O 15	Ramsay clo Grnfd
52	C 11	Ramsay rd E7
73	V 7	Ramsay rd W3
18	C 4	Ramscroft clo N9
107	R 13	Ramsdale rd SW17
38	F 3	Ramsden dri Rom
15	Z 16	Ramsden rd N11
89	P 20	Ramsden rd SW12
81	Z 20	Ramsden rd Erith
122	E 13	Ramsey clo Croy
26	D 19	Ramsey clo NW9
135	T 16	Ramsey st E2
3	Y 16	Ramsey way N14
49	V 17	Ramsgate st E8
36	K 14	Ramsgill appr Ilf
36	K 14	Ramsgill dri Ilf
37	Z 12	Rams gro Rom
58	C 11	Ramus dr Grnfd
95	P 9	Rancliffe gdns SE9
66	D 7	Rancliffe rd E6
66	F 7	Rancliffe rd E6
44	C 8	Randall av NW2
81	Y 17	Randall clo Erith
88	J 2	Randall clo SW11
76	F 18	Randall pl SE10
149	N 8	Randall rd SE11
39	T 18	Randall rd Rom
149	N 8	Randall rd SE11
81	K 16	Randall st E16
132	L 3	Randell's rd N1
102	E 9	Randle rd Rich
111	R 7	Randlesdown rd SE6
65	Z 17	Randolph app E 16
129	Z 12	Randolph av W9
130	C 17	Randolph av W9
98	J 7	Randolph clo Bxly Hth
103	W 13	Randolph clo Kingst
130	B 17	Randolph cres W9
129	X 10	Randolph gdns NW6
130	C 18	Randolph ms W9
130	C 18	Randolph rd W9
3	S 15	Randolph rd E17
70	D 5	Randolph rd S'hall
132	B 1	Randolph st NW1
22	K 7	Randon clo Harrow
87	U 7	Ranelagh av SW6
86	G 5	Ranelagh av SW13
12	B 13	Ranelagh clo Edg
12	B 13	Ranelagh dri Edg
84	C 12	Ranelagh dri Twick
34	K 15	Ranelagh gdns E11
87	U 8	Ranelagh gdns SW6
73	U 18	Ranelagh gdns W4
53	U 3	Ranelagh gdns Ilf
147	V 9	Ranelagh gro SW1
118	A 10	Ranelagh pl New Mald
66	J 4	Ranelagh rd E6
51	Z 11	Ranelagh rd E11
65	O 6	Ranelagh rd E15
31	T 10	Ranelagh rd N17
30	C 6	Ranelagh rd N22
62	D 7	Ranelagh rd NW10
148	C 11	Ranelagh rd SW1
72	G 5	Ranelagh rd W5
70	A 1	Ranelagh rd S'hall
42	H 17	Ranelagh rd Wemb
153	Z 2	Ranfurly rd Sutton
111	Z 11	Rangefield rd Brom
112	C 13	Rangefield rd Brom
31	V 15	Rangemoor rd N15
21	R 2	Rangers rd E4
93	W 1	Rangers sq SE4
142	M 7	Rangoon st EC3
26	B 10	Rankin clo NW9
81	P 19	Ranleigh gdns Bxly Hth
89	T 20	Ranmere st SW12
23	R 14	Ranmoor clo Harrow
23	S 13	Ranmoor gdns Harrow
157	V 7	Ranmore av Croy
153	O 20	Ranmore rd Sutton
144	D 13	Rannoch rd W6
144	E 16	Rannoch rd W6
44	A 1	Rannock av NW9
44	A 2	Rannock av NW9
77	Y 12	Ransom rd SE7
130	K 20	Ransom st SW1
16	L 4	Ranulf rd NW2
63	X 4	Ranwell st E3
81	G 9	Ranworth clo Erith
19	O 10	Ranworth rd N9
39	S 9	Raphael av Rom

39	T 8	Raphael park Rom
139	N 19	Raphael st SW3
15	S 9	Rasper rd N20
107	X 3	Rastell av SW2
63	T 18	Ratcliffe Cross st E1
134	C 14	Ratcliff gro E1
63	U 18	Ratcliffe la E1
63	T 19	Ratcliffe orchard E1
63	N 20	Ratcliffe st E1
52	K 16	Ratcliff rd E7
140	E 3	Rathbone pl W1
65	O 16	Rathbone st E16
140	D 2	Rathbone st W1
30	D 15	Rathcoole av N8
30	D 15	Rathcoole gdns N8
110	M 2	Rathfern rd SE6
72	C 4	Rathgar av W13
27	V 6	Rathgar clo N3
90	J 7	Rathgar rd SW9
89	X 16	Rathmell dri SW4
77	V 13	Rathmore rd SE7
90	F 11	Rattray rd SW2
90	F 12	Rattray rd SW2
91	X 3	Raul rd SE15
47	U 13	Raveley st NW5
89	R 2	Ravenet SW11
108	M 8	Ravenfield rd SW17
65	Y 6	Ravenhill rd E13
87	P 12	Ravenna rd SW15
58	M 9	Ravenor park Grnfd
58	L 8	Ravenor Pk rd Grnfd
59	N 9	Ravenor Pk rd Grnfd
34	K 6	Raven rd E18
63	N 14	Raven row E1
143	X 1	Raven row E1
111	X 19	Ravensbourne av Brom
125	Y 1	Ravensbourne av Brom
60	A 15	Ravensbourne gdns W13
35	X 4	Ravensbourne gdns Ilf
36	A 5	Ravensbourne gdns Ilf
36	N 18	Ravensbourne pk SE6
92	M 18	Ravensbourne Pk cres SE6
92	K 20	Ravensbourne rd SE6
126	E 6	Ravensbourne rd Brom
99	V 7	Ravensbourne rd Drtfrd
84	D 14	Ravensbourne rd Twick
120	D 11	Ravensbury av Mordn
121	N 4	Ravensbury clo Mitch
120	F 9	Ravensbury gro Mitch
120	F 8	Ravensbury path Mitch
105	Z 3	Ravensbury rd SW18
106	A 3	Ravensbury rd SW18
111	Z 10	Ravenscar rd Brom
126	C 5	Ravens clo Brom
8	D 9	Ravens clo Enf
74	G 11	Ravenscourt av W6
74	F 10	Ravenscourt gdns W6
74	G 11	Ravenscourt pk W6
74	H 11	Ravenscourt pl W6
74	H 11	Ravenscourt rd W6
74	F 9	Ravenscourt sq W6
16	G 14	Ravenscraig rd N11
45	V 1	Ravenscourt av NW11
27	W 20	Ravenscroft av NW11
42	L 3	Ravenscroft av Wemb
65	S 14	Ravenscroft clo E16
4	D 13	Ravenscroft pk Barnt
4	D 12	Ravenscroft Pk rd Barnt
65	T 14	Ravenscroft rd E16
73	W 11	Ravenscroft rd W4
124	F 1	Ravenscroft rd Becknhm
135	P 10	Ravenscroft st E2
15	S 14	Ravensdale av N12
109	P 19	Ravensdale gdns SE19
31	V 20	Ravensdale rd N16
82	B 7	Ravensdale rd Hounsl
148	U 11	Ravensdon st SE11
55	X 12	Ravensfield clo Dgnhm
152	B 10	Ravensfield gdns Epsom
45	W 17	Ravenshaw st NW6

Q

R

Ref	Name
127 Y 2	Ravenshill Chisl
26 L 12	Ravenshurst av NW4
88 M 19	Ravenslea rd SW12
74 D 12	Ravensmeade way W4
111 X 18	Ravensmead rd Brom
30 E 11	Ravenstone rd N8
26 E 19	Ravenstone rd NW9
107 R 2	Ravenstone st SW12
94 E 12	Ravens way SE12
115 Z 1	Ravenswood Bxly
125 T 20	Ravenswood av W Wkhm
156 J 6	Ravenswood clo Croy
103 U 16	Ravenswood ct Kingst
40 D 7	Ravenswood cres Harrow
125 T 19	Ravenswood cres W Wkhm
83 T 1	Ravenswood gdns Islwth
33 T 14	Ravenswood rd E17
89 S 19	Ravenswood rd SW12
156 J 6	Ravenswood rd Croy
62 K 8	Ravensworth rd NW9
113 T 8	Ravensworth rd SE9
149 P 5	Ravent rd SE11
134 J 16	Ravey st EC2
79 U 17	Ravine gro SE18
147 N 6	Rawlings st SW3
158 K 16	Rawlins clo S Croy
27 S 9	Rawlins clo N3
120 G 10	Rawnsley av Mrdn
89 R 3	Rawson st SW11
65 S 6	Rawston wlk E13
133 W 12	Rawstorne pl EC1
133 W 12	Rawstorne st EC1
4 M 18	Raydean rd Barnt
55 Z 14	Raydons gdns Dgnhm
55 Y 15	Raydons rd Dgnhm
56 A 14	Raydons rd Dgnhm
47 S 7	Raydon st N19
127 P 14	Rayfield clo Brom
94 C 19	Rayford av SE12
68 A 6	Ray gdns Bark
11 P 16	Ray gdns Stanm
96 Z 2	Raylens clo SE9
18 A 10	Rayleigh clo N13
117 O 3	Rayleigh ct Kingst
157 X 14	Rayleigh ri S Croy
17 Z 10	Rayleigh rd N13
18 A 10	Rayleigh rd N13
105 U 20	Rayleigh rd SW19
21 X 20	Rayleigh rd Wdfd Grn
34 L 1	Rayleigh rd Wdfd Grn
21 Z 18	Ray Lodge rd Wdfd Grn
27 N 11	Raymead NW4
122 G 11	Raymead av Thntn Hth
79 T 19	Raymere gdns SE18
34 B 9	Raymond av E18
71 Z 8	Raymond av W13
110 C 11	Raymond clo SE26
65 X 2	Raymond rd E13
105 T 15	Raymond rd SW19
124 H 10	Raymond rd Becknhm
54 D 2	Raymond rd Ilf
151 X 6	Raymouth rd SE16
34 C 12	Rayne ct E18
50 C 19	Rayner st E9
40 F 4	Rayners la Harrow
22 F 20	Rayners la Pinn
87 R 13	Rayners rd SW15
52 L 1	Raynes av E11
18 K 18	Raynham av N18
18 K 16	Raynham rd N18
74 J 10	Raynham rd N18
18 K 17	Raynham ter N18
70 D 3	Raynor clo S'hall
42 G 14	Raynors clo Wemb
40 B 3	Raynton clo Harrow
19 P 15	Rays av N18
19 P 15	Rays rd N18
133 U 18	Ray st EC1
89 T 1	Raywood st SW8
42 Z 19	Reading la E8
50 A 18	Reading la E8
40 L 14	Reading rd Grnfd
154 D 12	Reading rd Sutton
14 D 16	Reading way NW7
83 R 13	Reapers wy Islwth
75 N 3	Reardon path E1
143 X 15	Reardon path E1
75 N 3	Reardon st E1
143 X 13	Reardon st E1
75 R 19	Reaston st SE14
75 P 9	Rebecca ter SE16
73 Z 14	Reckitt rd W4
75 O 15	Record st SE15
106 J 12	Recovery rd SW17
38 L 17	Recreation av Rom
110 E 9	Recreation rd SE26
126 B 3	Recreation rd Brom
70 A 10	Recreation rd S'hall
121 Y 8	Recreation way Mitch
134 A 5	Rector st N1
20 B 10	Rectory clo E4
27 W 6	Rectory clo N3
118 M 4	Rectory clo SW20
99 R 11	Rectory clo Drtfrd
11 R 10	Rectory clo Stanm
11 O 17	Rectory clo Stanm
116 C 20	Rectory clo Surb
34 K 18	Rectory cres E11
77 X 18	Rectory Field cres SE7
30 A 12	Rectory gdns N8
89 V 7	Rectory gdns SW4
58 F 2	Rectory gdns Grnfrd
124 M 1	Rectory grn Becknhm
89 V 7	Rectory gdns SW4
56 J 4	Rectory gro Croy
100 F 12	Rectory gro Hampt
107 P 13	Rectory la SW17
2 C 17	Rectory la Edg
115 R 11	Rectory la Sidcp
115 U 11	Rectory la Sidcp
11 O 17	Rectory la Stanm
116 C 20	Rectory la Surb
59 T 15	Rectory la Wallgtn
58 B 7	Rectory park Grnfd
58 D 8	Rectory Pk av Grnfd
78 J 11	Rectory pl SE18
53 U 16	Rectory rd E12
33 R 12	Rectory rd E17
30 A 14	Rectory rd N8
49 V 9	Rectory rd N16
86 G 4	Rectory rd SW13
73 U 2	Rectory rd W3
111 O 20	Rectory rd Becknhm
124 M 2	Rectory rd Becknhm
56 F 20	Rectory rd Dgnhm
70 E 9	Rectory rd S'hall
153 Z 7	Rectory rd Sutton
18 K 14	Reculver ms N18
75 S 13	Reculver rd SE16
146 H 15	Redanchor clo SW3
137 Y 6	Redan pl W2
144 G 1	Redan st W14
90 K 5	Redan ter SE5
110 C 6	Redberry gro SE26
27 Z 4	Redbourne av N3
150 A 20	Redbridge gdns SE5
35 N 14	Redbridge la S11
35 N 18	Redbridge la East Ilf
34 L 18	Redbridge la West E11
147 N 12	Redburn st SW3
40 K 16	Redcar clo Grnfd
150 A 19	Redcar st SE5
63 N 20	Redcastle clo E1
135 N 16	Redchurch st E2
145 W 10	Redcliffe clo SW5
145 Y 10	Redcliffe gdns SW10
146 B 14	Redcliffe gdns SW10
53 V 3	Redcliffe gdns Ilf
145 Z 12	Redcliffe ms SW10
146 A 15	Redcliffe pl SW10
146 C 13	Redcliffe rd SW10
145 Z 13	Redcliffe sq SW10
145 Z 13	Redcliffe st SW10
119 X 12	Redclose av Mrdn
65 Y 4	Redclyffe rd E6
59 N 18	Redcroft S'hall
58 M 18	Redcroft S'hall
142 D 14	Redcross wlk SE1
142 C 15	Redcross way SE1
13 S 12	Reddings clo NW7
13 S 11	Reddings the NW7
157 R 20	Reddington clo S Croy
110 G 18	Reddons rd Becknhm
137 V 8	Rede pl W11
71 X 19	Redesdale gdns Islwth
146 M 12	Redesdale st SW3
82 G 19	Redfern av Hounsl
62 B 1	Redfern rd NW10
145 W 6	Redfield la SW5
122 D 9	Redford av Thntn Hth
155 Z 14	Redford av Wallgtn
133 Z 4	Redford wlk N1
87 R 15	Redgate ter SW15
87 P 9	Redgrave rd SW15
113 Y 13	Red Hill Chisl
25 U 8	Redhill dri Edg
131 Y 11	Redhill st NW1
97 Y 11	Red House la Bxly Hth
121 X 13	Red Ho rd Croy
46 B 11	Redington gdns NW3
46 A 10	Redington rd NW3
9 N 4	Redlands rd Enf
90 B 19	Redlands way SW2
81 R 17	Red Leaf clo Blvdr
83 W 9	Redlees park Islwth
83 Y 11	Redless clo Islwth
141 U 5	Red Lion ct EC4
28 F 8	Red Lion hill N2
78 J 20	Red Lion la SE18
95 W 1	Red Lion la SE18
95 W 2	Red Lion pl SE18
117 O 20	Red Lion rd Surb
150 D 14	Red Lion row SE17
141 N 2	Red Lion sq WC1
141 O 2	Red Lion st WC1
84 H 13	Red Lion st Rich
139 W 13	Red Lion yd W1
125 V 17	Red Lodge rd W Wkhm
63 P 14	Redmans rd E1
143 U 13	Redmead la E1
74 J 10	Redmore rd W6
139 T 8	Red pl W1
80 K 7	Redpoll way Blvdr
91 N 11	Red Post hill SE24
65 R 5	Redriff rd SE13
75 U 8	Redriff rd SE16
38 J 7	Redriff rd Rom
30 C 2	Redruth clo N22
53 S 3	Redruth rd E9
30 F 7	Redston rd N8
50 G 13	Redvers rd N22
83 O 19	Redway dri Twick
16 L 3	Redwood clo N14
104 F 2	Redwood SW15
146 E 6	Reece ms SW7
65 S 16	Reed clo E16
94 F 13	Reed clo SE12
56 G 16	Reede gdns Dgnhm
56 D 17	Reede rd Dgnhm
56 J 16	Reede rd Dgnhm
56 G 17	Reede way Dgnhm
31 Z 12	Reedham clo N17
91 W 6	Reedham st SE15
49 F 12	Reedholm vlls N16
47 U 19	Reed pl N17
39 U 7	Reed Pond wlk Rom
31 W 9	Reed rd N17
149 T 7	Reedworth st SE11
11 U 13	Reenglass rd Stanm
123 U 14	Rees gdns Croy
53 W 17	Reesland clo E12
134 D 5	Rees st N1
26 B 18	Reets Farm clo NW9
43 X 1	Reeves av NW9
156 J 4	Reeves cnr Croy
139 U 10	Reeves ms W1
64 D 10	Reeves rd E3
31 V 7	Reform row N17
88 M 5	Reform st SW11
60 H 16	Regal clo W5
18 H 16	Regal clo N18
155 S 5	Regal cres Wallgtn
131 V 5	Regal la NW1
24 K 19	Regal way Harrow
134 J 9	Regan way N1
89 R 18	Regarth av Rom
60 K 18	Regency clo W5
100 E 11	Regency clo Hampt
83 T 14	Regency ms Islwth
148 F 4	Regency pl SW1
148 F 8	Regency pl SW1
97 X 9	Regency wy Bxly Hth
124 L 15	Regency wlk Croy
15 R 17	Regent clo N12
24 J 19	Regent clo Harrow
140 C 9	Regent pl W1
90 J 14	Regent pl SE24
117 O 12	Regent rd Surb
64 C 9	Regent sq E3
17 S 17	Regents av N13
157 S 13	Regents clo S Croy
11 X 14	Regents ct Edg
27 V 11	Regents Park rd N3
47 O 20	Regent's Park rd NW1
131 U 4	Regent's Park rd NW1
131 W 4	Regent's Park ter NW1
131 T 8	Regent's Park Zoological gdns NW1
94 E 4	Regents pl SE3
132 L 14	Regents sq WC1
81 U 11	Regent sq Blvdr
128 G 14	Regent st NW10
139 Z 4	Regent st W1
140 B 10	Regent st W1
73 P 15	Regent st W4
4 B 11	Regina clo Barnt
52 D 19	Reginald rd E7
76 B 20	Reginald rd SE8
48 D 4	Regina rd N4
123 Y 6	Regina rd SE25
71 Z 3	Regina rd W13
70 B 10	Regina rd S'hall
72 A 3	Regina ter W13
132 C 15	Regnart bldgs NW1
79 U 10	Reidhaven rd SE18
120 B 19	Reigate av Sutton
112 D 6	Reigate rd Brom
54 J 8	Reigate rd Ilf
156 B 10	Reigate way Wallgtn
49 Y 8	Reighton rd E5
136 D 12	Relay rd W12
91 X 7	Relf rd SE15
154 G 10	Relko gdn Sutton
146 L 1	Relton ms SW7
147 S 8	Rembrandt clo SW1
93 Y 11	Rembrandt rd SE13
25 P 6	Rembrandt rd Edg
31 P 18	Remington rd N15
133 Y 10	Remington st W2
141 N 4	Remnant st WC2
64 A 1	Remus rd E3
49 V 10	Rendlesham rd E5
7 X 4	Rendlesham rd Enf
75 R 7	Renforth st SE16
66 H 19	Renfrew clo E6
82 A 5	Renfrew rd Hounsl
149 N 6	Renfrew rd SE11
82 A 4	Renfrew rd Hounsl
103 U 17	Renfrew rd Kingst
106 M 15	Renmuir st SW17
32 J 11	Renness rd E17
96 F 13	Rennets clo SE9
96 E 14	Rennets Wood rd SE9
141 V 12	Rennie st SE1
156 J 1	Renown clo Croy
38 F 4	Renown clo Rom
32 F 17	Rensbury rd E17
81 P 16	Renshaw clo Blvdr
26 M 19	Renters av NW4
27 O 19	Renters av NW4
68 E 10	Renwick rd Bark
58 B 11	Repens wy Grnfd
105 W 1	Replingham rd SW18
38 G 15	Repository rd SE18
39 W 11	Repton av Rom
42 D 13	Repton av Wemb
154 H 12	Repton clo Carsh
111 R 20	Repton ct Becknhm
35 U 4	Repton clo Ilf
39 W 12	Repton gdns Rom
35 U 4	Repton gro Ilf
144 M 20	Repton rd SW6
25 N 14	Repton rd Harrow
63 V 16	Repton st E14
38 F 4	Repulse clo Rom
6 G 16	Reservoir rd N14
92 H 5	Reservoir rd SE4
77 N 16	Restell clo SE10
138 B 20	Reston pl SW7
96 G 16	Restons cres SE9
47 T 6	Retcar clo NW5
20 D 9	Retingham way E4
24 F 16	Retreat clo Harrow
50 D 18	Retreat pl E9
84 G 13	Retreat rd Rich
25 X 15	Retreat the NW9
86 B 8	Retreat the SW13
82 B 3	Retreat the SE15
40 J 2	Retreat the Harrow
117 N 15	Retreat the Surb
123 N 8	Retreat the Thntn Hth
152 K 4	Retreat the Worc Pk
86 L 10	Rettivard clo Carsh
79 X 17	Revell ri SE18
177 U 2	Revell rd Kingst
153 U 13	Revell rd Sutton
92 H 9	Revelon rd SE4
91 S 16	Revstoke rd SW18
114 B 2	Reventlow rd SE9
151 R 6	Reverdy rd SE1
120 H 15	Revensby rd Carsh
44 E 6	Review rd NW2
69 T 4	Review rd Dgnhm
146 A 19	Rewell st SW6
120 F 15	Rewley rd Carsh
38 H 3	Rex clo Rom
139 W 11	Rex pl W1
34 K 17	Reydon av E11
127 W 5	Reynard clo Brom
109 T 18	Reynard dri SE19
30 M 2	Reynardson rd N17
31 N 2	Reynardson rd N17
53 Y 15	Reynolds av E12

R

R

37	U 19	Reynolds av Rom
55	T 1	Reynolds av Rom
46	A 2	Reynolds clo NW11
121	N 20	Reynolds clo Carsh
155	N 1	Reynolds clo Carsh
52	C 9	Reynolds ct E11
25	N 9	Reynolds dri Edg
84	M 17	Reynolds pl Rich
17	W 19	Reynolds pl SE15
92	D 12	Reynolds pl SE15
73	W 7	Reynolds rd W4
117	Z 17	Reynolds rd New Mald
157	S 8	Reynolds way Croy
133	Z 7	Rheidol ter N1
31	V 6	Rheola clo N17
135	O 15	Rhode st E2
29	T 5	Rhodes av N22
51	X 6	Rhodesia rd E11
90	A 5	Rhodesia rd SW9
48	D 16	Rhodes st N7
119	Y 14	Rhodes Moorhouse ct Mrdn
63	X 6	Rhodeswell pl E3
63	X 15	Rhodeswell rd E14
63	X 17	Rhodeswell rd E14
63	X 9	Rhondda gro E3
63	X 6	Rhyl st NW5
47	P 17	Rhyl st NW5
29	Y 1	Rhys av N11
121	P 2	Rialto rd Mitch
21	Z 17	Ribble clo Wdfd Grn
40	L 18	Ribblesdale av N11
30	C 14	Ribblesdale rd N8
107	S 14	Ribblesdale rd SW16
98	W 8	Ribchester av Grnfd
64	C 18	Ricardo st E14
105	W 12	Ricards rd SW19
73	U 3	Richard cotts W3
38	L 17	Richards av Rom
23	Y 16	Richards clo Harrow
	M 6	Richardson rd E15
132	A 19	Richardson's ms W1
33	O 11	Richards pl E17
146	M 5	Richard's pl SW3
143	W 7	Richard st E1
5	S 15	Richard st E16
133	N 20	Richbell pl WC1
9	P 18	Richbourne ter SW8
45	R 13	Richborough rd SE9
10	B 3	Richfield rd Bushey Watf
10	B 4	Richfield rd Bushey Watf
65	P 3	Richford rd E15
74	L 7	Richford st W6
83	B 19	Richford st W6
144	B 1	Richford st W6
152	H 9	Richlands av Epsom
20	J 16	Richmond av E4
133	O 3	Richmond av N1
44	L 19	Richmond av NW10
119	U 2	Richmond av SW20
84	G 14	Richmond br Rich
140	E 6	Richmond bldgs W1
32	M 19	Richmond clo E17
20	K 16	Richmond cres E4
18	K 5	Richmond cres N9
26	H 15	Richmond gdns NW4
10	H 20	Richmond gdns Harrow
23	V 1	Richmond gdns Harrow
156	B 6	Richmond gro N1
133	X 1	Richmond gro N1
116	L 15	Richmond gro Surb
84	K 17	Richmond hill Rich
84	J 15	Richmond Hill ct Rich
140	E 7	Richmond ms W1
57	T 17	Richmond park Rich
85	X 10	Richmond Pk rd SW14
102	K 19	Richmond Pk rd Kingst
79	O 11	Richmond pl SE18
20	K 5	Richmond rd E4
52	J 15	Richmond rd E7
49	U 20	Richmond rd E8
50	A 19	Richmond rd E8
51	V 6	Richmond rd E11
28	D 8	Richmond rd N2
17	N 20	Richmond rd N11
31	R 19	Richmond rd N15
118	J 1	Richmond rd SW20
72	J 4	Richmond rd W5
5	P 17	Richmond rd Barnt
5	R 17	Richmond rd Barnt
156	B 5	Richmond rd Croy
54	B 9	Richmond rd Ilf
83	Z 8	Richmond rd Islwth
102	J 19	Richmond rd Kingst
122	J 7	Richmond rd Thntn Hth
156	B 5	Richmond rd Thntn Hth
84	D 19	Richmond rd Twick
65	U 7	Richmond st E13
140	K 16	Richmond ter SW1
140	K 17	Richmond Ter ms SW1
52	E 6	Richmond way E11
136	G 19	Richmond way W14
94	F 9	Richmond gdns SE3
12	J 14	Richmond gdns Edg
63	Z 19	Rich st E14
90	E 20	Rickard clo SW2
145	U 13	Rickett st SW6
68	K 10	Rickman st E1
48	A 7	Rickthorne rd N14
95	R 10	Rickyard path SE9
41	V 14	Ridding la Grnfd
112	L 7	Riddons rd SE12
78	F 12	Rideout st SE18
72	C 13	Ride the Brentf
9	R 13	Ride the Enf
64	C 7	Ridgdale st E3
17	Y 2	Ridge av N21
18	A 2	Ridge av N21
99	T 16	Ridge av Drtfrd
94	L 9	Ridgebrook rd SE3
94	M 8	Ridgebrook rd SE3
27	P 8	Ridge clo NW4
25	Z 13	Ridge clo NW9
7	R 5	Ridge crest Enf
45	T 3	Ridge hill NW11
158	G 1	Ridgemount av Croy
109	Z 17	Ridgemount clo SE20
132	E 19	Ridgemount gdns WC1
7	U 10	Ridgemount gdns Enf
88	B 14	Ridgemount rd SW18
30	E 19	Ridge rd N8
18	A 4	Ridge rd N21
45	W 9	Ridge rd NW2
107	S 17	Ridge rd Mitch
119	V 20	Ridge rd Sutton
153	U 1	Ridge rd Sutton
98	B 18	Ridge the Bxly
117	O 12	Ridge the Surb
83	P 18	Ridge the Twick
4	C 20	Ridgeview clo Barnt
15	P 10	Ridgeview rd N20
99	T 16	Ridge way Drtfrd
96	J 13	Ridgeway East Sidcp
7	T 6	Ridgeway Enf
100	A 7	Ridge way Felt
17	N 8	Ridgeway N14
96	H 12	Ridgeway West Sidcp
21	Z 15	Ridge way Wdfd Grn
5	Y 20	Ridgeway dri Barnt
112	H 10	Ridgeway dri Brom
35	R 14	Ridgeway gdns Ilf
20	P 8	Ridgeway park E4
71	T 20	Ridgeway pl Islwth
83	U 1	Ridgeway rd Islwth
71	T 18	Ridgeway rd North Islwth
20	G 5	Ridgeway rd E4
20	G 5	Ridgeway the E4
28	A 3	Ridgeway the N3
15	Y 14	Ridgeway the N11
13	U 11	Ridgeway the NW7
13	V 13	Ridgeway the NW7
14	B 16	Ridgeway the NW7
25	Z 14	Ridgeway the NW9
45	V 3	Ridgeway the NW11
73	P 7	Ridgeway the W3
156	C 7	Ridgeway the Croy
22	J 19	Ridgeway the Harrow
40	K 2	Ridgeway the Harrow
24	O 20	Ridgeway the Harrow
39	V 13	Ridgeway the Harrow
11	R 19	Ridgeway the Stanm
69	V 3	Ridgewell clo Dgnhm
12	J 14	Ridgmont gdns Edg
88	B 14	Ridgemount rd SW18
132	F 20	Ridgmount st WC1
105	P 16	Ridgway SW19
105	O 17	Ridgway gdns SW19
105	S 16	Ridgway pl SW19
90	J 8	Ridgway rd SW9
154	G 14	Ridgway the Sutton
65	Z 14	Ridgwell rd E16
140	A 2	Riding House st W1
7	X 15	Ridings av N21
60	M 11	Ridings the W5
61	N 12	Ridings the W5
45	V 2	Ridings the Surb
117	R 11	Ridings the Surb
45	V 2	Riding the NW11
8	F 4	Ridler rd Enf
72	B 8	Ridley av W13
39	Z 4	Ridley clo Rom
52	K 11	Ridley rd E7
49	U 16	Ridley rd E8
62	H 5	Ridley rd NW10
106	A 17	Ridley rd SW19
126	D 6	Ridley rd Brom
97	O 2	Ridley rd Welling
97	P 2	Ridley rd Welling
96	D 14	Riefield rd SE9
158	C 14	Riesco dri Croy
44	L 15	Riffel rd NW2
148	U 13	Rifle ct SE11
136	H 12	Rifle pl W11
148	U 13	Rifle st E14
87	U 5	Rigault rd SW6
156	F 4	Rigby clo Croy
53	X 7	Rigby ms Ilf
64	C 18	Rigden st E14
62	H 8	Rigeley rd NW10
50	G 4	Rigg appr E10
107	W 11	Higgindale rd SW16
142	M 19	Riley rd SE1
9	R 4	Riley rd Enf
146	F 16	Riley st SW10
48	F 16	Ringcroft st N7
112	J 17	Ring clo Brom
126	F 6	Ringer's rd Brom
87	X 15	Ringford rd SW18
87	T 3	Ringmer av SW6
	A 7	Ringmer gdn N4
8	B 18	Ringmer pl Enf
92	B 19	Ringmore ri SE23
30	D 7	Ringslade rd N22
93	S 18	Ringstead rd SE6
154	G 10	Ringstead rd Sutton
70	B 14	Ringway S'hall
16	G 19	Ringway N11
8	M 8	Ringwell clo Enf
28	M 9	Ringwood av N2
122	B 16	Ringwood av Croy
104	G 3	Ringwood gdns SW15
32	K 18	Ringwood rd E17
17	V 4	Ringwood way N21
	H 10	Ringwood way Hampt
159	U 15	Ripley clo Croy
85	Z 7	Ripley gdns SW14
154	C 8	Ripley gdns Sutton
85	Y 17	Ripley rd E16
81	P 10	Ripley rd Blvdr
7	Y 4	Ripley rd Enf
100	G 18	Ripley rd Hampt
54	J 8	Ripley rd Ilf
35	P 20	Ripon gdns Ilf
29	N 4	Ripon rd N9
31	O 12	Ripon rd N17
78	L 17	Ripon rd SE18
97	N 3	Rippersley rd Welling
67	P 2	Ripple rd Bark
68	C 4	Ripple rd Bark
69	N 5	Ripple rd Dgnhm
82	R 2	Ripplevale gro N1
79	X 13	Rippolson rd SE18
42	J 16	Rippon clo Grnfd
44	A 1	Rippoth rd E3
118	H 17	Risborough dri Worc Pk
141	Z 16	Risborough st SE1
75	P 7	Risdon st SE16
39	U 1	Risebridge chase Rom
39	U 6	Risebridge rd Rom
39	J 6	Risedale rd Bxly Hth
92	H 17	Riseldine rd SE23
33	U 2	Rise park Rom
39	S 5	Rise park blvd Rom
39	P 7	Rise Park pl Rom
34	D 15	Rise the E11
17	V 15	Rise the N13
13	S 20	Rise the NW7
43	Z 11	Rise the NW10
99	U 11	Rise the Drtfrd
12	E 15	Rise the Edg
41	Y 15	Rise the Grnfd
57	T 19	Rise the Sidcp
158	C 20	Rise the S Croy
23	R 8	Risinghill st N1
23	T 6	Risinghome clo Harrow
23	T 6	Risingholme rd Harrow
33	X 13	Risings the E17
141	Y 1	Rising Sun ct EC1
30	M 5	Risley av N17
15	O 5	Risley av N17
148	M 16	Rita rd SW8
149	N 17	Rita rd SW8
30	L 16	Ritches rd N15
124	A 15	Ritchie rd Croy
133	T 7	Ritchie st N1
32	H 12	Ritchings av E17
107	P 4	Ritherdon rd SW17
49	W 17	Ritson rd E8
78	J 17	Ritter st SE18
50	C 18	Rivaz pl E9
34	B 13	Rivenhall gdns E18
17	V 9	River av N13
17	Y 3	River bank N21
76	K 6	River bank SE10
76	L 11	River bank SE10
34	L 18	River clo E11
74	H 12	Rivercourt rd W6
84	E 14	Riverdale gdns Twick
79	W 13	Riverdale rd SE18
79	W 14	Riverdale rd SE18
27	Z 17	Riverdale rd Bxly
98	A 17	Riverdale rd Bxly
81	W 14	Riverdale rd Erith
84	E 15	Riverdale rd Twick
100	C 9	Riverdale rd Twick
12	J 12	Riverdene Edg
53	X 10	Riverdene rd Ilf
8	C 12	River front Enf
155	O 5	River gdns Carsh
124	M 1	River Gro pk Becknhm
32	E 7	Riverhead clo E17
152	A 19	Riverholme dri Epsom
102	H 1	River la Rich
84	H 20	River la Twick
102	C 14	Rivermead clo Tedd
100	J 6	River Meads av Felt
111	X 17	River Pk gdns Brom
30	D 7	River Park rd N22
133	Z 1	River pl N1
102	E 14	River reach Tedd
67	Y 14	River rd Bark
68	B 14	River rd Bark
48	K 10	Riverside rd N5
38	F 2	Riversdale rd Rom
8	E 11	Riversfield rd Enf
44	J 1	Riverside NW4
77	V 8	Riverside SE7
102	A 1	Riverside Twick
59	U 12	Riverside clo W7
116	G 8	Riverside clo Kingst
155	R 6	Riverside clo Wallgtn
86	B 1	Riverside dri W4
120	J 11	Riverside dri Mitch
102	C 4	Riverside dri Rich
74	J 12	Riverside gdns W6
8	A 10	Riverside gdns Enf
60	K 6	Riverside gdns Wemb
64	H 7	Riverside rd E15
31	Y 18	Riverside rd N15
106	D 8	Riverside rd SW17
115	Z 5	Riverside rd Sidcp
141	N 17	Riverside wlk SE1
97	W 19	Riverside wlk Bxly Hth
83	U 7	Riverside wlk Islwth
133	T 12	River st EC1
74	L 14	River ter W6
144	B 11	River ter W6
74	K 16	Riverview gdns SW13
144	A 14	Riverview gdns SW13
101	W 5	River View gdns Twick
73	T 18	Riverview gro W4
111	N 3	Riverview pk SE6
73	T 18	Riverview rd W4
17	U 14	Riverway N13
77	O 7	River wlk SE10
152	A 11	River way Epsom
100	J 9	River way Twick
35	N 6	Rivington av Wdfd Grn
26	C 3	Rivington cres NW9
134	K 14	Rivington pl EC2
134	L 14	Rivington pl EC2
30	K 2	Rivulet rd N17
31	N 2	Rivulet rd N17
39	S 5	Rix Park rd Rom
53	R 15	Rixsen rd E12
51	O 20	Roach rd E3
64	B 1	Roach rd E3
48	B 6	Roads pl N4
76	F 18	Roan st SE10
10	M 19	Robb rd Stanm
139	T 4	Robert Adam st W1
135	T 13	Roberts st E2
130	D 18	Robert clo W9
75	U 19	Robert Lowe clo SE14
126	L 1	Roberton dri Brom
72	G 7	Robert's all NW7
14	D 18	Roberts clo NW7
120	E 18	Robertsbridge rd Carsh
39	Z 4	Roberts clo Rom
147	T 2	Roberts ms SW1
64	H 3	Robertson rd E15
89	S 6	Robertson st SW8
133	U 16	Robert's pl EC1
33	R 4	Roberts rd E17
81	T 14	Roberts rd Blvdr
78	K 4	Robert st E?

131 Y 13	Robert st NW1
132 A 13	Robert st NW1
79 R 11	Robert st SE18
140 L 11	Robert st WC2
156 M 5	Robert st Croy
97 X 10	Robina clo Bxly Hth
38 M 1	Robin clo Rom
38 M 2	Robin clo Rom
160 C 5	Robin ct EC2
47 O 6	Robin gro N6
72 D 17	Robin gro Brentf
26 O 19	Robin gro Harrow
113 R 14	Robin Hill dri Chisl
121 V 7	Robin Hood clo Mitch
23 V 3	Robin Hood dri Harrow
64 G 19	Robin Hood la E14
104 A 11	Robin Hood la SW15
97 Z 12	Robin Hood la Bxly Hth
121 W 7	Robin Hood la Mitch
153 Y 11	Robin Hood la Sutton
104 C 11	Robin Hood rd SW15/SW19
104 A 8	Robin Hood way SW15
41 X 17	Robin Hood way Grnfd
112 K 7	Robins ct SE12
125 V 2	Robins ct Becknhm
63 P 6	Robinson rd E2
106 K 16	Robinson rd SW17
56 D 11	Robinson rd Dgnhm
147 N 13	Robinsons clo W3
103 Y 9	Robin Wood pl SW15
90 E 4	Robsart st SW9
62 H 1	Robson av NW10
7 V 9	Robson clo Enf
108 K 7	Robson rd SE27
25 N 6	Roch av Edg
51 N 1	Rochdale rd E17
80 B 13	Rochdale rd SE2
75 Z 18	Rochdale wy SE8
88 E 11	Rochelle clo SW11
135 N 14	Rochelle st E2
122 B 1	Roche SW16
63 X 4	Rochester av E13
126 J 4	Rochester av Brom
94 K 7	Rochester clo SE3
8 F 7	Rochester clo Enf
97 P 15	Rochester clo Sidcp
108 B 19	Rochester dri SW16
98 F 15	Rochester dri Bxly Hth
157 T 5	Rochester gdns Croy
53 T 2	Rochester gdns Ilf
47 V 19	Rochester ms NW1
47 U 19	Rochester pl NW1
155 N 8	Rochester rd Carsh
148 C 5	Rochester row SW1
47 W 20	Rochester sq NW1
148 E 4	Rochester st SW1
47 U 19	Rochester ter NW1
94 H 1	Rochester way SE3
94 K 6	Rochester way SE3
95 V 8	Rochester way SE9
96 C 9	Rochester way SE9
99 O 19	Rochester way Bxly
120 F 15	Roche wlk Carsh
37 T 14	Rochford av Rom
66 A 6	Rochford clo E6
57 Y 19	Rochford clo Hornch
121 Z 15	Rochford way Croy
25 Z 8	Rock av SW14
110 E 2	Rockburn rd SE23
92 A 17	Rockell's pl SE22
60 A 7	Rockford av Grnfd
62 G 15	Rock gdns Dgnhm
45 O 13	Rockhall rd NW2
108 F 10	Rockhampton clo SE27
108 F 9	Rockhampton rd SE27
157 R 14	Rockhampton rd S Croy
109 U 10	Rock hill SE26
39 Z 20	Rockingham av Hornch
86 D 11	Rockingham clo SW15
150 B 2	Rockingham st SE1
24 C 8	Rocklands dri Stanm
138 F 18	Rockley rd W14
79 Y 13	Rockmount rd SE18
86 G 8	Rocks la SW13
59 S 2	Rockware av Grnfd
111 W 18	Rockwell gdns SE19
56 G 15	Rockwell rd Dgnhm
136 C 17	Rockwood pl W12

133 Y 9	Rocliffe st W2
94 C 7	Rocque la SE3
45 W 4	Rodborough rd NW11
123 R 15	Roden gdns SE25
89 Y 14	Rodenhurst rd SW4
48 C 11	Roden rd N7
53 X 9	Roden way Ilf
46 M 13	Roderick rd NW3
66 M 1	Roding av Bark
35 O 8	Roding la North Wdfd Grn
35 N 12	Roding la South Ilf
35 M 13	Roding la South Ilf
34 M 13	Roding la South Ilf
50 G 13	Roding rd E5
66 L 14	Roding rd E6
21 Y 19	Rodings the Wdfd Grn
139 R 2	Rodmarton st W1
14 H 15	Rodmell slope N12
77 O 14	Rodmere st SE10
90 A 20	Rodmill la SW2
118 A 10	Rodney clo New Mald
32 J 7	Rodney pl E17
150 C 5	Rodney pl E17
106 C 20	Rodney pl SW19
34 G 13	Rodney rd E11
150 D 6	Rodney rd SE17
150 F 7	Rodney rd SE17
120 H 5	Rodney rd Mitch
118 A 10	Rodney rd New Mald
82 G 17	Rodney rd Twick
133 P 8	Rodney st N1
78 L 8	Rodney st SE18
38 F 6	Rodney way Rom
86 G 18	Rodway rd SW15
112 H 19	Rodway rd Brom
12 B 19	Rodwell pl Edg
91 V 14	Rodwell rd SE22
78 J 4	Roebourne way E16
18 H 20	Roebuck la N17
21 Y 4	Roebuck la Buck Hl
9 O 4	Roedean av Enf
9 O 4	Roedean clo Enf
86 A 14	Roedean cres SW15
25 V 12	Roe end NW9
86 G 11	Roehampton clo SW15
114 C 16	Roehampton dri Chisl
86 B 15	Roehampton ga SW15
86 H 18	Roehampton High st SW15
86 F 11	Roehampton la SW15
104 K 1	Roehampton la SW15
104 C 6	Roehampton vale SW15
25 T 12	Roe la NW9
156 B 14	Roe wy Croy
76 F 6	Roffey st E14
56 F 15	Rogers gdns Dgnhm
66 R 17	Rogers rd E16
106 H 9	Rogers rd SW17
56 F 17	Rogers rd Dgnhm
133 O 18	Roger st WC1
110 E 1	Rojack rd SE23
34 F 4	Rokeby gdns Wdfd Grn
92 L 3	Rokeby rd SE4
92 L 3	Rokeby st E15
96 F 4	Rokesby clo Welling
30 A 15	Rokesly av N8
146 C 9	Roland gdns SW7
93 W 14	Roland rd E17
150 F 12	Roland way SE17
146 C 9	Roland way SW7
37 X 12	Roles gro Rom
5 X 15	Rolfe clo Barnt
127 Z 15	Rolleston av Brom
127 Z 16	Rolleston clo Orp
157 O 17	Rolleston rd S Croy
95 W 16	Roll gdns Ilf
75 R 16	Rollins st SE15
48 E 14	Rollit st N7
82 H 13	Rollit cres Hounsl
141 S 5	Rolls bldgs EC4
90 L 13	Rollscourt av SE21
20 C 18	Rolls Park av E4
20 D 17	Rolls Park rd E4
141 S 4	Rolls pas EC4
151 R 9	Rolls rd SE1
75 X 15	Rolt st SE8
113 O 18	Rolvenden gdns Chisl
125 Z 9	Romanhurst av Brom
126 A 10	Romanhurst av Brom
125 Y 9	Romanhurst gdns Brom
109 P 14	Roman ri SE19
63 U 7	Roman rd E3

66 E 12	Roman rd E6
29 R 2	Roman rd N10
74 C 10	Roman rd W4
53 Z 17	Roman rd Ilf
54 A 17	Roman rd Ilf
48 C 19	Roman way N7
8 H 16	Roman way Enf
158 J 2	Roman way Croy
32 G 4	Romany gdns E17
119 X 18	Romany gdns Sutton
32 J 10	Rona rd E17
107 O 7	Romberg rd SW17
93 T 13	Romborough gdns SE13
57 S 2	Rom cres Rom
94 K 11	Romero sq SE9
108 D 7	Romeyn rd SW16
52 K 16	Romford rd E7
51 Z 19	Romford rd E12
37 Z 1	Romford rd Rom
143 U 3	Romford st E1
48 H 8	Romilly rd N4
140 G 7	Romilly st W1
109 N 8	Rommany rd SE22
31 Z 4	Romney clo N17
46 B 4	Romney clo NW11
40 J 1	Romney clo Harrow
22 H 20	Romney dri Harrow
40 J 1	Romney dri Harrow
113 O 18	Romney dri Chisl
98 C 1	Romney gdns Bxly Hth
76 J 17	Romney rd SE10
68 J 3	Romney rd Dgnhm
117 Y 15	Romney rd New Mald
148 H 3	Romney st SW1
108 H 1	Romola rd SE21
68 J 2	Romsey gdns Dgnhm
71 Y 1	Romsey rd W13
65 N 10	Ronald av E15
124 M 10	Ronald clo Becknhm
48 G 15	Ronalds rd N5
112 F 20	Ronalds rd Brom
96 J 15	Ronaldstone rd Sidcp
63 R 18	Ronald st E1
47 N 13	Rona rd NW3
45 S 14	Rondu rd NW2
94 D 20	Roneo corner Hornch
94 D 20	Ronver st SE12
142 J 9	Rood la EC3
57 Y 20	Rook clo Hornch
57 X 20	Rook clo Hornch
26 D 15	Rookery clo NW9
69 V 1	Rookery cres Dgnhm
127 M 14	Rookery la Brom
126 L 14	Rookery la Brom
89 U 11	Rookery rd SW4
26 C 16	Rookery way NW9
29 U 12	Rookfield av N10
29 U 12	Rookfield clo N10
106 L 13	Rookstone rd SW17
118 F 9	Rookwood av New Mald
155 X 8	Rookwood av Wall
21 O 7	Rookwood gdns E4
31 W 20	Rookwood rd N16
57 O 18	Roosevelt way Dgnhm
63 X 20	Ropemakers fields E14
142 F 1	Ropemaker st EC2
160 F 1	Ropemaker st EC2
20 G 17	Ropers av E4
146 J 16	Ropers gdns SW3
95 V 14	Roper st SE9
121 P 2	Roper way Mitch
63 Y 12	Ropery st E3
78 L 8	Rope Yd rails SE18
144 L 19	Rosaline rd SW6
109 Z 8	Rosamund st SE26
82 B 5	Rosary clo Hounsl
146 C 8	Rosary gdns SW7
145 O 19	Rosaville rd SW6
49 U 19	Rosebery pl E8
134 C 18	Roscoe st EC1
25 T 3	Roscoff clo Edg
60 A 13	Roseacres clo W13
97 S 9	Roseacre rd Welling
142 B 12	Rose all SE1
140 C 13	Rose and Crown yd SW1
34 J 7	Rose av E18
106 M 20	Rose av Mitch
120 D 11	Rose av Mitch
144 E 19	Rose Bank
41 V 13	Rosebank av Wemb
63 X 7	Rosebank gdns E3
32 L 11	Rose bank gro E17
33 P 19	Rosebank rd E17

71 U 6	Rosebank rd W7
109 Z 17	Rose Bank st SE20
33 O 14	Rosebank vlls E17
61 X 16	Rosebank way W3
118 C 5	Roseberry av New Mald
30 J 18	Roseberry gdns N4
18 K 10	Roseberry rd N9
29 U 7	Roseberry rd N10
29 U 8	Roseberry rd N10
89 Z 16	Roseberry rd SW2
151 W 7	Roseberry st SE16
133 T 14	Roseberry av EC1
31 Z 7	Roseberry av N17
40 C 11	Rosebery av Harrow
53 R 18	Rosebery av E12
118 C 5	Rosebery av New Mald
96 H 18	Rosebery av Sidcp
122 M 3	Rosebery av Thntn Hth
119 O 15	Rosebery clo Mrdn
30 A 16	Rosebery gdns N8
59 Z 19	Rosebery gdns W13
18 J 10	Roseberry rd N9
83 O 13	Rosebery rd Hounsl
117 S 4	Rosebery rd Kingst
153 V 14	Rosebery rd Sutton
90 A 16	Rosebery rd SW2
117 R 4	Rosebery rd Kingst
83 R 19	Rosebine av Twick
88 B 6	Rosebury rd SW6
122 C 15	Rosecourt rd Croy
45 Z 10	Rosecroft av NW3
44 G 10	Rosecroft gdns NW2
83 R 20	Rosecroft gdns Twick
58 H 12	Rosecroft rd S'hall
80 C 8	Rosedale clo SE2
11 O 20	Rosedale clo Stanm
48 J 13	Rosedale ct N5
68 C 1	Rosedale gdns Dgnhm
52 L 16	Rosedale rd E7
68 C 1	Rosedale rd Dgnhm
152 G 10	Rosedale rd Epsom
84 J 9	Rosedale rd Rich
38 L 10	Rosedale rd Rom
108 D 7	Rosedene av SW16
122 B 17	Rosedene av Croy
64 A 19	Rosefield gdns E14
11 Y 18	Rosegarden clo Edg
72 H 8	Rose gdns W5
58 H 11	Rose gdns S'hall
25 X 12	Rose glen NW9
57 P 4	Rose glen Rom
37 W 10	Rosehatch av Rom
82 E 12	Roseheath rd Hounsl
154 B 2	Rose hill Sutton
120 C 19	Rosehill av Sutton
41 W 13	Rosehill gdns Grnfd
154 C 1	Rosehill gdns Sutton
154 A 1	Rosehill park Sutton
154 C 1	Rosehill pk W Sutton
42 C 15	Rosehill rd SW18
37 Z 2	Rose la Rom
31 O 2	Roseland clo N17
10 A 6	Rose lawn Bushey Watf
84 F 17	Roselieu clo Twick
28 B 8	Rosemary av N3
18 M 6	Rosemary av N9
19 N 7	Rosemary av N9
8 D 5	Rosemary av Enf
82 A 6	Rosemary av Hounsl
37 T 10	Rosemary av Rom
35 O 16	Rosemary dri Ilf
56 B 4	Rosemary gdns Dgnhm
85 W 7	Rosemary la SW14
151 X 18	Rosemary rd SE15
96 L 2	Rosemary rd Welling
134 F 4	Rosemary st N1
121 V 4	Rosemead av Mitch
42 L 4	Rosemead av Wemb
15 R 19	Rosemont av N12
46 C 17	Rosemont rd NW3
61 S 20	Rosemont rd W3
73 T 1	Rosemont rd W3
117 V 6	Rosemont rd New Mald
84 L 16	Rosemont rd Rich
60 K 3	Rosemont rd Wemb
147 N 6	Rosemoor st SW3
127 U 8	Rosemount dri Brom

R

59	Z 16	Rosemount rd W13
88	K 1	Rosenau rd SW11
90	K 19	Rosendale rd SE21
108	M 1	Rosendale rd SE21
17	V 5	Roseneath av N21
89	O 15	Roseneath rd SW11
8	C 14	Roseneath wlk Enf
12	F 11	Rosen's wlk Edg
93	S 17	Rosenthal rd SE6
92	E 13	Rosenthorpe rd SE15
76	G 8	Roserton st E14
124	E 14	Rosery the Croy
34	C 1	Roses the Wdfd Grn
140	J 8	Rose st WC2
148	K 18	Rosetta st SW8
112	L 9	Roseveare rd SE12
82	G 13	Roseville av Hounsl
118	M 1	Rosevine rd SW20
117	T 10	Rose wlk Surb
159	W 2	Rose wlk W Wkhm
91	P 17	Roseway SE21
82	L 9	Roseway SE12
41	V 17	Rosewood av Grnfd
57	X 15	Rosewood av Hornch
115	S 6	Rosewood clo Sidcp
115	U 13	Rosewood gdns Wallgtn
154	E 2	Rosewood gro Sutton
64	H 1	Rosher clo E15
50	E 16	Rosina st E9
87	O 7	Roskell rd SW15
73	T 8	Roslin rd W3
112	F 14	Roslin way Brom
120	F 3	Roslyn clo Mitch
39	S 7	Roslyn gdns Rom
31	P 15	Roslyn rd N15
136	M 9	Rosmead rd SW11
88	K 2	Rosnau cres SW11
133	T 16	Rosoman st EC1
133	U 15	Rosoman st EC1
39	W 19	Rossall rd Hornch
60	M 9	Rossall cres Wemb
56	A 5	Ross av Dgnhm
14	E 17	Ross av NW7
23	N 1	Ross clo Harrow
154	K 9	Rossdale Sutton
19	O 2	Rossdale dri N9
43	U 4	Rossdale dri NW9
9	O 20	Rossdale dri Enf
N 9		Rossdale rd SW15
94	G 1	Rosse ms SE3
H 12		Rossindel rd Hounsl
49	Y 6	Rossington st E5
107	T 1	Rossiter rd SW12
98	F 13	Rossland clo Bxly Hth
21	O 8	Rosslyn av E4
86	C 8	Rosslyn av SW13
15	W 1	Rosslyn av Barnt
56	D 2	Rosslyn av Dgnhm
23	W 14	Rosslyn cres N Harrow
23	W 14	Rosslyn cres S Harrow
42	J 12	Rosslyn cres Wemb
46	H 14	Rosslyn hill NW3
10	U 14	Rosslyn rd E17
23	S 1	Rosslyn rd Bark
67	S 1	Rosslyn rd Bark
84	D 16	Rosslyn rd Twick
130	L 17	Rossmore rd NW1
131	N 16	Rossmore rd NW1
155	T 12	Ross pde Wallgtn
123	S 4	Ross rd SE25
99	V 17	Ross rd Drtfrd
100	L 2	Ross rd Twick
155	V 12	Ross rd Wallgtn
9	R 7	Ross way SE9
106	G 10	Rostella rd SW17
31	V 19	Rostrevor av N15
70	C 14	Rostrevor gdns S'hall
87	U 2	Rostrevor rd SW6
105	X 13	Rostrevor rd SW19
141	X 20	Rotary st SE1
77	Z 20	Rothbury gdns Islwth
50	M 20	Rothbury rd E9
31	Y 3	Rothbury wlk N17
155	P 10	Rotherfield rd Carsh
9	T 1	Rotherfield rd Enf
134	B 1	Rotherfield st N1
97	Y 16	Rotherhill av SW16
75	R 11	Rotherhithe New rd SE16
151	V 11	Rotherhithe New rd SE16
75	S 10	Rotherhithe Old rd SE16
75	T 2	Rotherhithe st SE16
143	X 18	Rotherhithe st SE16
55	S 1	Rotherhithe tunnel E1
156	E 12	Rothermere rd Croy
61	O 13	Rotherwick hill W5
45	X 2	Rotherwick rd NW11
87	O 7	Rotherwood rd SW15
133	X 4	Rothery st N1
123	P 9	Rothesay av SE25
119	T 2	Rothesay av SW20
41	O 18	Rothesay av Grnfd
85	S 9	Rothesay av Rich
52	L 19	Rothesay av E7
150	H 2	Rothsay st SE1
73	V 9	Rothschild rd W4
108	K 10	Rothschild st SE27
68	G 2	Rothwell gdns Dgnhm
68	G 3	Rothwell rd Dgnhm
131	R 3	Rothwell st NW1
78	E 14	Rotunda clo SE18
151	S 5	Rouel rd SE16
119	X 15	Rougemont av Mrdn
124	G 17	Round gro Croy
110	E 5	Roundhay clo SE23
7	R 3	Roundhedge way Enf
110	B 6	Round hill SE26
7	P 15	Roundhill dri Enf
112	D 6	Roundtable rd Brom
42	A 19	Roundtree rd Wemb
30	M 4	Roundway N17
31	O 3	Roundway N17
35	T 6	Roundway rd Ilf
62	F 2	Roundwood park NW10
44	C 19	Roundwood rd NW10
64	B 11	Rounton rd E3
90	E 20	Roupell rd SW2
108	D 1	Roupell rd SW2
141	U 15	Roupell st SE1
132	B 1	Rousden st NW1
109	R 9	Rouse gdns SE21
88	D 19	Routh rd SW18
151	R 3	Rovel rd SE16
144	K 19	Rowallan rd SW6
19	Z 19	Rowan av E4
121	V 1	Rowan clo SW16
118	A 4	Rowan clo New Mald
72	L 6	Rowan clo W5
121	V 1	Rowan cres SW16
26	F 11	Rowan dri NW4
157	V 4	Rowan gdn Croy
121	V 2	Rowan st SW16
144	F 6	Rowan rd W6
97	Z 8	Rowan rd Bxly Hth
98	A 8	Rowan rd Bxly Hth
72	B 20	Rowan rd Brentf
17	X 11	Rowans the N13
144	F 6	Rowan ter W6
18	B 4	Rowantree clo N21
7	W 9	Rowantree rd N20
18	B 4	Rowantree rd N21
28	E 17	Rowan wlk N2
37	U 11	Rowan way Rom
15	N 5	Rowben clo N20
151	O 10	Rowcross pl SE1
151	O 9	Rowcross st SE1
58	H 2	Rowdell rd Grnfd
20	C 20	Rowden rd E4
110	K 20	Rowden rd Becknhm
89	N 4	Rowditch la SW11
44	K 20	Rowdon av NW10
159	Z 20	Rowdon cres Croy
69	O 1	Rowdown rd Dgnhm
67	Z 7	Rowe gdns Bark
88	J 5	Rowena cres SW11
40	G 9	Rowe wlk Harrow
107	O 2	Rowfant rd SW17
50	H 12	Rowhill rd E5
129	X 19	Rowington clo W2
24	E 11	Rowland av Harrow
65	O 12	Rowland ct E1
18	A 20	Rowland Hill av N17
46	J 14	Rowland Hill st NW3
22	J 1	Rowlands av Pinn
26	F 2	Rowlands gro NW7
56	B 8	Rowlands st Dgnhm
106	A 20	Rowland way SW19
97	P 19	Rowley av Sidcp
43	N 20	Rowley clo Wemb
61	N 1	Rowley gdns N4
30	L 16	Rowley rd N15
117	O 5	Rowlls rd Kingst
55	S 18	Rowney rd Dgnhm
55	R 18	Rowney rd Dgnhm
101	S 1	Rowntree rd Twick
64	G 2	Rowse clo E15
26	L 9	Rowsley av NW4
47	Z 16	Rowstock gdns N7
79	P 18	Rowton rd SE18
41	S 1	Roxborough av Harrow
71	W 19	Roxborough av Islwth
23	S 20	Roxborough pk Harrow
41	T 2	Roxborough pk Harrow
40	A 19	Roxborough Grnfd
40	A 19	Roxbourne clo Grnfd
40	A 4	Roxbourne park Rom
108	H 11	Roxburgh rd SE27
145	V 13	Roxby pl SW6
25	O 9	Roxden clo NW9
40	L 7	Roxeth Green av Harrow
40	A 10	Roxeth gro Harrow
41	R 6	Roxeth hill Harrow
93	S 16	Roxley rd SE13
159	N 12	Roxton gdns Croy
74	G 5	Roxwell rd W12
68	B 7	Roxwell rd Bark
34	M 1	Roxwell way Wdfd Grn
37	S 20	Roxy av Rom
140	B 11	Royal Academy W1
138	E 20	Royal Albert hall SW7
81	U 12	Royal Alfred home Blvdr
140	A 11	Royal arcade W1
147	O 9	Royal av SW3
83	B 3	Royal av Worc Pk
84	K 5	Royal Botanic gardens Rich
108	H 7	Royal cir SE27
47	U 20	Royal College st NW1
132	C 3	Royal College st NW1
152	A 3	Royal clo Worc Pk
136	J 15	Royal cres W11
40	A 11	Royal cres Ruis
136	H 15	Royal Cres ms W11
43	O 13	Royal ct Wemb
160	G 6	Royal Exchange bldgs EC2
141	O 14	Royal Festival Hall SE1
76	G 19	Royal hill SE10
76	F 20	Royal hill SE10
147	P 12	Royal Hospital rd SW3
78	F 14	Royal Military repository SE18
143	P 9	Royal Mint EC3
143	P 9	Royal Mint st E1
76	H 16	Royal Naval College SE10
49	Y 18	Royal Oak rd E8
98	C 12	Royal Oak rd Bxly Hth
76	K 19	Royal Observatory SE10
140	F 13	Royal Opera arcade SW4
94	B 5	Royal pde SE3
60	K 10	Royal pde W5
114	C 19	Royal pde Chisl
76	G 20	Royal pl SE10
65	Z 18	Royal rd E16
66	A 19	Royal rd E16
149	W 14	Royal rd SE17
115	V 6	Royal rd Sidcp
101	R 15	Royal rd Tedd
141	P 20	Royal rd Wallgtn
63	T 6	Royal Victor pl E3
155	S 4	Royal wlk Wallgtn
67	X 7	Roycraft av Bark
67	X 6	Roycraft clo Bark
67	X 6	Roycraft gdns Bark
34	H 5	Roycroft clo E18
79	N 14	Roydene rd SE18
36	J 14	Roy gdns Ilf
100	K 14	Roy gro Hampt
39	Y 17	Royle clo Rom
79	Y 12	Royle cres W13
20	C 17	Royston av E4
154	G 5	Royston av Sutton
155	Y 8	Royston av Wallgtn
35	N 19	Royston gdns Ilf
154	F 5	Royston park Sutton
124	F 1	Royston rd SE20
110	F 20	Royston rd Becknhm
99	S 15	Royston rd Drtfrd
84	L 14	Royston rd Rich
11	S 11	Roystons the Surb
63	P 7	Royston st E2
63	R 8	Royston st E2
89	U 6	Rozel rd SW4
110	M 5	Rubens st SE6
9	Y 11	Ruberoid rd Enf
33	O 10	Ruby rd E17
151	W 15	Ruby st SE15
55	S 10	Ruckholt clo E10
51	N 12	Ruckholt rd E10
22	E 6	Rucklidge av NW10
46	F 12	Rudall cres NW3
75	W 19	Ruddigore rd SE14
79	N 11	Rudd st SE18
98	H 8	Rudland rd Bxly Hth
89	U 17	Rudloe rd SW12
65	R 7	Rudolph rd E13
12	H 18	Rudyard gro NW7
157	Z 15	Ruffetts clo S Croy
158	A 16	Ruffetts the S Croy
23	Z 19	Rufford clo Harrow
132	K 3	Rufford st N1
40	A 10	Rufus dri Ruis
40	A 10	Rufus clo Ruis
134	J 14	Rufus st EC1
18	G 5	Rugby av N9
41	S 17	Rugby av Grnfd
42	C 14	Rugby av Wemb
23	S 14	Rugby clo Harrow
55	S 19	Rugby gdns Dgnhm
153	P 20	Rugby la Sutton
25	S 12	Rugby rd NW9
73	Z 6	Rugby rd W4
38	U 15	Rugby rd Dgnhm
83	U 15	Rugby rd Twick
133	N 19	Rugby st WC1
58	K 11	Ruislip clo Grnfd
59	P 11	Ruislip rd East Grnfd
58	L 11	Ruislip rd Grnfd
106	M 9	Ruislip rd SW17
145	Y 19	Rumbold rd SW6
75	O 2	Rum clo E1
143	Z 10	Rum clo E1
100	E 15	Rumsey clo Hampt
90	D 7	Rumsley rd SW9
43	Y 6	Runbury cir NW9
136	J 9	Runcorn pl W11
26	J 17	Rundell cres NW4
41	T 10	Runnefield Harrow
141	W 14	Running Horse yd
106	F 20	Runnymede SW19
82	L 17	Runnymede clo Twick
107	Z 20	Runnymede cres SW16
59	T 6	Runnymede gdns Grnfd
82	K 17	Runnymede gdns Twick
82	L 16	Runnymede rd Twick
75	P 6	Rupack st SE16
42	K 16	Rupert av Wemb
140	F 9	Rupert ct W1
90	J 6	Rupert gdns SW9
129	R 10	Rupert rd NW6
74	B 9	Rupert rd W4
140	E 8	Rupert st W1
107	T 17	Rural way SW16
65	P 17	Ruscoe rd E16
152	F 1	Rush ct Worc Pk
88	M 17	Rusham rd SW12
89	N 17	Rusham rd SW12
32	M 6	Rushbrook cres E17
114	A 5	Rushbrook rd SE9
33	P 1	Rushcroft dri E4
33	R 1	Rushcrof rd E4
90	F 11	Rushcroft rd SW2
109	P 18	Rushden clo SE19
80	G 9	Rushdene SE2
15	X 3	Rushdene av Barnt
14	A 18	Rushden gdns NW7
35	X 10	Rushden gdns Ilf
120	G 19	Rushen wlk Carsh
116	A 19	Rushett clo Surb
116	A 18	Rushett rd Surb
117	X 10	Rushey clo New Mald
93	S 18	Rushey grn SE6
7	P 15	Rushey hill Enf
93	O 14	Rushey mead SE4
92	M 16	Rushford rd SE4
158	L 3	Rush Green gdns
156	K 4	Rush Green rd Rom
26	D 13	Rushgrove av NW9
78	H 12	Rush Gro st SE18
89	P 8	Rush Hill rd SW11
102	B 8	Rushmead Rich
157	U 8	Rushmead clo Croy
12	G 7	Rushmead clo Edg
127	R 7	Rushmore clo Brom
50	E 12	Rushmore cres E5
50	C 12	Rushmore rd E5
56	E 9	Rusholme av Dgnhm
87	R 13	Rusholme rd SW15
24	A 19	Rushout av Harrow
134	G 8	Rushton st N1
26	G 11	Rushworth av NW4
26	G 12	Rushworth gdns NW4
141	Y 18	Rushworth st SE1
53	T 17	Ruskin av E12
73	R 20	Ruskin av Rich
97	N 6	Ruskin av Welling
28	A 18	Ruskin clo NW11
97	N 6	Ruskin dri Welling
152	L 2	Ruskin dri Worc Pk

60 F 11	Ruskin gdns W5
24 M 15	Ruskin gdns Harrow
25 N 13	Ruskin gdns Harrow
39 Y 4	Ruskin gdns Rom
97 N 6	Ruskin gro Welling
31 U 4	Ruskin rd N17
81 R 11	Ruskin rd Blvdr
155 O 11	Ruskin rd Carsh
156 K 2	Ruskin rd Croy
83 V 8	Ruskin rd Islwth
58 A 20	Ruskin rd S'hall
18 J 8	Ruskin wlk N9
90 L 14	Ruskin wlk SE24
127 T 13	Ruskin wlk Brom
120 F 1	Ruskin wy SW19
23 T 14	Rusland Pk rd Harrow
11 S 14	Rusper clo Stanm
30 L 9	Rusper rd N22
55 U 18	Rusper rd Dgnhm
30 H 8	Russell av N22
61 V 1	Russell clo NW10
125 S 5	Russell clo Becknhm
98 D 10	Russell clo Bxly Hth
99 W 9	Russell clo Drtfrd
77 W 19	Russell clo SE7
140 B 15	Russell ct SW1
15 X 8	Russell gdns N20
27 T 19	Russell gdns NW11
144 L 1	Russell gdns W14
102 C 4	Russell gdns Rich
136 K 20	Russell Gdns ms W14
13 N 14	Russell gro NW7
15 X 8	Russell la N20
16 A 6	Russell la N20
23 V 2	Russell mead Harrow
148 F 9	Russell pl SW1
19 X 14	Russell rd E4
33 R 20	Russell rd E10
65 U 17	Russell rd E16
32 K 11	Russell rd E17
17 O 18	Russell rd N13
31 R 16	Russell rd N15
15 X 7	Russell rd N20
26 E 19	Russell rd NW9
105 X 17	Russell rd SW19
144 M 2	Russell rd W14
21 X 6	Russell rd Buck Hl
21 Y 6	Russell rd Buck Hl
8 G 3	Russell rd Enf
41 N 13	Russell rd Grnfd
120 K 6	Russell rd Mitch
83 V 17	Russell rd Twick
108 C 12	Russells footpath SW16
132 J 19	Russell sq WC1
140 M 8	Russell st WC2
26 E 19	Russel rd NW9
48 C 14	Russet cres N7
20 J 13	Russets clo E4
160 C 5	Russia ct EC2
63 O 6	Russia la E2
135 Z 8	Russia la E2
73 Y 8	Russia row EC2
124 C 13	Rusthall av W4
107 T 17	Rusthall clo Croy
42 F 11	Rustic pl Wemb
119 V 16	Rustington wlk Mrdn
117 S 17	Ruston av Surb
136 K 5	Ruston ms W11
63 Z 3	Ruston st E3
150 D 17	Rust sq SE5
108 A 12	Rutford rd SW16
24 M 11	Ruth clo Stanm
154 F 13	Rutherford clo Sutton
148 F 4	Rutherford st SW1
10 D 5 ·	Rutherford way Bushey Watf
79 Z 15	Rutherglen rd SE2
152 G 14	Rutherwyke clo Epsom
77 T 16	Ruthin rd SE3
63 T 3	Ruthven st E9
97 N 18	Rutland av Sidcp
85 U 7	Rutland clo SW14
106 H 16	Rutland clo SW19
115 W 3	Rutland clo Bxly
119 W 15	Rutland dri Mrdn
30 J 18	Rutland gdns N4
138 L 19	Rutland gdns SW7
59 Y 15	Rutland gdns W13
157 T 9	Rutland gdns Croy
55 S 14	Rutland gdns Dgnhm
138 L 19	Rutland Gdns ms SW7
138 K 19	Rutland ga SW7
14 U 14	Rutland ga Blvdr
126 D 9	Rutland ga Brom
138 K 20	Rutlnd Ga ms SW7
74 K 14	Rutland gro W6
144 A 10	Rutland gro W6

146 K 1	Rutland Ms south SW7
146 K 1	Rutland ms W SW7
45 N 18	Rutland pk NW2
110 H 5	Rutland pk SE6
63 S 3	Rutland rd E9
34 J 14	Rutland rd E11
53 N 20	Rutland rd E12
33 O 18	Rutland rd E17
106 J 16	Rutland rd SW19
9 N 18	Rutland rd Enf
23 N 18	Rutland rd Harrow
53 Z 11	Rutland rd Ilf
54 A 11	Rutland rd Ilf
58 G 14	Rutland rd S'hall
101 P 4	Rutland rd Twick
146 K 1	Rutland st SW7
110 M 4	Rutland wlk SE6
105 Y 20	Rutlish rd SW19
120 E 9	Rutter gdns Mitch
92 E 4	Rutts ter SE14
10 D 5	Rutts the Bushey Watf
87 O 7	Ruvigny gdns SW15
115 X 15	Ruxley clo Sidcp
115 X 16	Ruxley corner Sidcp
94 J 10	Ryan clo SE9
91 W 18	Rycott path SE22
94 C 4	Ryculff sq SE3
27 R 5	Rydal clo NW4
60 C 7	Rydal cres Grnfd
98 H 3	Rydal dri Bxly Hth
26 B 15	Rydal gdns NW9
104 A 12	Rydal gdns SW15
82 K 16	Rydal gdns Hounsl
42 E 3	Rydal gdns Wemb
107 X 11	Rydal rd SW16
9 R 19	Rydal way Enf
84 F 15	Ryde pl Twick
112 H 13	Ryder clo Brom
140 B 13	Ryder ct SW1
66 K 17	Ryder gdns E6
57 U 18	Ryder gdns Rainhm
130 · A 8	Ryders ter NW8
140 C 13	Ryder st SW1
140 C 12	Ryder yd SW1
107 T 3	Rydevale rd SW12
95 P 7	Rydons clo SE9
134 C 4	Rydon st N1
48 B 20	Rydston clo N7
98 G 15	Rye clo Bxly
109 S 1	Ryecotes mead SE21
35 Z 7	Ryecroft av Ilf
82 L 20	Ryecroft av Twick
100 L 2	Ryecroft N1
93 V 13	Ryecroft rd SE13
108 G 15	Ryecroft rd SW16
87 Z 3	Ryecroft rd SW6
31 V 10	Ryecroft way N17
91 Z 19	Ryedale SE22
108 M 15	Ryefield rd SE19
92 B 11	Rye Hill pk SE15
91 X 3	Rye la SE15
92 E 12	Rye rd SE15
16 J 2	Rye the N14
12 A 19	Rye way Edg
87 P 14	Rye wlk SW15
105 X 6	Ryfold rd SW19
16 F 13	Ryhope rd N11
47 S 17	Rylandes rd NW2
47 S 17	Ryland rd NW5
94 J 16	Rylands cres SE12
74 D 7	Rylett cres W12
74 F 8	Rylett rd W12
18 A 11	Rylston rd N13
145 O 16	Rylston rd SW6
88 B 12	Rymer rd SW18
123 T 17	Rymer rd Croy
90 J 15	Rymer st SE24
78 J 4	Rymill st E16
139 O 20	Rysbrack st SW3

S

65 O 18	Sabbarton st E16
89 N 7	Sabine rd SW8
88 M 7	Sabine rd SW11
48 J 20	Sable st N1
50 A 6	Sach rd E5
126 E 19	Sackville av Brom
41 P 10	Sackville clo Harrow
53 T 3	Sackville gdns Ilf
153 X 17	Sackville rd Sutton
140 B 11	Sackville st W1
14 K 16	Saddlescombe way N12
120 L 3	Sadler clo Mitch
112 H 4	Sadstone rd SE12
27 V 17	Saffron clo NW11

133 U 19	Saffron hill EC1
141 V 1	Saffron hill EC1
38 L 7	Saffron rd Rom
133 U 19	Saffron st EC1
66 A 18	Sagasso clo E16
149 P 4	Sail st SE11
107 P 4	Sainfoin rd SW17
109 R 12	Sainsbury rd SE19
97 O 3	St Abb's st Welling
103 N 16	St Agathas clo Kingst
63 P 4	St Agnes clo E9
149 V 15	St Agnes pl SE11
91 Z 14	St Aidans rd SE22
72 C 6	St Aidan's rd W13
101 Z 12	St Alban's gdns Tedd
66 J 9	St Alban's av E6
73 Y 10	St Albans Av W4
30 F 6	St Albans cres N22
34 E 3	St Albans cres Wdfd Grn
145 Z 1	St Alban's gro W8
146 A 1	St Alban's gro W8
120 K 18	St Alban's gro Carsh
45 Y 4	St Alban's la NW11
138 N 1	St Albans ms W2
133 V 5	St Alban's pl N1
47 P 9	St Alban's rd NW5
62 A 3	St Alban's rd NW10
4 C 4	St Albans rd Barnt
54 K 2	St Alban's rd Ilf
102 K 16	St Alban's rd Kingst
153 U 9	St Alban's rd Sutton
34 D 3	St Alban's rd Wdfd Grn
140 F 12	St Albans st SW1
144 K 12	St Alban's ter W6
37 W 15	St Aldrew's av Hornch
76 G 17	St Alfege pas SE10
78 B 15	St Alfege rd SE7
142 C 2	St Alphage gdn EC2
160 C 2	St Alphage gdn EC2
19 O 3	St Alphage rd N9
25 W 7	St Alphage wlk Edgw
89 W 11	St Alphonsus rd SW4
8 C 12	St Andrew rd Enf
41 Y 12	St Andrew's av Wemb
15 P 13	St Andrew's clo N12
44 J 10	St Andrew's clo NW2
24 E 7	St Andrew's clo Stanm
41 Y 11	St Andrew's clo Wemb
106 C 3	St Andrews ct SW18
24 E 5	St Andrews dri Stanm
49 O 4	St Andrew's gro N16
141 Y 7	St Andrews hill EC4
49 R 3	St Andrew's ms N16
131 X 16	St Andrew's pl NW1
63 N 4	St Andrews rd E2
33 Z 19	St Andrews rd E11
32 G 9	St Andrew's rd E17
19 P 4	St Andrew's rd N9
43 X 5	St Andrew's rd NW9
44 J 19	St Andrew's rd NW10
27 W 19	St Andrew's rd NW11
62 B 18	St Andrew's rd W3
71 S 5	St Andrew's rd W7
144 M 12	St Andrews rd W14
154 K 4	St Andrew's rd Carsh
156 L 8	St Andrew's rd Croy
53 U 1	St Andrew's rd Ilf
39 O 18	St Andrews rd Rom
115 X 7	St Andrews rd Sidcp
115 Y 18	St Andrew's rd Surb
116 F 14	St Andrew's sq Surb
136 J 6	St Andrews Sq W11
141 V 3	St Andrew st EC4
47 P 8	St Annes clo N6
140 E 6	St Annes ct W1
60 L 8	St Annes gdns Wemb
63 Y 19	St Annes pas E14
51 V 5	St Annes rd E11
42 H 15	St Anne's rd Wemb
63 Z 18	St Anne's row E14
63 Z 18	St Anne st E18
31 T 18	St Ann's clo N15
88 C 15	St Ann's cres SW18
47 O 18	St Ann's gdns NW5
88 C 17	St Ann's hill SW18
48 G 2	St Anns la SW1
88 C 17	St Ann's Pk rd SW18
86 C 7	St Anns pas SW13
30 B 13	St Anns rd N8
18 G 7	St Ann's rd N9
30 J 16	St Ann's rd N15
86 D 3	St Ann's rd SW13

136 H 13	St Ann's rd W11
23 U 18	St Ann's rd Harrow
148 G 1	St Ann's st Bark
67 R 4	St Ann's st Bark
130 G 8	St Ann's ter NW8
136 J 14	St Anns vlls W11
156 K 14	St Ann's way Croy
139 V 7	St Anselm's pl W1
34 K 1	St Anthony's av Wdfd Grn
106 J 4	St Anthony's clo SW17
65 U 1	St Anthony's rd E15
52 G 20	St Anthony's rd E7
157 T 5	St Arvan's clo Croy
92 F 7	St Asaph rd SE4
105 U 12	St Aubyn's av SW19
82 G 14	St Aubyn's av Hounsl
109 T 16	St Aubyn's st SE19
98 F 4	St Audrey av Bxly Hth
60 L 7	St Augustine's av W5
127 R 12	St Augustine's av Brom
156 L 15	St Augustine's av S Croy
42 K 9	St Augustine's av Wemb
47 V 19	St Augustine's rd NW1
81 P 9	St Augustine's rd Blvdr
24 M 8	St Austell clo Edg
93 V 4	St Austell rd SE10
67 S 2	St Awdry's rd Bark
67 P 1	St Awdrys wlk Bark
125 T 3	St Barnabas clo Becknhm
33 N 18	St Barnabas rd E17
107 P 18	St Barnabas rd Mitch
154 F 10	St Barnabas rd Sutton
21 X 20	St Barnabas rd Wdfd Grn
34 J 2	St Barnabas rd Wdfd Grn
147 V 10	St Barnabas st SW1
41 S 1	St Barnabas vlls SW8
66 F 5	St Bartholomews rd E6
133 Z 19	St Barts Medical School EC1
107 P 13	St Benedicts clo SW17
106 J 4	St Benet clo SW17
120 C 18	St Benet's gro Carsh
66 B 4	St Bernard's rd E6
52 Y 2	St Bernards Croy
126 G 3	St Blaise av Brom
143 N 5	St Botolph st EC3
24 M 5	St Bride's av Edg
141 W 7	St Bride's pas EC4
141 V 5	St Bride's st EC4
15 C 17	St Catherines clo SW17
9 F 5	St Catherines dri SE14
20 B 9	St Catherines rd E4
55 Y 1	St Chads gdns Rom
37 V 18	St Chads park Rom
132 M 11	St Chad's pl WC1
37 X 20	St Chad's rd Rom
132 L 12	St Chad's st WC1
136 K 2	St Charles pl W10
136 H 2	St Charles sq W10
128 J 20	St Charles sq W10
83 R 2	St Christophers clo Islwth
139 V 5	St Christopher's pl W1
152 J 7	St Clair dri Worc Pk
35 V 7	St Claire clo Ilf
37 V 18	St Clair rd E13
157 S 3	St Clairs rd Croy
143 N 7	St Clare st EC3
160 G 8	St Clement's ct EC3
141 P 6	St Clement's la WC2
48 E 19	St Clement st N7
109 N 9	St Cloud rd SE27
58 F 16	St Crispin's clo S'hall
133 U 20	St Cross st EC1
22 F 1	St Cuthberts gdns Pinn
45 U 17	St Cuthbert's rd NW2
106 L 10	St Cyprians's st SW17
125 S 18	St David's clo W Wkhm
43 V 10	St David's clo Wemb
24 M 4	St David's dri Edg
26 J 20	St David's pl NW4
109 N 9	St Denis rd SE27

R
S

Page	Ref	Name
87	W 3	St Dionis rd SW6
92	K 3	St Donatts rd SE14
61	Y 18	St Dunstans av W3
141	U 6	St Dunstans ct EC4
61	Y 19	St Dunstan's gdns W3
142	J 10	St Dunstans hill EC3
153	T 11	St Dunstan's hill Sutton
125	T 13	St Dunstan's la Becknhm
52	K 16	St Dunstan's rd E7
123	V 8	St Dunstan's rd SE25
144	F 12	St Dunstan's rd W6
71	T 6	St Dunstan's rd W7
106	J 4	St Edmunds clo SW17
131	N 6	St Edmunds clo NW8
23	Z 4	St Edmunds dri Stanm
24	A 4	St Edmunds dri Stanm
82	K 19	St Edmund's la Twick
18	J 3	St Edmund's rd N9
35	V 19	St Edmunds rd Ilf
130	M 7	St Edmund's ter NW8
131	N 5	St Edmund's ter NW8
27	X 19	St Edwards clo NW11
39	O 15	St Edward's way Rom
20	F 5	St Egberts way E4
74	E 5	St Elmo rd W12
67	R 2	St Erkenwald rd Bark
140	E 20	St Ermins hill SW1
129	N 20	St Ervan's rd W10
137	O 1	St Ervan's rd W10
7	Z 4	St Faiths clo Enf
108	J 2	St Faith's rd SE21
93	V 20	St Fillans rd SE6
45	P 15	St Gabriel's rd NW2
52	J 20	St George's av E7
47	X 11	St George's av N7
25	W 12	St George's av NW9
72	F 5	St Georges av W5
70	E 1	St George's av S'hall
141	W 20	St George's cir SE1
27	U 19	St George's clo NW11
41	Z 10	St Georges clo Wemb
66	G 10	St George ct E6
147	Y 7	St George's dri SW1
148	B 9	St George's dri SW1
96	F 6	St Georges gro SW17
130	H 9	St Georges la EC3
131	P 2	St George's ms NW1
52	H 19	St George's rd E7
51	U 8	St George's rd E10
18	L 10	St George's rd N9
17	P 9	St Georges rd N13
27	V 18	St George's rd NW11
149	X 3	St George's rd SE1
105	U 16	St George's rd SW19
73	Z 6	St George's rd W4
71	W 3	St George's rd W7
125	P 1	St George's rd Becknhm
127	T 6	St George's rd Brom
55	Y 14	St Georges rd Dgnhm
56	A 12	St Georges rd Dgnhm
8	G 3	St Georges rd Enf
100	A 10	St George's rd Felt
53	T 1	St George's rd Ilf
103	O 19	St George's rd Mitch
121	S 6	St George's rd Mitch
85	N 9	St George's rd Rich
115	X 14	St George's rd Sidcp
84	B 13	St George's rd Twick
155	R 11	St George's rd Wallgtn
127	S 2	St George's rd West Brom
52	J 20	St George's sq E7
148	D 10	St George's sq SW1
148	E 11	St George's sq SW1
148	E 11	St George's Sq ms SW1
75	X 10	St George's stairs SE16
131	P 2	St Georges ter NW8
139	Z 8	St George st W1
156	M 4	St George's wlk Croy
150	K 15	St George's way SE15
151	O 15	St George's way SE15
148	F 13	St George's Wharf SW1
94	E 2	St German's pl SE3
92	J 20	St Germans rd SE23
56	H 19	St Giles av Dgnhm
56	H 19	St Giles clo Dgnhm
140	H 5	St Giles High st WC2
140	H 6	St Giles pas WC2
91	R 1	St Giles rd SE5
150	H 20	St Giles rd SE5
109	N 10	St Gothard rd SE27
133	S 13	St Helena st WC1
122	O 1	St Helen's cres SW16
136	G 4	St Helen's gdns W10
142	J 5	St Helen's pl EC3
75	R 12	St Helen's rd SE16
122	D 2	St Helen's rd W13
72	C 2	St Helen's rd W13
35	U 19	St Helens rd Ilf
80	J 5	St Helens rd SE2
120	C 13	St Helier av Mrdn
82	G 14	St Heliers av Hounsl
33	T 19	St Heliers rd E10
128	H 4	St Hildas clo NW6
74	H 16	St Hildas rd SW13
109	Z 19	St Hugh's rd SE20
39	V 12	St Ivians dri Rom
92	J 2	St James' SE14
71	Y 3	St James av W13
124	J 6	St James av Becknhm
106	L 3	St James clo SW17
90	G 7	St James cres SW9
136	J 13	St James gdns W11
88	M 4	St James gro SW11
140	E 11	St James mkt SW1
140	F 18	St James park SW1
18	M 9	St James rd N9
151	U 11	St James rd SE1
107	P 19	St James rd Mitch
116	G 13	St James rd Surb
115	Z 19	St James way Sidcp
63	R 6	St James'av E3
15	N 11	St James'av N20
15	W 11	St James'av N20
100	M 13	St James'av Hampt
153	X 10	St James'av Sutton
15	W 12	St James clo N20
79	N 13	St James's clo SE18
118	C 12	St James's clo New Mald
84	J 12	St James's ct Rich
106	L 2	St James's dri SW17
60	J 1	St James's gdns Wemb
29	S 12	St James's la N10
140	B 15	St James's palace SW1
122	L 17	St James's pk Croy
140	B 14	St James's pl SW1
9	U 18	St James's pl Enf
52	C 15	St James's rd E7
151	T 1	St James's rd SE16
154	K 5	St James's rd Carsh
123	O 19	St James's rd Croy
100	L 12	St James's rd Hampt
116	H 14	St James's rd Kingst
153	Y 13	St James's rd Sutton
140	D 13	St James's sq SW1
140	B 13	St James's st SW1
74	M 14	St James's st W6
144	C 11	St James's st W6
131	N 7	St James's ter NW1
131	N 6	St James's Ter ms NW8
133	W 16	St James's wlk EC1
133	V 17	St James's wlk EC1
18	H 7	St Joans rd N9
15	Z 18	St John's av N11
62	D 3	St John's av NW10
87	P 13	St Johns av W5
50	S 5	St John's Church rd E9
42	K 15	St John's clo Wemb
21	X 5	St Johns ct Buck Hl
83	V 5	St John's ct Islwth
90	F 7	St John's cres SW9
110	C 18	St John's cts SE20
148	H 4	St John's gdns SW1
136	M 11	St John's gdns W11
137	N 11	St John's gdns W11
47	W 8	St John's gro N19
84	J 9	St John's gro Rich
88	H 11	St John's hill SW11
88	F 11	St John's Hill gro SW11
133	X 19	St John's la EC1
133	X 7	St Johns ms W11
57	S 20	St Johns pk SE3
133	X 19	St Johns path EC1
133	W 19	St John's pl EC1
20	E 13	St John's rd E4
66	E 4	St John's rd E6
65	S 17	St John's rd E16
33	T 9	St John's rd E17
19	N 11	St John's rd N15
27	W 19	St Johns rd NW11
110	C 16	St John's rd SE20
88	K 10	St John's rd SW11
105	R 16	St John's rd SW19
67	U 5	St John's rd Bark
154	K 5	St John's rd Carsh
156	J 5	St John's rd Croy
100	C 10	St John's rd Felt
23	V 18	St John's rd Harrow
36	H 20	St John's rd Ilf
54	G 1	St John's rd Ilf
83	W 5	St John's rd Islwth
116	E 2	St John's rd Kingst
117	V 7	St John's rd New Mald
84	K 10	St John's rd Rich
115	P 10	St John's rd Sidcp
70	B 8	St John's rd S'hall
153	Z 3	St John's rd Sutton
97	P 8	St John's rd Welling
42	H 13	St John's rd Wemb
133	W 15	St John's sq EC1
52	J 17	St Johns ter E7
79	R 15	St John's ter SE18
128	H 15	St John's ter W10
8	B 1	St John's ter Enf
133	W 19	St John st EC1
93	O 4	St John's vale SE4
47	X 5	St John's vlls N19
47	X 4	St John's way N19
130	G 7	St John's Wood barrack NW8
130	K 11	St John's Wood High st NW8
130	G 14	St Johns Wood rd NW8
130	J 8	St John's Wood ter NW8
130	G 3	St John's Wood pk NW8
70	D 3	St Joseph's dri S'hall
30	B 13	St Josephs rd N8
19	O 5	St Joseph rd N9
89	S 1	St Joseph's st SW8
63	N 7	St Jude's rd E2
135	X 11	St Judes rd E2
49	S 16	St Jude st N16
108	F 11	St Julian's clo SW16
108	H 9	St Julian's Farm rd SE27
129	S 3	St Julians rd NW6
131	W 8	St Katherine's precinct NW1
80	J 6	St Katherines rd SE2
143	O 12	St Katharine's wy E1
113	S 10	St Keverne rd SE9
71	Z 4	St Kilda rd W13
49	O 4	St Kilda's rd N16
23	S 18	St Kilda's rd Harrow
24	M 1	St Lawrence clo Edgw
76	H 1	St Lawrence st E14
136	L 2	St Lawrence st W10
20	L 18	St Leonards av E4
24	C 15	St Leonards av Harrow
97	O 8	St Leonard's clo Welling
82	A 1	St Leonards gdns Hounsl
54	B 16	St Leonards gdns Ilf
64	G 18	St Leonard's rd E14
61	Z 11	St Leonard's rd NW17
85	U 8	St Leonards rd SW14
60	C 19	St Leonard's rd W13
156	H 6	St Leonards rd Croy
116	F 12	St Leonard's rd Surb
47	P 18	St Leonards sq NW5
147	O 11	St Leonards ter SW3
147	P 10	St Leonards ter SW3
108	C 18	St Leonard's wk SW16
146	M 14	St Loo av SW3
90	N 10	St Louis rd SE27
31	T 9	St Loys rd N17
89	X 10	St Luke's av SW4
8	B 3	St Luke's av Enf
53	Z 15	St Luke's av Ilf
124	A 14	St Lukes clo SE25
137	P 4	St Lukes ms W11
102	L 20	St Luke's pas Kingst
137	P 3	St Lukes rd W11
65	P 17	St Luke's sq E16
146	K 9	St Luke's st SW3
129	O 11	St Luke's yd W9
19	O 9	St Malo av N9
67	R 3	St Margarets Bark
30	J 13	St Margaret's av N15
15	R 6	St Margaret's av N20
40	M 8	St Margaret's av Harrow
114	E 6	St Margaret's av Sidcp
153	S 5	St Margaret's av Sutton
86	K 13	St Margaret's cres SW15
84	B 12	St Margaret's dri Twick
79	O 15	St Margaret's gro SE18
83	Z 15	St Margaret's gro Twick
84	A 15	St Margaret's gro Twick
93	Z 9	St Margaret's pas SE13
52	L 7	St Margaret's rd E12
31	S 9	St Margaret's rd N17
62	L 8	St Margaret's rd NW10
128	A 11	St Margaret's rd NW10
124	F 9	St Margaret's rd Becknhm
12	E 17	St Margaret's rd Edg
84	A 13	St Margaret's rd Twick
92	L 11	St Margaret's sq SE4
79	P 14	St Margaret's ter SE18
140	K 19	St Mark's clo SW1
5	N 13	St Mark's clo Barnt
131	U 4	St Mark's cres NW1
63	Y 1	St Mark's ga E9
116	K 13	St Mark's hill Surb
105	V 15	St Marks pl SW19
138	M 6	St Mark's pl W11
49	V 15	St Mark's ri E8
123	Z 9	St Mark's rd SE25
72	K 5	St Marks rd W5
71	T 5	St Mark's rd W7
128	F 20	St Mark's rd W11
136	G 2	St Mark's rd W11
126	G 7	St Marks rd Brom
8	H 19	St Mark's rd Enf
121	N 4	St Mark's rd Mitch
102	B 17	St Mark's rd Tedd
131	T 5	St Mark's sq NW1
143	P 7	St Mark st E1
66	A 7	St Martin's av E6
132	A 4	St Martin's clo NW1
8	M 5	St Martin's clo Enf
140	H 9	St Martin's ct WC2
140	J 9	St Martin's la WC2
142	A 4	St Martin's Le Grand EC1
160	A 4	St Martins Le Grand EC1
140	H 11	St Martin's pl WC2
18	M 8	St Martin's rd N9
90	C 4	St Martin's rd SW9
140	G 11	St Martin's rd WC2
106	C 8	St Martin's wy SW17
145	P 3	St Mary Abbot's pl W8
145	P 2	St Mary Abbots ter W14
142	J 10	St Mary At hill EC3
155	R 6	St Mary av Wallgtn
142	K 4	St Mary axe EC3
75	P 5	St Marychurch st SE16
143	Z 18	St Mary Ch st SE16
33	P 14	St Mary rd E17
67	S 5	St Marys Bark
63	T 16	St Mary's appr E12
34	H 20	St Mary's av N3
27	U 7	St Mary's av N3
125	Z 6	St Mary's av Brom
126	A 7	St Mary's av Brom
70	K 11	St Mary's av S'hall
101	W 15	St Mary's av Tedd
31	W 6	St Marys clo N17
152	E 17	St Mary's clo Epsom
62	F 5	St Marys ct W5
66	G 10	St Marys cres E6
26	J 11	St Marys cres NW4
71	R 19	St Marys cres Islwth
149	U 5	St Marys gdns SE11
48	K 19	St Mary's gro SW13
86	J 18	St Mary's gro SW13
73	T 17	St Mary's gro W4
85	N 11	St Mary's gro Rich
129	X 2	St Marys gro Rich
133	X 4	St Mary's path N1
51	U 8	St Mary's rd E10
30	B 14	St Mary's rd N8
19	O 5	St Mary's rd N9
62	C 2	St Mary's rd NW10

S

Ref	Name
27 S 20	St Mary's rd NW11
92 C 3	St Mary's rd SE15
123 R 7	St Mary's rd SE25
105 U 13	St Mary's rd SW19
72 G 5	St Mary's rd W5
15 Y 3	St Mary's rd Barnt
54 D 8	St Mary's rd Ilf
116 E 18	St Mary's rd Surb
152 C 3	St Mary's rd Worc Pk
138 F 1	St Mary's sq W2
138 E 1	St Marys ter W2
78 H 10	St Mary st SE18
149 U 5	St Marys wlk SE11
116 K 19	St Matthew's av Surb
127 U 6	St Matthew's dri Brom
90 E 12	St Matthew's rd SW2
72 K 3	St Matthews rd W5
135 S 15	St Matthew's row E2
148 F 2	St Matthew st SW1
26 D 15	St Matthias clo NW9
87 V 2	St Maur rd SW6
79 S 18	St Merryn clo SE18
15 V 16	St Michael clo N12
19 R 4	St Michael's av N9
43 R 17	St Michael's av Wemb
93 Z 9	St Michael's clo SE13
127 P 6	St Michael's clo Brom
22 C 18	St Michael's cres Pinn
128 K 1	St Michael's gdns W10
44 L 12	St Michael's rd NW2
90 C 4	St Michael's rd SW9
122 M 20	St Michael's rd Croy
156 M 1	St Michael's rd Croy
155 V 2	St Michael's rd Wallgtn
97 P 8	St Michael's rd Welling
138 J 3	St Michaels st W2
30 B 6	St Michaels ter N13
160 E 6	St Mildred's ct EC2
24 C 19	St Mildred's rd SE12
57 X 11	St Nicholas av Hornch
107 N 13	St Nicholas glebe SW17
127 S 1	St Nicholas la Chisl
79 Y 12	St Nicholas rd SE18
154 B 11	St Nicholas rd Sutton
92 M 3	St Nicholas rd SE14
154 A 8	St Nicholas way Sutton
92 J 8	St Norbert grn SE4
92 H 10	St Norbert gro SE4
92 G 12	St Norbert rd SE4
144 M 20	St Olaf's rd SW6
66 J 3	St Olave's ct E6
121 W 1	St Olave's wlk SW16
149 O 11	St Oswald's pl SE11
108 H 20	St Oswald's rd SW16
148 H 7	St Oswulf st SW1
132 J 11	St Pancras station NW1
47 V 20	St Pancras way NW1
132 E 6	St Pancras way NW1
44 M 17	St Paul's av NW2
75 U 2	St Paul's av SE16
24 M 15	St Paul's av Harrow
141 Z 6	St Paul's Cathedral EC4
160 A 7	St Pauls Churchyard EC2
141 Z 6	St Paul's Church yd EC4
82 C 6	St Pauls clo Hounsl
114 E 20	St Pauls Cray rd Chisl
47 Y 19	St Paul's cres NW1
51 X 16	St Pauls dri E15
49 N 17	St Paul's pl N1
48 L 17	St Paul's rd N1
49 N 18	St Paul's rd N1
31 Y 3	St Paul's rd N17
67 P 3	St Paul's rd Bark
72 G 17	St Paul's rd Brentf
81 W 19	St Paul's rd Erith
44 M 8	St Paul's rd Rich
122 M 6	St Paul's rd Thntn Hth
72 L 4	St Paul's rd W5
49 N 17	St Paul's shrubbery N1
126 D 3	St Paul's sq Brom
134 C 1	St Paul st N1
149 T 18	St Paul's ter SE17
63 Z 15	St Pauls way E3
64 A 14	St Paul's way E14
28 A 3	St Paul's way N3
130 H 6	St Peter's all EC3
33 Y 12	St Peter's av E17
18 L 14	St Peter's av N18
137 X 10	St Petersburgh ms W2
137 X 9	St Petersburgh pl W2
135 U 11	St Peter's clo E2
94 D 1	St Peter's clo SE3
10 C 5	St Peters clo Bushey
36 J 13	St Peter's clo Ilf
14 E 18	St Peter's clo Chisl
106 J 4	St Peter's clo SW17
27 N 15	St Peter's ct NW4
74 F 12	St Peter's gro W6
19 O 6	St Peter's rd N9
74 G 13	St Peter's rd W6
157 O 9	St Peter's rd Croy
117 O 4	St Peter's rd Kingst
58 H 15	St Peter's rd S'hall
84 C 12	St Peter's rd Harrow
74 F 12	St Peter's sq W6
133 X 5	St Peter's st N1
157 O 12	St Peter's st S Croy
145 N 20	St Peters ter SW6
74 F 12	St Peters vills W6
60 H 14	St Peter's way W5
49 W 19	St Philip's rd E8
116 G 14	St Philip's rd Surb
89 S 8	St Philips st SW8
152 J 2	St Phillip's av Worc Pk
96 L 17	St Quentin rd Welling
136 D 2	St Quintin av W10
65 V 8	St Quintin rd E13
43 X 16	St Raphaels way NW10
5 U 4	St Ronans clo Barnt
34 E 2	St Ronans cres Wdfd Grn
88 U 5	St Rule st SW8
90 C 14	St Saviours rd SW2
122 L 16	St Saviour's rd Croy
52 M 14	Saints dri E7
37 Y 7	St Silas pl NW5
87 N 14	St Simons av SW15
33 T 17	St Stephens av E17
74 K 4	St Stephens av W12
60 A 16	St Stephen's av W13
33 S 16	St Stephens clo E17
130 L 6	St Stephens clo NW8
58 F 16	St Stephen's clo S'hall
137 V 4	St Stephen's cres W2
122 E 6	St Stephens cres Thntn Hth
87 V 13	St Stephens gdns SW15
137 U 3	St Stephen's gdns W2
84 D 17	St Stephen's gdns Twick
93 U 7	St Stephens gro SE13
137 U 3	St Stephen's ms W2
84 E 17	St Stephen's pas Twick
63 X 4	St Stephen's rd E3
65 Z 1	St Stephens rd E6
33 S 16	St Stephen's rd E17
60 C 16	St Stephen's rd W13
4 B 17	St Stephen's rd Barnt
9 S 1	St Stephen's rd Enf
82 H 14	St Stephen's rd Hounsl
160 E 7	St Stephen's row EC4
149 N 20	St Stephens ter SW8
160 F 8	St Swithin's la EC4
93 W 14	St Swithun's rd SE13
98 D 19	St Thomas ct Bxly
22 C 5	St Thomas dri Pinn
58 B 17	St Thomas gdns Ilf
65 S 17	St Thomas rd E16
16 L 3	St Thomas rd N14
73 U 18	St Thomas rd W4
81 W 5	St Thomas rd Blvdr
47 O 17	St Thomas rd NW5
58 B 20	St Thomas's pl E9
48 G 9	St Thomas's rd N4
62 B 3	St Thomas's rd N10
50 B 20	St Thomas's sq E9
142 F 14	St Thomas st SE1
145 P 17	St Thomas' way SW6
22 A 17	St Ursula gro Pinn
58 H 16	St Ursula rd S'hall
82 M 17	St Vincent rd Twick
139 U 2	St Vincent st N1
5 V 17	St Wilfreds clo Barnt
5 V 16	St Wilfrid's clo Barnt
102 C 14	St Winifred's rd Tedd
53 U 15	St Winifride's av E12
149 N 7	Salamanca pl SE1
138 M 7	Salamanca st SE1 & SE11
139 N 7	Salamanca st SE1 & SE11
11 N 19	Salamond clo Stanm
119 P 19	Salcombe dri Mrdn
38 C 20	Salcombe dri Rom
13 Z 20	Salcombe gdns NW7
50 M 1	Salcombe rd E17
49 T 14	Salcombe rd N16
88 L 13	Salcott rd SW11
158 B 7	Salcott rd Croy
24 K 16	Salehurst clo Harrow
92 L 16	Salehurst rd SE4
156 K 6	Salem pl Croy
137 Y 8	Salem rd W2
138 J 3	Sale pl W2
107 X 2	Salford rd SW2
27 U 9	Salisbury av N3
67 S 1	Salisbury av Bark
93 V 9	Salisbury av Sutton
150 F 6	Salisbury clo SE17
141 V 6	Salisbury ct EC4
105 T 18	Salisbury gdns SW19
145 O 18	Salisbury ms SW6
131 P 20	Salisbury pl W1
20 C 11	Salisbury rd E4
52 E 18	Salisbury rd E7
51 V 7	Salisbury rd E10
53 O 14	Salisbury rd E12
33 T 16	Salisbury rd E17
30 K 17	Salisbury rd N4
18 J 10	Salisbury rd N9
30 G 6	Salisbury rd N22
123 X 16	Salisbury rd SE25
105 S 19	Salisbury rd SW19
72 B 6	Salisbury rd E13
4 E 12	Salisbury rd Barnt
98 E 20	Salisbury rd Bxly
127 P 12	Salisbury rd Brom
144 M 13	Salisbury rd Carsh
56 H 19	Salisbury rd Dgnhm
9 Z 1	Salisbury rd Enf
23 R 16	Salisbury rd Harrow
54 H 6	Salisbury rd Ilf
117 Y 5	Salisbury rd New Mald
84 K 10	Salisbury rd Rich
39 Z 16	Salisbury rd Rom
70 D 11	Salisbury rd S'hall
152 C 5	Salisbury rd Worc Pk
150 E 6	Salisbury row SE17
141 V 6	Salisbury sq EC4
73 W 4	Salisbury st W3
47 S 6	Salisbury wlk N19
63 U 17	Salmon la E1
63 X 17	Salmon la E14
65 R 7	Salmon rd E13
81 T 14	Salmon rd Blvdr
18 K 5	Salmons rd N9
25 V 20	Salmon st NW9
43 U 3	Salmon st NW9
65 X 14	Salomons rd E13
32 F 18	Salop rd E17
153 U 19	Saltash clo Sutton
107 P 14	Saltash rd SW17
36 D 1	Saltash rd Ilf
97 U 2	Saltash rd Welling
74 A 6	Salt Coats rd W4
75 T 3	Salter rd SE16
109 N 13	Salter's hill SE19
33 X 13	Salter's rd E17
63 Z 20	Salter st E14
62 G 11	Salter st NW10
88 B 10	Salterton rd N7
90 F 11	Saltoun rd SW2
31 V 12	Saltram clo N15
129 R 12	Saltram cres W9
64 B 19	Saltwell st E14
128 M 4	Salusbury rd NW6
129 N 8	Salusbury rd NW6
106 K 11	Salvador pl SW17
87 O 8	Salvia gdns Grnfd
34 D 2	Salway clo Wdfd Grn
51 Y 19	Salway pl E15
51 X 19	Salway rd E15
77 Z 13	Sam Bartram clo SE7
130 H 18	Samford st NW8
77 O 19	Samos clo SE3
124 A 3	Salmos rd SE20
4 C 18	Sampson av Barnt
143 U 14	Sampson st E1
65 X 7	Samson st E13
78 E 10	Samuel st SE18
44 K 10	Sancroft clo NW2
23 X 9	Sancroft rd Harrow
149 P 8	Sancroft st SE11
142 B 18	Sanctuary st SE1
97 V 17	Sanctuary the Bxly
60 K 11	Sandall clo W5
47 W 18	Sandall rd NW5
60 J 11	Sandall rd W5
18 K 18	Sandall rd N18
117 Z 10	Sandal rd New Mald
118 A 10	Sandal rd New Mald
64 L 3	Sandal st E15
49 O 9	Sandale clo N16
63 V 12	Sandalwood clo E1
119 Z 4	Sandbourne av SW19
92 H 4	Sandbourne rd SE4
12 M 18	Sandbrook clo NW7
49 R 10	Sandbrook rd N16
95 R 8	Sandby grn SE9
111 Z 12	Sandcliff rd Erith
141 T 16	Sandell st SE1
26 M 1	Sanders la NW7
27 N 1	Sanders la NW7
27 O 1	Sanders la NW7
45 S 8	Sanderstead av NW2
89 V 18	Sanderstead clo SW12
50 J 3	Sanderstead rd E10
157 O 18	Sanderstead rd S Croy
42 A 15	Sanderton rd Wemb
47 R 14	Sanderson N5
122 K 6	Sandfield gdns Thntn Hth
122 K 6	Sandfield rd Thntn Hth
30 L 3	Sandford av N22
66 F 11	Sandford clo E6
49 R 3	Sandford ct N16
66 E 9	Sandford rd E6
66 F 9	Sandford rd E6
46 A 20	Sandford rd SW6
97 Z 9	Sandford rd Bxly Hth
28 G 9	Sandford rd Brom
150 F 9	Sandford row SE17
80 F 18	Sandgate rd Welling
151 V 13	Sandgate st SE15
97 Y 7	Sandhills Wallgtn
47 Z 5	Sanders way N19
12 L 19	Sandhurst av Harrow
117 S 17	Sandhurst av Surb
25 O 10	Sandhurst clo NW9
157 T 18	Sandhurst clo S Croy
54 L 13	Sandhurst rd Ilf
19 S 1	Sandhurst rd N9
25 P 11	Sandhurst rd NW9
111 X 1	Sandhurst rd SE6
97 V 14	Sandhurst rd Bxly
9 R 20	Sandhurst rd Enf
114 M 7	Sandhurst rd Sidcp
157 T 18	Sandhurst way S Croy
153 U 3	Sandiford rd Sutton
157 X 3	Sandilands Croy
88 A 3	Sandilands rd SW6
91 W 6	Sandison st SE15
141 O 2	Sandiland st WC1
113 V 7	Sandling ri SE9
89 S 4	Sandmere rd SW4
90 A 10	Sandmere rd SW4
56 J 18	Sandown av Dgnhm
55 Y 7	Sandown Wallgtn
155 N 19	Sandown dri Carsh
123 Z 11	Sandown rd SE25
124 A 11	Sandown rd SE25
40 C 17	Sandown way Grnfd
111 Y 13	Sandpit rd Brom
158 F 7	Sandpits rd Croy
102 H 3	Sandpits rd Rich
64 K 14	Sandra clo Hounsl
23 U 12	Sandridge clo Harrow
119 T 2	Sandringham av SW20
8 E 8	Sandringham clo Enf
36 C 10	Sandringham clo Ilf
40 H 8	Sandringham cres Harrow
9 H 4	Sandringham dri Welling
30 B 19	Sandringham gdns N8
15 T 19	Sandringham gdns N12
36 C 10	Sandringham gdns Ilf
52 K 16	Sandringham rd E7
49 W 15	Sandringham rd E8
33 X 19	Sandringham rd E10
30 L 9	Sandringham rd N22

44 J 17 Sandringham rd NW2
45 S 2 Sandringham rd NW11
54 L 16 Sandringham rd Bark
112 F 13 Sandringham rd Brom
122 M 12 Sandringham rd Croy
40 H 20 Sandringham rd Grnfd
152 H 5 Sandringham rd Worc Pk
158 F 8 Sandrock pl Croy
93 P 7 Sandrock rd SE13
88 B 1 Sand's End la SW6
78 C 10 Sands st SE18
47 T 7 Sandstone pl NW5
77 V 16 Sandtoft rd SE7
45 Y 17 Sandwell cres NW6
132 J 14 Sandwich st WC1
85 O 8 Sandycombe rd Rich
84 C 17 Sandycombe rd Twick
79 Z 16 Sandycroft SE2
78 L 13 Sandy Hill rd SE8
78 L 15 Sandy Hill rd SE18
53 Y 13 Sandyhill rd Ilf
155 V 19 Sandy Hill rd Wallgtn
121 P 1 Sandy la Mitch
156 Z 11 Sandy la North Wallgtn
115 X 18 Sandy la Orp
102 E 5 Sandy la Rich
155 X 15 Sandy la South Wallgtn
153 T 18 Sandy la Sutton
101 Y 17 Sandy la Tedd
102 A 19 Sandy la Tedd
11 T 17 Sandymount av Stanm
113 V 15 Sandy ridge Chisl
46 B 6 Sandy rd NW3
142 L 1 Sandys row E1
158 K 5 Sandy way Croy
49 U 8 Sanford la N16
75 U 16 Sanford st SE14
49 V 8 Sanford ter N16
75 U 17 Sanford wlk SE14
93 R 20 Sangley rd SE6
111 U 1 Sangley rd SE6
123 T 8 Sangley rd SE25
88 G 11 Sangora rd SW11
52 B 8 Sansom rd E11
51 P 1 Sansom st SE5
150 F 20 Sansom st SE5
52 B 7 Sansom st E11
133 V 16 Sans wlk EC1
90 B 10 Santley st SW4
87 X 13 Santos rd SW18
10 E 17 Santway the Stanm
75 W 12 Sapphire rd SE8
123 O 13 Saracen clo Croy
142 M 7 Saracen's Head yd EC3
64 B 18 Saracen st E14
134 K 12 Sarah st N1
50 C 11 Saratoga st E5
141 O 5 Sardinia st WC2
23 O 7 Sarita clo Harrow
8 A 13 Sarnesfield rd Enf
45 V 14 Sarre rd NW2
82 F 4 Sarsen av Hounsl
106 M 2 Sarsfeld rd SW12
107 N 2 Sarsfeld rd SW12
60 C 5 Sarsfield rd Grnfd
105 R 5 Sarjant clo SW19
26 D 4 Satchell mead NW9
70 H 20 Sark clo Hounsl
65 V 15 Sark wlk E16
92 E 11 Sator rd SE15
52 A 9 Sauls Green E11
100 L 13 Saunders clo Hampt
100 M 13 Sanders clo Hampt
76 J 12 Saunders Ness rd E14
79 X 13 Saunders rd SE18
68 D 20 Saunders way SE2
42 B 15 Saunderton gdns Wemb
57 V 7 Saunton rd Hornch
66 H 18 Savage gdns E6
142 M 9 Savage gdns EC3
18 K 1 Savernake rd N9
47 N 12 Savernake rd NW3
118 B 12 Savile gdns New Mald
157 V 3 Savile gdns Croy
118 H 5 Savill gdns New Mald
78 D 3 Saville rd E16
73 Y 8 Saville rd W4
38 B 20 Saville rd Rom
101 V 2 Saville rd Twick
140 A 10 Saville row W1
9 S 10 Saville row W1
21 R 16 Savill row Wdfd Grn

105 R 17 Savona clo SW19
148 A 19 Savona st SW8
140 M 9 Savoy bldgs WC2
12 B 16 Savoy clo Edg
141 N 10 Savoy hill WC2
141 N 11 Savoy pl WC2
141 N 10 Savoy pl WC2
141 N 10 Savoy row WC2
141 N 10 Savoy steps WC2
141 N 10 Savoy st WC2
140 M 10 Savoy way WC2
105 R 4 Sawkin clo SW19
74 F 2 Sawley rd W12
120 H 17 Sawtry clo Carsh
56 J 18 Sawyers clo Bark
59 Y 18 Sawyers lawn W7
141 Z 16 Sawyer st SE1
142 A 16 Sawyer st SE1
90 A 17 Saxby rd SW2
67 V 5 Saxham rd Berk
20 L 11 Saxingham rd E4
120 F 5 Saxon av Felt
116 E 20 Saxonbury gdns Surb
93 X 9 Saxon clo SE13
61 T 15 Saxon dri W3
100 E 4 Saxon ho Felt
62 X 7 Saxon rd E3
66 F 12 Saxon rd E6
30 J 4 Saxon rd N22
123 O 12 Saxon rd SE25
112 D 18 Saxon rd Brom
53 Z 17 Saxon rd Ilf
54 A 17 Saxon rd Ilf
70 C 1 Saxon rd S'hall
43 U 9 Saxon rd Wemb
6 J 19 Saxon way N14
58 C 20 Saxon gdns S'hall
115 T 14 Saxon and Mallard wlk Sidcp
150 A 4 Sayer st SE17
84 M 18 Sayers wk Rich
75 Z 15 Sayes Ct st SE8
114 L 16 Scadbury pk Chisl
140 D 1 Scala st W1
31 W 10 Scales st N17
136 G 5 Scamps ms W10
143 W 14 Scandrett st E1
51 W 4 Scarborough rd E11
48 G 3 Scarborough rd N4
19 P 2 Scarborough rd N9
6 J 19 Scarborough rd N14
156 L 5 Scarbrook rd Croy
42 H 18 Scarle rd Wemb
111 Y 6 Scarlet rd SE6
95 O 7 Scarsbrook rd SE3
40 M 11 Scarsdale rd Harrow
145 U 3 Scarsdale vlls W8
86 F 7 Scarth rd SW13
75 V 13 Scawen rd SE8
135 P 9 Scawfell st E2
14 K 14 Scaynes link N12
63 P 9 Sceptre rd E2
14 K 14 Scaynes link N12
47 Y 6 Scholfield rd N19
20 J 6 Scholar's rd E4
107 U 2 Scholar's rd SW12
63 S 20 School House la E1
102 C 19 Schoolhouse la Tedd
116 D 1 School la Kingst
22 B 12 School la Pinn
97 S 7 School la Welling
70 G 1 School pass S'hall
70 F 1 School pass S'hall
63 N 12 School pl E1
53 T 13 School rd E12
61 Z 12 School rd NW10
114 C 19 School rd Chisl
69 T 3 School rd Dgnhm
100 M 14 School rd Hampt
83 N 8 School rd Hounsl
116 E 1 School rd Kingst
31 P 19 School rd N15
100 M 14 School Rd av Hampt
15 U 13 School way N2
76 G 13 Schooner st E14
87 V 13 Schubert rd SW15
146 G 2 Science museum SW7
135 O 17 Sclater st E1
49 V 12 Scobie pl N16
141 X 15 Scoresby st SE1
59 Y 6 Scorton av Grnfd
59 Z 13 Scotch comm W13
60 A 13 Scotch comm W13
22 A 2 Scott gro Pinn
34 J 1 Scoter clo Wdfd Grn
31 W 6 Scotland grn N17
91 T 17 Scotland Green rd Enf
9 U 15 Scotland Green rd N Enf
140 K 14 Scotland pl SW1

21 Y 6 Scotland rd Buck Hl
153 T 15 Scotsdale clo Sutton
94 J 15 Scotsdale rd SE12
133 V 16 Scotswood st EC1
31 Y 1 Scotswood wlk N15
122 B 1 Scott clo SW16
99 T 2 Scott cres Erith
40 J 5 Scott cres Harrow
130 E 14 Scott Ellis gdns NW8
55 W 3 Scottes la Dgnhm
143 T 20 Scott Lidgett cres SE16
125 Y 3 Scotts av Brom
100 K 17 Scotts dri Hampt
125 W 7 Scotts la Brom
51 T 4 Scott's rd E10
74 K 6 Scott's rd W12
136 A 18 Scott's rd W12
112 E 19 Scotts rd Brom
65 R 17 Scoulding rd E16
64 H 20 Scouler st E14
12 M 13 Scout way NW7
53 Z 9 Scrafton rd Ilf
68 J 5 Scrattons ter Bark
135 P 3 Scriven st E8
93 R 17 Scrooby st SE6
62 H 10 Scrubbs la NW10
89 X 19 Scrutton clo SW12
134 J 17 Scruttons st EC2
125 U 12 Scudamore la NW9
92 C 14 Scutari rd SE22
91 Y 7 Scylla rd SE15
91 Y 5 Scylla rd SE15
159 Z 3 Seabrook dri W Wkhm
56 E 2 Seabrook gdns Rom
55 V 9 Seabrook rd Dgnhm
141 X 5 Seacol la EC4
80 H 6 Seacourt rd SE2
16 K 15 Seafield rd N11
33 R 11 Seaford rd E17
31 P 14 Seaford rd N15
72 A 3 Seaford rd Enf
8 F 14 Seaford rd Enf
132 M 14 Seaford st WC1
118 K 9 Seaforth av New Mald
39 R 1 Seaforth clo Rom
48 L 15 Seaforth cres N5
17 S 4 Seaforth gdns N21
152 D 9 Seaforth gdns Epsom
21 Y 17 Seaforth gdns Wdfd Grn
54 U 13 Seagrave rd SW6
34 G 20 Seagry rd E11
49 V 13 Seal st E8
146 L 20 Searles clo SW11
150 F 4 Searles rd SE1
150 E 18 Sears st SE5
54 J 14 Seaton av Ilf
65 T 13 Seaton clo E13
99 W 19 Seaton rd Drtfrd
120 J 4 Seaton rd Mitch
83 O 16 Seaton rd Twick
80 F 20 Seaton rd Welling
60 J 5 Seaton rd Wemb
18 K 17 Seaton rd N18
18 K 12 Sebastian st EC1
67 N 9 Sebastopol rd N9
133 X 1 Sebbon st N1
52 L 3 Sebert rd E7
135 U 9 Sebright pas E2
4 D 10 Sebright rd Barnt
22 M 6 Secker cres Harrow
141 S 19 Secker st SE1
53 S 14 Second av E12
65 T 9 Second av E13
33 P 15 Second av E17
19 P 14 Second av N18
27 O 12 Second av NW4
82 A 7 Second av SW14
74 D 3 Second av W3
129 N 15 Second av W10
69 V 5 Second av Dgnhm
9 G 17 Second av Enf
37 T 15 Second av Rom
42 G 6 Second av Wemb
101 S 3 Second Cross rd Twick
43 T 13 Second way Wemb
150 H 9 Sedan way SE17
9 S 16 Sedcote rd Enf
147 S 6 Sedding st SW1
120 G 12 Seddon rd Mrdn
95 P 6 Sedgebrook rd SE3
24 E 16 Sedgecombe av Harrow
74 E 2 Sedgeford rd W12
111 R 12 Sedgehill st SE6
28 D 10 Sedgemere av N2
80 G 9 Sedgemere rd SE2
150 J 20 Sedgement pl SE5

56 E 11 Sedgemoor dri Dgnhm
112 B 2 Sedgeway SE6
51 T 7 Sedgwick rd E10
50 F 16 Sedgwick st E9
87 W 15 Sedleigh rd SW18
145 S 14 Sedlescombe rd SW6
139 X 7 Sedley pl W1
109 T 9 Seeley dri SE21
44 F 2 Seelig av NW9
107 S 16 Seely rd SW17
142 L 9 Seething la EC3
116 E 15 Seething Wells la Surb
12 K 18 Sefton av NW7
25 R 5 Sefton av Harrow
123 Y 20 Sefton rd Croy
157 Z 1 Sefton rd Croy
86 M 6 Sefton st SW15
92 H 20 Segal clo SE23
133 W 16 Sekforde st EC1
5 O 13 Selbie av NW10
32 M 15 Selborne av E17
115 Y 1 Selborne av Bxly
26 G 13 Selborne gdns NW4
59 T 5 Selborne gdns Grnfd
33 O 14 Selborne rd E17
8 M 10 Selborne rd N14
17 O 10 Selborne rd N14
30 C 5 Selborne rd N22
30 C 6 Selborne rd N22
157 T 7 Selborne rd Croy
53 W 8 Selborne rd Ilf
118 A 3 Selborne rd New Mald
115 R 10 Selborne rd Sidcp
33 N 14 Selborne rd E17
53 W 11 Selborne av E12
113 W 14 Selby clo Chisl
58 H 12 Selby gdns S'hall
120 K 16 Selby grn Carsh
51 Z 10 Selby rd E11
52 A 11 Selby rd E11
65 V 14 Selby rd E13
18 D 20 Selby rd N17
31 R 1 Selby rd N17
123 Y 3 Selby rd SE20
60 C 12 Selby rd W5
120 J 16 Selby rd Carsh
135 U 18 Selby st E1
77 P 13 Selcroft rd SE10
92 D 5 Selden rd SE15
123 R 14 Selhurst New rd SE25
123 R 15 Selhurst pl SE25
18 C 11 Selhurst rd N9
123 T 10 Selhurst rd SE25
56 A 2 Selinas la Dgnhm
100 K 10 Selkirk rd SW17
100 M 3 Selkirk rd Twick
101 N 2 Selkirk rd Twick
27 X 2 Sellers Hall clo N3
106 K 13 Sellincourt rd SW17
110 M 19 Sellindge clo Becknhm
149 O 6 Sellon ms SE11
62 E 4 Selous av NW10
4 C 17 Sellwood dr Barnt
4 C 18 Sellwood dr Barnt
132 C 5 Selous st NW1
157 O 13 Selsdon av S Croy
38 J 14 Selsdon clo Surb
159 J 19 Selsdon Pk rd S Croy
65 Y 4 Selsdon rd E6
34 E 20 Selsdon rd E11
65 Y 6 Selsdon rd E13
44 F 8 Selsdon rd NW2
108 H 8 Selsdon rd SE27
157 O 12 Selsdon rd S Croy
97 V 2 Selsdon rd Welling
49 T 14 Selsey pl N16
64 A 15 Selsey st E14
12 K 14 Selvage la NW7
146 E 9 Selwood pl SW7
124 A 20 Selwood rd Croy
119 V 19 Selwood rd Sutton
146 E 9 Selwood ter SW7
34 D 17 Selworthy clo E11
110 L 7 Selworthy rd SE6
20 H 19 Selworthy rd E4
36 J 18 Selwyn av Ilf
84 L 8 Selwyn av Rich
82 B 9 Selwyn clo Hounsl
25 R 3 Selwyn ct Edg
97 O 9 Selwyn cres Welling
63 X 7 Selwyn rd E3
65 U 4 Selwyn rd E13
117 Y 11 Selwyn rd New Mald
147 W 7 Semley pl SW1
122 C 2 Semley rd SW16
122 L 9 Seneca rd Thntn Hth
121 P 20 Senga rd Wallgtn
153 N 6 Senhouse rd Sutton

S

129 X 20 Senior st W2
112 H 2 Senlac rd SE12
18 F 2 Sennen rd Enf
113 R 7 Sennen wlk SE9
63 S 16 Senrab st E1
27 N 14 Sentinel sq NW4
11 P 19 September way Stanm
10 G 3 Sequoia clo Bushey Watf
51 V 2 Serbin clo E11
141 P 5 Serle st WC2
141 Z 7 Sermon la EC4
113 N 19 Serviden dri Chisl
151 N 5 Setchell rd SE1
75 R 6 Seth st SE16
68 G 1 Seton gdns Dgnhm
65 S 6 Settle rd E13
143 U 4 Settles st E1
87 Z 6 Settrington rd SW6
36 L 19 Seven Kings pk Ilf
54 J 6 Seven Kings rd Ilf
98 H 11 Sevenoaks clo Bxly Hth
92 K 15 Sevenoaks rd SE4
115 S 19 Sevenoaks way Sidcup
48 J 5 Seven Sisters rd N4
48 B 10 Seven Sisters rd N7
31 P 18 Seven Sisters rd N15
63 N 20 Seven Star all E1
53 U 12 Seventh av E12
39 Z 9 Seven av Rom
8 L 2 Severn dri Enf
44 C 15 Severn way NW10
88 J 10 Severus rd SW11
26 H 19 Sevington rd NW4
129 W 18 Sevington st W9
71 Y 5 Seward rd W7
124 F 3 Seward rd Becknhm
63 R 5 Sewardstone rd E2
20 C 1 Sewardstone rd E4
133 Y 15 Seward st EC1
134 A 14 Seward st EC1
50 E 11 Swedley st E5
80 B 6 Sewell rd SE2
65 T 9 Sewell st E13
39 O 10 Seymour rd Rom
31 X 7 Seymour av N17
119 P 17 Seymour av Epsom
21 P 8 Seymour av Mrdn
44 H 7 Seymour ct E4
53 T 4 Seymour ct NW2
177 O 12 Seymour gdns Surb
84 A 19 Seymour gdns Twick
139 N 3 Seymour hall W1
139 T 5 Seymour ms W1
123 Z 9 Seymour pl SE25
139 N 4 Seymour pl W1
20 D 4 Seymour rd E4
66 A 5 Seymour rd E6
50 L 4 Seymour rd E10
28 B 2 Seymour rd N3
30 H 16 Seymour rd N8
19 N 8 Seymour rd N9
97 W 17 Seymour rd SW18
105 P 6 Seymour rd SW19
73 W 9 Seymour rd W4
155 O 11 Seymour rd Carsh
101 N 11 Seymour rd Hampt
102 F 20 Seymour rd Kingst
116 F 1 Seymour rd Kingst
121 O 18 Seymour rd Mitch
139 R 6 Seymour st W1
123 Z 1 Seymour ter SE20
123 Z 1 Seymour vlls SE20
146 A 13 Seymour wlk SW10
76 H 11 Syssel st E14
73 Z 1 Shaa rd W3
101 U 10 Shacklegate la Tedd
70 F 1 Shackleton rd S'hall
58 F 20 Shackleton rd S'hall
49 V 13 Shacklewell grn E8
49 V 13 Shacklewell la E8
49 U 12 Shacklewell rd N16
49 U 13 Shacklewell row E8
135 P 15 Shacklewell st E2
152 D 3 Shadbolt clo Worc Pk
143 P 18 Shad thames SE1
58 E 7 Shadwell dri Grnfd
63 O 19 Shadwell pl E1
143 Z 7 Shadwell pl E1
10 A 2 Shadybush clo Bushey Watf
101 Z 17 Shaef way Tedd
56 J 17 Shafter rd Dgnhm
140 F 9 Shaftesbury av W1
9 S 3 Shaftesbury av Enf
5 S 9 Shaftesbury av Enf
24 H 19 Shaftesbury av Harrow

40 M 3 Shaftesbury av Harrow
41 O 6 Shaftesbury av Harrow
42 J 1 Shaftesbury av Harrow
70 H 9 Shaftesbury av S'hall
145 U 4 Shaftesbury ms W8
20 K 5 Shaftesbury rd E4
52 M 20 Shaftesbury rd E7
65 X 1 Shaftesbury rd E7
51 O 5 Shaftesbury rd E10
33 R 17 Shaftesbury rd E17
18 F 19 Shaftesbury rd N18
48 A 3 Shaftesbury rd N19
124 M 4 Shaftesbury rd Becknhm
120 H 16 Shaftesbury rd Carsh
84 J 19 Shaftesbury rd Rich
39 U 17 Shaftesbury rd Rom
67 O 5 Shaftesburys the Bark
134 D 9 Shaftesbury st N1
101 S 7 Shaftesbury way Twick
147 O 3 Shafto ms SW1
63 T 3 Shafton rd E9
16 H 16 Shakespeare av N11
61 Y 3 Shakespeare av NW10
25 O 20 Shakespeare clo Harrow
25 O 20 Shakespeare ct Harrow
53 T 19 Shakespeare cres E12
61 Y 3 Shakespeare cres NW10
25 N 20 Shakespeare dri Harrow
28 M 13 Shakespeare gdns N2
32 G 8 Shakespeare rd E17
13 T 14 Shakespeare rd NW7
90 J 10 Shakespeare rd SE24
73 W 1 Shakespeare rd W3
59 W 19 Shakespeare rd W7
97 Y 2 Shakespeare rd Bxly Hth
39 U 18 Shakespeare rd Rom
49 R 12 Shakespeare wlk N16
146 D 15 Shalcomb st SW10
119 S 11 Shaldon dri Mrdn
24 M 7 Shaldon rd Edg
61 U 19 Shaleimar rd W3
136 F 8 Shalfleet dri W10
61 U 19 Shallimar gdns W3
113 Y 9 Shallons rd SE9
116 L 19 Shalston vlls Surb
85 T 7 Shalstone rd SW14
122 C 14 Shamrock st Croy
89 W 7 Shamrock st SW4
16 E 5 Shamrock way N14
89 V 15 Shandon rd SW4
142 K 16 Shand st SE1
63 T 13 Shandy st E1
31 X 13 Shanklin rd N8
31 X 13 Shanklin rd N15
90 D 10 Shannon gro SW9
130 L 8 Shannon pl NW8
120 L 19 Shap cres Carsh
135 N 8 Shap st E2
90 K 13 Shardcroft av SE24
92 K 3 Shardeloes rd SE14
151 U 14 Shard's sq SE15
114 M 10 Sharman clo Sidcp
63 S 16 Sharman st E14
97 T 8 Sharnbrooke clo Welling
116 E 19 Sharon clo Surb
83 P 2 Sharon gdns E9
73 Y 13 Sharon rd W4
9 U 8 Sharon rd Enf
131 R 2 Sharpleshall st SW1
75 P 16 Sharratt st SE15
33 T 17 Sharsted st SE17
140 F 10 Shaver's pl SW1
68 L 6 Shaw ab Bark
94 M 12 Shawbrooke rd SE9
95 N 11 Shawbrooke rd SE9
91 V 19 Shawbury rd SE22
10 D 8 Shaw clo Bushey
80 D 3 Shaw clo SE18
127 O 2 Shaw clo Brom
146 M 11 Shawfield st SW3
86 H 19 Shawford ct SW15
68 L 6 Shaw gdns Bark
112 B 8 Shaw rd Brom
32 J 5 Shaw rd Enf
54 H 13 Shaw rd E17
155 Z 15 Shaw way Wallgtn
159 V 20 Shaxton cres Croy
48 A 17 Shearling way N7

94 B 9 Shearman rd SE3
99 V 7 Shearwood cres Drtfrd
26 B 13 Sheavesfield av NW9
135 P 18 Sheba st E1
85 R 12 Sheen Comm dri Rich
85 B 10 Sheen Ct rd Rich
85 V 10 Sheen Gate gdns SW14
84 M 9 Sheendale rd Rich
110 A 11 Sheenewood SE26
133 R 4 Sheen ga N1
85 W 7 Sheen la SW14
4 L 11 Sheen pk Rich
84 L 11 Sheen rd Rich
95 P 12 Sheen rd Rich
167 C 10 Sheen way Wallgtn
85 V 13 Sheen wood SW14
88 M 5 Sheepcote la SW11
89 N 5 Sheepcote la SW11
23 W 19 Sheepcote rd Harrow
37 X 13 Sheepcotes rd Rom
117 Z 18 Sheephouse way New Mald
118 A 18 Sheephouse way New Mald
135 W 5 Sheep la E8
63 Z 8 Sheffield sq E3
141 O 6 Sheffield st WC2
137 U 15 Sheffield ter W8
38 G 1 Sheila clo Rom
38 G 1 Sheila la Rom
22 D 11 Shelbourne clo Pinn
31 Z 6 Shelbourne rd N17
48 D 12 Shelburne rd N7
115 N 9 Shelbury clo Sidcp
92 B 14 Shelbury rd SE22
28 M 17 Sheldon av N6
46 K 1 Sheldon av N6
35 Y 7 Sheldon av Ilf
45 P 13 Sheldon rd NW2
98 B 3 Sheldon rd Bxly Hth
55 Y 20 Sheldon rd Dgnhm
18 F 14 Sheldon rd N18
156 L 6 Sheldon st Croy
137 S 17 Shelford rd SE19
120 F 2 Sheldrick clo Mitch
109 T 19 Shelford ri SE19
4 A 20 Shelford rd Barnt
88 L 12 Shelgate rd SW11
127 S 15 Shell clo Brom
53 P 18 Shelley av E12
59 P 8 Shelley av Grnfd
57 U 6 Shelley av Hornch
12 B 15 Shelley clo Edg
12 C 15 Shelley clo Edg
59 P 9 Shelley clo Grnfd
58 F 18 Shelley cres S'hall
96 H 2 Shelley dri SE18
42 D 8 Shelley gdns Wemb
61 Y 4 Shelley rd NW10
93 P 7 Shell rd SE13
93 P 8 Shell rd SE13
88 M 6 Shellwood rd SW11
105 Y 19 Shelton rd SW19
J 7 Shelton st WC2
34 G 11 Shenfield rd Wdfd Grn
34 G 2 Shenfield rd Wdfd Grn
134 K 10 Shenfield st N1
91 S 2 Shenley rd SE5
82 B 2 Shenley rd Hounsl
98 L 11 Shenstone clo Bxly Hth
99 N 5 Shepard clo Rom
134 D 12 Shepherdess pl N1
134 B 8 Shepherdess wlk N1
138 X 13 Shepherd mkt W1
136 D 17 Shepherds Bush grn W12
136 F 17 Shepherds Bush grn W12
74 M 5 Shepherds Bush mkt W12
136 C 16 Shepherds Bush mkt W12
136 G 18 Shepherds Bush pl W12
136 E 19 Shepherds Bush rd W6
144 D 5 Shepherds Bush rd W6
136 G 18 Shepherds Bush shopping centre W12
29 T 19 Shepherd's clo N6
114 E 18 Shepherds grn Chisl
29 S 19 Shepherds hill N6
50 E 16 Shepherds la E9
99 Z 19 Shepherd's la Drtfrd

40 C 19 Shepherds path Grnfd
139 T 8 Shepherds pl W1
139 X 14 Shepherd st W1
158 E 17 Shepherds way S Croy
155 O 4 Shepley clo Carsh
65 P 12 Sheppard st E1
134 C 3 Shepperton rd N1
55 U 20 Sheppey gdns Dgnhm
55 P 20 Sheppey rd Dgnhm
66 K 19 Shepstone st E6
95 S 12 Sherard rd SE9
140 D 6 Shereton st W1
70 G 10 Sherborne av S'hall
120 H 17 Sherborne cres Carsh
25 P 10 Sherborne gdns NW9
60 B 15 Sherborne gdns W13
160 F 8 Sherborne la EC4
153 X 1 Sherborne rd Sutton
134 E 3 Sherborne st N1
31 T 18 Sherboro rd N15
9 O 8 Sherbourne av Enf
60 B 15 Sherbourne gdns W13
98 D 9 Sherbrooke clo Bxly Hth
68 H 16 Sherbrooke gdns E6
144 L 19 Sherbrooke rd SW6
17 W 3 Sherbrook gdns N21
31 T 17 Shereboro rd N17
12 C 10 Sheredan rd E4
35 Y 16 Shere rd Ilf
86 C 18 Sherfield gdns SW15
24 E 19 Sheridan gdns Harrow
52 D 10 Sheridan rd E7
53 T 16 Sheridan rd E12
119 W 1 Sheridan rd SW19
81 R 9 Sheridan rd Blvdr
97 Z 7 Sheridan rd Bxly Hth
102 D 8 Sheridan rd Rich
143 Z 6 Sheridan st E1
154 L 12 Sheridan wlk Carsh
27 X 18 Sheridan wlk NW11
53 U 12 Sharingham av E12
6 K 18 Sheringham av N14
100 F 2 Sheringham av Twick
54 L 16 Sheringham dri Bark
48 E 17 Sheringham rd N7
124 B 5 Sheringham rd SE20
22 H 1 Sherington av Pinn
77 V 17 Sherington rd SE7
83 X 20 Sherland rd Twick
101 X 1 Sherland rd Twick
147 X 9 Sherland rd SW1
126 G 1 Sherman rd Brom
64 F 8 Sherman st E3
33 T 13 Shernhall st E17
52 K 17 Sherrard E7
53 O 16 Sherrard rd E12
5 O 16 Sherrards way Barnt
44 J 15 Sherrick Green rd NW10
45 Y 19 Sheriff rd NW6
31 X 7 Sherringham av N17
38 L 19 Sherringham av Rom
26 H 20 Sherrock gdns NW4
92 F 4 Sherwin rd SE14
34 H 11 Sherwood av E18
107 Y 19 Sherwood av SW16
108 A 20 Sherwood av SW16
41 U 16 Sherwood av Grnfd
86 K 8 Sherwood clo SW15
97 T 16 Sherwood clo Bxly
72 A 3 Sherwood clo W13
64 E 20 Sherwood gdns Bark
97 S 16 Sherwood Pk av Sidcp
121 V 8 Sherwood Pk rd Mitch
153 Y 12 Sherwood Pk rd Sutton
26 M 10 Sherwood rd NW4
27 N 9 Sherwood rd NW4
105 V 19 Sherwood rd SW19
123 Z 18 Sherwood rd Croy
100 M 11 Sherwood rd Hampt
40 M 8 Sherwood rd Harrow
41 N 8 Sherwood rd Harrow
36 D 14 Sherwood rd Ilf
96 G 6 Sherwood rd Welling
15 S 10 Sherwood st N20
140 D 9 Sherwood st W1
15 T 10 Sherwood st N20
159 T 2 Sherwood way W Wkhm
63 Y 6 Shetland rd E13
71 Z 17 Shield dr Brentf
72 A 16 Shield dr Brentf

S

80 E 11 Shieldhall st SE2
138 M 1 Shilliber pl W1
133 X 2 Shillingford st N1
88 K 6 Shillington st SW11
17 X 6 Shillitoe rd N13
62 M 17 Shinfield st W12
136 B 5 Shinfield st W12
110 G 6 Shinford path SE23
81 R 18 Shinglewell rd Erith
78 M 8 Ship & Half Moon pas SE18
142 H 17 Ship and Mermaid row SE1
107 S 1 Shipka rd SW12
85 W 6 Ship la SW14
65 X 18 Shipman rd E16
110 G 4 Shipman rd SE23
93 N 2 Ship st SE4
160 H 7 Ship Tavern pas EC3
55 V 9 Shipton clo Gdnhm
139 R 11 Shipton st E2
142 H 14 Shipwright yd SE1
64 C 19 Shirbutt st E14
95 O 6 Shirebrook rd SE3
27 P 18 Shirehall clo NW4
27 P 18 Shirehall gdns NW4
27 P 17 Shirehall la NW4
27 P 19 Shirehall pk NW4
102 J 10 Shires the Rich
129 R 15 Shirland ms W9
129 P 14 Shirland rd W9
97 V 20 Shirley av Bxly
158 C 1 Shirley av Croy
153 U 20 Shirley av Sutton
154 H 8 Shirley av Sutton
158 F 5 Shirley Ch rd Croy
82 M 14 Shirley clo Hounsl
124 G 10 Shirley cres. Becknhm
82 H 19 Shirley dri Hounsl
71 X 2 Shirley gdns W7
54 G 17 Shirley gdns Bark
19 S 2 Shirley gro N9
89 P 7 Shirley gro SW11
158 E 8 Shirley Hills rd Croy
77 Y 18 Shirley Ho dri SE7
124 B 19 Shirley Pk rd Croy
52 A 20 Shirley rd E15
73 Z 7 Shirley rd W4
158 B 1 Shirley rd Croy
7 Y 12 Shirley rd Enf
114 H 7 Shirley rd Sidcp
155 U 19 Shirley rd Wallgtn
65 P 17 Shirley st E16
133 P 4 Shirley st N1
158 L 4 Shirley way Croy
159 K 9 Shirley way Croy
46 M 12 Shirlock rd NW3
47 N 13 Shirlock rd NW3
31 O 5 Shobden rd N17
53 U 20 Shoebury rd E6
141 V 5 Shoe la EC4
24 E 12 Shooters la Harrow
94 C 4 Shooters hill SE18
77 Y 20 Shooters Hill rd SE3
94 A 2 Shooters Hill rd SE3
95 N 1 Shooters Hill rd SE18
7 V 5 Shooters Enf
48 T 17 Shoot Up hill NW2
100 C 14 Shore clo Hampt
134 L 15 Shoreditch High st EC2
100 F 4 Shore gro Felt
115 W 2 Shoreham clo Bxly
124 C 13 Shoreham clo Croy
88 A 13 Shoreham clo SW18
126 D 15 Shoreham way Brom
63 P 1 Shore pl E9
63 P 1 Shore rd E9
120 E 1 Shore st SW19
150 M 10 Shorncliffe rd SE1
93 U 20 Shorndean st SE6
97 R 15 Shorne clo Sidcp
127 W 5 Shornefield clo Brom
80 E 12 Shornells way SE2
145 R 18 Shorrold's rd SW5
152 E 16 Shortcroft rd Epsom
56 B 17 Shortcrofts rd Dgnhm
14 J 12 Short ga N12
82 H 3 Short hedges Hounsl
144 G 8 Shortlands W6
18 C 12 Shortlands clo N18
126 A 2 Shortlands gdns Brom
125 X 5 Shortlands gdns Brom
51 P 1 Shortlands rd E10
125 Y 5 Shortlands rd Brom
102 M 19 Shortlands rd Kingst
103 O 18 Shortlands rd Kingst
51 Y 6 Short rd E11
64 J 2 Short rd E15
74 A 16 Short rd W4

25 U 13 Shorts croft NW9
140 J 6 Shorts gdns WC2
154 K 10 Shorts rd Carsh
141 V 16 Short st SE1
67 P 3 Short st Bark
64 G 8 Short wall E15
15 X 19 Short way N12
95 P 8 Short way SE9
83 N 19 Short way Twick
155 S 14 Shortfield Wallgtn
87 X 1 Shottendane rd SW6
113 R 6 Shottery clo SE9
86 A 10 Shottfield av SW13
139 N 3 Shouldham st W1
95 T 8 Shrapnel rd SE9
85 X 11 Shrewsbury av SW4
24 K 14 Shrewsbury av Harrow
61 Z 3 Shrewsbury cres NW10
95 Z 3 Shrewsbury la SE18
137 T 3 Shrewsbury ms W2
79 R 20 Shrewsbury pk SE18
53 N 20 Shrewsbury rd E7
53 N 16 Shrewsbury rd E12
16 J 18 Shrewsbury rd N11
137 T 5 Shrewsbury rd W2
124 J 6 Shrewsbury rd Becknhm
120 K 18 Shrewsbury rd Carsh
106 M 16 Shrewton rd SW17
111 Z 9 Shroffold rd Brom
112 B 8 Shroffold rd Brom
122 A 9 Shropshire clo Mitch
132 D 19 Shropshire pl W1
30 C 1 Shropshire rd N22
130 L 19 Shroton st NW1
34 F 7 Shrubberies the E18
17 W 3 Shrubbery gdns N21
18 J 12 Shrubbery rd N9
108 A 10 Shrubbery rd SW16
70 F 1 Shrubbery rd S'hall
152 L 6 Shrubland gro Worc Pk
135 R 2 Shrubland rd E8
33 P 20 Shrubland rd E10
33 N 18 Shrubland rd E17
159 O 7 Shrublands av Croy
15 U 7 Shrublands clo N20
15 V 1 Shurland av Barnt
5 U 20 Shurland av Barnt
96 K 19 Shuttle clo Sidcp
98 B 18 Shuttlemead Bxly
99 V 8 Shuttle clo Drtfrd
135 S 18 Shuttle st E1
88 H 4 Shuttleworth rd SW11
89 X 6 Sibells rd SW4
97 Y 13 Sibley clo Bxly Hth
53 R 20 Sibley gro E12
94 J 18 Sibthorpe rd SE12
120 L 3 Sibthorpe rd Mitch
120 J 17 Sibton rd Carsh
140 L 2 Sicilian av WC1
69 W 10 Sickle corner Dgnhm
87 S 1 Sidbury st SW6
114 J 12 Sidcup By Pass rd Sidcp
115 U 17 Sidcup By Pass rd Sidcp
114 M 9 Sidcup High st Sidcp
115 S 13 Sidcup hill Sidcp
115 S 14 Sidcup Hill gdns Sidcp
113 X 4 Sidcup rd SE9
114 C 6 Sidcup rd SE9
94 J 14 Sidcup rd SE12
131 P 18 Siddons la NW1
31 X 5 Siddons rd N17
110 G 5 Siddons rd SE23
156 G 4 Siddons rd Croy
32 K 16 Side rd E17
114 E 1 Sidewood rd SE9
149 R 2 Sidford pl SE1
51 V 3 Sidings, the E11
83 T 4 Sidmouth av Islwth
51 T 7 Sidmouth rd E10
45 N 19 Sidmouth rd NW2
62 M 1 Sidmouth rd NW10
128 C 1 Sidmouth rd NW10
87 F 20 Sidmouth rd Welling
132 M 15 Sidmouth st WC1
17 R 18 Sidney av N13
129 W 1 Sidney Boyd ct NW6
72 F 16 Sidney gdns Brentf
133 W 11 Sidney rd EC1
52 E 16 Sidney rd E7
123 W 11 Sidney rd SE25
90 D 5 Sidney rd SW9
124 J 2 Sidney rd Becknhm
23 O 11 Sidney rd Harrow
83 Z 16 Sidney rd Twick

63 O 16 Sidney sq E1
143 Z 3 Sidney sq E1
135 O 17 Sidney st E1
135 Z 20 Sidney st E1
143 Z 1 Sidney st E1
63 O 16 Sidney St east E1
63 N 1 Sidworth st E8
135 X 2 Sidworth st E8
77 T 17 Siebert rd SE3
78 B 9 Siemens rd SE18
49 Y 15 Sigdon rd E8
78 M 8 Sigrist sq SE10
136 H 7 Silchester rd W10
98 F 3 Silecroft rd Bxly Hth
141 Y 19 Silex st SE1
94 E 14 Silk clo SE12
26 C 15 Silkfield rd NW9
93 T 5 Silk Mills path SE13
25 X 6 Silkstream rd Edg
142 D 1 Silk st EC2
10 D 10 Silsoe rd N8
19 Y 19 Silver Birch av E4
20 A 19 Silver Birch clo E4
5 W 15 Silvercliffe gdns Barnt
23 P 2 Silver clo Harrow
73 T 12 Silver cres W4
110 D 10 Silverdale SE26
40 E 16 Silverdale clo Grnfd
7 O 15 Silverdale Enf
36 J 17 Silverdale av Ilf
153 U 8 Silverdale clo Sutton
57 X 16 Silverdale dri Hornch
20 K 19 Silverdale rd E4
98 G 6 Silverdale rd Bxly Hth
156 J 14 Silverdale rd Croy
83 Y 6 Silverhall st Islwth
42 J 2 Silverholme Harrow
40 L 18 Silver join St Clo Grnfd
78 G 3 Silverland st E16
159 X 2 Silver la W Wkhm
121 E 11 Silverleigh rd Thntn Hth
93 P 17 Silvermere rd SE6
140 C 8 Silver rd W12
136 E 12 Silver rd W12
81 V 16 Silver Spring clo Erith
11 S 19 Silverston clo Stanm
11 S 19 Silverston way Stanm
18 B 15 Silver st N18
88 C 12 Silver st Enf
37 T 5 Silverthorne rd SW8
20 C 7 Silverthorne gdns E4
144 F 16 Silverton rd W6
78 B 3 Silvertown By-pass SW16
65 O 18 Silvertown way E16
77 S 3 Silvertown way E16
59 R 8 Silvertree la Grnfd
38 F 11 Silver way Rom
75 X 3 Silver wlk SE16
91 V 14 Silvester st SE22
142 D 18 Silvester st SE1
75 R 12 Silwood st SE16
75 V 18 Silwood st SE16
15 X 7 Simmons clo N20
20 K 9 Simmons la E4
78 L 13 Simmons rd SE18
15 W 7 Simmons way N20
154 J 3 Simms clo Carsh
94 H 18 Simnel rd SE12
137 S 9 Simon clo W11
51 O 6 Simonds rd E10
127 P 1 Simone clo Brom
51 X 16 Simons wlk E15
82 E 17 Simpson rd Hounsl
57 U 19 Simpson rd Rainhm
107 C 9 Simpson rd Rich
64 E 20 Simpsons rd E14
126 F 7 Simpson's rd Brom
88 H 5 Simpson st SW11
87 Y 14 Simrose ct SW18
94 B 10 Sims wlk SE3
57 Z 9 Sinclair clo Enf
136 H 19 Sinclair gdns W14
27 R 18 Sinclair gro NW11
10 A 17 Sinclair rd E4
19 X 18 Sinclair rd E4
136 J 19 Sinclair rd W14
144 K 1 Sinclair rd W14
71 Z 1 Singapore rd W13
134 G 15 Singer st EC2
122 K 16 Singleton clo Croy
106 L 16 Singleton clo SW17
66 C 16 Singleton rd Dgnhm
14 L 15 Singleton scarp N12
32 F 4 Sinnott rd E17
84 A 20 Sion rd Twick
21 S 17 Sir Alexander clo W3

64 D 2 Sir Alexander rd W3
30 K 8 Sirdar rd N22
136 J 11 Sirdar rd W11
160 D 6 Sise la EC4
67 X 3 Sisley rd Bark
87 V 15 Sisparb gdns SW18
123 Y 17 Sissinghurst rd Croy
89 N 8 Sisters av SW11
107 T 1 Sistova rd SW12
8 C 20 Sittingbourne av Enf
18 B 11 Sittingbourne av Enf
10 H 17 Sitwell gro Stanm
56 H 20 Siviter way Dgnhm
31 O 5 Siward rd N17
106 C 7 Siward rd SW17
126 J 7 Siward rd Brom
53 U 14 Sixth av E12
128 J 15 Sixth av W10
100 M 6 Sixth Cross rd Twick
101 O 8 Sixth Cross rd Twick
45 S 14 Skardu rd NW2
87 T 19 Skeena hill SW18
66 F 3 Skeffington rd E6
106 C 4 Skelbrook st SW18
87 V 11 Skelgill rd SW15
65 O 1 Skelly rd E15
52 G 19 Skelton rd E7
51 S 1 Skelton la E10
144 D 15 Skelwith rd W6
75 S 13 Sketchley gdns SE16
8 H 12 Sketty rd Enf
64 M 4 Skiers st E15
90 G 20 Skiffington clo SW2
142 A 12 Skin Mkt pl SE1
147 T 7 Skinner pl SW1
160 C 8 Skinners la EC4
133 V 15 Skinner st EC1
66 H 10 Skipsey av E6
63 R 3 Skipworth rd E9
33 W 3 Sky Peals rd Wdfd Grn
95 O 7 Slacebrook rd SE3
79 V 14 Sladedale rd SE18
99 U 1 Slade gdns Erith
99 T 1 Slade Green rd Erith
7 T 11 Slades clo Enf
114 B 9 Slades dri Chisl
7 S 10 Slades gdns Enf
5 U 11 Slades hill Enf
7 T 11 Slades ri Enf
79 U 16 Slade the SE18
150 C 19 Slade wk SE5
93 P 12 Slagrove pl SE13
146 C 16 Slaidburn st SW10
148 L 13 Slaithwaite rd SE13
148 L 13 S Lambeth pl SW1
48 E 14 Slaney rd N7
148 B 18 Sleaford st SW8
140 J 8 Slingsby pl WC2
146 K 6 Sloane av SW3
147 R 9 Sloane Ct east SW3
147 R 9 Sloane Ct west SW3
147 S 7 Sloane gdns SW1
147 R 6 Sloane sq SW1
139 P 19 Sloane st SW1
147 R 4 Sloane st SW1
147 R 5 Sloane ter SW1
124 K 14 Sloane wlk Croy
25 V 17 Slough la NW9
143 W 6 Sly st E1
44 W 4 Smallberry av Islwth
138 E 7 Smallbrook ms W2
49 U 8 Smalley clo N16
106 F 10 Smallwood rd SW17
88 C 12 Smardale rd SW18
81 R 12 Smarden clo Blvdr
113 T 8 Smarden gro SE9
39 Z 4 Smart clo Rom
140 L 4 Smarts pl WC2
63 T 8 Smart st E2
87 X 19 Smeaton rd SW18
89 Y 14 Smedley st SW8 & SW4
64 A 1 Smeed rd E3
141 X 2 Smithfield st EC1
72 K 17 Smith hill Brentf
51 T 14 Smithies ct E15
80 C 11 Smithies rd SE2
31 O 4 Smithson rd N17
148 J 3 Smith sq SW1
147 N 10 Smith st SW3
116 L 15 Smith st Surb
147 N 11 Smith ter SW3
105 S 3 Smithwood clo SW19
63 P 15 Smithy st E1
122 M 15 Smock wlk Croy
82 G 10 Smoothfield Hounsl
150 L 9 Smyrk's rd SE17
129 U 2 Smyrna rd NW6
64 E 19 Smythe st E14
6 G 11 Snakes la Barnt
35 S 17 Snakes la Wdfd Grn
21 T 18 Snakes la Wdfd Grn

S

11 V 14 Snaresbrook dri Stanm
34 E 11 Snaresbrook hall E18
33 Z 14 Snaresbrook rd E11
34 C 14 Snaresbrook rd E11
62 M 16 Snarsgate st W10
136 C 3 Snarsgate st W10
27 U 20 Sneath av NW11
18 H 18 Snells pk N18
44 M 13 Sneyd rd NW2
88 B 5 Snowbury rd SW6
134 J 19 Snowden st EC2
141 W 3 Snow hill EC1
142 G 17 Snowsfields SE1
53 N 15 Snowshill rd E12
53 P 14 Snowshill rd E12
91 U 8 Soames st SE15
118 A 1 Soames wlk New Mald
141 O 3 Soane Museum WC2
126 G 15 Socket la Brom
140 F 5 Soho sq W1
140 E 5 Soho st W1
45 X 10 Solent rd NW6
133 S 12 Soley ms WC1
86 L 14 Solna av SW15
18 A 3 Solna rd N21
92 A 9 Solomon's pass SE15
90 A 1 Solon rd SW4
82 C 7 Solway clo Hounsl
30 H 4 Solway rd N22
91 X 10 Solway rd SE22
5 U 19 Somaford gro Barnt
45 U 14 Somali rd NW2
54 D 20 Somerby rd Bark
48 J 7 Somerfield rd N4
49 U 13 Somerford gro N16
31 Y 2 Somerford gro N17
135 X 17 Somerford st E1
97 O 18 Somerhill av Sidcp
97 R 4 Somerhill av Welling
90 G 10 Somerleyton rd SW9
35 T 15 Somersby gds Ilf
132 F 9 Somers clo NW1
138 J 6 Somers cres W2
118 J 3 Somerset av SW20
96 L 11 Somerset av Welling
34 G 4 Somerset clo E18
118 B 13 Somerset clo New Mald
93 P 5 Somerset gdns SE13
122 D 6 Somerset gdns SW16
101 T 12 Somerset gdns Tedd
47 R 1 Somerset gdns N6
141 O 9 Somerset House WC2
33 O 17 Somerset rd E17
31 V 11 Somerset rd E17
18 F 16 Somerset rd N18
26 L 13 Somerset rd NW4
105 R 5 Somerset rd SW19
73 X 7 Somerset rd W4
72 C 3 Somerset rd W13
5 O 16 Somerset rd Barnt
72 F 17 Somerset rd Brentf
99 Z 17 Somerset rd Drtfrd
22 M 16 Somerset rd Harrow
117 N 4 Somerset rd Kingst
58 H 15 Somerset rd S'hall
101 U 12 Somerset rd Tedd
5 R 16 Somerset rd Barnt
70 A 18 Somerset ways Hounsl
137 N 19 Somerset sq W14
97 Z 5 Somersham rd Bxly Hth
90 C 17 Somers pl SW2
32 L 14 Somers rd E17
90 C 17 Somers rd SW2
85 S 8 Somerton av Rich
45 S 9 Somerton av NW2
92 A 10 Somerton rd SE15
112 H 5 Somertrees av SE12
40 J 14 Somervell rd Harrow
110 F 17 Somerville rd SE20
37 U 15 Somerville rd Rom
48 E 9 Sonderburg rd N7
150 F 13 Sondes st SE17
23 V 20 Sonia ct Harrow
15 P 14 Sonia gdns N12
44 D 12 Sonia gdns NW10
70 G 20 Sonia gdns Hounsl
123 X 15 Sonnng gdns SE25
48 C 18 Sophia clo N7
51 P 2 Sophia rd E10
65 V 16 Sophia rd E16
64 C 16 Sophia st E14
39 S 10 Sorrel wlk Rom
28 C 18 Sorrento rd Sutton
154 A 6 Sorrento rd Sutton
145 N 5 Sotheby rd N5
145 Z 20 Sotheron rd SW5

145 Z 20 Sotheron rd SW6
88 M 3 Souden st SW11
144 H 4 Souldern rd W14
32 H 19 South Access rd E17
26 C 8 South acre NW9
62 L 20 South Africa rd W12
74 J 1 South Africa rd W12
142 E 19 South Africa rd W12
89 S 2 Southall pl SE1
89 S 2 Southam st SW11
141 R 3 Southampton bldgs WC2
121 Z 8 Southampton gdns Mitch
140 L 2 Southampton pl WC1
46 M 14 Southampton rd NW5
132 K 19 Southampton row WC1
140 L 9 Southampton st WX2
91 T 1 Southampton way SE5
150 G 18 Southampton way SE5
150 K 19 Southampton way SE5
128 M 19 South av W10
139 V 12 South Audley st W1
20 E 1 South av E4
155 N 17 South av Carsh
85 O 3 South av Rich
58 D 20 South av S'hall
58 D 20 South Av gdns S'hall
114 A 8 Southbank Chisl
116 A 17 Southbank Surb
116 K 14 South Bank Surb
116 K 15 South Bank ter Surb
51 X 10 South Birkbeck rd S11
74 F 14 South Black Lion la W6
146 A 10 South Bolton gdns SW5
25 X 8 Southborne av NW9
116 X 19 Southborough clo Surb
127 U 12 Southborough la Brom
63 S 2 Southborough rd E9
127 S 10 Southborough rd Brom
116 J 20 Southborough rd Surb
126 F 18 Southbourne Brom
22 B 20 Southbourne clo Pinn
27 S 13 Southbourne cres NW4
94 H 12 Southbourne gdns SE12
54 B 16 Southbourne gdns Ilf
156 K 7 Southbridge pl Croy
156 M 8 Southbridge rd Croy
70 D 6 Southbridge way S'hall
94 C 15 Southbrook rd SE12
122 A 1 Southbrook rd SW16
74 K 6 Southbrook st W12
136 A 19 Southbrook st W12
8 K 14 Southbury av Enf
8 G 13 Southbury rd Enf
17 H 16 Southbury rd N13
66 G 7 Southchurch rd E6
29 R 17 South rd N6
4 H 12 South clo Barnt
97 W 11 South clo Bxly Hth
69 S 5 South clo Dgnhm
119 X 14 South clo Mrdn
40 E 2 South clo Pinn
100 H 6 South clo Twick
144 L 6 Southcombe st W14
117 S 18 Southcote av Surb
32 F 15 Southcote rd E17
47 V 12 Southcote rd N19
124 B 13 Southcote rd SE25
32 K 10 South Countess rd E17
140 F 1 South cres WC1
159 U 3 Southcroft av W Wkhm
96 H 7 Southcroft av Welling
107 N 14 Southcroft rd SW17
36 A 15 South Cross rd Ilf
109 O 6 South Croxted rd SE21
105 U 3 Southdean gdns SW19
12 L 12 South dene NW7
71 X 9 Southdown av W7
40 L 5 Southdown cres Harrow
36 G 15 Southdown cres Ilf

105 G 19 Southdown dri SW20
105 R 20 Southdown rd SW20
155 O 19 Southdown rd Carsh
57 X 2 Southdown rd Hornch
153 S 20 South dri Sutton
72 G 9 South Ealing rd W5
18 G 11 South Eastern av N9
147 V 6 South Eaton pl SW1
125 R 16 South End Pk rd Becknhm
145 S 3 South Edwardes sq W8
145 X 1 South end W8
156 M 8 south end Croy
46 K 13 South End clo NW3
95 Y 15 Southend clo SE9
95 Y 15 Southend cres SE9
46 K 14 South End grn NW3
110 L 9 Southend la SE16 & SE26
111 O 10 Southend la SE16 & SE26
53 T 19 Southend rd E6
34 H 6 Southend rd E18
46 J 11 South End rd NW3
111 P 17 Southend rd Becknhm
57 Z 14 South End rd Hornch
35 N 8 Southend rd Wdfd Grn
33 X 5 Southend rd E17
145 Y 1 South End row W8
32 G 9 Southerland rd E17
77 T 16 Southern appr SE10
123 V 6 Southern av SE25
63 Y 10 Southern gro E3
65 X 6 Southern rd E13
28 T 12 Southern rd N2
123 K 18 Southern row W10
133 N 9 Southern st N1
38 F 19 Southern way Rom
74 L 10 Southerton rd W6
144 B 5 Southerton rd W6
52 K 19 South Esk rd E7
31 S 15 Southey rd N15
90 E 1 Southey rd SW9
52 Z 18 Southey rd SW19
110 E 18 Southey st SE20
4 B 20 Southfield Barnt
71 W 5 Southfield cotts W7
101 V 8 Southfield gdns Twick
22 J 14 Southfield pk Harrow
73 X 6 Southfield rd W4
74 H 7 Southfield rd W4
9 P 19 Southfield rd Enf
26 H 9 Southfields NW4
87 X 16 Southfields rd SW18
106 G 18 South gdns SW19
134 G 1 Southgate gro N1
49 P 18 Southgate rd N1
134 G 3 Southgate rd N1
32 K 16 South gro E17
47 P 4 South gro N6
31 P 16 South gro N15
113 S 16 South hill Chisl
41 O 10 South Hill av Harrow
41 T 12 South Hill gro Harrow
46 K 12 South Hill pk NW3
46 K 11 South Hill pk NW3
125 Z 8 South Hill rd Brom
126 A 9 South Hill rd Brom
113 T 17 South Hill rd Chisl
149 S 19 South Island gro SW8
149 O 19 South Lambeth est SW8
148 L 17 South Lambeth rd SW8
79 Z 18 Southland rd SE18
127 R 7 Southlands gro Brom
26 M 10 Southlands rd Brom
127 P 8 Southlands rd Brom
83 P 13 Southland way Hounsl
116 G 6 South la Kingst
117 Z 15 South la New Mald
118 A 15 South la New Mald
117 X 9 South La w New Mald
121 Z 8 South Lodge av Mitch
122 A 8 South Lodge av Mitch
6 K 13 South Lodge cres Enf
6 J 14 South Lodge dr N14
7 N 17 South Lodge dr N14
153 X 6 Southly clo Sutton
152 C 16 Southmead Epsom
42 L 15 Southmeadows Wemb

26 D 3 South mead NW9
87 S 20 Southmead rd SW19
139 W 7 South Molton la W1
65 T 16 South Molton rd E16
139 W 7 South Molton st W1
139 W 7 South Molton pas W1
123 T 10 South Norwood hill SE25
113 V 8 Southold ri SE9
14 K 11 Southover N12
14 L 14 Southover N12
112 F 14 Southover Brom
94 A 20 South Park cres SE6
112 B 1 South Park cres SE6
54 F 9 South Park cres Ilf
54 G 9 South Park dri Ilf
54 G 9 South Pk gro New Mald
157 R 10 South Park Hill rd S Croy
105 X 16 South Park rd SW19
106 B 15 South Park rd SW19
54 F 11 South Park rd Ilf
145 G 10 South pde SW3
73 Y 10 South pde W4
142 G 1 South pl EC2
160 F 1 South pl EC2
116 L 16 South pl Surb
142 G 1 South pl ms EC2
160 G 1 South pl ms EC2
79 S 11 Southport rd SE18
154 X 19 South ri Carsh
18 L 5 South rd N9
110 E 4 South rd SE23
106 D 16 South rd SW19
72 G 10 South rd W5
72 C 10 South rd Edg
100 A 14 South rd Felt
100 D 16 South rd Hampt
37 X 18 South rd Rom
70 E 3 South rd S'hall
101 R 8 South rd Twick
94 C 4 South row SE3
116 J 8 Southsea rd Kingst
74 D 9 Southside W6
105 O 14 Southside comm SW19
96 F 18 Southspring Sidcp
27 Z 18 South sq NW11
141 R 1 South sq WC1
139 T 12 South st W1
126 F 2 South st Brom
9 S 17 South st Enf
39 R 16 South st Rainhm
39 R 16 South st Rom
143 P 7 South ter Enf
146 J 5 South ter SW7
116 K 13 South ter Surb
109 R 16 South vale SE19
41 U 12 South vale Harrow
94 A 5 Southvale rd SE3
126 J 3 South view Brom
99 O 13 South view Drtfrd
44 D 14 Southview av NW10
98 B 17 South View clo Bxly
35 Y 18 South View cres Ilf
34 J 11 South View dri E18
155 V 17 Southview gdns Wallgtn
29 Z 1 South View rd N8
111 X 9 Southview rd Brom
47 V 18 South vills NW1
89 Y 2 Southville SW8
159 Z 5 South wlk W Wkhm
142 C 11 Southwark Br SE1
142 B 16 Southwark Br rd SE1
142 A 14 Southwark gro SE1
143 X 20 Southwark Pk rd SE16
151 T 5 Southwark Pk rd SE16
151 X 2 Southwark Pk rd SE16
142 C 14 Southwark st SE1
63 Y 17 Southwater clo E14
19 R 9 South way N9
14 M 7 South way E12
14 L 5 Southway N20
28 B 17 Southway NW11
119 N 10 Southway SW20
126 E 18 Southway Brom
158 K 5 South way Croy
22 H 14 South way Harrow
155 V 9 Southway Wallgtn
42 P 14 South way Wemb
74 L 6 Southway clo W12
40 J 16 Southwell av Grnfd
146 C 3 Southwell gdns SW7
51 Z 7 Southwell Gro rd E11
90 A 4 Southwell rd SE5
122 F 14 Southwell rd Croy

S

24	H 18	Southwell rd Harrow
83	Z 15	South Western rd Twick
84	A 16	South Western rd Twick
51	X 3	Southwest rd E11
138	G 4	South Wharf rd W2
138	J 5	Southwick pl W2
138	J 7	Southwick pl W2
138	J 5	Southwick st W2
55	N 15	Southwold dri Bark
50	A 7	Southwold rd E5
98	G 17	Southwold rd Bxly
29	R 20	Southwood av N6
103	W 20	Southwood av Kingst
153	P 1	Southwood clo Worc Pk
117	X 18	Southwood dri Surb
35	Z 14	Southwood gdns Ilf
29	P 20	Southwood la N6
37	P 2	Southwood la N6
29	S 20	Southwood Lawn rd N6
47	S 1	Southwood Lawn rd N6
47	R 1	Southwood pk N6
113	Y 4	Southwood rd SE9
114	A 3	Southwood rd SE9
80	D 3	Southwood rd SE18
86	A 8	South Worple av SW13
85	Y 8	South Worple way SW14
86	A 8	South Worple way SW14
60	D 15	Sovereign clo W13
95	T 14	Sowerby clo SE9
57	U 17	Sowerey av Rainhm
133	T 15	Spafield st EC1
109	O 19	Spa hill SE19
107	S 13	Spalding rd E3
46	B 12	Spanby rd E3
46	E 3	Spaniards clo NW11
46	F 4	Spaniards end NW3
46	E 6	Spaniards rd NW3
139	U 3	Spanish pl W1
88	E 12	Spanish rd SW18
123	R 2	Spar clo SE25
23	T 13	Sparkbridge rd Harrow
151	O 2	Spa rd SE16
151	S 2	Spa rd SE16
152	J 19	Sparrow Farm rd Epsom
56	G 8	Sparrow grn Dgnhm
96	B 20	Sparrows la SE9
114	C 1	Sparrows la SE9
10	B 4	Sparrows way Bushey Watf
48	B 3	Sparholt rd N4
67	V 4	Sparsholt rd Bark
93	T 3	Sparta st SE10
78	K 17	Spearman st SE18
145	V 7	Spear ms W8
36	K 14	Spearpoint gdns Ilf
48	A 4	Spears rd N19
70	B 20	Speart la Hounsl
46	B 10	Spedan clo NW3
76	A 20	Speedwell st SE8
132	K 14	Speedy pl WC1
113	U 8	Speke hill SE9
123	N 3	Speke rd Thntn Hth
126	D 13	Speldhurst rd E9
63	S 2	Speldhurst rd E9
73	Z 7	Speldhurst rd W4
135	R 20	Spelman st E1
143	R 1	Spelman st E1
17	R 19	Spencer av N13
61	N 7	Spencer clo NW10
123	P 17	Spencer clo Croy
21	Y 17	Spencer clo Wdfd Grn
28	D 19	Spencer dri N2
95	T 13	Spencer gdns SW14
105	S 17	Spencer hill SW19
105	T 17	Spencer Hill rd SW14
88	F 13	Spencer pk SW18
47	T 11	Spencer ri NW5
66	B 3	Spencer rd E6
33	U 6	Spencer rd E17
16	D 14	Spencer rd N11
31	X 5	Spencer rd N17
88	G 12	Spencer rd SW18
118	K 1	Spencer rd SW20
73	V 2	Spencer rd W3
73	V 20	Spencer rd W4
112	B 13	Spencer rd Brom
23	U 8	Spencer rd Harrow
54	L 4	Spencer rd Ilf
83	O 3	Spencer rd Islwth
121	N 18	Spencer rd Mitch
157	S 11	Spencer rd S Croy
101	T 5	Spencer rd Twick
42	C 6	Spencer rd Wemb
133	X 13	Spencer st EC1
87	O 10	Spencer wlk SW15
49	R 13	Spencer gro N16
90	G 14	Spencer rd SE24
148	C 1	Spenser st SW1
49	P 8	Spensley wlk N16
79	X 13	Speranza st SE18
31	T 9	Spert st N17
63	V 20	Spert st E14
5	T 9	Spey side N14
39	P 2	Spey way Rom
62	G 6	Spezia rd NW10
118	E 13	Spiers clo New Mald
31	N 3	Sigurnell rd N17
58	C 18	Spikes Br rd S'hall
26	A 7	Spilsby clo NW9
79	V 14	Spindle clo SE18
157	R 8	Spindlewood gdns Croy
79	Y 14	Spinel clo SE18
40	D 4	Spinnells rd Harrow
118	A 11	Spinney clo New Mald
56	A 14	Spinney gdns Dgnhm
127	S 3	Spinney oak Brom
127	T 3	Spinneys the Brom
17	S 2	Spinney the N21
107	E 7	Spinney the SW16
5	O 10	Spinney the Barnt
115	Y 2	Spinney the Sidcp
11	X 14	Spinney the Stanm
152	M 9	Spinney the Sutton
41	X 10	Spinney the Wemb
134	M 20	Spitalfields market E1
134	L 20	Spital sq E1
135	R 19	Spital st E1
31	W 13	Spondon rd N15
15	O 15	Spooner wlk Wallgtn
93	U 20	Spratts st SE6
30	L 3	Spottons gro N17
159	O 11	Spout hill Croy
34	F 18	Spratt Hall rd E11
83	R 14	Spray la Islwth
78	M 10	Spray st SE18
79	N 10	Spray st SE18
147	N 8	Sprimont pl SW3
75	N 20	Springalls st SE15
151	X 19	Springall st SE15
17	P 1	Springbank N14
93	Z 17	Springbank rd SE13
111	U 20	Springbourne ct Becknhm
60	G 19	Spring Br rd W5
153	S 12	Spring Clo la Sutton
72	H 13	Springdale av Brentf
49	N 12	Springdale rd N16
49	Y 4	Springfield E5
50	A 3	Springfield E5
10	C 4	Springfield Bushey Watf
29	V 11	Springfield av N22
119	U 5	Springfield av SW20
100	K 14	Springfield av Hampt
10	L 11	Springfield clo Stanm
36	B 17	Springfield dri Ilf
50	A 4	Springfield gdns E5
25	Z 16	Springfield gdns NW9
127	U 9	Springfield gdns Brom
159	T 2	Springfield gdns W Wkhm
34	L 2	Springfield gdns Wdfd Grn
77	Y 17	Springfield gro SE7
129	W6	Springfield la NW6
26	A 15	Springfield mt NW9
49	Z 2	Springfield pk E5
109	Z 8	Springfield ri SE26
20	L 4	Springfield rd E4
53	U 19	Springfield rd E6
65	N 8	Springfield rd E15
32	K 19	Springfield rd E17
16	G 17	Springfield rd N11
31	X 12	Springfield rd N15
130	A 5	Springfield rd NW8
110	B 14	Springfield rd SE26
105	W 13	Springfield rd SW19
71	T 2	Springfield rd W7
98	G 10	Springfield rd Bxly Hth
127	U 9	Springfield rd Brom
23	T 18	Springfield rd Harrow
116	K 7	Springfield rd Kingst
101	Y 13	Springfield rd Tedd
108	L 20	Springfield rd Thntn Hth
122	L 1	Springfield rd Thntn Hth
82	H 20	Springfield rd Twick
155	S 11	Springfield rd Wallgtn
97	P 7	Springfield rd Welling
129	W 5	Springfield wlk NW6
140	H 13	Spring gdns SW1
57	Y 13	Spring gdns Hrnch
48	L 16	Spring gdns N5
38	J 17	Spring gdns Rom
155	U 11	Spring gdns Wallgtn
34	J 1	Spring gdns Wdfd Grn
148	M 11	Spring Gdns wlk SE11
73	O 15	Spring gro W4
82	M 2	Spring Grove cres Hounsl
52	L 3	Spring Grove rd Hounsl
83	N 3	Spring Grove rd Hounsl
84	M 12	Spring Grove rd Rich
85	N 12	Spring Grove rd Rich
49	X 2	Spring hill E5
91	P 8	Springhill clo SE5
11	N 13	Spring lake Stanm
123	Z 14	Spring la SE25
124	A 15	Spring la SE25
50	A 2	Spring la E5
139	R 1	Spring ms W1
159	T 7	Spring park Croy
158	G 4	Spring Pk av Croy
48	M 3	Springpark dri N4
125	V 5	Springpark dri Becknhm
158	F 3	Spring Pk rd Croy
47	R 16	Spring pl NW5
56	Z 15	Spring Pond rd Dgnhm
93	W 16	Spring Rice rd SE13
138	F 7	Spring st W2
152	O 20	Spring st Epsom
98	H 10	Spring vale Bxly Hth
144	G 2	Spring Vale ter W14
25	P 1	Spring Villa rd Edg
95	W 2	Springwater clo SE18
62	E 4	Springwell av NW10
108	D 10	Springwell clo SW16
108	E 11	Springwell rd SW16
70	A 20	Springwell rd Hounsl
12	F 7	Springwood cres Edg
12	G 7	Springwood cres Edg
39	V 16	Springwood way Rom
52	F 16	Sprowston ms E7
52	F 16	Sprowston rd E7
158	F 8	Sprucedale gdn Croy
155	Z 20	Sprucedale gdns Wallgtn
33	T 9	Spruce Hills rd E17
92	H 6	Sprules rd SE4
109	O 19	Spurgeon av SE19
109	O 19	Spurgeon rd SE19
150	E 1	Spurgeon st SE1
91	V 10	Spurling rd SE22
56	C 17	Spurling rd Dgnhm
32	Q 13	Spur rd N15
140	B 19	Spur rd SW1
67	O 8	Spur rd Bark
67	O 9	Spur rd Bark
11	Y 12	Spur rd Edg
77	Z 20	Spur rd Islwth
49	Z 18	Spurstowe rd E8
49	Y 16	Spurstowe ter E8
155	N 10	Square the Carsh
21	R 17	Square the Wdfd Grn
53	W 1	Square the Ilf
106	E 7	Squarey st SW17
28	E 4	Squire's la N3
48	F 9	Squires mt NW3
113	S 18	Squires Woor ces Chisl
15	P 13	Squirrels clo N12
152	E 2	Squirrels grn Worc Pk
39	Y 11	Squirrels Heath av Rom
22	E 11	Squirrels the Pinn
135	T 13	Squirries st E2
21	Y 2	Stables the Buck HI
149	S 10	Stables way SE11
58	G 4	Stable cr Grnfd
28	G 4	Stable wk N2
140	B 16	Stable yd SW1
140	B 16	Stable Yd rd SW1
19	P 15	Stacey av N18
33	W 17	Stacey clo E10
140	H 6	Stacey st WC2
139	T 20	Stackhouse st SW3
78	E 18	Stadium rd SE18
99	R 13	Stadium rd Drtfd
146	O 19	Stadium st SW10
43	P 13	Stadium way Wemb
50	G 3	Staffa rd E10
6	H 17	Stafford clo N14
153	T 13	Stafford clo Sutton
129	T 13	Stafford clo NW6
156	O 10	Stafford gdns Croy
140	A 20	Stafford pl SW1
84	L 18	Stafford pl Rich
63	Y 7	Stafford rd E3
52	M 19	Stafford rd E7
129	S 11	Stafford rd NW6
156	D 11	Stafford rd Croy & Wallgtn
23	N 3	Stafford rd Harrow
117	V 6	Stafford rd New Mald
114	H 9	Stafford rd Sidcp
155	U 14	Stafford rd Wallgtn
156	B 12	Stafford rd Wallgtn
91	Y 1	Staffordshire st SE15
140	A 12	Stafford st W1
137	U 20	Stafford ter W8
132	E 15	Sta fore ct NW1
25	U 7	Stag clo Edg
25	V 10	Stag la NW9
104	E 5	Stag la SW15
21	V 7	Stag la Buck HI
148	A 1	Stag pl SW1
121	S 5	Stainbank rd Mitch
31	V 12	Stainby rd N15
142	G 15	Stainer st SE1
142	H 15	Stainer st SE1
153	P 3	Staines av Sutton
82	E 10	Staines rd Hounsl
54	D 14	Staines rd Ilf
100	H 7	Staines rd Twick
101	O 4	Staines rd Twick
115	U 15	Staines wlk Sidcp
33	P 13	Stainforth rd E17
36	F 20	Stainforth rd Ilf
160	B 4	Staining la EC2
114	E 20	Stainmore clo Chisl
63	R 7	Stainsby st E2
64	A 16	Stainsby rd E14
64	A 16	Stainsby rd E14
93	W 18	Stainton rd Se6
9	R 5	Stainton rd Enf
130	L 20	Stalbridge st NW1
51	Y 3	Stalham st SE16
75	N 9	Stalham st SE16
109	S 19	Stambourne way SE19
159	V 4	Stambourne way W Wkhm
145	Y 18	Stamford Bridge stadium SW6
74	E 10	Stamford Brook av W6
74	E 9	Stamford Brook rd W6
148	M 18	Stamford bldgs SW8
31	X 14	Stamford clo N15
23	T 1	Stamford clo Harrow
70	H 1	Stamford clo S'hall
126	D 10	Stamford dri Brom
49	W 3	Stamford Grn east N16
49	W 4	Stamford Grn west N16
49	U 4	Stamford hill N16
66	C 3	Stamford rd E6
31	W 14	Stamford rd N15
68	D 2	Stamford rd Dgnhm
55	U 20	Stamford rd Dgnhm
141	T 13	Stamford st SE1
54	F 1	Stamforth rd Ilf
15	O 11	Stamp pl E2
100	E 15	Stanborough clo Hampt
83	R 7	Stanborough rd Hounsl
87	N 7	Stanbridge rd SW15
80	C 6	Stanbrook rd SE2
92	B 4	Stanbury rd SE15
26	A 15	Stancroft NW9
61	X 10	Standard rd NW10
81	R 14	Standard rd Blvdr
8	A 1	Standard rd Bxly Hth
9	W 1	Standard rd Enf
82	C 7	Standard rd Hounsl
87	X 20	Standen rd SW18
65	V 10	Standish rd W6
106	B 19	Stane clo SW19
107	Z 11	Stane pas SW16
63	X 7	Stanfield rd E3
56	F 15	Stanfield rd Dgnhm
38	G 18	Stanford clo Rom
100	E 15	Stanford clo Hampt

S

Page	Ref	Name
16	A 16	Stanford rd N11
145	Y 2	Stanford rd W8
148	E 6	Stanford st SW1
121	X 3	Stanford way SW16
11	O 14	Stangate gdns Stanm
123	X 10	Stanger rd SE25
99	X 11	Stanham pl Drtfrd
27	W 10	Stanhope av N3
126	E 20	Stanhope av Brom
23	P 5	Stanhope av Harrow
30	K 18	Stanhope gdns Harrow
29	U 19	Stanhope gdns N6
13	R 17	Stanhope gdns SW7
146	D 6	Stanhope gdns SW7
56	A 8	Stanhope gdns Dgnhm
53	T 3	Stanhope gdns Ilf
139	U 13	Stanhope ga W1
124	L 10	Stanhope gro Becknhm
146	D 5	Stanhope Ms east SW7
146	C 6	Stanhope Ms south SW7
146	C 5	Stanhope Ms west SW7
59	N 10	Stanhope Pk rd Grnfd
139	N 7	Stanhope pl W2
33	R 16	Stanhope rd E17
29	V 20	Stanhope rd N6
47	V 1	Stanhope rd N6
16	D 15	Stanhope rd N11
15	S 16	Stanhope rd N12
4	B 19	Stanhope rd Barnt
97	Z 4	Stanhope rd Bxly Hth
94	A 4	Stanhope rd Bxly Hth
155	O 17	Stanhope rd Carsh
157	R 7	Stanhope rd Croy
56	A 8	Stanhope rd Dgnhm
69	N 13	Stanhope rd Grnfd
114	M 8	Stanhope rd Sidcp
139	W 15	Stanhope row W11
132	A 12	Stanhope st NW1
138	G 8	Stanhope ter W2
145	R 11	Stanier clo SW6
74	L 3	Stanlake ms W12
74	K 2	Stanlake rd W12
136	A 14	Stanlake rd W12
74	L 3	Stanlake vlls W12
136	A 15	Stanlake vlls W12
56	K 8	Stanley av Bark
125	U 5	Stanley av Becknhm
56	C 3	Stanley av Dgnhm
58	M 3	Stanley av Grnfd
59	N 3	Stanley av Grnfd
118	F 11	Stanley av New Mald
39	W 14	Stanley av Rom
60	K 1	Stanley av Wemb
149	N 16	Stanley clo SW8
39	X 12	Stanley clo Rom
60	K 1	Stanley clo Wemb
137	O 9	Stanley cres W11
83	R 3	Stanleycroft clo Islwth
45	N 16	Stanley gdns NW2
107	N 16	Stanley gdns SW17
74	A 5	Stanley gdns W3
137	P 9	Stanley gdns W11
155	U 15	Stanley gdns Wallgtn
101	T 11	Stanley Gdns rd Tedd
89	R 5	Stanley gro SW8
122	F 15	Stanley gro Croy
60	M 2	Stanley Pk dri Wemb
154	M 16	Stanley Pk rd Carsh
155	S 14	Stanley Pk rd Wallgtn
132	J 9	Stanley pas NW1
20	K 4	Stanley rd E4
33	R 19	Stanley rd E10
33	R 16	Stanley rd E12
42	J 4	Stanley rd E15
34	C 6	Stanley rd E18
28	G 12	Stanley rd N2
18	F 7	Stanley rd N9
29	R 2	Stanley rd N10
16	L 17	Stanley rd N11
30	K 13	Stanley rd N15
105	T 10	Stanley rd SW14
137	T 16	Stanley rd SW19
73	U 8	Stanley rd W3
126	K 8	Stanley rd Brom
155	O 18	Stanley rd Carsh
122	G 15	Stanley rd Croy
8	F 13	Stanley rd Enf
60	M 7	Stanley rd Harrow
41	N 8	Stanley rd Harrow
147	N 16	Stanley rd Hounsl
83	N 9	Stanley rd Hounsl
54	D 8	Stanley rd Ilf
119	Y 8	Stanley rd Mrdn
115	O 8	Stanley rd Sidcp
58	A 20	Stanley rd S'hall
153	Z 16	Stanley rd Sutton
154	A 16	Stanley rd Sutton
101	U 13	Stanley rd Tedd
43	N 17	Stanley rd Wemb
155	N 19	Stanley sq Carsh
66	L 19	Stanley st E6
75	Y 19	Stanley st SE8
48	A 8	Stanley ter N4
88	K 4	Stanmer st SW11
88	N 8	Stanmore gdns Rich
154	D 6	Stanmore gdns Sutton
10	L 11	Stanmore hill Stanm
11	O 14	Stanmore hill Stanm
52	C 4	Stanmore rd E11
30	K 12	Stanmore rd N15
81	Y 10	Stanmore Blvd
84	M 7	Stanmore rd Rich
133	N 3	Stanmore st N1
125	P 2	Stanmore ter Becknhm
66	K 17	Stannard cres E8
49	W 17	Stannard rd E8
149	U 12	Stannary pl SE11
149	U 12	Stannary st SE11
90	D 7	Stansfield rd SW9
56	E 9	Stansgate rd Dgnhm
126	C 13	Stanstead clo Brom
57	Z 19	Stanstead clo Hornch
34	H 15	Stanstead rd E11
110	J 1	Stanstead rd SE23
115	W 2	Stansted cres Bxly
107	Z 11	Stanthorpe rd SW16
108	A 1	Stanthorpe rd SW16
101	T 14	Stanton av Tedd
153	O 1	Stanton clo Worc Pk
86	D 4	Stanton rd SW13
119	O 1	Stanton rd SW20
122	L 18	Stanton rd Croy
91	W 1	Stanton st SE15
110	K 9	Stanway way SE26
73	P 1	Stanway gdns Edg
12	G 17	Stanway gdns Edg
134	K 9	Stanway st N1
145	O 7	Stanwick rd W14
150	K 20	Stanwood gdns SE5
42	A 9	Stapenhill rd Wemb
22	A 1	Staple Field clo Pinn
108	A 1	Staplefield clo SW2
36	H 17	Stapleford av Ilf
87	R 20	Stapleford clo SW19
42	G 20	Stapleford clo Kingst
68	D 8	Stapleford way Bark
93	Y 14	Staplehurst rd SE13
154	J 17	Staplehurst rd Carsh
141	S 3	Staple Inn WC1
141	S 3	Staple Inn bldgs WC1
142	G 19	Staple st SE1
57	W 19	Stapleton cres Rainhm
156	F 10	Stapleton gdns Croy
30	F 20	Stapleton Hall rd N4
48	D 3	Stapleton Hall rd N4
107	N 7	Stapleton rd SW17
8	H 5	Stapley rd Blvdr
4	F 12	Staplyton rd Barnt
63	N 20	Star & Garter rd E1
142	K 8	Star all EC3
84	L 20	Star and Garter hill Rich
76	C 8	Starboard way E14
36	E 7	Starch Ho la Ilf
132	C 14	Starcross st NW1
74	G 6	Starfield rd W12
99	O 12	Star hill Drtfrd
64	M 12	Star la E16
65	N 13	Star la E16
21	U 6	Starling clo Buck HI
79	S 6	Starling ms SE18
145	N 12	Star rd W14
83	P 5	Star rd Islwth
138	J 4	Star st W2
65	P 13	Star st E16
141	S 5	Star yrd WC2
101	W 1	Staten gdns Twick
83	W 20	Staten gdns Twick
49	N 11	Statham gro N16
18	D 15	Statham gro N18
16	D 16	Station appr N11
87	U 7	Station appr SW16
107	Y 12	Station appr SW16
98	F 20	Station appr Bxly
98	J 5	Station appr Bxly Hth
127	W 2	Station appr Chisl
113	R 16	Station appr Drtfrd
95	S 12	Station appr SE9
113	T 1	Station appr SE9
162	F 11	Station appr Epsom
100	H 20	Station appr Hampt
23	U 20	Station appr Harrow
117	R 2	Station appr Kingst
22	B 12	Station appr Pinn
85	D 2	Station appr Rich
153	T 16	Station appr Sutton
97	O 5	Station appr Wemb
42	C 7	Station appr Wemb
73	W 20	Station appr rd W4
90	K 7	Station av SW9
152	C 19	Station av Epsom
85	O 3	Station av Rich
118	C 6	Station av New Mald
27	Z	Station clo N3
100	K 20	Station clo Hampt
31	N 14	Station cres N15
77	S 15	Station cres SE3
42	B 17	Station cres Wemb
141	Y 5	Stationers Hall ct EC4
73	W 20	Station gdns W4
42	J 17	Station gro Wemb
44	N 17	Station pde NW2
45	N 17	Station pde NW2
57	Y 13	Station pde Hornch
85	O 2	Station pde Rich
25	N 10	Station pde NW9
48	G 7	Station pl N4
108	J 3	Station ri SE27
20	K 3	Station rd E4
52	F 13	Station rd E7
51	V 10	Station rd E10
53	O 13	Station rd E12
51	W 18	Station rd E15
32	J 17	Station rd E17
27	Y 5	Station rd N3
28	A 7	Station rd N11
16	E 17	Station rd N11
31	Y 11	Station rd N17
47	V 10	Station rd N19
17	W 5	Station rd N21
30	A 1	Station rd N22
30	D 7	Station rd N22
28	G 18	Station rd NW4
13	P 18	Station rd NW7
110	C 15	Station rd SE20
123	V 9	Station rd SE25
86	E 4	Station rd SW13
86	D 9	Station rd SW13
106	F 20	Station rd SW19
61	N 17	Station rd W5
71	T 2	Station rd W7
81	T 9	Station rd Blvdr
97	Z 6	Station rd Bxly Hth
98	A 6	Station rd Bxly Hth
126	A 3	Station rd Brom
155	N 7	Station rd Carsh
122	L 20	Station rd Croy
157	P 3	Station rd Croy
99	T 15	Station rd Drtfrd
12	D 18	Station rd Edg
100	H 20	Station rd Hampt
22	K 15	Station rd Harrow
23	V 19	Station rd Harrow
42	K 12	Station rd Hounsl
36	F 11	Station rd Ilf
53	Z 8	Station rd Ilf
117	P 1	Station rd Kingst
118	J 12	Station rd New Mald
81	U 8	Station rd North Blvdr
22	D 12	Station rd Pinn
55	W 1	Station rd Rom
101	X 14	Station rd Tedd
125	U 20	Station rd W Wkhm
159	U 1	Station rd W Wkhm
51	W 20	Station st E15
78	L 4	Station st E16
128	E 9	Station ter NW10
90	M 2	Station ter SE5
59	P 2	Station view Grnfd
153	S 15	Station way Sutton
83	X 19	Station way Twick
102	L 17	Staunton rd Kingst
52	A 8	Staunton st SE8
48	B 14	Staveley clo N7
92	A 1	Staveley clo SE5
85	Z 1	Staveley gdns W4
73	X 18	Staveley rd W4
44	M 19	Staverton rd NW2
48	G 13	Stavordale rd N5
120	C 18	Stavordale rd Carsh
53	X 4	Stayton rd Sutton
50	D 7	Stead st SE17
81	S 10	Stean st E8
68	B 6	Stebbing way Bark
76	H 10	Stebondale st E14
41	W 1	Stedham pl WC1
28	M 6	Steeds rd N10
52	Z 12	Steele rd E11
31	T 9	Steele rd N17
61	W 7	Steele rd NW10
73	X 8	Steele rd W4
83	Y 11	Steele rd Islwth
63	R 18	Steele la E1
46	M 18	Steel's ms NW3
36	M 18	Steel's rd NW3
91	S 12	Steen way SE22
107	Y 8	Steep hill SW16
87	T 6	Steeple clo SW6
105	T 11	Steeple clo SW19
17	Y 17	Steeplestone clo N18
106	C 5	Steerforth st SW18
106	L 20	Steers mead Mitch
120	K 1	Steers mead Mitch
107	N 4	Stella rd SW17
123	Z 4	Stembridge rd SE20
124	A 4	Stembridge rd SE20
57	V 17	Stephen av Rainhm
88	B 6	Stephendale rd SW6
46	E 3	Stephen ms W1
98	K 9	Stephen rd Bxly Hth
59	W 16	Stephenson rd W7
64	M 15	Stephenson st E16
62	C 8	Stephenson st NW10
132	C 15	Stephensons way NW1
64	M 5	Stephen's rd E15
65	O 4	Stephen's rd E15
140	E 3	Stephen st W1
63	T 19	Stepney causeway E1
63	R 13	Stephney grn E1
63	U 16	Stepney High st E1
63	R 15	Stepney way E1
143	W 2	Stepney way E1
11	Z 13	Sterling av Edg
12	A 13	Sterling av Edg
8	A 5	Sterling rd Enf
138	L 20	Sterling st SW7
18	C 15	Sterling way N18
144	E 2	Sterndale rd W14
136	F 16	Sterne st W12
91	Y 6	Sternhall la SE15
107	Y 3	Sternhold av SW2
40	A 4	Sternhold av SW2
56	D 14	Sterry cres Dgnhm
152	A 8	Sterry gdns Dgnhm
56	E 17	Sterry gdns Dgnhm
67	X 4	Sterry rd Bark
56	D 12	Sterry rd Dgnhm
92	J 20	Steucers La SE23
15	O 16	Stevedale rd Welling
53	V 18	Stevenage rd E6
87	O 3	Stevenage rd SW6
144	E 20	Stevenage rd SW6
50	D 17	Stevens av E9
100	D 14	Stevens clo Hampt
10	B 6	Stevens grn Bushey Watf
55	R 9	Stevens rd Dgnhm
74	E 1	Steventon rd W12
134	M 20	Steward st E1
142	L 1	Steward st E1
39	R 16	Steward wlk Rom
100	C 15	Stewart clo Hampt
25	W 19	Stewart clo NW9
51	V 13	Stewart rd E15
17	X 17	Stewartsby clo N18
146	J 9	Stewart's gro SW3
147	Z 20	Stewart's la SW8
89	W 3	Stewart's rd SW8
148	A 20	Stewart's rd SW8
76	H 6	Stewart st E14
73	T 2	Steyne rd W3
113	T 10	Steyning gro SE9
14	K 17	Steynings way N12
115	X 3	Steynton av Bxly
81	S 10	Stickland rd Blvdr
58	K 10	Stickleton clo Grnfd
42	B 11	Stilecroft gdns Wemb
73	P 14	Stile Hall gdns W4
127	U 13	Stiles clo Brom
74	G 18	Stillingfleet rd SW13
148	C 6	Stillington st SW1
92	K 17	Stillness rd SE23
58	B 11	Stipulakis dr Grnfd
65	V 7	Stirling rd E13
32	G 9	Stirling rd E17
31	X 5	Stirling rd N17
30	H 4	Stirling rd N22
90	A 6	Stirling rd SW9
73	T 8	Stirling rd W3
23	V 9	Stirling rd Harrow
82	H 20	Stirling rd Twick
32	G 9	Stirling rd path E17
117	T 14	Stirling wlk Surb
122	A 18	Stirling wy Croy
40	E 10	Stites Hall la
124	B 14	Stockbury rd Croy
56	B 6	Stockdale rd Dgnhm
59	X 9	Stockdove way Grnfd
108	D 6	Stockfield rd SW16
87	L 3	Stockhurst clo SW15

S

Page	Grid	Name
9	X 10	Stockingswater la Enf
38	M 19	Stockland rd Rom
48	C 14	Stock Orchard cres N7
48	C 15	Stock Orchard st N7
107	X 20	Stockport rd SW16
121	X 1	Stockport rd SW16
33	V 11	Stocksfield E17
65	T 8	Stock st E13
30	L 3	Stockton gdns N17
12	M 10	Stockton gdns NW7
13	N 10	Stockton gdns NW7
30	L 3	Stockton rd N17
18	L 18	Stockton rd N18
90	D 8	Stockwell av SW9
90	C 3	Stockwell gdns SW9
90	C 6	Stockwell ms SW9
90	C 6	Stockwell gro SW9
90	C 5	Stockwell la SW9
90	D 4	Stockwell Pk cres SW9
90	D 4	Stockwell Pk rd SW9
90	E 7	Stockwell Pk wlk SW9
90	C 5	Stockwell rd SW9
90	B 2	Stockwell st SE10
110	B 20	Stodart rd SE20
124	B 1	Stodart rd SE20
37	S 20	Stoford clo SW19
87	Z 3	Stockenchurch st SW6
49	O 9	Stoke Newington Ch st N16
49	V 8	Stoke Newington comm N16
49	U 9	Stoke Newington High st N16
49	T 13	Stoke Newington rd N16
62	D 9	Stoke pl NW10
103	V 18	Stoke rd Kingst
62	E 17	Stokesley st W12
66	D 3	Stokes rd E6
124	G 15	Stokes rd Croy
17	U 9	Stonard rd N13
55	R 13	Stonard rd Dgnhm
92	H 16	Stondon pk SE23
61	Y 1	Stoneale pk NW10
31	U 16	Stonebridge rd N15
31	T 16	Stonebridge rd N17
43	T 18	Stonebridge way Wemb
141	R 3	Stone bldgs WC2
56	C 8	Stone clo Dgnhm
119	S 20	Stonecot clo Sutton
81	X 20	Stonecroft rd Erith
122	A 16	Stonecroft way Croy
141	V 4	Stonecutter st EC4
98	E 8	Stonefield cio Bxly Hth
40	A 14	Stonefield clo Ruislip
133	T 4	Stonefield st N1
78	B 19	Stonefield way SE7
40	B 14	Stonefield way Ruislip
11	Z 15	Stone gro Edg
11	Y 16	Stonegrove gdns Edg
35	R 19	Stonehall av Ilf
17	S 2	Stone Hall rd N21
16	J 18	Stoneham rd N11
85	V 13	Stonehill clo SW14
85	X 13	Stonehill rd SW14
73	R 14	Stonehill rd W4
109	T 6	Stonehills ct SE21
2	H 6	Stonehorse rd Enf
142	K 3	Stone House ct EC2
2	N 5	Stoneleigh av Enf
152	G 7	Stoneleigh av Worc Pk
152	E 10	Stoneleigh cres Epsom
124	G 13	Stoneleigh pk Croy
152	F 10	Stoneleigh Pk rd Epsom
136	H 10	Stoneleigh pl W11
31	V 9	Stoneleigh rd N17
120	H 16	Stoneleigh rd Carsh
35	S 11	Stoneleigh rd Ilf
136	H 10	Stoneleigh st W11
88	M 5	Stonells rd SW11
48	D 5	Stonenest st N4
125	P 8	Stone Pk av Becknhm
152	C 2	Stone pl Worc Pk
126	D 10	Stone rd Brom
142	A 19	Stones End st SE1
156	E 12	Stone st Croy
95	Y 4	Stoney all SE18
94	C 18	Stoneycroft clo SE12
32	H 13	Stoneydown av E17
32	G 13	Stoneydown yd E17
12	J 14	Stonefields gdns Edg
12	J 13	Stoneyfields la Edg
142	M 4	Stoney la E1
109	T 17	Stoney la SE19
142	D 13	Stoney st SE1
89	W 9	Stonhouse st SW4
145	P 7	Stonor rd W14
65	T 3	Stopford rd E13
149	Z 11	Stopford rd SE17
78	H 5	Store rd E16
51	Y 16	Store st E15
140	F 1	Store st WC1
32	L 14	Storey rd E17
29	N 18	Storey rd N6
140	H 18	Storeys gate SW1
78	K 4	Storey st E16
91	R 7	Stories rd SE5
52	D 19	Stork rd E7
26	A 2	Storksmead rd Edg
28	I 20	Stormont rd N6
46	L 1	Stormont rd N6
89	O 10	Stormont rd SW11
123	U 19	Storrington rd Croy
133	N 2	Story st N1
63	P 12	Stothard st E1
153	S 10	Stoughton av Sutton
104	G 1	Stoughton clo SW15
70	H 9	Stour av S'hall
139	N 5	Stourcliffe st W1
118	H 5	Stourhead gdns New Mald
64	A 2	Stour rd E3
56	F 7	Stour rd Dgnhm
99	V 8	Stour rd Drtfd
100	D 9	Stourton av Felt
76	C 16	Stowage the SE8
32	K 3	Stow ct E17
18	H 6	Stowe gdns N9
31	S 11	Stowe rd N15
74	J 6	Stowe rd W12
23	P 5	Stoxmead Harrow
52	G 13	Stracey rd E7
61	Z 3	Stracey rd NW10
61	Z 4	Stracey rd NW10
104	M 16	Stracham pd SW19
35	S 9	Stradbroke gro Ilf
48	L 13	Stradbroke rd N5
90	L 16	Stradella rd SE24
35	X 7	Strafford av Ilf
73	U 6	Strafford rd W3
4	E 11	Strafford rd Barnt
82	F 8	Strafford rd Hounsl
83	Z 18	Strafford rd Twick
84	A 19	Strafford rd Twick
63	W 8	Straham rd E3
76	G 18	Straightsmouth SE10
70	B 6	Straight the S'hall
66	G 19	Straight rd E6
91	Z 11	Straker's rd SE15
92	A 11	Straker's rd SE15
140	L 10	Strand WC2
141	P 7	Strand WC2
73	S 17	Strand-On-The-green W4
79	V 13	Strandfield clo SE18
18	D 15	Strand pl N18
145	O 1	Strangeways ter W14
132	M 3	Stranraer way N1
67	Z 2	Stratford clo Bark
56	J 20	Stratford clo Dgnhm
77	Y 8	Stratford ct New Mald
87	R 10	Stratford gro SW15
139	V 6	Stratford pl W1
65	S 5	Stratford rd E13
27	O 13	Stratford rd NW4
145	V 4	Stratford rd W8
70	A 11	Stratford rd S'hall
122	G 7	Stratford rd Thntn Hth
145	W 3	Stratford studios W8
47	W 20	Stratford vlls NW1
87	U 16	Stratham clo SW18
114	H 15	Strathaven rd SE12
88	H 12	Strathblaine rd SW11
108	C 17	Strathbrook rd SW16
42	F 7	Strathcona rd Wemb
108	D 12	Strathdale SW16
106	F 8	Strathdon dri SW17
82	M 20	Strathearn av Twick
100	L 1	Strathearn av Twick
138	J 8	Strathearn pl W2
97	Y 11	Strathearn rd SW19
153	Y 10	Strathearn rd Sutton
37	S 20	Stratheden pl SE3
94	E 1	Stratheden pl SE3
	F 18	Strathfield gdns Bark
90	A 12	Strathleven rd SW2
28	A 6	Strathmore gdns N3
137	V 13	Strathmore gdns W8
25	S 7	Stratmore gdns Edg
57	U 5	Strathmore gdns Hornch
105	Y 6	Strathmore rd SW19
123	N 17	Strathmore rd Croy
101	S 9	Strathmore rd Tedd
151	T 7	Strathnairn st SE1
46	H 19	Strathray gdns NW3
88	H 11	Strath ter SW11
105	Z 2	Strathville rd SW18
106	A 2	Strathville rd SW18
122	E 6	Strathyre av SW16
8	C 2	Stratton av Enf
155	X 20	Stratton av Wallgtn
119	W 3	Stratton clo SW19
97	Z 7	Stratton clo Bxly Hth
11	Z 20	Stratton clo Edg
82	F 4	Stratton clo Hounsl
76	F 8	Strattondale st E14
54	J 16	Stratton dri Bark
58	F 17	Stratton gdns S'hall
119	X 3	Stratton rd SW19
97	Z 8	Stratton rd Bxly Hth
98	A 8	Stratton rd Bxly Hth
139	Z 13	Stratton st W1
73	Y 7	Strauss rd W4
101	V 6	Strawberry Hill Twick
101	V 7	Strawberry Hill clo Twick
101	V 6	Strawberry Hill rd Twick
155	N 5	Strawberry la Carsh
28	F 5	Strawberry vale N2
101	X 6	Strawberry vale Twick
80	B 17	Streamdale SE2
126	F 8	Streamside clo Brom
81	R 16	Stream way Blvdr
66	F 4	Streatfeild av E6
24	G 10	Streatfield rd Harrow
108	B 4	Streatham clo SW16
108	C 14	Streatham Comm north SW16
108	B 15	Streatham Comm south SW16
108	A 6	Streatham ct SW16
107	Z 12	Streatham High rd SW16
108	A 17	Streatham High rd SW16
108	B 3	Streatham hill SW2
90	A 20	Streatham pl SW2
107	P 19	Streatham rd Mitch
140	J 3	Streatham rd WC1
107	W 18	Streatham vale SW16
101	O 5	Streathbourne rd SW17
46	E 12	Streatley pl NW3
129	P 1	Streatley rd NW6
64	H 6	Streimer rd E15
62	A 19	Strelly way W3
123	S 17	Stretton rd Croy
102	C 5	Stretton rd Rich
88	F 19	Strickland row SW18
93	O 3	Strickland st SE4
65	P 7	Stride rd E13
29	P 1	Strode clo N10
52	F 12	Strode rd E7
31	S 9	Strode rd N17
44	H 19	Strode rd NW10
144	K 17	Strode rd SW6
52	K 19	Strone rd E7
52	O 17	Strone rd E12
95	T 13	Strongbow cres SE9
95	U 13	Strongbow rd SE9
40	H 3	Strongbridge clo Harrow
74	D 5	Stronsa rd W12
135	O 11	Stronts pl E2
56	M 4	Strood av Rom
104	F 6	Stroud cres SW15
118	C 18	Stroudes clo Worc Pk
40	B 19	Stroudfield clo Grnfd
40	K 13	Stroud ga Harrow
124	B 16	Stroud Grn gdns Croy
48	D 3	Stroud Green rd N4
124	B 15	Stroud Green way Croy
124	B 16	Stroud Grn way Croy
123	Y 15	Stroud rd SE25
105	X 6	Stroud rd SW19
64	D 9	Stroudley wlk E3
134	B 10	Strut st N1
148	E 3	Strutton ground SW1
142	M 2	Strype st E1
44	G 2	Stuart av NW9
73	N 4	Stuart av W5
126	E 19	Stuart av Brom
40	D 10	Stuart av Harrow
30	E 5	Stuart cres N22
158	L 6	Stuart cres Croy
97	T 7	Stuart Evans clo Welling
101	U 12	Stuart gro Tedd
106	L 20	Stuart pl Mitch
92	D 11	Stuart rd SE15
105	X 5	Stuart rd SW19
73	V 1	Stuart rd W3
67	X 2	Stuart rd Bark
15	X 3	Stuart rd Barnt
23	W 10	Stuart rd Harrow
129	U 13	Stuart rd NW6
102	C 5	Stuart rd Rich
122	M 8	Stuart rd Thntn Hth
97	R 1	Stuart rd Welling
120	F 1	Stubbs wy SW19
70	M 20	Stucley rd Hounsl
131	Y 1	Stucley st NW1
87	Y 5	Studdridge st SW6
133	W 4	Studd st N1
75	N 19	Studholme st SE15
151	X 18	Studholme st SE15
139	R 18	Studio pl SW1
114	L 7	Studland clo Sidcup
110	E 14	Studland rd SE26
59	S 16	Studland rd W7
102	K 16	Studland rd Kingst
74	J 11	Studland st W6
20	J 20	Studley av E4
33	W 1	Studley av E4
115	S 12	Studley ct Sidcp
35	O 18	Studley dri Ilf
71	U 6	Studley Grange dri W7
52	H 18	Studley rd E7
90	A 3	Studley rd SW4
90	A 4	Studley rd SW4
68	K 2	Studley rd Dgnhm
65	V 1	Studley rd E7
140	L 4	Stukeley st WC2
111	O 16	Strumps hill la Becknhm
92	A 6	Sturdy rd SE15
33	T 8	Sturge av E17
52	Z 11	Sturgeon rd SE17
114	E 16	Sturges field Chisl
26	K 20	Sturgess av NW4
54	M 1	Sturgess av NW4
141	Z 17	Sturge st SE1
54	C 14	Sturmer way N7
31	O 14	Sturrock clo N15
64	D 18	Sturry st E14
143	O 17	Stutfield st E1
135	P 9	Styles gdns SW9
125	U 20	Styles way Becknhm
90	C 12	Sudbourne rd SW2
89	O 17	Sudbrooke SW12
102	H 7	Sudbrook gdns Rich
102	J 2	Sudbrook la Rich
42	F 11	Sudbrook park Rich
41	X 9	Sudbury Ct dri Harrow
41	X 10	Sudbury Ct rd Harrow
112	E 13	Sudbury cres Brom
42	B 15	Sudbury cres Wemb
41	X 11	Sudbury croft Wemb
157	T 7	Sudbury gdns Croy
157	T 8	Sudbury gdns Croy
41	Z 15	Sudbury Heights av Grnfd
42	A 16	Sudbury Heights av Grnfd
41	U 10	Sudbury hill Harrow
41	X 10	Sudbury Hill clo Wemb
54	K 15	Sudbury rd Bark
133	X 9	Sudeley st N1
87	Y 12	Sudlow rd SW18
142	A 18	Sudrey st SE1
59	W 6	Suez av Grnfd
9	W 13	Suez rd Enf
20	E 13	Suffield rd E4
31	T 15	Suffield rd N15
124	B 5	Suffield rd SE20
51	O 2	Suffolk ct E10
36	H 10	Suffolk ct Ilf
160	E 9	Suffolk la EC4
32	J 13	Suffolk rd E13
140	F 12	Suffolk rd SW1
65	R 10	Suffolk rd E13
31	N 17	Suffolk rd Enf
31	O 17	Suffolk rd N15
44	B 20	Suffolk rd NW10
62	B 1	Suffolk rd NW10
123	V 7	Suffolk rd SE25
74	F 20	Suffolk rd SW13
67	U 2	Suffolk rd Bark
56	J 15	Suffolk rd Dgnhm
22	F 17	Suffolk rd Harrow
36	H 18	Suffolk rd Ilf
115	T 15	Suffolk rd Sidcup

Page	Grid	Name
152	E 3	Suffolk rd Worc Pk
52	E 14	Suffolk st E7
140	F 12	Suffolk st SW1
64	G 6	Sugar House la E15
63	P 8	Sugar Loaf wk E2
89	O 10	Sugden rd SW11
116	A 20	Sugden rd Surb
150	E 16	Sugden st SE5
67	Y 6	Sugden way Bark
74	M 8	Sulgrave rd W6
136	D 19	Sulgrave rd W6
144	C 1	Sulgrave rd W6
90	A 19	Sulina rd SW2
48	M 18	Sullivan av E16
88	H 7	Sullivan clo SW11
87	Y 6	Sullivan ct SW6
87	Y 8	Sullivan ct SW6
11	S 1	Sullivan way Boreham Wd
34	G 14	Sultan rd E11
150	A 18	Sultan st SE5
124	G 3	Sultan st Becknhm
45	X 17	Sumatra rd NW6
91	V 1	Summer av SE15
63	R 17	Summercourt rd E1
128	M 8	Summerfield av NW6
129	N 8	Summerfield av NW6
60	B 12	Summerfield rd W5
94	D 20	Summerfield st SE12
113	Z 20	Summer hill Chisl
127	X 2	Summer hill Chisl
18	D 1	Summerfield gro Enf
31	P 13	Summerhill rd N15
82	B 1	Summerhouse av Hounsl
49	T 7	Summerhouse rd N16
29	S 11	Summerland gdns N10
73	V 1	Summerland av W3
28	L 12	Summerlee av N2
28	L 13	Summerlee gdns N2
106	C 4	Summerley st SW18
29	R 17	Summersby rd N6
153	Y 17	Summers clo Sutton
15	X 19	Summers la N12
28	F 1	Summers la N12
15	X 19	Summers row N12
133	T 18	Summers S EC1
106	D 8	Summerstown SW17
153	U 14	Summerville gdns Sutton
83	W 14	Summerwood rd Islwth
25	Y 15	Summit av NW9
16	G 8	Summit clo N14
45	S 17	Summit clo NW2
25	Y 14	Summit clo NW9
25	P 2	Summit clo Edgw
35	O 6	Summit dri Wdfd Grn
33	T 13	Summit rd E17
58	H 1	Summit rd Grnfd
16	F 8	Summit way N14
109	T 19	Summit way SE19
122	G 19	Sumner gdns Croy
146	G 7	Sumner pl SW7
146	G 6	Sumner Pl ms SW7
91	V 1	Sumner rd SE15
151	O 15	Sumner rd SE15
122	H 19	Sumner rd Croy
41	N 1	Sumner rd Harrow
122	G 20	Sumner rd South Croy
141	Z 12	Sumner st SE1
142	A 13	Sumner st SE1
43	S 9	Sumpter clo NW3
61	X 12	Sunbeam rd NW10
89	P 15	Sunburgh rd SW12
12	L 15	Sunbury av NW7
85	Z 11	Sunbury av SW14
12	L 15	Sunbury gdns NW7
84	H 10	Sun alley Rich
153	R 9	Sunbury rd Sutton
78	H 9	Sunbury st SE18
160	H 6	Sun ct EC2
99	U 4	Suncourt Erith
110	B 7	Suncroft pl SE26
88	G 2	Sunbury la SW11
158	F 20	Sundale av S Croy
110	F 2	Sunderland rd SE23
72	G 8	Sunderland rd W5
137	W 5	Sunderland ter W2
53	N 5	Sunderland way E12
62	G 19	Sundrew av W12
74	F 1	Sundrew av W12
123	V 5	Sundial av SE25
127	N 1	Sundorne rd SE7
96	F 6	Sundridge av Welling
113	O 15	Sundridge park Chisl
113	N 17	Sundridge Park mansion Chisl
123	W 19	Sundridge rd Croy
77	V 19	Sunfields pl SE3
97	Z 11	Sunland av Bxly Hth
77	V 20	Sun la SE10
60	K 3	Sunleigh rd Wemb
59	Y 4	Sunley gdns Grnfd
62	B 19	Sunningdale av W3
67	R 2	Sunningdale av Bark
100	B 4	Sunningdale av Felt
10	M 20	Sunningdale clo Stanm
25	U 17	Sunningdale gdns NW9
127	R 10	Sunningdale rd Brom
153	V 8	Sunningdale rd Sutton
26	L 9	Sunningfields cres NW4
26	L 11	Sunningfields rd NW4
93	R 6	Sunninghill rd SE13
123	Y 7	Sunny bank SE25
61	V 1	Sunny cres NW10
123	V 7	Sunnycroft rd SE25
82	K 5	Sunnycroft rd Hounsl
58	H 13	Sunnycroft st S'hall
94	H 12	Sunnydale rd SE12
20	L 16	Sunnydale av E4
54	M 18	Sunnydale gro NW7
42	E 20	Sunnydene gdns Wemb
110	G 10	Sunnydene st SE26
13	H 12	Sunnyfield NW7
26	L 9	Sunny gdns NW4
26	J 10	Sunny hill NW4
26	J 8	Sunny Hill park NW7
108	A 9	Sunnyhill rd SW16
153	Y 5	Sunnyhurst clo Sutton
121	W 5	Sunnymead av Mitch
25	Y 20	Sunnymead rd NW9
86	J 14	Sunnymead rd SW15
152	A 18	Sunnymede av Epsom
35	Z 13	Sunnymede dri Ilf
157	O 13	Sunny Nook gdns S Croy
9	U 7	Sunny Rd the Enf
105	S 15	Sunnyside SW19
20	G 3	Sunnyside dri E4
51	N 3	Sunnyside rd E10
47	Y 1	Sunnyside rd N19
45	W 9	Sunnyside rd NW2
72	F 4	Sunnyside rd W5
101	R 10	Sunnyside rd Tedd
18	J 12	Sunnyside Rd east N9
18	J 11	Sunnyside Rd north N9
18	J 12	Sunnyside Rd south N9
25	Y 14	Sunny view NW9
28	J 1	Sunny way N12
91	O 10	Sunray av SE24
127	T 13	Sunray av Brom
100	E 7	Sunrise clo Felt
145	O 11	Sun rd
20	E 4	Sunset av E4
91	O 15	Sunset av Wdfd Grn
123	T 3	Sunset gdns SE19
90	M 10	Sunset rd SE5
91	N 10	Sunset rd SE5
27	S 8	Sunset view Barnt
120	M 2	Sunshine way Mitch
134	H 20	Sun st EC2
134	J 20	Sun St pas EC2
142	J 1	Sun St pas EC2
91	Z 2	Sunwell clo SE15
116	F 14	Surbiton ct Surb
116	H 9	Surbiton cres Kingst
116	H 10	Surbiton Hall clo Kingst
116	M 12	Surbiton Hill Surb
116	M 14	Surbiton Hill pk Surb
117	P 11	Surbiton Hill pk Surb
116	J 10	Surbiton Hill rd Kingst
116	K 8	Surbiton rd Kingst
128	V 18	Surgeon st E13
75	P 15	Surrendale pl W9
154	G 4	Surrey Canal rd SE14
91	U 1	Surrey gro SE5
88	J 2	Surrey gro SE17
109	P 10	Surrey la SW11
110	A 1	Surrey mews SE27
92	E 12	Surrey mount SE23
67	U 2	Surrey rd SE15
56	J 14	Surrey rd Bark
22	M 16	Surrey rd Dgnhm
125	S 20	Surrey rd W Wkhm
141	X 17	Surrey row SE1
150	K 8	Surrey sq SE17
65	X 10	Surrey st E13
141	P 8	Surrey st WC2
156	L 4	Surrey st Croy
109	O 16	Surridge gdns SE19
48	A 16	Surr st N7
38	J 11	Susan clo Rom
78	F 18	Susannah st E14
94	J 5	Susan rd SE3
113	X 20	Susan wood Chisl
127	Y 1	Susan wood Chisl
83	S 8	Sussex av Islwth
84	B 15	Sussex clo Twick
35	T 17	Sussex clo Ilf
40	G 18	Sussex cres Grnfd
30	K 17	Sussex gdns N4
138	H 6	Sussex gdns W2
138	H 8	Sussex ms E W2
138	G 9	Sussex ms W W2
131	O 16	Sussex pl NW1
138	H 6	Sussex pl W2
74	L 13	Sussex pl W6
144	C 9	Sussex pl W6
81	V 19	Sussex pl Erith
118	B 8	Sussex pl New Mald
14	L 16	Sussex ring N12
66	J 5	Sussex rd E6
154	M 15	Sussex rd Carsh
81	V 19	Sussex rd Erith
22	M 16	Sussex rd Harrow
23	N 17	Sussex rd Harrow
118	B 8	Sussex rd New Mald
118	R 13	Sussex rd Sidcup
70	A 8	Sussex rd S'hall
157	P 13	Sussex rd S Croy
125	S 20	Sussex rd W Wrhm
138	H 8	Sussex sq W2
65	W 10	Sussex st E13
147	Z 10	Sussex st SW1
48	A 7	Sussex way N4
47	Z 5	Sussex way N19
6	D 16	Sussex way Barnt
28	B 16	Sutcliffe clo NW11
94	J 13	Sutcliffe park SE9
79	U 17	Sutcliffe rd SE18
97	U 4	Sutcliffe rd Welling
129	V 19	Sutherland av W9
130	B 15	Sutherland av W9
60	A 18	Sutherland av W13
96	L 12	Sutherland av Welling
	F 14	Sutherland clo Barnt
25	S 14	Sutherland ct NW9
86	B 9	Sutherland gdns SW13
118	J 19	Sutherland gdns Worc Pk
87	U 20	Sutherland gro SW18
101	U 12	Sutherland gro Tedd
137	T 5	Sutherland pl W2
32	F 9	Sutherland rd pth E17
63	Y 6	Sutherland rd E3
32	G 9	Sutherland rd E17
18	L 5	Sutherland rd N9
23	N 17	Sutherland rd N17
74	A 16	Sutherland rd W4
59	Z 18	Sutherland rd W13
81	S 7	Sutherland rd Blvdr
122	F 18	Sutherland rd Croy
17	N 14	Sutherland rd Enf
58	E 17	Sutherland rd S'hall
147	Y 9	Sutherland row SW1
150	A 12	Sutherland sq SE17
147	Z 11	Sutherland st SW1
150	B 12	Sutherland wlk SE17
77	Z 19	Sutlej rd SE7
48	B 19	Sutterton st N7
119	U 18	Sutton Comm rd Sutton
153	Y 2	Sutton Comm rd Sutton
154	A 3	Sutton Comm rd Sutton
73	V 17	Sutton ct W4
65	Y 9	Sutton Ct rd E15
73	W 16	Sutton Ct rd W4
154	C 13	Sutton Ct rd Sutton
4	D 16	Sutton cres Barnt
82	J 3	Sutton dene Hounsl
67	V 5	Sutton gdns Bark
154	G 10	Sutton gro Sutton
70	G 20	Sutton Hall rd Hounsl
73	W 13	Sutton la W4
82	K 6	Sutton la Hounsl
73	U 16	Sutton La south W4
154	A 13	Sutton Pk rd Sutton
50	C 15	Sutton pl E9
65	R 12	Sutton rd E13
32	F 6	Sutton rd E17
29	P 5	Sutton rd N10
67	U 5	Sutton rd Bark
67	W 4	Sutton rd Bark
82	J 1	Sutton rd Hounsl
140	G 5	Sutton row W1
82	F 2	Sutton sq Housnl
63	O 18	Sutton st E1
128	B 19	Sutton way NW10
62	M 13	Sutton way Hounsl
82	F 1	Sutton way Hounsl
106	D 3	Swaby rd SW18
17	X 20	Swaffam way N13
30	J 1	Swaffam way N22
88	C 18	Swain rd SW18
122	M 10	Swain rd Thnth Hth
47	R 4	Swain's la N6
74	C 4	Swainson rd W3
106	L 16	Swain's rd SW17
99	T 13	Swaislands dri Drtfrd
99	Z 15	Swaisland rd Drtford
81	U 14	Swalecliffe rd Blvdr
99	V 9	Swale rd Drtfrd
111	P 9	Swallands rd SE8
58	F 5	Swallow dri Grnfd
158	G 20	Swallowdale S Croy
92	E 2	Swallow clo SE14
77	W 14	Swallowfield rd SE7
139	Z 6	Swallow pas W1
140	C 11	Swallow pl W1
57	X 19	Swallow wlk Hornch
33	U 2	Swanage rd E4
88	D 16	Swanage rd SW18
98	F 3	Swanbridge rd Bxly Hth
100	B 10	Swan clo Felt
135	O 15	Swanfield st E2
160	F 10	Swan la EC4
15	R 9	Swan la N20
99	S 19	Swan la Drtfrd
90	C 3	Swan ms SW9
86	E 4	Swan pl SW13
97	U 3	Swanley rd Welling
150	J 3	Swan mead SE1
75	R 5	Swan rd SE16
100	B 11	Swan rd Felt
61	K 7	Swan rd S'hall
74	B 13	Swanscombe rd W4
136	H 14	Swanscombe rd W11
9	O 14	Swansea rd Enf
32	G 4	Swansland gdns E17
142	C 19	Swan st E3
84	A 7	Swan st Islwth
105	R 1	Swanton gdns SW19
81	T 19	Swanton rd Erith
147	O 14	Swan wlk SW3
39	R 15	Swan wlk Rom
15	R 9	Swan way N20
9	S 8	Swan way Enf
142	F 10	Swan wharf EC4
34	V 15	Swanwick clo SW15
48	H 19	Swan yd N1
64	C 11	Swaton rd E3
81	S 17	Swaylands clo Blvdr
143	U 9	Swedenborg gdns E1
143	O 19	Sweeney cres SE1
18	G 12	Sweet Briar grn N9
18	F 11	Sweet Briar gro N9
18	F 14	Sweet Briar Wlk N18
15	T 9	Sweets way N20
65	T 8	Sweete st E13
94	G 5	Sweyn pl SE3
40	K 7	Swift clo Harrow
112	A 15	Swiftsden way Brom
100	A 9	Swift rd Felt
67	F 7	Swift rd S'hall
87	U 2	Swift st SW6
137	N 1	Swinbrook rd W10
124	C 16	Swinburn cres Croy
86	H 12	Swinburne rd SW15
42	H 18	Swinderby rd Wemb
54	H 6	Swindon clo Ilf
74	K 2	Swindon st W12
136	A 14	Swindon st W12
100	A 8	Swinfield clo Felt
90	H 7	Swinford gdns SW9
79	W 17	Swingate la SE18
50	J 16	Swinnerton st E9
43	T 5	Swinton clo Wemb
133	N 13	Swinton pl WC1
133	O 12	Swinton st WC1
113	V 9	Swithland gdns SE9
72	C 12	Swyncombe av W5
90	L 2	Sybourn st E17
72	G 8	Sycamore av W5
96	L 15	Sycamore av Sidcp
58	C 4	Sycamore clo Grnfd
154	L 8	Sycamore clo Carsh
120	G 4	Sycamore gdns Mitch
136	A 20	Sycamore gdns W6
74	L 7	Sycamore gro NW9
43	W 1	Sycamore gro NW9

S

117 Z 5 Sycamore gro New Mald
118 A 4 Sycamore gro New Mald
109 Y 20 Sycamore gro SE20
104 M 15 Sycamore rd SW19
134 A 17 Sycamore st EC1
122 E 10 Sycamore way Thntn Hth
110 A 12 Sydenham av SE26
109 Y 7 Sydenham hill SE26
110 B 8 Sydenham pk SE26
110 C 7 Sydenham Pk rd SE26
108 J 6 Sydenham pl SE27
109 Z 3 Sydenham ri SE23
110 A 2 Sydenham ri SE23
110 G 11 Sydenham rd SE26
123 P 15 Sydenham rd Croy
157 N 1 Sydenham rd Croy
49 V 11 Sydner rd N16
146 H 8 Sydney clo SW3
26 L 16 Sydney gro NW4
146 H 7 Sydney ms SW3
146 H 7 Sydney pl SW7
30 F 12 Sydney rd N8
29 R 5 Sydney rd N10
80 H 8 Sydney rd SE2
119 P 3 Sydney rd SW20
71 Z 3 Sydney rd W13
72 A 5 Sydney rd W13
97 X 10 Sydney rd Bxly Hth
8 B 14 Sydney rd Enf
36 B 8 Sydney rd Ilf
84 K 11 Sydney rd Rich
114 J 9 Sydney rd Sidcup
101 V 13 Sydney rd Tedd
84 A 16 Sydney rd Twick
21 S 15 Sydney rd Wdfd Grn
146 J 8 Sydney st SW3
27 Z 7 Sylvan av N3
30 E 1 Sylvan av N22
13 P 18 Sylvan av NW7
38 C 18 Sylvan av Rom
116 F 19 Sylvan gdns Surb
75 N 17 Sylvan gro SE15
151 Y 16 Sylvan gro SE15
109 S 19 Sylvan hill SE19
52 G 17 Sylvan rd E7
34 E 15 Sylvan rd E11
33 N 15 Sylvan rd E17
123 V 1 Sylvan rd SE19
54 A 7 Sylvan rd Ilf
109 V 20 Sylvan Rd est SE19
55 P 11 Sylvan way Dgnhm
159 Z 8 Sylvan way W Wkhm
113 T 16 Sylvester av Chisl
50 A 18 Sylvester path E8
50 A 17 Sylvester rd E8
28 F 7 Sylvester rd N2
42 E 14 Sylvester rd Wemb
43 S 20 Sylvia gdns Wemb
147 P 6 Symons st SW3
84 D 3 Syon house Islwth
72 A 20 Syon la Brentf
71 X 20 Syon la Islwth
84 D 2 Syon park Islwth
71 V 18 Syon Pk gdns Islwth

T

142 D 18 Tabard st SE1
150 F 1 Tabard st SE1
65 T 12 Tabernacle av E13
134 G 18 Tabernacle st EC2
89 W 12 Tableer av SW4
47 Z 11 Tabley rd N7
153 T 15 Tabor gdns Sutton
105 U 17 Tabor gro SW19
74 K 9 Tabor rd W6
148 B 6 Tachbrook ms SW1
148 E 9 Tachbrook rd SW1
146 C 18 Tadema rd SW10
136 E 15 Tadmor st W12
118 D 10 Tadworth av New Mald
57 Y 13 Tadworth pde Hornch
44 G 7 Tadworth rd NW2
120 K 5 Taffeys how Mitch
64 F 8 Taft st E3
143 P 2 Tailworth st E1
123 R 16 Tait rd Croy
38 L 7 Takeley clo Rom
47 R 18 Talacre rd NW5
28 F 11 Talbot av N2
31 U 13 Talbot clo N15
26 G 16 Talbot cres NW4
54 M 7 Talbot gdns Ilf

94 A 3 Talbot place SE3
93 Z 3 Talbot pl SE13
94 A 3 Talbot pl SE13
66 H 4 Talbot rd E6
52 E 12 Talbot rd E7
29 O 19 Talbot rd N6
31 V 13 Talbot rd N15
29 W 6 Talbot rd N22
137 U 4 Talbot rd W2
137 P 6 Talbot rd W11
71 Y 2 Talbot rd W13
126 H 7 Talbot rd Brom
56 B 19 Talbot rd Dgnhm
23 X 9 Talbot rd Harrow
83 Z 10 Talbot rd Islwth
70 C 10 Talbot rd S'hall
123 O 9 Talbot rd Thntn Hth
83 U 20 Talbot rd Twick
101 U 1 Talbot rd Twick
42 G 17 Talbot rd Wemb
138 G 6 Talbot sq W2
142 F 15 Talbot yd SE1
91 U 2 Talfourd pl SE15
91 T 2 Talfourd rd SE15
144 J 9 Talgarth rd W14
109 W 9 Talisman sq SE26
42 L 9 Talisman way Wemb
23 Y 9 Tallack clo Harrow
50 M 4 Tallack rd E10
126 C 10 Tall Elms clo Brom
77 W 16 Tallis gro SE7
141 U 8 Tallis st EC4
15 R 17 Tallyho' corner N12
83 T 17 Talma gdns Twick
90 G 12 Talma rd SW2
64 E 10 Talwin st E3
62 E 20 Tamarisk sq W12
78 B 10 Tamar st E7
19 W 19 Tamar sq Wdfd Grn
31 W 10 Tamar way N17
129 S 16 Tamplin ms W9
21 N 18 Tamworth av Wdfd Grn
121 R 4 Tamworth la Mitch
121 S 7 Tamworth pk Mitch
145 T 14 Tamworth st SW6
121 T 8 Tamworth vlls Mitch
121 T 8 Tamworth Lodge est Mitch
30 J 20 Tancred rd N4
34 D 11 Tanfield av NW2
156 L 18 Tanfield rd Croy
85 T 9 Tangier rd Rich
7 F 10 Tanglewood clo Stanm
158 D 5 Tanglewood clo Croy
86 E 17 Tangley gro SW15
57 Z 19 Tangmere cres Hornch
26 B 7 Tangmere dri NW9
100 E 13 Tangley Pk rd Hampt
107 Y 17 Tankerville rd SW16
44 K 7 Tankridge rd NW2
18 E 15 Tanner end N18
92 M 3 Tanners hill SE8
93 N 1 Tanners hill SE4
58 C 10 Tanners la Ilf
142 K 18 Tanner st E1
143 O 18 Tanner st SE1
54 B 18 Tanner st Bark
56 G 8 Tannery clo Dgnhm
110 E 12 Tannsfeld rd SE26
47 Z 15 Tansley clo N7
141 T 18 Tanswell st SE1
89 N 20 Tantallon rd SW12
65 P 16 Tant av E16
37 X 11 Tantony gro Rom
156 K 3 Tanworth pl Croy
156 K 3 Tanworth rd Croy
46 L 11 Tanza rd NW3
154 A 16 Tapestry clo Sutton
134 B 10 Taplow st N1
92 B 7 Tappersfield rd SE15
135 X 17 Taps gdns E1
44 L 7 Tapp wlk NW2
4 G 13 Tapster st Barnt
91 T 12 Tarbert rd SE22
20 L 20 Tariff rd N17
110 A 3 Tarleton gdns SE23
115 R 8 Tarling clo Sidcp
65 R 19 Tarling rd E16
28 E 6 Tarling rd N2
143 Y 6 Tarling st E1
7 O 15 Tarn bank Enf
95 U 20 Tarnwood pk SE9
107 X 8 Tarrington clo SW16
149 Y 10 Tarver rd SE17
76 E 18 Tarves way SE10
16 E 16 Tash pl N11
46 M 16 Tasker rd NW3
17 Z 19 Tasmania ter N18
90 A 8 Tasman rd SW9

66 A 18 Tasman wk E16
144 K 14 Tasso rd W6
43 X 19 Tatam rd NW10
148 J 7 Tate gallery SW1
78 E 3 Tate rd E16
153 X 12 Tate rd Sutton
92 H 16 Tatnell rd SE23
95 R 12 Tattersall clo SE9
150 G 7 Tatum st SE17
118 K 3 Taunton av SW20
82 M 4 Taunton av Hounsl
83 N 3 Taunton av Hounsl
99 O 6 Taunton clo Bxly Hth
119 X 20 Taunton clo Sutton
7 T 11 Taunton dri Enf
131 O 18 Taunton ms NW1
131 N 17 Taunton pl NW1
94 C 13 Taunton rd SE12
58 K 2 Taunton rd Grnfd
24 K 8 Taunton way Stanm
24 K 9 Taunton way Stanm
136 K 15 Taverners clo W11
48 K 13 Taverner sq N5
59 Z 7 Tavistock av Grnfd
60 A 6 Tavistock av Grnfd
32 G 11 Tavistock av E17
137 O 2 Tavistock cres W10
121 Z 9 Tavistock cres Mitch
122 A 9 Tavistock cres Mitch
54 H 13 Tavistock gdns Ilf
123 N 18 Tavistock gro Croy
137 N 5 Tavistock ms W11
34 F 11 Tavistock pl E18
16 E 1 Tavistock pl N4
132 H 16 Tavistock pl WC1
52 B 11 Tavistock pl E7
52 B 19 Tavistock pl E15
34 E 11 Tavistock rd E18
31 N 19 Tavistock rd N4
62 D 5 Tavistock rd NW10
137 O 3 Tavistock rd W11
126 D 8 Tavistock rd Brom
120 G 20 Tavistock rd Carsh
123 N 19 Tavistock rd Croy
25 O 5 Tavistock rd Edg
97 T 2 Tavistock rd Welling
132 G 16 Tavistock sq WC1
140 M 9 Tavistock st WC2
141 N 7 Tavistock st WC2
47 Z 9 Tavistock ter N19
132 F 16 Taviton st WC1
68 E 19 Tawney rd SE2
75 T 10 Tawny way SE16
83 U 16 Tayben av Twick
90 D 10 Taybridge rd SW8
64 F 17 Tayburn clo E14
85 S 4 Taylor av Rich
31 X 1 Taylor clo N17
101 N 12 Taylor clo Hampt
38 E 1 Taylor clo Rom
106 K 18 Taylor rd Mitch
155 R 11 Taylor rd Wallgtn
62 B 16 Taylors grn W3
44 A 20 Taylor's la NW10
109 Y 10 Taylors la SE26
5 A 6 Taylors la Barnt
78 M 11 Taylor st SE18
110 B 3 Taymount ri SE23
132 M 2 Tayport clo N1
39 S 4 Tay way Rom
58 E 9 Taywood rd Grnfd
135 U 8 Teale st E2
64 M 8 Teasal way E15
31 T 3 Tebworth rd N17
158 E 18 Tedder rd South Croy
101 X 17 Teddington lodge Tedd
101 W 11 Teddington pk Tedd
101 W 10 Teddington Pk rd Tedd
147 N 11 Tedworth gdns SW3
147 N 11 Tedworth sq SW3
59 V 6 Tees av Grnfd
83 Z 2 Teesdale av Islwth
83 Z 2 Teesdale gdns Islwth
34 B 20 Teesdale rd E11
135 V 10 Teesdale yd E2
62 A 17 Tee the W3
123 X 17 Teevan clo Croy
123 X 18 Teevan rd Croy
25 N 8 Teignmouth clo SE9
89 X 11 Teignmouth clo SW4
45 O 16 Teignmouth gdns NW2
107 O 17 Teignmouth rd Mitch
97 T 3 Teignmouth rd Welling
45 Z 10 Telegraph hill NW3
55 N 2 Telegraph ms Ilf
86 K 17 Telegraph rd SW15
160 F 4 Telegraph st EC2
94 W 3 Telemann sq SE16
107 W 1 Telferscot rd SW12

107 Y 2 Telford av SW2
108 A 2 Telford av SW2
114 D 5 Telford rd SE9
128 K 20 Telford rd N11
58 K 18 Telford rd S'hall
84 A 15 Telford way W3
66 J 7 Telham rd E6
91 U 11 Tell gro SE22
95 P 1 Tellson av SE18
89 P 18 Temperley rd SW12
57 W 18 Tempest way Rainhm
10 B 19 Templars dri Harrow
45 U 17 Templar ho NW2
100 H 17 Templar pl Hampt
27 W 19 Templars av NW11
27 X 19 Templars cres N3
90 J 3 Templar st SE5
141 U 8 Temple av EC4
15 T 3 Temple av N20
158 L 4 Temple av Croy
56 D 3 Temple av Dgnhm
27 V 8 Temple clo N3
63 O 3 Temple clo Enf
135 Z 3 Templecombe rd E9
119 R 11 Templecombe way Mrdn
27 Y 16 Temple Fortune hill NW11
27 X 17 Temple Fortune la NW11
17 W 9 Temple gdns N21
27 W 18 Temple gdns NW11
27 X 19 Temple gdns Dgnhm
27 X 17 Temple gro NW11
7 W 10 Temple gro Enf
44 M 1 Templehof av NW4
141 U 7 Temple la EC4
59 W 19 Templeman rd W7
11 N 20 Temple Mead clo Stanm
62 A 18 Temple Mead clo W3
51 R 13 Temple Mill la E15
51 P 13 Temple Mill rd E15
141 P 9 Temple pl WC2
66 C 3 Temple rd E6
30 C 13 Temple rd N8
44 M 11 Temple rd NW2
45 N 10 Temple rd NW2
73 V 9 Temple rd W4
72 F 9 Temple rd W5
157 O 9 Temple rd Croy
82 L 3 Temple rd Hounsl
85 N 6 Temple rd Rich
85 U 12 Temple sheen SW14
85 T 11 Temple Sheen rd SW14
135 V 9 Temple st E2
20 C 12 Templeton av E4
123 P 1 Templeton clo SE19
145 U 6 Templeton pl SW5
31 O 18 Templeton rd N15
154 G 6 Temple way Sutton
60 B 14 Templewood W13
46 B 10 Templewood av NW3
46 B 10 Templewood gdns NW3
22 M 8 Temsford clo Harrow
89 Z 20 Tenbury ct SW2
24 B 8 Tenby av Harrow
37 Y 19 Tenby clo Rom
32 G 15 Tenby rd E17
31 V 13 Tenby rd N15
25 N 6 Tenby rd Edgw
9 P 13 Tenby rd Enf
37 Y 19 Tenby rd Rom
97 V 1 Tenby rd Welling
143 W 13 Tench st E1
51 V 8 Tenda rd SE16
37 T 15 Tendring way Rom
40 H 18 Tendy gdns Grnfd
107 X 2 Tenham av SW2
140 B 8 Tenison ct W1
141 R 14 Tenison way SE1
138 A 8 Tenniel clo W2
57 T 10 Tennison rd SE25
142 E 17 Tennis st SE1
8 E 7 Tenniswood rd Enf
52 F 1 Tennyson av E11
5 P 20 Tennyson av E12
25 V 11 Tennyson av NW9
118 K 12 Tennyson av New Mald
101 W 2 Tennyson av Twick
96 H 2 Tennyson clo SE18
54 S 5 Tennyson clo Ilf
97 V 8 Tennyson clo Welling
32 L 18 Tennyson rd E17
13 T 15 Tennyson rd NW7
129 P 5 Tennyson rd NW6
57 S 20 Tennyson rd SE20
106 C 14 Tennyson rd SW19

59 V 20 Tennyson rd W7
82 M 3 Tennyson rd Hounsl
89 S 5 Tennyson st SW8
57 U 6 Tennyson way Hornch
70 G 8 Tensing rd S'hall
70 H 12 Tentelow la S'hall
56 B 5 Tenterden av Dgnhm
27 O 10 Tenterden clo NW4
123 Y 16 Tenterden rd Croy
27 R 11 Tenterden dri NW4
27 P 11 Tenterden gdns NW4
27 O 11 Tenterden gro NW4
31 T 2 Tenterden rd N17
139 Y 6 Tenterden st W1
143 N 2 Tenter ground E1
123 Y 16 Tenterden rd Croy
135 V 17 Tent st E1
91 R 13 Terborch way SE22
64 M 9 Terial way E15
52 B 9 Terling clo E11
56 D 5 Terling rd Dgnhm
147 Z 4 Terminus pl SW1
86 C 5 Terrace gdns SW13
84 K 17 Terrace la Rich
50 D 20 Terrace rd E9
65 U 4 Terrace rd E13
21 S 18 Terrace the Wdfd Grn
129 S 3 Terrace the NW6
147 P 16 Terrace wlk SW11
55 Z 16 Terrace wlk Dgnhm
56 A 16 Terrace wlk Dgnhm
133 W 2 Terretts pl N1
107 S 5 Terrapin rd SW17
30 A 6 Terrick rd N22
62 K 18 Terrick st W12
22 E 10 Terrilands Pinn
30 L 14 Terront rd N15
75 V 11 Terry la SE8
90 A 1 Teversham la SW8
133 V 6 Tetbury pl N1
29 P 10 Tetherdown N10
126 E 4 Tetty way Brom
97 R 1 Teviot rd Welling
64 F 13 Teviot st E14
92 A 20 Tewkesbury av SE23
22 C 17 Tewkesbury av Pinn
31 O 19 Tewkesbury clo N15
25 U 10 Tewkesbury gdns SE9
31 O 19 Tewkesbury rd N15
120 F 19 Tewkesbury rd Carsh
16 H 18 Tewkesbury ter N11
79 V 13 Tewson rd SE18
8 B 20 Teynham av Enf
30 M 5 Teynton ter N17
31 X 8 Thackeray av N17
40 J 4 Thackeray clo Harrow
105 P 18 Thackeray clo SW19
55 O 2 Thackeray dri Rom
66 B 6 Thackeray rd E6
89 S 5 Thackeray rd SW8
137 Y 20 Thackeray st W8
109 Z 11 Thakeham clo SE26
76 K 16 Thalia clo SE10
69 U 12 Thames av Dgnhm
59 V 6 Thames av Grnfd
85 W 5 Thames bank SW14
102 B 10 Thamesgate clo Rich
38 L 8 Thames Hill av Rom
80 G 3 Thamesmead spine rd SE2
75 Z 1 Thames pl E1
84 B 11 Thames promenade Twick
78 A 4 Thames rd E16
73 R 17 Thames rd W4
67 W 9 Thames rd Bark
68 A 8 Thames rd Bark
99 W 8 Thames rd Drtfrd
102 G 17 Thames side Kingst
116 G 2 Thames side Kingst
76 E 16 Thames st SE10
82 H 6 Thamesville clo Hounsl
157 T 6 Thanescroft gdns Croy
156 M 3 Thanet pl Croy
157 N 7 Thanet pl Croy
98 E 19 Thanet rd Bxly
132 J 14 Thanet st WC1
48 D 9 Thane vlls N7
155 X 11 Tharp rd Wallgtn
15 R 3 Thatcham gdns N20
83 R 13 Thatchers way Islwth
37 Y 12 Thatches gro Rom
141 U 3 Thavies in EC4
105 O 18 Thaxted clo SW20
114 B 5 Thaxted rd SE9
145 R 13 Thaxton rd SW6
124 J 1 Thayers Farm rd Becknhm
139 U 4 Thayer st W1
88 M 8 Theatre st SW11
133 V 4 Theberton st N1
141 N 18 The County Hall SE1
141 U 17 The Cut SE1
21 W 8 The Drummonds Buck Hl
141 T 14 Theed st SE1
145 Z 10 The Little Boltons SW5
95 P 2 Thelma gdns SE3
101 X 14 Thelma gro Tedd
22 L 5 Theobald cres Harrow
156 J 2 Theobald rd Croy
150 E 3 Theobald st SE1
15 P 14 Theobalds av N12
133 O 20 Theobald's rd WC1
93 V 15 Theodore rd SE13
144 L 12 The Queen's Club W14
121 X 17 Therapia la Croy
122 A 15 Therapia la Croy
92 C 15 Therapia rd SE22
74 G 12 Theresa rd W6
74 G 12 Theresa st W6
76 E 11 Thermopylae ga E14
110 F 17 Thesiger rd SE20
89 X 3 Thessally rd SW8
148 A 19 Thessally rd SW8
17 X 20 Thetford clo N13
68 K 2 Thetford gdns Dgnhm
68 K 2 Thetford rd Dgnhm
118 A 12 Thetford rd New Mald
117 Z 13 Thetford rd New Mald
21 X 19 Theydon gro Wdfd Grn
50 C 5 Theydon rd E5
50 L 9 Theydon st E19
154 E 8 Thicket cres Sutton
109 X 17 Thicket gro SE20
55 U 17 Thicket gro Dgnhm
109 Y 18 Thicket rd SE20
110 A 16 Thicket rd SE20
154 E 7 Thicket rd Sutton
53 S 13 Third av E12
65 T 9 Third av E13
33 P 15 Third av E17
74 C 3 Third av W3
128 M 15 Third av W10
69 V 5 Third av Dgnhm
8 G 17 Third av Enf
37 T 17 Third av Rom
42 G 6 Third av Wemb
101 S 4 Third Cross rd Twick
43 U 13 Third way Wemb
25 X 4 Thirleby rd SE18
148 C 3 Thirleby rd SW1
60 C 8 Thirlmere av Grnfd
42 E 4 Thirlmere gdns Wemb
112 C 16 Thirlmere ri Brom
29 T 6 Thirlmere rd N10
107 X 10 Thirlmere rd SW16
98 K 3 Thirlmere rd Bxly Hth
40 J 17 Thirsk clo Grnfd
123 P 8 Thirsk rd SE25
89 N 8 Thirsk rd SW11
107 P 17 Thirsk rd Mitch
40 C 10 Thisledene av Harrow
24 G 6 Thistlecroft gdns Stanm
146 C 9 Thistle gro SW5
50 B 10 Thistlewaite rd E5
48 D 7 Thistlewood clo N7
71 P 18 Thistleworth clo Islwth
41 W 11 Thomas A 'beckett clo W11
88 H 9 Thomas Baines rd SW11
149 X 1 Thomas Doyle st SE1
93 P 19 Thomas la SE6
143 S 11 Thomas More st SE1
28 C 9 Thomas More wy N3
63 Z 16 Thomas rd E14
64 A 16 Thomas rd E14
78 K 10 Thomas st SE18
85 S 6 Thompson av Rich
91 V 16 Thompson rd SE22
56 C 10 Thompson rd Dgnhm
150 A 17 Thompsons av SE5
122 F 19 Thomson cres Croy
156 F 1 Thomson cres Croy
23 U 9 Thomson rd Harrow
151 S 7 Thorburn sq SE1
134 B 11 Thoresby st N1
116 A 17 Thorkhill rd Surb
18 L 18 Thornaby gdns N18
10 A 6 Thorn av Bushey Watf
12 D 20 Thorn bank Edg
71 P 20 Thornbury av Islwth
89 Z 16 Thornbury rd SW2
90 A 17 Thornbury rd SW2
71 R 19 Thornbury rd Islwth
83 R 4 Thornbury rd Islwth
50 C 10 Thornby rd E5
89 Z 17 Thorncliffe rd SW4
70 E 12 Thorncliffe rd S'hall
127 X 14 Thorn clo Brom
58 E 8 Thorn clo Grnfd
91 T 12 Thorncombe rd SE22
39 Y 18 Thorncroft Hornch
153 Z 10 Thorncroft rd Sutton
154 A 9 Thorncroft rd Sutton
148 J 19 Thorncroft st SW8
106 C 5 Thorndean st SW18
16 A 7 Thorndene av N11
146 B 18 Thorndike clo SW10
152 C 9 Thorndon gdns Epsom
51 Y 11 Thorne clo E11
65 R 17 Thorne clo E16
81 W 16 Thorne clo Erith
117 V 8 Thorne clo New Mald
156 H 12 Thorneloe gdns Croy
86 B 6 Thorne pas SW13
148 L 20 Thorne rd SW8
117 V 8 Thorne rd New Mald
125 T 6 Thornes clo Becknhm
65 R 17 Thorne st E16
86 B 6 Thorne st SW13
127 X 7 Thornet Wood rd Brom
31 Z 1 Thorney clo N15
73 T 12 Thorney Hedge rd W4
148 J 6 Thorney st SW1
27 S 3 Thornfield av NW7
74 K 5 Thornfield rd W12
136 A 17 Thornfield rd W12
93 U 14 Thornford rd SE13
129 W 17 Thorngate rd W9
65 W 3 Thorngrove rd E13
51 W 16 Thornham gro E15
132 H 19 Thornbaugh st WC1
79 V 19 Thornhill av SE18
133 O 7 Thornhill bridge N1
133 O 1 Thornhill cres N1
51 S 7 Thornhill gdns E10
54 H 20 Thornhill gdns Bark
116 A 19 Thornhill gdns Surb
133 R 2 Thornhill gro N1
51 R 7 Thornhill rd E10
48 F 20 Thornhill rd N1
133 S 2 Thornhill rd N1
122 M 17 Thornhill rd Croy
133 O 2 Thornhill sq N1
108 J 9 Thornlaw rd SE27
40 L 7 Thornley dri Harrow
76 L 13 Thornley pl SE10
111 U 3 Thornsbeach rd SE6
123 Z 4 Thornsett pl SE20
123 Z 4 Thornsett rd SE20
124 A 5 Thornsett rd SE20
106 B 3 Thornsett rd SW18
107 Y 2 Thornton av SW2
74 B 11 Thornton av W4
122 C 15 Thornton av Croy
125 O 3 Thornton dene Becknhm
107 X 1 Thornton gdns SW12
105 R 18 Thornton hill SW19
51 X 6 Thornton rd E11
89 W 19 Thornton rd SW12
85 X 9 Thornton rd SW14
4 E 13 Thornton rd Barnt
81 T 9 Thornton rd Blvdr
112 F 12 Thornton rd Brom
120 J 18 Thornton rd Carsh
53 Y 13 Thornton rd Ilf
122 E 13 Thornton rd Thntn Hth
105 P 17 Thornton rd SW19
122 F 11 Thornton row Thntn Hth
56 M 5 Thorntons Farm av Rom
90 E 5 Thornton st SW9
28 B 17 Thornton way NW11
78 B 14 Thorntree rd SE7
93 N 3 Thornville st SE4
34 J 7 Thornwood clo E18
93 Z 13 Thornwood rd SE13
94 A 13 Thornwood rd SE13
52 A 16 Throogood gdns E15
30 B 2 Thorold rd N22
53 Z 7 Thorold rd Ilf
54 C 4 Thorold rd Ilf
148 G 20 Thorparch rd SW8
89 Y 1 Thorparch rd SW8
74 G 3 Thorpebank rd W12
32 L 6 Thorpe cres E17
35 Y 12 Thorpedale gdns Ilf
48 B 5 Thorpedale rd N4
33 V 6 Thorpe Hall rd E17
136 M 4 Thorpe ms W10
66 F 4 Thorpe rd E6
52 C 11 Thorpe rd E7
33 T 7 Thorpe rd E17
31 T 19 Thorpe rd N15
54 D 20 Thorpe rd Bark
102 K 18 Thorpe rd Kingst
110 B 5 Thorpewood av SE26
109 R 11 Thorsden way SE19
45 R 10 Thorverton rd NW2
63 V 7 Thoydon rd E3
107 U 13 Thrale rd SW16
142 C 14 Thrale st SE1
142 G 6 Threadneedle st EC2
160 G 6 Threadneedle st EC2
63 N 11 Three Colts la E2
135 Y 16 Three Colts la E2
63 Y 19 Three Colt st E14
98 J 6 Three corners Bxly Hth
121 N 6 Three Kings rd Mitch
139 W 8 Three Kings' yd W1
64 F 9 Three Mill la E3
143 N 17 Three Oak la SE1
142 E 16 Three Tuns ct SE1
136 J 9 Threshers pl W11
110 D 8 Thriffwood SE23
65 W 18 Throckmorton rd E16
160 G 4 Throgmorton av EC2
142 G 5 Throgmorton st EC2
80 E 8 Throwley clo SE2
154 C 11 Throwley rd Sutton
154 B 8 Throwley way Sutton
121 T 3 Thrupp clo Mitch
149 Z 9 Thrush st SE17
111 R 12 Thurbarn rd SE6
151 S 1 Thurland rd SE16
108 G 9 Thurlby rd SE27
89 P 16 Thurleigh av SW12
88 L 17 Thurleigh rd SW12
89 O 16 Thurleigh rd SW12
119 R 11 Thurleston av Mrdn
15 Y 19 Thurlestone av N12
54 K 14 Thurlestone av Ilf
108 H 9 Thurlestone rd SE27
146 J 4 Thurloe clo SW7
39 S 19 Thurloe gdns Rom
146 H 4 Thurloe pl SW7
146 G 4 Thurloe Pl ms SW7
146 H 5 Thurloe sq SW7
146 G 5 Thurloe st SW7
42 H 16 Thurlow gdns Wemb
108 K 2 Thurlow hill SE21
108 K 3 Thurlow Pk rd SE21
46 G 14 Thurlow rd NW3
71 Y 6 Thurlow rd W7
150 H 10 Thurlow st SE17
47 N 17 Thurlow ter NW5
115 Y 14 Thursland rd Sidcup
159 W 16 Thursley cres Croy
105 P 5 Thursley gdns SW19
113 S 8 Thursley rd SE9
106 G 9 Thurslo st SW17
93 S 6 Thurston rd SE13
104 J 17 Thurston rd SW20
58 F 18 Thurston rd S'hall
135 O 7 Thurtle rd E2
81 W 16 Thwaite clo Erith
15 O 19 Thyra gro N12
42 H 19 Thyrlby rd Wemb
64 D 11 Tibbatt's rd E3
134 A 2 Tibberton sq N1
87 O 17 Tibbets ride SW15
105 O 2 Tibbets clo SW19
110 J 5 Ticehurst rd SE23
80 E 5 Tickford clo SE2
65 R 20 Tidal Basin rd E16
157 T 5 Tidenham gdns Croy
87 N 12 Tideswell rd SW15
158 M 5 Tideswell rd Croy
102 B 10 Tideway clo Rich
64 B 13 Tidey st E3
96 K 4 Tidford rd Welling
64 A 11 Tidworth rd E3
90 A 20 Tierney rd SW2
108 A 1 Tierney rd SW2
75 R 8 Tiger bay SE16
126 H 8 Tiger la Brom
49 Y 11 Tiger wy E5
94 M 8 Tilbrook rd SE3
66 G 7 Tilbury rd E6
51 T 2 Tilbury rd E10
58 A 14 Tilbury sq Grnfd
86 L 15 Tidesley rd SW15
106 G 2 Tilehurst rd SW18

153	R 11	Tilehurst rd Sutton
47	U 3	Tilekiln la N6
17	Y 16	Tile Kiln la N13
47	Z 20	Tileyard rd N1
159	U 18	Tilford av Croy
105	P 2	Tilford gdns SW19
50	A 13	Tilia rd E5
76	B 8	Tiller rd E14
43	V 19	Tillett clo NW10
135	T 12	Tillet way E2
27	W 11	Tillingbourne gdns N3
27	W 12	Tillingbourne way N3
14	M 13	Tillingham way N12
27	O 20	Tilling rd NW11
133	N 2	Tilloch st N1
18	F 7	Tillotson rd N9
22	K 3	Tillotson rd Harrow
53	W 1	Tillotson rd Ilf
63	S 15	Tillotson st E1
143	Y 7	Tilman st E1
109	U 12	Tilney av SE19
134	C 17	Tilney ct EC1
21	U 18	Tilney dri Buck Hl
49	O 18	Tilney gdns N1
56	B 19	Tilney rd Dgnhm
139	U 13	Tilney st W1
89	Z 18	Tilson gdns SW2
31	X 5	Tilson rd N17
144	M 15	Tilton st SW6
61	X 20	Tiltwood the W3
95	T 16	Tiltyard appr SE9
W 2		Timber clo Chisl
152	A 8	Timbercroft Epsom
79	U 18	Timbercroft la SE18
27	R 7	Timberdene NW4
63	N 18	Timberland rd E1
134	A 17	Timberland st EC1
89	Y 7	Timbermill wy SW4
31	Y 19	Timberwharf rd N16
154	B 11	Times sq Sutton
63	X 14	Timothy rd E3
86	G 20	Timsbury wlk SW15
90	J 1	Tindal st SW9
149	X 20	Tindal st SW9
85	Z 7	Tinderbox all SW14
63	R 14	Tinsley rd E1
91	U 10	Tintagel cres SE22
11	V 15	Tintagel dri Stanm
25	T 10	Tintern av N18
87	R 14	Tintern clo SW15
106	D 16	Tintern clo SW19
17	N 2	Tintern gdns N14
30	L 5	Tintern rd Carsh
120	F 20	Tintern rd Carsh
90	B 10	Tintern rd SW4
40	K 4	Tintern way Harrow
65	T 13	Tinto rd E13
65	T 13	Tinto rd E16
148	M 8	Tinworth st SE11
149	N 9	Tinworth st SE11
7	Z 7	Tippetts clo Enf
89	O 7	Tipthorne rd SW11
157	S 8	Tiptown dri Croy
35	X 9	Tiptree cres Ilf
156	L 15	Tirlemont rd S Croy
122	L 15	Tirrell rd Croy
26	D 20	Tirrel way NW9
140	E 9	Tisbury ct W1
121	Z 3	Tisbury rd SW16
150	G 8	Tisdall pl SE17
138	K 6	Tichbourne row W2
130	M 7	Titchfield rd NW8
131	N 7	Titchfield rd NW8
120	F 19	Titchfield rd Carsh
9	U 1	Titchfield rd Enf
120	G 18	Titchfield wlk Carsh
88	G 20	Titchwell rd SW18
147	P 13	Tite st SW3
26	F 4	Tithe clo NW7
40	G 9	Tithe Farm av Harrow
40	G 9	Tithe Farm clo Harrow
26	G 3	Tithe wlk NW7
10	E 3	Titian av Bushey Watf
20	B 16	Titley clo E4
80	F 2	Titmuss av SE2
35	W 9	Tiverton av Ilf
96	B 20	Tiverton dri SE9
114	B 1	Tiverton dri SE9
31	O 18	Tiverton rd N15
18	D 19	Tiverton rd N18
128	H 6	Tiverton rd NW10
24	M 9	Tiverton rd Edg
82	M 4	Tiverton rd Hounsl
60	K 5	Tiverton rd Wembl
150	A 2	Tiverton st SE1
78	D 10	Tivoli gdns SE18
109	L 13	Tivoli rd SE27
82	B 11	Tivoli rd Hounsl
35	W 9	Tivotron rd Ilf
76	A 5	Tobago st E14
46	K 19	Tobin clo NW3
63	V 12	Toby la E1
20	A 14	Tofton rd E4
160	F 5	Tokenhouse yd EC2
43	P 18	Tokyngton av Wemb
86	G 14	Toland sq SW15
42	K 2	Toley av Wemb
36	D 9	Tollesbury gdns Ilf
63	S 11	Tollet st E1
109	T 5	Tollgate dri SE21
129	W 8	Tollgate gdns NW6
66	E 15	Tollgate rd E6
65	Y 15	Tollgate rd E16
47	V 6	Tollhouse way N19
48	D 5	Tollington pk N4
48	C 6	Tollington pl N4
48	C 12	Tollington rd N7
48	A 9	Tollington way N7
132	C 15	Tolmers sq NW1
83	Y 8	Tolson rd Islwth
118	M 1	Tolverne rd SW20
37	X 15	Tolworth gdns Rom
117	V 19	Tolworth ri S Surb
117	V 19	Tolworth ri N Surb
117	V 19	Tolworth ri S Surb
95	R 10	Tom Coombs clo SE9
79	P 9	Tom Crabb rd SE18
101	Y 1	Tomlins av Twick
64	B 9	Tomlin's gro E3
135	P 13	Tomlinson clo E2
73	T 13	Tomlinson clo W4
67	O 4	Tomlins orchard Bark
51	T 14	Tomlins ter E14
133	X 14	Tompion st EC1
36	C 5	Tomswood clo Ilf
36	A 2	Tomswood hill Ilf
36	C 5	Tomswood hill Ilf
132	J 12	Tonbridge st WC1
119	V 19	Tonfield rd Sutton
125	O 12	Tonge clo Becknhm
88	B 13	Tonsley hill SW18
88	B 13	Tonsley pl SW18
88	B 13	Tonsley rd SW18
88	B 13	Tonsley st SW18
121	O 3	Tonstall rd Mitch
22	A 4	Tooke clo Pinn
141	S 4	Took's ct EC4
142	K 15	Tooley st SE1
143	N 18	Tooley st SE1
23	O 7	Toorack rd Harrow
23	P 7	Toorack rd Harrow
107	T 7	Tooting Bec common SW16
107	X 9	Tooting Bec gdns SW16
107	P 8	Tooting Bec rd SW17
106	J 12	Tooting gro SW17
106	J 12	Tooting High st SW17
125	Z 10	Tootswood rd Brom
126	A 10	Tootswood rd Brom
30	M 4	Topham sq N17
133	S 17	Topham st EC1
20	H 3	Tophouse rise E4
84	M 8	Topiary sq Rich
94	M 9	Topley st SE9
125	Y 11	Top pk Becknhm
29	Z 15	Topsfield rd N8
107	N 8	Topsham rd SW17
129	O 2	Torbay rd NW6
40	C 5	Torbay rd Harrow
47	T 20	Torbay st NW1
24	L 2	Torbridge clo Edg
97	Z 16	Torbrook clo Bxly
110	C 4	Torcross dri SE23
137	U 16	Tor gdns W8
112	C 17	Tormead clo Brom
79	U 15	Tormount rd SE18
53	T 11	Toronto av E12
51	X 12	Toronto rd E11
54	A 3	Toronto rd Ilf
35	P 13	Torquay gdns Ilf
137	W 2	Torquay st W2
52	B 18	Torrens rd E15
90	C 13	Torrens rd SW2
52	B 19	Torrens sq E15
133	N 1	Torrens st N1
120	H 19	Torre wlk Carsh
47	X 17	Torriano av NW5
47	W 16	Torriano cotts NW5
92	B 10	Torridge gdns SE15
122	J 11	Torridge rd Thntn Hth
93	Y 18	Torridon rd SE6
111	Y 3	Torridon rd SE6
15	U 16	Torrington av N12
40	L 11	Torrington dri Harrow
16	H 20	Torrington gdns N11
60	D 2	Torrington gdns Grnfd
15	W 16	Torrington gro N12
15	S 15	Torrington pk N12
132	D 19	Torrington pl WC1
34	F 10	Torrington rd E18
56	C 3	Torrington rd Dnghm
60	D 3	Torrington rd Grnfd
119	Y 16	Torrrington way Mrdn
97	T 1	Tor rd Welling
110	F 18	Torr rd SE20
23	U 14	Torver rd Harrow
86	H 14	Torwood rd SW15
138	G 20	Tothill st SW1
80	E 20	Totnes rd Welling
28	G 14	Totnes wlk N2
17	V 18	Tottenhall rd N13
132	C 18	Tottenham Court rd W1
140	F 2	Tottenham Court rd W1
31	U 13	Tottenham Grn east N15
31	V 12	Tottenham Grn South side N17
30	C 15	Tottenham la N8
140	C 1	Tottenham ms W1
49	P 18	Tottenham rd N1
140	C 1	Tottenham st W1
106	M 11	Totterdown st SW17
13	W 9	Totteridge common N20
14	K 7	Totteridge grn N20
15	N 7	Totteridge la N20
14	F 5	Totteridge village N20
24	E 16	Totternhoe clc Harrow
122	G 6	Totterdown rd Thntn Hth
63	U 7	Totty rd E3
142	A 18	Toulmin st SE1
145	R 17	Tournay rd SW6
123	Y 3	Tovil clo SE20
64	E 12	Towcester rd E3
143	N 14	Tower br E1
143	O 11	Tower Br appr E1
142	M 18	Tower Br rd SE1
150	J 3	Tower Br rd SE1
109	Z 17	Tower clo SE20
140	H 7	Tower ct WC2
30	M 6	Tower gdns N17
31	O 6	Tower Gdns rd N17
52	D 14	Tower Hamlets rd E7
33	O 11	Tower Hamlets rd E17
142	L 10	Tower hill EC3
143	N 10	Tower hill EC3
33	O 14	Tower ms E17
142	M 11	Tower of London EC3
142	L 10	Tower pl EC3
84	J 7	Tower ri Rich
45	G 20	Tower rd NW10
81	X 12	Tower rd Blvdr
98	F 10	Tower rd Bxly Hth
101	W 6	Tower rd Twick
84	J 12	Towers pl Rich
22	A 4	Towers rd Pinn
58	H 10	Towers rd S'hall
57	W 14	Tower st WC2
30	C 8	Tower ter N22
124	H 19	Tower view Croy
100	D 4	Towfield rd Felt
48	M 3	Towncourt path N4
58	E 7	Towney mead Grnfd
12	U 12	Town Hall Appr rd N15
73	X 13	Town Hall av W4
88	M 8	Town Hall rd SW11
77	V 7	Townholm cres W7
52	C 19	Townley rd E15
91	S 13	Townley rd SE22
98	B 14	Townley rd Bxly Hth
98	D 11	Townley rd Bxly Hth
150	D 8	Townley st SE17
72	H 18	Town mead Brentfd
88	D 4	Townmead rd SW6
85	T 4	Townmead rd Rich
67	N 4	Town quay Bark
18	M 8	Town rd N9
19	D 11	Town rd N9
16	L 13	Townsend av N14
25	Y 18	Townsend la NW9
43	Z 2	Townsend la NW9
31	U 16	Townsend la N15
70	B 2	Townsend rd S'hall
150	H 6	Townsend st SE17
130	L 8	Townshend rd NW8
113	Z 13	Townshend rd Chisl
84	M 11	Townshend rd Rich
85	O 10	Townshend ter Rich
108	L 5	Townson rd SE27
105	S 20	Toynbee rd SW20
135	U 5	Toynbee st E1
44	L 14	Tracey av NW2
24	D 2	Tracey st Stanm
148	M 20	Tradescant rd SW8
61	V 11	Trading Estate rd NW10
18	D 20	Trafalgar av N17
151	O 11	Trafalgar av SE15
119	P 20	Trafalgar av Worc Pk
63	T 13	Trafalgar gdns E1
76	K 16	Trafalgar gro SE10
76	L 15	Trafalgar rd SE10
106	C 17	Trafalgar rd SW19
101	R 4	Trafalgar rd Twick
140	H 12	Trafalgar sq SW1
140	H 12	Trafalgar sq WC2
150	F 10	Trafalgar st SE17
51	S 16	Trafford clo E15
122	D 11	Trafford rd Thntn Hth
51	Y 20	Tramway av E9
19	O 4	Tramway av N9
121	N 12	Tramway path Mitch
50	F 15	Tranby pl E9
46	K 13	Tranley ms NW3
18	G 4	Tranmere rd N9
106	D 4	Tranmere rd SW18
82	L 19	Tranmere rd Twick
94	A 5	Tranquil vale SE3
138	K 2	Transept st NW1
72	B 16	Transport av Brentf
103	Z 19	Traps la Kings
118	A 1	Traps la New Mald
48	E 9	Travers rd N7
10	B 7	Treacy clo Bushey Watf
136	H 9	Treadgold st W11
135	W 9	Treadway st E2
82	K 9	Treaty rd Hounsl
132	M 6	Treaty st N1
139	X 14	Trebeck st W1
145	U 9	Trebovir rd SW5
63	Y 12	Treby st E3
47	Y 13	Trecastle way N7
102	H 1	Tree clo Rich
63	Y 8	Tredegar rd E3
64	A 5	Tredegar rd E3
29	Y 3	Tredegar rd N11
63	Y 9	Tredegar sq E3
63	X 8	Tredegar ter E3
135	U 3	Trederwen rd E8
110	D 13	Tredown rd SE26
127	P 9	Tredwell clo Brom
86	C 8	Treen av SW13
65	Y 17	Tree rd E16
147	R 16	Tree wlk SW11
112	H 10	Treewall gdns Brom
56	E 7	Trefgarene rd Dgnhm
48	B 12	Trefil wlk N7
88	E 14	Trefoil rd SW18
30	A 20	Tregaron av N8
89	P 10	Tregarvon rd SW11
40	G 11	Tregenna av Harrow
6	H 16	Tregenna ct N14
50	M 20	Trego rd E9
90	A 7	Tregothnan rd SW9
146	A 12	Tregunter rd SW10
36	E 1	Trehearn rd Ilf
85	Z 8	Trehearn rd Ilf
107	P 8	Treherne ct SW17
50	H 14	Trehurst st E5
51	U 10	Trelawn rd E10
90	F 13	Trelawn rd SW2
36	E 1	Trelawney rd Ilf
63	Z 8	Trellis sq E3
109	O 16	Treloar gdns SE19
89	Y 9	Tremadoc rd SW4
93	O 6	Tremaine clo SE4
124	A 4	Tremaine rd SE20
47	U 8	Tremlett gro N19
47	U 9	Tremlett ms N19
54	L 9	Trenance gdns Ilf
11	N 19	Trenchard clo Stanm
119	Y 14	Trenchard ct Mrdn
76	K 15	Trenchard st SE10
109	Z 18	Trenholme clo SE20
109	Z 18	Trenholme rd SE20
62	K 9	Trenmar gdns NW10
4	W 5	Trent av W5
14	B 16	Trent gdns N14
105	X 2	Trentham st SW18
6	E 6	Trent park Barnt
90	C 14	Trent rd SW2
21	V 6	Trent rd Buck Hl
152	L 4	Trent way Worc Pk
7	O 10	Trentwood side Enf
88	B 18	Treport st SW18
111	Z 16	Tresco clo Brom
54	L 8	Tresco gdns Ilf
40	C 2	Trescoe gdns Harrow
92	B 9	Tresco rd SE15
67	X 1	Tresham rd Bark
135	P 15	Tressillian cres SE4
92	M 9	Tressillian rd SE4
93	O 6	Tressillian rd SE4
63	C 16	Trestis clo Grnfd

T

68 M 3 Treswell rd Dgnhm
69 N 3 Treswell rd Dgnhm
13 P 12 Tretawn gdns NW7
13 O 12 Tretawn pk NW7
144 M 8 Trevanion rd W14
41 O 2 Treve av Harrow
53 U 14 Trevelyan av E12
24 H 20 Trevelyan cres Harrow
42 J 1 Trevelyan cres Harrow
62 M 4 Trevelyan gdns NW10
128 C 5 Trevelyan gdns NW10
52 B 13 Trevelyan rd E15
106 J 14 Trevelyan rd SW17
141 X 14 Treveris st SE1
128 J 19 Treverton st W10
86 J 18 Treville st SW15
110 G 3 Treviso rd SE23
76 B 15 Trevithick st SE8
22 C 18 Trevone gdns Pinn
5 U 18 Trevor clo Barnt
126 D 18 Trevor clo Brom
23 W 1 Trevor clo Harrow
83 V 12 Trevor clo Islwth
25 Y 4 Trevor gdns Edg
138 M 20 Trevor pl SW7
105 T 19 Trevor rd SW19
25 Y 4 Trevor rd Edg
34 G 1 Trevor rd Wdfd Grn
138 M 20 Trevor sq SW7
139 N 19 Trevor sq SW7
138 M 19 Trevor st SW7
33 W 4 Trevose rd E17
118 M 1 Trewince rd SW20
106 B 4 Trewint st SW18
110 F 12 Trewsbury rd SE26
58 C 12 Triandra wy Grnfd
65 Z 15 Triangle ct E16
66 A 14 Triangle ct E16
89 X 10 Triangle pl SW4
135 W 3 Triangle rd E8
117 U 4 Triangle the New Mald
75 U 10 Trident st SE16
75 V 10 Trident st SE16
149 P 16 Trigon rd SW8
110 G 3 Trilby rd SE23
48 B 3 Trinder gdns N4
48 B 3 Trinder rd N4
4 A 17 Trinder rd Barnt
73 N 3 Tring av W5
58 E 16 Tring av S'hall
43 P 18 Tring av Wemb
36 D 17 Tring clo Ilf
69 Z 1 Trinidad gdns Dgnhm
63 Z 20 Trinidad st E14
28 F 11 Trinity av N2
8 J 20 Trinity av Enf
74 K 17 Trinity Church rd SW13
142 C 20 Trinity Church sq SE1
52 A 6 Trinity clo E11
93 W 11 Trinity clo SE13
46 F 13 Trinity clo NW3
82 B 9 Trinity clo Hounsl
157 T 19 Trinity clo S Croy
106 M 5 Trinity cres SW17
107 N 5 Trinity cres SW17
65 P 13 Trinity gdns E16
93 T 2 Trinity gdns SE10
90 C 10 Trinity gdns SW9
98 B 10 Trinity pl Bxly Hth
90 H 20 Trinity ri SW2
28 F 9 Trinity rd N2
30 A 2 Trinity rd N22
106 L 3 Trinity rd SW17
107 N 6 Trinity rd SW17
88 G 17 Trinity rd SW18
105 Z 16 Trinity rd SW19
36 A 9 Trinity rd Ilf
85 N 9 Trinity rd Rich
70 A 2 Trinity rd S'hall
142 M 9 Trinity sq EC3
142 C 20 Trinity st SE1
7 Y 8 Trinity st Enf
62 D 20 Trinity way W3
142 C 20 Trio pl SE1
94 A 8 Tristan sq SE3
33 W 10 Tristram clo E17
112 D 9 Tristram rd Brom
132 A 16 Triton sq NW1
156 A 7 Tritton av Croydon
109 O 7 Tritton rd SE21
156 D 4 Trojan way Croy
81 R 17 Trosley rd Blvdr
91 T 12 Trosslachs rd SE22
151 T 6 Trothy rd SE1
29 N 2 Trott rd N10
88 H 3 Trott st SW11
77 W 13 Troughton rd SE7
92 G 2 Troutbeck rd SE14
89 U 16 Trouville rd SW4
50 M 18 Trowbridge rd E9
102 E 15 Trowlock av Tedd
102 F 15 Trowlock wy Tedd
109 P 15 Troy rd SE19
91 X 7 Troy town SE15
31 X 1 Trulock ct N17
31 X 2 Trulock rd N17
75 N 7 Truman st SE16
122 K 10 Trumble gdns Thntn Hth
71 V 7 Trumpers way W7
52 B 11 Trumpington rd E7
160 C 5 Trump st EC2
10 E 5 Trundlers way Bushey Watf
142 A 17 Trundle st SE1
75 U 14 Trundley's rd SE8
53 R 2 Truro gdns Ilf
32 L 14 Truro rd E17
30 A 3 Truro rd N22
47 O 19 Truro st NW1
108 H 12 Truslove rd SE27
74 L 8 Trussley rd W6
144 B 2 Trussley rd W6
57 W 2 Truston's gdns Hornch
35 P 15 Tryfan clo Ilf
147 N 9 Tryon st SW3
79 R 17 Truam rd SE18
62 E 7 Tubbs rd NW10
57 W 18 Tucks rd Rainhm
86 E 18 Tuckton wlk SW15
100 H 17 Tudor av Hampt
39 W 11 Tudor av Rom
152 L 9 Tudor av Worc Pk
46 J 16 Tudor clo NW3
13 V 20 Tudor clo NW7
43 W 6 Tudor clo NW9
113 V 20 Tudor clo Chisl
127 V 1 Tudor clo Chisl
99 Y 16 Tudor clo Drtfrd
153 P 12 Tudor clo Sutton
155 W 17 Tudor clo Wallgtn
21 V 16 Tudor clo Wdfd Grn
32 K 20 Tudor ct E17
43 R 16 Tudor Ct north Wemb
43 R 17 Tudor Ct south Wemb
7 X 4 Tudor cres Enf
102 H 11 Tudor dri Kingst
103 N 14 Tudor dri Kingst
119 T 17 Tudor dri Mrdn
39 V 12 Tudor dri Rom
43 W 7 Tudor gdns NW9
86 C 8 Tudor gdns SW13
101 W 1 Tudor gdns Twick
61 R 15 Tudor gdns W3
39 W 12 Tudor gdns Rom
159 T 6 Tudor gdns W Wkhm
63 O 1 Tudor gro E9
135 Z 2 Tudor gro E9
140 F 3 Tudor pl W1
106 K 19 Tudor pl Mitch
20 E 19 Tudor rd E4
65 Z 4 Tudor rd E6
63 O 2 Tudor rd E9
135 Y 3 Tudor rd E9
19 O 4 Tudor rd N9
109 U 18 Tudor rd SE19
124 B 13 Tudor rd SE25
67 X 3 Tudor rd Bark
4 M 11 Tudor rd Barnt
5 N 11 Tudor rd Barnt
125 S 6 Tudor rd Becknhm
100 H 18 Tudor rd Hampt
23 P 8 Tudor rd Harrow
83 P 10 Tudor rd Hounsl
103 P 18 Tudor rd Kingst
58 B 20 Tudor rd S'hall
141 U 8 Tudor st EC4
97 Z 15 Tudor wlk Bxly
16 K 5 Tudor way N14
73 O 6 Tudor way W3
11 P 17 Tudor Well clo Stanm
94 K 9 Tudway rd SE9
48 A 11 Tufnell Park rd N7
47 V 11 Tufnell Pk rd N19
20 A 14 Tufton rd E4
148 H 2 Tufton st SW1
123 O 14 Tugela rd Croy
110 M 4 Tugela st SE6
135 S 9 Tuilerie st E2
125 U 6 Tulse clo Becknhm
90 F 18 Tulse hill SW2
108 G 1 Tulse hill SW2
108 M 4 Tulsmere rd SE27
18 D 12 Tuncombe rd N18
74 L 3 Tunis rd W12
136 A 14 Tunis rd W12
62 B 2 Tunley rd NW10
107 N 3 Tunley rd SW17
65 X 10 Tunmarsh la E13
63 T 19 Tunnel appr E1
76 L 6 Tunnel appr SE10
76 L 6 Tunnel av SE10
77 O 11 Tunnel av SE10
75 P 6 Tunnel entrance SE16
29 V 2 Tunnel gdns N11
90 D 10 Tunstall rd SW19
123 T 20 Tunstall rd Croy
157 T 1 Tunstall rd Croy
25 V 19 Tunworth clo NW9
86 C 17 Tunworth cres SW15
100 L 20 Tudinghall la Felt
19 P 4 Turin rd N9
135 S 14 Turin st E2
109 R 19 Turkey oak clo SE19
147 R 9 Turks row SW3
133 W 19 Turks Head yd EC1
48 C 5 Turle rd N4
121 Z 2 Turle rd SW16
48 C 5 Turleway clo N4
65 N 4 Turley clo E15
141 W 4 Turnagain la EC4
55 Y 5 Turnage rd Dgnhm
89 S 8 Turnchapel ms SW4
31 R 14 Turner av N15
106 L 20 Turner av Mitch
101 O 6 Turner av Twick
28 A 19 Turner clo NW11
28 A 19 Turner dri NW11
33 U 11 Turner rd E17
24 L 8 Turner rd Edg
117 Z 16 Turner rd New Mald
63 Y 15 Turners rd E3
65 P 17 Turner st E16
46 D 2 Turners wood NW11
35 O 13 Turneville rd E2
145 O 13 Turneville rd W14
90 M 19 Turney rd SE21
91 O 18 Turney rd SE21
145 O 13 Turney rd
74 A 11 Turnham Green ter W4
92 H 12 Turnham rd SE4
133 V 19 Turnmill st EC1
75 Y 18 Turnpike clo SE8
30 F 12 Turnpike la N8
157 S 4 Turnpike link Croy
147 X 11 Turpentine la SW1
38 E 1 Turpin av Rom
65 T 7 Turpin est E13
47 X 5 Turpin way N19
155 T 16 Turpin way Wallgtn
127 T 16 Turpington clo Brom
127 R 15 Turpington la Brom
150 C 8 Turquand st SE17
89 U 6 Turret gro SW4
42 J 16 Turton rd Wemb
79 T 14 Tuscan rd SE18
76 M 15 Tuskar st SE10
75 O 18 Tustin st SE15
21 U 8 Tuttlebee la Buck Hl
51 S 14 Tweedale ct E15
120 F 19 Tweedale rd Carsh
65 V 7 Tweedmouth rd E13
39 O 2 Tweed way Rom
39 O 3 Tweed way Rom
126 F 2 Tweedy rd Brom
141 R 8 Tweezer's all WC2
64 F 11 Twelve Trees ct E14
21 U 15 Twentyman clo Wdfd Grn
84 D 13 Twickenham br Twick
156 B 5 Twickenham clo Croy
41 X 15 Twickenham gdns Grnfd
23 T 2 Twickenham gdns Harrow
51 V 6 Twickenham rd E11
83 X 10 Twickenham rd Islwth
84 A 1 Twickenham rd Islwth
84 F 11 Twickenham rd Rich
101 Y 9 Twickenham rd Tedd
88 A 18 Twilley st SW18
14 M 13 Twineham green N12
101 O 6 Twining av Twick
14 E 19 Twinn rd NW7
47 S 11 Twisden rd NW5
61 W 1 Twybridge way MW10
60 M 9 Twyford Abbey rd Wemb
28 L 11 Twyford av N2
29 N 10 Twyford av N2
61 P 19 Twyford av W3
73 P 1 Twyford av W3
73 R 2 Twyford cres W3
141 N 4 Twyford pl WC2
120 F 19 Twyford rd Carsh
40 J 2 Twyford rd Harrow
54 B 14 Twyford rd Ilf
133 N 4 Twyford st N1
65 O 13 Tyas rd E16
119 X 5 Tybenham rd SW19
9 O 10 Tyberry rd Enf
139 O 8 Tyburn way W1
142 J 18 Tyers gate SE1
149 O 8 Tyers st SE11
149 O 10 Tyers ter SE11
81 O 14 Tyeshurst clo SE2
121 Z 3 Tylecroft rd SW16
122 C 3 Tylecroft rd SW16
54 B 14 Tylehurst gdns Ilf
111 R 20 Tyler rd Becknhm
24 L 19 Tylers ga Harrow
77 N 14 Tyler st SE10
52 K 11 Tylney rd E7
127 N 3 Tylney rd Brom
48 J 20 Tyndale ter N1
51 T 7 Tyndall rd E10
96 L 8 Tyndall rd Welling
89 O 6 Tyneham rd SW11
8 L 3 Tynemouth dri Enf
31 W 13 Tynemouth rd N15
107 O 17 Tynemouth rd Mitch
88 C 4 Tynemouth st SW6
54 A 7 Tyne rd Ilf
63 S 6 Type st E2
87 Z 1 Tyrawley rd SW6
41 U 12 Tyrell clo Harrow
154 M 8 Tyrell ct Carsh
66 H 7 Tyrone rd E6
114 J 11 Tyron way Sidcp
97 P 13 Tyrrell av Welling
91 X 11 Tyrell rd SE22
93 O 6 Tyrwhitt rd SE4
133 T 15 Tysoe st EC1
92 D 19 Tyson rd SE23
49 U 17 Tyssen pas E8
49 V 17 Tyssen st E8
47 X 10 Tytherton rd N19

U

64 E 14 Uamvar st E14
107 P 19 Uckfield gro Mitch
9 U 1 Uckfield rd Enf
148 D 6 Udall st SW1
101 Z 13 Udney Pk rd Tedd
62 H 3 Uffington rd NW10
108 G 9 Uffington rd SE27
22 L 2 Ufford clo Harrow
22 L 2 Ufford rd Harrow
141 W 17 Ufford st SE1
49 P 20 Ufton gro N1
49 R 20 Ufton rd N1
134 H 2 Ufton rd N1
107 V 10 Ullathorne rd SW16
17 P 11 Ulleswater rd N13
103 Y 10 Ullswater clo SW15
103 Y 9 Ullswater cres SW15
104 A 10 Ullswater cres SW15
108 J 5 Ullswater rd SE27
74 G 20 Ullswater rd SW13
57 W 14 Ullswater way Hornch
17 X 13 Ulster gdns N13
48 C 12 Ulster ms N7
131 V 18 Ulster pl NW1
131 W 18 Ulster ter W1
77 N 16 Ulundi rd SE3
87 P 12 Ulva rd SW15
91 W 13 Ulverscroft rd SE22
108 J 5 Ulverstone rd SE27
33 X 7 Ulverston rd E17
45 W 14 Ulysses rd NW6
143 V 5 Umberton st E1
86 G 17 Umbria st SW15
30 H 19 Umfreville rd N4
9 W 10 Under Bridge way Enf
93 P 6 Undercliff rd SE13
4 K 16 Underhill Barnt
131 Z 5 Underhill pas NW1
91 Z 17 Underhill rd SE22
131 Z 5 Underhill st NW1
16 F 9 Underne av N14
77 V 20 Underpass SE3
142 J 6 Undershaft EC3
112 B 8 Undershaw rd Brom
159 U 12 Underwood Croy
135 S 19 Underwood rd E1
20 E 15 Underwood rd E4
134 D 11 Underwood st N1
113 V 5 Underwood the SE9
106 L 12 Undine st SW17
59 R 3 Uneeda dri Grnfd
142 L 15 Unicorn pas SE1

63 W 12 Union dr E1
89 X 4 Union gro SW8
16 L 18 Union rd N11
89 X 4 Union rd SW8
127 O 11 Union rd Brom
122 M 16 Union rd Croy
123 N 16 Union rd Croy
58 H 5 Union rd Grnfd
42 J 18 Union rd Wemb
18 H 20 Union row N17
134 B 6 Union sq N1
64 H 4 Union st E15
141 X 16 Union st SE1
142 A 15 Union st SE1
4 F 13 Union st Barnt
116 H 3 Union st Kingst
134 M 11 Union wlk SE2
78 A 8 Unity way SE18
132 E 17 University college WC1
26 C 2 University clo NW9
132 H 20 University of London WC1
106 G 15 University rd SW19
132 C 18 University st WC1
151 R 16 Unwin rd SE15
83 U 7 Unwin rd Islwth
138 D 7 Upbrook ms W2
26 C 19 Upcerne rd SW10
110 A 18 Upchurch clo SE20
12 H 14 Upcroft av Edg
157 Z 5 Upfield Croy
158 A 3 Upfield Croy
59 V 13 Upfield rd W7
53 Z 16 Uphall rd Ilf
74 B 11 Upham Pk rd W4
13 O 15 Uphill dri NW7
25 W 16 Uphill dri NW9
13 P 13 Uphill gro NW7
13 P 14 Uphill gro NW7
22 D 1 Up Hill view rd Pinn
65 R 12 Upland rd E13
91 X 12 Upland rd SE22
91 X 18 Upland rd SE22
98 B 8 Upland rd Bxly Hth
157 O 12 Upland rd S Croy
54 G 14 Upland rd Sutton
125 N 4 Uplands Becknhm
32 F 9 Uplands av E17
85 T 13 Uplands clo SW14
35 P 2 Uplands end Wdfd Grn
7 U 9 Uplands Pk rd Enf
30 E 17 Uplands rd N8
16 B 6 Uplands rd Barnt
37 U 11 Uplands rd Rom
35 P 2 Uplands rd Wdfd Grn
7 T 16 Uplands way N21
54 L 20 Upney la Bark
67 Y 1 Upney la Bark
36 C 18 Uppark dri Ilf
81 R 10 Up Abbey rd Blvdr
136 J 17 Up Addison gdns W14
147 V 1 Up Belgrave st SW1
139 P 5 Up Berkeley st W1
109 R 20 Up Beulah hill SE19
116 G 16 Up Brighton rd W1
139 S 9 Up Brook st W1
72 F 17 Upper butts Brentf
116 G 16 Up Cavendish av N3
146 K 14 Up Cheyne row SW3
49 Y 4 Up Clapton rd E5
50 A 8 Up Clapton rd E5
124 J 10 Up Elmers end Becknhm
125 P 13 Up Elmers End rd Becknhm
18 J 17 Up Fore st N18
120 L 4 Upper green Mitch
139 T 10 Up Grosvenor st W1
101 V 4 Up Grotto rd Twick
41 S 13 Up ground SE1
141 V 12 Up ground SE1
123 T 9 Up Grove SE25
81 O 16 Up Grove of Blvdr
102 G 8 Up Ham rd Rich
131 U 17 Up Harley st NW1
81 V 13 Up Holly Hill rd Blvdr
140 C 8 Up James st W1
140 C 9 Up Johns st W1
74 H 14 Up mall W6
41 P 20 Up marsh SE1
139 O 1 Up Montagu st W1
153 T 16 Up Mulgrave rd Sutton
64 B 15 Up North st E14
16 G 17 Up Park rd N11
46 L 17 Up Park rd NW3
81 U 12 Up Park rd Blvdr
112 K 20 Up Park rd Brom
103 O 16 Up Park rd Kingst
137 T 19 Up Phillmore gdns W8

57 T 11 Up Rainham rd Hornch
86 K 10 Up Richmond rd SW15
87 N 11 Up Richmond rd SW15
85 T 10 Up Richmond Rd w SW14
65 R 9 Upper rd E13
155 Z 11 Upper rd Wallgtn
157 T 17 Up Selsdon rd S Croy
81 R 10 Up Sheridan rd Blvdr
158 D 4 Up Shirley rd Croy
48 H 20 Upper st N1
133 V 8 Upper st N1
133 W 2 Upper st N1
140 J 8 Up St Martins la WC2
82 G 2 Up Sutton la Hounsl
102 D 19 Up Teddington rd Kingst
46 D 10 Upper ter NW3
141 Z 8 Up Thames st EC4
142 B 9 Up Thames st EC4
160 C 9 Up Thames st EC4
160 F 10 Up Thames st EC4
48 F 4 Up Tollington pk N4
90 D 20 Up Tulse hill SW2
114 M 12 Upperton Rd Sidcp
65 X 9 Upperton Rd west E13
65 Y 8 Upperton Rd west E13
106 M 4 Up Tooting pk SW17
107 N 4 Up Tooting pk SW17
106 L 9 Up Tooting rd SW17
107 N 6 Up Tooting rd SW17
58 J 12 Up Town rd Grnfd
154 F 10 Up Vernon rd Sutton
33 W 11 Up Walthamstow rd E17
97 P 4 Up Wickham la Welling
131 V 20 Up Wimpole st W1
132 G 15 Up Woburn pl WC1
24 E 19 Uppingham av Stanm
17 S 19 Upsdell av N13
90 L 3 Upstall st SE5
52 G 20 Upton av E7
98 B 15 Upton clo Bxly
52 G 20 Upton dene Sutton
24 C 17 Upton gdns Harrow
52 G 19 Upton la E7
52 H 1 Upton la E7
52 H 20 Upton Pk rd E7
65 V 1 Upton Park rd E7
18 L 16 Upton rd N18
79 P 18 Upton rd SE18
97 Y 10 Upton rd Bxly Hth
98 A 14 Upton rd Bxly Hth
82 H 9 Upton rd Hounsl
123 N 2 Upton rd Thntn Hth
15 V 20 Upway N12
94 D 16 Upwood rd SE12
122 A 1 Upwood rd SW16
150 B 16 Urlwin st SE5
105 T 1 Urmston dri SW19
88 J 3 Ursula st SW11
68 K 1 Urswick gdns Dgnhm
50 C 15 Urswick rd E5
68 K 1 Urswick rd Dgnhm
63 Z 5 Usher rd E3
63 S 8 Usk st E2
65 P 20 Usk st E16
56 B 9 Ulvedale rd Dgnhm
8 B 17 Uvedale rd Enf
146 B 18 Uverdale rd SW10
60 K 20 Uxbridge rd W5
73 O 2 Uxbridge rd W5
74 G 3 Uxbridge rd W12
136 B 16 Uxbridge rd W12
72 C 1 Uxbridge rd W13
100 L 13 Uxbridge rd Hampt
22 L 1 Uxbridge rd Harrow
23 O 1 Uxbridge rd Harrow
116 G 10 Uxbridge rd Kingst
70 L 2 Uxbridge rd S'hall
10 K 18 Uxbridge rd Stanm
11 O 17 Uxbridge rd Stanm
137 S 13 Uxbridge st W8
42 K 4 Uxendon cres Wemb
42 M 3 Uxendon hill Wemb
43 N 2 Uxendon hill Wemb

V

21 O 6 Valance av E4
125 Z 7 Valan leas Brom
130 B 13 Vale clo W9

126 F 6 Vale cotts Brom
104 B 8 Vale cres SW15
22 A 15 Vale croft Pinn
4 K 16 Vale dri Barnt
30 L 20 Vale gro N4
73 Y 4 Vale gro W3
61 P 15 Vale lane W3
55 W 3 Valence av Dgnhm
55 X 10 Valence cir Dgnhm
55 Y 8 Valence park Dgnhm
55 X 10 Valence wood Dgnhm
56 A 9 Valence Wood rd Dgnhm
11 S 14 Valencia rd Stanm
115 Y 2 Valentine av Bxly
110 E 5 Valentine ct SE23
141 V 18 Valentine pl SE1
52 E 19 Valentine rd E9
40 L 10 Valentine rd Harrow
141 W 18 Valentines park Ilf
53 Y 2 Valentine's rd Ilf
53 Y 4 Valentine's rd Ilf
55 Y 9 Valentine's way Rom
64 M 9 Valerian way E15
45 V 4 Vale ri NW11
17 H 17 Vale rd E7
30 M 20 Vale rd N4
31 N 19 Vale rd N4
127 V 2 Vale rd Brom
52 E 8 Vale rd Epsom
121 W 8 Vale rd Mitch
153 Z 8 Vale rd Sutton
152 F 5 Vale rd Worc Pk
48 J 10 Vale row N5
132 J 1 Vale royal N1
13 Q 13 Valeswood rd Brom
30 L 20 Vale ter N4
74 C 3 Vale the N3
29 O 4 Vale the N10
17 N 1 Vale the N14
16 L 3 Vale the N20
45 T 6 Vale the NW11
146 G 14 Vale the SW3
158 G 3 Vale the Croy
78 B 17 Vale the Hounsl
34 F 3 Vale the Wdfd Grn
65 R 5 Valetta gro E13
74 C 4 Valetta rd W3
58 B 18 Valette st E9
38 F 7 Valliant clo Rom
143 U 1 Vallance rd E1
135 U 14 Vallance rd E2
29 V 6 Vallance rd N22
33 U 12 Vallentin rd E17
15 U 14 Valley av N12
99 U 15 Valley clo Drtfrd
25 R 18 Valley dri NW9
99 P 4 Valleyfield rd SW16
7 T 9 Valley Fields cres Enf
106 G 17 Valley gdns SW19
42 L 20 Valley gdns Wemb
77 Y 13 Valley gro SE7
101 X 13 Valley ms Twick
108 D 10 Valley rd SW16
81 X 11 Valley rd Blvdr
126 A 4 Valley rd Brom
99 U 16 Valley rd Drtfrd
115 R 20 Valley rd Orp
20 B 5 Valley side E4
20 A 7 Valley side parade E4
158 C 2 Valley wlk Croy
62 H 8 Valliere rd NW10
114 G 2 Valliers Wood rd Sidcp
59 V 13 Vallis way W13
90 M 3 Valmar rd SE5
91 N 2 Valmar rd SE5
106 M 12 Valnay st SW17
32 H 4 Valognes av E17
87 V 15 Valonia gdns SW18
79 O 16 Vamberry rd SE18
94 C 1 Vanborough ter SE3
77 O 18 Vanbrugh fields SE3
77 O 17 Vanbrugh hill SE3
77 P 19 Vanbrugh pk SE3
77 P 20 Vanbrugh Pk rd SE3
77 O 18 Vanbrugh Pk rd west SE3
73 Z 8 Vanbrugh rd W4
94 C 1 Vanbrugh ter SE3
110 L 3 Vancouver rd SE23
25 T 5 Vancouver rd Edg
58 C 20 Vanderbilt rd SW18
65 U 18 Vandome clo E16
140 D 20 Vandon pas SW1
140 D 1 Vandon st SW1
117 Z 17 Van Dyck av New Mald
87 V 17 Vandyke clo SW15
95 P 14 Vandyke cross SE9
46 F 14 Vane clo NW3
24 M 14 Vane clo Harrow

81 S 13 Vanessa clo Blvdr
148 D 5 Vane st SW1
38 E 8 Vanguard clo Rom
93 O 2 Vanguard st SE4
156 A 16 Vanguard way Wallgtn
156 A 17 Vanguard way Wallgtn
112 E 8 Vanoc gdns Brom
52 D 12 Vansittart rd E7
75 W 18 Vansittort st SE14
145 U 18 Vanston pl SW6
106 M 13 Vant rd SW17
107 N 13 Vant rd SW17
75 O 15 Varcoe rd SE16
151 Z 12 Varcoe rd SE16
88 G 12 Vardens rd SW11
63 N 16 Varden st E1
143 W 3 Varden st E1
56 W 16 Varley rd E16
132 A 12 Varndell st NW1
31 P 19 Varty rd N15
149 V 20 Vassall rd SW9
151 P 3 Vauban st SE16
100 D 15 Vaughan clo Hampt
26 G 16 Vaughan av NW4
74 E 10 Vaughan av W6
53 T 1 Vaughan gdns Ilf
52 C 19 Vaughan rd E15
90 L 6 Vaughan rd SE5
22 M 19 Vaughan rd Harrow
23 R 20 Vaughan rd Harrow
116 A 17 Vaughan rd Surb
96 L 5 Vaughan rd Welling
76 A 19 Vaughan Williams clo SE8
148 J 10 Vauxhall br SW1 & SE11
148 C 6 Vauxhall br SW1 & SE11
156 M 15 Vauxhall gdns S Croy
148 M 13 Vauxhall gro SW8
149 N 13 Vauxhall gro SW8
148 M 15 Vauxhall Park SE11
148 L 13 Vauxhall stn SE1
149 P 8 Vauxhall st SE11
148 M 10 Vauxhall wlk SE11
149 N 8 Vauxhall wlk SE11
63 O 13 Vawdrey clo E1
107 R 16 Vectis rd SW17
93 P 11 Veda rd SE13
10 A 3 Vega rd Bushey Watf
91 S 12 Velde way SE22
130 H 19 Venables st NW8
74 C 12 Vencourt pl W6
90 M 5 Venetian rd SE5
30 J 20 Venetia rd N4
72 F 7 Venetia rd W5
110 D 14 Venner rd SE26
99 P 4 Venners clo Bxly Hth
89 W 9 Venn st SW4
24 C 6 Ventnor av Stanm
15 N 9 Ventnor dri N20
54 G 17 Ventnor gdns Bark
75 T 19 Ventnor rd SE14
154 B 17 Ventnor rd Sutton
97 Y 18 Venture clo Bxly
78 F 8 Venus rd SE18
7 U 18 Vera av N21
87 T 2 Vera rd SW6
74 F 14 Verbena gdns W6
112 A 2 Verdant la SE6
158 F 2 Verdayne av Croy
80 A 18 Verdun rd SE2
74 F 19 Verdun rd SW13
145 N 12 Vereker rd W14
139 X 6 Vere st W1
109 P 16 Vermont rd SE19
88 B 16 Vermont rd SW18
154 A 4 Vermont rd Sutton
55 Y 13 Verney gdns Dgnhm
75 O 14 Verney rd SE16
151 V 12 Verney rd SE16
55 Y 12 Verney rd Dgnhm
43 Y 10 Verney way SE16
151 V 11 Verney way SE16
79 O 16 Vernham rd SE18
53 T 13 Vernon av E12
119 O 3 Vernon av SW20
34 G 1 Vernon av Wdfd Grn
24 A 4 Vernon ct Stanm
6 B 18 Vernon cres Barnt
23 Z 4 Vernon dri Stanm
24 A 4 Vernon dri Stanm
144 L 6 Vernon ms W14
140 L 2 Vernon pl WC1
133 P 12 Vernon rise WC1
41 P 16 Vernon ri Grnfd
63 Z 6 Vernon rd E3
51 Z 4 Vernon rd E11
52 A 5 Vernon rd E15
51 Z 19 Vernon rd E15
32 L 14 Vernon rd N8
30 G 11 Vernon rd N8
85 V 13 Vernon rd SW14

54 K 5 Vernon rd Ilf
154 E 10 Vernon rd Sutton
133 O 11 Vernon sq WC1
144 L 6 Vernon st W14
97 Y 5 Veroan rd Bxly Hth
52 F 20 Verona rd E7
107 S 5 Veronica rd SW17
36 A 15 Veronique gdns Ilf
89 R 19 Verran rd SW12
109 X 19 Versailles rd SE20
32 K 20 Verulam av E17
58 J 11 Verulam rd Grnfd
133 S 20 Veralum st EC1
22 M 8 Verwood rd Harrow
74 F 4 Vespan rd W12
92 J 5 Vesta rd SE4
110 G 4 Vestris rd SE23
91 R 2 Vestry ms SE5
33 B 14 Vestry rd E17
91 S 2 Vestry rd SE5
134 F 12 Vestry st N1
110 K 5 Vevey st SE6
56 D 9 Veysey gdns Dgnhm
141 V 2 Viaduct bldgs EC1
135 W 14 Viaduct pl E2
135 W 14 Viaduct st E2
34 G 8 Viaduct the E18
93 S 8 Vian st SE13
90 D 20 Vibart gdns SW2
132 L 4 Vibart wk N1
17 T 20 Vicarage av SE3
81 X 18 Vicarage clo Erith
68 G 3 Vicarage cres SW11
85 X 12 Vicarage dri SW14
67 R 2 Vicarage dri Bark
70 C 20 Vicarage Farm rd Hounsl
82 C 3 Vicarage Farm rd Hounsl
137 W 15 Vicarage gdns W8
120 J 7 Vicarage gdns Mitch
137 W 16 Vicarage ga W8
91 P 1 Vicarage gro SE5
66 K 8 Vicarage la E6
52 B 19 Vicarage la E15
66 O 2 Vicarage la E15
152 G 19 Vicarage la Epsom
54 D 5 Vicarage la Ilf
79 P 14 Vicarage pk SE18
47 Z 1 Vicarage path N19
51 O 1 Vicarage rd E10
52 B 20 Vicarage rd E15
31 X 3 Vicarage rd N17
26 G 20 Vicarage rd NW4
85 Y 12 Vicarage rd SW14
156 G 4 Vicarage rd Croy
56 F 20 Vicarage rd Dgnhm
57 X 4 Vicarage rd Hornch
116 G 2 Vicarage rd Kingst
153 Z 7 Vicarage rd Sutton
101 X 12 Vicarage rd Tedd
101 T 4 Vicarage rd Twick
35 S 2 Vicarage rd Wdfd Grn
88 G 2 Vicarage wlk SW11
43 Z 10 Vicarage way NW10
40 G 1 Vicarage way Harrow
63 O 4 Vicars clo E8
65 S 3 Vicars clo E15
8 F 10 Vicars clo Enf
93 P 9 Vicars hill SE13
17 U 3 Vicars Moor la N21
14 O 14 Vicar's rd NW5
55 R 10 Vicars wlk Dgnhm
90 A 1 Viceroy rd SW8
148 J 7 Vickers Building SW1
41 L 20 Victor go Wemb
146 H 3 Victoria And Albert Museum SW7
66 A 3 Victoria av E6
142 K 2 Victoria av EC2
27 W 5 Victoria av N3
5 U 15 Victoria av Barnt
82 G 12 Victoria av Hounsl
116 F 16 Victoria av Surb
155 P 5 Victoria av Wallgtn
5 V 15 Victoria av Barnt
85 O 3 Victoria cotts Rich
43 P 17 Victoria cres N15
31 R 16 Victoria cres N15
109 R 14 Victoria cres SE19
90 W 17 Victoria cres SW19
65 N 17 Victoria Dock rd E16
65 T 19 Victoria Dock rd E16
105 R 3 Victoria dri SW19
105 S 4 Victoria dri SW19
140 L 16 Victoria emb EC4/WC2/SW1
141 S 9 Victoria emb EC4/WC2/SW1
137 S 12 Victoria gdns W11
82 A 1 Victoria gdns Hounsl
15 T 15 Victoria gro N12

146 A 1 Victoria gro W8
137 V 10 Victoria Gro ms W2
4 H 14 Victoria la Barnt
129 S 4 Victoria ms NW6
129 T 4 Victoria ms NW6
49 T 10 Victorian gro N16
49 T 11 Victorian rd N16
63 W 2 Victoria park E9
63 P 3 Victoria Pk rd E9
135 Y 5 Victoria Pk rd E9
63 O 8 Victoria Pk sq E2
135 Z 11 Victoria Pk sq E2
84 H 13 Victoria pl Rich
89 S 10 Victoria ri SW4
20 M 5 Victoria rd E4
21 N 4 Victoria rd E4
65 S 7 Victoria rd E13
33 T 7 Victoria rd E17
34 H 8 Victoria rd E18
48 E 3 Victoria rd N4
18 J 9 Victoria rd N9
31 W 14 Victoria rd N15
29 W 5 Victoria rd N22
27 N 13 Victoria rd NW4
129 O 8 Victoria rd NW6
129 T 4 Victoria rd NW6
13 R 15 Victoria rd NW7
62 A 12 Victoria rd NW10
85 X 7 Victoria rd SW14
61 Y 13 Victoria rd W3
60 C 14 Victoria rd W5
138 A 19 Victoria rd W8
53 Z 18 Victoria rd Bark
54 A 18 Victoria rd Bark
5 U 15 Victoria rd Barnt
98 D 12 Victoria rd Bxly Hth
127 P 12 Victoria rd Brom
113 X 12 Victoria rd Chisl
56 J 14 Victoria rd Dgnhm
32 Z 15 Victoria rd Ilf
36 A 15 Victoria rd Ilf
117 N 3 Victoria rd Kingst
106 K 19 Victoria rd Mitch
59 S 18 Victoria rd Rom
40 A 13 Victoria rd Ruis
114 M 8 Victoria rd Sidcp
70 D 9 Victoria rd S'hall
116 G 15 Victoria rd Surb
154 F 12 Victoria rd Sutton
101 X 15 Victoria rd Tedd
84 A 18 Victoria rd Twick
147 Y 1 Victoria sq SW1
147 Y 2 Victoria sq SW1
147 Y 5 Victoria station SW1
51 Y 20 Victoria st E15
140 G 20 Victoria st SW1
138 D 2 Victoria st SW1
81 P 14 Victoria st Blvdr
48 F 4 Victoria ter N4
41 S 4 Victoria ter Harrow
148 L 1 Victoria Tower Gardens SW1
85 N 10 Victoria vlls Rich
77 W 15 Victoria way SE7
62 K 7 Victor rd NW10
110 F 17 Victor rd SE20
23 O 11 Victor rd Harrow
101 T 11 Victor rd Tedd
18 C 10 Victor vlls N9
20 D 11 Victory av Mrdn
150 D 5 Victory pl SE17
117 T 16 Victory pl SE19
106 B 18 Victory rd E11
63 G 17 Victory sq SE5
38 F 7 Victory way Rom
93 O 2 Victory wlk SE4
26 P 12 View clo Harrow
87 V 16 Viewfield rd SW18
97 T 20 Viewfield rd Sidcp
79 W 14 Viewland rd SE18
28 M 20 View rd N6
29 N 19 View rd N6
81 N 13 View the SE2
7 U 19 Viga rd N21
109 X 9 Vigilant clo SE26
140 B 10 Vigo st W1
58 C 19 Viking rd S'hall
80 A 18 Villacourt rd SE18
20 H 16 Village clo E4
99 U 11 Village Green rd Drtfrd
27 S 7 Village rd N3
8 D 19 Village rd Enf
153 X 15 Village row Sutton
77 Z 16 Village the SE7
78 A 16 Village the SE7
43 Z 12 Village way NW10
44 A 12 Village way NW10
91 O 15 Village way SE21
125 N 3 Village way Becknhm
40 F 1 Village way E Harrow
40 D 1 Village way Pinn
90 F 7 Villa rd SW9
79 P 12 Villas rd SE18

150 F 10 Villa st SE17
150 G 12 Villa st SE17
116 L 11 Villiers av Surb
100 F 2 Villiers av Twick
51 O 6 Villiers clo E10
117 N 9 Villiers clo Surb
15 X 4 Villiers ct SW1
116 L 11 Villiers path Surb
44 G 17 Villiers rd NW10
124 F 4 Villiers rd Becknhm
83 S 4 Villiers rd Islwth
116 M 6 Villiers rd Kingst
140 K 12 Villiers rd WC2
70 F 4 Villiers rd S'hall
82 H 18 Vincam clo Twick
4 M 11 Vincent clo Barnt
114 F 2 Vincent clo Sidcp
44 E 10 Vincent gdns NW2
20 K 20 Vincent rd N15
30 L 13 Vincent rd N15
30 F 7 Vincent rd N22
79 N 11 Vincent rd SE18
73 U 8 Vincent rd W3
123 S 18 Vincent rd Croy
68 L 2 Vincent rd Dgnhm
83 P 3 Vincent rd Islwth
117 P 5 Vincent rd Kingst
61 D 1 Vincent rd Wemb
100 M 14 Vincent row Hampt
40 B 18 Vincents path Grnfd
148 E 5 Vincent sq SW1
65 P 16 Vincent st E16
148 F 6 Vincent st SW1
133 X 9 Vincent ter N1
134 G 14 Vine ct E1
143 U 2 Vine ct E1
24 K 17 Vine ct Harrow
33 T 13 Vinegar all E17
54 B 15 Vine glns Ilf
133 S 18 Vine hill EC1
142 L 15 Vine la SE1
82 J 10 Vine pl Hounsl
13 X 16 Vineries bank NW7
6 H 18 Vineries the N14
9 Vineries the Enf
130 K 14 Vinery vlls NW8
28 A 5 Vines av N3
143 N 7 Vine st EC3
140 C 11 Vine st W1
38 L 14 Vine st Rom
133 U 18 Vine St br EC1
142 B 18 Vine yd SE1
27 S 2 Vineyard av NW2
105 X 9 Vineyard Hill rd SW19
84 J 13 Vineyard pas Rich
85 X 7 Vineyard path SW14
84 K 14 Vineyard the Rich
133 T 16 Vineyard wlk EC1
158 L 18 Viney bank Croy
117 N 13 Vine clo Surb
154 C 5 Vine clo Sutton
93 S 8 Viney rd SE13
90 F 10 Vining st SW9
160 C 9 Vinters pl EC4
80 C 12 Viola av SE2
62 E 20 Viola sq W12
8 B 3 Violet av Enf
156 J 12 Violet gdns Croy
130 B 10 Violet hill NW8
156 J 9 Violet la Croy
64 C 12 Violet rd E3
33 P 19 Violet rd E17
34 H 7 Violet rd E18
139 N 1 Virgil pl W1
149 R 1 Virgil st SE1
36 D 8 Virginia gdns Ilf
134 M 14 Virginia rd E2
108 J 20 Virginia rd Mitch
143 T 10 Virginia st E1
90 D 16 Virginia wlk SW2
56 F 1 Vignoles rd E2
134 B 19 Viscount st EC1
7 T 9 Vista av Enf
35 O 16 Vista dri Ilf
95 P 19 Vista the SE9
24 J 19 Vista way Harrow
26 J 17 Vivian av NW4
43 S 17 Vivian av Wemb
43 O 15 Vivian gdns Wemb
63 V 6 Vivian rd E3
31 Z 7 Vivian sq SE15
84 F 17 Vivienne clo Twick
79 T 20 Voce rd SE18
96 F 1 Voce rd SE18
118 D 14 Voewood clo New Mald
89 X 3 Voltaire rd SW4
34 E 18 Voluntary pl E11
47 V 7 Vorley rd N19
108 B 16 Voss ct SW16
135 U 14 Voss st E2
156 C 15 Vulcan clo Croy

7 U 9 Vulcan ga Enf
92 K 5 Vulcan rd SE4
92 L 4 Vulcan rd SE4
48 D 17 Vulcan way N7
61 Z 20 Vyner rd W3
63 N 4 Vyner st E2
98 H 8 Vyne the Bxly Hth

W

65 Y 19 Wada rd E16
150 D 7 Wadding st SE17
51 X 16 Waddington rd E15
51 X 17 Waddington st E15
98 F 11 Waddington ter Bxly Hth
108 M 19 Waddington way SE19
109 N 20 Waddington way SE19
156 G 4 Waddon clo Croydon
156 E 6 Waddon Ct rd Croy
122 C 20 Waddon Marsh way Croy
156 H 4 Waddon New rd Croy
157 F 7 Waddon Pk av Croydon
156 H 5 Waddon rd Croydon
156 F 14 Waddon way Croydon
17 T 3 Wades gro N21
7 T 19 Wades hill N21
17 U 3 Wades hill N21
63 O 5 Wadeson st E2
135 Y 7 Wadeson st E2
64 C 19 Wade's pl E14
38 A 20 Wadeville av Rom
81 S 15 Wadeville clo Blvdr
33 S 3 Wadham av E17
130 J 2 Wadham gdns NW3
41 P 17 Wadham gdns Grnfd
33 T 3 Wadham rd E17
87 T 11 Wadham rd SW15
123 Z 3 Wadhurst clo SE20
73 Y 9 Wadhurst rd W4
89 U 1 Wadhurst rd SW8
33 Z 20 Wadley rd E11
60 D 6 Wadsworth clo Grnfd
74 J 9 Wadsworth mansion SE14
60 C 6 Wadsworth rd Grnfd
65 T 15 Watford rd E16
63 Y 13 Wager st E3
18 J 20 Waggon la N17
64 X 4 Waghorn rd E13
7 Z 20 Waghorn rd Harrow
91 X 7 Waghorn st SE15
5 W 1 Wagon rd Barnt
38 K 8 Wainfleet av Rom
94 C 19 Wainford clo SW19
94 Waite Davies rd SE12
151 O 13 Wake st SE15
109 S 18 Wakefield gdns SE19
35 P 20 Wakefield gdns Ilf
16 L 17 Wakefield rd N11
31 U 15 Wakefield rd N15
84 H 13 Wakefield rd Rich
66 E 3 Wakefield st E6
18 K 17 Wakefield st N18
132 L 15 Wakefield st WC1
22 E 11 Wakehams hill Pinn
49 O 18 Wakeham st N1
88 L 13 Wakehurst rd SW11
39 N 12 Wakehurst rd SW11
59 W 15 Wakeling rd W7
63 U 18 Wakeling st E14
64 M 6 Wakelin rd E15
128 D 13 Wakeman rd NW10
25 Y 14 Wakemans Hill av SE9
54 B 19 Wakering rd Bark
133 X 11 Wakley st EC1
148 M 19 Walberswick st SW8
160 E 8 Walbrook EC4
150 C 8 Walcorde av SE17
149 U 4 Walcot sq SE11
9 X 8 Walcot rd Enf
148 D 5 Walcott st SW1
108 H 7 Waldeck gro SE27
30 J 12 Waldeck rd N15
85 W 7 Waldeck rd SW14
73 P 15 Waldeck rd W4
84 H 13 Waldeck rd W13
101 V 5 Waldegrave gdns Twick
101 W 9 Waldegrave pk Twick
30 G 10 Waldegrave rd N8

W

109 V 18 Waldegrave rd SE19
60 M 18 Waldegrave rd W5
127 S 10 Waldegrave rd Brom
55 T 6 Waldegrave rd Dgnhm
101 V 8 Waldegrave rd Twick
157 U 7 Waldemar av Croy
87 T 3 Waldemar av SW6
72 D 4 Waldemar av W13
105 X 11 Waldemar rd SW19
17 Z 13 Walden av N13
113 V 10 Walden av Chisl
69 Z 7 Walden av Rainhm
81 O 13 Walden clo Blvdr
122 D 7 Walden gdns Thntn Hth
31 O 5 Walden rd N17
113 U 14 Walden rd Chisl
143 V 3 Walden st E1
110 C 2 Waldenshaw rd SE23
36 H 1 Walden way Ilf
106 K 19 Waldo pl Mitch
62 J 9 Waldo rd NW10
126 M 7 Waldo rd Brom
156 J 17 Waldorf clo S Croy
110 D 2 Waldram cres SE23
110 E 2 Waldram Pk rd SE23
110 D 2 Waldram pl SE23
125 W 6 Waldrom gdns Brom
156 K 9 Waldronhyrst Croy
146 H 14 Waldron ms SW3
106 D 5 Waldron rd SW18
41 S 4 Waldron rd Harrow
156 K 9 Waldrons path S Croy
156 K 8 Waldrons the Croy
10 J 17 Walerand clo Stanm
93 V 6 Walerand rd SE13
154 K 12 Wales av Carsh
61 Y 15 Wales Farm rd W3
63 U 14 Waley st E1
15 O 1 Walfield av N20
49 T 12 Walford rd N16
56 A 20 Walfrey gdns Dgnhm
145 X 19 Walham grn ct SW6
145 T 17 Walham gro SW6
145 T 16 Walham yd SW6
113 X 11 Walkden rd Chisl
79 O 10 Walker clo SE18
99 S 7 Walker clo Drtfrd
140 E 8 Walker's ct W1
87 R 9 Walkers pl SW15
108 M 1 Walkerscroft mead SE21
109 N 2 Walkerscroft mead SE21
99 Y 14 Walkley rd Drtfrd
28 G 9 Walks the N2
139 T 4 Wallace collection W2
154 L 11 Wallace cres Carsh
64 M 9 Wallace rd E15
48 M 17 Wallace rd N1
92 H 6 Wallbutton rd SE4
45 P 3 Wallcote av NW2
46 H 2 Wall End rd E6
39 Z 11 Wallenger av Rom
92 E 3 Waller rd SE14
74 E 1 Wallflower st W12
145 W 6 Wallgrave rd SW5
136 E 4 Wallingford av W10
36 L 20 Wallington rd Ilf
155 U 14 Wallington sq Wallgtn
88 F 8 Wallis clo SW11
50 M 19 Wallis rd E9
51 N 18 Wallis rd E9
58 K 17 Wallis rd S'hall
85 Z 10 Wallorton gdns SW14
64 J 20 Wall rd E14
49 P 19 Wall st N1
51 X 2 Wallwood rd E11
63 Z 15 Wallwood st E14
90 M 3 Walmar clo Rom
71 Z 7 Walmer gdns W13
139 N 1 Walmer pl W1
139 N 1 Walmer st W1
79 R 11 Walmer ter SE18
60 B 4 Walmgate rd Grnfd
14 K 18 Walmington rd N12
45 R 15 Walm la NW2
154 K 14 Walnut clo Carsh
36 C 12 Walnut clo Ilf
154 C 16 Walnut clo Sutton
8 B 18 Walnut gro Enf
120 J 4 Walnut Tree av Mitch
72 K 16 Walnut Tree clo SW15
114 D 20 Walnut Tree clo Chisl
105 R 12 Walnut Tree cotts SW19
77 O 15 Walnut Tree rd SE10

72 K 17 Walnut Tree rd Brentf
55 X 7 Walnut Tree rd Dgnhm
70 F 17 Walnut Tree rd Hounsl
149 S 4 Walnut Tree wlk SE11
84 M 5 Walpole av Rich
85 N 5 Walpole av Rich
72 D 4 Walpole clo W13
101 V 13 Walpole cres Tedd
73 V 13 Walpole gdns W4
101 U 6 Walpole gdns Twick
101 V 13 Walpole pl Tedd
65 Y 2 Walpole rd E6
32 J 12 Walpole rd E17
34 B 6 Walpole rd E18
30 M 7 Walpole rd N17
106 G 15 Walpole rd SW19
127 N 11 Walpole rd Brom
157 N 2 Walpole rd Croy
116 H 16 Walpole rd Surb
101 V 13 Walpole rd Tedd
101 T 4 Walpole rd Twick
147 O 9 Walpole st SW3
42 L 17 Walrond av Wemb
92 E 4 Walsham rd SE14
152 C 10 Walsingham gdns Epsom
49 Y 10 Walsingham rd E5
8 B 16 Walsingham rd Enf
120 M 10 Walsingham rd Mitch
123 S 10 Walters rd SE25
9 R 16 Walters rd Enf
63 T 9 Walters st E2
116 J 1 Walter st Kingst
126 E 2 Walters yd Brom
63 T 16 Walter ter E1
129 R 17 Walterton rd W9
12 J 20 Walter wlk Edg
25 R 18 Waltham av NW9
49 V 15 Waltham clo Drtfrd
25 P 9 Waltham dri Edg
33 N 3 Waltham Pk way E17
120 G 19 Waltham rd Carsh
70 B 8 Waltham rd S'hall
33 X 11 Walthamstow rd E17
105 S 14 Waltham ri SW19
19 X 12 Waltham way E4
20 B 5 Waltham way E4
31 N 5 Waltheof av N17
31 N 4 Waltheof gdns N17
40 E 12 Walton av Harrow
118 D 10 Walton av New Mald
153 U 5 Walton av Sutton
44 K 7 Walton clo NW2
23 R 12 Walton clo Harrow
40 E 12 Walton cres Harrow
23 R 13 Walton dri Harrow
61 T 15 Walton gdns W3
42 J 7 Walton gdns Wemb
159 U 14 Walton grn Croy
147 O 1 Walton pl SW3
53 W 12 Walton rd E12
53 W 13 Walton rd E12
65 X 6 Walton rd E13
31 V 14 Walton rd N15
23 R 12 Walton rd Harrow
38 C 2 Walton rd Rom
115 S 8 Walton rd Sidcp
146 L 5 Walton st SW3
147 N 3 Walton st SW3
8 A 6 Walton st Enf
148 K 17 Walton ter SW8
61 T 15 Walton way W3
121 U 9 Walton way Mitch
150 C 19 Walworth pl SE17
150 B 9 Walworth rd SE17
127 N 7 Walwyn av Brom
86 J 20 Wanborough dri SW15
104 H 1 Wanborough dri SW15
106 L 18 Wandle bank SW19
155 Z 6 Wandle bank Wallgtn
155 Z 6 Wandle Ct gdns Wallgtn
106 K 3 Wandle rd SW17
106 L 18 Wandle rd SW19
156 A 5 Wandle rd Croy
156 L 6 Wandle rd Croy
120 E 10 Wandle rd Mrdn
155 R 3 Wandle rd Wallgtn
156 E 6 Wandle side Croy
155 R 5 Wandle side Wallgtn
121 L 11 Wandle way Mitch
145 Z 18 Wandon rd SW6
88 A 5 Wandsworth Br rd SW6
88 G 15 Wandsworth common SW18

88 G 13 Wandsworth Comm North side SW18
88 E 15 Wandsworth Comm West side SW18
87 Y 14 Wandsworth High st SW18
87 Y 13 Wandsworth hill SW18
87 V 10 Wandsworth park SW15
87 Z 13 Wandsworth plain SW18
89 T 6 Wandsworth rd SW8
148 H 18 Wandsworth rd SW8
25 S 5 Wandsworth stadium SW18
55 V 1 Wangey rd Rom
91 P 9 Wanlay rd SE5
90 L 8 Wanless rd SE24
65 W 11 Wanlip rd E13
50 M 20 Wansbeck rd E9
68 Z 1 Wansbeck rd E9
145 W 18 Wansdown pl SW6
150 A 7 Wansey st SE17
34 A 7 Wansford rd Wdfd Grn
126 L 3 Wanstead clo Brom
35 N 18 Wanstead gdns Ilf
52 K 2 Wanstead house E11
35 S 19 Wanstead la Ilf
53 N 7 Wanstead Pk av E12
52 M 5 Wanstead Pk av E12
35 O 20 Wanstead Pk rd Ilf
53 S 3 Wanstead Pk rd Ilf
34 F 17 Wanstead pl E11
126 K 3 Wanstead rd Brom
98 L 20 Wansunt rd Bxly
94 B 13 Wantage rd SE12
56 G 15 Wantz rd Dgnhm
143 Z 14 Wapping Dock st E1
75 O 3 Wapping High st E1
143 T 14 Wapping High st E1
143 X 10 Wapping la E1
75 N 1 Wapping la SE8
75 P 2 Wapping wall E1
74 K 4 Warbeck rd W12
30 D 6 Warberry rd N22
103 U 14 Warboys app Kingst
20 H 17 Warboys cres E4
103 X 16 Warboys rd Kingst
10 B 19 Warburton clo Harrow
135 X 3 Warburton rd E8
100 J 1 Warburton rd Twick
53 N 2 Warburton ter E17
63 N 2 Warburtoss rd E8
75 O 9 Wardale clo SE16
81 Z 7 Ward clo Erith
26 B 2 Wardell clo NW9
26 C 4 Wardell field NW9
40 E 4 Warden av Harrow
47 N 4 Warden rd NW5
142 A 15 Wardens gro SE1
143 X 3 Warden st E1
50 F 15 Wardle st E9
63 S 9 Wardley st E2
88 A 19 Wardo av SW6
87 R 2 Wardo av SW6
75 R 12 Wardour st SE16
140 D 6 Wardour ms W1
140 E 7 Wardour st W1
64 H 2 Ward rd E15
47 V 11 Ward rd N19
141 Y 7 Wardrobe pl EC4
141 Y 7 Wardrobe ter EC4
54 F 1 Wards rd Ilf
149 P 8 Ward st SE11
82 J 10 Wareham clo Hounsl
35 Y 16 Waremead rd Ilf
128 F 14 Warfield rd NW10
100 L 20 Warfield rd Hampt
128 F 14 Warfield yd NW10
9 V 19 Warf rd Enf
31 V 18 Wargrave av N15
40 M 10 Wargrave rd Harrow
30 M 16 Warham rd N4
23 W 8 Warham rd Harrow
156 M 10 Warham rd S Croy
149 X 18 Warham st SW9
115 R 7 Waring park Sidcp
115 T 15 Waring rd Sidcp
71 Y 19 Warkworth gdns Islwth
31 P 3 Warkworth rd N17
79 T 20 Warland rd SE18
56 C 2 Warley av Dgnhm
79 P 8 Warley rd N9
35 X 4 Warley rd Ilf
34 H 2 Warley rd Wdfd Grn
122 J 8 Warlingham rd Thntn Hth
129 R 16 Warlock rd W9
48 B 12 Warlters

48 B 12 Warlters ms N7
48 A 2 Waltersville rd N4
90 M 15 Warmington rd SE24
65 T 11 Warmington rd E13
123 W 4 Warminster gdns SE25
123 W 6 Warminster rd SE25
123 X 3 Warminster sq SE25
121 T 2 Warminster way Mitch
24 H 11 Warneford rd Harrow
135 Y 4 Warneford st E9
153 S 2 Warner av Sutton
52 A 16 Warner clo E15
135 T 10 Warner clo E9
32 J 13 Warner rd E17
29 X 13 Warner rd N8
90 M 2 Warner rd SE5
112 C 18 Warner rd Brom
133 R 17 Warner st WC1
133 S 18 Warner st EC1
21 S 16 Warners clo Wdfd Grn
154 M 16 Warnham Ct rd Carsh
15 V 17 Warnham rd N12
74 A 4 Warple way W3
85 T 9 Warren av Rich
51 V 9 Warren av E11
111 Z 17 Warren av Brom
158 E 17 Warren av S Croy
19 S 5 Warren clo N9
98 E 12 Warren clo Bxly Hth
111 N 19 Warren ct Becknhm
18 H 3 Warren clo N9
103 X 17 Warren cutting Kingst
47 V 11 Warrender rd N19
58 L 11 Warren dri Grnfd
57 X 10 Warren dri Hornch
117 S 20 Warren dri N Surb
117 U 20 Warren dri S Surb
52 K 1 Warren Dri the E11
51 X 16 Warren gdns E15
103 W 15 Warren house Kingst
11 N 10 Warren house Stanm
78 M 9 Warren la SE18
78 L 8 Warren la SE18
10 K 9 Warren la Stanm
23 Z 18 Warren ms W1
103 X 16 Warren Pk rd Sutton
154 H 12 Warren Pk rd Sutton
21 P 3 Warren Pond rd E4
100 Y 20 Warren ri Kingst
20 G 8 Warren rd E4
51 V 9 Warren rd E10
34 K 19 Warren rd E11
52 L 1 Warren rd E11
44 E 8 Warren rd NW2
106 J 16 Warren rd Bushey Watf
10 B 5 Warren rd Bushey Watf
98 D 12 Warren rd Bxly Hth
123 T 19 Warren rd Croy
36 D 15 Warren rd Ilf
103 V 15 Warren rd Kingst
115 T 8 Warren rd Sidcp
83 O 17 Warren rd Twick
137 B 17 Warren st W1
37 X 14 Warren ter Rom
53 R 12 Warren the E12
154 H 20 Warren the Carsh
70 D 20 Warren the Hounsl
14 E 18 Warren the NW7
77 Y 16 Warren wlk SE7
12 F 6 Warrens Shawe la Edg
89 N 2 Warriner gdns SW11
130 A 17 Warrington cres W9
130 A 19 Warrington gdns W9
156 H 6 Warrington rd Croy
55 X 7 Warrington rd Dgnhm
23 T 16 Warrington rd Harrow
55 X 7 Warrington sq Dgnhm
149 Z 18 Warrior rd SE5
53 V 12 Warrior sq E12
78 C 8 Warspite rd SE18
64 G 3 Warton rd E15
129 Y 17 Warwick av W9
130 A 19 Warwick av W9
12 G 11 Warwick av Edg
40 D 13 Warwick av Harrow
5 V 16 Warwick clo Barnt
10 F 3 Warwick clo Bushey Watf
100 M 18 Warwick clo Hampt
141 R 2 Warwick ct WC1
138 B 1 Warwick cres W2
72 K 33 Warwick dene W5
86 J 9 Warwick gdns SW15
129 V 20 Warwick gdns Ilf

145 P 3 Warwick gdns W14
54 A 5 Warwick gdns Ilf
40 Z 5 Warwick gro E5
50 A 5 Warwick gro E5
116 L 16 Warwick gro Surb
140 F 13 Warwick Ho st SW1
141 Y 5 Warwick la EC4
129 Z 18 Warwick ms W9
72 G 4 Warwick pl W5
130 A 20 Warwick pl W9
147 Z 8 Warwick Place north SW1
20 A 16 Warwick rd E4
34 J 15 Warwick rd E11
53 R 16 Warwick rd E12
52 D 18 Warwick rd E15
32 K 6 Warwick rd E17
16 L 17 Warwick rd N11
18 F 15 Warwick rd N18
124 B 6 Warwick rd SE20
145 S 8 Warwick rd SW5
102 D 20 Warwick rd Tedd
72 G 4 Warwick rd W5
145 P 5 Warwick rd W14
5 N 15 Warwick rd Barnt
9 Z 1 Warwick rd Enf
117 U 5 Warwick rd New Mald
115 R 13 Warwick rd Sidcp
70 E 8 Warwick rd S'hall
154 C 10 Warwick rd Sutton
122 E 7 Warwick rd Thntn Hth
101 U 1 Warwick rd Twick
97 T 7 Warwick rd Welling
147 Z 2 Warwick row SW1
148 A 1 Warwick row SW1
75 Z 18 Warwickshire path SE8
141 Y 5 Warwick sq EC4
148 A 8 Warwick sq SW1
148 A 8 Warwick Sq ms SW1
140 C 9 Warwick st W1
79 T 16 Warwick ter SE18
147 X 9 Warwick way SW1
8 B 6 Warwick way SW1
53 S 11 Washington av E12
65 Y 2 Washington rd E6
34 C 7 Washington rd E18
74 G 19 Washington rd SW13
117 O 4 Washington rd Kingst
117 O 4 Washington rd Kingst
152 J 1 Washington rd Worc Pk
64 E 9 Washington st E3
110 G 1 Wastdale rd SE23
73 P 17 Watcombe cotts Rich
123 Z 11 Watcombe rd SE25
124 A 10 Watcombe rd SE25
27 N 16 Waterbrook la NW4
111 T 18 Waterbank rd SE6
55 T 18 Waterbeach rd Dgnhm
80 A 17 Waterdale rd SE2
51 P 18 Waterden rd E15
10 C 14 Waterfall clo N14
16 F 14 Waterfall rd N11
106 H 15 Waterfall rd SW19
106 J 14 Waterfall ter SW17
80 C 2 Waterfield clo SE18
88 A 1 Waterfield clo Stanm
11 O 19 Water gdns Stanm
141 W 8 Watergate EC4
76 A 15 Watergate st SE8
140 L 12 Watergate wlk EC4
20 L 13 Waterhall av E4
144 H 8 Waterhouse clo W6
52 A 18 Water la E15
54 J 10 Water la Ilf
62 G 2 Water la Kingst
84 G 13 Water la Rich
101 Z 1 Water la Twick
74 C 11 Waterloo pl SW1
39 O 18 Waterloo gdns Rom
63 P 6 Waterloo gdns E2
129 R 1 Waterloo pas NW6
140 F 13 Waterloo pl SW1
84 J 12 Waterloo pl Rich
65 Y 2 Waterloo rd E6
52 D 14 Waterloo rd E7
51 N 2 Waterloo rd E10
44 G 5 Waterloo rd NW2
141 U 18 Waterloo rd SE1
36 B 7 Waterloo rd Ilf
39 O 17 Waterloo rd Rom
154 F 10 Waterloo station SE1
141 R 16 Waterloo station SE1
32 J 12 Waterloo ter N1
47 U 4 Waterlow rd N19
102 H 18 Watermans clo Kingst
87 R 9 Waterman st SW15

120 M 15 Watermeade la Carsh
111 T 9 Watermead rd SE6
102 C 8 Watermill clo Rich
18 D 17 Water mill la N18
100 G 5 Water Mill way Felt
155 T 14 Water rd Wallgtn
61 N 4 Water rd Wemb
24 H 2 Watersfield way Edg
56 E 16 Waters gdns Dgnhm
124 M 1 Waterside Becknhm
99 S 12 Waterside Drtfrd
131 U 3 Waterside pl NW1
70 G 7 Waterside rd S'hall
134 L 12 Waterson st N1
111 Y 7 Waters rd SE6
112 B 6 Waters rd SE6
117 S 5 Waters rd Kingst
117 S 5 Waters sq Kingst
141 R 8 Water st WC2
157 R 9 Water Tower hill
30 M 5 Waterville rd N17
50 E 8 Waterworks la E5
90 B 15 Waterworks rd SW2
156 L 5 Water Works yd Croy
119 V 2 Watery la SW20
115 S 17 Watery la Sidcp
120 L 14 Wates way Mitch
10 M 1 Watford By pass Borhm Wd
11 P 3 Watford By pass Borhm Wd
88 K 1 Watford rd SW11
41 Y 4 Watford rd Harrow
42 B 13 Watford rd Harrow
13 O 14 Watford way NW7
26 E 4 Watford way NW7
43 S 11 Watkin rd Wemb
48 C 17 Watkinson rd N7
25 U 6 Watling av SE9
26 A 1 Watling av Edg
160 B 7 Watling ct EC4
11 R 5 Watling Fm clo Borhm Wd
142 B 7 Watling st EC4
160 B 7 Watling st EC4
98 J 11 Watling st Bxly Hth
99 X 15 Watling st Drtfrd
110 H 12 Watlington gro SE26
143 Y 6 Watney market E1
85 U 9 Watney pas SE1
85 V 6 Watney rd SW14
121 W 12 Watneys rd Mitch
63 N 18 Watney st E1
143 Y 8 Watney st E1
53 W 20 Watson av E6
153 S 2 Watson av Sutton
106 K 16 Watson clo SW19
30 D 6 Watsons rd N22
75 Z 20 Watson's st SE8
65 U 5 Watson st E13
49 P 14 Watson st N16
44 F 6 Watsons yd NW2
50 C 9 Watsfield rd E5
64 C 13 Watts gro E3
113 Z 20 Watts la Chisl
114 A 20 Watts la Chisl
101 Y 12 Watt's la Tedd
75 N 3 Watts st E1
143 X 13 Watts st E1
30 K 11 Watt way N17
93 W 3 Wat Tyler rd SE10
17 V 15 Wauthier clo N13
96 J 15 Wavell dri Sidcp
129 W 2 Wavel ms NW6
73 Y 14 Wavendon av W4
92 A 10 Waveney av SE15
19 X 15 Waverley av E4
33 W 10 Waverley av E17
117 U 14 Waverley av Surb
154 C 4 Waverley av Sutton
82 E 20 Waverley av Twick
100 G 1 Waverley av Wemb
34 K 6 Waverley clo E18
127 N 12 Waverley clo Brom
79 R 15 Waverley gdns NW10
61 N 7 Waverley gdns Bark
67 U 7 Waverley gdns Ilf
36 D 8 Waverley gro N3
27 S 10 Waverley gro N3
130 F 8 Waverley pl NW8
33 V 10 Waverley rd E17
34 K 6 Waverley rd E18
29 Z 20 Waverley rd N8
31 V 8 Waverley rd N17
31 Y 2 Waverley rd N17
79 R 14 Waverley rd SE18
123 Z 8 Waverley rd SE25
124 A 8 Waverley rd SE25
7 X 12 Waverley rd Enf
152 J 11 Waverley rd Epsom
40 C 4 Waverley rd Harrow

58 H 19 Waverley rd S'hall
54 K 14 Waverley way Carsh
88 C 19 Waverton rd SW18
139 W 12 Waverton st W1
34 F 7 Wavertree rd E18
108 B 2 Wavertree rd SW2
58 G 17 Waxlow cres S'hall
61 X 6 Waxlow rd NW10
22 A 8 Waxwell clo Pinn
22 A 9 Waxwell la Pinn
141 P 20 Waxwell ter SE1
58 A 9 Wayfarer rd Grnfd
88 K 6 Wayford st SW11
49 X 15 Wayland av E8
108 J 6 Waylett pl SE27
42 F 11 Waylett pl Wemb
136 F 6 Wayneflete sq W10
156 J 7 Waynflete av Croy
106 D 4 Wayneflete st SW18
45 T 4 Wayside NW11
85 W 12 Wayside SW14
10 C 1 Wayside av Bushey Watf
6 J 19 Wayside clo N14
39 S 10 Wayside clo Rom
84 D 15 Wayside ct Twick
56 D 14 Wayside gdns
113 T 10 Wayside gdns SE9
113 T 10 Wayside gdns SE9
23 S 5 Weald la Harrow
23 V 3 Weald rd Harrow
49 Y 6 Weald sq E5
153 V 3 Wealdstone rd Sutton
113 U 15 Weald the Chisl
38 G 19 Weald way Rom
20 K 10 Weale rd E4
8 C 6 Weardale gdns Enf
93 X 11 Weardale rd SE13
135 W 13 Wear pl E2
63 Z 14 Weatherley clo E3
147 S 4 W Eaton pl ms SW1
142 L 15 Weavers la SE1
135 S 18 Weaver st E1
108 K 10 Weaver wlk SE27
141 V 19 Webber row SE1
141 X 18 Webber st SE1
88 L 12 Webbs rd SW11
150 J 3 Webb st SE1
77 P 17 Webb rd SE3
88 M 14 Webbs rd SW11
72 G 3 Webster gdns W5
51 V 11 Webster rd E11
151 U 2 Webster rd SE16
46 G 15 Wedderburn rd NW3
67 T 4 Wedderburn rd Bark
108 L 16 Wedgewood way SE19
58 M 17 Wedlake st W10
35 W 4 Wedmore av Ilf
58 B 19 Wedmore gdns N19
47 X 8 Wedmore ms N19
59 R 10 Wedmore rd Grnfd
47 Y 9 Wedmore st N19
45 X 13 Weech rd NW6
47 O 15 Weedington rd NW5
76 L 8 Weetman st SE10
143 T 5 Wehill rd E1
94 F 12 Weigall rd SE12
138 V 7 Weighhouse st W1
123 Z 3 Weighton rd SE20
23 R 4 Weighton rd Harrow
124 A 3 Weighton rd SE20
154 G 11 Weihurst gdns Sutton
87 R 9 Weimar st SW15
15 Z 7 Weirdale av N11
15 Z 8 Weirdale av N20
18 B 19 Weir Hall av N18
139 N 15 Weir Hall gdns N15
18 A 18 Weir Hall gdns N18
31 P 1 Weir Hall rd N17
18 C 17 Weir Hall rd N18
89 V 19 Weir rd SW12
98 B 9 Weir rd Bxly
106 B 9 Weir rd SW19
14 Y 1 Weir's pas NW1
87 P 8 Weiss rd SW15
112 G 10 Welbeck av Brom
115 N 2 Welbeck av Sidcp
15 T 15 Welbeck clo N12
152 F 17 Welbeck clo Epsom
118 C 11 Welbeck clo New Mald
66 A 8 Welbeck rd E6
5 V 19 Welbeck rd Barnt
120 H 20 Welbeck rd Carsh
40 K 3 Welbeck rd Harrow
154 G 2 Welbeck rd Sutton
139 W 4 Welbeck way W1
311 V 1 Welbourne rd N17
90 K 3 Welby st SE5
16 F 17 Weld pl N11

105 T 10 Welford pl SW19
107 R 13 Welham rd SW17
154 H 1 Welhouse rd Carsh
24 C 18 Wellacre rd Harrow
97 P 13 Wellan clo Welling
59 V 7 Welland gdns Grnfd
4 A 16 Well appr Barnt
34 K 19 Well Cottage clo E11
40 B 10 Well clo Ruis
143 T 8 Wellclose sq E1
143 T 10 Wellclose st E1
160 C 6 Well ct EC4
23 T 17 Welldon cres Harrow
132 J 10 Wellers ct NW1
142 A 17 Wellers st SE1
74 H 8 Wellesley av W6
157 N 3 Wellesley Ct rd Croy
101 S 5 Wellesley cres Twick
157 O 3 Wellesley gro Croy
34 F 16 Wellesley rd E11
53 O 18 Wellesley rd E17
30 F 7 Wellesley rd N22
47 O 14 Wellesley rd NW5
73 P 14 Wellesley rd W4
122 M 20 Wellesley rd Croy
156 M 2 Wellesley rd Croy
157 N 3 Wellesley rd Croy
23 T 17 Wellesley rd Harrow
53 Y 6 Wellesley rd Ilf
54 B 4 Wellesley rd Ilf
54 D 13 Wellesley rd Sutton
101 S 6 Wellesley rd Twick
63 R 16 Wellesley rd N10
29 S 9 Wellfield av N10
108 B 10 Wellfield rd SW16
108 D 11 Wellfield wlk SW16
90 K 8 Wellfit rd SE24
42 A 18 Wellgarth gdns Grnfd
46 A 4 Wellgarth rd NW11
95 S 10 Well Hall rd SE9
4 B 14 Wellhouse la Barnt
125 N 9 Wellhouse rd Becknhm
97 R 8 Welling High st Welling
20 C 9 Wellington av E4
19 N 10 Wellington av N9
31 W 18 Wellington av N15
82 G 13 Wellington av Hounsl
22 E 4 Wellington av Pinn
97 N 15 Wellington av Sidcp
152 M 6 Wellington av Worc Pk
137 S 6 Wellington clo W11
69 X 1 Wellington clo Dgnhm
92 E 3 Wellington clo SE14
117 W 7 Wellington cres New Mald
69 Y 1 Wellington dri Dgnhm
77 X 14 Wellington gdns SE7
101 P 9 Wellington gdns Hampt
130 H 12 Wellington pl NW8
66 G 5 Wellington rd E6
52 D 14 Wellington rd E7
50 M 3 Wellington rd E10
34 G 14 Wellington rd E11
32 J 12 Wellington rd E17
130 G 10 Wellington rd NW8
128 G 14 Wellington rd NW10
105 Z 5 Wellington rd SW19
72 D 9 Wellington rd W5
81 P 12 Wellington rd Blvdr
97 V 14 Wellington rd Bxly
126 L 9 Wellington rd Brom
122 J 17 Wellington rd Croy
8 E 18 Wellington rd Enf
18 E 4 Wellington rd Enf
101 P 10 Wellington rd Hampt
23 T 9 Wellington rd Harrow
82 E 10 Wellington rd North Hounsl
22 D 4 Wellington rd Pinn
82 G 14 Wellington rd South Hounsl
135 R 12 Wellington row E2
147 N 10 Wellington sq SW3
64 L 14 Wellington st E16
78 K 11 Wellington st SE18
140 M 8 Wellington st WC2
141 N 8 Wellington st WC2
67 O 2 Wellington st Bark
137 W 11 Wellington ter W2
41 R 4 Wellington ter Harrow
64 A 11 Wellington way E3
96 D 7 Wellington way SE9
85 V 12 Well la SW14
111 Z 3 Wellmeadow rd SE6
93 Z 18 Wellmeadow rd SE13

71	Y 10	Wellmeadow rd W7
120	G 20	Wellow wlk Carsh
46	G 10	Well rd NW3
4	A 17	Well rd Barnt
43	X 5	Wells dri NW9
56	G 16	Wells gdns Dgnhm
53	R 1	Wells gdns Ilf
57	U 18	Wells gdns Rainhm
62	B 13	Wells House rd NW10
4	A 15	Wellside clo Brentf
85	V 12	Wellside gdns SW14
70	J 1	Wells la S'hall
140	B 3	Wells ms W1
127	W 5	Wellsmoor gdns Brom
110	A 8	Wells Park gro SE26
109	X 8	Wells Park rd SE26
43	U 9	Wellsprings cres Wemb
131	O 6	Wells ri NW8
74	M 7	Wells rd W12
136	C 19	Wells rd W12
127	U 3	Wells rd Brom
140	B 3	Wells st W1
19	R 4	Wellstead av N9
66	J 7	Wellstead rd E6
48	F 6	Wells ter N4
16	L 4	Wells the N14
50	D 20	Well st E9
63	P 1	Well st E9
135	Z 1	Well st E9
51	Y 17	Well st E15
76	G 17	Well st SE10
150	H 16	Wells way SE5
48	E 15	Wells yd N7
46	G 10	Well wlk NW3
55	N 2	Wellwood rd Ilf
88	D 13	Wellwood st SW18
151	S 8	Welsford st SE1
65	R 10	Welsh clo E13
135	U 4	Welshpool st E8
74	G 13	Weltje rd W6
79	U 20	Welton rd SE18
63	P 8	Welwyn st E2
42	L 10	Wembley Hill rd Wemb
43	N 13	Wembley Hill rd Wemb
42	M 12	Wembley Pk dri Wemb
43	O 10	Wembley Pk dri Wemb
100	G 19	Wembley rd Hampt
43	U 17	Wembley way Wemb
47	U 1	Wembury rd N6
94	C 5	Wemyss rd SE3
41	S 8	Wendella ct Harrow
74	C 7	Wendell rd W12
154	F 1	Wendling rd Sutton
63	Z 3	Wendon st E3
118	E 14	Wendover dri New Mald
62	D 6	Wendover rd NW10
95	O 7	Wendover rd SE9
126	H 7	Wendover rd Brom
97	O 11	Wendover way Welling
8	G 19	Wendy clo Enf
60	K 4	Wendy way Wemb
134	B 10	Wenlock rd N1
12	G 20	Wenlock rd Edg
134	D 10	Wenlock st N1
63	T 6	Wennington rd E3
34	D 1	Wensley av Wdfd Grn
35	S 5	Wensleydale av Ilf
100	K 18	Wensleydale gdns Hampt
100	J 20	Wensleydale pass Hampt
100	J 17	Wensleydale rd Hampt
18	M 19	Wensley rd N18
111	Y 4	Wentland clo SE6
111	Y 5	Wentland rd SE6
14	M 20	Wentworth av N3
27	Z 1	Wentworth av N3
119	W 17	Wentworth clo Mrdn
99	V 17	Wentworth dri Drtfrd
17	V 12	Wentworth gdns N13
42	M 3	Wentworth hill Wemb
43	N 3	Wentworth hill Wemb
63	X 11	Wentworth ms E3
27	Z 2	Wentworth pk N3
53	N 14	Wentworth rd E12
27	V 19	Wentworth rd NW11
4	D 11	Wentworth rd Brentf
122	F 18	Wentworth rd Croy
143	P 3	Wentworth st E1
22	A 13	Wentworth way Pinn

98	F 4	Wenvoe av Bxly Hth
24	E 3	Wernborough rd Stanm
79	P 15	Wernbrook st SE18
123	X 10	Werndee rd SE25
35	V 10	Werneth Hall rd Ilf
132	D 10	Werrington st NW1
87	R 11	Werter rd SW15
47	R 12	Wesleyean pl NW5
61	X 8	Wesley av NW10
82	D 4	Wesley av Hounsl
41	N 6	Wesley clo Harrow
48	D 8	Wesley clo N7
51	U 2	Wesley clo E10
61	X 3	Wesley rd NW10
139	V 1	Wesley st W1
57	Y 3	Wessex av SW19
36	H 18	Wessex clo Ilf
117	S 2	Wessex clo Kingst
99	S 3	Wessex dri Erith
22	B 3	Wessex gdns NW11
59	R 7	Wessex la Grnfd
63	P 10	Wessex st E2
45	S 2	Wessex way NW11
47	Y 3	Westacott clo N19
63	R 17	West Arbour st E1
33	R 15	West av E17
14	L 19	West av N3
27	O 15	West av NW4
22	D 19	West av Pinn
58	D 19	West av S'hall
56	B 12	West av Wallgtn
33	P 14	West Avenue rd E17
49	S 2	West bank N16
66	M 3	West bank Bark
7	Y 10	West bank Enf
100	M 15	Westbank rd Hampt
118	L 9	West Barnes la New Mald
30	G 9	West Beech rd N22
11	U 15	Westbere dri Stanm
45	T 14	Westbere rd NW2
61	X 18	Westbourne av W3
153	S 1	Westbourne av Sutton
138	E 8	Westbourne cres W2
110	E 3	Westbourne dri SE23
137	X 4	Westbourne gdns W2
137	W 6	Westbourne gro W2
137	T 3	Westbourne Gro ms W11
137	X 5	Westbourne Gro ter W2
137	X 5	Westbourne Pk ms W2
137	X 4	Westbourne Pk rd W2
137	R 4	Westbourne Pk rd W11
137	W 3	Westbourne Pk vlls W2
19	N 11	Westbourne pl N9
48	D 17	Westbourne rd N7
110	E 14	Westbourne rd SE26
80	K 19	Westbourne rd Bxly Hth
123	V 15	Westbourne rd Croy
138	G 9	Westbourne st W2
138	A 1	Westbourne ter W2
138	A 3	Westbourne ter W2
138	C 5	Westbourne Ter ms W2
88	H 2	Westbridge rd SW11
146	J 20	Westbridge rd SW11
100	E 17	Westbrook av Hampt
5	U 11	Westbrook av Barnt
5	T 12	Westbrook cres Barnt
97	T 6	Westbrooke cres Welling
114	F 5	Westbrooke rd Sidcp
97	T 7	Westbrooke rd Welling
94	H 2	Westbrook rd SE3
70	E 19	Westbrook rd Hounsl
123	O 2	Westbrook rd Thntn Hth
5	T 11	Westbrook sq Barnt
32	M 12	Westbury E17
30	H 10	Westbury av N22
30	L 6	Westbury av N22
58	G 12	Westbury av S'hall
42	K 20	Westbury av Wemb
14	L 18	Westbury gro N3
21	Y 7	Westbury la Buck Hl
72	U 15	Westbury pl Brentf
52	J 16	Westbury rd E7
33	N 13	Westbury rd N11
29	N 11	Westbury rd N12
14	M 17	Westbury rd N12
124	E 1	Westbury rd SE20

60	J 18	Westbury rd W5
67	S 3	Westbury rd Bark
124	J 6	Westbury rd Becknhm
127	O 1	Westbury rd Brom
21	V 6	Westbury rd Buck Hl
113	O 20	Westbury rd Chisl
123	O 15	Westbury rd Croy
100	A 2	Westbury rd Felt
53	V 7	Westbury rd Ilf
117	Z 11	Westbury rd New Mald
42	K 20	Westbury rd Wemb
52	J 17	Westbury ter E7
140	K 4	West Central st WC1
22	J 4	West chantry Harrow
27	O 10	Westchester dri NW4
18	H 11	West clo N9
6	B 14	West clo Barnt
59	N 6	West clo Grnfd
100	C 15	West clo Hampt
43	N 4	West clo Wemb
42	M 4	West clo Wemb
118	E 1	Westcombe av SW20
122	B 16	Westcombe av Croy
4	L 17	Westcombe dri Barnt
77	T 18	Westcombe hill SE3
77	T 14	Westcombe hill SE7
77	R 18	Westcombe Pk rd SE3
77	N 15	Westcombe Pk rd SE10
107	V 13	Westcote rd SW16
159	T 19	Westcott clo Croy
31	T 18	Westcott clo N17
59	U 16	Westcott cres W7
149	X 12	Westcott rd SE17
45	Y 15	West cotts NW6
14	L 20	West ct N3
42	D 8	West ct Wemb
45	S 12	Westcroft clo NW2
119	U 8	Westcroft gdns Mrdn
155	P 8	Westcroft sq W6
74	F 11	Westcroft sq W6
45	S 12	Westcroft way NW2
145	T 6	West Cromwell rd SW5
72	A 17	West cross wy Brentf
71	Z 18	West cross wy Brentf
112	K 2	Westdean av SE12
51	U 12	Westdown rd E15
93	N 18	Westdown rd SE6
107	U 9	West dri SW16
10	C 19	West dri Harrow
153	P 19	West dri Suttton
10	C 20	West Drive gdns Harrow
147	S 4	West Eaton pl SW1
62	A 1	West Ella rd NW10
33	W 16	West End av E10
22	A 13	West End av Pinn
45	Z 15	West End av NW6
45	Z 20	West End la NW6
129	V 4	West End la NW6
4	C 14	West End la Barnt
22	A 15	West End la S'hall
70	B 2	West End rd S'hall
48	J 12	Westerdale rd N5
77	S 14	Westerdale rd SE10
31	T 15	Westerfield rd N15
18	D 11	Westerham av N9
97	S 15	Westerham dri Sidcp
33	S 20	Westerham rd E10
73	O 17	Westerley ware Rich
110	L 11	Westerley cres SE26
62	B 19	Western av N3
27	R 19	Western av NW11
61	U 13	Western av W3
60	F 8	Western av W5
56	L 17	Western av Dgnhm
57	N 17	Western av Dgnhm
58	F 3	Western av Grnfd
59	S 7	Western av Grnfd
60	F 8	Western av Grnfd
137	V 2	Western Av extension W2
14	M 20	Western ct N3
61	O 19	Western gdns W5
89	O 18	Western la SW2
129	R 19	Western ms W9
65	X 5	Western rd E13
33	U 16	Western rd E17
27	L 12	Western rd N2
28	L 12	Western rd N2
30	C 9	Western rd N22
61	U 11	Western rd NW10
90	G 8	Western rd SW9
60	H 20	Western rd W5
72	H 1	Western rd W5
120	J 2	Western rd Mitch
39	S 15	Western rd Rom
58	H 11	Western rd S'hall

153	X 12	Western rd Sutton
36	B 20	Westernville gdns Ilf
14	M 1	Western way N20
79	T 9	Western way SE18
76	D 12	West Ferry rd E14
9	V 11	Westfield clo Enf
153	U 8	Westfield clo Sutton
24	H 14	Westfield dri Harrow
24	G 13	Westfield gdns Harrow
24	G 13	Westfield la Harrow
22	E 1	Westfield pk Pinn
30	B 14	Westfield rd N8
12	M 11	Westfield rd NW7
71	Z 3	Westfield rd W13
72	A 4	Westfield rd W13
124	L 3	Westfield rd Becknhm
98	L 7	Westfield rd Bxly Hth
156	J 3	Westfield rd Croy
56	A 13	Westfield rd Dgnhm
120	K 4	Westfield rd Mitch
116	F 13	Westfield rd Surb
153	U 8	Westfield rd Sutton
86	D 7	Westfields SW3
86	C 7	Westfields av SW13
61	U 15	Westfields rd W3
78	B 9	Westfield st SE18
68	N 20	West gdns E1
143	Z 10	West gdns E1
106	J 15	West gdns SW17
80	L 15	Westgate rd SE2
123	Z 9	Westgate rd SE25
124	A 9	Westgate rd SE25
111	T 19	Westgate rd Becknhm
125	S 2	Westgate rd Becknhm
135	X 3	Westgate st E8
145	Y 12	Westgate ter SW10
24	F 16	Westglade ct Harrow
30	K 13	West Green rd N15
31	P 14	West Green rd N15
21	Z 17	West gro Wdfd Grn
93	V 2	Westgrove la SE10
147	S 1	West Halkin st SW1
113	P 1	West hallowes SE9
149	Z 19	Westhall rd SE5
85	S 3	West Hall rd Rich
64	M 2	West Hamm la E15
65	R 1	West Hamm park E15
45	Z 19	West Hampstead ms NW6
141	T 5	West Harding st EC4
85	U 12	Westhay gdns SW14
45	Y 5	West Heath av NW11
45	Y 9	West Heath clo NW3
99	U 16	West Heath clo Drtfrd
45	Y 4	West Heath dri NW11
45	Y 8	West Heath gdns NW3
45	Y 7	West Heath rd NW3
46	B 9	West Heath rd NW3
80	H 17	West Heath rd SE2
99	U 16	West Heath rd Drtfrd
44	H 3	West Hendon bdwy NW9/NW2
87	P 18	West hill SW15
41	P 5	West hill Harrow
47	S 6	West hill N6
157	S 19	West hill S Croy
42	M 4	West hill Wemb
43	O 4	West hill Wemb
87	W 16	West Hill rd SW18
15	N 6	West Hill rd SW18
28	A 14	Westholm NW11
98	L 1	West holme Erith
95	P 12	Westhorne av SE9
94	G 17	Westhorne av SE12
27	O 10	Westhorpe gdns NW4
87	N 8	Westhorpe rd SW15
105	X 1	Westhouse clo SW19
114	A 12	Westhurst dri Chisl
64	A 20	West India Dock rd E14
17	T 11	Westlake clo N13
134	D 12	Westland pl N1
89	U 17	Westlands ter SW12
143	W 19	West la SE16
71	X 8	Westlea rd W7
85	O 15	Westleigh av SW15
86	L 14	Westleigh av SW15
127	R 2	Westleigh dri Brom
25	P 6	Westleigh gdns Edg
73	P 3	West lodge av W3
137	V 12	West mall W8
86	J 17	Westmead SW15
38	B 14	West mead Epsom

Ref	Street
154 H 9	Westmead rd Sutton
12 K 10	Westmere dri NW7
147 Z 8	West ms SW1
140 J 20	Westminster abbey SW1
122 H 2	Westminster av Thntn Hth
140 L 18	Westminster br SW1
141 P 18	Westminster Br rd SE1
148 B 3	Westminster cathedral SW1
36 E 18	Westminster clo Ilf
101 X 12	Westminster clo Tedd
17 N 17	Westminster dri N13
67 U 7	Westminster gdns Bark
36 D 8	Westminster gdns Ilf
19 N 6	Westminster rd N9
71 U 4	Westminster rd W7
154 E 1	Westminster rd Sutton
111 U 18	West Moat clo Becknhm
9 T 8	Westmoor rd Enf
9 S 9	Westmoor rd Enf
78 A 10	Westmoor st SE7
96 H 9	Westmoreland av Welling
53 N 4	Westmoreland clo E12
84 B 15	Westmoreland clo Twick
154 B 18	Westmoreland dri Sutton
147 Y 11	Westmoreland pl SW1
60 F 14	Westmoreland pl W5
33 O 19	Westmoreland rd E17
25 N 11	Westmoreland rd NW9
86 F 2	Westmoreland rd SW13
126 B 10	Westmoreland rd Brom
139 V 1	Westmoreland st W1
147 Y 10	Westmoreland ter SW1
22 L 16	Westmorland rd Harrow
121 Z 10	Westmorland way Mitch
95 W 10	Westmount rd SE9
111 W 20	West oak Becknhm
19 N 10	Westoe rd N9
55 N 15	Weston dri Bark
24 C 5	Weston dri Stanm
83 R 3	Weston gdns Islwth
56 A 11	Weston grn Dgnhm
112 D 19	Weston gro Brom
30 C 17	Weston pk N8
133 O 11	Weston rise WC1
73 U 9	Weston rd W4
112 D 19	Weston rd Brom
55 Z 11	Weston rd Dgnhm
8 C 8	Weston rd Enf
142 H 17	Weston st SE1
135 Z 1	Weston wlk E9
88 E 17	Westover rd SW18
45 Y 7	Westover hill NW2
109 T 15	Westow hill SE19
109 T 17	Westow st SE19
113 R 2	West park SE9
85 R 2	West Park av Rich
37 X 16	West Park clo Rom
85 P 3	West Park rd Rich
104 L 12	West pl SW19
6 F 15	Westpole av Barnt
63 T 17	Westport rd E1
63 T 15	Westport rd E13
65 V 13	Westport rd E13
141 W 2	West Poultry av EC1
141 X 1	West Poultry av EC1
58 M 6	West Ridge gdns Grnfd
65 R 3	West rd E15
18 M 20	West rd N17
31 Z 1	West rd N17
89 Z 12	West rd SW4
60 J 14	West rd W5
16 B 5	West rd Barnt
103 W 20	West rd Kingst
37 X 17	West rd Rom
56 M 3	West rd Rom
128 J 17	West row W10
54 L 11	Westrow dri Bark
54 M 14	Westrow dri Bark
54 L 9	Westrow gdns Ilf
85 U 5	West Sheen vale Rich
26 H 6	Westside NW4
104 M 13	West Side comm SW19
105 N 15	West Side comm SW19
141 X 2	West Smithfield EC1
149 W 3	West sq SE11
63 N 7	West sq E2
51 Z 8	West st E11
33 R 16	West st E17
140 H 7	West st WC2
98 A 9	West st Bxly Hth
126 E 2	West st Brom
154 L 9	West st Carsh
156 M 7	West st Harrow
14 A 11	West st Sutton
154 M 8	West St la Carsh
122 T 12	West Temple sheen SW14
143 O 7	West Tenter st E1
26 M 15	West view NW4
44 C 14	Westview clo NW10
18 D 3	West View cres N9
35 N 6	Westview dri Wdfd Grn
74 G 6	Westville rd W12
60 J 15	West wlk W5
16 B 4	West wlk Barnt
19 Y 18	Westward rd E4
20 A 18	Westward rd E4
24 K 19	Westward way Harrow
147 Z 8	West Warwick pl SW1
18 C 15	West way N18
43 Z 10	West way NW10
118 K 7	Westway SW20
62 G 19	West way W12
136 B 7	Westway W12
12 G 19	West way Edg
82 D 1	West way Hounsl
125 Y 15	West way W Wkhm
118 K 6	Westway clo SW20
158 G 2	West Way gdns Croy
152 E 8	Westways Epsom
107 Z 15	Westwell rd SW16
136 E 19	Westwick gdns SW14
109 N 19	Westwood av SE19
40 L 12	Westwood av Harrow
86 D 8	Westwood gdns SW13
110 B 10	Westwood hill SE26
96 L 10	Westwood la Welling
92 N 13	Westwood la Welling
123 N 12	Westwood pk SE23
110 B 1	Westwood rd E16
77 V 3	Westwood rd E16
86 D 8	Westwood rd SW13
54 L 4	Westwood rd Ilf
24 D 6	Wetheral dri Stanm
40 J 17	Wetherby clo Grnfd
146 A 8	Wetherby gdns SW5
145 Y 9	Wetherby ms SW5
146 B 7	Wetherby pl SW7
7 Z 4	Wetherby rd Enf
50 L 1	Wetherden st E17
63 T 3	Wetherell rd E9
29 P 4	Wetherill rd N10
88 L 19	Wexford st SW12
106 C 6	Weybourne st SW18
122 G 10	Weybridge rd Thntn Hth
105 S 2	Weydown clo SW19
56 B 10	Weyland rd Dgnhm
94 M 2	Weyman rd SE3
13 O 15	Weymouth av NW7
72 E 8	Weymouth av W5
153 Z 16	Weymouth ct Sutton
139 X 1	Weymouth ms W1
135 O 8	Weymouth pl E2
131 X 20	Weymouth st W1
139 W 1	Weymouth st W1
135 O 9	Weymouth ter E2
10 L 20	Weymouth wlk Stanm
48 F 7	Whadcoat st N4
156 D 1	Whaddon Marsh way Croy
38 A 18	Whalebone av Rom
160 F 4	Whalebone ct EC2
38 A 18	Whalebone gro Rom
64 M 1	Whalebone la E15
37 Y 3	Whalebone la N Rom
38 A 7	Whalebone la N Rom
56 B 3	Whalebone la S Dgnhm
38 A 17	Whalebone la S Rom
132 L 8	Wharfdale rd N1
122 D 7	Wharfedale gdns Thntn Hth
145 X 11	Wharfedale st SW10
101 Y 2	Wharf la Twick
135 U 7	Wharf pl E2
64 J 3	Wharf rd E15
134 A 9	Wharf rd N1
134 B 11	Wharf rd N1
19 V 1	Wharf rd N9
9 W 18	Wharf rd Enf
L 15	Wharf st E16
71 P 2	Wharncliffe dri S'hall
123 R 4	Wharncliffe gdns SE25
123 R 4	Wharncliffe rd SE25
44 B 17	Wharton clo NW10
133 R 13	Wharton cottages WC1
126 H 1	Wharton rd Brom
P 13	Wharton st WC1
110 F 17	Whateley rd SE22
91 U 13	Whateley rd SE22
119 R 5	Whatley av SW20
92 G 19	Whatman rd SE23
9 U 7	Wheatfields Enf
9 U 8	Wheatfields Enf
123 Z 5	Wheathill rd SE20
124 A 6	Wheathill rd SE20
70 H 17	Wheatlands Hounsl
107 O 7	Wheatlands rd SW17
18 C 9	Wheatley gdns N9
83 V 7	Wheatley rd Islwth
139 V 1	Wheatley st W1
E 18	Wheatsheaf la SW6
148 K 17	Wheatsheaf la SW8
39 T 18	Wheatsheaf rd Rom
145 R 20	Wheatsheaf ter SW6
128 L 20	Wheatstone rd W10
132 K 4	Wheeler gdns N1
54 S 7	Wheelers cross Bark
56 K 9	Wheel Farm dri Dgnhm
48 C 20	Wheelwright st N7
135 N 18	Wheler st E1
74 A 7	Whellock rd W4
80 H 1	Whernside clo SE2
15 S 8	Whetstone clo N20
141 O 3	Whetstone pk WC2
94 L 4	Whetstone rd SE3
48 A 7	Whewell rd N4
132 K 13	Whidborne st WC1
68 G 19	Whimbrel clo SE2
107 X 11	Whinfell clo SW16
95 R 8	Whinyates rd SE9
33 W 15	Whipps cross E17
33 X 16	Whipps Cross rd E11
34 B 18	Whipps Cross rd E11
133 U 14	Whiskin st EC1
25 N 7	Whistler gdns Edg
34 H 14	Whistler st N5
135 S 6	Whiston rd E2
134 M 7	Whiston rd N1
92 K 11	Whitbread rd SE4
93 S 11	Whitburn rd SE13
61 S 8	Whitby av NW10
25 R 10	Whitby gdns NW9
156 F 1	Whitby gdns Sutton
40 M 10	Whitby rd Harrow
41 N 10	Whitby rd Narrow
15 N 16	Whitby st E1
75 V 17	Whitcher clo SE14
47 V 19	Whitcher pl NW1
24 M 2	Whitchurch av Edg
11 Z 19	Whitchurch clo Edg
11 Z 20	Whitchurch gdns Edg
12 B 20	Whitchurh la Edg
24 K 2	Whitchurh la Edg
136 G 9	Whitchurch rd
47 O 7	Whitchurch st WC2
26 C 7	White acre NW9
51 X 17	Whitall way E15
103 P 5	White Ash lodge Rich
69 S 3	Whitebarn la Dgnhm
77 W 15	Whitebeam av Brom
T 19	White Bear st EC1
143 R 3	Whitechapel High st E1
35 X 20	Whitechapel rd E1
143 U 2	Whitechapel rd E1
143 S 4	White Ch la E1
136 B 10	White City clo W12
62 L 20	White City clo W12
62 L 19	White City la W12
A 9	White City rd W12
136 B 9	White City Stadium W10
133 T 7	White Conduit st N1
L 18	Whitecote rd S'hall
125 W 8	Whitecroft clo Becknhm
125 V 9	Whitecroft way Becknhm
134 H 20	Whitecross pl EC2
134 C 11	Whitecross st EC2
45 N 2	Whitefield av NW2
87 T 17	Whitefield clo SW18
112 A 7	Whitefoot la Brom
112 B 7	Whitefoot ter Brom
23 S 8	Whitefriars av Harrow
23 S 7	Whitefriars dri Harrow
141 U 6	Whitefriars st EC4
56 D 17	White gdns Dgnhm
23 V 2	White Ga gdns Harrow
140 J 15	Whitehall SW1
140 K 14	Whitehall ct SW1
20 L 6	Whitehall gdns E4
140 K 15	Whitehall gdns SW1
73 R 3	Whitehall gdns W3
73 T 16	Whitehall gdns W4
21 U 8	Whitehall la Buck Hl
99 Y 3	Whitehall la Erith
47 V 3	Whitehall la N19
73 T 16	Whitehall Pk rd W4
140 K 13	Whitehall pl SW1
155 R 9	Whitehall pl Wallgtn
71 Y 7	Whitehall rd W7
127 O 10	Whitehall rd W7
23 S 20	Whitehall rd Harrow
122 F 13	Whitehall rd Thntn Hth
21 O 7	Whitehall rd Wdfd Grn
31 U 2	Whitehall st N17
142 J 3	White Hart ct EC2
31 S 1	White Hart la N17
30 J 2	White Hart la N22
86 B 6	White Hart la SW14
38 E 4	White Hart la Rom
79 V 11	White Hart rd SE18
128 F 3	Whiteheart slip Brom
149 V 9	White Hart st SE11
142 F 15	White Hart st SE1
130 J 19	Whitehaven st NW8
87 T 17	Whitefield clo SW18
88 B 19	Whitehead clo SW18
146 M 8	Whitehead's gro SW3
99 W 14	Whitehill rd Drtfrd
113 V 10	White Horse hill Chisl
63 T 13	White Horse la E1
123 P 8	Whitehorse la SE25
63 U 17	White Horse rd E1
66 G 8	White Horse rd E6
122 M 17	Whitehorse rd Croy
123 N 13	Whitehorse rd Croy
139 Y 14	White Horse st W1
160 D 3	White Horse yrd EC2
11 S 14	White Ho dri Stanm
7 Z 5	White Ho la Enf
16 L 9	Whitehouse ct N14
16 E 10	Whitehouse way N14
142 M 4	White Kennett st E1
60 D 17	Whiteledges W13
65 P 7	Whiteleg rd E13
65 P 7	Whitelegg rd E13
109 P 12	Whiteley rd SE19
145 P 7	Whiteleys cotts
100 H 7	Whiteley's way Felt
160 H 6	White Lion ct EC2
133 S 9	White Lion st N1
139 Y 8	White Lion yd W1
108 K 17	White lodge SE19
103 V 1	White lodge Rich
28 H 19	White Lodge clo N2
154 E 15	White Lodge clo Sutton
16 E 17	Whitemore clo N11
125 V 3	Whiteoak dri Becknhm
59 R 8	Whiteoaks la Grnfd
14 G 3	White orchards N20
8 K 17	White orchards Stanm
50 M 19	White Post la E9
51 N 19	White Post la E9
93 O 8	Whitepost la SE13
75 P 19	White Post st SE15
52 A 20	White rd E15
36 G 17	Whites av Ilf
142 L 17	Whites grounds SE1
143 N 2	White's row E1
89 Y 10	Whites sq SW4
89 Y 10	White's sq SW4
72 E 13	Whitestile rd Brentf
46 E 9	Whitestone la NW3
158 A 1	Whitethorn gdns Croy
8 A 16	Whitethorn gdns Enf
64 B 13	Whitethorn st E3
132 B 18	Whitfield pl W1
65 Z 2	Whitfield rd E6
93 X 3	Whitfield rd SE3
81 N 18	Whitfield rd Bxly Hth
132 B 18	Whitfield st W1
140 D 1	Whitfield st W1
120 L 6	Whitford gdns Mitch
156 L 11	Whitgift av S Croy

W

156	M 2	Whitgift sq Croy
149	N 6	Whitgift st SE11
156	L 5	Whitgift st Croy
67	N 1	Whiting av Bark
4	A 18	Whitings rd Barnt
154	G 1	Whitland rd Carsh
31	T 7	Whitley rd N17
87	T 20	Whitlock dri SW19
63	V 10	Whitman rd E3
62	M 6	Whitmore gdns NW10
128	C 8	Whitmore gdns NW10
124	L 6	Whitmore rd Becknhm
40	M 3	Whitmore rd Harrow
41	O 2	Whitmore rd Harrow
87	O 14	Whitnell way SW15
35	N 12	Whitney av Ilf
51	P 1	Whitney rd E10
115	Y 16	Whitney wlk Sidcp
115	Z 16	Whitney wlk Sidcp
65	Z 2	Whittaker rd E6
153	V 5	Whittaker rd Sutton
147	S 7	Whittaker st SW1
110	C 8	Whittall gdns SE26
53	O 12	Whitta rd E12
40	L 15	Whitten av Grnfd
87	V 2	Whittingstall rd SW6
142	J 7	Whittington av EC3
17	O 20	Whittington rd N22
30	A 1	Whittington rd N22
22	C 16	Whittington way Pinn
155	N 17	Whittlebury clo Carsh
58	K 17	Whittle clo S'hall
22	M 3	Whittlesea clo Harrow
22	M 4	Whittlesea path Harrow
22	M 3	Whittlesea rd Harrow
23	N 3	Whittlesea rd Harrow
23	N 4	Whittlesea rd Harrow
141	T 15	Whittlesey st SE1
41	W 16	Whitton av East Grnfd
41	P 16	Whitton av West Grnfd
42	B 19	Whitton clo Grnfd
82	M 14	Whitton dene Hounsl
83	T 13	Whitton dene Islwth
41	Z 17	Whitton dri Grnfd
83	O 14	Whitton Manor rd Islwth
82	L 12	Whitton rd Hounsl
83	T 16	Whitton rd Twick
82	H 16	Whitton waye Hounsl
65	S 10	Whitwell rd E13
78	K 18	Whitworth rd SE18
123	U 8	Whitworth rd SE25
77	N 13	Whitworth st SE10
91	Y 8	Whorlton rd SE15
30	G 10	Whymark av N22
52	H 18	Whyteville rd E7
89	P 7	Wickersley rd SW11
143	V 7	Wicker st E1
159	O 11	Wicket the Croy
63	O 11	Wickford st E1
135	Z 17	Wickford st E1
32	E 12	Wickford way E17
158	H 1	Wickham av Croy
152	M 10	Wickham av Sutton
153	O 11	Wickham av Sutton
125	X 18	Wickham chase W Wkhm
126	A 16	Wickham chase W Wkhm
9	O 11	Wickham clo Enf
118	C 13	Wickham clo New Mald
159	Y 9	Wickham ct W Wkhm
159	V 2	Wickham Ct rd W Wkhm
159	V 2	Wickham cres W Wkhm
92	L 8	Wickham gdns SE4
79	Z 15	Wickham la SE2
80	B 18	Wickham la SE2
33	U 1	Wickham rd E4
92	M 6	Wickham rd SE4
93	N 4	Wickham rd SE4
125	S 5	Wickham rd Becknhm
158	F 3	Wickham rd Croy
159	N 1	Wickham rd Croy
23	R 8	Wickham rd Harrow
149	O 9	Wickham st SE11
96	M 3	Wickham st Welling
97	P 1	Wickham st Welling
125	T 9	Wickham way Becknhm
64	A 3	Wick la E3
27	T 9	Wickliffe av N3
43	R 6	Wickliffe gdns Wemb
132	M 12	Wicklow st WC1
133	N 12	Wicklow st WC1
50	E 18	Wick rd E9
89	P 5	Wick rd SW11
102	C 19	Wick rd Tedd
113	N 8	Wicks clo SE9
90	K 5	Wickwood st SE5
48	C 13	Widdenham rd N9
40	B 7	Widdicombe av Harrow
48	C 13	Widdenham rd N9
64	L 1	Widdin st E15
35	R 12	Widecombe gdns Ilf
113	S 7	Widecombe rd SE9
28	F 15	Widecombe way N2
142	L 2	Widegate st E1
121	X 6	Wide way Mitch
129	V 15	Widley rd W9
127	O 4	Widmore Lodge rd Brom
126	K 2	Widmore rd Brom
127	O 3	Widmore rd Brom
43	R 19	Wigginton av Wemb
26	D 3	Wiggins mead NW9
102	C 4	Wiggins Pointers cotts Rich
30	G 17	Wightman rd N4
100	A 2	Wigley rd Felt
139	X 4	Wigmore pl W1
154	H 1	Wigmore rd Carsh
139	X 4	Wigmore st W1
154	G 2	Wigmore wlk Carsh
34	K 18	Wigram rd E11
33	V 9	Wigram sq E17
65	W 11	Wirston rd E13
24	J 5	Wigton gdns Stanm
149	T 11	Wigton pl SE11
32	L 5	Wigton rd E17
48	H 6	Wilberforce rd N4
26	F 19	Wilberforce rd NW9
65	W 11	Wilberforce way SW19
147	R 5	Wilbraham pl SW1
18	B 17	Wilbury way N18
137	P 12	Wilby ms W11
148	J 18	Wilcox rd SW1
153	Z 9	Wilcox rd Sutton
101	R 9	Wilcox rd Tedd
140	M 5	Wild ct WC2
11	U 20	Wildcroft gdns Edg
86	M 20	Wildcroft rd SW15
87	N 17	Wildcroft rd SW15
87	O 17	Wildcroft rd SW15
113	Z 18	Wilderness rd Chisl
100	K 10	Wilderness the Hampt
49	T 2	Wilderton rd N16
91	P 8	Wildfell rd SE6
92	D 3	Wild Goose dri SE14
27	Z 20	Wild hatch NW11
142	H 20	Wilds rents SE1
150	H 1	Wild's rents SE1
140	M 6	Wild st WC2
94	D 18	Wildwood clo SE12
46	E 5	Wildwood gro NW3
46	C 19	Wildwood rd NW11
46	C 2	Wildwood rd NW11
8	A 12	Wilford cl Enf
148	B 1	Wilfred st SW1
61	V 13	Wilfrid gdns W3
109	U 11	Wilkers oak SE19
135	P 18	Wilkes st E1
143	O 1	Wilkes st E1
65	Y 16	Wilkinson rd E16
149	N 20	Wilkinson st SW8
73	X 6	Wilkinson way W3
47	R 17	Wilkin st NW5
17	V 18	Wilk pl N13
134	K 9	Wilks pl N1
31	P 8	Wilks rd N17
65	O 19	Willan wall E16
89	S 7	Willard st SW8
73	R 3	Willcott rd W3
94	M 10	Will Crooks gdns SE9
95	N 10	Will Crooks gdns SE9
5	P 20	Willenhall av Barnt
78	L 15	Willenhall rd SE18
96	L 19	Willersley av Sidcp
114	K 2	Willersley av Sidcp
114	K 1	Willersley clo Sidcp
45	O 19	Willesden la NW6
128	M 1	Willesden la NW6 & NW2
129	R 2	Willesden la NW6 & NW2
47	S 17	Willes rd NW5
122	F 11	Willett pl Thntn Hth
122	F 11	Willett rd Thntn Hth
113	X 5	William Barefoot dri SE9
109	Y 20	William Booth rd SE20
38	L 6	William clo Rom
140	J 11	William IV st WC2
139	R 18	William ms SW1
65	Z 3	William Morley clo E6
32	K 10	William Morris clo E17
131	Z 14	William rd NW1
132	A 15	William rd NW1
105	T 18	William rd SW19
154	E 10	William rd Sutton
32	K 5	Williams av E17
30	F 5	Williams gro N22
85	V 6	Williams la SW14
120	D 12	Williams la Mrdn
14	F 18	Williamson NW7
48	A 13	Williamson st N7
70	B 12	Williams rd S'hall
156	F 13	Williams ter Croy
33	T 19	William st E10
15	R 15	William st N12
31	U 1	William st N17
139	R 18	William st SW1
54	A 20	William st Bark
154	L 5	William st Carsh
27	Y 17	Willifield way NW11
21	Z 20	Willingale clo Wdfd Grn
30	J 8	Willingdon rd N22
47	W 15	Willingham clo NW5
47	V 15	Willingham Ter NW5
90	A 8	Willington rd SW9
117	P 4	Willingsham way Kingst
154	H 14	Willis av Sutton
65	P 5	Willis rd E15
122	M 16	Willis rd Croy
81	V 10	Willis rd Erith
64	E 17	Willis st E14
28	G 11	Willmott clo N2
156	C 8	Willoughby av Croy
19	N 20	Willoughby la N9
32	A 2	Willoughby la N17
31	Z 1	Willoughby Pk rd N17
30	G 12	Willoughby rd N8
46	F 12	Willoughby rd NW3
103	N 20	Willoughby rd Kingst
84	F 14	Willoughby rd Twick
140	H 2	Willoughby st WC1
86	E 6	Willow av SW13
97	N 15	Willow av Sidcp
87	T 7	Willow bank SW6
102	B 6	Willow bank Rich
48	L 19	Willow Bridge rd N1
151	P 17	Willowbrook rd SE15
70	G 9	Willowbrook rd S'hall
98	B 17	Willow clo Bxly Hth
72	E 17	Willow clo Brentf
127	U 13	Willow clo Brom
57	Y 10	Willow clo Hornch
122	H 14	Willow clo Thntn Hth
49	U 6	Willow cotts N16
73	O 17	Willow cotts Rich
24	B 16	Willowcourt av Harrow
10	D 4	Willowdene Bushey Watf
82	M 18	Willowdene clo Twick
4	F 15	Willow dri Barnt
14	K 8	Willow end N20
116	J 19	Willow end Surb
82	G 3	Willow gdns Hounsl
65	S 5	Willow gro E13
113	Z 15	Willow gro Chisl
152	M 7	Willow Hayne gdns Worc Pk
120	M 12	Willow la Mitch
60	F 13	Willowmead clo W5
157	T 7	Willow mt Croy
148	C 5	Willow pl SW1
46	G 11	Willow rd NW3
72	K 6	Willow rd W5
8	E 9	Willow rd Enf
99	X 3	Willow rd Erith
117	V 8	Willow rd New Mald
37	Y 18	Willow rd Rom
155	T 16	Willow rd Wallgtn
120	A 12	Willows av Mrdn
134	H 15	Willow st E3
20	K 4	Willow st E4
38	L 14	Willow st Rom
58	A 12	Willowtree la Grnfd
120	F 1	Willow vw SW19
106	B 1	Willowtree clo SW18
74	G 3	Willow vale W12
113	Y 15	Willow vale Chisl
120	F 1	Willow view SW19
32	L 15	Willow wlk E17
28	G 8	Willow wlk N2
30	J 12	Willow wlk N15
7	P 20	Willow wlk N21
150	L 5	Willow wlk SE1
151	N 6	Willow wlk SE1
153	V 4	Willow wlk Sutton
28	A 3	Willow way N3
80	B 7	Willow way SE26
100	K 5	Willow way Twick
41	Z 10	Willow way Wemb
123	R 14	Willow Wood cres SE25
80	E 12	Willrose cres SE2
82	J 17	Wills cres Hounsl
13	V 16	Wills gro NW7
49	Y 20	Wilman gro E8
125	R 20	Wilmar gdns W Wkhm
103	O 13	Wilmer cres Kingst
134	K 6	Wilmer gdns N1
64	H 1	Wilmer Lea clo E15
16	L 15	Wilmer way N14
73	X 20	Wilmington av W4
54	E 19	Wilmington gdns Bark
54	G 20	Wilmington gdns Bark
133	S 15	Wilmington sq WC1
133	S 14	Wilmington st WC1
120	A 1	Wilmore end Mitch
28	F 7	Wilmot clo N2
47	V 19	Wilmot pl NW1
71	U 4	Wilmot pl W7
51	R 7	Wilmot rd E10
31	O 10	Wilmot rd N17
154	L 11	Wilmot rd Carsh
99	Y 14	Wilmot rd Drtfrd
135	X 14	Wilmot st E2
78	M 11	Wilmount st SE18
88	B 20	Wilna rd SW18
88	C 19	Wilna rd SW18
136	J 12	Wilsham st W11
93	N 1	Wilshaw st SE14
40	C 16	Wilsmere dri Grnfd
23	U 1	Wilsmere dri Harrow
106	K 20	Wilson av Mitch
57	N 18	Wilson clo
22	M20	Wilson gdns Harrow
143	V 19	Wilson gro SE16
65	Z 8	Wilson rd E6
51	W 4	Wilson rd E6
65	R 5	Wilson rd SE5
91	P 3	Wilson rd SE5
22	M 20	Wilson rd Harrow
52	U 1	Wilson rd Ilf
35	T 15	Wilsons av N17
65	R 5	Wilson st E13
33	T 15	Wilson st E17
134	G 19	Wilson st EC2
142	G 1	Wilson st EC2
160	G 1	Wilson st EC2
17	U 3	Wilson st N21
56	H 20	Wilthorne gdns Dgnhm
74	B 14	Wilton av W4
133	S 19	Wilton cres SW1
105	V 20	Wilton cres SW19
38	L 2	Wilton dri Rom
105	V 20	Wilton gro SW19
118	D 13	Wilton gro New Mald
147	V 1	Wilton ms SW1
139	S 18	Wilton pl SW1
29	P 6	Wilton rd N10
147	Z 4	Wilton rd SW1
148	A 6	Wilton rd SW1
106	J 6	Wilton rd SW19
5	Y 13	Wilton rd Barnt
53	Y 11	Wilton rd Ilf
80	G 10	Wilton rd SE2
139	T 19	Wilton row SW1
134	E 4	Wilton sq N1
147	W 1	Wilton st SW1
137	T 20	Wilton ter SW1
134	D 4	Wilton vils N1
49	Y 18	Wilton way E8
50	A 18	Wilton way E8
101	O 1	Wiltshire gdns Twick
90	G 7	Wiltshire rd SW9
90	G 4	Wiltshire rd SW9
122	G 7	Wiltshire rd Thntn Hth
118	B 15	Wilverley cres New Mald
90	C 18	Wimbart rd SW2
104	E 13	Wimbledon common SW19
105	U 14	Wimbledon Hill rd SW19
87	X 17	Wimbledon Pk rd SW18
105	U 3	Wimbledon Pk rd SW19
105	O 3	Wimbledon Pk side SW19

		...SW17
		...S'hall
		...lo Buck
		...e clo SE12
		...mborne dri Pinn
		...mborne gdns W13
B 15		Wimborne gdns W13
18 H 8		Wimborne rd N9
31 S 7		Wimborne rd N17
124 G 8		Wimborne way Becknham
134 E 8		Wimbourne st N1
117 O 4		Wimpole clo Kingst
139 W 1		Wimpole ms W1
139 W 4		Wimpole st W1
90 E 6		Winans wlk SW9
40 J 15		Wincanton cres Grnfd
35 Z 9		Wincanton gdns Ilf
87 V 18		Wincanton rd SW18
79 S 7		Winchat rd SE18
120 G 18		Winchcombe rd Carsh
154 J 1		Winchcombe rd Carsh
95 P 8		Winchcombe gdns SE9
81 O 20		Winchelsea av Bxly Hth
87 O 14		Winchelsea clo SW15
52 D 11		Winchelsea rd E7
31 U 10		Winchelsea rd N17
61 Z 3		Winchelsea rd NW10
157 U 14		Winchelsey ri Croy
87 V 1		Winchendon rd SW6
101 R 10		Winchendon rd Tedd
128 M 2		Winchester av NW6
25 P 12		Winchester av NW9
70 F 16		Winchester av Hounsl
126 B 7		Winchester clo Brom
8 D 19		Winchester clo Enf
103 T 17		Winchester clo Kingst
45 G 20		Winchester ms NW3
126 B 7		Winchester pk Brom
49 U 16		Winchester pl E8
47 T 3		Winchester pl N6
26 H 20		Winchester rd E4
33 V 2		Winchester rd E4
47 T 2		Winchester rd N6
18 H 5		Winchester rd N9
46 G 20		Winchester rd NW3
130 H 1		Winchester rd NW3
97 W 4		Winchester rd Bxly Hth
126 B 7		Winchester rd Brom
100 D 6		Winchester rd Felt
24 L 12		Winchester rd Harrow
54 D 10		Winchester rd Ilf
84 A 16		Winchester rd Twick
142 E 12		Winchester sq SE1
147 Y 9		Winchester st SW1
148 A 10		Winchester st SW1
73 W 4		Winchester st W3
142 E 13		Winchester wlk SE1
24 E 17		Winchfield clo Harrow
110 J 11		Winchfield rd SE26
16 L 5		Winchmore Hill rd N14
17 P 2		Winchmore Hill rd N21
149 T 6		Wincott st SE11
96 E 10		Wincrofts dri SE9
155 O 17		Windborough rd Carsh
159 Z 2		Windermere rd W Wkhm
27 Y 9		Windermere av N3
128 M 6		Windermere av NW6
119 Z 6		Windermere av SW19
57 W 14		Windermere av Hornch
42 E 3		Windermere av Wemb
35 S 17		Windermere gdns Ilf
42 E 4		Windermere gro Wemb
29 S 6		Windermere rd N10
47 W 7		Windermere rd N19
104 A 11		Windermere rd SW15
121 W 2		Windermere rd SW16
72 D 7		Windermere rd W5
98 J 4		Windermere rd Bxly Hth
123 U 19		Windermere rd Croy
58 F 13		Windermere rd S'hall
88 H 4		Winders rd SW11
110 D 10		Windfield clo SE26
85 N 7		Windham rd Rich
55 U 9		Winding way Dgnhm
41 S 11		Winding way Harrow
75 X 12		Windlass pl SE8
105 P 1		Windlesham gro SW19
110 C 4		Windley clo SE23
116 C 19		Windmill clo Surb
89 S 13		Windmill dri SW4
7 S 10		Windmill gdns Enf
46 C 10		Windmill hill NW3
7 X 11		Windmill hill Enf
51 X 17		Windmill la E15
10 E 5		Windmill la Bushey Watf
59 N 12		Windmill la Grnfd
116 B 17		Windmill la Surb
18 C 12		Windmill rd N18
88 F 15		Windmill rd SW18
104 K 11		Windmill rd SW19
74 A 11		Windmill rd W4
72 D 10		Windmill rd W5
72 D 13		Windmill rd W5
122 L 7		Windmill rd Croy
100 L 13		Windmill rd Mitch
121 U 11		Windmill rd Mitch
149 S 11		Windmill row SE11
140 E 2		Windmill st W1
10 F 4		Windmill st Bushey Watf
141 U 16		Windmill wlk SE1
25 Y 12		Windover av NW9
110 F 6		Windrush la SE23
88 F 9		Windrush clo SW11
32 J 7		Windsor av E17
120 D 1		Windsor av SW19
12 E 12		Windsor av Edg
117 W 13		Windsor av New Mald
153 T 6		Windsor av Sutton
71 Z 17		Windsor clo Brentf
27 T 8		Windsor clo N3
40 H 11		Windsor clo Harrow
16 G 3		Windsor cl N14
40 G 11		Windsor cres Harrow
43 R 9		Windsor cres Wemb
5 Y 19		Windsor dri Barnt
99 X 15		Windsor dri Drtfrd
108 L 10		Windsor gro SE27
148 C 4		Windsor pl SW1
20 D 13		Windsor rd E4
52 H 15		Windsor rd E7
51 R 7		Windsor rd E10
52 F 6		Windsor rd E11
27 T 8		Windsor rd N3
48 A 10		Windsor rd N7
17 U 12		Windsor rd N13
31 X 7		Windsor rd N17
44 J 17		Windsor rd NW2
60 H 20		Windsor rd W5
72 J 1		Windsor rd W5
4 D 19		Windsor rd Barnt
97 Y 11		Windsor rd Bxly Hth
55 Z 10		Windsor rd Dgnhm
23 O 6		Windsor rd Harrow
54 B 12		Windsor rd Ilf
102 K 18		Windsor rd Kingst
85 N 5		Windsor rd Rich
115 S 16		Windsor rd Sidcp
70 E 8		Windsor rd S'hall
101 R 11		Windsor rd Tedd
122 K 4		Windsor rd Thntn Hth
152 H 3		Windsor rd Worc Pk
133 Y 4		Windsor st N1
91 P 5		Windsor wlk SE5
49 U 5		Windus rd N16
49 V 5		Windus wlk N16
127 R 1		Windyridge Brom
105 P 11		Windy Ridge clo SW19
75 O 2		Wine clo E1
143 Z 11		Wine clo E1
141 V 5		Wine Office ct EC4
93 U 1		Winforton st SE10
100 G 9		Winfred rd Hampt
88 C 20		Winfrith rd SW18
121 Z 13		Wingate cres Croy
53 Z 15		Wingate rd Ilf
73 Z 8		Wingate rd W6
52 Z 15		Wingate rd Ilf
15 T 14		Wingate rd Sidcp
51 Y 13		Wingfield rd E15
33 R 15		Wingfield rd E17
103 O 14		Wingfield rd Kingst
91 W 7		Wingfield st SE15
90 A 16		Wingford rd SW2
90 L 8		Wingmore rd SE24
114 E 15		Wingrave rd W6
112 A 5		Wingrove rd SE6
89 N 10		Winifred gro SW11
105 Y 20		Winifred rd SW19
56 A 5		Winifred rd Dgnhm
99 Y 14		Winifred rd Drtfrd
78 G 3		Winifred st E16
18 G 3		Winifred ter N9
65 U 8		Winkfield rd E13
30 G 5		Winkfield rd N22
25 N 1		Winkley clo SE9
111 Y 10		Winlaton rd Brom
56 A 10		Winmill rd Dgnhm
79 W 15		Winncommon rd SE18
140 E 8		Winnett st W1
40 B 18		Winnings wlk Grnfd
28 F 18		Winnington clo N2
28 G 17		Winnington rd N2
46 F 2		Winnington rd N2
9 O 1		Winnington rd Enf
94 F 20		Winn rd SE12
122 J 1		Winn rd SE12
32 K 10		Winns av E17
33 N 9		Winns av E17
33 N 9		Winns ter E17
33 W 9		Winsbeach E17
60 F 12		Winscombe cres W5
47 T 8		Winscombe st N19
10 M 15		Winscombe way Stanm
110 L 6		Winsford rd SE6
18 A 16		Winsford rd N18
89 O 13		Winsham gro SW11
138 G 5		Winslade ms W2
90 B 13		Winslade rd SW2
93 R 19		Winslade way SE6
138 F 4		Winsland st W2
140 B 4		Winsley st W1
20 M 9		Winslow gro E4
144 E 12		Winslow rd W6
100 A 7		Winslow way Felt
66 J 20		Winsor ter E6
88 G 8		Winstanley rd SW11
56 K 14		Winstead gdns Dgnhm
44 A 1		Winston av NW9
10 H 20		Winston clo Harrow
38 H 13		Winston clo Rom
22 J 3		Winston ct Harrow
49 O 12		Winston rd N16
73 X 10		Winston wlk W4
66 E 4		Winter av E6
92 L 20		Winterbourne rd SE6
55 T 7		Winterbourne rd Dgnhm
122 F 8		Winterbourne rd Thntn Hth
90 L 16		Winterbrook rd SE24
105 S 4		Winterfold clo SW19
116 B 16		Winters rd Surb
13 U 16		Winterstoke gdns NW7
110 L 1		Winterstoke rd SE6
146 D 13		Winterton pl SW10
90 B 13		Winterwell rd SW2
87 N 13		Winthorpe rd SW15
30 W 13		Winthrop st E1
29 V 2		Winton av N11
19 S 4		Winton clo N9
25 N 1		Winton gdns Edg
65 X 19		Winton rd E16
108 G 13		Winton way SW16
123 P 11		Wisbech rd Croy
157 V 20		Wisborough rd South Croy
56 H 5		Wisdons clo Rom
13 N 7		Wise la NW7
13 X 19		Wise la NW7
51 N 6		Wiseman rd E10
3 V 8		Wise rd E15
106 K 1		Wiseton rd SW17
95 N 3		Wishart rd SE3
89 N 14		Wisley rd SW11
115 P 18		Wisley rd Orp
93 W 11		Wisteria rd SE13
135 Y 15		Witan st E2
124 C 5		Witham rd SE20
56 A 15		Witham rd Dgnhm
83 R 3		Witham rd Islwrth
39 Y 15		Witham rd Rom
157 S 10		Witherby clo Croy
12 O 13		Witherington rd N5
26 D 4		Withers mead NW9
113 V 5		Witherstone way SE9
87 P 19		Withycombe rd SW19
20 K 12		Withy Mead E4
159 U 15		Witley cres Croy
70 E 11		Witley gdns S'hall
47 N 19		Witley rd N19
110 F 6		Witney path SE23
20 K 10		Wittenham way E4
112 B 12		Wittersham rd Brom
91 Z 6		Wivenhoe clo SE15
68 C 6		Wivenhoe rd Bark
110 D 14		Wiverton rd SE26
68 J 3		Wix rd Dgnhm
89 R 10		Wix's la SW4
57 W 12		Woburn av Hornch
106 D 16		Woburn clo SW19
132 H 17		Woburn pl WC1
154 J 1		Woburn rd Carsh
122 M 20		Woburn rd Croy
123 N 20		Woburn rd Croy
132 G 18		Woburn sq WC1
132 G 15		Woburn wlk WC1
102 D 19		Woffington clo Kingst
86 D 11		Woking clo SW15
126 K 7		Woldham rd Brom
70 F 10		Wolf br S'hall
126 F 14		Wolfe clo Brom
78 A 14		Wolfe cres SE7
53 V 12		Wolferton rd E12
52 B 18		Wolffe gdns E15
108 J 9		Wolfington rd SE27
93 Y 12		Wolfram clo SE13
88 H 7		Wolftencroft clo SW11
12 D 12		Wolmer clo Edg
12 C 10		Wolmer gdns Edg
32 L 11		Wolseley av E17
105 X 4		Wolseley av SW19
73 T 15		Wolseley gdns W4
52 H 10		Wolseley rd E7
29 X 17		Wolseley rd N8
30 C 6		Wolseley rd N22
73 W 10		Wolseley rd W4
23 T 9		Wolseley rd Harrow
121 O 17		Wolseley rd Mitch
57 N 2		Wolseley rd Rom
143 R 18		Wolseley st SE1
66 K 9		Wolsey av E6
30 N 11		Wolsey clo Hounsl
103 T 20		Wolsey clo Kingst
117 T 1		Wolsey clo Kingst
152 F 7		Wolsey clo Worc Pk
159 V 19		Wolsey cres Croy
119 T 16		Wolsey cres Mrdn
102 J 14		Wolsey dri Kingst
55 Z 1		Wolsey gro Edg
47 U 16		Wolsey ms NW5
49 P 15		Wolsey rd N1
9 N 9		Wolsey rd Enf
100 L 14		Wolsey rd Hampt
143 Z 1		Wolsey st E1
14 J 16		Wolsley clo Drtfrd
14 J 16		Wolstonbury N12
80 H 6		Wolvercote rd SE2
117 R 1		Wolverton av Kingst
103 R 20		Wolverton av Kingst
73 N 1		Wolverton gdns W5
144 E 6		Wolverton gdns W6
11 P 20		Wolverton rd Stanm
24 C 1		Wolverton rd Stanm
17 J 20		Wolverton way N14
30 G 2		Wolves la N22
30 C 19		Womersley rd N8
153 O 19		Wonersh way Sutton
104 B 20		Wonford clo New Mald
107 N 3		Wontner rd SW17
64 E 19		Woodall clo E14
9 U 19		Woodall rd Enf
15 O 12		Woodbank N12
112 C 7		Woodbank rd Brom
110 G 14		Woodbastwick rd SE26
17 U 8		Woodberry av N21
22 M 13		Woodberry av Harrow
23 N 13		Woodberry av Harrow
29 R 9		Woodberry cres N10
48 L 3		Woodberry down N4
15 P 20		Woodberry gdns N12
48 L 2		Woodberry gro N4
49 N 2		Woodberry gro N4
15 R 19		Woodberry gro N12
20 G 3		Woodberry way E4
15 P 20		Woodberry way N12
116 H 7		Woodbine av Kingst
101 P 5		Woodbine clo Twick
110 B 19		Woodbine gro SE20
8 C 3		Woodbine gro Enf
152 L 5		Woodbine la Worc Pk
34 G 18		Woodbine pl E11
110 A 19		Woodbine pl SE20
96 G 20		Woodbine rd Sidcp
50 C 17		Woodbine ter E9
86 K 10		Woodborough rd SW15

s W5
hs Ilf
rd E11
rd E17
ville rd E18
Woodville rd NW6
Woodville rd N16
Woodville rd NW11
Woodville rd W5
N 14 Woodville rd Barnt
X 8 Woodville rd Mrdn
C 6 Woodville rd Rich
122 M 8 Woodville rd Thntn Hth
123 N 7 Woodville rd Thntn Hth
26 G 17 Woodward av NW4
91 T 16 Woodward rd SE22
55 S 20 Woodward gdns Dgnhm
55 U 20 Woodward rd Dgnhm
68 C 1 Woodward rd Dgnhm
83 O 16 Woodwards Foot path Twick
23 Z 17 Woodway cres Harrow
76 F 16 Wood wharf SE10
91 S 19 Woodyard la SE21
94 D 16 Woodyates rd SE12
J 4 Woolacombe rd SE3
150 F 10 Wooler st SE17
80 D 3 Woolf clo SE18
30 H 19 Woolaston rd N4
44 F 2 Woolmead av NW9
18 L 18 Woolmer gdns N18
18 L 17 Woolmer rd N18
64 G 19 Woolmore st E14
88 A 7 Woolneigh st SW6
87 Z 7 Woolneigh st SW6
94 K 16 Wool rd SW20
32 E 7 Woolston clo E17
110 J 4 Woolstone rd SE23
78 G 9 Woolwich Ch st SE18
78 H 8 Woolwich comm SE18
78 H 8 Woolwich High st SE18
78 L 4 Woolwich manorway SE18
78 K 13 Woolwich New rd SE18
98 E 6 Woolwich rd Bxly Hth
80 K 15 Woolwich rd SE2
81 P 13 Woolwich rd SE2
77 Y 12 Woolwich rd SE7
78 B 10 Woolwich rd SE7
77 O 13 Woolwich rd SE7
98 D 10 Woolwick rd Bxly Hth
64 J 17 Wooster gdns E14
27 Y 6 Wootton gro E3
141 U 15 Wootton st SE1
124 B 3 Worbeck rd SE20
31 W 1 Worcester av N17
158 M 3 Worcester clo Croy
159 N 3 Worcester clo Croy
121 R 5 Worcester clo Mitch
13 O 10 Worcester cres NW7
21 X 14 Worcester cres Wdfd Grn
41 O 18 Worcester gdns Grnfd
35 R 20 Worcester gdns Ilf
152 C 5 Worcester gdns Worc Pk
160 C 9 Worcester pl EC4
53 T 11 Worcester rd E12
32 F 6 Worcester rd E17
105 V 13 Worcester rd SW19
153 Z 15 Worcester rd Sutton
154 A 15 Worcester rd Sutton
K 3 Worcester av Enf
53 P 19 Wordsworth av E12
34 C 9 Wordsworth av E18
59 P 7 Wordsworth av Grnfd
153 N 9 Wordsworth dri Sutton
30 H 13 Wordsworth pde N16
49 S 13 Wordsworth rd N16
116 H 2 Wordsworth rd SE20
91 E 18 Wordsworth rd SE20
100 E 10 Wordsworth rd Hampt
155 W 15 Wordsworth rd Wallgtn
27 X 14 Wordsworth wlk NW11

146 M 19 Worfield st SW11
149 N 9 Worgan st SE11
134 G 8 Worgate st N1
7 S 13 World's End la Enf
74 L 13 Worlidge st W6
144 C 10 Worlidge st W6
91 V 10 Worlingham rd SE22
74 G 3 Wormholt rd W12
142 H 3 Wormwood st EC2
128 K 18 Wornington rd W10
128 M 19 Wornington rd W10
137 N 1 Wornington rd W10
130 H 5 Woronzow rd NW8
105 P 19 Worple av SW19
83 Y 13 Worple av Islwth
40 E 3 Worple clo Harrow
105 T 18 Worple rd SW19
118 M 2 Worple rd SW20
119 O 1 Worple rd SW20
83 Z 8 Worple rd Islwth
105 U 16 Worple Rd mews SW19
85 Y 7 Worple st SW14
40 E 4 Worple way Harrow
84 L 12 Worple way Rich
134 G 19 Worship st EC2
106 E 17 Worslade rd SW17
110 M 11 Worsley Br rd SE26
111 N 13 Worsley Br rd SE26
51 Z 11 Worsley rd E11
52 A 11 Worsley rd E11
89 V 12 Worsopp dri SW4
64 M 4 Worthing clo E15
70 D 17 Worthing rd Hounsl
116 M 20 Worthington rd Surb
117 N 19 Worthington rd Surb
66 A 1 Wortley rd E6
122 E 16 Wortley rd Croy
83 P 4 Worton gdns Islwth
83 R 9 Worton rd Islwth
83 P 5 Worton way Islwth
44 M 11 Wotton rd NW2
52 A 10 Wouldham rd E11
18 K 7 Wrampling pl N9
35 W 10 Wray av Ilf
48 B 6 Wray cres N4
153 P 7 Wrayfield rd Sutton
153 U 19 Wray rd Sutton
79 P 18 Wrekin rd SE18
44 M 13 Wren av NW2
70 F 10 Wren av S'hall
55 W 14 Wren gdns Dgnhm
57 S 5 Wren gdns Hornch
91 N 2 Wren rd SE5
55 W 14 Wren rd Dgnhm
115 U 7 Wren rd Sidcp
133 O 16 Wren st WC1
128 F 7 Wrentham av NW10
111 Z 10 Wrenthorpe rd Brom
64 B 7 Wrexham rd E3
94 J 3 Wricklemarsh rd SE3
95 P 2 Wricklemarsh rd SE3
75 S 19 Wrigglesworth st SE14
49 S 17 Wright rd N1
105 N 16 Wrights clo SE13
93 W 11 Wrights clo SE13
137 W 20 Wright's la W8
145 W 1 Wrights la W8
63 X 5 Wrights rd E3
123 S 6 Wrights rd SE25
155 R 9 Wrights row Wallgtn
85 X 7 Wrights way SW14
132 C 1 Wrotham rd NW1
47 U 3 Wrotham rd W13
4 E 9 Wrotham rd Barnt
97 U 3 Wrotham rd Welling
62 H 6 Wrottesley rd NW10
79 N 16 Wrottesley rd SE18
89 N 15 Wroughton rd SW11
26 K 12 Wroughton ter NW4
55 U 17 Wroxall rd Dgnhm
29 W 2 Wroxham gdns N11
92 B 5 Wroxton st SE15
154 L 5 Wrythe av Carsh
154 M 5 Wrythe Grn Carsh
120 C 19 Wrythe Grn rd Carsh
154 G 1 Wrythe la Carsh
16 L 15 Wulfstan st W12
97 Z 20 W woodside Bxly
60 K 2 Wyatt ct Wemb
108 B 3 Wyatt Pk rd SW2
99 T 8 Wyatt rd N5
52 F 18 Wyatt rd E7
48 K 9 Wyatt rd N5
33 U 11 Wyatt's la E17
43 V 20 Wybourne way NW10
4 H 11 Wyburn av Barnt
157 N 18 Wyche gro S Croy
102 M 19 Wych Elm pas Kingst
5 N 19 Wycherley cres Barnt

11 U 19 Wychwood av Edg
122 K 6 Wychwood av Thntn Hth
11 U 19 Wychwood clo Edg
12 T 19 Wychwood clo Edg
11 T 19 Wychwood wlk Edg
96 K 3 Wycliffe clo Welling
106 B 16 Wycliffe rd SW19
90 J 1 Wycliffe rd SW11
133 W 14 Wyclif st EC1
45 X 6 Wycombe gdns NW11
31 Y 5 Wycombe rd N17
35 U 16 Wycombe rd Ilf
61 R 2 Wycombe rd Wemb
123 Z 17 Wydehurst rd Croy
119 N 15 Wydell clo Mrdn
112 H 9 Wydeville Mnr rd SE12
20 M 7 Wymead cres E4
88 G 8 Wye st SW11
35 Z 5 Wyfields Ilf
36 A 5 Wyfields Ilf
87 S 1 Wyfold rd SW6
144 L 20 Wyfold rd SW6
56 J 19 Wyhill wlk Dgnhm
71 X 9 Wyke gdns W7
55 U 17 Wykeham av Dgnhm
Wykeham grn Dgnhm
42 M 3 Wykeham hill Wemb
43 N 3 Wykeham hill Wemb
14 F 5 Wykeham rise N20
26 L 16 Wykeham rd NW4
24 A 12 Wykeham rd Harrow
64 A 1 Wyke rd E3
119 N 2 Wyke rd SW20
46 C 4 Wyldes clo NW11
18 G 8 Wyldfield gdns N9
43 T 17 Wyld way Wemb
92 H 17 Wyleu st SE23
70 H 8 Wylie rd S'hall
63 O 12 Wyllen clo E1
129 V 14 Wymering rd W9
87 N 7 Wynan rd SW15
96 J 20 Wyncham av Sidcp
114 J 1 Wyncham av Sidcp
16 L 5 Wynchgate N14
17 N 4 Wynchgate N14
23 Z 17 Wynchgate Harrow
158 E 20 Wyncote way S Croy
25 R 17 Wyndale av NW9
34 H 4 Wyndcliff rd SE7
77 Y 15 Wyndcliff rd SE7
7 V 12 Wyndcroft clo Enf
47 U 10 Wyndham cres N19
82 F 15 Wyndham cres Hounsl
139 O 2 Wyndham ms W1
139 O 2 Wyndham pl W1
65 Z 1 Wyndham rd E6
149 Z 19 Wyndham rd SE5
150 B 19 Wyndham rd SE5
72 A 7 Wyndham rd W13
15 Z 6 Wyndham rd Barnt
103 O 17 Wyndham rd Kingst
139 O 1 Wyndham st W1
91 O 13 Wyndham rd SE24
110 G 6 Wynell rd SE23
133 O 7 Wynford rd N1
133 R 8 Wynford rd N1
116 N 0 Wynford way SE9
90 E 6 Wynne rd SW9
96 L 13 Wynns av Sidcp
146 U 1 Wynnstay gdns W8
88 E 9 Winter st SW11
123 T 10 Wynton gdns SE25
61 T 16 Wynton pl W3
149 R 10 Wynyard ter SE11
133 W 12 Wynyatt st EC1
12 F 11 Wyre gra Edg
59 W 8 Wyresdale Cres Grnfd
139 O 5 Wythburn pl W1
56 F 10 Wythenshawe rd Dgnhm
95 Y 15 Wythens wlk SE9
127 T 3 Wythes clo Brom
78 C 3 Wythes rd E16
95 S 16 Wythfield rd SE9
95 T 15 Wythfield rd SE9
40 M 11 Wyvenhoe rd Harrow
148 J 17 Wyvil est SW8
148 K 16 Wyvil rd SW8
64 E 14 Wyvis st E14

Y

76 H 2 Yabsley st E14
151 R 5 Yalding rd SE16

57 V 13 Yale way Hornch
120 E 1 Yarborough rd SW19
133 S 14 Yardley st WC1
31 Z 15 Yarmouth cres N15
139 X 14 Yarmouth pl W1
80 H 6 Yarnton way Belvdr
78 B 10 Yateley st SE18
40 B 5 Yeading av Harrow
22 G 16 Yeading wlk Harrow
134 E 1 Yeete st N1
29 N 19 Yeatman rd N6
93 V 6 Yeats clo SE13
144 E 10 Yeldham rd W6
88 G 5 Yelverton rd SW11
119 Y 15 Yenston clo Mrdn
83 S 14 Yeomans ms Islwth
146 L 3 Yeomans' row SW3
75 V 11 Yeoman st SE8
9 O 9 Yeomans way Enf
143 R 8 Yeomans yd E1
64 C 14 Yeo st E3
47 Y 9 Yetbury rd N19
113 S 19 Yester dri Chisl
113 U 16 Yester pk Chisl
113 U 17 Yester rd Chisl
112 A 16 Yewdale clo Brom
44 D 19 Yewfield rd NW10
45 R 13 Yew gra NW2
17 T 4 Yew Tree clo N21
97 N 3 Yew Tree clo Welling
118 B 19 Yew Tree clo Worc Pk
37 Z 15 Yew Tree gdns Rom
39 O 16 Yew Tree gdns Rom
62 F 20 Yew Tree rd W12
124 K 5 Yewtree rd Becknhm
82 E 13 Yew Tree wlk Harrow
41 S 3 Yew wlk Harrow
49 P 6 Yoakley rd N16
48 B 18 Yoke clo N7
95 R 13 Yolande gdns SE9
48 E 8 Yonge pk N4
85 W 12 York av SW14
71 U 2 York av W7
114 J 4 York av Sidcp
24 B 6 York av Stanm
140 L 11 York bldgs WC2
71 U 2 York clo W7
119 Z 9 York clo Mrdn
16 M 2 York ga N14
131 U 18 York ga NW1
92 C 2 York gro SE15
108 J 5 York Hill SE27
137 X 17 York Ho pl W8
96 J 8 Yorkland av Welling
47 T 15 York ms NW5
53 X 8 York ms Ilf
88 E 7 York pl SW11
71 T 2 York pl W7
140 K 11 York pl WC2
53 X 8 York pl Ilf
47 S 10 York ri NW5
19 Z 18 York rd E4
52 E 19 York rd E7
51 T 9 York rd E10
32 F 17 York rd E17
16 L 19 York rd N11
16 M 2 York rd N14
18 M 17 York rd N18
18 B 3 York rd N21
141 P 16 York rd SE1
88 E 8 York rd SW11
106 B 15 York rd SW19
61 X 16 York rd W3
72 E 9 York rd W5
5 S 16 York rd Barnt
72 G 15 York rd Brentf
122 F 16 York rd Croy
82 K 8 York rd Hounsl
53 X 8 York rd Ilf
103 N 19 York rd Kingst
84 M 13 York rd Rich
153 X 16 York rd Sutton
101 T 10 York rd Tedd
18 M 17 Yorkshire gdns N18
63 V 17 Yorkshire rd E14
112 A 9 Yorkshire rd Mitch
121 Z 10 Yorkshire rd Mitch
122 A 9 Yorkshire rd Mitch
63 V 14 York sq E14
139 R 1 York st W1
67 N 4 York st Bark
121 O 18 York st Mitch
83 Z 20 York st Twick
7 Z 3 York ter Enf
98 J 1 York ter Enf
131 T 17 York Ter east NW1
131 T 17 York Ter west NW1
135 R 9 Yorkton st E2
132 K 4 York way N1
47 Z 19 York way N7
15 Y 10 York way Felt
100 D 7 York way Felt

Z